1001 BOOKS
YOU MUST READ BEFORE YOU DIE

1001 BOOKS
YOU MUST READ BEFORE YOU DIE

GENERAL EDITOR PETER BOXALL

PREFACE BY PETER ACKROYD

A Quintessence Book

First published in Great Britain in 2008 by Cassell Illustrated
A division of Octopus Publishing Group Limited
Endeavour House, 189 Shaftesbury Avenue, London, WC2H 8JY
www.octopusbooks.co.uk

An Hachette UK Company
www.hachette.co.uk

A CIP catalogue record for this book is available from the British Library.

ISBN-13: 978-1-84403-740-7
QSS.BIE5

This book was designed and produced by
Quintessence Editions Limited
230 City Road, London, EC1V 2TT
www.1001beforeyoudie.com

Update Editor	Elspeth Beidas
Update Designer	Tea Aganovic
Project Editor	Jenny Doubt
Assistant Editors	Marianne Canty, Catherine Osborne, Ruth Patrick, Frank Ritter, Tobias Selin Tara Woolnough
Editorial Director	Jane Laing
Publisher	Mark Fletcher

Manufactured in Singapore by Pica Digital Pte Ltd.
Printed in China by Midas Printing International Ltd.

Contents

Preface to the second edition

By Peter Boxall, General Editor

The response to the first edition of *1001 Books* has been overwhelming. Since its publication in March 2006, the book has generated a huge amount of discussion and passionate debate about what it means to read, about what we read for, and about what we should and shouldn't read. If ever proof were needed that the novel is not dead, that it is a thriving and essential part of contemporary culture, then the response to the publication of *1001 Books* has provided it. From public discussions of the book in the media and on the internet, to private emails sent to me from around the world, I have been both heartened and moved by the strength and the depth of the commitment to the novel that the response to this book has evidenced.

Of course, the form that this public response has taken has not always been consensual. While I have received many emails that enthuse about the list, the most common reaction to the book has been to engage critically with it. Typically, readers will have four responses. They will welcome the fact that some of their cherished titles are on the list; they will tell me about novels that they did not know, which the book has inspired them to read; they will ask why certain titles are on the list that they believe do not deserve to be; and they will demand to know why some titles that they think do deserve to be included have been omitted. Inevitably, every reader strikes a slightly different balance between these four responses, and every reader suggests a different list. I have come to the realization that the omission of a title from the list has been as much of a provocation to re-read it as its inclusion would have been, as readers match their priorities and their critical sensibility against that implied by the book. It has been this kind of engagement, and the debate that has ensued from it, that has been, for me, the most exciting consequence of the book, and its most worthwhile contribution.

With the publication of this new, international edition, this debate can only become fiercer. The publication of this book poses some important and difficult questions, to add to those put by the first edition. Perhaps the most pressing of these relates to the question of the relationship between nationality and the canon. What does it mean to have an "international" edition of this kind of book? In what ways would the book look different to a Czech audience, or a Spanish or German audience, than it would to an audience in the United States, or in the United Kingdom? Does a body of writing, a canon of essential texts, emerge from a national context, or does it in some way transcend nationality, rising above the contexts that generate it? What does it mean to try to respond to all of these different national contexts at the same time? Is it possible to produce a list that can speak at once to readers in Turkey and in Greece, in Serbia and Croatia?

I do not think I would be able to answer these questions adequately if I had 1001 pages for this preface, rather than just two. But what I hope that the publication of this new edition will do is extend the terms of the debate, reach out and engage with a fuller and more diverse readership. Rather than answering any questions about the vexed relationship between nationality, reading, and the canon, I hope that this book will bring the questions themselves to life, for a new, international generation of readers. And, as with the first edition of *1001 Books*, I hope that this debate will take place in the context of an inclusive passion for reading, a love of what the novel can do. As with the first edition, the contributors to this book are not interested in producing an exclusive list, a list that can achieve a transnational and transcultural consensus about which books we should read before we die. The books that have been excised from the list in the move from the first edition to this second, international edition have been done so regretfully; it has not suddenly become safe to die without having read Coetzee's *Elizabeth Costello*, or Bunyan's *Pilgrim's Progress*. Similarly, non-Anglophone books that are included here—for example Uwe's *Jahrestage*, Rojas's *Celestina*—have not been chosen because, in an "international" context, they somehow annihilate the significance of the books they replaced. On the contrary, I hope that this book will build on the success of the first edition by increasing and stimulating debates about reading in a plethora of national contexts, rather than offering itself as a definitive list. Above all, I hope that people will disagree with the selection in this book passionately, and vocally. It is from such disagreement about what constitutes our international fictional heritage, from such critical and urgent discussion about the books that continue to define us, that the future of the novel will emerge.

Introduction

By Peter Boxall, General Editor

There is an ancient connection between death, storytelling, and the number 1001. Since *The Thousand and One Nights*, the number has had a mythical, deathly resonance. Sheherezade, the storyteller of the *Nights*, recounts her tales, over a thousand and one long Arabian evenings, to her king and would-be executioner, as a means of staving off the moment of her own death. Each night the king intends to kill her, but Scheherezade conjures such succulent fragments of prose that he is compelled to let her live another day, so that he can steal from her another, subsequent night, and another instalment in her endless, freewheeling fiction. The infinitely open, unresolvable quality of Scheherezade's storytelling continues to lend the number 1001 something of the mathematical sublime, of the countless or the unlimited. But at the same time, the number also maintains the mortal urgency of Scheherezade's plight. As much as it suggests endless expanse, the number speaks also of precision, and of a cramped, urgent brevity. Scheherezade's stories are still often translated as *The Thousand Nights and One Night*, emphasizing this uneasy proximity, in the number itself, between the expansive and the contracted, the many and the one. Over the great stretch of the thousand and one nights, Scheherezade always has only one night to live; as the evenings glide smoothly away, death is a constant companion, lending to each passing night the peculiar vividness of the final moment, lending the whole, living, proliferating work the unmistakable savor of last things.

In compiling the following list of 1001 books you must read before you die, I have found myself very much in the grip of this Scheherezadian paradox. The story of the novel, as it is told here, is a long and rambling affair, full of surprising turns, and unlikely subplots. Weaving this multi-layered tale through reference to 1001 titles has seemed, from the beginning, to be a gargantuan task, and a task that could never end. The final list, including all the novels that one must read and excluding all the ones that it is safe to leave unread, could of course never be drawn up, just as Scheherezade's stories still have not ended, and will never end, this side of the knowable. But at the same time, the limits that the number has pressed upon me are cruel and narrow. One thousand and one is after all such a small number, given the extent of the subject matter. Each title here has to fight for its slender berth, and each entry is fueled by a certain concentrated energy, a struggle to make room for itself as desperate as if life depended upon it. Each novel is a work that you must read before you die, and while death is always a distant prospect, it is also always imminent, lurking in the shadows of every instant. Something you must do before you die might feel like a lazy aspiration, but it is also something you have to do in a hurry, or even now.

This contradiction between the roomy and the constricted can be felt moving throughout this book. The novel is represented here in all its variety, its inventiveness, its wit, as it stretches from the ancients—from Aesop, Ovid, Chariton—to the contemporary fiction of Amis, DeLillo, or Houellebecq. But at the same time the novel as a complete entity is forever beyond our grasp, refusing to be fully systematized, always something more than the sum of its parts. Indeed, it might be argued that the novel, as a stable, recognizable object, does not really exist. There is no consensus among readers and critics about when the novel as a form came into being; there is no definite boundary that separates a novel from a short story, from a novella, from a prose poem, from autobiography, witness testimony, or journalism, from a fable, or a myth, or a legend. And there is certainly no consensus concerning how one distinguishes between the trashy novel and the literary masterpiece. Rather, the novel as a form, and as a body of work, is an inspired idea that we can only grasp fleetingly, fragmentarily; an idea that makes prose fiction possible, but that is also itself something of a fiction.

The list that is offered here, then, does not seek to be a new canon, and does not claim to define or exhaust the novel. Rather, it is a list that lives in the midst of the contradiction between the comprehensive and the partial. It is a list that is animated by the spirit of the novel, by a love for what the novel is and does, but which nevertheless does not hope or aim to capture it, to sum it up, or put it to bed. Prose fiction lives in so many guises and different languages, across so many nations and centuries, that a list like this will always, and should always, be marked, formed, and deformed by what it leaves out. Rather than defending its borders against that which it excludes, this book offers itself as a snapshot of the novel, one story among others that one can tell about its history. The book is made up of entries from over 100 contributors—a cross-section of the international reading community, including critics, academics, novelists, poets, literary journalists—and the list is generated to a large degree from what this diverse group of readers tells us about what the novel looks like today. As such, this book reflects a set of priorities that are shared by today's readers, a certain understanding of where the novel comes from, a particular kind of passion for reading. But it does so in a spirit of love for the diversity and endlessness of the possibilities of fiction, rather than in any desire to separate the quality from the rabble, the wheat from the chaff. It speaks of a thousand and one things, but with a breathless urgency that derives partly from the haunting knowledge of how many other things there are to be said, how many other novels there are to be read, how short even the longest story can feel when faced with the endlessness of storytelling.

This combination of the long and the short, the exhaustive and the partial, is perhaps nowhere more evident in this book than at the level of each individual entry. There is clearly something insane about writing 300 words—the approximate length of each of these entries—on something as many-mansioned and multi-textured as a novel. Even a thin slip of prose, such as Charlotte Perkins Gilman's *The Yellow Wallpaper*, surely cannot be condensed into 300 words, so what of Dorothy Richardson's *Pilgrimage*, or Samuel Richardson's *Clarissa*, or Proust's *À la recherche*—novels that run into thousands of pages? What can 300 words hope to do in the face of such monsters? This is a question that vexed me, somewhat, at the start of this project. But as the book goes to press, it strikes me that the brevity of each of these entries is this book's greatest strength. What these entries seek to do is neither to offer a full critique of each title, nor to give us a flavor of the prose, nor even simply to provide a canned plot synopsis. What each entry does is to respond, with the cramped urgency of a deathbed confession, to what makes each novel compelling, to what it is about each novel that makes one absolutely need to read it. There is no other format that I can think of that could deliver this kind of entreaty more effectively, or with a more thrilling intensity. One contributor, in discussing with me what these entries might hope to achieve, hit upon a phrase that for me has come to define what this book does. He said that each entry might be thought of as a "micro-event," a miniaturized but complete reading experience that contains within it something of the boundlessness of the novel.

I have many people to thank for their help over the last months. Working on this project has been an extraordinary pleasure, mostly because of the incredible enthusiasm and goodwill shown by everybody who has been a part of it. My first debt of gratitude is to all of the contributors. I have been moved by how promptly and willingly all of the contributors have responded to the demands of this book, and I have been staggered by the sheer quality and imaginative exuberance of the work that has been produced. This really has been a labor of love and friendship, so thank you. There are also many, many people who contributed to the production of this book, but who are not listed as contributors. Maria Lauret was unable to be in the book, but I thank her for her help, and remember Paul Roth with love and sorrow. I have had countless discussions, over unnumbered kitchen tables, about what titles should be in this list, and I thank everybody who has made suggestions to me. I would particularly like to thank Alistair Davies, Norman Vance, Rose Gaynor, members of my family in Cardiff and London, in the U.S. and Turkey, and the entirety of the Jordan family. I am deeply grateful to Liz Wyse, whose clear intelligence and calm good humor made even the difficult moments a pleasure. Jenny Doubt saw this book through to publication with an extraordinary, unflappable professionalism, and with imaginative flair. Witnessing her ability to deal with the manifold pressures that a project like this produces in its final stages has left me gasping with admiration. The Art Director Tristan de Lancey and Picture Researcher Maria Gibbs have done an incredible job, and I am grateful to everybody at Quintet, in particular Jane Laing and Judith More. As always, my love and thanks go to the Boxall Jordans; to Hannah, who has been a central part of this project from the beginning, and to Ava and Laurie, for whom reading is a transformative pleasure that is only now beginning.

Working on this book has taught me a great deal about the novel. It has also taught me something about how contagious the love of books is, how much excitement, friendship, and pleasure they produce. I hope that some of the excitement, and some of the love and friendship, that went into making this book will be communicated in the reading of it.

Contributors

Vance Adair (VA) is a Teaching Fellow in the Department of English Studies at the University of Stirling. He has written on critical theory and early modern drama.

Rhalou Allerhand (RA) is a journalist who studied English at the University of the West of England. She also writes fiction.

Jordan Anderson (JA) is a postgraduate student at King's College London and a graduate of Harvard University. He has published on the work of Thomas Hardy.

Carlos G. Aragón (CA) is a PhD candidate at the University of Birmingham. He is working on a dissertation about Pedro Juan Gutiérrez's "Cycle of Havana Centre."

Susanna Araujo (SA)

Derek Attridge (DA) has published books on the works of James Joyce. He is a Professor in the Department of English and Related Literature at University of York.

Sally Bayley (SB)

Lorenzo Bellettini (LB) is completing a PhD on Arthur Schnitzler at Cambridge University. He is president of Cambridge University Creative Writing Club.

Alvin Birdi (ABi) is a former economist and has held lecturing posts at the Universities of Manchester and Middlesex. He is completing a DPhil on Samuel Beckett and J.M. Coetzee at the University of Sussex.

Laura Birrell (LBi)

Andrew Blades (ABl) is undertaking a DPhil on masculine identity in AIDS literature. He reviews theater for the *Stage* newspaper.

Maria-Dolores Albiac Blanco (M-DAB) is Professor of Spanish Literature at the Univesity of Zaragoza and has published works mainly on eighteenth-century subjects.

María del Pilar Blanco (MPB) is completing her doctorate on American literature and film in the Department of Comparative Literature at New York University.

Vicki Blud (VB) received a Masters degree in English Literature from King's College London. She will now specialize in medieval literature and critical theory.

Anna Bogen (AB) is a DPhil candidate at the University of Sussex. She is currently writing her doctoral thesis on early twentieth-century fiction and women's education. She has published extensively on children's literature, the nineteenth-century *bildungsroman*, and the work of Virginia Woolf.

Dr. Peter Boxall (PB) is a Senior Lecturer in English literature at the University of Sussex. He has published widely on twentieth-century fiction and drama.

Dr. Kate Briggs (KB) is a Research Fellow in Modern Languages and Literatures at Trinity College, Dublin.

Marko Cindric (MCi)

Monika Class (MC) is a doctoral student at Balliol College, Oxford, working on a thesis on nineteenth-century British writers.

Liam Connell (LC) teaches literature at the University of Hertfordshire. His research interests are in postcolonial writing, modernism and popular literature.

Clare Connors (CC) is Lecturer in English at the Queen's College, Oxford, where she teaches and writes about Victorian and modern literature and literary theory.

Philip Contos (PC) studied English and Italian literature at Columbia and Oxford universities. He currently works as an editor in London.

Jennifer Cooke (JC) is completing a thesis on the plague in texts and culture.

Ailsa Cox (ACo)

Vybarr Cregan-Reid (VC-R)

Abi Curtis (AC) is completing a PhD at the University of Sussex. She has published fiction and poetry and was awarded an Eric Gregory Award for poetry in 2004.

Ulf Dantanus (UD) is Director of Studies for the Gothenburg Program at the University of Sussex. He has postgraduate degrees from Trinity College Dublin and Göteborg University.

Jean Demerliac (JD) is a writer and editor who has written and translated Herman Melville. He has contributed to many publications and multimedia projects at the Bibliothèque nationale de France.

Sarah Dillon (SD)

Lucy Dixon (LD) studied English literature and Afrikaans at Stellenbosch University.

Margaret Anne Doody (MD) is John and Barbara Glynn Family Professor of Literature at the University of Notre Dame. She has written six novels and many critical works.

Jenny Doubt (JSD) completed her MA at the University of Sussex in postcolonial literature. She is one of the Founding Editors of *Transgressions*, a twentieth-century interdisciplinary humanities journal.

Karen D'Souza (KDS)

Lizzie Enfield (LE) worked for BBC radio before going freelance, and now contributes to various national newspapers and magazines. Her novels, *What You Don't Know* and *Uncoupled*, are published by Headline.

Martin Paul Eve (MPE) is an Associate Tutor and researcher at the University of Sussex. His work focuses primarily upon the fiction of Thomas Pynchon in relation to various schools of European philosophy.

Fabriano Fabbri (FF) is lecturer in contemporary art techniques at the University of Bologna. He has always been interested in the connections between art and mass culture.

Anna Foca (AF)

Seb Franklin (SF)

Daniel Mesa Gancedo (DMG) is a Lecturer in Latin American literature at the University of Zaragoza. His works include *Similar Strangers; the Artificial Character and the Narrative Contrivance in Latin American literature* (2002).

Andrzej Gasiorek (AG) is a Reader in twentieth-century English literature at the University of Birmingham, where he has been teaching for the last twelve years. He is the author of *Postwar British Fiction: Realism and After* (1995), *Wyndham Lewis and Modernism* (2004), and *J. G. Ballard* (2005).

Diana Gobel (DG) completed her DPhil in Russian History at Oxford, and has since worked as a freelance copy editor, researcher, and translator.

Richard Godden (RG) teaches American Literature in the Department of American Studies at the University of Sussex. He has published *Fictions of Capital: The American Novel from James to Mailer* (1990), and *Fictions of Labor: William Faulkner and the South's Long Revolution* (1997).

Jordi Gracia (JGG) is Professor of Spanish Literature at the University of Barcelona and works mainly on twentieth-century Spanish literature. Among his works is *The Silent Resistance: Fascism and Culture in Spain* (Anagrama Essay Prize, 2004).

Reg Grant (RegG) is a freelance writer. He has an extensive knowledge of modern European literature, especially post–Second World War French fiction.

Frederik Green (FG) is a PhD candidate in East Asian Languages and Literatures at Yale University. He is currently writing a dissertation on the Republican-period writer Xu Xu.

Christopher C. Gregory-Guider (CG-G) teaches twentieth-century literature and culture at the University of Sussex. He has published articles on W. G. Sebald, Iain Sinclair, photography, trauma, and memory. Other interests include narrative and filmic representation of mental illness and the cultural history of walking.

Eleanor Gregory-Guider (EG-G) received a BA (Hons) in English and History from the University of Texas and a MA in eighteenth-century studies, focusing on literature and art history from the University of York.

Agnieszka Gutthy (AGu) is an Associate Professor of Spanish in the Department of Foreign Languages and Literatures at Southeastern Louisiana University. She specializes in comparative literature, Basque, and Kashubian studies. She also writes on Polish and Spanish literature.

Andrew Hadfield (AH) is Professor of English at the University of Sussex where he teaches Renaissance literature and contemporary literature and theory. His most recent book is *Shakespeare and Republicanism* (2005). He has written essays on Saul Bellow and T. H. White, and is a reviewer for the *Times Literary Supplement*.

Friederike Hahn (FH) has an MA in Shakespearean Studies and is currently completing her PdD at King's College London.

Esme Floyd Hall (EH) is a writer who lives and works in Brighton. She has published three nonfiction titles with Carlton Books and has contributed to various newspapers and magazines, including *Sunday Times Style*, *Observer*, *She*, and *Zest*.

Philip Hall (PH) was born in New Zealand, where he earned a degree in English literature and a Masters degree in Law. He currently lives and works in London, and writes on a variety of subjects.

James Harrison (JHa) is a writer and book editor who now only reads hardbacks with large type and generous spacing. Thus, he has read (with pleasure) Cervantes's *Don Quixote* and Gore Vidal's *Palimpsest*.

Doug Haynes (DH) is a Lecturer in American Literature at Sussex University. He specializes in late twentieth-century American writing. He has published work on the novelists Thomas Pynchon and William Burroughs and has written on Surrealist black humor.

Thomas Healy (TH) is Professor of Renaissance Studies at Birkbeck College, University of London. He is the author of three critical studies, editor of two collections of essays, and co-editor of *The Arnold Anthology of British and Irish Literature in English*.

Jon Hughes (JH) is a Lecturer in German at Royal Holloway, University of London. He is the author of a monograph on the work of Joseph Roth, and has published on twentieth-century German/Austrian literature and film.

Rowland Hughes (RH) is a Lecturer in English literature at the University of Hertfordshire. His interests lie in eighteenth- and nineteenth-century American literature and Anglo-American cinema.

Jessica Hurley (JHu) is a doctoral student at the University of Pennsylvania. She specializes in contemporary American and British fiction, performance, and theory.

Haewon Hwang (HH) When studying Russian literature, Haewon was forewarned that she would end up a plumber. She is now gladly exploring sewers in the course of researching underground spaces.

Bianca Jackson (BJ) is a doctoral candidate writing on the sexually dissident subject in contemporary Indian Anglophone literature at the University of Oxford.

David James (DJ) is associate tutor in the Department of English at the University of Sussex, where he wrote a DPhil on the evolution of a poetics of place and perception in British fiction from 1970 to the present.

Dr. Meg Jensen (MJ) is Head of the Department of Creative Writing at Kingston University, where she also lectures on nineteenth- and twentieth-century English and American literature.

Iva Jevtic (IJ)

Carole Jones (CJ) teaches in the School of English, Trinity College. She has published articles on Scottish fiction and the representation of masculinity in recent writing.

Gwenyth Jones (GJ) has completed a PhD on the literature of Budapest and teaches Hungarian literature to undergraduates.

Thomas Jones (TEJ) is an editor at the *London Review of Books*.

Michael Jones (MJo)

Hannah Jordan (HJ) is a freelance writer and critic. She is working on a children's novel, entitled *A Bohemian Christmas*.

Jinan Joudeh (JLSJ) has studied English and American Literature at Duke, Sussex, and Yale universities. She is currently working on modernist American fiction in the context of friendship, marriage, and theory.

Lara Kavanagh (LK) is currently completing an MA in Twentieth Century Literature at King's.

Christine Kerr (CK) was born in England and received her PhD from the University of Sussex. She has taught English literature in Europe, Africa, and Asia and is a faculty member at Champlain College in Montréal.

Kumiko Kiuchi (KK) is a DPhil student in the English Literature Department at the University of Sussex. She was awarded her BA and one of her MAs in Japan. Her research interests include the problem of translation, modernism, the philosophy of language, and the work of Samuel Beckett.

Joanna Kosty (JK)

Andrea Kowalski (AK) is a journalist working for the BBC World Service. In 2000, she received a Masters degree from the Institute of Latin American Studies (ILAS) in London.

Katya Krylova (KKr) is a PhD student in the Department of German at Cambridge University. Specializing in post-war German literature, her thesis focuses on the legacy of the Second World War, topography and identity in the works of Ingeborg Bachmann and Thomas Bernhard.

Karl Lampl (KL) was born in Lilienfeld, Austria and studied at the University of Vienna. After moving to Canada he settled in Montreal, where he graduated from Concordia University.

Laura Lankester (LL) has a MA in English Literature from University College London. She currently works for a London publisher and writes reviews.

Anthony Leaker (AL) is studying twentieth-century America and European literature. He has taught at the University of Paris.

Vicky Lebeau (VL) is Reader in English at the University of Sussex. She is the author of *Lost Angels: psychoanalysis and cinema* (1995), *Psychoanalysis and cinema: the play of shadows* (2001).

Hoyul Lee (Hoy)

Maria Lopes da Silva (ML) specializes in critical theory and Portuguese, Brazilian, and Lusophone African literature. She received a MA from the University of Cambridge and is completing a PhD on Florbela Espanca.

Sophie Lucas (SL) studied Philosophy at the University of Bordeaux. Based in Paris, she now teaches French as a foreign language.

Graeme Macdonald (GM) is Lecturer in nineteenth- and twentieth-century literature in the Department of English and Comparative Literary Studies at The University of Warwick, England.

Heidi Slettedahl Macpherson (HM) is Reader in North American literature at the University of Central Lancashire. She is the author of *Women's Movement* (2000) and the co-editor of *Transatlantic Studies* (2000), and *Britain and the Americas* (2005).

Martha Magor (MaM)

Muireann Maguire (MuM)

José-Carlos Mainer (JCM) is Professor of Spanish Literature at the University of Zaragoza. Among his publications are *The Silver Age 1902–1939* (1975, re-edited in 1987), *Modernism and 98* (1979), *History, Literature, Society* (1990), *Uncontrolled Literature* (2000), and *Philology in Purgatory (2003)*.

Peter Manson (PM)

Laura Marcus (LM) is Professor of English at the University of Sussex. She has published on nineteenth and twentieth-century literature. She has co-edited *The Cambridge History of Twentieth-Century English Literature*.

Victoria Margree (VM) received her DPhil in English Literature from the University of Sussex. She lectures at Sussex and the University of Brighton.

Nicky Marsh (NM) works at the University of Southampton, where she is director of the Center for Cultural Poetics. Her published work has appeared in journals including *New Formations, Postmodern Culture, Feminist Review*, and *Wasafari*.

Louise Marshall (LMar) is a Lecturer in Restoration and eighteenth-century literature at the University of Wales. Her research focuses on drama.

Rosalie Marshall (RMa) has a BA in French and Scandinavian Studies, and she has returned to higher education to do a PhD in French Caribbean Literature. Her career has included teaching modern languages.

Andrew Maunder (AM)

Maren Meinhardt (MM) is Science and Psychology Editor at the *Times Literary Supplement*. She is writing a biography of Alexander von Humboldt.

Dr. Ronan McDonald (RM) is Director of the Samuel Beckett International Foundation and Lecturer in the School of English at the University of Reading. His publications include *Tragedy and Irish Literature* (2002) and the *Cambridge Introduction to Samuel Beckett* (2005), as well as articles and reviews.

Dr. Patricia McManus (PMcM) teaches courses on English literary and cultural history at the University of Sussex. She is currently writing a book on the English novel from 1920–1940.

Lisa McNally (LMcN)

Geoffrey Mills (GMi) studied English at Reading and London Universities and currently works as an English teacher in Worcestershire. He writes both poetry and prose, some of which has been published.

Drew Milne (DM) is the Judith E. Wilson Lecturer in Drama and Poetry, Faculty of English, University of Cambridge. He has edited *Marxist Literary Theory* and *Modern Critical Thought*. His novel is entitled *The Prada Meinhof Gang*.

Jacob Moerman (JaM)

Pauline Morgan (PMB) completed a doctoral thesis on Elizabeth Bowen at the University of Sussex. Her literary research has explored psychoanalysis, ghosts, and music.

Jonathan Morton (JM) is a History teacher living in Oxford. He studied History and English literature and creative writing at U.E.A in Norwich and did an MA in Modern European History.

Domingo Ródenas de Moya (DRM) is Professor of Spanish and European Literature at the Universitat Pompeu Fabra, Barcelona. He has published *The Mirrors of the Novelist* and has edited many contemporary classics.

Alan Munton (AMu) is Archivist at the University of Plymouth, and a Lecturer in English. His Cambridge doctorate on Wyndham Lewis featured the first full discussion of Lewis' *The Childermass*, summarized here.

Robin Musumeci (RMu)

Salvatore Musumeci (SMu) received an Masters degree in history from Trinity College (Hartford, Connecticut). He is currently completing a PhD dissertation at Queen Mary, University of London.

Paul Myerscough (PMy) is an editor at the *London Review of Books*.

Stratos C. Myrogiannis (SMy) received his MPhil from the University of Thessaloniki, Greece, and started his PhD on the Greek Enlightenment at Cambridge in 2005.

María Ángeles Naval (MAN) is a Professor at the Department of Spanish Philology (Spanish and Hispanic Literatures) of the University of Zaragoza. Her research has concentrated on the Spanish literature of the nineteenth and twentieth centuries.

Stephanie Newell (SN) lectures in postcolonial literature at the University of Sussex. She specializes in West African literature and African popular culture, and her publications include *Literary Culture in Colonial Ghana: "How to Play the Game of Life"*, *West African Literatures: Ways of Reading*.

Caroline Nunneley (CN)

Julian Patrick (JP) is a Professor of English and Comparative Literature at the University of Toronto where he teaches early modern

literature, literary theory, and psychoanalysis in the Department of English and the Literary Studies Program.

Andrew Pepper (AP) is a Lecturer in English and American literature at Queen's University Belfast. He is the author of *The Contemporary American Crime Novel* (2000) and the co-author of *American History and Contemporary Hollywood Film* (2005). His first novel is *The Last Days of Newgate*.

Irma Perttula (IP) is researching the grotesque and carnivalization in Finnish literature. She teaches Finnish literature courses at the University of Helsinki and the Open University.

Roberta Piazza (RPi) is a Lecturer in Modern Languages at the University of Sussex, where she has taught translation and modern Italian and European literatures. After completing an American doctorate and an MPhil in Linguistics, she is now working on a DPhil on the dialogue of Italian cinema.

Fiona Plowman (FP) studied English literature at the University of London. She is a former commissioning editor and reviewer for *The Good Book Guide* magazine. She currently works as a freelance editor and writer.

David Punter (DP) is Professor of English at the University of Bristol, where he is also Research Director for the Faculty of Arts. He has published extensively on Gothic and Romantic literature; on contemporary writing; and on literary theory, psychoanalysis, and the postcolonial, as well as four small volumes of poetry.

Robin Purves (RP) is a Lecturer in English literature at the University of Central Lancashire. He has published articles on nineteenth-century French writing, contemporary poetry, and philosophy. Along with Peter Manson, he runs a press, *Object Permanence*.

Vincent Quinn (VQ)

Santiago del Rey (SR) is an editor, cultural journalist, and literary critic.

Vera Rich (VR) is a writer and translator, specializing in the literature of Ukraine and Belarus. She is a former General Secretary of the Anglo-Ukrainian Society and Deputy Editor of The Ukrainian Review.

Oscar Rickett (OR) is a freelance writer from London. He has written on twentieth-century American literature, nineteenth-century English literature, and modern Argentina.

Dr. Ben Roberts (BR) teaches at the University of Bradford. His main areas of interest are cultural theories of technology and counterfeit money in literature.

Dr. Anne Rowe (AR) is a Senior Lecturer at Kingston University. She is the author of *Salvation by Art: The Visual Arts and the Novels of Iris Murdoch* and is also the

Director of the Center for Iris Murdoch Studies at Kingston University. In addition to her teaching, she is the European Director of the Iris Murdoch Society and European Editor of the *Iris Murdoch News Letter*.

Nicholas Royle (NWor) is Professor of English Literature at the University of Sussex. His major works include *E. M. Forster* (1999) and *The Uncanny* (2003). He is joint editor of the *Oxford Literary Review*.

David Rush (DR)

Martin Ryle (MR) teaches English and Cultural Studies at the University of Sussex, and has particular research interests in Irish writing and contemporary fiction. His critical writing includes work on George Gissing and Michel Houellebecq.

Darrow Schecter (DSch) completed a doctorate on Antonio Gramsci at the University of Oxford. He was a British Academy Post-Doctoral Fellow, and is currently a Reader in Intellectual History in the School of Humanities at the University of Sussex. He has written several books on the subjects of European intellectual history and political theory.

Lucy Scholes (LSc)

Tobias Selin (TSe) was born in Sweden and studied Mechanical Engineering and the Philosophy of Science. After working as an editor in London for a couple of years, he returned to Sweden and currently works in engineering.

Christina Sevdali (CSe) is currently finishing her PhD in Linguistics at the University of Cambridge. Her first degree was in Ancient and Modern Greek literature. She enjoys writing about cinema and singing jazz.

Elaine Shatenstein (ES) is a freelance book reviewer, newspaper columnist, and feature writer, as well as a guest speaker for literary groups, a writing instructor, and an editor. She has previously worked in broadcasting and film as a writer and producer, and was published in an anthology of social satire.

John Shire (JS) is a writer and photographer, and his short fiction has appeared in a number of UK and U.S. publications. In addition to this work, he has a virtual hand in two websites; www.libraryofthesphinx. co.uk and Invocations Press. Sadly, a degree in English Literature and Philosophy has done him very little good.

Tom Smith (TS) is a Lecturer at the Faculty of International Business, in the University of Applied Sciences Furtwangen. His short stories have appeared in numerous magazines and anthologies and he has also won an Ian St. James Award. He has an MA in Creative Writing and is currently working toward a DPhil at Sussex University.

Daniel Soar (DSoa) works as an editor at the *London Review of Books*.

Matthew Sperling (MS)

David Steuer (DS)

Simon Stevenson (SS) is an Assistant Professor of English at National Dong Hwa University, Taiwan where he teaches literature and literary theory.

Esther MacCallum Stewart (EMcCS)

Luis Sundqvist (LS)

Céline Surprenant (CS) is a Senior Lecturer in French in the English Department at the University of Sussex. She is the author of *Freud's Mass Psychology: Questions of Scale* (2003). She has also translated Jean-Luc Nancy's *The Speculative Remark* (2001).

Theodora Sutcliffe (TSu) is a journalist and copywriter who also writes fiction.

Julie Sutherland (JuS) completed her PhD in English studies and seventeenth-century studies at the University of Durham. She was born in Canada and returned there to become Professor of Early Modern Drama at Atlantic Baptist University.

Keston Sutherland (KS) is a Lecturer in English at the University of Sussex. He is the author of *Antifreeze*, *The Rictus Flag*, *Neutrality* and several other books of poetry. He edits the occult leftist journal *Quid*, the *Q?* series of noise, and rant CD-Rs, and co-edits Barque Press.

Bharat Tandon (BT) is College Lector and Director of Studies in English Literature at Jesus College, Cambridge, and teaches British and American literature. Aside from his teaching duties, he writes regularly on contemporary British and American fiction and cinema for the *Times Literary Supplement* and the *Daily Telegraph*.

Jenny Bourne Taylor (JBT) is a Reader in English at the University of Sussex. She has written extensively on nineteenth-century literature and culture. Recent publications include *George Gissing: Voices of the Unclassed* (2005), which she edited with Martin Ryle, and editing *The Cambridge Companion to Wilkie Collins* (2006).

Philip Terry (PT)

Samuel Thomas (SamT) completed his DPhil in English Literature at the University of Sussex. His research interests include Thomas Pynchon, the Frankfurt School of Critical Theory, and contemporary Eastern European writing.

Sophie Thomas (ST) is a Lecturer in English at the University of Sussex, where she teaches a range of subjects, including eighteenth and nineteenth-century literature, and on MA programs in Critical Theory, and Literature and Visual Culture.

Dale Townshend (DaleT) is Thesia Stuftung Research Fellow in the Department of English Studies at the University of Stirling. He has co-edited four volumes in the *Gothic: Critical Concepts in Literary and Cultural Studies* series (2004). His monograph, *The Orders of Gothic*, is published by AMS Press.

David Towsey (DT) is a Lecturer in English Literature at Hertford College, Oxford University, and he also teaches for the Oxford University Department of Continuing Education. He has previously published on literary theory and Romantic literature, and is currently working on late Victorian and Edwardian writings as part of a larger study of Walter de la Mare's short stories.

David Tucker (DTu)

Garth Twa (GT) is the author of a short story collection called *Durable Beauty*. He is also an award-winning filmmaker, and is currently hard at work on his second book, *My Ice Age*, which describes both his youth in an Eskimo settlement on the Arctic Circle and his years struggling on the outer fringes of Hollywood.

Miriam van der Valk (MvdV) gained an MA in Philosophy at Amsterdam University, specializing in the theory of psychoanalysis and feminist politics.

Cedric Watts (CW) is Research Professor of English Literature at the University of Sussex. His many publications include books on Shakespeare, Keats, Cunninghame Graham, Joseph Conrad, and Graham Greene. He is also the co-author (along with John Sutherland) of *Henry V, War Criminal? and Other Shakespeare Puzzles*.

Claire Watts (ClW) is a writer and a freelance editor with a degree in French from the University of London. She also runs her local school library.

Manuela Wedgwood (MWd)

Andreea Weisl (AW)

Gabriel Wernstedt (GW)

Juliet Wightman (JW) has taught English Studies at the University of Stirling for several years. Her research focuses closely on language and violence, making particular reference to Renaissance literature and drama.

Ilana Wistinetzki (IW) received an MPhil degree in classical Chinese literature from Yale University in 2000. She then went on to teach modern Hebrew at both Yale and Beijing universities.

Tara Woolnough (TW) lives and works in London. She obtained a degree in Classics, and an MA. She now works as an editor and writer in book publishing.

Marcus Wood (MW)

Title Index

Il faut vous fuir, Ma...
... Sens bien. J'aurois dû b...
...ttendre ; ou plustôt, il f...
...oir jamais. Mais que j...
...n'y prendre aujourdui
...romis de l'amitié : Soy...
...h conseillez-moi.

Vous Savez que je n...
...ans vôtre maison que...
...e Madame vôtre mér...
...'avois cultivé quelques...
...lle a cru qu'ils ne Se...

1800

PRE

The Thousand and One Nights

Anonymous

Original Title | *Alf laylah wa laylah*
Original Language | Arabic
First Published | *c.* 850
Source | from *Hazar Afsanah* (*A Thousand Tales*)

The tales that make up the collection known to us as *The Thousand and One Nights* are some of the most powerful, resonant works of fiction in the history of storytelling. The tales, told over a thousand and one nights by Sheherazade to King Shahryar, include foundational narratives such as "Sinbad," "Aladdin," and "Ali Baba and the Forty Thieves." These stories have an uncanny capacity to endure. But while the tales of *The Thousand and One Nights* are remarkable for their familiarity and their currency, perhaps their most important legacy is the concept of narrative itself that emerges from them.

It is in the *Nights* that an underlying, generative connection is fashioned between narrative, sex, and death—a connection that has remained at the wellspring of prose fiction ever since. King Shahryar is in the unseemly habit of deflowering and killing a virgin on a nightly basis, and the *Nights* opens with Sheherazade lining up to be the king's next victim. Determined not to meet with such a fate, Sheherazade contrives to tell the king stories; in accordance with her plan, they prove so compelling, so erotic, so luscious and provocative, that at the end of the night, he cannot bring himself to kill her. Each night ends with a tale unfinished, and each night the king grants her a stay of execution, so that he might hear the conclusion. But the storytelling that Sheherazade invents, in order to stay alive, is a kind of storytelling that is not able to end, that never reaches a climax. Rather, the stories are inhabited by a kind of insatiable desire, an open unfinishedness that keeps us reading and panting, eager for more, just as King Shahryar listens and pants. The eroticism of the tales, their exotic, charged texture, derives from this desirousness, this endless trembling on the point both of climax, and of death. **PB**

◉ The binding from a 1908 edition of the *Nights* stylishly captures the exoticism that attracted Westerners to tales of the East.

◉ Leon Bakst designed the costumes for the Ballet Russes version of Rimsky-Korsakov's *Sheherazade*, performed in Paris in 1910.

The Tale of the Bamboo Cutter

Anonymous

Original Language | Japanese
First Published | 10th century
Alternate Title | *The Tale of Princess Kaguya*
Original Title | *Taketori Monogatari*

The Tale of the Bamboo Cutter is referred to in *The Tale of Genji* as the "ancestor of all romances." It is also the oldest surviving Japanese work of fiction. There are various theories regarding the exact date of its writing, but it is believed to have appeared late in the ninth century or early in the tenth century. Yasunari Kawabata, one of Japan's finest modern novelists, unveiled his modern re-telling in 1998.

The story is of Kaguya-hime, an exceptionally beautiful princess who was found by an old bamboo cutter when only a baby. Her beauty takes possession of the men of Japan and, in an attempt to see her married, her bamboo-cutter guardian chooses five suitors for her. The coldhearted Kaguya-hime, unwilling to marry, sets these suitors impossible tasks. The largely devious suitors use their money and position to try to convince the princess that they have completed their tasks. One prince sets a team of workers to work day and night to make the princess a golden branch; another pays a man in China to find a robe that will not burn.

Each incidence of failure provides a proverb. An ill-starred adventure is "plum foolish" because the grand counselor, on failing to bring a dragon's jewel back to the princess, replaces his eyes with stones that look like plums. Masayuki Miyata's illustrations of the Kawabata version are wonderful and almost warrant a reading of the book alone. **OR**

The Tale of Genji

Murasaki Shikibu

Lifespan | *b. c.* 973 (Japan), *d. c.* 1014
First Published | 11th century
Original Language | Japanese
Original Title | *Genji Monogatari*

The Tale of Genji is the earliest work of prose fiction still read for pleasure by a substantial audience today. Written at least in part by Murasaki Shikibu, a woman at the imperial court at Kyoto, its loose structure revolves around the love life of an emperor's son, the handsome, cultured Genji. The young man undergoes complex emotional and sexual vicissitudes, including involvement with the mother-figure Fujitsubo and with Murasaki, whom he adopts as a child and who becomes the true love of his life. Forced into exile as the result of a politically ill-judged sexual adventure, Genji returns to achieve wealth and power, then, grieving after Murasaki's death, retires to a temple. With Genji sidelined, the book moves on to a darker portrayal of the succeeding generation, before ending apparently arbitrarily—opinions differ as to whether the work is unfinished or deliberately inconclusive.

The Tale of Genji opens a window upon a distant, exotic world—the aestheticized, refined court life of medieval Japan. In this lies much of its enduring appeal. Fiction works its magic to bridge the historical, cultural, and linguistic gulf between Murasaki's world and our own. Much may be lost in translation, but modern readers are charmed to identify with familiar emotions in such a remote context, and fascinated when characters' responses and attitudes prove startlingly unexpected. **RegG**

Romance of the Three Kingdoms

Luó Guànzhong

Lifespan | *b. c.* 1330 (China), *d.* 1400
First Published | 14th century
Original Language | Chinese
Original Title | *Sanguó Yanyì*

Romance of the Three Kingdoms is one of the four foundational classic novels of Chinese literature. Spanning over a hundred years of Chinese history (184–280), this epic saga of the last days of the Hàn dynasty is a compilation of history and legend based on ancient storytelling traditions. It is attributed to a fourteenth-century scholar, Luó Guànzhong, who combined the many extant sources and stories into a continous capitivating epic.

The story begins with the outbreak of the rebellion against Emperor Líng led by a Taoist wizard, Zhang Jiao, and ends with the fall of Hàn (220) and the founding of the Jin dynasty. Much of the action takes place within the rival kingdoms of Wei, Shu, and Wu inhabited by magicians, monsters, powerful warlords, and legendary immortal heroes fighting for control over China. With its gripping plot, its classic heroes and villains, intricate intrigues, and spectacular battle scenes, the *Romance* is a literary masterpiece and can be considered the Chinese equivalent of *The Illiad*. The book has been translated into many languages, including French, English, Spanish, and Russian. The novel remains one of the most popular books in East Asia, cherished for its traditional wisdom, fantastic fairy tales, historical detail, and insights into war strategy. As a popular Korean proverb says: "One can discuss life after reading *Romance of the Three Kingdoms*." **JK**

The Water Margin

Shi Nai'an & Luo Guanzhong

Lifespan | *b. c.* 1296 (China), *d. c.* 1370
First Published | 1370
Alternate Title | *Outlaws of the Marsh*
Original Title | *Shuihu Zhuàn*

This novel is loosely based on exploits of the early twelth-century bandit Song Jiang and his group of outlaws. The text passed through centuries of professional storytelling and was edited, expanded, and revised before being printed in differing versions, the earliest surviving consisting of 120 chapters and dating from the early sixteenth century. This not only explains the textual inconsistency of the work, but also makes the exact dating and attribution of authorship impossible.

The first part of the novel describes in varying detail how the 108 heroes are brought together at their stronghold in the Liangshan marshes under their leader Song Jiang. United by their respect for the emperor who is misled by corrupt officials, the outlaws adhere to a strict code of chivalry: robbing the rich while helping the poor and showing fierce loyalty to their sworn brothers. In the latter part of the novel, the outlaws are granted an imperial amnesty and they help to suppress an uprising, a feat during which most of the outlaws are killed.

Although at times extremely violent and misogynous by today's standards, the novel captivates the reader's imagination through its multi-dimensional characters and the lively, colorful language. Read as a glorification of peasant revolution, the novel was eulogized in post-1949 China and was a favorite of Mao Zedong. **FG**

The Golden Ass

Lucius Apuleius

Written in the second century, *The Transformations of Lucius Apuleius of Madaura*, more commonly known as *The Golden Ass*, is the only Latin novel to survive in its entirety. Its style is racy, boisterous, and irreverent, as was the mode of professional storytellers of the time, but ultimately the story is a moral one.

The Golden Ass recounts the often ludicrous adventures of Lucius, a young member of the Roman aristocracy who is obsessed with magic, and who is accidentally turned into an ass. In his new guise, he witnesses and shares the misery of the slaves and destitute freemen who, like Lucius, are reduced to little more that animals by the treatment of their wealthy owners.

The book is the only surviving work of literature from the ancient Greco-Roman world that examines first-hand the conditions of the lower classes. Despite its serious subject matter, the tone is bawdy and sexually explicit, as Lucius spends time in the company of bandits and eunuch priests, witnesses adulterous wives, and is called upon to have intercourse with a beautiful woman. It is also a work that examines the contemporary religions of the time. In the final chapters of the book, Lucius is eventually turned back into a man by the goddess Isis. Lucius is subsequently initiated in the mystery cults of Isis and Osiris, and dedicates his life to them. At this point the rowdy humor of the earlier segments of the novel is exchanged for equally powerful and beautiful prose. *The Golden Ass* is a precursor to the literary genre of the episodic picaresque novel, in which Voltaire, Defoe, and others have followed, and its entertaining mixture of magic, farce, religion, and mythology make for a compelling read. **LE**

Lifespan | *b. c.* 123 (Madauros, modern Algeria), *d.* 170
First Published | 1469
First Published by | C. Sweynheim & A. Pannartz
Original Title | *Metamorphoses*

◔ Apuleius is candid and uproarious on the subject of sex, handled without a trace of Judaeo-Christian guilt or romantic sensibility.

◔ This illustration by Jean de Bosschere, from a 1923 edition of *The Golden Ass*, shows a woman being attacked with a firebrand.

Tirant lo Blanc

Joanot Martorell

Lifespan | *b.* 1413 (Spain), *d.* 1468
First Published | 1490
First Published by | Nicolou Spindeler (Valencia)
Original Language | Catalan

Cervantes wrote that this novel of chivalry was "a treasury of enjoyment and a mine of recreation." Joanot Martorell managed to combine his real-life experience as a knight with literary sources (such as Ramón Llull, Boccaccio, and Dante), enriching the whole with a fertile imagination that was nonetheless true to life. Consequently, *Tirant lo Blanc* is a vindication of chivalry and a literary corrective to the fiction, prone to fantasy, that glorified it. Realistic incidents of war and love predominate over shorter imaginary episodes, such as that of the maiden turned into a dragon.

Tirant himself is forged from the iron of the legendary knights, but his victories are the result of his skill as a strategist, his wisdom, and his fortitude, not of superhuman qualities. So he is thrown from his horse, he becomes exhausted, and he suffers wounds. His itinerary traces the actual geography of England, France, Sicily, Rhodes, and Constantinople, and the military campaigns are historical ones, such as the blockade of the island of Rhodes in 1444 and the attempt to reconquer Constantinople.

Today the novel retains its freshness due to its humor and the mischievous sensuality of many episodes: for example, a scene in which the maiden Plaerdemavida sends Tirant to the bed of his beloved Carmesina so that he can caress her as much as he likes. Plaerdemavida puts her head between the two of them so that the princess thinks that it is her servant who is lying next to her. **DRM**

La Celestina

Fernando de Rojas

Lifespan | *b. c.* 1465 (Spain), *d.* 1541
First Published | 1499
First Published by | Fadrique de Basilea (Burgos)
Original Language | Spanish

The title of the earliest editions of this book, *The Comedy or Tragicomedy of Calisto and Melibea*, referred to two young lovers, but very soon it was replaced by *La Celestina*, which is the name of an old witch who gives Melibea a magic potion that makes her fall in love with Calisto. The enigmas of the text do not end there. Its author, Fernando de Rojas, a scholar of Jewish descent, declared that he was continuing an incomplete, anonymous work, and this appears to be true. Indeed, all this mystery contributes to the profound impression made by the piece, which was read with passion and treated as common property.

The work has a theatrical arrangement designed to be read aloud (in public and in private), but not to be performed: it is what is known as a humanistic comedy. But the freedom and frankness of its dialogs, the psychological penetration of its many characters, the variety of its moods (from the educated and sophisticated to the very coarse), meant that this masterpiece influenced the emerging novel form much more than it did the theatre. Although it is proclaimed as a moral work, about illicit love and its punishments, as well as the evils of witchcraft and ambition, the book reveals a bitter perception of human nature and, often, a profound nihilism. Cervantes, who read it closely, accurately summed it up in a famous couplet with the last syllables missing: "A book of divine truth, if more of the human was hidden." **JCM**

Amadis of Gaul

Garci Rodríguez de Montalvo

Lifespan | *b. c.* 1450 (Spain), *d.* 1505
First Published | 1508
First Published by | Jorge Coci (Saragossa)
Original Language | Spanish

Amadis of Gaul is a primitive novel, a romance, and a book of chivalry, and it is the most relevant and original Spanish contribution to the Arthurian legend of adventures of knights-errant. There is evidence that the story has been popular since the mid-fourteenth century. The adventures circulated in three books that Rodríguez de Montalvo abridged and re-presented between 1470 and 1492, making room for his new saga of chivalry about the son of Amadis and Oriana, *The Exploits of Esplandian* (1510).

The debt of *Amadis* to the Arthurian legend is evident in actual incidents, such as the investiture of the knight, and in the prophecies and the appearance of magic. For example, Merlin and Morgan have their Castilian counterparts in Urganda the Unknown and Arcalaus the Magician. As in the genre of chivalry, the driving force is love and marriage. But *Amadis* remains remote from the troubadour theme of adulterous love for a married woman, which is at the heart of the chivalrous adventures that most influenced *Amadis*: Tristan of Leonis and Lancelot of the Lake. Oriana, with whom Amadis was in love, was the daughter, not the wife, of the King of Brittany. The cycle of Amadis, continued in *The Exploits of Esplandian*, incorporates moralizing elements, which make the text close to the theoretical treatise *School of Princes*. Montalvo's work is a Christianization of the knightly code, making the worn-out folkloric Arthurian model believable in the Spain of the Catholic kings. **MAN**

EL RAMO
QVE DE LOS QVA
TRO LIBROS DE AMADIS
DE GAVLA SALE.

LLAMADO LAS SERGAS DEL MVY
Esforçado Cauallero: Esplandian hijo del excelente Rey
Amadis Gaula.

AORA NVEVAMENTE ENMENDADAS
en esta impression, de muchos errores que en las
impressiones passadas auia.

CON LICENCIA.
Impresso en Alcala de Henares, por los herederos de IuanGracia
que sea en gloria, Año **M. D. LXXXVIII.**

A costa de Iuan de Sarria mercader de libros.

". . . and holding his shield in front of him, sword in hand, he advanced towards the lion; for the great shouts the King Garinter uttered could not deter him."

◉ On the title page of a 1588 edition of *Amadis of Gaul*, the amorous hero sets forth in search of chivalrous adventures.

The Life of Lazarillo de Tormes

Anonymous

First Published | 1554
First Published by | Alcalá de Henares, Spain
Original Title | *La vida de Lazarillo de Tormes y de sus fortunas y adversidades*

It is likely that it will never be known who wrote this work. For a long time it was suggested that the author was a nobleman, Diego Hurtado de Mendoza; recently, it has been suggested that it was Alfonso de Valdés, a highly educated imperial official with Erasmian tendencies. No one would think that this story was written by the participant himself. The tale concerns the life of the son of a woman who ended up living with a black slave—the child becomes a blind man's guide, the servant of several masters, and, finally, Toledo's town crier as a result of the influence of an archpriest who was certainly his mother's lover. Yet this short book would have us believe that, in all honesty, it is a letter in which Lázaro explains the "situation" that has aroused so much attention in the anonymous man or woman ("Your worship") to whom the text is addressed.

Everything the author wrote was already the material of folklore or from the repertory of anti-clerical tales; but what was radically new was the uninhibited tone and the skill with which he turned the whole collection into the experiences of just one life. This work was the start of the picaresque story, but it was also much more: the modern novel as a personal expression of the world. **JCM**

○ Lazarillo is subjected to an oral examination by a grotesque blind man in Goya's painting inspired by the picaresque novel.

Gargantua and Pantagruel

François Rabelais

Lifespan | *b. c.* 1494 (France), *d.* 1553
First Published | 1532–1564, by F. Juste (Lyon)
Full Title | *Grands annales tresueritables des gestes merveilleux du grand Gargantua et Pantagruel*

Published under the anagrammatic pseudonym of Alcofribas Nasier, *Pantagruel* established a whole new genre of writing, with a riotous mix of rhetorical energy, linguistic humor, and learned wit. In creating a comedy of sensory excesses, playing off various licentious, boozy, and lusty appetites, Rabelais also prefigures much in the history of the novel, from *Don Quixote* to *Ulysses*. Perhaps his greatest achievement is his free-spiritedness, which combines high-jinking vulgar materialism with a profound, skeptical mode of humanist wit.

The novel itself tells the story of the gigantic Gargantua and his son Pantagruel. The first book details fantastic incidents in the early years of Pantagruel and his roguish companion Panurge. The second, *Gargantua*, tracks back in time to the genealogy of Pantagruel's father, while satirizing scholasticism and old-fashioned educational methods. The third develops as a satire of intellectual learning, mainly through the heroic deeds and sayings of Pantagruel. In the fourth book, Pantagruel and Panurge head off on a voyage to the Oracle of the Holy Bottle in Cathay, which provides scenes for satire on religious excess. The fifth and most bitter book takes them to the temple of the Holy Bottle, where they follow the oracle's advice to "Drink!" The plot hardly rises to the level of picaresque, but there is a feast of mirth in the telling. **DM**

The Lusiad

Luís Vaz de Camões

Lifespan | b. c. 1524 (Portugal), d. 1580
First Published | 1572
First Published by | Antonio Gôçaluez (Lisbon)
Original Title | Os Lusíadas

The central thread of Camões's Portuguese national epic *The Lusiad* is a narrative of the voyage of Vasco da Gama, pioneering the sea route from Portugal to India in 1498. As a man of the Renaissance, besotted with the Latin and Greek classics, the author embroiders this story with a profusion of history and legend, giants and nymphs, and disputes of the gods on Olympus. Yet *The Lusiad* is grounded in the author's hard-won experience of the world. Camões lost an eye as a young man fighting the Moors in Morocco and spent seventeen years on travels around Portuguese outposts in India and East Asia.

There can be no pretence that *The Lusiad* is an easy read, yet its prolix verse reveals a novelistic imagination convinced that historical fact can be made more dramatic than romantic heroics. Da Gama is a surprisingly downbeat hero, wily and sensible, prone to error, and owing much to luck. Camões was a man of his time; he views the voyage to India as bringing civilization to the barbarians, and encourages his king to embark on a crusade to destroy Islam. Yet the author is no one's fool. He can see the horrors perpetrated under the disguise of spreading Christianity, the corruption that empire breeds, and the illusions of heroic conquest. English critic Maurice Bowra described *The Lusiad* as "the first epic poem which in its grandeur and universality speaks for the modern world." **RegG**

Monkey: A Journey to the West

Wú Chéng'en

Lifespan | b. c. 1500 (China), d. 1582
First Published | 1592, anonymously
Alternate Title | Monkey
Original Title | Xi You Ji

Monkey is an abridged translation of the popular Chinese folk novel *A Journey to the West*, attributed to a scholar and poet of the Ming dynasty, Wú Chéng'en. Based on traditional folktales, with its background in Chinese popular religion, mythology, and philosophy—in particular Taoism, Confucianism, and Buddhism—*A Journey to the West* became one of the four classical novels of Chinese literature.

The novel is based on the story of a famous Chinese Buddhist monk, Xuánzàng, who undertook a pilgrimage to India during the Tang Dynasty (618–907) in order to obtain Sanskrit texts called Sutras. Xuánzàng is accompanied by three disciples—Monkey, Pig, and Friar Sand—who help the monk to defeat various monsters and demons before they finally bring the Sutras back to the Chinese capital. Monkey himself reflects many traditional values in his quest for immortality, enlightment, atonement, and spiritual rebirth.

The book is unique in its combination of adventure, comedy, poetry, and spiritual insight. Working on many levels, it is thought to be at once an allegory for a spiritual journey toward enlightenment and a satire on inefficient and absurd bureaucracy, ancient or modern. **JK**

❯ The cunning and playful Monkey is a thorn in the side of the gods and a most useful companion on the journey to India.

Unfortunate Traveller

Thomas Nashe

Lifespan | b. 1567 (England), d. 1601
First Printed | 1594, by T. Scarlet for C. Burby
Full Title | The Unfortunate Traveller; or,
The Life of Jacke Wilton

The Unfortunate Traveller is perhaps the most brilliant of the Elizabethan novellas. Thomas Nashe tells the complex and disturbing story of Jack Wilton, an amoral young recruit in Henry VIII's army in France. Wilton has a series of dangerous adventures, starting when he worms his way into the good offices of the army's Lord of Misrule, a cider seller. He convinces the man that the king regards him as an enemy spy, and receives a great deal of free drink. Eventually the king is confronted and the plot is exposed, resulting in a whipping for Wilton (although we are aware that in the real world a harsher punishment would have befallen him). Wilton then travels throughout Europe, witnessing the destruction of the Anabaptist Utopia established in Münster, before reaching Italy where he witnesses even more spectacular vice and cruelty—specifically the executions of two criminals, Zadoch and Cutwolfe. Wilton returns to England, horrified at what he has seen, and vows to remain at home in the future.

The Unfortunate Traveller is disturbing and funny by turns, with every description undercut by a powerful irony, so we remain unsure whether travel is an enlightening or a pointless process. Nashe's descriptions, especially those of violence, are a brilliant and unsettling combination of the ordinary and the extraordinary—notably when the dying Zadoch has his fingernails "half raised up, and then underpropped . . . with sharp pricks, like a tailor's shop window half-open on a holiday." **AH**

Thomas of Reading

Thomas Deloney

Lifespan | b. c. 1543 (England), d. c. 1600
First Published | c.1600
Full Title | Pleasant Historic of Thomas of Reading;
or, The Sixe Worthie Yeomen of the West

In its diversity, Thomas of Reading parallels Chaucer's Canterbury Tales. It caters for all tastes: comic anecdotes, folk wisdom, reveling, adultery, murder, a journey, doomed love, rivalry between royal siblings, and a thief's cunning escape from punishment. Roughly following the fates of six West Country clothiers, Deloney interweaves their largely comic adventures with the tragic story of Margaret, a noblewoman whose father has fallen from grace and who works with one of the clothiers' wives until she falls in love with the king's brother.

On the surface an innocent collection of anecdotes, Thomas of Reading is also an astute social critique. It celebrates the clothiers but disparages their social superiors. Virtuous and generous, the clothiers form a close-knit community. The nobility, however, fails to live up to that ideal. When her aristocratic friends shun her, Margaret realizes that "the meane estate is best." She finds happiness among the clothiers until she consents to elope with the king's brother, a reentry into the nobility that is ruinous for the lovers.

Though often referred to as a novel, Thomas of Reading is hard to categorize because it lacks generic unity and does not focus on a central event or figure. But it is precisely the narrative's deviation from familiar literary patterns that makes it appear refreshingly new today. Thomas of Reading was written over four centuries ago, but its celebration of individual merit is modern. **FH**

Don Quixote

Miguel de Cervantes Saavedra

Lifespan | *b.* 1547 (Spain), *d.* 1616
First Published | 1605–1615, by Juan de la Cuesta
Full Original Title | *El ingenioso hidalgo Don Quixote de la Mancha*

Don Quixote has read himself into madness by reading too many books of chivalry, and so sets out to emulate the knights of old, first by getting himself some armour (out of pasteboard) and a steed (a broken-down nag), and then by getting himself knighted. He goes to an inn, which he thinks a castle, meets prostitutes whom he thinks high-born ladies, addresses them and the innkeeper, who is a thief, in language so literary that they cannot understand it, and then seeks to get himself knighted by standing vigil all night over his armour. The ludicrous transformation of the sacred rituals of knighthood into their ad hoc material equivalents parallels a similar desacralizing going on Europe at the time.

In all this it is the knowing reader, rather than the characters or the action, that is the implied subject of address. Cervantes here invents the novel form itself, by inventing the reader. Reading begins with the Prologue's address to the "idle" reader, and by implication extends throughout the first book, as Quixote's friends attempt to cure his madness by burning his books to stop him reading. In the process we meet readers, and occasions for reading, of all kinds. In 1615, Cervantes published a second book in which Don Quixote becomes not the character reading but the character read, as many of the people he meets have read Book I and know all about him. Indeed this combination of the always already read and the force of perpetual reinvention is what continues to draw the reader in. **JP**

> *"All kinds of beauty do not inspire love; there is a kind which only pleases the sight, but does not captivate the affections."*

The first part of *Don Quixote* was originally published in Madrid in 1605; fewer than twenty copies of the first edition survived.

The Travels of Persiles and Sigismunda

Miguel de Cervantes Saavedra

> *"The desires of this life are countless and linked together in an endless chain, a chain that sometimes reaches all the way up to Heaven and at others sinks into Hell."*

⊙ Painted by Jauregui y Aguilar in 1600, Cervantes was a man whose experience of life included maiming and enslavement.

Lifespan | *b.* 1547 (Spain), *d.* 1616
First Published | 1617
Original Title | *Los trabajos de Persiles y Sigismunda, historia septentrional*

Cervantes wrote the emotional dedication of this novel when he was close to death, having received the last rites, and he died without seeing it published. It is a Byzantine novel, an artificial, moralizing genre that was popular in the second half of the sixteenth century. With it Cervantes believed he would win the literary glory that could not be granted to a parody such as his *Don Quixote*.

The novel tells the story of the travels of Persiles, Prince of Thule, and his beloved Sigismunda, Princess of Finland, on their long and eventful journey to Rome, where the Pope blesses their love and joins them in marriage. Pretending to be siblings called Periander and Auristela, the heroes travel the icy Nordic wastes, overcoming numerous setbacks (separation, abduction, and shipwrecks), after which they continue their journey, still encountering many obstacles, through Portugal, Spain, France, and finally Italy, the capital of which symbolizes the unity and supremacy of the Church. The protagonists display perfect moral qualities: honor, virtue, fortitude, and chastity.

In this "northern story" Cervantes wrote a completely new kind of novel, combining intrigue with moral example, adventure with instruction, and he sought to encode within it an allegory of human life, a blend of good and evil, of chance and free will, in the human journey toward salvation. **DRM**

The Conquest of New Spain

Bernal Díaz del Castillo

Lifespan | b. 1495 (Spain), d. 1582 (Guatemala)
First Published | 1632
Original Title | Verdadera historia de la conquista de Nueva España

A large number of historical works written in the sixteenth century were devoted to the discovery and conquest of America, and were classified as "general," "natural," or "moral." This history by Bernal Díaz stands out for the words "true history" in its original title: that is, the events have been "seen and experienced." Aware that his position as a soldier made him vulnerable to the criticism of learned historians trained in rhetoric and fine writing, the author makes clear from the start his criterion of personal experience, one that is likely to become increasingly highly respected. He omits the imperialistic, ideological plan of the official histories in favor of experience.

This work is seen by some as the first novel of Spanish-American literature. It is a powerful exercise of memory that, written over three decades later, reconstructed the days leading to the discovery of the Aztec empire and the conquest of Mexico. The author brings his writing to life through a remarkable narrative skill, based on attention to detail and not excluding irony. His text, moreover, is constructed as a demanding, polemical argument; he strongly questions the inaccuracies of other historians of the same events and, instead of the unctuous panegyrics they wrote about the hero Cortés, he defends the work of the self-sacrificing soldiers who accompanied him. **DMG**

The Adventurous Simplicissimus

Hans von Grimmelshausen

Lifespan | b. 1622 (Germany), d. 1676
First Published | 1668
Original Title | Der abenteuerliche Simplicissimus
Pseudonym | German Schleifheim von Sulsfort

Unlike Cervantes' Don Quixote (with which this fascinating novel might be contrasted), The Adventurous Simplicissimus remains a relatively undiscovered gem of a picaresque novel. Indeed, it is a mystery why this portrait of a war-torn Europe nearly 400 years ago has not been "optioned" as a major Hollywood movie or Broadway musical.

Perhaps the first truly native German novel, it tells the partly autobiographical tale of a farm boy caught up in the Thirty Years War (1618–48), when lawless troopers laid the German countryside to waste and the population was decimated by battle, murder, famine, and fire. Grimmelhausen was only a child when he was caught up by warring Hessian and Croatian troops. As the boy narrator, he pulls no punches as he describes his family and other hapless peasants being captured and tortured by marauding mercenaries. The boy fails to understand the grim tableaux of extreme violence, rape, and pillage going on around him but nevertheless describes everything he sees with an engaging, ribald wit.

Laid out in episodic chapters, Simplicus's misadventures are engrossing and his descriptions of warfare are particularly gripping, not unlike a war reporter's dispatches. Farther, his occasional forays into fantasy and philosophy (this at a time when witchcraft, soothsaying, and prophecy were very much to the fore) brim with historical interest. **JHa**

The Princess of Clèves

Marie-Madelaine Pioche de Lavergne, Comtesse de La Fayette

Dates | *b*. 1634 (France), *d*. 1693
First Published | 1678
First Published by | C. Barbin (Paris)
Original Title | *La Princesse de Clèves*

M^rse M^lle^ne PIOCHE DE LA VERGNE.

Comtesse de la Fayette

"The Duc de Nemours was a masterpiece of Nature."

⏾ The Comtesse de La Fayette helped found the modern French literary tradition of the refined analysis of sentiments.

This profound story of a forbidden love that is enflamed and then resisted until it dies an unnatural death takes place in the court of Henry II of France during the last years of his reign (*c*. 1558). The young heroine of the title enters a society in which the adulterous love affairs of the powerful and beautiful constitute the only important action. Determined to protect the princess from this world even as she introduces her to it, her mother agrees to an early marriage with the Prince of Clèves whom the princess respects but cannot love passionately. She then falls deeply in love with the Duc de Nemours, the most sought after man at court, who returns her favors. Their love is never consummated, nor is it determined by accident or fate; it is both encouraged and resisted in the course of a series of scandalous scenes of intimacy and betrayal that were themselves received as a literary scandal by La Fayette's own society, not merely because they were regarded as implausible, but because of their evident singularity of purpose.

In one scene, Nemours, aware that the Princess is watching, steals a portrait of her belonging to her husband. Nemours watches the Princess' reaction, noting that she does nothing to intervene. In a second, the Princess confesses to her husband that she is in love with another man, while Nemours, that man, looks on unobserved and listens to her confession. In a third, Nemours, spied on by a servant of her husband, follows the Princess to her country house, where he sees her contemplating a picture in which he is represented. All of these scenes provoke overwhelming and unresolvable turmoil in the Princess but offer the modern reader an experience of compelling narrative and emotional complexity. **JP**

Oroonoko

Aphra Behn

The order of the original title indicates the direction of the narrative: from fictional romantic beginnings in the west African country of Coramantien, to the hero's enslavement, to the subsequent events in Surinam that Behn herself may very well have witnessed during the 1660s. The movement chronicled by the title chronicles also suggests the importance of Behn's text to the history of the novel, as well as its interest for modern readers.

Oroonoko is a noble warrior-prince, the grandson of the king, with whom he clashes over the beautiful Imoinda, Oroonoko's lover and the object of the king's jealous and impotent affections. In revenge for the lovers' persistence, the king sells Imoinda as a slave, while Oroonoko is betrayed into slavery. The two lovers meet again in Surinam, where they are renamed Clemene and Caesar. Anxious to be free, Caesar persuades the slaves to revolt against their tormentors; the slaves are caught and Caesar is whipped almost to death. Clemene is now pregnant and, fearing that their child will also become a slave, they make a murder-suicide pact that concludes in tragedy, though not quite as Caesar had envisaged.

Behn's extended short story gives a uniquely participatory role to the narrator, who is not only an "eyewitness" to many of the events she recounts as "true history," but refers to herself as an actor in the story. As a female, however, she is unable to save Oroonoko from the "obscure world" he has fallen into. The result is an oddly skewed general uncertainty that is still profoundly affecting: exotic romance mixes with an acute account of the slave trade and, in Surinam, the relations between the local Carib Indians, the English plantation owners, the slaves, and the Dutch. Historical, readerly, and authorial consciousness are here joined. **JP**

Lifespan | *b.* 1640 (England), *d.* 1689
First Published | 1688
First Published by | W. Canning (London)
Full Title | *Oroonoko; or, The Royal Slave*

"He had nothing of barbarity in his nature . . ."

○ Probably Britain's first female professional author, Aphra Behn was also by turns a merchant's wife and inmate of a debtors' prison.

Robinson Crusoe

Daniel Defoe

Robinson Crusoe is thought by many to be the first English novel. It has haunted the literary and critical imagination since its publication, returning in guise after guise: in *The Swiss Family Robinson*; in Luis Bunuel's 1954 film *The Adventures of Robinson Crusoe*, in Robert Zemeckis's 2000 movie *Castaway*; in J. M. Coetzee's novel *Foe*. The novel presents the reader with a fundamental, and fascinating, scenario. The prolonged and intense solitude of Robinson, shipwrecked on a desert island, strips him of the tools that have enabled him to live, returning him to a naked confrontation with the essential problems of his existence, including his personal connection with God, his relationship with the natural world that surrounds him, and with civilization as he knew it. In the vast silence even words begin to desert him. He tries to keep a diary in order to stay in touch with his civilized self, but as time goes by the small supply of ink that he salvages from the shipwreck starts, inevitably, to fail. He waters the ink down so that it might last him a little longer, but the words that he writes become fainter and fainter, until they disappear altogether, leaving the pages of Robinson's diary as blank as his horizon.

This encounter with total solitude does not lead Robinson to madness, to silence, or to despair. Rather, Robinson discovers in his enforced solitude the basis for a new kind of writing, and for a new kind of self-consciousness. Just as he fashions new tools for himself from the materials that he has at hand, so too does he invent a new way of telling himself the story of his life and of his world. It is this newly forged narrative form that Robinson bequeaths to a world on the brink of Enlightenment, the narrative form in which we continue, even now, to tell ourselves the stories of our lives. **PB**

Lifespan | *b.* 1660 (England), *d.* 1731
First Published | 1719, by W. Taylor (London)
Full Title | *The Life and Strange Surprising Adventures of Robinson Crusoe of York, Mariner, Written by Himself*

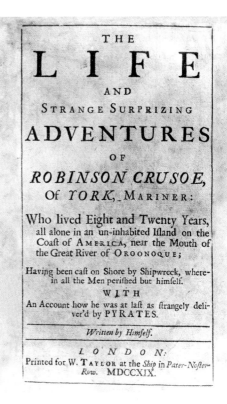

THE

LIFE

AND

STRANGE SURPRIZING

ADVENTURES

OF

ROBINSON CRUSOE,

Of *YORK*, MARINER:

Who lived Eight and Twenty Years,
all alone in an un-inhabited Ifland on the
Coaft of AMERICA, near the Mouth of
the Great River of OROONOQUE;

Having been caft on Shore by Shipwreck, wherein all the Men perifhed but himfelf.

WITH

An Account how he was at laft as ftrangely deliver'd by PYRATES.

Written by Himfelf.

LONDON:
Printed for W. TAYLOR at the *Ship* in *Pater-Nofter-
Row*. MDCCXIX.

◉ The first edition of the novel was published as the memoirs of a mariner, with no mention of the name of the actual author.

◉ John Hassall produced this cover image for a 1908 edition of *Robinson Crusoe*, designed primarily to appeal to children.

Love in Excess

Eliza Haywood

Lifespan | b. 1693 (England), d. 1756
First Published | 1719
First Published by | W. Chetwood (London)
Full Title | Love in Excess; or, The Fatal Enquiry

Eliza Haywood's three-volume tale recounts the experiences of one Count D'elmont as he finds—and loses—his way along the often treacherous path to romantic and sexual fulfillment. Part the dashing hero and part the profligate rake, through the fault of others as well as his own, D'elmont becomes enmeshed in a series of compromising relationships. D'elmont's devotion to the lovely Melliora is the object of dispute throughout, and when this relationship is not directly under threat from such ambitious women as Alovisa, D'elmont himself indirectly threatens it through his participation in a range of complex ménages à trois. Letters intended to circulate privately between lovers are continuously intercepted, and lovers are farcically substituted to comic and tragic effect. However, as the title of the piece suggests, it is not long before D'elmont and others learn the importance of romantic moderation in a world otherwise characterized by passionate excess. When he replaces the mercenary marital ambitions of his early years with the mature embracing of conjugal affection, the hero eventually chooses his spouse based upon moderation, fidelity, and reserve.

Along with Robinson Crusoe, Love in Excess was one of the most popular early eighteenth-century novels. Haywood's frank treatment of desire and sexual passion renders her a key figure in the feminine tradition of amatory fiction that runs from Aphra Behn to Delarivier Manley and beyond. **DT**

Moll Flanders

Daniel Defoe

Lifespan | b. 1660 (England), d. 1731
First Published | 1722, by W. Chetwood (London)
Full Title | The Fortunes and Misfortunes of the Famous Moll Flanders

Appearing three years after Defoe's most famous work, Robinson Crusoe, Moll Flanders stands as one of the important precursors to the modern novel. Narrated in the first person, it is the autobiography of Moll Flanders. Moll leads an eventful life, which includes travel with gypsies, five marriages, incest, prostitution, and twelve years as one of London's most notorious and successful thieves. When she is finally caught, she escapes the death sentence with the help of a minister who encourages her to repent her evil ways. Transported to Virginia with one of her husbands, she buys her freedom, sets up as a planter, and increases her amassed wealth with the income from a plantation. In her old age, she returns to England, where she resolves to spend the rest of her years in penitence for the life she has led.

Defoe paints an unforgettable picture of the seamy underside of England. A masterful gold digger, conniver, and survivor, Moll exploits her formidable talents to evade poverty. The novel's power lies in the force and attraction of Moll's character, which catches the reader's imagination and sympathy. But it also lies in the delightfully subversive moral of the tale that seems not to be that wickedness will be punished, but rather that one can live a profligate life and not only get away with it, but in fact prosper from it too. **JSD**

⬤ Defoe was a prolific journalist who wrote over 500 works on crime, economics, politics, and the supernatural, as well as novels.

Gulliver's Travels

Jonathan Swift

Everyone knows at least something about *Gulliver's Travels*. Variously read and rewritten as a children's story, a political satire, a travel text, an animated film, and a BBC television series, Swift's perennial classic has been bowdlerized, added to, argued over, and adapted, but remains a constant presence in any widely accepted canon of English Literature.

The narrative follows the adventures of innocent abroad, Lemuel Gulliver, from misguided youth, through the distorting mirrors of Lilliput and Brobdignag, onto the more enigmatic islands of Laputa, Balnibarbi, Glubbdubdrib, Luggnagg, and Japan, followed by the crucially important land of the Houyhnhms and the Yahoos. Swift masterfully inserts such locations into the blank spaces of eighteenth-century maps (actually included in the first edition) and follows the conventions of the contemporary travel narrative with such precision that the real and the fantastical coalesce. Our only guide is Gulliver, whose unwavering confidence in the superiority of the Englishman and of English culture is slowly and inevitably picked apart by the assorted characters he encounters on his travels—some minute, some huge, some misguided, some savage, others guided entirely by reason. All offer comments to and perspectives on Gulliver, which force readers to question their own assumptions. It is a satire that may have lost some of its immediate political force, but one that still has a sting in its tail for us today, made all the more effective as Swift stages the climax of the tales within the bounds of the English nation-state. The vehemence with which Gulliver eschews the company of his fellows for his horses is an image that will remain with readers forever—for it is here that it becomes clear that he is not the main target of the satire. We are. **MD**

Lifespan | *b.* 1667 (Ireland), *d.* 1745
First Published | 1726, by B. Motte (London)
Full Title | *Travels Into Several Remote Nations of the World, by Lemuel Gulliver*

A page from Swift's manuscript of *Gulliver's Travels* displays a clear and disciplined hand at the service of a lucid brain.

Self-consciously superior, Gulliver enjoys terrifying the Lilliputians with a demonstration of English firepower.

A Modest Proposal

Jonathan Swift

Lifespan | *b.* 1667 (Ireland), *d.* 1745
First Published | 1729
First Published by | S. Harding (Dublin)
Pseudonym | Isaac Bickerstaff

The full title of *A Modest Proposal* is *A Modest Proposal for Preventing the Children of Poor People from Being a Burden to Their Parents, Or the Country, and for Making Them Beneficial to the Public*. The title is long but Swift's propagandizing pamphlet is as succinct and excoriating a work of satire as is possible to conceive. Penned after its author returned to Dublin to become Dean of St. Patrick's, the work expresses in equal measure contempt for English policy in Ireland and for Irish docility in taking it. A prolific writer, political journalist, and wit, Swift was skilled at transforming outrage to glacial irony.

The proposal here is anything but modest: Irish children can become less burdensome to their families and the state by being eaten by the rich. Children might become quality livestock for poor farmers. Young children, Swift suggests, are "nourishing and wholesome" whether they are "stewed, roasted, baked, or broiled," while older, less obviously tasty offspring might be spared for breeding purposes. The advantages of Swift's proposal include reducing the numbers of "Papists," providing much-needed funds for the peasantry, boosting national income, and stimulating the catering trade. Swift also satirizes the callousness of the English protestant absentee landowners whose economics value mercantilism ahead of labor power. While, across his oeuvre, Swift is notoriously complicated in his politics, in this memorable pamphlet, we find him at his savage best. **DH**

Joseph Andrews

Henry Fielding

Lifespan | *b.* 1707 (England), *d.* 1754
First Published | 1742, by A. Millar (London)
Full Title | *The History of the Adventures of Joseph Andrews, and of his Friend Mr. Abraham Adam*

Joseph Andrews actually begins as a "sequel" to *Shamela*, Fielding's short burlesque of Richardson's sensationally popular *Pamela*. However, it quickly surpasses the original, displaying Fielding's progress toward an original fictional voice and technique, and revealing his moral preoccupation with the question of "good nature" as the basis for real virtue.

In a comic inversion of typical gender roles, Joseph (Pamela's brother and a servant in the Booby household) virtuously resists the lustful advances of Mrs. Booby, not because he lacks masculine vigor (unthinkable for a Fielding hero), but because he faithfully loves the beautiful Fanny Goodwill. When he is dismissed by his frustrated mistress, Joseph embarks on a picaresque series of adventures with Parson Abraham Adams, who overshadows Joseph as the most vigorous presence in the novel. Adams' virtue is matched by his naivety, continually entangling him and his companions in difficulties that test his good nature. Nabokov, among others, noted the cruelty of *Joseph Andrews*; Fielding seems to relish placing his virtuous heroes and heroines in compromising positions. The foolishness and eccentricity of both the Parson and Joseph, however, are vindicated by their physical and moral courage, their loyalty, and their benevolence—the comic morality of *Don Quixote* is an obvious model. Fielding manipulates the conventions of romance to bring about a happy ending, with a wink to his readers to acknowledge its artificiality. **RH**

Memoirs of Martinus Scriblerus

J. Arbuthnot, J. Gay, T. Parnell, A. Pope, J. Swift

Lifespan | births from 1667, deaths from 1745
Born | Ireland, Scotland, England
Full Title | *Memoirs of the Extraordinary Life,
Works, and Discoveries of Martin Scriblerus*

The seventeen short chapters of the *Memoirs of Scriblerus*, finalized by Pope, offer a series of narratives that originated in a project begun in 1713, and continued at informal meetings of the Scriblerus Club, which met in the lodgings occupied by Dr. Arbuthnot in St. James's Palace. The club began to break up with the departure of Swift from London, and completely disbanded with the Queen's death in 1714. The project was, however, continued by correspondence, making early use of the recently established postal service.

The *Memoirs* draw on the rich store of satirical writing in Europe: from classical sources such as Horace and Lucian to later writers such as Rabelais, Erasmus, and Cervantes. The "learned phantome" Martinus Scriblerus has with "capacity enough, dipped into every art and science, but injudiciously." The Scriblerians target the modern age as the site of vaunting, false taste, corruption, and bad faith. In their critique of modern writing in the expanding print culture, they contrast ancient grandeur, passion, dignity, reason, and common sense with modern excess and venal behavior.

Here many strategies are employed: direct narrative, comic analysis, and exposition. Some of the works of the Scriblerians are themselves related to the *Memoirs*: for instance, Pope's *Dunciad*, Swift's *Gulliver's Travels*, Gay's *The Beggar's Opera*. Nor are the *Memoirs* without modern descendants, such as J. K. Toole's *A Confederacy of Dunces* (1980). **AR**

The PHIZ *and* CHARACTER *of an* ALEXANDRINE Hyper-critick & Comentator.

Nature her self shrunk back when thou wert born,
And cry'd the Work's not mine ——
The Midwife stood agast; and when she saw
Thy Mountain back, and thy distorted legs,
Thy face half minted with the stamp of Man,
And half o'ercome with Beast, stood doubting long,
Whose right on Thee were more:
—— then art all ov'r, Error, Soul and Body,
The first young tryal of some unskill'd Power,
Rude in the making Art, an Ape of Jove. &c.

| Awd by no Shame, by no Respect controul'd, | Spleen to Mankind his envious Heart possest, |
| In Scandal busy, in Reproaches bold. | And much he hated All, but most the Best. |

"Ye gods! annihilate but space and time, And make two lovers happy."

⬤ An anonymous 1729 print represents Pope as a monkey in a papal tiara, and below cites his own satirical verses against him.

Pamela

Samuel Richardson

Lifespan | *b.* 1689 (England), *d.* 1761
First Published | 1742
First Published by | C. Rivington (London)
Full Title | *Pamela: or, Virtue Rewarded*

Pamela sparked an unprecedented degree of public debate. The novel consists of letters written by fifteen-year-old Pamela Andrews, the beautiful servant of wealthy Mr. B—. Pamela resists Mr. B—'s increasingly forceful efforts to seduce her, until, chastened by her virtue, he marries her. *Pamela* does not end with the heroine's marriage, however, but follows her struggle to establish herself in her new role, and to gain acceptance from Mr. B.—'s peers.

Pamela is a novel about the abuse of power and the correct way to resist. For all Pamela's insistence that "virtue" is her only defense, she is really empowered by language—something that makes her resistance to her social superior a political as well as a moral act. Despite plotting a provincial servant girl as his heroine, Richardson's critique of the upper classes is limited; Pamela's "reward," after all, is to ascend into their ranks. Pamela herself suggests that Mr. B—'s crime is not merely his sexual incontinence, but his failure to fulfill his pastoral role as her "Master."

Pamela was praised by some as a handbook of virtuous behavior, while others denounced it as thinly disguised pornography. A slew of parodies appeared in *Pamela*'s wake (most notably Fielding's *Shamela*), arguing that Pamela manipulates her sexuality for personal gain; that Richardson's moral intentions for the novel had been corrupted by the titillating subject matter. These ambiguities are what make *Pamela* so fascinating, for the modern reader no less than Richardson's contemporaries. **RH**

Clarissa

Samuel Richardson

Lifespan | *b.* 1689 (England), *d.* 1761
First Published | 1749
First Published by | Samuel Richardson (London)
Full Title | *Clarissa: or, The History of a Young Lady*

Richardson's ambitious narrative of tragic seduction is traced through the hundreds of letters written between Clarissa Harlowe, her confidante Anna Howe, the charming, but also cruel and duplicitous seducer Lovelace, and a supporting cast of family and acquaintances. In reading them, we find ourselves slowly absorbed into their individual personalities. Meaning is thus accumulated in each successive letter, but their sequence has its own dramatic structure and tension, maintained for the novel's length. Through this we are made to confront not only Lovelace's terrible manipulations, but also his power of allusive evocation, which flow from the same source. In a similar manner, Clarissa triumphantly claims her constant self, virtuous through and beyond death, but is reliant on a complementary capacity for self-deception that uses the measure of her pen to calculate the distance between thought and action in those she observes. Henry James perhaps found in *Clarissa* a model for his own prose of suspicion.

Like Marcel Proust's *Remembrance of Things Past* (1913–27), the sheer scale of *Clarissa* means that it can seem a novel that is more talked about than read. Yet for those readers who are prepared to spend time with it, *Clarissa* offers a proportionate amount of satisfaction. **DT**

⊙ Vice triumphant: a smug Lovelace carries off the virtuous Clarissa, as depicted by French Romantic artist Edouard Dubufe.

Tom Jones

Henry Fielding

Lifespan | *b.* 1707 (England), *d.* 1754
First Published | 1749
First Published by | A. Millar (London)
Full Title | *The History of Tom Jones, a Foundling*

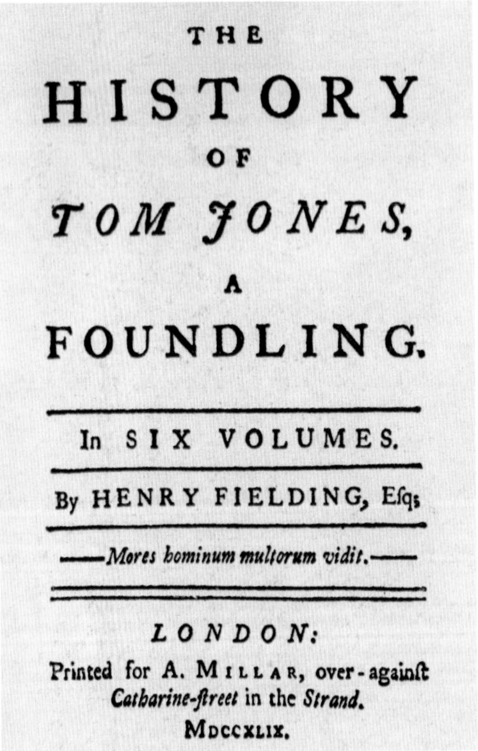

THE

HISTORY

OF

TOM JONES,

A

FOUNDLING.

In SIX VOLUMES.

By HENRY FIELDING, Efq;

——*Mores hominum multorum vidit.*——

LONDON:

Printed for A. MILLAR, over-againſt
Catharine-ſtreet in the *Strand*.
MDCCXLIX.

🔘 The title page of the first edition of *Tom Jones*, published in 1749, bears the Latin tag, "He saw the customs of many men."

🔘 Michael Angelo Rooker's illustration of 1780 captures the essentially benign comic verve of Fielding's satire.

Tom Jones is a picaresque comic novel in which we follow the wanderings and vicissitudes of the engaging hero as he, born illegitimate, grows up, falls in love, is unjustly expelled from his foster-father's home, and roams England. Warmhearted but impetuous, Tom is repeatedly involved in fights, misunderstandings, and bawdy adventures. However, he is eventually narrowly saved from the gallows and happily united with his true love, Sophia, while his enemies are variously humiliated.

This is not only a long and complicated novel but also a great one. Anticipating Dickens at the peak of his powers (Dickens reportedly said, "I have been Tom Jones"), Fielding describes, with gusto, glee, mock-heroic wit, and sometimes satiric scorn, the rich variety of life in eighteenth-century England, from the rural poor to the affluent aristocrats. Like the paintings of his friend William Hogarth, Fielding's descriptions betray the sharp observation of a moralist who is well aware of the conflict between Christian standards, which are supposed to govern social conduct, and the competing power of selfishness, folly, and vice in the world. In the society he depicts, Good Samaritans are few and far between, and snares await the innocent at every turn. Nevertheless, like an ironic yet benevolent Providence, Fielding guides the deserving lovers through the world's corruption to their happiness.

Following the example of Chaucer, Fielding relished farcical entanglements and sexual comedy: his hero is no virgin. Fielding was a brilliant experimentalist (influencing Sterne), and *Tom Jones* is surprisingly postmodern: the narrator repeatedly teasingly interrupts the action to discuss with the reader the work's progress—while critics are urged to "mind their own business." **CW**

Fanny Hill

John Cleland

Lifespan | *b.* 1709 (England), *d.* 1789
First Published | 1749
First Published by | G. Fenton (London)
Original Title | *Memoirs of a Woman of Pleasure*

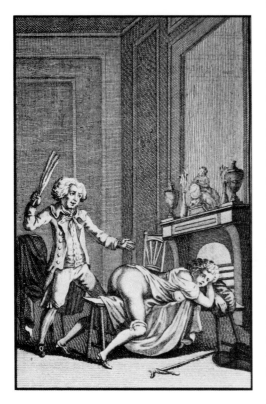

"Truth! Stark naked truth ..."

⊛ Like Cleland himself, the illustrator of *Fanny Hill* presents
erotic acts in a style calculated both to stimulate and amuse.

This book is undoubtedly the most famous erotic novel in English. Published in 1749 (though possibly written, in part, some time earlier), it is set in a realistically depicted eighteenth-century London, firmly connecting John Cleland's work with that of his contemporaries, Richardson, Fielding, and Smollett.

At the beginning of the work, Fanny Hill is a beautiful fifteen-year-old country girl. Having lost her "innocence," she learns to exploit her sexuality to survive and advance herself in the world. In fashioning this controversial and illicitly popular work, Cleland drew on the largely French fashion for erotic fiction, and the existing genre of the "whore's autobiography," which tended to present the whore's life as a warning against the miseries attendant on sexual indulgence. Strikingly, Cleland feels no compulsion to punish Fanny for her promiscuity, and she ends the novel happily married.

Aware that much pornography suffered from repetitiveness, Cleland eschews "crude" or slang terminology for sexual acts or organs, instead producing a dazzling array of metaphors and similes from a seemingly endless supply. Although he unflinchingly depicts the physiological pleasure of sex, for both men and women, Fanny's sexual appetites are surprisingly conservative—while relishing various heterosexual acts, she is conflicted about her own lesbian encounter, and repeatedly speaks with disgust about male homosexuality.

After surviving more than two centuries' worth of moral opprobrium, Cleland's masterpiece has now emerged as an important work in the development of the novel. It still, however, divides readers, between those who find its vibrant depiction of sexuality liberating, and those who see it as a transparent vehicle for male gratification. **RH**

Peregrine Pickle

Tobias George Smollett

The exploits of the egotistical Peregrine Pickle are the subject of Tobias Smollett's second novel. While the episodic construction and interpolated narratives are reminiscent of *Roderick Random*, *Peregrine Pickle* is more than a repetition of an earlier narrative. Peregrine is a fallible hero and this is emphasized by the frequently critical tone of the third-person omniscient narrator. The son of a short line of moderately successful merchants, Peregrine is despised by his own mother and adopted by his eccentric uncle, whose exploits provide much of the humor in the early part of the novel. Peregrine enjoys a privileged education that compounds his own misguided sense of self-importance. He undertakes the Grand Tour, traveling through Europe amid a profusion of excess, sexual intrigue, and rakish conduct and, on his return to London, attempts to ingratiate himself into fashionable society and political circles. He aspires to marriage with an heiress as a way of rising to the ranks of the nobility. However, Peregrine's ambitions are thwarted by his own destructive and corrupt behavior, demonstrating his inability to conduct himself in a manner appropriate to his financial standing. Eventually, during his incarceration in the Fleet prison, Pickle reforms. He marries Emilia and adopts the life of a country gentleman removed from the evils of fashionable society.

Despite the work's scatological humor, Smollett's satire engages with some serious concerns, such as the arbitrariness of French justice and the threat posed to social order by contemporary commercialization. Peregrine has to learn the responsibilities and privileges of social position before he can truly value his ultimate reward: a quiet life of felicity with his beloved Emilia. **LMar**

Lifespan | *b.* 1721 (Scotland), *d.* 1771
First Published | 1751 (revised 1758)
First Published by | T. Smollett (London)
Full Title | *The Adventures of Peregrine Pickle*

"... a pert jackanapes."

⬥ Peregrine rescues the scantily clad Emilia from a burning inn, a typical picaresque episode from Smollett's satire.

The Female Quixote

Charlotte Lennox

Lifespan | *b.* 1727 (U.S.), *d.* 1804
First Published | 1752
First Published by | A. Millar (London)
Alternate Title | *The Adventures of Arabella*

Charlotte Lennox's second novel, *The Female Quixote*, is a forerunner of Jane Austen's *Northanger Abbey*. In the absence of any broader education, the understanding of Lennox's heroine Arabella about the world around her has been drawn entirely from seventeenth-century French romances. Lennox comically displays the pitfalls of Arabella's failure to distinguish between fiction and reality. She expects lovers to fall at her feet, sees danger and disguise in commonplace situations, and breaks social strictures regarding appropriate female behavior. Arabella's illusion that the world conforms to the conventions of the romance novel gives her a confidence in herself and her position that is overturned by her eventual re-education. By showing the absurdity of Arabella's fantasy, Lennox subtly exposes how little power women in eighteenth-century society actually enjoyed. Rationalism triumphs over fantasy in the novel, and Arabella learns about her real position in society.

Although modern readers may find Lennox's comedy repetitive at times, the novel is still saved by the likeability of its main character—readers are disappointed when she finally succumbs to social convention, and touched by the genuine hilarity of the situations she creates for herself. Yet while readers may laugh at Arabella's naivety, Lennox's exposure of the dangers of letting the imagination run wild does bring into question the eighteenth-century practice of limiting women's education. **EG-G**

Candide

Voltaire

Lifespan | *b.* 1694 (France), *d.* 1778
First Published | 1759, by G. & P. Cramer (Geneva)
Original Title | *Candide; ou, L'Optimisme*
Given Name | François-Marie Arouet

Voltaire's *Candide* was influenced by various atrocities of the mid-eighteenth century, most notably an earthquake in Lisbon, the outbreak of the horrific Seven Years' War in the German states, and the unjust execution of the English Admiral John Byng. This philosophical tale is often hailed as a paradigmatic text of the Enlightenment, but it is also an ironic attack on the optimistic beliefs of the Enlightenment. Voltaire's critique is directed at Leibniz's principle of sufficient reason, which maintains that nothing can be so without there being a reason why it is so. The consequence of this principle is the belief that the actual world must be the best of all possible worlds.

At the opening of the novel, its eponymous hero, the young Candide, schooled in this optimistic philosophy by his tutor Pangloss, is ejected from the magnificent castle in which he is raised. The rest of the novel details the multiple hardships and disasters that Candide and his various companions meet in their travels. These include war, rape, theft, hanging, shipwrecks, earthquakes, cannibalism, and slavery. As these experiences gradually erode Candide's optimistic belief, the novel mercilessly lampoons science, philosophy, religion, government, and literature. A caustic and comic satire of the social ills of its day, *Candide's* reflections remain as pertinent now as ever. **SD**

⊙ A romantic illustration from an 1809 edition of *Candide* is captioned: "My captain . . . killed all that stood in the path of his fury."

Mon capitaine.... tuait tout ce qui s'opposait à sa rage.

Candide, Ch. XI.

Rasselas
Samuel Johnson

Lifespan | *b.* 1709 (England), *d.* 1784
First Published | 1759
First Published by | R. & J. Dodsley (London)
Full Title | *The Full History of Rasselas, Prince of Abissinia*

Dr. Samuel Johnson undoubtedly achieved greatest renown, and earned his place in history, with his seminal *Dictionary of the English Language*. But less well known is his first and only novel, *Rasselas*, published four years later, which tells the story of its eponymous hero, the Prince of Abissinia. Rasselas lives in the happy valley in which he and the other royal sons and daughters are kept secluded from the vagaries of human life, with their every want and desire provided for, until they succeed to the throne. By the age of twenty-six, however, Rasselas is dissatisfied and restless with this life in which he wants for nothing. Guided by a learned man, Imlac, he escapes from the valley in the company of his sister, Nakayah, and sets out to explore the world and discover the source of true happiness.

A parable in the literary tradition of Bunyan's *Pilgrim's Progress*, Rasselas's adventures and lengthy conversations provide a vehicle for Johnson's moral reflections on an astonishingly broad range of topics. These include poetry, learning, solitude, reason and passion, youth and age, parents and children, marriage, power, grief, madness, and desire.

Although Dr. Johnson's abilities as a novelist are overshadowed by his strengths as a moralist in this book, *Rasselas* remains of interest today both as a testament to the predominant concerns of the Enlightenment, and for the humor and universality of Johnson's reflections on these topics. **SD**

"Human life is everywhere a state in which much is to be endured, and little to be enjoyed."

🔊 Johnson's princely hero looks uncomfortable with a tool of manual labor as he explores a wider experience of life.

Julie; or, The New Eloise

Jean-Jacques Rousseau

Lifespan | *b.* 1712 (Switzerland), *d.* 1778 (France)
First Published | 1760
First Published by | Duchesne (Paris)
Original Title | *Julie; ou, la nouvelle Héloïse*

Julie, Jean-Jacques Rousseau's first novel, is modeled on the medieval story of *Eloise*, and the forbidden love between herself and her tutor, Abelard. Yet in *Julie*, Rousseau transforms secrecy and sinfulness into renunciation and redemption, in which it is the pupil and not the master who makes the central claim on our attention. Julie's relationship with her teacher, Saint-Preux, reformulates the twelfth-century conflict between bodily desire and religious purpose into a characteristically eighteenth-century study of right behavior. In this epistolary novel, Rousseau links the classical tradition of civic virtue with its Enlightenment counterpart of domestic order and the new birth of individual feeling, which was to eventually culminate in the Romantic movement.

As befits this apparently paradoxical transition, the thematic structure of *Julie* is both rigorous and odd. In the first half, Julie alternately resists and is consumed by Saint-Preux's passion, which leads to his banishment from her father's house. By the second half, he has returned to the new estate formed by Julie and her husband, Wolmar, where all three happily co-exist in the cultivation of both mind and landscape. In this static Elysium, the dangerous desires of the novel's first part are ethically recapitulated. For readers, this allegorical mirroring of virtue and desire makes Julie's triumph somewhat suspect. However, the irreducibility of the problem makes the difficulty of Rousseau's novel a persistently contemporary one. **DT**

Émile; or, On Education

Jean-Jacques Rousseau

Lifespan | *b.* 1712 (Switzerland), *d.* 1778 (France)
First Published | 1762
First Published by | Duchesne (Paris)
Original Title | *Émile; ou, De l'Éducation*

Jean-Jacques Rousseau's philosophical novel charts the ideal education of an imaginary pupil, Émile, from birth to adulthood. Émile is not taught to read until he himself thirsts for the knowledge, and his experience of literature is deliberately limited. According to Rousseau, *Robinson Crusoe* supplies the best treatise on an education according to nature, and it is the first book Émile will read.

Rousseau's educational philosophy regarding religion was also radical. He advocates delaying a child's religious education to prevent indoctrination or ill-conceived notions about divinity. Émile is thus not taught according to one doctrine but is equipped with the knowledge and reason to choose for himself. Early adolescence is a time which demands learning by experience rather than academic study. Émile is seen to pose and answer his own questions based on his observations of nature. During the transition between adolescence and adulthood Rousseau begins to focus on Émile's socialization and his sexuality.

In the final book, "Sophie: or Woman," Rousseau turns his attention toward the education of girls and young women. In this book, he disapproves of serious learning for girls on the basis that men and women have different virtues. Men should study truth; women should aim for flattery and tact. Rousseau's novel concludes with the marriage of Émile and Sophie, who intend to live a secluded but fruitful life together in the country. **LMar**

The Castle of Otranto

Horace Walpole

Lifespan | *b.* 1717 (England), *d.* 1797
First Published | 1765
First Published by | W. Bathoe & T. Lowndes (London)
Pseudonym | Onuphrio Muralto

The Castle of Otranto, Horace Walpole's only novel, enjoys pride of place as the founding text of the gothic genre. The central narrative revolves around the prince of Otranto (the tyrannous Manfred) and his family, and develops from a mysterious incident at the inception of the story: the death of Conrad, Manfred's son and heir, crushed under the weight of a gigantic plumed helmet. This supernatural occurrence unleashes a train of events that leads to the restoration of the rightful heir to the title of Otranto. These events take place principally in the family castle, well appointed with vaults and secret passageways, which becomes the scene, as well as the embodiment, of mysterious deaths and hauntings. Largely a fantasy set in the chivalric Middle Ages, the novel nevertheless deals in violent emotions, and places its characters in psychological extremis. Cruelty, tyranny, eroticism, usurpation—all have become, along with the setting, the common currency of gothic narratives.

Walpole claimed that the basic story first came to him in a dream, and that he had been "choked by visions and passions" during its composition. Concerned for the reception his work might receive, he not only first published it under a pseudonym, but went so far as to pretend that it was the translation of a sixteenth-century Italian manuscript. The whimsy of Walpole's literary experiment is mirrored in the construction of his own gothic revival mansion, Strawberry Hill, which can still be visited today. **ST**

The Vicar of Wakefield

Oliver Goldsmith

Lifespan | *b.* 1730 (Ireland), *d.* 1774 (England)
First Published | 1766
First Printed by | B. Collins for F. Newbury (London)
Written | 1761–1762

The Vicar of Wakefield, as the title suggests, tells the story of Dr. Primrose and his large family, who on the surface live an idyllic life in a rural parish. This tranquillity is disrupted by sudden impoverishment, which sets the plot in motion. The plot, though thin, includes thwarted marriages, unscrupulous behavior, lost children, fire, imprisonment, various disguises, and mistaken identity. Vulnerability attenuates the situation of all the characters who, like the vicar himself, are generally virtuous, but also susceptible to foolish and naive behavior. The vicar is the novel's main narrator, which in itself produces a number of comic ironies; to fill in gaps, however, there are numerous stories within stories. The novel contains sentimental set pieces, but its overall register is richly comic. Both the disasters that befall the characters and the equally dramatic reversals of fortune are amusing.

One of the most striking aspects of Goldsmith's minor classic, clearly, is its heterogeneity. Not only is the plot untidy and digressive, but the text itself includes non-fictional elements, such as poems, sermons, and various disquisitions on politics, legal punishment, and poetics. All this reflects the diversity of Goldsmith's output as a writer: he was a poet, a playwright, and a novelist, but also took on a great deal of hack work to make a living. **ST**

❯ Among the book illustrators of the time, Thomas Rowlandson made twenty-four illustrations for Goldsmith's masterpiece.

TRISTRAM SHANDY. VOL.II.Ch. 6.P.12
Corporal Trim reading the Sermon to
Shandy's Father, Dr. Slop & Uncle Toby.

W. Hogarth delin.   Printed for C. Cooke, Paternoster Row May 25. 1793.   C. Grignion sculp.

Tristram Shandy

Laurence Sterne

The book's full title, *The Life and Opinions of Tristram Shandy, Gentleman*, suggests a loosely biographical work, but the eponymous author-narrator scarcely gets so far as his third year of life, and remains studiously circumspect about his own opinions. While little of Tristram's life is divulged, the book generates an intimate relationship between the processes of reading and writing. Through digressions and interruptions, narrative expectations are dismantled with a freedom and vivacity that eliminates the very notion of plot. With its inventive conversation between spoken idiom and written circumspection, it is mischievously friendly, and as lewdly suggestive as anything that had ever been written. This book is the archetypal "experimental" novel, prefiguring modern and postmodern fiction. From Rabelais, Laurence Sterne develops comic fantasy, bawdy grotesque, and learned wit. From Cervantes, Sterne takes the picaresque combustion of narrative form, modulating into a more quixotic, but nevertheless realistic, dissection of human folly. Portraits of Tristram's father, his mother, Uncle Toby, and others build up an oblique but intimate representation of family life. The comic brilliance of the literary surface obscures Sterne's deeper psychological realism, his almost Proustian analysis of sentimentality, notably the well-meant but ridiculous erudition of Tristram's father. The modulation of Toby's interest in warfare into his love affair offers a fine comic characterization of the links between speech, personality, and the groin.

For all its garrulous intimacy, Sterne leaves much to the imagination. The book's diplomatic irony provides a subtle critique of the English gentleman, from class and sexuality to all the unacknowledged delicacies of property and propriety. **DM**

Lifespan | *b.* 1713 (Ireland), *d.* 1768 (England)
First Published | 1759–1767
First Published by| J. Dodsley (London)
Serialized | Nine volumes

○ Laurence Sterne's complex imagination found expression through wit, lewdness, sentiment, and garrulous rhetoric.

○ William Hogarth produced prints of scenes from *Tristram Shandy* in the 1760s that have defined visualization of the book ever since.

A Sentimental Journey

Laurence Sterne

Lifespan | *b.* 1713 (Ireland), *d.* 1768 (England)
First Published | 1768, by G. Faulkner (Dublin)
Full Title | *A Sentimental Journey Through France and Italy by Mr. Yorick*

Overshadowed by *Tristram Shandy*, Sterne's shorter novel is nevertheless a comic gem. Combining autobiographical anecdote, incidental fiction, and pastiche of travel writing, the book chronicles the journey of Yorick and his servant La Fleur through France. The Grand Tour, that education in continental manners and art so important to the English gentleman, figures as an implied object of satire. However, there is not much grand about this journey; rather, we are confronted with a belittling and microscopic investigation of sensibility.

More than a mere story, the principal pleasure of this novel is its playful manipulation of conversational intimacy. The manner of the telling takes priority, while the author-narrator leaves different incidents suspended between sentimental interpretations and a more knowing realism. One notable example is a man lamenting his dead ass, related as an allegory from nature of how feeling toward an animal might provide an edifying example of humane fellow-feeling. The mourner has nevertheless overworked and starved the ass he mourns. Swiftly juxtaposing this with the unfeeling lash given to the animals on which the author's transport depends, the allegory is shot through with double entendres. Such gulfs between sentiment, material conditions, and narrative point of view are always close to the surface, even if financial considerations, earthly passions, and a continuously implied eroticism are politely deflected. **DM**

The Man of Feeling

Henry Mackenzie

Lifespan | *b.* 1745 (Scotland), *d.* 1831
First Published | 1771
First Published by | T. Cadell (London)
First Published | Anonymously

The first anonymously published edition of *The Man of Feeling* sold out in little more than six weeks, likening its cataclysmic effects to the stir caused by the publication of Rousseau's *The New Eloise* a decade earlier. Marking a crucial cultural moment in the history of literature, the "editor" of *The Man of Feeling* purports to offer his readers an historical account of the experiences of young Harley, the eponymous man of feeling himself. Each fictional episode that follows is designed with the express intention of exploring a particular emotive reaction, be it an emphatically non-erotic identification of a London prostitute, or the circulation of affection between a father and his estranged offspring. The represented emotions range broadly from pity, sympathy, and empathy to charity and benevolence.

The turns of plot in *The Man of Feeling* seem secondary to the careful cultivation of emotional response. Each tableau is linked to the next without much discernible concern for the generation of narrative suspense, while other sections, the editor informs his reader, are either missing or incomplete. Even so, the emphasis that this fiction brought to bear on the emotional responses of both character and reader alike would prove crucial to a range of eighteenth-century writers, but would also provide much of the aesthetic foundation that later novelists could safely take for granted. As Dickens so well understood, the reader of fiction was there primarily to be moved. **DT**

Humphry Clinker

Tobias George Smollett

Lifespan | *b.* 1721 (Scotland), *d.* 1771
First Published | 1771
First Published by| W. Johnston & B. Collins (London)
Full Title | *The Expedition of Humphry Clinker*

Smollett's last novel is an epistolary narrative detailing the travels through Britain of Matt Bramble and his company, including the servant hero, the impoverished Humphry Clinker. The letters reveal the characters of their very different authors. Matt Bramble is a hypochondriac misanthrope, his sister Tabitha, an aging husband-hunter, Jery Melford their nephew, an exuberant Oxford student, his sister Lydia a naive sentimental romantic, and Tabitha's maid, Wyn Jenkins, a virtually illiterate social climber. These varied points of view provide a lively and wide-ranging narrative that engages the reader directly in deciphering not only the progress and adventures of the party but also the targets of Smollett's satire. The narrative allows for multiple interpretations of the events that unfold, and there is no one authoritative version. However, Clinker's moral integrity and religious zeal are constant throughout the accounts.

The party continually encounters mishap, with Clinker invariably at the center. Such mishaps include duels, romantic intrigues, jealous encounters, a false imprisonment, and innumerable disputes both large and small. Finally the love matches are made, and the plot tied up. Unlike Smollett's other titular heroes, Clinker reaps a reward that is unquestionably deserved. His naivety regarding the ways of the world and his morality are admirable traits, against which the flaws of his companions and his society are clearly exposed. **LMar**

"The capital is become an overgrown monster; which like a dropsical head, will in time leave the body and extremities without nourishment and support."

⊙ A suitably caricatural representation of the hypochondriac Matt Bramble engaged in a close encounter with a young widow.

The Sorrows of Young Werther

Johann Wolfgang von Goethe

Lifespan | *b.* 1749 (Germany), *d.* 1832
First Published | 1774
First Published by | Weygandsche Buchhandlung
Original Title | *Die Leiden des Jungen Werthers*

"I shall perish under the splendor of these visions!"

🔺 German artist Johan Tischbein's famous portrait of his friend Goethe in the Roman Campagna was painted in 1786.

▶ French composer Jules Massenet's late nineteenth-century operatic version of *Werther* is tender and romantic.

The Sorrows of Young Werther, the novel that first made Goethe internationally famous, tells a story of a young man afflicted by a rather extreme dose of eighteenth-century sensibility: Werther is a case study of over-reliance on emotion, imagination, and close introspection. Our hero is sent to the fictional village of Walheim on family business, where he meets and promptly falls in love with Lotte. This attractive young woman, meanwhile, is engaged to another, the rational and rather dull local official Albert. Once established, this triangle places Werther at a complete impasse, and the impossibility of a happy resolution drives him to take his own life. Part of the novel's intrigue has always been its loose relation to actual events: Goethe's relationship with Charlotte Buff, who was engaged to his close friend, Kestner, and the love-related suicide of another friend, Karl Jerusalem (who borrowed pistols from an unsuspecting Kestner for the deed). Another element of the novel's success was its effective use of the epistolary form. The narrative unfolds initially through Werther's letters to a single correspondent. When Werther's psychological state deteriorates, a fictive editor steps in, and the last part of the novel is his arrangement of Werther's final scraps and notes.

The novel struck a powerful chord in its own time, and its appearance was followed by what can only be called Werther mania: would-be Werthers wore his trademark blue jacket and yellow waistcoat; there was even Werther eau de cologne, and china depicting scenes from the novel. Legend also has it that there were copycat suicides, which alarmed Goethe, because his depiction of Werther was more critical than laudatory. The novel was extensively revised in 1787 for a second version, which has become the basis for most modern editions. **ST**

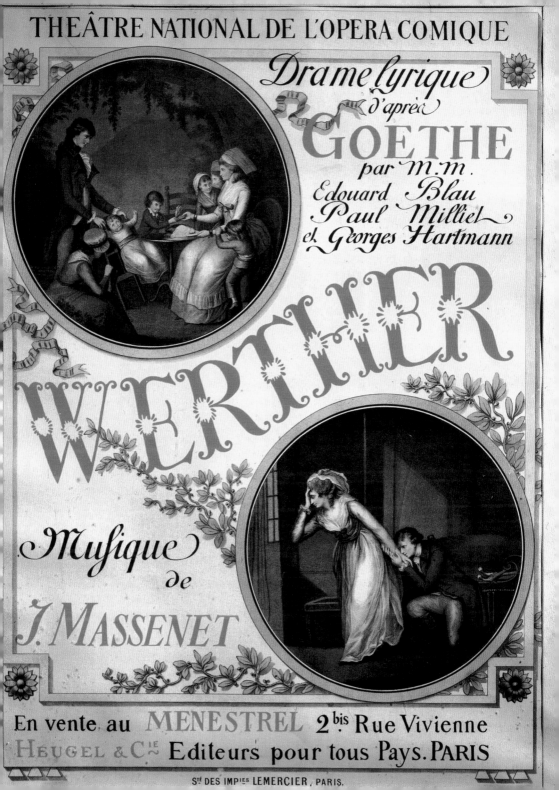

Evelina

Fanny Burney

Lifespan | *b.* 1752 (England), *d.* 1840
First Published | 1778, anonymously
Full Title | *Evelina; or, The History of a Young Lady's Entrance into the World*

🌑 Fanny Burney was a diarist as well as a novelist, recording memorable experiences of life at the court of George III.

Samuel Johnson remarked of the twenty-six-year-old Fanny Burney's debut novel, *Evelina*, that it "seems a work that should result from long experience and deep and intimate knowledge of the world." Her sense for character psychology and awkward social comedy are amply on show in *Evelina*. Adapting the form of the epistolary novel from predecessors such as Samuel Richardson, Burney traces the fortunes of her young heroine as she travels up from the country to negotiate the social world of London for the first time. Here she encounters a stream of suitors and some long-lost relatives, whose grotesque lack of breeding drives her to the brink of physical collapse. She is eventually acknowledged as her absent father's true daughter. One of the novel's great strengths is the way in which Burney filters the bustle of London society through the shy consciousness of Evelina. In addition, the growth of her feelings toward the righteous Lord Orville is subtly and ironically rendered. Love-struck teenagers often enjoy writing down the names of their crushes, and there is a charming naturalism in the way Burney has Evelina mention Lord Orville slightly more often than necessary.

Evelina's comedy of manners may itself feel a little "mannered" at times, especially when set next to the novels of the writer she influenced most directly, Jane Austen. Burney is vulnerable to the same accusations about the limits of her social scene as are sometimes leveled at Austen—there is no urban squalor here. But for its depiction of psychological interactions in a solidly imagined social setting, *Evelina* marks a high point in late eighteenth-century fiction—one that proves that this kind of wit did not suddenly begin in 1811 with Austen's *Sense and Sensibility*. **BT**

Reveries of a Solitary Walker

Jean-Jacques Rousseau

Jean-Jacques Rousseau—philosopher, social and political theorist, novelist, and proto-Romantic—was one of the eighteenth century's leading intellectuals. *Reveries of the Solitary Walker*, the last book he wrote, is a wonderfully lyrical, heartfelt, and somewhat obsessive account of an aging man's reckoning with his past. Rousseau achieved a great deal of notoriety during his lifetime from a succession of popular and hugely important works. By attacking the state religion and denouncing contemporary society as morally corrupt, he not only challenged the establishment but also the Enlightenment thought that prevailed in the Parisian salons. Rousseau became the subject of a long-lasting campaign of derision and humiliation, and eventually was forced into exile.

The *Reveries of the Solitary Walker* finds Rousseau, "alone and neglected," torn between his love of solitude and his yearning for company, trying to assuage his crippling self-doubt and irrepressible need to address his persecutors. The novel's lasting appeal stems from this compelling tension between his sober, meditative philosophizing and his impassioned rage against the ills of society. Rousseau wants to show that he is at peace with himself, blissfully disengaged from society, and yet he is also constantly betrayed by his sense of injustice and pride. The combination of his circumstances and his inner turmoil make him one of the first—and most fascinating—modern examples of the prototype of the literary outsider.

Reveries is therefore a vital precursor to the great works of isolation and despair by writers such as Dostoevsky, Beckett, and Salinger, which have had such an enormous impact on the development of the novel in the twentieth century. **AL**

Lifespan | *b*. 1712 (Switzerland), *d*. 1778 (France)
First Published | 1782
First Published in | *Oeuvres Complètes* (Poinçot)
Original Title | *Les Rêveries du Promeneur Solitaire*

CHOCOLAT POULAIN
GOUTEZ ET COMPAREZ! QUALITÉ SANS RIVALE

98. JEAN-JACQUES ROUSSEAU

◉ Rousseau is depicted as the "solitary walker" on this card, one of a series on French writers given away with Poulain chocolate.

Dangerous Liaisons

Pierre Choderlos de Laclos

Lifespan | *b.* 1741 (France), *d.* 1803 (Italy)
First Published | 1782
First Published by | Durand (Paris)
Original Title | *Les Liaisons Dangereuses*

A recent series of successful film, theater, and ballet adaptations suggest that this gripping tale of love, deceit, and the art of seduction still holds a powerful grip on our collective imagination. Written by a lieutenant in the French army, *Dangerous Liaisons* manages to shock and delight in equal measure. The action takes place among the aristocratic circles of pre-revolutionary France and centers on the ruthless, charming libertine Valmont and his rival, one-time lover, and partner in crime, Merteuil. Valmont is gifted with wealth, wit, and intelligence, and leads an idle life guided by a self-imposed code of conduct: to seek ever-greater glory in his seduction of unsuspecting society women. Merteuil is a sexually liberated young widow but, unlike Valmont, she has to play the role expected of her by society. Together, they create a complex web of relationships based on betrayal, lies, and sexual misconduct. Their attempts to outdo the other have disastrous consequences as jealousy and hubris undermine their own deeply flawed principles.

Laclos makes exemplary use of the popular epistolary form, because it is precisely in the delicious recounting of the events that his two leading characters derive their pleasure—a pleasure shared by the reader as we indulge in the eloquence and exquisite cruelty of this captivating masterpiece. **AL**

🌕 Laclos's novel, illustrated here by Georges Barbier, presents a
harsh vision of savage relationships conducted in civilized tones.

Confessions

Jean-Jacques Rousseau

Lifespan | *b.* 1712 (Switzerland), *d.* 1778 (France)
First Published | 1782, in *Oeuvres Complètes*
First Published by | Poinçot (Paris)
Part 2 Published | 1788, by P. Du Peyrou

Unpublished until after his death, Rousseau's *Confessions* are a landmark of European literature, and perhaps the most influential autobiography ever written. This is a work that had a defining impact not only on the novel, but on the development of the autobiography as a literary genre. Although Rousseau predicts having no imitators in this vein, he was seriously mistaken. Goethe, Tolstoy, and Proust all acknowledged their debt to Rousseau's pioneering attempt to represent his life truthfully—warts and all.

Rousseau famously argued that man's innate good nature was corrupted by society. Yet in *Confessions* Rousseau acknowledges that he often behaved appallingly. One incident in particular stands out. When working as a young servant in the household of a wealthy Geneva aristocrat, Rousseau describes how he stole valuable old ribbon and then blamed the theft on a servant girl, Marion. Rousseau comments that he was "the victim of that malicious play of intrigue that has thwarted me all my life," simultaneously accepting responsibility for his actions and denying it.

Rousseau freely admits the contradictory nature of his character, one he felt was forced on him by circumstances beyond his control. Indeed, in line with his desire not to mislead the reader, he undoubtedly exaggerates his own sins and misdemeanors just to prove his point, which serves as yet another paradox of this compelling, frustrating, and vitally important work. **AH**

The 120 Days of Sodom

Marquis de Sade

Lifespan | *b.* 1740 (France), *d.* 1814
First Composed | 1785
Original Title | *Les 120 Journées de Sodome, ou l'École du libertinage*

The Marquis de Sade composed *The 120 Days of Sodom* while confined in the Bastille, and his only manuscript was lost to him forever when the revolutionary mob stormed the prison on July 14, 1789. Without his knowledge, it passed into the hands of an aristocratic French family and remained there until a corrupt German edition appeared in 1904. The first accurate publication was printed in several volumes between 1931 and 1935.

The book's stated intention is to appall propriety, morality, and the law. It is set at the end of the reign of Louis XIV, a time when war profiteers were gathering vast fortunes quickly and covertly. A group of wealthy libertines decides to pool the female members of their families as sexual resources to be held in common, and they minutely plan an immense and prolonged debauchery. Cycles of suppers devoted to a particular sexual vice are inaugurated, before the participants formalize their perversions in a festival of absolute criminal licence in a remote, impregnable, and luxurious château. A complex set of statutes are formulated to preserve order in the midst of myriad acts of rape and murder, and it is the arithmetical and permutational aspect of the sexual violence that is perhaps the novel's key. Alone in his cell, de Sade worked out a meticulous, purely imaginative, masturbatory economy of gradual gratification, fixated on images of debasement and cruelty that have been studied as much by clinicians as by gourmands of extremity. **RP**

Anton Reiser

Karl Philipp Moritz

Lifespan | *b.* 1756 (Germany), *d.* 1793
First Published | 1785
First Published by | Friedrich Maurer (Berlin)
Last Part Published | 1790

In many ways, the autobiographical protagonist of *Anton Reiser* can be seen as a less fortunate "brother" of Wilhelm Meister, the hero of Goethe's famous 1796 novel, *The Apprenticeship Years of Wilhelm Meister*. Both young men are theater enthusiasts and have unrealistically high hopes of what they will achieve as actors on the stage; but, while Wilhelm, the son of a wealthy patrician, wins friends for his theatrical enterprise quite easily, Anton Reiser has to struggle against poverty and real and imagined humiliations that undermine his self-confidence.

The first two parts of Moritz's "psychological novel"—as he called it himself—deal with Anton's unhappy childhood: how he is sent off to work for a pietist but ruthlessly exploitative hatter; and how, even after he is allowed to attend a grammar school in Hannover and makes good progress there, he is tortured by thoughts of having to depend on public charity and being made fun of by the other pupils. The last two parts show Anton seeking consolation in solitary reading, but also yearning to make a name for himself as an actor, for which he sacrifices the less glamorous prospects that studying at university would have opened up for him.

Anton Reiser provides valuable insights into a world that was previously neglected by literature—that of the town artisans and apprentices, and their working and living conditions. It is also a moving account of an individual's struggle against obstacles outside of, and within, himself. **LS**

Vathek

William Beckford

Lifespan | *b*. 1760 (England), *d*. 1844
First Published | 1786, by J. Johnson (London)
Original Language | French
Original Title | *Vathek, Conte Arabe*

Originally written in French, when its author was only twenty-one, *Vathek* was inspired in part by William Beckford's sumptuous coming-of-age celebrations at his magnificent country estate of Fonthill in 1781.

Vathek is at once a comic farce and a tragic parable, drawing on a prodigious body of learning in order to both revel in and parody the "oriental tale" popular in England since the translation of the *Arabian Nights*. The tale follows the exploits of the Caliph Vathek and his variously grotesque associates on an inexorable journey to damnation—a gloriously inevitable fate given the excesses of his court and his complete disregard for conventional morality. Beckford consciously fabricates a fantastical "eastern" setting to explore individual freedoms in a way that parallels his own controversial predilections—his sexual intemperance culminated in European exile soon after completing the text, following a scandal with a young aristocrat.

Described on its publication in England as a combination of "the sombrous grotesque of Dante" with "the terrific greatness of Milton," *Vathek* influenced numerous literary figures including Hawthorne, Poe, Swinburne, and Byron. While it offers a remarkable insight into early orientalist fantasies of the "east," it is this quality, perhaps, that ensures its longevity; the potent combination of sexual and sensory inquiry with a prevailing sense of childlike wonder offers potentially instructive parallels with our own contemporary obsessions. **MD**

WILLIAM BECKFORD ESQ.ᴬ

London published as the Act directs April 19, 1798 by J.Willon

"Being much addicted to women and the pleasures of the table, he sought by his affability, to produce agreeable companions . . ."

◔ This flattering 1798 portrait endows the decadent Beckford with a look of fierce independence and passionate intensity.

Justine

Marquis de Sade

Lifespan | *b.* 1740 (France), *d.* 1814
First Published | 1791
First Published by | Nicolas Massé (Paris)
Original Title | *Justine, ou Les Malheurs de la vertu*

🔺 The Marquis de Sade is presented in portrait and at his prison writing table in this nineteenth-century allegorical sheet.

▶ De Sade's unfortunate and virtuous heroine prepares to submit to one of a series of acts of violent abuse and sexual degradation.

It is in this novel's full title, *Justine, ou les malheurs de la vertu*, that we can perhaps find the most cogent definition of its continuing power to shock and absorb. De Sade's heroine is good, and because she is good, she suffers without redemption. Like Rochester's earlier poetry in England, De Sade's novels take human bodies and transform them into components within a copulating machine. In the case of *Justine*, it is a device that mathematically converts virtue into suffering with a remainder of readerly pleasure. Justine declares her scruples, flees, pleads for the lives of others, and professes her faith. In return, she is stripped, bitten, slapped, whipped, and penetrated, orally, anally, and vaginally.

In this way, de Sade makes explicit what is only implicit in the eighteenth-century novels of sentiment such as Richardson's *Clarissa*, and Rousseau's *Julie; or, the new Héloïse*. The woman's capacity to feel purely and empathetically makes her an object of fascination and degradation, perpetually brought down and renewed. This violent eroticism in the relationship between reader and heroine is properly named "sadistic." As Roland Barthes observed, where we wish to imply, to suggest, to create meaning through metaphors, de Sade asserts, combines, exposes. Yet, in doing so, he draws us into a desirous complicity: we feel the compulsive rhythm of what is performed on Justine's body, even as she does not. The signs of our spiritual existence, our religion, morality and self-governance, are relentlessly translated into our corporeal body: limbs, lips, breasts, and buttocks. That radical reduction saw de Sade committed to an asylum and his texts destroyed; the continuing challenge *Justine* offers to the comforts of our authority will not so easily be erased. **DT**

A Dream of Red Mansions

Cao Xueqin

Lifespan | *b. c.* 1715 (China), *d.* 1764
First Published | 1791
Original Title | *Hóng lóu mèng*
Given Name | Cao Zhan

Considered the greatest masterpiece of traditional Chinese fiction, this huge, largely autobiographical novel chronicles in detail the decay of an aristocratic family in eighteenth-century Beijing. Also known as *The Story of the Stone*, it is, all at the same time, a Bildungsroman, a novel of sentiment, a repository for Taoist, Buddhist, and Confucian traditions, and, with its more than 400 characters, a mosaic of society at the height of the Qing dynasty. Its author, Cao Xueqin, died after completing only eighty chapters, but although this left most strands of the complex plot unresolved, the unfinished manuscript soon gained considerable popularity.

The novel begins with a prologue telling of a sentient stone that enters the mortal realm with the help of a Buddhist monk and a Taoist priest, and which is reincarnated as Jia Baoyu, the capricious heir of the mighty Jia clan and protagonist of the novel. The stone's fateful entanglement with a crimson flower is mirrored in Baoyu's relationship to his frail cousin Daiyu, who later dies when Baoyu is married to a different cousin against his will.

The novel and especially its twelve main female characters have widely featured in poetry and painting. More recently, a theme park, feature movies, television series, and computer games have paid homage to the lasting popularity and cultural significance of this novel in China. **FG**

The Adventures of Caleb Williams

William Godwin

Lifespan | *b.* 1756 (England), *d.* 1836
First Published | 1794, by B. Crosby (London)
Alternate Title | *Things as They Are; or,*
The Adventures of Caleb Williams

William Godwin's *Caleb Williams*, one of the most important and widely read novels of the 1790s, offers readers a potent mixture of personal history and political commentary. As a young man, self-educated and orphaned, Caleb finds himself in the employ of an enigmatic but apparently honorable local aristocrat, Falkland. Caleb's curiosity, however, leads him to uncover an unsavory fact about Falkland, namely that he had been the murderer of a tyrannous neighboring noble, a crime for which he allowed two innocent members of the local peasantry to be tried and executed. The stories of all these men illustrate the novel's central critique of an ossified class system that sanctions oppression and makes a mockery of the law. Falkland's response to Caleb's discovery of his secret is to follow, frame, and persecute him. This had its historical analogue in the suspension of civil liberties when England declared war on Revolutionary France, including those of writers suspected of holding seditious views.

Readers have sometimes felt that the novel suffers to the extent that it is a fictional vehicle for Godwin's radical political philosophy, articulated in his *Enquiry Concerning Political Justice* (1793). Yet because of the psychological drama at the center of the plot, it has also been received as a gothic novel. For modern readers, the extreme nature of Caleb's persecution has distinctly Kafkaesque overtones. **ST**

The Interesting Narrative

Olaudah Equiano

Lifespan | *b.* 1745 (Nigeria), *d.* 1797 (England)
First Published | 1794, by T. Wilkins (London)
Full Title | *The Interesting Narrative of the Life of Equiano; or, Gustavus Vassa, the African*

Olaudah Equiano's *The Interesting Narrative* is a landmark text and a crucial read for anyone seeking to understand the complex issue of race in Britain and the lineage of Afro-British writing. This is the earliest first-hand account in English of the trans-Atlantic slave trade, presenting the full horror of the experience in order to justify and promote the abolitionist agenda. In a hostile political and literary climate, the success and popularity of Equiano's text succeeded in furthering this agenda.

The text follows Equiano's journey from his kidnapping in Africa, and incorporates slavery in the British navy; work on slave ships; the purchase of his own freedom; work on plantations; and finally a return to England. It is an explicitly religious meditation that simultaneously forges an identity for the author that is self-consciously both British and African. This is highlighted in his choice of names. While on abolitionist tours, in publications, and in public, he referred to himself as Gustavus Vassa; in this text his African identity is brought to the foreground, while the narrator is acutely conscious of his existence as both. The recent revelation that Vassa/Equiano may have been born in South Carolina, and that consequently he constructed his African identity, only enhances the remarkable insights the text offers into the ambiguities of such experience. As a result, it is as relevant now as it has ever been. **MD**

Olaudah Equiano,
or
GUSTAVUS VASSA,
the African.

Published March ... 1789 by G. Vasa

> "*I offer . . . history of neither a saint, a hero, nor a tyrant.*"

⬥ This portrait of the ex-slave author as an impeccable eighteenth-century gentleman appeared in the first edition of the book.

The Mysteries of Udolpho

Ann Radcliffe

Lifespan | *b.* 1764 (England), *d.* 1823
First Published | 1794
First Published by | P. Wogan (Dublin)
Original Language | English

An essential gothic novel, *The Mysteries of Udolpho* remains a classic today. It tells the story of Emily St. Aubert, who is imprisoned by her evil guardian, Montoni, in his grand gothic castle, Udolpho. Terror and suspense dominate Emily's life within Udolpho, as she struggles to withstand Montoni's perfidious schemes and her own psychological breakdown. The narration has a dream-like quality, which reflects Emily's confusion and horror, and lends emphasis to the psychological battle she must engage in to survive her nightmares. Radcliffe's spectacular descriptions of landscapes are used partly to reflect emotion in the novel, particularly melancholia and dread—but also tranquillity and happiness. Radcliffe's characters are varied and well drawn, but where she really succeeds is in the creation of a likable and strong heroine.

Although rarely considered a feminist, Radcliffe conveys a significant underlying message about the importance of female independence. Despite her apparent weakness and the extremity of her fears, Emily ultimately defeats Montoni through the strength of her own free will and her moral integrity. *The Mysteries of Udolpho* offers not just the supernatural horrors created by the imagination; the true horror that Emily must face is the dark side of human nature, a more potent terror than anything conjured by the mind. **EG-G**

Wilhelm Meister's Apprenticeship

Johann Wolfgang von Goethe

Lifespan | *b.* 1749 (Germany), *d.* 1832
First Published | 1795–1796
First Published by | Unger (Berlin)
Original Title | *Wilhelm Meisters Lehrjahre*

Despite Goethe's forbidding stature, this is a delightful novel. Goethe is engagingly worldly and wry, telling a story of intellectual development and education with warmth, in what is often considered the classic example of the Bildungsroman.

Initially disillusioned by unrequited love, Wilhelm Meister travels forth on various adventures, and joins a group of itinerant players who afford him apprenticeship in life. Offering a group portrait of the life of theater, much imbued with Shakespeare, the novel celebrates and then undermines the theatrical vocation. The humane realism of the early parts of the novel deepens and modulates into something altogether more unusual once the surfaces of theatricality and social performance are penetrated, and mysterious characters hint at a different kind of literary symbolism and intellectual purpose. Goethe builds a richly ironic account of human self-development across its knowingly flimsy plot structure, somehow combining the ironizing good humor of Fielding's *Tom Jones* with something more philosophical. Not to be confused with *Wilhelm Meister's Travels*, this novel is especially recommended reading for deluded thespians and wannabe aesthetes. **DM**

> Mignon, the heroine of Goethe's *Wilhelm Meister*, represented by early twentieth-century Czech artist Franz Doubek.

The Monk

M. G. Lewis

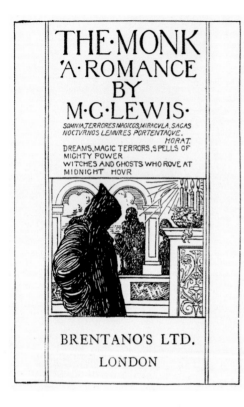

THE·MONK
'A·ROMANCE
BY
M·G·LEWIS·

SOMNIA,TERRORES MAGICOS,MIRACVLA, SACAS
NOCTVRNOS LEMVRES PORTENTAQVE.
HORAT.
DREAMS,MAGIC TERRORS,SPELLS OF
MIGHTY POWER
WITCHES AND GHOSTS WHO ROVE AT
MIDNIGHT HOVR

BRENTANO'S LTD.
LONDON

"Who but myself has passed the ordeal of youth, yet sees no single stain upon his conscience? . . . I seek for such a man in vain."

⊙ A 1913 edition updates Lewis's eighteenth-century horror story to appeal to the taste of early twentieth-century decadents.

Lifespan | *b.* 1775 (England), *d.* 1818 (at sea)
First Published | 1796
First Published by | J. Bell (London)
Full Title | *The Monk: A Romance*

An extravagantly, possibly gratuitously, dark gothic novel, M. G. Lewis's *The Monk* caused controversy when it was first published, and remains shocking and chilling today. Unlike Ann Radcliffe, whose gothic fiction always comes with rational explanations, Lewis embraces the supernatural alongside the most extreme and gruesome acts of human depravity and cruelty. The monk of the title is Ambrosio, who is admired for his piety. As we discover, however, Ambrosio is truly the most hypocritical and evil representative of the Catholic church imaginable. His crimes begin relatively modestly but quickly escalate into the darkest and most blasphemous acts possible. Nor is he the only character so perfidious—the prioress of a nearby convent shows that she, too, is capable of barbaric excesses of cruelty. The novel offers an extreme picture of how power, perhaps especially the power held by spiritual figures, can corrupt absolutely.

Despite a convoluted plot, the novel moves at a good pace and the story flows easily. Although Lewis does not employ extravagant descriptions of landscape, *The Monk* is nonetheless a highly visual novel, conjuring vivid and thus memorable images of horror and destruction. This is ultimately a story of the complete crushing of innocence, with no softening redemptive message to lighten the horror. *The Monk* continues both to fascinate and to shock today, and few modern novelists could compete with the sheer grotesqueness of Lewis's vision. **EG-G**

Camilla

Fanny Burney

Lifespan | *b.* 1752 (England), *d.* 1840
First Published | 1796
First Published by | T. Payne and T. Cadell (London)
Original Language | English

The full title of this novel is *Camilla; or, A Picture of Youth* and this is precisely what Burney gives us in this, her third novel. *Camilla* tells the story of a lively and spirited young girl's entry into the world, of her eventual coming of age. Camilla's story and those of her sisters—the beautiful Lavinia and the angelic, though disfigured and scarred, Eugenia—display the ideals, temptations, loves, doubts, and jealousies that both inform and trouble the passage from youth to adulthood. Burney's characters, especially the women, are realistic, enabling the reader to be easily drawn in to their joys, sorrows, and concerns.

Burney's novel also gives a wonderful depiction of public entertainment and pleasure in late eighteenth-century England as well as the manners and fashions that made up the social theater—in particular, the social restrictions and even dangers that confronted young women. Burney uses the emotional extremes of popular gothic fiction to show that danger can be found close to home.

In *Northanger Abbey*, Jane Austen's narrator alludes to Burney's novels *Camilla* and *Cecilia*, saying they are "work in which the greatest powers of the mind are displayed, in which the most thorough knowledge of human nature, the happiest delineation of its varieties, the liveliest effusions of wit and humour, are conveyed to the world in the best-chosen language." Austen's high praise is well deserved, and makes the strongest case yet for reading this novel. **EG-G**

Jacques the Fatalist

Denis Diderot

Lifespan | *b.* 1713 (France), *d.* 1784
First Published | 1796 (written 1773)
First Published by | Buisson (Paris)
Original Title | *Jacques le Fataliste et son maître*

Diderot's *Jacques the Fatalist* is among those very few extraordinary novels that seem to anticipate the distant future of the genre, leaping ahead of itself by 150 years, into the company of Samuel Beckett's anti-fictional transgressions of the novel form. It is an exceptionally interesting novel with an exceptionally uninteresting plot. Like metafiction of the twentieth century, it comments continually on its own procedures of composition and guesses continually at the reasons why its story might have turned out as it did, satirizing the reader's appetite for romantic tales or the thrills of an improbable adventure. Diderot sprinkles a few such thrills into the narrative recounted by Jacques to his characterless Master as they roam about, but he is always sure to announce their arrival.

Diderot was a polymath—philosopher, critic, and political essayist; hence, perhaps, his distrust and comedic handling of the novel form. His most famous literary labor, taking him almost twenty-five years, was on the *Encyclopédie ou Dictionnaire raisonné des Sciences, des Arts et des Métiers*, the great expression of French Enlightenment rationality co-authored, among others, by the mathematician D'Alembert. *Jacques the Fatalist*, which Diderot wrote around 1770 but never published during his lifetime, was a curious departure into a parallel zone of philosophical thinking, in which the so-called "problems of existence" can be staged as farces of self-expression and storytelling. **KS**

J'étais à terre et l'on me traînait

The Nun

Denis Diderot

Lifespan | *b* 1713 (France), *d*. 1784
First Published | 1796 (written 1760)
First Published by | Buisson (Paris)
Original Title | *La Religieuse*

The playful origins of this epistolary novel, published posthumously, are intriguing. In 1760, Denis Diderot and his friends wrote a series of letters to the Marquis de Croismare. The letters purported to come from Suzanne Simonin, an illegitimate child who had been forced to take religious vows to expiate her mother's guilt. Having escaped from the convent, she apparently wanted the Marquis to help her annul her binding vows. In her letters, the nun recounts the details of her confinement against her will and describes its effect on her understanding of religion and her faith. The novel's reputation as a *succès de scandale* is due in great part to its unashamed and explicit depiction of the narrator's encounter with the cruelty prevalent in monastic institutions, and her attendant discovery of eroticism and spirituality.

The Nun has been considered an attack on Catholicism, typifying the French Enlightenment's attitude toward religion. It stirred public opinion anew when, in 1966, the Jacques Rivette movies version was banned for two years. More recently, *The Nun* has been much discussed for its emphatic portrayal of lesbianism and sexuality. Aimed at exposing the oppressive and unnatural structure of life in religious institutions, the narrator's fate at the hands of monastic power provides a striking model for narrative and, indeed, life reversals. **CS**

🔵 Nuns take the offensive in an illustration to Diderot's novel, captioned: "I was on the ground and they were dragging me."

Hyperion

Friedrich Hölderlin

Lifespan | *b*. 1779 (Germany), *d*. 1843
First Published | 1797 (vol. 1), 1799 (vol. 2)
First Published by | J. Cotta (Tübingen)
Full Title | *Hyperion, oder der Eremit in Griechenland*

Friedrich Hölderlin's *Hyperion* appeared in two volumes between 1797 and 1799, and is a kind of autobiography written in letters from Hyperion mostly to his friend Bellarmin, but with some to Diotima. The text is set in ancient Greece, yet some 200 years after it was written, the words that describe invisible forces, conflicts, beauty, and hope are still relevant.

The novel works on several levels as a fictional reflection on, and interpretation of, the Enlightenment and the French Revolution. On the philosophical level, it can be interpreted as an investigation into the separation between subject and object, between individual and individual, man and nature, as a condition of their unity. On the political level, it expresses the ambivalence toward reason and revolutionary force as possible instruments of social and historical progress—elements that still exist in various twentieth-century forms.

Hölderlin's critical description of the German society of his day is still broadly applicable to bourgeois Western European existence in the third millennium. And those who have never felt Hyperion's Utopian longing for harmony with nature and God, free of all alienation, should ask the divine cashier for their money back. The inexplicable reasons have to do with love, language, and Diotima. But for this one has to delve into the experience of reading the novel oneself. **DS**

1) [illegible]

2) [illegible], что оборот. 1–

[illegible] объявит.

4) [illegible],

[illegible]

удивленія [illegible] —

[illegible]: Что, что [illegible]

Как было [illegible]

[illegible]

[illegible] с Генераломъ, Через [illegible]

[illegible] властельн[illegible]

[illegible] ему

Странникъ, ([illegible]

Сестра — [illegible]

ся, [illegible]

[illegible] 300 т[illegible]

[illegible]

Fyodor Dostoevsky, *Crime and Punishment*, 1886

Castle Rackrent

Maria Edgeworth

Lifespan | *b.* 1767 (England), *d.* 1849 (Ireland)
First Published | 1800
First Published by | J. Johnson (London)
Full Title | *Castle Rackrent: An Hibernian Tale*

Though little known and read, Maria Edgeworth's first novel is a small gem—several gems, perhaps, because it tells four stories of successive generations of the Rackrent family and their estate, linked by their narrator, Thady Quirk, loyal steward to the last three. The novel's subtitle indicates the nature of its humor: "An Hibernian tale taken from facts, and from the manners of the Irish Squires, before the year 1782." Sir Patrick is devoted to drink and wild living, while the debt-ridden Sir Murtagh lives for the law. Sir Kit is an inveterate gambler who dies in a duel, while the last squire, Sir Condy Rackrent, is a spendthrift politician and philanderer. Through varying degrees of neglect, profligacy, and obsession, the estate is finally run into the ground; or rather, it ends up in the hands of a canny young lawyer, Jason Quirk, none other than old Thady's son. Once the reader's ear is tuned to the vernacular idiom of Thady Quirk (because he is illiterate, the novel affects to be the transcription of an oral narrative), the ironic comedy of the old butler's tale is easy to appreciate. Nevertheless, Edgeworth thought it necessary to include a glossary for her English readers.

Castle Rackrent has been long regarded as the first regional novel—it capitalizes on Edgeworth's first-hand knowledge of Anglo-Irish relations in the late eighteenth century—as well as the first historical novel. It had a strong influence on Walter Scott, who greatly admired Edgeworth and referred to her as "the great Maria." **ST**

Henry of Ofterdingen

Novalis

Lifespan | *b.* 1772 (Germany), *d.* 1801
First Published | 1802, by G. Reimer (Berlin)
Given Name | Friedrich Leopold von Hardenberg
Original Title | *Heinrich von Ofterdingen*

Henry of Ofterdingen, the most representative work of early German Romanticism, is an extraordinarily light and profound fusion of novel, fairy tale, and poem. Young Henry is a medieval poet who seeks the mysterious "blue flower" that, in his dreams, acquires the beautiful traits of the yet unknown Mathilda. He sets out on a long journey to gain his poetic and philosophical education. The novel, which reflects, in part, events in the life of its author, remained unfinished and was published posthumously. Its impact on the history of German literature and, in the long term, of European literature, was, however, remarkable.

Novalis originally thought of his novel as an answer to Goethe's *Wilhelm Meister*, a work that he initially read with enthusiasm but later judged as being highly unpoetical; he disliked the victory of the economical over the poetic that Goethe's work, in Novalis's opinion, so conspicuously celebrates. Unlike Goethe's text, Novalis's simple narrative, interspersed with lyrical tales and exquisitely chiseled songs, ingeniously presents in literary form the mysticism of Johann Gottlieb Fichte, which was to influence Romantic thought considerably and with which he expressed the idea of describing a universal harmony with the help of poetry. The symbol of the blue flower, which is central in Henry's quest, later became an emblem for the whole of German Romanticism, a symbol of longing and the search for the unattainable. **LB**

Rameau's Nephew

Denis Diderot

Lifespan | b. 1713 (France), d. 1784
First Published | 1805 (composed 1761–1784)
First Published by | Goeschen (Leipzig)
Original French Title | Le Neveu de Rameau

Denis Diderot is one of the most important figures of the French Enlightenment, a contemporary of Rousseau and Voltaire. As well as editing the world's first encyclopedia, he managed to create a body of work that includes novels, philosophical dialogues, scientific essays, art, and drama criticism. Diderot was a polymath of verve and originality, and nowhere is this more visible than in Rameau's Nephew. Part novel, part essay, part Socratic dialogue, it expanded the boundaries of what is possible in fiction.

The action is straightforward. While taking a stroll in the Palais-Royal gardens, the narrator, a philosopher, bumps into the nephew of the great composer Rameau, and they become engaged in conversation. Underlying their discussion is the question of morality and the pursuit of happiness, which they approach from opposite poles. The prudish philosopher argues for the Greek ideal of virtue being equal to happiness. The nephew, witty cynic and lovable scoundrel, shows that conventional morality is nothing other than vanity, that the pursuit of wealth is society's guiding principle, and that what matters is how you are perceived, not how you actually are. The book is not a simple morality tale, however. Like its tragicomic hero, it is a complex challenge to all forms of reactionary thought and behavior. Too controversial to be published in Diderot's lifetime, it is also a savage indictment of the moral hypocrisy, intellectual pretensions, and spiritual vacuity of eighteenth-century Parisian society. **AL**

Elective Affinities

Johann Wolfgang von Goethe

Lifespan | b. 1749 (Germany), d. 1832
First Published | 1809
First Published by | J. F. Cotta (Tübingen)
Original Title | Die Wahlverwandtschaften

The phrase "elective affinities" is both precise and rich with ambiguity. It evokes a condition ripe with emotional and romantic possibilities. When Goethe chose Wahlverwandtschaften as his title, however, it was a technical term used solely in chemistry. That it subsequently came to have the connotations it does—both in German and in English—is in large part due to the power of Goethe's elegantly rigorous novel.

Using both a scientific configuration of desire and the symbolism of nature, Goethe's novel is a complex, yet measured and smoothly impersonal exploration of love. The marriage of Charlotte and Eduard is used to examine the perceptions of morality, fidelity, and self-development inscribed deeply within the concept of love. When this marriage is interrupted and challenged by the advent of the Captain and Ottilie, the state of marriage takes on a pastoral hue, at once idyllic and unreal. Through the reserved courtship between Charlotte and the Captain, and the consuming passion forged between Eduard and Ottilie, the novel lingers on the irresistible chaos of desire.

The novel was condemned at first for its immoral thesis that love had a chemical origin. But it is rather a sustained reflection on the complications arising out of human intercourse and demonstrates the ways in which our experience of other people makes our experience of love and desire fluid and unreliable. Just as love cannot be caught and immobilized in marriage, desire cannot rest with one person. **PMcM**

Michael Kohlhaas

Heinrich von Kleist

Lifespan | *b.* 1777 (Germany), *d.* 1811
Partly Featured | 1808, in *Phöbus*
First Published | 1810, in *Erzählungen*
Full Name | Bernd Heinrich Wilhelm von Kleist

Heinrich von Kleist's short tale, based on a true chronicle, tells of an honest man who, after being wronged, becomes an outlaw and a murderer. Michael Kohlhaas, a hardworking horse dealer, is one day mistreated by an arrogant local aristocrat. He seeks redress through the courts, only to find that the powerful lord's influence blocks him at every turn. Despairing, he agrees that his wife should petition the highest representative in the land, but she dies after being hurt by over-zealous bodyguards.

The initial trivial incident now becomes a cause for vengeance. Kohlhaas decides that, because the law has failed him, he has the right to claim justice through other means; so he razes the lord's castle and kills his servants. He amasses a small army and rampages through the land, following the escaping aristocrat with fire and violence. Upon the intervention of Martin Luther, an amnesty is forged, and Kohlhaas is promised the legal justice he desires. But corruption and nepotism are rife, and Kleist complicates the tale by describing yet more twists and turns in Kohlhaas's case.

The themes of justice, the right to obtain it, and the right to resist corruption are still relevant today, making *Michael Kohlhaas* a surprisingly contemporary read. The tale pivots on the ambiguity between justice and vengeance, from both the official political side and that of the powerless individual. Kohlhaas's eventual fate is at once logical and absurd, fitting and deeply unsatisfying. **JC**

Sense and Sensibility

Jane Austen

Lifespan | *b.* 1775 (England), *d.* 1817
First Published | 1811
First Published by | T. Eggerton (London)
Original Language | English

Like Jane Austen's other novels, this is a marriage plot: its principal protagonists are all, eventually, united with the partners they deserve. Important as this resolution is, however, it is not where the chief satisfaction of Austen's narrative lies. Elinor and Marianne, the two sisters at its center, may well correspond to the sense and sensibility of the novel's title, but a simple identification of reason and passion as their enduring qualities would be unwise.

The creation of perspective, the transition between apparent extremes, is achieved primarily through language, in the precise placement and patterning of phrase, clause, and sentence to create character. As a result, her prose charts exactly the movement between the distortions and blindness of passion, and the reasonable good sense that always seems to succeed it. *Sense and Sensibility* was developed from an earlier novel in letters called *Elinor and Marianne*, but it was only by abandoning the epistolary form of her eighteenth-century precursors that Austen was able to achieve such analytical precision. Her shift in titles is instructive: we no longer move from one viewpoint to another, but remain within a common syntax that propagates the implications created by patterns of ideas. The novelist now writes with one voice, but in doing so, she speaks for all the voices she creates. **DT**

> Charles Brock's illustration of *Sense and Sensibility* sentimentalizes Austen's work to match the patronizing image of her as "gentle Jane."

"The enjoyment of Elinor's company"

Chapter XLIX

Pride and Prejudice

Jane Austen

Lifespan | *b.* 1775 (England), *d.* 1817
First Published | 1813
First Published by | T. Eggerton (London)
Original Language | English

This unflattering sketch by Jane Austen's sister Cassandra is the only existing image of Austen taken from real life.

In the 1940 film version, Laurence Olivier opposes Mr. Darcy's pride to the prejudice of Greer Garson's Elizabeth Bennett.

Pride and Prejudice is the second of four novels that Jane Austen published during her lifetime. As widely read now as it was then, Austen's romance is indisputably one of the most enduringly popular classics of English literature. Written with incisive wit and superb character delineation, *Pride and Prejudice* tells the story of the Bennett family, its ignorant mother, negligent father, and five very different daughters, all of whom Mrs. Bennett is anxious to see married off. Set in rural England in the early nineteenth century, its major plot line focuses on the second eldest daughter, Elizabeth, and her turbulent relationship with the handsome, rich, but abominably proud Mr. Darcy. Slighted by him when they first meet, Elizabeth develops an instant dislike of Darcy, who, however, proceeds to fall in love with her, despite his own better judgement. Subsequent to a disastrous and rejected marriage proposal, both Elizabeth and Darcy eventually learn to overcome their respective pride and prejudice.

Although the novel has been criticized for its lack of historical context, the existence of its characters in a social bubble that is rarely penetrated by events beyond it is an accurate portrayal of the enclosed social world in which Austen lived. Austen depicts that world, in all its own narrow pride and prejudice, with unswerving accuracy and satire. At the same time, she places at its center, as both its prime actor and most perceptive critic, a character so well conceived and rendered that the reader cannot but be gripped by her story and wish for its happy dénouement. In the end, Austen's novel remains so popular because of Elizabeth, and because of the enduring appeal to men and women alike of a well-told and potentially happily-ending love story. **SD**

Mansfield Park

Jane Austen

Lifespan | *b.* 1775 (England), *d.* 1817
First Published | 1814
First Published by | T. Eggerton (London)
Original Language | English

One of Austen's more sober novels, *Mansfield Park* deals with her trademark themes—marriage, money, and manners. It tells the familiar story of a young woman, Fanny Price, and her pursuit of the right husband. Fanny is the archetypal poor relative, who is "rescued" from her large and impoverished family to be raised in her aunt's household, the seat of Sir Thomas Bertram, Mansfield Park. Effectively orphaned and an outsider, Fanny is variously tolerated and exploited, and suffers excruciating humiliations at the hands of her other aunt, the mean-spirited Mrs. Norris. Her cousins, with the exception of the warm and principled Edmund, are shallow characters who court the attentions of any visiting gentry, such as the rakish Crawfords, with disastrous consequences. Fanny, by contrast, is stronger on virtue than vice, and her sterling qualities are steadily revealed, though readers sometimes find her conventional femininity off-putting.

Typically, Austen mocks the pretensions of the rich and idle—their double standards, their condescension, and, indeed, their claims to moral legitimacy. Also typical are Austen's allusions to the darker side of the Mansfield Park idyll, made through a few strategically placed details. The Bertram family fortune, it turns out, comes—on the backs of slaves—from plantations in Antigua. Intriguingly, how much attention we must give Jane Austen's attention to these details has recently placed the novel at the center of bitter critical dispute. **ST**

Emma

Jane Austen

Lifespan | *b.* 1775 (England), *d.* 1817
First Published | 1816
First Published by | T. Eggerton (London)
Original Language | English

Austen said of her fourth published novel that it would contain a heroine no one would like but herself—and as if to prove her wrong, generations of readers have warmed to the flawed protagonist of *Emma*. "Handsome, clever and rich," Emma is a young woman used to ruling over the small social world of the village of Highbury. The comedy as well as the psychological interest of the novel lies in seeing what happens when people fail to act as she hopes and ordains. She attempts to pair her protégée Harriet Smith with two unsuitable candidates, and completely fails to read the true direction of the men's affections. She also fails to decipher, until it is almost too late, the nature of her own feelings for Mr. Knightley, her wise neighbor who functions throughout as Emma's only critic. Some recent readers view the novel as dangerously paternalistic in its intertwining of romance and moral education, but it should be said that *Emma* is less concerned with teaching a lesson than in exploring the mortifying effects of learning one.

Austen's trademark blending of an omniscient and ironic third-person narrative voice with a more indirect style that renders individual points of view comes into its own. A form suited both to the novel's concerns with individual, solipsistic desires and to its overarching moral commitment to the importance of frankness and mutual intelligibility, it points the way toward later nineteenth-century works of novelistic realism. **CC**

Rob Roy

Sir Walter Scott

Lifespan | *b.* 1771 (Scotland), *d.* 1832
First Published | 1817
First Published by | A. Constable & Co. (Edinburgh)
Original Language | English

Despite its title, this novel recounts more of the experiences of Francis ("Frank") Osbaldistone than any sustained history of the life of its eponymous outlaw, the legendary "Scottish Robin Hood." And yet, this distinctly Scottish romance was influential not only in consolidating the disparate accounts of the life of Rob Roy MacGregor, but also in mythologizing the Scottish Highlands as the place of sublime but barbaric attraction for many nineteenth-century English tourists. The novel is set against the backdrop of the Jacobite Rebellion of 1715, which sought to restore the ascendancy forfeited by the Stuarts in 1688. Scott tracks Frank's experiences as he journeys from his family home in London, to his uncle's residence in Northumbria, and on to Glasgow and the highlands of Scotland. Frank crosses the Scottish border in order to retrieve the assets of his father. Frank's progress northward brings with it exposure to a range of colorful personalities, not least the legendary Rob Roy, who assists Frank in the recovery of the assets.

Much of the narrative impetus of *Rob Roy* derives from the social and political conflicts and divisions that had plagued Great Britain ever since the Act of Union of 1707. But the vision that Scott ultimately offers up in the novel is one in which the various tensions between commerce and poetry, English and Scottish, Jacobite and Hanoverian, highland and lowland, Catholic and Protestant, have been successfully reconciled. **DaleT**

"You have requested me, my dear friend, to bestow some of that leisure, with which Providence has blessed the decline of my life, in registering the hazards and difficulties which attended its commencement."

◔ Sir Edwin Landseer's portrait of Scott hints at romantic wildness behind the exterior of a nineteenth-century gentleman.

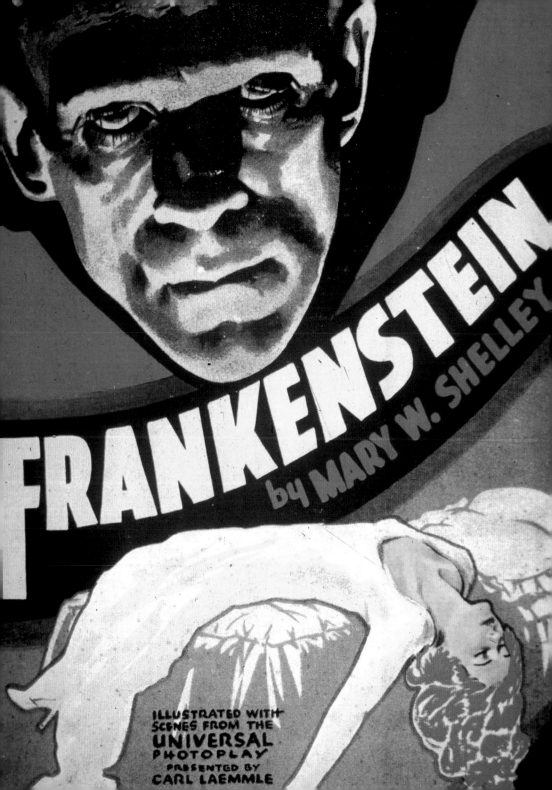

FRANKENSTEIN

by MARY W. SHELLEY

ILLUSTRATED WITH
SCENES FROM THE
UNIVERSAL
PHOTOPLAY
PRESENTED BY
CARL LAEMMLE

Frankenstein

Mary Wollstonecraft Shelley

Frankenstein has far more in common with *Dracula* than with any of the novels of generic late-gothicism. Both are commonly cited as early examples of the horror genre, and both have introduced a character to popular culture that has become distorted beyond all recognition, mainly through their representations in the Hammer, and earlier Universal, movie franchises. *Frankenstein,* and *Dracula* also, seems now more akin to the ultra-modern strain of science-fiction technohorror than any classical version of the genre. At the center of the story is the idea that our understanding of science can be developed and controlled, to the point that the tendency of Nature toward dissolution can be arrested; the impossibility of this desire is at the center of its "horror."

The subtitle of the novel, *The Modern Prometheus*, makes clear the connection with Greek mythology, but it is evident that *Frankenstein* is a novel that looks forward as well as back. The Swiss scientist and philosopher Frankenstein is inspired by occult philosophy to create a human-like figure, and give it life. The idea of reanimation is at the heart of much modern horror—the attempted violation of chaotic natural order in favor of linear certainty is something that modern society takes for granted, from the construction of unnatural environments to the continual attempts to postpone death and decline. *Frankenstein* is a novel that addresses such concerns from a point in history where the developments could only be imagined. Yet it remains, in all sorts of ways, an inescapable part of the culture it examines and foresees, and for these reasons alone it must continue to be read and reassessed. Effortless prose, grotesque imagery, and surreal imagination will ensure that it continues to be enjoyed. **SF**

Lifespan | *b.* 1797 (England), *d.* 1851
First Published | 1818
First Published by | Lackington et al. (London)
Full Title | *Frankenstein; or, The Modern Prometheus*

"The fallen angel becomes a malignant devil."

◉ Daughter of the radical feminist Mary Wollstonecraft, the author of *Frankenstein* married poet Percy Bysshe Shelley in 1816.

◉ The dominant images of Frankenstein in the popular imagination are supplied by James Whale's 1931 movie version.

Ivanhoe

Sir Walter Scott

Lifespan | *b*. 1771 (Scotland), *d*. 1832
First Published | 1820
First Published by | A. Constable & Co. (Edinburgh)
Full Title | *Ivanhoe; or, The Jew and his Daughter*

Walter Scott's historical romance details the political and cultural enmity between the subjugated Saxons and their Norman-French overlords during the reign of Richard the Lionheart in the twelfth century. Wilfred of Ivanhoe, a brave Saxon knight, returns from the Crusades to assist King Richard in recovering his throne from his usurping brother Prince John. To this endeavor, the assistance of a range of other personages, both historical and imaginary, is central—even the famed mythological outlaw Robin Hood makes an appearance. The narrative is urged forward by three confrontations of epic proportions: the tournament at Ashby-de-la-Zouche, the siege of Torquilstone Castle, and the rescuing of the heroine Rebecca from Templestowe, the seat of the Knights Templar. In each instance, conflict and bloody warfare ensue; at other moments, elements gleaned from gothic romance take precedence. Yet for all the delight that he takes in the adventure and the sheer vitality of chivalry, Scott also subtly critiques warfare.

With its focus on medieval England, *Ivanhoe* signalled a change from the Scottish subject-matter of Scott's earlier *Waverley* novels. As a sustained examination of the political, chivalric, and romantic practices of old, this fiction not only galvanized for a number of later writers and readers their impression of the medieval past, but also pioneered the genre of the historical novel, the literary form most often used to express it. **DaleT**

Melmoth the Wanderer

Charles Robert Maturin

Lifespan | *b*. 1782 (Ireland), *d*. 1824
First Published | 1820
First Published by | A. Constable & Co. (London)
Original Language | English

Melmoth occupies a curiously transitional position in literary history. As the final, belated representative of the gothic tradition in literature, it contains many of the key features of the genre: wild and remote, or otherwise exotic locations, a succession of strange stories, labyrinthine entrapments, and the dangerous lure, for the Protestant, of Catholic Europe. The question of identity is in the foreground from the outset, as we are introduced to John Melmoth, a young student who inherits his uncle's legacy. The estate includes a manuscript that relates the story of an ancestor, also called John Melmoth, who becomes the guiding thread for the novel. We discover that he has attained satanic immortality in exchange for his soul, yet he now uses this duration in order to seek his release from eternity by trying to drive another to take on his burden.

Melmoth's appeal to modernity resides not so much in the surprise and tension of the action that keeps us engaged, but in its reflection on the nature of temptation and torment. The satanic Melmoth is always fated to fail; his victims doomed to endure the hardships of their lives. The human mind is portrayed as both vanquisher and vanquished, and it is for this reason that, though quickly forgotten by his own generation, Maturin became a model for the twilight explorations of Poe, Wilde, and Baudelaire, among others. It is only in realizing this that we have begun to acknowledge Maturin's fundamental contribution to literary history. **DT**

The Life and Opinions of the Tomcat Murr

E. T. A. Hoffmann

Lifespan | *b.* 1776 (Germany), *d.* 1822
First Published | 1820–22
Full Name | Ernest Theodor Amadeus Hoffman
Original Title | *Lebensansichten des Katers Murr*

In E. T. A. Hoffmann's bizarre novel, comprising an autodidactic feline's "life and opinions" accidentally interspersed with "a fragmentary biography of Kappellmeister Johannes Kriesler on random sheets of waste paper," the reader is taken on a fantastical journey through the mundanities of everyday life in early nineteenth-century Germany. Murr, the tomcat, cuts a gregarious figure that contrasts markedly with the anxious composer Kriesler. The confident and eclectic talents of Murr, a creature modeled on Hoffmann's own adored tabby cat, render him a true Renaissance feline, whereas Kriesler, Hoffmann's alter ego, is a character saturated in the Romantic sensibility, ravaged, as he regularly is, by the extremes of emotional experience.

Hoffmann's mesmerizing tale invokes everything from the supernatural, to the operatic, the musical, and the psychiatric in a narrative populated by characters who traverse the borders between madness and sanity, in a style that mirrors this uncertainty. It has even been suggested that Hoffmann's work laid the foundations of magic realism. Following in the traditions of Rabelais, Cervantes, and Sterne, Hoffmann's work went on to impact upon such a varied group as Gogol, Dostoevsky, Kafka, Kierkegaard, and Jung, and in many ways his writing prefigured Freud's thinking about the uncanny. This is an immensely inventive and unusual read that both stimulates and confounds in turn. **JW**

"Bashfully—with trembling breast—I lay before the world some leaves from my life: its sorrows, its hopes, its yearnings—effusions which flowed from my inmost heart in sweet hours of leisure and poetic rapture."

◉ A composer as well as an author, Hoffmann cast Kriesler, the human hero of *Tomcat Murr*, in his own Romantic image.

The Private Memoirs and Confessions of a Justified Sinner

James Hogg

Lifespan | *b.* 1770 (Scotland), *d.* 1835
First Published | 1824
First Published by | Longman et al. (London)
Original Language | English

○ Originally a poverty-stricken shepherd, James Hogg educated himself and gained valuable patronage as a poet and essayist.

James Hogg was born into poverty in the Scottish Lowlands and worked as a shepherd before teaching himself to read and write. He put some of his previous work experience to good use in writing a textbook on sheep diseases, before composing poetry as the "Ettrick Shepherd," and moving onto his most famous work, *The Private Memoirs and Confessions of a Justified Sinner*.

Hogg presented this metaphysical thriller as a true story. Purporting to be a historical reconstruction of the life of two brothers, George and Robert, narrated by the book's editor, along with the confessional manuscript of Robert, the novel offers a series of doubles and doublings. The editor's account, some hundred years after the actual events, is contrasted with the confessional religiosity of the sinner's account. These different stylistic perspectives give the book its bifocal structure, revealing the public and private sides of a killer who styles himself a "justified sinner."

Abusing Calvinist doctrines of predestination—if you are born one of God's elect, then you can do no wrong—the confession reveals an orgy of confused fanaticism, through which Hogg conducts his satire on religious fanaticism. Throughout the book, extremism is contrasted with healthier, more honorable and humane good sense, particularly in the resistance shown by the lower classes to their "betters." Robert is haunted by a shape-shifting stranger who could be either a manifestation of the devil or a symptom of intense psychological trauma. At once gothic comedy, religious horror story, mystery thriller, and psychological study, the novel is both terrifying and terrific. **DM**

The Life of a Good-for-Nothing

Joseph von Eichendorff

A young man lies in the grass, thinking of this and that. His exasperated father, taking a break from a hard day's work, tells his "good-for-nothing" son to get on his feet and do something. At that, our young hero takes up his fiddle and sets off into the wide world, singing a song as he goes. So begins the delightful picaresque novella *The Life of a Good-for-Nothing* by the nineteenth-century German Romantic Joseph Von Eichendorff. Better known for his lyrical poetry, Eichendorff, who was a leader of the late Romantics, secured his place as a key figure in Germany's literary heritage with this brief but vibrant coming-of-age story.

The young protagonist is picked up on the road by two aristocratic ladies who take him to their castle, where he works as a gardener and then, once his eccentricities have endeared him to those around him, as a bookkeeper. He falls in love with one of the ladies, but when he sees her with another man, he picks up his fiddle and, once more defying social conventions, heads back to the road, guided only by serendipity and a longing for adventure. From his lady's castle, chance takes him to Italy and Prague, through good times and bad, from one adventure to another. Eventually the road takes him back to the castle and to the arms of his true love.

Eichendorff, whose poems have been set to music by such illustrious composers as Robert Schumann and Felix Mendelssohn, infuses his novella with the kind of lyrical prose rarely found outside of the very best poetry. His hero, the ideal "Romantic man," is the most sympathetic of characters and his whimsical story is never less than fascinating and refreshing. **OR**

Lifespan | *b*. 1788 (Poland), *d*. 1857
First Published | 1826, by Vereinsbuchhandlung
First Chapter Published | 1823
Original Title | *Aus dem Leben eines Taugenichts*

Eichendorff combined a career as a Prussian government official with the writing of Romantic lyric poetry and prose.

Last of the Mohicans

James Fenimore Cooper

Lifespan | *b.* 1789 (U.S.), *d.* 1851
First Published | 1826
First Published by | J. Miller (London)
Full Title | *The Last of the Mohicans, a Narrative of 1757*

The pivotal set piece of *The Last of the Mohicans* is the massacre at Fort William Henry during the French and Indian War. This is the "factual" event around which Cooper, the first internationally renowned American novelist, builds a compelling tale of wilderness adventure. Drawing heavily on the American genre of the Native American captivity narrative, he creates a template for much American popular fiction, particularly the Western.

Frontiersman Natty Bompo had already been introduced as an old man in *The Pioneers* (1823); here he appears in middle age, as Hawkeye, a scout working for the British, with two Delaware Native American companions, Chingachgook and his son, Uncas. Having crossed paths with Cora and Alice Munro, the daughters of a British colonel, Bompo and friends spend the rest of the novel rescuing them from captivity, escorting them to safety, or pursuing them through the wilderness.

Cooper's racial politics are conservative; though the novel raises the possibility of interracial romance between Uncas and the genteel Cora (who has a black mother), the prospect is quashed. Cooper laments the destruction of the wilderness, and of the Native Americans who inhabit it, but all are shown to succumb inevitably to progress, typical of the ideology of nineteenth-century America. **RH**

⊙ American landscape artist Thomas Cole painted this scene from *The Last of the Mohicans: Cora Kneeling at the Feet of Tamenund.*

The Betrothed

Alessandro Manzoni

Lifespan | *b.* 1785 (Italy), *d.* 1873
First Published | 1827
First Published by | Pomba; Trameter; Manini
Original Title | *I Promessi Sposi*

Written in the Florentine dialect, *The Betrothed* was Alessandro Manzoni's attempt to put forward an authoritative model for a standardized Italian language as a condition for the cultural and political unification of the country. The novel is set during the seventeenth-century Spanish occupation of the Italian peninsula, and based on an allegedly authentic manuscript that the author reproduces in perfectly baroque style. Manzoni is able to draw on parallels from history to depict his own era, when Italy was under Austrian domination.

From a peaceful little village in Lombardy, where two humble peasants are preparing for their wedding, the story introduces a circus of characters, who scheme to prevent or expedite that union. There is an impressive variety of actors, powerless and powerful, modest and aristocratic, religious and secular. Inspired by the new Romantic culture, *The Betrothed* examines the abuse of power in all its many forms. Priests use their knowledge of Latin to outwit their parishioners; fathers abuse their paternal authority to force their daughters into a nunnery; crooks kidnap a simple girl who has found refuge in a convent. But, above all, obtuse foreign governments oppress and prevaricate without sympathy for the local population. Nevertheless, the novel's message is positive: people's faith in overcoming difficulties and their determination to pursue their goals facilitates a favorable resolution of the story with the union of the betrothed. **RPi**

The Red and the Black

Stendhal

Lifespan | *b.* 1783 (France), *d.* 1842
First Published | 1831
First Published by | Hilsum (Paris)
Original Title | *Le Rouge et le Noir*

LE ROUGE

ET LE NOIR

CHRONIQUE DU XIXᵉ SIÈCLE,

PAR M. DE STENDHAL.

TOME PREMIER.

PARIS.

A. LEVAVASSEUR, LIBRAIRE, PALAIS-ROYAL.

1831.

⊙ The front cover of the first edition of Stendhal's *The Red and the Black* carries the subtitle "Chronicle of the 19th century."

❯ Fellow author Alfred de Musset produced this striking drawing of Stendhal dancing at an inn at Pont Saint-Esprit.

Set in France in the 1830s, *Le Rouge et le Noir* chronicles Julien Sorel's duplicitous rise to power and his subsequent fall. The son of a carpenter, Julien seeks initially to realize his Napoleonic ambitions by joining the priesthood. Despite some torrid liaisons during his training, Julien succeeds in becoming a priest and eagerly accepts the invitation of the Marquis de la Mole to become his personal secretary. Even Julien's affair with the Marquis' daughter, Mathilde, is the occasion of his ennoblement so that he can marry her without scandal. Before Julien has an opportunity to enjoy his aristocratic life, however, the Marquis receives from Mme de Renal (another of Julien's conquests when he was training for the priesthood) a letter that exposes him as a fraud. Prevented from marrying Mathilde, Julien exacts revenge.

Sometimes perceived as being a bit too melodramatic to appeal to modern literary taste, *The Red and the Black* is immensely important in terms of the development of the novel as an art form. On the one hand, it is a story told very much in the Romantic tradition. Sorel may be unscrupulous and roguish in the pursuit of his ambitions, yet set against a petty and constraining bourgeois French society, his energy and sheer gumption often lure the reader into a reluctant rapport. It is in Stendhal's narrative style, however, that this novel has proved to be most influential. In largely being told from the vantage point of each character's state of mind, the novel's convincing psychological realism prompted Émile Zola to proclaim it the first truly "modern" novel. It is for this reason, quite apart from the fact that it remains a rollicking good yarn, that *The Red and the Black* should be reserved a place on every serious reader's bookshelf. **VA**

The Hunchback of Notre Dame

Victor Hugo

Lifespan | *b.* 1802 (France), *d.* 1885
First Published | 1831
First Published by | Flammarion (Paris)
Original Title | *Notre-Dame de Paris*

"*The owl goes not into the nest of the lark.*"

● Victor Hugo was by far the most prolific and versatile author of the French Romantic school, both in poetry and prose.

● Nicolas Maurin's contemporary illustration shows a disgusted Esmerelda feeding the grotesque hunchback Quasimodo.

Victor Hugo's *The Hunchback of Notre-Dame* is a historical novel in the tradition of Scott's *Ivanhoe*. It presents a vivid tableau of life in fifteenth-century Paris, a city teeming with noble festivities, grotesque revelries, mob uprisings, and public executions, all of which take place around Notre-Dame. Hugo devotes two chapters to the description of the Gothic church, bringing the reader into the very soul of Notre-Dame. From the dizzying heights of its stony gaze, he offers the reader a subjective view of Paris. The word *anankhe* ("fate"), etched on one of the walls, reveals the driving force of the gothic plot.

Quasimodo's fate is sealed when he is abandoned at birth by his mother on the steps of Notre-Dame. Adopted by the Archdeacon Claude Frollo, Quasimodo becomes bellringer of the tower, hiding his grotesque, hunchbacked figure away from prying Parisian eyes. Frollo is consumed by forbidden lust for the beautiful gypsy Esmeralda, who dances on the square below the cathedral. He convinces Quasimodo to kidnap her, but his attempts are foiled by the captain of the King's Archers, Phoebus, who also falls for Esmeralda. Quasimodo is imprisoned for the crime, and is abused and humiliated by his captors. After a particularly brutal flogging, he is tended to by Esmeralda, who gives him water. From this point on, Quasimodo is hopelessly devoted to her. With all three characters under her spell, a dramatic tale of love and deceit ensues. The love-obsessed Frollo spies on Phoebus and Esmeralda, stabbing the former in a jealous rage. Esmeralda is arrested and condemned to death for his murder, and, despite a brave rescue attempt by Quasimodo, is later hanged. Quasimodo, seeing Esmeralda hanging lifeless from the gallows, cries out, "There is all I loved." The theme of redemption through love struck a universal chord. **KL**

Eugene Onegin

Alexander Pushkin

Described by Gorki as "the beginning of all beginnings," and written, in the words of Gogol, by "the most singular manifestation of the Russian spirit," Pushkin's novel in verse occupies a crucial place in the Russian literary canon. It is about the jaded sophisticate Eugene Onegin—who spurns the love of the simple provincial girl Tatiana, only relenting when it is too late—who kills his friend in a duel provoked by himself.

The reasons for the novel's success are disputed. According to Vladimir Nabokov, it lies in its language, "verse melodies the likes of which had never been known before in Russia." If Nabokov is right, an intuitive appreciation of *Eugene Onegin*'s seminal significance will be difficult for those who are unable to read the novel in the original; but without it, any understanding of Russian literary culture will miss a vital reference point. Yet even in translation, the way Pushkin achieves a sense of seriousness through irony and playfulness is striking. Narrative convention is subverted, the literary project itself refracted in a series of delightful digressions, inventions, and jokes. Not despite but because of all this richness, the tale acquires a depth of meaning that is hard to account for given the simplicity of its plot of spurned love and sacrificed friendship.

Extremely funny and deeply serious, Pushkin's lightness of touch combines with an astonishing, funambulist freedom of language within a sophisticated, strictly executed poetic form (the fourteen-verse so-called "Onegin-stanza"). Even if you choose not to take Nabokov's advice and learn Russian before beginning the novel, it is certainly worth reading the work in more than one translation, preferably with the benefit of Nabokov's detailed commentary. **DG**

Lifespan | *b.* 1799 (Russia), *d.* 1837
First Published | 1833
Written and Serially Published | 1823–31
Original Title | *Yevgeny Onegin*

"The illusion which exalts us is dearer to us than ten-thousand truths."

◉ Pushkin is portrayed by Wassili Tropinin in 1827—a writer of genius destined to die in a duel at the age of thirty-seven.

◉ Tatiana writes a letter confessing her love in an illustration based on Tchaikovsky's 1879 opera version of Pushkin's tale.

Eugénie Grandet

Honoré de Balzac

Lifespan | *b*. 1799 (France), *d*. 1850
First Published | 1834
First Published by | Charles-Béchet (Paris)
Original Language | French

Like Sir Walter Scott, Honoré de Balzac wrote novels in part to clear debts and the pains of debt—capital accumulation and attendant moral corruption run right through *Eugénie Grandet*, which later became part of Balzac's larger grouping of novels, *La Comédie Humaine*. Amid robust, moral critique of greed, and the poverty of provincial experience, this novel combines convincingly drawn human characters with a sociological grasp of deeper changes in French society. The realist representation of Eugénie's father as a tyrannical miser shows the workings of avarice not just as an individual "sin," but as a reflection of the secular nihilism of financial calculation in nineteenth-century capitalism.

The plot has a classical simplicity and causal circularity, unfolding a bourgeois tragedy that the narrator declares more cruel than any endured by the house of Atreus in Greek tragedy. Eugénie's father's fixation on money limits her experience, and ultimately destroys the family. The novel unveils the full damage done to Eugénie, though she asserts some moral dignity through acts of precise generosity. With a grasp of temporal cycles that prefigures Proust, Balzac dramatizes both the critical framework of individual actions and the wheels of generational change. Comic bathos tempers the stark social realism; the entertainment Balzac wrings from the judgments of his more or less omniscient narrator is surprising. An ideal introduction to one of the great realist novelists. **DM**

> *"Narrow minds can develop as well through persecution as through benevolence; they can assure themselves of their power by tyrannizing cruelly or beneficently over others."*

⬆ This Jules Leroux illustration, taken from a 1911 edition of the novel, depicts Nanon and a manservant carrying a keg.

Le Père Goriot

Honoré de Balzac

Lifespan | *b.* 1799 (France), *d.* 1850
First Published | 1834–1835
First Published by | Werdet (Paris)
Original Language | French

This is the story of a wealthy businessman, Goriot, who bequeaths a fortune to his two ungrateful daughters. Living alone in a shabby boarding house, so that he can continue to give what little he has to his avaricious offspring, he also befriends an ambitious young man named Rastignac, who exploits their association to further his own social aspirations. As intrigue, betrayal, and even murder become implicated in the daughters' rise into high society, various villains ensure that the narrative is enlivened by some sensational plot twists. Essentially, though, it is Goriot's unreciprocated love for his daughters that is the central tragedy around which Balzac chronicles the broader social malaise.

Constituting one of the works in Balzac's epic series, *La Comédie Humaine*, *Le Père Goriot* essentially transposes Shakespeare's *King Lear* to 1820s Paris. Against Goriot's selfless devotion to his family, the novel explores in myriad ways how it is no longer filial bonds or ideals of community that sustains the social edifice, but a corrupt pseudo-aristocracy that is based on aggressive individualism and greed.

Although some may become impatient with the overly sinuous plot structure, it is Balzac's eye for detail and his gift for psychological realism that continue to inspire admiration. The sheer breadth of his artistic vision locates him firmly within the nineteenth-century tradition, but his narrative technique and attention to character still make Balzac a hugely important figure in modern fiction. **VA**

The Nose

Nikolay Gogol

Lifespan | *b.* 1809 (Ukraine), *d.* 1852
First Published | 1836 (Russia)
Original Title | *Nos*
Original Language | Russian

One of Gogol's best-known stories, *The Nose* is quite possibly also one of the most absurd, and as such is the forerunner of a tradition that almost a century later would become very strong, not only in Russia, but all over Europe. It has also served as the basis for a wonderfully inventive and funny opera of the same name by Shostakovich.

Kovalev is a junior civil servant with a consciousness of his own importance and an equally acute sense of his place in the bureaucratic hierarchy. Alarmingly, he wakes up one morning to find his nose gone. While on his way to the relevant authorities to signal this loss, he is astonished to meet his nose dressed in the uniform of a civil servant several ranks above him. He attempts to address the errant nose, but is rebuffed on the grounds of rank. He tries to place a notice in the newspaper to ask for help in catching his nose, but fails. When his nose is later brought back to him by the police, the doctor says it cannot be put back on. Some time later, and for no apparent reason, Kovalev wakes up to find his nose mysteriously back in its place. The whole story is related in considerable detail, only to end with a list of all the implausibilities in this literally incredible story. Gogol even goes so far as to make the indignant statement that the greatest of these implausibilities is "how authors can choose such subjects" at all. Readers may well wonder why Gogol did choose to write *The Nose*, but they are unlikely to regret that he did. **DG**

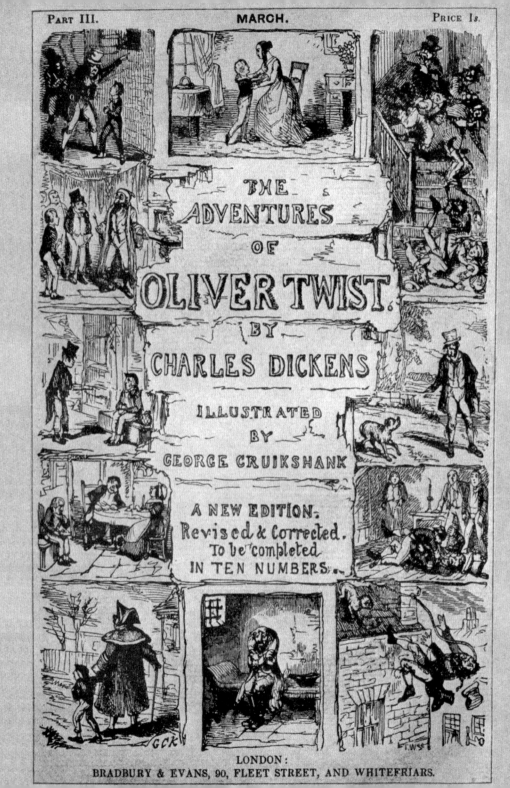

THE ADVENTURES OF OLIVER TWIST.

BY CHARLES DICKENS

ILLUSTRATED BY GEORGE CRUIKSHANK

A NEW EDITION.
Revised & Corrected.
To be completed
IN TEN NUMBERS.

LONDON:
BRADBURY & EVANS, 90, FLEET STREET, AND WHITEFRIARS.

Oliver Twist

Charles Dickens

Oliver Twist started life as one of Dickens's "Mudfog" sketches, a series of papers written for the early numbers of *Bentley's Miscellany*. The first two monthly parts, depicting Oliver's birth and upbringing in the workhouse, formed part of a series of radical melodramatic attacks on the 1834 New Poor Law. *Oliver Twist* is at once a picaresque story, a melodrama, and a fairy-tale romance in which the foundling is revealed to have noble origins. It is also one of the first novels to feature a child as the central character; though, in contrast with Dickens's later children, Oliver both stays a prepubescent and remains untouched by the traumas he experiences. Oliver's curious blankness is central to Dickens's multiple purposes. It enables him to remain the passive victim of institutionalized violence in the workhouse—even the famous scene where he asks for more gruel is not an act of self-assertion, but the result of drawing lots. It allows him to remain free of corruption when he falls in with Fagin's criminal gang (in contrast with the "Artful Dodger") so that he can be recast as a middle-class child by his rescuer, Mr. Brownlow. The conspiracy between the wicked master of the den of underage thieves, Fagin, and Oliver's half-brother, Monks, to turn Oliver into a criminal produces the tension between imprisonment and escape that drives and unites the novel. Oliver escapes from the workhouse and from Fagin's underworld den, only to be recaptured until he is finally united with his aunt, Rose Maylie, and adopted by Brownlow. The fact that this dismal pattern is eventually broken is entirely due to the intervention of the prostitute Nancy, who brings the two worlds together—but at the price of her violent murder by her lover, Bill Sykes, in one of Dickens's most bloodthirsty scenes. **JBT**

Lifespan | *b.* 1812 (England), *d.* 1870
First Published | 1838 by R. Bentley (London)
Full Title | *The Adventures of Oliver Twist; or, The Parish Boy's Progress*

○ George Cruikshank, the illustrator of *Oliver Twist*, created unforgettable images of Fagin and the Artful Dodger.

○ The cover of the 1846 edition: by then *Oliver Twist* had already taken up an immovable place at the heart of Victorian culture.

The Lion of Flanders

Hendrik Conscience

Lifespan | *b.* 1812 (Belgium), *d.* 1883
First Published | 1838
First Published by | L. J. de Cort (Antwerp)
Original Title | *De leeuw van Vlaanderen*

Hendrik Conscience is a key figure in the modern history of the Flemish-speaking population of Flanders, now a part of Belgium. When he began his prolific writing career in the 1830s, Flemish literature did not exist. Conscience forged a sophisticated literary language out of the speech of an underclass in a kingdom ruled by francophone Walloons.

The Lion of Flanders, probably the best of the hundred novels Conscience wrote, is one of the few still read today. A historical romance in the tradition established by Sir Walter Scott, it describes a crucial moment in the history of Flemish resistance to the dominance of the French at the start of the fourteenth century. The merchants and artisans of the Flemish guilds rise in revolt against the king of France and his supporters in Flanders. When the French knights invade Flanders to restore their king's authority, they are defeated in the battle of Kortrijk (or Courtrai), the climax of Conscience's tale.

The novel has all the necessary trappings of romantic medievalism, including choleric or chivalric armored knights, sturdy men of the people with bluff manners and wholesome sentiments, and a beautiful demoiselle to be saved from peril. It is not a work of subtlety or startling originality, but the storytelling is robust and the subject matter of interest to anyone with a glimmer of curiosity about European history and nationalism. **RegG**

The Charterhouse of Parma

Stendhal

Lifespan | *b.* 1783 (France), *d.* 1842
First Published | 1839
First Published by | Ambroise Dupont (Paris)
Original Title | *Le Chartreuse de Parme*

Movement is the operative principle of this story, which shifts quickly between several countries and decades. Many readers have remarked on the disconcerting rapidity of these transitions, bringing narrative enjoyment to the foreground, but also perplexing us as to the overall shape of the story.

The novel's sense of movement is achieved not by progression, but by a constantly managed undercutting, which extends to character, theme, and judgement. We are told at the outset that this is the story of the Duchess Sanseverina, but, at least initially, its hero appears to be her idealistic nephew, Fabrice. Yet his principled bravery is not allowed to stand either; arriving at Waterloo his expectation of the camaraderie of war is undermined when his compatriots steal his horse. In the parts of the novel where summaries of a period of years alternate with passages spanning only hours, limpidity of duration is matched by an elevation of perspective—these range from the bell tower of Fabrice's childhood church, to the Farnese Tower in which he is incarcerated at the heart of the story. With imprisonment as its central theme, Stendhal's extreme freedom with the narrative seems resonantly undermining. As theme defeats theme, and one aspect of narrative technique shows up the limitations of another, the novel operates according to its own exhilarating logic. **DT**

The Fall of the House of Usher

Edgar Allan Poe

Lifespan | *b.* 1809 (U.S.), *d.* 1849
First Published | 1839 by W. Burton (Philadelphia)
First Serialized | *Burton's Gentleman's Magazine*
Original Language | English

It seems to be stretching the definition of the word to its very limits to describe *The Fall of the House of Usher* as a "novel." However, despite the characteristic brevity of the narrative, the work deserves inclusion here, because it is simply impossible to imagine the modern novel without considering Poe's masterful writing, and this seminal tale in particular. The story is imbued with an atmosphere of foreboding and terror, underpinned by an equally strong exploration of the human psyche.

Roderick and Madeline Usher are the last of their distinguished line. They are, therefore, the "House of Usher," as is the strange, dark mansion in which they live. The narrator of Poe's tale is a childhood friend of Roderick's, summoned to the decaying country pile by a letter pleading for his help. He arrives to find his friend gravely altered, and through his eyes, we see strange and terrible events unfold. The reader is placed in the position of the narrator, and as such we identify strongly throughout with the "madman" watching incredulous as around him reality and fantasy merge to become indistinguishable. The unity of tone and the effortlessly engaging prose are mesmerizing, enveloping both subject matter and reader. For one who died so young, Poe left an incredible legacy, and it adds a resonance to this tale that his own house was to fall so soon. **DR**

"When the clouds hung oppressively low in the heavens, I had been passing alone, on horseback, through a singularly dreary tract of country."

◉ Irish illustrator Harry Clarke produced this suitably disturbing visual interpretation of Poe's famous horror story in 1923.

CAMERA OBSCURA

HILDEBRAND

Camera Obscura

Hildebrand

Lifespan | *b.* 1814 (Netherlands), *d.* 1903
First Published | 1839
First Published by | Erven F. Bohn (Haarlem)
Given Name | Nicolaas Beets

The young Nicolaas Beets was a theology student at the University of Leiden when, under the pseudonym Hildebrand, he published the first version of the loosely linked collection of stories and sketches entitled *Camera Obscura*. Beets's prose work was realist in style and mildly satirical in intention. Its gently humorous, ironic portrayal of Dutch bourgeois society was an instant success with a public ready to laugh at its own foibles.

Like the works of his English contemporary Charles Dickens, Beets's book is never entirely free of sentimentality. However critical of its characters, it never strays far from sympathy; the flashy parvenu Kegge or the stilted student Pieter Stastok are ridiculed, yet without malice. There are true villains—such as van der Hoogen in the Stastok family stories—but these always get their due reward, for Beets's comfortable moral universe has no place for unrewarded virtue or unpunished vice.

Camera Obscura has established itself as a classic of Dutch literature because it is sharp and shrewd in its observations of human behavior and is written in a prose that fulfills Beets's declared aim to present the Dutch language in its everyday clothing instead of its Sunday best. Beets's rich cast of characters may have dated, but they can still inspire amused affection and offer fodder for reflection. **RegG**

🔵 A 1950s cover of the book shows the eponymous optical device, used by painters in quest of an exact representational art.

A Hero of Our Times

Mikhail Yurevich Lermontov

Lifespan | *b.* 1814 (Russia), *d.* 1841
First Published | 1840
First Chapter Published | 1839
Original Title | *Geroy nashego vremeni*

A collection of five tales connected by an intricate narrative structure centering on one protagonist, this work simultaneously exemplifies two recurrent themes of Russian nineteenth-century literature—the Caucasian adventure story and the "superfluous" antihero. Pechorin, Lermontov's "hero," is a young Russian officer disillusioned with life and mankind, who describes his own soul as half-dead and happiness as the ability to have power over others. Unlike Pushkin's Eugene Onegin, who suffers from the absence of a meaningful spiritual life, Pechorin's disappointment stems from a failure of the world to live up to his high ideals. In consequence, his egotism is of a more active and more vengeful kind—he abducts a young Circassian girl and then tires of her; he makes a young Russian noblewoman fall in love with him to spite an acquaintance; and he kills that same acquaintance in a duel.

Set in Russian "frontier" country, populated by smugglers, wild mountain tribes, marvelous horses, and drunk Cossacks, Pechorin's adventures are told against the backdrop of a spectacular Caucasian landscape, beautifully evoked by Lermontov. This landscape and the effect it has both on his characters and his readers contradicts the jadedness with which Pechorin regards his life, and the men and women around him, and is one source of vital tension in the work; another is the contrast between Pechorin's spiritual and metaphysical yearnings and his callous and even vicious behavior. **DG**

Dead Souls

Nikolay Gogol

Lifespan | *b*. 1809 (Ukraine), *d*. 1852
First Published | 1842 (Russia)
Original Title | *Myertvye dushi*
Original Language | Russian

The writing of *Dead Souls* drove Gogol mad. It started off as a humorous idea for a story, the conceit being that Chichikov, a scheming opportunist, would travel through Russia buying up the rights to dead serfs (souls), who had not yet been purged from the census and could therefore—like all chattels—still be mortgaged. As the novel grew, so did Gogol's aspirations; his goal became no less than to rekindle the noble yet dormant core of the Russian people, to transform the troubled social and economic landscape of Russia into the gleaming great Empire that was its destiny. He no longer wanted to write about Russia: he wanted to save it. He was driven into messianic obsession and, having burned Part Two—twice—after ten years of labor, he committed suicide by starvation.

Chichikov's travels across the expanse of Russia in a troika provided the opportunity for Gogol to shine as a satiric portrait artist, a caricaturist of the panoply of Russian types. He makes Russian literature funny—tragically funny. In Chichikov he created a timeless character, a huckster not unrecognizable in today's dotcom billionaires, able to exploit the stupidity and greed of landowners eager to get even richer themselves. Although Gogol was unable to deliver the key to Russian salvation he had envisaged, with what remains he has inarguably succeeded in writing his "great epic poem," which, hauntingly, did finally "solve the riddle of my existence." **GT**

Lost Illusions

Honoré de Balzac

Lifespan | *b*. 1799 (France), *d*. 1850
First Published | 1843
First Published by | G. Charpentier (Paris)
Original Title | *Illusions Perdues*

A kind of westernized *Arabian Nights*, *Lost Illusions* is one of the central works of Balzac's seventeen-volume *Human Comedy* (1842–46), set during the period of restored monarchy in France. As self-appointed record-keeper of his epoch, Balzac was interested in "all of society," but, most significantly, the upheavals related to money. Balzac's fictions draw our attention to the many contrasts that define different cultural domains: between the royalists and the liberals, the aristocracy and the bourgeoisie, the hoarders and the squanderers, the virtuous and the depraved, Paris and the provinces.

Steeped in the imagery of the theater, the three parts of *Lost Illusions* tell the story of the provincial poet Lucien de Rubempré, who languishes in provincial Angoulême in the company of his alter ego, David Séchard, nurturing his ambitions. He is initiated into the Parisian literary, journalistic, and political world, and suffers successive disillusions. Marcel Proust praised the way in which Balzac's style aims "to explain," and is marked by its beautiful "naiveties and vulgarities." Some critics, on the other hand, while they celebrate Balzac's powers of observation, denigrate his "clumsy and inelegant style." From the first pages to the last, *Lost Illusions* provides ample opportunity to share Proust's admiration for the writer. **CS**

❯ This title page of *Les Illusions Perdues*—*Lost Illusions*—bears the author's own comments and annotations scrawled in ink.

Illusions perdues

The Pit and the Pendulum

Edgar Allan Poe

This claustrophobic tale of horror and suspense has earned Edgar Allan Poe a prominent place at the forefront of the Romantic tradition, alongside Bram Stoker's *Dracula* and Mary Wollstonecraft Shelley's *Frankenstein*. As one of America's first serious literary critics, he was dismissive of art and literature that was preoccupied with the mundane or the everyday, preferring to deal with the unexpected and the puzzling in his own narratives—specifically, the terrifying and the supernatural.

Poe was highly regarded as a writer of poetry and prose, but his life was plagued by ill health, money problems, and bouts of depression and mental illness that were aggravated by alcohol. Two years after the death of his wife (he had notoriously married his thirteen-year-old cousin), he fell into a state of despair and, at the age of forty, died after drinking himself into a coma.

It is therefore not surprising to find that so many of his stories feature the plight of desperate protagonists brought by terror to the brink of insanity. However, much of the popular criticism of Poe and his work, including attempts to seek out symbols for psychoanalytical interpretation, has confused the writer's own torment with that of his narrators. In *The Pit and the Pendulum* there is an overpowering atmosphere of dread—the dark chamber reeking of putrefaction and death, the frenzied rats, the immobilized victim's horror of the descending razor-edged pendulum—that has prompted much discussion about the writer's mental state. But this masterpiece, which draws on so many of the distinctive and recurring motifs spawned by writers of the horror genre, should be read as the finely wrought and compelling work of a gifted imagination. **TS**

Lifespan | *b.* 1809 (U.S.), *d.* 1849
First Published | 1843
First Serialized | *The Gift for 1843* (Philadelphia)
Original Language | English

"The sentence, the dread sentence of death, was the last of distinct accentuation which reached my ears."

◉ Poe's portrait decorates a late nineteenth-century cigar box, reflecting the enduring popularity of his horror stories

◉ An illustration of Poe's *The Pit and the Pendulum* represents the victim's hallucinations as well as his horrific predicament.

LES TROIS MOUSQUETAIRES. — *Un mousquetaire, placé sur le degré supérieur, l'épée nue à la main, empêchait, ou, du moins, s'efforçait d'empêcher les trois autres de monter. Ces trois autres s'escrimaient contre lui de leurs épées fort agiles.* (Page 34.)

The Three Musketeers

Alexandre Dumas

Lifespan | *b*. 1802 (France), *d*. 1870
First Published | 1844
First Published by | Baudry (Paris)
Original Title | *Les Trois Mousquetaires*

The Three Musketeers is the most famous of around two hundred and fifty books to come from the pen of this prolific author and his seventy-three assistants. Alexandre Dumas worked with the history professor Auguste Maquet, who is often credited with the premise for, and even the first draft of, *Les Trois Mousquetaires*, although the text, like all his others, plays very fast and loose with the historical narrative.

D'Artagnan, the hero, is a Gascon, a young man who embodies in every aspect the hotheaded stereotype of the Béarnais people. Armed with only a letter of recommendation to M. de Tréville, head of King Louis XIV's musketeers, and his prodigious skill with a sword, this incomparable youth cuts a swathe through seventeenth-century Paris and beyond, seeking his fortune. The enduring quality of Dumas's texts lies in the vitality he breathes into his characters, and his mastery of the *roman feuilleton*, replete as it is with teasers and cliffhangers. *The Three Musketeers* is a romance par excellence, and the pace of the narrative carries the reader on a delirious journey. The strength of the characters, from the "Three Musketeers" themselves, to Cardinal Richelieu and the venomous "Milady," need scarcely be highlighted, so entrenched have they all become in Western culture. The charisma of Dumas's swaggering young Gascon certainly remains undimmed. **DR**

🔇 The Musketeers display their swashbuckling skill with the sword in an early twentieth-century illustration of Dumas's romance.

Facundo

Domingo Faustino Sarmiento

Lifespan | *b*. 1811 (Argentina), *d*. 1888 (Paraguay)
First Published | 1845, serialized in *El Progreso*
Original Title | *Civilización y Barbarie: Vida de Juan Facundo Quiroga*

Facundo; or, Civilization and Barbarism in the Argentine Pampas—the title of the last edition published in the author's lifetime—is not a novel. But this hybrid of biography, history, geography, recollections, Utopian accounts, diatribes, and political programs has greater narrative strength than any Spanish-American fiction of its time.

The life of Juan Facundo Quiroga (1793–1835), a Caudillo gaucho during the civil wars that marked the independence of Argentina, is used by Sarmiento as a vehicle for his interpretation of the state. An imaginary Argentina is turned into the main protagonist: visualized as oriental, medieval, and African (models that must be given up), but also as Roman and French (models to aspire to). Argentina is a heroine fought over by two colossi: that of civilization (the city, the future, Europe) and that of barbarism (the pampas, the present, America). Facundo represents the second and he is a disguised version of Rosas, the dictator in power when the book was written, who forced Sarmiento into exile in Chile. The book's main literary value lies in Facundo himself, a fascinating, monstrous creature, thanks to the skill of Sarmiento's writing. The complex additions that surround the text (titles, epigraphs, and notes), the symbolic and allegorical depth of many passages, the powerful and often self-aware style, which seeks to win the agreement of the reader, reveal a modern quality that still nourishes the best Argentine novelists. **DMG**

The Devil's Pool

George Sand

Lifespan | *b.* 1804 (France), *d.* 1876
First Published | 1845, by Desessart (Paris)
Given Name | Amandine-Aurore-Lucile Dupin
Original Title | *La mare au diable*

"To tell the truth, this chant is only a recitative, broken off and taken up at pleasure."

◆ George Sand's adoption of a male *nom de plume* was typical of her determined stand against social and marital conventions.

In her lifetime, George Sand was a cultural celebrity, known as much for her liberated lifestyle as for her novels. After a failed early marriage, she had a number of highly scrutinized affairs; Chopin and De Musset were among her lovers. Her most famous early novel, *Indiana*, was a graphic proto-feminist depiction of the fate of a woman abused as much by her husband as by her lover.

In the 1840s, however, Sand turned to writing a series of novels of rural life, set in the countryside of Berry, where she lived on her country estate of Nohant. The hero of *The Devil's Pool* is Germain, a widowed ploughman. Left by his wife's death with sole responsibility for three young children, he reluctantly accepts the logic of courting a rich widow, Catherine Leonard, in a neighboring region. He travels to meet the widow in the company of a young shepherdess, Marie, who has found work on a farm in the widow's neighborhood. On their journey, they stop by the pool of the title and bond under its magical influence. Both Germain and Marie find disillusion on arrival—the widow is vain and proud, and Marie's employer attempts to abuse her. After many vicissitudes, ploughman and shepherdess recognize their mutual love.

The tone and intention of the novel is idyllic. Sand consciously serves up the countryside for a sophisticated readership as an escape from urban complexity and corruption. Although she never flinches from country life's harsher realities—this is a world of endemic poverty and low life expectancy— these are implicitly accepted as part of the unchanging natural order. Sand's rural novels were immensely popular in her own day, and they have retained a real freshness and charm as an authentic expression of the Romanticism of their era. **RegG**

The Count of Monte-Cristo

Alexandre Dumas

Alexandre Dumas's very well-known serialized novel begins with the incarceration of the hero, Edmond Dantès, in the Château d'If, as a result of the denunciation by his rivals of his purported Napoleonic allegiance, just before Napoléon's return from Elba in 1815. During his fourteen-year imprisonment, the hero fortuitously meets the Abbé Faria, who educates him and reveals to him the secret of the great wealth hidden in the Island of Monte-Cristo. Edmond is able to make a dramatic escape, substituting himself for the Abbé's dead body, which—enclosed in a bag—is thrown into the sea. The transformation of Edmond into the Count of Monte-Cristo begins.

Now wealthy, the Count is able to make those whose denunciations condemned him to prison suffer for their evil slander. Each of them will be subjected to a series of imaginative punishments, as the setting of the novel moves from Rome and the Mediterranean to Paris and its surroundings. The ingenious plots involve concealment and revelation, sign language, use of poisonous herbs, and all manner of other things. But beyond the exciting narrative, Dumas focuses on the corrupt financial, political, and judicial world of France at the time of the royal restoration, and on the marginal figures, such as convicts, that infiltrate it.

Finally, the Count wonders if his program of retribution has not led him to usurp God's power in order to see justice done. This apparently fantastic and passionate tale of revenge is a historical narrative in the manner of Sir Walter Scott; that is, one that is not wholly accurate. Unfolding gradually, *The Count of Monte-Cristo* offers an unusual reflection on happiness and justice, omnipotence, and the sometimes fatal haunting return of the past. **CS**

Lifespan | *b.* 1802 (France), *d.* 1870
First Published | 1845–1846
First Published by | Pétion (Paris)
Original Title | *Le Comte de Monte-Cristo*

"Only a man who has felt ultimate despair is capable of feeling ultimate bliss."

Alexandre Dumas earned a fortune from his popular novels, but his profligate spending ensured that he died in poverty.

Jane Eyre

Charlotte Brontë

Lifespan | b. 1816 (England), **d.** 1855
First Published | 1847
First Published by | Smith, Elder & Co. (London)
Pseudonym | Currer Bell

"Reader, I married him."

George Richmond's 1850 chalk sketch of Charlotte Brontë captures her intelligence and unflinching personal integrity.

This is the first page of the original manuscript of *Jane Eyre*, which was published under the pseudonym Currer Bell.

Charlotte Brontë's first published novel tells a story common to her later novel, *Villette*, of a young woman who must struggle for survival, and subsequently fulfillment, without the support of money, family, or obvious class privilege. The orphaned Jane is caught between two often conflicting sets of impulses. On the one hand, she is stoical, self-effacing, and self-sacrificial. On the other, she is a passionate, independently minded, and dissenting character, rebellious in the face of injustice, which seems to confront her everywhere. As a child, Jane Eyre suffers first as the ward of her aunt, the wealthy Mrs. Reed, and her abusive family, then under the cruelly oppressive regime at Lowood School, where Mrs. Reed finally sends her. As a young governess at Thornfield Hall, questions of class thwart her course toward true love with the Byronic Mr. Rochester, with whom she has forged a profound connection while caring for his illegitimate daughter.

Class, however, is less of a barrier to their union—and both characters are in any case contemptuous of its dictates—than the fact that Mr. Rochester already has a wife. She is the infamous madwoman imprisoned in the attic (the Creole Bertha Mason from Spanish Town, Jamaica, whose story is imaginatively reconstructed by Jean Rhys in *Wide Sargasso Sea*). Bertha's plight has been seen to offer a counterpoint to Jane's, as well as raising questions about the representation of women in nineteenth-century fiction. Strong elements of coincidence and wish fulfillment lead ultimately to the resolution of the central romantic plot, but *Jane Eyre* still speaks powerfully for the plight of intelligent and aspiring women in the stiflingly patriarchal context of Victorian Britain. **ST**

Jane Eyre

by Currer Bell

Vol. 1st

Chap. 1st

re was no possibility of taking a walk that day.
had been wandering indeed in the leafless shrubb
hour in the morning, but since dinner (Mrs R
there was no company, dined early) the cold w
d had brought with it clouds so sombre, a rain
ting that further out-door exercise was now out
stion.

I was glad of it; I never liked long walks — espe
chilly afternoons; dreadful to me was the coming
the raw twilight with nipped fingers and toes and
dened by the chidings of Bessie, the nurse, and hum
the consciousness of my physical inferiority to Eliza,
Georgiana Reed.

Vanity Fair

William Makepeace Thackeray

For many, the defining moment of *Vanity Fair* occurs in its opening chapter. Becky Sharp, prospective governess, emerges from Miss Pinkerton's academy and flings her parting gift of Doctor Johnson's *Dictionary* back through the gates. This "heroical act" is our first indication of Becky's irreverent power to shape her own destiny, but in dispensing with that monument of eighteenth-century control and classification, William Thackeray also symbolically, if not literally, inaugurates Victorian fiction.

Thackeray's novel is historical: set in the Regency period, it explores the limits of that world, as well as the constitutive conditions laid down for its own. Becky is central to this achievement, as her literary creation draws on the dualistic possibilities of that transitional moment. A constantly calculating adventuress who, devoid of all sentimentality, is thus the perfect mistress of a society in which everything is for sale and nothing possesses lasting value. Yet our perception of the way in which she operates sets her quite apart from any of the satirical heroines of contemporary literature. She is seductive because of her constant power to surprise, balancing often conflicting emotions such as ambition, greed, and selfishness, with poise, warmth, and admiration. Becky makes her way through a hollow world with the Battle of Waterloo at its center, diagnosing the hypocrisies she exploits as well as acting as a foil to illuminate the few moments of generosity that are in evidence, her own included. As a result, she not only makes possible Tolstoy's *Anna Karenina*, formed directly under Thackeray's influence, but also Eliot's Gwendolen Harleth and Hardy's Sue Bridehead. Placed at the shifting heart of *Vanity Fair*, she causes its universe to be glitteringly compelling, and uncomfortably familiar. **DT**

Lifespan | *b.* 1811 (India), *d.* 1863 (England)
First Published | 1847
First Published by | Bradbury & Evans
Full Title | *Vanity Fair: A Novel Without a Hero*

Becky Sharp, Thackeray's self-willed anti-heroine, is visualized in period dress by *Vanity Fair*'s original illustrator, Frederick Barnard.

Photographed here by Ernest Edwardes in the 1860s, Thackeray was a satirist who despised the hypocrisies of Victorian society.

Wuthering Heights

Emily Brontë

Lifespan | *b.* 1818 (England), *d.* 1848
First Published | 1847
First Published by | T. C. Newby (London)
Pseudonym | Ellis Bell

There has been a great obsession with solitude in modern writing, and Emily Brontë's *Wuthering Heights* must stand as the most violent expression of the products of extreme austerity and isolation ever written. It is an utterly psychotic love story, as far removed both from the novels of her two sisters and William Wyler's 1939 film adaptation as imaginable.

Emily Brontë was brought up with great simplicity, encountering only her father, an Irish pastor, and her sisters, with whom she traded stories to pass the time on their remote Yorkshire wasteland. Given her situation, she could not possibly have acquired any true experience of love, so how could she possibly have distilled such unaffected beauty and crazed, passionate fury into a novel? There is a kind of awful modernity in the story of doomed lovers Catherine and Heathcliff, a model of society at its most efficient, squeezing out the elemental and the innocent freedom of childhood in favor of a calculated reason, and it is this process that plunges the two lovers into disaster. Catherine is able to deny the freedom of her youth for a place in adult society, Heathcliff is driven to a furious retribution that will stop at nothing. *Wuthering Heights* is a model of catastrophe as envisaged by an innocent woman able to express pure desperation. Doubtless this is the reason that compelled Georges Bataille to judge it "one of the greatest books ever written." **SF**

The Tenant of Wildfell Hall

Anne Brontë

Lifespan | *b.* 1820 (England), *d.* 1849
First Published | 1848
First Published by | T. C. Newby (London)
Pseudonym | Acton Bell

A sensational story of alcoholism and domestic abuse, *The Tenant of Wildfell Hall* scandalized reviewers on its publicaton. As *The American Review* put it, the book takes the reader "into the closest proximity with naked vice, and there are conversations such as we had hoped never to see printed in English." Nevertheless, the book sold remarkably well, and in a Preface to a second edition of the book, Anne Brontë (writing as Acton Bell) defended herself against her critics, by citing the novelist's moral duty to depict "vice and vicious characters ... as they really are."

The Tenant of Wildfell Hall, with its feminist themes, is a powerful portrayal of a young woman's marriage to a Regency rake, her pious struggle to reform him, and, finally, her flight in order to protect their son against his father's corruption. Told largely from Helen Huntingdon's point of view, through letters and journals, the novel recounts an abusive relationship at a time in English history when married women had few legal rights. As the novelist May Sinclair wrote in 1913: "The slamming of Helen's bedroom door against her husband reverberated throughout Victorian England"—a reverberation that continues to resound for readers today. **VL**

◗ A close-up of Anne and Emily Brontë, taken from Branwell's original portrait of all three Brontë sisters.

David Copperfield

Charles Dickens

Lifespan | *b.* 1812 (England), *d.* 1870
First Published | 1850, by Collins (London)
Full Title | *The Personal History, Experience, and Observation of David Copperfield*

Regarded as Charles Dickens's most autobiographical work, David's account of his childhood ordeal working in his stepfather's warehouse, and his training as a journalist and parliamentary reporter certainly echoes Dickens's own experience. A complex exploration of psychological development, *David Copperfield*—a favorite of Sigmund Freud—succeeds in combining elements of fairy tale with the open-ended form of the Bildungsroman. The fatherless child's idyllic infancy is abruptly shattered by the patriarchal "firmness" of his stepfather, Mr. Murdstone. David's suffering is traced through early years, his marriage to his "child-wife" Dora, and his assumption of a mature middle-class identity as he finally learns to tame his "undisciplined heart."

The narrative evokes the act of recollection while investigating the nature of memory itself. David's development is set beside other fatherless sons, while the punitive Mr. Murdstone is counterposed to the carnivalesque Mr. Micawber. Dickens also probed the anxieties that surround the relationships between class and gender. This is particularly evident in the seduction of working-class Emily by Steerforth, and the designs on the saintly Agnes by Uriah, as well as David's move from the infantilized sexuality of Dora to the domesticated rationality of Agnes in his own quest for a family. **JBT**

🔴 Dickens was photographed by Herbert Watkins in this relaxed pose at around the time *David Copperfield* was written.

The Scarlet Letter

Nathaniel Hawthorne

Lifespan | *b.* 1804 (U.S.), *d.* 1864
First Published | 1850
First Published by | Ticknor, Reed & Fields (Boston)
Original Language | English

The scarlet letter of the title is a gold-bordered, embroidered "A" that the puritanical community of seventeenth-century Boston forces adulteress Hester Prynne to wear. It is both a badge of shame and a beautifully wrought human artifact.

The Scarlet Letter, rich in a symbolism that contradicts its puritanical subject matter, seeks to demonstrate a community's failure to permanently fix signs and meanings. This waywardness lies at the heart of a series of oppositions in the novel between order and transgression, civilization and wilderness, the town and the surrounding forest, adulthood and childhood. The more this society strives to keep out wayward passion, the more it reinforces the split between appearance and reality. The members of this community who are ostensibly the most respectable are often the most depraved, while the apparent sinners are often the most virtuous. The novel crafts intriguing symmetries between social oppression and psychological repression. Dimmesdale's sense of torment at his guilty secret, and the physical and mental manifestations of his malaise reflects the pathology of a society that needs to scapegoat and alienate its so-called sinners. Eventually, personal integrity is able to break free from social control. Perhaps more so than any other novel, *The Scarlet Letter* effectively encapsulates the emergence of individualism and self-reliance from America's puritan and conformist roots. **RM**

Moby-Dick

Herman Melville

Lifespan | *b.* 1819 (U.S.), *d.* 1891
First Published | 1851
First Published by | Harper (New York)
Full Title | *Moby-Dick; or, The Whale*

"A whaleship was my Yale College and my Harvard."

⊙ Pictured here is the astute Herman Melville in 1850, at the age of thirty-one, captured in paint by Asa W. Twitchell.

❯ Rockwell Kent's illustration for a 1937 edition of *Moby Dick* shows the great white whale upending a boatful of whalers.

Moby-Dick is often cited as "the Great American Novel," the high watermark of the nineteenth-century literary imagination. A huge, monstrous, and yet exquisitely refined creation, the novel continues to confound, enthrall (and often defeat) generations of readers around the world. Narrated by Ishmael, a Massachusetts schoolteacher who has forsaken his old life for the romance of the high seas, the novel chronicles the long sea voyage of the *Pequod*, a whaling ship led by the demonic Captain Ahab. Ahab is hunting for the white whale that has robbed him of one of his legs. All other considerations (including the safety of his crew) become secondary concerns compared with his monomaniacal quest.

No simple plot summary can do justice to the breadth and complexity of Melville's novel. One can almost feel the book fighting with itself—balancing the urge to propel the narrative forward with the urge to linger, explore, and philosophize. *Moby-Dick* is a turbulent ocean of ideas, one of the great meditations on the shape and status of America—on democracy, leadership, power, industrialism, labor, expansion, and nature. The *Pequod* and its diverse crew become a microcosm of American society. This revolutionary novel borrowed from a myriad literary styles and traditions, switching with astonishing ease between different bodies of knowledge. Quite simply, no one in American literature had written with such intensity and such ambition before. In *Moby-Dick* are abstruse metaphysics, notes on the technicalities of dissecting a whale's foreskin, and mesmerizing passages of brine-soaked drama. *Moby-Dick* is an elegy, a political critique, an encyclopedia, and a ripping yarn. Reading the novel constitutes an experience every bit as wondrous and exhausting as the journey it recounts. **SamT**

The House of the Seven Gables

Nathaniel Hawthorne

Lifespan | *b.* 1804 (U.S.), *d.* 1864
First Published | 1851
First Published by | Ticknor, Reed & Fields (Boston)
Original Language | English

Nathaniel Hawthorne draws heavily on his New England roots in this novel, which is marked by an extreme determinism, punctuated by withering observations of contemporary materialism, as the residual effects of familial guilt are traced through several generations. Nearly two centuries ago, Colonel Pyncheon constructed the eponymous house on land he had illegally confiscated from the Maule family, incurring a dreadful curse. As a result, the spring that had made the land valuable became stagnant, and the house was never a place of happiness. In the mid-nineteenth century the Colonel's descendant, Judge Jaffrey Pyncheon, has inherited the Colonel's power, greed, and hypocrisy. His lodger, Holgrave, is the novel's crucial unifying figure; the revelation of his true identity offers hope that the sins of the past need not endlessly pollute the future.

The surprising sentimentality of the conclusion palliates the bleak notion of inherited sin, but cannot efface it entirely. Hawthorne's acute historical consciousness meant that, for him, the past was always near at hand, shaping the physical, moral, and spiritual texture of the present; he felt out of step with nineteenth-century America's forward-looking faith in "progress," measured largely in economic terms. *The House of the Seven Gables* acknowledges this tension and explores the possibility of escaping from the burden of the past. **RH**

Uncle Tom's Cabin

Harriet Beecher Stowe

Lifespan | *b.* 1811 (U.S.), *d.* 1896
First Published | 1852
First Published by | J. P. Jewett (Boston)
Full Title | *Uncle Tom's Cabin; or, Life Among the Lowly*

The first American novel to sell more than a million copies, *Uncle Tom's Cabin* has a claim to be the most influential piece of fiction ever written. Stowe was galvanized by the passing of the Fugitive Slave Act in 1850 into writing what the poet Langston Hughes has called "America's first protest novel."

The saintly slave Uncle Tom, having lived most of his life with kindly owners, is sold for financial reasons at the novel's outset. Refusing to escape, Uncle Tom responds with Christian tolerance and forgiveness, maintaining his faith consistently until his brutal death. Although "Uncle Tom" has become a byword for black complicity in white oppression, for Stowe, Tom displays Christian virtues, and his Christ-like death positions him as the chief moral exemplar of the novel. Besides the overt emotional and physical suffering of slaves, Stowe emphasizes how slavery damages the morality and humanity of white slave owners themselves. The diverse cast of strong females, black and white, displayed how women, too, could help to achieve abolition.

Stowe surely achieved her political aims with this phenomenally successful novel that was to play a significant role in the forthcoming American Civil War, inspiring anti-slavery activism, and deeply antagonizing slave-holding. **RH**

> Like any bestseller, *Uncle Tom's Cabin* fed off its own success, attracting new readers on the basis of numbers already sold.

135,000 SETS, 270,000 VOLUMES SOLD.

UNCLE TOM'S CABIN

FOR SALE HERE.

AN EDITION FOR THE MILLION, COMPLETE IN 1 Vol., PRICE 37 1-2 CENTS.

"   "   IN GERMAN, IN 1 Vol., PRICE 50 CENTS.

"   .   "   IN 2 Vols,. CLOTH, 6 PLATES, PRICE $1.50.

SUPERB ILLUSTRATED EDITION, IN 1 Vol., WITH 153 ENGRAVINGS,

PRICES FROM $2.50 TO $5.00.

The Greatest Book of the Age.

CRANFORD

by
Mrs
Gaskell

George G. Harrap & Co. Ltd. London.

Cranford
Elizabeth Gaskell

At first glance, *Cranford* might seem insubstantial, but Elizabeth Gaskell has provided a remarkable insight into the ideas and actions behind social change in a small, fictional country town in the early nineteenth century. Gaskell depicts a set of wholly credible characters, with a delicacy fully worthy of Jane Austen. *Cranford* engrosses the reader in the lives of these characters even as they go about their mundane daily business.

Cranford is essentially a town—and a society—ruled by women, mostly single or widowed. The narrator, Mary, who no longer lives in Cranford and can thus see it from the outside, describes the occasional arrivals, departures, and deaths as seen through their impact on the town's women. Mary adopts an attitude of amused indulgence toward her friends, but never allows herself to tip toward scorn or mockery. There is a strong sense that life in Cranford is locked into a spiral of genteel decline; even though the women no longer possess the necessary wealth, they stoically attempt to adhere to the traditional rules of social decorum. The men who should be here have defected to the nearby industrial town of Drumble, which, although never seen in the novel, exerts a powerful influence on life in Cranford. What is exceptional about the book is that, although the main characters often seem involved in events and squabbles of the most petty variety, we never lose our sympathy either for their struggles to make ends meet, or for their unceasing attempts to conceal the fragility of their circumstances; indeed, there is an astonishing bravery half-hidden within this tale of domestic incident. The reader is made to see that, as this way of life passes away, something valuable beyond the more obvious social facades is being lost. **DP**

Lifespan | *b*. 1810 (England), *d*. 1865
First Published | 1853
First Published by | Chapman & Hall (London)
Original Language | English

"'I'll not listen to reason,' she said, now in full possession of her voice, which had been rather choked with sobbing. 'Reason always means what someone else has got to say.'"

◉ The ladies of Cranford pursue their lives of genteel poverty as satirically visualized by Irish illustrator Hugh Thomson.

◐ A 1940 edition of Gaskell's *Cranford* uses a portrait of the author herself as the centerpiece of its elaborate title page.

Bleak House

Charles Dickens

Lifespan | *b.* 1812 (England), *d.* 1870
First Published | 1853
First Published by | Bradbury & Evans (London)
Original Language | English

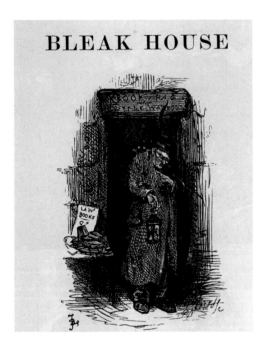

"The butterflies are free. Mankind will surely not deny to Harold Skimpole what it concedes to the butterflies."

⬤ H. K. Browne ("Phiz") produced suitably somber illustrations for Dickens's dark portrayal of fog-bound London in *Bleak House*.

Bleak House begins with fog: "Fog everywhere. Fog up the river, where it flows among green aits and meadows; fog down the river, where it rolls defiled among the tiers of shipping, and the waterside pollutions of a great (and dirty) city." And at the center of the fog, but murkier still, is the High Court. Legal corruption permeates this novel like a disease, issuing in particular from the Byzantine lawsuit of Jarndyce and Jarndyce, with which all the book's characters have a connection. This suit, the narrator tells us, has become so complicated and of such longevity "that no man alive knows what it means." People live and die as plaintiffs in the case. Structured around Chancery's tortuous machinations, Dickens's narrative is less picaresque than other of his works but nevertheless provides his customary, witty dissection of the layers of Victorian society. Whether they live in the sunny aristocratic milieu of the Dedlocks in Lincolnshire or in the slums of Tom-All-Alone's in London, there is always someone with a stake in the Jarndyce case.

In reality, it is the public sphere as a whole that is satirized in *Bleak House*. Everything resembles Chancery: Parliament, the provincial aristocracy, and even Christian philanthropy is caricatured as moribund and self-serving. At some unconscious level, all public life is tainted with a complicity between class, power, money, and law. Private and inner life is affected too. The narrative, which is split between the third person and the novel's heroine, Esther Summerson, concerns moral disposition as much as social criticism. Characters—from the wearyingly earnest to the brilliantly shallow, from the foolish and foppish to the vampiristic and dangerous—are all illuminated in the darkness of Dickens's outraged, urbane opus. **DH**

Walden

Henry David Thoreau

Walden is not exactly a novel, but it is indisputably a cornerstone of American literature. Between July 1845 and September 1847, Henry David Thoreau lived a solitary, austere, self-sufficient life in a simple cabin on the shore of Walden Pond, near Concord, Massachusetts, where he developed and practiced his personal and political philosophy. In a series of eighteen essays, distilled from his voluminous journal entries, *Walden* records Thoreau's thoughts and experiences of this time.

Convinced that "the mass of men lead lives of quiet desperation," Thoreau sought to "simplify" his life in every way, eating only what he found in the wild, or could cultivate himself. Apart from physical exercise such as walking, fishing, and swimming, the remainder of his time was devoted to observing the natural world around him, writing, reading, and thinking. His greatest luxury was the leisure to pursue these ends; he notes that "a man is rich in proportion to the number of things he can afford to let alone." Deeply influenced by the transcendental philosophy of Emerson, Thoreau rejected religious orthodoxy, seeking instead a personal bond with God, discovered through Nature. For Thoreau, however, Nature is not only spiritual; he describes with equal reverence his occasional approach toward primal savagery. He also refuses to feel hidebound by tradition, encapsulating the untapped potential of youth in the image of the West. This ethos underpins the appeal of *Walden* to generations of Americans, despite its rejection of aggressive capitalism. Thoreau's experiment was neither misanthropic nor revolutionary. Practical, honest, and beautiful, it is the record of one man's efforts to live "a life of simplicity, independence, magnanimity, and trust." **RH**

Lifespan | *b.* 1817 (U.S.), *d.* 1862
First Published | 1854
First Published by | Ticknor & Fields (Boston)
Full Title | *Walden; or, Life in the Woods*

> "*I went to the woods because I wished to live deliberately, to front only the essential facts of life . . .*"

◉ This frontispiece from the first edition of Thoreau's *Walden* emphasizes the return to a simplified lifestyle.

Green Henry

Gottfried Keller

Lifespan | *b.* 1819 (Switzerland), *d.* 1890
First Published | 1854
First Published by | Friedrich Vieweg und Sohn
Original Title | *Der grüne Heinrich*

A seminal example of the Bildungsroman, *Green Henry* is written in the tradition of Goethe's *Wilhelm Meisters Lehrjahre*, presenting the reader with a sensitive and thoughtful portrait of childhood, adolescence, and maturity. Called "Green Henry" because of the color of his clothes, Henry Lee grows up in a small Swiss village with his doting mother. Keller documents the passing joys and tragedies of childhood in painstaking detail, emphasizing the freshness and innocence of Henry's response to village life and the natural world, as well as his strong bond with his mother.

Henry grows older, moves to town, and begins to attend school, and Keller focuses on his moral and philosophical development, which leads to a desire to become an artist and to an attraction toward two women, the pure and innocent Anna and the earthy, sexually experienced Judith. Driven by these two forces, Henry confronts love, loss, and eventually artistic defeat, finally experiencing maturity through the putting-aside of his artistic ambitions in favor of a small but useful career in the provinces. Although the lessons that Henry learns growing up are painful, they are none the less instructive. Displayed throughout *Green Henry* is a skillful merging of larger social concerns with the vagaries of personal life. Often compared to Hardy's *Jude the Obscure*, it features vivid and realistic characters, whose place on the novel's stage, while often tragic, is ennobled by Keller's sympathy for the human condition. **AB**

North and South

Elizabeth Gaskell

Lifespan | *b.* 1810 (England), *d.* 1865
First Published | 1855, by Harper (New York)
First UK Edition | Chapman & Hall
First Serialized | 1854–55, by Household Words

North and South is, as its title suggests, a study in contrasts. Its heroine, the daughter of a clergyman who resigns because of his religious doubts, is displaced from the southern village of Helstone (a pastoral, traditional backwater) to the bustling manufacturing city of Milton Northern, a fictionalized Manchester in northwest England. The city teems with the energy of industrialization, its rising capitalist class, and all that comes with it: pollution, worker unrest, illness, atheism, and a host of other apparent evils. In this environment, the Hale family are truly foreigners, with their country-gentry habits and values. It is a "condition of England" novel that looks unflinchingly at the plight of factory workers, and at worker–"master" relations.

To this end, we find our heroine, Margaret Hale, befriending struggling families such as the Higginses, and speaking out for reconciliation between millhands and millowners. Interwoven in opposition to this story is the narrative of Margaret's coming of age, worked out in the romance plot between Margaret and her ideological antithesis, Mr. Thornton, a prominent factory owner and self-made man. Margaret loses her parents and the apparent certainty of her youthful rural values, but gains a more nuanced understanding of change, political as well as personal, and its possibilities. **ST**

❯ Gaskell was deeply concerned with social issues in Victorian society, such as the exploitation of child labor in cotton mills.

Madame Bovary

Gustave Flaubert

Madame Bovary is a revelation; almost 150 years old, it feels as fresh as if it were tomorrow's novel. Readers who are accustomed to think of nineteenth-century novels as rambling, digressive, plot-driven stories will have a shock when they encounter a novel from that long century that is digressive and has a compelling plot but wraps all these up in a prose style so exquisite that the book feels fragile and sturdy all at once.

Flaubert takes the story of adultery and presents it as banal, an unheroic element of the unheroic provincial petit bourgeois world he is immersed in. But he also makes it beautiful, sordid, melancholy, and joyous, revels in emotions run amok and the mess of feelings that clichés can neither hide nor contain. Emma Bovary, a beauty confined to a marriage that bores her, yearns for the gigantic and gorgeous emotions she finds in the romance novels she devours. Her life, her husband, her imagination is not enough; she takes a lover and then another, but they, too, fail to sate her appetites. She shops, using an array of material objects as a means of fulfillment; when these also give way before the depths of her yearning, she finally kills herself, in debt and in despair.

Flaubert does not mock Emma Bovary; neither does he sentimentalize, moralize, or treat her joy or desperation as heroic. The impersonal, prosaic narrator—a monster of precision and detachment yet endearing, almost charming—mocks all with his aloofness, and cherishes all with his lavish and meticulous attention to detail. The result is a rich context—not just for Emma Bovary but for the novel, for writing itself. For so much scrupulous care to be given to something, that something must be precious. Flaubert makes this novel precious. **PMcM**

Lifespan | *b.* 1821 (France), *d.* 1880
First Published | 1857
First Published by | Charpentier (Paris)
Original Language | French

For writing *Madame Bovary*, Flaubert was prosecuted for offences against public morality—ensuring the book's notoriety.

The follies of the novel's eponymous heroine are presented mercilessly, yet without alienating the reader's sympathy.

Indian Summer
Adalbert Stifter

Lifespan | *b.* 1805 (Austria), *d.* 1868
First Published | 1857
First Published by | Gustav Heckenast (Budapest)
Original Title | *Der Nachsommer*

🔵 The title page of the first edition of Stifter's *Indian Summer* is illustrated with a restrained etching by Peter Johann Geiger.

Adalbert Stifter's *Indian Summer* is a novel that defies many expectations of the genre. For a work of such length, its plot does not seem very exciting at first glance, and the style is deliberately plain. The novel offers few of the majestic scenes of Bohemian forests and mountains otherwise found in Stifter's stories, which have been well known to many generations of schoolchildren in Central Europe.

It is characteristic of the novel's design that the name of the young narrator, Heinrich, is not revealed until quite some way into the text, after his scientific expeditions have already taken him several times to the Freiherr von Risach's remote country house. Heinrich, for his part, is never curious to find out his kind host's name. Like Heinrich, the reader is not told the story of Risach's youth—the only tragic episode that interrupts the novel's serene course—until near the end, when the love between Heinrich and Natalie, benignly watched over by his parents, her mother, and Risach, has blossomed into marriage.

The rewards of this novel lie not in sudden revelations or dramatic conflicts but in the fruits borne by diligent work of the kind to which Risach dedicates himself—cultivating roses, restoring old furniture. Thus, the flowering of a delicate cactus in Risach's greenhouse is one of several late scenes in the novel that reward the reader's patience. Equally, Risach allows Heinrich's artistic sense to mature gradually, enabling Heinrich in another late "blossoming" scene to appreciate fully the beauty of a statue that he had previously overlooked.

This is a novel that may not appeal to everyone. On its first appearance, it was widely criticized, but Nietzsche, significantly, regarded it as one of the few gems of German prose because its serenity so defied the hectic spirit of its time. **LS**

Adam Bede

George Eliot

George Eliot's first full-length novel is at once a fine example of, and contains a passionate artistic manifesto for, literary realism. Set in the English Midlands, in the early nineteenth century, the eponymous character, a carpenter, is in love with the flighty, shallow, and vain Hetty Sorel. She, in turn, is seduced by the likeable but irresponsible local squire, Arthur Donnithorne, who leaves town shortly after getting her pregnant.

The main drama lies in the gripping rendition of Hetty's lonely and unsuccessful journey to find her lover, her eventual infanticide, and her moving confession to her cousin, Dinah Morris. The confession, in its charged moment of interpersonal communication and sympathy, provides the symbolic and moral climax of the book.

Eliot's agnostic humanism enables her to retain—without any spiritual belief—the Christian ethical schema of confession, forgiveness, and redemption. It is at this moment that Eliot's writing moves away from documentary fidelity of the Dutch realists, whose paintings, she suggests, are analogous to her own work, to a heightened diction that conjures with the unknown and the sublime. Indeed, while the novel is peopled with lovingly sketched rural characters, it is almost more compelling at times such as this, when the language of realism develops into something stranger. Despite its suggestion of something that lies beyond the everyday life of human affairs, the novel's "realist" impulse is to suggest that one should subdue one's own desires to an acceptance of duty and the here and now. Contemporary readers might find the conclusion somewhat hard to swallow, but there remains much to relish in this vividly narrated and emotionally convincing novel. **CC**

Lifespan | *b.* 1819 (England), *d.* 1880
First Published | 1859
First Published by | W. Blackwood & Sons (London)
Given Name | Mary Ann Evans

'There's Adam Bede a-carrying the little un.'

⬣ The high-minded village carpenter Adam Bede has less impact on the reader than Eliot's more rounded female characters.

Oblomov

Ivan Goncharov

Lifespan | *b.* 1812 (Russia), *d.* 1891
First Published | 1859
Movie Adaptation | 1981
Original Language | Russian

One of the world's great novels, *Oblomov* came to be seen as the definitive representation of the lethargic and myopic Russian aristocracy of the nineteenth century. A principal target of the novel is the institution of serfdom; like many Russian intellectuals, Goncharov felt that Russia could not modernize and compete with the rest of the developed world unless it abolished the institutions and social practices that hampered it so severely.

But *Oblomov* would not be a remarkable novel if it were only a critique of an important, but now long gone, problem. A bittersweet tragicomedy, it centers on one of the most charming but ineffectual protagonists in literature. Oblomov is good-natured but lacks the willpower to put his ideas into practice. He relies on his much more able servant, Zakhar, to organize his pointless existence, in an updated version of the relationship between Don Quixote and Sancho Panza. Falling in love with the beautiful Olga, he simply cannot take the necessary actions to secure her affections, and he loses her to his practical but rather less appealing friend, Stolz. After this predictable failure Oblomov sinks further into lethargy, rarely leaving his bedroom, despite the good offices of his well-intentioned landlady. *Oblomov* is a brilliant and unusual novel about wasted opportunity: how many works of literature tell the story of a hero who fails to secure the object of his affections through inactivity? And how many can convince most readers that he is still a good man? **AH**

The Woman in White

Wilkie Collins

Lifespan | *b.* 1824 (England), *d.* 1889
First Published | 1860
First Published by | S. Low, Son & Co. (London)
Original Language | English

Opening with the hero Walter Hartright's thrilling midnight encounter with the mysterious fugitive from a lunatic asylum, *The Woman in White* was an instant hit when it first appeared as a weekly serial.

Different narrators present their accounts like witnesses in a trial. The plot investigates how a "legitimate" identity is built up and broken down through a set of doublings and contrasts. The rich, vapid heiress Laura, married to the villain Sir Percival Glyde, is substituted by her uncanny double, the woman in white, Anne Catherick. While Laura is drugged and placed in a lunatic asylum, Anne dies of a heart condition and is buried in Laura's place. The plot, mastermined by the engaging rogue Count Fosco, is narrated by Laura's feisty half-sister Marian, a character probably based on George Eliot. From the sensational moment when Walter Hartright sees his beloved Laura standing by her own grave, the story turns into a quest to reconstruct her. Walter's increasingly obsessive drive to prove Laura's identity leads to two disclosures of illegitimacy.

This book defined the sensation novel of the 1860s. Wild and uncanny elements of gothic fiction are transposed into the everyday world of the upper-middle-class family, appealing directly to the nerves of the reader and exploiting modern anxieties about the instability of identity. **JBT**

> Frederick Waddy's caricature shows a furtive Wilkie Collins pasting up a poster for his stage adaptation of the novel in 1872.

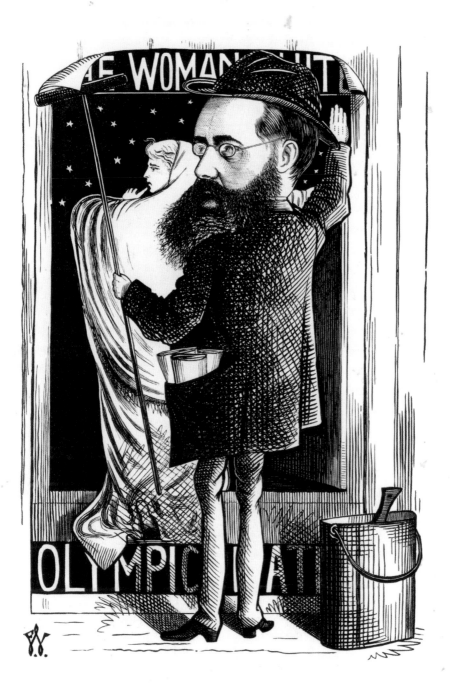

The Mill on the Floss

George Eliot

Lifespan | *b.* 1819 (England), *d.* 1880
First Published | 1860
First Published by | W. Blackwood & Sons (London)
Given Name | Mary Ann Evans

The Mill on the Floss reworks elements of George Eliot's own history into a study of childhood and of how a woman's identity is shaped and constrained by circumstance. Following the development of Maggie and Tom Tulliver, the two children of the miller of Dovecote Mill, it stresses the unpredictability of family inheritance. Stolid Tom takes after his mother, while his sister Maggie—dark, impulsive, and imaginative—favors her father. Unlike Tom, Maggie is intellectually sharp, and is a tomboy in contrast to her cousin, Lucy Deane. The story is set in the 1840s, within the wider provincial middle-class community of St. Oggs, and explores the competing forces of continuity and change. Tulliver is financially ruined by the modernizing lawyer Wakem; and while Tom labors to reclaim the family property, Maggie strives to overcome past feuds through her friendship with Philip, Wakem's disabled son. However, it is the brother–sister bond and the conflict between the claims of family ties that drive the novel. In a moment of impulse, Maggie gives way to her suppressed desire for Lucy's fiancé, Stephen, drifting with him down the stream, before returning, disgraced, to her family. In a tragic denouement, Maggie is ultimately reconciled with Tom; however, as the narrator comments on the aftermath of the flood, "Nature repairs her ravages—but not all." **JBT**

🔵 Tom and Maggie Tulliver are about to be overwhelmed by the flood in a late-Victorian visualization of the novel's climax.

Max Havelaar

Multatuli

Lifespan | *b.* 1820 (Netherlands), *d.* 1887
First Published | 1860
First Published by | De Ruyter (Amsterdam)
Given Name | Eduard Douwes Dekker

When it first appeared in print, *Max Havelaar* caused a stir that saw its author challenging the Dutch government to refute its essential truth: that colonial policy as practiced in Java at the time was nothing more than a series of extortions and cruel tyrannies that oppressed the peoples of the Dutch Indies by forcing them to forego planting rice crops in order to supply their overseas masters with coffee and tea. No one took up the challenge at the time, although much later, the main substance of the book was found to be accurate.

This notoriety, and the book's success in provoking some positive changes in the region, much as *Uncle Tom's Cabin* helped to focus attention on the plight of, and consequently improve the situation for, American slaves, does not relegate it to the status of a worthy tract that has attained its purpose. Beyond the missionary service accomplished, *Max Havelaar* remains a work to be read and enjoyed for its satirical humor. Recounting the adventures of a colonial administrator at odds with the government he serves, it takes on and renders laughable the bourgeois businessman and colonial administrator alike.

Multatuli, which means "I have suffered greatly" is now the name of both a Dutch literary prize and a museum in the Netherlands, and the Max Havelaar Foundation is a fair-trade labeling organization. While these homages are fitting, they remain only facets of a more complex novel. **ES**

Great Expectations

Charles Dickens

> *"I never had one hour's happiness in her society, and yet my mind all round the four-and-twenty hours was harping on the happiness of having her with me unto death."*

⊙ Miss Havisham, in her bridal gown, intimidates the young Pip in Marcus Stone's illustration of *Great Expectations*.

Lifespan | *b.* 1812 (England), *d.* 1870
First Published | 1861
First Published by | Chapman & Hall (London)
Original Language | English

Great Expectations works on numerous levels: as a political fairy tale about "dirty money," an exploration of memory and writing, and a disturbing portrayal of the instability of identity.

Looking back from some undistinguished and unspecified future, Pip recalls his childhood, living with his fierce sister and her gentle, blacksmith husband in the Thames marshland, and the fateful effects of his encounter with the escaped convict, Magwitch, by his parents' graveside. When Pip later comes into a mysterious financial inheritance, he assumes that it can only have come from the mummified Miss Havisham, preserved eternally at the moment of her own altarside jilting. But Dickens's great stylistic coup is to make ceiling and floor change places—as in an Escher picture.

Shorter and more quickly composed than Dickens's giant social panoramas of the 1850s, *Great Expectations* gains from this pacing, as it unfolds like a fever-dream. Victorian writers were fond of "fictional autobiographies," but Dickens's novel has another layer of unsettling irony, in that it tells of someone who has been constructing himself as a fictional character. And as Pip shamefully reviews his past life on paper, it often seems that the act of writing is the only thing holding his fractured identities together. Perhaps autobiography should ideally be an act of recovery, but *Great Expectations* dramatizes instead the impossibility of Pip's lending his life coherence, or atoning for the past. **BT**

Silas Marner

George Eliot

Lifespan | *b.* 1819 (England), *d.* 1880
First Published | 1861
First Published by | W. Blackwood & Sons (London)
Full Title | *Silas Marner: The Weaver of Raveloe*

Silas Marner weaves elements of fairy tale and traditional ballad into an exploration of the meaning of the family and the nature of belonging. Set in a "far-off time" when "superstition clung easily around every person or thing that was at all unwonted," it charts the moral, psychological, and social transformation of Silas, the weaver. He is cast out of his northern primitive Methodist community, and arrives as a stranger in the rural Midlands village of Raveloe. Isolated and feared, the weaver is reduced to miserly obsession and mechanical repetition. His fractured identity is recreated when he adopts Eppie, the abandoned child of an opium addict. The story of Silas's social assimilation into the community, and of Eppie's upbringing, contains some of George Eliot's most powerful writing. Set within this redemptive tale is the disclosure of Eppie's origins as the child of a disastrous secret marriage: that of the son of the local squire, Godfrey Cass, who finally acknowledges Eppie as his own. Eppie, however, decides to stay with her adoptive father and her working-class community, and the novel profoundly reworks the "family romance" that underpins so much English fiction, in which the child discovers noble origins and a "true self." Here, the family is seen primarily as a set of emotional and social bonds, rather than a genetic inheritance. Community takes the place of individual aspiration, and for all its static, pastoral quality, *Silas Marner* is a moving exploration of how social selves are made. **JBT**

Fathers and Sons

Ivan Turgenev

Lifespan | *b.* 1818 (Russia), *d.* 1883 (France)
First Published | 1862
Original Title | *Otti I deti*
Original Language | Russian

Published only a year after the emancipation of the Russian serfs, and during a period when Russia's young intellectuals were increasingly agitating for revolution, *Fathers and Sons* was very much a novel of the time in its depiction of two generations with widely differing political and social values.

The central and most memorable character in the novel is the self-proclaimed nihilist, Bazarov, who claims to accept no form of authority, and is only interested in ideas that can be verified by scientific materialism. The narrative follows Bazarov and his acolyte, Arkady, as they visit their parental homes: what results is a confrontation between the old order of the traditional fathers and its new challengers, their idealistic sons. As well as the contemporary political resonances, this antagonism demonstrates the timeless conflict between youth and its elders. Tensions are also explored within the relationship of the charismatic, domineering Bazarov and his initially star-struck disciple, with their differences becoming manifest when they fall in love with the same woman.

Turnegev's skill lies at the level of characterization: the profound (mis)communication that operates between the main protagonists ensures that, even when their actions and rhetoric may appear misguided, they are ultimately understandable and extremely human. *Fathers and Sons* remains a classic and beautifully drawn examination of the necessity and power of youthful idealism, and its pitfalls. **JC**

Les Misérables

Victor Hugo

Lifespan | *b.* 1802 (France), *d.* 1885
First Published | 1862
First Published by | A. Lacroix & Verboeckhoven
Original Language | French

🔵 The image of Cosette created by Hugo's illustrator, Emile Bayard, is now famous as the logo for the musical based on the novel.

🔵 An illustration shows the costumes designed for a French theatrical version of *Les Misérables,* performed in 1878.

Les Misérables is one of only a few novels that have taken on a vivid afterlife long after their initial publication. There have been (horribly) abridged versions, rewritings, movies, and, of course, the world-famous musical, yet in order to understand the true scale of Victor Hugo's achievement, one must return to the text itself.

Like Tolstoy's *War and Peace*, this novel is concerned with the way in which individual lives are played out in the context of epoch-defining historical events. What is "History"? Hugo asks us. Who creates "History"? To whom does it happen? What role does the individual play in such events? The character of Jean Valjean is thus the key to *Les Misérables*, an escaped convict whose desperate need to redeem himself through his adopted daughter, Cosette, lies at the heart of the novel. Valjean is pursued throughout by the extraordinary Inspector Javert, with whose life his becomes irrevocably entwined, and who is relentless in his determination to uphold the law and to apprehend him. This personal drama of hunter and prey is then cast into the cauldron of revolutionary Paris as Cosette falls in love with the radical idealist Marius and Valjean grapples with the possibility of losing all that he has ever loved. The novel draws the reader into the politics and geography of Paris with a vividness that is unparalleled, and then leads on, incorporating Hugo's characteristic meditations upon the universe, to the Battle of Waterloo, and the final, astonishing denouement. There are not many texts that can be termed national classics, but *Les Misérables* is one, and is a landmark in the development of the historical novel that stands alongside the greatest works of Dickens and Tolstoy. It is also a deeply compelling read. **MD**

Acte I. Jean Valjean. Jacquin. Une Femme. (2 T) Mme Magloire. Melle Baptistine. Un Brigadier. Mr Miriel

(5e T) _ Javert. Fantine. (4e T) La Tenardier Fantine. Tenardier. (3e T) _ Petit Gervais.

(5e T) Fauchelevent. Un Ouvrier. (6e T) Jean Valjean. (8e T) Sœur Simplice. Fantine. (9e T.) _ Cosette.

(10e T) Claquesous. Tenardier. Montparnasse Eponine. (11e T) _ Cosette. (12e T) Fauchelevent.

The Water-Babies

Charles Kingsley

Lifespan | *b.* 1819 (England), *d.* 1875
First Published | 1863
First Published by | Macmillan & Co. (Cambridge)
Full Title | *The Water-Babies: A Fairy Tale for a Land-Baby*

Often mistakenly thought of as a children's book, Charles Kingsley's masterpiece, *The Water-Babies*, was first published in *Macmillan's Magazine* just four years after Darwin's *The Origin of Species*. A ten-year-old chimneysweep named Tom, cruelly exploited by his master, Grimes, falls down the wrong chimney at Sir John Harthover's country estate into little Ellie's bedroom. There is a great hue and cry, and Tom, supposed to be a burglar, is chased through the grounds and drowns in a pond, but does not die. His memory of his land-dwelling life has gone and he is transmogrified into a water-dweller. He begins a voyage of physical and psychological exploration in this new world, rediscovering his own identity as he interacts with, and learns from, the other various sea creatures. In this watery realm, Tom learns the teachings of Mrs. Doasyouwouldbedoneby, and evolves from a dirt-encrusted chimneysweep into a clean Victorian gentleman.

The Water-Babies touches on most of Kingsley's favorite themes: the impact of poverty, education, sanitation, pollution, and evolution. In Tom's spiritual regeneration, Kingsley presents a vision of nature as at once the tool and the expression of divine reality. It is this aspect of the novel, where he shows that he is able to present Darwin's theory of evolutionary development as a series of parables, that we see Charles Kingsley at his best. More interestingly, Kingsley is also able to articulate and interact with notions of the degeneration of the species that would not become a common currency in the novel for another quarter of a century. In 1887, a special edition of the novel was published to commemorate Kingsley's death. The marvelous illustrations by Linley Sambourne are as violent, shocking, and completely unexpected as Kingsley's prose. **VC-R**

Charles Kingsley's concern with the fate of the poor—he was a Christian Socialist—permeated many of his fictional writings.

Tom the chimneysweep becomes an object of curiosity to his fellow water-dwellers in J. W. Smith's 1920s illustration.

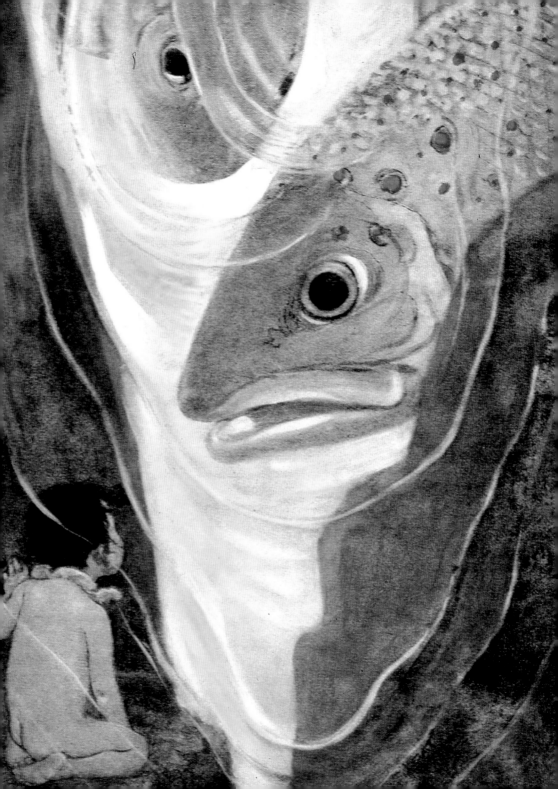

Notes from the Underground

Fyodor Dostoevsky

Lifespan | *b.* 1821 (Russia), *d.* 1881
First Published | 1864
First Published by | *Epokha* magazine
Original Title | *Zapiski iz podpolya*

"The more conscious I was of goodness . . . the more ready I was to sink in it altogether."

● This powerful photograph of Dostoevsky presents the image of a deeply serious individual haunted by inner demons.

As the title suggests, the anonymous narrator of Fyodor Dostoevsky's *Notes from the Underground* is a voice from beneath the daylight world—a troubled consciousness leaking out from a crack in the floorboards of Russian society. The novel is both the apology and the confession of a bitter, misanthropic civic official living alone in St. Petersburg. Divided into two sections, it reflects two key stages in Russian intellectual life during the nineteenth century: the rationalist utilitarianism of the 1860s and the sentimental, literary romanticism of the 1840s. Across these two parts, the narrator launches a series of dazzling, provocative attacks on the many changing orders of his lifetime—aesthetic, religious, philosophical, and political. He is a highly educated but deeply disillusioned soul, savaging both the "beautiful and lofty" romanticism of his youth and the new socialist principles that correspond with his middle age. No target is immune from scorn.

Notes from the Underground is Dostoevsky's darkest and strangest work. On the one hand, it is a kind of "case study"—an analysis of alienation and self-loathing, a novel that situates itself distinctly on the faultline between society and the individual. On the other hand, it is a tragicomic theater of ideas. It offers a powerful rebuttal to both enlightenment idealism and the promises of socialist utopianism. It bravely rejects notions of "development" and a "higher consciousness" and instead depicts human beings as persistently irrational, defiant, and uncooperative. According to Nietzsche, it is a work that expresses "the voice of the blood." *Notes from the Underground* is a shadowy, difficult, and compelling novel, which deserves to be recognized as forming much more than simply a critical prelude to Dostoevsky's later, more celebrated works. **SamT**

Uncle Silas

Sheridan Le Fanu

Uncle Silas arises principally from the genre of Victorian sensationalist fiction, and, like the works of Wilkie Collins, combines the interest of a hidden mystery with the compulsion of a determined investigation. Yet this story about the inheritance of a Derbyshire country house has also been shown to be a political allegory for the dissolution of Anglo-Irish society, and a metaphysical version of Emanuel Swedenborg's speculations about death and the afterlife.

The compelling heroine, Maud Ruthyn, functions as both an investigator and victim, enquiring into her father's secrets, and then suffering the consequences in her uncle's house. Silas's estate, Bartram-Haugh, represents one aspect of a poisonous paralysis of Protestant culture, but is also "a dream of romance," populated by the fantastic and the grotesque. There is nothing supernatural in *Uncle Silas*: all of its events can be accounted for purely by human malignity. Evil is not represented as spiritually evanescent but instead is manifest in physical characteristics: we are led to suspect characters because of their excessive appetites, "fat-faced" appearance, and dull, cunning expressions. A lexicon of corporeality leads the reader from the merely unconventional or malicious, to those "lean," white-faced figures who, like Uncle Silas himself, are merely deathly visiters in the world of the living. As such, these creations lie behind the unsettling ghost stories of the Edwardian age.

Sheridan Le Fanu's astute diagnosis of the Anglo-Irish tradition meant that his texts were also powerfully resonant for William Butler Yeats and James Joyce, arguably making *Uncle Silas* one of the less frequently acknowledged antecedents of the great works of twentieth-century modernism. **DT**

Lifespan | *b.* 1814 (Ireland), *d.* 1873
First Published | 1864
First Published by | R. Bentley (London)
Full Title | *Uncle Silas: A Tale of Bartram-Haugh*

"Later in life he married, and his beautiful young wife died."

◉ Le Fanu, photographed here around 1850, was a member of Anglo-Irish society—Anglican by religion but Irish by birth.

Alice's Adventures in Wonderland
Lewis Carroll

Lifespan | *b*. 1832 (England), *d*. 1898
First Published | 1865
First Published by | Macmillan & Co. (London)
Given Name | Charles Lutwidge Dodgson

Sir John Tenniel's original illustrations for *Alice in Wonderland* are an integral part of the book's imaginative universe.

Preceded by the white rabbit, Alice falls into the underworld in this illustration by W. H. Walker for a 1907 edition of the book.

Wholly familiar as an integral part of our culture, Lewis Carroll's trip down the rabbit hole is a children's book containing enough bizarre satire, wordplay, and comedy to satisfy any adult reader. Indeed, the Surrealist André Breton wrote of *Alice* that here, "accommodation to the absurd readmits adults to the mysterious realm inhabited by children." Far from patronizing children, the book is positively educative for jaded adults. Published in 1865, the same year as Lautréamont's infernal *The Songs of Maldoror* and Rimbaud's *A Season in Hell*, *Alice* may be a radically English, genteel journey into a dream landscape, yet it is not without its dark side.

Dozing on the bank of the River Isis, seven-year-old Alice spies the waistcoated White Rabbit anxiously checking his watch and decides to follow him underground. In her pursuit of the punctilious bunny, she stumbles into an assortment of odd predicaments. As she tipples potions and nibbles fungi she grows and shrinks from the size of a mouse to the size of a house, or sprouts a neck as long as a snake's. She encounters characters now inscribed on all our consciousnesses: the Mouse, bobbing in the "Pool of Tears," whose tale is typographically rendered as a tail; the hookah-puffing Caterpillar; the horrifying Duchess, nursing a pig; the disappearing grin of the Cheshire Cat; the tea-drinking Mad Hatter and March Hare squeezing Dormouse into a teapot; the murderous Queen of Hearts, who plays croquet with flamingo-mallets; and the dolorous Mock Turtle, who teaches her the Lobster Quadrille. Ever the prim ingénue, Alice tries to confront madness with logic, in a story that digs gently at the unsympathetic puritanism of Victorian bourgeois child-rearing practice. This is a book that must be read with Tenniel's original illustrations. **DH**

Journey to the Center of the Earth

Jules Verne

Lifespan | *b.* 1828 (France), *d.* 1905
First Published | 1866
First Published by | P-J. Hetzel (Paris)
Original Title | *Le Voyage au Centre de la Terre*

E. Riou's illustration for *Journey to the Center of the Earth* is captioned: "We descended a kind of winding stairs."

Jules Verne wrote other imaginary tales, a selection of which were published in this elaborately bound edition.

Journey to the Center of the Earth revives the literary tradition of the descent into hell, completely renewed in the form of science fiction. One of the great scientific questions of the mid-nineteenth century, which the novel explores, concerned the geothermic temperature deep within the earth's core, and the question of whether hot or cold temperatures prevail under the earth's crust. In the character of Axel, a kind of intellectual alter-ego, the novelist creates a defender of the theory of a central fire, who is opposed to his uncle, the woolly-minded professor Lindenbrock, defender of Humphry Davy's theory of a cool center. With extraordinary imaginativeness, the novel adopts the latter hypothesis and takes place in a Gruyère-like Cold Earth, where the volcanoes and the sea are linked by a series of channels.

Having managed to enter the earth through an extinguished volcano in Iceland, named the Sneffels, the characters find themselves in a huge cavity, sheltering an "inner Mediterranean sea," which they explore until they are ejected by the volcanic lava flow of the erupting Stromboli chimney. Their journey can be divided into two main parts. The first takes the heroes back through time, through successive geological layers, until they reach the "primitive granite." The second is the discovery of the inner sea—that is, of a paleontological space populated with "living fossils," where all periods of biological classification are mixed. The discovery of a human jaw in Abbeville, in 1863, prompted the writer to introduce into his narrative an "antediluvian shepherd," recalling the great anthropoids, who were—for the Darwinians who were debating the issue of evolution at the time—the ancestors of modern man. **JD**

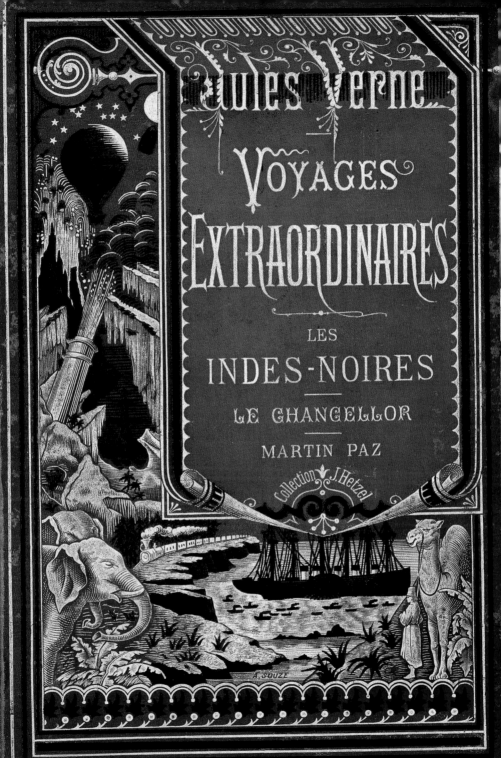

JULES VERNE

VOYAGES
EXTRAORDINAIRES

LES
INDES-NOIRES

LE CHANCELLOR

MARTIN PAZ

Collection J. Hetzel

A. SOUZE

LENEGRE. REL.

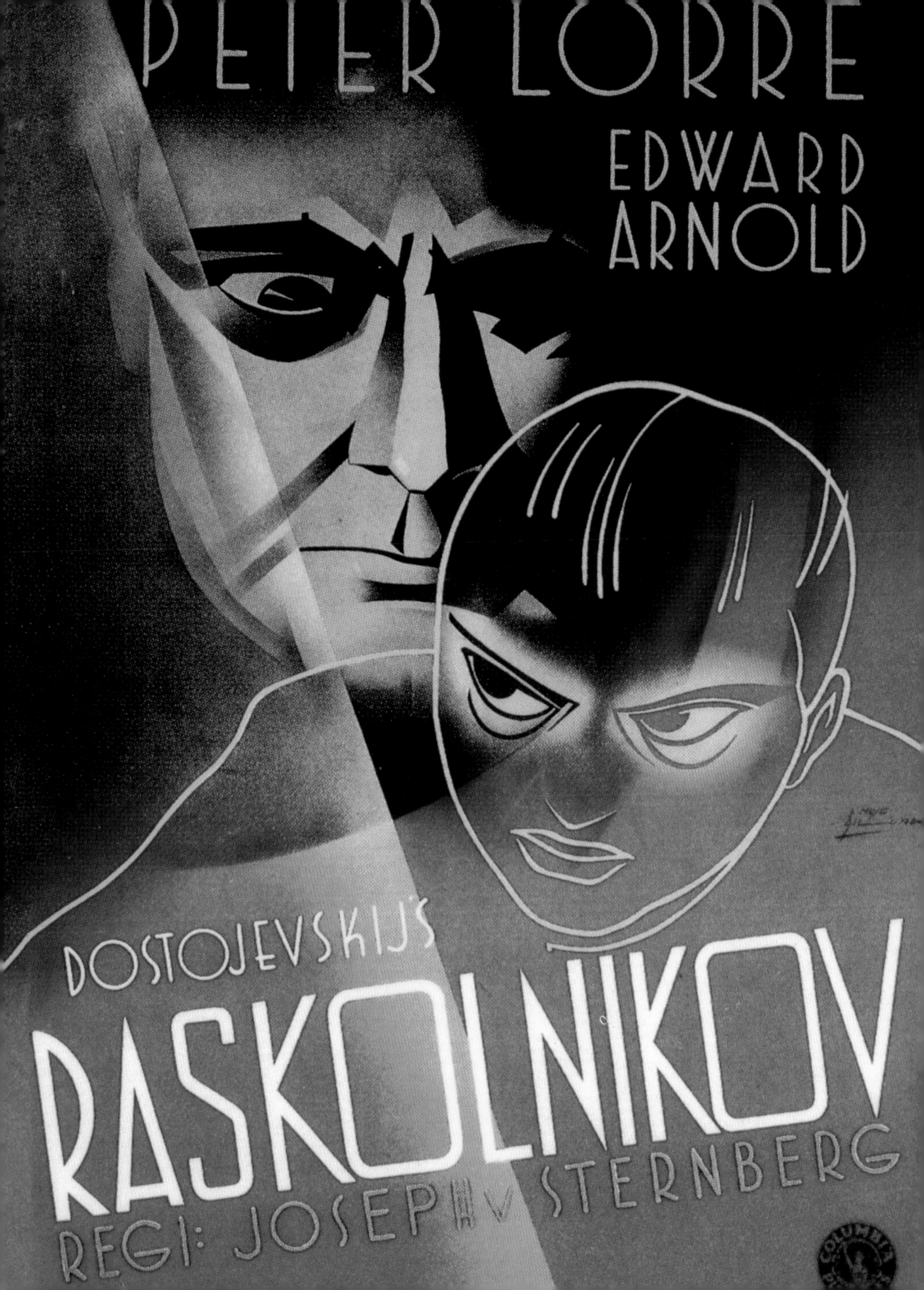
PETER LORRE
EDWARD ARNOLD
DOSTOJEVSKIJ'S
RASKOLNIKOV
REGI: JOSEPH v. STERNBERG

Crime and Punishment

Fyodor Dostoevsky

Lifespan | *b.* 1821 (Russia), *d.* 1881
First Published | 1866
First Serialized in | *Russkii Vestnik* periodical
Original Title | *Prestupleniye i nakazaniye*

Crime and Punishment is a masterpiece of Russian and world fiction, as captivating as it is, in the end, mysterious. Quite near the novel's beginning, the protagonist Raskolnikov commits, for reasons opaque to himself and to the reader, a double murder. For the rest of the book he walks, rambles, or staggers through the streets of St. Petersburg. He doubts whether his crime—which he barely regards as a crime at all—will be discovered. The concrete world around him is dissolving into the stuff of dreams.

It is often said that *Crime and Punishment* is a study of guilt, but this is not strictly accurate: Raskolnikov does not feel guilt, but he does feel terror and an extraordinary depth of alienation from the rest of humanity. Even though friends make their best efforts to help him, he is unable to accept their help. He is even unable to understand their feelings of love and sympathy, because he regards himself as an outcast—his ability to kill is the embodiment of that alienation rather than its cause or effect.

As readers, we are plunged into one man's delirium, a symbol for the incomprehension that might overtake us all if we looked closely enough at our fellow human beings. Although written in 1866, *Crime and Punishment* stands as the great antecedent to the twentieth-century literature of alienation of such figures as Camus and Beckett. **DP**

🔵 A Swedish poster for Josef von Sternberg's 1935 movie version of Dostoevsky's novel, with Peter Lorre as murderer Raskolnikov.

Last Chronicle of Barset

Anthony Trollope

Lifespan | *b.* 1815 (England), *d.* 1882
First Published | 1867
First Published by | Smith, Elder & Co. (London)
Original Language | English

Written between 1855 and 1867, the six novels that form the so-called *Barsetshire Chronicles* are a reflection of Anthony Trollope's fascination with everyday provincial life, together building up a panoramic view of the Church, marriage, politics, and country life in mid-Victorian England. *The Last Chronicle of Barset* has always held a special place among Trollope's novels. Its scope and scale, together with Trollope's masterly evocation of his famous mythical county, has meant that it is regarded as one of the most ambitious Victorian novels, and seems to sum up Trollope's work as a whole. It revisits the lives of some of Trollope's much-loved characters who appear in earlier Barsetshire novels. These include the poverty-stricken clergyman, Josiah Crawley, whose humiliation after being charged with stealing a check (wrongly as it turns out) forms the central crisis. Crawley, a proud, exasperatingly unsociable man, revels in his status as victim-martyr.

Parallel to the Crawley plotline, heroine Lily Dale clings onto the memory of the man who, some years before, had jilted her. Lily, a younger and prettier version of Dickens's Miss Havisham, now refuses to consider marrying anyone else, and at only twenty-four she determines to remain an "Old-Maid." Lily's obstinacy exasperated contemporary readers, but some recent critics have read Lily as a kind of protofeminist, whose strong sense of selfhood allows her to refuse to marry merely to conform to the expectations of her day. **AM**

Thérèse Raquin

Émile Zola

Lifespan | *b.* 1840 (France), *d.* 1902
First Published | 1867
First Published by | A. Lacroix (Paris)
Serialized Title | *Un Mariage d'Amour* (1867)

Thérèse Raquin is not the best of Émile Zola's novels; it has the hesitancy of a beginning and the dogmatism of a defense, rather than the assured scope of his later masterpiece *Germinal* (1885). Yet it is precisely the properties of uncertainty and of extravagance that make *Thérèse Raquin* significant.

In keeping with the developing creed of naturalism, Zola chose two "specimens" to enact his theories about sexual desire and remorse. But Raquin and Laurent, her lover, are so heavily invested with the responsibility of embodying Zola's mechanical determinism that they become strange, tortured creatures. The result is a novel seemingly divided against itself, a wonderful amalgam of wild eroticism and meticulous detachment. The impersonality of the third-person narrator is pushed to outrageous extremes as the would-be "scientific" narrator is forced to provide ever more elaborate explanations for the conduct of the two lovers. Thérèse Raquin herself is a magnificent creation; she enters the text as a site of mute desires and fears, as the "human animal" without free will, subject to the inexorable laws of her physiology. Gradually, however, and then volcanically, her history cumulates to give her voice and movement, and a superb consciousness of herself as a woman and of the bodily pleasures of being a woman. **PMcM**

Parodying a scene from *Thérèse Raquin*, caricaturist Lebourgeois shows Zola confronting a French officer over the Dreyfus affair.

The Moonstone

Wilkie Collins

Lifespan | *b.* 1824 (England), *d.* 1889
First Published | 1868
First Published by | Tinsley Brothers (London)
Original Language | English

The Moonstone is often regarded as the first—and, by some, the greatest—English detective novel. It concerns the theft of an invaluable diamond, but from this starting point it ranges across the whole history of the gem, from its original position adorning a Hindu god, through a succession of lootings, until it reappears in the nineteenth century as a wedding gift, and is immediately stolen. At this point, Sergeant Cuff is brought in and, with a little help, he eventually unfolds the mystery.

One of the remarkable features of the novel is that it is told in the first person from a variety of viewpoints, which compounds the mystery because it is not always clear whose account the reader should trust. Much of the novel is composed of dialogue between characters, which enables the reader to move surprisingly rapidly through the intricacies of the plot. Over the course of this long novel, Collins displays a remarkable ability to unpack the workings of people's minds; unusually, perhaps, for a nineteenth-century male writer, the minds of women as much as of men. There is a remarkable vividness to the scenes in which the novel is set, and a force of action that holds the reader spellbound from start to finish. Considered a landmark in English literature, *The Moonstone* is a mystery to be unravelled, but it is also a presentation of the essentials of nineteenth-century society, related with the lightest of touches and with the utmost realism of dialogue and characterization. **DP**

Little Women

Louisa May Alcott

Lifespan | *b*. 1832 (U.S.), *d*. 1888
First Published | 1868
First Published by | Roberts Bros. (Boston)
Full Title | *Little Women; or, Meg, Jo, Beth, and Amy*

A timeless evocation of idealized family life, *Little Women* was an instant success, and became one of America's best-loved classic novels. Originally a story for young girls, its appeal has since transcended the boundaries of time and age.

Little Women chronicles the lives of the four March sisters, growing up in New England against the backdrop of the American Civil War. The story details their struggles with poverty and hardship, their moral failings, and personal disappointments. While their father is away with the Union armies, the sisters, Meg, Jo, Amy, Beth, and their mother are left to fend for themselves, under the watchful eyes of their wealthy neighbors. The routine of their daily lives is punctuated by their letters and plays, misdemeanors and acts of kindness, as well as by their dreams and aspirations. The girls' progress into womanhood is marked by Meg's departure to be married, Jo's struggles to become a writer, Beth's untimely death, and Amy's unexpected romance. Partially autobiographical, *Little Women* offers a representation of Alcott and her own sisters. Perhaps it is this immediacy that gives this evocative portrait of nineteenth-century family life a lasting vitality, endearing it to generations of readers and inspiring new women writers, from Simone de Beauvoir to Joyce Carol Oates and Cynthia Ozick. **LE**

◷ The publication of *Little Women* brought Louisa Alcott fame, but also led her to be stereotyped as a children's author.

The Idiot

Fyodor Dostoevsky

Lifespan | *b*. 1821 (Russia), *d*. 1881
First Published | 1868–1869
First Serialized in | *Russkii Vestnik* periodical
Original Title | *Idiot*

Fyodor Dostoevsky's second long novel reworks the "holy fool" motif: the apparently naive person who may secretly be wise. The "idiot" in this case is the saintly Prince Myshkin, an epileptic (like the author himself), whom we encounter returning to Russia from a Swiss sanatorium to stay with his distant relative, Mrs. Yepanchin, the wife of a wealthy general. Set in the rapidly developing St. Petersburg of the 1860s, the narrative follows Myshkin's impact on the Yepanchins and the social milieu they inhabit. The prince serves as a catalyst for conflict between social hypocrisy and the emotions it masks, dealing with money, status, sex, and marriage. Like any good Russian novel, *The Idiot* includes a long list of characters with difficult names, and roils with intrigue and passion against the backdrop of an emergent bourgeois modernity.

At the outset, Myshkin befriends rich, wilful young buck Rogozhin, his opposite in every way. But the two men subsequently become rivals for the affections of Nastasya Filippovna. She is an orphan adopted by a General Totsky, who, it is strongly hinted, raped her in her adolescence. Her status is thus dubious, a fallen woman, but Myshkin, who can eerily divine inner characters, perceives in her a suffering soul; a spiritual bond forms between them, in sharp contrast to Rogozhin's fierce desire for her. How, Dostoevsky asks, does the ethereal, frequently insufferable spirituality of a Myshkin sit in relation to the more primitive drives of a Rogozhin? **DH**

Maldoror

Comte de Lautréamont

Lifespan | *b.* 1846 (Uruguay), *d.* 1870 (France)
First Published | 1868–1869
First Published by | Albert Lacroix (Paris)
Original Title | *Les Chants de Maldoror*

Although Lautréamont was unknown during his lifetime, his narrative prose poem *Les Chants de Maldoror* is now recognized as one of the earliest and most unsettling works of Surrealist fiction. The first canto of *Maldoror* was published anonymously in Paris just two years before the author's early death aged twenty-four. However, it was not until a Belgian literary journal took the bold step of republishing Lautréamont's work, in 1885, that he began to find an audience among the European avant-garde.

Maldoror tells the tale of the eponymous "hero" who rebels against God by committing an extraordinary succession of depraved and immoral acts. This is a wild, hallucinatory, poetic, and disturbing work—radical not only for its stylistic innovation (which the Surrealists so admired) but also for its blasphemous content. The tale encompasses murder, sadomasochism, putrefaction, and violence. It is a celebration of evil, a work that depicts Christ as a rapist and includes a protracted fantasy about intercourse with sea creatures. Each new act of inhumanity fails to bring Maldoror any kind of respite or satisfaction, and his fury increases as the book progresses. *Maldoror* retains its power to shock and bewilder, but perhaps its most interesting feature is the lyrical power of Lautréamont's prose, which succeeds in making the utterly repellent appear beautiful and enchanting—a disorienting effect that challenges both conventional morality and our assumptions about language itself. **SamT**

Phineas Finn

Anthony Trollope

Lifespan | *b.* 1815 (England), *d.* 1882
First Published | 1869
First Published by | Virtue & Co. (London)
Full Title | *Phineas Finn, the Irish Member*

Like the eponymous Irish hero of this novel, Anthony Trollope also had political ambitions, standing (unsuccessfully) as the Liberal candidate for Beverly in 1868. Chastened by his experiences, he channeled them into a series of six novels (the *Palliser* series), which analyzes the lives and loves of government ministers and their families, set against the backdrop of parliamentary intrigue and real-life politicians.

Phineas Finn MP is a familiar Trollopian hero: handsome, well mannered, impressionable, but weak and easily flattered. As he rises up the political greasy pole, attracting the notice of powerful government men, his private life grows more complicated. Although already engaged, Phineas becomes entangled with three different but equally alluring women—the brilliant Lady Laura Standish, the heiress Violet Effingham, and the mysterious Madame Max Goesler—all outstanding matches for the ambitious politician. Phineas's tendency to dither is typical of Trollope's young men and much of the novel is about how he reconciles his conscience with his ambitions and love of the bright lights. The capital of a great, self-confident empire, London is also a place where principled behavior is always threatened by political expediency, and good connections are much more important than mere ability. Trollope's interest lies not in political philosophy but rather in psychology, and in what makes mid-Victorian people "tick." His penetrating insights are much on display here. **AM**

Sentimental Education

Gustave Flaubert

Lifespan | *b.* 1821 (France), *d.* 1880
First Published | 1869, by M. Lévy Frères (Paris)
Original Title | *L'Education sentimentale: Histoire d'un jeune homme*

Sentimental Education is surely one of the greatest novels yet written, possibly even the greatest triumph in literary realism ever accomplished. It is a novelist's novel: though at first condemned as immoral by the Parisian reviewers on its publication in 1869, it was greatly admired by younger aspiring novelists. In the early twentieth century it stood as the measure to be matched by James Joyce and Ezra Pound. Gustave Flaubert was a tremendous laborer in his craft, obsessively preoccupied with the exactitude of every detail of social observation, as well as with literary style. He was the mythical master novelist, devoted beyond comprehension—the modern novelist, writing to a commercially imposed deadline, is the complete antithesis.

Sentimental Education follows Frédéric Moreau, an idle young man living on a grand inheritance. His ambitions and principles are discarded and dimmed in a thrillingly observed satire on the mentality of affluent consumers in a mid-nineteenth-century Paris defined by its ubiquitous exhibition of luxury goods and attitudes. But this is also the Paris of the July revolution of 1848. Frédéric drifts through the uprising, scintillated by death on the barricades as much as he is by a proprietorial relationship with a courtesan chosen to help him forget his true passion for another man's wife. The novel is at once gigantic in its historical perception, and minutely attentive to the slow suffocation of emotional and political idealism in a single heart. **KS**

> *"The artist must be in his work as God is in creation, invisible and all-powerful; one must sense him everywhere but never see him."*
>
> *Gustave Flaubert, 1857*

◉ Eugène Giraud's caricature of Flaubert catches the air of misanthropic superiority with which he viewed the world.

War and Peace

Leo Tolstoy

Lifespan | *b.* 1828 (Russia), *d.* 1910
First Serialized | 1865–1869, in *Russkii Vestnik*
First Published | 1869, by M. N. Katkov (Moscow)
Original Title | *Voyna i mir*

"Our body is a machine for living. It is organized for that, it is its nature. Let life go on in it unhindered and let it defend itself, it will do more than if you paralyse it by encumbering it with remedies."

⬧ Tolstoy achieved enormous prestige among the Russian people, revered as a spiritual leader and as a friend of the poor.

⬧ In his later years, Tolstoy gave away his fortune and lived like a peasant, condemning his great novels as worthless.

Leo Tolstoy's *War and Peace* is one of those few texts—James Joyce's *Ulysses* is another—that are too often read as some kind of endurance test or rite of passage, only to be either abandoned halfway or displayed as a shelf-bound trophy, never to be touched again. It is indeed very long, but it is a novel that abundantly repays close attention and re-reading. Like the movies of Andrei Tarkovsky, who was greatly influenced by Tolstoy, once you enter into his Russia, you will not want to leave: and in this sense, the length of the text becomes a virtue, since there is simply more of it to read.

Based primarily on the members of two prominent families, the Bolkonskys and the Rostovs, *War and Peace* uses their individual stories to portray Russia on the brink of an apocalyptic conflict with Napoleon Bonaparte's France. Events swiftly move the central characters toward this inevitable confrontation. No other writer surpasses Tolstoy in the scale of his epic vision, which encompasses the mood of whole cities, the movement of armies, and the sense of foreboding afflicting an entire society. The skirmishes and battles are represented with astonishing immediacy, all crafted from interlinked individual perspectives. The interconnected nature of the personal and the political, and of the intimate and the epic, are masterfully explored. As Tolstoy examines his characters' emotional reactions to the rapidly changing circumstances in which they find themselves, he uses them to represent Russian society's responses to the demands of both war and peace. One final note: if you are going to read *War and Peace*, then opt for an unabridged version. Tolstoy may be unjustly famed for his ability to digress, but to compromise the unity of the full version is to undermine the reading experience. **MD**

King Lear of the Steppes

Ivan Turgenev

Lifespan | *b.* 1818 (Russia), *d.* 1883 (France)
First Published | 1870 (Russia)
Original Title | *Stepnoy korol Lir*
Original Language | Russian

King Lear of the Steppes, a little-known novella, is Ivan Turgenev's literary appropriation of Shakespeare. It begins, in a narrative framing device, with a group of old friends discussing types of people they have known: everyone has met a Hamlet; someone once knew a potential Macbeth. But one speaker grabs their attention by saying that he once knew a King Lear—as though this were the ultimate impossibility and the ultimate storytelling challenge.

Turgenev's Lear, Martin Petrovich Harlov, is a plain-speaking, aristocratic country landowner who commands fear and respect from his peasants. He is mythically enormous, with a back that is "two yards long," and "as Russian as Russian could be." Among the symptoms of his Russianness are his bouts of superstitious gloom; he spends hours in his study pondering his mortality. This belief that death is imminent is his motive for dividing his estate between his two daughters; his only requirement for himself being that they look after him in his dotage. He is, of course, betrayed by both daughters and their scheming husbands, first manipulated and cowed, then driven out into the night.

The story represents the ideal mythic vehicle for Turgenev's visual imagination, and it enables him to experiment with a narrative that fluently combines onstage set pieces with the sense of Russian history progressing behind the scenes. **DSoa**

Alice Through the Looking Glass

Lewis Carroll

Lifespan | *b.* 1832 (England), *d.* 1898
First Published | 1871
First Published by | Macmillan & Co. (London)
Given Name | Charles Lutwidge Dodgson

In 1871, six years after *Alice in Wonderland*, Lewis Carroll returned to the Alice character with a new idea: to follow her into the world behind the mirror. Having recently taught the real Alice (Liddell) how to play chess, he used the game as a narrative device. The Looking Glass world is set out like a chessboard; Alice begins as a pawn and becomes a queen, with each chapter of the story dedicated to a move toward this end. As events progress, a chess problem, shown in a diagram at the start of the book, is solved correctly.

More schematic than *Wonderland*, this novel is nevertheless equally full of memorable characters and ideas, many of which involve contradiction and inversion. In order to get anywhere in this topsy-turvy place, Alice must walk in the opposite direction. Memory does not only go "backward"; the White Queen remembers things "that happened the week after next." We meet the "Contrariwise" twins Tweedledum and Tweedledee. Language also seems slippery, and meaning is elusive. Most famously, in the poem "Jabberwocky," we find Carroll's "portmanteau words," running together associations and meanings: "frumious," "mimsy," "slithy," and "brillig," among many others. **DH**

◉ Dodgson alias Carroll took this photo, with its playful mirror imagery; the girls may be Alice Liddell and one of her sisters.

Middlemarch

George Eliot

Lifespan | *b.* 1819 (England), *d.* 1880
First Published | 1871–1872, by Blackwood & Sons
Full Title | *Middlemarch, a Study of Provincial Life*
Given Name | Mary Ann Evans

"People glorify all sorts of bravery except the bravery they might show on behalf of their nearest neighbours."

⬥ In an early photograph, George Eliot is posed with an awkward expression that gives little idea of her high seriousness.

In *Middlemarch*, George Eliot focuses on the minutiae of ordinary lives led in a provincial English town, mapping in intricate detail the interior worlds of her many characters as a scientist might examine the tiny, interconnecting veins of a leaf through the lens of a microscope. It is through such insight and precision that Eliot achieves the measured realism for which *Middlemarch* is acclaimed, considered at the time of its publication, as it is today, to be one of the greatest English novels.

Middlemarch's impassioned heroine, Dorothea, is, like Lydgate—the young doctor whose story connects in vital ways with her own—an idealist. Convinced that a form of heroism can be found in even the smallest of gestures, she mistakes her first husband's intellectual pursuits for a work of such grandiose proportions. But Mr. Causabon's deathly project aspires to reduce to a single, simplified principle the Darwinian diversity that constitutes the very life force of the novel.

One of *Middlemarch's* central concerns is the way in which women adapt to the roles they have been allotted by society. We feel for Dorothea, painfully aware of her lack of education and financial dependency, as she strives bravely for heroism while her sister tinkles away contentedly on the piano. Struggling with their failings and wrong choices, trying to live well and to love well, the stories of Dorothea and Lydgate, interwoven with so many others, are at once intensely moving and acutely real. Eliot deftly spins her web of densely plotted suspense, and manages to lay bare the basic motivations of her characters with such compassion and understanding that we find ourselves soon caught up in the narrative, as their overlapping lives become entwined with ours. **KB**

Spring Torrents

Ivan Turgenev

The tone of *Spring Torrents* is perfectly poised between bitter regret for youth's lost passions and ironic awareness of their largely illusory quality. Dreading the approach of old age and the end of his rather aimless life, Dimitry Sanin finds "a tiny garnet cross" packed away in a drawer of his desk. The discovery evokes the wonderful, shameful story of his double love affair thirty years ago, when he was in Frankfurt, on his way back from the Grand Tour.

His intimate memories return in a series of vivid tableaux. First he recalls falling in love with Gemma, the daughter of an Italian pastry cook, who has a devoted brother and protective widowed mother, an operatically loyal family servant, Pantaleone, and a dull German fiancé. Sanin fights a ridiculous duel with an officer who has spoken insultingly about Gemma, displaces the dull fiancé, and even overcomes the mother's doubts. All seems set for a happy ending. But then, seeking a buyer for his estate to raise money for the wedding, Sanin falls into the company of decadent Russians: an old school friend, Polozov, and his magical, dominant wife, Maria Nikolaevna. Soon Maria, riding some way ahead of Sanin, is leading him deep into the woods: "She moved forward imperiously, and he followed, obedient and submissive, drained of every spark of will and with his heart in his mouth."

Sanin is a commonplace man, and his romance, with its ingenuous virgin and experienced femme fatale, replays a familiar tale. Turgenev's theatrical treatment brings to the foreground the affair's predictable and almost absurd aspect. But his precise, lucid, and sympathetic observation makes us aware at the same time that to Sanin, who is young, this is intolerably real, and that nothing in his later life will count for anything in comparison. **MR**

Lifespan | *b.* 1818 (Russia), *d.* 1883 (France)
First Published | 1872 (Russia)
Original Title | *Veshniye vody*
Original Language | Russian

"To desire and expect nothing for oneself . . . is genuine holiness."

Ivan Turgenev, 1862

⊘ A friend of writers such as Flaubert and Zola, Turgenev was better appreciated in western Europe than in his native Russia.

Erewhon

Samuel Butler

Lifespan | *b.* 1835 (England), *d.* 1902
First Published | 1872
First Published by | Trübner & Co. (London)
Full Title | *Erewhon; or, Over the Range*

As with many good science fiction texts, particularly utopian ones, *Erewhon* is more a comment on its own time that goes on to reflect prophetically on events of the future, than a genuinely futuristic text. Like More's "no place" of *Utopia*, *Erewhon's* reversed "nowhere" is a reflection on social unease and political development in the Victorian era, and its meditations on extreme and often contradictory social practices have as much currency today as they did then. As an allegory, *Erewhon* is at once reflective and disturbing, more so perhaps, as its dominant fears still lie at the heart of contemporary unease.

Butler's traveler Higgs finds himself in the world of Erewhon where everything is turned on its head. No machines are allowed—it is feared they will take over the world, a common science fiction theme. Criminals are sent to hospitals to recover from their misdeeds, education consists of studying anything as long as it has no relevance, and the sick are incarcerated.

Erewhon is a book that reflects directly on the implications of Darwinism, registering the shock that followed the publication of *The Origin of Species* (1859) among the reading public. *Erewhon* transposes these evolutionary ideas into a social context, once again identifying them with fear and distrust. Butler himself was profoundly influenced by Darwin's text, but, like many science fiction writers, also saw the potential for development of such themes along unsettling lines. **EMcCS**

"When I die at any rate I shall do so in the full and certain hope that there will be no resurrection, but that death will give me quittance in full."

Samuel Butler, Notebooks, 1912

🔘 Photographed here in 1898, Samuel Butler was a competent composer, painter, and translator as well as a satirical novelist.

The Devils

Fyodor Dostoevsky

Lifespan | *b.* 1821 (Russia), *d.* 1881
First Published | 1872 (Russia)
Original Title | *Besy*
Original Language | Russian

Though *The Devils* is quite possibly the most violent of Dostoevsky's novels, it also brims with buffoonery and trenchant social satire. Set in the late 1860s, the story concerns the fortunes of a group of insurgents committed to unleashing anarchy in Russia. As a series of betrayals inevitably consumes the group, the novel portrays the catastrophic consequences that can ensue from abstract political theorizing.

The orgy of destruction depicted in the closing pages has often been cited as an example of the author's proneness to sensationalism. As its title suggests, however, this is a novel about purgation, and in the Dostoevskian universe, the recuperation of society often comes at a heavy price. For example, the life is spared of the most dangerous character of the story, Peter Verhovensky (a psychopath who was loosely based on the ringleader of the so-called Nechaevists brought to trial in Russia). The fact that the innocent sometimes have to be sacrificed in order to regenerate society is only one of a series of provocative moral positions taken up by the novel.

The Dionysian frenzy that grips the action not only erases any easy understanding of the relationship between good and evil, it also points to the essential fragility of a society increasingly estranged from the moral certainties of the church. Within a generation Russia would surrender to convulsive social change; the novel offers a prescient and terrifying glimpse into the future of a society that has collectively lost its soul. **VA**

In a Glass Darkly

Sheridan Le Fanu

Lifespan | *b.* 1814 (Ireland), *d.* 1873
First Published | 1872
First Published by | R. Bentley (London)
Original Language | English

These five short stories of malign and supernatural forces were originally brought out in periodicals, but were later published together, united by the guiding narrative of the "German physician" Martin Hesselius, from whose casebooks the tales are drawn. His function, and hence that of the collection as a novel, could be regarded as regulative, bringing coherence and clarity—"the work of analysis, diagnosis and illustration"—to the darkness he observes.

If this truly is Sheridan Le Fanu's intention in this work, we must regard the book as a failure. Nobody is cured, no theory identified, no line of meaning uncovered. The stories are united instead by the lurid and persistent, figures of the preying imagination. These range from the avenging victims of a cruel judge to a small, black monkey of "unfathomable malignity," maddeningly singing through the head of the clergyman he tracks and corrupts. Whatever their origin, they all follow their targets with inexplicable determination. Yet they also have the power exemplified by the vampiric lesbian seductress Carmilla, perhaps the book's most memorable visitant. A specter of the body, not the soul, she absorbs the tale's narrator with "gloating eyes" that combine pleasure and hatred, physical excitement and disgust in equal measure. In confronting us with our own hitherto unapprehended fears and desires, Le Fanu shows these apparitions of ourselves to be the most modern, and enduring, of ghosts. **DT**

JULES·VERNE'S·WORKS

LOW'S AUTHORISED & ILLUSTRATED EDITION

AROUND THE WORLD
IN
EIGHTY DAYS

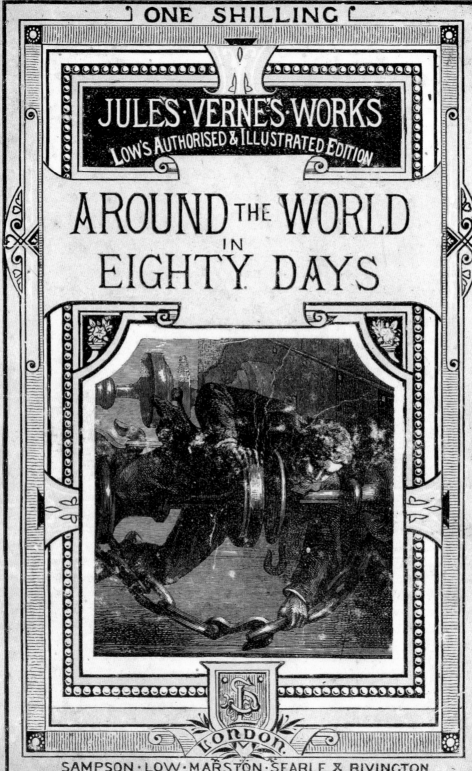

LONDON.

SAMPSON·LOW·MARSTON·SEARLE & RIVINGTON

Around the World in Eighty Days

Jules Verne

Lifespan | *b.* 1828 (France), *d.* 1905
First Published | 1873
First Published by | P. J. Hetzel (Paris)
Original Title | *Le Tour du monde en quatre-vingt jours*

Around the World in Eighty Days won Jules Verne worldwide renown, and was a fantastic success for the times, selling 108,000 copies, with translations into English, Russian, Italian, and Spanish as soon as it was published. The book's new subject was bound to cause a great sensation: making a bet with the members of the Reform Club, Phileas Fogg, a rich British eccentric who lives as a recluse, lays his entire wealth as a wager that he can go around the world in eighty days.

Accompanied by his valet, Passepartout, he sets out on a journey that first takes him to Suez, and on to meet a series of characters—cruel Hindus, a company of Japanese acrobats, Sioux Indians, and so on. Much of the richness and poetry of the novel depends on the antagonism between the characters Fogg and Passepartout. The geometric and impassive Phileas Fogg, a man of the "fog," who does everything as regularly as clockwork, and for whom the world is reduced to twenty-four time zones, contrasts with the emotive and lively Passepartout, who is forever in sympathy with places and people whom he meets. Yet numerous accidents and unpredictable events will finally get the better of the bachelor's little quirks. **JD**

This dramatic cover image for Verne's novel was created by illustrator Louis Dumont for the first English edition in 1876.

The Enchanted Wanderer

Nicolai Leskov

Lifespan | *b.* 1831 (Russia), *d.* 1895
First Published | 1873 (Russia)
Original Title | *Ocharovanny strannik*
Original Language | Russian

Nicolai Leskov is the least well known of the giants of the Russian novel. In the English-speaking world, he has been eclipsed by others such as Tolstoy and Gogol, possibly because his are the most purely Russian stories of them all, defying incorporation into the western European realist or psychological novel traditions. English translations of his stories are liable to be read as parodies of some stereotyped fable, or even as comedies, in places approaching the manner of Beckett. This is a great part of his appeal: to read him requires that we abandon all anticipation of plot and reader-style empathy with "real" characters. We must submit to the logic of the storyteller who knows by heart but not, apparently, by head, what he wants to tell us.

The Enchanted Wanderer is a vast reel of improbable misfortunes and adventures narrated by the hero to an audience on board a ship. The wanderer is enchanted, because at every step of his life some new adventure befalls him, from the most exotic and magical to the most ludicrously mundane. The great German literary critic Walter Benjamin wrote that the now almost lost craft of storytelling always depended on stories excluding psychological explanations for the actions of their characters: the lack of explanation sets the imagination free. Leskov is the great practitioner of that wonderful and beguiling craft. **KS**

Far from the Madding Crowd

Thomas Hardy

Lifespan | *b.* 1840 (England), *d.* 1928
First Published | 1874
First Published by | Smith, Elder & Co. (London)
Original Language | English

◉ Photographer Frederick Hollyer made this portrait of Thomas Hardy in 1884, a novelist then at the height of his powers.

◉ Joseph Poorgrass wheels a barrow of apples to Bathsheba's residence in this idyllic illustration by Ditz of Hardy's novel.

The pressures of late Victorian modernity, felt acutely in Thomas Hardy's later work, barely touch the world of *Far from the Madding Crowd*. The minor rustic characters seem to come from an earlier age, and Hardy here first applies the name "Wessex" to the topographical and imaginative landscape where his greatest novels are set.

However, Hardy's vision already encompasses injustice and tragedy. Fleeing from her husband, Bathsheba Everdene spends a foggy night beside a swamp, and shivers to see at sunrise its "rotting tree stumps" and the "clammy tops" and "oozing gills" of the fungi growing there. Nature has its poisons, as humanity has its ills. Of the five main characters, two are pathologically destructive: Sergeant Troy is dashing, but selfish and heartless, and Farmer Boldwood is in love only with his own obsessional desire. Fanny Robin, an innocent betrayed, prefigures Hardy's vindication of the "fallen woman" in *Tess of the d'Ubervilles*, but where Tess becomes defiant, Fanny remains passive. Even Bathsheba, independently minded, kind-hearted, and inconstant, causes more sorrow than joy. Only Gabriel Oak is thoroughly good, and he must wait until the last chapter for his reward. Plot and characters are strongly rather than subtly drawn, but the vivid presence of the natural and cultural background is striking. Among the memorable images: Gabriel's shepherd's van, like Noah's ark in the fields; a sheared ewe rising from her fleece "like Aphrodite from the foam"; the Weatherbury church, with its gargoyles; and the great medieval threshing and shearing barn nearby. This world, encompassed within a few square miles, is so intimately known and powerfully depicted that it makes our current global landscape feel drab and featureless. **MR**

Pepita Jiménéz

Juan Valera

Lifespan | *b.* 1824 (Spain), *d.* 1905
First Printed | 1874, by J. Noguera for M. Martínez
First Serialized | 1874, in *Revista de España*
Original Language | Spanish

Among the consequences of the Spanish Revolution of September 1868 were philosophical polemics that opposed, on the one hand, traditional religious experience, and, on the other, the new vitalist and even materialist moral principles, of which diplomat and novelist Juan Valera was a firm upholder.

The theme of *Pepita Jiménez*—also the name of the protagonist—is a literary depiction of the religious climate in which Spaniards of the middle and upper classes existed in the last third of the nineteenth century. In a social world of landowners, Don Luis de Vargas, a would-be mystic who is training to be a priest, meets the beautiful Pepita, widow of an octogenarian, who is being courted by his father, Don Pedro de Vargas. The young pair fall in love and "sin," creating a moral conflict with profound theological ramifications. The Church demands remorse, loyalty to their earlier vows, and the renunciation of lustful human love. Pepita demands the restoration of her virtue and marries Luis. In an added psychological twist, Luis, the recognized natural son of Don Pedro, wishes through his priesthood to wash away the sin of his father.

The narrative structure is free and imaginative; it incorporates the devices of discovered documents, written correspondence, and a narrator who completes what the letters fail to do, rounding off the figure of the vindicated Pepita. **M-DAB**

The Crime of Father Amado

José Maria Eça de Queirós

Lifespan | *b.* 1845 (Portugal), *d.* 1900 (France)
First Published | 1876, by Tipografia Castro Irmão
First Serialized | 1875, in Revista Ocidental
Original Title | *O crime do Padre Amaro*

The first and most famous novel by Portugal's foremost nineteenth-century writer, *The Crime of Father Amaro* is a scathing attack on religious hypocrisy and the narrowness of provincial life.

The priest of the title is a weak young man forced into the priesthood without faith or vocation. He arrives in the provincial town of Leiria, a small-minded haunt of petty vice and malicious gossip. Bored and irked by celibacy, Amaro soon finds an outlet for his lively lust with an attractive young parishioner. Although the reader may identify with the lovers, José Queirós ultimately permits no illusions about an affair that is satisfyingly torrid but crude and exploitative. Amaro is a mediocrity, priggish at heart and keen for personal advancement. He is learning the ropes of corruption and his lover must eventually pay the price for this education.

As the plot unfolds to its brutal, unsentimental conclusion, the author shows some sympathy for his limited and hopeless characters, but none for the society and the church that have made them what they are. The continuing power of the story to shock, at least in Catholic countries, was shown in 2002 when a Spanish-language movie version caused a first-rate scandal in Mexico. **RegG**

❯ Eça de Queirós modeled himself upon Parisian fashions in personal appearance as well as in his realist literary style.

THÉÂTRE DE L'AMBIGU
L'ASSOMMOIR

DRAME EN 9 TABLEAUX TIRÉ DU ROMAN
DE M¹ E. ZOLA
PAR M²⁵ W. BUSNACH & O. GASTINE

Drunkard

Émile Zola

Lifespan | *b.* 1840 (France), *d.* 1902
First Published | 1877
First Published by | A. Lacroix (Paris)
Original Title | *L'Assommoir*

In Émile Zola's own words, this is "a work of truth, the first novel about the common people that does not lie and that smells of the common people." The narrative details the fluctuating fortunes of Parisian laundrywoman Gervaise Macquart, whose determination to transcend the slum milieu through hard work is ultimately thwarted by circumstance. Gervaise's roofer husband suffers a fall and stops working. His ensuing alcoholism drains Gervaise's assets and seduces her into the fatal *l'assommoir* (bar), affecting her moral and physical dissolution. Urban vicissitude is linked with moral improbity; individual misfortune linked with environmental disintegration. Gervaise's tragic, pathetic decline is inexorable, as her alcoholism leads to infidelity, inertia, squalor, alienation, and prostitution.

Zola's insistence on his novel's ethnographic credentials deflected accusations that it actually caricatured working-class life. Its authentic and innovative use of street language; its lewd, sexual frankness; anti-clericalism; anti-officialdom; its general filth, deprivation, and bad manners, were deemed immoral, unpalatable, and potentially inflammatory by conservative critics. *L'Assommoir* stakes a serious claim for working-class experience and popular culture as aesthetically worthy, formally challenging material for the artist. And in overthrowing artistic conventions and inciting debate on the appropriate form and material for modern art, it earns its place as one of the first truly modern novels. **GM**

N° 4   LES HOMMES D'AUJOURD'HUI   10 c.
DESSINS DE GILL

ÉMILE ZOLA

"She was a mattress for the soldiers to lie on before she was twelve—and she's left one leg down there . . ."

◉ André Gill's caricature suggests mutual respect between Balzac, old master of realism, and Zola, new master of naturalism.

◉ Zola considered the 1879 stage adaption of *L'Assomoir* at the Théâtre de l'Ambigu in Paris to be a great success.

METRO-GOLDWYN-MAYER PRÆSENTERER:

NY
KOPI

GRETA
GARBO

FREDRIC
MARCH

ANNA KARENINA

ISCENESÆTTELSE: CLARENCE BROWN

PRODUCENT: DAVID O. SELZNICK

Anna Karenina

Leo Tolstoy

Lifespan | *b*. 1828 (Russia), *d*. 1910
First Serialized | 1873–1877, in *Russkii Vestnik*
First Published | 1877, by M. N. Katkov (Moscow)
Original Language | Russian

Anna Karenina is claimed by many to be the world's greatest novel. Whether or not that is the case, it is one of the finest examples of the nineteenth-century psychological novel. Leo Tolstoy analyzes the motivation behind the actions of the characters, though without any moral judgement. Alongside the omniscient narration, Tolstoy frequently employs interior monologue, a stylistic innovation for the novel form that enables him to present his characters' thoughts and feelings in intimate detail.

Rebellious Anna Karenina succumbs to her attraction to a dashing officer, Count Vronsky, and leaves her loveless marriage to embark on a fervent and ultimately doomed love affair. In doing so, she sacrifices her child and subjects herself to the condemnation of Russian high society. Anna's tragic story is interwoven with the contrasting tale of the courtship and marriage of Konstantin Levin and Kitty Shcherbatskaya, which closely resembles that of Tolstoy and his own wife. In his search for the truth, Levin expresses views about contemporary society, politics, and religion that are often taken to be those of the author himself.

The novel is valuable for its historical as well as its psychological aspects. Despite its length, *Anna Karenina* draws readers into a breathtaking world that is vital and all-consuming in its realism. **SD**

❺ The success of Greta Garbo's 1935 movie portrayal of Tolstoy's heroine made her the face of Anna Karenina around the world.

Martín Fierro

José Hernández

Lifespan | *b*. 1834 (Argentina), *d*. 1889
First Published | 1872–1879, by Imprenta La Pampa (Buenos Aires)
Original Language | Spanish

Martín Fierro is a narrative poem raised to the level of an epic in the literature and identity of Argentina. The name of the protagonist appears in the titles of the two original parts, *Martín Fierro the Gaucho* and *The Return of Martín Fierro*. In the first part, the gaucho's life in the pampas is evoked in the course of more than 7,000 verses. Happy and free until he is recruited to fight against the Indians on the frontier, his days then become so miserable that he decides to run away. Having found his house torn down, he embarks on the life of a drifter, which leads him to crime. He escapes from the police with the help of Cruz, a providential character with whom he decides to live among the Indians; they turn their backs on a world that has no place for them.

The second part describes their lives among the Indians, but Cruz dies and Fierro, having killed an Indian in Part One, has to flee again. A chance meeting with his children and Cruz's son turns the poem into a succession of parallel stories that take a picaresque and uplifting direction. The epic poem comes to its end after a contrapuntal song between Fierro and a dark-skinned character, the brother of the man Fierro had killed.

The interest of the unexpected events, the originality of meter, and the skillful narrative (the complexity of which is only revealed at the end) transforms into poetry this ideological critique of the treatment of the gauchos during the founding of the Argentine nation. **DMG**

The Red Room

August Strindberg

Lifespan | b. 1849 (Sweden), d. 1912
First Published | 1880
First Published by | A. Bonniers Förlag
Original Title | Röda rummet

The Red Room is often described as the first modern Swedish novel. Using Zola's naturalism and Dickens's social criticism Strindberg revitalized a stale, conventional tradition. Because its social and political satire was a little too close to the bone, its initial reception was controversial, but the novel is now recognized as a watershed in Swedish literature. In the opening chapter, with its famous bird's-eye view of Stockholm, Strindberg's vivid prose sparkles with energy and invention. The hero of the novel, the young and idealistic Arvid Falk, resigns from the Civil Service in disgust at the corruption he sees everywhere in the Establishment. He wants to become a writer and joins a group of bohemian artists, but struggles to free himself from his own prim and puritan inclinations. Falk's radical and reforming spirit is gradually softened, and he is tempted to adopt the selfish view of life advocated by the conservative journalist Struve. As so often in Strindberg, it is the tension between irreconcilable opposites that provides the narrative energy.

The subtitle, Scenes of Literary and Artistic Life, reveals a series of satirical excursions into the worlds of the arts, religion, government, and finance. The focus is on man in society, sometimes at the expense of in-depth characterization. But many of the minor characters—like the carpenter who threatens to reclaim the lost beds of the working classes from affluent middle-class ladies who offer him charity—are memorable in an eccentric Dickensian way. **UD**

Ben-Hur

Lew Wallace

Lifespan | b. 1827 (U.S.), d. 1905
First Published | 1880
First Published by | Harper & Bros. (New York)
Original Language | English

Prompted by a casual discussion about the life of Jesus, Lew Wallace began writing his epic tale of revenge and adventure with religious themes in mind, and Ben-Hur was the result; a parable that counterpoises Judah Ben-Hur, a Jew from Jerusalem, with the concurrent life of Jesus Christ.

When Ben-Hur accidentally dislodges a roof tile and it hits a Roman official, he is wrongly accused of murder and sent to the galleys by his former friend, Messala, a Roman noble. The seeds of epic struggle and redemption are sown when a stranger offers Ben-Hur a glass of water, and from this point his struggle to attain citizenship and Christ's mission are inextricably linked. The popularity of the 1959 Hollywood epic, with its spectacular chariot race, perhaps overrides the blend of religious parable and adventure that obviously adapted itself so well to the stage (it was adapted for the theater in 1899, and proved enduringly popular) and then the screen. However, the film is that unusual breed, a strong adaptation of the text that takes on its key motifs without losing the religious intensity. Ben-Hur is characteristically remembered for elements that comprise only a tiny part of the text itself: an event rather than a narrative, and a set piece rather than a gradually unfolding epic. However, the text has lost none of its forceful message, while simultaneously representing the author's desire to appraise some of the central tenets of Christian belief through the figure of an apparently ordinary man. **EMcCS**

Nana

Émile Zola

Lifespan | *b.* 1840 (France), *d.* 1902
First Published | 1880
First Published by | A. Lacroix (Paris)
Original Language | French

Nana exposes a licentious Parisian sexual economy, hooked on prostitution and promiscuity. The respectable classes indulge in drunken orgies, homosexuality, sadomasochism, voyeurism, and more. An influential aristocrat, Count Muffat, is the epitome of this degradation and chastisement. His familial, political, and religious status is compromised by his infatuated devotion to Nana. She is an ostensibly luminous yet inherently tainted figure: debt, misogynistic violence, a dysfunctional family, class background, and an ultimately fatal sexual disease temper her success. Her eventual physical corrosion is horrific, reflecting the total corruption and disfigurement of both state and society. It is no coincidence that Nana's death throes take place against the backdrop of a screaming mob galvanized by the Franco-Prussian War, where the ultimate violent ruin, collapse, and purification of this stage of French history is completed.

Today's readers will discover an extraordinary prescience in the correlation in *Nana* of society's obsession with sex, celebrity, and power. A conscious emphasis on exploitation and disgraceful revelation is paramount in a novel that opens with a theatrical striptease, before going on to revisit connected themes of sexual and economic exhibitionism. Determinedly realist and deliberately explicit, *Nana* is a spectacular novel, which indicts a public appetite for voyeurism and sensationalism that is still alive and healthy in the modern world. **GM**

The Portrait of a Lady

Henry James

Lifespan | *b.* 1843 (U.S.), *d.* 1916 (England)
First Published | 1881
First Published by | Macmillan & Co. (London)
Original Language | English

Portrait of a Lady epitomizes Henry James's favorite "international" theme: the relationship of naive America and cultured Europe, and the contrast between their moral and aesthetic values.

Isabel Archer is a beautiful and spirited young American woman, seeking aesthetic enrichment in Europe. She is not wealthy, but refuses two financially advantageous proposals of marriage, fearing they would curtail her imaginative and intellectual freedom. Yet ironically, when she receives a large inheritance, she realizes she has no actual aims or purpose with which to fill her future. Moreover, it brings with it the sinister attentions of the charismatic, urbane aesthete Gilbert Osmond. When Isabel marries him, she discovers that she has been manipulated for her fortune. Escaping from the captivity of enforced domestic convention, she finds herself embroiled in a scene of complex sexual and moral emotions, which even Isabel herself struggles to understand. But she chooses instead to accept the responsibility of her own free choice, even when that means knowingly renouncing the greater liberty she so cherished. Despite her vanity and self-delusion, Isabel is steadfast in her effort to lead a noble life.

Beneath the melodrama of the novel's plot, James masterfully reveals the more subtle tragedy of lost innocence and curtailed dreams. "The world's all before us—and the world's very big," Goodward entreats at the end of the novel. "The world's very small," Isabel now replies. **DP**

The House by the Medlar Tree

Giovanni Verga

Lifespan | *b.* 1840 (Sicily), *d.* 1922
First Published | 1881
First Published by | Treves (Milan)
Original Title | *I Malavoglia*

"Be content to be what your father was, then you'll be neither a knave nor an ass."

⊙ Giovanni Verga was born in Sicily and wrote about its people
and their sufferings with a pessimism based on experience.

The House by the Medlar Tree constitutes the first part of a grand enterprise intended to portray the fight for life at all levels of social reality, from the dispossessed to the powerful. Giovanni Verga surpassed the French naturalists' commitment to depicting reality faithfully, and created a narrative in which the author disappears to leave space for the characters, who speak in a new style that directly reflects their sentiments and inner thoughts. The story is that of a tightly knit family of fishermen in a small Sicilian village, held together by their obedience to old traditions and patriarchal customs. The Toscanos represent the losers, who, like clams, hold on tightly to the sea-beaten rocks in a desperate attempt to resist the cruel waves of life, but in the end are swept away by the rough waters. Owners of a fishing boat, Padron 'Ntoni and his family are not utterly poor. Therefore, the catastrophe that hits them is a pitiless punishment for attempting to improve their life by engaging in an unfortunate entrepreneurial effort. The author's message is absolutely clear: change and progress in Sicily are simply inconceivable.

Written especially for the bourgeoisie, Verga's novel expresses the disillusionment inherent in the national unification of the Kingdom of the Two Sicilies in 1861, which it was believed would solve the problems of Italy's southern regions. But the reality in the mid nineteenth century proved to be more complex. While the north thrived, the poor in the south were more destitute than ever, repressed by new customs regulations and an onerous obligatory requirement to serve in the military. *The House by the Medlar Tree* is an eye-opening representation of the crude and passionless life that was endured in southern Italy, and is a valuable contribution to realist narrative. **RPi**

The Posthumous Memoirs of Brás Cubas

Joaquim Maria Machado de Assis

Described by American critic Susan Sontag as "the greatest author ever produced in Latin America," Machado de Assis was a writer of romantic fiction before this radically original book propelled him into the first rank of novelists of his time. Influenced by the anarchic comedy of Laurence Sterne's *Tristram Shandy*, the Brazilian writer subverted the form of the nineteenth-century Realist novel while triumphantly achieving the Realists' objective—a brutally honest depiction of contemporary society.

As in Billy Wilder's movie *Sunset Boulevard*, the narrator is dead. This voice from beyond the grave sardonically surveys a lifetime of futility. Brás Cubas has belonged to the privileged elite of Rio de Janeiro, living off inherited wealth. His mediocre existence has been without sense or purpose, epitomized by a lengthy adulterous affair with a politician's wife, which is as dull as the worst conventional marriage. Machado de Assis's acerbic graveyard humor makes of this unpromising material a lacerating comedy. The fragmented narrative, circuitous and digressive, allows room for every variety of fantasy, meditation, and comic riff. The notion of human progress is mercilessly satirized in the person of Quincas Borba, an amateur positive philosopher whose optimism drifts into insanity.

Casual vignettes of the cruelty of Brazil's inegalitarian society strike home like a slap in the face. In the last decades of his life, Machado became the intellectual doyen of Rio society and a Brazilian national hero. His later works include a partial sequel to *Posthumous Memoirs*, the novel *Quincas Borba*. Machado's dark sense of humor, pessimistic view of human nature, and abandonment of conventional narrative make him seem today one of the least dated of nineteenth-century writers. **RegG**

Lifespan | *b.* 1839 (Brazil), *d.* 1908
First Published | 1881
First Serialized | 1880, in Revista Brasileira
Original Title | *Memórias Póstumas de Brás Cubas*

"Life without struggle is a dead sea in the center of the universal organism."

◉ The son of a house painter and a domestic servant, Machado de Assis knew Brazilian society from the bottom to the top.

Bouvard and Pécuchet

Gustave Flaubert

Lifespan | b. 1821 (France), d. 1880
First Published | 1881
First Published by | A. Lemerre (Paris)
Original Title | Bouvard et Pécuchet

On a hot summer's day, two clerks named Bouvard and Pécuchet meet on the Boulevard Bourdon in Paris, and discover that not only have they written their names on exactly the same spot on their hats, but they also have the same liberal political opinions, and, most importantly, the same yearning for knowledge. Thanks to an inheritance, they retire to the countryside, where they propose to test all existing theories in all areas of knowledge. As they challenge the received ideas, the protagonists become more and more aware of inconsistencies that are spread everywhere in their manuals. Bouvard and Pécuchet enter into a repetitive cycle of events: they consult numerous encyclopedias and monographs, apply their knowledge, fail catastrophically in their experiments, regret the falsity and defects of their chosen field, and move on to a new one. They investigate all topics, from archeology to theology, before giving up their quests and deciding to become copyists again.

This "grotesque epic," unfinished and published posthumously, stands out in the history of the novel. It encapsulates a dramatic passion for knowledge, embodied by the heroes' enthusiasm for every kind of problem. Conveyed in Flaubert's economical style, Bouvard and Pécuchet's episodic enthusiasms, earnest endeavors, and recurring disillusions are an exceptionally disquieting and comical affair. **CS**

Treasure Island

Robert Louis Stevenson

Lifespan | b. 1850 (Scotland), d. 1894 (Samoa)
First Published | 1883
First Published by | Cassell & Co. (London)
Original Language | English

"If this don't fetch the kids, why, they have gone rotten since my day," Robert Louis Stevenson said on publication of his children's classic. With its evocative atmosphere, peopled with fantastic characters and set pieces, Treasure Island has spawned countless imitations. Films such as Pirates of the Caribbean still encourage the romanticism of piracy, and Stevenson's classic remains true to form despite various literary attempts to dispute his role in the popular canon.

However, Stevenson's text contains few of the elements commonly associated with it. The rip-roaring tale of pirates and parrots is there, but perhaps some of the romanticism is due not to the nominal hero, Jack Hawkins, who staidly adheres to law and order, but to the turncoat ship's cook, Long John Silver. Silver is a wonderful villain: erratic, bombastic, and deadly, and his obvious intelligence and relationship with Hawkins are both gripping and unpredictable. All the elements of a classic adventure are exaggerated by buried treasure, curses, strange meetings, storms, mutiny, and subterfuge. However, this tale of quest, siege, and recovery has one final trick in its rather unformed ending. Even though the villain escapes and the hero returns rich and prosperous, there is a feeling that all has only just begun. **EMcCS**

⟩ A map drawn by author Robert Louis Stevenson depicts his fictional but impeccably realized Treasure Island.

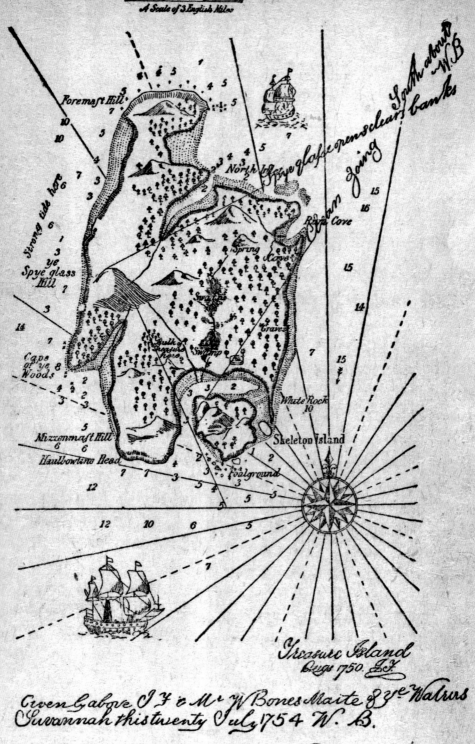

A Scale of 3 English Miles

Foremast Hill

North Inlet

Spye glaſs opens clear banks

Strong tide here

ye
Spye glaſs
Hill

Skeleton Island opens cove going South about W.B

Spring Cove

Swan

Graves

Bulk of
Treasure here

Cape
of ye
Woods

Swamp

White Rock

Skeleton Island

Mizzenmast Hill

Haulbowline Head

Foalground

Treasure Island
Augt 1750. J.F.

Given above J.F. & Mr. W. Bones Maite of yͤ Walrus
Suvannah this twenty July 1754 W. B.

Facsimile of Chart, latitude and
longitude struck out by J. Hawkins

A Woman's Life

Guy de Maupassant

Lifespan | *b.* 1850 (France), *d.* 1893
First Published | 1883
First Published by | Corbeil (Paris)
Original Title | *Une Vie: l'humble vérité*

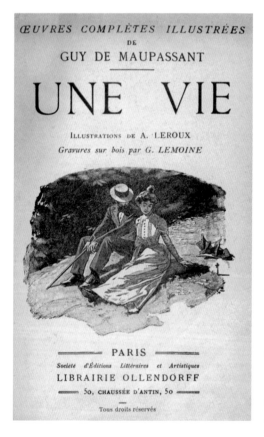

● Despite its pessimistic depiction of a woman's life, Maupassant's novel also incorporates lyrical evocations of nature.

Guy de Maupassant wrote *A Woman's Life* over more than six years. Even though the story is set in the period that extends from the Restoration of the French monarchy to the 1848 Revolution, it shows a complete disregard for political history. Instead, it focuses exclusively on the life of a provincial aristocrat, Jeanne Le Perthuis des Vauds, from the moment when she leaves the convent to her death in the Caux country. Maupassant was strongly encouraged by Flaubert, who found the subject "excellent," and this story is the inverse of Flaubert's *Madame Bovary*. It recounts the story of a pious woman who suffers from a series of disillusions in her life, beginning with the unfaithfulness of a miserly, and ruthlessly ambitious husband. Jeanne's progressive descent into resignation, if not her actual sense of masochism toward the series of misfortunes that she must suffer (miscarriage, the mothering of a premature child who becomes a swindler, the death of her parents, solitude, poverty, and so on), recalls Flaubert's *Un Coeur Simple*.

A seminal work of naturalism, *A Woman's Life* is also the cruel story of life's traps and pitfalls, and the natural and animal "force" of its indifferent perpetuation. Maupassant's criticism of marriage, which he believed restrained the natural sexual instincts of emotive women, and the pessimistic outlook of the story, show Schopenhauer's decisive influence on the so-called naturalist or determinist ideas of the time. Even though the distribution of the book was provisionally blocked by the publisher Hachette, who deemed that its content was "pornographic," *A Woman's Life* was generally well received by the critics, even by the opponents of naturalism, who were swayed by the emotion and the lyricism of certain of its descriptions. **JD**

The Death of Ivan Ilyich

Leo Tolstoy

The Death of Ivan Ilyich is a short novel but not a modest one. As the spiritual crisis of Levin, Leo Tolstoy's self-portrait, had been left unresolved in *Anna Karenina*, here he describes the agony of ambivalence that led to that resolution, albeit through the story of a less complicated man, a man less liable to crises of self-understanding than Levin.

Ivan Ilyich is an ambitious bureaucrat jostling his way up the ladder of advantages in a corrupt Russia still harnessed by the czar's bureaucratic apparatus. He slides gracefully into the roles offered to him, adjusting the attitudes and ethics of his youth to fit with the exigencies of his career, and accepting gladly the circus of perks and consolations offered by fashionable society and its luxuries. He particularly enjoys playing cards, a pastime evidently despised by Tolstoy as much as by the German philosopher Schopenhauer, who thought it the most degraded, senseless and "automatic" behavior imaginable.

Following what seems like an unremarkable injury, Ivan becomes gradually more incapacitated until finally he is unable to rise from the couch in his drawing room. Tolstoy describes with ferocious zeal the intensity of Ivan's physical suffering, which so exhausts him that eventually he gives up speaking and simply screams without remission, horrifying his attendant family. In the end, death proves not to be the destination of Ivan's tormented and ignorant spiritual journey. Instead, it is simply the wasted province of all that he leaves behind by relinquishing his life, all the possessions and affectations, and even the human intimacies that he permitted himself in order to pass off his life as a reality worth settling for. Without a doubt, *The Death of Ivan Ilyich* represents Tolstoy's most concerted denunciation of a pre-revolutionary corrupted social existence. **KS**

Lifespan | *b.* 1828 (Russia), *d.* 1910
First Published | 1884 (Russia)
Original Title | *Smert Ivana Ilyitsha*
Original Language | Russian

◉ A signed portrait of Tolstoy depicts a stern moralist who has renounced the frivolities of existence in conventional society.

Against the Grain

Joris-Karl Huysmans

Lifespan | *b.* 1848 (France), *d.* 1907
First Published | 1884
First Published by | Charpentier (Paris)
Original Title | *À rebours*

Joris-Karl Huysmans's *Against the Grain* is a sensuous joy of a novel. It guts the aesthetic, spiritual, and physical desires of the late nineteenth-century high bourgeoisie and feasts on the remains. Luxuriating in self-disgust and self-love, *Against the Grain* has been called "the breviary of Decadence," the mirror in which writers of the fin de siècle could recognize their own elegant longings for a world other than the coarsely materialistic one they inhabited.

Politically, "Decadence" incorporated sexual dissidence and stressed the sacredness of the body as a sensual matrix, but it was locked into a chronic antagonism with bourgeois materialism. Huysmans, Wilde, and Valéry all needed the bourgeoisie as much as they scorned them; without the utilitarian materialism and sentimentality of "respectable society," their love affair with debauchery and excess had nothing against which to define itself.

Against the Grain embodies and exploits this political slipperiness. The Duc Jean des Esseintes is a frail aesthete, a lover of ecstasies both debauched and spritual, and the lone descendant of his once forbiddingly manly family, founded by medieval warriors and patriarchs. He is a "degenerate," his lonely vices the consequence of the physical degeneration of the aristocracy. But the narrative lingers delicately over his experiments and despairs. The result is a lush, stylized study in intensity, a fascinating portrayal of an age through the eyes of one who abandoned it. **PMcM**

The Regent's Wife

Clarín Leopoldo Alas

Lifespan | *b.* 1852 (Spain), *d.* 1901
First Published | 1884–1885
First Published by | Daniel Cortezo (Barcelona)
Original Title | *La Regenta*

Clarín Leopoldo Alas here composed a romantic narrative in a naturalistic structure set in the Levitical society of Vetusta (Oviedo). As in so many nineteenth-century novels, the subject is adultery, but while in *Madame Bovary* Flaubert created an anti-romantic novel about a degraded romantic sensibility, in *The Regent's Wife* Alas did the opposite.

Ana Ozores, orphaned by her mother and separated from her nonbelieving father, is brought up by strict aunts. She is disgraced by an innocent childhood incident that forces her to spend the night in the company of a boy, and, as a result of her guilt, she suffers from morbid hypersensitivity. The positivist Frígilis "scientifically" arranges her marriage to the much older Quintanar, the Regent of the Audiencia (president of the court), who can give the impressionable Ana support and security. The positivist theories break down in the face of the unsatisfied needs of Ana, who is tied to an inadequate, fatherly husband.

Ana is courted both by her confessor, Fermin de Pas, a canon who relishes his influence in the city and is under the influence of his avaricious mother, and by the seducer Alvaro Mesía. Eventually, the hypocritical society of Vetusta witnesses the fall of Ana who, after years of fidelity and spiritual anxiety, falls into the arms of Mesía. He rounds matters off by killing the Regent in a duel and abandoning Ana, who is defeated and humiliated by Vetusta and rejected by everyone, apart from Frígilis. **M-DAB**

Bel-Ami

Guy de Maupassant

Lifespan | *b.* 1850 (France), *d.* 1893
First Published | 1885
First Published by | V. Harvard (Paris)
Original Language | French

Guy de Maupassant is perhaps best known as a writer of short fiction, and he utilizes the shorter form as a structuring principle for his longer productions. The hero of *Bel-Ami*, Georges Duroy, arrives in Paris as an innocent from the provinces, but in realizing the ascendant power of journalism, rapidly apprehends (and cheerfully exploits) the amorality and decadence at its heart. This discovery occurs impressionistically, giving us lasting images of the cafés, boulevards, and newspaper offices of Maupassant's city. But everything has a price and a limitation, so that the attempt to inscribe it with authenticity or infinite worth only shows up its absence of value, and devalues its possessor.

In *Bel-Ami*, individual stories are women to be seduced, whose bodily presence is described with phenomenological exactitude. However, each woman also represents a calculation, where sexual desire is measured against practical benefit. The "bright silky kimono" of Clotilde de Marelle thus translates into a need that is "brutal" and "direct," a woman to be quickly discarded. But her successor's "loose white gown," represents the longer rhythm of his desire for social worth: she will be ravaged equally, but in a process that exploits her political as well as erotic value. Love, or authentic emotion, moves in inverse proportion to the cynical force of ambition. Maupassant encourages us to enjoy the latter for what it is, as long as we are not tempted to draw any more lasting lessons from his work. **DT**

Marius the Epicurean

Walter Pater

Lifespan | *b.* 1839 (England), *d.* 1894
First Published | 1885, by Macmillan & Co. (London)
Full Title | *Marius the Epicurean: His Sensations and Ideas*

Walter Pater is perhaps best known as the author of *The Renaissance* (1873), ostensibly an overview of art and culture from that period, but in effect a manifesto for aesthetic existence that was to profoundly influence the artistic temperament of the fin de siècle. His contemporary, Oscar Wilde, enthusiastically adopted "the love of art for its own sake," as the principle that art never expresses anything but itself. Pater wrote *Marius the Epicurean* not only to imply the inadequacy of this Wildean reading, but also to provide a general model for the experience of art within the form of a life.

The subject matter of *Marius* is less important than the ideas with which it is concerned. It describes the education of the young Roman of its title, through several varieties of pagan philosophy, culminating in Christian faith and martyrdom. Marius develops, however, not through the events of his life, but as a reader, and the form of the novel sets out to reproduce that readerly experience. Reading, in this case, meaningfully connects past, present, and future, becoming itself a process of redemptive moral growth. The carefully constructed temporal simultaneity of Pater's novel makes us feel this as readers, as well as observing its effects in his hero. The relative neglect of *Marius* is demonstrated by the fact that no modern edition of the work exists. But if we are to see literature as a process of spiritual as well as sensual formation, respecting both sides of Pater's equation, then reading it remains crucial. **DT**

Adventures of HUCKLEBERRY Finn.

(Tom Sawyer's Comrade.)

BY

MARK TWAIN.

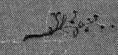

ILLUSTRATED.

The Adventures of Huckleberry Finn

Mark Twain

Like many of the titles found in the "Children's Classics" section of bookstores, *The Adventures of Huckleberry Finn* is not a children's book as we understand the term these days, and it is not surprising that adaptations of Twain's work aimed at children are usually quite heavily edited. Sharing with *Tom Sawyer* (1876) a vivid portrayal of Mississippi small-town life, replete with colorful characters, superstitions, slang, and river lore, these adventures are of a different kind. The contrast becomes clear quite early on, when the bloodthirsty boys' game of "highwaymen" and ransom organized by Tom is echoed in Huck's escape from his drunken, violent father. In order to avoid being followed, Huck fakes his own murder. Early on in his flight, he links up with the escaped slave Jim, and together they travel down the Mississippi. Along the way they meet an assortment of locals, river folk, good and bad people, and get mixed up with a pair of con men. Many of their adventures are comic, and Huck's naivety in describing them is frequently used to humorous effect. However, the straightforwardness with which Huck relates his experiences allows the narrative to shift unexpectedly from absurdity into much darker terrain, as when he witnesses a young boy of his own age die in a pointless and ridiculous feud with another family.

It is these sudden shifts and the contrasts they produce that make this more than an adventure novel. Huck is not necessarily an innocent, but in telling his story he tends to take conventional morals and social relations at face value. By doing so, he brings a moral earnestness to bear on them which exposes hypocrisy, injustice, falsehood, and cruelty more subtly and more scathingly than any direct satire could. **DG**

Lifespan | *b*. 1835 (U.S.), *d*. 1910
First Published | 1885
First Published by | Dawson (Montreal)
Given Name | Samuel Langhorne Clemens

Mark Twain excelled at the ironic criticism of hypocrisy and injustice seen through the innocent eyes of childhood.

The first edition of *Huckleberry Finn* was illustrated by Edward Kemble, who created an unforgettable image of the young hero.

Germinal

Émile Zola

Lifespan | *b.* 1840 (France), *d.* 1902
First Published | 1885
First Published by | Charpentier (Paris)
Original Language | French

Anyone interested in the intersection between literature and politics should know this famous, explosive novel of class conflict and industrial unrest, set in the coalfields of northern France in the 1860s. Émile Zola's uncompromising presentation of an impoverished, subterranean, and vulnerable working existence, paralleled by bourgeois luxury, leisure, and security, provoked controversy.

The title recalls the seventh month of the French revolutionary calendar, associated with mass insurrection, rioting, violence, poverty, and starvation. All feature in *Germinal*'s central story: the eruption and failure of a general strike and its universally negative outcome. The main narrative charts Étienne Lantier's emotional and political assimilation into a mining community, illuminating a dark disenfranchized world, ripe for revolt. His progression from neutral outsider to committed strike leader mobilizes a collective struggle, subtly presented in tandem with the contradictions and compromises of individual belief and aspiration. The narrative is permeated with significant oppositions, but capitalism subjugates all of the protagonists.

Germinal's much-debated ending resonates with a challenging question: what is the potential for social change and transition? The final images of destruction and renewal suggest possible political evolution through the germination of individual and collective working-class endeavor. It is significant though, that this remains inconclusive. **GM**

> *"He was unemployed and homeless, and had only one thought in his head; the hope that the cold would be less keen after daybreak."*

◉ Émile Levy's poster for a stage version of *Germinal* expresses the melodramatic quality of Zola's apocalyptic vision of class war.

King Solomon's Mines

H. Rider Haggard

Lifespan | *b.* 1856 (England), *d.* 1925
First Published | 1885
First Published by | Cassell & Co. (London)
Original Language | English

H. Rider Haggard's phenomenal best seller was intended to rival *Treasure Island*, and its hero, Allan Quartermain, has proved an enduring figure in popular literature, being memorably recreated as an opium-raddled wreck in Alan Moore's *The League of Extraordinary Gentlemen* (2002). The tale itself is classic fantasy; Quartermain and his aides venture into uncharted reaches of Central Africa to discover the infamous King Solomon's Mines, repository of a legendarily huge treasure. Of course, the journey is fraught with peril and excitement. Quartermain encounters the Kukuanas, ruled by King Twala and the witch Gagool, who become increasingly more villainous as tension between the tribe and those intending to purloin the diamond mines intensifies.

Haggard's writing displays a deep knowledge of African, especially Zulu, cultures, which he had observed, and often admired, firsthand. Quartermain is an imperialist, but he is more tolerant and open to change than other contemporary characters, and it is notable that several of his adventures, including this one, involve attempts to save tribes from disappearing. This is possibly why his texts have survived—they identify a more generic threat to mankind through the destruction of an entire race. Haggard's central characters are bombastic and brash, yet Haggard makes the reader aware of this, and it is Quartermain who emerges as the culturally resourceful hero rather than his less observant, and more stereotypically belligerent colleagues. **EMcCS**

The Quest

Frederik van Eeden

Lifespan | *b.* 1860 (Netherlands), *d.* 1932
First Published | 1885
First Published by | De Nieuwe Gids (Amsterdam)
Original Title | *De kleine Johannes*

Frederik van Eeden was one of the founders of a psychotherapeutic clinic in Amsterdam. Both as a writer and as a doctor he concerned himself with social wrongs. *The Quest* was first published in *De Nieuwe Gids* (*The New Guide*), an epoch-making and innovative literary periodical started by the Tachtigers (Eighties Movement). Van Eeden's ideas, however, diverged from the guidelines of the Tachtigers, which favored pieces conforming to the principle of *l'art pour l'art*: art for art's sake. Van Eeden distinguished himself through his religio-ethical sympathies and he focused more on content than on form, an outlook that eventually led to a rift.

Van Eeden's novel describes the experiences of Johannes, a protagonist who displays many similarities to himself. As a child, Johannes has every opportunity to play and to give his unbridled imagination free rein. His primary interest is in nature and animals, but in the course of time, he also experiences less pleasant aspects of life, such as illness and death. Johannes makes a spiritual journey in which he learns that most people's lives contrast sharply with his idyllic childhood.

The Quest is constructed as a symbolic fairy tale, in which imagination eventually loses out to rationalism and materialism. The religio-ethical undertones resolve toward the end of the novel, where Johannes is given a task among mankind. Read against the background of the Aesthetic Movement, *The Quest* an extraordinary and poignant tale. **JaM**

The Strange Case of Dr. Jekyll and Mr. Hyde

Robert Louis Stevenson

Lifespan | *b*. 1850 (Scotland), *d*. 1894 (Samoa)
First Published | 1886
First Published by | Longmans, Green & Co. (Lon.)
Original Language | English

This novel begins, quietly enough, with an urbane conversation between the lawyer, Mr. Utterson, and his friend, Mr. Enfield. The latter tells how, returning home in the early hours of the morning, he witnessed a "horrible" incident: a small girl, running across the street, is trampled by a man who leaves her screaming on the ground. "It sounds nothing to hear," Enfield concludes, "but it was hellish to see."

Such reticence is characteristic of Robert Louis Stevenson's retelling of this classic gothic story of "the double," the notion of a man pursued by himself, of a second personality inhabiting the true self. Stevenson gradually discloses the identity of the "damned Juggernaut," Mr. Hyde, who disappears behind the door of the respectable, and well liked, Dr. Jekyll. But identifying Hyde is not the same as knowing how to read the conflict, the double existence, unleashed by Jekyll's experiments with the "evil side of my nature." Notably, in 1888, the psychological phenomenon explored here was invoked to explain a new, and metropolitan, form of sexual savagery in the tabloid sensationalism surrounding the Ripper murders. This is an early example of the ongoing role in public of Stevenson's story, and its critical reflection on the many discontents of modern cultural life. **VL**

🔇 In this illustration from the first edition, Dr. Jekyll transforms into his evil other self, to the horror of the unfortunate Dr. Lanyon.

The Manors of Ulloa

Emilia Pardo Bazán

Lifespan | *b*. 1852 (Spain), *d*. 1921
First Published | 1886
First Published by | Daniel Cortezo (Barcelona)
Original Title | *Los pazos de Ulloa*

With this scabrous novel, continued a year later in *Mother Nature*, the Countess de Pardo Bazán achieved her best work and one of the peaks of Spanish naturalism. In it she contrasts the barbarism and primitiveness of rural Galicia with the standards that regulate civilized life. The young priest Julián Álvarez arrrives at the ancestral home of Don Pedro Moscoso, the illegitimate Marquis of Ulloa and authentic feudal overlord. Don Pedro has found out that the effective running of the estate depends on the brutal Primitivo, whose daughter, Sabel, works as a maid. The marquis indulges his erotic affection with Sabel, the result of which is a child, Perucho.

Soon the well-behaved Julián, who is trying to tidy up the organization of the estate, clashes with the violent Primitivo. Julián remains at the house and tries to redeem the marquis through marriage. To this end they travel to Santiago, where Don Pedro can select a wife from among his four cousins. He chooses Nucha, the favorite of the priest. The first months of marriage are happy, until Nucha gives birth to a girl. The marquis, who wanted a boy, quickly resumes his relationship with Sabel. Julián's plan for Nucha and the girl to flee is discovered, and he is expelled from the house. Ten years later, he returns to find the tomb of Nucha and two children playing: the boy, Perucho, elegantly dressed, and the girl, dirty and ragged. **DRM**

The People of Hemsö

August Strindberg

Lifespan | *b.* 1849 (Sweden), *d.* 1912
First Published | 1887
First Published by | A. Bonniers Förlag (Stockholm)
Original Title | *Hemsöborna*

◉ Strindberg in holiday mood with two of his daughters: *The People of Hemsö* shows the sunnier side of his somber nature.

◉ Strindberg, portrayed here in 1899, endured three unhappy marriages and suffered long periods of mental instability.

A feat of straightforward, folksy storytelling, *The People of Hemsö* is set on an island in August Strindberg's beloved Stockholm archipelago. Written during a difficult period in exile from Sweden, the novel, paradoxically, has a strong sense of place, and is like a sunny, carefree summer holiday in comparison with some of Strindberg's more psychologically intense work. Its mood is generous and forgiving, and the naturalism, so often used for painting in bleak colors, is here affirmative and bright.

The detailed description of nature and characters is authentic and genuine, and free from social and political indignation. Mrs. Flod, a widow of some means, hires Carlsson to run the farm on the island. As a newcomer and a landlubber among sailors and fishermen, who prefer the boat to the field, Carlsson is immediately and implicitly distrusted by the locals. His main rival is Gusten, the son and heir, and a struggle for control of the farm develops between them. Although it may be possible to see traces of a Nietzschean power struggle in their confrontation, the novel is far too light and happy to carry any sustained philosophical weight. Nevertheless, this contest is a clever, page-turning device: is Carlsson a slippery confidence trickster preying on the lonely widow, or an honest, hard-working man revitalizing the neglected farm? This question, also debated by the other characters in the novel, still enthrals readers today. Together with the magnificent passages describing the sea and the islands, the broad rustic comedy, and the dramatic final twists and turns of the plot, the lure of this fundamental question is why *The People of Hemsö* retains its prominent position in Strindberg's oeuvre, and why it has achieved its status as one of the most popular Swedish novels. **UD**

AVG · STRINDBERG
VRVSVND · JVLI · 1899 ·   RITADT AT HAN
                          GAMLE VÄN
                                  O.L

Pierre and Jean

Guy de Maupassant

Lifespan | *b.* 1850 (France), *d.* 1893
First Published | 1888
First Published by | V. Harvard (Paris)
Original Title | *Pierre et Jean*

Set in 1880s Le Havre, *Pierre and Jean* is a highly charged, gripping tale of a family breakdown. The title refers to two brothers, children of a respectable middle-class ex-jeweler and his wife, whose lives are torn apart by an unexpected inheritance. Jean, the younger son and an aspiring lawyer, discovers he is the sole beneficiary of a family friend's estate. All of the family except for Pierre are overjoyed at this sudden godsend. Pierre is at first plagued by simple feelings of jealousy, but his morose condition worsens when he begins to question his mother's honor and fears Jean may be the benefactor's illegitimate son. He is tormented by doubts and the jealousy turns to fear, guilt, and anger. He becomes deeply confused and his anguish forces him to probe deep within himself, thereby furthering his isolation from both his family and society at large. The port of Le Havre and the Normandy coastline form an integral, illustrative backdrop to Pierre's fear, agony, and ultimate yearning for escape.

Widely considered to be one of the masters of the short story, Guy de Maupassant was a highly prolific and successful writer. *Pierre and Jean*, his fourth novel, is illustrative of a shift in both Maupassant's own work and in French literature generally; a shift away from the social realism typified by authors such as Balzac and Zola, and toward a greater concern with the fundamental workings of human psychology. **AL**

"Jean . . . was as fair as his brother was dark, as deliberate as his brother was vehement, as gentle as his brother was unforgiving . . ."

⊙ As a disciple of Flaubert, Maupassant cultivated an ironic vision of life, but with a vein of warmth and sympathy his master lacked.

Under the Yoke

Ivan Vazov

Lifespan | *b.* 1850 (Bulgaria), *d.* 1921
First Published | 1889, in Odessa
Original Language | Bulgarian
Original Title | *Pod Igoto*

Under the Yoke: A Romance of Bulgarian Liberty is a nineteenth-century historical drama written with patriotic fervor and a fiery passion that has been compared to Longfellow and even Tolstoy. The story is set in 1875–76 around the town of Bela Cherkva (Ivan Vazov's hometown of Sopot) in a corner of Bulgaria struggling to throw off the Turkish "yoke." But it is a false dawn (real emancipation did not come till 1886), ending in an abortive insurrection when help from Russia fails to materialize and the leading patriots find only martyrdom.

But it is not all doom and gloom: the heroes, including Dr. Sokoloff and the orphan girl Rada and Boicho Ognianoff (heroically in love too), are all caught up in the excitement of the uprising. Vazov chronicles their story against a backdrop of the meadows of the Balkan valleys, the watercourses and mills, the walnut and pear groves, as well as the cafés, the monasteries, and the farmsteads. There are many memorable set pieces, not least the final slaughter of the bandits at the mill.

Vazov was born before Bulgarian Liberation and died after the First World War, so his life was very much part of Bulgaria's modern history. He was an unabashed patriot and Bulgaria's national poet; his poems and prose revered the heroes who had made the liberation possible. This does not make him overly "domestic" for international readers; there is plenty to delight in this novel, which revealed Bulgaria's artistic potential to the West. **JHa**

The Child of Pleasure

Gabriele D'Annunzio

Lifespan | *b.* 1863 (Italy), *d.* 1938
First Published | 1898
First Published by | Treves (Milan)
Original Title | *Il piacere*

The Italian writer D'Annunzio—whose political ideas are frequently questioned as being possible precursors to Mussolini's fascism—seems to write this first novel from the perspective of a Romantic poet. The book is lushly written, combining the author's gorgeous, tightly crafted prose and, through the story's main character, his poetry; it is also well worth reading for its descriptions of Rome.

The Child of Pleasure is both an examination and a criticism of the wealthy Italian upper classes and the transience of that rarefied social world. The protagonist, Andrea, is a young poet and aristocrat from distinguished lineage who has fallen in love with two women; after a duel leaves him with diminished health, he is torn by his desire for both, as well as by a spiritual rebirth gained through having nearly been killed in the duel. When the husband of one of the women falls into a great scandal, she is suddenly threatened with losing everything, including the passion for which she has compromised herself in order to be with Andrea.

The story's strength comes from its assertion that the lifeblood of the characters is their reputation, without which they are barred from Rome's pleasurable life. It is partly their maintenance of reputation and avoidance of scandal that serve to destroy them, physically and emotionally. The characters are rigidly confined within their social rules, and their desires are constantly thwarted; they are tormented by unfulfilled needs. **JA**

Eline Vere

Louis Couperus

Lifespan | *b.* 1863 (Netherlands), *d.* 1923
First Published | 1889
First Published by | Van Kampen & Zoon
Original Title | *Eline Vere. Een Haagsche Roman*

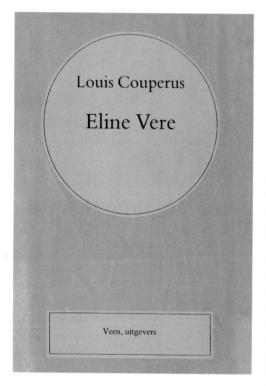

Louis Couperus

Eline Vere

Veen, uitgevers

"Eline, naturally that is me."

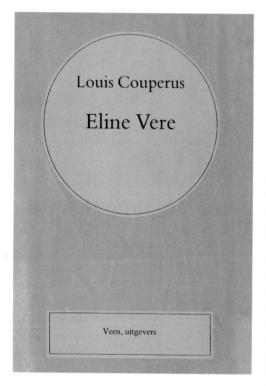 Couperus's first novel was an immediate success on publication in 1889; this is the jacket of an edition published in 1990.

First appearing as a serial in the journal *Het Vaderland*, Louis Couperus's novel tells the story of the young and talented Eline Vere, who discovers a reality quite unlike what she has learned from her books. Falling in love with an opera singer, she finds that her passion dies out as quickly as it came, leaving her disillusioned. Yet shortly thereafter, Eline accepts another man's proposal of marriage and, for a while, they experience an honest mutual affection. But her cousin Vincent is not convinced. As a determinist, to him such love equals childish idealism and nothing but a poetic flight from the truth that there is no free will and that no one is any more than a product of their specific time and place. Eline eventually breaks off her engagement.

In the spirit of Flaubert, Tolstoy, and Wilde, Couperus uses psychological realism to investigate the constant longing that threatens to consume the subject. What is it that we are, ever dissatisfiedly, looking for—and what if there is nothing to find? Who is more treacherous, the cynic or the romantic? And what do we do when we have lost the battle against reality? As Eline starts to question these things, her health deteriorates and she becomes depressed; she considers suicide but cannot find the courage to take her own life. When she dies accidentally of a morphine overdose, no questions are answered but we wonder whether there could be an alternative ending to the terror of loss, and whether there is any possibility of truthfulness.

Having achieved international acclaim early in life, in the Netherlands Couperus remained an ambivalently received dandy until the end of his life. The twentieth century saw a revival of public and academic interest in his work, and *Eline Vere* was made into a movie in the 1990s. **MvdV**

Hunger

Knut Hamsun

Knut Hamsun's reputation has suffered from his Nazi sympathies in and around the Second World War, but his early, semi-autobiographical portrait of the writer as a hungry young man is a seminal modernist classic, to be placed among Dostoevsky's *Notes from the Underground* and Beckett's *Malone Dies*. Hamsun, who won the Nobel Prize in 1920, was himself influenced by Dostoevsky, developing a kind of Nietzschean individualism that rebelled against both naturalism and the progressive literary politics associated with Ibsen. Set in Kristiania, the urban angst of *Hunger* prefigures the alienated cityscapes of Kakfa, but with an insistence on tensions between everyday economics and colloquial reverie worthy of James Kelman.

Told with the urgency of a breathless and starved present tense, the novel traces the various degradations of the narrator as he attempts to sustain himself through writing. Sometimes feverish from lack of food, other times merely contemptuous of humanity, the narrator has an overdeveloped sense of personal worth. The resulting encounters and misperceptions are both darkly existential and hilarious. Hunger gradually pulls apart the relation between need and dignity, inducing representations of madness that have an almost hallucinatory effect. The reading experience can become as delirious and confusing as the narrator's condition. Juxtaposing his fantasies and petty crimes with no less petty strategies of revenge and dreams of respect, the novel is carefully balanced between affirming this writer as exceptional and revealing him as a deluded soul, comically lost to spite and stupidity. In ways that prefigure the intellectual down-and-outs of Beckett's work, *Hunger* is an antidote for anyone planning a career as a starving writer. **DM**

Lifespan | *b.* 1859 (Norway), *d.* 1952
First Published | 1890, by Philipsen (Copenhagen)
Original Title | *Sult*
Nobel Prize for Literature | 1920

"This happened while I was walking around starving . . ."

⊘ The jacket of *Hunger—Sult* in Norwegian—published as the first volume of Knut Hamsun's *Collected Works* (*Samlede Werker*).

By the Open Sea

August Strindberg

Lifespan | *b.* 1849 (Sweden), *d.* 1912
First Published | 1890
First Published by | A. Bonniers Förlag (Stockholm)
Original Title | *I havsbandet*

When August Strindberg wrote *By the Open Sea*, he had fallen under the influence of Nietzsche's "Superman" theories. He researched the fields of biology, geology, and geography to implement and authenticate the scientific method and to describe accurately a strong, intellectual man of science.

The novel has two main characters, Axel Borg, a fisheries inspector sent to investigate the dwindling supplies of herring, and the natural landscape of sea and islands, a constant source of fascination for the author. Snobbish and superior, Borg alienates the simple and down-to-earth fishermen, and assumes the stronger man's right to oppress the weak. Taught by his father to suppress the feminine within him, he dominates and conquers a young woman, Maria, but in his own unconscious she takes on the role of anima, exposing the dark recesses of his mind. When under pressure from the locals and the locality, cracks begin to appear in his ego and his confidence begins to look like insecurity. His ideas become increasingly grandiose, and he experiments on himself in an attempt to control and conquer nature.

Borg is clearly Strindberg's alter ego, a sensitive and lonely genius dragged down by the mediocrity of the common rabble. Pointing forward to his "Inferno" crisis of the 1890s, this psychological novel, which charts the frightening degeneration of a proud and intellectual man into a persecuted wreck, gives an interesting insight into Strindberg's own state of mind at the time. **UD**

La Bête Humaine

Émile Zola

Lifespan | *b.* 1840 (France), *d.* 1902
First Published | 1890
First Published by | Charpentier (Paris)
Original Language | French

La Bête Humaine was the seventeenth novel in Émile Zola's twenty-novel series, *Les Rougons-Macquart*, through which he sought to follow the effects of heredity and environment on a single family, using the "scientific" terms central to late nineteenth-century Naturalism and to contemporary theories of degeneration and "hereditary taint." *La Bête Humaine* was also a vehicle through which Zola explored the power and impact of the railway, bringing together his twin fascinations with criminality and railway life. The impersonal force of the train becomes inextricably linked in the novel with human violence and destructiveness, and in the character Jacques Lantier, a train driver tormented by his pathological desire to kill women, Zola depicted what a later generation would define as a serial killer. Murder is made inseparable from machine culture, and accident and psychopathology become indivisible. Lantier's violent desires are stimulated when he glimpses the murder, driven by sexual jealousy, of Grandmorin, one of the directors of the railway company. His "itch for murder intensified like a physical lust at the sight of this pathetic corpse." The effects of this murderous desire are played out in the rest of the novel.

Zola's meticulous observation of the physical world is shown in his depictions of the railways, which paint in words the qualities of light and shadow, fire and smoke, that also acted as a magnet to the Impressionist painters of his time. **LM**

Thaïs

Anatole France

Lifespan | *b.* 1844 (France), *d.* 1924
First Published | 1890
First Published by | Calmann-Lévy (Paris)
Nobel Prize for Literature | 1921

Thaïs, a historical romance set in fourth-century Egypt, tells the story of two very different early Christians, and in doing so examines both the early church and the accepted conventionalities of piety in a new and provocative light. The novel describes the interaction of Paphnuce, the pious and ascetic Abbot of Aninoë, with the beautiful actress and courtesan Thaïs. Inspired by what he thinks is a vision from God, Paphnuce travels to Alexandria in order to convert Thaïs to Christianity, a religion she was baptized into but has since ignored. In the heady atmosphere of fourth-century Alexandria, Paphnuce argues the case for Christianity. The conversion a success, Thaïs retires to a convent to live out a life of purity and renunciation, but Paphnuce, his duty seemingly done, finds himself unexpectedly facing a host of new temptations. In his desire to become holy, his own motives become increasingly dubious until, in a dramatic conclusion, he is reunited with Thaïs and finally forced to question his own previously unshakable faith.

In its nuanced exploration of morality and human will, *Thaïs* exposes the inevitable contradictions inherent in the idea of purity, and challenges the reader's expectations of both saints and sinners. Written in a dreamy, evocative style, the novel merges the exotic atmosphere and excitement of the historical romance with a philosophic exploration of the effects of trying to renounce desires in favor of spiritual salvation. **AB**

"Such was the sanctity of these holy men that even wild beasts felt their power. When a hermit was about to die, a lion came and dug a grave with its claws."

◉ Italian soprano Lina Cavalieri appears as Thaïs in Massenet's operatic version of France's novel, first performed in 1894.

The Kreutzer Sonata

Leo Tolstoy

Lifespan | *b*. 1828 (Russia), *d*. 1910
First Published | 1890 (Russia)
Original Title | *Kreitserova sonata*
Original Language | Russian

> *"In our day marriage is only a violence and falsehood."*

◉ Inspired by Tolstoy's novel, René Prinet painted this image of a couple roused to passion by performing the Kreutzer Sonata.

The Kreutzer Sonata proffers a blistering attack on the "false importance attached to sexual love." It argues in favor of sexual abstinence (even within marriage), against contraception, and against sentimental ideas of romantic attachment. These morals are, in many respects, alien to the West today, but the novel cannot be simply dismissed as a reactionary rant. The idea that women will never enjoy equality with men while they are treated as sexual objects resonates with ongoing feminist debates. Here is the late Tolstoy at his most puritanical, following his famous late "conversion" to Christianity. If we were in any doubt that he shares the views advanced by the tormented protagonist, Pozdnyshev, he wrote a famous "Epilogue" the following year, an elaboration of his apologia for chastity and continence as befitting human dignity. The novel caused a scandal on its publication and attempts were made in Russia to ban it, though copies were widely circulated. Mere extracts were prohibited in America, and Theodore Roosevelt called Tolstoy a "sexual moral pervert."

Set during a train journey, Pozdnyshev tells the narrator the story of how he came to kill his wife, blaming his actions on the sexual ethos of the times. Readers of *Anna Karenina* will know that the train in Tolstoy's world can often be seen as a symbol of degraded modernity. The most compelling aspect of this novella is the psychological acute depiction of obsessive male jealousy. Like Shakespeare's Othello, Pozdnyshev's conviction that his wife is having an affair with her music partner finds confirmation in trifles. The barrier between his inner pain and his polished, scrupulously polite social exterior, between private passion and public decorum, ultimately breaks down in his final murderous outburst. **RM**

The Picture of Dorian Gray

Oscar Wilde

"There is no such thing as a moral or an immoral book. Books are well written, or badly written. That is all." The series of aphorisms that make up the "Preface" of Oscar Wilde's only novel was his response to those critics who had questioned the immorality and unhealthiness of the story after its scandalous first appearance in *Lippincott's Monthly Magazine*. However, for all its transgressive delights, *The Picture of Dorian Gray* could easily be read as a profoundly moral book, even a cautionary tale against the dangers of vice. Dorian's descent into moral squalor is neither admirable, as can be seen in his peremptory rejection of his fiancée, the actress Sybil Vain, nor enviable. Indeed the beautiful boy is the least interesting character in the book that bears his name.

After the artist Basil Hallward paints Dorian's picture, his subject's frivolous wish for immortality comes true. As the picture of him grows old and corrupt, Dorian himself continues to appear fresh and innocent for decades, despite the lusts and depravity of his private life. To be sure, it is the epigrammatic wit of Lord Henry Wotton that encourages Dorian on his quest for sensuality and sensation, but Dorian's values pervert the deeply serious Wildean ethic that they superficially resemble. Whereas Oscar Wilde's essays advocate individualism and self-realization as a route to a richer life and a more just society, Dorian follows a path of hedonism, self-indulgence, and the objectification of others. It is, nonetheless, a story that poignantly reflects Wilde's own double life and anticipates his own fall into ignominy and shame. The conceit on which it is based—the painting in the attic—seems immediately to mutate from fiction into the stuff of myth. **RM**

Lifespan | *b*. 1854 (Ireland), *d*. 1900
First Published | 1891
First Published by | Ward, Lock & Co. (London)
Given Name | Fingal O'Flahertie Wills

"How sad it is! I shall grow old, and horrid, and dreadful."

⊙ A lounging Dorian Gray contemplates the portrait that is destined to grow old while its subject enjoys eternal youth.

Down There

Joris-Karl Huysmans

Lifespan | *b.* 1848 (France), *d.* 1907
First Published | 1891, by Tresse & Stock (Paris)
UK Title | *The Damned*
Original Title | *Là Bas*

A cynical aesthete of the late nineteenth-century "decadence," Joris-Karl Huysmans was inexorably led by his disgust at bourgeois materialism to an interest in spiritual life and the occult. *Down There*, his most commercially successful novel, handles the sensational topic of satanism with a light, sardonic touch, while sparing the reader none of its horrors or vileness. The result is a multilayered work rich in imagination and humor, abstruse information, and lurid detail. Durtal, the author's alter ego, is researching a book about Gilles de Rais, the fifteenth-century "Bluebeard," satanic criminal and companion of the saintly Joan of Arc. This leads him to investigate at first hand the cult of satanism in contemporary Paris. Gilles's tortured search for spiritual powers is contrasted with the vulgarity of a Parisian black mass at which society ladies degrade themselves with the sinister Canon Docre.

Despite the dark material, there is plentiful humor, especially in descriptions of the indignities and everyday miseries of Durtal's bachelor existence. But Gilles's descent into horror at his chateau in Brittany ultimately dominates the book. A startling passage in which the Breton countryside is obscenely eroticized by Gilles's sex-obsessed gaze, prefigures Dali and Surrealism. For Huysmans, satanism was a step on the road to religious belief. *Down There* ends with Durtal failing to commit to Catholicism, but the author himself embraced the monastic life before his death in 1907. **RegG**

Tess of the D'Urbervilles

Thomas Hardy

Lifespan | *b.* 1840 (England), *d.* 1928
First Published | 1891, by Osgood, McIlvaine & Co.
Full Title | *Tess of the D'Urbervilles: A Pure Woman Faithfully Presented*

Tess of the D'Urbervilles is as famous for its heroine as for its notoriously tragic plot. Originally shunned by critics upon its publication in 1891 because of "immorality," the novel traces the difficult life of Tess Durbeyfield, whose victimization at the hands of men eventually leads to her horrific downfall. *Tess* spares the reader none of the bitterness inherent in English country life, and Hardy's often romanticized love for the landscape of Wessex is balanced by the novel's grimly realistic depiction of social injustice.

When Tess's father discovers that his own family, the Durbeyfields, are related to a prominent local dynasty, he agrees that his daughter should contact the heir, Alec D'Urberville, with tragic results. He seduces her, and soon abandons her, leaving her an unmarried single mother. While she briefly finds happiness with another man, the seemingly upright Angel Clare, he too rejects her upon hearing of her sexual past, leaving her in poverty and misery. Forced back into the arms of Alec, Tess must sacrifice her personal happiness for economic survival, but when her feelings of injustice overwhelm her in a moment of passion, the consequences are tragic.

In *Tess*, Hardy presents a world in which the human spirit is battered down by the forces, not of fate, but of social hierarchy. Tess's eventual death, one of the most famous in literature, is a direct result of human cruelty and as such represents one of the most moving indictments of the lives of nineteenth-century English women in all of literature. **AB**

Gösta Berling's Saga

Selma Lagerlöf

Lifespan | *b.* 1858 (Sweden), *d.* 1940
First Published | 1891, by Hellberg (Stockholm)
Original Title | *Ur Gösta Berlings Saga: Berättelse från det gamla Värmland*

In 1909, Selma Lagerlöf became the first woman to receive the Nobel Prize for Literature. Although written at the dawn of the modern era, her *Gösta Berling's Saga*, steeped in the local lore and legend of the mountainous and sparsely populated province of Värmland in the Swedish midwest, represents a return to traditional storytelling about glorious manor houses, beautiful women, gallant men, and extraordinary and romantic adventures.

In the bachelors' wing at Ekeby Manor, the generous and hospitable major's wife gives refuge to twelve homeless "cavaliers" led by Gösta Berling, a defrocked priest who is also a handsome and romantic Don Juan. These men represent old-fashioned, traditional values of chivalry and romance, but are also weak characters, dangerously devoted to bohemian living and reckless revelry. In a pact with the evil Sintram, the devil's local representative, the major's wife is evicted and the cavaliers take over Ekeby for a year, threatening to run it to rack and ruin. Fantastic events take place, and the Great Ball at Ekeby, in particular, is a classic episode of eventful drama.

The wish to recapture a golden age is offset by an interest in the nature of memory and reality. The novel is written in an old-fashioned, allegorical, and slightly mannered style, but the beginning, where the protagonist's state of mind and his dependence on the bottle is described, anticipates the modern novel in its intense focus on the human mind. **UD**

> *"For what is a man's soul but a flame? It flickers in and around the body of a man as does the flame around a rough log."*
>
> Selma Lagerlöf

⊙ Swedish novelist Selma Lagerlöf intertwined fairy tale and legend with realistic portrayal of rural life in a patriarchal society.

New Grub Street

George Gissing

Lifespan | *b*. 1857 (England), *d*. 1903 (France)
First Published | 1891
First Published by | Smith, Elder & Co. (London)
Original Language | English

Among the earliest and best novels about the business of authorship, *New Grub Street* draws a map of the late-Victorian publishing industry. George Gissing highlights the split between literary writing and popular journalism, typified in magazines such as the newly launched *Tit-Bits*, anticipating a hundred years of subsequent debate about art and mass culture. He gives a coolly realistic appraisal of the market, but still affirms that fiction can express its own kind of truth. Among a memorable, psychologically convincing cast of characters, the most fully drawn is Edwin Reardon, whose struggles to complete his novel *Margaret Home* are shown in detail. Desperate work gets the book finished, but it is feeble and full of padding, and Reardon, marked for failure, dreads seeing it reviewed. Jasper Milvain, by contrast, a shrewd, breezily assured literary operative with no aesthetic scruples, prospers. Harold Biffen is a garret-dwelling perfectionist who lives on bread and dripping. Biffen's novel *Mr. Bailey, Grocer*, a hyperrealist study of "ignobly decent" everyday life, is Gissing's intriguing guess at what twentieth-century avant-garde fiction might be like. Minor characters include, among others, the irascible Alfred Yule and his daughter, Marian.

Gissing was a cannier author than Reardon or Biffen, and a more serious writer than Milvain. *New Grub Street*, commercially and artistically his most successful book, shows that good fiction sometimes thrives in the marketplace. **MR**

News from Nowhere

William Morris

Lifespan | *b*. 1834 (England), *d*. 1896
First Published | 1891, by Reeves & Turner (London)
Full Title | *News from Nowhere; or, an Epoch of Rest, being some chapters from a Utopian Romance*

As prophecy, William Morris's dream of a utopian future, in which there is no private property, no government, no legal system, no penal system, and no formal education, can seem comically unlikely. Morris imagines a future London that has been reforested, and in which the clothes, the crockery, the buildings, and the bridges have all been designed by William Morris. The ideal that Morris is imagining here belongs much less to the future than it does to a specifically nineteenth-century fantasy steeped in an agrarian past. But the value of this dream is not found in its representation of an imagined future, so much as in its characterization of the limits of contemporary political imagination. Morris's vision of a life that is not governed by an oppressive state-apparatus brings a sharp, satirical focus to bear on the irrationality and the contradictions of his own time, and indeed present-day political conditions. Morris leads us to see with a new clarity the rank injustices that are produced by an unequal distribution of wealth.

The novel's bright, witty prose makes it just as much an entertaining tale as it is a socialist manifesto. It is also surprisingly sensual. An image of social justice is here entwined with an erotic delight in the possibilities of human beauty. **PB**

❯ The art nouveau cover of an issue of *Art Journal* magazine devoted to William Morris reflects his wide-ranging interests.

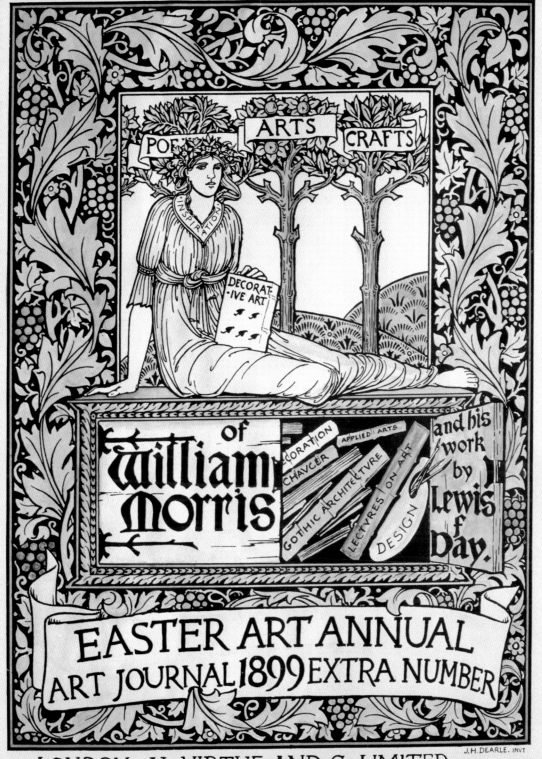

POE... ARTS CRAFTS

·INSPIRATION·

DECORAT-IVE ART

of
William
Morris
...oration
CHAVCER
applied arts
GOTHIC ARCHITECTVRE
LECTVRES ON ART
DESIGN
and his
work
by
Lewis
F.
Day.

EASTER ART ANNUAL
ART JOURNAL 1899 EXTRA NUMBER

J.H.DEARLE. INVT

LONDON: H VIRTUE AND Co LIMITED

Collier's

Household Number for November

Sherlock Holmes

In this Number Solves
The Mystery of

The
Norwood Builder

VOL XXXII NO 5   OCTOBER 31 1903   PRICE 10 CENTS

The Adventures of Sherlock Holmes

Sir Arthur Conan Doyle

Between 1891 and 1893 twenty-four of Arthur Conan Doyle's *Sherlock Holmes* stories were published in *The Strand*, of which the first twelve were republished in book form as *The Adventures of Sherlock Holmes*.

"To Sherlock Holmes she is always 'the woman.'" So begins "A Scandal in Bohemia," the first story in the collection. Irene Adler is "the" woman because she is the only person ever to have outwitted Holmes. The King of Bohemia fears that he will be blackmailed by Adler, his former lover, who has kept some compromising love letters and a photograph. However, she manages to turn the tables on the detective, retaining the photograph to ensure her own safety. Other highlights in the collection are the eerie "The Red-Headed League," where a red-headed man is offered employment by the League as a ruse to keep him occupied while criminals dig a tunnel from the cellar of his premises to a bank. In "The Man with the Twisted Lip," Holmes's help is enlisted to solve the mystery of the disappearance of Mr. Neville St. Clair. His wife has seen him at a window in a rougher part of town, but the police are unable to find anyone but a beggar. A number of enigmas follow before Holmes is able to reach a conclusion.

The first appearance of Sherlock Holmes in 1887 is particularly interesting in historical terms. For the first time, European cities had proliferated to the point where it was impossible to know more than a small percentage of their inhabitants. Yet the London that features in these stories manages to resist the idea that the city is sublime, that it is too large for any one person to be able to comprehend. Holmes and Watson represent Conan Doyle's bourgeois remedy to the terrifying and seemingly endless late nineteenth-century expansion of urban and industrial civilization. **VC-R**

Lifespan | *b*. 1859 (Scotland), *d*. 1930 (England)
First Published | 1892
First Published by | G. Newnes (London)
Original Language | English

"HOLMES GAVE ME A SKETCH OF THE EVENTS."

◉ Illustrator Sydney Paget was responsible for establishing the original appearance of Sherlock Holmes and Dr. Watson.

◉ Frederick Door Steele created this image of Conan Doyle's great detective for the cover of *Collier's Weekly* magazine in 1903.

Diary of a Nobody

George and Weedon Grossmith

Lifespan (George) | *b.* 1847 (England), *d.* 1912
Lifespan (Weedon) | *b.* 1852 (England), *d.* 1919
First Serialized | 1892, by *Punch* magazine (London)
First Published | 1892, by J. W. Arrowsmith (Bristol)

One of the great English comic novels, *Diary of a Nobody* bridges the world of Dickens to that of Waugh and Wodehouse. Straitlaced London clerk Charles Pooter records his daily life, both in the office and at home in suburban Holloway: a life involving insolent junior employees, his long-suffering wife, Carrie, and the serial amours of his son, Lupin. The masterstroke of the novel is the ironic distance between Pooter's sense of himself and the world, and his dim recognition that matters might be otherwise; readers will enjoy tracing how events conspire to outwit Pooter's attempts at maintaining a certain kind of genteel English decorum.

Both Grossmith brothers had strong theatrical connections, and stage comedy certainly influences the *Diary's* best set pieces. The more neurotic Pooter becomes about the smallest matters of domestic order, the more life seems to fling banana skins in his path, as when the new boots he buys for a dance send him sliding over the dance floor. Like Dickens's Micawber, Pooter is a comic figure who transcends his immediate context, largely through the *Diary's* surreally funny style; a reader does not need to know much about the 1890s to luxuriate in Pooter's absurd obsession with red enamel paint, which even leads him to repaint the spines of the family Shakespeare. At the same time, he is a supreme example of anxious Englishness, and Helen Fielding's Bridget Jones and John Cleese's Basil Fawlty might not exist without his example. **BT**

> *"He left the house, slamming the door after him, which nearly broke the fanlight; and I heard him fall over the scraper, which made me feel glad I hadn't removed it."*

In one of Weedon Grossmith's original illustrations, Pooter is surprised by the maid while executing an impromptu polka.

The Viceroys

Federico De Roberto

Lifespan | *b.* 1861 (Italy), *d.* 1927
First Published | 1894
First Published by | Galli (Milan)
Original Language | *I viceré*

"The Viceroys" is the nickname by which the aristocratic Uzeda family is known in Catania, because their forebears were viceroys of Sicily during the era of Spanish government. Their personal history, characterized by ferocious clashes of interests and an irreducible family pride, mirrors around thirty years of the history of Sicily, from the Bourbon period until the unification of Italy.

When the novel was published, it was far from successful. Reasons for this include the decline of *verismo*—De Roberto applied its principles rigorously, taking such devices as the impersonal narrator and a meticulous observation of facts to their extreme consequences, to the effect of slowing down the narrative rhythm. Also, the novel's pessimism and deliberately inelegant language had become unfashionable at a time of aestheticism.

Despite all this, *The Viceroys* is a novel of the first rank for the psychological subtlety of its characterization, the vastness of its scope, and the vividness of its descriptions. The author undertakes a lucid, acute critique of Sicilian society and thus distinguishes his work from other contemporary Sicilian novels. In De Roberto's narrative there is no room for good sentiments or the elegiac praise of patriarchal life. Its ultimate message, which anticipates Tomasi di Lampedusa's celebrated novel *The Leopard*, is that a principle of tragic fatalism inheres in the things and the people of Sicily to the effect that nothing can change. **LB**

Jude the Obscure

Thomas Hardy

Lifespan | *b.* 1840 (England), *d.* 1928
First Published | 1895
First Published by | Osgood, McIlvaine & Co. (Lon.)
Original Language | English

Jude the Obscure is the angriest and most experimental of Hardy's novels, preoccupied with themes of desire and displacement. When Jude Fawley leaves rural Marygreen and Alfredston behind him for the spires of Christminster City, a university town, he chooses to walk rather than ride the last four miles. He is physically pacing out the distance he is traveling, a distance only accurately measured in ambition and hope, or in the beautiful enthusiasm of one who knows not the obstacles on the path ahead.

When the stonemason Jude enters the city, he brings with him his class and its history. At first it enriches him; when he reads the monumental architectural pages of the college buildings, he does so through an artisan's eyes. Gradually, his class works to define limits for his ambition—the letter from the Master of "Biblioll College" warning Jude to remain "in your own sphere" provides one cruelly pragmatic moment of discovery. Jude's own broken marriage and his unconventional relationship with a free-spirited cousin ends in cruel tragedy, and the nature of Jude's response is telling.

Interwoven with despair, resentment, anger, and pride is a sense of exile all the more painful for being inarticulate. Forbidden access to the "world of learning," yet knowing such a world exists, Jude Fawley is doubly exiled, displaced by his desires from his social roots and hobbled by those roots in achieving his desires. **PMcM**

Effi Briest

Theodor Fontane

Lifespan | *b*. 1819 (Germany), *d*. 1898
First Published | 1895
First Published by | F. Fontane & Co. (Berlin)
Original Language | German

Thomas Mann declared *Effi Briest* among the six most significant novels ever written. Even more powerful testimony to its power comes from Krapp in Beckett's play *Krapp's Last Tape*: "Scalded the eyes out of me reading Effie again, a page a day, with tears again." Effi Briest is indeed scalding and anyone worried about appearing red-eyed should take appropriate precautions.

Widely thought the finest of Theodor Fontane's novels, *Effi Briest* exemplifies the realist novel, combining acute and moving characterizations with a critical portrait of social dynamics. Free of judgmental moralism, the novel—loosely based on a true story—nevertheless focuses its sympathies on the plight of the eponymous Effi, married too young to a much older man. In an otherwise conventional tale of love and adultery, Fontane weaves a beautiful and allusive sense of personal and social tragicomedy. Contrasting nature and culture, the naïvety of Effi shines through the troubling world she inhabits. Worthy of comparison with Eugénie Grandet, Emma Bovary, or Anna Karenina, Effi's character acts as a vehicle for exploration into the historical and social structure of society. The disruption of Effi's fragile humanity by the sexual and political undercurrents of the novel's social critique is particularly subtle. Sensitive to the risks of anything approaching melodrama, this novel, although told directly and with symbolic concentration, is built of oblique hints, acidic tangents, and dramatic ironies. **DM**

The Time Machine

H. G. Wells

Lifespan | *b*. 1866 (England), *d*. 1946
First Published | 1895
First Published by | W. Heinemann (London)
Full Title | *The Time Machine: An Invention*

The Time Machine, H. G. Wells's first novel, is a "scientific romance" that inverts the nineteenth-century belief in evolution as progress. The story follows a Victorian scientist, who claims that he has invented a device that enables him to travel through time, and has visited the future, arriving in the year 802,701 in what had once been London. There, he finds the future race, or, more accurately, races, because the human species has "evolved" into two distinct forms. Above ground live the Eloi—gentle, fairy-like, childish creatures, whose existence appears to be free of struggle. However, another race of beings exists— the Morlocks, underground dwellers who, once subservient, now prey on the feeble, defenseless Eloi. By setting the action nearly a million years in the future, Wells was illustrating the Darwinian model of evolution by natural selection, "fast-forwarding" through the slow process of changes to species, the physical world, and the solar system.

The novel is a class fable, as well as a scientific parable, in which the two societies of Wells's own period (the upper classes and the "lower orders") are recast as equally, though differently, "degenerate" beings. "Degeneration" is evolution in reverse, while Wells's dystopic vision in *The Time Machine* is a deliberate debunking of the utopian fictions of the late nineteenth century, in particular William Morris's *News from Nowhere*. Where Morris depicts a pastoral, socialist utopia, Wells represents a world in which the human struggle is doomed to failure. **LM**

The Island of Dr. Moreau

H. G. Wells

Lifespan | b. 1866 (England), d. 1946
First Published | 1896
First Published by | W. Heinemann (London)
Full Name | Herbert George Wells

A prophetic science fiction tale, *The Island of Doctor Moreau* takes on an even more sinister light, given contemporary debates about cloning and genetic experimentation, as well as the contentious issues that still surround Moreau's modus operandi—vivisection.

As with Wells's *The Time Machine* and *The War of the Worlds*, *Moreau* confronts readers with a gruesome extrapolation of evolution theory, which embodies many of the concerns arising from the publication of Darwin's *The Origin of Species* (1859). *Moreau* also represents a series of fundamental anxieties about the role of science and human responsibility. Here, the archetypal mad scientist who creates without due care or any apparent concern for the consequences of his work, is as vile as the beasts he manipulates. This orgiastic society of half-men, half-beasts, with their deliberately mutilated commandments—"Not to suck up Drink; that is the Law. Are we not Men?"—reflects contemporary society clearly enough, without needing the final sting. The barbarism of Moreau's methods is as horrific as the issues that lie beneath; developments in science mean that the text has as much capacity to shock now as on first publication, as Moreau flays his animals alive and slowly molds them into humans. This may be a far cry from the infinite delicacy of genetic manipulation, but it still succeeds in arousing all of the classic fears of "unknown" scientific methods. **EMcCS**

Quo Vadis

Henryk Sienkiewicz

Lifespan | b. 1846 (Poland), d. 1916 (Switzerland)
First Published | 1896, by Gebethner & Wolff
Original Title | *Quo vadis: Powieść z czasów Nerona*
Nobel Prize for Literature | 1905

An epic depiction of the cruelty and corruption of ancient Rome, *Quo Vadis* was an international best seller in the decade after its publication. Its lurid scenes of decadent carousing at the court of Nero and of the persecution of early Christians made it highly suitable for screen adaptation.

The central plot traces the ill-starred love between Ligia, a Christian girl from the area that is now Poland, and a Roman officer, Marcus Vinicius, who is eventually converted to the new faith after meeting the apostles Peter and Paul. This somewhat hackneyed storyline is much enlivened by the presence of Vinicius's uncle, the Roman author Petronius, a cynical aesthete who provides a witty insider's view of life at Nero's court. Nero himself emerges as a complex villain, who deliberately sets fire to Rome to clear the way for his architectural ambitions. He then blames the fire on the Christians, unleashing a wave of persecution. Henryk Sienkiewicz's strong Catholic faith shines through, as the love and spirituality of the early Christians are pitted against the power and materialism of Rome. There is also a subtext of Polish nationalism—at the time the book was written, Polish citizens were under the oppressive rule of three neighboring empires.

A fellow Polish Nobel Prize winner, Czeslav Milosz, wrote that Sienkiewicz displayed "a rare narrative gift," and although this kind of novel has long been out of fashion, the author's superb craftsmanship ensures that it remains an excellent read. **RegG**

Dracula

Bram Stoker

Lifespan | *b.* 1847 (Ireland), *d.* 1912 (England)
First Published | 1897
First Published by | A. Constable & Co. (London)
Original Language | English

"I trust . . . you will enjoy your stay in my beautiful land."

● Bram Stoker's was far from being the first vampire horror story, as is shown by this 1847 book illustration of the "feast of blood."

◗ A French poster for the 1958 film *Horror of Dracula*, one of the better movie exploitations of Dracula's potential to thrill.

Dracula is a true horror novel, as firmly rooted in the reality of the world where it takes place as it is in the forces of the supernatural that invade it. The blurring between these points is doubled in the story's telling, wherein the era's most cutting-edge modes of communication are corrupted, transmitting an ancient evil. Englishman Jonathan Harker travels to a remote castle in Transylvania to conduct a real estate deal with Count Dracula, whose fatal appetite for blood is unleashed. As the Count boards a ship for England in search of fresh prey, Dr. Van Helsing embarks on a complex plan to thwart the vampire. The narrative progresses through a series of eyewitness reports, diary entries, and technical notes from doctors and scientists. Each of these narrative modes should represent a degree of accurate "truth," yet across them the figure of Dracula is a constant presence, lurking out of sight, contravening laws of physics. The fascination and prevailing horror of *Dracula* lie in the prospect that even the most advanced of technologies, developed in search of some ultimate rationality and truth, still cannot eradicate the forces of the irrational, regardless of the particular period in history or the advancement in question.

The bloodthirsty Count has become a popular icon, the figurehead of both Universal and Hammer Horror movies throughout the twentieth century. Critics have carried out extensive psychoanalytical and postcolonial readings of the text. As a result, the strengths of the work as a horror novel, let alone a revolutionary one, have been flattened, reduced to almost nothing throughout the century that lies between its creation and the present day. This must not be the case, regardless of what vast and repetitive mileage it has already generated. **SF**

Universal Film, Inc. présente:

LE CAUCHEMAR DE DRACULA

(HORROR OF DRACULA)

Universal International

AVEC **PETER CUSHING** · **MICHAEL GOUGH** ET **MELISSA STRIBLING**
ET **CHRISTOPHER LEE** DANS LE RÔLE DE **DRACULA**
NE PRODUCTION **HAMMER FILM EN COULEURS** · MISE EN SCÈNE **TERENCE FISHER**

What Maisie Knew

Henry James

Lifespan | *b.* 1843 (U.S.), *d.* 1916 (England)
First Published | 1897
First Published by | W. Heinemann (London)
Original Language | English

When Beale and Ida Farange get divorced, their daughter Maisie is "disposed of in a manner worthy of the judgment seat of Solomon. . . . They would take her, in rotation, for six months at a time." The actual arrangements are altogether messier, as Maisie is passed back and forth between parents, new spouses, and lovers. Yet because everything is refracted through Maisie's consciousness, she appears as the still center of the novel, while the monstrous adults loom in and out of view.

"Small children have many more perceptions than they have terms to translate them," Henry James says in his "Preface" to the New York edition of the novel (1909). Maisie sees more than she understands. But she also knows more than she knows. At the root of her parents' tangled and unedifying relationships are sex and money, two subjects that Maisie, in a straightforward sense, knows nothing about. Yet she witnesses their effects in the behavior of the adults surrounding her, and in that way comes to know a very great deal about what sex and money mean.

Maisie's clarity of perception, uncluttered by the preoccupations of the grown-ups she is watching, and James's supple articulation of what she sees, provide a rich account of the fall out of an unhappy marriage. The activities of the adults are also thrown into sharp relief by the dignified figure of Maisie herself. And yet she is not unscathed by her experience: no one who knows as much as Maisie could be described as an innocent child. **TEJ**

Compassion

Benito Pérez Galdós

Lifespan | *b.* 1843 (Spain), *d.* 1920
First Published | 1897
First Published by | Viuda e Hijos de Tello (Madrid)
Original Title | *Misericordia*

Compassion, one of the most popular of this author's novels, belongs to a time in the life of Benito Pérez Galdós marked by an intense preoccupation with social questions and the possibility of a return to a morality of charity and generosity. The social world of this novel, set in Madrid, includes a middle-class family (the Zapatas, who are destined to fall into poverty) and a sea of wretched individuals, all of them victims of the sovereignty and volatility of money, who are permanently condemned to beg at the doors of churches and move from place to place in search of money and food.

From among these unfortunates emerge two unforgettable figures: a blind Moroccan beggar called Almudena and an old maid, Benigna (Nina) de Casia, who begs for alms for the secret purpose of feeding her ruined mistress. All survive through daydreams that carry them to another, preferable, reality: Almudena surrenders himself to his love for Benigna (which is very similar to the passion of Don Quixote for Dulcinea); Benigna gathers together the lies which people have to tell each other; the ruined bourgeoisie live on the memory of better times. Eventually, when Benigna and his beloved are abandoned because the Zapatas have received an unexpected inheritance, the dignity of these two characters is raised to a dimension of almost miraculous saintliness, although very typical, on the other hand, of the radical European imagination at the end of the nineteenth century. **JCM**

Pharaoh

Boleslaw Prus

Lifespan | *b*. 1847 (Russia), *d*. 1912 (Poland)
First Published | 1897, by Gebethner i Wolff (Warsaw)
Given Name | Alexander Glowacki
Original Title | *Faraon*

The story of *Pharaoh* opens 3,000 years ago, at the close of the New Kingdom period in Egypt. The nation is in decline, encroached on by desert to the west and to the east by the rising threat of the Assyrian army. Young Prince Ramses is the official heir to his dying father's throne. On his accession, Ramses is determined to restore the powers of the pharaoh, rebuild the army, and make Egypt's people prosperous again. But he stands to inherit an empty treasury and a population weakened by greedy priests and tax-gatherers. The high priests control Egypt in all but name, and they have no intention of allowing a brash young ruler to challenge their supremacy. Ramses relies on the support of the military and loyal nobles to implement his reforms. But the priests are dangerous enemies, especially when Ramses threatens to appropriate the treasure of the sacred Labyrinth in Thebes.

Pharaoh, praised as the greatest novel ever written in Polish, is a Bildungsroman for the eleventh century B.C.E. Ramses's self-imposed quest to discover how to rule his nation matures him from an ambitious boy to a wise and noble statesman. His very human failings—such as untimely passions for unsuitable women—interact with his genuine concern for social and agricultural reform. Rich in symbolic detail, *Pharaoh* is also an allegory for Poland or any country whose nationhood is threatened by powerful neighbors, and a meditation on historical inevitability. **MuM**

"Don't think about happiness. If it doesn't come, there's no disappointment; if it does come, it's a surprise."

◉ Prus's novel is set in ancient Egypt, but explores the machinations of power politics in terms equally applicable to modern times.

Fruits of the Earth

André Gide

Lifespan | *b.* 1869 (France), *d.* 1951
First Published | 1897, by Mecure de France (Paris)
Original Title | *Les Nourriture Terrestres*
Nobel Prize for Literature | 1947

André Gide's espousal of paganism in *Fruits* was linked to a desire to give free expression to his own homosexuality.

The title page of a 1920 edition of Gide's work is illustrated with a sympathetic woodcut portrait of the author by Louis Jou.

André Gide wrote *Fruits of the Earth* while suffering from tuberculosis. It takes the form of a long letter or address written to an imagined correspondent —Nathaniel, a disciple and idealized companion— and it is apparently a hymn to the heady pleasures of daily life that can be absolutely appreciated only by someone near to death, to whom every breath is miraculous. There are asides on the common blackberry and the taste of lemons, and on the particular feeling that can be found only in the shade of certain well-tended gardens.

The book's mode—a startling combination of the didactic and the euphoric, incorporating verses and songs—caused it to be read as an alternative or additional gospel, and it was for a long time Gide's most popular book, not least for its radical position on homosexuality. The new gods are sensation, desire, and instinct; the goals are adventure and excess. But an essential part of the book's doctrine is the necessity of renunciation. There is little pleasure in possession, and desire is dulled by consummation. Conventions are inimical because they are constraining, but also because they involve false consciousness.

This aspect of the book's message was taken up by Jean-Paul Sartre and Albert Camus, and was explored more elaborately by Gide himself in *The Immoralist* (1902). It would be easy to argue that *Fruits of the Earth* is not itself a novel, but in it Gide discovered at their barest some of the most fundamental principles of novel writing, and in the relation between the narrator and his ideal reader— "I should like to speak to you more intimately than anyone has ever yet spoken to you"—he found a way of charging a work of fiction with a sense of urgency that few writers have matched. **DSoa**

·A· GIDE·
LES·NOURRI
TURES·TE
RRESTRES

Gravures sur bois de LOUIS JOU.

(Claude Aveline, éditeur.)

The War of the Worlds

H. G. Wells

Lifespan | b. 1866 (England), d. 1946
First Published | 1898
First Published by | W. Heinemann (London)
Original Language | English

Like so many of H. G. Wells's pioneering science fiction texts, *The War of the Worlds* introduces a theme that was to find countless imitations. His work has been reproduced directly in film, comic book, and even progressive rock, but perhaps the most well-known exploration is Orson Welles's infamous radio broadcast of 1938. Interspersed with music from "Ramón Raquello and his orchestra," it reported a full-scale Martian invasion. That the initial transmission provoked panic in America, though of course exaggerated by the media, is testament to the greatness of Wells's fiction.

The plot is simple: a strange disk lands on Horsell Common, Surrey, and eventually hatches. The alien inside is malevolent, destroying all with its "heat ray" and striking terror in the heart with the eerie battle cry of "ulla." Humanity seems powerless in its wake and the Martians easily seize control.

The grandeur of Wells's vision is at once simple and deeply complex, suggesting humanity's inherent fallibility and lack of control over its destiny. At the same time, Wells introduces a series of underlying motifs that question prevailing social and moral beliefs. Finally, the spectacle of the Martians is both awe- and fear-inspiring, and the nature of the aliens themselves has been continually reinterpreted since the novel's first publication. **EMcCS**

🔘 Orson Welles is photographed shortly after his broadcast of *The War of the Worlds* that panicked America.

As a Man Grows Older

Italo Svevo

Lifespan | b. 1861 (Austria-Hungary), d. 1928 (Italy)
First Published | 1898, by Libreria Ettore Vram
Given Name | Aron Ettore Schmitz
Original Title | *Senilitá*

In Italo Svevo's beloved home city of Trieste lives a man called Emilio Brentani. He is a person who harbors literary ambitions. He is also a man in love with a modest but beautiful girl called Angiolina, "little angel." Although intended by Emilio to be an understanding free of sentimental impediments, their relationship swiftly changes, becoming passionate. The relationship soon evolves into a comedy of emotional errors, however, and Emilio's ineptitude forces him into ever greater compromises, exposing him to an uneven contest with his self-possessed friend Balli, a sculptor. In the end, the protagonist's plight culminates in tragedy as he disrupts the life of his sister Amalia, the one person who, too late, he realizes he truly loves.

Although now considered by some critics to be Svevo's great masterpiece and often regarded as being a more consummate and balanced work than *The Confessions of Zeno*, this novel was a failure when it was first published. Written in a simple, sometimes clumsy language that is a mixture of old-fashioned vocabulary and dialect expressions (Svevo learned Italian as his second language), it passed almost completely unnoticed before its "rediscovery" decades later. Characterized by a deep humanity, as well as by its humor, and profound psychological insight, *As a Man Grows Older* (the English title was the suggestion of Svevo's friend and admirer James Joyce) is a brilliant study of hopeless love and hapless indecision. **LB**

Dom Casmurro

Joaquim Maria Machado de Assis

Lifespan | *b.* 1839 (Brazil), *d.* 1908
First Published | 1899
First Published by | H. Garnier (Rio de Janeiro)
Founder of | Brazilian Academy of Letters

By the time Machado de Assis wrote *Dom Casmurro*, he was the acknowledged master of Brazilian literature, who had been teasing his respectable public with a subtly hostile depiction of their vices and hypocrisies for more than three decades. This funny, innovative, disturbing novel is the consummation of his idiosyncratic art.

The novel's eponymous hero and narrator is an elderly man telling his life story. He is building a house like the one in which he grew up, and his narrative has a similar function: to join the beginning of his life satisfyingly to its end. But the reader becomes aware that the missing middle of his existence poses some serious problems. The focus of the story is supposedly the narrator's love for Capitu, the adored childhood sweetheart whom he marries and who bears his son. Gradually, though, Capitu begins to appear as a monster of infidelity, the focus of her husband's jealousy.

Dom Casmurro is the most unreliable of narrators. Insinuating and confiding, he addresses his readers directly at every turn, at one moment begging them to believe his every word, at the next admitting to yawning lapses of memory. At times, Dom Casmurro imagines his reader tossing the book away in boredom or disgust. But Machado knows the hypnotic power of his own creation. Hooked by that sly, elusive conversational voice, readers may throw the book down, but they will always pick it up again. **RegG**

The Awakening

Kate Chopin

Lifespan | *b.* 1851 (U.S.), *d.* 1904
First Published | 1899
First Published by | H. S. Stone & Co. (Chicago)
Given Name | Katherine O'Flaherty

The Awakening was initially met with condemnation and outrage, forcing its author into financial crisis and literary obscurity. Coming back from this apparent literary death-at-birth, the effects of this novel live on, inveterate and relentless. Now widely read, *The Awakening* is critically acclaimed as an American version of *Madame Bovary*. When Edna Pontellier finds her position as young wife and mother in New Orleans unbearably stifling, her refusal to go by the laws and mores of society drives her up against a world at once disapproving and uncannily precognizant of her struggles, in a provoking and often progressive critique of marriage and motherhood in Creole society.

Chopin provides a startling account of what it might mean to "awaken" into a better understanding of one's position. The novel invites us to wonder if it might not be better to carry on "sleeping" through life, as well as dealing with the complicated ways in which different kinds of "production" and "destruction" merge with one another. Chopin's subject matter and observations are engrossing and, in many respects, ahead of their time. But what is most remarkable about *The Awakening* is the way in which it forces us to think about the very notion of time, of being ahead or outside of one's time, and of the time of reading. Reading, like awakening, is identified with a strange present; here the reader is left uncertain whether the awakening is still happening or, perhaps, has not yet begun. **JLSJ**

The Stechlin

Theodor Fontane

Lifespan | *b.* 1819 (Germany), *d.* 1898
First Published | 1899
First Published by | F. Fontane & Co. (Berlin)
Original Title | *Der Stechlin*

"In the end, an old person dies, and two young people get married; that's about all that happens over five hundred pages". This is Theodor Fontane's own laconic comment on the novel of his old age. In contrast to *Effi Briest's* intricate psychological motivation, there is a new type of realism, where a technique of extensive dialogue is used to characterize a society on the brink of profound changes.

The old person is Major Dubslav, called "the Stechlin," owner of a castle as well as lake Stechlin—the latter is, according to myth, said to boil whenever a major catastrophic event occurs anywhere in the world. The two young people are Woldemar, the Stechlin's son, and Armgard, the slightly colorless sister of the brilliant and lively Melusine. The Stechlin, warm, humane, and skeptical toward radicalism of any kind, is persuaded to stand as Conservative candidate for the Reichstag, though his phlegmatic approach to politics means that he is easily defeated by his Social Democrat rival. As the crumbling of the old elites, makes it necessary for the relationship between individual and society to be redefined, the Stechlin welcomes the changing times, even though the approach of democracy will do away with the privilege of those such as himself. It is left to Melusine, who shares the name of the seductive water fairy of legend, to point out the connection between the lake, so mysteriously linked to the rest of the world, and the importance of keeping in touch with a changing world. **MM**

Theodor Fontane.

"Books have a sense of honor. If they are lent out, they will not come back."

Theodor Fontane, 1895

◔ Theodor Fontane was fifty-six when he first turned to writing novels and *Effi Briest* was produced in his seventies.

Eclipse of the Crescent Moon

Géza Gárdonyi

Lifespan | b. 1863 (Hungary), d. 1922
First Published | 1899
First Published by | Légrády (Budapest)
Original Title | Egri csillagok

A compulsory text in Hungarian high schools until this day and re-read by many throughout adulthood, *Eclipse of the Crescent Moon* was voted the nation's favorite book in a 2005 survey. Set in the years following the Hungarians' defeat by the Turks at the Battle of Mohács (1526), the novel interweaves meticulously researched historical detail with romance, adventure, and skullduggery, not to mention fictionalized events from the author's life, into a masterpiece of patriotic prose.

The novel opens in 1533 with our heroes Gergely Bornemissza, an orphan boy, and Éva Cecey, the daughter of a wealthy family, frolicking in a stream. Kidnapped by Yumurdjak, a one-eyed Turk, they escape capture and return to defend their village. Gergely's strategic command and skill with explosive devices bring him under the wing of the nobleman Bálint Török but later land him in jail, while his love for Éva takes them both to Constantinople incognito, to free Török from the Sultan's imprisonment. Following the siege of Eger in 1552, in which the people of the city successfully fought off the numerically far superior Turks, Gergely and Éva are reunited together with their son.

Gárdonyi's research took him from Vienna to Constantinople. His grave lies inside the fortress of Eger, honored for his unforgettable narrative of one of Hungary's battles to remain free. **GJ**

Some Experiences of an Irish R. M.

Somerville and Ross

Lifespan (Somerville) | b. 1858 (Greece), d. 1949 (Ire)
Lifespan (Ross) | b. 1862 (Ireland), d. 1915
First Published | 1899
First Published by | Longmans & Co. (London)

A series of comic tales of late nineteenth-century Anglo-Irish life, dealing largely with hunting, shooting, and horse riding, might seem unlikely to have many attractions for readers today. The poorer characters play minor roles, while the foreground is occupied by the elite and their hangers-on. The authors were members of the landowning "Ascendancy," and the artifices and conventions of the storytelling reflect the angle, and the limits, of their vision. The fictitious narrator, Major Sinclair Yeates, is resident magistrate at Skebawn. Being "of Irish extraction," Yeates is not quite English—but he is certainly not Irish. We hear the wit and music of English as it was spoken in rural Ireland, and west Cork is pleasantly evoked in descriptions of rivers, coasts, bogs, and fields.

One of the best stories among these witty, well-observed tales, "Lisheen Races, Second-hand," recounts the visit to Skebawn of Yeates's college friend Leigh Kelway, an Englishman and a well-intentioned bore. When Yeates takes him to some "typical country races," Kelway (much to the reader's delight) endures countless indignities and disasters, culminating in a collision with a mail coach. Yeates will always remain an outsider in Cork, but he knows and loves it as a foreigner in a way that Kelway never can. **MR**

> Edith Somerville wrote the *Irish R. M.* tales with her cousin and companion, Violet Martin, who took the pseudonym Martin Ross.

1// It was a /cold, blowy .day in early Apr
were striking thirteen, Winston Smith, pushe
Victory Mansions, turned to the right down
ed the button of the lift. Nothing happened
second time when a door at the end of the p
a smell of boiled greens and old rag mats,
acted as porter and caretaker thrust out a
for a moment sucking his teeth and watching

"Lift ain't working," he announced at
"Why isn't it working?"
"No lifts ain't working. The currents
The 'eat ain't working neither. All current
daylight hours. Orders!" he barked in milit
door again, leaving it uncertain whether th
felt was against Winston, or against the au
the current.

Winston remembered now. It was part o
preparation for Hate Week. The flat was sev

1900s

George Orwell, *Nineteen Eighty-Four*, 1949

Sandokan: The Tigers of Mompracem

Emilio Salgari

Lifespan | *b.* 1862 (Italy), *d.* 1911
First Published | 1900
First Published by | A. Donath (Genoa)
Original Title | *Le Tigri di Mompracem*

The Tigers of Mompracem, Emilio Salgari's most famous novel and the greatest Italian bestseller of all time, features the first adventure of Sandokan, Salgari's enduring creation that spawned a whole legion of sequels. The Tigers are a band of rebel pirates fighting against the colonial power of the Dutch and British empires. They are led by Sandokan, the indomitable Tiger of Malaysia, and his loyal friend, Yanez de Gomera, a Portuguese wanderer and adventurer (his bearing a Spanish name was an error of the writer). After twelve years of spilling blood and spreading terror throughout Malaysia, Sandokan has reached the height of his power, but when the pirate learns of the existence of the Pearl of Labuan, his fortunes begin to change.

In the dozen novels that comprise the Sandokan series, Salgari's pen transformed the bloodthirsty pirate into a noble warrior, a kind of Malay Robin Hood, imbuing his character with a strong sense of idealism, passion, and loyalty. Though popular with the masses, Salgari was shunned by critics throughout his life and for most of the twentieth century. It was not until the late 1990s that his writings began to be revisited and new translations appeared in print, becoming very popular, especially in Italy, Spain, and Latin America. The adventurous flair of the books has inspired numerous writers, from Umberto Eco, who would read Salgari as a way to explore the world, to Gabriel Garcia Marquez, who devoured his books as a young man. **LB**

"On December 20th 1849, a violent hurricane raged over Mompracem . . . home to the most feared pirates in the Sea of Malaysia."

◉ Indian actor Kabir Bedi plays Sandokan in one of several mini-series based on Salgari's novels and made in Italy in the 1970s.

Sister Carrie

Theodore Dreiser

Lifespan | *b*. 1871 (U.S.), *d*. 1945
First Published | 1900
First Published by | Doubleday, Page & Co.
Original Language | English

Sister Carrie is a gripping and grim novel that charts the fortunes of three main characters making their way at the turn of the nineteenth century. Carrie Meeber moves from the Midwest to Chicago to live with relatives who feel obliged to take her in. She takes a menial job and then moves in with the raffish salesman, Charles Drouet. However, she soon tires of him and attaches herself to the more socially elevated George Hurstwood. He leaves his wife and family for her, steals a large sum of money from his employers, and they run off to New York. There, Carrie rises while George falls. She becomes a celebrated actress and dancer, while he lapses into poverty after she leaves him.

Theodore Dreiser's novel is a major landmark in American fiction, which helped to establish a distinctly American literary identity. *Sister Carrie* is significant for a number of reasons. Dreiser's sparse, journalistic style depicts the realities of everyday city life in a powerful language that seems to hide nothing, so that we feel we see characters as they really are. Equally important, the novel does not serve as a fable, and no serious judgments are offered on the protagonists' behavior. Carrie is a woman dealt a bad hand, who determines to make the most of what she has, seizing opportunity when it is offered. Charles is a pleasure-seeker, a mixture of the vulgar and the appealing. And George, a tormented and unhappy man, loses all he has in pursuit of a modest, but unobtainable, goal. **AH**

None but the Brave

Arthur Schnitzler

Lifespan | *b*. 1862 (Austria), *d*. 1931
First Published | 1901
First Published by | S. Fischer Verlag (Berlin)
Original Title | *Lieutenant Gustl*

Utterly bored at the opera, egocentric young Lieutenant Gustl prefers to look around in search of pretty women and potential flirts. In tune with the growing anti-Semitism of the time, he thinks that there are too many Jews in the army, and later contemplates an upcoming duel with a doctor who made an unflattering remark about the military.

In a cloakroom argument after the show, a baker, reacting to Gustl's attempt to jump the queue, grabs the soldier's sword and threatens to snap it. Convinced he has been completely dishonored but unable to challenge the baker to a duel because of the latter's lower social status, Gustl ponders suicide and spends the night wandering through the streets of Vienna wishing for the baker's death. In the morning he resolves to have his last breakfast. It is while sitting in a café that he learns the baker died of a stroke just after their encounter, thus freeing Gustl from his suicidal thoughts.

Despite its simplicity, this narrative quickly became famous because of the scandal it provoked with its sarcastic portrayal of an Austrian officer and because of its questioning the rationality of dueling. What assures its lasting fame, however, is its innovative structure and language. Written entirely in the form of an interior monologue, the text borrows its technique from Freud's early psychoanalytical studies on mental associations. Schnitzler's approach was highly influential with later writers such as James Joyce in *Ulysses*. **LB**

Kim

Rudyard Kipling

Lifespan | *b.* 1865 (India), *d.* 1936 (England)
First Published | 1901
First Published by | Macmillan (London)
Nobel Prize for Literature | 1907

In this imperialist Bildungsroman the young hero, Kim, an Irish orphan, matures from a Lahore street urchin into an invaluable member of the British Secret Service. Rudyard Kipling equates Kim's personal maturity with a wider cultural maturity, linking the boy's journey into manliness with one from native childishness to an adult European civilization. These two ideas are deeply entwined in the novel as Kim must trade in the education of the street for that of a military boarding school, and the languages of India for his native tongue. Kipling's own language fully supports this hierarchy, so that the supposedly immature cultures of Asia are expressed through a deliberately archaic idiom.

Kipling has been rightly seen as an apologist for British imperialism; in *Kim* there is little doubt that British rule is the best thing for India. Moreover, as a Sahib who is a master of disguise, able to successfully appear as a Hindu, a Muslim, or a Buddhist-mendicant, Kim embodies the notion of Western mastery over the Asiatic cultures.

Nevertheless, this view of Kipling's writing does not do justice to the complexity of his vision of India. Kipling frequently identifies similarities between the cultures of India and those of the Europeans-in-India. The Irish soldiers who discover Kim are just as superstitious and credulous as the Indian travelers on the Grand Trunk Road, and the Buddhist priest who shares responsibility for Kim's education with Creighton, the English surveyor and spy master, presents a perspective on India remarkably similar to Creighton's own. One of the charms of this novel is as a survey of India, and, though it repeatedly lumps together the "oriental" as an undifferentiated mass, its descriptions of individual Indians stresses the brightness and diversity of Indian public life. **LC**

Rudyard Kipling, photographed here in 1890, was born in Bombay and learned his craft as a journalist in Lahore.

Printmaker William Nicholson made this portrait of Kipling in his mid-thirties, by then Britain's acknowledged bard of empire.

Buddenbrooks
Thomas Mann

Lifespan | *b.* 1875 (Germany), *d.* 1955
First Published | 1901, by S. Fischer Verlag (Berlin)
Original Title | *Buddenbrooks: Verfall einer Familie*
Nobel Prize for Literature | 1929

Buddenbrooks: The Decline of a Family is among the last and greatest achievements of the European realist novel. The book spans forty-odd years during the mid-nineteenth century.

Set in the Hanseatic city of Lübeck, the novel follows the fortunes of one of the leading families of the city's ruling merchant class. Its focus is on the growth of three siblings from childhood to midlife. Christian Buddenbrook, lacking the self-discipline (or perhaps the self-repression) required to become a businessman and solid citizen, performs instead the self-destructive role of half-licensed fool. By contrast, his elder brother, Thomas, adapts himself fully, but at great physical and psychological cost, to his position as head of the firm, Consul and Senator. Their sister, Tony, passionately values the prestige of the family, but her infelicitous adventures in love and marriage show that she is incapable of playing the dutiful daughter and wife. The final chapters are devoted to Thomas's son, Hanno, who inherits from his Dutch mother an exceptional musical talent and an estrangement from the masculine, public shows of the Hanseatic state. With Hanno, we realize, the Buddenbrook line will take a new direction, or come to its end.

The novel's tapestry of closely observed scenes is seemingly inexhaustible—among them are family feasts and arguments, deathbeds and childbirth, weddings, seaside holidays, schoolrooms, and ship launchings. Mann's detailed analysis of the interplay between public and private self, and between a declining ethic of civic and commercial propriety and a new spirit of aesthetic self-cultivation, is remarkable, not only for its subtlety and objectivity, but for the wider historical resonances evoked by his characters and their fates. **MR**

◈ The cover of an early twentieth-century German edition of Mann's family saga suggests a cosier vision than the book presents.

The Hound of the Baskervilles

Sir Arthur Conan Doyle

Arguably one of the best Sherlock Holmes stories and one of the all-time classical mysteries, the atmosphere of *The Hound of the Baskervilles* is ghoulish, full of suspense and fear, and Sherlock Holmes is at his most brilliant. When Sir Charles Baskerville dies suddenly from heart failure, there are rumors that his death was caused by the gigantic ghostly hound of the title, said to have haunted his family for generations. When the estate's heir, Sir Henry Baskerville, arrives in England from Canada to take up his inheritance, Watson accompanies him to Baskerville Hall, and a skeptical Holmes is called in to investigate. Situated on the edge of Dartmoor, the Baskerville estate borders a vast, brooding, misty moor, containing features such as Grimpen Mire, a deadly quicksand-like bog. It is the descriptions of the moor and the oppressive Baskerville Hall that provide much of the chilling atmosphere that pervades the novel. Into this setting Sir Conan Doyle weaves the sounds of a wailing woman, a mysterious butler, an escaped killer, and the specter of the ghostly, fire-breathing, murderous hound.

The Hound of the Baskervilles draws the reader in, not only to the world of the misty moor and strange goings-on, but also to the works of Conan Doyle. In this novel he displays his own interest in the occult, alongside Sherlock Holmes's talent for keen scientific detection, in a story that is full of atmosphere, suspense, and unexpected turns. It is a novel that keeps the reader fearful and guessing until the very last page, and then leaves them wanting more. Arguably the most popular of all the Sherlock Holmes mysteries, since its original serialization in 1901–1902, *The Hound of the Baskervilles* has been set to film no fewer than eighteen times, beginning with a German silent production of 1914. **LE**

Lifespan | *b.* 1859 (Scotland), *d.* 1930
First Published | 1902, by G. Newnes (London)
Original Title | *The Hound of the Baskervilles: Another Adventure of Sherlock Holmes*

Sydney Paget created this image of the ghostly hound for the original serialized version of the novel in *Strand* magazine.

Heart of Darkness

Joseph Conrad

Based on Joseph Conrad's own venture into Africa in 1890, *Heart of Darkness* is the best of his shorter novels and is the most brilliant of all his works. Eloquent, audacious, experimental, recessive, satiric, yet deeply humane, since its serialization in 1899 it has continued to provoke controversy and reward analysis. Charles Marlow, one of Conrad's "transtextual" characters (for he appears also in *Youth*, *Lord Jim*, and *Chance*), tells a group of British friends about his journey into a part of central Africa identifiable as the "Congo Free State," which was then the private property of Leopold II, King of the Belgians. Marlow recalls the absurdities and atrocities that he witnessed: a French warship shelling the continent, the cruel treatment of enslaved black laborers, and the remorseless rapacity of the white colonialists who are impelled by the desire for profits from ivory. He looks forward to meeting Mr. Kurtz, the greatly talented and idealistic European trader; but, when he reaches the dying adventurer, he finds that the idealist has become deranged and depraved. Virtually a savage god, Kurtz sums up his view of Africans in the phrase "Exterminate all the brutes!" The "heart of darkness," we learn, is not simply the jungle at the center of the "Dark Continent"; it is also the corrupt heart of Kurtz, and it may even be European imperialism itself. "All Europe contributed to the making of Kurtz," and London is depicted as the center of brooding gloom.

Written when imperialism was "politically correct," this brilliantly anti-imperialist and largely anti-racist work shows Conrad at the peak of his powers as a challenging innovator in ideas and techniques. *Heart of Darkness* has proved immensely influential, and numerous adaptations include the movie *Apocalypse Now* (1979). **CIW**

Lifespan | *b*. 1857 (Ukraine), *d*. 1924 (England)
First Published | 1902
First Published by | W. Blackwood & Sons (London)
Original Language | English

Conrad held a sternly pessimistic view of the world, suggesting no encouraging alternative to the corruption of imperialism.

Marlon Brando's Colonel Kurtz embodies the darkness at the heart of the Vietnam War in the 1979 movie *Apocalypse Now*.

The Wings of the Dove

Henry James

Lifespan | *b.* 1843 (U.S.), *d.* 1916 (England)
First Published | 1902
First Published by | A. Constable & Co. (London)
Original Language | English

The Wings of the Dove is perhaps Henry James's darkest moral drama, the story of a passionate love triangle between the enigmatic Kate Croy, her secret fiancé Merton Densher, and Milly Theale, the young and fatally ill American heiress. All is played out against the symbolic backdrops of London materialism and Venetian beauty and decay. Milly's desperate desire to experience "the sense of having lived" provides both the sympathetic and self-serving motivations for Kate's scheme. She wants Densher to seduce Milly, filling her final days with happiness, in the knowledge that the fortune the girl will surely leave him after her death will enable him to marry Kate herself. James is a master of the complex moral situation, and combines the melodrama of his plot with nuanced values. Though elaborate and self-conscious, the narrative style lacks neither realism nor intensity. The sexual attraction between Kate and Densher, his developing feelings for Milly, her determined resistance of her fate, and Kate's jealousy, are vividly and powerfully portrayed.

When Milly finally learns the truth of her friends' deception but leaves them her fortune nevertheless, her own capacity for manipulation through moral victory becomes clear. For in renouncing the spoils of corruption, Densher also rejects Kate for Milly's idealized memory, with which she knows she cannot compete. In the very success of her plan Kate realizes that she has brought about her own downfall. "We shall never be again as we were," she declares. **DP**

The Immoralist

André Gide

Lifespan | *b.* 1869 (France), *d.* 1951
First Published | 1902
First Published by | Mercure de France (Paris)
Original Title | *L'Immoraliste*

A thought-provoking work that still has the power to challenge complacent attitudes and unfounded cultural assumptions, *The Immoralist* recounts a young Parisian man's attempt to overcome social and sexual conformity.

Michel is a young, puritanical scholar, who has recently married solely to please his dying father. On his honeymoon in North Africa he becomes very ill and almost dies. His brush with death gives him an all-consuming desire to live, and his convalescence has the force of a religious awakening. Experiencing things with a heightened awareness, he is sexually drawn to the Arab boys he surrounds himself with. Sensually aroused, he realizes that conventional social morality and the trappings of bourgeois civilization—education, church, and culture—have alienated him from his true self. But the selfish pursuit of authenticity and pleasure he embarks on causes him to neglect his wife as well as important practical matters. When she falls ill, he persuades her they should go south, doing so merely in order to gratify his own desires, which he is incapable of resisting. His once radical freedom has turned to base enslavement. Michel's attempt to access a deeper truth by repudiating culture, decency, and morality results in confusion and loss. In being true to himself, Michel has harmed others. Yet the novel remains as much an indictment of the arbitrary constraints of a hypocritical society as it is of Michel's misguided behavior. **AL**

The Ambassadors

Henry James

Lifespan | *b.* 1843 (U.S.), *d.* 1916 (England)
First Published | 1903
First Published by | Methuen & Co. (London)
Original Language | English

Henry James regarded *The Ambassadors* as his best novel, and it is certainly held to be his greatest artistic achievement. In the character of Lambert Strether, a middle-aged New Englander confronted with the social and aesthetic attractions of a beguiling Paris, he brought to perfection his style of first-person narrative.

Strether has been sent to Europe on behalf of his fiancée, the redoubtable Mrs. Newsome, charged with retrieving her son Chad from the clutches of a liaison which, it is assumed, is corrupting him with European moral laxness. But upon his arrival, Strether discovers a much more complicated affair, which leads him to re-evaluate both American and European cultures. Although he fails as an ambassador, he comes to a better understanding of the strengths and weaknesses of both European and American society, and he quickly accedes to the suggestion that Chad's relationship with the beautiful Marie de Vionnet is not a shameful affair but actually a "virtuous attachment."

Overall, *The Ambassadors'* vision is tragic: its most sensitive characters are largely victims of a seemingly inescapable social regulation. Indeed, with *The Ambassadors*, James excels at representing figures who are aware of their loss of youth, and who seem increasingly out of pace with the world. In the figure of Strether, he has developed a character who proves capable of choosing his own destiny, though hardly a triumphant one. **DP, TH**

"Live all you can; it's a mistake not to. It doesn't so much matter what you do in particular, so long as you have your life. If you haven't had that what HAVE you had?"

Henry James based his novels on the subtle psychological observation of characters in intense emotional situations.

The Riddle of the Sands

Erskine Childers

Lifespan | *b.* 1870 (Ireland), *d.* 1922
First Published | 1903, by Smith, Elder & Co. (Lon.)
Full Title | *The Riddle of the Sands: A Record of Secret Service . . .*

Erskine Childers wrote *The Riddle of the Sands* after returning home wounded from the Second Boer War, where he fought for the British. The narrator, Carruthers, who works for the Foreign Office, receives a mysterious invitation from an old friend, Davies, to join him on his yacht in the Baltic. The *Dulcibella* is not what Carruthers was expecting. For a start, there is no crew—or, rather, Carruthers is the crew—and Davies is not on a pleasure cruise. He is systematically mapping the shallows of the German North Sea coast, having realized that Germany could exploit the apparently unnavigable waters to launch a surprise large-scale invasion of Britain using shallow-draught troop-carriers.

Carruthers and Davies's activities attract the attention of the German authorities, and they soon face more serious threats than those presented by the treacherous seas. Matters are further complicated by Davies's having fallen in love with a German girl: perhaps Childers was able to dramatize Davies's conflict of loyalties as vividly as he does because it reflected his own divided sense of duty toward Ireland and Britain (which would eventually lead to his execution). This novel was intended to make a serious point about a potential threat to British national security. But just as Davies and Carruthers commit themselves to their adventure not only out of a sense of duty but also for the sheer excitement it brings, so *The Riddle of the Sands* easily transcends its role as propaganda. **TEJ**

The Call of the Wild

Jack London

Lifespan | *b.* 1876 (U.S.), *d.* 1916
First Published | 1903
First Published by | Macmillan (New York)
First Serialized | 1903, in *Saturday Evening Post*

Set against a backdrop of winter in northwest Canada during the Klondike Gold Rush of the 1890s, *The Call of the Wild* is the story of a dog's transformation from pet to leader of a wolf pack.

The dog, Buck, has been raised as part of a human household. When he is stolen to join a sled-dog pack, he is transformed into a mere servant of humans. This is a Darwinian world, where only those most fitted to the situation will survive. London describes dogfights, beatings, and Buck's growing blood lust with a lyrical touch that highlights the romantic appeal of the wilderness and wildness itself. When the traces binding Buck to the sled are cut, Buck becomes the equal of his rescuer, John Thornton, but is bound to Thornton by love. It is only with Thornton's death, when Buck kills some Yeehat Indians, that he realizes that humans have no power over him, so he turns his back on the human world to embrace the wild.

Buck's adaptation is not just a matter of learning to cope with new situations, but an atavistic rekindling of wild instincts within him. In the most anthropomorphic moments of the book, Buck has visions of men in animal skins cowering by a fire in the dark. These visions make Buck's transformation seem more than just instinctive. The call of the wild becomes a mystical, spiritual force. **CW**

❯ Jack London's best-selling novels earned him a fortune, but he clung to the attitudes of his roustabout background.

Memoirs of my Nervous Illness

Daniel P. Schreber

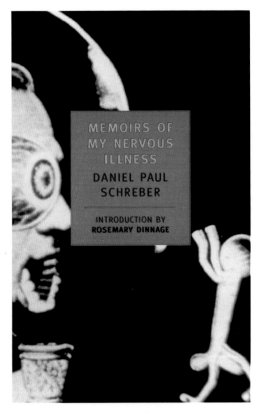

Lifespan | *b.* 1842 (Germany), *d.* 1911 (Italy)
First Published | 1903
First Published by | Oswald Mutze (Leipzig)
Original Title | *Denkwürdigkeiten eines Nervenkranken*

In 1884, Senatspräsident Daniel Paul Schreber, a distinguished judge, suffered the first in a series of mental collapses that would mark his life with psychosis and eventually lead to his permanent committal to a psychiatric hospital. Throughout his trials Schreber kept a diary, which he then, in his more lucid periods, turned into a book of memoirs.

Because of a rift in the miraculous structure of things, Schreber tells us, he is now the only man left alive and thus has sole attention of an ignorant God, who can neither learn nor understand, and so deals with people as if they were "corpses." This brutal God wants to "unman" Schreber in order to repopulate the world from his womb. Schreber's account is as much an autobiographical story written from the margins of madness as a primer in the work of a creative mind unraveling—layer after layer—the fabric of the ordinary world. It does this through a poetic vision that insists on the correspondences between the world and man, who is presented as being at once victim and miracle worker.

Finally, this work is also a historical document on modernity. Moritz Schreber, Paul's authoritarian father, was an eminent expert on child-rearing who, among other things, advised ignoring the cries of babies, bathing them in cold water, and touching children as little as possible. The *Memoirs* are thus a tragic testimony of a whole generation raised in absence of contact, any contact—with psychosis as its only recourse to touch and poetry. **IJ**

"The sun has for years spoken with me in human words and . . . reveals herself as . . . the organ of a still higher being."

◉ Schreber's description of the world as interpreted by a psychotic mind influenced Sigmund Freud's formulation of psychoanalysis.

The Way of All Flesh

Samuel Butler

Lifespan | *b.* 1835 (England), *d.* 1902
First Published | 1903
First Published by | Grant Richards (London)
Original Language | English

Most critics of *The Way of All Flesh* note, with surprise, the savagery of its satirical bite. It is, after all, a thinly veiled autobiography, based on Butler's relationship with his overbearing father. What's more, the book was written between 1873 and 1883, when Victorian values of decorum and hierarchy were arguably strongest. All in all, you might expect some restraint.

Far from it: Butler delights in revealing the self-righteous hypocrisy of those who say they hold traditional values dear. Little wonder he insisted the manuscript remain unpublished until after his death; until 1903, *The Way of All Flesh* remained locked in a drawer. V. S. Pritchett famously described the book as a time bomb. "One thinks of it lying in Samuel Butler's desk for thirty years, waiting to blow up the Victorian family and with it the whole great pillared and balustraded edifice of the Victorian novel."

The story follows three generations of the Pontifex family, focusing on the aptly named Ernest. Ernest's father and grandfather are both prominent clergymen, and it is expected that Ernest will follow suit. However, a crisis of faith sees him abandon this career for an altogether less certain future; his father, who excels in pompous moralizing and little else, is particularly dismayed. Ernest's attempts to build a new life repeatedly founder—an alcoholic wife, broken marriage, and failed business bring him to near collapse. Despite this, he perseveres and eventually escapes from the malign influence of his past to become a new—and modern—man. **PH**

Hadrian the Seventh

Frederick Rolfe

Lifespan | *b.* 1860 (England), *d.* 1913 (Italy)
First Published | 1904
First Published by | Chatto & Windus (London)
Original Title | *Hadrian The Seventh: A Romance*

Frederick Rolfe shortened his first name to "Fr" because he wished to be thought a priest; in this novel, he imagines himself appointed Pope. Hadrian is the first English Pope since Adrian IV, and he is also a version of Rolfe, an eccentric and penurious Catholic convert. As Pontiff, Hadrian sets Europe to rights, merging religious authority with political skill in a skewed but sometimes grimly prescient way. Pro-German in an anti-German period, the novel imagines a federal Europe under German hegemony. Hadrian is pursued by Jerry Sant, a member of a combined Liblab (Liberal and Labour) political group. Snubbed in his hope that the Pope will support Socialism, Sant shoots Hadrian: "The world sobbed, sighed, wiped its mouth; and experienced extreme relief. . . . He would have been an ideal ruler if He had not ruled."

These concluding ironies show that *Hadrian* is a peculiar but not a deluded fiction. A delightful, innocent, but unmistakably male sensuality, mitigates the novel's puritan impulse to clean up the Catholic Church. In an episode of unexpected charm, he teaches one of his lithe young guards the key to color photography (then unknown). This hints at the novel's interest in new technologies, such as the Marconigraph. Above all, Hadrian is obsessed by the new journalism; he regularly consults thirty-seven newspapers, and organizes his political moves to satisfy them. For all its archaism, *Hadrian* identified significant components of modernity. **AMu**

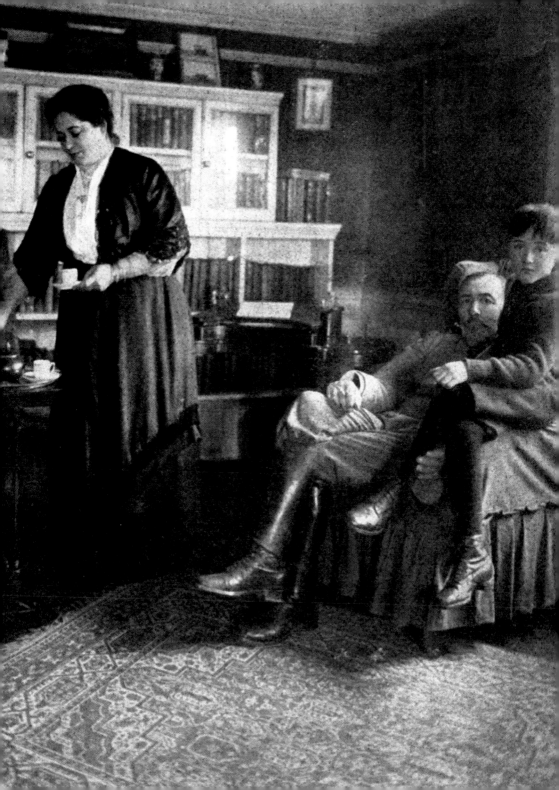

Nostromo

Joseph Conrad

Lifespan | *b.* 1857 (Ukraine), *d.* 1924 (England)
First Serialized | 1904, by *T. P.'s Weekly*
First Published | 1904, by Harper & Bros. (Lon. & N.Y.)
Full Title | *Nostromo: A Tale of the Seaboard*

Experimental in its shifting perspectives, *Nostromo* describes the turbulent history of a South American region as it develops through an unstable period of predatory dictatorships to a modern era of democracy and flourishing capitalism. The fictional state of Sulaco fights to secure its secession from Costaguana, becoming an apparently independent state. This brilliantly prophetic novel shows how economic imperialism, led by the United States, proves a mixed blessing in Sulaco.

Thanks partly to Joseph Conrad's friendship with R. B. Cunninghame Graham, well-traveled in those regions, and partly to his assiduous reading of memoirs and histories, he was able to confer vivid realism on his fictional Sulaco, despite having visited South America himself only briefly, and twenty years prior. Conrad interweaves large matters with small, political struggles with familial tensions, and the global with the intimate. As we follow the experiences of Nostromo, the foreman of the dockworkers, and of the diversity of people whose lives are connected with his deceptive character, we see the price exacted in human terms by historical evolution. Like Higuerota, the snow-capped mountain that dominates the region, this novel provides "the utmost delicacy of shaded expression and a stupendous magnificence of effect." **CW**

🔵 The Polish novelist and sailor Joseph Conrad, photographed at home with his wife, Jessie, and his son, Jack, in the early 1900s.

The House of Mirth

Edith Wharton

Lifespan | *b.* 1862 (U.S.), *d.* 1937 (France)
First Published | 1905
First Published by | Macmillan & Co. (London)
Original Language | English

Part love story, part social critique, *The House of Mirth* begins hopefully with a flirtation. Lily Bart, while settling her serious matrimonial sights on a more lucrative target, allows herself the pleasure of an infatuation with Lawrence Selden, a shabbily genteel intellectual. With a lightness of touch and arch wit reminiscent of Austen, Edith Wharton creates a heroine at the height of her sexual power: beautiful, fashionable, and well connected.

While retaining the external elements of a traditional romance, however, Wharton has an altogether less comforting vision to offer. The feminine power that Lily represents is cast as a barrier to intellectual freedom. Lily's perfection as an object of desire, beautifully imagined in an episode where she displays herself to an enraptured audience as the tableau vivant of a Reynolds painting, is presented as a futile waste of female creativity and becomes, rather than a triumph, an emblem of women's commodified status.

The novel's strength lies in Wharton's deft control of the versions of Lily as alternately architect of her own destiny and hapless pawn in a society governed by capital, power, and sexual inequality. Lily's love of surface and luxury is reflected in the fabric of a novel that delights in producing one of fiction's most enthralling heroines, whose potent mixture of power and powerlessness, poise and vulnerability, breathes life into the very myths it seeks to undermine. **HJ**

Professor Unrat

Heinrich Mann

Lifespan | *b.* 1871 (Germany), *d.* 1955 (Switzerland)
First Published | 1905, by A. Langen (Munich)
Original Title | *Professor Unrat, oder das Ende eines Tyrannen*

A socialist who believed in politically committed literature, Heinrich Mann was at one time Thomas's more famous brother.

Based on *Professor Unrat*, Von Sternberg's movie *The Blue Angel* made a star of Marlene Dietrich as the fatal seductress.

Elder brother of the great German writer Thomas Mann, Heinrich, an equally prolific novelist and essayist, differed from his brother in his commitment to political rather than aesthetic issues. Exiled by the Nazis for his attacks on their militarist-nationalist ideology, he was also a passionate critic of imperial bourgeois capitalism and a staunch supporter of democracy and various forms of socialism. *Professor Unrat* is his best-known novel, having been successfully adapted for screen, most famously as Josef von Sternberg's 1930 movie *The Blue Angel*, with Marlene Dietrich in the lead role, which launched her into international stardom.

The novel concerns an authoritarian, repressed, socially inept schoolteacher who falls in love with a young dancer named Rosa Frohlich. After an arbitrary meeting, Professor Unrat is soon enthralled by Rosa's compelling charm, and he determines that no one else shall have anything further to do with her. Unrat's close association with such a woman scandalizes the small-town community and he loses his job at the school. But he is unperturbed and with Rosa's help reinvents himself as a high-society player. They establish a successful salon and he delights in watching the downfall of former pupils and enemies, as they lose their fortunes at the gambling table or their reputations in inappropriate liaisons. But the greatest downfall will be Unrat's own as he gradually learns the full extent of Rosa's suspect behavior, losing control of his all-consuming rage.

Professor Unrat is a fascinating examination of the social values of imperial Germany and of the power of desire to transform and control even the most iron-willed of men. Unrat's slow demise under the influence of one of literature's great femme fatales is a captivating cautionary tale. **AL**

Solitude

Víctor Català

Lifespan | *b*. 1869 (Spain), *d*. 1966
First Published | 1905, by Publicació Joventut
Given Name | Caterina Albert i Paradís
Original Language | *Solitut*

In the case of Caterina Albert i Paradís, the adoption of "Víctor Català" as a pseudonym for her works of fiction was a daring concealment, and it also gave her an opportunity to masculinize her authorial voice. During her time, the fashionable literary treatment of the rural environment was to present it as bucolic and idyllic—that is, fundamentally false. Víctor Català was aiming for exactly the opposite with novels such as *Rural Dramas* of 1902 and her little masterpiece, *Solitude*, of 1905, which were far from the sugary taste of the middle classes. Nature lacks compassion and makes demands on people without forgiveness or mercy: it establishes human fates at the limits of desire, as if every person is subject to the rule of a superior, insensitive power.

Caterina Albert was herself a landowner, but a good education brought her close to the literary naturalism of Zola. She came to favor the direct reality of the narrator's voice, and was disinclined to sweeten the harshness of rural life by falsifying it. On the contrary, both the solitude of her characters and their feeling of powerlessness before fate emerge undisguised in dramatic personae who are almost always primitive, basic, and integrated like animals in the dominant space of nature. Víctor Català applied a crude perspective to the rural environment and its pain that she knew so well. Her work is the origin of the extraordinary wealth of the idiom used in reflecting the morality of remote regions implacably subject to the superior laws of nature. **JGG**

Young Törless

Robert Musil

Lifespan | *b*. 1880 (Austria), *d*. 1942 (Switzerland)
First Published | 1906, by Wiener Verlag (Vienna)
Original Title | *Die Verwirrungen des Zöglings Törless*
(*The Confusions of Young Törless*)

Caught in an ominous spiral of introspection and experimentation, Törless and three of his fellow cadet pupils at a military academy move from pondering and playing with abstractions to the creation of situations in which they push the abstractions into a feverish life. A sense of power is already alive, but mute, in the structures of the academy and in the pupils' unquestioning assumption of their social destiny as rulers. The thoughtful sadism practiced by the boys turns power inside out, makes it feral and pungent and intoxicating. Their exploration of power in the ritualized humiliation of one of their peers spreads also to encompass an unfolding of the ideas of pity, honor, superiority, justice, will, and desire as the boys use each other to test out and shape their undefined identities. The coldness and clarity of cruelty becomes the raw material and the medium of their self-fashioning.

The beauty of Robert Musil's writing is its capacity to infuse the novel with a duality that allows events their stark brutality while simultaneously existing as anxieties, possibilities, desires, precisely as perplexities (the "*Verwirrungen*" of Musil's original title) in Törless' mind. This is the power of *Young Törless*, and the mindset and world it so memorably describes. The reader comes away possessed not with the trite conclusion that we are all capable of terrible things, but with an enriched sense of how difficult it is to know what it is to be human. **PMcM**

The Forsyte Saga

John Galsworthy

Lifespan | *b.* 1867 (England), *d.* 1933
First Novel of Saga Published | 1906
(*The Man of Property*)
Compiled as Saga | 1929, (entitled *A Modern Comedy*)

First published in 1922, *The Forsyte Saga* comprises three novels: *The Man of Property* (1906), *In Chancery* (1920) and *To Let* (1921). Keenly ironic, deeply engaged in the "state of England" from the 1880s to the 1920s (though tellingly withdrawn during the First World War), *The Forsyte Saga* is also John Galsworthy's exploration of "the disturbance that Beauty effects in the lives of men." Beauty is a counter to, and incitement of, the urge to possession, to property, at the heart of the Forsyte family story. This tension is embodied by Soames Forsyte, in whom the quest for beauty dovetails violently with the passion to possess (passion that culminates in the rape of his wife).

Chronicling three generations of the Forsyte family, the *Saga* is a monument to the Edwardians, and was received as a quintessentially English book by enraptured readers. Its vision of the "tribal instinct," of the "swarmings of savage hordes" embedded in the everyday lives of a respectable middle-class family, sustains the tension and dramatic conflict of Galsworthy's narrative: the Forsyte family is a spectacle of "almost repugnant prosperity," a "reproduction of society in miniature." As such, the Forsytes are also Galsworthy's means to pursue, in extraordinary and patient prose, the creative violence of family life: the "deprivation and killing of reality" at the heart of family intimacy, its imposition of a shared history, and a spirit of ruthlessly collective enterprise. **VL**

"But no Forsyte had as yet died . . . death being contrary to their principles, they took precautions against it."

⬤ John Galsworthy, here photographed in 1912, depicted with critical irony the affluent class to which he himself belonged.

The Jungle

Upton Sinclair

Lifespan | *b.* 1878 (U.S.), *d.* 1968
First Published | 1906
First Published by | Doubleday, Page (New York)
Original Language | English

The Jungle was not the first muckraking novel, although it is easily one of the most influential books of the twentieth century—Roosevelt used it to push through the stalled Pure Food and Drug Act and Meat Inspection Act. It is a raw and sometimes nauseating chronicle based on the real incidents of the 1904 stockyard workers' strike in Chicago. A manifesto for social change, it savagely reveals the American dream gone sour. Sinclair strips away the myth of America as a boon to the tired, the poor, the huddled masses yearning to breathe free. Instead, the golden land of manifest destiny is shown to be a Dickensian nightmare, where wage slaves can barely survive, where powerless immigrants are chewed up by a capitalist machine oiled by corruption and bald greed.

But it is more than a polemic; it is a gripping and harrowing tale. Jurgis Rudkus, a recent immigrant from Lithuania, comes to a new and promising land in an attempt to build a family. His life is permeated by the stink of ordure and offal of a primitive meat industry and the struggle for daily bread. Systematically Jurgis's dreams, along with his family, are annihilated. Embittered by the brutal crimes wrought upon his family, Jurgis gradually descends into crime himself. But Jurgis does return from hell. The novel ends with a beacon of hope in the form of socialism; the last sentence, in upper case, is "CHICAGO WILL BE OURS!" A more socially important novel is hard to imagine. **GT**

The Secret Agent

Joseph Conrad

Lifespan | *b.* 1857 (Ukraine), *d.* 1924 (England)
First Published | 1907, by Methuen & Co. (London)
First Serialized | 1906, by *Ridgway's: A Militant Weekly for God and Country*

The Secret Agent tells of subversive politics, crime, and detection. The setting is late Victorian London, depicted predominantly as a dank and murky metropolis. In the parlor of Adolf Verloc's seedy shop in Soho, a grotesque band of revolutionaries meets to pursue futile political arguments. Michaelis is grossly corpulent; Karl Yundt is totteringly decrepit; and Ossipon has the cranial features (including frizzy hair and Mongoloid eyes) that, according to his mentor Cesare Lombroso, signify the criminal degenerate. All these enemies of society are lazy, notes the slothful Verloc; and all, including Verloc himself, are dependent on women for support.

At an embassy clearly intended to be Russian, Mr. Vladimir, an elegant diplomat, urges Verloc to bomb Greenwich Observatory. Vladimir thinks that such an outrage will be blamed on foreigners in England, so that the British Government will be less hospitable in future to refugees, particularly enemies of czarist Russia. Verloc obtains a bomb from the diminutive "Professor" (a nihilistic anarchist) and directs his mentally immature brother-in-law, Stevie, to plant it. However, this ill-measured move sparks a series of cumulatively tragic events, as the story advances toward its conclusion.

This masterpiece of ruthlessly ironic narration looks back to such atmospheric Dickensian works as *Bleak House*, and forward to Greene's sleazy *It's a Battlefield*. Particularly relevant to present times is its anticipation of the era of the suicide bomber. **CW**

Mother

Maxim Gorky

Lifespan | *b.* 1868 (Russia), *d.* 1936
First Published | 1907
Original Title | *Mat*
Original Language | Russian

Tracing the life of a working-class woman in late nineteenth-century provincial Russia, *Mother* powerfully evokes the cruelty, absurdity, and bitterness of life under an increasingly oppressive czarist regime. In an anonymous factory town, a middle-aged mother, Pelagea Nilovna, is left to face what she assumes will be a life of loveless drudgery after the death of her abusive husband. She is slowly awakened, however, to the presence of her maturing son, Pavel, who, in an apparently sober and modest life, spends his evenings reading philosophy and economics. As Pavel and his mother become closer, he begins to let her into his secret world—one in which these apparently harmless texts represent radical new ideas, the spread of which ensures that Pavel is in almost constant mortal danger. Pelagea is gradually drawn into a revolutionary socialist group; and while she is radicalized by Pavel and his friends' conversation, at the same time she provides them with a valuable human perspective that stresses the value of kindness, mercy, and love.

Often described as socialist realism, such a term does not cover the breadth of Gorky's skill in a novel that, despite its ideological bent, resists becoming propaganda. Political goals are interwoven with passages of lyrical beauty, occasional humor, and vivid and memorable characters. Moving and often painful to read, it remains an important perspective on the cultural and political extremes that existed in Russia at the time. **AB**

"The accumulated exhaustion of years had robbed them of their appetites, and to be able to eat they drank, long and deep, goading on their feeble stomachs with the biting, burning lash of vodka."

◉ Forced into exile because of his opposition to czarist rule, Gorky is welcomed by Russian revolutionaries in London in 1907.

The House on the Borderland

William Hope Hodgson

Lifespan | *b.* 1877 (England), *d.* 1918
First Published | 1908
First Published by | Chapman & Hall (London)
Original Language | English

In this elusive novel, a recovered manuscript tells the broken tale of the Recluse and his sister who live in isolation, apparently under constant threat from glowing swine creatures. The Recluse has visions of incomprehensible cosmic landscapes, peopled by immobile ancient gods, menacing and indistinct. He tries to protect his home and his sister, but she does not seem to see the creatures and fears him instead. He barricades the house against attacks. Here the manuscript stumbles. Left open to the elements, several pages are indecipherable. Finally, fragments concerning love and loss give way to a helpless trip into the future, a pre-psychedelic vision of souls in flight and the death of the universe. Then, under renewed attacks, the manuscript breaks off.

"The inner story must be uncovered, personally, by each reader," William Hope Hodgson suggests. This remains a work of vast imagination, unfettered by logic, plot, or traditional resolutions. In the position of the house, the character of the Recluse, even the recovery of the manuscript, there is an instinctive significance, but none of it is explained. The Recluse's visions of the future are imbued with a profound resonance that lurks just beneath the threshold of conscious comprehension. We feel he knows more than he will tell us or even admit to himself. Whatever is really going on, we can only try to imagine. There are many wonderful clues but no certainties. **JS**

The Old Wives' Tale

Arnold Bennett

Lifespan | *b.* 1867 (England), *d.* 1931
First Published | 1908
First Published by | Chapman & Hall (London)
Original Language | English

The Old Wives' Tale shares with many of Bennett's books its major setting in the Staffordshire potteries, the sleepy "Five Towns." At the same time it describes in vivid detail expatriate life in mid-nineteenth century Paris during a time of extraordinary political upheaval. This divided setting reflects the general scheme of the novel, which tells the story of the two "old wives," Constance and Sophia Baines, who grow up as the daughters of a modest tradesman. Their destinies, guided by their marriages, take them in vastly different directions. Demure Constance marries her father's assistant, outwardly leading the conventional life of a Victorian wife and mother. This is in sharp contrast to Sophia's disastrous elopement with a traveling salesman, who leaves her abandoned and penniless in Paris. Neither sister's life is wholly positive or negative; the excitement of Paris under siege is balanced by Sophia's constant struggle for survival in a hostile foreign culture, while the domestic harmony of Constance's family life also suffers from smothering boredom.

Overall, *The Old Wives' Tale* is a compassionate novel, and the two sisters' touching reunion shows the importance of family love and loyalty in what might otherwise be seen as blighted lives. **AB**

❯ E. O. Hoppe depicts English author Arnold Bennett in a woodcutting carved in 1900.

The Inferno

Henri Barbusse

Lifespan | *b.* 1873 (France), *d.* 1935 (Russia)
First Published | 1908, by Mondiale (Paris)
Alternate Title | *Hell*
Original Title | *L'Enfer*

Henri Barbusse began his writing career with *The Inferno*. This absorbing yet disquieting novel is an early modern example of the literature of alienated, disaffected manhood. Colin Wilson later used it in his introduction to *The Outsider* (1956), showing *The Inferno's* direct influence on existentialist writers.

A nameless man checks into a hotel in Paris. He is thirty years old and is without any ties. Other than this, we only know that he is jaded, disillusioned, indifferent to and weary of life. He writes, "I don't know who I am, where I am going, what I am doing . . . I have nothing and deserve nothing," and yet he suffers from an obsessive, almost religious yearning for the unattainable. On his first night in the hotel his attention is drawn to noises emanating from next door. Finding a hole that grants him a view of the adjoining room, he remains transfixed for days, observing the changing occupants. His voyeurism becomes compulsive as he derives a strange feeling of omnipotence and psychosexual fervor from watching the many different aspects of private life that are on display: adulterous couples, single women undressing, homosexuality, childbirth, and death. However, he achieves little real satisfaction from this activity and it is this voyeuristic compulsion that ultimately destroys him.

Scandalous at the time of publication, it still has the power to shock today; candid, explicit, and full of philosophical musings, *The Inferno* is a fascinating insight into one man's inner struggle. **AL**

> *"I was thirty years old. I had lost my father and mother eighteen or twenty years before, so long ago that the event was now insignificant."*

Barbusse failed to make an impression with *The Inferno*, but later won fame through his powerful anti-war novel *Under Fire*.

A Room with a View

E. M. Forster

Lifespan | *b.* 1879 (England), *d.* 1970
First Published | 1908
First Published by | E. Arnold (London)
Original Language | English

A Room with a View is a classic coming-of-age novel. Forster introduces us to Lucy Honeychurch, who, accompanied by her anxious and over-protective guardian, Charlotte Bartlett, is touring Italy in her first introduction to a wider world far removed from the English countryside of her childhood. Lucy is a spirited piano player and her playing of Beethoven gives the reader the first hint of her real emotional depth. The great question of this novel is what will Lucy choose: a room with a view, or the closed walls of conventional society? This question is embodied by the two rivals for her affection. There is the thoughtful and passionate George Emerson, who understands and fully appreciates what he is seeing, whether it is the Italian people or Lucy herself. The sophisticated and arrogant Cecil Vyse, on the other hand, treats Lucy more as a work of art or a project than as a living, thinking individual. This novel is about the pains and crossroads of growing up—the temptation of self-deception, the pull between family and one's own desires.

Forster's novel offers a brilliant satire of early twentieth-century middle England and its rigorously upheld social conventions. The novel is also remarkably sensual—the scenery, both in the Italian and the English settings, is perfectly drawn with exquisite visual detail, and when Lucy plays the piano or the weather turns violent, the reader can almost hear the crescendo of the notes or the thunder. A simply delightful read. **EG-G**

Strait is the Gate

André Gide

Lifespan | *b.* 1869 (France), *d.* 1951
First Published | 1909, by Mercure de France (Paris)
Original Title | *La Porte Étroite*
Nobel Prize for Literature | 1947

There is something irresistible, even seductively perfect about André Gide's *Strait is the Gate*. Technically the story is about love; as family comfort is withdrawn from them, two cousins find in each other resources of virtue and of beauty. Jerome loses his father before he is twelve years old. An only child, he watches his mother cherish her grief as he experiences his own in the too-early maturing of an already aged sensibility. His cousin, Alyssa, is despised by her adulterous mother because of her loyalty to her father, whose confidante she becomes. But to summarize thus puts undue emphasis on what is only a beginning; the facts of Jerome and Alyssa's existence—their high-bourgeois lives in a France that seems an endless round of luxuriantly flowered summers, but also scornful of the crudity of material change—have but a skeletal presence.

It is their doomed, delicate, intense and difficult love that fills the text, and which, establishing itself as the only reality, explains Jerome and Alyssa. As a love that remains unconsummated, indeed that remains devoid of any physical engagement, it therefore remains a yearning, a mutual and declared yet lonely striving for one another. It is the prolonged and seemingly pointless trajectory from youthful uncertainty and caution to considered postponement then denial, that fascinates. With exquisite control, Gide has created an exploration of love that manages to capture the absolute yet open-ended nature of yearning itself. **PMcM**

The Notebooks of Malte Laurids Brigge

Rainer Maria Rilke

Lifespan | *b.* 1875 (Czech Republic), *d.* 1926 (Swit.)
First Published | 1910, by Insel Verlag (Leipzig)
Original Title | *Die Aufzeichnungen des Malte Laurids Brigge*

> *"All the soarings of my mind begin in my blood."*
>
> *Rainer Maria Rilke*

🔵 Rilke was painted by Helmut Westhoff in 1901 as a young poet inspired by misty intuitions about love, sex, pain, and death.

🔵 By the time he wrote *The Notebooks*, Rilke had learned to look at the modern world, even if with a terrified sense of alienation.

Few of the many champions of Rainer Maria Rilke's sole novel admit that it is only great in parts; its purely intermittent ability to astonish is forceful enough to help us forget that the work as a whole is an awkward composite of narrative fiction, diary, and commonplace book. Odd passages of aimless depiction or idling histrionics should perhaps be expected, however, in what is, nominally, the journal of a young Danish aesthete of aristocratic stock, now penniless, fragile, and unmoored in Paris. Reports of disturbing encounters in the street (with, for example, an intrusive old woman whose "bleary eyes ... looked as though some diseased person had spat a greenish phlegm under the bloody lids") vie with intensely re-experienced memories of Malte's strange infancy and adolescence. The novel extends itself with Rilkean meditations on themes like faith, illness, and art, and speculations concerning the inner lives of the obscure historical personae with whom Malte is obsessed.

The novel's prose seldom approaches the sublimity of Rilke's greatest lyrics, but it sometimes appears to emerge from a similar place. Just as Rilke's poetry is strewn with questions, rhetorical ones directed toward himself and unanswerable questions aimed at anyone else, Malte's artistry takes a thin kind of sustenance from his cultivated ignorance about the world and everyone in it. Deliberate nurturing of an insatiable curiosity, and the determined curtailment of the urge to satisfy it, fuels Rilke's art and his hero's thought. Despite and because of this lack of knowledge, the novel is extremely beautiful and not much like anything else: the sentences or paragraphs with which Rilke ends each of its sections are often the most remarkable of all. You must change your life. **RP**

Howards End

E. M. Forster

Lifespan | *b*. 1879 (England), *d*. 1970
First Published | 1910
First Published by | E. Arnold (London)
Original Language | English

Reflecting on the social upheaval that characterized the Edwardian period, *Howards End* introduces the reader to two very different families, the Schlegels and the Wilcoxes. While the Schlegels are idealistic and intellectual, the Wilcoxes are materialistic and practical. The novel documents the connection that develops between these two families and the clashing of their very different worldviews.

The two Schlegel sisters, Margaret and Helen, respond to the Wilcoxes in contrasting ways. While Helen remains idealistic and passionately opposed to the materialism and pragmatism of the Wilcoxes, Margaret hopes to reconcile the two approaches to life and nurture an appreciation for both. In her writing she hopes to "only connect," in order to exalt both her prose and her passion. *Howards End* documents Margaret's attempt to connect, detailing its successes and its failures.

Truly a masterpiece, the novel has moments of real beauty and optimism. As with all of Forster's novels, the characters are brilliantly drawn, and the dialogue is realistic and moving. Although this novel deals with extreme emotions and actions, it never becomes melodramatic or absurd. Instead, it remains all too real a picture of human emotion, and the disasters that can result from pride, anger, miscommunication, and hypocrisy. **EG-G**

🔘 Forster is portrayed in 1940 by Vanessa Bell, sister of Virginia Woolf and a member, like Forster, of the Bloomsbury Group.

Impressions of Africa

Raymond Roussel

Lifespan | *b*. 1877 (France), *d*. 1933 (Sicily)
First Published | 1910
First Published by | Librairie Alphonse Lemerre
Original Title | *Impressions d'Afrique*

The first nine chapters of *Impressions of Africa* describe a series of seemingly impossible feats against the backdrop of an imaginary African city. A marksman separates the yolk from the white of a soft-boiled egg with a single bullet; a statue made from corset stays tilts back and forth, its mechanism operated by a tame magpie. In the second half of the novel, we learn that a group of shipwrecked passengers has been captured by an African king, and that to entertain him and ensure their freedom, the prisoners must perform elaborate theatrical tasks or build the fantastical machines that we have already seen in the first half.

In an essay published after his suicide in 1935, Raymond Roussel reveals that the starting point for his novel was not an impression of Africa at all, but a particular linguistic resource: the way in which a single word can have two or more different meanings. In one variation on his key writing technique, Roussel would start out with a homonym and then assign himself the task of writing a story, or inventing a scenario, which would get us from *baleines* (corset stays) to *baleines* (whales). This is a travelogue that takes us nowhere because, however far away from the initial term we go, the narrative only ever contrives to get us back to where started—from *baleines* to *baleines*. Language is no longer at the service of fiction. Rather, fiction is at the mercy of language; novels are generated in the dark space between a word and its repetition. **KB**

Fantômas

Marcel Allain and Pierre Souvestre

Lifespan (Allain) | b. 1885 (France), d. 1970
Lifespan (Souvestre) | b. 1874 (France), d. 1914
First Published | 1911, by A. Fayard (Paris)
Original Language | French

First published in 1911, *Fantômas* was a sensation in the authors' native France and, although still relatively unknown to the English-speaking world, it continues to occupy a prominent place in the popular imagination across Europe and the globe. With the original *Fantômas* serving as inspiration for an extraordinary thirty-one sequels, various movie versions, and a successful comic book in Mexico, this mysterious creation lives on.

The eponymous "hero" of the novel is a masked arch-criminal, an amoral genius at war with bourgeois society. Fantômas is without history and without motive, a nightmare made flesh, an enigma whose physical existence is only confirmed by the trail of corpses he leaves in his wake, or the tantalizing swish of a cape at an open window. He is pursued by the brilliant but perpetually frustrated Inspector Juve. As Fantômas rapes, murders, and swindles his way through the Paris night, the very mention of his name comes to inspire fear in the hearts of all God-fearing citizens.

It is strange that this violent, crudely written tale should enjoy such staying power, as well as being a notable inspiration to both the Dada movement and the Surrealists. An uncanny work that reflects the paranoia, confusion, and thrill of the modern city, it communicates a feeling of Old World morals under threat, and exploits ongoing concerns. *Fantômas* casts a long shadow; it appeals to both the primal and the intellectual imagination. **SamT**

Ethan Frome

Edith Wharton

Lifespan | b. 1862 (U.S.), d. 1937 (France)
First Published | 1911
First Published by | Macmillan & Co. (London)
Original Language | English

Ethan Frome is a limpid account of mental isolation, sexual frustration, and moral despair in a turn-of-the-century New England farming community. The novel recounts the story of Frome's burgeoning desire for the mercurial Mattie Silver, a destitute relative of his wife, Zeena, and traces the logic whereby the two lovers attempt to destroy themselves, with unexpected and harrowing consequences.

Frome stands at the heart of the story; his withered personality is the bitter fruit of a harsh environment and an inward-looking community. He is a man of hidden depths who intuits an abundant reality beneath the surface of prosaic life, and whose sociability is granted no outlet in an isolated community. An interplay between external environment and inner psyche is dramatized here; the inarticulacy of the characters is central to the novel, which is framed by the words of a narrator whose knowledge of the history he recounts is unreliable. We are left with disconcerting questions about moral choice and agency, the role of environment in determining behavior, and the conflict between social mores and individual passions. *Ethan Frome* focuses primarily on the suffering of its eponymous protagonist, but it also depicts the social conditions that enable the formation of so manipulative a figure as Zeena. **AG**

⬤ This photograph of Edith Wharton was taken before she became a novelist, but already suggests a determined personality.

The Charwoman's Daughter

James Stephens

Lifespan | *b.* 1882 (Ireland), *d.* 1950 (England)
First Published | 1912
First Published by | Macmillan (London)
Original Language | English

The poet and novelist James Stephens was born and reared in a Dublin slum, and started his adult life as a clerk in a solicitor's office. All of his work carries with it an edge of claustrophobia, a haunting sense of loneliness amid overcrowding. But Stephens was in love with the idea of the imagination, and the Dublin of his work is at once a place of confines and of liberation, of small rooms and open streets, of the press of necessity and the beauty of a silk dress glimpsed in a shop window.

The Charwoman's Daughter is the strange, wistful story of sixteen-year-old Mary, the only child of her fiercely protective widowed mother. It is also a story about Dublin and about how we see that city. Usually depicted in Irish fiction as a man's town, a place trapped in its history, and home to big, busy conversations and random, unregulated encounters, this Dublin is both domestic and urban.

Mary and her mother live in a one-room tenement flat that is home to the rituals of their bitter love. By day her mother cleans the houses of the Dublin rich, while Mary makes observations as she walks through the city. The imaginative richness of her insights makes the city come alive as a place that is both strange and wonderful, remote yet friendly. It is this sense of discovery and the bittersweet richness it brings with it that makes this such an unusual but compelling Dublin novel. **PMcM**

Death in Venice

Thomas Mann

Lifespan | *b.* 1875 (Germany), *d.* 1955 (Switzerland)
First Published | 1912, by Hyperionverlag (Munich)
Original Title | *Der Tod in Venedig*
Nobel Prize for Literature | 1929

When renowned author Gustave von Aschenbach, with uncharacteristic spontaneity, travels to Venice, his attention is captivated by a young boy whose blond curls and exquisite proportions seem to embody the Greek ideal of beauty. Watching Tadzio soon becomes the focus of Aschenbach's days; and then, of his existence. On board the ship to Venice, Aschenbach looks on with horror as a simpering old man with a painted face mingles with a group of young men. But by the close of the story, Aschenbach has become that man, as, intoxicated, he pursues Tadzio through the passages and canals of an infected city.

Death in Venice, as Mann maintained, is about the artist's loss of dignity, but Mann also examines the relationship between art and life. Aschenbach believes that with labor and discipline he can master life and even mold it into art. But Tadzio's Dionysus, inspiring unstructured emotion and unruly passion, forces him to recognize the fallacy of that belief. The mythical elements of the novel offer a context for the portrayal of homosexuality. Written with subtlety and profound psychological insight, *Death in Venice* is a vivid account of what it is like to fall in love.

The novella was perhaps Mann's ideal artistic form (*Death in Venice* runs to a mere seventy pages): from the first hints of foreboding to the final pathetic climax, this is a masterwork of its genre. **KB**

Sons and Lovers

D. H. Lawrence

Lifespan | *b*. 1885 (England), *d*. 1930
First Published | 1913
First Published by | Duckworth & Co. (London)
Original Language | English

In *Sons and Lovers*, D. H. Lawrence compellingly describes the Nottinghamshire countryside and the mining community with which he felt such a deep connection. Bold in the honesty with which it tackles the subjects of family, domestic strife, class struggle, gender conflict, sexuality, industrialism, and poverty, *Sons and Lovers* is also alive to the natural world that it evokes with an intensity verging on mysticism.

The novel's key theme is the relationship between the boy Paul Morel and his mother, a ubiquitous maternal presence with great ambitions for her gifted son. Their powerful bond excludes the father, a poorly educated miner, who is treated with disdain by the mother, an attitude the boy internalizes as his own as he becomes a man. Urgent class issues thus overlap with volatile psychosexual questions. Paul lives out his mother's frustrated aspirations through education and art; but the almost incestuous relationship between mother and son threatens to prevent him from developing a separate adult identity and from forging mature sexual relationships with other women.

Sensitive to the social position of an intelligent woman such as Gertrude Morel, who is as trapped by the mining community as her embittered husband, it also captures the frustrations of adolescent love, the confusing allure of different kinds of sexual relationships, and the violence of male rivalries. **AG**

The Ragged Trousered Philanthropists

Robert Tressell

Lifespan | *b*. 1870 (Ireland), *d*. 1911
First Published | 1914
First Published by | G. Richards (London)
Original Language | English

This book remains perhaps the pre-eminent classic of English working-class literature, yet the first-time reader may well be surprised at its tone. Although at the heart of the novel there is an intelligent, passionate, and sustained attack on capitalism, there is also a violent bitterness directed at those workers who fail to see the necessity of socialism, and in this way, deliver their children into exploitation.

This is a strange kind of novel, where the reader's attention is held not by any trick of suspense or narrative flow but rather by the minute exploration of lives led under the heel of profit. The whole story is vividly fuelled by anger, directed mainly at those who are duped by their bosses; it is implied that the employers themselves can hardly behave in any other way. But the book is not only about the working class in a conventional sense, it is also about the nature of work itself, and how the possibility of pride in one's work is destroyed and ridiculed by the demands of greater "efficiency." Inevitably, the worker is forced to perform rapid, slapdash work, which removes all genuine satisfaction through labor, as with the protagonist who has much to give to his chosen "craft," but who is constantly denied by "the system." *The Ragged Trousered Philanthropists* is thus in tune with the broader socialist movements of Edwardian England that we now tend to associate with such figures as Ruskin and Morris. **DP**

Platero and I

Juan Ramón Jiménez

Lifespan | *b*. 1881 (Spain), *d*. 1958 (Puerto Rico)
First Published | 1914, by La Lectura (Madrid)
Complete Edition | 1917, by Editorial Calleja
Original Title | *Platero y yo*

The subtitle of this book, *An Andalusian Elegy*, and the fact that its author chose to dedicate it to the great teacher Francisco Giner de los Ríos (who read it with admiration), together provide two important keys to its interpretation. First, *Platero and I* is a personal recollection of a part of Andalusia (the surroundings of Moguer, near Huelva), amounting to a full display of aesthetic Spanish regionalism; and second, it is a demonstration of the intention to teach sensibility to both children and adults.

This story succeeds in both of its aims. It is the simple (but only apparently so) tale of a poet on holiday ("dressed in mourning, with my Nazarene beard") and Platero, his "little, furry, soft" donkey. The text is written in the form of short pieces (some would see them as prose poems), while the story summons up a joyful world of children, the boisterous life of animals in the fields, a frieze of peasants ranging from the entertaining to the mischievous, and some unforgettable landscapes described with adjectives of almost Fauvist colors. But not everything is so happy: "Platero" and his owner are also witnesses of gratuitous cruelty, incomprehension, and sorrow. And in the end the little donkey dies. Few works of Spanish letters are so clearly associated with the aesthetic enjoyment and the ethical imperatives: morality and beauty. **JCM**

◉ Joaquin Vaquero Turcios's painting shows an aging Jiménez, sadly distant from the fresh boyhood he shared with Platero.

Tarzan of the Apes

Edgar Rice Burroughs

Lifespan | *b*. 1875 (U.S.), *d*. 1950
First Published | 1914
First Published by | L. Burt Co. (New York)
Original Language | English

Ideologically, the *Tarzan* series has so little to commend it that it is surprising the books have not been subject to a more severe pounding. It is also perhaps ironic that, while factions are liable to ban or even burn more recent fictions, *Tarzan* still happily occupies a position in the popular canon, even becoming the subject of a Disney movie and subsequent ongoing cartoon series. Narratively, it is exciting, dynamic, often surprisingly well written, and full of all the classic tropes one expects from good pulp fiction—survival against the odds, an unknown land, fierce adversaries, dramatic fights, and beautiful women. That said, the underlying subtexts of the book are racist, sexist, utterly formulaic, and overridingly imperialist, ultimately championing the figure of the white supremacist male. In *Tarzan of the Apes*, the eponymous hero conquers (in order) the apes, lions, and elephants, black tribesmen, degenerate sailors, professors of theology, women, and the British, before returning his ire to the tribesmen again.

Today *Tarzan*, like W. E. John's *Biggles* series, goes largely unread, with its considerable strengths largely forgotten—early discussions of ecology, the importance of Burroughs's writing on heroic texts, and the often piercing social commentary. Overall, the mythology of Tarzan, who first communicates with Jane Porter via written notes, and then in French, eschewing the sexually primal "Me Tarzan, you Jane," has superseded the real text. **EMcCS**

Locus Solus

Raymond Roussel

Lifespan | *b.* 1877 (France), *d.* 1933 (Sicily)
First Published | 1914
First Published by | Librairie Alphonse Lemerre
Original Language | French

Strange and extremely difficult, Ramond Roussel's self-published novels and poems were ridiculed in his lifetime. Now, though, Roussel is enjoying fame for his solitary adventures into language, which have had a decisive impact on a number of key thinkers and writers of the twentieth century, from Michel Foucault to New York poet John Ashbery.

Locus Solus is marked by a macabre theatricality, and proceeds by unveiling a series of fantastical scenes: cats, teeth, diamonds, and dancing girls are showcased among a host of complex mechanisms. Our guide is the brilliant scientist and inventor Martial Canterel, who is taking a group of colleagues on a tour of his lonely estate—the solitary place of the title. The impressive central exhibit is a huge glass cage, in which eight elaborate tableaux vivants are on display. Only, the actors that we suppose are playing dead are, in fact, dead. Canterel has transformed corpses into automata by injecting them with a fluid of his own invention: revived by "resurrectine," the dead players are doomed to re-enact the key moments of their lives. Moments, of course, that were meaningful precisely because they were thought to be unique and unrepeatable. The kind of language machine that Roussel invented to write this and other novels operates at the switch-point where a word divides to mean two different things. His fiction is always dangerously close to mimicking the show of meaninglessness that is the central spectacle of his strikingly peculiar novel. **KB**

Kokoro

Natsume Soseki

Lifespan | *b.* 1867 (Japan), *d.* 1916
First Published | 1914
First Published by | Iwanami Shoten (Tokyo)
Original Language | Japanese

Kokoro is a novel that captures the changes in mentality that Japan experienced during a period of rapid modernization at the end of the nineteenth century. Set in Tokyo, in around 1910, this three-part novel traces the relationship between a young man, the narrator, and an old man, whom he calls *Sensei* (meaning "teacher," but suggesting the relationship of master and disciple). Sensei is haunted by a stigma in his past, which hangs over the entire novel.

Parts one and two of the novel revolve around the deaths of the narrator's father and of Sensei's friend, and his frequent visits to the graveyard where they lie buried. The narrator becomes preoccupied by Sensei's secret, and his anxiety grows. One day a letter arrives, delivering Sensei's confession of his guilt in a tragic love triangle, and his sense of multiple self-contradictions. He is torn between morality and possessiveness, intellect and emotion, death and life. He suffers from the impossibility of understanding his and others' *kokoro* (the soul or the inner workings of the mind).

In its depiction of Sensei's malaise the novel is not only a testament to the rapid modernization of Japan, but also an examination of a tortured sense of failure and responsibility. Natsume, who established the form of the first-person novel, is one of the greatest writers in modern Japanese literature. **KK**

❱ The building of a railway from Tokyo to Yokahama was typical of the modernization of Japan in the Meiji era observed by Natsume.

Handcuffed TO THE GIRL WHO DOUBLE-CROSSED HIM

The "Monte Cristo" hero..
The MAN who put
the MAN in roMANce...

ROBERT **DONAT** MADELEINE **CARROLL**
in

THE **39** STEPS

Directed by ALFRED HITCHCOCK

Director of The Man Who Knew Too Much

A *GB* PRODUCTION

A HUNDRED STEPS AHEAD OF ANY PICTURE THIS YEAR

The Thirty-Nine Steps

John Buchan

Lifespan | *b.* 1875 (Scotland), *d.* 1940 (Canada)
First Published | 1915
First Published by | W. Blackwood & Sons (London)
Original Language | English

A forerunner of the modern spy thriller, *The Thirty-Nine Steps* revolves around a German plot to declare war on an unprepared Britain through a secret invasion. Although this storyline was clearly topical and drew on the brutal conflict of the First World War, it also reflected Buchan's deep distaste for German culture. The narrative centers on Richard Hannay, an almost superhuman and ridiculously lucky South African engineer who rescues a hunted British spy, only to find himself the focus of a manhunt orchestrated by agents of the German state. Believing himself to be too visible in London, Hannay escapes to the Scottish Highlands in the hope of hiding out in what he takes to be an unpopulated wilderness. But Hannay is quickly disabused, when he finds that the "isolated" Highland landscape is overpopulated by motorcars and German agents posing as pillars of British society.

The novel is important in establishing a formula for the spy thriller: car chases, elaborate disguises, and an urgent quest to avert disaster. The dramatic turns of the plot rely upon a sense of paranoia, where every potential ally is also a potential enemy. Buchan's own war work involved running the newly formed Department of Information, responsible for producing propaganda to support the war effort, and his novels clearly complement this work. **LC**

🔄 Alfred Hitchcock's movie version of Buchan's spy thriller, released in 1935, is now far more widely known than the original novel.

The Rainbow

D. H. Lawrence

Lifespan | *b.* 1885 (England), *d.* 1930
First Published | 1915
First Published by | Methuen & Co. (London)
Original Language | English

Central to D. H. Lawrence's break from well-established fictional conventions is his conviction that human subjectivity could no longer be described in terms of what he called "the old stable ego," and that a different way of presenting character was required in art. He considers the "realism" with which fictional characters had hitherto typically been presented as, paradoxically, essentially unrealistic, and in *The Rainbow* he moves to a presentation of human individuals and their vexed relationships that draws on unconscious impulses.

Written in the shadow of the First World War, the novel contrasts the stretches of time in which the Brangwen family was rooted to the soil, against the far-reaching changes to human life (especially the inexorable destruction of communities) now occurring. Issues such as adolescent sexuality, marital relations, intergenerational conflict, exile, colonialism, national identity, education, upward social mobility, the New Woman, lesbianism, and psychological breakdown (the precursor of a necessary rebirth and regeneration) are woven together. Sexually explicit and brutally honest about relationships, *The Rainbow* delineates the breakdown of an established social order; focusing on the shifting balance of power in parent–child and male–female relations; at the same time it situates epochal transformations within a mythic frame of reference, which is indebted to Lawrence's rendering of biblical cadences and pantheistic traditions. **AG**

Of Human Bondage

William Somerset Maugham

Lifespan | *b.* 1874 (France), *d.* 1965
First Published | 1915
First Published by | W. Heinemann (London)
Original Language | English

"It is cruel to discover one's mediocrity only when it is too late."

◉ Here photographed by Claude Harris in 1927, Maugham was bullied as a child for his stutter, a bitter torment he never forgot.

One of the most well known and influential writers of his time, William Somerset Maugham's experiences as a miserable, stuttering medical student ultimately shaped his fiction. His best-known novel, *Of Human Bondage*, is squarely based on his own life. An Edwardian Bildungsroman, the novel utilizes the technique of third-person narration, but filters everything through the presiding consciousness of its central character, Philip Carey. Characterized by a leisurely pace and an episodic structure, the novel traces Carey's history from childhood to young adulthood. It describes his difficult early years, the harsh conditions of his life at school (where he is relentlessly tormented because of his clubfoot), the gradual loss of his religious faith, and his experiences as a young man hungry to encounter the world on his own terms.

The novel is preoccupied, above all, with the search for meaning in a human existence that appears to have none. Carey is convinced, through his glimpses into the lives of other people around him, that their existences are mostly full of suffering, frequently sordid, and generally futile. His own experiences, in turn, seem only to confirm his cynical diagnosis. Yet he does not lose his desire to confront life's vicissitudes nor to search for a personal philosophy. The viewpoint he develops refuses the limiting categories of virtue and vice in favor of a Darwinian view of life. The terms "good" and "evil" are seen as labels deployed by society to make the individual conform—existence is in itself insignificant and futile. Carey's stoical conclusion, explored through loosely linked episodes in the novel, is that the thinking individual can only really find a measure of freedom by rejoicing in the aesthetic pattern of life's random events. **AG**

The Good Soldier
Ford Madox Ford

Critical opinion on *The Good Soldier* is divided. Some regard it as a wholly improbable novel, in which substance is sacrificed to style, and others see it as one of the most finely crafted novels of the twentieth century, in which Ford Madox Ford examines whether it is possible to create a narrative of the modern world through aesthetic experimentalism. Ford was a chief exponent of the literary style known as impressionism, in which an emphasis is placed on the way a narrator experiences events, and on how this impression shapes our understanding of reality. This book is the best example of this style.

In *The Good Soldier*, Ford aims to demonstrate how thoroughly our experience of reality is shaped by the limits of our knowledge. Narrated solely from the point of view of an idle, rich American, John Dowell, *The Good Soldier* illustrates the extent to which Dowell's consciousness of reality alters as he acquires new knowledge and understanding of past events. Through the course of the novel, we realize that Florence, Dowell's wife, has been conducting a long affair with the "good soldier" of the title, Edward Ashburnham. Dowell is the ultimate unreliable narrator, unaware of his wife's true nature and the passionate coupling that has been taking place. He describes his idyllic friendship with the Ashburnhams, but following his realization of the affair, he must begin again, and attempt to retell the story of this friendship. The first section of the novel is in a sense rewritten, since everything that Dowell believed to be true is the product of his lack of understanding. Throughout the novel, Dowell tries and fails to conceive of a narrative method that can faithfully recount these contradictory perspectives: one of self-deluding innocence and one of tortured enlightenment. **LC**

Lifespan | *b.* 1873 (England), *d.* 1939 (France)
First Published | 1915
First Published by | The Bodley Head (London)
Given Name | Ford Hermann Hueffer

"I had never sounded the depths of an English heart. I had known the shallows."

◉ Madox Ford served in the First World War and is photographed in uniform at about the time that *The Good Soldier* was published.

老婆鬼腕を
持去る図

Rashomon

Akutagawa Ryunosuke

Lifespan | *b.* 1892 (Japan), *d.* 1927
First Published | 1915 in *Teikoku Bungaku* magazine
Alternate Title | *The Rasho Gate*
Real Name | Chokodo Shujin

Rashomon and Other Stories comprises six short stories, written by Akutagawa in the early and middle period of his career between 1915 and 1921. "Remaking" or imitation is an important element in his work; in this collection he retells a number of historical fables. Akutagawa defends imitation against the ideology of the original, considering it not as a mere reproduction but as a subtle process of digestion and transformation.

Akutagawa applies a parabolic style and tone to these stories, which contrasts with their unexpected endings and creates curious emotional effects. Some of the stories are simply delightful, while others suspend our simplistic moral judgment and invite us to reflect further on the impulsive nature of human beings. Akutagawa is also a master of structure. "Dragon" and "Yam Gruel" effectively use the report form and create an amusing atmosphere by contrasting the narrow perspective of the characters with a broader perspective of the world as a whole. "Kesa and Morito" and "In a Grove" cleverly juxtapose multiple quasi-Dostoevskian monologues without background explanation, creating a faltering sense of reality. Akutagawa is one of the most widely read modernist writers in Japan. His timeless stories are perceptive and witty investigations into the very nature of literature itself. **KK**

◀ The demon of *Rashomon*, disguised as an old woman, carries off his arm that had been severed by the hero Watanabe no Tsuna.

Under Fire

Henri Barbusse

Lifespan | *b.* 1873 (France), *d.* 1935 (Russia)
First Published | 1916
First Published by | Flammarion (Paris)
Original Title | *Le Feu*

The members of the squad celebrated in Henri Barbusse's story of front-line fighting in the early years of the First World War, are the French army's *poilus* or "hairy ones," and there is not a liberal or an intellectual present among them. Yet Barbusse was a journalist with a purpose. His voluntary two years in the trenches led him to pacifism and Communism, and *Under Fire* is an early step on that road.

As the experience of war is primarily one of disintegration, it is difficult to construct the purposive narrative required for a pacifist polemic, and Barbusse does not try. Chapters describe life behind the lines or on leave, or express *poilu* anger at the "Rear," where soldier-administrators are able to avoid the bloodbath at the front. There are anecdotes within anecdotes, stories of crossing accidentally into enemy lines to return with a box of matches taken from a slaughtered German. Above all, there is the fighting, in which men die in so many appalling ways: crushed, shot, split open, rotting, buried, unburied. The stories are orchestrated by a participant narrator who directs the reader from above the struggle. In the final chapter, the squad—now much diminished—begins a discussion that disparages nationalism, exalts the soldiers' latent political power, and recognizes the need for equality and justice. This "dream of fumbling thought" is the beginning of a learning process for these ordinary working men, which is validated by the novel's unforgettable accounts of the front line. **AMu**

A Portrait of the Artist as a Young Man

James Joyce

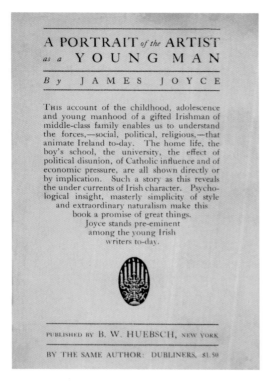

A PORTRAIT *of the* ARTIST
as a YOUNG MAN

By JAMES JOYCE

THIS account of the childhood, adolescence and young manhood of a gifted Irishman of middle-class family enables us to understand the forces,—social, political, religious,—that animate Ireland to-day. The home life, the boy's school, the university, the effect of political disunion, of Catholic influence and of economic pressure, are all shown directly or by implication. Such a story as this reveals the under currents of Irish character. Psychological insight, masterly simplicity of style and extraordinary naturalism make this book a promise of great things. Joyce stands pre-eminent among the young Irish writers to-day.

PUBLISHED BY B. W. HUEBSCH, NEW YORK

BY THE SAME AUTHOR: DUBLINERS, $1.50

"The artist, like the God of the creation, remains within or behind or beyond or above his handiwork, invisible, refined out of existence, indifferent, paring his fingernails."

The front cover of the first edition of *A Portrait of the Artist as a Young Man* neatly summarises the main themes of the novel.

Lifespan | *b.* 1882 (Ireland), *d.* 1941
First Published | 1916
First Published by | B. W. Huebsch (New York)
First Serialized | 1914–1915, in *The Egoist* (London)

First published in serial form between 1914 and 1915, *A Portrait of the Artist as a Young Man* is the novel that established James Joyce as one of the most innovative literary talents of the twentieth century.

Portrait traces the development of Stephen Dedalus from childhood, through adolescence, to the first flushes of manhood. Over time, he gradually begins to rebel against his devout Catholic upbringing—questioning the values of his family, church, history, and homeland. At the same time, Stephen's interest in art and literature intensifies as he struggles to come to terms with his adult self. This, however, is no ordinary coming-of-age story. The language used at each stage of the narrative is skillfully manipulated in order to reflect Stephen's age and intellectual maturity. *Portrait* begins with "moocows" and ends with Stephen expressing his desire to "forge in the smithy of my soul the uncreated conscience of my race."

Portrait remains a work of startling invention and imaginative richness, in which Joyce began to hone his revolutionary "stream of consciousness" technique. It is the work in which the hallmarks of Joyce's writing are truly established: the broad sexual humor, the blasphemous fantasies, the erudite wordplay, the simultaneous eradication and exposure of authorial personality, the infinitely complex push–pull relationship with Ireland and Irishness. In *Portrait*, Joyce redefines both himself and the parameters of modern writing. **SamT**

The Underdogs

Mariano Azuela

Lifespan | b. 1873 (Mexico), d. 1952
First Published | 1916, by El Paso del Norte (Texas)
First Serialized | Cuadros de la Revolución Mexicana
Original Title | Los de abajo

This picture of the Mexican revolution inaugurated a genre of fiction that still flourishes today. A chronicle of historical events, written within a very short time of their occurrence, it is also an epic poem of the dispossessed, with its main character a fictitious, idealized hero, Demetrio Macías. A victim of the abuse of power, he abandons home and family and launches himself into a revolt that only ends with his death. For two years, he harasses the army as the leader of a gang of renegades. What at first is a disorganized rebellion is quickly given ideological justification and collective protection as a result of the speech (cynical and self-interested, however) of the doctor and journalist Luis Cervantes. With this mentor, Maías becomes a legendary revolutionary leader, but soon the coexistence of the two men is degraded by jealousy and greed. Abandoned by his backer and having lost the support of the peasants and the meaning of the struggle, which only continues through inertia, culminating in revenge, he finds his family again, only to die immediately.

Within the novel's linear, realist approach, direct interventions by the narrator denounce some issues of the nineteenth century. But the agility of a dialog that changes register according to the situation of each character; the alternations of verbal pace that give each scene an appropriate rhythm; and the impressionistic description of nature and the characters give the novel a modernity that influenced the best of later Mexican fiction. **DMG**

Pallieter

Felix Timmermans

Lifespan | b. 1886 (Belgium), d. 1947
First Published | 1916
First Published by | Van Kampen (Amsterdam)
Original Language | Flemish

During the period between the two World Wars, Felix Timmermans was one of Flanders' most successful authors. He made his debut with Schemeringen van de dood (Shimmerings of Death) in 1910, a collection of mysterious and melancholy stories. After a serious illness he changed his style with Pallieter, a novel that can be interpreted as an ode to life. In it he also dealt with the social and religious establishment of his day, but not without consequences; the Roman Catholic Church compelled Timmermans to adapt the sexually tinged passages. It was not until 1966 that the unexpurgated version was published.

The novel follows the mental evolution of Pallieter who, after having fallen in love with a young woman, experiences various disillusionments and disappointments. He chooses to turn his back on both city and society in order to dedicate himself completely to nature. Gradually he starts to enjoy life, and joyfully he accepts each day as a gift from God. And that is what makes Pallieter, above all, a hymnal ode to all the good things on earth.

Timmermans himself expressly warned readers against interpreting his novel as a faithful rendition of reality. Rather, it should be seen as an expression of desire. Pallieter is a work of imagination and its emphasis on metaphors, distorted reality, and a lyrical worldview, also marked the beginning of Expressionism. At first glance, the novel is a marvel of simplicity, but behind the images lies a rich layer of a still fascinating, archetypical world. **JaM**

Home and the World

Rabindranath Tagore

Lifespan | *b.* 1861 (India), *d.* 1941
First Published | 1916
Nobel Prize for Literature | 1913
Original Title | *Ghare Baire*

Played out against the backdrop of *Swadeshi* (part of India's home-rule movement, *Swadeshi* involved setting up a self-sufficient state and boycotting British products), *The Home and the World* charts the relationship between love, nation, and revolution. Nikhil, an enlightened landlord who has progressive ideas about women and nationalism, marries Bimala, a local girl. The couple live happily together until Nikhil's childhood friend, Sandeep, arrives, bringing with him the radical fervor of *Swadeshi*. Hypnotized by Sandeep and his passionate beliefs, Bimala contemplates deserting her husband for Sandeep and the promotion of *Swadeshi*. Nikhil becomes aware of the attraction between his wife and his friend but, being a liberal thinker, he allows Bimala the freedom to decide for herself.

Originally written in Bengali, and composed as three first-person narratives, the novel creates an objective account of differing political ideals and a marriage under threat. *The Home and the World* (as the title suggests) is a meditation on the invasion of the private sphere by the public and political world; it also discusses the relationship of women to the nation. In his Nobel Prize acceptance speech in 1919, Rabindranath Tagore criticized nationalistic arbitrary drawing of divides between countries. This belief is illuminated in *The Home*, where Tagore, decrying the hubris of *Swadeshi* and the limitations of Indian nationalism, suggests through Nikhil's serenity a wiser route toward political freedom and unity. **LL**

Growth of the Soil

Knut Hamsun

Lifespan | *b.* 1859 (Norway), *d.* 1952
First Published | 1917 by Gyldendal (Oslo)
Given Name | Knut Pederson
Original Title | *Markens grøde*

Growth of the Soil, which led to Knut Hamsun's Nobel Prize win in 1920, strives for a plain and uncomplicated prose suitable to the simplistic lifestyles of the farming community it describes. Beginning with one man's lone arrival in the Norwegian wilds, the narrative follows him as he clears the land, builds up his farm, marries, and has a family. This sense of the solitary hero forging his life gives an epic trajectory to a novel that seeks to explore the hardships facing those who live on the land, and to portray the isolation felt in small, rural communities.

Although no paean to rural idylls, Hamsun's narrative gently prizes the qualities of hard-working, plain-thinking people whose lives follow the rhythm of nature's cycles. Repetition is indeed one of the keys to the novel, which is not without its dark underbelly of selfishness and even infanticide. In following two generations, it tracks the alterations wrought by man upon the land, and records the inevitable technological changes that slowly come to transform farming methods. As a family saga, it also traces the troubles, tensions, and love within familial life, as the younger generation matures and the parents age. *Growth of the Soil* evinces an almost romantic nostalgia for the slow-changing earthy lives of the rural wilderness; this came at a time when the culture and celebrity of city living had come to make such communities seem archaic. In this winning, if strangely sad, novel, it is a now obsolete way of life that Hamsun portrays. **JC**

The Return of the Soldier

Rebecca West

Lifespan | *b.* 1892 (England), *d.* 1983
First Published | 1918
First Published by | Nisbet & Co. (London)
Given Name | Cicily Isabel Fairfield

West's short novel, published when she was twenty-four, is one of the most compelling literary responses to the horrors of the First World War, told from the perspective of those left at home. At its opening, the narrator, Jenny, and her cousin Chris's decorative but vacuous wife, Kitty, are living in a beautiful English house, Baldry Court, awaiting Chris's return from the Front. He comes back suffering from memory loss brought about by shell shock. Everything that has happened in the last fifteen years is erased from his mind, including his marriage and the death of his infant son, and Baldry Court and its inhabitants have become meaningless to him. He is infatuated with a working-class woman, Margaret, whom he had known when she was a girl, and who becomes the only figure who can give him solace, as both a lover and mother figure. At the close of the novel, he is cruelly "cured" by being forcefully reminded of his dead child, a dead son in a society now full of dead sons. The "return" of memory will return him to the Front, and we must assume, to an almost certain death in the trenches, in "No Man's Land where bullets fall like rain on the rotting faces of the dead."

The novel is bitterly ironic and yet lyrical, particularly in its representation of the lost world in which Chris' amnesia, the "hysterical fugue" brought about by shell shock, has enabled him to take refuge. It is a love story of a kind, through which West explores some of the most complex and difficult questions arising out of the war experience. **LM**

Rebecca West

"She was not so much a person as an implication of dreary poverty, like an open door in a mean house that lets out the smell of cooking cabbage and the screams of children."

◉ West made her name as a journalist campaigning in support of the suffragette movement before turning to the writing of fiction.

Tarr

Wyndham Lewis

Lifespan | *b.* 1882 (Canada), *d.* 1957 (England)
First Published | 1918
First Published by | Alfred A. Knopf (New York)
First Serialized | 1916–1917, in *The Egoist* (London)

Like Joyce's *A Portrait of the Artist as a Young Man*, *Tarr* was originally serialized in *The Egoist* magazine before its publication as a book. Alongside Joyce's work, *Tarr* signaled a new era in English literary writing. Wyndham Lewis stands a long way removed from the modernism of more "accepted" writers. Nevertheless, *Tarr* equals (if not exceeds) anything the period has to offer in terms of stylistic radicalism and imaginative scope. Although the novel was later rewritten, in 1928, the 1918 version remains definitive—retaining the experimental punctuation that gives the work such a distinctive appearance. Drawing heavily on Lewis's own experiences in Montparnasse between 1903 and 1908, *Tarr* is an account of expatriate bohemian life in Paris before the First World War. The novel dismantles the ideals of European art by tracking the decline of its central character, Otto Kreisler, whose pretentious gestures, frustrations, and sordid sexual conquests are the basis for an iconoclastic critique of the modern intellectual world.

What makes *Tarr* so striking is its emphasis on exteriority (as opposed to the interior life that so preoccupied the likes of Joyce and Woolf), on ways of seeing, and images of language. The novel is an exercise in "visual writing," an attempt to employ the principles of "Vorticist" painting in print. Lewis's characters are rendered as strange, abstracted forms —as gargoyles chiseled out of human matter. *Tarr* is a difficult, provocative, and extraordinarily crafted work, outside the familiar modernist canon. **SamT**

> *"He must get his mouth on hers; he must revel in the laugh, where it grew. She was néfaste. She was in fact evidently 'the Devil.'"*

⬤ Wyndham Lewis was a painter as well as a writer and founded the Vorticist art movement, an English version of Italian Futurism.

The Storm of Steel

Ernst Jünger

Lifespan | *b*. 1895 (Germany), *d*. 1998
First Published | 1920
First Published by | Verlag Robert Meier (Leisnig)
Original Title | *In Stahlgewittern*

"I had to leap into a water-filled, wire-laced mine crater. Dangling over the water on the swaying wire I heard the bullets rushing past me like a huge swarm of bees, while scraps of wire and metal shards sliced into the rim of the crater." You might expect this slice of trench warfare *vérité* to be the relatively recent work of Pat Barker, Sebastian Faulks, or Niall Ferguson, but you would be wrong. It comes from the pen of a German who joined up on the first day of the First World War (1914–18) as a teenager, kept a diary of all four years of ritual slaughter in sixteen notebooks, and survived. Two years later, Ernst Jünger self-published his experiences, and the novel later appeared in myriad revised editions.

Effectively a memoir (though Jünger does not mention his rank or name), Jünger writes a German soldier's account of out-and-out warfare on the Western Front. It is all here: the camaraderie, the patriotism, and the bloody, harrowing tests of bravery and foolhardiness against the "Britisher" that are as much a personal challenge as a nationalistic struggle. It is a brutally honest take on life in the dugouts and death in the craters, told with fascination, pace, and ultimately a feeling that Germany's tribulations are a precursor to rebirth and victory. Undoubtedly the war made the man and the man created *Storm of Steel*, which has survived and outclassed many rivals in a crowded genre by its powerful handling of the "normality" of modern warfare's mechanistic violence. **JHa**

Women in Love

D. H. Lawrence

Lifespan | *b*. 1885 (England), *d*. 1930 (France)
First Published | 1920 (private subscription only)
First Published by | M. Secker (London) in 1921
Full Name | David Herbert Lawrence

Women in Love, one of the greatest English twentieth-century novels, was written in a mood of rage and despair against an increasingly decadent, mechanical civilization. It offers an apocalyptic reading of English society in which a cleansing cataclysm is positively desired. A dream of annihilation animates this pessimistic text, which is very much a war novel, even though the war is not ostensibly its subject.

A profoundly unsettling work, *Women in Love* was refused publication for four years after it was completed. This was due to the candid appraisal of sexuality, the violence endemic to relationships, the instability of identity (portrayed as prey to unconscious drives and motives), and the seeming cynicism of several of the characters. In the novel, D. H. Lawrence continued to develop his modernist style, evolving an imagistic language to evoke the ineffable nature of human subjectivity, as well as a fragmented form to depict the chaos of contemporary social existence. The text is a heartfelt exploration of the struggle toward a new mode of being—one that would reject alike the dead hand of obsolete cultural traditions and the iron cage of modern rationality in favor of openness to what Lawrence called "the creative soul, the God-mystery within us." *Women in Love* is an unresolved text that nonetheless boldly avers the writer's conviction that "nothing that comes from the deep, passional soul is bad, or can be bad." **AG**

Main Street

Sinclair Lewis

Lifespan | *b.* 1885 (U.S.), *d.* 1951(Italy)
First Published | 1920
First Published by | Harcourt, Brace & Howe (N. Y.)
Full Title | *Main Street: the Story of Carol Kennicott*

Sinclair Lewis's *Main Street* presents a searing portrait of small-town America. The premier satirist of his day, Lewis delivers a scathing social commentary that also becomes, through the story of protagonist Carol Kennicott, an urgent humanist manifesto that cries out for change in the American way of life.

Carol, a new bride, finds herself locked in a new relationship and trapped in the stifling world of Gopher Prairie, Minnesota. Confronted by suspicion and hostility, Carol at first tries to change the town through many of the "improvement" schemes typical of the era, including the Chautauqua (a summer adult education school). As she struggles, the town itself inevitably changes with the expansion of modern suburban culture and the coming of the First World War. *Main Street* is filled with incidents of exaggerated social hypocrisy and downright cruelty; however, despite Lewis's satiric tone, the human relations within the world of *Main Street* manage to retain a dignity and pathos that are intensely moving. Carol's eventual defeat by the forces of small-minded convention urges the reader to contemplate the dangers of isolationist thinking, but at the same time acknowledge the strength of the flawed human ties that bind her to Gopher Prairie.

Lewis's prose is by turns caustic and emotionally charged, making the novel at once very funny and extremely serious. *Main Street* demonstrates Lewis's power as an important chronicler of American society in the early twentieth century. **AB**

The Age of Innocence

Edith Wharton

Lifespan | *b.* 1862 (U.S.), *d.* 1937 (France)
First Published | 1920
First Published by | D. Appleton & Co. (N.Y.)
Pulitzer Prize | 1921

Winner of the 1921 Pulitzer Prize for fiction, *The Age of Innocence* was written in the fragmented aftermath of the First World War, which Edith Wharton experienced first-hand in Paris. Newland Archer, the ambivalent protagonist, represents the apogee of good breeding. He is the ultimate insider in post-Civil War New York society. His upcoming marriage to young socialite May Welland will unite two of New York's oldest families. From the novel's opening pages, however, May's cousin, the Countess Ellen Olenska, imports a passionate intensity and mysterious Old World eccentricity that disrupt the conventional world of order-obsessed New York. Ellen's hopes of being set free from her past are dashed when she is forced to choose between conformity and exile, while Newland's appointment by the Welland family as Ellen's legal consultant begins an emotional entanglement the force of which he could never have imagined.

Drawing on the distinct observational style of anthropology, then a burgeoning science, Wharton narrates a romance doomed by duty in 1870s "Old New York." Though Wharton's is a critical eye, mindful of the suffering often inflicted by the unimaginative, oppressive enforcement of arbitrary mores, the equation of greater liberty with unqualified happiness does not go unquestioned. **AF**

❯ Actress Katharine Cornell appears in a 1929 stage production of
The Age of Innocence, which was also made into a movie in 1993.

Crome Yellow

Aldous Huxley

Lifespan | *b.* 1894 (England), *d.* 1963 (U.S.)
First Published | 1921
First Published by | Chatto & Windus (London)
Original Language | English

"The proper study of mankind is books."

⌾ Aldous Huxley's father and brother were both biologists, but his poor eyesight prevented him from following a scientific career.

Crome Yellow, Aldous Huxley's first and highly successful novel, would probably be better loved and more often read if it were not for the dystopian *Brave New World*. *Crome Yellow* is an altogether lighter, wittier, more amusing book, which takes up with the novel the country-house literary satire pioneered by Thomas Love Peacock's *Nightmare Abbey*. Huxley's thinly disguised satirical portraits of his contemporaries fall somewhere between D. H. Lawrence's romances of exploratory sincerity and the more acerbic asperity of Wyndham Lewis.

The plot is pleasingly perfunctory, but also functional, seeing the reader through the hopeless love muddle of one rather shy Dennis Stone, sensitive plant, aspiring poet, and his clumsy amours for Anne Wimbush. Anne's uncle hosts a party on his country estate, Crome Yellow, and this theater allows Huxley to introduce a variety of more or less ridiculous characters, among them Priscilla Wimbush, the hostess with the mostest and occult leanings; the painters Gombauld and Tschuplitski, whose work verges on blank canvas; and the self-help guru Mr. Barbecue-Smith. A distinguishing feature of Huxley's early satire, a prototype for Evelyn Waugh's early novels, is its relaxed but verbally acute derision of the pretensions of Huxley's peers, not least their clumsy emotional entanglements and "modern" sensibilities. Where satire often tends to foster reactionary contempt, Huxley's stylized mockery allows a sense of social wit, existential exploration, and verbal play. This, then, is a novel of high spirits lightly deflated. *Crome Yellow* has the edge on Huxley's subsequent and similar novel *Antic Hay* (1923), perhaps because the comedy is rougher, and more deliberately absurd, but both are entertaining. **DM**

Life of Christ

Giovanni Papini

Hailed as a great master by Henri Bergson, and praised as a friend and disciple by William James, Giovanni Papini was a journalist, vitriolic critic, poet, and novelist, whose avant-garde polemics made him one of the most controversial Italian literary figures in the early and mid-twentieth century. After years of religious turbulence and vocal atheism, this enfant terrible of the Florentine avant-garde sprung the ultimate surprise on those who thought they had him safely pigeonholed by turning to the simple faith of Christ. In 1921, Papini officially announced his newly found Roman Catholicism, publishing a book that became Italy's best seller in the 1920s and an international best seller after having been swiftly translated into more than thirty languages.

Papini's *Life of Christ* was in part a religious novel, in part a historical essay, and in part an exquisite example of dramatic literature. Its overwhelming theme is the poetic plea for the human race to return to a simple religion of brotherly love—a plea that won international fame for the book and its author. It is also important, however, to recognize Papini's achievement in stripping away the layers of embellishment and ceremony with which literature, theological systems, and skeptical critics had obscured the picture of Christ's life and times. He wrote with a simplicity that makes the story clear to every mind, and with a burning passion that brings it home to every heart. What also contributed to the success of the novel was its extraordinarily rich language. Papini's energetic, vibrant, and colorful tone, his love of images, and his penchant for paradoxes and provocations distinguished his prose from that of any other academic writer of his time. **LB**

Lifespan | *b.* 1881 (Italy), *d.* 1956
First Published | 1921
First Published by | Vallecchi Editore (Florence)
Original Title | *Storia di Cristo*

"There are those who have a desire to love, but do not have the capacity to love"

⊙ Papini was an intellectual prominent in debate on the cultural issues of his day; his adoption of Christianity was controversial.

Ulysses

James Joyce

Ulysses is one of the most extraordinary works of literature in English. At the literal level, it explores the adventures of two characters, Stephen Dedalus and Leopold Bloom, over the course of a single day in Dublin. But this is merely a peg onto which to hang all manner of streams-of-consciousness, on topics ranging from such generalities as life, death, and sex through to the contemporary state of Ireland and Irish nationalism. Threaded through this work is a continuing set of allusions to the *Odyssey*—the original Homeric account of Ulysses' wanderings. Occasionally illuminating, at other times these allusions seem designed ironically to offset the often petty and sordid concerns which take up much of Stephen's and Bloom's time, and continually distract them from their ambitions and aims.

The book conjures up a densely realized Dublin, full of details, many of which are—presumably deliberately—either wrong or at least questionable. But all this merely forms a backdrop to an exploration of the inner workings of the mind, which refuses to acquiesce in the neatness and certainties of classical philosophy. Rather, Joyce seeks to replicate the ways in which thought is often seemingly random and there is no possibility of a clear and straight way through life.

Ulysses opened up a whole new way of writing fiction that recognized that the moral rules by which we might try to govern our lives are constantly at the mercy of accident, chance encounter, and byroads of the mind. Whether this is a statement of a specifically Irish condition or of some more universal predicament is throughout held in a delicate balance, not least because Bloom is Jewish, and is thus an outsider even—or perhaps especially—in the city and country he regards as home. **DP**

Lifespan | *b*. 1882 (Ireland), *d*. 1941 (Switzerland)
First Published | 1922
First Published by | Shakespeare & Co. (Paris)
First Serialized | 1918–21, in *The Little Review* (N. Y.)

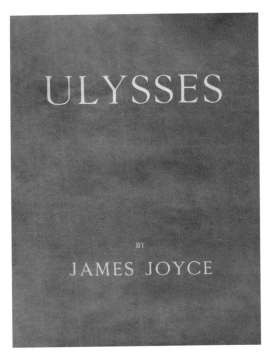

"*Love loves to love love.*"

◔ Published in Paris by Sylvia Beach's Shakespeare & Co., the first edition incurred huge losses for the company's owner.

◔ The original manuscript of the Circe section of *Ulysses* shows the extensive revisions to which the author subjected his first draft.

Babbitt

Sinclair Lewis

Lifespan | *b.* 1885 (U.S.), *d.* 1951 (Italy)
First Published | 1922
First Published by | Harcourt, Brace & Co. (N. Y.)
Original Language | English

After the enormous success of his novel *Main Street*, Sinclair Lewis turned to another icon of American life, this time the archetypal middle-class businessman, immortalized in the figure of George F. Babbitt. Babbitt is a real-estate salesman who lives and works in the fictional Midwestern town of Zenith. His story is that of suburban life in a city that is filled with "neither citadels nor churches, but frankly and beautifully office-buildings." Lewis's novel satirically but lovingly details Babbitt's routines and rituals as he goes to and from work, socializes, plays golf, goes to the club, and becomes involved in local politics. In the midst of his contented and prosperous life, however, an event occurs that turns Babbitt's world upside down and forces him to examine his comfortable existence. Babbitt's resulting lurch from one uncertainty to another allows the reader to see beyond the shining office towers of Zenith to a grittier, more sobering but ultimately more human kind of American life.

Lewis's triumph here lies in taking a character that no one could possibly like—the self-important, conformist, and aggressively bigoted American businessman—and evoking not only barbed humor but vivid human feeling. *Babbitt* works as a political critique, piercing the smug veil worn by interwar American capitalism, but transcends mere amusing satire. Life in Zenith has a surprising depth; as such, it reminds us of the redemptive power of looking past ideology to the human relations beneath. **AB**

Claudine's House

Colette

Lifespan | *b.* 1873 (Italy), *d.* 1954
First Published | 1922, by Ferenczi (Paris)
Alternate Title | *My Mother's House*
Original Title | *La Maison de Claudine*

In this semiautobiographical tale, France's most adored female author reminisces on her rural upbringing as a child with her wise and wondrous mother and Mother Nature. It is a beautiful observation of a girl on the cusp of innocence and knowingness set in a magical woodscape. Colette's evocation of nature's enigmatic goings-on is very much in evidence: the cat purrs like "the rumble of a distant factory," tame swallows land on her hair, and a spider regularly climbs down from its web to collect sipfuls of drinking chocolate from her mother's bedside bowl. But the world of adults is never far away, be it local villagers or more urbane visitors, and Colette describes both worlds with her trademark sensuality, recalling the sounds, smells, tastes, textures, and colors of her past.

Ironically, this idyllic childhood was also a world away from her real life at the time of writing. The innocent girl had been a libertine in the Paris demi-monde, a music-hall dancer performing transvestite pieces, and a woman more at home with gossip, pleasures of the flesh, and scandal. Her writing career began bizarrely when her first husband forced her to ghostwrite four incredibly popular "Claudine" novels (1900–04) under his pen name "Willy." However, despite its title, *Claudine's House* is not one of that series. **JH**

❯ Colette became an erotic stage actress after leaving her husband in 1905; her writing often plays off sensuality against innocence.

Life and Death of Harriett Frean

May Sinclair

Lifespan | *b.* 1862 (England), *d.* 1946
First Published | 1922
First Published by | W. Collins & Sons (London)
Given Name | Mary Amelia St. Clair

Brief, bare, and cruelly ironic, this novel marked a turning point in Sinclair's career, reflecting her engagement with psychoanalysis as a (then new) theory of the unconscious mind, and the conflict between sexuality and social identity. On one level, it is a case history, inviting the reader to share the consciousness of Harriett Frean literally from cradle to grave. As the story opens, Harriett is in her cot, her parents amusing her with nursery rhymes, and wondering at her laughter: "Each kissed her in turn, and the Baby Harriett stopped laughing suddenly." It is a foreboding moment in a book that returns compulsively to the destruction written into parental love, to the demand for self-sacrifice embedded in their wish for their daughter to "behave beautifully."

Enraptured by the image of herself reflected by her parents, Harriett embarks on a life of renunciation. Its destructiveness is Sinclair's key theme, a critique of virtue that uncovers the fundamental attack on desire, on life itself, at work in the conventionally beautiful behavior of the Victorian middle classes. Sinclair's complex relation to modernity, and to literary modernism, is at the heart of this novel, which she uses to explore the "life" of a woman who cannot bring herself to destroy her parents' child. **VL**

Sinclair became a novelist after the First World War, in which she served as an ambulance driver, a formative experience in her life.

The Forest of the Hanged

Liviu Rebreanu

Lifespan | *b.* 1885 (Romania), *d.* 1944
First Published | 1922
First Published by | Cartea românească (Bucharest)
Original Title | *Padurea spânzuratilor*

The Forest of the Hanged is the first psychological novel of Romanian literature. It examines the painful position of Romanian Transylvanian soldiers in the First World War: politically still part of the Austro-Hungarian empire, they were forced to fight against their own co-nationals. The novel is based on the true story of Emil Rebreanu, brother of the writer, hanged in 1917 for trying to defect to the Romanian side. The literary hero, Apostol Bologa, lieutenant in the Austro-Hungarian army, meets a similar fate; through his experience, Liviu Rebreanu illustrates the struggle between allegiances and the call of duty.

Hanging, seen as the vilest and most humiliating death, was the punishment for deserters in the war, and the image of the gallows, often improvised from trees, haunts Rebreanu's book. Bologa changes radically throughout the novel. At first totally devoted to his military duty, he serves on the jury that convicts a deserter to death; but, filled with inexplicable guilt at the sight of the hanged man, his Romanian nationalistic conscience awakens and his military ideals are exposed as void. Unable to take arms against his co-nationals when moved to the Transylvanian front, Bologa chooses the gallows, becoming the deserter he initially despised.

The Forest of the Hanged is a war testimony of universal relevance that will still makes a strong impression on the modern reader. **AW**

Siddhartha

Hermann Hesse

Lifespan | b. 1877 (Germany), d. 1962 (Switzerland)
First Published | 1922
First Published by | S. Fischer Verlag (Berlin)
Nobel Prize | 1946

As the son of a Brahmin, Siddhartha enjoys comfort and privilege while sequestered in his home village. However, as he grows older, his heart is moved by a burning desire to acquire wisdom and new experiences. Telling his father his intentions, Siddhartha and his childhood friend, Govinda, leave the safety of home to join the Samanas, a group of wandering ascetics. As Hermann Hesse's novel unfolds, we follow Siddhartha in his search for meaning and truth in a world of sorrow and suffering.

Drawing on both Hindu and Buddhist teachings, Siddhartha expertly explores the tension between the doctrinal dictates of organized religion and the inner promptings of the soul. As Siddhartha grows older, a fundamental truth gradually becomes apparent both to him and to us: there is no single path to self-growth, no one formula for how to live life. Hesse challenges our ideas of what it means to lead a spiritual life, to strive after and to achieve meaningful self-growth through blind adherence to a religion, philosophy, or indeed any system of belief. We should, rather, seek to seize hold of the reality of each moment, which is always new, alive, and forever changing. Hesse uses the potent symbol of a river to convey this sense of vibrancy and flux.

The particular brilliance of this novel is the way in which its profound message is delivered through a prose that flows as naturally and shimmeringly as the surface of the river beside which Siddhartha spends the final years of his life. **CG-G**

The Enormous Room

e. e. cummings

Lifespan | b. 1894 (U.S.), d. 1962
First Published | 1922
First Published by | Boni & Liveright (New York)
Full Name | Edward Estlin Cummings

This autobiography came about because cummings and his friend B. (William Slater Brown) preferred, when in France, in 1917, the company of French soldiers to that of their fellow Americans. They were working as volunteer drivers for the Norton-Harjes section of the American Red Cross when they were arrested and detained in Normandy. B. had written home to his family in Massachusetts indiscreet letters concerning rumors of French mutinies that the authorities had intercepted, and cummings was implicated. The eponymous room is where these interim prisoners live and sleep.

cummings celebrates the oddity and sheer peculiarity of his fellow detainees. They are given extraordinary names. He likes the Wanderer, Mexique, the Zulu, and, above all, Jean Le Nègre. He does not like The Sheeney With the Trick Raincoat or Bill the Hollander. Against these individuals, liked or not, stands (in irony) "the inexorable justice of le gouvernement français." This classic anarchist structure sets individuals against all authority. cummings asserts the values of a new, modernist art, which will require "that vast and painful process of Unthinking which may result in a minute bit of purely personal Feeling. Which minute bit is Art." For the rest of his life, a more focused cummings was to remain in his art an instinctive anarchist. **AM**

⊘ Despite modernist techniques, cummings belongs to the U.S. populist tradition, lauding love, individualism, and the underdog.

Kristin Lavransdatter

Sigrid Undset

Lifespan | *b.* 1882 (Denmark), *d.* 1949 (Norway)
First Published | 1920–1922
First Published by | H. Aschehoug & Co. (Oslo)
Nobel Prize for Literature | 1928

"Lavrans and Ragnfrid were more than commonly pious and God-fearing folk."

⊙ Sigrid Undset was awarded the Nobel Prize for Literature in 1928, a tribute to the international success of her historical novels.

The proud and independent Kristin Lavransdatter (meaning Laurence's daughter, surnames not being much used in fourteenth-century Norway) is the heroine of this door-stopping saga steeped in ancient folk tales, royal power struggles, and courtly, old-worldy language. Her father Lavrans is a rich farmer and devout Christian who adores Kristin. She is expected to marry Simon Darre, heir to the neighboring estate, but she falls in love with the handsome but irresponsible Erlend Nikulausson who owns the great manor Husaby. In true soap-opera style he has a lover, Eline, with whom Kristin vies for his attention—in one scene Kristin suggests, "Shall we throw dice for our man, we two paramours?" Murder, marriage, plots against the monarchy, and trials and tribulations encircle Kristin, who is driven by love and loyalty. She emerges through all this a strong but self-sacrificing woman.

Originally published in three volumes (*The Garland*; *The Mistress of Husaby*; *The Cross*), *Kristin Lavransdatter* evokes the medieval milieu strikingly (Sigrid Undset's father was an archaeologist and the family home steeped in folklore and legend). The author became a Roman Catholic in 1924 and religion is a constant theme in this and her other novels. The subarctic Scandinavian landscape is painted beautifully, but Undset's greatest achievement is in the characterization of a woman for all times. Kristin Lavransdatter has been compared with Anna Karenina, Tess, and Emma Bovary as one of the great characters of female literature. She is certainly a woman of universal and timeless appeal and the trilogy remains Undset's lasting masterpiece. Awarded the Nobel Prize for Literature in 1928, Undset's work was labeled "an Iliad of the North" for its faithfulness to early Scandinavian culture. **JHa**

Amok

Stefan Zweig

Stefan Zweig was a prolific novelist, biographer, translator, and world traveler. A notable pacifist, he fled his native Austria in 1934 to London and then Brazil, where, disillusioned by the rise of fascism, he and his wife committed suicide. *Amok* is a short, intense story of a troubled doctor who loses his mind in the tropics. It is narrated by a worldly passenger who meets the mysterious doctor on board a ship returning to Europe from Calcutta. The doctor is in desperate need of human contact and has a chilling secret to confess. Written as reported speech that, like the colonial setting, recalls Joseph Conrad, it is a gripping tale of passion, moral duty, and uncontrollable unconscious forces.

The doctor has been forced to travel to Asia following a misdemeanor committed at a German hospital, where he was in thrall to a beautiful but domineering woman. Having set off full of romantic ideals of bringing civilization to the indigenous people, he finds himself isolated in a remote station, and his condition slowly deteriorates as the tropical torpor and solitude become too much for him. He becomes estranged from his European self and utterly dispirited. When an English lady arrives at his station requesting an abortion, he is provoked by her arrogance and domineering manner to such an extent that he loses control of his conscious will. At first he struggles to gain the upper hand in a veiled sado-masochistic scenario, but when she laughs in his face he can do nothing but pursue her in a manic attempt to appease his infatuation.

A Freudian exploration of the power of the unconscious and latent sexuality, *Amok* is a finely wrought story full of psychological insight. As such, it is an ideal introduction to Stefan Zweig's impressive body of work. **AL**

Lifespan | *b.* 1881 (Austria), *d.* 1942 (Brazil)
First Published | 1922
First Published by | S. Fischer Verlag (Berlin)
Original Language | German

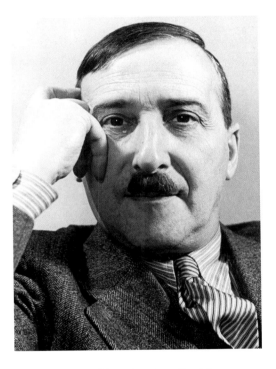

"We are all criminals if we remain silent . . ."

Stefan Zweig, 1918

◉ Zweig's work is notable for its psychological insight, which he applied in biographies of authors such as Stendhal and Tolstoy.

The Devil in the Flesh

Raymond Radiguet

Lifespan | *b.* 1903 (France), *d.* 1923
First Published | 1923
First Published by | Grasset (Paris)
Original Title | *Le Diable au Corps*

Written only five years after the First World War, the story of a love affair between a sixteen-year-old boy and a young woman married to a soldier fighting on the front shocked public sensitivity. Raymond Radiguet himself added to the polemic by publishing an article on the novel just days after its appearance, in which he calls his "false autobiography" all the more real for not being real. The youth of the author, his great promise, and the scandalous content of the story brought quick success to *The Devil in the Flesh*.

Because of his tempestuous life and early death, Radiguet is often linked to Rimbaud. Radiguet denounced the label of "child prodigy" in his characteristically terse style, admitting, however, to an artistic affinity with both Rimbaud and Baudelaire. The anonymous protagonist of the story and his lover are thus initially brought together by their liking of *Les Fleurs du Mal*. Despite association with the Surrealists and his love relationship with Jean Cocteau, Radiguet's influences can be traced back to French classicism. Consequently, *The Devil in the Flesh* is elegant and compact, often presenting psychological insight into the workings of ill-fated love in the form of short maxims. The novel is also an indictment of the petit-bourgeois morals that left generations of young men and women tragically unprepared for the logic of both love and war. **IJ**

⊙ Modigliani painted this portrait of the teenage Radiguet in 1919; the talented author died four years later aged twenty.

Zeno's Conscience

Italo Svevo

Lifespan | *b.* 1861 (Italy), *d.* 1928
First Published | 1923, by Cappelli (Bologna)
Given Name | Ettore Schmitz
Original Title | *La Coscienza di Zeno*

In the life of Italo Svevo, the pen name of Ettore Schmitz, writing never took the place of a profession, but remained the secret passion he pursued when not involved in his office job or playing the violin. Two elements mark his life: his friendship with James Joyce, and his acquaintance with psychoanalysis through Freud, whose *Über der Traum* he translated.

This novel is protagnist Zeno's autobiography, written at the instigation of Doctor S. as part of his psychoanalysis. Zeno's account of his life is far from a tribute to Freud's science; rather, it is an opportunity to portray the transient and ephemeral character of people's desires. A typical anti-hero, Zeno has zero willpower and laughs at his incapacity to retain control of his existence. When he decides that marriage could cure his malaise, he proposes to the beautiful Ada, but accidentally ends up marrying Augusta, her unattractive sister. Zeno's neurosis becomes apparent in the account of his repeated and frustrated attempts to quit smoking. Helplessly dominated by the habit, Zeno fills his days with thousands of resolutions to ban cigarettes. Significant dates in his life are magical reminders of the possibility of a new smokeless life: "the ninth day of the ninth month of 1899," "the third day of the sixth month of 1912 at 12." Zeno needs to give himself prohibitions that he ritually infringes. His volatility and spinelessness always make his last cigarette the penultimate one, while he relishes the pleasure he derives from his own failure. **RPi**

A Passage to India

E. M. Forster

Lifespan | b. 1879 (England), d. 1970
First Published | 1924
First Published by | E. Arnold & Co. (London)
Full Name | Edward Morgan Forster

E. M. Forster's last novel achieves a seriousness not evident in his earlier works. While he represents the British in India as stuffy caricatures of prejudice, Forster does not make them into the sustained parodies that we find in *Howard's End* or *A Room with a View*. At the heart of this liberal study of Anglo-Indian relations sits the vast emptiness of the booming Marabar caves, which Forster establishes as a site of ambiguity and uncertainty. Visitors to the caves are never sure what it is they have witnessed, if anything at all. Adele Quested, a British woman who is newly arrived in India, is accompanied to the caves by the Indian Dr. Aziz, and what happens between them there is never clearly established. Although the British assume that she was attacked by Aziz, Adele herself never confirms this. In fact, she spectacularly withdraws the allegation in court, and earns herself the opprobrium of her fellow countrymen. However, even this retraction fails to clarify the episode, which remains an example of the indeterminacy that characterizes Forster's modernist aesthetic.

If the rape trial is the center of the novel's plot, the friendship between Aziz and the sympathetic British humanists, Mrs. Moore and Cyril Fielding, represents the potential for connection across national lines (a central concept in Forster's writing). For some, the novel stands as a benevolent portrayal of the early nationalist campaign in India. Others, however, have pointed to Forster's inability to avoid exotic fantasy in his depiction of Indians. **LC**

We

Yevgeny Zamyatin

Lifespan | b. 1884 (Russia), d. 1937 (France)
First Published | 1924
First Published by | E. P. Dutton (New York)
Original Russian Title | *My*

The first novel to be banned by the Soviet censorship bureau in 1921, *We* is a prototypical dystopian novel, bearing similarities to later such fictions. The novel consists of a series of diary entries by D-503, a mathematician and a thoroughly orthodox citizen of the authoritarian, futuristic state to which he belongs. The diary sets out as a celebration of state doctrine, which dictates that happiness, order, and beauty can be found only in unfreedom, in the cast-iron tenets of mathematical logic and of absolute power. As the diary and novel continue, however, D-503 comes under the subversive influence of a beautiful dissident, named I-330. Enthralled by a wild desire for I, D loses his faith in the purity of mathematical logic, and in the capacity of a perfectly ordered collective to satisfy all human needs. Gradually, he finds himself drawn toward the poetic irrationality of $\sqrt{-1}$, and the anarchism of a private love. He no longer identifies with "we," and starts to think of himself, in an ironic reflection of the name of his guerrilla lover, as "I."

What sets the novel apart is the intellectual subtlety of his understanding of authoritarianism. The novel is not a straightforward denunciation of communism, but a moving, blackly comic examination of the contradictions between freedom and happiness that state socialism produces. **PB**

⊗ A poster from the early days of Bolshevik rule in Russia: Zamyatin's novel was later interpreted as an attack on Soviet totalitarianism.

Российская Социалистическая Федеративная Советская Республика

ПРОЛЕТАРИИ ВСЕХ СТРАН СОЕДИНЯЙТЕСЬ

ВСЕМИРНАЯ РЕВОЛЮЦИЯ

ДА ЗДРАВСТВУЕТ

N° 30

1ое МАЯ ПРАЗДНИК ТРУДА
ДА ЗДРАВСТВУЕТ МЕЖДУНАРОДНОЕ
ЕДИНЕНИЕ ПРОЛЕТАРИАТА!

The Magic Mountain

Thomas Mann

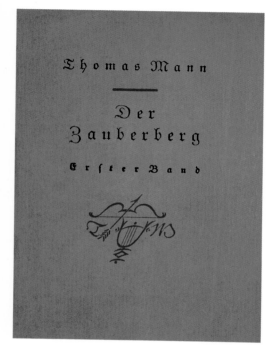

"*Waiting we say is long. We might just as well—or more accurately—say it is short, since it consumes whole spaces of time without our living them or making any use of them as such.*"

● Thomas Mann drew material for *The Magic Mountain* from a period his wife Katia spent in a tuberculosis sanatorium in 1913.

Lifespan | *b.* 1875 (Germany), *d.* 1967 (Switzerland)
First Published | 1924
First Published by | S. Fischer Verlag (Berlin)
Original Title | *Der Zauberberg*

The Magic Mountain opens with Hans Castorp making the journey from Hamburg to a tuberculosis sanatorium in the Swiss mountains. The first three weeks of what was supposed to be a temporary visit pass by achingly slowly. But Castorp is soon seduced by the repetitive, strangely enchanted existence of the patients. His imagination is caught by a series of vividly drawn characters who come to recuperate, and to die, on the mountain.

The novel belongs to the Bildungsroman tradition, though Castorp's initiation is not into the world of action and events—the clamor of the approaching First World War is consigned to somewhere below the quiet of the sanatorium—but into the world of ideas. Thomas Mann uses the debates between patients as a way of exploring the philosophical and political concerns of his time: humanism versus the very real threat of absolutism. Castorp must also struggle to understand what it means to fall in love in a place marked by illness and death—the troublingly intimate memento that Clavdia Chauchat confers upon her lover is an X-ray photograph of her clouded lungs.

The prospect of Castorp's return to the flatland is deferred, and as the weeks stretch into months and then into years, time seems not to pass by at all. We experience with Hans Castorp the intensity of the formative moments—tragic, erotic, mundane, absurd—of his seven years in the sanatorium, all suspended in a heightened present. **KB**

The Green Hat

Michael Arlen

Lifespan | b. 1895 (Bulgaria), d. 1956 (U.S.)
First Published | 1924
First Published by | W. Collins & Sons (London)
Former Name | Dikran Kouyoumdjian

The Green Hat tells the story of the seductive Iris Storm—allegedly based on Nancy Cunard—whose forbidden love for her childhood sweetheart, Napier Harpenden, leads her through a series of tragic marriages and disastrous love affairs, culminating in her dramatic suicide. The novel made Michael Arlen a celebrity, but this flamboyantly public figure also had close connections to some major figures of British modernism, such as D. H. Lawrence and Osbert Sitwell. Although *The Green Hat* remains a popular romance, its modernism is evident, for example, in an affectionate parody of Sitwell's magazine, *The New Age*; the novel can also be read as a popular rewrite of Ford's *The Good Soldier*, which Iris describes as an "amazing romance." Arlen's writing style, with its ambiguous, elliptical descriptions, is clearly influenced by modernism, while the imagery offers some particularly stark, oddly dislocated depictions resembling imagism.

These modernist elements combine with the conventional features of the romance, particularly where the novel comments on the pace of fashion and the modern age. For instance, Iris commits suicide by driving her car into the tree under which she and Napier declared their love. Clearly the grand romantic gesture is one of the clichés of the genre, but the use of the motor car, which figures as a symbol of high-speed modernity and is described through the image of a giant insect, seems an almost futurist diversion from convention. **LC**

The New World

Heruy Wäldä-Sellassé

Lifespan | b. 1878 (Ethiopia), d. 1939
First Published | 1925
First Published in | Addis Ababa
Original Language | Ethiopic

Ethiopia was one of the very few African countries to escape takeover by European colonial powers, and in 1923, it was accepted into the League of Nations. As the director of the government press, Heruy Wäldä-Sellassé was responsible for the promotion of an Ethiopian national culture and Amharic as a printed language, and as a diplomat he sought ideas and aid from the developed world.

The New World, Wäldä-Sellassé's second novel, is situated unreservedly in the perspective of the desirability of modernization along Western lines. The novel's central character is an Ethiopian who takes an opportunity to study in Europe, and then returns inspired with a mission to transform his home country. But his aspirations are thwarted by the ignorance and prejudice of the Ethiopian people. They resist his efforts to persuade them to abandon their traditional practices and beliefs. They are hostile to the wonders of modern European technology, and they give allegiance to a traditional priesthood that is corrupt and reactionary.

To today's reader, Wäldä-Sellassé's modernizer is almost certain to appear unbearably patronizing and startlingly politically incorrect in his assumption of the unquestionable superiority of Western civilization. Yet the book describes a significant moment in the evolving relationship between African aspirations and European power, as well as contributing largely to the establishment of a modern Amharic literature. **RegG**

The Professor's House

Willa Cather

Lifespan | *b.* 1873 (U.S.), *d.* 1947
First Published | 1925
First Published by | A. Knopf (New York)
Full Name | Willa Siebert Cather

*"He had never learned
to live without delight."*

🌐 Famous mostly for her portrayals of pioneer life in the American
West, Cather made it onto the cover of *Time* magazine in 1931.

The opening and closing sections of *The Professor's House* are chronologically sequential narratives of history professor Godfrey St. Peter's current domestic and professional lives. They flank an autobiographical confession made years before to St. Peter by his student, Tom Outland. As Outland describes his discovery of an ancient civilization on New Mexico's Blue Mesa, a revelation of almost religious intensity, he imparts the dry, luminous clarity of his Southwestern origins. Tom Outland's seemingly boundless scientific and spiritual potential, and the paternal affection that St. Peter feels for him, sanctify him as a figure of lyrical perfection rendered complete by his early death in the First World War.

The professor's house is in fact two houses. On the one hand, there is the homely, perennially dilapidated house, now emptied and mostly uninhabited, where St. Peter raised his family and forged his career. On the other hand, there is the house that he had custom-built for his retirement, financed with a prestigious academic prize, which represents a comfortable future he has, until recently, resisted. When he first met Outland, St. Peter was an unorthodox young academic with financial and professional concerns, but by the time of the narrative, he has achieved renown and even wealth by virtue of the same work that, years ago, was deemed unpublishable. St. Peter's daughter, who was engaged to Outland at the time of his death, capitalizes ruthlessly with her husband on Outland's tragic story and lucrative inventions. Though Outland has suffered, he has nevertheless been spared the petty indignities St. Peter endures as his sense of self is slowly usurped by institutional forces beyond his influence. **AF**

The Artamonov Business

Maxim Gorky

The Artamonov Business, one of Maxim Gorky's longest and most ambitious novels, tells the story of the merchant Artamonov family through three generations. Ilya Artamonov, a liberated serf, starts his own factory and tries to pass on what he sees as the bourgeois values of hard work and humility to his heirs, his son, Pyotr, and nephew, Alexei. Ascending into the ranks of the middle classes brings only disaster for the Artamonovs, however, as Pyotr's weakness and Alexei's cold business sense lack the warmth and humanity that characterized Ilya's generation. In the third generation, the Artamonovs are visited by what seems to them to be disaster when their factory is taken over by the workers as part of the October Revolution. But as Gorky makes plain, the process of degeneration that has accompanied the family's rise to bourgeois status ensures the necessity of their downfall and paves the way for the possibility of a better world.

Here Gorky presents a sweeping family saga in the manner of *War and Peace*, but with Tolstoy's historical background replaced by a much more urgent and contemporary setting. The characters, both the damaged Artamonovs and the shifting cast of factory workers who coexist with them, are vivid and lifelike. As in all of his novels, Gorky avoids the trap of political propaganda, treating all of the figures—workers and capitalists alike—with a sardonic although ultimately sympathetic eye. Readers of the novel will find themselves catching a glimpse of the fervor of revolutionary Russia that allowed many, including Gorky, to be swept away on a wave of new hope for societal change. The Artamonov Business remains a valuable novel, both for its literary skill and for its value as the product of a poignant moment in Russian history. **AB**

Lifespan | *b.* 1868 (Russia), *d.* 1936
First Published | 1925, in *Russkaia Kniga* (Berlin)
Given Name | Aleksey Maksimovich Peshkov
Original Title | *Delo Artamonovic*

"When everything is easy one quickly gets stupid."

Maxim Gorky, 1926

⊙ Gorky had an often difficult relationship with Russia's Bolshevik rulers; this novel was written during a period of self-exile in Italy.

The Trial

Franz Kafka

"Somebody must have made a false accusation against Josef K., for he was arrested one morning without having done anything wrong."

As in Franz Kafka's long story *Metamorphosis*—which begins with the line "Gregor Samsa awoke one morning from uneasy dreams to find himself transformed in his bed into a gigantic insect"—the entire narrative of *The Trial* emerges from the condition that announces itself in the opening sentence. The protagonist, Josef K., never discovers what he is being charged with, and is never able to understand the principles governing the system of justice in which he finds himself ensnared. Instead, the narrative follows his exhausting determination to understand and to protest his innocence in the complete absence of any doctrine that would explain to him what it would mean to be guilty, or indeed, of what he actually stands accused. In following Josef K.'s struggle toward absolution, the novel presents us with an astonishingly moving account of what it is to be born naked and defenseless into a completely incomprehensible system, armed only with a devout conviction of innocence.

Intimacy with this novel has a peculiar effect on the reader. If the first response to K.'s grappling with the authorities is a sense of familiarity and recognition, there is soon a strange reversal. It begins to seem that our world merely resembles Kafka's; that our struggles are a faint likeness of the essential struggle that is revealed to us in K.'s endless plight. For this reason, *The Trial*, in all its inconclusion, its impossibility, and its difficulty, is a wildly exhilarating book, which takes us to the very empty heart of what it is to be alive in a world of everyday trials pushed to the extreme. **PB**

Lifespan | *b*. 1883 (Czechoslovakia), *d*. 1924 (Austria)
First Published | 1925
First Published by | Die Schmiede (Berlin)
Original Title | *Der Prozeß*

Franz
Kafka
Der
Prozeß
Roman

This *Man at Table* sketch forms part of a series taken from Kafka's 1905 lecture notes from the Kierling Sanatorium (Vienna).

Anthony Perkins starred as the bewildered K. in Orson Welles's darkly expressionistic film version of *The Trial*, made in 1962.

The Counterfeiters

André Gide

Lifespan | *b.* 1869 (France), *d.* 1951
First Published | 1925
First Published by | Gallimard (Paris)
Original Title | *Les Faux-Monnayeurs*

Significantly, Andre Gide's only novel worthy of the name is an investigation into the possibilities of the novel. Edouard, one of the many narrative voices in *The Counterfeiters*, is also a struggling novelist. He, like Gide, keeps a diary documenting the process of novel writing. He, too, is trying to write a novel called *The Counterfeiters*. In a vertiginous effect of *mise en abyme*, we are reading a novel about a novelist writing a novel about a novelist writing a novel . . . This is one of the many devices that Gide employs to wrongfoot the reader. Another is the deception of the title. Just as Gide flirts with recognized genres such as the romance and the Bildungsroman, the possibility of a detective fiction with schoolboys passing off fake gold coins is hinted at but never followed through. Counterfeit coins serve as a metaphor for false values more generally—those put into circulation by the state, the family, the Church, and the literary establishment.

The Counterfeiters does not make things easy for us: we are deprived of a reassuringly impersonal narrative voice, we are introduced to characters who turn out to have no role to play, and the threads of the novel's many different plots are left hanging. But this is also why it is so important. Reading *The Counterfeiters*, all of our certainties as readers of nineteeth-century novels are called in question, which means that we are also uncertain of Gide: in the midst of all this inauthenticity, what actually guarantees the value of *The Counterfeiters*? **KB**

The Great Gatsby

F. Scott Fitzgerald

Lifespan | *b.* 1896 (U.S.), *d.* 1940
First Published | 1925
First Published by | C. Scribner's Sons (New York)
Full Name | Francis Scott Key Fitzgerald

The Great Gatsby is an American literary classic. Nick Carraway's enraptured account of the rise and fall of his charismatic neighbor during a single summer came to evoke the pleasurable excesses and false promises of a whole decade. The novel's extraordinary visual motifs—the brooding eyes of the billboard, the ashen wasteland between metropolitan New York and hedonistic Long Island, the blues and golds of Gatsby's nocturnal hospitality—combined the iconography of the "jazz age" and its accompanying anxieties about the changing social order characteristic of American modernism. Gatsby, infamously created out of a "platonic conception of himself," came to be synonymous with nothing less than the American Dream.

Gatsby's lavish and hedonistic lifestyle is a construct, we quickly learn, erected in order to seduce Daisy, the lost love of his youth who is now married to the millionaire Tom Buchanan. Fitzgerald's easy conjuring of Gatsby's shimmering fantasy world is matched by his presentation of its darker and more pugnacious realities. The novel frequently hints at the corruption that lies behind Gatsby's wealth, and Tom is shown to be a crude and adulterous husband. The novel's violent climax is a damning indictment of the careless excess of the very privileged, yet it concludes ambivalently. **NM**

❯ Fitzgerald and his wife, Zelda, during Christmas, 1925, disguise the strains that soon brought their lives to breaking point.

(Jan 3rd 1924)

There was an age when the pavement was grass; another
when it was swamp; an age of tusk & mammoth; a
age of silent sunrise; & through them all the battered
woman — for she wore a skirt — with her right
hand exposed, her left clutching at her knees stood
singing of love; which love unconquerable in battle;
which she sang after looking for millions of years
after a while had lasted a million years, yes, a million years
so she sang, her lover, & which she sang was immortal
through her lover, & millions of years ago her lover,
in May, her lover, who had been dead three centuries,
had walked, she crooned, with her in May; but
in the course of ages, when long as summer days, &
being flaming, so she remembered with nothing but
red flowers, he had gone; death's enormous sickle had
swept over those tremendous hills; & when,
she laid her hoary & immensely she laid her
hoary & immensely aged head on the earth
now become a mere cinder of ice, it would have
outlived everything — her memory of happiness even — the
she implored that "lay by my side a branch of
purple heather"; there where on that high burial
place which the last rays of the last sun
caressed a branch of purple heather; for then
the pageant of the universe would be over.

at last

Mrs. Dalloway

Virginia Woolf

Virginia Woolf's novel *Mrs. Dalloway* takes place over the course of a single day, and is one of the defining texts of modernist London. It traces the interlocking movements around Regent's Park of the two main protagonists: Clarissa Dalloway is a socialite, and wife of Richard Dalloway, a Conservative MP, while Septimus Warren Smith is a veteran and shell-shocked victim of the First World War. The passage of time in the novel, punctuated by the periodic striking of a giant, phallic Big Ben, ultimately takes us to a double climax; to the success of Mrs. Dalloway's illustrious party, and to the suicide of Septimus Warren Smith, who finds himself unable to live in the post-war city.

Much of the effect of this novel derives from the irreconcilability of its two halves, an irreconcilability that is reflected in the space of the city itself. Different people go about their different lives, preparing for suicide and preparing for dinner, and there is no way, the novel suggests, of building a bridge between them. Septimus and Clarissa are separated by class, by gender, and by geography, but at the same time, the novel's capacity to move from one consciousness to another suggests a kind of intimate, underground connection between them, which is borne out in Clarissa's response to the news of Septimus's death. A poetic space, which does not correspond to the clock time meted out by Big Ben, underlies the city, suggesting a new way of thinking about relations between men and women, between one person and another. *Mrs. Dalloway* is a novel of contradictions—between men and women, between rich and poor, between self and other, between life and death. But despite these contradictions, in the flimsy possibility of a poetic union between Septimus and Clarissa, the novel points toward a reconciliation we are still waiting to realize. **PB**

Lifespan | *b.* 1882 (England), *d.* 1941
First Published | 1925
First Published by | Hogarth Press (London)
First U.S. Edition | Harcourt, Brace & Co. (N. Y.)

Woolf was always dogged by bouts of depression, attempting suicide in her early thirties and finally drowning herself in 1941.

Woolf's draft notes for *Mrs. Dalloway* explore the experience of a reality she found "very erratic, very undependable."

Chaka the Zulu

Thomas Mofolo

Lifespan | b. 1875 (Lesotho), d. 1948
First Published | 1925
First Published by | Morija Sesuto Book Depot
Original Title | Chaka

Thomas Mofolo, a native of Basutoland in South Africa, wrote *Chaka the Zulu*, an undisputed masterpiece of Sesotho literature, in 1910. The novel tells the story of Chaka, the illegitimate son of a minor South African chief and the man who, at the beginning of the nineteenth century, created the Zulu nation through ten years of continuous war.

Sent away from his father's palace along with his mother, Chaka is bullied as a child. The rejection by his father and his peers causes Chaka to see life as nothing more or less than the exercise of might. Banished from his tribe, Chaka encounters a witchdoctor, Isanusi, in the desert. With Isanusi's help Chaka wins the chieftainship of his tribe and the love of a beautiful woman. But his desire for fame and ambition are too strong and Chaka, in a diabolical pact with Isanusi, kills the woman he loves in order to become the greatest chief of all time.

Mofolo, a Christian writer with a keen eye for sin, methodically chronicles the deterioration of his protagonist's soul. Chaka is, in the end, unable to distinguish war and murder; he has sacrificed his conscience to become a dictator. But, given that Chaka's story began in his troubled childhood, we are able to see Chaka as a brilliant and alienated teenager as well as a savage tyrant. Mofolo, blending historical truth with romance, creates a fascinating novel that sheds light on pre-colonial Africa. **OR**

The Making of Americans

Gertrude Stein

Lifespan | b. 1874 (U.S.), d. 1946 (France)
First Published | 1925
First Published by | Contact Editions (Paris)
Original Language | English

Gertrude Stein's innovative prose has a measured beauty that is best enjoyed with the rhythm and pace of the spoken word. This epic novel reinvents and simultaneously challenges the form of the traditional family saga, as it follows several generations of four families, but to summarize it in such a way fails to do it justice. Moving back and forth in time with fluidity, Stein traces the internal, emotional development of people as they mature, as they relate to their spouses and their community, and, ultimately, as they become American; this is done with an almost cubist desire to show the events in all their facets and from many angles. *The Making of Americans* also takes time to comment on its own composition, and contains some of Stein's most comprehensive comments upon her conception of writing and her unique style.

Somewhat underrated as a modernist classic, the novel certainly has all the hallmarks of a text that forges a new and idiomatic use of language while challenging the previous Victorian concept of realism. It is also an epic interpretation of the Americans' psychological development, reaching back to the founding families and the generations they produce and nurture. Challenging, beautifully written, and rightfully a literary masterpiece, *The Making of Americans* deserves to be ranked among the forefront of modernist achievements. **JC**

The Murder of Roger Ackroyd

Agatha Christie

Lifespan | *b.* 1890 (England), *d.* 1976
First Published | 1926
First Published by | W. Collins & Sons (London)
Full Name| Agatha Mary Clarissa Christie

All detective novels have twists, but the masterpiece of Agatha Christie's extensive oeuvre trumps them all, reverting on some of the fundamental principles of the genre in its startling denouement.

This novel contains many of the ingredients for which Christie became famous: a couple of bodies, a country-house setting, a small group of suspects, and the moustache-twirling Belgian detective Hercule Poirot. As narrated by the local doctor, Sheppard, there is a veritable profusion of possibilities as to who murdered Roger Ackroyd: is it the parlormaid, the retired major, Ackroyd's stepson, or a mysterious stranger seen lurking about the grounds? This (partial) list suggests some of the incidental interest of Christie's novel, which conveys social and class structures in rural 1920s England. Everyone, as Poirot says, has a secret, and the novel teasingly unveils an illegitimate son, a secret marriage, blackmail, and drug addiction as possible motives for the stabbing.

Red-herrings and dubious alibis abound: the actual time of the murder has been ingeniously concealed, Ackroyd's voice being heard from beyond the grave, recorded on a dictaphone, the disappearance of which provides Poirot with a vital clue. For the reader, deducing the true criminal is almost impossible; this is one of the few detective novels that compels a second reading, to see how the murderer's tracks are so masterfully obscured. **CC**

One, None and a Hundred Thousand

Luigi Pirandello

Lifespan | *b.* 1867 (Italy), *d.* 1936
First Published | 1926, by R. Bemporad (Florence)
Original Title | *Uno, nessuno e centomila*
Nobel Prize for Literature | 1934

Being the object of a friend or relative's close scrutiny may, at times, come as a surprise, especially if the observer is cruelly right in highlighting some of our minor physical imperfections. But for Moscarda, the protagonist of Luigi Pirandello's novel, his wife's unexpected comment about his nose, slightly bent to the right, triggers a sensational change in his life. His wife sees Moscarda totally at variance with his self-image. Moscarda suddenly realizes that he lives with an inseparable stranger and that for others—his wife, his friends, and his acquaintances—he is not at all who he is for himself. Moscarda is forced to live with a thousand strangers, the thousand Moscardas that others see, who are inseparable from his own self and yet whom, dramatically, he will never know.

Pirandello's favorite theme of the relativity of perception and the fragmentation of reality into incomprehensible pieces is his philosophical core. Closely connected to it is the reflection on language and the impossibility of objective and satisfactory communication between speakers, due to the fact that we all charge words with our own meanings. As Moscarda obsesses over the painful realization that he is only what others make of him, he tries to subvert others' reality by reinventing himself as a new, different, Moscarda. But his attempt to possess his own self is in vain, and his only way out is self-denial, starting with a refusal to look at mirrors. **RPi**

Under Satan's Sun

Georges Bernanos

Lifespan | *b*. 1888 (France), *d*. 1948
First Published | 1926
First Published by | Plon (Paris)
Original Title | *Sous le soleil de Satan*

French Catholic writer Georges Bernanos's first novel is a passionate statement of belief, the intensity of which is barely contained within the fictional frame.

The novel opens with the story of Mouchette, a teenage girl in rural France revolted by the hypocrisy and stupidity of her social environment. Among other heinous sins, she murders her rakish lover. Bernanos then introduces his hero, Father Donissan, a clumsy and uncultivated young priest who practices self-flagellation and has a strangely inspirational impact on local people. His extremism is naturally disapproved by the Catholic hierarchy. On a road at night, Donissan tussles with Satan incarnated as a horse dealer. He also encounters Mouchette and recognizes that she is under Satan's power. The girl's subsequent fate involves Donissan in an extreme reaction, which provokes church and secular authorities to unite in diagnosing him as suffering mental illness. By the end of the novel, Donissan has achieved a subtly martyred sainthood.

Bernanos succeeds in endowing these supernatural events with a concrete imaginative reality. His aggressive rejection of the complacent "bourgeois" world has recommended him to many non-believers as a fellow spirit. However, although Bernanos's own political beliefs at one time veered to the far right, his books explicitly deny any connection between an assertion of Catholic faith, even in an almost medieval form, and support for the existing social order. **RegG**

The Good Soldier Švejk

Jaroslav Hašek

Lifespan | *b*. 1883 (Czechoslovakia), *d*. 1923
First Published | 1926, by A. Synek (Prague)
First Published in four volumes | 1921–1923
Original Title | *Osudy dobrého vojáka Švejka*

The Good Soldier Švejk is, in the original, a monumental and unfinished collection (Jaroslav Hašek died before he could complete the last two volumes) of comically epic adventures, involving an accidental soldier in the Austro-Hungarian army during the First World War. The brilliance of the novel depends on the hapless but well-meaning central figure Švejk—walking on the margins of history, yet somehow constantly altering its outcome. This he achieves by doggedly doing precisely what is required of him, while frustrating the system's expectations by being always and entirely himself.

In Švejk, Hašek—who had himself variously been a soldier, dog-stealer, drunkard, and cabaret performer—invented and perfected a fictional type. A prototypical Forrest Gump, Švejk was taken up in Czechoslovakia as a national hero, capable because of his (apparent) artlessness of exposing the assertive lies of power. The batman to a Czech lieutenant, Švejk was dragooned into service for idle remarks uttered in a tavern about the assassination of Archduke Ferdinand. Throughout his adventures, and perhaps because of their multiplicity, it is never clear how much of Švejk's character is calculation and how much wide-eyed innocence. Along the way he manages to attack propaganda, bureaucratic self-servingness, and an all-pervading secret state. **DSoa**

⊙ Illustrator Josef Lada's original images of Švejk's misadventures have imposed his vision of the characters on readers ever since.

Alberta and Jacob

Cora Sandel

Lifespan | *b.* 1880 (Norway), *d.* 1974 (Sweden)
First Published | 1926, by Gyldendal (Oslo)
Given Name | Sara Fabricius
Original Title | *Alberte og Jakob*

The first part of Cora Sandel's "Alberta" trilogy, *Alberta and Jacob* was hailed as a masterpiece by the women's emancipation movement. Set in a small provincial town in northern Norway, the novel focuses on Alberta, a girl from a middle-class family in financial difficulties. Unable to go to school or to go south for the gay social life of the city of Christiania, Alberta has nothing to do but dust and mend, or attend dull social events. The novel probes the stifling emptiness of Alberta's life, her hopes and fears, her secret yearnings and inner rebellion.

The narrative is framed by evocative descriptions of the intense contrasts of Norway's seasons, starting in the constantly dim light of early winter, when Alberta's world shrinks to the confines of her own house. As the days lengthen, rich young people appear in her town, and her world expands and is filled with parties and outings. However, trapped by her sense of unattractiveness and social inadequacy, Alberta stands on the outside of almost all the events, an observer, unable to act. When the days grow shorter again, Alberta is left trapped.

In contrast, Alberta's outgoing and rebellious brother, Jacob, openly fights for his right to go to sea, and eventually manages to escape the family. Finally, as even her outspoken friend, Beda Buck, is forced to conform, Alberta contemplates suicide. But at the last moment she feels the life within her assert itself, and she drags herself home, determined "to live in spite of it all, to live on as best as she could." **CIW**

The Castle

Franz Kafka

Lifespan | *b.* 1883 (Czechoslovakia), *d.* 1924 (Austria)
First Published | 1926
First Published by | K. Wolff (Munich)
Original Title | *Das Schloss*

It stands as testament to the achievements of Franz Kafka that the unfinished state of *The Castle* is in no way detrimental to its effectiveness. Unlike *The Trial* and *The Metamorphosis*, the literal entirety of the story is not contained in the first line; whether this is due to the unfinished nature of the novel is impossible to know, but *The Castle* is certainly a more miasmic, elusive work than even these. In this respect it seems somehow right that there is no ending, that the events recounted seemingly form part of an infinite series, of which a small segment has found its way onto the pages of a novel.

The arrival of the land surveyor K in the village that surrounds the castle, and the discovery that he is not wanted, and cannot stay, constitutes the total narrative, but the progression through the relatively straightforward points is typically nightmarish. Kafka's integration of absurdity and realism is at its most subtle here; events never veer from the apparently literal, but somehow remain totally alien. Despite the apparent fixedness of characters on a page, the feeling of detachment, that everyone is self-consciously playing a part, is inescapable. More than it tells a story, *The Castle* evokes an atmosphere of perpetual unease. There is a suggestion of fear lurking just out of sight, with all else obscured by the interminable obstacles of bureaucracy. The entirety of the novel is akin to that final moment in a dream when you try to speak and find no air to carry your voice, time slowed to a crawl. **SF**

Blindness

Henry Green

Lifespan | *b.* 1905 (England), *d.* 1973
First Published | 1926
First Published by | J. M. Dent & Sons (London)
Given Name | Henry Vincent Yorke

Henry Green was to gain considerable renown as a writer's writer, and all of his novels are in some sense "experimental." His singular prose style inverts conventional word order, utilizes curious parenthetic constructions, deploys unnecessary demonstratives, and omits a whole range of words normally used to connect clauses. Green's first novel, *Blindness*, already reveals his fascination with language as a means of communication and his modernist desire to shape it anew.

The novel tells the story of John Haye, a young man who is accidentally blinded and must learn to live with the loss of vision. Haye gradually comes to realize that there are other ways of processing sensation, experiencing life and construing reality. Haye is preoccupied with the nature of language and with writers who are known as original literary stylists. His interest in the problem of expression marks him out as someone who is not content with the surface aspect of social life; phenomena observed from the outside and accepted as "reality" are shown to be products of a deeper blindness than that which afflicts the novel's protagonist.

Narrated from a range of viewpoints, *Blindness* draws on the technique of "stream of consciousness" for its presentation of different perspectives. Here Green explored the inner world of the mind and suggested that the death of sight perhaps presaged the birth of a more profound form of experience and a deeper mode of knowledge. **AG**

> *"[A] kind of informal diary would be rather fun."*

⊙ Henry Green's novels are often described as being among the most important works of English modernist literature.

The Sun Also Rises

Ernest Hemingway

Lifespan | *b.* 1899 (U.S.), *d.* 1961
First Published | 1926, by C. Scribner's Sons (N. Y.)
Alternate Title | *Fiesta*
Nobel Prize | 1954

The cynical irony of the title—an oblique reference to narrator Jake's mysterious First World War wound, and what no longer rises because of it—sets the apathetic tone for this "Lost Generation" novel. A band of cynical, hard-living expatriates swirls like a hurricane around a comparatively peaceful eye, Jake. In its depiction of the group's journey from *l'entre deux guerres* Paris to Pamplona for July's *fiesta*, *The Sun Also Rises* captures a war-shaken culture losing itself in drink and drama, and eschewing all but the occasionally comforting illusion of meaningful experience. Quixotically irascible, Robert Cohn dramatizes the romantic hero's final crash into absurdity, as he cultivates a disruptive infatuation with Jake's former lover, Brett, who shares neither Cohn's intense affection nor his fraught-with-significance outlook (though she does share his bed).

Ernest Hemingway's first major novel represented a stylistic breakthrough. Though its influence on later writing has slightly obscured its radical character, comparing the style of *The Sun Also Rises* with those more established contemporaries, such as Ford Madox Ford and Theodore Dreiser, gives a sense of Hemingway's innovation. The spare prose creates a language seemingly devoid of histrionics, allowing characters and dynamics to come through cleanly and clearly, to a perhaps still unequaled degree. **AF**

🔾 Hemingway stands with Sylvia Beech outside her bookshop, Shakespeare & Co., a focus for expatriate writers in Paris.

Amerika

Franz Kafka

Lifespan | *b.* 1883 (Czechoslovakia), *d.* 1924 (Austria)
First Published | 1927, by K. Wolff (Munich)
Composed | 1912–1914
Original Language | German

At the tender age of sixteen, Karl Rossmann finds himself in exile, shipped to the New World after shaming his family by getting a serving girl pregnant. Despite being alone and vulnerable in a strange land, he has youthful optimism and irrepressible good humor on his side. Karl sets out to seek his fortune, and finds work as an elevator boy in a hotel. He gets fired and drifts on again, meeting a succession of bizarre characters, and in the final chapter joins a mysterious traveling theater.

This is an unsettling and disorienting vision of America. On arrival, Karl observes the Statue of Liberty holding a huge sword aloft. This and other puzzling details—a bridge across the Hudson conveniently connects New York with Boston—may simply reveal that Franz Kafka never visited America, but they also create a paradoxical world that is fascinating and sinister, boundlessly open and broodingly claustrophobic. Here is a place where success can bring vast wealth and fine mansions, where failure can lead to misery and rootlessness.

Familiar Kafkaesque themes are already developing—the implied threat of nameless authority, the fear of being singled out, the sense of identity slipping away. *Amerika* was never finished, but there is enough to tantalize us into speculating about its conclusion. The final scene, in which Karl heads west on a train through spectacular scenery, is a paean to the American Dream. Was this intended as a Kafka novel with a happy ending? **TS**

The Case of Sergeant Grischa

Arnold Zweig

Lifespan | *b.* 1887 (Poland), *d.* 1968 (Germany)
First Published | 1927
First Published by | Kiepenheuer (Potsdam)
Original Title | *Der Streit um den Sergeanten Grischa*

The Case of Sergeant Grischa is a multi-angled study of the social forces that perpetuate war. Its protagonist, Grischa, is a Russian soldier in the twilight of the First World War who is captured by the German military and imprisoned. Wanting to go to his wife and their child—whom he has never seen—Grischa escapes from the prison in hope of getting to Russia. To conceal his identity, he wears the abandoned clothes of a German soldier found in the forest. He is caught once more, and is believed to be the man whose clothes he is wearing. Grischa suddenly learns that the soldier whose identity he has assumed is known as a deserter, and that the penalty for desertion is execution. The fate of the other man now seems to have him by the throat.

Despite the fact that Grischa is ultimately able to prove his identity and his innocence, he realizes that the soldiers who have understood his situation are so afraid of disobeying orders that they are prepared to execute him regardless. The meaninglessness of Grischa's condemnation comes to represent the wider numbers of innocent men and women killed through war, in battle or otherwise, by soldiers who are merely following orders—men who are not judged, by Grischa, to be good or bad, but to be under the heel of a chain of superiors, each with their own motivations. Zweig's accomplishment as an author is to examine this complex system, almost scientifically, and to draw from his observations a tragic view of morality and human nature. **JA**

"In the whole company of prisoners . . . there were not two who would refuse any request or disobey any order of Sergeant Grischa . . ."

⊙ The cover of the first edition of the book accentuates the fact that the "gripping tale" is written from personal experience.

Tarka the Otter

Henry Williamson

Lifespan | b. 1895 (England), d. 1977
First Published | 1927
First Published by | G. P. Putnam's Sons (London)
Original Language | English

An otter is born, grows up in the waterways of Devon, is hunted by men and dogs as well as facing a number of man-made hazards, and eventually, probably, dies by their hand. This is the essence of *Tarka the Otter*, but it is not its whole. *Tarka* is notable for its lack of anthropomorphic identification and its meticulous, sometimes pedantic, depictions of pastoral life through the eyes of a wild animal.

This is not a comfortable tale of humanized creatures, and it avoids the rural idyll while skillfully exploiting it. Henry Williamson's great strength in this book is the alienation of Tarka, who is, and always remains, feral. This refusal to succumb to personalization, a strong reflection of Williamson's sense of introversion following the First World War, makes *Tarka the Otter* stand apart from its successors. *Tarka* often shows disdain for both human and mechanized intervention; metal and guns are the enemy, providing rude interruptions in the steady life of the Devon waterways. This is not an easy or simple life—Williamson presents it as a neutral space of great pastoralism, yet this space is interrupted continually by man or his creations; traps, wires, and the great hunting dog "Deadlock," who pursues Tarka throughout the text. This disdain for metal and man is testimony to Williamson's post-war disgust with his fellow man, a disillusionment later echoed in his wartime novel *The Patriot's Progress*, and the epic series *The Chronicles of Ancient Sunlight*, which saw him return to the subject of the human world. **EMcCS**

To the Lighthouse

Virginia Woolf

Lifespan | b. 1882 (England), d. 1941
First Published | 1927
First Published by | Hogarth Press (London)
Full Name | Virginia Adeline Woolf

To the Lighthouse was Virginia Woolf's most autobiographical novel, in which she represented her parents, Julia and Leslie Stephen, through the fictional characters of Mr. and Mrs. Ramsay. The novel's structure is that of two days separated by a passage of ten years. In the first part, "The Window," the Ramsay family and assorted guests are depicted during a day on the Hebridean island on which they have their summer home. The novel's central section, "Time Passes," is an experiment in modernist narration, as Woolf absorbed into her fiction the representational forms suggested to her by the new art of the cinema; Mrs. Ramsay dies and the world war intervenes to fracture history and experience. In the final section, "The Lighthouse," the artist figure Lily Briscoe finishes the painting of Mrs. Ramsay whose "vision" had formerly eluded her, and Mr. Ramsay and his two youngest children, James and Cam, reach the lighthouse, having made the journey planned with the first words of the novel.

The novel is a ghost story of a kind, in which Woolf explored the impact of death, representing it indirectly as it resonates throughout the narrative. She reversed the priorities of the novel, bracketing off death and marriage in the novel's central section, and focusing instead on the changes wrought by time on matter. It is a profound exploration of time and memory, of Victorian conventions of masculinity and femininity, and of the relationship between art and what it seeks to record. **LM**

Remembrance of Things Past

Marcel Proust

It has often been said that the importance of Marcel Proust's monumental novel lies in its pervasive influence on twentieth-century literature, whether because writers have sought to emulate it, or attempted to parody and discredit some of its traits. However, it is equally important that readers have enjoyed the extent to which the novel itself unfolds as a dialogue with its literary predecessors.

Remembrance of Things Past (or *In Search of Lost Time*) is the daunting and fashionable 3,000-page "story of a literary vocation," on which Proust worked for fourteen years. In it, he explores the themes of time, space, and memory, but the novel is, above all, a condensation of innumerable literary, structural, stylistic, and thematic possibilities. The most striking one is the structural device whereby the fluctuating fortunes of the bourgeoisie and the aristocracy from the mid-1870s to the mid-1920s are narrated through the failing memories of an aspiring writer, Marcel, who succumbs to many distractions. This defect of memory entails misperceptions of all sorts, partly corrected, bringing rare moments of joy by the faculty of "involuntary" memory. These moments of connection with the past are brought about by contingent encounters in the present, which reawaken long-lost sensations, perceptions, and recollections. It is these moments that give the novel its unique structure, which, no doubt more than any other novel, calls for careful reading.

Appropriately, the publication of this epic novel in French is still evolving, as scholars continue to work on notes and sketches. The novel has also recently attracted new translators into English, long after the first translation into English between 1922 and 1930. Proust's "mass of writing," as it has sometimes been described, continues to expand. **CS**

Lifespan | *b.* 1871 (France), *d.* 1922
First Published | 1913-27 in seven volumes
First Published by | *Nouvelle Revue Française* (Paris)
Original Title | *À la recherche du temps perdu*

A hypersensitive, neurotic asthma sufferer, Proust had many characteristics in common with his novel's fictional narrator.

Proust handwrote his massive masterpiece in school exercise books, endlessly crossing out and rewriting as he went along.

Steppenwolf

Hermann Hesse

Lifespan | *b.* 1877 (Germany), *d.* 1962 (Switzerland)
First Published | 1927, by S. Fischer Verlag (Berlin)
Original Title | *Der Steppenwolf*
Nobel Prize for Literature | 1946

Harry Haller, the protagonist of *Steppenwolf*, feels himself painfully divided into two diametrically opposed personas. One is associated with his intellect and the noble ideals to which he aspires, while the other consists of the baser instincts and desires of the flesh. *Steppenwolf* chronicles this tension that dominates Haller's inner life from three distinct perspectives: his bourgeois landlady's nephew, a psychoanalytic tract, and Haller's own autobiographical account. With the help of some of the novel's other characters, Haller gradually learns that "every ego, so far from being a unity is in the highest degree a manifold world, a constellated heaven, a chaos of forms . . ." He determines to explore the multiple aspects of his being, experimenting with his sexuality, frequenting jazz clubs, where he learns to dance the fox-trot, and socializing with groups of people whom he formerly regarded with condescension and derision. Thus he realizes that these pursuits are to be valued as much as the thrill of intellectual discovery. The highly experimental, perplexing nature of the conclusion goes some way to explaining why *Steppenwolf* is the most misunderstood of Hesse's works.

In addition to a brilliant and thought-provoking meditation on the tumultuous process of self-discovery, *Steppenwolf* is a scathing and prescient critique of the complacency of Germany's middle class amid the escalating militarism that preceded and made possible Hitler's rise to power. **CG-G**

Nadja

André Breton

Lifespan | *b.* 1896 (France), *d.* 1966
First Published | 1928
First Published by | Gallimard (Paris)
Original Language | French

André Breton's *Nadja* is the most well known and most enduring example of the "Surrealist novel." This semi-autobiographical work is an account of Breton's relationship with a strange and unconventional young woman in Paris. Nadja is an enigmatic, haunting presence; she is both material and immaterial, modern and ancient, artificial and carnal, sane and mad. She is a state of mind, a projection that disrupts the structures of everyday reality, a metaphor for "the soul in limbo." Using the figure of Nadja, perhaps rather questionably, Breton channels the key elements of Surrealist thought: accident, shock, desire, eroticism, magic, and radical freedom. The narrative consists of a series of chance encounters around the city, jumping from point to point with its own unconscious logic. Notionally a "romance," *Nadja* is really a meditation on Surrealism as a way of life, overturning the distinctions between art and world, dream and reality.

A literary collage, the prose is supplemented by images, including sketches by Nadja herself, prints of Surrealist paintings, and numerous photographs. *Nadja* is a rich, textured surface of ideas, a repository of what the critic Walter Benjamin calls "profane illuminations." From the mainstream to the avant-garde, and from literature to advertising, *Nadja's* influence continues to be felt. **SamT**

> Breton wearing a crown of thorns. Although not seen here, above is a quote from his Surrealist Manifesto headed "auto-prophecy."

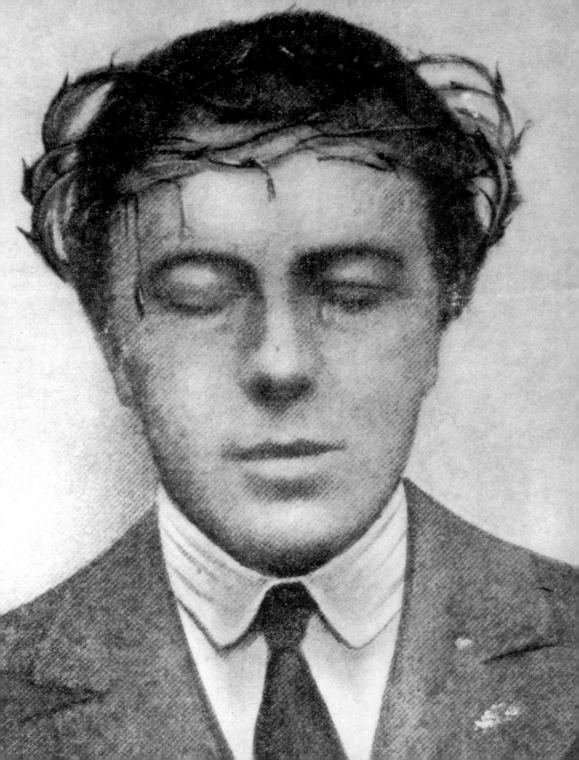

Quicksand

Nella Larsen

> "Authors do not supply imaginations, they expect their readers to have their own, and to use it."
>
> *Nella Larsen, 1926*

Larsen, right, receives a Harmon Foundation award in 1929; like the heroine of her novel, she was a mixed-race woman in a racist world.

Lifespan | *b.* 1891 (U.S.), *d.* 1964
First Published | 1928
First Published by | A. Knopf (New York)
Original Language | English

Helga Crane is the protagonist in Nella Larsen's compelling and loosely autobiographical novel, *Quicksand*. Born of a white Danish mother and a West Indian father, Helga Crane is a restless and rootless figure in search of sexual and social acceptance. The novel begins in the claustrophobic atmosphere of "Naxos," a black college in the South, then moves north, first to Chicago and on to Harlem, where Helga is initially welcomed by the emerging intellectual class. Next she travels to Denmark, where her blackness is celebrated in problematically exotic and erotic ways. In each of these locations, Helga is forced to reject both the proposals of unsuitable lovers, and her own growing desire. In the end, she marries a preacher and returns to the American South, where she sinks into a "quagmire" of harsh reproductive and domestic labors.

The novel is an honest examination of the contradictory promises that twentieth-century America held out to women. Helga Crane is socially vulnerable, yet she is also able to hesitatingly articulate a desire for pleasure and self-fulfillment. The novel makes clear the particular tribulations faced by the "mulatto" woman who can claim no community. The promise of the future is suggested by depictions of the pleasures of urban anonymity and of the relations between gender and desire. But it is this future's utter failure to materialize, and Helga's acceptance of a blind sacrifice in its place, that makes the ending so bitterly damning. **NM**

Decline and Fall

Evelyn Waugh

Lifespan | b. 1903 (England), d. 1966
First Published | 1928
First Published by | Chapman & Hall (London)
Full Name | Evelyn Arthur St. John Waugh

Evelyn Waugh's debut novel, *Decline and Fall*, introduced the world to the acerbic and hilarious style for which he became famous. The story is of the "mysterious disappearance" of Paul Pennyfeather, a young middle-class everyman, into "extraordinary adventures" that are as absurd as they are arresting. The appeal of the book, however, lies not in its plot, but in its relentless and caustic wit, and the biting satire it aims at swathes of British society.

Among the abysses that pepper Paul's "disappearance" are a ludicrous expulsion from Oxford, an appointment as a master at a carnivalesque boarding school in North Wales, an engagement to a wealthy socialite, and a spell in prison. Surrounding the roller-coaster rise and fall of this hapless protagonist are a cast of recurring characters that are intoxicating in their colorful absurdities. From a pedophilic lush with a peg leg, to a "modern churchman" destined to have his head hacked off by a crazed religious visionary, *Decline and Fall* teems with a host of unforgettable characters.

Underneath this incredible abundance lies a not-so-thinly veiled attack on a variety of targets. From the vicissitudes of modern architecture to the moral turpitude of the upper classes, Waugh casts satirical barbs with ruthless accuracy. Although a sense of hopelessness seems to underlie these critiques, it is impossible to criticize the direction of the moral compass of this novel, which remains unremittingly superb in its comic intensity. **DR**

Some Prefer Nettles

Junichiro Tanizaki

Lifespan | b. 1886 (Japan), d. 1965
First Published | 1928
Original Title | *Tade kuu mushi*
Imperial Prize in Literature | 1949

Often compared to Junichiro Tanizaki's own failed marriage and his retreat from Tokyo to the more traditional Osaka-Kyoto region after the great earthquake of 1923, this novel tells the story of Kaname, a man whose own domestic rupture stems from his sensual desire for the Western "other" embodied in a Eurasian prostitute. Meanwhile, his wife, Misako, also eschews her traditional role and turns outward for emotional fulfillment by taking a lover, subscribing to Western ideals of beauty, and listening to jazz. In this seemingly unbridgeable gulf that defines the crisis of modernity, Misako's father, a traditionalist, attempts to resolve the situation by turning the couple inward, back to the classical art forms and Japanese aesthetic values that connect them to a larger inner and historical meaning.

Through the display of *bunraku*, traditional Japanese puppetry, and the precise gestures of the father's geisha, O-hisu, Tanizaki paints an alternate landscape within modern Japan and offers a return to the past as an option for reinventing the present. Through glimpses at theaters, reflections on walks, and an evocation of nature, Tanizaki gestures at a possibility of reconciliation between two people and two traditions. *Some Prefer Nettles* is known as a hallmark of Tanizaki's sparing prose style, a treatise on beauty, and a revaluation of Japanese culture. Above all, it is a meditation on the fragility of relationships, the difficulty of letting go, and the paralysis of indecision. **HH**

Parade's End

Ford Madox Ford

Lifespan | *b.* 1873 (England), *d.* 1939 (France)
Last Volume of Tetralogy Published | 1928
First Published by | Duckworth & Co. (London)
Tetralogy Published as Single Volume | 1950

Ford Madox Ford's gargantuan *Parade's End*, one of many First World War classics, is frequently hailed as the "best war book." This may be because it is both one of the most comprehensive and yet most understated of the war books, using Ford's characteristic modernism to subtly portray a world falling into deceit. Civilian concerns and activities are subtly investigated, as Ford charts the passage of Christopher Tietjen's wartime service and the breakdown of his marriage to the villainous Sylvia.

As with so many of the war books, it is often difficult to separate the author from their fictional counterpart, and Ford, who was blown up and partially deafened by a shell in the trenches while shaving, is no exception. The last of the *Parade's End* books were published slightly before the more aggressive diatribes against war formed a seemingly cohesive voice. As such, Ford's is perhaps a more well-mannered war. Tietjen's shock and lack of comprehension of his circumstances is symptomatic of the confused responses of veterans, and the quartet's impressionist atmosphere adds to this inability to fully comprehend the impact of the war on even one person. Yet Ford's work now stands as a rather dense investigation, and his indirect war message is less clearly received by the present generation, accustomed as it is to a more stereotypical vision of mud, guts, and poppies. "No more hope, no more glory, not for the nation, not for the world I dare say, no more parades." **EMcCS**

The Well of Loneliness

Radclyffe Hall

Lifespan | *b.* 1880 (England), *d.* 1943
First Published | 1928
First Published by | Jonathan Cape (London)
Given Name | Marguerite Radclyffe-Hall

On its publication in 1928, *The Well of Loneliness* prompted one of the most famous legal trials for obscenity in the history of British law, resulting in a twenty-year ban. At the same time, it brought the existence of lesbians to the attention of the public and each other in an unprecedented way.

The Well of Loneliness tells the story of the "invert" Stephen (named by a father desperate for a son) who is painfully aware of her "queerness" from an early age. Following her first love affair, Stephen is thrown out of her beloved family home in the secure and wealthy Midlands, and travels to London and then Paris, becoming a successful writer. Serving with the ambulance corps on the front line in the First World War, Stephen meets and falls in love with a young girl called Mary—the final part of the novel tells the story of their relationship.

For some modern readers, the novel is outdated with its almost gothic melodrama, its nineteenth-century theories of sexual orientation, and its deep pessimism with regard to the fate of those who choose lovers from their own sex. But there are others for whom the novel still strikes a painfully resonant chord. The book's power derives from its unerring and possibly unnerving perception of heterosexual society, and the devastating effects of both its prejudices and its norms. **SD**

> ⏵ Radclyffe Hall published poems and two other novels before *The Well of Loneliness* brought her notoriety.

Lady Chatterley's Lover

D. H. Lawrence

The publication history of *Lady Chatterly's Lover* provides a plot itself worthy of a novel. Published privately in 1928 and long available in foreign editions, the first unexpurgated edition did not appear in England until Penguin risked publishing it in 1960. Prosecuted under the Obscene Publications Act of 1959, Penguin was acquitted after a notorious trial, in which many eminent authors of the day appeared as witnesses for the defense.

Due to this infamous history, the novel is most widely known for its explicit descriptions of sexual intercourse. These occur in the context of a plot that centers on Lady Constance Chatterly and her unsatisfying marriage to Sir Clifford, a wealthy Midlands landowner, writer, and intellectual. Constance enters into a passionate love affair with her husband's educated gamekeeper, Oliver Mellors. Pregnant by him, she leaves her husband and the novel ends with Mellors and Constance temporarily separated in the hope of securing divorces in order to begin a new life together.

What remains so powerful and so unusual about this novel is not just its honesty about the power of the sexual bond between a man and a woman, but the fact that, even in the early years of the twenty-first century, it remains one of the few novels in English literary history that addresses female sexual desire. It depicts a woman's experience of the exquisite pleasure of good sex, her apocalyptic disappointment in bad sex, and her fulfillment in truly making love. As if all this were not enough to mark *Lady Chatterly's Lover* as one of the truly great English novels, it is also a sustained and profound reflection on the state of modern society and the threat to culture and humanity of the unceasing tide of industrialization and capitalism. **SD**

Lifespan | *b.* 1885 (England), *d.* 1930 (France)
First Published | privately in 1928 (Florence)
First English-Language Publication | 1932
Published by | M. Secker (London)

Penguin's jacket for the first 1960 edition bears the emblem of the phoenix, which beckons to Lawrence's *Phoenix Essays*.

Eager purchasers of *Lady Chatterley* look for the dirty bits after the obscenity trial that cleared the book for sale in Britain in1960.

Orlando

Virginia Woolf

Lifespan | *b.* 1882 (England), *d.* 1941
First Published | 1928
First Published by | Hogarth Press (London)
Original Language | English

For a demonstration of the sheer vitality of Virginia Woolf's writing, *Orlando* is unsurpassed. The novel is a provocative exploration of gender and history, as well as of the nature of biography itself; perhaps surprisingly, given these highly intellectual concerns, it was highly popular when first published.

Following Orlando over a 400-year life full of adventure, love, and a shift in gender, the character was apparently based on Woolf's lover, Vita Sackville-West. In the court of Elizabeth I, Orlando is a dazzlingly handsome sixteen-year-old nobleman. There follows a frost fair on the Thames, at which a love affair with a Russian princess begins, only to end in heartache. Later Orlando is sent by Charles II as ambassador to the Ottoman court in Constantinople, where he becomes a woman, before returning to England to reside in the company of Pope and Dryden. A marriage in the nineteenth century leads to a son and a career as a writer, and the story ends in 1928, as Woolf's text was published.

This extraordinary tale is augmented by a series of writerly flourishes, questioning our conception of history, of gender, and of biographical "truth." If these are constructs, then who constructs them? What do they mean for individuals living and telling their lives? Woolf uses a series of devices to facilitate this kind of speculation: clothes are prominent, as is their role in shaping perceptions of gender; the narrative voice, too, is brilliantly conscious of itself, and of us as readers. It is a remarkable text. **MD**

"Better was it to go unknown and leave behind you an arch, than to burn like a meteor and leave no dust."

⬤ Aristocratic bisexual novelist Vita Sackville-West was the model for the character of the androgynous Orlando in Woolf's novel.

Story of the Eye

Georges Bataille

Lifespan | *b*. 1897 (France), *d*. 1962
First Published | 1928
Original Title | *Histoire de l'oeil*
Pseudonym | Lord Auch

This classic of literary pornography also happens to be a significant surrealist novel. Georges Bataille—French librarian, sometime Marxist thinker, and literary critic—also wrote a classic, non-fictional study of eroticism. *Story of the Eye* synthesizes traditions of French literary-pornographic writing, abandoning the complications of libertine plotting or the notorious encyclopedia of body parts and orifices associated with de Sade. Bataille instead offers a quicker, more associative kind of pornographic dream. There are sexual acts and various defilements, but Bataille's erotic novel is as much dominated by death, language, and literary analysis as it is by action. Here we have pornography, but pornography for intellectuals.

Told in the first person, this short novel's plot moves between fantasies and the subsequent acting out of various erotic obsessions involving an array of objects, ranging from a cat's saucer to an antique wardrobe. The story invests more meaning in objects than in characters, while narrative situations emerge as rhetorical conceits linking objects to contexts in a string of metaphorical displacements, characteristic of literary Surrealism. Bataille's prose poetics, however, have a stringency and clarity very different from the arbitrary reverie characteristic of other Surrealists. Overall, the novel is rounded off by Bataille's remarkable analysis of the book's confessional account of coincidences between memories and obscene images. **DM**

Retreat Without Song

Shahan Shahnoor

Lifespan | *b*. 1903 (Turkey), *d*. 1974 (France)
First Published | 1929
First Published by | Tparan Masis (Paris)
Original Title | *Nahanje arhants ergi*

Retreat Without Song first appeared in serialized form in the Parisian daily *Haratch*, to violent protests from the newspaper's mainly Armenian readership. Shahan Shahnoor's critics objected to what they regarded as the novel's pornographic character, to the perceived distortion of Armenian values, and to the defeatist tone predominating in the descriptions of the Armenian diaspora. The writer, then barely twenty-six years old, almost lost an eye in a brawl with disapproving co-nationals.

For anyone reading Shahnoor's novel today, it is hard to see what could have provoked such upheaval. Bedros is a young Armenian who makes a living in Paris as a fashionable photographer. As is common in artistic circles, he has a rapidly changing sequence of girlfriends, all actresses, models, or singers. This rhythm is interrupted when two women enter his life: Madam Jeanne, or Nenette, the woman he loves, and little Lise, the girl who loves him. Caught in the thoroughly Parisian lures of the one, and careful to spare the innocence of the other, Bedros finds his way back to an unadulterated self, more oriental in its passion and depth.

Even though it takes up most of the narrative, the love story functions as a backdrop for the fate of exiles who are parted from their previous existence and their families. Little by little, their non-European selves and national identity succumb to the assimilating pressures of European sophistication until little remains but café patriotism. **MWd**

GAUMONT DISTRIBUTION présente un Film de MELVILLE-PRODUCTIONS

Une Réalisation de **JEAN-PIERRE MELVILLE**

Les Enfants Terribles

d'après le Roman célèbre de

JEAN COCTEAU

avec **NICOLE STEPHANE, EDOUARD DERMITHE**

RENÉE COSIMA, JACQUES BERNARD

MEL MARTIN, MARIA CYLIAKUS, JEAN-MARIE ROBAIN, MAURICE REVEL, ADELINE AUCOC, RACHEL DEVYRIS

et

ROGER GAILLARD

Les Enfants Terribles

Jean Cocteau

Lifespan | *b.* 1889 (France), *d.* 1963
First Published | 1929, by Grasset (Paris)
Alternate Title | *Children of the Game*
U.S. Title | *The Holy Terrors*

Les Enfants Terribles is a claustrophobic tale of love and attraction transformed into jealousy and malice, a comment on the potentially destructive and unstable nature of human relationships that was written in the wake of discoveries about the unconscious inaugurated by Freud and others. The book can also be read as a child's nightmare. Virtually all the story takes place within one room, after the book's famous opening scene when Paul, a sensitive young man, is injured by a snowball thrown by the sexually charismatic bully, Dareglos, with whom he is infatuated. He is forced to take to his bed in the cluttered and oppressive room that he shares with his sister, Elisabeth. Here they play a series of games, alternately arguing and making up. When Elisabeth brings Agathe to stay with them, Paul develops a crush on her because of her resemblance to Dareglos, which inflames Elisabeth's jealousy.

Many find the novel's portrayal of damaged and obsessive adolescence prophetic of the roles played out by young Europeans and Americans after the Second World War. Paul and Elisabeth have few connections with life outside, retreating into a fantasy world in which they consume each other with their over-heated emotions and unrestrained needs. They are simultaneously tragic figures who stand for the fate of humanity and irritating, immature youths whose behavior is both comic and ridiculous. Cocteau also wrote the screenplay for Jean-Pierre Melville's celebrated film (1950). **AH**

"Wealth is an inborn attitude of mind, like poverty. The pauper who has made his pile may flaunt his spoils, but cannot wear them plausibly."

◉ This portrait of Cocteau is by Picasso, one of a galaxy of cultural superstars with whom he was associated in the course of his career.

◉ In Melville's 1950 movie of Cocteau's novel, Nicole Stéphane and Edouard Dermithe played the over-intimate siblings.

Berlin Alexanderplatz

Alfred Döblin

Lifespan | b. 1878 (Poland), d. 1957 (Germany)
First Published | 1929
First Published by | S. Fischer Verlag (Berlin)
Original Language | German

"This awful thing which was his life acquires a meaning."

⬥ Phil Jutzi directed a successful movie version of the novel in 1932; it was made into a TV serial by Rainer Fassbinder in the 1980s.

Berlin Alexanderplatz ranks alongside the work of James Joyce and John Dos Passos both as one of the great urban epics of the 1920s and as an attempt to innovate the novel genre. Utilizing a montage style that owes much to cinema, the novel is as much about a place as it is about a "story."

At one level, the novel can be thought of as a morality tale; its main protagonist is the ex-convict Franz Biberkopf, and his vain attempt to become a "decent" human being. Biberkopf is an archetypally naïve "little man," around whom the playful narrator constructs a complex narrative of crime, temptation, and betrayal. Franz attempts a variety of jobs, loses his arm in a bungled robbery, becomes a pimp, falls in love, and is finally betrayed and framed for murder by his nemesis, Reinhold. Alfred Döblin populates working-class eastern Berlin with a memorable cast of shady underworld characters, and is wonderfully sensitive both to the rhythms of their speech and to the patterns of their lives.

However, the novel is chiefly remembered for its style. The narration incorporates and evokes the sensations of the city, and suggests a sense of the speed, contrasts, and bewildering simultaneity that define it. In a conscious rejection of traditional conceptions of the novel, the multilayered narrative gives free rein to the competing discourses of the metropolis. The reader is greeted with newspaper reports, exchanges between random characters, advertising hoardings, street signs (literally, in the form of illustrations), and lines from popular songs. Additionally, biblical and classical allusions suggest, again in playful manner, Döblin's desire to create a modern epic. The effect is exhilarating, and what one initially assumes will simply form the setting—the city of Berlin—becomes the star of the show. **JH**

All Quiet on the Western Front

Erich Maria Remarque

The epigraph of *All Quiet on the Western Front* states that the intention of the book is to be neither an accusation nor a confession, but an account of a generation, including the survivors, "destroyed by the war." But rather than a warning, or even a statement of self-defense, this epigraph, marked by its simplicity and clarity, is a one-sentence declaration, however quiet, that what follows is a story of destruction.

In the polarized political debates of the Weimar Republic, the First World War was not a topic but a touchstone for all else. How you understood the war, its origins, its conduct, surrender, and defeat, was the index to your understanding of the past and to your understanding of how liveable or damaged the future could be. Given this interpretive context, the pacifism of the novel could satisfy neither left nor right ends of the critical spectrum in inter-war Germany. But Erich Remarque's text does not assume or argue for pacifism; it simply enacts it as an appalled response to the daily efficiencies of organized slaughter. It is this quiet, certain, yet exploratory demonstration of the utter inhumanity of war that constitutes the magnificence of *All Quiet on the Western Front* as an anti-war novel.

Central to Remarque's achievement is the voice of Paul Bäumer, the novel's nineteen-year-old narrator. He is one of a band of front-line soldiers whose experience of war strips the mythology of heroism bare, leaving the tedium, the earth-shaking fear, the loneliness, and the anger of men whose bodies are neither protected nor honored by military uniforms. The novel ends with the disappearance of Bäumer's voice; it is replaced by the polite brevity of the report of his death on a day in which all was quiet on the Western front. **PMcM**

Lifespan | *b*. 1898 (Germany), *d*. 1970 (Switzerland)
First Published | 1929, by Propyläen (Berlin)
Original Title | *Im Westen nichts Neues*
Given Name | Erich Paul Remark

"One could sit like this forever . . ."

⬙ Lew Ayres starred as Paul Bäumer in the well-regarded 1930 movie version of *All Quiet on the Western Front*.

The Time of Indifference

Alberto Moravia

Lifespan | *b.* 1907 (Italy), *d.* 1990
First Published | 1929, by Alpes (Milan)
Original Title | *Gli indifferenti*
Given Name | Alberto Pincherle

Alberto Moravia's early masterpiece, produced when he was eighteen, was written after the murder of Matteotti, who openly opposed Mussolini in parliament, when the Fascist regime enjoyed popular consensus. Although the work does not contain explicit references to the Italian political situation, the story of a middle-class family, depicted as helpless victims of the corruption of their social entourage, clearly has a political message.

The central motif highlights the inadequacy and incapacity of the characters to deal with reality, marked by an indelible and congenital weakness. Mariagrazia, her son, Michele, and daughter, Carla, although afflicted by a serious financial crisis, keep up appearances and carry on a life of ostentatious bourgeois wealth. Slowly but inexorably they drift toward a miserable end. Michele, the central character, is oblivious to the dramas around him, indifferent to a reality that is disintegrating before his eyes. He is painfully unable to play by the social rules of his class, or find the moral energy to react and rebel against them. He tries to eliminate Leo, his mother's—and later his sister's—loathsome lover, but (farcically) his gun is not loaded. With this novel, Moravia commenced his long-term investigation into the human condition. He went on to pursue the themes of conformism, contempt, and tedium as he portrayed the limitations of a social class at the end of its historical trajectory, yet profoundly unable to renovate and transform itself. **RPi**

". . . it also seemed to her, because of some fatalistic taste for moral symmetries, that this almost familial affair was the only epilogue her life deserved."

After his precocious debut in 1929, Alberto Moravia remained a prominent figure in Italian cultural life for over half a century.

Living

Henry Green

Lifespan | *b.* 1905 (England), *d.* 1973
First Published | 1929
First Published by | J. M. Dent & Sons (London)
Given Name | Henry Vincent Yorke

By any standard, Henry Green was a precocious writer. He began his first novel, *Blindness*, while at school, and completed it while still a student. His next novel, *Living*, was published in 1929, before his twenty-fifth birthday. It is the story of a working-class community in Birmingham, or rather, a story about the self-expression of that community in the largest sense, with "expression" considered both as the inventiveness of colloquial and workplace speech, and as the optimistic social or antisocial behavior of working people.

Partly because it is a story about expression and not simply about people's lives, Green took on the challenge of finding a prose style through which the difficulties of expression could be expressed. As a result, this is Green's most linguistically adventurous novel, and readers may at first find themselves baffled by the omissions of definite articles and the strange disappearance of nouns. The prose reads jerkily, as though it had been composed under the duress of an artificial word limit and constrained to skip the decorum of grammar. However, Green did not intend to imitate the lives of workers; rather, he aimed to evoke—through the atmosphere of grammatical compression—the economy of expectations and desires characteristic of the working-class community, and the dependence on simplicity of self-expression. Green conveys this effectively and movingly, allowing his narrative to carry the constrained language along with it. **KS**

I Thought of Daisy

Edmund Wilson

Lifespan | *b.* 1895 (U.S.), *d.* 1972
First Published | 1929
First Published by | Scribner (New York)
Original Language | English

Edmund Wilson is remembered mainly as an influential literary critic and editor (he worked at both *Vanity Fair* and *The New Yorker*) who was among the first to recognize the emerging talent of writers such as Vladimir Nabokov and Ernest Hemingway. However, like many—if not most—critics and editors, he always aspired to be a writer.

I Thought of Daisy is only barely fictional; the story is really a thinly disguised *roman à clef*. It starts out by following the anonymous narrator as he returns to New York from a long stay in 1920s Paris. He quickly falls in love with both the literary scene in Greenwich Village and one of the scene's most talented writers, the poet Rita. The character Rita is, in fact, based on Edna St. Vincent Millay, who in 1923 became the first woman to win the Pulitzer Prize for Poetry, and with whom Wilson had a short-lived affair. In the book, the affair falls apart as the narrator becomes disillusioned with left-wing, Modernist values. Deciding that his life lacks a moral core, he returns to an old mentor from his college days, Professor Grosbeake. The Professor leads him toward a less cerebral approach to life, which in turn leads him to fall in love with the titular Daisy, an all-American chorus girl.

The book's significance is widely thought to lie in the way it attempts to bring Proustian sensibilities to bear on the American literary scene. Given Wilson's stature as a literary critic, this attempt was to have lasting influence. **PH**

A Farewell to Arms

Ernest Hemingway

Lifespan | *b.* 1899 (U.S.), *d.* 1961
First Published | 1929
First Published by | C. Scribner's Sons (New York)
Nobel Prize for Literature | 1954

A Farewell to Arms is set in Italy and Switzerland during the First World War. The very sparse and unadorned style of Ernest Hemingway's narrator, Frederic Henry, provides a realistic and unromanticized account of war on the Italian front and is typical of the writing style that was to become the hallmark of Hemingway's later writing. Henry's descriptions of war are in sharp relief to the sentimental language of his affair with Catherine, an English nurse he meets while recovering from an injury in Turin.

The novel has been particularly praised for its realistic depiction of war; this has often been attributed to personal experience. However, while there are strong autobiographical elements in the novel, Hemingway's combat experience was more limited than that of his protagonist. He did work as an ambulance driver on the Italian front, but for the Red Cross and only for a few weeks in 1918. Hemingway also fell in love with a nurse, Agnes von Kurowsky; but, unlike Frederic Henry, Hemingway's advances were subsequently rebuffed.

A Farewell to Arms established Hemingway as a successful writer and also as a spokesman of "The Lost Generation," a group of American intellectuals who lived in Paris in the 1920s and 1930s and whose outlook—shaped by the experience of the First World War—was cynical and pessimistic. **BR**

◅ Gary Cooper, star of the 1932 movie of *A Farewell to Arms*, refreshes his knowledge of the book during a break in filming.

Passing

Nella Larsen

Lifespan | *b.* 1891 (U.S.), *d.* 1964
First Published | 1929
First Published by | A. Knopf (London & New York)
Original Language | English

Nella Larsen's novel explores the complexities of racial identity in early twentieth-century New York. Its central character, Irene Redfield, is a member of the African-American bourgeoisie that became increasingly fashionable and visible in New York during the Harlem Renaissance era of the 1920s. Irene is married to a doctor and dedicates her life to charitable and social causes. However, her accidental meeting with childhood friend Claire Kendry—who has concealed her mixed parentage in order to assume a white identity—serves to reveal the insecurities and anxieties that lie beneath this seemingly complacent and comfortable life.

At its most obvious, the novel offers a satire of the mores, pretensions, and ambitions of the Harlem Renaissance. The novel's main concern is with exploring the consequences of Claire Kendry's deliberate subversion of early twentieth-century America's stridently enforced desire for racial purity, which both confounds and demonstrates its power. Claire has married a wealthy, racist white American and many of her subsequent actions—from bearing his child to introducing him to Irene—involve the risk that her "true" identity will be revealed. Larsen explores this difficult territory, which is fraught with assumptions about authenticity, purity, and knowledge, by skillfully providing the reader with a silhouette of what cannot be said. In the end, it seems that Irene's own deep ambivalence about Claire is the most dangerous and unstable force of all. **NM**

Look Homeward, Angel

Thomas Wolfe

"Men will often say they have 'found themselves' when they have really been worn down into a groove by the brutal and compulsive force of circumstance."

◉ Thomas Wolfe is revered in the United States for his lyrical invocations of American life in the early twentieth century.

Lifespan | *b.* 1900 (U.S.), *d.* 1938
First Published | 1929, by Grosset & Dunlap (N.Y.)
Full Title | *Look Homeward, Angel: A Story of the Buried Life*

On one level, *Look Homeward, Angel* is a portrait of the artist as a young man writ large, with the action transferred to a small but affluent hill town in North Carolina. Thomas Wolfe is no modernist, however, and lacks Joyce's subtle, ironic touch and Flaubertian control of his material. Yet in these shortfalls lie his distinct qualities, for instead he gives us sheer exuberant expression. Wolfe is an old-fashioned writer in the tradition of Whitman and Melville; he "tried the hardest to say the most," wrote Faulkner, who considered him the greatest writer of his generation, as well as the "best failure."

The narrator is budding artist Eugene Gant, an idealistic young man governed by an active imagination and a yearning for transcendence. Yet he is incapable of belief in the conventional idea of God, and equally unable to shake off a firmly held determinist view of the human condition. Eugene's growth from infancy to early manhood is a journey characterized by his quest for self-knowledge and his resultant loneliness and frustration. The real quality of the novel, however, lies not in the portrayal of Eugene's struggle to find a place in the world, but in the rich, vivid account of the life that surrounds him. At the heart of the family saga lies a compelling tension between Eugene's parents; his father is a heavy-drinking, womanizing, yet lovable man, while his mother is practical and hard-working, keeping their family of ten afloat despite her husband's hell-bent intention to destroy it. **AL**

The Maltese Falcon

Dashiell Hammett

Lifespan | *b.* 1894 (U.S.), *d.* 1961
First Published | 1930
First Published by | A. Knopf (London & New York)
First Serialized in | *Black Mask* magazine, 1929

Along with Raymond Chandler, Dashiell Hammett is more or less synonymous with the change in the detective story from the model of the master detective trying to solve the apparently insolvable crime to a more "everyday" approach. This change was evidently influenced by factors such as the rapid growth of urban space, big business, and corruption, all of which seem to characterize the era following the First World War in North America.

Taking a broad scope, Hammett introduces throughout his work a number of different protagonists, a series of locations both real and fictional, and very "open" descriptions. Hammett's style revels in increasingly convoluted plotting of its crimes, favoring an apparently endless series of twists and turns, in contrast to Chandler's all-enveloping miasma of corruption.

Hammett's character Sam Spade is only one in a series of detective protagonists. Spade moves through a violent, sleazy world, where the characters are all selfish, two-timing double-crossers. Spade is as prone to strokes of insight and masterfulness, in the vein of Sherlock Holmes or Dupin, as he is to brawling, cussing, and outbluffing thugs. Above all else, *The Maltese Falcon* mirrors this composite nature; it is at heart a fusion of detective stories, where elements from the reverential past of the genre meet scenes of action and adventure, played out in a world where reverence is only going to get you either robbed or killed. **SF**

Her Privates We

Frederic Manning

Lifespan | *b.* 1882 (England), *d.* 1935
First Published | 1930 by P. Davies (London)
Original Title | *The Middle Parts of Fortune*
Pseudonym | Private 19022

The uncensored (and original) version of this novel, called *The Middle Parts of Fortune*, is rumored to have come about when the publisher, Peter Davies, locked his recalcitrant and inebriated author in his study and demanded he write a war novel before he was released. During the War Books Controversy, a series of novels were published that irrevocably altered the way the war was depicted in literature; this is one of the most lucid of these graphic, uncompromising, and scandalous texts.

Frederic Manning's novel was originally published in two volumes under his army serial number: Private 19022 (his name did not appear on the spine until 1943). In contrast to the officer-experience theme that became popular through the writing of Graves, Sassoon, and Blunden, Manning's semi-autobiographical text follows the life of Private Bourne: drunk, freeloader, and raconteur. It is perhaps this emphasis on the lower ranks of the army that has led to the continued success of the book, alongside concentration on the mundanities and discomforts of trench life. Unlike the more dynamic constructions of the other war books, ostensibly very little happens here, concerned as it is with the aftermath of battle and the gradual preparation for another attack, in which most of Bourne's companions are killed. In this way, *The Middle Parts of Fortune* is a far more accurate depiction of wartime life and one that still has the potential to subvert the war experience. **EMcCS**

The Apes of God

Wyndham Lewis

Lifespan | *b.* 1882 (Canada), *d.* 1957 (London)
First Published | 1930
First Published by | Arthur Press (London)
Original Language | English

◉ The front cover of the first edition features a striking depiction of one of the artistic "Apes" Lewis satirizes in his novel.

◗ This self-portrait by Lewis, painted in the early 1920s, conveys the satirical aggression that he brought to his writing.

A monstrous, exhaustive, and, some would argue, exhausting work of English modernism, Wyndham Lewis's *The Apes of God* has an exuberant, infectious energy nevertheless. The novel is a satirical group portrait of the artistic pretensions of London upper-class society during the 1920s, a period described by Lewis as "the insanitary trough between the two great wars." The book's critique is specifically aimed at the self-delusions of the "art world" and those who think they live in it. With hints of Pope and Swift, Lewis reworks the standard features of eighteenth-century satire, reveling in physical exaggeration, building up some characters to mock heroic heights, and reducing everything else to absurdity. However, Lewis goes farther than simply reheating 200-year-old satire by inventing a fresh and unusual prose style—almost a Cubist reinvention of fiction—to support his belief that art must do more than passively ape existing forms.

The book follows an impressionable young innocent, Dan Boleyn, as he is guided by his mentor, Horace Zagreus, on a voyage through London's gallery of pseudo-artists—the "Apes" of the title—who subject him to confusing, misleading diatribes on the meaning and practice of art. Once the reader becomes accustomed to Lewis's unique style, the plot gathers pace, as the various characters are assembled at Lord Osmund's Lenten party. Lewis's satire engages physical and ideological prejudices with a zest that is hard to condone, not least the continual racist, especially anti-Semitic, and sexist stereotyping. If it is often difficult to like Lewis's severity and the limited space it leaves for humans to distinguish themselves from apes of ideology, there is nevertheless plenty to relish in his style and his satirical provocations. **DM**

Monica

Saunders Lewis

Lifespan | *b.* 1893 (Wales), *d.* 1985
First Published | 1930, by Gwasg Aberystwyth
Given name | John Saunders Lewis
Original Language | Welsh

Saunders Lewis's novel *Monica* is a frank and poignant portrayal of sexual obsession and the shortcomings of a relationship based on physical passion. Monica is a sexually frustrated young woman, shut away in the family home taking care of her sick mother. When Monica's outgoing sister, Hannah, brings home a fiancé, Bob, Monica is overcome with jealousy and lust. She encourages Bob's secret attraction to her, until Hannah catches them kissing and Monica and Bob are forced to leave town to get married.

Throughout, the reader is aware of Monica dissembling, from her claim that her nighttime walks around the city streets were not aimed at catching a man, to her contention that she did not break up the relationship between Hannah and Bob. At last, when falling pregnant removes the sexual attraction that binds Bob to her, Monica begins to see her own behavior in a different light.

Lewis's novel has been considered one of the earliest existential novels—even the first—as Monica's soul-searching leads her to realize that "her vacuous fantasies had been a veil between her and the nothingness of existence." The novel was accused of immorality for its openness about sex, prostitutes, and venereal disease, and because of the author's apparent objectivity. But to the modern reader, the novel seems explicitly moral; Monica despairs and meets her death, and Bob catches venereal disease after one night of infidelity. **CIW**

Insatiability

Stanisław Ignacy Witkiewicz

Lifespan | *b.* 1885 (Poland), *d.* 1939 (Ukraine)
First Published | 1930, by Dom Ksiazki Polskiej
Pseudonym | Witkacy
Original Title | *Nienasycenie*

Described by Czesław Miłosz as "a study of decay; mad, dissonant music, erotic perversion," *Insatiability* is Stanisław Witkiewicz's second novel and his diagnosis of the state of Poland before the Second World War. Poland has become a military dictatorship, staffed by cynical, pleasure-seeking aristocrats: morally vacant, intellectually decadent, and doomed. But Poland is also Europe's last firewall before a truly insatiable enemy, the horde of Chinese Communists that has already overrun Russia. The Chinese owe their invincibility to Murti-Bingism, a mystical cult whose followers take a pill inducing contentment, passivity, and obedience.

The novel's hero, Baron Genezyp Kapen, is a handsome and vital young officer, greedy for experience and adventure. But he cannot reconcile himself to life's earthy realities. His erotic initiation by the aging but magnetic Princess di Ticonderoga leaves him both fascinated and repelled by sex. Stripped of both his romantic and political illusions, Genezyp begins a series of infatuations and assaults that culminate in his murder of his bride—a virginal aristocrat and dedicated Murti-Bingist—on their wedding night. Genezyp's decline into madness parallels Poland's submission to Chinese invasion and the chemical panacea of Murti-Bing

Genezyp's combination of naive lust and disgust for reality foreshadows the crises of existentialism, and—like many of Witkiewicz's works—*Insatiability* greatly influenced the Theatre of the Absurd. **MuM**

The Waves

Virginia Woolf

Lifespan | *b.* 1882 (England), *d.* 1941
First Published | 1931
First Published by | Hogarth Press (London)
Given Name | Adeline Virginia Stephen

The Waves, though Virginia Woolf's most experimental piece of writing, is nevertheless endlessly rewarding. It shares many of the preoccupations of her other novels: experiments with time and narrative; the representation of lives in biographical writing; and the unfixing of identities. It also pushes the "stream of consciousness" in new directions: becoming an exploration of the relationship between inner life and the "impersonal" elements of waves and water, rather than a narrative technique.

Woolf uses the time span of a day to explore the temporality of a life, or lives—the movement of the waves defines the passage from dawn to dusk and provides a structure for the novel. It was conceived as "prose yet poetry"—the six selves of the novel are represented by "dramatic soliloquies," and interspersed with "poetic interludes" that describe the passage of the sun across the sky and the rhythms of the tide.

The Waves traces the six lives from childhood to middle age, but seeks to show continuities rather than developments. "We are not single," as Bernard (the novel's chief chronicler) remarks. The characters speak their thoughts as separate entities, rarely in dialogue, yet the novel brings them together by listening in at synchronous moments in their lives and by regrouping them at various stages. *The Waves* is concerned with the experience and articulation of identity through a fascinating discourse that cannot be named either as speech or as thought. **LM**

"I have outlived certain desires; I have lost friends, some by death—Percival—others through sheer inability to cross the street."

◉ The cover for the first edition of Woolf's poetic novel was designed by the novelist's elder sister, the painter Vanessa Bell.

To the North

Elizabeth Bowen

Lifespan | *b.* 1899 (Ireland), *d.* 1973 (England)
First Published | 1932
First Published by | Constable & Co. (London)
Original Language | English

With its manically driven characters, consumed by a new age of locomotion, and a plot that is hurled forth by car, bus, and plane, Elizabeth Bowen's mid-career novel offers startling insights into the effects of technological acceleration on the fabric of everyday lives. From the opening setting (in a house on the Abbey Road before a "funnel of traffic and buses"), to the narrative's apocalyptic climax, Emmeline Summers seems knowingly committed to the most destructive uses of travel, ever hurdling stability in favor of the unknown. This willing attraction to peril leads to her surrender to the sadistic Mark Linkwater—an escape from one form of domestic claustrophobia to a relationship at best glacial, at worst insufferably cruel. Her sister-in-law Cecilia finds herself suffocated with a similar inevitability, which only serves to highlight "how precious had been her solitude."

Bowen invites the reader into a denatured realm, conveying the most intimate consequences of mechanization on her protagonists as they become gradually estranged from one another. *To the North* anticipates the fallout of modernity's love affair with the machine, evoking the sinister reification of transport as an inherently positive force. Stylistically, too, the novel's austere timbre complements this pattern of encroachment. The book's impersonal narrative voice seems to impersonate the harmful pressure of mechanical networks on the basis of human will. **DJ**

The Thin Man

Dashiell Hammett

Lifespan | *b.* 1894 (U.S.), *d.* 1961
First Published | 1932
First Published by | A. Barker (London)
Movie Adaptation Released | 1934

At the center of what marks out *The Thin Man* from the mass of hard-boiled fiction is the detective, or in this case, detectives. The investigator of old, the Sam Spade or Marlowe, is defined solely in negative relief by the crimes he deals with; when there is no crime, he is reduced to near invisibility, returned to the office, waiting for the phone to ring and bring the next case. In contrast to this, the investigators of *The Thin Man*, Nick and Nora Charles, are not only married, but married to each other, with a beloved schnauzer in tow, and the vibrancy of their social life is clearly detailed. They are far removed from the mythical solitaries of conventional film noir investigation, living it up in a luxury hotel room, and attending glittering parties as a backdrop to the case they are working on.

What Dashiell Hammett clearly realizes is that the corruption he sees as characterizing America is at work everywhere, in every space and strata of society, and is represented as such. This is a novel where the deception, mistaken identity, and extreme narrative convolution of the genre do not form the entire world, but are moved beyond its parameters, juxtaposed with social and personal relationships. It must be seen as marking the culmination of Hammett's writing, where the world of the cynical meets the vibrant American fantasy city of F. Scott Fitzgerald. **SF**

❯ A Pinkerton Agency detective before he became a writer,
  Dashiell Hammett looked like a character from his own novels.

Journey to the End of the Night

Louis-Ferdinand Céline

Lifespan | *b.* 1894 (England), *d.* 1961 (U.S.)
First Published | 1932, by Denoël & Steele (Paris)
Original Title | *Voyage au bout de la nuit*
Given Name | Louis-Ferdinand Destouches

Journey to the End of the Night is a groundbreaking masterpiece that has lost none of its startling power and ability to shock. Loosely autobiographical, the first-person narrative traces the experience of the young narrator, Bardamu, from being a twenty-year-old volunteer in the army at the start of the First World War to becoming a qualified doctor at the beginning of the 1930s. During this period, he has a nervous breakdown, travels to Central Africa and the United States, then returns to France to complete his medical studies. The novel is characterized by a brash, vibrant, gritty prose, a deeply sardonic wit, and scathing cynicism. Still lyrical and eloquent throughout, it is full of slang, obscenities, and colloquialisms. Bardamu has an uncompromisingly bleak view of humanity—"mankind consists of two very different races, the rich and the poor," he claims—and although he is mostly concerned with the latter he has little but contempt for both. All we can be sure of is pain, old age, and death. From such an unpromising outlook, however, Céline extracts incredible humor that never ceases to entertain.

The influence of Céline's original, anarchic, and corrosive novel is inestimable; William Burroughs was a noted admirer. In Céline's mordant view of lowlifes we can see an obvious precursor to Beckett's pessimistic antiheroes. This book is vital to our understanding of the development of the novel. **AL**

> *"Love, Arthur, is a poodle's chance of attaining the infinite, and personally I have my pride."*

Céline's darkly comic masterpiece is a savage attack on patriotism, colonialism, and life in general; this is the jacket of a 1935 edition.

The Return of Philip Latinowicz

Miroslav Krleža

Lifespan | *b*. 1893 (Croatia), *d*. 1981
First Published | 1932
First Published by | Minerva (Zagreb)
Original Title | *Povratak Filipa Latinovicza*

After twenty-three years of absence, Philip Latinowicz returns home. The idea of return disturbs the progression of this novel, making its narrative move in several directions at the same time. Miroslav Krleža sustains the temporal complexity of the novel by writing in a strikingly visual manner, a mode that is reflected in the fact that the main character is an accomplished painter, who thinks about his art incessantly. At the beginning of the novel, however, Philip's experience of life is as isolated, fragmented, and alienated as his own past. Philip never knew his father, and during his childhood his mother was a cold, distant figure, who eventually turned him away from home after he stole some of her money and spent a feverish night in a brothel.

The novel is shockingly candid in its portrayal of sex and physicality. Ultimately, however, it is not sensuality that redeems Philip, but his art. As the novel progresses, Philip is able to reestablish his artistic vision, especially through his relationship with Bobochka, femme fatale and former wife of a minister, who is stranded in the provinces with the man she once ruined. And yet art has limited powers—even though Krleža in the end rebuilds his main character, Philip's return to life is effected through an almost ritual slaying (one suicide, one murder) of characters that could neither conform nor escape the confines of provincial morality. **IJ**

The Radetzky March

Joseph Roth

Lifespan | *b*. 1894 (Ukraine), *d*. 1939 (France)
First Published | 1932
First Published by | G. Kiepenheuer Verlag (Berlin)
Original Title | *Radetzkymarsch*

The Radetzky March ranks as one of the finest European historical novels of the twentieth century. In evoking a specific milieu—the provinces of the Habsburg Empire during its final years of ceremonial grandeur and political instability—the text draws in part on Joseph Roth's childhood at the empire's periphery and on memories of a supranational pride in an almost abstract conception of "Austria." The prototypically Austrian march of Strauss the Elder recurs as a leitmotif in the narrative, symbolizing tradition, order, and belonging—qualities that are gradually lost as the infrastructure of the Empire begins to crumble.

When Lieutenant Trotta saves the life of the Emperor at the battle of Solferino, he becomes the "Hero of Solferino." Neither he nor the generations that follow are able to live up to the expectations his legend creates. His grandson, Carl Joseph, is an undistinguished soldier who feels most at home in the borderlands of Galicia, in which parochial definitions of both nationality and identity seem irrelevant. Carl Joseph's death during the First World War represents not so much a personal tragedy as the end of an era. This novel explores the complexities of family and friendship, translating a sense of nostalgia for a lost age into an unsentimental historical narrative. The atmosphere of imperial Austria has rarely been so convincingly and lovingly evoked. **JH**

The Forbidden Realm

J. J. Slauerhoff

Lifespan | *b.* 1902 (England), *d.* 1990
First Published | 1932, by Nijgh & Van Ditmar
First Serialized in | Forum
Original Title | *Het verboden rijk*

The works of Dutch poet and novelist J. J. Slauerhoff are a late flowering of the decadent Romantic tradition, with the artist cast as an alienated outsider futilely wandering the face of the Earth—a role Slauerhoff literally fulfilled through a career as a ship's surgeon. Innovative in technique and original in its imaginative conception, *The Forbidden Realm* dramatizes the author's uncomfortable relationship with himself and the late imperialist world.

The novel tells the stories of two men separated by centuries of history. One is the sixteenth-century Portuguese poet Camões, a seafaring bard of empire. The other is a nameless wireless operator on a contemporary merchant ship, an obvious alter ego for the author. The two men's lives develop a strange mirroring: the wireless operator is shipwrecked, as Camões had been, and then travels to the Portuguese colony of Macao, where Camões spent years of exile. The wireless operator ends up alone in Macao undergoing a total loss of identity that he welcomes as a liberation from his hated self.

The Forbidden Realm belongs alongside Conrad's *Heart of Darkness* as one of the novels of the agony of colonialism, the disintegration of European self-confidence and morals in an alien environment. But it is a disintegration that Slauerhoff embraces rather than deplores. The novel is short on characterization and its plot sometimes wanders, but Slauerhoff's identification with his subject gives it a haunting, hallucinatory quality. **RegG**

Cold Comfort Farm

Stella Gibbons

Lifespan | *b.* 1902 (England), *d.* 1990
First Published | 1932
First Published by | Longmans & Co. (London)
Femina Vie Heureuse Prize | 1933

Cold Comfort Farm is a viciously funny novel and by far the most famous of Stella Gibbons's numerous works. Published in 1932, it is a parody of the rural novel, and in particular the work of Mary Webb, but also of many writers now considered part of the canon of great "English literature."

It tells the story of Flora Poste, a young London socialite who finds herself confronted with a long-estranged branch of her family, the Starkadders, after her parents' death. The novel is peopled with a cornucopia of fantastic characters, from the brassiere-collecting Mrs. Smiling, to the tiresome Mr. Mybug, and the wonderful menagerie that is Cold Comfort Farm itself. The Starkadders are a truly remarkable creation, from Judith's obsession with her son, the smoldering Seth, to Elfine's wildness and the sermons of Reuben—and, of course, that something nasty in the woodshed. Far from being intimidated by the stern rusticity of her new location and family, Flora sets about transforming them, one by one, and the scenes that these various processes encompass are, without exception, delightful.

The targets of *Cold Comfort Farm*'s biting satire range from the social machinations of Austen to the melodramatic doom of Hardy and the overblown romanticism of Lawrence. The irreverence and sheer wit of the book are endlessly engaging. **DR**

◗ Gibbons, photographed a half-century after writing *Cold Comfort Farm*, was a prolific author who had no other major success.

Brave New World

Aldous Huxley

Aldous Huxley's futuristic dystopia depicts a world in which state power has grafted itself so thoroughly and so effectively to the psyche of its citizenry that the boundaries of exploitation and fulfillment seem irremediably blurred. The World State's professed ideal of social stability has been achieved through the proliferation of consumption and myriad sophisticated technologies. These include the State's monopolistic manufacture of human beings, enforced by making contraception mandatory and promiscuity a virtue. Each of five hierarchically arranged social castes undergoes its own complex pre- and post-natal conditioning to encourage self-satisfaction. The desire for unattainable social mobility within the lowest castes is eradicated, allowing the controlling upper class to maintain its power.

This hybridized philosophy of the World State draws on aspects of Plato's stratified Republic, and utilitarianism's focus on the concept of "happiness." The State facilitation of no-strings-attached pleasure may strike some readers as counterintuitive, given the vehemence with which sexuality is marketed today as the ultimate expression of individuality. Yet the uncoupling of sex from taboo and reproduction dismantles its emotional significance, which aids the World State in eliminating all private allegiances that do not contribute to tightening its stranglehold. In the end, the indiscriminate cultivation of what we might consider "adult" pursuits like drugs and sex renders them completely innocuous. For the childlike denizens of *Brave New World*, order is an end in itself, codified by the organized consumption of goods and services. But it is their conviction that they have been successful in achieving the fullest expression of human aspiration that should give contemporary readers everywhere the deepest shudder of recognition. **AF**

Lifespan | *b.* 1894 (England), *d.* 1963 (U.S.)
First Published | 1932
First Published by | Chatto & Windus (London)
Inspired by | *Men Like Gods* by H. G. Wells (1921)

The bold jacket design for the first edition of *Brave New World* reflects the author's dystopian vision of fractured futurity.

Huxley in 1935: his rejection of technological materialism led him later to embrace mysticism and consciousness-expanding drugs.

Vipers' Tangle

François Mauriac

Lifespan | *b.* 1885 (France), *d.* 1970
First Published | 1932, by Bernard Grasset (Paris)
Original Title | *Le nœud de vipères*
Nobel Prize for Literature | 1952

"Ask those who know me . . . why, malevolence is my leading characteristic!"

Mauriac regarded human passions as counter to his religious beliefs—the hope of salvation lay in overcoming them.

The snakes in the title of François Mauriac's novel *Vipers' Tangle* (also known as *The Knot of Vipers*) refer both to the tangled and vicious emotions in the heart of its narrator, Louis, and to the struggles and machinations of his grasping family, with whom he is locked in a seemingly never-ending combat. No one is guiltless in this text, which has been called the "classic example" of the Catholic novel.

Set in Paris and the beautiful vineyard country surrounding Bordeaux, the novel takes the form of a two-part confession, written by Louis as he lies dying from heart disease, describing the progressive decline of his family relationships toward what appears to be certain tragedy. Mauriac's novel is a skillful examination of the devastating effects of societal disapproval and the resulting insecurity of the sensitive human soul. Louis, wounded early in his marriage by what he perceives to be the disregard of his new wife and her family, embarks on a self-defensive campaign of cruelty that inevitably spreads from his wife through his children and eventually to his grandchildren, poisoning his family life through several generations.

For Mauriac, however, this coldly-calculated suffering—horrible as it is—serves to suggest the possibility of Louis's salvation. As he confesses his transgressions to the reader, Louis is forced to consider the feelings and motivations of others, gradually leading to a change of heart that is all the more moving because of its origins. Written in spare, elegant prose, *Vipers' Tangle* is a novel that deftly exposes the seemingly limitless and infectious spread of the effects of a cruel action, but also holds out the possibility of eventual redemption and peace, offering, at the end, a moving portrait of both divine mercy and human fallibility. **AB**

The Man Without Qualities

Robert Musil

Although Robert Musil's unfinished, multivolume novel, *The Man Without Qualities*, is a staggering 2,000 pages long, it is written in short, digestible chapters, and amply repays the reader willing to invest the time. It was undoubtedly Musil's most important body of work and is frequently ranked in the same stratum as the masterpieces of Marcel Proust and James Joyce. It is considered a definitive portrait of fin-de-siècle Austrian society, as well as of the political situation leading to the outbreak of the First World War and the end of the Austro-Hungarian empire.

Considering the novel's length, Musil's plot is surprisingly insubstantial. Ulrich, the protagonist, is a trained mathematician who lacks any purpose in life. He is being pushed by his father to find a useful place in society; Musil reminds us that just because a man has no "qualities" of his own, it does not mean that his family and friends will not try to impose their own qualities on him. Ulrich consistently fails to make any progress in this quest for societal standing, and instead he catches a succession of new lovers in the way that one catches successive colds. Through the intervention of his father, he joins the *Parallelaktion*, an attempt to find a suitable way of celebrating the sixtieth anniversary of the emperor's reign. The deliberations of the planning committee, in their utter vacuity, reflect the wider vacuity at large. Ulrich finally forms an incestuous relationship with his sister, Agathe, and enters into a different plane of existence, which has variously been labeled as opening the door to totalitarianism, or as an immoralist critique of totalitarian rationalism.

Whatever the judgment, Musil's style is unique and mesmerizing, and the novel is nothing short of the embodiment of an entire philosophy. **DS**

Lifespan | *b.* 1880 (Aust.-Hungary), *d.* 1942 (Switz.)
Last Completed Volume Published | 1933
First Published by | Publikationsvermerk (Zurich)
Original Title | *Der Mann ohne Eigenschaften*

"Ultimately a poem, and the mystery of it, cuts the meaning of the world clear . . ."

◉ Musil lived through the collapse of the Austrian Empire and the rise of Nazism, which forced him into exile after 1938.

Cheese

Willem Elsschot

Lifespan | *b.* 1892 (Belgium), *d.* 1960
First Published | 1933, by P. N. Van Kampen & Zoon
Given Name | Alfons-Jozef de Ridder
Original Title | *Kaas*

Willem Elsschot is the pseudonym of Alfons-Jozef de Ridder, the head of a successful advertising business who wrote his bestselling novels and short stories secretly in his spare time. Elsschot considered *Cheese*, written in less than a fortnight, to be his masterpiece. It is the tragicomic tale of a fifty-year-old clerk, Frans Laarmans, who decides to leave the job he has held for decades and go into the cheese business. Laarmans's obsession with what people think of him dictates his every move, from whether to sit or to stand at his mother's deathbed to his ill-fated venture into business.

Ignored by friends of his new acquaintance, the lawyer Van Schoonberg, Laarmans seeks to improve his status by accepting Van Schoonberg's offer to establish him in the cheese business. Laarmans throws himself into the details of setting up his office, ordering the right stationery, and deciding on a name for his enterprise. But when the first large batch of Edam arrives, he is taken by surprise and has no idea what to do with the cheese. Laarmans's hopelessly inadequate attempts to succeed in a business he knows nothing about, selling a product he finds disgusting, are related with masterly comic pacing and understated pathos. In prose often so laconic as to appear artless, Elsschot has created a convincing portrait of the 1930s, from the status-obsessed middle classes to the desperate people applying to be cheese salesmen, as well as a succinct satire on the perils of social climbing. **CIW**

Man's Fate

André Malraux

Lifespan | *b.* 1901 (France), *d.* 1976
First Published | 1933
First Published by | Gallimard (Paris)
Original Name | *La condition humaine*

In the 1930s, André Malraux was the quintessential politically committed intellectual. *Man's Fate*, winner of the Prix Goncourt in 1933, belongs firmly to that heroic period of revolutionary politics, before a full understanding of the horrors of Stalinism diminished wholehearted left-wing commitment.

The book is set amid the complex political upheavals that rocked Shanghai in 1927—from a Chinese Communist insurrection to the repression and massacre of the Communists by their supposed allies, the Nationalist Guomindang. Malraux deploys personal knowledge of China and of the workings of international communism to good effect. His characters are endowed with complex inner lives, especially the political assassin Ch'en, haunted by a sense of alienation generated by his murders. Yet each character perhaps too clearly exemplifies a particular attitude to life and the revolution.

The climactic moment of the book has the Communist agent Katow, in the hands of Guomindang torturers, compassionately pass his cyanide suicide pills to two terrified Chinese prisoners and accept with unwavering courage an agonizing death in the boiler of a steam train. Such heroics mark *Man's Fate* as, in essence, an intellectual version of a boys' action-adventure story. It is hardly the profound examination of the human condition that Malraux intended, but, packed with dramatic incident and powerfully evoked detail, it remains a highly readable and informative period piece. **RegG**

A Day Off

Storm Jameson

Lifespan | *b.* 1891 (England), *d.* 1986
First Published | 1933
First Published by | Nicholson & Watson (London)
Full Name | Margaret Storm Jameson

Having "a day off" from working in the gritty, impersonal, urban world of Storm Jameson's interwar fiction scarcely affords any kind of lasting consolation or reprieve from everyday toil. Haunted by the "gaunt Yorkshire valley" from whose memory she seeks distraction in the "colored dusty circus of London," the pitiable heroine shifts about the streetscape clutching at chance re-encounters that rekindle the flame of past relationships. Over the course of one afternoon's wandering London's commercial West End, events resolutely testify to all that this woman cannot possess in her own domestic isolation—mean, cramped, and perpetually on the brink of psychological exhaustion. Jameson shadows her with a sense of crystalline immediacy, referring to this character anonymously with "she" and "her": abstracted pronouns complementing the alienation this woman feels unrelievedly at the bustling heart of that world-metropolis.

Jameson advocated a new, central role for the social novelist as a silent witness, for whom stylistic economy should always prevail over needless embellishment. In *A Day Off*, it is her depersonalized commentary that so pervasively implicates the reader, constantly testing the reader's capacity for empathic comprehension of the protagonist's inner world. Jameson makes us continually aware of our implied position as observers participating in her heroine's futile quest for belonging. **DJ**

Testament of Youth

Vera Brittain

Lifespan | *b.* 1893 (England), *d.* 1990
First Published | 1933, by V. Gollancz (London)
Full Title | *Testament of Youth: An Autobiographical Study of the Years 1900–1925*

Vera Brittain quickly became the spokesperson of her generation for this emotive account of her experiences in the First World War, during which all of her close male friends—brother, fiancé, and best friend—were killed in combat.

At first it might seem odd that a female pacifist should produce the definitive literary account of the First World War, until Brittain's forward-thinking perspectives are considered. During the rethinking of the First World War in the 1960s, Brittain's writing appeared to reflect perfectly the changing attitudes to war, which correlated more with the Peace Movement than the ideals of 1914–18. *Testament of Youth* collects all the ideas of the war "mythology," imaginatively presenting "the pity of war," the Lost Generation, and the idea that after 1918 nothing was ever the same again. Historical detail is then combined with these highly charged, emotive perceptions. Her intention was to inform a generation who still lacked the tools to describe war. But *Testament of Youth* has been instrumental in encouraging a negative perception of the war as unrelentingly grim, especially in the latter stages of the twentieth century, when the role of women during wartime was given greater attention. As an active participant who served in the Voluntary Aid Detachment, and as a woman, Vera Brittain brings a valid alternative perspective to the "horror of the trenches." Her evolution from naïve patriotism to disillusion is compelling. **EMcCS**

The Autobiography of Alice B. Toklas

Gertrude Stein

Lifespan | *b.* 1874 (U.S.), *d.* 1946 (France)
First Published | 1933, by J. Lane (London)
First U.S. Publisher | Harcourt Brace & Co. (N.Y.)
Original Publication Source | *The Atlantic Monthly*

"I like a view but I like to sit with my back turned to it."

⊙ Gertrude Stein (left), her companion, Alice B. Toklas, and dog Basket photographed at the author's French home in the 1940s.

⊙ Stein's image is posthumously reinterpreted by Andy Warhol as part of his 1980 series *Ten Portraits of Jews of the 20th Century*.

This is Gertrude Stein's best selling and most accessible work. An "autobiography" written in the voice of her long-time companion, it is a work of sublime modernism, experimenting with voice and point of view, the nature of objectivity, and, above all, a superlative act of unabashedly unreliable narration.

Alice, or Gertrude, claims to have met only three geniuses in her life; the foremost, of course, is Gertrude herself. This is an astonishing claim, considering that the women's lives crossed with virtually every great and influential figure of the early twentieth century. Stein was at the forefront of modernism, arguably its midwife. Her atelier on the Rue de Fleurus in Paris was the centerpoint of art and ideas at a time when, in the mornings, you could choose between buying a new Gauguin or a pot of jam. Picasso and his varying wives are ever-present, as is the young Hemingway. Juan Gris also wanders in, puppy-dogging Picasso. Guillaume Apollinaire (who coined the term "Surrealism") is an intimate, and Jean Cocteau, Lytton Strachey, Erik Satie, Ezra Pound, and Man Ray—to name a mere few—make appearances. It is a delirious time, and this ringside account by an unreliable witness, with all its various contradictions, paradoxes, and repetitions, is captivating. Gertrude was there as den mother to the birth of Cubism and the Fauves. She nurtured a renaissance of letters, was there for the birth of Dadaism, and when the Futurists came to town. She was also there when Nijinsky first danced *Le Sacre du Printemps* and created a scandal.

This is a mischievous act of ventriloquism, capturing the breathless, slightly dotty rambling of Alice, companion to the wives of geniuses. But, like the couple themselves, there is very little of Alice and a whole lot more of Gertrude. **GT**

Murder Must Advertise

Dorothy L. Sayers

Lifespan | *b.* 1893 (England), *d.* 1957
First Published | 1933
First Published by | V. Gollancz (London)
Adapted for Television | 1973

In *Murder Must Advertise*, Dorothy L. Sayers sends her private detective hero Lord Peter Wimsey into an advertising agency to investigate the death of one of its employees. Wimsey, working under the alias Death Bredon, adopts with gusto the role of a copy writer, as he uncovers a plot involving a cocaine-dealing ring. The chief pleasure of the novel is its vivid realization of the advertising world, for which Sayers drew on her own years of experience as a copywriter. Sayers, like Joyce, was entranced by this language of persuasion, which allowed her fascination with word games full play, yet discomforted by a culture that had recourse to the easy slogan. "Advertise, or go under," are the last words of the novel.

Advertising, too, becomes the means through which the drug dealers operate, so that Sayers is able to intertwine her detailed depiction of the office world with her detective plot. Wimsey (the name fully intended to conjure up "whimsy") is a chameleon figure in this as well as Sayers's other detective novels. He is a monocled and rather effete aristocrat with shades of P. G. Wodehouse's Bertie Wooster, a champion cricketer and athlete, and a detective whose involvement with crime and death is part of a moral universe. Sayers, for all her wit and whimsy, rarely lets her readers forget that the discovery of the murderer, at the heart of the detective novel's game, was at that time shadowed by the state hangman's noose. **LM**

Miss Lonelyhearts

Nathanael West

Lifespan | *b.* 1903 (U.S.), *d.* 1940
First Published | 1933, by Liveright (New York)
First Translation | French, 1946
Given Name | Nathan Weinstein

Miss Lonelyhearts, the male protagonist of Nathanael West's novel, answers newspaper readers' despairing questions about how to handle their lives, which range from the mildly amusing to the genuinely grotesque. Known around town as a male "Dear Abby," Miss Lonelyhearts feels emasculated. The vast chasm between his ambivalent aspirations to Christianity and the Depression-weary hedonism of 1930s New York, precludes him from offering anything more than the feeblest clichés to inspire his readers. He would like to offer a vision of meaningful living through the redemptive power of Christ, but is silenced by his editor, Shrike, who mocks religious belief and sarcastically recommends alternatives such as art, sex, and drugs. Miss Lonelyhearts's own behavior throughout the novel swings between extremes. He makes halfhearted attempts to stabilize his life—for example, through a marriage proposal to his dependable girlfriend, Betty (whom he then avoids for weeks)—but also engages in ridiculously ill-advised escapades, including personal involvement with his readers.

The protagonist's lack of empathy for his readers exposes his failure to emulate Christ, while the extent to which suffering believers are able to confess their darkest secrets and fervent requests in the prayer of their letters is diminished to a function of the journalism market. *Miss Lonelyhearts* is an interesting examination of the problematic role of Christianity in the modern world. **AF**

Call it Sleep

Henry Roth

Lifespan | *b.* 1906 (Ukraine), *d.* 1995 (U.S.)
First Published | 1934
First Published by | R. O. Ballou (New York)
Original Language | English

Long overlooked until it was reissued in the 1960s, at a time when issues of cultural identity were highly prominent in American life, *Call it Sleep* is now widely recognized as one of the masterpieces of twentieth-century American fiction. The novel is an exuberant, visceral portrait of a slum childhood and the immigrant experience in New York's Lower East Side at the start of the century. It is written from the perspective of the developing consciousness of David Schearl, a young Jewish boy recently arrived from Austria-Hungry with his mother to join his previously settled father. The novel charts the early years of his childhood as he learns to live in a foreign culture and deal with his personal fears, troubling family relationships, and challenging social adjustments. A key element of the narrative is the drastic change between speaking Yiddish and English, the associated problems of assimilation, and being caught between two cultures. This is reflected in the combination of gritty urban realism and a modernist focus on consciousness. Henry Roth's virtuoso prose brilliantly captures the child's confused but magical view of his strange surroundings and constant fear.

One of the most authentic, moving accounts of childhood terror in literature, *Call it Sleep* is a poignant, lyrical, and compelling tale of a child's rude awakening to a radically new world and an essential contribution to our understanding of American social history. **AL**

The Street of Crocodiles

Bruno Schulz

Lifespan | *b.* 1892 (Austria-Hungary), *d.* 1942
First Published | 1934
First Published by | *Rój (Warszawa)*
Original Title | *Sklepy Cynamonowe*

In this collection of short stories, Bruno Schultz reworks memories of his childhood in Drohobycz, Galicia, into a series of labyrinthine narratives that bring together the captivatingly prosaic and the fancifully absurd. The dilapidated decadence of his home in Market Square—with countless rooms let to lodgers and countless more left unoccupied and forgotten for months on end—serves as the backdrop for his recollections of an unconventional upbringing by an indolent mother and disengaged father.

The lengthy and convoluted "lectures" delivered by his mentally wandering father to bemused but intrigued household audiences, appear to anticipate many of the concerns of postmodernism. And, while the lectures progressively degenerate in terms of their own internal coherence, they function as a unifying narrative thread that is picked up at various points in the stories. Throughout the book, Schultz depicts his father's failing mental and physical health, and the impact that this has upon the family; however, the gentle comedy with which he does so allows an unsentimental realism to sit congenially alongside a rather more surreal sensibility.

Schultz was influenced by Surrealism and Expressionism and as such can rightly be considered alongside writers such as Gogol and Kafka. A Polish Jew, he was killed by the S.S. in 1942. He left only two published collections of stories, which, until recently, have not received the widespread attention and critical acclaim they richly merit. **JW**

Thank You, Jeeves

P. G. Wodehouse

Lifespan | *b.* 1881 (England), *d.* 1975 (U.S.)
First Published | 1934
First Published by | H. Jenkins (London)
Full Name | Sir Pelham Grenville Wodehouse

"I just sit at a typewriter and curse a bit."

P. G. Wodehouse, 1956

🔹 The comic butler, a stock figure in fiction, reaches its supreme realization in Wodehouse's most famous creation, Jeeves.

People seem not to know how to read Wodehouse. Readers tend to see him as a comic writer and expect jokes—but there are none, just as there is little as regards an engaging plot or interesting characterization. P. G. Wodehouse is now somewhat unfashionable, as the world that he created, an everlasting midsummer England untouched by either of the World Wars, peopled with characters endowed with the psychology of a prepubescent, has long gone—even in the realms of fantasy. The reactionary politics of his novels have not stood the test of time. However, to go to Wodehouse for politics, plot, characterization, or jokes is to miss the sheer wonder of his prose. He was a writer of fine and peerless talent whose literary creativity spoke to a popular audience in a way that no other novelist could. His ability to weave from nothing a supremely comic metaphor or simile is still unmatched in the novel form.

He is of course most famous for the *Jeeves and Wooster* series (of which *Thank You, Jeeves* is the first full-length novel). The condescending butler Jeeves had appeared in short stories since 1917. Wodehouse was to have great success with Jeeves in the novel form, but the plots of the novels are practically indistinguishable from one another. The stories seem to turn upon Jeeves' dislike of Wooster's clothing or music. Wooster always seems to get mistakenly engaged to someone frighteningly serious and intelligent, whereupon he is then victim to the violent suitor whose place he has usurped. All such events will be set in train by the unpleasant combination of purple socks and red cummerbund, or ownership of a stolen cow creamer. Floating serenely on the surface of all this silliness, though, is Wodehouse's utterly inimitable prose. **VC-R**

Tender is the Night

F. Scott Fitzgerald

F. Scott Fitzgerald is recognized as the ultimate chronicler of the American post-war boom and Jazz era, drawing on his own life to describe the extravagant nonstop, alcohol-fueled party of the pre-Depression years. *Tender is the Night* sold well and was generally well received, attracting praise from Fitzgerald's peers, Ernest Hemingway among them.

Set in the 1920s, the book tells the story of beautiful eighteen-year-old movie star Rosemary Hoyt, who is on holiday with her mother on the French Riviera when she meets Dick Diver, an American psychologist, and his wealthy wife, Nicole. Nicole had been abused by her father, commited to a sanitarium, and subsequently rescued by her doctor, who is now her husband. Entering their sophisticated, high-society world, Rosemary falls in love with Dick, and he with her. They are blissfully happy for a while, but tragedy soon strikes when a friend of the Divers kills a man in a drunk-driving accident, and Nicole has a nervous breakdown. At this point in the novel, the Divers's idyll disintegrates as a series of unfortunate events begins to unfold.

This is Fitzgerald's most autobiographical work, drawing on his own experiences living with the expatriate fast set in the south of France. The Divers were based on Gerald and Sara Murphy, a glamorous American couple that he and his wife Zelda knew. The novel also features the same sort of psychological treatments that the schizophrenic Zelda sought in Switzerland; the high costs of the treatment drove Fitzgerald away from novel writing and into the life of heavy drinking and Hollywood screenwriting that led to his early death. And, unlike the novel, real life doesn't have a happy ending—in contrast to Nicole, Zelda never recovered, remaining institutionalized until her death in 1948. **EF**

Lifespan | *b*. 1896 (U.S.), *d*. 1940
First Published | 1934
First Published by | C. Scribner's Sons (New York)
Revised Edition Published | 1948

"If you're in love it ought to make you happy."

The first-edition cover reflects the beauty of *Tender is the Night*'s Riviera setting, with no suggestion of the book's darker themes.

Tropic of Cancer

Henry Miller

Lifespan | *b.* 1891 (U.S.), *d.* 1980
First Published | 1934, by Obelisk Press (Paris)
First Published | 1961
Original Language | French

⊘ Like many other American artists and writers between the wars, Miller found Paris both morally liberating and usefully cheap.

❯ The actress Maria de Medeiros in the movie *Henry & June*, based on the romance between Anaïs Nin and Henry Miller.

Henry Miller's infamous autobiographical novel was first published in the 1930s by the risqué Parisian press Obelisk. Because of its sexually explicit themes and language, the book was banned for the following thirty years in both America and Britain. When it was finally published, in America in 1961 and in the UK in 1963, the novel gained cult status. In the book, Miller explores the seedy underbelly of Paris, where he lived as an impoverished expatriate in the 1930s, with a unique sensuality and freedom. Unshackled by moral and social conventions, Miller peppers his book with philosophical musings, fantasies, and a series of explictly described anecdotes about his sexual encounters with women.

The novel is, as Samuel Beckett remarked, "a momentous event in the history of modern writing," and undoubtedly did much to break down societal taboos about sex and the language used to talk about sex. The novel inspired the Beat generation, whose rejection of middle-class American values led to a search for truth through the extremes of experience. However, feminist critics, most notably Kate Millet, have identified the irrepressibly misogynistic character of the work. Women are frequently represented as passive and anonymous receptacles, whose only role is to satisfy men's physical desires. It is certainly true that the sheer violence of Miller's prose overshadows any putative eroticism or titillation that the novel's reputation may lead the reader to expect.

Although Miller's work has achieved great popularity, this is perhaps a result of his reputation as a writer of "dirty books" rather than as a writer of good literature, and, indeed, there has been a good deal of critical disagreement about the "literary" quality of his work. **JW**

The Postman Always Rings Twice

James M. Cain

Lifespan | *b.* 1892 (U.S.), *d.* 1977
First Published | 1934
First Published by | A. Knopf (New York)
First Adapted for Screen | 1946

This pulp masterpiece is a doomed gothic romance, an account of the grim conditions of life in Depression-era California. Cain asks to what extent his protagonists, Frank and Cora, are able to act independently of the larger sexual, political, and economic forces that appear to determine their lives. Frank's self-knowledge is severely limited; although he would like to see himself as unattached and free, he quickly becomes embroiled in a passionate and destructive relationship. Cora's *petit-bourgeois* aspirations involve murdering her "dirty" Greek husband and thereby "inheriting" his roadside café. Bereft of all morality and even any sense of self, Frank readily agrees to assist Cora in her plans. On a clifftop road they ply Cora's husband with alcohol, place him in his car, and dispatch him to his death.

As Frank and Cora turn on each other, both are placed at the mercy of the law, which is shown to be even more amoral and skewed than the two lovers. The novel's ending underlines the extent to which human existence, and indeed happiness, is both fleeting and arbitrary. Though *The Postman* was filmed three times, Cain's cinematic influence extends well beyond this, and it is hard to imagine the Coen brothers, for example, without him. **AP**

🔘 John Garfield carries bikini-clad actress Lana Turner off Laguna Beach in the 1946 movie adaptation of the novel.

On the Heights of Despair

Emil Cioran

Lifespan | *b.* 1911 (Romania), *d.* 1995 (France)
First Published | 1934, by Editura "Fundatia pentru Literatura si Arta" (Bucharest)
Original Title | *Pe culmile disperarii*

Written at twenty-two years old, after months of debilitating depression accompanied by insomnia, *On the Heights of Despair* is more a cry than a work of philosophical reflection. In sixty-six short essays, sometimes only a paragraph long, with suggestive titles such as "On Not Wanting to Live," "The World in Which Nothing is Solved," "On Individual and Cosmic Loneliness," "Ecstasy," and "The Beauty of Flames," Emil Cioran explores topics such as futility, irrationality, and the downright agony of existence.

This series of poignant ruminations functions as a stay in the narrator's seeming drive toward suicide, a death wish that is, paradoxically, a result of too much plenitude: "I could die of life." The solution lies in confession—one is driven to expression by necessity. Writing, as life, is the contrary of systematic thought. A philosopher turned poet therefore writes to mislead, not to organize understanding but to expose its sordid underbelly, the relentless, dull affair of day-to-day existence. In the course of such a shift from philosophical (un)concern to poetic expression, this "drama" opens up paradoxes, which offer, in turn, a kindly region in which it is possible to live both earnestly and ironically. Despite being an ostensibly gloomy book about the merits of life and suicide respectively, *On the Heights of Despair* is tinged with a most unlikely humor that cherishes, above all, life's incomprehensibility. **IJ**

The Bells of Basel

Louis Aragon

Lifespan | *b*. 1897 (France), *d*. 1982
First Published | 1934
First Published by | Denoël et Steele (Paris)
Original Title | *Les Cloches de Bâle*

"Love is made by two people, in different kinds of solitude."

⊙ Aragon photographed in 1920: he was then a Surrealist, but in the 1930s committed himself to communism and social realism.

❯ Aragon is number 12 in Max Ernst's depiction of the Surrealist group in 1922; André Breton is 13, and 15 is the artist De Chirico.

Despite its title, most of the action of Louis Aragon's *The Bells of Basel* takes place in Paris. The title is more than appropriate, however, because it is the passionate and fiery last chapter, set in Basel, Switzerland, at the 1912 International Congress Against War, that gives the novel its emotional and political energy; telling us, in effect, how to interpret its earlier depictions of life in bourgeois Paris.

The Bells of Basel focuses on two strong female characters whose lives are loosely connected: Diane de Nettencourt, the elegant, seemingly amoral wife of the financier Brunel and mistress to the capitalist automobile magnate Wisner; and Catherine, a beautiful Georgian emigrée torn between her bourgeois upbringing and a rising consciousness of social injustice. Through the lives of Diane and Catherine, Aragon paints a picture of pre-war Paris society as corrupt, depraved, and desperately cynical, where human relationships function as a mere façade for the more important ebb and flow of capitalist profit and loss. Aragon sets this scene against the background of a humane workers' movement that is in the process of gradually gaining in both consciousness and militancy, culminating in the congress in Basel and the appearance of the middle-aged communist character Clara. In this heroine's revolutionary posture and unapologetically militant stance, so different from the manipulative beauty of Diane and Catherine, Aragon triumphantly discovers the modern woman.

The tone throughout most of the novel is sardonic and understated, yet *The Bells of Basel* ends on a note of touching faith in human progress. If the rot at the heart of French society is unsparingly documented in the novel, so, too, are the tools required to transform it. **AB**

The Nine Tailors

Dorothy L. Sayers

Lifespan | *b.* 1893 (England), *d.* 1957
First Published | 1934
First Published by | V. Gollancz (London)
Full Name | Dorothy Leigh Sayers

The Nine Tailors reaches beyond Sayers's earlier work in its scope and ambition, creating a rich cast of characters in a vividly realized setting. The action takes place in a Fenland village and is centered on the parish church, Fenchurch St Paul. While the closed community setting is typical of the "Golden Age" detective fiction of the 1920s and 1930s, Sayers does not succumb to cozy and comfortable Englishness, instead depicting a rural world shadowed by secrecy and guilt, and a desolate landscape, whose flooding has deliberately Biblical overtones. The novel also uses campanology, or bell ringing, in highly ingenious ways, as regards both structure and content, interweaving with it the detective plot and its subsequent unravelling.

Unfortunately, Sayers never completed her biography of the nineteenth-century writer Wilkie Collins, author of *The Moonstone*, which has been described as the first English detective novel. A great admirer of Collins as a "plot maker" who managed to draw together romance and realism, Sayers was inspired by his example; *The Nine Tailors* has strong echoes of *The Moonstone*, not only in the details of the crime, which again revolves around a jewelry theft, but in the skillful orchestration of subplots. *The Nine Tailors* was the novel that secured Sayers's growing reputation as one of the finest twentieth-century detective novelists and as a writer who brought the "clue puzzle" into the broader traditions of the English novel. **LM**

Auto-da-Fé

Elias Canetti

Lifespan | *b.* 1905 (Bulgaria), *d.* 1994 (Switzerland)
First Published | 1935
First Published by | Herbert Reichner Verlag (Vienna)
Original Title | *Die Blendung*

This neglected masterpiece of German modernism offers a mysterious and indirect analysis of the perils of bookishness, and the darkness that ensues when the bookworm turns. Prophetically, this bonfire of the vanities attempts to dissect the social madness that was engulfing the German-speaking world. Echoing the dark comedy of Kafka, Elias Canetti's "K"—Peter Kien—is a creature of the mind, determined to resist socialization in preference for a life of scholarship, but lacking worldly defenses. The novel details his series of encounters with creatures whose rapacious interests generate an extraordinary comedy of competing delusions.

Peter Kien, an obsessive scholar of sinology, has a large personal library. Beset by nightmares of his library going up in smoke, he stupidly marries Therese, the scheming and deluded housekeeper he has employed to look after the library. Descending into varieties of hallucinatory mania, Kien is ejected from his library by his "wife" and enters a nightmare underground world. After sundry misadventures at the hands of Fischerle, a crooked, hunchbacked dwarf with delusions of becoming the world chess champion, he becomes embroiled again with Therese and Bendikt Pfaff, proto-Nazi caretaker and retired policeman. Kien's brother, a Parisian psychologist, adds interpretative confusion to the dark brew before the book's violent logic of disintegration precipitates the final inferno. Dark, terrifying, disturbing, and funny. **DM**

They Shoot Horses, Don't They?

Horace McCoy

Lifespan | *b.* 1897 (U.S.), *d.* 1955
First Published | 1935
First Published by | A. Barker (London)
Movie Adaptation Released | 1969

Overlooked at the time of its initial publication, *They Shoot Horses, Don't They?* was critically rehabilitated in the 1940s by the Parisian noirist Marcel Duhamel, who favorably compared Horace McCoy to Hemingway. The novel's protagonists, Robert and Gloria, dream of Hollywood stardom, but in the bleak tawdriness of Depression-era Los Angeles they find only monotony, emptiness, and ultimately death. In the guise of the dance marathon, a form of spectacle in which contestants endlessly circulate around an arena over a period of days in the hope of being the last pair standing, McCoy found the perfect metaphor for life's randomness, absurdity, and meaninglessness. Battling exhaustion, Robert and Gloria fail in their pursuit of the cash prize when the event is ended by a bizarre accidental shooting. Set adrift, Gloria's insistence that life has no meaning persuades Robert to realize her morbid ambition.

The dance marathon is used to comment on the exploitative nature of popular forms of entertainment and on the ways in which human life has been organized and debased under capitalism. Unlike the sugarcoated banality of most Hollywood movies, the dance marathon is unpredictable, painful, violent, and nihilistic. The dance contestants are commodities—cattle, or rather horses, who can be shot once their value has been utilized. Here are the seeds of McCoy's social critique but, like the dance marathon itself, it is a critique that leads nowhere and yields nothing. **AP**

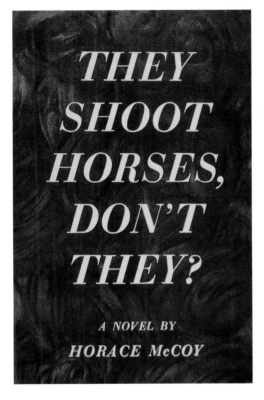

"We throw ourselves on the mercy of the court. This boy admits killing the girl, but he was only doing her a personal favor."

⬧ McCoy's Depression-era novels earned him an enthusiastic following in Europe, but were little admired in America.

The Last of Mr. Norris

Christopher Isherwood

Lifespan | *b.* 1904 (England), *d.* 1986 (U.S.)
First Published | 1935
First Published by | Hogarth Press (London)
Original Title | *Mr. Norris Changes Trains*

This intriguing novel portrays a series of encounters in 1930s Berlin between the narrator, William Bradshaw, and the mysterious and sinister Mr. Norris. When Bradshaw first meets Arthur Norris on a train bound for Germany, he notes that his eyes were "the eyes of a schoolboy surprised in the act of breaking one of the rules." Always on the move, always involved in shady deals, Mr. Norris somehow manages to elude the scrutiny of the authorities.

The tone of the book is comical, at times farcical, but it is set in the final years of the Weimar Republic, and the rise of Nazi power provides an ominous counterpoint to the carefree café society that Isherwood depicts. This atmospheric evocation of a world on the very brink of ruin introduces us to a gallery of damned souls, prisoners in their own city, hounded by a ruthless new social order determined to expose and eradicate them. Their only hope resides in flight, but even this option is fraught with the risk of arrest. As the communists are driven underground, the rise in the tally of beatings and shootings fuels a feverish proliferation of gossip and rumor. Against the backdrop of Berlin's descent into civil war, Bradshaw's position remains one of detachment—he positions himself as an observer, passively witnessing the collapse of civilization from the shadowy wings of a theater of the absurd. **TS**

🄌 Isherwood (left) and his lifelong friend and literary collaborator, poet W. H. Auden, embark on a trip to war-torn China in 1938.

Untouchable

Mulk Raj Anand

Lifespan | *b.* 1905 (Pakistan), *d.* 2004 (India)
First Published | 1935
First Published by | Wishart Books (London)
Founding Editor of | Marg

"*Untouchable* could only have been written by an Indian . . . no European, however sympathetic, could have created the character of Bakha because he would not have known enough of his troubles." So wrote Mulk Raj Anand's friend E. M. Forster in the preface of this simply told tale of a day in the life of a sweeper from the lowest caste in India's class system who collects human excrement, making him and his like ritually unclean and therefore not to be touched. "They think we are dirt because we clean their dirt," says Bakha. But bumping into someone from a higher caste becomes a catastrophe in social terms, poisoning the untouchable's life.

The story follows Bakha's search to make some sense of his low-born position. After meeting and then rejecting the message of a Salvationist missionary called Hutchinson, he talks to a follower of Gandhi who says all Indians are equal and gives great hope to the sweeper. But it is the third, more technological, solution that potentially can be his salvation. The flushing toilet with mains drainage can get rid of such appalling epithets as "low-caste vermin" once and for all. The sweeper wonders whether Machine or Mahatma might be his savior.

This was the first of several works depicting the lives of India's poorer castes, while attacking the social yoke under which they burdened. Anand's prose translates Punjabi and Hindi streettalk into a sympathetic English style, which has led many reviewers to call him India's Charles Dickens. **JHa**

Independent People

Halldór Laxness

Lifespan | b. 1902 (Iceland), d. 1998
First Published | 1935 (Reykjavík)
Original Title | Sjálfstætt fólk
Nobel Prize for Literature | 1955

Lost in a blizzard and close to death, Bjartur, the proud, stubborn, brutal, and often idiotic hero of this extraordinary novel, begins to hallucinate. As the snowstorm tears at him, its claws become those of Grimur, the mythical demon from Icelandic sagas. He fights his way, step by step, reciting all the poetry and ballads he can remember in a desperate attempt to stay awake. Finally, close to collapse, he reaches the safety of another crofter's hut, exhausted but victorious.

In essence, this novel is a reclamation of Iceland's mythical past, an attempt to redefine the sense of nation and history through those most often ignored. It gives voice to the ancient farming communities, their wit, their sufferings, and their conflicts. Full of tough realism, the novel's pages reek with the stink of sheep dung, of smoke and stone, and of deep, endless drifts of snow. It focuses on Bjartur and his fight to remain independent and free from debt during the early years of the twentieth century, through the prosperity of the war years to the economic crisis and growth of socialism after the war has ended. In hard, poetic, and often beautiful prose Laxness charts the struggles of Bjartur's growing family, the death of his first and second wives, and the longings and unfulfilled dreams of his three children.

Laxness, who spent much of his childhood on farms similar to those described, wrote over sixty literary works and is considered the undisputed master of Icelandic fiction. **JM**

Nightwood

Djuna Barnes

Lifespan | b. 1892 (U.S.), d. 1982
First Published | 1936
First Published by | Faber & Faber (London)
Introduction to the Original Edition by | T. S. Eliot

Nightwood has the reputation of a great novel written by a poet, a reputation partly fostered by T. S. Eliot's suggestion that the book will appeal primarily to readers of poetry. The prose style of the book is indeed remarkable, possessing varieties of urbane wit and a kind of modernist baroque seemingly schooled in Jacobean dramatic poetry. A pioneering representation of love between women, Nightwood makes uncomfortable reading for anyone looking for positive images of lesbian identity, but however troubling, this is a hilarious and stylish book.

Set mostly in Paris and New York, the novel suggests a cosmopolitan drift of bohemians and exiles in Europe. At the center of the novel is the dangerous figure of Robin Vote, who more or less ruins her husband, Felix Volkbein, their child Guido, and the two women who love her, Nora Flood and Jenny Petherbridge. Counterbalancing the destructive allure of Robin Vote, Doctor Matthew O'Connor administers the healing power of distractingly outlandish monologues. What at first seem like windy exercises in rhetoric for rhetoric's sake are gradually revealed as humane deflections of the suffering otherwise threatening to break out. The doctor's unorthodox efforts are finally reduced to drunken rubble by the wheels of this dark fable. A book to reread many times. **DM**

❯ Barnes wrote about lesbian relationships, which she saw as narcissistic: "A man is another person—a woman is yourself."

At the Mountains of Madness

H. P. Lovecraft

H. P. Lovecraft's most effective novel begins as a tale of exploration at the cutting edge of science. Airplanes and drilling devices are shipped to Antarctica in 1930, just as the mapping of the continent begins in earnest. But this "awful place," more ancient than any other continent, is not so easily opened up to materialist exploitation. Soon enough, an entirely new history of the world is in evidence, one that undermines all previously held views of science and nature, a vision that contains vast alien cities buried beneath the ice and the awesome and awful survivors of its heyday.

The positive and efficient first-person narrative of the geologist, Dyer, patiently and didactically explains the wonders of new technology. Only when the first survey group, isolated by a storm, begins to radio back of highly unusual finds in a cavern beneath the surface, do events begin to unravel. From then on, Dyer and his companion, the student Danforth, are on a downward spiral of discovery that attacks every notion of time, space, and life, until Danforth's speech is reduced to disconnected fragments, recalled only in dreams.

Deeply influenced by Poe, Lovecraft's horror tends to be implied and offstage, but this effectively deepens the abounding philosophical horror felt by the protagonists. This intriguing blend of gothic horror and lost-world scenarios within a more modern genre framework can be rediscovered in many contemporary narratives, especially film. Lovecraft achieved little success in his lifetime but his work resonates with themes that consistently inspire later generations of writers, science fiction as much as horror. Largely due to his *Cthulhu* stories, called *Cthulhu Mythos* by August Derleth, Lovecraft is today the subject of a large cult following. **JS**

Lifespan | *b*. 1890 (U.S.), *d*. 1937
First Serialized | 1936
First Serialized in | *Astounding Stories* magazine
Full Name | Howard Phillips Lovecraft

Lovecraft, who was often ill as a child, claims that his work was often inspired by the experience of horror through nightmares.

Lovecraft's association with and influence on the genres of horror, occult, and the macabre continues to be perpetuated.

Absalom, Absalom!

William Faulkner

Lifespan | *b.* 1897 (U.S.), *d.* 1962
First Published | 1936
First Published by | Random House (New York)
Nobel Prize for Literature | 1949

Told five times between 1835 and 1910 (while Sutpen rests from hunting his absconded French architect with a pack of slaves), this is the peasant-to-planter story of Thomas Sutpen, of his plantation (called "the Hundred"), and of Bon, his possible son who may be black and who, if black and acknowledged, will bring the house down.

The gaps and contradictions exposed by multiple narration beg epistemological questions concerning how we know what we know of historical matters. But given that in *Absalom, Absalom!* the questions arise from a regionally specific labor problem—that of the denied black body within the white, whose coerced work gives substance to the face, skin, sex, and land of the white owning class—those questions must be recast. "Who knows what and how do they know it?" is reformed as, "How, knowing that their face, skin, sex, and land are made by African-American labor (the good inside their goods), can they go on denying what they know?" Faulkner's answer would seem to be that to acknowledge their knowledge (or for Sutpen to face Bon as his son), would be to cease to be themselves.

That William Faulkner should begin to think such unthinkable thoughts about his own ancestors in *Absalom, Absalom!*, even as his region continued to depend for its substance on bound black workers (bound by debt peonage rather than chattel slavery), may explain the structure of this work, undoubtedly one of the greatest of modernist novels. **RG**

War with the Newts

Karel Capek

Lifespan | *b.* 1890 (Czech Republic), *d.* 1938
First Published | 1936
First Published by | Fr. Borový (Prague)
Original Title | *Valka s mloky*

This science-fiction dystopia begins with the discovery, by a portly sea captain, of some peculiar salamanders, or newts, that he is able to train. The amphibians are exceedingly intelligent, stand upright, and are able to develop the powers of speech. With financial backing, the captain sails around the Pacific with his newts, fishing for pearls. The newts multiply rapidly and soon the business is a huge international concern. Within years there are considerably more newts than people—some have even graduated from universities—and they are beginning to run out of the shallow water areas they inhabit. The newts are slaves, exploited second-class citizens, until one day they present the world with their own demands.

Karel Capek was well known in his native Czechoslovakia for his journalism, plays, and novels. *War with the Newts* is generally considered to be his best narrative tale. At a time when Europe was watching with dismay the developments in Germany, Capek was a committed anti-Nazi but also had an antipathy to the Communist Party. The novel parodies both movements, as well as commenting on the selfishness inherent in nation states and their dealings with each other. Capek handles human interaction and political machinations with a combination of warm interest and distinctly comic irony. Poignant, funny, and politically astute, Capek's novel presented a twentieth-century moral warning that still has resonance today. **JC**

Keep the Aspidistra Flying

George Orwell

Lifespan | *b*. 1903 (India), *d*. 1950 (England)
First Published | 1936
First Published by | V. Gollancz (London)
Given Name | Eric Arthur Blair

The changes George Orwell was forced to make by his publisher, together with the weaknesses he himself saw in it, left him disappointed with this novel. But for all that, it is still a powerful and savagely satirical portrait of literary life. Very much a London novel, and perhaps even more a 1930s one, *Keep the Aspidistra Flying* describes the struggles of hapless Gordon Comstock. In Comstock's indictment of capitalism, access to culture is seen as inseparable from the possession of wealth and privilege, while the domination of contemporary life by advertising points to an all-embracing commodification of the everyday. These are the signs of a futile existence, a dying civilization; the threat of an impending cataclysm—a theme Orwell would develop further in *Coming Up for Air*—hangs over the action.

Comstock, however, appears to be trapped as much by his own weak character as by the system he deplores. He refuses to accept the respectability of middle-class life, represented by the potted plants of the novel's title, which, in Comstock's eyes, symbolize "mingy, lower-class decency." Yet he rejects revolutionary politics as a means of bringing about change, and his own attempt to embrace poverty by living like an anchorite among the destitute merely assuages his sense of guilt. Moreover, the novel nags away at Comstock's ambiguous character, asking whether his anger and despair should be read as a self-pitying drama or as a genuine rejection of capitalist exploitation. **AG**

"Suddenly a double knock deep below made the whole house rattle. Gordon started. His mind fled upwards from the abyss. The post! London Pleasures was forgotten."

◉ Eric Blair, pictured here after having adopted his pseudonym, which he did in order not to embarrass his parents by his work.

Gone with the Wind

Margaret Mitchell

Lifespan | *b*. 1900 (U.S.), *d*. 1949
First Published | 1936
First Published by | Macmillan & Co. (London)
Pulitzer Prize | 1937

🔘 Margaret Mitchell was a shy and private individual who had great difficulty coping with the fame her novel brought her.

🔘 A poster advertising the novel in 1936 is surprising, as the iconography of *Gone with the Wind* is set by the 1939 movie.

Gone with the Wind's romanticized setting in Civil War and Reconstruction-era Georgia, as well as its central characters, the fiery Southern belle Scarlett O'Hara and her dashing husband, Rhett Butler, have become the stuff of American mythology. Although David O. Selznick's 1939 film helped to immortalize Mitchell's novel, the book had already enjoyed phenomenal sales on first publication and went on to win the Pulitzer Prize, a year later, in 1937.

A sweeping historical saga, it follows Scarlett and her friends and relatives through a period of major upheaval in American social and economic history. The novel traces the transition from the agricultural society of the early 1860s, represented by Tara, the family plantation, to the beginnings of Southern industrialization in the 1880s. While it is famously a tale about Scarlett, Rhett, and Ashley's love triangle, *Gone with the Wind* is also a love letter to a place, the city of Atlanta, Georgia. Margaret Mitchell was born in Atlanta and grew up hearing stories of the antebellum city and the battles fought by the Confederate army. She lovingly details Atlanta's expanding and changing society in carefully constructed passages that reveal the extent of her historical research.

However, *Gone with the Wind* is not an uncontroversial novel, and Margaret Mitchell's own sympathies with Southern slave owners and idyllic portrayal of pre-war plantation society have exposed the book to an expansive cultural debate, producing critical analysis, protest, and even parody that continues today. Nevertheless, it remains an ambitious, gripping novel, and, far more importantly, an undisputed cultural phenomenon that not only helped to shape the direction of the American novel, but that has had a significant effect on America's popular conception of its own history. **AB**

GONE WITH THE WIND

The Thinking Reed

Rebecca West

Lifespan | *b.* 1892 (England), *d.* 1983
First Published | 1936
First Published by | Hutchinson & Co. (London)
Given Name | Cicily Isabel Fairfield

Rebecca West was well known throughout the twentieth century for her progressive and feminist politics, and her fifth novel, *The Thinking Reed*, sensitively examines the limitations of the life led by many middle-class women during the 1920s.

It follows the fortunes of Isabelle Torrey, an intelligent young American widow who is prematurely thrust onto the European social scene. Disappointed in a love affair, she impulsively marries the immensely wealthy Marc Sallafranque, only to experience emotional swings from love to hate and back again over the course of their violent and passionate marriage. Charting an evolving relationship against the background of the decadent social scene of the very wealthy, *The Thinking Reed*, like Fitzgerald's *Tender is the Night,* highlights the disintegration of not only a class but an entire way of life. Strikes and industrial unrest grow daily more violent at Marc's automobile factory outside of Paris, while the stock market crash looms across the ocean. Marc and Isabelle's carefree lifestyle is clearly doomed, but in losing their fortune, the novel implies, they will gain the human dimension missing from their increasingly desperate and empty social maneuverings. Eventually Isabelle comes to feel only revulsion for the vapid and cruel social circle that she once embraced so enthusiastically.

The Thinking Reed remains an important and thoughtful exploration of relationships, class, and marriage for today's reader. **AB**

> *"Writing has nothing to do with communication between person and person, only . . . between different parts of a person's mind."*
>
> Rebecca West, "The Art of Skepticism," 1952

West appeared on the cover of *Time* magazine in 1947—her fame in America rested primarily on her work as a journalist.

Eyeless in Gaza

Aldous Huxley

Lifespan | *b*. 1894 (England), *d*. 1963 (U.S.)
First Published | 1936
First Published by | Chatto & Windus (London)
Original Language | English

The title, which quotes Milton's Samson Agonistes ("Eyeless in Gaza at the Mill with slaves"), inaugurates Aldous Huxley's partly autobiographical narrative of Anthony Beavis's quest for enlightenment. The novel traces his life from his English boyhood in 1902 to his risky commitment to pacifism in 1935. We encounter his predominantly upper-middle-class and highly articulate friends, relatives, and partners. The novel is chronologically experimental, moving to and fro in time, creating a range of ironic links between past and present. It is experimental, too, in the boldness with which customary plot development gives way to intellectual meditations, providing a range of witty or provocative reflections on topics such as sociology, democracy, and totalitarianism, particularly the problem of reconciling individual freedom with social harmony. In the most notorious passage in the novel, a live dog is dropped from an airplane and hits the flat rooftop where Anthony and his partner, Helen, are lying naked in the sun. It bursts, spraying them with its blood. Typically, the well-read Anthony says to Helen: "You look like Lady Macbeth." Ironies multiply: he feels tenderness, while she decides to leave him. Huxley's sense of the tragicomedy created by the entrapment of the human self is brilliantly encapsulated here.

Huxley's writing in *Eyeless in Gaza* may in places appear prolix and didactic. Nevertheless, in his lifetime, Huxley, like Lawrence and H. G. Wells, was for many readers an emancipatory influence. **CW**

Summer Will Show

Sylvia Townsend Warner

Lifespan | *b*. 1893 (England), *d*. 1978
First Published | 1936
First Published by | Chatto & Windus (London)
Original Language | English

How does one tell the story of revolution, when writing in the early 1930s? The Soviet revolution is too close and too unmanageable, yet there has been no revolution in Western Europe since the nineteenth century. Sylvia Townsend Warner—not yet a Communist—turns back to the year of revolutions, 1848, specifically to Paris, when a popular revolt removed the Orléanist Louis Philippe. Her heroine is Englishwoman Sophia Willoughby.

Personal tragedy prepares Sophia for revolution when she loses her children to smallpox, her home to legal trickery, and her husband to adultery. Following her husband, Frederick, to Paris, she falls in love with his mistress, Minna Lemuel. But in the violent summer of 1848, Minna is killed at the barricades by Caspar, whom Sophia has brought up in England. Sophia kills Caspar, yet refuses to believe Minna is dead. These melodramatic events are dissolved in a detached but involving prose.

Sophia is then employed by the revolutionary Ingelbrecht, a version of Engels, to distribute a mysterious pamphlet—*The Communist Manifesto*. The defeat of the summer of 1848 has shown that she will live on as a revolutionary. *Summer Will Show* tells three stories: Sophia as a *flâneuse* on the streets of radicalized Paris; Sophia in love with Minna, a subtle, almost impalpably sensitive lesbian romance; and Sophia's gradual discovery of what it means to be a revolutionary. Autobiographically speaking, the last two are Warner's own stories. **AMu**

Rickshaw Boy

Lao She

Lifespan | *b.* 1899 (China), *d.* 1966
First Published | 1936, by Renjian Shuwu (Beijing)
Given Name | Shu Qingchun
Original Title | *Luotuo xiangzi*

This socio-critical novel describes the physical and moral decline of its young protagonist, the rickshaw-puller Xiangzi. It was praised both for its depiction of Xiangzi's struggle in an unjust society and its lively language, which captured the Beijing vernacular.

Arriving in Beijing from the northern countryside, Xiangzi becomes an aspiring rickshaw-puller with the sole ambition of owning a rickshaw. His zeal is soon rewarded, but before long his rickshaw is snatched away by marauding warlord armies that draft him as a coolie. When Xiangzi escapes, he manages to steal and sell three camels, a feat resulting in his being nicknamed "Camel." But the theft also marks the first step in his moral and physical decline: he is robbed by a crafty detective; cheated into marriage by Tiger Liu, the tyrannical daughter of a rickshaw renter; abuses his health and succumbs to drinking and gambling after Tiger's death in childbirth; and finally betrays the rickshaw union organizer to the secret police. His tragedy is accentuated by the suicide of Fuzi, a girl forced into prostitution whom Xiangzi had decided to marry.

Some Chinese post-1949 editions censored the ending, and the first English translation was even given a happy ending. Yet it is precisely Lao She's uncompromising and realistic depiction of the working man's plight—partly self-inflicted, partly brought about by a hostile society—that allows *Rickshaw Boy* to be read as a parable of the fate of the Chinese people in the twentieth century. **FG**

Out of Africa

Isak Dinesen (Karen Blixen)

Lifespan | *b.* 1885 (Denmark), *d.* 1962
First Published | 1937, by Putnam (London)
Given Name | Karen Christence Dinesen
Original Title | *Den afrikanske Farm*

Karen Blixen only narrowly missed out on the Nobel Prize for Literature, and *Out of Africa* is her most famous novel, both a memoir of her time on a coffee farm in Kenya and a vivid portrait of the beginning of the waning of European imperialism.

Dinesen recounts her struggles to make a success of the coffee plantation in the years before and after the First World War, fighting poverty and natural disasters to keep her farm, with the ghost of failure always a step behind her. Her reminiscences are peppered with references to God, lions (believed to be symbolic of nature's aristocracy), the violence of Africa, racism, and decency. Dinesen was in love with the African landscape and the descriptive passages in this book are at times exquisite, although some of her references to Africans will make modern readers uncomfortable. She hints at the differences between European and African culture—believing that men exist in a truer form in Africa—and recounts how she, as a woman, tried to bridge the chasm between them. In the end, she loses the farm and leaves for Europe, but she never stops loving the country she called home for twenty years. This is a novel about the death of imperialism and displacement, savagery, beauty, and the human struggle. Hailed as perhaps the greatest pastoral elegy of modernism, most of all, it is a book about Africa. **EF**

◗ Karen Blixen is shot by photographer Carl van Vechten in a setting that suggests a loving remembrance of Africa.

In Parenthesis

David Jones

Lifespan | b. 1895 (England), d. 1974
First Published | 1937, by Faber & Faber (London)
Full Title | In Parenthesis: Impressions, in a fictitious form, of life on the Western Front

Often heralded as the unsung classic of the First World War, this lyrical tale is written from the point of view of an ordinary Welsh private. Jones's tale follows the journey of one man into a baffling, dangerous but often frighteningly beautiful world. Jones was also attempting to universalize the war experience; to portray his "truth" of the war in a new voice that gave it proper tongue and moved it away from the pretensions of modernism and the rhetoric of high diction. He did so within a form that has had a lasting impact on the understanding of the First World War: poetry. His work also encompasses long sections of lyric prose, and perhaps in these respects he was no different from writers such as Brooke, Sassoon, Brittain, and Graves, all of whom looked for new ways to describe the war they saw in a manner befitting their experiences.

Critics have often had positive things to say about the work, from Stephen Spender, who thought the text was "probably the World War I monument most likely to survive," to Julian Mitchell in 2003, who extolled In Parenthesis as a classic waiting to be rediscovered. What they often forget is the sheer inaccessibility of the novel. This is not a recent trend; Jones's work has always been marginalized because so few people are able to survive its depths. Yet it has always had its champions. Whether this makes it a good book that will endure as long as predicted remains to be seen, but it is certainly not, nor is it ever likely to be, a popular one. **EMcCS**

Ferdydurke

Witold Gombrowicz

Lifespan | b. 1904 (Poland), d. 1969 (France)
First Published | 1937
First Published by | Rój (Warszawa)
Movie Adaptation Released | 1991

This extraordinarily funny, crude, and subversive novel was banned by the Nazis, suppressed by the Communists, and has since become a set text in most Polish high schools. It is a novel about identity, the power of time and place, adolescence, and the brutality of childhood.

Joey Kowalski narrates the story of his transformation from a thirty-year-old man into a teenage boy, or a man seen by the rest of society as a teenage boy. For, while he is taken by a strange professor to a local school and becomes part of that world, he still maintains his adult memories and opinions. This gives him a unique perspective on the social, political, and cultural complexities present in the colliding worlds of students and teachers. He is frustrated by his desires, patronized by the adults around him, and forced to take part in the games and rituals of the playground.

The dark, repressed, and often damaged areas of the human psyche that exist in the boundary between "maturity" and "immaturity" are explored in a narrative of great power, wit, and philosophical sophistication. The novel is almost celebratory in its use, and abuse, of language and in its pastiche of the rose-tinted, nostalgic novels of childhood. It was written at a time of great change and crisis for Poland and for Europe, and reflects the uncertainties and frustrations of that time. Witold Gombrowicz is now recognized as one of the greatest Polish authors of the twentieth century. **JM**

The Blind Owl

Sadegh Hedayat

Lifespan | b. 1903 (Iran), d. 1951 (France)
First Published | 1937 (Iran)
First Serialized | 1941, in the newspaper *Iran*
Original Title | *Bouf-e Kour*

This claustrophobic novella is narrated by a tormented young artist who feels himself trapped in a hypnagogic limbo between sleep and wakefulness, sanity and madness. He describes a world of vivid and disturbing hallucinations, fueled by wine and opium, evoking the images from the classic Persian miniatures that he paints on pen-boxes for a living. A sensuous and intimidating woman, who is at once his life's inspiration and the source of all his despair, is juxtaposed with a dark cypress tree, a winding brook, and a squatting yogi. Morbidly fascinated by these endlessly recurring motifs, and helpless to escape his obsessive desire and terror, he can now only communicate with his shadow, cast like an owl on the wall.

This is Sadegh Hedayat's best-known work of prose. Originally banned from publication in his homeland during the oppressive rule of Reza Shah, it appeared in Tehran only after the Shah's abdication in 1941, as a serial in a daily newspaper. Hedayat was a scholar of Persian history and folklore, but his writing was also influenced by the works of de Maupassant, Chekhov, Edgar Allan Poe, and Franz Kafka. He spent the last ten years of his life as an exile in Paris, studying philosophy with Sartre.

The Blind Owl is Hedayat's legacy, a masterly exploration into the very darkest inner landscapes—clouded with horror and sinisterly mocking *momento mori*, but illuminated with flashes of dazzling description and deeply moving insight. **TS**

The Hobbit

J. R. R. Tolkien

Lifespan | b. 1892 (South Africa), d. 1973 (England)
First Published | 1937
First Published by | G. Allen & Unwin (London)
Full Title | *The Hobbit: or, There and Back Again*

Although it stemmed from stories he had been writing about his fictional world, Middle Earth, for a decade, *The Hobbit* was J. R. R Tolkien's first published work, which was to be followed, over a decade later, by its sequel, *The Lord of the Rings*. The plot and characters combined the ancient heroic Anglo-Saxon and Scandinavian epics Tolkien studied at Oxford University with the middle-class rural England in which he lived and felt comfortable.

Bilbo Baggins, the hero of the story, is a hobbit—a race of small people about half the size of humans with hairy feet and a passion for food and drink. Encouraged by the wizard Gandalf, Bilbo leaves his village, Hobbiton, for the first time and sets off on an adventure with a group of dwarves seeking to reclaim their treasure from a dragon. When Bilbo meets the tormented Gollum, he finds himself the bearer of a magic ring that makes the wearer disappear. After a series of adventures, Bilbo and Gandalf return to the village, but Bilbo is no longer accepted, his adventurous behavior being deemed unhobbitlike. Bilbo is an unlikely hero, who achieves metamorphosis through pools of inner strength he did not know he possessed. Some critics have tried to read metaphors for England's heroism during the war or the inherent evil in some nationalities. But Tolkien was known to dislike allegory, and it is more likely simply the heroic story of a small, charming person who has no idea how resourceful he is until his abilities are put to the test. **EF**

Their Eyes Were Watching God

Zora Neale Hurston

Lifespan | *b.* 1903 (U.S.), *d.* 1960
First Published | 1937
First Published by | J. B. Lippincott Co. (Philadelphia)
Movie Adaptation | 2005 (Harpo Studios)

"They sat in company with the others. . . . They seemed to be staring at the dark, but their eyes were watching God."

● Hurston trained as an anthropologist, developing a fine ear for speech patterns through the study of Afro-American oral culture.

Brutal experiences of slavery prompt sixteen-year-old Janie's maternal grandmother to marry her off to a respectable man. She hopes to insulate Janie from the potentially ruinous burdens she and other black women have had to bear. Yet Janie's fearless idealism leaves her feeling unfulfilled, and she abandons her emotionally stingy husband for Joe, an extravagant dreamer with whom she heads farther south to build a thriving, all-black town out of little more than overwhelming ambition and some roadside land. Joe elevates Janie's socio-economic status, but she becomes a trapping of his success rather than a respected partner. By the time of Joe's death, Janie is a middle-aged woman confident enough to withstand the town's persistent, speculative gossip and trust her instincts with Tea Cake, a mysterious younger man. By the novel's end, though she has lost everything, Janie has realized her vision of love like a blossoming pear tree in the intense, volatile bond she and Tea Cake shared.

Zora Neale Hurston was the mayor's daughter in America's first incorporated black town, where her social and political experience of African-American autonomy afforded a unique perspective on race. She eventually trained as an anthropologist, researching African-American folklore and oral culture in her native Florida. The dialogue in *Their Eyes Were Watching God* is written primarily in the strong Southern African-American dialect (framed by a standard English narrative), the pronunciation, rhythm, and playfulness of which Hurston renders in rich detail using almost phonetic spelling. This celebration of colloquial language and life was harshly criticized by contemporaries such as Richard Wright, but Hurston is now regarded as a highly significant figure in African-American literature. **AF**

Of Mice and Men

John Steinbeck

The title of quite possibly John Steinbeck's best-known work refers to a line from a Robert Burns's poem, *To a Mouse*, hinting simply at the tragedy of the tale. The novella tells the story of George and Lennie, two migrant workers who have been let off the bus miles from the California ranch where they work. George is a small, sharp man with dark features, and Lennie a mentally subnormal, shapeless giant who is deeply devoted to George and relies on him for protection and guidance. Camped out for the night, this unlikely couple share a dream of starting a farm together. Back on the ranch, the men meet Slim, the mule driver who admires their friendship. He gives Lennie one of his puppies and convinces the two men to include him in their dreams of buying a piece of land and setting up home. But the dream is shattered when Lennie accidentally kills the puppy and, without meaning to, breaks the neck of a woman on the ranch. Fleeing a terrible death at the hands of a lynch mob, Lennie encounters George, who gently reminds him of the idyllic life they will share together, before shooting his friend in the back of his head. When the mob arrives, Slim realizes that George has killed his friend out of mercy and leads him away to safety.

This is a story about brotherhood and the harsh reality of a world that refuses to allow such idealized male bonds to be nurtured. George and Lennie's unique relationship approaches that ideal, but it is misunderstood by the rest of the world, who cannot comprehend true friendship, instead undermining one another and exploiting weakness wherever it can be found. But perhaps the real tragedy of the novel lies in the depiction of the death of the great American dream as a reality, exposing it as exactly what it purports to be: merely a dream. **EF**

Lifespan | *b.* 1902 (U.S.), *d.* 1968
First Published | 1937
First Published by | Covici Friede (New York)
Nobel Prize for Literature | 1962

"Might jus' as well spen' all my time tellin' you things and then you forget 'em, and I tell you again."

Steinbeck based most of his best writing on observation of life among the lower levels of rural society in his native California.

Murphy

Samuel Beckett

Lifespan | *b.* 1906 (Ireland), *d.* 1989 (France)
First Published | 1938
First Published by | G. Routledge & Sons (London)
Nobel Prize for Literature | 1969

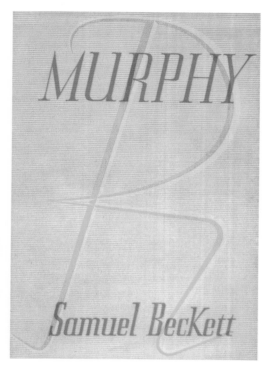

*"Let our conversation now
be without precedent . . ."*

⬤ Largely ignored when first published, *Murphy* was relaunched on
the back of the success of the play *Waiting for Godot* in the 1950s.

In a writing career that produced many masterpieces, *Murphy* is perhaps the most continuously delightful and engagingly disengaged Samuel Beckett ever wrote. Almost a conventional novel, lacking the rigorous austerity and reflexivity of Beckett's later novels, *Murphy* is closer in spirit to the play and pseudo-erudition of *Tristram Shandy*, with more than occasional hints of Joycean wit and Rabelaisian materialism. From the off, the novel takes lapidary strikes at the lazy pomp of the omniscient narrator. Dead phrases are turned over with amused scorn— "And life in his mind gave him pleasure, such pleasure that pleasure was not the word." Between arcane referentiality and lexical flicks, the jokes come thick and fast, so fast that thick is not the word.

The novel describes the adventures of Murphy in London, with a particularity of specified urban geography unusual in Beckett's work. Aspiring to freedom and a quality of stillness in a rocking chair, Murphy resolutely attempts to avoid getting caught up in anything remotely resembling a plot, but nevertheless finds himself propelled into misadventures with sundry implausible creations. Among other escapades, Murphy runs away from his betrothed, shacks up with a prostitute, and finds relatively gainful employment in a mental institution, where he plays a peculiar brand of pacifist chess. Murphy dies in an accident, the revelation of which would only spoil what little suspense and final uplift the novel can offer. Notably buoyant among many bits of bravura narration is the description of Murphy's "mind," but perhaps the most lasting glow to emanate from this comic romance is the brio with which it resists the temptations and literary tedium of its darker leanings. A great way into Beckett, and a great way out. **DM**

U.S.A.

John Dos Passos

The three novels collected as *U.S.A.* are the most successful of many twentieth-century attempts to write the inclusive story of American life. Dos Passos covers the years 1900 to 1930, describing the rise of the labor movement, the inner workings of capitalism, life at sea, the American experience of the First World War, the rise of Hollywood, and the decline into the great Depression. These events are skillfully evoked in the lives of the novels' twelve main characters, six men and six women. The centrality of violence to American life is firmly established, particularly in the accounts of attacks on the Wobblies (International Workers of the World) as they attempt to organize a union.

"But mostly *U.S.A.* is the speech of the people," Dos Passos writes, and his impeccable ear for the many voices of America puts these voices into conflict, or collusion, or concurrence, building up an overview that is also a socialist critique. Dos Passos is not a nineteenth-century naturalist but a modernist, and the speech of the people is embedded in a narrative that derives from James Joyce, Gertrude Stein, and Ernest Hemingway. The autobiographical "Camera Eye" sections are in the style of Joyce's *A Portrait of the Artist*, and the "Newsreel" sections quoting actual newspaper headlines are a satirical documentary device. Stein's continuous present is here the model for the main text. This method works to convey equally the political hopes of working people, the social innocence of young women and men, and the inevitability of events when power intervenes. It also allows skips and jumps in consciousness that Dos Passos uses to push the narrative forward. The irruption of American voices into this process-language makes for a complex but unquestionably successful mix. **AMu**

Lifespan | *b*. 1896 (U.S.), *d*. 1970
First Published | 1938, by Constable & Co. (London)
Trilogy | *The 42nd Parallel* (1930); *1919* (1932); *The Big Money* (1936)

"non nein nicht englander amerikanisch americain" [sic]

The Big Money was the final novel to be published in the *U.S.A* trilogy; it covers the postwar years leading up to the Depression.

Brighton Rock

Graham Greene

The two main characters in Graham Greene's gripping reflection on the nature of evil are the amateur detective Ida and the murderous Pinkie, a Roman Catholic who chooses hell over heaven. Responsible for two murders, he is forced to marry the hapless Rose to prevent her from giving evidence. A good Catholic, Rose seems to represent Pinkie's lost innocence. Although Ida is ostensibly the heroine of the novel, her heroism belongs to the blank morality of the detective novel, where the measure of goodness is in the ability to solve the mystery. By contrast, through his contemplation of his own damnation, Pinkie's evil achieves a sense of moral seriousness that Ida's agnosticism can never obtain. Rose is Pinkie's counterpart here, sharing his Catholic faith and prepared to corrupt herself in order to protect a man that she believes loves her. For Pinkie, the part he plays in Rose's corruption will ensure his damnation much more clearly than his role in the murders that punctuate the novel.

Brighton Rock began life as a detective novel, and the mark of that genre remains in Ida's pursuit of Pinkie. However, the structure of the detective novel merely contains the moral framework seen here. The contrast between Pinkie's theological morality and its insubstantial counterparts is reinforced using various narrative techniques. Principally, the language through which Pinkie's contemplation of hell is expressed contrasts vividly with the comparatively frivolous considerations of Ida and the other characters. What finally distinguishes Pinkie's tragic mode from the generic patterns of the detective story is a critique of commercialized popular culture in which, with the exception of Pinkie, almost every character is associated with the limited imaginative potential of mass culture. **LC**

Lifespan | *b.* 1904 (England), *d.* 1991 (Switzerland)
First Published | 1938
First Published by | W. Heinemann (London)
Movie Adaptation Released | 1947

GRAHAM GREENE

Brighton Rock

A story of murder and love, of guilt and faith, of the perpetual conflict between evil and good, BRIGHTON ROCK is one of the most powerful and exciting novels the publishers have handled ☞

Greene converted to Catholicism in the late 1920s, an event that profoundly affected his subsequent fiction.

Richard Attenborough plays Pinkie in the 1947 movie *Brighton Rock*, which makes an excellent thriller out of Greene's drama.

Cause for Alarm

Eric Ambler

Lifespan | *b.* 1909 (England), *d.* 1998
First Published | 1938
First Published by | Hodder & Stoughton (London)
Postwar Pseudonym | Eliot Reed

In the late 1930s, Eric Ambler reinvented the British thriller, a genre that had been teeming with unconvincing villains pitted against, as he put it, heroes of "abysmal stupidity." His first novel, *The Dark Frontier* (1936), began as a parody. A scientist regains consciousness after a car crash believing himself to be a tough hero, and foils a charismatic Countess's dastardly plan for world domination. Five more followed in the next five years, of which the best is *Cause for Alarm*.

Nicholas Marlow—an engineer, as Ambler himself was—loses his job on the day he proposes to his girlfriend. Ten weeks later, still unemployed, he accepts a position in the Milan office of a British company that manufactures machines for making artillery shells. In Italy, he is approached by various spies of ambiguous affiliation, eager for information about how the Fascist government is arming itself. Caught up in a tangle of espionage and counter-espionage, Marlow eventually falls foul of the authorities. Trapped on the wrong side of a continent rolling toward war, with a price on his head, he has to flee. The last third of the novel is taken up by an impressively sustained and exhilarating chase across northern Italy. *Cause for Alarm* is the extremely exciting story of an innocent abroad who finds that his innocence is a kind of culpability, of a man who is forced to recalibrate his loyalties to his employers, to his country, to science, and to the world at large. **TEJ**

Alamut

Vladimir Bartol

Lifespan | *b.* 1903 (Italy), *d.* 1967 (Slovenia)
First Published | 1938
First Published by | *Modra ptica* (Ljubljana)
First English Edition | 2004, by Scala House Press

The Slovenian writer Vladimir Bartol languished out of print and unpublished for many years. A man so much of his time as to transcend his time, he was savagely censored in the Soviet era. Yet *Alamut*, his masterpiece, is one of those rich works that acquires new meaning as it journeys into its futurity: what was, in part, a satire on the rising fascist movements that would envelop its author only a year after publication acquires new and deeper levels in a world of militant Islam.

Alamut reimagines the story of the eleventh-century Ismaili leader Hasan ibn Sabbah, the "Old Man of the Mountain" who created the original assassins—elite suicide attackers motivated by religious passion and a carefully nurtured vision of the paradise that awaited them. Set in Alamut, Sabbah's hilltop fortress, and seen primarily through the eyes of the young slave girl Halima and the elite, if naive, warrior Ibn Tahir, the narrative raises potent questions about faith, belief, rhetoric, and the nature and purpose of power.

Yet there is much, much more to this novel than politics and religion. The life of the girls and ageing women in the initially idyllic harem are explored; the moral complexities at the heart of Sabbah's ascent to power are painfully exposed; the contrasting landscape of medieval Iran and the savage beauty of isolated Alamut are intensely imagined. The whole, despite the occasional longueur, still has the power to shock, to move, and to provoke. **TSu**

Rebecca

Daphne du Maurier

Lifespan | *b.* 1907 (England), *d.* 1989
First Published | 1938
First Published by | V. Gollancz (London)
Movie Adaptation Released | 1940

Rebecca still captivates readers today, nearly seventy years after its first publication, when it became an immediate best seller, spawning many adaptations, serializations, movies, stage shows and copycat narratives. The novel's resilience lies in Du Maurier's combination of fairy-tale elements with aspects of gothic romance and thriller.

The shy narrator is chosen for marriage by a wealthy, mysterious, upper-class widower and thus saved from her life as the paid companion to an ill-mannered European woman. She moves to Manderley, an ancient English mansion filled with forbidden rooms, shrouded furniture, and labyrinthine passageways, only to find that both house and owner, the aristocratic Maximilian de Winter, are haunted and oppressed by the memory of the first Mrs. de Winter, Rebecca. Maxim himself bears a distinct literary resemblance to Mr. Rochester in *Jane Eyre*, and as with Rochester, Maxim's "secret self" masks the revelation around which the plot of the novel revolves. In a subtle twist, Du Maurier's novel is named after the first, rather than the second wife. *Jane Eyre*'s madwoman in the attic is replaced here by the body of a murdered woman bobbing in the sea, refusing to be washed away. *Rebecca*'s unnamed narrator breaks the Victorian mold of the novel with her neurotic, Oedipal fantasies, and she raises more questions than she answers. One of Du Maurier's achievements is to secure readers' loyalty to this jealous, insecure narrator. **SN**

"*Last night I dreamt I went to Manderlay again. It seemed to me I stood by the iron gate leading to the drive, and for a while I could not enter, for the way was barred to me.*"

Du Maurier's fascination with her initially abandoned and neglected house "Menabilly" inspired the house in *Rebecca*.

Nausea

Jean-Paul Sartre

Lifespan | *b.* 1905 (France), *d.* 1980
First Published | 1938, by Gallimard (Paris)
Original Title | *La Nausée*
Nobel Prize for Literature | 1964 (declined)

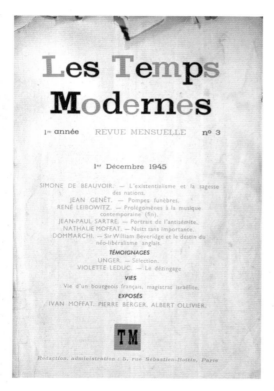

Sartre was an editor for the journal *Les Temps Modernes*, first published in 1945, which he used to develop his ideas.

By 1946, when this photo of Sartre was taken, his existentialism was being popularized as a hip attitude to life for young radicals.

Jean-Paul Sartre's *Nausea* is that rare thing in literary history—a "philosophical" novel that succeeds in both of its endeavors. The novel is at once a manifesto for existentialist philosophy and a convincing work of art. In fact, it succeeds to such an extent that it blurs the distinction between literature and philosophy altogether. *Nausea* details the experiences of thirty-year-old Antoine Roquentin, a researcher who has settled in the French port of Bouville (a thinly disguised Le Havre) after several years of travel. Settling down, however, produces a series of increasingly strange effects. As Roquentin engages in simple, everyday activities, his understanding of the world and his place in it is fundamentally altered. He comes to perceive the rational solidity of existence as no more than a fragile veneer. He experiences the "nausea" of reality, a "sweetish sickness," a ground-level vertigo. He is appalled by the blank indifference of inanimate objects, yet acutely conscious that each situation he finds himself in bears the irrevocable stamp of his being. He finds that he cannot escape from his own overwhelming presence.

This is a delicately controlled examination of freedom, responsibility, consciousness, and time. Influenced by the philosophy of Edmund Husserl and the literary stylings of Dostoevsky and Kafka, *Nausea* is the novel that announced existentialism to the world—a system of ideas that would go on to become one of the most significant developments in twentieth-century thought and culture. The notion that "existence precedes essence" is writ large for the first time here, several years before Sartre "formalized" his ideas in *Being and Nothingness* (1943) and before the horrors of the Second World War had intensified their impact. **SamT**

Miss Pettigrew Lives for a Day

Winifred Watson

Lifespan | b. 1907 (England), d. 2002
First Published | 1938
First Published by | Methuen & Co. (London)
Radio Adaptation Released | 2000 (BBC Radio 4)

"Miss Pettigrew pushed open the door of the employment agency and went in as the clock struck a quarter past nine. She had, as usual, very little hope . . ." So begins Winifred Watson's recently rediscovered, enchanting tale. The story unfolds over twenty-four hours in the life of neglected spinster Guinevere Pettigrew. Sent to the wrong address by her employment agency, Miss Pettigrew, a governess, is mistaken for the new housekeeper by the glamorous and rather amoral nightclub singer Miss La Fosse. Thrown into a world of cocktails before noon, cocaine that must be disposed of, and fistfights between dangerously handsome suitors, perhaps most shocking of all to Miss Pettigrew is the wicked thrill of makeup. As first-time readers, we worry for the frightened and sheltered Guinevere, but there is more to her than meets the eye. Over the course of the day, in a series of deft interventions, witty misunderstandings, brilliant repartee, and enough gin to sink a lesser woman, Guinevere is revealed not only to her newfound friends, but more importantly to herself, as a lifesaver, in more ways than one. A delightful, intelligent, and naughty novel, which reminds us that it is never too late to have a second chance; it is never too late to live. **MJ**

🔾 Writing "a book that was fun" was a new departure for Watson, whose reputation had been established with dramatic novels.

On the Edge of Reason

Miroslav Krleža

Lifespan | b. 1893 (Croatia), d. 1981
First Published | 1938
Original Title | Na rubu pameti
NIN Prize | 1962

Miroslav Krleža's novel delivers a brilliant critique of contemporary bourgeois society on the southern brinks of the Austro-Hungarian empire in the period between the two World Wars. It exposes the social hierarchy of a nameless Croatian town ridden by corruption, dishonesty, conformism and consumerism, from the petit bourgeois shopkeepers, civil servants, aspiring "intellectuals," and "torchbearers" to the industrial magnates at the top of the Austro-Hungarian socioeconomic elite.

The novel concerns the downfall of an unremarkable, middle-class, middle-aged legal adviser leading a dull life in an unhappy marriage and unsatisfactory job, yet unable to escape the general apathy and small-mindedness of his surroundings. One day he stirs these stagnant waters when he accidentally insults a local potentate, rousing scandal across the entire society.

Erudite, picturesque, and with a keen eye for detail, Krleža's style has been described as baroque, rendering his characters with great mastery, sensitivity, and imagination. *On the Edge of Reason* remains in the forefront of socially conscious and innovative literature comparable to that of Joyce, Zola, and Svevo. The novel represents the world with uncompromising realism, although bearing some traces of Krleža's romantic infatuation with the Marxist idealism of his earlier literary career. **JK**

The Big Sleep

Raymond Chandler

Lifespan | *b.* 1888 (U.S.), *d.* 1959
First Published | 1939
First Published by | Hamish Hamilton (London)
Movie Adaptation Released | 1946

🔵 *The Big Sleep* was Chandler's first novel, and would be the first in a series of books to feature the detective Philip Marlowe.

🔵 Novelist William Faulkner was one of the screenwriters for the impressively witty 1946 movie version of Chandler's novel.

The Big Sleep represents some major departures in the nature of the detective genre, changes that necessarily reflect the world in which it was written. Corrupt networks map out Raymond Chandler's post-Prohibition era, be they explicitly criminal or nominally official, and it is the gray areas in between that allow the detective Philip Marlowe to exist. The gray, claustrophobic urban space is a major constituent of the novel; set in Southern California, the location could really be any major city given that exteriors are almost entirely absent. Rooms, cars, and even phone booths represent a series of divided compartments in which the story develops, a series of points with no connections.

This is Chandler's first Marlowe story, but there is no introduction to the character; rather, we leap straight into the investigation as it gets underway. This is essential to the nature of the world and the character, a new kind of "hero" who seems only to become active when there is a crime to solve. We know nothing of his background and only ever see him return to his office, and this only when a trail is exhausted. Like Sergio Leone's *Man With No Name*, Marlowe combines a kind of shabby fallibility—a hard drinker who seems to be constantly beaten up by men and women alike—with an almost supernatural authority whereby he seems to serenely coast over the jumbled twists and turns of the case, observing and randomly following leads and providence, until a solution is finally reached. That this is in such contrast to the Sherlock Holmes school of detective work—where central to the plot is the immense intellectuality of the detective that allows him to simply consider at length the facts in order to succeed—is perhaps the most significant factor in the novel's literary importance. **SF**

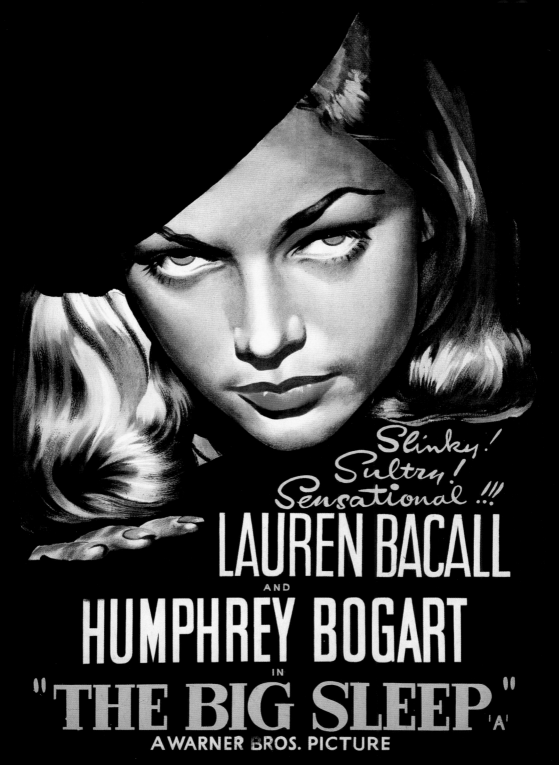

Goodbye to Berlin

Christopher Isherwood

"I am a camera," Christopher Isherwood writes, "with its shutter open, quite passive, recording, not thinking." What he offers us are snapshots and newsreels of Berlin during the last days of the Weimar Republic. The city is caught in the eerie calm of an apocalyptic hurricane, the brief gap wedged between the First World War and the distant thunder of the all-powerful Third Reich.

Isherwood, the narrator and observer, is detached and numb as though shell-shocked—what he is witnessing has never been witnessed before. The demimonde he inhabits is a fatalistic free-for-all, fueled by a growing despair so great that the only recourse is a dance of abandon, the last and most memorable song of the dance band on the *Titanic* as the iceberg looms. It is a world of lost souls, where the great have fallen, where the good do what they can to make ends meet, where everything is for sale and virtue is an unaffordable luxury. Former socialites must take in lodgers, prostitutes mingle with opera singers, and Isherwood stumbles through opportunities with his fellow expatriate and co-lodger, the aspiring nightclub singer, Sally Bowles. Sally is a perfect emblem of the time: tragic and blind to consequences, capricious and predatory, and deadened by alcohol and sex. This is a melancholic though unsentimental novel about a world that will soon no longer exist. The hedonism of the Weimar is fading and soon will be eradicated. Sally grows distracted and disagreeable. The Jewish Landauers' tenuous safety will soon be destroyed. Rudi, the communist youth, will have his idealism prove fatal. Innocence will be lost.

With his understated and dispassionate prose, Isherwood throws the massive and terrifying events of 1930s Berlin into relief; his genius is chilling. **GT**

Lifespan | *b*. 1904 (England), *d*. 1986 (U.S.)
First Published | 1939
First Published by | Hogarth Press (London)
Compiled as | *The Berlin Stories* (1946)

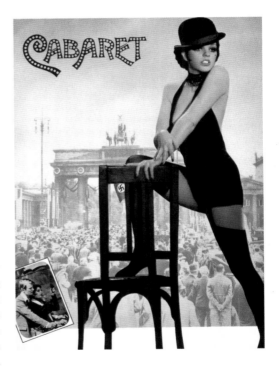

The musical *Cabaret*, based on Isherwood's novel, was filmed in 1972 with Liza Minnelli cast as nightclub singer Sally Bowles.

When Isherwood moved to Berlin, the sexual freedom depicted here influenced both his personal life and his writing.

The Grapes of Wrath

John Steinbeck

It is something of a commonplace these days to talk of *The Grapes of Wrath* as a novel that has become profoundly ingrained in the consciousness of America, and yet no other writer chronicled the catastrophic period of the Great Depression in the 1930s with the same passion and political commitment. As John Steinbeck's masterpiece, its place in the canon of great American literature is confirmed by the Pulitzer Prize it was awarded in 1940 (the same year it was adapted for film) and the Nobel Prize for Literature that the author received in 1962. It is concerned with the Joad family, who lose their Oklahoma farm and head west with dreams of a better life in California. As the journey unfolds, they and thousands of other "Okies" flocking westward converge along Highway 66, telling each other tales of injustice and relishing the plenty that lies ahead. What they find in California is exploitation, greed, low wages, hunger, and death. In a stunning indictment of the savage divisions that those with money seek to extend and exploit, Steinbeck represents the desperation of the family as the threat of violence, starvation, and death begin to eat away at them. It is only wrath, a defiant solidarity, and constant sacrifice that allow them to maintain their dignity.

Steinbeck has been criticized in the past for a perceived sentimentality in his characterization of the Joads, but while a reader is inevitably drawn into their plight, they are only ever actors in a tragedy that is bigger than they are. This is, above all, a political novel, and the defeats, the mud, the hunger, and the maltreatment all carry a political charge, a condemnation of injustice (and of those in positions of power who create the injustice), and a validation of the quiet anger and dignified stoicism of the common man in response. **MD**

Lifespan | *b.* 1902 (U.S.), *d.* 1968
First Published | 1939, by Viking (New York)
Pulitzer Prize | 1940
Nobel Prize for Literature | 1962

Californian photographer Peter Stackpole snapped this casual, unposed image of Steinbeck for *Life* magazine in 1937.

Steinbeck described Ford's 1940 movie version of his novel as "a hard, straight picture," although it ended with an optimistic twist.

Good Morning, Midnight

Jean Rhys

Lifespan | b. 1890 (Dominica), d. 1979 (England)
First Published | 1939
First Published by | Constable & Co. (London)
Given Name | Ella Gwendolen Rees William

The title of Jean Rhys's somber fifth novel is taken from an Emily Dickinson poem. *Good Morning, Midnight* is set between the World Wars and centers on Sasha, a middle-aged woman who has returned to the Paris of her youth. The fragmented narrative slips between Sasha's past and present in exploring the paradoxical limitations of the life of a woman who has sought to free herself from convention.

As the novel opens, and Sasha attempts to locate herself among Paris's familiar landmarks, we are deluged with the bittersweet memories of her youth. We learn how she escaped from the strictures of a working-class London life by marrying the artistic Enno and moving with him to Europe. But Enno's reluctance to protect his wife from degrading social and economic transactions makes her profoundly aware of how "cheap" she is to society, and how vulnerable she is. As we move further into the novel and into Sasha's past we learn of the trauma—the death of her child in early infancy and her subsequent abandonment by her husband—that led to her rejection by even unconventional society. It is Sasha's rapid and poignant decline, her steady drinking and drifting between jobs that seem to value feminine youth and beauty above all, that offers a continuity between the novel's past and the present. As the novel ends, we see Sasha stumbling to accept how the inevitable and harsh combinations of poverty and age have rendered her only more vulnerable. **NM**

"I'm a bit of automation, but sane, surely—dry, cold and sane. Now I have forgotten about dark streets, dark rivers, the pain, the struggle, the drowning . . ."

Rhys, born to a Welsh father and Creole mother in Dominica, often wrote about the effects of women being uprooted.

At Swim-Two-Birds

Flann O'Brien

Lifespan | b. 1911 (Ireland), d. 1966
First Published | 1939
First Published by | Longmans & Co. (London)
Given Name | Brian O'Nuallain

Ireland in the 1930s, with its censorship and church domination, was hardly a hotbed for the avant-garde or experimental novel. But it was precisely the pieties and stifling atmosphere of Ireland at the time that impelled this delightfully transgressive, antiauthoritarian, and satirical experimental novel. Literary exuberance contrasted with the mundanity of social life is one of the anomalies within the novel that gives it such potent comic power.

This is a novel about a novelist writing a novel about the writing of novel. The frame story is narrated by a student living sullenly under his nagging uncle's roof, while engaged in writing a book about an author called Dermot Trellis. The student has firmly democratic and revolutionary ideas on the form: the novel should not be confined to one beginning and ending, nor should the characters be under any compulsion to be good or bad. They should, rather, be "allowed a private life, self-determination and a decent standard of living." Furthermore, the "entire corpus of existing literature" is simply a storehouse from which an author can draw whatever characters he wishes. The narrator and Trellis draw on cowboy stories, popular romances, folklore, and (mercilessly lampooned) figures from Irish mythology. Eager for revenge against his despotic creator, one character begins his own novel in which Trellis becomes trapped as a fictional creation. If ever a novel was before its time, undoubtedly this was it. **RM**

Finnegans Wake

James Joyce

Lifespan | b. 1882 (Ireland), d. 1941 (Switzerland)
First Published | 1939
First Published by | Faber & Faber (London)
Extracts Published | 1928–1939

James Joyce's last book is perhaps the most daunting work of fiction ever written. Yet it is also one of the funniest, bringing pleasure to generations of readers willing to suspend the usual assumptions that govern the novel. Instead of a single plot, *Finnegans Wake* has a number of kernel stories, some of them occurring in hundreds of versions, from a word or two long to several pages. The most ubiquitous is a story of a fall that turns out not to be entirely negative, including the Fall of Man; an indiscretion in Phoenix Park, Dublin, involving an older man and two girls; and a tumble from a ladder by an Irish builder, Tim Finnegan.

In place of characters, the novel has figures who go by many different names, each figure consisting of a cluster of recognizable features. In place of settings, it merges place names from around the globe. Joyce achieves this condensation through the "portmanteau": the fusing together of two or more words in the same or different languages. Thus "kissmiss" is both the festive season and something that might happen during it, with a suggestion of fatefulness; the Holy Father becomes a "hoary frother"; and an old photo is a "fadograph." Reading *Finnegans Wake*—best done aloud and if possible in a group—means allowing these suggestions to resonate, while accepting that many will remain obscure. The work's seventeen sections have their own styles and subjects, tracing a slow movement through nightfall and dawn to a final unfinished sentence that returns us to the beginning of the book. **DA**

Native Son

Richard Wright

Lifespan | *b.* 1908 (U.S.), *d.* 1960 (France)
First Published | 1940
First Published by | Harper & Row (New York)
Movie Adaptations Released | 1951, 1986

Richard Wright's novel leaped onto the American literary scene as a warning to white America of the violence that the country was harboring within it. The novel's opening presents its central protagonist, Bigger Thomas, beating a rat to death in front of his frightened sister, cowed mother, and admiring brother. Wright's identification of Bigger with the rat allows us to see him as both perpetrator and victim, and it is from this uneasy position that the reader views the ensuing, disturbing events.

This realist novel is divided into three parts. The first section describes Bigger's introduction into the middle-class world of the Daltons and his accidental killing of their daughter, Mary. The second sees a desperate Bigger pursued across the Chicago landscape and records the punitive effects of his crime on the wider African-American community. The final section focuses on Bigger's court case and Wright's attempt to defend his broken humanity.

The explicit and sexualized violence of the novel, in particular the decapitation and burning of the dead Mary Dalton, brought the book its initial notoriety. Wright was both celebrated for his fearless honesty and castigated for providing white America with the stereotype it most loved to fear. Seeking to avoid a sentimental view of black America, Wright was exploring the meaning of freedom. His commitments to black nationalism and communism are qualified finally by his commitment to the existential desire to truly know oneself. **NM**

The Tartar Steppe

Dino Buzzati

Lifespan | *b.* 1906 (Italy), *d.* 1972
First Published | 1940
First Published by | Rizzoli (Milan)
Original Title | *Il deserto dei Tartari*

In this mysterious and disquieting novel, soldiers at a garrison await the attack of the enemy, the Tartars, due to arrive from the north any day. The fortress where the action takes place belongs to an undifferentiated past, and the atmosphere within the fortress, situated at the bottom of harsh and inaccessible mountains at the border of a stony desert, is suspended between reality and dream. The soldiers prepare continuously for that moment, although no one knows how and when the attack will take place. No one even knows who the enemy really is. Destiny is in charge of the lives of these men, especially Lieutenant Drogo, who finds himself at the fortress against his will, after an exhausting journey overshadowed by the enigmatic fortress and the threatening harshness of the landscape. In the surreal atmosphere within the garrison, life is disciplined by strict military routines. Sentries patrol nobody knows what to defend the fortress from nobody knows whom. Military maneuvers have no apparent meaning, while the soldiers' unreal life is dominated by an absurd wait.

Strongly existentialist in its themes, the novel remains elusive today, but it seems ironic that not long after publication the soldiers' long wait was ultimately met with a conflict far larger than they could ever have hoped for. **RPi**

> ◗ *The Tartar Steppe* depicts the futility of military tactics such as that shown in this 1917 Italian poster: "Everyone must do his duty!"

A. MAUZAN
Fate tutti
il vostro dovere!
LE SOTTOSCRIZIONI AL PRESTITO SI RICEVONO PRESSO IL
CREDITO ITALIANO

The Power and the Glory

Graham Greene

Lifespan | b. 1904 (England), d. 1991 (Switzerland)
First Published | 1940
First Published by | W. Heinemann (London)
Movie Adaptation Released | 1962

The Power and the Glory, with its account of a priest's desperate flight from arrest and execution, is set against the bleak backdrop of the persecution of the Catholic Church in Mexico in the 1920s. The terrain Graham Greene describes—whether physical, social, or psychological—is suitably desolate. The protagonist, described but never named, is a "whisky priest" and the father of an illegitimate child, whom he briefly and unhappily encounters on his journey. The psychological and spiritual avenues available to him for making sense of his fate seem as unpromising as his options for escaping from the secular authorities. He has a price on his head and his pursuers are liable to execute the villagers who come to his assistance. But through the despair, and despite Greene's resistance to various weightless forms of redemption (he is much exercised by the fraudulent, pride-sustaining qualities of piety), lies the hazily grasped apprehension of God's goodness. The priest comes to realize that conditions of suffering and sinfulness are, perhaps, the only means by which God's presence can be manifested in this world.

There are many triumphs in this novel: the priest's night-long incarceration in an overcrowded jail; his quest to buy wine for sacramental purposes; and the ideological and personal cat-and-mouse encounters between the priest and the zealous lieutenant. Greene succeeds in fashioning a fallen world marked, strikingly, by the twin poles of intense claustrophobia and unbounded emptiness. **RM**

For Whom the Bell Tolls

Ernest Hemingway

Lifespan | b. 1899 (U.S.), d. 1961
First Published | 1940
First Published by | C. Scribner's Sons (New York)
Nobel Prize for Literature | 1954

Set in 1937 during the Spanish Civil War, *For Whom the Bell Tolls* follows the struggles of an American college instructor who has left his job to fight for the Republicans. Robert Jordan has been dispatched from Madrid to lead a band of *guerrilleros* that operates in a perpetual state of leadership crisis. Pablo, the ostensible head of the group, has lost his robust commitment to the hardships of war and wistfully dreams of living peacefully in the company of his horses. Pilar, Pablo's superstitious, half-gypsy companion, has kept the group cohesive with her darkly agitated care for both the guerrilleros themselves and the fight that has brought them together. Jordan finds an instant bond with Maria, a young woman who was raped by Fascist soldiers before being taken in by the Republican camp.

Jordan feels a creeping ambivalence toward the Republican cause and a more general self-alienation as he wrestles with his own abhorrence of violence. His inability to integrate his belief systems is dramatized through his relationship with Maria, for whom he bears a painfully intense love, although he shuns her while strategizing the risky bridge-blowing mission. Ultimately Jordan is forced to reassess his personal, political, and romantic values as his insistence on a coherent and orderly hierarchy of beliefs and experiences is shattered. **AF**

❯ Director Frank Capra (right) discusses the novel with Hemingway in 1941; the film version was eventually directed by Sam Wood.

The Man Who Loved Children

Christina Stead

Lifespan | *b.* 1902 (Australia), *d.* 1983
First Published | 1940
First Published by | Simon & Schuster (New York)
Patrick White Award | 1974

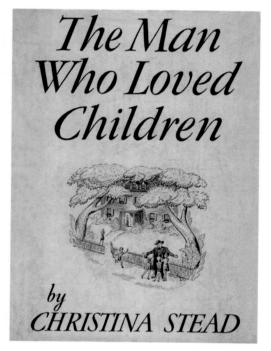

The Man Who Loved Children

by

CHRISTINA STEAD

"A self-made man is one who believes in luck and sends his son to Oxford."

⌃ At the age of two Stead lost her mother, and much of *The Man Who Loved Children* was based on her childhood experiences.

Like the book itself, the title of Christina Stead's masterful novel points toward both emotional honesty and bitter irony. The novel tells the story of the large Pollit family, the product of a disastrous marriage between Sam Pollit, a working-class naturalist, and the querulous Baltimore heiress Henny Collyer. Set in and around Washington D.C. in the 1930s, the novel examines family life through the lens of Stead's painfully revealing microscope, reflecting the naturalism of writers like Zola, whom Stead admired greatly.

The result is a rich tapestry of scenes that shift from the comic to the gruesome with a rapidity that reflects the swift emotional changes of real life. The characters produced by Stead's exhaustive technique are both lifelike and fascinating. Sam, the self-proclaimed lover of children, emerges as the dominant force of the book, a charismatic but infuriating mix of egocentric bravado and creativity, leading the reader to watch with fascination his attempts to manipulate and control his children, sisters, wife, and colleagues in the service of what he sees as political and moral good. His wife, Henny, disappointed in love and forced to live in a declining financial situation, provides her children with a bitter counterpoint to their father's high spirits.

As the text goes on, a battle develops between Sam and his awkward adolescent daughter, Louie, whose gropings after independence and nascent adult consciousness eventually lead directly to the novel's shocking conclusion. Clear-eyed and unforgiving, this novel presents a picture of family life as seen from the inside, and spares neither characters nor readers from realizing the often uncomfortable truths that lie behind the innocuous personas we assign to family members. **AB**

Broad and Alien is the World

Ciro Alegría

As the emblematic title suggests, this is the story of endless wanderings of the dispossessed. The Peruvian community of Rumi, consisting of powerless, uneducated, but above all impoverished Indians and half-castes, clashes with the insatiable expansion of big landowners. Constructed from the memories of the elderly Rosendo Maqui, the origin of this forsaken community is described as a prologue to the main story, which concerns the lawsuit brought by the covetous landowner Álvaro Amenábar to seize the community's lands. The novel presents the legal process as a pure sham that conceals greed and consigns the Indians to a much smaller territory, where, incredibly, they continue to be exploited. Their leaders are systematically destroyed; the peaceable Rosendo dies in prison, while Fiero Vásquez, the bandit who could have led an armed resistance, is beheaded.

Immediately before the brutal end of *Broad and Alien is the World* the horror increases with the description of the treatment of indigenous communities in other parts of Peru, particularly in the mines and the forest rubber plantations, where oppression is endemic. At the same time, the native cause is expressed increasingly explicitly. The charismatic, messianic rebel Benito Castro is introduced to take up his position in the community and to embark on armed resistance, but, almost inevitably, this proves equally unsuccessful.

In spite of a formal approach that was somewhat archaic even in its own day—an omnipresent narrator spends too long in presenting events and historical parallels—Ciro Alegría has created a whole gallery of characters incorporated in a natural landscape and, overall, a convincing novel about the struggle against injustice. **DMG**

Lifespan | *b.* 1909 (Peru), *d.* 1967
First Published | 1941
First Published by | Ediciones Ercilla (Santiago)
Original Title | *El mundo es ancho y ajeno*

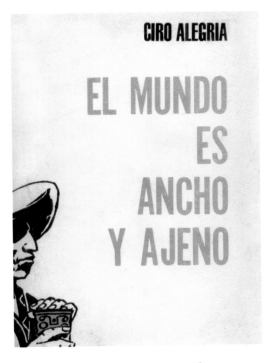

"Nearer, ever nearer, the explosion of the Mausers continues to resound."

◉ The cover of this 1970 paperback edition suggests the uncertain fate of Indians in the Peruvian highlands.

The Living and the Dead

Patrick White

"During the early . . . months I hovered between London and New York writing too hurriedly a second novel."

Patrick White, 1973

⬥ The Spanish Civil War plays a central role in this novel set in 1930s London about relationships within the Standish family.

Lifespan | *b.* 1912 (England), *d.* 1990 (Australia)
First Published | 1941
First Published by | Routledge & Kegan Paul
Nobel Prize for Literature | 1973

Set in London during the 1930s, the plot of *The Living and the Dead* focuses on the fraught relationship between Catherine Standish and her two children, Elyot and Eden. Having been abandoned by her husband, Catherine is an emotionally distant mother. Elyot is a writer and critic who, while given to ruminating on his lack of belonging in the world, willfully insulates himself from it through books. Eden, his sister, who at first appears to be a more expansive character, seeks fulfillment through her political activism and dalliances with men, only to meet with disappointment on both fronts.

While this summary may make the novel sound an unremittingly bleak affair, it is in those passages where Patrick White so penetratingly inhabits the minds of his characters that he deservedly earns his reputation as a writer of the very first rank. In these truthful yet compassionate glimpses into the self-doubts and self-delusions that motivate each life, White introduces some of the thematic concerns that came to dominate his later fiction: what is the value of self-sacrifice in a world increasingly indifferent to human suffering? What is the purpose of imagination in a universe vacated by God?

Some readers may find the frequent longueurs in the narrative a little cumbersome. Yet White's loftiness is never contrived in this moving account of how the socially inhibited struggle with, and are imprisoned by, an inability to give imaginative surrender to their own vision. **VA**

The Harvesters

Cesare Pavese

Lifespan | *b.* 1908 (Italy), *d.* 1950
First Published | 1941
First Published by | Einaudi (Torino)
Original Title | *Paesi Tuoi*

The Harvesters is a novel in which the plot is closely underwritten by nature—oppressive heat is broken by great storms, burning sunshine is contrasted with eerie moonlight. In the raging, sun-scorched hills of the dry northern Italian countryside, there is a sense that Italy itself, the actual land, is a stable, eternal, natural reality in a shifting world of danger, passion, and death.

Cesare Pavese begins his story in the aftermath of Talino and Berto's release from a Fascist prison. Talino convinces Berto to accompany him home to his country farm for the harvest. At the farm, Berto finds a world wholly alien to his native Turin, a place where morality is obscured and everything is not as it appears. The plot unfolds in half-truths and falsehoods, with stories, unfinished or never begun, that Berto, as an outsider, can barely comprehend. Upon arriving at the farm, Berto finds a large family, impoverished and brutalized, yet he is quickly attracted to Gisella, one of Talino's four sisters. They have a brief affair, but Berto only begins to guess at the truth of Gisella and Talino's relationship before, savagely and abruptly, tragedy strikes.

Pavese moved in anti-Fascist circles, yet always felt torn, wanting to join the fight but incapable of doing so. His writing expresses his inner conflict, perhaps reflecting Italy's own struggles at that time. Celebrated after the war as a model of anti-Fascist thinking, his work has been hailed as a brilliant depiction of humanity in times of hardship. **RMu**

Conversations in Sicily

Elio Vittorini

Lifespan | *b.* 1908 (Italy), *d.* 1966
First Published | 1941, by Bompiani (Milan)
Alternate Title | *In Sicily*
Original Title | *Conversazione in Sicilia*

The opening of *Conversations in Sicily* contains emblematic references to the events of 1936 that marked the beginning of the Spanish Civil War. Silvestro, the protagonist and narrator, has plunged into despondency and disillusionment at the realization of his powerlessness when confronted by the loss of humanity. He embarks on a metaphorical journey to his native Sicily. During a rediscovery of his origins and subsequent psychological transformation, Silvestro converses with numerous people. There is the orange picker who, unable to sell his produce, evokes southern poverty. There is the courageous man who feels he has a moral duty to humanity and would be ready to renounce all his possessions to fight in its defense. A knife sharpener laments the indolence of people who do not give him swords, daggers, or even cannons to sharpen.

The abstract words of these conversations are a symbolic incitement to fight against the suppression of liberty and democracy. In the middle of the novel, Silvestro converses with his mother, Concezione, and recalls his youth. A strong woman, unscathed by her husband's abandonment and unafraid of solitude, Concezione is a symbol of womanly and motherly strength. At the end of his three-day journey, which can be interpreted as a Christian metaphor for inner rediscovery, Silvestro has been "resurrected" to a higher human understanding. The author's anti-Fascism, therefore, acquires a dimension that is not so much historical or political as it is moral. **RPi**

The Outsider

Albert Camus

Lifespan | *b.* 1913 (Algeria), *d.* 1960 (France)
First Published | 1942, by Gallimard (Paris)
U.S. Title | *The Stranger*
Original Title | *L'Étranger*

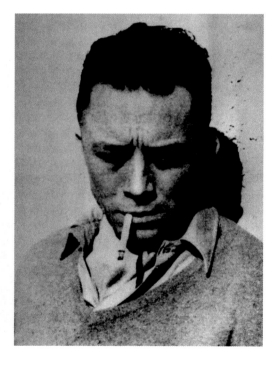

◉ Like his antihero, Meursault, in *The Outsider*, Albert Camus was the son of European settlers in Algeria, then under French rule.

◉ Albert Camus's watercolor portrait, entitled "Alberic," is detailed with a furrowed brow reminiscent of his own.

The Outsider is a novel of absolute flatness. The events of the story, despite taking in a murder and subsequent trial, seem to have no weight to them whatsoever, as if they simply float past on the page. This, it becomes clear, is absolutely essential to both the story's purpose, its much-discussed relationship with the philosophy of existentialism, and, oddly, to its readability. Albert Camus's careful simplicity roots the story at once in the everyday and in the fable, and it is left up to the reader to resolve this ambiguity.

This is a novel that displays an unwavering discipline in expounding a life where conventional self-conduct is undermined. There is no technical "cleverness" in the illustration of its themes; we are simply presented with a period of time in the life of a blank man named Meursault, a social outcast who chooses to live a private and solitary life. During this period, a number of significant events take place in his life—the death of his mother, the murder of a man, and a judgment that condemns Meursault to death—but each of these fails to rouse the expected emotional response from him.

On first impression, there appear to be certain parallels with Kafka, in the suggestion that vast complexities lurk behind a visibly spare style and in the general dreamy detachment that surrounds it. But there is nothing of the surreal and everything of the mundane in Meursault's world, over which he has little control. Dislocated from others as well as from his own life, Meursault's character demonstrates the meaninglessness of life, beyond the meaning one is willing to ascribe to it. It is the realization of and resignation to this essential meaninglessness that for Camus constitutes the absurd, a theme that he went on to develop more fully in his later work. **SF**

Celui-ci c'est Albéric, le "Jeune-homme-qui-croyait-que-c'était-arrivé-et-qui-s'aperçut-que-ce-n'était-pas-au..."

(Quelle chaleur)

Embers

Sándor Márai

Lifespan | *b.* 1900 (Hungary), *d.* 1989 (U.S.)
First Published | 1942
First Published in | Budapest
Original Title | *A gyertyák csonkig égnek*

Embers is a rediscovered jewel of Central European literature—originally published in Budapest in 1942, but virtually unknown to a wider audience until its translation into English in 2001. Against the odds, the novel has gone on to become an international bestseller, although its author, who committed suicide while in exile in the United States in 1989, will never bear witness to its unexpected popularity.

Set in Hungary just after the outbreak of the Second World War, in a remote castle at the base of the Carpathian mountains, Henrik, a 75-year-old retired general, dines with an old friend, Konrad, who he has not seen for over forty years. There are many unresolved issues between the pair, and what follows is a wonderfully controlled standoff—an unfolding series of anecdotes, reminiscences, silences, rebuttals, denials, and obfuscations. Sándor Márai paces his work with skill and precision, allowing each new revelation to emerge just as one feels some kind of reconciliation may be possible. Years of smoldering resentment are condensed into a single night.

Embers is a brief and remarkably intense work, a novel still steeped in the lore and atmosphere of the Austro-Hungarian empire. It is a novel of long shadows and vintage wine, of candlelight, ancient forests, and creaking mahogany. Márai maintains this atmosphere without ever resorting to cheap theatrics. For all its old-world charm, the novel remains an intricately observed study of class, friendship, betrayal, and masculine pride. **SamT**

Chess Story

Stefan Zweig

Lifespan | *b.* 1881 (Austria), *d.* 1942
First Published | 1942, by Bermann-Fischer (Sthlm)
Alternate Titles | *Royal Game*; *Chess*
Original Title | *Schachnovelle*

Chess Story is set on an ocean liner, where a young and illiterate—but amazingly talented—chess world champion plays for money with a complete unknown. The stranger's knowledge of chess is extensive, but his practical ability is almost untested at the board. The reason behind this imbalance is what drives the unfolding of the story, and sets the backdrop for a tense and surprising tournament.

Published posthumously in 1943, a year after his tragic double suicide with his wife, *Chess Story* is one of Stefan Zweig's best-known pieces of fiction. The author was also popular as a biographer, essayist, playwright, and poet, and was known to Sigmund Freud, Thomas Mann, and Romain Rolland. As an Austrian Jew, the growth of Nazi influence caused him to leave his homeland in 1934; he subsequently gained British citizenship, but died in Brazil, hopeless and disillusioned about the state of Europe.

Chess Story is a small, powerful text, confidently staging large themes, including Gestapo torture, the nature of obsession, the foolishness of hubris and greed, and political manipulation. In this tale, chess operates as a poison, a dangerous psychological addiction, but also as a cure for the mental barrenness of solitary confinement and as a ticket to fame. Zweig's narrator is never named, but it is through his eyes that we observe the match, and it is to him alone that the stranger reveals his curious secret. *Chess Story* is a short but fast-paced and fascinating narrative gem. **JC**

The Glass Bead Game

Hermann Hesse

Lifespan | *b.* 1877 (Germany), *d.* 1962 (Switzerland)
First Published | 1943, by Fretz & Wasmuth (Zürich)
Alternate Title | *Magister Ludi*
Original Title | *Das Glasperlenspiel*

The Glass Bead Game purports to be the biography of Joseph Knecht, a member of an elite group of intellectuals in twenty-third-century Europe who live and carry out their work in isolation from the rest of society. The novel follows Knecht from his early schooling to his eventual attainment of the revered title of Magister Ludi, or "Master of the Game." This Glass Bead Game is the raison d'être of the intellectual community of which Knecht becomes the head. Although the game's exact nature is never fully explained, it becomes clear that it involves the synthesis of diverse branches of human knowledge; from philosophy, history, and mathematics, to music, literature, and logic. Despite the exquisite nature of the game, Knecht grows increasingly discontent with its players' complete detachment from worldly affairs.

Written amid the events of early 1940s Europe, *The Glass Bead Game* is an eloquent and powerful meditation on the relationship between the spheres of politics and the contemplative life. Hermann Hesse's novel is a passionate argument for a more symbiotic relationship between thought and action. Powerfully illustrating this very union, Knecht leaves the enclosed community in order to experience those aspects of life neglected by his studious existence. This novel is thus a continuation of one of Hesse's enduring themes: the importance of self-reflection as a means of discerning the ever-changing path toward self-growth and renewal. **CG-G**

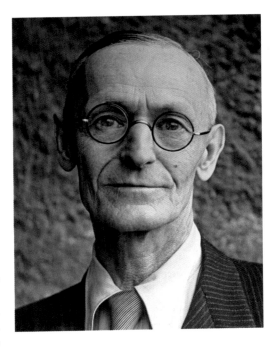

"[T]he Master and the boy followed each other as if drawn along the wires of some mechanism, until soon it could no longer be discerned which was coming and which going . . ."

● This photograph of Hesse was taken in 1962, the year of his death. He was awarded the Nobel Prize for Literature in 1946.

Joseph and His Brothers

Thomas Mann

Lifespan | b.1875 (Germany), d. 1955 (Switzerland)
First Published in four parts | 1933–1943
First Published by | S. Fischer Verlag (Berlin)
Original Title | Joseph und seine Brüder

Thomas Mann intended this retelling of the Old Testament story of Joseph to be the monumental culmination of his distinguished writing career. By the time its first volume appeared in October 1933, however, the Nazis had taken power in Germany and Mann had been forced into exile. Largely denied an audience in his home country, he found few foreign readers for a Biblical epic with no obvious relevance to the political or intellectual issues of the day.

The four volumes of the work—The Stories of Jacob, The Young Joseph, Joseph in Egypt, and Joseph the Provider—follow faithfully the outline of the familiar tale from Genesis. Joseph, eleventh son of Jacob, is driven out of his family, rises to be the right-hand man of the pharaoh of Egypt, and returns at last to lead his people. Mann's epic version expands brief Biblical episodes into richly detailed stories, illuminated with emotional insights, character sketches, and flashes of humor. The author's dense meditations on myth and history lie dauntingly across the reader's path, but fresh narrative delights are always only a few pages away.

The work is a vast compendium of information about ancient civilizations, but the author achieves a complex statement about life that is timeless rather than historical. Joseph ultimately emerges as Mann's image of a fully enlightened human being, blending sophisticated intelligence with respect for tradition, the visionary inspiration of the dreamer's imagination with critical scientific realism. **RegG**

The Little Prince

Antoine de Saint-Exupéry

Lifespan | b.1900 (France), d. 1944 (in the air)
First Published | 1943
First Published by | Reynal & Hitchcock (New York)
Original Title | Le Petit Prince

This charming fable tells the story of an adult's encounter with his inner child. Set in the heart of the Sahara, the tale unfolds after Antoine Saint-Exupéry's pilot-narrator finds himself stranded with a "broken" engine, facing the prospect of "life or death." The very largest question of all lies at the heart of the tale: one's life and how one spends it. The relationship between adult and child unfolds against a backdrop of human emergency, and its nature is one of acute questioning: the inimitable questioning of a child in the form of the "little prince," who asks his adult mentor so "many questions." The dialogue between narrator and child is a form of self-address: the adult engaging with his inner child through the unfettered imaginings and demands of a young child. The little prince and our narrator initially engage through the act of drawing, when the little prince first appears with his demand, "If you please, draw me a sheep."

Saint-Exupéry's tale is a surreal one, defying the conventions of reality and entering into the realm of dreamscape, where the imagination can run riot. The narrator is gently led into a rediscovery of his capacity for imagining. And so the role reversal begins, and the child tutors the adult in the sacred art of wondering. Written during the final year of his life, Saint-Exupéry's The Little Prince reads as a manifesto on how the adult life can and should be lived. **SB**

> Saint-Exupéry wrote Le Petit Prince at this desk at the home of French painter Bernard Lamotte in Connecticut.

Dangling Man

Saul Bellow

Lifespan | *b.* 1915 (Canada), *d.* 2005 (U.S.)
First Published | 1944
First Published by | Vanguard Press (New York)
Nobel Prize for Literature | 1976

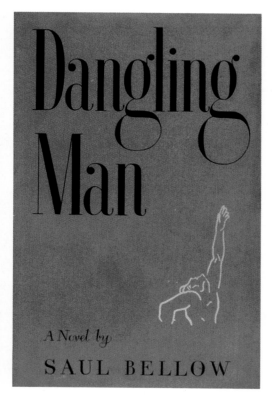

🌑 Published in 1944, *Dangling Man* reflected contemporary intellectual preoccupations with the nature of freedom.

Dangling Man was Saul Bellow's first novel, and it established him as one of the major American writers of the period. The novel is written in the form of the diary of its protagonist, Joseph. Having given up his job at the Inter-American Travel Bureau, Joseph, a "dangling man," is confined to a Chicago boarding house while he waits to be drafted for the Second World War. He rarely leaves the confines of his room, immersing himself instead in the writing of the Enlightenment. His increasingly solipsistic lifestyle alienates both his wife, Iva, and his other intellectual friends. The novel ends with Joseph finally being called up and leaving his friends and family to begin life in the army. He hopes that his new regimented life will relieve his current mental suffering; a hope that one assumes will be in vain.

In Joseph's search for the meaning of his "dangling" life, the novel testifies to the influence of French existentialism on the intellectual life of 1940s America. Sections of Joseph's diary are given over to a dialogue with an imaginary interlocutor, which he calls the Spirit of Alternatives or *Tu As Raison Aussi* ("You Are Also Right"). The existential concerns of *Dangling Man* can perhaps be thought of in the context of Sartre's *Nausea* and Camus's *L'Étranger*. It also prefigures Bellow's later writings in its juxtaposition of low life and high culture; Joseph's diary mixes the banality of everyday life with references to Goethe and Diderot.

In Joseph's lonely wanderings through the city streets, we see Bellow beginning to combine the concerns of European literature with an authentically American urban experience. *Dangling Man* has been described as an "apprentice" work, as it bears witness to the birth of one the most important and influential voices of the modern American novel. **BR**

The Razor's Edge

William Somerset Maugham

Social satire, philosophical novel, and saint's life, *The Razor's Edge* describes the spiritual quest of an extraordinary young American. After seeing his best friend die in order to save his life while serving as an airman during the First World War, Larry Darrell questions the meaning of his life. He returns to America with the need to find out more about the nature of good and evil, and leaves behind his home, his fiancée, and his social set. After meeting a venerated maharishi high in the mountains of India, Larry experiences enlightenment. Maugham's narrator reports on his quest as observed from afar, "at long intervals," and sometimes secondhand. In the process he also follows the lives of a number of characters who are connected to Larry, travelling from America to India and France.

The Razor's Edge should preferably be read not only before you die, but also before you turn twenty and while you are still capable of truly falling in love with a fictional character. As you get older, you may appreciate Maugham's art more: the subtle, sharp, yet kind irony with which he, or rather his narrator, treats his characters and their social setting—with the exception of Larry, who is described simply and forthrightly. You may be in a better position to understand the cultural and philosophical background to the novel's discussions on the nature of God, the existence of good and evil, and the meaning of life. But you are less likely to feel actual yearning for the protagonist and the quality Maugham admirably seeks to recreate in his portrait of him: his goodness.

To be fully appreciated, this is a work of fiction that presupposes the reader has faith, or at least a longing for it. There are certainly worse things that can be said of a novel. **DG**

Lifespan | *b*. 1874 (France), *d*. 1965
First Published | 1944
First Published by | W. Heinemann (London)
Original Language | English

Maugham was living in the United States when he wrote *The Razor's Edge*; while there he also worked on Hollywood scripts.

Transit

Anna Seghers

Lifespan | *b*. 1900 (Germany), *d*. 1983
First Published | 1944
First Published by | Nuevo Mundo (Mexico)
Given Name | Netti Reiling

Transit, one of the greatest treatments of flight and exile in modern German writing, is a powerful blending of documentary with fiction. Written on Anna Seghers's own flight from the Nazis (she was Jewish, as well as a member of the Communist Party), it was begun in France and finished in Mexico, where it was first published in Spanish (the German version was not published until 1948). This experience is mixed with a dramatized account of the fate of the Austrian writer and doctor Ernst Weiß. Weiß, unaware that a U.S. visa had been prepared for him, through Thomas Mann's intercession with President Roosevelt, killed himself in his hotel room, where Seghers attempted to visit him just afterward. Lines are blurred, and it is never clear how much of the real Weiß is present in his fictional counterpart.

The narrator of *Transit*, Seidler, flees a German concentration camp, only to be interned in France; he escapes again, this time to Marseille, outside the occupation. Joining the throng of those scrambling for passage to America, he attempts to get a message to an acquaintance, a writer named Weidel: on arrival at Weidel's hotel, Siedler learns that he has killed himself the night before. Among the dead man's effects is a transit visa to America; Seidler assumes his identity in order to make use of it. Complications arise when Weidel's wife arrives on the scene. At last Seidler comes to realize that his own identity is being eroded, and he turns down his chance of passage, opting instead to join the French Resistance. **MM**

Pippi Longstocking

Astrid Lindgren

Lifespan | *b*. 1907 (Sweden), *d*. 2002
First Published | 1945
First Published by | Rabén och Sjögren
Original Title | *Pippi Långstrump*

Pippi is a nine-year-old with definite "attitude." With her red braids sticking out sideways, a strength "that no policeman in all the world can match," and her total lack of parental supervision, the children's book heroine Pippi Longstocking sets up home at Villekulla Cottage by a beautiful orchard. She is rich (with a big suitcase full of gold pieces), independent (her mother is in heaven, her father shipwrecked with the cannibals), and has her monkey, Mr. Nelson, her horse, and her neighbors for company. The next-door children, Tommy and Annika, are well brought-up and never fuss or bite their nails—so they are quite unlike the anarchic, assertive, adventure-seeking Pippi. Not surprisingly, they are completely mesmerized by the heroine in their various escapades as she leads them to defy conventions and poke fun at the grown-ups they encounter.

Astrid Lindgren was prompted to write *Pippi* after making up the story to entertain her daughter in bed with pneumonia. Published in 1945, when straitlaced, "seen-and-not-heard" attitudes to children were beginning to be questioned by Swedish society, Pippi burst onto the children's fiction scene, her outlook as unconventional as her clothes. Lindgren told her story from a child's-eye view but above all she instilled in Pippi a fiery and quirky spirit that kids latched onto in droves. **JHa**

❯ Pippi Longstocking demonstrates her superhuman strength on this Swedish cover of Lindgren's subversive children's classic.

KÄNNER DU

PiPPi

LÅNGSTRUMP?

BILDERBOK AV ASTRID LINDGREN OCH INGRID NYMAN

Loving

Henry Green

Lifespan | b. 1905 (England), d. 1973
First Published | 1945
First Published by | Hogarth Press (London)
Given Name | Henry Vincent Yorke

Henry Green's fifth novel, *Loving*, tells the uneventful story of an English aristocratic household in Ireland during the Second World War. The narrative of its little round of daily events is split between the servants of the house and their masters. Upstairs we follow the comedy of well-bred, largely hypocritical emotionalism played out by the lady of the house, Mrs. Tennant, and her daughter-in-law, Mrs. Jack. Downstairs the parallel comedy of restricted hopes and sensational fears is acted out by the star of the drama, the butler, Charley Raunce, and his staff. Raunce falls in love with a servant girl, Edith, and their daily round of flirtations and confessions of desire leads to a fairy-tale ending capped by the cliché "happily ever after."

What sets this book apart from other comedies of manners is the great sensitivity with which Green, the son of a rich Birmingham industrialist, reveals that the experience of loving is rooted in and cannot escape the experience of class relations. The novel exposes the contradictions of class society by tracing the limits imposed on even the most passionate longing by the accidents of birth and social status, and by the deep impression of emotional habits accumulated through physical labor or the freedom from it. To each social class, there belongs its own experience of love and its own manner of believing that love transcends class. Far from reducing the love story to sociology or historical analysis, Green's novel is suffused with a beautiful and implicit pathos. **KS**

Animal Farm

George Orwell

Lifespan | b. 1903 (India), d. 1950 (England)
First Published | 1945
First Published by | Secker & Warburg (London)
Given Name | Eric Arthur Blair

George Orwell's fable of the animals who take over Manor Farm but are betrayed by their leaders has become a powerful myth of freedom for the post-Second World War generation. Its purpose was to destroy another myth, that the Soviet Union was a socialist state; the difficulties that Orwell faced in getting his book published confirmed his view that the British intelligentsia was in thrall to the Soviet system. *Animal Farm* was based on Orwell's own experience in the Spanish Civil War, when the left-wing militia in which he fought was ruthlessly eliminated for not being communist.

Animal Farm is a masterpiece of controlled irony, focused on essential developments in the rise of the Soviet state, but tied to Orwell's knowledge of rural life. Major, an elderly white boar representing Karl Marx, declares the animals' "duty of enmity towards Man and all his ways." When revolution comes, all animals shall be equal. Unfortunately, the pig Napoleon (Stalin) and his fierce dogs (secret police) take over, working to death the carthorse Boxer (the Soviet people) and exiling Snowball (Trotsky). There is pathos in the carthorse Clover's realization that the seven founding commandments are now one: "All animals are equal but some animals are more equal than others." Such irony confirms the book's support of genuine revolution. **AMu**

❷ The cover of a 1954 Latvian translation of *Animal Farm*: the book was banned in Soviet bloc countries, but circulated clandestinely.

DŽ. ORVELS

DZĪVNIEKU
FARMA

The Bridge on the Drina

Ivo Andrić

Lifespan | b. 1892 (Bosnia), d. 1975 (Yugoslavia)
First Published | 1945, by Prosveta (Belgrade)
Original Title | *Na Drini ćuprija*
Nobel Prize for Literature | 1961

Ivo Andrić's work *The Bridge on the Drina* recounts the turbulent history of the famous Mehmed-pasha Sokolovich Bridge in Visegrad, Bosnia. In the novel, Andrić chronicles the period from the building of the bridge in the sixteenth century to the start of the First World War in 1914 and the complete dissolution of the Austro-Hungarian Empire.

Strictly speaking, *The Bridge on the Drina* is more a chronicle than a novel, organized into a series of vignettes describing the life of the local population in Bosnia and Herzegovina, and its transformations over the course of centuries. Given the recent Bosnian bloodshed, the novel provides a fascinating insight into the dynamics and the history of tensions between the local Christians, Muslims, and Jews. A beautiful piece of writing set in a rich local dialect, the book is also a story of language itself. The social and cultural changes brought on by successive rule of the Ottoman and Austro-Hungarian empires are reflected in the populace's vocabulary, their thoughts, bodies, and attitudes. Throughout, the bridge endures as a symbol of continuity.

Even though the novel concludes in 1914 with the retreat of the Austro-Hungarian forces, the bridge itself witnessed further historical strife during the 1990s. This, perhaps, is an incentive for a more cautious reading of Andrić, where the bridge emerges not so much as a metaphor of possible coexistence among nations but simply as a stage for the relentless flow of history. **IJ**

"Theories such as yours only satisfy the eternal need for games, flatter your own vanity, deceive yourself and others. That is the truth, or at least how it appears to me."

Ivo Andrić was the first Bosnian recipient of the Nobel Prize for Literature, which he was awarded in 1961.

Christ Stopped at Eboli

Carlo Levi

Lifespan | b. 1902 (Italy), d. 1975
First Published | 1945
First Published by | G. Einaudi (Turin)
Original Title | Cristo si è fermato a Eboli

Christ Stopped at Eboli has been variously described as a diary, a documentary novel, a sociological study, and a political essay. Its author is equally difficult to categorize. Carlo Levi trained as a doctor, but later devoted himself to politics, literature, and painting. Between 1935 and 1936, during the Abyssinian war, he was exiled to Gagliano, a remote hill town in the "foot" of Italy, because of his opposition to Mussolini and the Fascist regime. *Christ Stopped at Eboli*, Levi's account of the exile, refers to Eboli, the central town of the region, which he was occasionally allowed to visit.

The title of the book is a metaphor for the isolation of the people of this remote region, their poverty and deprivation of little concern to the middle-class Fascist party. Levi chronicles his life in the malaria-ridden village, while painting unsentimental portraits of the inhabitants, from the Fascist mayor to Giulia, a woman who had more than a dozen pregnancies with more than a dozen men. To the stoical peasant community, Levi is a figure of authority to whom they turn for support in their daily struggles against disease and poverty. But his attempts to help them with limited medical supplies is mostly in vain; in a world where a stethoscope has never been seen, the impact of his medical knowledge proves negligible. His novel, however, was an international sensation and, in a move toward social realism in postwar Italian literature, brought to the attention of the Italian public a long-neglected part of their own country. **LE**

Arcanum 17

André Breton

Lifespan | b. 1896 (France), d. 1966
First Published | 1945
First Published by | Brentano (New York)
Original Title | Arcane 17

The high point of the Surrealist movement, which André Breton had headed in France, was over by 1944, and Europe was in the midst of an exhausting war. Written from Québec in the months following D-Day, *Arcanum 17* has much to say about the role of the artist during war, and the role of war in the work that will follow its aftermath. Yet Breton's text is neither gloomily pessimistic nor nostalgic; it has a quiet, if cautionary, optimism for the future of Europe and her artists. This is reflected in the title, which refers to the major arcana tarot card, the Star, that depicts a beautiful young woman emptying upon the earth two urns, labeled love, and intelligence.

Arcanum 17 is neither an essay nor a narrative, although it combines musings and opinions on art and war with a variety of literary themes. These include personalized accounts of Breton's life and his lover during this period, and evocative, poetic descriptions of the dramatic Canadian landscape. The main literary leitmotiv is the legend of Melusina, which A. S. Byatt was to draw on later in her novel *Possession* (1990). Melusina keeps her fidelity to the man whose curiosity banishes her from the human realm; from this stems Breton's call for women to take the reins of power from the destructive hands of men. *Arcanum 17* is a poignant exploration of personal and European loss; it is also a testament to the fascinating maturation of a thinker whose youthful writings had been at the forefront of artistic change in France. **JC**

Brideshead Revisited

Evelyn Waugh

Lifespan | *b.* 1903 (England), *d.* 1966
First Published | 1945
First Published by | Chapman & Hall (London)
Full Name | Evelyn Arthur St. John Waugh

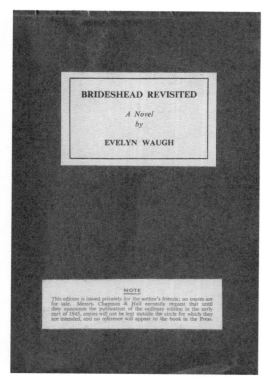

BRIDESHEAD REVISITED

A Novel
by

EVELYN WAUGH

NOTE

This edition is issued privately for the author's friends; no copies are for sale. Messrs. Chapman & Hall earnestly request that until they announce the publication of the ordinary edition in the early part of 1945, copies will not be lent outside the circle for which they are intended, and no reference will appear to the book in the Press.

"'I have been here before . . .'"

◐ Written toward the end of the Second World War, *Brideshead* was partly a nostalgic tribute to an upper-class world.

Arguably Evelyn Waugh's best novel, and certainly his most famous, *Brideshead Revisited* follows the aristocratic Flyte family from the 1920s through to the Second World War. The novel is subtitled "The Sacred and Profane Memories of Captain Charles Ryder," and the narrator first meets Sebastian, an aesthete from the Catholic Flyte family, at Oxford University. The two form an intense friendship. Charles is a serious, earnest student, but there is a tension between the scholasticism of his undergraduate pursuits and his artistic ambitions. His friendship with Sebastian enables him to loosen his grip on the conventional values that had until then structured his life, and the pair's decadent lifestyle encourages Charles's artistic development. During their breaks from Oxford, they spend time together at Brideshead Castle, the home of the Flyte family, and Charles comes to realize that Sebastian's faith is one that he cannot always understand: to him it seems naive and inconsistent.

Sebastian's continual heavy drinking increasingly drives a wedge between him and Charles; however, Charles's relationship with the Flyte family overall remains strong. Years later, after they have both married unhappily, Charles falls in love with Sebastian's sister, Julia. But Julia's strong Catholic beliefs eventually become insurmountable to a continuing relationship.

Waugh had converted to Catholicism himself in 1930, and in many ways *Brideshead Revisited* can be seen as a public expression of his own belief, and an exposition of divine grace. Within the novel he explores a complex interdependency of relationships and, in particular, the overarching importance of religious faith, which, although not always prominent, ultimately prevails. **JW**

Bosnian Chronicle

Ivo Andrić

Bosnian Chronicle is part of the Nobel Prize-winning author Ivo Andrić's *Bosnian Trilogy*. Comprising three novels published in 1945, the only common factor between them is the setting. *Bosnian Chronicle*, like Andrić's other masterpiece *The Bridge on the Drina*, deals with Bosnia and her history.

The novel, subtitled "The Age of the Consuls," tells of the rivalry between the French and Austrian consuls in an out-of-the-way, old-fashioned Bosnian town called Travnik, at the beginning of the nineteenth century. We watch as the two once gifted men compete for the attentions of the Turkish vizier-in-residence, while at the same time pettily sabotaging the plans of their rival. Two men with a great deal in common, the consuls are forced to act out in microcosm the war their two nations are waging in Europe. Andrić moves, Tolstoy-like, across the vast political and emotional domains that form the canvas of his novel. Discontent stirs in the bazaars in Travnik and Serbo-Croatian peasants revolt. Mohammedans, Christians and Jews take arms against one another. Tension builds and explodes. All the while, the two consuls are gradually destroyed by their hard life in the East.

Andrić masterfully portrays the two consuls as fish out of water; he shows the bonds that connect the East and the West but, crucially, shows Bosnia as a land that will remain forever alien to the consuls. Just as poignantly, he emphasizes their similarities and the tragedy that is their inability to take comfort in one another. On a grander level, *Bosnian Chronicle* is a far-reaching, dense, epic, and lyrical meditation on the history and condition of the author's homeland. On a more detailed level, it is a moving portrait of cultural misunderstanding and energy needlessly crushed and wasted. **OR**

Lifespan | *b.* 1892 (Bosnia), *d.* 1975 (Yugoslavia)
First Published | 1945, by Drzavni zavod Jugoslavije
Alternate Title | *The Days of the Consuls*
Original Title | *Travnicka hronika*

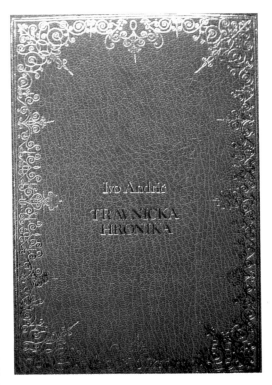

"'. . . we don't want visitors.'"

🔾 Andrić's novel explores the ethnic complexities of his native region; although he was born in Bosnia, his parents were Croats.

The Tin Flute

Gabrielle Roy

Lifespan | *b.* 1909 (Canada), *d.* 1966
First Published | 1945
First Published by | Société des Éditions Pascal
Original Title | *Bonheur d'occasion*

French Canadian author Gabrielle Roy's first novel, *The Tin Flute*, centers on the lives of Florentine Lacasse and her mother, Rose-Anna, in the slums of Montréal in the final years of the Depression. It paints a harshly realistic picture of the everyday struggle of the poor, and their ardent dreams of a better life. With a wealth of observational detail, Roy weaves a compassionate drama of the family's battle for everything from food, clothing, and a place to live to self-respect and life itself.

Central to the story is Florentine. The only member of her family with a regular job, she sees in her mother the image of a life she is determined to avoid at all costs. Desperate when she find herself pregnant and abandoned, Florentine discards her romantic dreams and marries a man she does not love. It is only on the last pages of the novel, when Florentine glimpses the man she once loved, that she realizes that she has escaped her poverty, and is now loved, cared for, and secure.

As they communicate and interact with each other, each of Roy's characters seems isolated within their own inner struggle. Roy penetrates this inner turmoil, showing up the contradictions within each. *The Tin Flute*'s stark realism and focus on urban life formed a remarkable departure from Quebec's literature of the time, heralding a move away from the sentimental, romanticized image of the province that had dominated French-Canadian literature for the previous three centuries. **CIW**

Andrea

Carmen Laforet

Lifespan | *b.* 1921 (Spain), *d.* 2004
First Published | 1945
First Published by | Ediciones Destino (Barcelona)
Original Title | *Nada*

In its time, Carmen LaForet's *Andrea* was new and daring, because it recreates the sordid, hostile environment of a great city and of family relationships marked by suspicion and egoism. The novel was even classified as alarmist, and although the plot and viewpoint are simple and even flat, the young author, at age twenty-three, displayed remarkable ability in creating an atmosphere of sordid passions, cruelty, and hatred, perplexing and astonishing the main character, Andrea.

Andrea travels, full of hopes and illusions, to Barcelona to study philosophy and literature. She lives in the house of her grandmother with her mother's family, individuals who are not only incapable of affection but who are also of restricted mental and moral equilibrium: the music lover Román, a sinister maniac mixed up in smuggling activities that end in his suicide; an unsuccessful painter who mistreats his wife; and the unbalanced Angustias, who seeks to suppress her frustrations in a convent. All are unwelcoming, reproaching Andrea for the debt she owes them for taking her in.

The expressiveness of the style and the description of the setting meant that this novel was received by Spanish exiles as a social denunciation, something that was not intended by the author. Today the novel stands out for its naive narrative power (which won it the first Nadal Prize) and the fact that it was an essential part of the regeneration of the novel in Spain's postwar era. **M-DAB**

The Death of Virgil

Hermann Broch

Lifespan | *b.* 1886 (Austria), *d.* 1951 (U.S.)
First Published | 1945
First Published by | Pantheon Books (New York)
Original Title | *Der Tod des Virgil*

A great masterpiece of European modernism, this exploration of the relationship between life and death moves like a great prose poem through its four sections entitled "water," "fire," "earth," and "air." It was begun during the author's internment in a concentration camp and continued during his exile from Nazi Vienna.

The novel takes place over the last twenty-four hours of the life of Virgil and is located primarily in the palace of Augustus in Brundisium. Virgil has returned to Italy to die and brought with him the newly completed *Aeneid*. During his descent into death he debates with himself, the emperor, and his friends about the use of poetry, the relationship between religion and the state, and the nature of totalitarianism. His decision to burn the manuscript mirrors Hermann Broch's own concerns as he carried the half-completed novel with him to America.

The novel is written in almost endless, flowing sentences that are masterpieces of construction. The essence of the style was characterized as "one thought, one moment, one sentence" and it allows the author to move beautifully through intricate, multilayered thoughts, without becoming simply essayistic. It embraces an entire world and an entire discourse with a profound and sensual immediacy that allows the reader to enter into discussions of considerable intellectual complexity. Pushing language to extremes, Broch created an experience for the reader unlike anything else in literature. **JM**

"Overstrong was the command to hold fast to each smallest particle of time, to the smallest particle of every circumstance, and to embody all of them in memory . . ."

⊙ Hermann Broch photographed in Vienna in 1937, the year before the Nazi takeover drove him into exile in America.

Titus Groan

Mervyn Peake

Lifespan | *b.* 1911 (China), *d.* 1968 (England)
First Published | 1946, by Eyre & Spottiswoode (Lon.)
Titus Groan Novels | *Titus Groan* (1946),
Gormenghast (1950), *Titus Alone* (1959)

Packed with delicious grotesques and delirious prose, *Titus Groan* centers on the dark behemoth of Gormenghast, the walled ancestral home of the line of Groan. Crumbling, malignant, with corridors and towers and forgotten wings housing misplaced occupants, it is a living, seething universe. Its inhabitants—hostage to its mind-numbing routine, the original meaning of which is long forgotten—scurry to perform a ceaseless flow of rituals.

The players are a delightful menagerie of archetypes and caricatures. Lord Sepulchrave, 76th Earl of Groan, is morose, exhausted by endless duty; his career wife, Gertrude, is increasingly detached, comfortable only with the birds that nest in her hair and the sea of cats that surrounds her. Sourdust and Barquentine, the librarians, are keepers of the ritual, and Swelter, the demonic porcine cook, is despot in the steaming hell of the Great Kitchens. Mr. Flay is Sepulchrave's major-domo, willing to defend tradition to the death. Driving the narrative is Steerpike, low-born and opportunistic, who wheedles, flatters, and manipulates in his Machiavellian quest for power. He will stop at nothing in his relentless journey upward. To this house an heir is born, Titus, 77th Earl of Groan.

A novel of superb craft, full of intrigue and humor, it is a scathing allegory of British society, from blind deference, to tradition, to the merciless class system. There are no magic potions, no mythical beasts. The monsters are those we know: the boredom of routine, ruthless self-interest, and foolish vanity. **GT**

Zorba the Greek

Nikos Kazantzakis

Lifespan | *b.* 1883 (Greece), *d.* 1957 (Germany)
First Published | 1946
First Published by | Dim. Dimitrakou (Athens)
Original Title | *Vios kai politia tou Alexi Zormpa*

A twentieth-century Sancho Panza and Falstaff rolled into one, Alexis Zorba is one of the most exuberant "Everyman" creations of modern fiction. The Greek completely captivates the narrator (probably the author himself as a young intellectual) at a café in the port of Piraeus in Athens, "a living heart, a large voracious mouth, a great brute soul, not yet severed from mother earth."

Zorba's lust for life (and his revelation that he is an ex-foreman of mines) prompts an invitation to take charge of the men working a lignite mine. In the course of their friendship and picaresque adventures on the shimmering island of Crete, the robust Greek wreaks havoc and good feelings in equal measure, and calls the narrator to question his own orthodox and studious approach to life.

The book is fundamentally a philosophical sparring between Zorba's tour-de-force spontaneity, and the more rational and restrained "Ancient Greek" outlook adopted by the young narrator regarding what is right or wrong, good or evil. Add a backdrop of the warm and welcoming Aegean light, air, color, and odors, and you have a recipe for a superb alfresco fictional feast. Nikos Kazantzakis, who in 1957 was pipped by Albert Camus by one vote for the Nobel Prize for Literature, had an amazing output, from travel books to translations. But it was his *Zorba the Greek*, as well as *The Last Temptation of Christ* (1960), that helped put modern Greek writing into the international arena. **JHa**

Back

Henry Green

Lifespan | *b*. 1905 (England), *d*. 1973
First Published | 1946
First Published by | Hogarth Press (London)
Given Name | Henry Vincent Yorke

Back is a fascinating war novel, which portrays the consequences of the war on a character who has returned home. Charley Summers is a lost individual, a benumbed and disoriented former soldier traumatized by recent experiences. He finds himself unable to connect with people around him and unable to relate his present to his past. *Back* depicts the perplexities and anguish of its central character with great subtlety. The loose narrative style adopted by Henry Green cleverly approximates the meandering nature of Charley's confused thoughts. Rendered childlike by the psychological trauma of war, he is an innocent abroad, a hapless enigma who is incapable of either confronting or making sense of reality.

Back is, however, an optimistic, almost magical, work, which offers Charley a specific form of personal redemption when he hesitantly begins to fall in love with Nancy, the half-sister of his prewar lover, Rose. Through Nancy, Charley is able not only to relive the past, but also to work through the trauma that shattered it, although there is no naive resolution of the psychological ills that beset him. In fact, he remains an enigma to himself and to others, as Nancy frankly admits toward the end of the novel: "She did not know if he didn't, or just couldn't, tell about himself, tell even something of all that went on behind those marvellous brown eyes." The novel concludes with a tear-stained scene in which love, pain, and self-sacrifice are mingled together in a wonderfully lyrical epiphany. **AG**

House in the Uplands

Erskine Caldwell

Lifespan | *b*. 1903 (U.S.), *d*. 1987
First Published | 1946
First Published by | Duell, Sloane & Pearce (N. York)
Original Language | English

Erskine Caldwell is best known for *Tobacco Road* (1932) and *God's Little Acre* (1933). Both were lauded and reviled in equal measure when first published, with Caldwell's social-realist portrayal of rural life bordering, for many, on pornographic. The publication of *God's Little Acre* led to Caldwell's arrest on obscenity charges; although he was exonerated, the trial simply increased his notoriety and served to sell more books. He was one of the first authors to reap the rewards of the then recent paperback phenomenon, as thousands of cheap copies were snapped up by readers eager to be scandalized.

Whereas his earlier books had dealt primarily with the working men and women of the American South, Caldwell turned his attention to the land-owning Southern aristocracy in *House on the Uplands*. The book paints a familiar portrait of rural degradation and despair, although Caldwell's often grotesque humour is notably lacking.

The protagonist is Grady Dunbar, the last scion of a formerly well-to-do family. He has drunk and gambled away all his money, and then, his pockets empty, mortgaged his house and land to further fund his debauched flings. Throughout it all, his young and naive wife loyally stays by his side, essentially a slave to her husband's passions. At the same time, Grady's field-workers, too, remain trapped, as they till his lands, unpaid but too scared to move on. All linked together, the book follows Grady's decline and inevitable fall. **PH**

The Path to the Nest of Spiders

Italo Calvino

Lifespan | *b.* 1923 (Cuba), *d.* 1985 (Italy)
First Published | 1947
First Published by | Einaudi (Turin)
Original Title | *Il sentiero dei nidi di ragno*

"Your first book already defines you . . . "

⬤ Italian novelist and journalist Italo Calvino photographed in
a café in 1981, the year he was awarded the Légion d'Honneur.

The fact that this is the first novel Italo Calvino wrote, when he was just twenty-three and at the start of a prodigious literary career, should alone be enough to recommend it. Within are the stirrings of what was later to mature into a unique and inimitable style and sophistication; however, the story also represents the attempt of a young writer to come to terms with the aftermath of the partisan movement in Italy. The precocious Pin is the child whom we follow through the adult world of a rural Italy riven by civil discontent and confusion.

Pin is an orphan—lazy, foulmouthed, and worldly enough to use local gossip to his advantage. He is also a child who craves adult attention, but only crudely and imperfectly understands how to capture or retain it. The irony is that the two things Pin utterly fails to comprehend—politics and women—are those that equally mystify most of the other characters. When Pin's home village is occupied by the Germans, the locals join the partisans, although Calvino makes it clear that this is more about resistance to change than the practice of a committed political ideology.

Interestingly, although *The Path to the Nest of Spiders* won Calvino a prize, he refused to authorize a re-edition until nearly a decade later, a third and definitive edition being finally published in 1964, along with an invaluably revealing preface. This reluctance, Calvino admits, was to do with how he had used and caricatured the comrades with whom he had formerly fought alongside. *The Path to the Nest of Spiders*, while it lacks the obsession with symmetry and order of Calvino's later works, is beautifully written and represents the response from one of Italy's most famous twentieth-century writers to a singular moment in the country's history. **JC**

Under the Volcano

Malcolm Lowry

Malcolm Lowry's *Under the Volcano* catapulted him to international literary fame after years as a struggling novelist. Lowry later claimed that the novel was the first volume of a trilogy based on Dante's *Divine Comedy*, *Under the Volcano* being a vision of hell.

The story tells of the last day in the life of Geoffrey Firmin, the alcoholic British consul in fictional Quauhnahuac (identifiable as Cuernavaca), Mexico; aptly enough, this day happens to fall on the macabre festival of the Day of the Dead. The novel is narrated in flashback by Firmin's former neighbor, Jacques Laruelle, who has had an affair with Firmin's wife, Yvonne. She returns to try to renew her troubled relationship with the consul, and together with her brother-in-law, Hugh, she visits the festival, which is haunted by an increasing threat of violence. When Geoffrey gets separated from Yvonne and Hugh by a terrible storm, the day ends with the deaths of the couple—Yvonne is killed by a runaway horse, and Geoffrey is murdered by fascist thugs, who throw him into a ditch beneath the volcano.

Lowry's work is more significant for its powerful symbolism and ornate prose style than for its characterization. The setting of the festival of the Day of the Dead under the volcano points to the inevitable death of the self-destructive protagonist, but it also suggests the wider eruptions of a culture in crisis—the novel is set in 1938 and was written during the Second World War. Firmin's death at the hands of the fascists anticipates a brutal world order that cannot be easily contained. Equally, like all Lowry's writing, *Under the Volcano* is autobiographical, and it charts the end of his relationship with former wife Jan Gabrial, caused largely by his own excesses and obsessions, principally alcohol, which would ultimately lead to his "death by misadventure." **AH**

Lifespan | *b.* 1909 (England), *d.* 1957
First Published | 1947
First Published by | Jonathan Cape (London)
Full Name | Malcolm Clarence Lowry

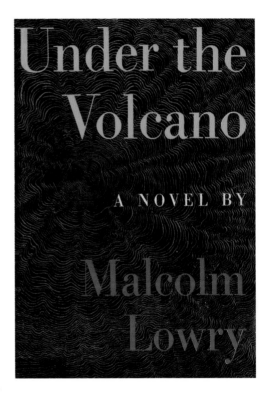

"I have no house, only a shadow."

⊙ The sober jacket of the first U.S. edition, published by Reynal & Hitchcock, carries no hint of the novel's macabre exuberance.

If This Is a Man

Primo Levi

"It was my good fortune," writes Primo Levi in his preface to *If This Is a Man*, "to be deported to Auschwitz only in 1944." It is a stark opening to this classic account of Levi's ten months in the horrific Nazi death camp, one that strikes the distinctive note of his writing on the Holocaust. Beginning with his capture by the Fascist militia in December 1943, the chapters of *If This Is a Man* were written, Levi explains, "in order of urgency." He is acknowledging that this is an attempt both to explain to his readers what life was like in Auschwitz, and to work his own way through the experience of life-in-death that emerges as the reality of the Lager ("The life of Ka-Be is a life of limbo").

What is a man in Auschwitz? What does an attrocity such as Auschwitz do to the idea of humanity? Levi delivers what has been described as a prose poem on this "exceptional human state"— thousands of individuals, enclosed together within barbed wire, yet "ferociously alone." In *If This Is a Man*, Levi introduces a number of important themes and categories that would return throughout his writing, notably those of *The Drowned and the Saved*. He reveals the pitiless division that holds sway in the world of the camp: the status of the "Organisator," the "Kombinator," and the "Prominent," and the lowly "musselman."

There is no third way—that is, no ordinary life—in the camp, and so Levi finds the image of evil that this book struggles to convey: "an emaciated man—on whose face and in whose eyes not a trace of a thought is to be seen." No thought, and no story: Auschwitz was an attack on the life of the mind against which Levi writes in this book, an attack that generates what he describes as the elemental need to tell the "unlistened-to story." **VL**

Lifespan | *b.* 1919 (Italy), *d.* 1987
First Published | 1947, by De Silva (Turin)
U.S. Title | *Survival in Auschwitz*
Original Title | *Se questo è un uomo*

As a young man Levi joined the Italian anti-Fascist resistance, but he was soon arrested as a partisan and subsequently deported.

Railway tracks leading to the Auschwitz concentration camp; Levi was one of the few Italian Jews to survive imprisonment.

Exercises in Style

Raymond Queneau

Lifespan | b. 1903 (France), d. 1976
First Published | 1947, by Gallimard (Paris)
Revised Edition | 1963
Original Title | Exercices de style

When Raymond Queneau's *Exercises in Style* first appeared in 1947, it led at once to his election to France's prestigious Académie Goncourt. Nothing quite like it had appeared in French or any other language before, nor has Queneau's feat been repeated successfully since. The book begins with a seemingly inconsequential anecdote. On a bus in rush hour, a man with a felt hat accuses another passenger of jostling him. Eventually, when a seat becomes vacant, the man sits down. Later, the man is encountered again in front of the Saint-Lazare station, in the company of a friend who is telling him to get an extra button put on his overcoat. Queneau spends the rest of the book retelling the story in ninety-nine different ways: as a dream, an ode, a sonnet, in the present, as an official letter, as a telegram, in reported speech, as blurb, in anagrams.

We tend to take it for granted that style is somehow subservient to story, offering a window through which the reader is able to perceive a given and incontrovertible reality. Queneau reveals that style never can be transparent, that language itself shapes and defines the underlying reality that we perceive. Queneau's work forces us to come face to face with this perception in many amusing and dazzling ways. It is reminiscent of a whole tradition of the antinovel, from Laurence Sterne to James Joyce to Alain Robbe-Grillet, a tradition that insists that what really matters is not the story, but the way in which you tell it. **PT**

The Plague

Albert Camus

Lifespan | b. 1913 (Algeria), d. 1960 (France)
First Published | 1947, by Gallimard (Paris)
Original Title | La Peste
Nobel Prize for Literature | 1957

This text has often been criticized for its "bleak existentialism," yet to do so is to miss the point of Albert Camus's masterpiece altogether. What stands out in this text, despite its unflinching view of human suffering and despair, is an overriding sense of common humanity. This is far from evident as the narrative opens, however, with the death of thousands of rats in the streets of the Algerian city of Oran. When people begin to sicken and die, despite the disorganization and initial denial of the mercenary city authorities, it becomes apparent that it is the bubonic plague that is afflicting the city. Strict quarantine is imposed, and it is in the suffocating claustrophobia of this enforced isolation—brilliantly captured by Camus—that individuals are forced to confront the apparent inevitability of death, and the bonds that bind the community together begin to collapse. Yet even at the darkest point, all hope is not lost. After an initial retreat into their own reflective solitude that would seem to suggest the lonely and unique nature of human despair, the efforts of a number of prominent characters serve to bring the community together gradually, in collective understanding of their plight.

The sensitivity and understanding with which a citywide cast of individuals is created is remarkably compelling and brings Oran to life. It is this that sets *The Plague* apart from Camus's other great work, *The Outsider*, and that makes it a timely and still relevant work today. **MD**

Doctor Faustus

Thomas Mann

Lifespan | *b*. 1875 (Germany), *d*. 1955 (Switzerland)
First Published | 1947
First Published by | Bermann Fischer (Stockholm)
Original Title | *Doktor Faustus*

Doctor Faustus tells the story of the rise and fall of the musician Adrian Leverkühn through the eyes of his friend, Serenus Zeitbloom. In this novel, Thomas Mann adapts the Faust myth to suggest that Leverkühn achieves his musical greatness as a result of a pact with the devil. Interwoven with the narration of this bargain and its repercussions is an exploration of how and why Germany chose to ally itself with dark forces in its embracing of fascism through Hitler.

Doctor Faustus engages with the ideas of many European philosophers and thinkers, elaborating its own unique vision. Particularly brilliant are Mann's meditations on the evolution of musical theory over the course of the nineteenth and twentieth centuries, including the advent of the twelve-tone system of Arnold Schönberg, the composer on whom Leverkühn is partly based. Also in strong evidence is Mann's preoccupation with the ruthless demands of creative life. Leverkühn suffers excruciating periods of pain, punctuated by short bouts of breathtaking genius. Many of the finest passages are those that explore the relationship between illness and creativity.

The novel's major achievement is its eloquent synthesis of complex ideas on art, history, and politics, as well as its elaborate meditation on the relationship between the artist and society. The final description of Leverkühn's fate is tinged with the despair and isolation that Mann himself endured as he pondered the future of his native Germany from the vantage point of his exile in California. **CG-G**

DOCTOR FAUSTUS

THE LIFE OF THE GERMAN COMPOSER
ADRIAN LEVERKÜHN
AS TOLD BY A FRIEND

THOMAS MANN

Lo giorno se n'andava e l'aere bruno
toglieva gli animai che sono in terra
dalle fatiche loro, ed io sol uno
m'apparecchiava a sostener la guerra
sì del cammino e sì della pietate,
che ritrarrà la mente que non erra.
O Muse, o alto ingegno, or m'aiutate,
o mente che scrivesti ciò ch'io vidi,
qui si parrà la tua nobilitate.

Dante: *Inferno*, Canto II

LONDON
SECKER & WARBURG

".. . a revered man sorely tried by fate, which both raised him up and cast him down."

◉ The cover of the first English edition carries lines from Dante, beginning: "Day was departing . . ." and calling on the Muses for aid.

Midaq Alley

Naguib Mahfouz

Lifespan | *b.* 1911 (Egypt), *d.* 2006
First Published | 1947, by Maktabat Misr (Kairo)
Original Title | *Zuqaq al-Midaqq*
Nobel Prize for Literature | 1988

Egypt's most famous novelist and winner of the 1988 Nobel Prize for Literature, Naguib Mahfouz has written forty novels in a prolific, varied, and highly controversial career. He is best known to Western readers for his realist portrayals of life in twentieth-century Cairo, early works whose narrative style and characterization recall European masters of the previous century, such as Dickens, Balzac, and Zola.

Midaq Alley is set in the Old Quarter of Cairo during the Second World War. There is an undeniable charm to its humorous evocation of the daily routines of a backstreet community, but the vision the narrative unfolds is harsh and critical. There is no cosiness to the portraits of individuals such as Kirsha, the homosexual drug-dealing café owner, who abandons his wife at night to trawl for young men, or the sinister Zaita, whose profession is mutilating the poorest of the poor so they can make a better living as crippled beggars.

Mahfouz is depicting a society in crisis, in which the only escape from frustration, poverty, and stagnation lies in the hazardous world of possibilities opened up by modernization—given concrete form in the presence of British and American troops in Egypt. When the heartless local beauty, Hamida, seduced by the lure of modernity, becomes a prostitute for the Allied forces, it precipitates the novel's tragic climax. Westerners visiting *Midaq Alley* are given a rare opportunity to view the modern world through Arab eyes. **RegG**

Froth on the Daydream

Boris Vian

Lifespan | *b.* 1920 (France), *d.* 1959
First Published | 1947
First Published by | Gallimard (Paris)
Original Title | *L'écume des jours*

This novel is a French surrealist tour de force, where even the original title, *L'écume des jours*, is fairly untranslatable (it was called *Mood Indigo* in the United States). The plotline, such as it is (somehow it was turned into a film and an opera), involves Colin, a wealthy young dilettante with a servant and pet talking mouse. All Colin wants is to fall in love. Enter Chloe and love blossoms (literally). Chloe develops "a water-lily on the lung," the remedy for which is to be surrounded by floral displays, which cripples Colin financially. He has already splashed out 25,000 "doublezoons" for the wedding of his best friends, Chick and Lisa, but the newly marrieds' lives disintegrate as Chick obsesses about collecting everything about Jean Pulse Heartre (say it out loud). Lisa goes into homicidal mode, the police do the dirty too, and the style becomes distinctly Chandleresque in the denouement—significantly, Vian was Raymond Chandler's French translator.

This work is a surreal, science-fictionlike, and at times very funny love story, but, above all, it is a poignant take on how young, optimistic, and frivolous daydreams become clouded by orthodoxy and conformity. In translation, some of the original French wordplay may be lost, but much of the poetry remains for the non-French speaker.

Vian also wrote shlock-horror titles, including the infamous *J'irai cracher sur vos tombes*. He is said to have died of a heart attack watching the movie version of *I Spit on Your Graves*, which he hated. **JHa**

Journey to the Alcarria

Camilo José Cela

Lifespan | b. 1916 (Spain), d. 2002
First Published | 1948, by Emecé (Buenos Aires)
Original Title | Viaje a la Alcarria
Nobel Prize for Literature | 1989

Journey to the Alcarria refreshed a genre that writers younger than Camilo José Cela were taking up again to denounce the backwardness of the Spanish countryside and its abandonment. What interested the future Nobel laureate, on the other hand, was to preserve the unusual aspects of places and their eye-catching locations in stories and styles that carried literary weight. In the book, there is an abundance of descriptions of local customs, traditions, and legends; of unknown, uncommon people, their behavior, and their extravagant names.

Critics tended to pillory Cela for triviality in preferring the adornment of style to the assessment of the conditions of life of the people, and for not having a more humanist point of view. However, he did not claim to be making a social denunciation, nor to be entering the area of sociology, but to be writing a text with the very marked imprint of his unusual style: "The oilcloth on the table is yellow, with the color worn off in places and the edges somewhat raveled. A 'girlie' calendar on the wall advertises anisette." Written in the third person and deliberately phenomenological in description, the frequent repetition of the rhetorical formula "the traveler" (the person who comes and goes, who reads, and who asks questions) was an effective device to replace the first-person narrative. Read today, the novel can give a slightly tiring and falsely modest point of view, but, in spite everything, this is probably Cela's best book. **M-DAB**

Ashes and Diamonds

Jerzy Andrzejewski

Lifespan | b. 1909 (Poland), d. 1983
First Published | 1948
First Published by | Czytelnik (Warsaw)
Original Title | Popiól i diament

Opening on the last day of the Second World War in Europe, Ashes and Diamonds traces three men—Szczuka, the district Communist Party secretary; Michael, a reluctant Resistance hitman; and Kossecki, a Nazi collaborator—over the next few days in a small Polish town. Kossecki hopes to forget his concentration-camp past, where he was one of the hated orderlies, wishing to return to his old life as a hardworking magistrate and family man. His elder son has entered the Resistance, which is now fighting Polish Communists, while the younger has joined an anarchist group and become an accessory to murder. Szczuka faces the task of instilling justice and self-respect into a currency-hungry town council, while silently grieving over his wife's almost certain death in the camps. Michael's Resistance cell has ordered him to assassinate Szczuka. But can he continue with killing after he falls in love with Kristina, a waitress in the town's hotel?

Jerzy Andrzejewski creates a vivid, cinematic portrait of Poland flung into chaos, morally stunned and economically shattered in the aftermath of liberation. Everyone is compromised: young people disillusioned and brutalized by war, the older generation implicated by the choices they made for survival. Even Szczuka's sincere faith in socialist utopia is tested by the grubby power-broking at a mayoral banquet. Meanwhile, the occupying Red Army is the unseen elephant in the room, shadowing Poland's past, present, and future. **MuM**

Disobedience

Alberto Moravia

Lifespan | *b*. 1907 (Italy), *d*. 1990
First Published | 1948
First Published by | Bompiani (Milan)
Original Title | *La disubbidienza*

One of Italy's most prominent literary figures of the past century, Alberto Moravia had a prolific and highly successful writing career. A great deal of his work concerns the obsessions and complexes of the Roman bourgeoisie, in particular the twinned themes of money and sex, seen as agents of power, rather than pleasure. It is characterized by an almost clinical clarity of expression, an open approach to sexuality, and a close attention to the psychological.

Disobedience is a highly original treatment of the coming-of-age theme. Luca is a disaffected only child of respectable middle-class parents who becomes increasingly dissatisfied with all that he previously cherished. He embarks on a process of what he perceives to be logical, calculated disobedience, relinquishing all worldly goods and love. Eventually he falls ill and is bedridden for several months, during which time he experiences troubling hallucinations. When he recovers, his convalescence is accompanied by a sexual initiation with his nurse. The experience is heavily symbolic, and Luca sees it as a rebirth through which he overcomes his destructive self-denial and gains an almost mythic sense of oneness with reality. A heavily charged, complex work dealing with teenage rebellion, sexuality, and alienation, *Disobedience* is a fascinating psychological portrait of an Oedipal awakening. **AL**

◉ Alberto Moravia, far left, enjoys a relaxed conversation with other Italian writers, including Elsa Moranti and, on her left, Carlo Levi.

All About H. Hatterr

G. V. Desani

Lifespan | *b*. 1909 (Kenya), *d*. 2001 (U.S.)
First Published | 1948, by F. Aldor (London)
Revised Edition Published | 1972, by Penguin UK
Full Name | Govindas Vishnoodas Desani

All About H. Hatterr is a singular book, unmatched in its sustained comedy of rhetoric and language. Models might be perceived in the idiomatic style and formal play of Laurence Sterne, James Joyce, or Flann O'Brien, but nothing can quite prepare you for this book's inventive play of rhetoric, innocence, and wit. Part of the joke is that the central character-narrator, the eponymous H. Hatterr, continually reveals an acutely intelligent grasp of the English language, life, and literary artifice, but is perceived as a simple-minded dupe. Linguistic sophistication is blended with quixotic innocence, as if Joyce's Leopold Bloom, having acquired English as a second language, had learned to write like Rabelais or Laurence Sterne. Exhibit one, the book's much fuller title: *The Autobiographical of H. Hatterr, being also a mosaic-organon of Life: viz., a medico-philosophical grammar as to this contrast, this human horseplay, this design for diamond-cut-diamond … H. Hatterr by H. Hatterr.*

The novel relates how the orphaned Hatterr, of multicultural and multilingual background, is adopted into "the Christian lingo (English)" as his "second vernacular" and goes "completely Indian to an extent few pure non-Indian blood sahib fellers have done." Hatterr's adventures mostly focus on a variety of unlikely spiritual encounters with the society, sages, and anglo-grotesques of India and England. Rumor has it that this Indo-Anglian classic much influenced Salman Rushdie, but Desani more than has the edge. **DM**

Cry, the Beloved Country

Alan Paton

Lifespan | *b.* 1903 (South Africa), *d.* 1988
First Published |1948
First Published by | Scribner (New York)
Full Name | Alan Stewart Paton

One of the greatest South African novels, *Cry, the Beloved Country* was first published in the United States, bringing international attention to South Africa's tragic history. It tells the story of a father's journey from rural South Africa to and through the city of Johannesburg in search of his son. The reader cannot help but feel deeply for the central character, a Zulu pastor, Stephen Kumalo, and the tortuous discoveries he makes in Johannesburg. It is in a prison cell that Kumalo eventually finds his son, Absalom, who is facing trial for the murder of a white man—a man who ironically cared deeply about the plight of the native South African population and had been a voice for change until his untimely death. Here we meet another father, that of the victim, whose own journey to understand his son eventually leads to his life and grief becoming strangely entwined with Kumalo's.

The novel captures the extremes of human emotion, and Alan Paton's faith in human dignity in the worst of circumstances is both poignant and uplifting. The novel shows the brutality of apartheid, but despite its unflinching portrayal of darkness and despair in South Africa, it still offers hope for a better future. The novel itself is a cry for South Africa, which we learn is beloved in spite of everything; a cry for its people, its land, and the tentative hope for its freedom from hatred, poverty, and fear. **EG-G**

In the Heart of the Seas

Shmuel Yosef Agnon

Lifespan | *b.* 1888 (Aust.-Hungary), *d.* 1970 (Israel)
First Published | 1948, Schocken (New York)
Original Title | *Bi-levav yamim*
Nobel Prize for Literature | 1966

In the Heart of the Seas established Agnon as one of the most important authors of modern Hebrew literature and earned him the Bialik Prize. Set in the late nineteenth century, the short novella in fourteen chapters carries the reader, in the company of a small group of pious Hassidic Jews, from the city of Buczacz in Eastern Galicia (now Ukraine) through Poland and Moldava to Constantinople and across "the heart of the seas" to Jaffa and Jerusalem. The companions "of good heart" overcome dangers and hardships on the road, as well as the temptations of Satan, by the power of their faith and their vibrant love for the Jerusalem and the land of Israel.

This picaresque novella is also Agnon's symbolic autobiography. It is written in his original and personal style, a weaving together of traditional Judaism, the language of the Scriptures and the rabbinical texts, and influences of German literature into a modern, intricate, and unique language that is distinctly his own. In his acceptance speech for the Nobel Prize for Literature that he was awarded in 1966 (with Nelly Sachs), Agnon succinctly summed up his view of his own work: "It is by the virtue of Jerusalem that I have written all that God has put into my heart and into my pen." To this day, Agnon remains the most studied author of modern Israeli literature, and *In the Heart of the Seas* has been translated into numerous languages. **IW**

This Way for the Gas, Ladies and Gentlemen

Tadeusz Borowski

Lifespan | *b.* 1922 (Ukraine), *d.* 1951 (Poland)
First Published | 1948
National Literary Prize | 1950
Original Title | *Pozegnanie z Maria*

Originally published as *Farewell to Maria*, the title of the English translation is indicative of the way in which Tadeusz Borowski depicts the existence of those imprisoned in a Nazi concentration camp.

In the story that provides the title of the collection, a group of prisoners anxiously await the arrival of next transport of Jews, knowing that their role in the Kommando—unloading people destined for the gas chambers—would provide them with food to supplement their grossly inadequate rations. They are repeatedly subjected to physically and morally emaciating conditions. By providing an unemotional representation of the actions of people forced into countless impossible situations, Borowski demonstrates the way in which all those involved with the camps were dehumanized.

The impact of Borowski's writing is derived in large part from the economy of his style. The stories are loosely autobiographical, as he was himself held at various concentration camps during the Second World War. After his release he embraced Communism, believing it provided the greatest guarantee that the horrors of the Nazi regime would never be repeated. When he came to realize that atrocities were similarly being committed in the name of Communism, he was left utterly disillusioned. Tragically, having survived both Auschwitz and Dachau, he took his own life by gassing himself. **JW**

Death Sentence

Maurice Blanchot

Lifespan | *b.* 1907 (France), *d.* 2003
First Published | 1948
First Published by | Gallimard (Paris)
Original Title | *L'Arrêt de mort*

The reclusive Maurice Blanchot exerted a profound influence on twentieth-century French thought, while at the same time maintaining a scrupulous reserve, both in life and in writing. The original French title can be translated as both "death sentence" and "stay of execution"—both a final, definitive judgment and an indefinite reprieve. This short novel reverberates in the suspension of meaning generated by its title.

The first of two narrative sections details the struggle and treatment of a terminally ill woman known only as "J." She dies, and mysteriously comes to life only to be killed again by an overdose administered by the narrator. The second narrative documents the narrator's interactions with three other women against the background of the occupation and bombing of Paris in 1940. Between the two parts occur many parallels and repetitions, which multiply and complicate interpretations.

As the narrator struggles to recount the events he relates, he senses that words always double back, consuming himself and the truth he is attempting to convey. For the narrator, this struggle is the condition of all writing; he feels the acute inability of words to capture adequately an event in all its complexity, and yet is overtaken by the insatiable desire to tell, condemned to explore the limits of what can be said by forever starting again. **SS**

Nineteen Eighty-Four

George Orwell

Lifespan | *b.* 1903 (India), *d.* 1950 (England)
First Published | 1949
First Published by | Secker & Warburg (London)
Given Name | Eric Arthur Blair

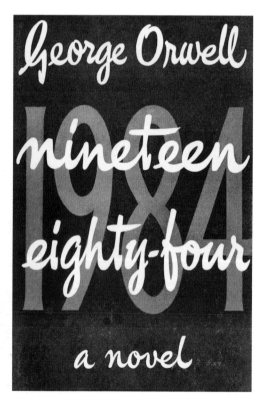

○ Published in London in 1949, Orwell's novel reflected the drabness of postwar Britain, beset by austerity and shortages.

◑ The vibrant cover of the German translation of *Nineteen Eighty-Four* depicts the all-seeing eye of the sinister Big Brother.

Nineteen Eighty-Four is one of George Orwell's most powerful politically charged novels, a beautifully crafted warning against the dangers of a totalitarian society, and one of the most famous novels in the dystopian genre.

Winston Smith is a low-ranking member of the ruling party in London whose every move is monitored by telescreens. Everywhere Winston goes, the party's omniscient leader, Big Brother, watches him. The party is trying to eradicate the possibility of political rebellion by eliminating all words related to it from the language, creating sanitized "Newspeak." "Thoughtcrime" (thinking rebellious thoughts) is illegal. Winston, who works at the Ministry of Truth altering historical records for the party's benefit, is frustrated and oppressed by the prohibitions on free thought, sex, and individuality. He illegally purchases a diary to record his thoughts and spends his evenings wandering the poor areas where the "proles" live, relatively free from monitoring. Winston starts an illicit affair with Julia, a fellow party employee, but they are caught by a party spy, and, in Room 101, Winston is forced to confront his worst fear. Giving up his love for Julia in terror, Winston is released, his spirit broken and his acceptance of the party complete.

In 1949, at the beginning of the nuclear age and before television was mainstream, Orwell's creation of a telescreen-monitored world just a single generation into the future was terrifying. This is an important novel not only for its stark warning against abusive authority (and its somewhat ironic contribution to modern television content), but also for its insights into the power of manipulating language, history, and the psychology of fear and control. These issues are perhaps even more pertinent today than when Orwell penned his novel. **EF**

GEORGE ORWELL

>1984<

ROMAN

The Man with the Golden Arm

Nelson Algren

FRANK SINATRA · ELEANOR PARKER · KIM NOVAK

THE MAN WiTH THE GOLDEN ARM

A FILM BY OTTO PREMINGER

Lifespan | *b.* 1909 (U.S.), *d.* 1981
First Published | 1949
First Published by | Doubleday & Co. (New York)
Movie Adaptation Released | 1955

Nelson Algren's best novel is perhaps first remembered through its cinematic adaptation in the movie starring Frank Sinatra as his hustling junkie antihero, Frankie Machine. This is as unjust a situation as the fact that Algren himself has, thanks to a biography of his lover, Simone de Beauvoir, come to be known principally as the man who helped the author of *The Second Sex* achieve her first orgasm.

The novel mingles the true-crime titillation of pulp fiction and low journalism with the crusading zeal of sociological investigation: a marketable blend of prurience and high-mindedness, lifted above its many rivals in the field by Algren's sustained poetic gift. His prose style, with its violently clashing registers, and the enduring resonance of its poetic voice, is indelibly marked by the influence of T. S. Eliot and James Joyce.

Chicago was the great subject of Algren's writing life and he dusted its dilapidated bars, damp flophouses, filthy holding tanks, and drenched sidewalks—all sites of the most harrowing indignity—with a dignified, perceptive language that he knew how to share with his central characters. If Algren's rhetorical style is occasionally portentous, Frankie Machine, Sparrow Saltskin, Sophie, Molly, and the chorus of weary Chicago policemen survive with their expressive intensities intact, even as the bunch of petty criminals are sent into unsustainable downward spirals by addiction, violence, and inescapable poverty. **RP**

"I had a great big habit. One time I knocked out one of my own teet' to get the gold for a fix. You call that bein' hooked or not?"

🔘 The poster for Otto Preminger's 1955 movie adaptation of the book, initially banned because it showed drug addiction.

Kingdom of This World

Alejo Carpentier

Lifespan | *b.* 1904 (Cuba), *d.* 1980 (France)
First Published | 1949, by Publicaciones
Iberoamericana (Mexico)
Original Title | *El reino de este mundo*

With this book, Alejo Carpentier declared war on the exhausted inheritance of European Surrealism and at the same time produced a defining text for the emergent magic realist movement. The novel is underpinned by a relatively straightforward historical narrative, which follows the major events of the only successful revolution in the Atlantic slave diaspora. Set in revolutionary Santo Domingo, the island that was to emerge in 1803 as Haiti, the first black ex-slave republic, the novel follows the fortunes of the central character, Ti Noël. Initially a servant to one of the *grand blanc* families before the revolution, Ti Noël forms an intense friendship with the charismatic Mandingo slave leader Macandal, then witnesses his execution and voodoo apotheosis. After the successful slave revolution, Ti Noël is re-enslaved as part of the immense labor force consigned by the black dictator Henri Christophe to erect his unearthly fortified mountaintop palace. The novel ends with a phantasmagoric account of the fall of Christophe, the sacking of Sans Souci, and Ti Noël's death.

Carpentier wrote *Kingdom of This World* in a state of near despair at what he saw as the unrelenting formulaic nature of fantasy literature. However, in this short, delicately wrought masterpiece, Carpentier fuses a precisely researched external history with a series of anthropomorphic transformations and metaphoric juxtapositions, which constantly achieve his ideal of a "marvellous reality," a new fiction of the "marvellous in the real." **MW**

The Heat of the Day

Elizabeth Bowen

Lifespan | *b.* 1899 (Ireland), *d.* 1973 (England)
First Published |1949
First Published by | A. Knopf (New York)
Full Name | Elizabeth Dorothy Cole Bowen

Elizabeth Bowen's *The Heat of the Day* is a beautiful novel: immersed in it, you do not want to leave it, but to stay encased in the symmetry and clarity of its vision. It is a love story set in wartime London. Stella discovers that her lover, Robert, is suspected of being a Nazi spy. He himself confesses to sympathy for the German vision of order and rule of law. Stella's delicately structured world slowly disintegrates.

This story and the strange hues of a summertime city at war give the novel its momentum and texture. There is, however, another level and another love story also at work, one that generates an intense and painful melancholy. This second love story is inarticulate, felt only as a sense of loss, a grieving for something loved and gone. What *The Heat of the Day* mourns would not have been mourned by many, nor will many today regret its passing. For it anticipates and lingers over the death of the cultural and social supremacy of the English property-owning class. Many of the sons of this class were slaughtered in the First World War, and in the interwar years the Great Depression had depleted their capital, while the existence of the Labour Party had drained their power and political prestige.

Bowen began writing *The Heat of the Day* in 1944, one year before the Labour landslide in the British general election of 1945. What enriches the text of this novel, enveloping and enlarging the individual stories of loss, is Bowen's elegy for an era even then already past. **PMcM**

Love in a Cold Climate

Nancy Mitford

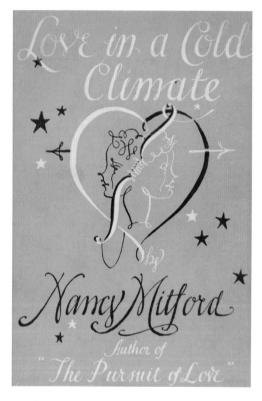

Lifespan | *b.* 1904 (England), *d.* 1973 (France)
First Published | 1949
First Published by | Hamish Hamilton (London)
Original Language | English

Love in a Cold Climate, set in roughly the same time and place as Nancy Mitford's earlier novel *The Pursuit of Love* (1945), delves into British aristocratic society between the wars with similarly hilarious results. It is the story of Polly Montdore, an heiress whose unconventional choice of husband not only shocks her own family, but also provides scandal enough to occupy all of her wealthy acquaintants. Told by her friend, Fanny, the sensible narrator of many of Mitford's novels, Polly's story expands to become a larger commentary on the comic and tragic elements inherent within society life. Light and witty in tone, the novel describes what would usually appear to be an ordinary round of social engagements in a world in which the ordinary is a surprisingly rare phenomenon. Mitford's characters often verge on the bizarre; "Uncle Matthew," modeled on Mitford's father, typifies the eccentric aristocrat, while the insufferable Lady Montdore, who undergoes a hilariously drawn affair with Canadian nephew and arch-aesthete Cedric, remains a cutting portrait of the domineering but gullible matriarch.

Mitford's novels, like those of Jane Austen, focus on the small social maneuverings of an exclusive family and their "set"; like Austen, she uses fond but mocking satire to gently send up the family, even while encouraging the reader to care about its fortunes. **AB**

> "To fall in love you have to be in the state of mind for it to take, like a disease."

Nancy Mitford

🌐 The title, *Love in a Cold Climate*, is a quotation from *Keep the Aspidistra Flying* by George Orwell.

The Case of Comrade Tulayev

Victor Serge

Lifespan | *b*. 1890 (Belgium), *d*. 1947 (Mexico)
First Published | 1949, by Editions du Seuil (Paris)
Given Name | Victor Lvovich Kibalchich
Original Title | *L' Affaire Toulaév*

The Case of Comrade Tulayev is about totalitarianism and hence is about defeat, enclosure, and the systematization of paranoia. It differs, however, from Orwell's *Nineteen Eighty-Four* or Koestler's *Darkness at Noon* in its determination to pay respect to the multiplicity and excesses of ordinary life. The novel takes the show trials and purges of Stalin's Russia as its core material. Serge himself had lived through the optimistic revolution of 1917 and the development of a total system of bureaucratic power in Stalinism. He had fought that development as part of Trotsky's Left opposition and had been deported to Central Asia between 1933 and 1936. It was at that time that Stalin's long waves of purges, the Great Terror, began.

There is a dense historical undercurrent in this novel, reaching back beyond Stalinism to incorporate, through memory, anecdote, and association, multiple varieties of Russian life. This is life as lived among the soldiers of the First World War, landless peasants, political activists in exiled or underground parties, the life of scholars, clerks, travelers, and enthusiasts.

Serge's narrative is rich with voices, while the plot condenses with a shocking coolness and clarity. Yet Serge still manages to keep the narrative poised at a level where Russia is an arena pulsating with life. While terror, death, betrayal, and a painful confusion are pervasive, so, too, are the small rhythms of work, fraternity, conversation, and hope. **PMcM**

The Garden Where the Brass Band Played

Simon Vestdijk

Lifespan | *b*. 1898 (Netherlands), *d*. 1971
First Published | 1950
First Published by | Gravenhage (Rotterdam)
Original Title | *De koperen tuin*

One of the giants among writers to come from the Netherlands, Vestdijk, who trained as a physician and published poetry as well as essays, was as prolific as he was versatile. His work had a major influence on the Dutch existentialists, and, if it were better known outside his own country, might be ranked with that of Joyce, Kafka, and Proust.

This novel, a moody study of the conflict between bourgeois society and the romantic ideal, is set in a fictional small town where Nol, a judge's son, first encounters enchantment. While still a child, he attends an outdoor concert with his mother and is seduced simultaneously by the music and dancing with the conductor's daughter. He subsequently takes piano lessons with the maestro, who opens his heart and mind to the mysteries of art. Nol's fascination and affinity for this way of knowing the world brings him into internal conflict with the milieu in which he has grown up and the class that claims him. His attachment to the musician Cuperus and especially to his daughter Trix, both of whom are quasi-outcasts in genteel society, is emblematic of the author's preoccupation with the unattainable beloved, and Nol's story is a sort of romantic quest that pits the ideal against social convention and the loss of innocence this entails. Vestdijk manages to combine rapture and suffering with comedy in a mix that is intensely realistic and completely engaging. **ES**

I, Robot

Isaac Asimov

Lifespan | *b.* 1920 (Russia), *d.* 1992 (U.S.)
First Published | 1950
First Published by | Gnome Press (New York)
Original Language | English

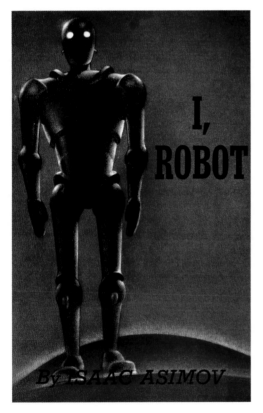

"Ninety-eight—ninety-nine . . ."

⬤ The classic image of the robot, as used on this jacket for *I Robot*, was influenced by 1920s movies such as Fritz Lang's *Metropolis*.

I, Robot is one of the great classics of science fiction. Ostensibly, it is a collection of short stories, but the fact that they are all linked together as they explore the twin subjects of robotics and philosophy warrants the book's inclusion in a list of literature's great novels. In *I, Robot*, Isaac Asimov coined the term "robotics" and set out the principles of robot behavior we know as the Three Laws of Robotics, followed by science fiction writers ever since. The three rules read: 1) A robot may not injure a human being or through inaction allow a human being to come to harm; 2) A robot must obey orders given by human beings except where such orders would conflict with the First Law; 3) A robot must protect its own existence as long as such protection does not conflict with the First or Second Law.

The stories are connected by robo-psychologist Dr. Susan Calvin, who works for the corporation that manufactures intelligent robots, and her discussions with a reporter who is putting together a profile of her career. Dr. Calvin reflects on robot evolution and discusses how little humanity really understands about the artificial intelligence it has created. Each story illuminates a problem encountered when a robot interprets the three fundamental laws, and something goes awry. Although *I, Robot* was published in 1950 and includes stories from the 1940s, when computing was in its embryonic stage, Asimov's vision of the future of software is startlingly accurate and insightful. Asimov's writing is certainly not top-drawer, and the characterization is often weak, but the scientific style, the blend between fact and fiction, and the stunning insights into the world of robotics, from which so much else has developed, make this one of the most important works of science fiction in the history of the genre. **EF**

The Grass is Singing

Doris Lessing

Doris Lessing's first novel, written in Africa, but not published until she was living in Europe, opens with the murder of the wife of a white Rhodesian farmer by her African servant. The novel's interest lies, however, in the story suppressed by the community of white farmers of the events that lead up to the tragedy. The retrospective narrative thus moves irrevocably toward an inevitable death.

From the first pages, it is clear that we are being asked to bear witness to a story of human relations that a colonial system of justice will not allow to be heard. Dick and Mary Turner are each possessed by need and a deluded idea of the other person. When they marry, city-girl Mary is brought to live on Turner's isolated and failing farm. As Mary is gradually disabused of her hopes about Dick and the future, she succumbs to torpor and hysteria in the sweltering heat of the veld. Only Moses, the latest in a series of native servants ill-treated by Mary, seems able to respond to her misery. But Moses's acts of kindness toward her violate the sacred colonial taboo—that separate races are not allowed to recognize one another as human beings. Desire and fear are inextricably intertwined as Mary feels herself surrendering to the authority of a man she associates with the surrounding bush, which threatens always to reconquer the land taken by the white farmers.

The portrait of lives destroyed is mitigated in its painful intensity only by the descriptions of the stark beauty of the African veld. *The Grass is Singing* is the first publication of a major literary figure, an angry denunciation of the hypocrisies of the colonial power known to Lessing from her youth in southern Africa, and a dissection of colonial mentality and the deformations it performs on both the colonizer and the colonized. **VM**

Lifespan | *b.* 1919 (Iran)
First Published |1950
First Published by | Michael Joseph (London)
Nobel Prize for Literature | 2007

"I'm not lonely."

⊙ This paperback edition of Lessing's novel was published by Heinemann in 1973 as one of its African Writers series.

A Town Like Alice

Nevil Shute

Lifespan | b. 1899 (England), d. 1960 (Australia)
First Published | 1950
First Published by | Heinemann (London)
Given Name | Nevil Shute Norway

Nevil Shute's *A Town Like Alice* received international acclaim and became an Australian classic. A love story set against the backdrop of the Second World War in the Far East and the postwar Australian outback, it is a tale of shifting societies and changing times, brought about by the impact of war. The novel is based on a real event, when the Japanese invaded Sumatra and captured eighty Dutch women and children, who were then forced to trek around the island for the next two and a half years.

The narrator tells the story of Jean Pagett, an English secretary in Malaysia. Captured along with other English women and children, she spends the next three years on a grueling "death march" around the Malay Peninsula. During this forced march, Jean strikes up a friendship with an Australian prisoner of war, Joe Harman, but later believes he has been killed. After the war Jean revisits Malaysia and discovers Joe is not dead. She travels to Australia, their romance is rekindled, and they turn the one-horse town in which Joe lives into a thriving community, based on Alice Springs. *A Town Like Alice* has all the elements of a great love story and was written when the British-born author had just embarked upon a love affair of his own—with his new country, Australia. **LE**

◖ Nevil Shute, an aeronautical engineer as well as a novelist, satisfied popular taste for moral dilemmas and happy endings.

The Moon and the Bonfires

Cesare Pavese

Lifespan | b. 1908 (Italy), d. 1950
First Published | 1950
First Published by | Einaudi (Turin)
Original Title | La luna e i falò

Cesare Pavese's last novel has been acclaimed as his best, a lyrical walk through the Langhe region of Piedmont. The story is minimal, as the author did not want to create a complex plot or explore the psychology of the characters.

After Italy is liberated from Fascism, Anguilla, who has spent twenty years in America, returns to his native village. He has traveled enough to know that all countries in the world are similar and one needs to settle somewhere. Consequently, he returns to the Langhe because "those villages were waiting for him." In a narrative that alternates between present and past, Anguilla—accompanied by his friend and guide, Nuto—rediscovers his homeland. Anguilla's desire is to find himself through the physical appropriation of Gaminella, the place where he spent his childhood, and Mora, where he worked during his adolescence. His idealized village has acquired the symbolic colors of an earthly paradise, but he soon finds that the trees have been cut down, and Santa, who was a young girl when he left, has been killed. Nuto shares with Anguilla the same faith in the value of the Resistance and the necessity of a social revolution and helps him to become aware of the deceptiveness of his search. He introduces Anguilla to the mythical essence of social revolution by affirming his belief in the peasants' traditions and superstitions, and in the regenerative power of the bonfires. **RPi**

Gormenghast

Mervyn Peake

Lifespan | *b.* 1911 (China), *d.* 1968 (England)
First Published | 1950
First Published by | Eyre & Spottiswoode (London)
Full Name | Mervyn Lawrence Peake

"Oh, wonderful. He's behaving his damn self."

🔵 Mervyn Peake, an illustrator as well as a writer, peruses some sketches in a photo published in *Picture Post* magazine (1946).

This is the second volume of Mervyn Peake's extraordinary *Gormenghast* trilogy and inarguably the apex of the series. It is also an outstanding feat of literature. *Gormenghast* takes up where *Titus Groan* left off. Lord Sepulchrave is dead, Swelter has been vanquished by Mr. Flay, and Steerpike, bald from his own arson—his disfiguring scars reflecting his progressive inner rot—continues his vicious ascent through the hierarchy. He has become a force to be reckoned with. Titus is approaching restless adolescence. As he closes in on manhood, he becomes a worthy adversary to the machinations of the increasingly powerful Steerpike. And Gormenghast itself, huge and malevolent, wheezes on.

The carnival of characters from *Titus Groan* returns with exhilarating vibrancy, coursing through the labyrinth of Great Halls and bedchambers, the dusty cellars and libraries. There are the lovelorn Fuschia, the nattering twin aunts having tea parties in the boughs outside their window, the toadying Dr. Prunesquallor, and his sister, Irma, with her preening, unearned vanity. Peake takes his original scathing allegory of British life and expands it with new targets for his sublime wit: an excoriating and hilarious examination of Titus's education in a system that is eerily familiar. The novel culminates with an apocalyptic flood, as Steerpike and Titus do battle for the very heart of Gormenghast. With an awareness of the outside world and the itch of adolescence, Titus finally decides to leave the craggy battlements of his home and sets out for the world beyond the crumbling walls.

Peake's prose is masterful; his characters so strange they become hyperreal. *Gormenghast* is as complex and dark as a Bosch triptych. It is a fairy tale without sugar, leaving only the skeletal nightmare. **GT**

The 13 Clocks

James Thurber

The 13 Clocks contains all the essential ingredients of a thrilling fairy tale. There is a prince disguised as a ragged minstrel, a tragic princess trapped in a castle by an evil duke, and the prospect of a daring task that must be completed within an impossible time frame. This constraint is a key element in the story because the duke claims to have "slain" time, and the thirteen clocks in the castle are frozen at ten minutes to five. The prince must find a priceless treasure and deliver it up as the clocks strike the hour. His only hope is the Golux, a tiny wizard possessed of a strange logic and an indescribable hat.

The castle is a dangerous place, noisily patrolled by huge metallic guards, silently controlled by the duke's velvet-hooded spies. Nightmarish creatures lurk in the darkest corners of the deepest dungeons. Playful counterpoints to these horrors are provided by touches of absurdity. Brightly colored balls come bouncing downstairs at unlikely moments—are there ghosts of murdered children playing above? Chimes of distant laughter hint at the possibility. There are also elements of parable: love conquers all, time is unfrozen, and evil meets inevitable nemesis. In the final pages the duke is pursued by "a blob of glup, that smells of old unopened rooms and makes a sound like rabbits screaming."

The language is dazzlingly inventive and the tone wickedly ironic—hallmarks of the most admired and controversial humorist of the first half of the twentieth century. At the time of writing *The 13 Clocks*, Thurber was rapidly losing his sight, and the descriptions of half-perceived figures moving in shadows, of shafts of sunlight piercing darkened rooms, and thickets of night lit by flashes of lightning, create hallucinatory landscapes that suggest a great preoccupation with encroaching blindness. **TS**

Lifespan | *b.* 1894 (U.S.), *d.* 1961
First Published | 1950
First Published by | Simon & Schuster (New York)
Full Name | James Grover Thurber

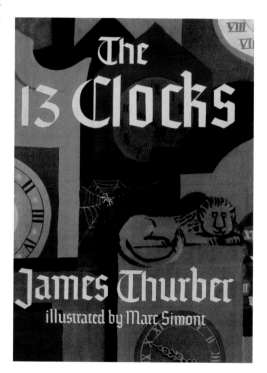

> *"He called himself Xingu, which was not his name . . ."*

Thurber was unable to draw the cartoons for *The 13 Clocks* after losing his sight, so enlisted his friend Marc Simont to illustrate it.

The Labyrinth of Solitude

Octavio Paz

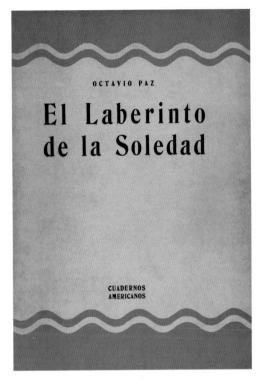

Lifespan | *b.* 1914 (Mexico), *d.* 1998
First Published |1950, by Cuadernos Americanos
Original Title | *El laberinto de la soledad*
Nobel Prize for Literature | 1990

A book made up of nine individual essay-chapters on aspects of Mexican national character might seem an odd choice in a list of indispensable novels, but *The Labyrinth of Solitude* also marks an advance in prose fiction. It is an analytical and intensely poetic Bildungsroman showing the formation not of an individual, but of a nation's identity.

Octavio Paz was already among the greatest Mexican poets of the twentieth century when he wrote *The Labyrinth of Solitude* in 1950. He was also a significant public figure: he traveled to Europe in the 1930s, fighting for the Republicans in the Spanish Civil War; he was an esteemed diplomat; and he went on to win the Nobel Prize for Literature in 1990. *Labyrinth* proved controversial with the Mexican establishment, because it held up a mirror to a nation that did not always like what it was shown. The book describes Mexico at a crucial moment of self-realization, but it is also often critical of aspects of Mexican identity: its machismo, dissimulation, harshness, and immovable gender roles.

In this work, Paz is part anthropologist and art semiologist, reading the signs through which Mexican culture was constructed, from the dress codes of disaffected Mexican-American youth gangs to the public rituals of the famous Day of the Dead. But he also brings all of his profound eloquence as a poet to bear on his subject, and the book resonates on every page with instinctive insights, connections, and verbal finesse. **MS**

"... what is he searching for? Perhaps he searches for his destiny. Perhaps his destiny is to search."

🔾 Paz's grandfather was also an author, and it was through his extensive library that Paz came into early contact with literature.

The Abbot C

Georges Bataille

Lifespan | b. 1897 (France), d. 1962
First Published | 1950
First Published by | Les Editions de Minuit (Paris)
Original Title | L'Abbé C

George Bataille's short novel *The Abbot C* follows the dangerously entangled relationship between twin brothers: Robert, a priest, who lives a life of such virtue that he has earned the sobriquet "the abbot," and his antipathetic brother Charles, who leads a dissolute life devoted to pleasure. The novel is comprised of various narrators and opens with the narrative of a mutual friend, who finds Robert in a state of anguish on account of his brother's grave ill health. As the story unfolds, the extent of the brothers' overlapping emotional lives becomes clear. Charles's involvement with Eponine, a woman who shares his decadent and licentious lifestyle, is complicated by her sexual desire for the abstemious Robert and, more sensationally, by Robert's uneasy physical desire for her. This painful triangulation puts unbearable strain upon the sibling relationship and causes the steady breakdown of Robert's sanity and simultaneous deterioration of Charles's physical health.

Fusing Bataille's familiar fascination with the relationship between eroticism, death, and sensuality, the novel explores the thin line between sexual desire and morbidity. In its concentration on the fissure between the moral code demanded by religious observance and the truth of individual conscience, it explores an intriguing dimension of human experience. Readers may find the treatment of this issue somewhat excessive and the contrived intention to shock rather heavy-handed, but this is still an engaging and unusual piece of writing. **JW**

The Guiltless

Hermann Broch

Lifespan | b. 1886 (Austria), d. 1951 (U.S.)
First Published | 1950
First Published by | Willi Weismann (Munich)
Original Title | Die Shuldlosen

A loosely connected set of short stories much like Christopher Isherwood's *Goodbye to Berlin*, Hermann Broch's *The Guiltless* paints a picture of interwar European society that is similarly bleak and ominous. Ranging in time between 1913 and 1933, the stories that make up *The Guiltless* describe characters not only destroyed by the impact of the First World War, but themselves seemingly intent on destroying any remnants of moral certainty.

Loosely focused on the fortunes of "Mr. A," a seemingly rootless young man living as a boarder in the run-down palace of an ageing baroness, the novel details a series of social failures that he either provokes or witnesses. Sexual relations turn to betrayal and violence; love for nature mutates into an inhuman indifference; family life becomes a grotesque parody of nonexistent prewar conventions. Broch inserts "explanations" preceding each group of stories, making it increasingly clear that the distorted values of this decadent society foreshadow the much more menacing norms of looming Nazism. None of the characters is overtly political but their inhuman actions lay the groundwork for the passive acceptance of fascism.

Arrestingly written in a mixture of understated prose and satiric verse, *The Guiltless* remains today a haunting and powerful novel that forces the reader to concede that, as one of the characters belatedly notes, "Our responsibility, like our wickedness, is bigger than ourselves." **AB**

Barabbas

Pär Lagerkvist

Lifespan | *b.* 1891 (Sweden), *d.* 1974
First Published | 1950
First Published by | Bonniers (Stockholm)
Nobel Prize for Literature | 1951

Condemned as a thief but released in place of Christ, Barabbas appears only fleetingly in the New Testament. In the skillful hands of Pär Lagerkvist, however, he becomes an enigmatic, haunted figure, an outcast compelled by a bewildering inner force to seek out a God whom he can neither fully accept nor reject. Unable to settle into his former existence after witnessing Christ's death, he becomes a drifter, then a slave, all the while encircling Christians wherever he finds them, in a dangerous dance of mutual incomprehension. Structured around three crucifixions, *Barabbas* offers an array of shifting parallels and contrasts—between Barabbas and Jesus, doubt and faith, darkness and light.

Having lost his own faith as a young man, Lagerkvist was profoundly interested in the anguish of those who, having no certainties, seek a sense of purpose in an apparently meaningless world. In *Barabbas* we find the perfect setting for these themes, where the unquestioning, peace-giving faith of the early Christians sits alongside the fearful loneliness of one man's nagging doubt.

In 1951, Lagerkvist was awarded the Nobel Prize for literature, principally for this novel. That *Barabbas* should have moved the Nobel Committee so deeply is unsurprising; in the aftermath of the Second World War and its horrors, "What does all this mean?" was a timely cry. *Barabbas* is a work of profound modernity, placing in the foreground man's growing sense of existential anguish. **RMa**

The End of the Affair

Graham Greene

Lifespan | *b.* 1904 (England), *d.* 1991 (Switzerland)
First Published | 1951
First Published by | Heinemann (London)
Full Name | Henry Graham Greene

Set in London during and after the Second World War, this is the tortured story of an affair between Maurice Bendrix, a novelist, and the married Sarah Miles. The lovers meet at a party and proceed to liberate each other from the confines of duty and unhappiness. After several years, the affair is still continuing, against the backdrop of London during the Blitz. The building in which the lovers meet is hit by a bomb, and Bendrix is knocked unconscious. Terrified that he is dead, Sarah makes a deal with God that if he lets him live, she will give up her lover. Bendrix recovers, and Sarah—true to her promise—ends the affair with no explanation, leaving Bendrix unhappy and confused. It is only years later that he finds out about her passionate vow to God.

Graham Greene is known for his Catholicism, and also for questioning religious faith in the light of his own adulterous affairs. This is the most autobiographical of Greene's novels, probably based on his own wartime affair. It is a story of love, passion, and religious faith, and how love of self, love of another, and love of God collide. The tension that pervades *The End of the Affair* comes from the interplay of doubt and faith, and Greene's underlying message that human love and passion are inadequate for relieving suffering—for that, he believes, one must turn to the love of God. **EF**

❯ Like many authors of his period, Greene was a heavy drinker—a characteristic with which he endows many of his heroes.

Molloy

Samuel Beckett

Lifespan | *b.* 1906 (Ireland), *d.* 1989 (France)
First Published | 1951
First Published by | Les Editions de Minuit (Paris)
Nobel Prize for Literature | 1969

Samuel Beckett is better known for his plays than for his novels, but his novels are the greater achievement. They are the funniest prose alive. *Molloy*, written initially in French, then translated into English by Beckett and Patrick Bowles, is the first novel in the trilogy finished off by *Malone Dies* and *The Unnamable*. Although they complete the trilogy, these two later novels proved inadequate to the job of putting an end to the decline begun in *Molloy*, which extends into everything that Beckett would go on to write.

Beckett is the great master of every possible shade of decline and its unrivalled comedian. *Molloy* is probably the funniest of all his writing. It is made up of two stories, each the doppelgänger of the other. In the first, the wretched cripple Molloy stumbles through a lost thread of episodes peopled by his insensible mother, a litter of comic citizens, a policeman, and a grotesque feminine captor named Lousse, before ending up dumped by Beckett in a ditch. His place is then surrendered to Moran, whom Beckett dispatches, together with his son, on a quest to find his predecessor, a quest that Moran pursues with furious inertia only to find that Beckett has declined to contrive a meeting between them. He trudges home to find his bees turned to ash.

Beckett nails all the perks of fiction (all the events, sympathies, and glitter of fiction's "real life") into their smorgasbord and buries it. His stories are all the confessions of a syntax addict whose phantom fix is total disagreement with himself. **KS**

The Rebel

Albert Camus

Lifespan | *b.* 1913 (Algeria), *d.* 1960 (France)
First Published | 1951
First Published by | Gallimard (Paris)
Original Title | *L'Homme révolté*

The Rebel recalls the dispute between Camus and Sartre in 1952. It also represents the dispute between metaphysical freedom and actual revolution. In the aftermath of the Second World War, the French yearned for social change and activism. The verdict of the day favored Sartre. *The Rebel* was accused of supporting the vision of right-wing reactionaries. But does it really? In the cultural context of our time, *The Rebel* appears to question the foundation of collectivist ideology and to present us with an acute insight into the preconditions of "being political." The thesis of the book can be summarized in the statement: "I revolt, therefore we are." However, in Camus, the absolute solitariness or freedom of the individual never allows the emergence of "we" to be the objective of individual revolt. Metaphysically speaking, we are already engaged with a political situation before the actual intended revolution. In the eyes of Camus, Sartrian left-wing existentialism dismisses the freedom of the individual. For Sartre, revolt means an actual engagement with politics so as to bring about changes, while for Camus it is a metaphysical condition of the inner life of the individual. Camus stands back from Sartrian activism, which promotes solidarity. How do we read *The Rebel* today? The way we read it will point to the political condition in which we live. **KK**

❯ Camus casts a mordant glance on a Parisian street in 1957,
  the year in which he was awarded the Nobel Prize for Literature.

The Catcher in the Rye

J. D. Salinger

a novel by **J. D. SALINGER**

" . . . I'm standing on the edge of some crazy cliff. What I have to do, I have to catch everybody if they start to go over the cliff . . ."

To escape the unwanted fame that *The Catcher in the Rye* brought him, Salinger became a recluse, vigorously defending his privacy.

Lifespan | *b.* 1919 (U.S.)
First Published | 1951
First Published by | Little Brown & Co. (Boston)
Full Name | Jerome David Salinger

The Catcher in the Rye presents the dazzling mock-autobiographical story of an American teenager, Holden Caulfield, charting his rebellious encounters with the "phoney" world around him. Shadowed by apocalyptic anxieties ("I'm sort of glad they've got the atomic bomb invented. If there's another war, I'm going to sit right the hell on top of it."), it is also an extraordinary study of refused or impossible mourning, above all Holden's for his dead younger brother, Allie. Once asked "who was the best war poet, Rupert Brooke or Emily Dickinson," Allie said Dickinson. Salinger's novel is itself a kind of war poetry. It is at war with "phoney" adult (affluent, middle-class, white, patriarchal, American) values, but also with itself: Holden brilliantly ridicules those around him, but in the process inevitably also makes himself ridiculous.

Hilarious and disturbing, satirical and strangely poignant by turns, *The Catcher in the Rye* is written in a deceptively simple and colloqiual style: "What really knocks me out is a book that, when you're all done reading it, you wish the author that wrote it was a terrific friend of yours and you could call him up on the phone whenever you felt like it." Novels to read before you die are novels like that. How phoney is *this* phone? Salinger's voice is enigmatically concealed in Holden's. There is the captivating ease and intimacy of someone directly speaking to us. At the same time, the reader is left with the remarkable sense that the tone of the entire work is perhaps really audible only to the dead brother. **NWor**

The Opposing Shore

Julien Gracq

Lifespan | *b.* 1910 (France)
First Published | 1951, by J. Corti (Paris)
Original Title | *Le Rivage des Syrtes*
Given Name | Louis Poirier

A strangely moody and distilled piece of writing, *The Opposing Shore* is set in decadent Orsenna, a fictional country long engaged in a phoney war with Farghestan, the neighboring barbarian state. In a permanently suspended stalemate, all battles having ceased some 300 years earlier, neither side can afford either to concede or to continue, or is prepared to negotiate terms of peace. Yet legends of the war have stimulated the poets to an output far beyond what the situation might be expected to inspire.

Aldo, a young and dissipated man, scion of an aristocratic family, is disappointed in love and weary of the pleasures of the capital; he longs for exile and asceticism. So he takes on the position of Observer at the military post on the frontier, where the Admiralty, a long-disused fortress, maintains a purely symbolic presence. There Aldo, poet and loner, attempts to shake off his torpor and invigorate his fatherland by launching a naval maneuver that regenerates the hostilities to disastrous effect.

The novel follows a graceful path of sumptuous imagery that slows the action to a timelessness that reads like myth. Gracq's writing has a strong affinity to the Surrealism of André Breton, although he was never part of this or any other literary movement.

Gracq, like his protagonist Aldo, disdained the effete cultural milieu of urban centers—in this case, Paris. Had he not categorically rejected the honor, *The Opposing Shore* would have been awarded the Prix Goncourt in 1951. **ES**

Foundation

Isaac Asimov

Lifespan | *b.* 1920 (Russia), *d.* 1992 (U.S.)
First Published | 1951, by Gnome Press (New York)
Trilogy | *Foundation* (1951), *Foundation and Empire* (1952), *Second Foundation* (1953)

Isaac Asimov's Foundation series, of which this is the first book, is one of his earliest and best-known works, which he began when he was only twenty-one. It helped to redefine the science fiction genre with its seamless interweaving of science fact with fiction.

Foundation is set in the future, when the world is barely remembered, and humans have colonized the galaxy. The book introduces Hari Seldon, a brilliant visionary and psychohistorian whose job is to use mathematics and probability to predict the future. Seldon does not have the ability to prevent the decline of humanity that he predicts. Instead, he gathers together the galaxy's top scientists and scholars on a bleak outer planet and sets out to preserve the accumulated knowledge of humankind, and begin a new civilization based on art, science, and technology. He calls his sanctuary the Foundation and designs it to withstand a dark age of ignorance, barbarism, and warfare he predicts will last for 30,000 years. But not even Hari has foreseen the intense barbarism lurking in space or the birth of an extraordinary creature whose mutant intelligence will destroy all he holds dear.

With his scientist-populated *Foundation*, Asimov became one of the first writers to theorize that atomic power would revolutionize society. In addressing the ways in which the Foundation responds to the problems Seldon has predicted, the author raises issues about traditional religion as the controlling drug of the masses, and the rise of science as the new faith for humankind. **EF**

Samuel Beckett

by

Malone Dies

Samuel Beckett

Lifespan | b. 1906 (Ireland), d. 1989 (Paris)
First Published | 1951
First Published by | Les Editions de Minuit (Paris)
Original Title | Malone meurt

For those readers who easily tire of colorful fiction, *Malone Dies* will be as revitalizing as anything in the language. It is Samuel Beckett's attempt to winnow down still more violently the nib of his fiction. The stories are what the language uses to get away from itself, and they are all going nowhere. Early on in *Malone Dies*, we are spoon-fed the story of the sorrows of young Sapo Saposcat, a fake and abortive Bildungsroman in a suite of ludicrously colorless episodes. Later he tries his hand at a love story, where the protagonists manage at great effort and discomfort to act out what are surely the most repulsive sex scenes in any comedy.

When the language of *Malone Dies* begins to resemble a novel, it is always faking it. As each consecutive excuse for a story is dumped, we are dragged back into the scene of syntax addiction and the parody of mystification over life and death, endlessly knocked on the head by casual remarks such as "ideas are so alike, when you get to know them," and endlessly restarted. So it goes until the book's brutal finish, in which Beckett is perhaps more nearly terrified than anywhere else in his fiction by the corner he has crushed himself into and by his failure to lose control of language even there. The horror and optimism of Beckett are that true claustrophobia is possible only in paradise. **KS**

⬅ A portrait of Beckett by fellow author J. P. Donleavy brings out the intense blank gaze and tight lips of a death-haunted man.

Day of the Triffids

John Wyndham

Lifespan | b.1903 (England), d. 1969
First Published | 1951, by Michael Joseph (London)
Full Name | John Wyndham Parkes Lucas Beynon Harris

Published in 1951 to moderate acclaim, this novel was later to become a science fiction classic (as well as a low-budget movie in 1963) and a defining novel of the post-disaster genre. The action opens with biologist Bill Masen in the hospital, bandages draped over his eyes after a poisonous plant (triffid) sting. Nurses describe to him the most spectacular meteorite shower England has ever seen, but when he awakens the next morning, the hospital routine he expects never starts. Overcoming his fear of damaging his eyes, he removes the bandages to find thousands of sightless people wandering the streets. He meets Josella, another sighted survivor, and the two leave the city together in an attempt to survive in a postapocalyptic world. The triffids, which can grow to seven feet, walk on their roots, and kill a man with a sting, have made their first attack and are now poised to prey on humanity. Masen eventually convinces other survivors to band together to try to defeat these intelligent plants. It is essentially the story of a normal man who must alter his social values in order to survive.

On the face of it, this seems to be a reasonably straightforward survival adventure, but it was the first of its time to anticipate disaster on a global scale. Wyndham predicts the technologies of biowarfare and mass destruction, offering a sophisticated account of Cold War paranoia that was well before its time in terms of its exploration of the psyche of individuals in the face of social change. **EF**

Memoirs of Hadrian

Marguerite Yourcenar

Lifespan | *b*. 1903 (Belgium), *d*. 1987 (U.S.)
First Published | 1951, by Librarie Plon (Paris)
Original Title | *Mémoires d'Hadrien*
Given Name | Marguerite de Crayencour

Marguerite Yourcenar will always be distinguished by becoming, in 1980, the first woman ever elected as a member of the Académie Française. And it is largely on the strength of work such as *Memoirs of Hadrian* that her literary reputation was built. The book is constructed as a long letter from the dying emperor to Marcus Aurelius, who was then an adolescent (and who succeeded as ruler of Rome following the intervening reign of his adoptive father, Antoninus Pius). The account relates the professional and historical aspects of Hadrian's two decades as Emperor, distilling from his worldly experience what he can transmit to the younger man of the judgment and insight he has attained. His reflections on the fundaments of life—the mysteries of love, the demands of the body, the question of human destiny—shared by all of us make this novel far more accessible to a contemporary reader than might be expected of the thoughts of a second-century titan.

Yourcenar's achievement is the thoroughness of her research; it is easy to forget that this is fiction written in a philosophical style, its tone that of a man of action examining and evaluating his existence. *Memoirs of Hadrian* has been admired equally by scholars of classical antiquity as by arbiters of literary art, and secured the author's international reputation when it appeared. **ES**

⊙ Marguerite Yourcenar is pictured in a portrait taken in Bordeaux, France, some ten years after *Memoirs* was published.

The Hive

Camilo José Cela

Lifespan | *b*. 1916 (Spain), *d*. 2002
First Published | 1951
First Published by | Emecé (Buenos Aires)
Nobel Prize for Literature | 1989

The title of *The Hive* refers to the teeming variety of Madrid, the great city where people looking to make a life congregate, like bees in a hive. The novel has no subject or main character; there are about 300 characters, most of them from the middle classes who have been ruined by the severity of the postwar period. Their lives are ordinary, beset by illness (tuberculosis) or debt, or they are falling into prostitution. They are obsessed by sex, and their conversations allude to wartime topics—firing squads, prison—or to conservative principles (that "class" comes with blood, that one must be Spanish, or Catholic). It is a Spain obsessed by denunciation and distrust. The structural connection of the episodes, told by "the narrator" with alleged objectivity, is rooted in the repetition of places and characters—the main ones are the Café of Doña Rosa and the fugitive "intellectual" Martín Marco.

This novel influenced writers of the so-called mid-century generation, who carried out the work of criticism and social denunciation that Cela did not attempt. Cela did not describe the essential sordidness of the inhabitants of the beehive, nor did he point to causes or culprits; he tended to see everything in a fatalistic way, seeing the piety that occurs as compatible with betrayal or cruelty. With a supreme command of language, Cela limits himself to relating the facts of a degraded reality, and thus he achieves a devastating statement that, in spite of its lack of censoriousness, was avidly read. **M-DAB**

Wise Blood

Flannery O'Connor

Lifespan | *b.* 1925 (U.S.), *d.* 1964
First Published | 1952
First Published by | Harcourt, Brace & Co. (N. Y.)
Full Name | Mary Flannery O'Connor

a novel by **Flannery O'Connor**

WISE

BLOOD

"Nothing matters but that Jesus was a liar."

◓ *Wise Blood* was O'Connor's first novel—on the jacket of the first
edition, the unknown author's name is given little prominence.

Since its publication in 1952, Flannery O'Connor's *Wise Blood* has become one of several American novels that have gone on to define the so-called "Southern Gothic" genre. It is a work deeply embedded in the intense humidity and religious fervor of the old South.

The story centers on a young man named Hazel Motes. Raised by an uncompromisingly conservative family, Hazel returns home after a spell in the military with his religious faith destroyed by the experience of war. As a way of coming to terms with his newfound sense of loss, Hazel creates his own church: the Church without Christ. It is a church where "the deaf don't hear, the blind don't see, the lame don't walk, the dumb don't talk, and the dead stay that way." Hazel becomes a kind of heretical antipriest, a renegade street preacher driven by an urge to save those around him from Christianity. The further away he tries to push himself from faith, however, the deeper his need for redemption becomes.

Wise Blood is populated by an eccentric collection of misfits, thieves, con artists, scumbags, and false prophets. It is partly a theological allegory, a meditation on the place of God in modern culture, and partly a grotesque, madcap comedy. It is a novel of miracles and murder, of lustful flesh and pure spirit, of blindness and vision, of violence and healing. O'Connor presents a complex vision of the rural South in which she was raised. The novel unravels many of the South's myths and prejudices, yet at the same time pays homage to its traditions, heritage, and defiance. The spare, economical prose finds insight and wonder in the smallest detail, acutely sensitive to the transformative power of both faith and doubt. The world of *Wise Blood* is tough, tarnished, and visceral, but it is also brushed with grace. **ST**

The Old Man and the Sea

Ernest Hemingway

Critical opinion tends to differ over *The Old Man and the Sea,* which moves away from the style of Ernest Hemingway's earlier works. Within the frame of this perfectly constructed miniature are to be found many of the themes that preoccupied Hemingway as a writer and as a man. The routines of life in a Cuban fishing village are evoked in the opening pages with a characteristic economy of language. The stripped-down existence of the fisherman Santiago is crafted in a spare, elemental style that is as eloquently dismissive as a shrug of the old man's powerful shoulders. With age and luck now against him, Santiago knows he must row out "beyond other men," away from land and into the deep waters of the Gulf Stream. There is one last drama to be played out, in an empty arena of sea and sky.

Hemingway was famously fascinated with ideas of men proving their worth by facing and overcoming the challenges of nature. When the old man hooks a marlin longer than his boat, he is tested to the limits as he works the line with bleeding hands in an effort to bring it close enough to harpoon. Through his struggle he demonstrates the ability of the human spirit to endure hardship and suffering in order to win. It is also his deep love and knowledge of the sea, in her impassive cruelty and beneficence, that allows him to prevail.

The essential physicality of the story—the smells of tar and salt and fish blood, the cramp and nausea and blind exhaustion of the old man, the terrifying death spasms of the great fish—is set against the ethereal qualities of dazzling light and water, isolation, and the swelling motion of the sea. And the narrative is constantly tugging, unreeling a little more, pulling again. It is a book that demands to be read in a single sitting. **TS**

Lifespan | *b.* 1899 (U.S.), *d.* 1961
First Published | 1952
First Published by | C. Scribner's Sons (New York)
Pulitzer Prize for Literature | 1953

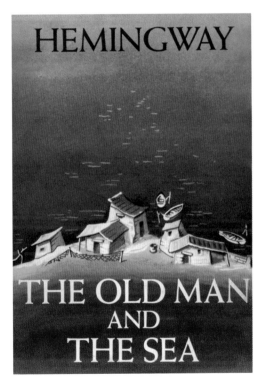

"A man can be destroyed but not defeated."

◉ The cover illustration of the British first edition, published by Jonathan Cape, depicts the novel's Cuban fishing village.

Invisible Man

Ralph Ellison

Lifespan | *b.* 1914 (U.S.), *d.*1994
First Published | 1952
First Published by | Random House (New York)
National Book Award | 1952

"I am an invisible man."

⊙ This is one of a series of photographs staged by Gordon Parks,
a friend of Ellison, as a visual interpretation of *The Invisible Man*.

⊙ Another of Parks's photographs illustrates Ellison's invisible hero
rising from underground: "I must come out, I must emerge . . ."

Invisible Man is Ralph Ellison's only novel and is widely acknowledged as one of the great novels of African-American literature. The invisibility of Ellison's protagonist is about the invisibility of identity—above all, what it means to be a black man—and its various masks, confronting both personal experience and the force of social illusions.

The novel's special quality is its deft combination of existential inquiry into identity as such—what it means to be socially or racially invisible—with a more sociopolitical allegory of the history of the African-American experience in America. The first-person narrator remains nameless, retrospectively recounting his shifts through the surreal reality of surroundings and people from the racist South to the no less inhospitable world of New York City. While *Invisible Man* bears comparison with the existentialist novels of Sartre and Camus, it also maps out the story of one man's identity against the struggles of collective self-definition. This takes the narrator-protagonist through the circumscribed social possibilities afforded to African-Americans, from enslaved grandparents through southern education, to models associated with Booker T. Washington, through to the full range of Harlem politics. Ellison's almost sociological clarity in the way he shows his central character working through these possibilities is skillfully worked into a novel about particular people, events, and situations, from the nightmare world of the ironically named Liberty Paints to the Marxist-Leninist machinations of the Brotherhood. In the process, Ellison offers sympathetic but severe critiques of the ideological resources of black culture, such as religion and music. Fierce, defiant, and utterly funny, Ellison's tone mixes various idioms and registers to produce an impassioned inquiry into the politics of being. **DM**

The Judge and His Hangman
Friedrich Dürrenmatt

Lifespan | *b.* 1921 (Switzerland), *d.* 1990
First Published | 1952
First Published by| Benziger (Einsiedeln)
Original Title | *Der Richter und sein Henker*

Written while he was flourishing in postwar Germany as a playwright, novelist, essayist, theater director, and painter, Friedrich Dürrenmatt's *The Judge and His Hangman* weaves a suspenseful tale of murder in a remote part of Switzerland. The stark minimalism of the author's Brechtian theatrical work is counteracted in this atmospheric novel, in which words paint foreboding and thrilling backdrops to the tale of Police Commissioner Bärlach, who is investigating the murder of a fellow police officer, Schmied. Bärlach, an ageing and dying man whose investigative faculties have not yet taken a backseat to his physical frailties, hands over the bulk of the detective work to his colleague, Tschanz. The two of them launch into a harrowing investigation (Bärlach is brain; Tschanz is brawn), but there are very few clues: a bullet on the side of the road, beside the car in which Schmied, dressed in evening clothes, was murdered, and an entry—a single "G"—in the victim's diary on the night he was killed. This last clue leads Bärlach and Tschanz to the home of the cold, mysterious, and brilliant Gastmann.

This novel, the first of Dürrenmatt's books to be published in America, addresses the theme of modern detective work in a way that is far from secondary to its mysterious plot. Critiquing policing methods is bound up inextricably both with the plot and with an equally important study of human imperfection. It is this last aspect, in particular, that truly distinguishes this piece of crime fiction. **JuS**

> *"The more human beings proceed by plan the more effectively they may be hit by accident."*
>
> *Friedrich Dürrenmatt, 1957*

◉ Friedrich Dürrenmatt was famous not only for his crime novels, but also for his avant-garde plays and satires.

Excellent Women

Barbara Pym

Lifespan | *b.* 1913 (England), *d.* 1980
First Published | 1952
First Published by | Jonathan Cape (London)
Original Language | English

Excellent Women is set in postwar London. Housing shortages bring handsome naval officer Rockingham Napier and his anthropologist wife, Helena, to a Pimlico flat. Here they share a bathroom with the narrator, Mildred Lathbury. Convinced of her own dreariness, Mildred lives in a modest world of jumble sales and charitable good works. As she becomes involved in the Napiers' very different lives, a disturbing hint of romance brings her frustrations to the surface. An emotional upheaval at the vicarage complicates the plot, while an odd relationship develops between Mildred and Helena's fellow anthropologist, the splendidly named Everard Bone.

All of Barbara Pym's early novels—six were published between 1950 and 1961—sparkle with wit and invention. She has a superb ear for the absurdities of everyday speech and her characters are observed with a sharp eye. What makes *Excellent Women* her finest work is the emotionally engaging first-person narration. Exploited and ignored by the selfish, insensitive individuals around her, Mildred spurns self-pity. It is hardly surprising that Pym became unpublishable in the 1960s. There is no place in her world for inflated gestures of liberation (even if Mildred allows herself to purchase an unsuitable shade of lipstick—"Hawaiian Fire"). Mildred endures her limited fate with decency and humor, drawing comfort and amusement from the minutiae of everyday life. Therein lies the poignancy and comedy of this exquisitely crafted work. **RegG**

A Thousand Cranes

Yasunari Kawabata

Lifespan | *b.* 1899 (Japan), *d.* 1972
First Published | 1952, by Kodansha (Tokyo)
Original Title | *Sembazuru*
Nobel Prize for Literature | 1968

The first Japanese novelist to win the Nobel Prize for Literature, in 1968, Yasunari Kawabata in this novel weaves a delicate web of sexual relations behind the veil of the traditional Japanese tea ceremony. After his father's death, Kikuji is lured into his world, becoming involved with his father's mistress, Mrs. Ota, as well as being controlled by his father's spurned lover, Chikako. In reliving the memory of his father through his women, Kikuji refuses to choose a young woman for himself, although an elusive girl and Mrs. Ota's daughter linger as potential partners.

As possessions are passed from one generation to the next, affections and passions are also transferred through the same hands, albeit through illicit relations and tainted ambitions. Kawabata noted that he did not intend to evoke the beauty of the ceremony, but rather the "vulgarity into which the tea ceremony has fallen." The line between clean and unclean, desire and disgust, is constantly raised and erased in a futile search for purity in this world.

The irony of the title encapsulates Kawabata's lament at the erosion of tradition and the difficulty of physical and spiritual fulfillment. A thousand cranes, traditionally signifying a long and prosperous marriage, is an unattainable illusion. Tragically, Kawabata suffered the same fate as one of his characters when he committed suicide, but his legacy introduced Japanese aesthetics to a wider Western audience and contributes to the shaping of a modern identity in Japanese literature. **HH**

Go Tell It on the Mountain

James Baldwin

Lifespan | b. 1924 (U.S.), d. 1987 (France)
First Published | 1953
First Published by | Knopf (New York)
Full Name | James Arthur Baldwin

". . . I ain't going to have that boy's blood on my hands."

⊙ Baldwin spent three years as a preacher when he was a teenager, and the influence of the church remained evident in his writing.

This semi-autobiographical Bildungsroman focuses on the complex and often fragile social bonds surrounding protagonist John as he celebrates his fourteenth birthday and, that night, falls to the "threshing-floor" of his stepfather Gabriel's Harlem church in a climactic adult initiation. Gabriel, whom John believes to be his biological father, is a volatile, domineering force who ran wild as a very young man before experiencing an early religious epiphany that prompted him to preach the wrath of God. Gabriel married John's mother to rescue her from the trials of single motherhood, but condemns her loving acceptance of John, which to Gabriel shows an unconscionable shamelessness over John's illegitimacy and her relationship with his father, her first love. Gabriel himself fathered an illegitimate child during his first marriage—a fact that he has continually guarded under the guise of repentance. He holds his silence regarding his orphaned son, who grew up hard and died violently and young.

While most of this history is not known to John, he is an intuitive boy who senses exactly the sorts of hazard that Harlem presents to black adolescents, especially those unprotected by an institution, usually the church. The loving support that John receives from Elisha, one of the church's young leaders, vibrates with an intensely joyful homoeroticism on which John can imagine building a fulfilling future in the church. Insofar as his stepfather is the figure responsible for doctrinal exegesis and enforcement, however, there is only a cruel vindictiveness that works to frighten and shame its believers into unquestioning obedience. The basic physical and emotional exhaustion of John's hallucinatory conversion allows him an early morning moment of triumphant respite, however brief. **AF**

Casino Royale

Ian Fleming

We have been let down, badly, by Cubby Broccoli's James Bond films. Sean Connery may have caught something of the thin-lipped coldness of Ian Fleming's creation, but there was, from the very first film, a refusal to take things too seriously, and Connery's arch one-liners found their camp culmination in Roger Moore's arched eyebrow. *Casino Royale*, Ian Fleming's first Bond story, was originally filmed only as a spoof, with David Niven as Bond, but it received a more serious interpretation with a 2006 version starring Daniel Craig. Everything in the novel—from the black-and-white of Cold War ideology, to Bond's then impossibly exotic choice of avocado and vinaigrette as a starter in the faded casino towns of northern France—is redolent of the early 1950s in which it was written.

The plot is simple, even elemental. The villain is Le Chiffre, a Russian spy operating in France, who has misappropriated KGB funds and turned to gambling to make good the loss. Bond, as the Secret Service's most accomplished gambler, is sent to Royale-les-Eaux to defeat Le Chiffre at the tables, thereby ruining him and his French network. There is an attempt on Bond's life, a game of baccarat over twenty-five pages, a car chase, a lovingly described scene of grotesque torture, and a rescue. The final chapters are a curiously distended account of Bond's convalescence with Vesper Lynd, the first "Bond girl"; the novel ends in a gratuitous burst of betrayal and misogyny. The prose is hard and unsparing, the detail minutely fetishistic (along the way we learn how—exactly—to make Bond's signature Martini). Only in the descriptions of gambling and flagellation—two of Fleming's most treasured pursuits—does the writing run away with itself. Otherwise, the book takes on the same aspect as its hero's face: "taciturn, brutal, ironical and cold." **PMy**

Lifespan | *b.* 1908 (England), *d.* 1964
First Published | 1953
First Published by | Jonathan Cape (London)
Full Name | Ian Lancaster Fleming

"Vodka dry Martini . . ."

Ian Fleming devised the artwork for the cover of his first Bond novel, using heart motifs to reference both Baccarat and love.

Junkie

William Burroughs

Lifespan | *b.*1914 (U.S.), *d.* 1997
First Published |1953, by Ace Books (New York)
Original Title | *Junkie: Confessions of an Unredeemed Drug Addict*

"... he kept it for himself."

◈ A 1959 photo of Burroughs captures the harrowed look of the
addict but gives no hint of the dry humor revealed in his writing.

William Burroughs is well remembered for a variety of reasons: the literary iconoclast, revered for the perceived experimentalism of his writing and art; his "coolness" in influencing a generation of artists, filmmakers, and musicians; and his legendary drug use. As a result, he has become reduced to a two-dimensional image. In today's environment, his legacy has inevitably been boiled down to so much aimless psychedelia and pottering "experimentation"; the actual breadth of his writing becomes almost irrelevant. Burroughs remains a writer who, far from simply employing surface-level gimmicks, writes about his life using whatever seems to be the most appropriate technique. Where *The Naked Lunch* employs a high degree of abstraction to describe both the polyglot, paranoid environment of middle-of-the-century Tangier and the process of opiate withdrawal, other works, notably *Junkie* and the later *Queer*, use far more simplistic narrative methods.

What *Junkie* seems to do is present the interior world of *The Naked Lunch* as a contemporary, exterior reality. A semi-autobiographical work, it outlines the author's relationship with opiates from early experiences to full-blown long-term addiction. In fact, Burroughs found the discipline required to write the novel with the help of a daily morphine injection. The Burroughs of *Junkie* is inescapably a man rather than the cartoon outlaw of hipster folklore. He openly describes addiction's vicious circle, while highlighting the way in which society holds addicts up as scapegoats to conceal its chronic failings and addictions. The book's real importance is in this candor; the way in which it props up the Burroughs canon with a truthful simplicity that stubbornly undermines attempts to position its author as the Mickey Mouse of a marketable "counterculture." **SF**

Lucky Jim

Kingsley Amis

Kingsley Amis had already published several collections of poetry when he achieved popular success with his first novel, *Lucky Jim*, which was influential in defining the direction of English postwar fiction. *Lucky Jim* is iconoclastic, satirical, and disrespectful of the norms of conservative society, and very funny. It tells the story of Jim Dixon, a mediocre but sharp-witted assistant lecturer at an uninspiring provincial university who realizes that he has made a terrible career choice. He decides that what he studies—medieval history—is dull and pedantic, and he can no longer stand the awful pretensions he encounters at his institution and in the grim town where he is forced to live. Jim pushes his luck more and more, barely disguising his contempt for his colleagues, especially the absurd Professor Welch, until he manages to lose his job when he delivers a lecture on "Merrie England," unprepared, blind drunk, and keen to parody the university authorities. Despite this, he leaves academia for a better job, and he manages to get the girl.

Lucky Jim has usually been seen as a very English novel. Jim Dixon has intellect, but, unwilling to fit in with the expectations of his social superiors, he is quite prepared to misuse it. The novel is really a story of frustrated ambition and talent, which exposes England as a drab wilderness that is ruled and run by colorless charlatans. *Lucky Jim* is written with considerable verve and a keen satirical eye. It contains numerous magnificent comic descriptions and sequences, especially at the start of the novel, when Jim reflects on the value of his utterly worthless research. The most celebrated passage is an account of a cultural weekend at Professor Welch's house, which ends with what is probably the best description of a hangover in English fiction. **AH**

Lifespan | *b.* 1922 (England), *d.* 1995
First Published | 1953
First Published by | V. Gollancz (London)
Somerset Maugham Award | 1953

LUCKY JIM

C. P. SNOW WRITES:
"It is humorous, self-mocking, hopeful endearing. For promise & achievement combined, it is the best first novel I've read in the last two years"

KINGSLEY AMIS

"Doing what you wanted . . ."

⊙ C. P. Snow, who gave this ringing endorsement to Amis's novel, had published his own campus novel, *The Masters*, two years earlier.

The Lost Steps

Alejo Carpentier

Lifespan | b.1904 (Switzerland), d. 1980 (France)
First Published | 1953, by Edición y Distribución
Iberoamericana de Publicaciones (Mexico City)
Original Title | Los pasos perdidos

The Lost Steps, the third novel by this Cuban author born in Lausanne, saw a change in his usual approach; it is one of his few nonhistorical works, and it is not set in the Caribbean world. Alejo Carpentier here tells the story of a contemporary pilgrimage in search of the origins of civilization and of personal identity. This is the most autobiographical of his works. Indeed, there is no absurdity in seeing a reflection of the author in the figure of the South American musicologist and composer, who gives up his comfortable position in the EU to begin a search for primitive musical instruments in the depths of the Venezuelan jungle.

Told in the form of an artificial diary, the journey is a flight from both creative sterility and sterile relationships with his wife and lover. In the forest, the protagonist finds the instruments he is looking for, as well as the telluric half-caste Rosario, his perfect complement. He also finds the inspiration to continue writing an unfinished cantata that would never be completed in the modern city. With passion and art at last within his grasp, there is only one thing missing: a reason to stay in the jungle. To yield to the temptation of returning would be a fatal error, but during his stay nature has closed off the route, and a return proves to be impossible. In a final image placing the erudite wanderer by a river that can tell him nothing, Carpentier manages to express the predicament of the modern artist, lost between two irreconcilable worlds. **DMG**

The Hothouse

Wolfgang Koeppen

Lifespan | b.1906 (Germany), d. 1996
First Published | 1953
First Published By | Scherz & Goverts (Stuttgart)
Original Title | Das Treibhaus

Set in Bonn in the early years of the West German government, *The Hothouse* describes the final days of an idealistic politician, Keetenhueve, before his dramatic suicidal leap into the Rhine. The novel caused a scandal in Germany when it was published, largely because of Koeppen's unsparing look at what were then extremely new corridors of power, and in which he diagnosed an already spreading web of compromise, cynicism, and even corruption.

Koeppen himself famously described the book as "a novel about failure," but Keetenhueve's failure moves the reader because it is a failure in which idealism and justice are equally defeated. The novel opens with the death of Keetenhueve's young wife, Elke, who, haunted by her family heritage and Keetenhueve's neglect, succumbs to alcoholism and dissipation. Like Elke, all of the novel's characters have difficulty in coming to terms with the past; guilt about Nazism hampers any efforts to change German society. Keetenhueve, for all his failure, offers a heroic side to the reader, fighting against a remilitarization of the country and arguing for the interests of peace. Although that argument ends in defeat, its eloquent and impassioned expression in the pages of Koeppen's novel make this a seminal work about early postwar Germany and the effects of political power on the individual. **AB**

⊙ Koeppen (on bike) wrote his final novel in 1954, forty-two years before his death; why he virtually ceased to write is unknown.

The Long Good-Bye

Raymond Chandler

Lifespan | *b.* 1888 (U.S.), *d.* 1959
First Published | 1953
First Published by | Hamish Hamilton (London)
Movie Adaptation Released | 1973

"No way has yet been invented to say goodbye to them."

⬤ The British first edition jacket plays up the thriller's traditional appeal to voyeurism, rather than more sophisticated literary aims.

A work of Raymond Chandler's maturity, written a good decade after Philip Marlowe first became a household name, *The Long Good-Bye* has a good claim to being his finest achievement. With *The Big Sleep* (1939), he began to graft mainstream literary sophistication onto the generic templates of pulp gumshoe fiction, and *The Long Good-Bye* can equally be read as a significant work of American fiction.

After helping Terry Lennox to escape to Mexico, private detective Philip Marlowe finds that he may have unknowingly abetted the flight of a murderer; not only that, Terry apparently kills himself as well, leaving Marlowe with a bewildering knot of unsolved problems and posthumous responsibilities. The puzzle aspect in Chandler's novels is often a pretext for a larger and more world-weary social observation, and this is particularly true here; as Marlowe's quest for solutions leads him into the corrupt, leisured world of Idle Valley, the novel's larger satirical purposes come into focus. Away from the downtown "mean streets," Chandler can indulge Marlowe's cultured side more (referencing Flaubert is not common in 1950s crime novels). And it is right that the initial detective premise somewhat recedes into the background: in Chandler's world, the solving of a crime cannot return us to innocence. If the detective genre is often turned to more serious and resonant literary purposes nowadays, this was a possibility opened up by the laconic, deadpan example of *The Long Good-Bye*. **BT**

The Go-Between

L. P. Hartley

Lifespan | *b.* 1895 (England), *d.* 1972
First Published | 1953
First Published by | Hamish Hamilton (London)
Movie Adaptation Released | 1971

L. P. Hartley's semi-autobiographical novel is constructed around the retrospective narrative of Leo Colston. Now an elderly man, Colston thinks back to his boyhood and the summer he spent at the affluent family home of his school friend. During his stay with the Maudsley family, Leo becomes embroiled in the socially unacceptable relationship between his friend's older sister, Marian, and Ted, a local farmer.

Leo becomes the "go-between" of the book's title, facilitating an illicit sexual relationship that defies the restrictive class conventions of Edwardian England. Made aware of sexual desires, he views them with a mixture of fascination and horror. His role in enabling this relationship is a catalyst for Leo's coming of age, precipitating a loss of childish innocence. In his adult revisitation of these events, Colston's disapproval of Marian and Ted is clear. But the sense of nostalgia is not limited to a loss of sexual naivety: the novel is heavily inflected with the class dynamics of Edwardian society, and inherent in Colston's reflections is a longing for a way of life permeated by class differences that function to his advantage. In this quintessentially English novel, Leo's epiphany occurs during a cricket match, which for him represents the "struggle between order and lawlessness, between obedience to tradition and defiance of it, between social stability and revolution."

This novel is of interest for its unusual take on the familiar theme of love divided by social barriers, but also for the studied honesty of Leo's narrative. **JW**

The Dark Child

Camara Laye

Lifespan | *b.* 1928 (Guinea), *d.* 1980 (Senegal)
First Published | 1953
First Published by | Plon (Paris)
Original Title | *L'Enfant noir*

African fiction mogulist Chinua Achebe once criticized *The Dark Child* by Laye Kamara (who is erroneously published as Camara Laye in the West) for being "too sweet." He was undoubtedly referring to the unpoliticized musings of its first-person narrator Fatoman, first as a child in a small Muslim village and then as a young man negotiating a new urban existence. But for Western audiences the novel was an early example of francophone African literature, recording for the first time aspects of local daily tribal life, including circumcision ceremonies and details of the goldsmithing trade.

Written when Kamara was in Paris studying mechanics, the novel is autobiographical, charting with a distinctly nostalgic tone Kamara's own childhood in Upper Guinea. As the child of parents reputed to have supernatural abilities, Kamara was a product of the esteemed Malinké tribe, and grew up in a Muslim community far from the influence of France. It was only when he traveled to Kouroussa and later to Conakry and Paris that he faced the dichotomies of village and city, Africa and Europe.

In 1956, Kamara returned to Africa and eventually took up a government post, where his disagreements with post-independence president Sekou Touré saw him in and out of prison, and eventually exiled. Kamara's inability to readjust to life in Africa is expressed in a sequel, *A Dream of Africa* (1966), which is distinctly political, and as such reinforces the novelty of *The Dark Child*. **JSD**

A Day in Spring

Ciril Kosmac

Lifespan | *b*.1910 (Slovenia), *d*. 1980
First Published | 1954
First Published by | Presernova druzba (Ljubljana)
Original Title | *Pomladni dan*

A few days after the end of the Second World War, Ciril Kosmac's protagonist wakes one May morning to his first day at home after fifteen years of exile and battle. Stirred by fresh encounters with sights and objects familiar from childhood and early youth, he undergoes emotional events in which memories, retaining all the purity of raw experience, weave through a present toned down and tinged with nostalgia, as if viewed through the wrong end of a telescope. The result is a portrait of delicate poignancy, threaded with a vitality that alternates with loss and sorrow in a mutually enriching flow.

The returning man finds himself suspended between two worlds—one is the world of banishment, mute and alien in spite of fifteen years of familiarity, the other is the world of village life on the shadowy side of a hill washed by the Idritsa river. This personal state of abeyance and reckoning unfolds against the backdrop of parallel uncertainties and internal resettlings in the wider social context, with Slovenia gaining part independence from Austro-Hungarian rule after the First World War, and finally, after the Second World War, gaining full autonomy from Italy and joining Yugoslavia. It is owing to Kosmac's masterly ability that his narrative, while retaining a light symbolism, never degenerates into allegory: the political world is so intimately welded with the personal world that they become indistinguishable, and individual fate seeps seamlessly into shared, communal destiny. **MWd**

A Ghost at Noon

Alberto Moravia

Lifespan | *b*. 1907 (Italy), *d*. 1990
First Published | 1954
First Published by | Bompiani (Milan)
Original Title | *Il Disprezzo*

Like most of Alberto Moravia's work, this novel is a political accusation: capitalist culture reduces the intellectual to a mere producer of goods. Riccardo Molteni, the protagonist, is a failed intellectual who betrays his ambition to become a playwright and sells his soul to consumerism to make money by writing screenplays. He convinces himself that he does this to pay for the apartment he bought to make his wife, Emilia, happy. Molteni increasingly loses sight of reality and becomes incapable of noticing what is happening around him, unable to see that his wife no longer loves him. In a nostalgic and regretful way, he carries on loving a semblance, or a "ghost," of what Emilia once was (hence the English translation of the novel's title).

Molteni takes refuge in Greek myths, with their protagonists who lived in a world where the relationship with reality was straightforward and unmediated. When faced with the challenging task of transforming the *Odyssey* into a movie, Molteni discovers that a text such as Homer's holds the key to his existence. Odysseus and Molteni are united by a similar destiny. Their wives, Penelope and Emilia, despise their passivity and self-assurance. Molteni is excessively confident that Emilia is faithful and disregards the producer's courtship of her. She is hurt, and feels she is being sold cheaply to secure her husband's occupation. Her contempt for him grows and is finally shouted into his face before she abandons him on the island of Capri. **RPi**

The Story of O

Pauline Réage

Lifespan | *b.* 1907 (France), *d.* 1998
First Published | 1954
First Published by | Pauvert (Sceaux)
Original Title | *Histoire d'O*

Pauline Réage is a complex mask. It is the pen name of Dominique Aury, itself the pen name of Anne Desclos, a French journalist and translator who became one of the most infamous pornographers of all time when she published *The Story of O* in Paris in 1954. "Réage"—a name invented specifically for *The Story of O*—was apparently told by her lover, Jean Paulhan, that no woman could ever write an erotic novel. *The Story of O* is her response. The novel is one of the most thorough and challenging ripostes ever made in a lovers' quarrel.

The novel is distinguished less by its plot than by the manner of its prose, in particular the control exercised by Réage in her depiction of O's private musings and reflections during and after her submission to acts of torture and humiliation. The intense erotic effect is achieved by a kind of mismatch between language and psychological content. If the language were made to imitate the full violence of O's mental and physical suffering, it would often be shattered and reduced to an incoherent scream. Instead, the prose is constrained by Réage and proceeds unruffled and at an unvarying pace through a series of degraded sexual episodes, leading eventually to the disappearance of O behind yet another mask, that of an owl. The most tightly fitted mask is style itself. *The Story of O* is a shocking novel and at the same time a masterfully boring one. The deep erotic joy of suffering, it tells us, is rooted in the terror of boredom. **KS**

Under the Net

Iris Murdoch

Lifespan | *b.* 1919 (Ireland), *d.* 1999 (England)
First Published | 1954
First Published by | Chatto & Windus (London)
Full Name | Dame Jean Iris Murdoch

Iris Murdoch's first published novel, *Under the Net*, captures the exuberant spirit of freedom in postwar Europe. Jake Donaghue, the novel's swashbuckling first-person narrator, is a rootless, impoverished young writer who relishes this freedom. He has no home, no commitments, and no permanent job and conducts relationships based only on a woman's ability to provide sex and shelter. But chance, misfortune, and a series of hilarious misunderstandings startle Jake into an awareness that others have existence outside his perception of them, and that the world holds mysteries that he can barely imagine. A stark period of depression and a candid renegotiation of his love life follows. Jake finally becomes an aspiring novelist committed to producing work that engages with the world that he has begun, at last, to see.

Beneath the surface of the fast-moving narrative lies a wealth of philosophical questioning: Murdoch contests existential ideas of freedom; she asks what it means to be in love; and she rigorously questions what makes a good writer and what constitutes good art. Underlying these ideas are the questions of how accurately thought can be translated into language (language is the "net" of the title) and how far art distances us from reality, rather than bringing us closer to it. But Jake's visits to *The Laughing Cavalier* at the Wallace Collection in London, and to the Fontaine de Médicis in Paris, illustrate Murdoch's belief that art is not divorced from the real world and that, in particular, "art and morality are one." **AR**

Lord of the Flies

William Golding

Lifespan | *b.* 1911 (England), *d.* 1993
First Published | 1954, by Faber & Faber (London)
First Movie Adaption Released | 1963
Nobel Prize for Literature | 1983

William Golding
Lord of the Flies

◉ The first edition of Golding's novel appeared at a time of public concern about the destructive nature of human beings.

◗ Peter Brook's 1963 movie version of the novel was filmed in an unsparing documentary style that suited the apocalyptic theme.

A staple of many a schoolroom, *Lord of the Flies* is a gripping examination of the conflict between the two competing impulses that exist within all human beings. On the one hand, there is the instinct to live peacefully, abide by rules, and value the moral good over the instinct for immediate gratification of desires. On the other, there is the impulse to seize supremacy through violence, sacrificing the individual at the expense of the group.

This is the story of a group of young schoolboys marooned on a tropical island after their plane is shot down during the war. Alone, without adult supervision, the boys begin by electing a leader, Ralph, who narrowly defeats Jack in the vote (Jack is elected head of the hunt). The moral conflict at the novel's heart—between good and evil, order and chaos, civilization and savagery, the rule of law and anarchy—is represented by the differing characters of sensible, levelheaded Ralph and savage, charismatic Jack. As the boys split into two different factions, their island society is plunged into chaos. While some behave peacefully, working together to maintain order and achieve common goals, others rebel, generating terror and violence. Frightened, the boys become convinced there is a monster on the island, and when one of them, Simon, realizes the beast is not an external figure, but exists within each and every one of them, he is murdered.

This thought-provoking exploration of human evil and original sin reflects the society of the time and is steeped in Golding's experiences of the Second World War, when he witnessed the isolated savagery of desperate men unconfined by the rules of civilized society. Although the gripping story is confined to a small group of boys on a small island, it explores issues central to the wider human experience. **EF**

The Mandarins

Simone de Beauvoir

Lifespan | *b.* 1908 (Paris), *d.* 1986
First Published | 1954
First Published by | Gallimard (Paris)
Original Title | *Les Mandarins*

Henri, the struggling writer at the center of *The Mandarins*, begins his new novel by wondering, "What truth do I want to express? My truth. But what does that really mean?" His words express the questioning that lies at the center of Simone de Beauvoir's novel, which probes the changing conceptions of identity and artistic practice in postwar France.

Focusing on a group of intellectuals in Paris in the immediate years after 1944, *The Mandarins* explores, on an almost epic scale, the repercussions inherent in coming to terms with both France's terrible legacies of war and Nazi occupation and the new concerns arising with the reconstruction of Europe and the beginnings of the Cold War. At the novel's center are Henri, editor of the left-wing magazine *L'Espoir*, and his former lover, Paula, who is struggling to cope with their separation. The other central figure is Anne, psychoanalyst and mother of Henri's new lover, Nadine, whose brief extramarital affair and growing sense of personal and political emptiness force her to the edge of suicide. The novel focuses on the interactions between Henri, Paula, Anne, and Nadine, as well as a host of minor characters, centered around the fortunes of *L'Espoir* and the continuing fallout of the war.

Unwavering in its determination to expose often uncomfortable truths about postwar society, *The Mandarins* is a richly rewarding and epic portrait that determinedly connects the personal and the political on every level. **AB**

Bonjour Tristesse

Françoise Sagan

Lifespan | *b.* 1935 (France), *d.* 2004
First Published | 1954
First Published by | Julliard (Paris)
Given Name | Françoise Quoirez

When Cécile, a precocious fifteen-year-old, leaves boarding school to live with her widowed libertine father, Raymond, she enters into a world of decadence that is a far cry from her strict convent-school days. Gallivanting between Paris and the French Riviera, the golden-skinned duo embraces a hedonistic existence, consisting of short-lived affairs, glittering characters, and every luxury imaginable. But their life of gay frivolity is threatened two years later when Raymond believes he has fallen in love with Anne Larsen, a former friend of Cécile's mother who moves within more staid, intellectual circles. Fearing for her freedom, Cécile, the quintessential enfant terrible, invokes the help of her lover, Cyril, and her father's former paramour, Elsa, to intervene. But her cunning plot proves to have tragic consequences, forever coloring her future happiness with tristesse.

Written when she was just eighteen years old, Françoise Sagan's first novel was an instant international best seller. With its description of overt sexuality, celebration of wealth and opulence, and intimation of same-sex desire, the novel shocked and titillated its first readers, paving the way for a permissive French society. Simmering beneath the façade of the jaded ingénue is the unsettling portrait of a child who will do anything to maintain the life outlined for her by the only parent she knows. **BJ**

⊚ The teenage Sagan shocked contemporary readers with her cool, non-judgmental approach to sex and relationships.

Death in Rome

Wolfgang Koeppen

Lifespan | *b*.1906 (Germany), *d*. 1996
First Published | 1954
First Published by | Scherz & Goverts (Stuttgart)
Original Title | *Tod in Rom*

Playfully alluding to Thomas Mann's *Death in Venice*, *Death in Rome* provides a satiric and chilling updating of Mann's masterpiece. Despite its setting, Wolfgang Koeppen's novel is designed to answer the question: what will become of postwar Germany?

That country is represented in the novel by four members of a single family. The patriarch, Gottlieb Judejahn, is an ex-SS officer who has run away from facing trial in Germany; his son, Adolf, is in the process of becoming a Catholic priest. Joining them are Gottlieb's brother-in-law, Friedrich Wilhelm Pfaffrath, a high-level bureaucrat, and his son, Siegfried, a composer. Siegfried, to whom all of his family represent the horror of a war he wants to forget, narrates, and Koeppen focuses on his inability to escape his childhood in Nazi Germany, even in his music. Adolf, similarly horrified by his father's actions, cannot achieve the absolution he looks for as a priest due to his own actions in childhood.

As the four characters interact in the setting of a chaotic postwar Rome, Koeppen paints a bleak picture of the aftereffects of the Third Reich. All are locked in a seemingly permanent state of inaction; ironically, it is only the monstrous Judejahn who is able to take comfort in continuing violence.

It may be that *Death in Rome* presents an almost uninhabitable world to the reader, but it is one in which justice, if not mercy, is highlighted and celebrated; the reader is never able to forget the seriousness of the sins of the past. **AB**

The Sound of Waves

Yukio Mishima

Lifespan | *b*.1925 (Japan), *d*. 1970
First Published | 1954, by Shinchosha (Tokyo)
Given Name | Hiraoka Kimitake
Original Title | *Shiosai*

This simple, intense love story is set on a remote Japanese island, and tells of the love between Shinji, a poor young fisherman, and Hatsue, a beautiful pearl diver. The lovers become the subject of jealous gossip, and Shinji is accused of having stolen Hatsue's virginity. Her furious father restricts Hatsue to the house, and forbids Shinji to see her again. He has promised her hand in marriage to Shinji's rival, Yasuo, the boorish and arrogant son of a wealthy family. But later he relents, and sets the two suitors a trial in which they have to pit themselves against a storm at sea. It is Shinji, noble and hardworking, who wins the test and regains the respect of the village and is reunited with his beloved Hatsue.

Although the likely setting of the story is the Shima Peninsula, home of Japan's famous female pearl divers, it was written after Yukio Mishima had visited the Mediterranean and become immersed in the literature of ancient Rome and Greece. *The Sound of Waves* thus represents an interesting fusion of styles—the plot is as sparely and delicately constructed as a Japanese miniature, but the lyrical descriptions of island life and the healing, redemptive power of the sea are suggestive of a more romantic tradition. This novel is much less graphically violent and sexually explicit than his later works, and captures the feelings of first love with an evocative tenderness that reveals a gentler side to the man hailed as one of the most important Japanese writers of the twentieth century. **TS**

The Unknown Soldier

Väinö Linna

Lifespan | *b*.1920 (Finland), *d*. 1992
First Published | 1954
First Published by | WSOY (Porvoo)
Original Title | *Tuntematon Sotilas*

This is *Band of Brothers* without the varnish. Linna has written a grim and gritty account of a Finnish machinegun company caught up in a doomed attempt to fight the onslaught of Stalin's tanks and infantry invading their motherland in 1941. Splattered bodies, piercing bullets, harrowing hand-to-hand trench warfare, summary executions, bullying upper-class officers, brief relief with booze and women—all this "explodes" the myth of honorable warfare. The coarse language and often cowardly, insolent, and terror-stricken behavior of the working-class soldiers was shunned by Finnish politicians, literary critics, and patriots more used to unquestioning depictions of warfare. Moreover, Linna had the gall to question why the Finns were fighting this war with the Nazis in the first place.

Linna's eye for realism in the warfare of the sub-Arctic forests, stems from his own experience as a squad leader of a machinegun unit on the Eastern Front. That, and being a factory worker himself, helps him imbue his colorful squaddies with very human fears and foibles. The earthy dialog also rings true, for example, "I'm a Finn, I eat metal and I shit chain," and one of the characters, Rokka, has come to mean an insubordinate but brilliant soldier in Finnish. That does not prevent them meeting pointless, random, and terrifying deaths—such is the nature of warfare. *The Unknown Soldier* became the country's biggest-selling novel, and was turned into a movie twice (1955 and 1985). **JHa**

I'm Not Stiller

Max Frisch

Lifespan | *b*. 1911 (Switzerland), *d*. 1991
First Published | 1954, by Suhrkamp (Frankfurt)
Original Title | *Stiller*
Original Language | German

Widely considered Switzerland's greatest literary figure of the last century, Max Frisch was a novelist, playwright, diarist, and journalist. The popular and critically acclaimed *I'm Not Stiller* is a remarkably sustained narrative, which combines anguish and humor to explore issues of identity, self-loathing, and humanity's intense longing for freedom.

The novel begins with the arrest at the Swiss border of a man traveling under a false identity. He claims to be Mr. White from America, but the Swiss authorities believe him to be Anatol Stiller, a famous sculptor from Zürich, who has been missing for six years. In prison, the man is asked to write down his life story in order to prove his identity. In the process he tells not only stories of the past few years of his life, but also of his meetings in the present with Stiller's wife, Julika, and other important people from his past. Through these accounts we learn about his life before the disappearance and are able to piece together a picture of this deeply troubled character. Stiller writes about himself as if he is another person— a self he has attempted to escape from, but which he now has to confront anew as he is slowly compelled to accept both his past and his real identity.

An ironic exploration of an extreme existential crisis, this is also a touching portrayal of a failed marriage and a social critique of Swiss conformity. Complex, psychologically profound, and intellectually challenging, it still manages to be entertaining, funny, and poignant at the same time. **AL**

The Ragazzi

Pier Paolo Pasolini

Lifespan | b. 1922 (Italy), d. 1975
First Published | 1955
First Published by | Garzanti (Milan)
Original Title | *Ragazzi di vita*

Ragazzi di vita, translated literally into English as *Boys of Life*, is the story of a group of boys who live in the slums of Rome during the years immediately following the Second World War. One of the notable aspects of the Italian edition is that it contains a glossary of words in the "Romano" dialect for the Italian reader unfamiliar with it. Those acquainted with the Italian cinematographic neorealism of the period will know that the use of regional dialects and of non-professional actors was common in the films of Rossellini, De Sica, Fellini, and other directors.

Pier Paolo Pasolini was an unorthodox Marxist who thought that the emphasis on exploitation, alienation, and marginalization needed to be supplemented by an analysis of the mechanism of integration in modern, liberal democracies. Hence the ambiguity of the sociopolitical condition of the sub-proletariat in Pasolini's novels of the later 1950s; the class occupies the unique position of running the simultaneous risk of complete integration or complete marginalization. But Pasolini's achievement here is his non-sentimental portrayal of the choice between joining a banal, all-encompassing mainstream, or accepting life on a hopelessly bleak periphery. Today better known as a director, Pasolini's literary status was established by *Ragazzi di vita*, and it is more than worthy of the best aspirations of the Italian neorealist movement. **DSch**

⊕ Pasolini's homosexuality, central to the writing of *The Ragazzi*, led to his expulsion from the Italian Communist Party in the 1940s.

The Recognitions

William Gaddis

Lifespan | b.1922 (U.S.), d. 1998
First Published | 1955
First Published by | Harcourt Brace (New York)
Original Language| English

It is in pursuit of the real that this immense novel explores every imaginable way that cultural products can be forged, or counterfeited. Paintings are faked, ideas for novels are stolen, plays are plagiarized, book reviews are paid for, and somebody in a Paris café has "a fake concentration camp number tattooed on her left arm." The main character, Wyatt Gwyon, is an artist whose skills are appropriated by an unscrupulous art dealer and a gallery owner to produce work by the nonexistent Flemish painter van der Goes. Feeling himself to be unreal, Wyatt insists to his wife, Esther, that being moral "is the only way we can know ourselves to be real." She asks him pointedly if women can afford to be moral. In this novel, no thought is effective, no discussion concludes, and no narrator intervenes on behalf of truth.

Almost every character here is an American, but the context is European high culture. You need to know Latin, French, Spanish, and Italian to get the many jokes. The same scenes recur at the end as at the beginning, so this novel resembles a snake swallowing its tail. Based on confused conversations—often at parties or in cafés—the word predominates, but the physical evidence of corruption is that the characters keep tripping up and falling down. Bodily incompetence eventually extends to the built environment when a hotel collapses and an organ-player brings down upon himself an entire church. *The Recognitions* was an influential "sleeper" novel: Thomas Pynchon is Gaddis Americanized. **AMu**

The Burning Plain

Juan Rulfo

Lifespan | *b.* 1917 (Mexico), *d.* 1986
First Published | 1955
First Published by | Fondo de Cultura Económica
Original Title | *El Llano en llamas*

With this collection of fifteen stories (which became seventeen in later editions), Juan Rulfo was recognized as a master. Post-revolutionary scenes in Llano Grande in the state of Jalisco overcome the rural limitations of these tales about the Mexican Revolution. The popular language is artistically developed and the life of the peasant appears representative of an archetype of neglect, at the margins of folklore.

Rulfo's stories are about what has happened and what cannot be changed (in "The Man" and "Tell Them Not to Kill Me!"). Rulfo explores the mechanisms of power and the faces of violence, often within the framework of family relationships being torn apart ("No Dogs Bark," "The Inheritance of Matilde Arcángel"). The majority of Rulfo's characters are alone and feel that they are culprits ("Macario," "The Hill of the Comrades"). As a result, they are traveling or wandering with no true purpose ("Talpa," "They Gave Us the Land"), and they speak ceaselessly in the face of dumb or nonexistent interlocutors ("Luvina," "Remember"). The skillful handling of temporal structure and narrative voices, together with the dexterous balance between reality and fantasy, remote from magical realism, means that the great originality of these stories and their author would be enough, with only one other novel (*Pedro Páramo*), for him to be considered one of the greatest writers of his time. **DMG**

The Quiet American

Graham Greene

Lifespan | *b.* 1904 (England), *d.* 1991 (Switzerland)
First Published | 1955
First Published by | Heinemann (London)
Movie Adaptations Released | 1958, 2002

This novel is, in some sense, an allegory for the end of paternalistic European colonialism in Indochina and the beginning of zealous American imperialism. Set in Vietnam during the early 1950s, it recounts the conflict between Fowler, the jaded English journalist, and Pyle, the idealistic American spy, for the affections of Phuong, a young Vietnamese woman anxious for a Western husband to provide shelter from poverty and prostitution. Phuong is constantly associated with the Vietnamese landscape and flora, but also with the intoxicating opium and an aura of unintelligibility. Pyle is young and wealthy and offers the promise of financial security, whereas Fowler is old and jaded, offering only the prospects of a continuing and unsatisfactory informal union. For these reasons, the book has most frequently been read as prophetic and critical of America's role in the Vietnam War.

Typically, Graham Greene's novel is not contained by the limitations of its genre and expands from this central allegory to offer a study of masculinity and responsibility. The novel is infested with references to what is manly. It seeks to puncture the mock heroics of soldiers and, by extension, journalists, in an attempt to undermine the reverence for physical action usually found in thrillers. Finally, it questions Fowler's desire for disengagement in the face of conflict, suggesting that to be a man requires him to take a moral responsibility for events. **LC**

The Trusting and the Maimed

James Plunkett

Lifespan | *b.* 1920 (Ireland), *d.* 2003
First Published | 1955
First Published by | The Devin-Adair Co. (New York)
Given Name | James Plunkett Kelly

The stories that make up *The Trusting and the Maimed*, originally published in the Dublin magazines *The Bell* and *Irish Writing*, share characters and locales to create an elegiac yet satirical portrayal of post-independence Ireland. Dublin is prominent, but it is a Dublin of dilapidated suburbs and of longed-for trips to the country, as much as it is a city of streets, offices, and pubs. A combination of evocative lyrical moments and precisely defined vignettes of everyday life build up a memorable account of a stagnating, crippled country. It is the harshness of the novel's conclusion and the gentleness of its method that constitute James Plunkett's achievement.

Ireland in the 1940s and the 1950s was a depressed, inward-looking, wounded place, and Plunkett captures this melancholy beautifully. While the stories' episodic structure needs no center, there is a dominant tone set by the recurrence of the lives of city clerks. Young, frustrated, and restless, they rot in their safe jobs from nine to five. They could be white-collar workers in any city. They save for "sin," for the weekends of liquor, sex, and bawdy humor they use to endure the working week. The book is steeped in an atmosphere of palpable decay, a religion reduced to self-parodying remnants, and a patriotism shrunk to disciplinary fetishes and pub songs. It eloquently expresses the pity and resentment that were the cultural hallmarks of post-colonial Ireland. **PMcM**

The Tree of Man

Patrick White

Lifespan | *b.* 1912 (England), *d.* 1990 (Australia)
First Published | 1955
First Published by | Viking Adult (New York)
Nobel Prize for Literature | 1973

The Tree of Man was the novel that established Patrick White as the most significant Australian novelist of the postwar period. White's chronicle of the lives of pioneers in the new country was a deliberate attempt to give Australia a work that would stand alongside Thomas Mann, Leo Tolstoy, or Thomas Hardy.

The *Tree of Man* tells the story of the Parker family. Stan Parker, a young penniless man sets up a camp in the wilderness with his wife, Amy. Their settlement grows into a prosperous farm and they have children and grandchildren. By the time both die the once isolated dwelling is part of suburbia, surrounded by brick houses. The novel concludes as Stan's grandson walks through the trees that survive on the farm, a link to the nature out of which this obscure society was created: "in the end there were the trees. . . . Putting out shoots of green thought. So that, in the end, there was no end." Life goes on, as the experience of the Parker family shows, and men and women adapt to whatever life throws at them. *The Tree of Man*, the title alluding to the tree in the Garden of Eden and the genealogies sketched out in the ancient world of the Bible, is an attempt to show how important and moving the lives of forgotten and ordinary people can be, how heroic their struggles against the elements invariably are, and how poetry can be discovered in the least likely places. **AH**

The Last Temptation of Christ

Nikos Kazantzákis

Lifespan | b. 1883 (Greece), d. 1957 (Germany)
First Published | 1955, by Diphros (Athens)
Movie Adaptation Released | 1988
Original Title | Ho teleutaíos peirasmós

This novel is a retelling of the life of Jesus Christ. Although Kazantzákis was a Christian, he was also a Nietzschean and a worshipper of nature, and his Jesus is intensely alive to his physical surroundings in Palestine and fully a man of flesh and blood. He is as much tormented by the divine call to become the Messiah as by his desire for Mary Magdalene.

The descriptions of Jesus's life are largely based on the New Testament. The full-blown prose of the narrative spills over into a sort of magic realism at times, as, for example, when flowers blossom around the feet of the Messiah. At the climactic moment of the crucifixion, Jesus is rescued, as he thinks, by an angel who leads him to an earthly contentment in which he marries both Martha and Mary, has children, and lives a good human life. Years later, he realizes that the angel is, in fact, Satan and that this earthly paradise is a dream. Waking up, he finds himself back on the cross and dies. This seems to be where the author finds Jesus's value: in a spiritual not a natural dimension. In spite of this, the Vatican condemned the novel, finding its Jesus too carnal and self-doubting, placing it on the index of forbidden books, while in Greece, Orthodox authorities sought Kazantzákis's prosecution, delaying the book's publication. **PM**

○ Willem Dafoe played Jesus in Martin Scorsese's movie version of Kazantzákis's novel, released to a scandalized reception in 1988.

The Devil to Pay in the Backlands

João Guimarães Rosa

Lifespan | b. 1908 (Brazil), d. 1967
First Published | 1955
First Published by | José Olympio (Rio de Janeiro)
Original Title | Grande Sertão: Veredas

While practicing medicine in the Brazilian state of Minas Gerais, and having later become a diplomat and a politician, João Guimarães Rosa became acquainted with the harsh reality of those inhabiting that vast territory. As Riobaldo, his novel's protagonist, narrates his life, the reader becomes both listener and viewer of the rhythm of the backlands. The novel's characters form a tapestry of human relations, and both individual and collective experiences are lyrically scrutinized. These are men that love and kill with the same intensity. Riobaldo himself is torn between not only the classical dichotomy of carnal and platonic love, but also of impossible affection in the shape of his companion in arms.

Language is immediately striking in this novel. Even when describing shocking episodes, poetic licence is granted by its vivacious originality. In making abundant use of neologisms, aphorisms, archaisms, onomatopoeias, and alliterations, the author generates a musical, quasi-undulating mood that confers on the prose a cinematic character.

This is a novel that simultaneously presents what is most specific about life in the backlands of Minas Gerais and what is most universal about the human condition. In bearing witness to the plight of individuals forced to look introspectively into their own existence, it becomes a metaphysical journey in which we cannot but participate. **ML**

Lolita

Vladimir Nabokov

Lifespan | *b.* 1899 (Russia), *d.* 1977 (Switzerland)
First Published | 1955
First Published by | Olympia Press (Paris)
Original Language | English

◉ Nabokov produced a whole body of work in Russian before transforming himself into an American novelist in the 1940s.

◉ Dominique Swain, playing Lolita in the 1998 movie version, was older than Nabokov's prepubescent nymphet.

The first publication of *Lolita*, by risqué Parisian press Olympia, caused widespread outrage. The violent erotic passion of the novel's protagonist and narrator, Humbert Humbert, for the twelve-year-old Lolita, and the intensity and extent of Humbert's abuse of her, remain genuinely shocking, particularly in a culture preoccupied with child abuse and the sexualization of children.

Written in Nabokov's characteristic immaculate style, this violent and brutal novel poses fascinating questions about the role of fiction. Is it possible for us to find beauty, pleasure, and comedy in a narrative that is ethically repugnant? Can we suspend moral judgment in favor of aesthetic appreciation of a finely tuned sentence or a perfectly balanced phrase? The answers to these questions remain unclear, but in pitting substance against style, in balancing the ethical so delicately against the aesthetic, Nabokov invents a new kind of literary fiction.

Humbert's abduction of Lolita, and his fleeing with her across America in a crazed attempt to outrun the authorities, make this novel an inaugural work of postmodern fiction, as well as a kind of proto-road movie. Humbert is an old-world European, a lover of Rimbaud and Balzac, who finds himself displaced in the shiny world of corporate 1950s America and entranced by the lurid charms of gum-chewing, soda-drinking Lolita. The story of this encounter between venerable age and crass youth, between Europe and America, between high art and popular culture, is the story on which many of the novels and films that come in the wake of *Lolita* are based. Without *Lolita*, it is difficult to imagine Pynchon's *The Crying of Lot 49* or Tarantino's *Pulp Fiction*. It is a mark of its originality and power that, after so many imitations, it remains so troubling, so fresh, and so moving. **PB**

The Talented Mr. Ripley

Patricia Highsmith

Lifespan | *b*. 1921 (U.S.), *d*. 1995 (Switzerland)
First Published | 1955
First Published by | Coward-McCann (New York)
Given Name | Mary Patricia Plangman

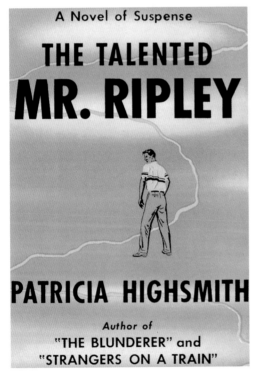

A Novel of Suspense

THE TALENTED
MR. RIPLEY

PATRICIA HIGHSMITH

Author of
"THE BLUNDERER" and
"STRANGERS ON A TRAIN"

*"There was no doubt the
man was after him."*

◉ As indicated on this 1955 first edition jacket, Patricia Highsmith's
preferred term for her genre of writing was "suspense fiction."

Tom Ripley is one of the great creations of twentieth-century pulp writing, a schizophrenic figure at once charming, ambitious, unknowable, utterly devoid of morality, and prone to outbursts of extreme violence. Indeed, the line that Highsmith draws between psychosis on the one hand, and class envy and sexual yearning on the other, means that it is possible to read his deviant behavior both in relatively straightforward terms as a symptom of mental illness and as a complex manifestation of bourgeois ambitions and repressed homosexual desire. At the story's center is the relationship between Tom and Dickie Greenleaf, a wealthy socialite who has taken up residence in the quiet Italian coastal village Mongibello with his girlfriend, Marge. Tom is at once appalled by Dickie's clumsy attempts to paint and by his "inexplicable" attachment to Marge, whom he clearly does not love, and attracted by his style, affluence, and good looks. This uneasy mixture of sentiments is brought into explosive conflagration when Tom murders Dickie and assumes his identity in a calculated bid to benefit financially.

In the hands of a lesser writer, *The Talented Mr. Ripley* might simply have been an enjoyable tale of "cat and mouse," as Tom is hunted down by the Italian police, Marge, and Dickie's father across a series of attractively rendered Italian settings. But Highsmith infuses her story with all kinds of moral, psychological, and philosophical complexities. How can we distinguish between different categories of desire—sexual and material? How can we talk about identity as something fixed or essential, if Tom can "become" Dickie with such effortlessness and success? How is sexual desire related to sexual disgust? And, for readers, is it morally aberrant to cheer quietly for a cold-blooded murderer? **AP**

The Lord of the Rings

J. R. R. Tolkien

The Lord of the Rings is actually three books—The Fellowship of the Ring, The Two Towers, and The Return of the King. It follows on from the story of The Hobbit, which J. R. R. Tolkien had published well over a decade earlier, further exploring the world of Middle Earth and war that would determine the fate of all men. Like The Hobbit, it is the story of an unlikely hero—a childlike, unassuming hobbit, Frodo—whom fate has destined for greater things. At the beginning, elves, dwarves, hobbits, and men come together under the wizard Gandalf's watchful eye to set off on a journey to destroy the magic ring, which Bilbo Baggins had found in The Hobbit. The ring holds inside it the essence of evil and therefore must be destroyed before Lord Sauron can find it and plunge Middle Earth into darkness. Through a series of misadventures, the fellowship either die or become separated. Only Frodo, his loyal friend Sam, and the wasted creature Gollum—who had fallen for many years under the ring's power and is now its slave—are left to return the ring to the fires of Mount Doom, which is the only way to destroy it.

The book is about power and greed, innocence, and enlightenment. Ultimately, it describes an old-fashioned battle of good against evil, of kindness and trust against suspicion, and of fellowship against the desire for individual power. Tolkien's evil is an internal force—most evident in the "good" and "bad" sides of the character Gollum, who epitomizes the struggle to be good. This is also a story about war, no doubt drawn from Tolkien's own experience, and how enemies in life are united in death, the one great equalizer. If there is a message, it is that there is little point to war and that the search for ultimate power is futile in a world where togetherness will always (justly) win out. **EF**

Lifespan | b. 1892 (South Africa), d. 1973 (England)
First Published | 1954–1956, by Allen & Unwin (Lon.)
Trilogy | The Fellowship of the Ring (1954), The Two Towers (1955), The Return of the King (1955)

"Even the wise cannot see all ends."

⬥ Tolkien's academic grounding in Anglo-Saxon, Celtic, and Norse mythology helped shape his personal imaginative world.

The Lonely Londoners

Sam Selvon

Lifespan | b. 1923 (Trinidad), d. 1994 (Canada)
First Published | 1956
First Published by | Allan Wingate (London)
Original Language | English

Often identified as part of Sam Selvon's Moses cycle of novels, *The Lonely Londoners* was one of the first attempts to narrate the life of black Caribbean men in London during the wave of mass migration to Britain during the 1950s. The novel takes the form of a modern picaresque, with an episodic structure where blackness is normalized and where the few peripheral white characters that we encounter are seen as exotic or strange. This is achieved primarily through the novel's innovative use of language—the book is written almost wholly in a version of Trinidadian Creole. Selvon never attempts to translate the language into standard English, and in this sense it can be felt to anticipate later novels such as Irvine Welsh's *Trainspotting*. The novel also centers on black experience through its construction of monumental London as a fantasy, projected through the colonial imaginings of Britain's imperial subjects.

While the central characters are overwhelmingly male and lower class, the book does attempt to raise challenging questions about gender politics. Issues of domestic violence and of women's roles within Caribbean family structures are vital to the way that Selvon seeks to represent the dizzying effects of migration, and the relative absence of black women in the novel is intimately connected to a pervasive sense of loss and longing for home. **LC**

⊙ West Indian immigrants disembark at a London railway terminus in 1956—the inspiration of Selvon's Trinidadian dialect novel.

The Roots of Heaven

Romain Gary

Lifespan | b. 1914 (Lithuania), d. 1980 (France)
First Published | 1956
First Published by | Gallimard (Paris)
Original Title | Les Racines du ciel

This fifth novel by Romain Gary, which brought him his first Prix Goncourt (he won the second under a different name to confound the prize's restrictions), conveys the author's ardent support of dignity and compassion with wry humor and brilliant insight.

Curiously contemporary, almost prescient, the story is set in French Equatorial Africa. Morally complex and compromised characters—doubting priests, aspiring revolutionaries, big-game hunters, colonial administrators, arms dealers—all revolve around the mysterious figure of Morel, who launches a campaign to save the elephant herds, the only free creatures on earth, from total destruction. The elephants represent the companionship that Morel craves in the absence of God, when a dog is simply no longer adequate to satisfy the need for friendship and comfort. His fight to conquer the despair of the human condition, his "Jewish idealism"—as the Nazi commander of his war camp had termed the belief in noble conventions and the primacy of spirituality—attracts pragmatists, eccentrics, men of good will and understanding, as well as schemers of all descriptions, who try to exploit Morel's defense of nature to further their own causes, projecting onto him the reflection of what is essential in themselves.

Richly deserving its great distinction, *The Roots of Heaven* pays tribute to an ancient, imperishable, and desperate gaiety that is itself a form of subversion and means of survival. The movie adaptation of the book was released in 1958. **ES**

The Floating Opera

John Barth

Lifespan | b. 1930 (U.S.)
First Published | 1956
First Published by | Appleton Century Crofts (N. Y.)
Full Name | John Simmons Barth Jr.

At the age of fifty-four, narrator and protagonist Todd Andrews, a successful small-town lawyer with a heart condition, a grumbling prostate, and an increasing penchant for "Sherbrook rye and ginger ale," reflects on the events seventeen years earlier that led him to contemplate suicide and works through the reasons why he subsequently decided not to carry out the act. He also recalls the protracted love affair that he pursued with the wife of his best friend and his unsuccessful attempts to discover why his father mysteriously hanged himself.

Such a simple plot outline of *The Floating Opera* cannot do it justice, however, because everything else that happens in John Barth's extraordinary debut novel is unpredictable, subversive, and riotous. The constantly shifting, unraveling, and reconfiguring narrative generates an unstoppable energy, unfolds a sequence of spectacles, calamities, and melodramas, and introduces a cast of characters drawn from a tidewater Maryland setting. When entertainment for the townspeople aboard the glittering showboat *Floating Opera* rapidly descends into chaos and disorder, we are provided with an appropriate metaphor for this postmodern "nihilistic comedy."

Underlying the perfectly sustained pitch of absurdity and ambiguity, and the sliding scale of humor from ribaldry and slapstick to dark chuckling cynicism, there is an inquiry into the arbitrary nature of existence and Barth's "tragic view" that its ultimate boundary is fragmentation and death. **TS**

Giovanni's Room

James Baldwin

Lifespan | b. 1924 (U.S.), d. 1987 (France)
First Published | 1956
First Published by | Dial Press (New York)
Full Name | James Arthur Baldwin

Giovanni's Room explores a struggle with the need for social approbation, in which the protagonist must ultimately abandon his dependence on conventional norms of success and worth. The white, middle-class narrator, David, quietly flees his home environment to live aimlessly in Paris, far from his father's wordless pressure to settle down. Facing financial difficulties, however, he proposes to another traveling American, Hella, who leaves Paris to think it over. While she is gone, David accompanies a friend to a gay bar, where he forms an instant, ecstatic connection with Giovanni, the mysterious Italian bartender. David immediately takes up residence in Giovanni's tiny room, but secretly longs for Hella's return, which he thinks will free him from his desperate love for Giovanni. When David leaves their room to continue his heterosexual charade, the consequences are tragic for all three points in his surreptitious love triangle.

Baldwin's spare prose unsentimentally exposes the cruelty and cynicism animating David's abject terror in the face of desire. Giovanni locates David's self-aversion in the American cult of cleanliness and distaste for the body. In the end, David's willingness to shield himself using the overwhelming authority of white American maleness, no matter how forged and self-destructive his claim to it may be, isolates him as much as the empty room in which he writes. **AF**

> Photographed by Carl Mydans for *Time* magazine in 1962, Baldwin's steady gaze makes no bid for public approbation.

Justine

Lawrence Durrell

Lifespan | *b*.1912 (India), *d*. 1980 (France)
First Published | 1957
First Published by | Faber & Faber (London)
U.S. Edition Published by | E. P. Dutton (New York)

Lawrence Durrell's novel, the opening gambit of his Alexandria Quartet, should be highly regarded for its extended passages of remarkable prose poetry. The author's impressionist treatments describe parts of a city that refuses to become a whole for its protagonist. The narrative appears to assume a suspect but romantic theory of physical causes, detecting a symbiosis between the landscape, the weather, and the city's women: sultry, enigmatic, and perhaps ultimately disappointing. Its first-person account of the dissatisfaction of an indolent déclassé English intellectual trying to make sense of a Mediterranean city and its citizens has him attributing their readable histories and personalities to the influence of the place they inhabit. The natives of the Egyptian city are seen as a set of intrinsic predispositions determined by racial inheritances, whereas his actions and emotions are put down to his mostly dire economic situation and a shameful lack of motivation.

Sexual promiscuity, the smoking of hashish, constant reference to Cafavy, and nods to decadent French novels of the fin de siècle make this a very different book from most English novels of its time. Essentially it is a superior kind of travel writing, constructed in often extraordinarily vivid and painterly language, but hobbled every once in a while by its dated sexual and racial politics. **RP**

❸ Durrell indulges his amateur interest in painting: much of his best writing consists of descriptions of places seen with an artist's eye.

The Glass Bees

Ernst Jünger

Lifespan | *b*.1895 (Germany), *d*. 1998
First Published | 1957
First Published by | Klett (Stuttgart)
Original Title | *Gläserne Bienen*

The Glass Bees has been claimed as a major contribution to the science fiction genre and as a precursor of magical realism, but Ernst Jünger's dense, reflective work is in truth too idiosyncratic for any categorization. The chief protagonist, Captain Richard, is an ageing war veteran—exactly like the author, who fought in both World Wars—and much of the book is a grim reflection on the veteran's alienation from the modern world.

The reader's interest quickens when Jünger turns from these obsessions to the corporation where his hero seeks employment. Run by the sinisterly benign Zapparoni, the business is a global communications and cybernetics empire making miniaturized robots and virtual reality entertainment. Some of the robots perform domestic tasks such as cleaning, while others are linked to sinister military programs. The book's climactic episode occurs in the garden of Zapparoni's establishment—a sort of idyllic Silicon Valley. In a passage that owes much to Junger's experiments with hallucinogenic drugs in the early 1950s, Captain Richard minutely observes the shiny, transparent, robotic bees of the title in action and is horrified to discover a pool scattered with severed ears. As a story, this is almost derisory. But the text crackles with ideas that fascinate us by their prescience, seeming to foresee the Internet, nanotechnology, and global warming, as well as a world discreetly dominated by technologically hip, morally ambivalent plutocrats. **RegG**

Doctor Zhivago

Boris Pasternak

Boris Pasternak's epic story of the love affair between Lara and Yuri, set against the historical and geographical vastness of revolutionary Russia, was banned in the USSR from its first publication in Italy until 1988. While Pasternak was silenced by the Soviets, he won extravagant plaudits in the West, receiving the Nobel Prize for Literature in 1958.

It is a bitter irony that this divergence between Soviet and Western responses to *Doctor Zhivago* has had such a profound influence on the way that the novel has been read. Pasternak has been caricatured by both the West and the East as a writer who prioritizes a romantic Western concept of individual freedom over the iron cruelties of the socialist state. In fact, rather than being in any simple sense counter-revolutionary, the book is a subtle examination of the ways in which revolutionary ideals can be compromised by the realities of political power. The relationship between Lara and Yuri, one of the most compelling in postwar fiction, grows out of a fascination with the possibilities of revolutionary justice and is closely interwoven with it. The novel is driven by the struggle to achieve some kind of perfect truth, in both personal and political terms, but its drama and pathos are found in the failure of this striving toward the ideal and in the extraordinary difficulty of remaining faithful to a personal, political, or poetic principle.

One of the most striking things about the novel is the Russian landscape itself, which emerges with a wonderful spaciousness and an extraordinary beauty. It is from its elegiac encounter with the vast landscape on which this drama is played out that *Doctor Zhivago* produces an extraordinary sense of happiness and a sense of the boundlessness of historical and human possibility. **PB**

Lifespan | *b.* 1890 (Russia), *d.* 1960
First Published | 1957, by Feltrinelli (Milan)
Nobel Prize for Literature| 1958 (declined)
Original Language | Russian

When this English paperback edition appeared in 1960, Pasternak's novel was hailed in the West as an attack on the Soviet system.

David Lean's 1965 film version, a huge box office hit, made *Doctor Zhivago* into a scenic epic of doomed romantic love.

Pnin

Vladimir Nabokov

Lifespan | *b.* 1899 (Russia), *d.* 1977 (Switzerland)
First Published | 1957
First Published by | Doubleday (New York)
Original Language | English

This short comic novel brought Vladimir Nabokov his first National Book Award nomination, widespread popularity, and first commercial success. An early example of the 1950s campus novel, it follows the experiences of the hapless Russian émigré Professor Timofey Pnin. As a teacher of Russian at Waindell College, he inhabits the rather strange and detached world of academia, and he struggles to adapt to American university life. Physically awkward and an implacable pedant, Pnin's greatest misfortune is his inability to marshal English idiom, and much of the comedy of the book arises from his idiosyncratic use of the language. However, his ultimately dignified conduct ensures that his character cannot be reduced to the pared-down stereotype offered by the somewhat uncharitable narrator, and in comparison with his other non-American colleagues he is an undeniably decent man.

Evolving out of a series of short stories originally published in the *New Yorker* between 1953 and 1955, the book has been criticized for appearing more as a series of discrete sketches than a novel. This criticism is unfair, however, as—in keeping with Nabokov's concern for thematic rather than plot-driven cohesion—the novel returns to Pnin's inability to feel physically or linguistically "at home" in North American culture. Above all, the unmistakably deft Nabokovian style, with its extended linguistic digressions and offbeat humor, make this novel a comic masterpiece and a real joy. **JW**

On the Road

Jack Kerouac

Lifespan | *b.* 1922 (U.S.), *d.* 1969
First Published |1957
First Published by | Viking Press (New York)
Screenplay by | Russell Banks

Jack Kerouac's *On the Road* has become a classic text in American literary counterculture. Set in the aftermath of the Second World War, Sal Paradise's account of his travels across America has become emblematic of the struggle to retain the freedom of the American dream in a more sober historical moment. Paradise's journey with the free and reckless Dean Moriarty (based on fellow Beat adventurer Neal Cassady) from the East to the West Coast of America is a celebration of the abundance, vitality, and spirit of American youth. The pair's rejection of domestic and economic conformity in favor of a search for free and inclusive communities and for heightened individual experiences were key constituents of the emerging Beat culture, of which Kerouac—along with literary figures such as Ginsberg and Burroughs—was to soon to become a charismatic representative.

Reputedly written by Kerouac in a three-week burst of Benzedrine and caffeine-fueled creativity on a single scroll of paper, the production of this loosely autobiographical novel became a legend of the sort that occurred within it. Yet the novel also holds within it an acknowledgement of the limitations of its vision, and Dean's gradual decline slowly reveals him to be something of an absurd and unlikely hero for Sal to follow into maturity. **NM**

❯ Jack Kerouac, left, glances away from his friend Neal Cassady, a folk hero of the Beats depicted in *On the Road* as Dean Moriarty.

The Manila Rope

Veijo Meri

Lifespan | *b.* 1928 (Finland)
First Published | 1957
First Published by | Otava (Helsinki)
Original Title | *Manillaköysi*

The Manila Rope introduces Joose, a naive, working-class soldier fighting in the Second World War, who is allowed some leave from the front to visit his family. Before leaving, he finds a manila rope in his camp and decides to take it home for a clothesline. He hides the rope by wrapping it around his body, but during his long journey by train, the rope tightens around his body and almost kills him.

This novel paints a wholly original picture of war. Little account is given of the war itself, more specifically the Finnish Continuation War (1941–44), which in the novel appears shapeless and incomprehensible. Instead, different narrators sharing Joose's train journey tell of their emotional and physical wartime experiences. The tone of the narration is humorous and hilarious, but the events in the stories are often terrifying and macabre. War is portrayed as destructive and pointless, with the soldiers passive, unheroic, and seeing themselves as merely "slaughter waste." Almost all of them are trying to gain from the war in one way or another, but invariably their attempts are failing. The suffering Joose has himself become a victim, his anguish and nausea caused by his own attempt to profit, however trivially, from war.

The black humor and absurdity of this work of metafiction recall Nikolai Gogol, Franz Kafka, and Jaroslav Hasek. The Manila Rope asks questions not only about war and human fate but also about narration and history writing, fact and fiction. **IP**

The Deadbeats

Ward Ruyslinck

Lifespan | *b.* 1929 (Belgium)
First Published | 1957, by A. Manteau (Brussels)
Given Name | Raymond Charles Marie De Belser
Original Title | *De ontaarde slapers*

In a small house on the edge of a Belgian town, a middle-aged married couple scratch out an existence on unemployment benefit. Filthy and indolent, they lie in bed all day, rising only to go to the labor exchange or let in the local baker. The husband, Silvester, once a respected soldier, is now nihilistic, afraid, and defeated. His wife fears the return of war with a hysterical intensity.

Written in the 1950s, Ward Ruyslinck's short novel recalls Camus in its existential depiction of lives with no purpose. Silvester sees life as simply the living out of days. He knows that those who have courage can take what they want in life but believes, or pretends to believe, that the gratitude one must show for taking things from life is not worth it. Unlike that of Camus's outsider, Silvester's nihilism is based on fear; he is unable to act decisively. Both husband and wife, on the day of their twenty-second anniversary, wonder how it is that the person they live with is now a shadow of the person they once found attractive. However, the arrival of an infantry unit carrying out exercises helps to define the character of the feelings they might still have for each other.

Ruyslinck chronicles the inner futility of his two protagonists, using them to make more universal points concerning unemployment, war, and the restlessness of humanity. For Ruyslinck, people have "war in their bodies," and this harrowing story of two people cast adrift is a deeply troubling picture of minds gone to seed and energy unused. **OR**

Homo Faber

Max Frisch

Lifespan | *b.* 1911 (Switzerland), *d.* 1991
First Published | 1957
First Published by | Suhrkamp (Frankfurt)
Original Language | German

Homo Faber is a tragicomic tale of the alienation of modern man and the dangers of rationalism. Walter Faber is a fifty-year-old Swiss émigré working as an engineer for UNESCO. He is a punctilious creature of habit with a strongly held view that science and reason can account for all things. The novel begins when, on a flight to Venezuela, his plane is forced to land in the Mexican desert. This disruption to his ordered life and a chance meeting with the brother of his erstwhile best friend are the beginnings of a series of events that force him to confront his past.

Before the war, Faber was in a relationship with a German Jew, Hanna, who became pregnant. He offered to marry her, but she refused, fearing he was simply making a political gesture. Faber leaves for a long-term work project with the understanding that she would terminate the pregnancy. But in Mexico he learns that Hanna, in fact, married another. This shock discovery creates a fissure in his rationalist armor that will crack completely by the time he is united with Hanna and the daughter he never knew he had. Walter's failure to address his emotional side, and his dogmatic belief that he can control his environment through logic and technology, make this reunion anything but happy. His hubris has disastrous consequences. Max Frisch is a master of irony, used here to full effect to produce a troubling, ambivalent work that leaves you torn between feelings of sympathy and contempt for his perfectly realized but deeply flawed creation. **AL**

Blue of Noon

Georges Bataille

Lifespan | *b.* 1897 (France), *d.* 1962
First Published | 1957
First Published by | Pauvert (Paris)
Original Title | *Le Bleu du ciel*

Despite having met his ideal woman in the wealthy, beautiful, and debauched "Dirty," Troppmann, the narrator of *Blue of Noon*, is impotent, forcing him to explore his insatiable appetites by other means. His sexual impotence reflects a wider sense of powerlessness that pervades this novel, written in 1935, but unpublished until 1957. Moving around Europe in 1934, Troppmann witnesses the first signs of the rise of Nazism, seemingly resigned to its eventual triumph. Convinced of the failure of politics in general, he remains resolutely disengaged from any political revolutionary activity. Instead, accompanied by Dirty, he embarks on a project of willful self-destruction. Georges Bataille wrote elsewhere about the state of "sovereignty" that is achieved precisely when the self is lost in a moment that exceeds any potential use, any recuperative "experience." Troppmann tries to attain this state through repeated acts of transgression, by negating values and violating taboos.

Mirroring Europe's descent into fascism in the drunk, sick, and decaying bodies of its protagonists, Bataille points to the fascination with a deathly sexuality that Nazism taps into. The novel is attuned to the allure of the ecstatic violence of fascism, while finally suggesting that it might be possible to turn these forces against themselves. Very few can match Bataille's willingness to search for a degree zero, the headlong pursuit of absolute nullity coupled with the acute knowledge of its ultimate unattainability. **SS**

The Midwich Cuckoos

John Wyndham

Lifespan | *b.* 1903 (England), *d.* 1969
First Published | 1957
First Published by | Michael Joseph (London)
First Movie Adaptation | *Village of the Damned* (1960)

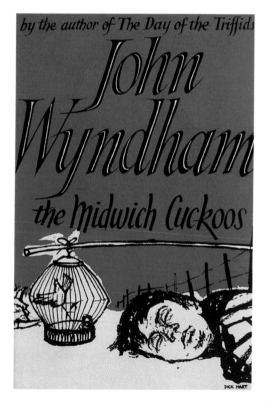

"Cuckoos lay eggs . . ."

🔵 *The Midwich Cuckoos* sets a science fiction story of hostile alien invasion in the apparently tranquil setting of an English village.

Midwich is a tiny and unexceptional rural village where very little ever happens, until a mysterious force envelops it, and everyone falls unconscious. Soon after, the inhabitants wake to find that everything remains normal, and most have no ill effects. However, it becomes clear that every woman of childbearing age is simultaneously pregnant. The resulting children are extraordinary: uncannily alike, remarkably well developed, and endowed with a telepathic sense that allows all to know exactly what one has learned. Unsurprisingly, they prompt a great deal of unease in the village and, in classic sci-fi style, a professor arrives to investigate the phenomenon. What follows is a compelling struggle between the children, the villagers, and the authorities around them that quickly takes on global proportions.

This synopsis may seem familiar, because although it was initially popular as a novel, the story is probably better known as a result of the two filmed versions (the first considerably superior), both rather unnecessarily titled *Village of the Damned*. This novel has also had an enduring influence on successive generations of science fiction writers. Although *The Midwich Cuckoos* has undeniably dated, as with many of Wyndham's novels—the most popular being *The Day of the Triffids*—it nevertheless powerfully epitomizes the concerns and questions that preoccupied writers following the end of the Second World War and during the Cold War that followed. The fear that is engendered in Midwich by the possibility of invasion, infiltration, and pollution is masterfully manipulated by Wyndham in terms of the domestic, the personal, and the body. He also brilliantly captures the uncomprehending intrusion of Cold War propaganda and politics into the most unlikely setting—little England. **MD**

Voss

Patrick White

The novel with which Patrick White first achieved international fame is both a love story and an adventure story, and yet it is neither. Set in Australia in the mid-nineteenth century, the novel dramatizes an expedition, led by Johann Ulrich Voss, into the center of the vast Australian continent. At the same time, it follows the growing relationship between Voss and Laura Trevelyan, wealthy daughter of one of the sponsors of Voss's voyage. Laura, like the colonial society to which she belongs, never leaves the fringes of the continent. But as Voss penetrates deeper and deeper into the dark heart of the country, Laura travels with him, telepathically or in spirit, so that a relationship which begins somewhat frigidly in the drawing rooms of colonial Australia reaches a passionate, feverish intensity in the harsh, otherworldly conditions of the interior.

This tale of love and exploration has many antecedents. Voss's dogged, driven attempt to penetrate the land resembles Marlow's journey in Joseph Conrad's *Heart of Darkness*. The precise attention to nineteenth-century sensibility lends the drawing-room scenes an unmistakable quality of Jane Austen; and the intensity of the personal relations sometimes reads like Lawrence transposed to the outback. But while Voss's journey and his difficult relationship with Laura have all these overtones, the most striking feature of this novel is its discordance, its unnavigable strangeness. The land itself is the most imposing presence, and the deadly vastness of the unmapped interior exerts an extraordinary influence on the European culture that the colonists bring to it. This culture is remade by the silent land that Voss seeks to penetrate, just as the novel form is refashioned from this confrontation with the hidden depths of the desert. **PB**

Lifespan | *b.* 1912 (England), *d.* 1961 (Australia)
First Published | 1957
First Published by | Eyre & Spottiswoode (London)
Nobel Prize for Literature | 1973

"His legend will be written . . ."

⊙ An artist's impression of White's dogged hero appears on the striking cover of the first edition, which made the novelist's name.

Jealousy

Alain Robbe-Grillet

Lifespan | *b.* 1922 (France)
First Published | 1957
First Published by | Les Editions de Minuit (Paris)
Original Title | *La Jalousie*

Alain Robbe-Grillet's *Jealousy* is one of the most famous examples of the *nouveau roman*, or "new novel," which tried to extend the limits of the realist approach to novelistic plotting, setting, and characterization. The style is one of rigorous objectivity that is restricted to the visual description of the planes and surfaces of the observable world and the stances and gestures of human figures. The reader is denied any direct access to the thoughts of either the nameless narrator or the people he observes. Looking through a venetian blind (*jalousie* in French), he watches his wife engaging in what looks like an affair with his neighbor, Franck. He makes no attempt to comment or reflect on what he is seeing—in fact he never uses the pronoun "I" at all.

The true originality of the novel lies in its ability to communicate the force of jealousy despite the self-imposed limitations of its objective style. The reader gradually becomes attuned to the repetitions and minute variations of the text and eventually forms the impression of a consciousness constituted and consumed by jealousy. The narrative style brilliantly captures the behavior of the jealous lover, whose obsessive attention to detail manages to see in every stray glance and unconscious gesture evidence of a hidden betrayal. The flat, filmic mode of narration perfected here has been tremendously influential for later postmodern writers attempting to describe the curious depthlessness of a world seen primarily through the lens of the camera. **SS**

The Birds

Tarjei Vesaas

Lifespan | *b.* 1897 (Norway), *d.* 1970
First Published | 1957
First Published by | Gyldendal (Oslo)
Original Title | *Fuglane*

Not to be confused with Daphne du Maurier's short story and screenplay for Hitchcock's shlock avian-horror movie, this is a far more restrained and poignant affair from one of Scandinavia's pre-eminent twentieth-century writers. And this—along with *The Ice Palace*—is probably Tarjei Vesaas's finest novel.

The Birds tells the tale of the sibling relationship of a simple-minded boy, Mattis, and his elder sister, Hege, who is his emotional and physical carer. They live together by a lake deep in the Norwegian hinterland, but Hege is wearying of her enclosed world of self-sacrifice. The catalyst for change comes when Mattis, role-playing the part of a ferryman, brings home his one and only genuine passenger. Jørgen is a traveling lumberjack who needs a roof for the night, especially as Mattis's leaking boat has left his rucksack partially soaked. Hege is at once flustered and attracted by this new arrival—much to the consternation of Mattis. The dynamics of their relationships are acutely observed and the denouement is particularly haunting, as well as revealing a partial clue to the title.

Vesaas was the foremost exponent of the style called *landsmål* or "country language," or *Nymorsk* ("New Norwegian"), as it was later known. Couched in a completely believable dialog, *The Birds* describes highly charged relationships and experiences in a stunningly primordial landscape. The novel can also be taken as allegorical and symbolic—a heartfelt plea for tolerance of outsiders. **JHa**

The Once and Future King

T. H. White

Lifespan | *b.* 1915 (India), *d.* 1964 (Greece)
First Published | 1958
First Published by | Collins (London)
Full Name | Terence Hanbury White

T. H. White's complex and often brilliant retelling of the Arthurian legends was written over a twenty-year period as a sequence of four novels and first published as a single volume in 1958. It is best known for the rather saccharine Disney cartoon of the first book, *The Sword in the Stone* (published in 1939; movie released in 1963). *The Once and Future King* was based on Thomas Malory's ambitious prose romance of the Arthurian court, *Le Morte d'Arthur*, written in the fifteenth century. White does not update the story, but he is always conscious of the parallels between the brutality of the dying Middle Ages and the rise of fascism in his own lifetime. In the course of the four published novels, Arthur grows from a gangly, nervous youth ("the Wart") into a vigorous military leader. He is eventually forced to emulate the actions of the Nazi-esque Celtic forces assembled by his nemesis, Mordred, in an attempt to try to preserve the innocence of England. The result is disastrous and, as he rides out to meet his death, Arthur concludes that only without nations can humankind be happy. There are some magnificent set pieces, notably when the Wart, transformed into a perch by Merlin, is nearly eaten by the pike, Mr. P., who warns him that the only reality is that of power.

The Once and Future King is a messy sequence of novels that is not properly integrated, as the author acknowledged. Still, it is a powerful, disturbing work about the evil that men can do and the desperate struggle for values in a hostile world. **AH**

EXCALIBVR RETURNS TO THE MERE

"Whoso pulleth Out This Sword of This Stone and Anvil, is Rightwise King Born of All England."

⊙ The return of the magic sword to the Lady of the Lake as visualized by British illustrator Henry Justice Ford in 1902.

The Bell

Iris Murdoch

Lifespan | b. 1919 (Ireland), d. 1999 (England)
First Published | 1958
First Published by | Chatto & Windus (London)
Original Language | English

The Bell is generally agreed to be Iris Murdoch's best early novel. The plot, which clearly belongs to the Anglo-Irish literary genre of the "big house" novel, involves the tense, unhappy relationships between a group of characters on a retreat at a Benedictine monastery, Imber Court. Here they hope to resolve the issues that trouble them in the world outside. They represent a cross section of weak and confused humanity whose spiritual needs prevent them from integrating properly with their fellow men and women, but whose lust for life precludes them from being able to accept a contemplative life cut off from the world. The main figure is Michael Meade, an ex-priest and schoolteacher struggling to suppress his homosexuality and who is racked with a mixture of guilt and frustration. The plot revolves around the plan to restore the cracked bell of the community, a labor that proves endless and futile. The unstable community starts to disintegrate after the arrival of two outsiders. Dora Greenfield is the unhappy wife of Paul, a scholar studying documents at the Abbey, who is unsure whether to end their marriage. Toby Gashe is a young man who finds himself attracted to both Dora and Michael.

The Bell established Iris Murdoch as a major figure in British fiction. It poignantly explores the tragic interaction of a group of people who need to balance their own needs and desires against those of others, as well as understand how far life can or should be lived in terms of spiritual ideals. **AH**

Borstal Boy

Brendan Behan

Lifespan | b. 1923 (Ireland), d. 1964
First Published | 1958
First Published by | Hutchinson (London)
Full Name | Brendan Francis Behan

Borstal Boy is Brendan Behan's account of life for a "paddy" in an English Borstal (young offender institution). From a working-class Republican family in Dublin, Behan was arrested in Liverpool in 1939 in possession of IRA explosives. Sentenced to three years' Borstal detention, he served two and was then expelled from England at the age of eighteen.

Part of the beauty of *Borstal Boy*, a novel he was to write seventeen years later, is the skill with which it recaptures the contradictions that make up the "young offender." Behan himself appears in the text as a riddle of pride, fear, loneliness, and aggression. He is at once a cynically knowing critic of the pieties of both Irish nationalism and English imperialism and a homesick boy; aggressively at home with his fists in the macho culture of his institution, and tempted to gentleness and desire by the bodies and strengths of his Borstal comrades.

Magistrates, screws, detainees, friends, foes, priests—all are drawn with a respect for both the differences that separate and those that unite. The result is a fine social history of interwar England, as well as a classic of prison literature. What sets *Borstal Boy* apart from other such classics is the generosity of Behan's anger and his skill as a writer in exposing the many ways in which prison dehumanizes all who come into contact with it. **PMcM**

❯ Behan poses in front of a poster for the French version of his 1956 play *The Quare Fellow*, which first established his reputation.

Gabriela, Clove and Cinnamon

Jorge Amado

Lifespan | *b.* 1912 (Brazil), *d.* 2001
First Published | 1958
First Published by | Livraria Martins Editora
Original Title | *Gabriela, Cravo e Canela*

*"I continue to firmly believe
in changing the world . . ."*

Jorge Amado

⊙ Amado's novels address major themes in a totally accessible form;
his *Gabriela* was adapted into a popular Brazilian TV soap opera.

In 1930, the newly elected president of Brazil, Getulio Vargas, publicly burned Jorge Amado's first six novels—intending to warn Brazil's intellectuals of the consequences of expressing dissident politics in literature. Amado eventually won a seat in congress for the Communist Party, but decided he was "of better use to the people as a writer than by spending my time on party activity."

Amado grew up on his grandfather's cocoa plantation at Itabuna, in the northeast province of Bahia. At this time, wealthy plantation-owning men were preoccupied with asserting their masculinity through promiscuity. Amado was exposed to the misery of female workers, a familiarity that he used to situate his portrayal of the intoxicating, sensual, and ever-happy Gabriela, whose skin looks like cinnamon and smells like cloves.

Gabriela is a modernist text, questioning the traditional double standard that requires married Brazilian men to be loyal to their masculinity and women to be loyal to their husbands. This double standard is played out in the love story between Gabriela and Nacib, who hires her to cook in his bar. Nacib's jealousy at finding his beloved Gabriela in bed with another leads him to pressure her into marriage, but the potential entrapment that this represents threatens to squash the innocence and freedom that makes Gabriela so potent.

Gabriela's situation became a platform for the inequality of women (who, according to the Brazilian constitution, only became equal to men in 1988). Gabriela's characterization reinforced the stereotype of Brazil as a Third World country, but it did so through a woman standing outside a society whose essence she nevertheless embodied, thus speaking of and to Brazil's most invisible citizens. **JSD**

Saturday Night and Sunday Morning

Alan Sillitoe

From the outset of his writing career, English author Alan Sillitoe found a vibrant catalyst for his imagination in Nottingham, the region he had grown to know intimately since birth. Yet his debut novel, *Saturday Night and Sunday Morning*, was more than simply an exercise in regional realism. In a narrative that makes nimble transitions between the naturalistic and the mythical, Sillitoe describes the progress of Arthur Seaton from factory floor to fractious love life, creating an unsentimental, pseudo-autobiographical picaresque novel. Arthur's riotous enjoyment of the "best and bingiest glad-time of the week," as he drinks in pubs and chases girls, is a "violent preamble to prostrate Sabbath." In his evocations of Arthur's everyday detailed perception of Nottingham's once resilient environment under change, Sillitoe does perfect justice to the local people and regional place, scrupulously mapping a townscape that is barely resisting the parasitic "empires" of suburbia, which are encroaching on it. Sillitoe returned to this "Seaton saga" in *Birthday*, published in 2001, aligning himself with Balzac in conducting across the decades what he described recently as a "Nottingham *comédie humaine*."

Central to this ongoing project, Sillitoe's imaginative geography has contributed richly to the postwar regional novel's stylistic and thematic scope. By using his personal acquaintance with Nottinghamshire's cartography, he articulates with formidable precision a prospective map of what the county could potentially become. Sillitoe's fiction is never straightforwardly realist: it often blends urban verisimilitude with visionary speculation in order to demonstrate how an author can allow factual experiences of indigenous place to inform a fable of social possibilities alive in its midst. **DJ**

Lifespan | *b*.1928 (England)
First Published | 1958, by W. H. Allen (London)
Movie Adaptation Released | 1960
Author's Club First Novel Award | 1958

"For it was Saturday night, the best and bingiest glad-time of the week . . ."

⬥ In 1960, when this photo was taken, Sillitoe's gritty regional realism appealed to a public eager for working-class heroes.

Things Fall Apart

Chinua Achebe

Lifespan | b.1930 (Nigeria)
First Published | 1958
First Published by | Heinemann (London)
Full Name | Albert Chinualumogu Achebe

Things Fall Apart is Chinua Achebe's first and most famous novel, written in response to the negative ways that Africans are represented in canonical English texts such as Joseph Conrad's *Heart of Darkness* and Joyce Cary's *Mister Johnson*. It has sold over eight million copies and been translated into more than thirty languages. The novel describes the historical tragedy caused by the arrival of the British in Igboland, in eastern Nigeria. In the first part of the novel, the local culture is shown to be complex and dynamic, pristine and untouched by Europe. The second section reveals the social transformations brought about by early imperialists and Christian missionaries. The final part dwells on the theme of African silence as a direct consequence of British colonial rule. The story of the protagonist, Okonkwo, is caught up in these broader historical currents.

Things Fall Apart is an anticolonial novel. It contains numerous scenes of African silence, or absence, in the face of Europe's speech, or presence. Over and against these acts of silencing, the novel as a whole works in the opposite direction, pulling against colonialism and celebrating the noisiness of an uncolonized Igbo world. It is shown to be filled with oral genres, including ceremonies, proverbs, folktales, debates, gossip, and conversations, overseen by the ubiquitous West African "talking drum." **SN**

○ Achebe's powerful critique of imperialism appeared just as African countries, including Nigeria, were winning independence.

The Bitter Glass

Eilís Dillon

Lifespan | b.1920 (Ireland), d.1994
First Published | 1958
First Published by | Faber & Faber (London)
Original Language | English

The Irish Civil War of 1922–23 pitted "free staters" against Republicans, those who accepted the partition of Ireland drawn out in the Treaty of 1921 against those who held out for a united Ireland. The war was as bitter and as personal as only a civil war can be, as the first Irish Free State Government authorized the execution of Republicans committed to a cause they had shared but two years before.

Eilís Dillon's *The Bitter Glass* is set in the west of Ireland in the hot summer of 1922 and uses the conflict to pinpoint the redundancy of the war to those in whose name it was being fought. A party of wealthy young Dubliners makes the journey to a remote summer house in Connemara, rich with memories of childhood alliances, hopes, and betrayals. Dillon uses the opening sections of the novel to build up a vivid sense of the ambiguous conflicts pulsing under the surface of the Dubliners' personal relationships. When the house and its inhabitants are taken prisoner by a flying column of IRA men on the run from Free State forces, the idyllic holiday home is turned into an arena of rage that explodes with an emancipatory shock.

Dillon crafts a poetic and sardonic narrative that identifies women as those who resent most strongly the lack of, and hope most keenly for, freedom. The freedom they yearn for, however, exceeds the political liberties being fought for around them, as it embraces liberation from both material want and emotional shame. **PMcM**

The Guide

R. K. Narayan

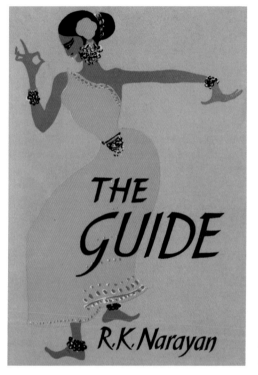

> "I knew that here was a lifelong customer for me. A man who preferred to dress like a permanent tourist was just what a guide passionately looked for all his life."

⦿ The first edition cover artwork reflected Narayan's ability to handle serious material with a light and humorous touch.

Lifespan | *b.* 1906 (India), *d.* 2001
First Published | 1958
First Published by | Methuen (London)
Full Name | Rasipuram Krishnaswami Narayan

There is a minor figure of a lawyer in R. K. Narayan's novel, *The Guide*, who can talk for hours without completing a sentence. This is the secret of his success because he can keep a jury fidgeting over minute details. It is also the reason why Railway Raju succeeds in a series of corrupt practices throughout this novel. As a tourist guide, he attains star status because he can fabricate local histories at a pinch for bored tourists. It is his work as a guide that leads him to meet the neglected dancer Nalini, wife of academic Marco. Nalini's dancing is denigrated by her husband and it is Raju's support for her that brings them together once Marco disowns his wife.

Nalini's success as a dancer and Raju's corrupt business sense lead to fortunes for the pair, but Raju falls into a trap laid by Marco and is sent to prison. On his release, Raju is mistaken for a holy man. He assumes this role willingly and once again attains fame through his deception. However, he is a victim of his own success as he inadvertently suggests that he might fast to bring rains to a drought-ridden village. Resentful at his self-imposed hunger and his body weakening, Raju finally resolves to complete the fast out of sincerity. On the eleventh day of the fast, he staggers and collapses. There is, however, the slightest suggestion that the rains may well arrive.

The Guide is one of the best loved of Narayan's works set in his fictitous town, Malgudi. Its success is no doubt due to its humor in depicting the irrestible urge to spin a yarn, and keep it spinning. **ABi**

The Leopard

Giuseppe Tomasi di Lampedusa

Lifespan | *b.* 1896 (Italy), *d.* 1957
First Published | 1958
First Published by | Feltrinelli (Milan)
Original Title | *Il gattopardo*

Appearing posthumously in 1958, one year after the author's death, *The Leopard* received unexpected international success. Translated into many languages, it became the subject of cinematographic epic by Visconti in 1963. *The Leopard* struck a new chord, as it deliberately ignored the Italian neorealist narrative tradition, both stylistically and thematically. While neorealism centered on low-class characters and unveiled the crude reality of Fascist Italy, *The Leopard* is the saga of the aristocratic Sicilian family of the Salinas (whose coat of arms bears a leopard).

From 1860 to 1910, a series of events affects the microcosm of the protagonist, Prince Fabrizio, and his relatives, as well as the macrocosm of the Italian nation. In Italy's south, the Bourbon kingdom is crumbling under Garibaldi, and the Kingdom of the Two Sicilies is being joined with the rest of the country; however, the end of Spanish colonization coincides with the death of the aristocracy, which had long been supported by the feudal system and which is being supplanted by the bourgeoisie. *The Leopard* portrays the melancholy of that loss. The most poignant pages are those in which Prince Fabrizio bemoans the harsh landscape of Sicily and the Sicilians, who have developed an irredeemable sense of indifference and vanity in the attempt to survive numberless foreign colonizations. The new course of history will not touch Sicily, Don Fabrizio predicts, as the national unification that is underway is for the Sicilians nothing but a new form of domination. **RPi**

Deep Rivers

José María Arguedas

Lifespan | *b.* 1911 (Peru), *d.* 1969
First Published | 1958
First Published by | Losada (Buenos Aires)
Original Title | *Los ríos profundos*

In *Deep Rivers*, José María Arguedas immerses himself in the reality of being Peruvian through the experience of an autobiographical character, Ernesto. His subject is the abandonment of innocence and identity brought about by the plight of the indigenous peoples. After traveling for years through the mountains in the company of his father, an obscure country lawyer, Ernesto enters a religious seminary in Abancay. This is where all his argument's tension is concentrated: from personal conflict (training in a violently racist environment), to universal conflict (the struggle against plague that by the end of the novel is hovering over the city), to social conflict (the rebellion of the native women).

At the seminary Ernesto learns the law of force and subjugation. He also finds out about the assimilation of Indian culture, with its potential for revolt and its redeeming vocation of helping the victims of plague. Eventually, he leaves the mountains and joins his destiny with those he has chosen as his own. The viewpoints of the adolescent, the adult, and the specialist in linguistic and cultural questions are married in a single awareness that finds meaning, in memory and imagination, in his experience. Paying special attention to nature, to Quechua singing, to the role of magic and ritual, and to some very well-known symbols, Arguedas makes an argument of high artistic quality in favor of indigenous Peru. This is his best text and one of the best novels of the indigenous movement. **DMG**

Breakfast at Tiffany's

Truman Capote

Lifespan | *b.* 1924 (U.S.), *d.* 1984
First Published | 1958
First Published by | Random House (New York)
Given Name | Truman Streckfus Persons

"You got to be rich to go mucking around in Africa."

◓ Truman Capote poses as a self-consciously sophisticated and hedonistic observer of life in this photograph dating from 1955.

▶ Blake Edwards's 1961 movie version of the story was toned down and sweetened up to meet Hollywood requirements of the time.

Breakfast at Tiffany's is a charmingly naughty fable, capturing in crystal a glorious moment of New York during the last gasp of American innocence. The story is the reminiscence of a writer in New York during the Second World War, closely echoing Isherwood's *Goodbye to Berlin*, in which a writer in a strange land struggles to make a name.

With Holly Golightly, Truman Capote has given us one of the most indelible heroines in fiction. Pushing the boundaries and paving the way for the revolution to come, Holly is a gamine—sexually free, hedonistic, and a prostitute. She lives for the moment, damns the consequences, and makes up her own morality as she goes along. Like her cat without a name, she is unfettered, untameable.

The novel's unnamed narrator meets Holly when she climbs through the writer's window, to escape an overzealous and unmuzzled john who intends to bite her. They become fast friends, and the narrator is swept up in Holly's thrill-seeking (albeit subsistence) living. At the core they want "happiness" and connection, dreams that seem like fate to those young enough to hope. But hints of darkness cloud their lives and the novel itself. Disaster strikes Holly's family, ultimately changing the relationship she has with the narrator, and her innocence is tested when her regular client, Mafia don "Sally" Tomato, uses her for more than just sex.

The novel was a turning point for Capote. Gone is the lyrical Southern Gothic of his early writing. With *Breakfast at Tiffany's*, he takes his place among New York's glitterati. Daring in its day—promiscuity and homosexuality are discussed openly—it may have lost its ability to shock, but its charm does not diminish. The novel is a fresh breeze off the East River—from a time when such a thing was still possible. **GT**

AUDREY
HEPBURN

PLAYS THAT DARING, DARLING
HOLLY GOLIGHTLY TO A NEW HIGH
IN ENTERTAINMENT DELIGHT!

BREAKFAST
AT TIFFANY'S

A JUROW-SHEPHERD
PRODUCTION

GEORGE PEPPARD · PATRICIA NEAL · BUDDY EBSEN · MARTIN BALSAM AND MICKEY ROONEY
TECHNICOLOR

A PARAMOUNT
RELEASE

BLAKE EDWARDS · MARTIN JUROW AND RICHARD SHEPHERD · GEORGE AXELROD

Pluck the Bud and Destroy the Offspring

Kenzaburo Oe

Lifespan | b. 1935 (Japan)
First Published | 1958 by Kodansha (Tokyo)
Original Title | Memushiri kouchi
Nobel Prize for Literature | 1994

Pluck the Bud and Destroy the Offspring vividly captures the devastating conditions that war can inflict on even the most innocent of victims. The novel is told from the view of a vulnerable boy determined to live, and presents us with a personal experience of Japan toward the end of the Second World War.

As bombs rain down daily on the cities of Japan, the coming end is foreshadowed. A group of boys, abandoned by their parents and incarcerated in a rehabilitation center, are about to take refuge in a country village. As outsiders, they are treated inhumanely by the villagers, but unity among them remains tight. Through the voice of the narrative "I" they are determined to become the "we," and to survive. When a deadly plague arrives, the villagers abandon the boys and flee, closing all the gates to the village. Although the boys find themselves locked in, they gain a transitory freedom. In the most devastating conditions, they set up a kind of paradise, occupying the villagers' houses and managing to create a life for themselves. Their happiness is short-lived, however, as their fear of the plague develops into larger conflicts and disputes. The villagers' eventual return brings the final blow. "Listen, someone like you should be throttled while they're still a kid. We squash vermin while it's small. We're peasants: we nip the buds early." Sadly, paradise is about to disappear. **KK**

Billiards at Half-Past Nine

Heinrich Böll

Lifespan | b. 1917 (Germany), d. 1985
First Published | 1959, by Kiepenheuer & Witsch
Original Title | Billard um Halbzehn
Nobel Prize for Literature | 1972

This family saga about three generations of architects living and working in a town in Catholic West Germany unfolds in conversations and inner monologues, all during one day, September 6, 1958. Over sixty years of German history are revealed through the lives of the family—from the Kaiser era through the Third Reich and into the West German economic miracle of the 1950s.

Billiards at Half-Past Nine is about the refusal to forgive and forget the failure of civilization and the Catholic Church's complicity in war, persecution, and torture. When the monastery that was the first great project of architect Heinrich Fähmel in 1907 is blown up at the end of the Second World War by his son, Robert, an explosions expert for the Wehrmacht, it is really in an act of protest against the civilization it represents. The grandson, Joseph, who is involved in the restoration of the monastery after the war, is deeply confused when he finds out about this. Family tensions, as well as the contradiction of living in a society to which one cannot be reconciled, find a strangely redemptive resolution in a symbolic act of violence. The novel is remarkable for its humanism, and its call to readers to share the characters' moral revulsion and their refusal to forget. **DG**

◖ Böll's writing is dominated by memories of the Second World War and by a critique of the moral vacuum of postwar Germany.

Down Second Avenue

Ezekiel Mphahlele

Lifespan | *b.* 1919 (South Africa), *d.* 1997
First Published | 1959
First Published by | Faber and Faber (London)
Given Name | Ezekiel Mphahlele

Ezekiel Mphahlele is one of the most pervasive voices in South African literature. *Down Second Avenue* is his first autobiographical novel. Mixing reminiscences with penetrating social criticism, Mphahlele paints a vivid picture of his own struggle against the racial segregation of the apartheid South African education system.

The book tells the story of a young black man, Eseki, growing up in a tribal village near Pretoria and making his way as a secondary school teacher of Afrikaans and English in the city. Like many young black idealists relocated to townships built only for black and colored people in the early 1940s, Eseki is quickly drawn into the world of politics and opposition to the country's ruling party. Patronized and bullied, he is consequently barred from teaching. He exiles himself to Nigeria, where he can finally breathe "the new air of freedom" and express his uncompromising critique of the apartheid regime: "Africa is no more for the white man who comes here to teach and to control her human and material forces and not to learn."

The story is told in a simple but evocative language. Pivoting on two central themes in black South African literature, alienation and exile, it presents Mphahlele's personal transformation from a provincial schoolboy from the rural "old Africa" into a socially and politically conscious writer, journalist, and activist shaping the new consciousness of modern, nationalist, black South Africa. **JK**

Cider With Rosie

Laurie Lee

Lifespan | *b.* 1914 (England), *d.* 1997
First Published | 1959
First Published by | Hogarth Press (London)
Original Language | English

An extremely vivid semi-autobiographical description of life in a small English village in the early part of the twentieth century, *Cider With Rosie* depicts a world that was soon to vanish: a world where transport was limited to the horse and cart, and where there were few reasons to travel away from one's home.

What is perhaps most remarkable about it, and has kept it a firm readers' favorite since it was first published, is the rich lushness of the description. The cottage garden, for example, as seen through the eyes and other senses of a young child, becomes a world of its own. Many of the episodes are richly comic, yet there is also a sense of tragedy, a sense that the certainty and routine that once controlled village life have now vanished. The protagonist's mother, abandoned by her husband with two families to cope with, leads a life of extraordinary drudgery, yet her longing for, and recognition of, the greater things in life rarely falters. Most of all, perhaps, Laurie Lee makes no attempt to prettify country life; although there are marvelous things to be found in the fields and hedgerows, there is also a commonplace brutality to country living, including incest, violent sexual relations, and even murder. The counterbalance to this is the sense of tradition, of belonging, which has disappeared as modernity has spread to the most distant places of England. **DP**

⊙ Lee takes the cash for the 1960 WH Smith Literary Award, won by *Cider With Rosie*, from actress Peggy Ashcroft flourishing an apple.

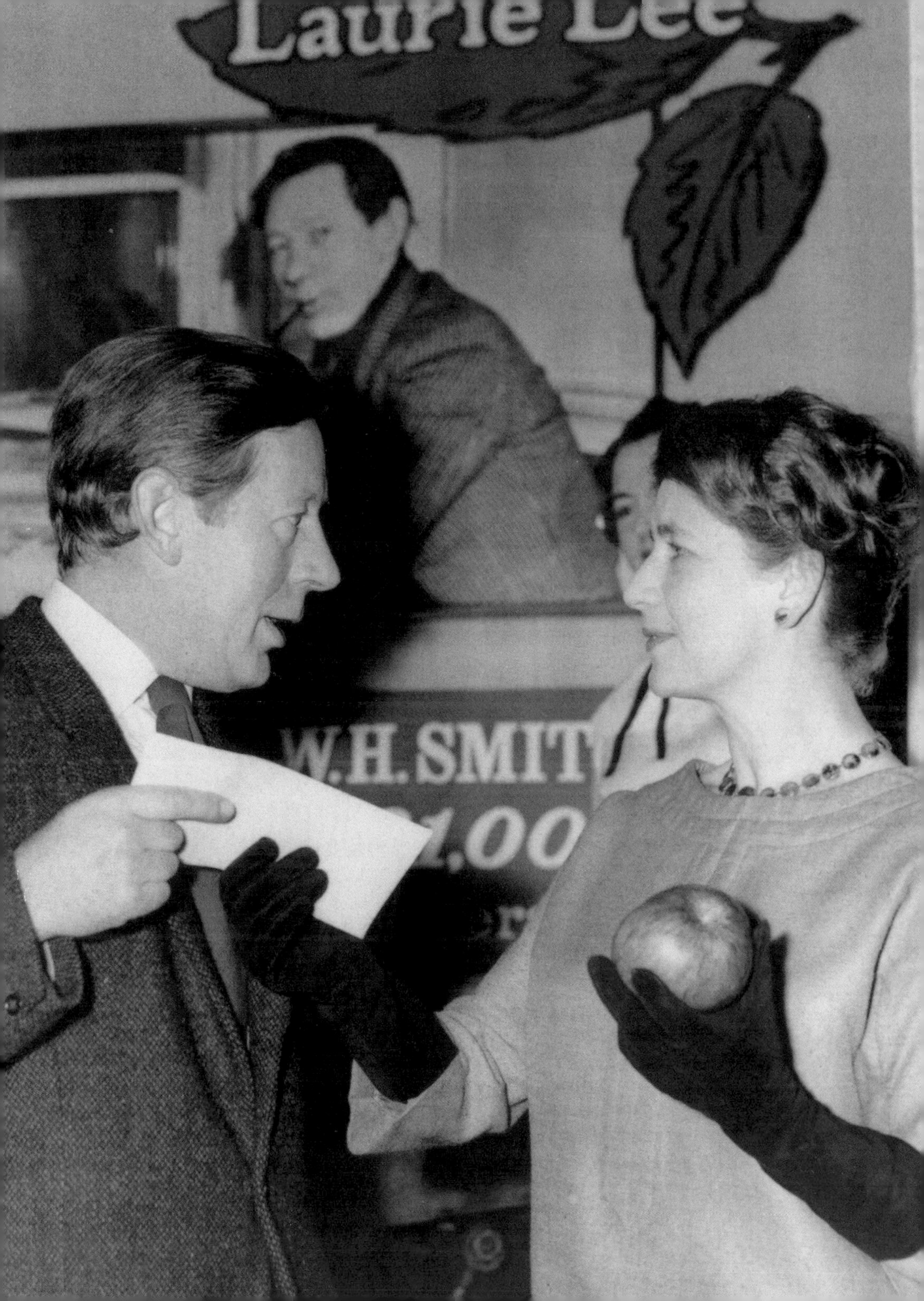
Laurie Lee
W.H.SMIT

The Tin Drum

Günter Grass

Oskar Matzerath is detained in a mental hospital for a murder he did not commit. His keeper watches him. His keeper also brings him the paper on which Oskar writes his autobiography. Oskar considers the keeper a friend, rather than an enemy, for the simple reason that the keeper has eyes that are the right shade of brown. Oskar Matzerath is a dwarf: he claims to have willed himself to stop growing at the age of four. He has a singing voice that can cut holes in glass at fifty paces. During the Second World War, Oskar was part of a traveling band of dwarves that entertained the troops. He also uses his tin drum to beat out the story of his life. That life story is also the story of prewar Poland and Germany, the rise of Hitler, the defeat of Poland, the Nazi onslaught on Europe, then the defeat and partition of Germany.

An important book in the exploration of postwar German identity, Günter Grass's novel is heartbreakingly beautiful. Oskar Matzerath's voice continues to haunt long after the novel itself is finished. It is the voice of an "asocial," those the Nazis considered to belong (along with criminals, homosexuals, and vagabonds) to "life unworthy of life." Grass draws on the picaresque tradition to map out his dwarf drummer's journey through a brutal and brutalizing era in European history, but he also reinvents the traditions of a popular culture despised by the Nazis as "degenerate art." Fairy tales, the carnivalesque, the harlequin, the mythological trickster—all jostle and combine in *The Tin Drum* to reveal the deathlike inhumanity of the rationalization of racial hygiene. The result is not a fetishization of the irrational, but rather an expansion and transformation of the normal, until the life Oskar inhabits ultimately becomes swollen to grotesque, yet all the more painfully human, proportions. **PMcM**

Lifespan | *b.* 1927 (Poland)
First Published | 1959, by Luchterhand (Neuwied)
Original Title | *Die Blechtrommel*
Nobel Prize for Literature | 1999

"How blind, how nervous and ill-bred they are!"

◔ A striking representation of "little Oskar," Grass's compulsive drummer, illustrates the jacket of the German first edition.

◔ Oskar was played by twelve-year-old David Bennent in Schlondorff's 1979 movie, which won an Oscar for Best Foreign Language Film.

The Naked Lunch

William Burroughs

Lifespan | *b.* 1914 (U.S.), *d.* 1997
First Published | 1959
First Published by | Olympia Press (Paris)
Full Name | William Seward Burroughs

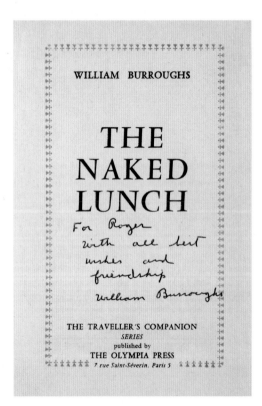

WILLIAM BURROUGHS

THE NAKED LUNCH

For Roger
with all best
wishes and
friendship
william Burroughs

THE TRAVELLER'S COMPANION
SERIES
published by
THE OLYMPIA PRESS
7 rue Saint-Séverin, Paris 5

◉ The Parisian Olympia Press issued the first edition of this and other novels thought too obscene for U.K. or U.S. publication.

◐ Burroughs called hard drugs ". . . the ultimate merchandise. No sales talk necessary. The client will crawl through a sewer and beg to buy."

William Burroughs has often been hailed as a celebrator of drug indulgence and (homo)sexual excess, but his best works, among which *The Naked Lunch* is preeminent, provide a far deeper and more complex account of Western culture. The novel's central argument is that drugs are not an accidental problem; the whole notion of addiction is deeply engrained in a society that fetishizes commodity and consumption. Furthermore, the line between so-called "prescription" drugs and illegal drugs is a narrow one, which can be manipulated by those in power to serve their need for ever-increasing profits.

But these arguments alone would not make *The Naked Lunch* a great book. What is more important is the tremendous energy and vividness that Burroughs brings to his scenes of violence and mayhem. He presents us with a cast of characters who are constantly tearing at the walls of the prisons their lives have become; they see something of the truth of "the system," but are too paralyzed by dependence to escape. Further, Burroughs invents his own style, here and in other novels, based on what he called the "cut-up technique," which serves to render the reader equally unable to make full sense of the surroundings. Narratives begin, interweave, become lost, and are found again; scenarios are glimpsed then vanish from sight.

There are plenty of postmodern texts that use unreliable narrators. Burroughs goes further than this, producing a world that seems to have no recognizable coordinates at all. Lost in the world of the junkie, we are sometimes painfully aware that the paranoid visions of the drug world may be more accurate about the systems of corporate and state power than the consoling fictions we tell ourselves in asserting the freedom of the individual will. **DP**

BILLY LIAR

Billy Liar

Keith Waterhouse

Lifespan | *b.* 1929 (England)
First Published | 1959
First Published by | Michael Joseph (London)
Stage Adaptation | 1960

When people refer to the "angry young men" of 1950s British fiction and drama, they will usually have in mind Kingsley Amis's Jim Dixon; perhaps John Braine's Joe Lampton and William Cooper's Joe Lunn; certainly John Osborne's Jimmy Porter. Billy Fisher, Keith Waterhouse's feckless antihero, gets less of a look-in. He would be the first to feel the injustice: Billy is every bit as thwarted and furious as his peers, and this novel is just as telling a document of the postwar crises of class and masculinity as *Lucky Jim* or *Room at the Top.*

Billy, maybe twenty years old, still lives with his parents in the English town of Stradhoughton, works as an undertaker's clerk, and dreams of escape. A compulsive fantasist, Billy has invented Ambrosia, an imaginary world where he can be prime minister, lover, revolutionary, and writer all at once. His life has become a tangle of increasingly elaborate lies, and *Billy Liar* is the story of the day when it all goes wrong. Much of the unraveling is hysterical, but only some of it is funny, reflecting as it does the impotence of a generation of British men born too late to have had their lives defined by the war, but too soon to enjoy the class mobility afforded by the postwar settlement. Billy's anxiety pierces every line, and at the end, the reader is left with the queasy sense that for him, finally, there can be no escape. **PMy**

❮ Tom Courtney played the lovable fantasy-prone undertaker's clerk Billy in John Schlesinger's 1963 movie version of the novel.

Absolute Beginners

Colin MacInnes

Lifespan | *b.* 1914 (England), *d.* 1976
First Published | 1959
First Published by | MacGibbon & Kee (London)
UK Musical Movie Adaptation Released | 1986

The best known of Colin MacInnes's London trilogy, which includes *City of Spades* (1957) and *Mr. Love and Justice* (1960), *Absolute Beginners* has had a curious afterlife, thanks to the David Bowie-featured 1980s movie musical, which culled large sections of the text. Frequently appearing on top-ten "hip lists" alongside Jack Kerouac's superficially similar *On the Road* (1957), the novel has as its star not its central character, a bohemian photographer "out for kicks and fantasy," but London in all its frenetic glory. It is narrated in a language replete with "spades," "daddy-os," "reefers," "oldies," and "oafos," yet behind the coming-of-age tale lies a society in the throes of radical transformation.

This is postwar London in the aftermath of the Suez crisis, in the year of the Notting Hill riots: previously ironclad certainties concerning the God-given destiny of the British Empire and the racial homogeneity of its metropolitan center are archaic irrelevancies. This is an emerging London entirely incomprehensible to the prewar "oldies" in positions of authority. It is also a city fizzing with excitement and tension—racial, generational, and sexual. When it finally breaks down in riots, it is not just law and order, nor the social bonds of community that begins to disintegrate, but the city itself begins to collapse.

Fresh, vital, and eternally relevant, *Absolute Beginners* offers extraordinary insight into the origins of contemporary society and a farewell to the society that was left behind. **MD**

Promise at Dawn

Romain Gary

Lifespan | *b.* 1914 (Lithuania), *d.* 1980 (France)
First Published | 1960
First Published by | Gallimard (Paris)
Original Title | *La Promesse de l'aube*

"Then she began to cry . . ."

🔵 Romain Gary with his wife, American actress Jean Seberg: she committed suicide in 1979, and he shot himself the following year.

A tribute to the woman who single-handedly, and single-mindedly, raised him to become the great artist that she believed to be her own destiny, *Promise at Dawn* is Romain Gary's memoir of his youth in Vilna and Nice. It reads as a self-portrait in double, reflecting the mix of East European and French cultures that shaped him.

Written with contagious humor and profound affection, it describes his formative experiences with a mother who, if she had not existed, would have certainly required being invented, and to some degree probably was. But this is only fair, as she herself went to such lengths to create her son's fate, her years of struggle and hard work recounted with a restraint that gives them poignant if often comic immediacy. Her unshakable desire that her son grow up as a Frenchman and not a Russian was one of many goals that she set—and he met.

Every facet of Gary's mother's life, every effort she made, was dedicated to the child she adored and to his future triumphs. This was the promise at the dawn of his life. She foresaw and directed him toward his accomplishments as author, officer, and diplomat, and he did his utmost to fulfill and reward her faith in him. Her unremitting devotion sustained him through law school, military training, and wartime service, as well as his early attempts at getting his fiction published. Hers was a love that would leave him forever hungry and longing to find its perfection again, but also one that served as inspiration for his courage and conviction in justice.

The story closes at the end of the Second World War, with Gary's formidable, indefatigable, and sometimes embarrassing mother, with her romantic and noble soul, demonstrating yet another surprising facet of the artistic genius she truly was. **ES**

Rabbit, Run
John Updike

In *Rabbit, Run*, John Updike's second novel, the author introduced one of the towering characters of postwar American fiction. Harry "Rabbit" Angstrom was a basketball star at school, famous throughout his hometown of Brewer, Pennsylvania. Now in his late twenties, he lives in a small apartment in one of the poorer parts of town with his pregnant wife, Janice, and young son, Nelson. He has a dead-end job selling vegetable peelers door to door. Alienated and estranged, desperate to escape, he drives away one night without telling anyone he is leaving. But he soon loses heart and turns back toward Brewer. His old basketball coach, one of the few who has not forgotten Harry's glory days, introduces him to a girl called Ruth, with whom he begins an affair.

Updike tells the story in the present tense: if it has become commonplace since, the technique was fairly innovative at the time, and Updike's use of it has rarely been bettered. The novel is also in the third person: although the bulk of the narrative takes place inside Harry's head, it is not Harry's voice that we hear, or not exactly. In sensuous, elegant, hyper-articulate prose, Updike represents Harry's consciousness in the language that Harry would use if only his mind moved as gracefully as his body once did on the basketball court.

Harry is not so much an everyman as a nobody and a far from admirable one: his impulsive and thoughtless behavior has appalling consequences. Yet our sympathy is secured by the quality of careful attentiveness that Updike brings to describing the intricacies of Harry's character. With its sequels— *Rabbit, Redux* (1971), *Rabbit Is Rich* (1981), and *Rabbit at Rest* (1990)—*Rabbit, Run* presents a detailed and extraordinary portrait of an ordinary American man in the second half of the twentieth century. **TEJ**

Lifespan | *b.* 1932 (U.S.), *d.* 2009
First Published | 1960
First Published by | A. Knopf (New York)
National Medal for Humanities | 2003

"Love makes the air light."

● The young John Updike, photographed here in 1960, published books of poetry and short stories before turning to novels.

To Kill a Mockingbird

Harper Lee

Lifespan | *b.* 1926 (U.S.)
First Published | 1960
First Published by | Lippincott (Philadelphia)
Pulitzer Prize | 1961

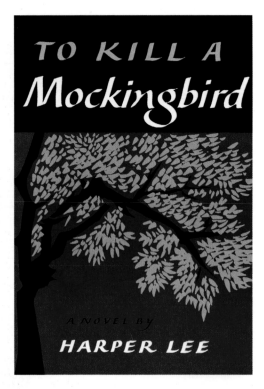

⌃ The jacket of the novel's first edition: it was an immediate success and was made into a movie within two years of publication.

⌄ Harper Lee was thirty-four years old when *Mockingbird*, her first book, was published; she has not written another novel.

Set in Depression-era Alabama, Harper Lee's Pulitzer-winning novel weaves together a young girl's coming-of-age story and a darker drama about the roots and consequences of racism, probing how good and evil can coexist within a single community or individual.

Scout, the novel's protagonist, is raised with her brother, Jem, by their widowed father, Atticus Finch. He is a prominent lawyer who speaks to them as competent interlocutors and encourages them to be empathetic and philosophical, rather than swept away by the superstition bred of ignorance. Atticus lives his convictions when a spurious rape charge is brought against Tom Robinson, one of the town's black residents. Atticus agrees to defend him, puts together a case that gives a more plausible interpretation of the evidence, then prepares for the town's attempts to intimidate him into abandoning his client to their lynch mob. As the furor escalates, Tom is convicted and Bob Ewell, the Robinson plaintiff, tries to punish Atticus with an unimaginably brutal act.

The children, meanwhile, play out their own miniaturized drama of prejudice and superstition centering on Boo Radley, a local legend who remains shut inside his brother's house. They have their own ideas about him and cannot resist the allure of trespassing on the Radley property. Their speculations thrive on the dehumanization perpetuated by their elders; Atticus reprimands them, however, and tries to encourage a more sensitive attitude. Boo then makes his presence felt indirectly through a series of benevolent acts, finally intervening in a dangerous situation to protect Jem and Scout. Scout's continuing moral education is twofold: to resist abusing others with unfounded negativity, but also the necessity of perseverance when these values are inevitably, and sometimes violently, subverted. **AF**

The Magician of Lublin

Isaac Bashevis Singer

Lifespan | *b.* 1904 (Poland), *d.* 1991 (U.S.)
First Published | 1960, by Noonday (New York)
Original Title| *Der Kunstnmakher fun Lublin*
Nobel Prize | 1978

" . . . Yasha was held in small esteem by the community."

⬤ Singer photographed by Walter Daran in 1962—a Yiddish writer then just starting to win recognition from anglophone America.

In *The Magician of Lublin*, set in late nineteenth-century Poland, Yasha Mazur is the David Blaine of Warsaw—without the financial wealth. Making a career out of escape, he is also adept at escaping his own Jewish faith, and (when he needs to) his barren and pious wife as well as the women he lusts after. He is hampered by lack of both money and moral courage, and concerns himself only with the superficial pursuits of getting his hands on money and having sex. But his life turns upside down when he bungles a robbery that was meant to finance a new life with one of his adoring women, while Magda, his faithful assistant, commits suicide because of his continuing infidelity. At the scene, Yasha "touched her forehead: it felt neither cold nor warm but beyond temperature."

Yasha, agonizing over his actions and dire situation, returns to his wife, but only with a typical Singer twist. He has himself bricked up as a penitent in a "cooler" with nothing but the barest essentials—candlestick, water jug, straw pallet to sleep on, pelisse, a few books, and a shovel to bury his excrement. Initially people think it must be merely another magician's stunt, but after three years of solitude, he has become a celebrity hermit with people seeking him out for answers to their problems. It is a curious resolution, but one that Singer obviously feels comfortable with in his continuous literary examination of the role of the Jewish faith in the lives of his Polish characters (largely before the Holocaust), pestered with passions, magic, and religious devotion. *The Magician of Lublin* was made into a movie in 1979, with Alan Arkin as the lusty Yasha and Louise Fletcher, Valerie Perrine, and Shelley Winters as three of his adoring women. **JHa**

Halftime

Martin Walser

The novel *Halftime* is the first part of the so-called Anselm Kristlein trilogy, in which the story of the social decline and fall of the protagonist unfolds against the backdrop of the historical developments of the Federal Republic of Germany in the 1950s and 1960s. *Halftime* focuses on the period of the economic boom of the 1950s and offers a critical view of the emergent consumer society.

Anselm Kristlein, a thirty-five-year-old married man and a father of three children, interrupts his studies and finds a job in the advertising industry. Within a year he becomes not only an admired, well-paid expert in his field, but also skilled in the art of social climbing. As he perceives his family as an obstacle to his career, he prefers to divide his time between friends, colleagues, and his many lovers. Thanks to the parameters of his job, he soon gains access to high society, where he displays an ability to adapt quickly. Soon, the fundamental laws of consumer society, especially that of merciless competition, take on universal applicability in his life. Accordingly, Anselm attempts to conquer a friend's fiancée using the tricks and techniques of the expert advertiser he has become.

The novel follows Anselm through a series of memories. His retrospective narration is interlaced with associations, where external events and the protagonist's meditations and flashbacks all merge into a vibrant verbal flow without the confines of a linear story line (but not without the critical distance that derives from the narrator's irony). Despite scattered hints of criticism, however, it remains unclear to the reader whether Anselm will choose his family as an alternative to the ladder-climbing social ambitions that ultimately make him—physically and metaphorically—ill. **LB**

Lifespan | *b*. 1927 (Germany)
First Published | 1960
First Published by | Suhrkamp (Frankfurt)
Original Title | *Halbzeit*

"Writing is organized spontaneity." Martin Walser

◉ Walser was a prominent left-wing intellectual in the 1960s, critical of West Germany and opposed to the Vietnam War.

The Country Girls

Edna O'Brien

Lifespan | b. 1932 (Ireland)
First Published |1960, by Hutchinson (London)
Trilogy Published | *Country Girls Trilogy*
and Epilogue (1986)

Sick of the privations and oppressions of the convent school where they have been sent to board, Caithleen, the narrator of *The Country Girls*, and her best friend, Baba, compose an obscene letter about one of the nuns and leave it where they know it will be found. Duly expelled and sent home, they are met by Caithleen's furious father, who strikes his daughter's face. Edna O'Brien's first novel shows girls growing up in the shadow of the patriarchal family and the Church, the twin powers that dominate gossip-ridden small-town east Clare, where it is largely set. The heroines' irreverent, pleasure-seeking temperament is irreconcilably at odds with the claustrophobic limitations of that world, vividly depicted in the novel, and their eventual departure for Dublin is inevitable.

In *The Country Girls* the author subtly conceals her own more complex understanding and brings her narrator's artless impulsiveness to the foreground. Caithleen's narrative is impressionistic rather than reflective, focused on the pains and pleasures of the everyday: the nastiness of the convent soup, her enjoyment of *Tender Is the Night*, and dressing up to go out on the town. Unlike Baba, Caithleen nurses romantic illusions, not least about the clammy-handed "Mr. Gentleman" who pursues her in Clare and tries to seduce her after her flight to the capital. She has yet to discover that to seek happiness through love, sex, and men is not necessarily to find it, as the two succeeding novels in O'Brien's trilogy were to show. **MR**

Bebo's Girl

Carlo Cassola

Lifespan | b. 1917 (Italy), d. 1987 (Monaco)
First Published | 1960
First Published by | Einaudi (Turin)
Original Title | *La ragazza di Bube*

Like most of Carlo Cassola's works, *Bebo's Girl*, his most celebrated novel, deals with the effects of the Fascist era after the Second World War. The young female protagonist, Mara, becomes engaged to an equally young partisan called Bebo, who is a hero of the anti-Fascist resistance. As the novel unfolds we learn that Bebo is involved in an armed struggle against fascism in Tuscany's rural villages. Ultimately, however, Bebo's political mentor, the Italian Communist Party, decides to engage in the politics of compromise with the bourgeoisie. Despite this, Bebo continues his struggle, until events overwhelm him and he becomes a murderer to avenge the death of a comrade.

Mara must then decide whether to move on to a life of forgetting and rebuilding for the future, or to remain faithful to Bebo, who is sentenced to fourteen years in prison. She opts for the path of dignity and commitment to her generation's tragedy, which is to have fought for social justice and to have been denied it.

Cassola exposes how the emerging order of the new Italian republic betrayed Mara's generation and he does not condemn Bebo's actions politically. Rather, Cassola asks why the Italian Communist Party allowed potential leaders like Bebo to be unaware of the complexities of the forces uniting to defeat Communism. Cassola's writing, stripped down and loaded with detail, made him a forerunner of the French nouveau roman. **LB**

God's Bits of Wood

Ousmane Sembène

Lifespan | *b.* 1923 (Senegal), *d.* 2007
First Published | 1960
First Published by | Presses Pocket (Paris)
Original Title | *Les bouts de bois de Dieu*

Based on the Senegalese railway workers' strike of 1947–48, Ousmane Sembène's *God's Bits of Wood* is the gripping and adventurous narrative of a community in transition, galvanized and struggling against injustice. There is no one hero in the text, but rather a tableau of players, from men such as the rock-solid Bakayoko, ideological leader of the strike, through to loyal followers, turncoats, collaborators, and a white managerial class that finds its world turning upside down. Most remarkable is the burgeoning social awareness among the women of the town, whose traditional docility is challenged by the threat facing their families. In fact, it is the growing engagement of the women that structures the narrative, and their growing self-confidence that drives the novel toward its climax.

Ousmane consistently sought to portray the social changes facing Senegalese communities on the cusp of and beyond decolonization. Western students of the postcolonial period have seen *God's Bits of Wood* as a key text but it is also widely read and well respected in West Africa itself. This is because it is one of the earliest and most impressive novels to affirm the place of Africans in determining their own fate, challenging assumptions about their reliance on European leadership, or on self-serving individuals within their own ranks. It soon became a model for African social history writers, thanks to its defiance of the colonial status quo and its heady evocation of unity among the urban poor. **RMa**

The Shipyard

Juan Carlos Onetti

Lifespan | *b.* 1909 (Uruguay), *d.* 1994 (Spain)
First Published | 1961
First Published by | Comp. General Fabril Editora
Original Title | *El astillero*

The first part of a diptych—completed by *The Body Snatchers* in 1964, which describes the background of events only alluded to here—*The Shipyard* has as its main character Larsen, an ageing man who has returned to Santa Maria, the city from which he had been expelled, a world inhabited by familiar shadows. He is hired as manager in a dilapidated shipyard, the property of Jeremías Petrus, a former tycoon who lives with Angélica Inés, his idolized daughter, and his maid, Josefina. The shipyard is a fantastic, absurd enterprise, run by Gálvez and Kunz, who do not know whether Larsen is a threat or an ally in their dilemma of either to support the sham or promote its irretrievable collapse.

The novel is organised in short chapters. The story runs between the town, the collapsing shipyard, the little home of Gálvez and his pregnant wife (whom Larsen, if he had had the will, would have wanted to seduce), the arbor where Larsen and Angélica Inés meet, and the house where Larsen, on one occasion before disappearing, goes to bed with Josefina. An eye-witness narrator tells the story, making conjectures and supplying information, sometimes with hidden irony, in meandering phrases that pinpoint qualities of the characters. The narrator's domination of the story is such that he ends up by putting forward two alternate endings. An apparently traditional story of disappointed encounters, *The Shipyard* has a boldness that only later would be exploited in Spanish fiction. **DMG**

Catch-22

Joseph Heller

First published in 1961, Joseph Heller's frenetic satire on the madness of war and the excesses of bureaucracy has now been canonized as a cult classic. The novel tells the story of Captain Joseph Yossarian, a member of a U.S. bomber crew stationed on the Mediterranean island of Pianosa during the Second World War. Unmoved by patriotic ideals or abstract notions of duty, Yossarian interprets the entire war as a personal attack and becomes convinced that the military is deliberately trying to send him to an untimely death. He therefore spends much of the book concocting evermore inventive ways of escaping his missions—faking various medical conditions, oscillating between sanity and insanity, trapped in the circular logic of his "Catch-22" situation (the phrase that has become Heller's gift to the English language). Heller inserts a cast of manic, cartoonish characters into the island's hothouse environment—from demented disciplinarian Colonel Scheisskopf to Milo Minderbinder, a ruthless profiteer.

Heller presents war as a form of institutional insanity, a psychosis that overtakes the machinery of public and private life. *Catch-22* turns its back on conventional notions of heroism and "fighting the good fight," in order to place war in a much broader psychological, sociological, and economic context. Hilariously funny, the novel's insights are also deadly serious, stretching far beyond the limits of peacenik propaganda. It marks a major departure from the austere, realist approach that had dominated U.S. war fiction until the sweeping changes of the 1960s. Alongside works by Roth, Vonnegut, and Pynchon, *Catch-22* opened the floodgates for a wave of U.S. fiction in which war was represented with a new, countercultural sensibility in a language every bit as wild, grotesque, and bizarre as the real thing. **SamT**

Lifespan | *b.* 1923 (U.S.), *d.* 1999
First Published | 1961
First Published by | Simon & Schuster (New York)
Sequel | *Closing Time* (1994)

The writing of *Catch-22* was a lengthy process: Heller wrote the first section in 1953 while working as an advertising copywriter.

Heller is shown here in 1974, when his second novel was published, thirteen years after *Catch-22*, a hard act to follow.

Solaris

Stanislaw Lem

Lifespan | *b.* 1921 (Poland), *d.* 2006
First Published | 1961, by Wydawnictwo (Warsaw)
Original Language | Polish
Movie Adaptation Released | 1972, 2002

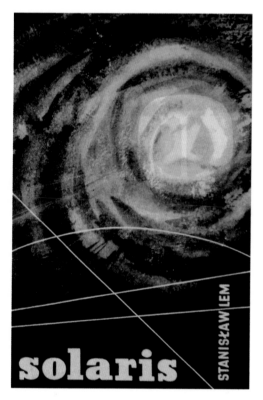

"I could not recognise a single constellation . . ."

🔘 Lem presents a pessimistic vision of humanity lost in a universe it can never understand and threatened by its own technology.

Science fiction has always been an obsessively debated literary category. For outspoken Polish writer Stanislaw Lem, who spent much of his career dismissing American science fiction as kitsch commercial fodder, its shortcomings were all too plain. It is no small irony then that his 1961 novel *Solaris* has become one of the undisputed classics of the genre, spawning two cinema adaptations (Andrei Tarkovsky's in 1972 and Steven Soderbergh's in 2002). Predictably, Lem poured scorn on them both.

The initial premise of *Solaris* is almost textbook: human scientists try and fail to make contact with an alien from the eponymous planet. Solaris is covered by an oceanlike organism whose intelligence outwits them continually. Their attempts to understand it are thrown back on themselves; their experiments reveal only their own psychological weaknesses. Kris Kelvin, the protagonist, is gradually destroyed by memories of his suicidal lover, whose image, regenerated by Solaris, haunts him. The other characters are, in turn, plagued by unspecified traumas.

Although well known and generally well-received, the movie versions of the book focussed almost exclusively on this psychological element. However, Lem is more concerned with hard science. Indeed, what the movies could never capture is the book's distinctive tone: dispassionate academic language describes inexplicable phenomena on the planet that our protagonists can never hope to comprehend.

By revealing the absolute alienness of that oft-imagined fantasy world beyond our own blue planet, Lem suggests a new literary hybrid. Part Franz Kafka, part Aldous Huxley, here is an unmapped mutation of sci fi that is compelling precisely because of its refusal to be explained. **ABI**

Cat and Mouse

Günter Grass

Günter Grass was born in Danzig in 1927 and with *Cat and Mouse*, the central work in the Danzig trilogy (the others being *The Tin Drum* and *Dog Years*), he attempts to recapture the past of that city and understand the impact of Naziism upon it. The novel presents wider historical events through the eyes of a small group of children, allowing the author to ground the narrative in his memory of the city and its people. Its central and elusive figure, Joachim Mahlke, dreams of becoming a clown and becomes instead a war hero. His performances and demonstrations of bravery for the other children seem more impressive and exciting than anything going on in the world around them. He is an outsider and possibly a Pole who refuses to bow to the pressure the regime places upon him to conform and to believe. His mysterious life satirizes Nazi preoccupation with heroism and hero worship; the other children hold him in awe and reverence, while he holds the regime in something approaching contempt. His desire to be a clown stems from his desire to perform for others, to be watched and admired, and it enables Grass to explore the contradictions at the heart of many of those raised to the rank of hero within the Nazi era.

The story, told by his friend, Pilenz, is written in the form of a confessional, a format that deliberately mirrors and engages with the postwar attempts to "confess" the Nazi past and thereby receive absolution. The novel shows the extraordinary technical abilities that Grass possesses by adeptly moving between comic fantasy, brutality, realism, and myth; between moments of almost lyrical beauty and horrific violence. It is also in constant dialogue with its own storytelling, the distorting power of memory, and the impossibility of reconciliation. **JM**

Lifespan | *b.* 1927 (Poland)
First Published | 1961, by Luchterhand (Neuwied)
Original Title | *Katz und Maus: eine Novelle*
Nobel Prize for Literature | 1999

"Still practicing, the cat came closer. Mahlke's Adam's apple attracted attention because it was large, always in motion . . ."

⊙ An outspoken participant in German politics, Grass wrote his Danzig novels partly as a critique of amnesia about the Nazi past.

The Prime of Miss Jean Brodie

Muriel Spark

Lifespan | *b.* 1918 (Scotland), *d.* 2006 (Italy)
First Published | 1961
First Published by | Macmillan & Co. (London)
Stage Adaptation | 1966

"'You will end up as a Girl Guide leader in a suburb like Corstorphine,' she said warningly to Eunice, who was in fact secretly attracted to this idea ..."

🌑 Maggie Smith won a Best Actress Oscar for her portrayal of Muriel Spark's quirky fascist-leaning teacher in the 1969 movie.

🌓 Spark, photographed here in 1960, was educated at an Edinburgh girl's school not unlike the one at which Miss Brodie is employed.

The qualities of Muriel Spark's *The Prime of Miss Jean Brodie* as a novel have been obscured by the popularity of the stage show and movie versions. Phrases such as the "crème de la crème" have entered popular consciousness, without the sophistication of Spark's overlapping purposes receiving the same recognition. From Miss Brodie's chilling Jesuitical assertion—"Give me a girl at an impressionable age, and she is mine for life"—through to the novel's dark conclusions, Spark poses a series of difficult questions about education, femininity, and authoritarianism. The very allure and asperity of Miss Brodie cut back into the elegant severity of Muriel Spark's own style and artifice. For all the minor trappings of glamour, Miss Brodie's deluded romanticizing is matter for this novel's inquiry into the authority of Spark's omniscient narrator. While maintaining an eminently readable narrative form, the novel is also as self-critical about its construction as any formalist could wish.

The story overlaps a number of time frames and alternative perspectives, notably the retrospective judgements of different members of the Brodie set that pepper the novel. This provides hints as to the ultimate unfolding of the modest rise and nasty downfall of an inspiring but dangerous teacher, the eponymous Jean Brodie. Miss Brodie teaches her charges with a reductive but inspiring severity that verges on criminal propaganda for authoritarianism, molding them as her *fascisti*. Tapping into the strange sadomasochistic fantasies of pedagogical crushes and schoolroom sexual tensions, the novel works through the curiously ineffective consequences of this "education" on the Brodie set, seen darkly through pupil Sandy Stranger's eyes. Satirical comedy as political diagnosis, it brings the morality of teaching and storytelling into stark relief: a delight. **DM**

A Severed Head

Iris Murdoch

Lifespan | *b.* 1919 (Ireland), *d.* 1999
First Published | 1961
First Published by | Chatto & Windus (London)
Married Name | Mrs. J. O. Bayley

As Martin Lynch-Gibbon enjoys a lazy afternoon in his mistress's apartment, he ponders his life. He has no intention of leaving his slightly older wife, Antonia, but nonetheless he relishes his liaisons with Georgie. Only blithely aware of Georgie's emotional needs, Martin is obtuse and complacent, despite his self-conscious civility and middle-class propriety—and ripe for moral education. This education comes in the form of the compelling, demonic Honor Klein, an anthropologist with something of the primitive about her, but who stands for truth and unmasking. Martin is shocked when he learns that his wife wishes to leave him for Klein's half brother, Palmer, but can readjust himself as a sort of a child to their surrogate parenting. Honor cuts through the cant and fake civility of this arrangement. When Martin learns that Antonia has also been having an affair with his brother, and when Honor exposes the truth about his relationship with Georgie, Martin's world comes undone.

A Severed Head has all the antic sexuality of a restoration comedy, yet chimes resonantly with the 1960s revolution in values and sexual mores. It uses surprise and suspense, incorporates farce and melodrama, balances its unlikely plot elements, integrates symbolism and imagery into its realist structure, and manages to comment wisely on the stupidities of human relationships. **RM**

⊙ Murdoch combined a flair for plot and character with an interest in currents of thought such as psychoanalysis and existentialism.

Franny and Zooey

J. D. Salinger

Lifespan | *b.* 1919 (U.S.)
First Published | 1961, by Little, Brown & Co. (Bost.)
Published as Short Stories | *Franny* (1955), *Zooey* (1957) in *New Yorker* magazine

The notoriety of *The Catcher in the Rye* has had the effect of deflecting attention both from J.D. Salinger's other writings and from what remains the essential quality of his writing in general: it is all about the details, rather than the broad strokes of disaffection and alienation. *Franny and Zooey* is almost entirely composed of details. A lopsided pair of stories about two children of the Glass family, the "novel" almost has the air of a minor work or sketch because of its deformed structure and apparently unfocused storytelling. Yet it deals throughout with ideas that are to be found at the edges of Salinger's other books, in particular the egotism and "phoniness" of people who, particularly as a result of intellectualism or religion, believe they can provide absolutes and remove the need to keep addressing daily the events of their lives.

Salinger's interest in Eastern religion—especially the rejection of absolutes and the refusal to provide anything as guaranteed—is at its clearest at the center of *Franny and Zooey*. The Glass family's youngest children are tormented by an idea that they move toward grasping as the novel progresses, the idea that learning, religion, and even happiness have been reduced to commodities. As such, each and every choice, irrespective of what it concerns, has the potential to be negative or positive. In the modern world, where all that many people desire is a lifestyle that removes the need to think constantly about their lives, the parallels with Salinger's apparently minor work are all too clear. **SF**

No One Writes to the Colonel

Gabriel García Márquez

Lifespan | b. 1928 (Colombia)
First Published | 1961
First Published by | Aguirre Editores (Medellín)
Original Title | El coronel no tiene quien le escriba

This novella, Gabriel García Márquez's second book, is a tale of violence and injustice, solitude and stagnancy. At the turn of the twentieth century, an unnamed colonel and civil war veteran lives with his asthma-ridden wife, starving and seemingly forgotten in a small village in Colombia. The colonel's life is fueled by the hope that he will one day receive the government pension, fifteen years overdue, that would end the poverty and hardship of his postwar existence. But every Friday his hopes for a better life are dashed when the mailman utters his weekly refrain: "No one writes to the colonel."

The irony of the colonel's plight—his blind faith in participating in a revolution only served to impoverish both himself and his countrymen farther—is juxtaposed with his central struggle: whether or not to sell his late son's sole legacy, the village's prize fighter-cock that may one day win him a fortune. Their son's life was taken as a result of his clandestine activities, circulating banned literature, but over time the cock comes to embody the potential for victory in the wake of loss. It also embodies the possibility of an alternative kind of battlefield in which citizens are remunerated for the madness of striving and hoping, and are shaken from the stagnancy that results from festering in solitude—a solitude that would soon become a trademark of García Márquez's literature. **JSD**

Faces in the Water

Janet Frame

Lifespan | b. 1924 (New Zealand), d. 2004
First Published | 1961
First Published by | Pegasus Press (Christchurch)
Order of New Zealand Awarded | 1990

Faces in the Water is one of the most powerful descriptions of mental illness ever written. Although a work of fiction, the novel is informed by Janet Frame's own experience as a patient (wrongly diagnosed with schizophrenia) in a New Zealand mental asylum.

Istina Mavet, the novel's main character, relates her experiences on the wards of Cliffhaven and Treecroft hospitals in a highly lyrical but disjointed fashion. Through her gaze, we see the deplorable conditions of these institutions, the horrible side effects of electroconvulsive shock therapy, insulin-induced comas, and lobotomies, as well as the kindnesses and cruelties of the psychiatric nurses.

The book is a biting critique of the gross power differential between medical "professional" and patient. While the skillful way in which the novel makes this point is enough to make it memorable, the prose's striking quality elevates it to a truly great novel. Istina's thoughts and narrative descriptions combine an accomplished lyricism with the fractured digressions symptomatic of psychological trauma. Istina's disturbance is unmistakable at times, but her ability to narrate these experiences is what sets her apart from her mostly inarticulate fellow patients. Frame herself won release from the mental institution in which she was a patient after eight years, an escape she attributed to publication of her book The Lagoon and Other Stories in 1951. **CG-G**

Memoirs of a Peasant Boy

Xosé Neira Vilas

Lifespan | *b*. 1928 (Spain)
First Published | 1961
First Published by | Follas Novas (Buenos Aires)
Original Title | *Memorias dun neno labrego*

This classic of Galician children's literature consists of an emotional description of the life of a poor child in rural Galicia. The main character is Balbino, who is presented as "a boy from a village. That's to say, a nobody." Through the boy's eyes and sensibility, the reader shares the experiences that build up his character as he matures. His encounters with death take place through two events: his godfather is run over, and his dog is accidentally caught in a snare set for foxes. But Balbino still has hope for the future and, as a symbol of this, he plants a cherry tree where the animal died. Another bitter experience is that of injustice, now exercised by his father, who hits him for dirtying the face of Manolito, a rich child. No less hard is his contact with love. At school, Balbino falls in love with the schoolmistress and this feeling drives him to study; but her marriage causes him such anguish that he refuses to return to school. His father makes him work for him as a punishment.

Wisdom on the one hand and friendship on the other combine to educate the youth. The first is delivered by a Jew, who teaches him about people and shows him that only honor and solidarity will pacify his conscience. Friendship is incarnate in Lelo, who has to emigrate and writes to him from America. As a result of this friendly correspondence, Balbino ceases to write his confidences in the notebook that we are reading. **DRM**

Stranger in a Strange Land

Robert Heinlein

Lifespan | *b*. 1907 (U.S.), *d*. 1988
First Published | 1961
First Published by | Putnam (New York)
Hugo Award | 1962

A strange and disturbing book, which won the 1962 Hugo Prize and rocked the science fiction world, Robert Heinlein's *Stranger in a Strange Land* not only gave science fiction books a place on mainstream bookshelves, but also became an emblem of the 1960s counterculture movement toward free love and unconstrained living. It tells the story of Valentine Michael Smith, the orphaned son of the first Mars explorers, who has been raised by Martians and returned to Earth by a second human mission. Although Smith is in his twenties by the time he comes back to Earth, he looks on the world with the eyes of a child, as he faces the arduous task of learning to be human. He has never seen a woman and has no knowledge of human culture or religions. Smith preaches his message of spirituality and free love and disseminates the psychic powers he learned on Mars. As time goes on, he converts many people to his way of thinking and becomes a messiah-like figure, with explosive results.

The story is a reflection on the conceits of its time, a sprawling satire of the human condition that takes in love, politics, sex, and, above all, organized religion, which is seen as a sham. The fact that, in reality, several religious movements emerged as a result of people reading the novel must have been alarming to an author whose message seems to reveal a frustration at people's desire to follow prophets and causes. **EF**

Labyrinths

Jorge Luis Borges

Lifespan | *b.* 1899 (Argentina), *d.* 1986 (Switzerland)
First Published | 1962
First Published by | New Directions (New York)
Original Language | English

Borges never wrote a novel. A novel would be either unnecessary or unfinished. Instead there are these "episodes," brought together in *Labyrinths*, a collection of his major works, comprising some of his most important short stories and most challenging essays. Here the reader can see the impact of vast ideas on tiny spots of history and individuals; the perspective of one person seeing the infinite for the first and only time. Borges's lucid prose, at once melancholy and scientific, is the ideal vehicle for tales of unending libraries, dreamers who are dreamed in turn, and men paralyzed by the inability to forget anything at all.

Fictions, essays, and parables—the range of Borges's reading and inspiration is evident. Pascal, Kafka, Judas, and Bernard Shaw all put in appearances. As André Maurois says: "Borges has read everything and especially what no one reads anymore." From Old Norse sagas to Arab philosophy, Borges favors the trick of reading between the lines, making the unseen connections and realizing the immense, sometimes terrible, implications. Despite separation into the three genres, all the pieces operate on similar levels. There is a constant wonder at the potential of both mankind and the universe, a certain irony about the actions of individuals and an elusive sadness at the ending of things. Magical realism, intertextuality, and postmodernist trickery are all here, fresh and absorbing, before the burden of such descriptions. Somewhere in Borges all the reading and writing in the world has already been done. **JS**

The Golden Notebook

Doris Lessing

Lifespan | *b.* 1919 (Iran)
First Published |1962
First Published by | Michael Joseph (London)
Prix Medicis | 1976

When, in 1972, Margaret Drabble characterized Doris Lessing as a "Cassandra in a world under siege," she brought into focus what has become a truism in the reception of Lessing's writing: namely, that we read her to find out "what's going on"—for an independent "diagnosis" of the dilemmas of our individual and collective lives.

First published in 1962, *The Golden Notebook* was immediately taken up—or, in Lessing's terms, "belittled"—as a crucial intervention in the so-called sex war. It was seen as a literary plea for psychic and political change in the lives of the "free women" at the book's heart. It is a complex novel, narrated through the four notebooks that divide, and contain, the life of the protagonist, Anna Wulf. As a struggling writer and single mother closely associated with the Communist Party through the 1950s, Wulf is the figure through whom Lessing writes about the conflicts of sexuality and sexual difference, politics and creativity—and, in particular, the theme of breakdown, which is omnipresent throughout the book. The crisis of political belief that shadowed the British Communist Party through the 1950s, the paranoia of the Cold War, is refracted through both the crisis of imagination that afflicts Anna Wulf as a writer and the disturbance in the relationship between the sexes that so preoccupies her as a "modern" woman. **VL**

❯ Lessing grew up in Southern Rhodesia—now Zimbabwe—where she learned the political activism that infuses her writing.

Time of Silence

Luis Martín-Santos

Lifespan | *b.* 1924 (Spain), *d.* 1964
First Published | 1962
First Published by | Seix-Barral (Barcelona)
Original Title | *Tiempo de silencio*

Luis Martín-Santos, the son of a military doctor, was a successful young psychiatrist, a friend of the best writers of his generation, and a clandestine militant of the Socialist Party. With *Time of Silence*, he blew apart the foundations of the realist, politically committed novel. He made free use of the internal monologue of the characters, he carefully broke up the structure of the story, and, above all, he employed a sarcastic style of narration, packed with wordplay, that came directly from James Joyce.

However, the problems he described were the same that were concerning his realist friends, and which had been a familiar part of Spanish writing since the time of the respected Pío Baroja: the hypocrisy of the traditional middle classes, the matriarchal aspect of Spanish society, the absurdity of any attempt at intellectual emancipation, and the impossibility of establishing links between a mindless proletariat and his own group of writers, who were committed to liberation.

With enthralling violence, the novel presents the environment in which the brief action unrolls—the family's rooming house, the brothel, the pretentious, aristocratic mansion, the nocturnal gatherings of the young intellectuals, and the shacks where the immigrants crowd together. It confers on Pedro, the young doctor who is the main character, more victim than agitator and always more astonished than aware, the distressing role of representative of the failure of a generation. **JCM**

Pale Fire

Vladimir Nabokov

Lifespan | *b.* 1899 (Russia), *d.* 1977 (Switzerland)
First Published | 1962
First Published by | Putnam (New York)
Original Language | English

Entering a web of reflections, imputations, madness, neighborliness, gayness, exiled royalty, murder, and literary criticism, it is hard to discern any stable world outside the text of Vladimir Nabokov's novel. With astonishing literary dexterity, Nabokov takes to considerable lengths here the notion that writing need be about nothing but itself.

The novel is divided into two parts: the four cantos of the poem "Pale Fire," attributed to invented author John Shade, and their annotated exegesis written, after Shade's death, by his friend, neighbor, and editor, Charles Kinbote. The poem and its notes, along with Kinbote's explanatory preface and index, form the novel's entire substance. Shade's poem is an apparently uncomplicated reflection on his life, his daughter's suicide, and his Christian thoughts on the nature of divine order. Kinbote's notes suggest that he believes himself to be Charles the Beloved, king of an obscure European country called Zembla. Escaping to the United States from revolution, Charles pseudonymously took up a post at Wordsmith University alongside his favorite poet, John Shade, whom he befriended and whose work he claims to understand. In his opinion, "Pale Fire" is really a coded history of Zembla. Is Kinbote an editor, a stalker, a madman, or an academic? Or is he a fiction supplied by a Shade writing his own annotations? **DH**

❯ Nabokov is photographed in 1958 on a butterfly hunt—he was a distinguished lepidopterist as well as an elusive novelist.

A Clockwork Orange

Anthony Burgess

A Clockwork Orange, Anthony Burgess's best-known work, shot to fame following Stanley Kubrick's controversial 1971 movie adaptation. The novel was inspired by a group of Russian teddy-boy ruffians Burgess encountered in St. Petersburg. It is narrated by teenage hooligan Alex and dotted with Russian-derived slang. Alex, along with his friends and followers Dim, Pete, and Georgie, leads a life of violence—beating up an old man and raping his wife as part of a normal night out. When Alex is set up, arrested, and sent to prison, he is chosen for a new, Pavlovian style anti-violence treatment called "Ludovico's technique." Soon, if so much as a violent thought passes through Alex's mind he feels ill, and his treatment is hailed as a great success. When Alex is released from prison, unable to fight back, he is beaten and left for dead in a field before being rescued by the very man he attacked at the beginning of the novel. Following his failed suicide attempt, while Alex is still unconscious, government psychologists reverse Ludovico's technique. For a time he reverts to his old violent ways, but by the end of the book, he is thinking about settling down. In the U.S. edition of *A Clockwork Orange*, the last chapter was removed—against Burgess's will—because it was thought to be too sentimental.

The novel is a comment on what the author saw as society's will to swallow up individual freedom and the rise of mass popular culture in the early 1960s, which brought a new rebellious conformism. Burgess rails against the psychological conditioning techniques of the time, which he thought were abhorrent. Alex's free choice of leaving the violence behind brings him to a final moral level infinitely higher than the forced harmlessness of his conditioning—a complete freedom. **EF**

Lifespan | *b.* 1917 (England), *d.* 1993
First Published | 1962
First Published by | W. Heinemann (London)
Movie Adaptation Released | 1971

Penguin's Pop Art-influenced cover for the novel offers a faceless, dehumanized image of Alex, the violent leader of the Droogs.

Burgess was an exceptionally prolific writer—*A Clockwork Orange* was one of five novels he published between 1960 and 1962.

One Flew Over the Cuckoo's Nest

Ken Kesey

Lifespan | *b.* 1935 (U.S.), *d.* 2001
First Published | 1962
First Published by | Viking Press (New York)
Movie Adaptation Released | 1975

"'I been silent so long now it's gonna roar out of me . . .'"

◆ Kesey became a hero of the 1960s hippie counterculture, leading the hallucinogen-inspired Pranksters in trips on the Magic Bus.

Ken Kesey's novel depicts a mental asylum in which repeated attempts to diagnose the patients as insane are conceived as part of a larger scheme to produce pliant, docile subjects across the United States. A key text for the antipsychiatry movement of the 1960s, it addresses the relationship between sanity and madness, conformity and rebellion. The novel remains finely balanced throughout. It is never clear, for example, whether the so-called "Combine" is, in actuality, a boundless authority designed to ensure social control across the whole population, or a projection of the narrator Chief Bromden's paranoid imagination. Also, the question of whether insanity, to quote R. D. Laing, "might very well be a state of health in a mad world," or at least an appropriate form of social rebellion, is raised but never quite answered.

Into the sterile, hermetically sealed world of the asylum wanders Randall P. McMurphy, a modern day "cowboy" with a "sideshow swagger" who disrupts the ward's smooth running and challenges the near-total authority of the steely Nurse Ratched. Insofar as McMurphy's acts of rebellion assume mostly self-interested forms, the novel's efforts at political mobilization fall short, and there remains something uneasy about its racial and gender politics. It takes the "cowboy" McMurphy to save the "Indian" Bromden and, in the era of civil rights and feminism, the white male patients are painted as "victims of a matriarchy," ably supported by a cabal of black orderlies. But Kesey's impressive attempts to come to grips with the amorphous nature of modern power—a power not necessarily tied to leaders or even institutions—make this a prescient, foreboding work. If McMurphy's fate is what awaits those who push too hard against the system, then Bromden's sanity depends on not turning a blind eye to injustice and exploitation. **AP**

Girl with Green Eyes

Edna O'Brien

Originally published as *The Lonely Girl*, this is the second novel of *The Country Girls* trilogy narrated by naïve convent girl Caithleen Brady. After moving to Dublin with her childhood friend, Baba, Caithleen (the shier and less streetwise of the two) becomes involved with Eugene, a filmmaker several years her senior, who is married but estranged from his wife. Perhaps inevitably, it is a fundamentally imbalanced romance, and Eugene exerts disproportionate control over their relationship.

On top of this, Caithleen's family's vehement disapproval forces a confrontation between the Catholic values of her upbringing and the changing cultural attitudes of the 1960s. Her desire to pursue a sexual relationship puts her at odds with strict Irish religious mores at the time, but Caithleen's moral conflict contrasts starkly with Eugene's inability to understand religious observance of any kind.

Upon its publication in 1962, the novel won critical acclaim for its frank, fresh, unpretentious portrayal of a young woman's experiences. Both the subject matter and O'Brien's explicit treatment of it were to prove contentious in her native Ireland, however, and the Irish Censorship Board banned all three novels of the trilogy, while copies of the books were burned in Irish churchyards in protest against the frank depiction of the sexual lives of the girls. In many ways, this reception proved O'Brien's point about the fundamental disjunct between an individual's desires and the oppressiveness of traditional mores, and reflected her own experience of growing up in rural Ireland. O'Brien's willingness to engage with culturally sensitive issues of the period makes her writing of the first importance. Her depiction of the realities of individual experience within a defined social milieu makes this novel unmissable. **JW**

Lifespan | *b.* 1932 (Ireland)
First Published | 1962
First Published by | Jonathan Cape (London)
Kingsley Amis Award | 1962

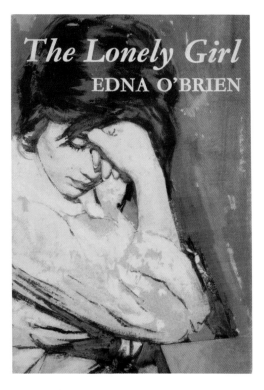

"My face in the mirror looked round and smooth."

⊙ *Girl with Green Eyes* was originally called *The Lonely Girl*; the title was changed in 1964 when the novel was republished.

The Death of Artemio Cruz

Carlos Fuentes

Lifespan | *b.* 1928 (Mexico)
First Published | 1962
First Published by | FCE (Mexico City)
Original Title | *La muerte de Artemio Cruz*

"If I think about what I did yesterday, I'll stop thinking about what's happening to me now. That's a good idea. Very good. Think yesterday."

◉ Fuentes translates his political commitment into a fictional
form combining technical experimentation and free fantasy.

While he is dying, Artemio Cruz multiplies himself in the form of three voices and three strictly alternated tenses: "I" speaks in the present and gives an account of the moment of his death agony, expanding concentrically throughout the whole novel; "you" is his imaginary twin, whose memories are expressed in an immediate or perhaps eternally postponed future; and finally "he" is the protagonist of twelve episodes or stages of his life had it been arranged as it should have been. In each case, other voices and other tenses appear in an extremely varied way.

The complex arrangement forms a complete biography: that of a Mexican tycoon who, from 1889 to 1959, represents the story of his country. It is a tale set during the Revolution and then fueled by his achievements. In his wake are loves left destroyed by the Revolution itelf; cowardice and betrayal; abuses, humiliation, and corruption. In the end, Cruz has a heart attack. Surrounded by his family, his secretary, a priest, and doctors—each of whom in turn delivers a different picture of the dying man—the tycoon faces the crossroads of a past and a future in which imagination and memory are mixed.

The intricate structural marquetry of the novel, its stylistic exuberance, and its historic and psychological density are unusual for its time. It makes demands that teach the reader to read in a different way, as is the case with any truly avant-garde work. **DMG**

The Time of the Hero

Mario Vargas Llosa

Lifespan | *b.* 1936 (Peru)
First Published | 1962
First Published in | Seix-Barral (Barcelona)
Original Title | *La ciudad y los perros*

This novel, Mario Vargas Llosa's first, dazzles with the scale of its experimentation with form and the risks it takes in tackling the dissection of a contemporary society. The story of the cadets of a Peruvian military college uses the author's own experience, but it transcends autobiography through the profound assimilation of literary models (Flaubert, Faulkner, and Sartre) and a rigorous construction based on fragmentation and a multiplicity of narrative voices. From the theft of an examination paper to the death of one of the cadets, the reader is at first presented with a depiction of the college's framework of races and social classes, whose relationships are governed by violence and deception. Then the novel progresses, like a criminal investigation, to expose the extent of moral corruption and the consequences of perverted education.

This is a fable about responsibility and determinism, the fundamental result of the structure formed by characters who are split between the world of the college and that of the city. The main characters exist in both (the cadets Alberto, Ricardo, and Jaguar, and Lieutenant Gamboa); from their outside position they are attracted and repelled by the evanescent Teresa, as well as their friends and families. These elements are ultimately brought together in the final part to reveal the faces of deceit and precarious truth. **DMG**

The Garden of the Finzi-Continis

Giorgio Bassani

Lifespan | *b.* 1916 (Italy), *d.* 2000
First Published | 1963, by G. Einaudi (Turin)
Movie Adaptation Released | 1970
Original Title | *Il giardino dei Finzi-Contini*

Bassani's novel is a moving story of Italy in the 1920s and 1930s, as Fascism takes hold and seeps into ordinary life. The narrator is a frequent visitor to the walled garden of the Finzi-Continis, a wealthy, cosmopolitan, and popular Jewish family in Ferrara. This town was also one of the key Fascist strongholds, but this dramatic irony escapes the narrator. He loves and admires the graceful, eccentric family and becomes increasingly absorbed in the garden's pleasures as events make the world outside more threatening; soon his world has shrunk to this small space. He falls in love with the beautiful, mysterious Micòl, but they both have to watch her brother, Alberto, waste away and die from a mysterious illness. Micòl, who grasps that she has no future, is forced to withdraw from all forms of public life, abandoning hopes of a brilliant career. Eventually even the myopic narrator starts to understand what is happening, and the novel reaches its sad, inevitable conclusion.

This novel of corrupted innocence and blighted talent and opportunity is also an indictment of ordinary citizens too blind to see the threat of creeping authoritarianism and prejudice. While affirming ordinary human values of friendship and kindness, it shows what happened to Italy when it made the fatal error of uniting with Nazi Germany—a moral vacuum rendered the beauty and intelligence of Italian culture vulnerable and delusive. **AH**

One Day in the Life of Ivan Denisovich

Aleksandr Isayevich Solzhenitsyn

Lifespan | *b*. 1918 (Russia), *d*. 2008
First Published |1963, by Sovetskii pisatel (Moscow)
Original Title | *Odin den Ivana Denisovicha*
Exiled from Soviet Union | 1974

"Better to . . . submit. If you were stubborn they broke you."

⊙ In the early 1960s, the Soviet authorities allowed Solzhenitsyn to address foreign journalists, but he soon fell out of favor again.

⊙ A rare photograph of Solzhenitsyn as an anonymous convict during the eight years that he spent in Soviet labor camps.

This contemporary literary classic is quite literally what it says it is: a single day in the life of a prisoner in a Stalinist labor camp in 1951. Ivan Denisovich Shukov is punished with three days in solitary confinement for not getting out of bed, but the threat is idle, and he only has to wash a floor before being taken back to breakfast. As the day goes on, the reader gains insight into the workers' suffering and companionship, and the uneasy coexistence between the prisoners and guards. At the end of the day, Ivan is lucky to be rewarded with a few extra mouthfuls of food from another inmate and thanks God for getting him through another day. This day, we find out at the end, is just one out of 3,653 of Ivan's prison existence. Ivan is an unlikely protagonist for Russian literature of this time, being a peasant, a normal man, and possibly illiterate. He represents the uneducated and persecuted mainstream of Soviet society. Despite his background, however, Ivan develops an inner dignity as he builds some meaning out of his mundane and degrading camp existence, transcending his surroundings with a spiritual intensity. Throughout, the story reverberates with the desperate dehumanization of the prisoners; the unjust punishments and arbitrary rules that reduce men to mere numbers. Yet despite the degradation a hope rings out as the twin strengths of camaraderie and faith help the men to survive.

Solzhenitsyn was arrested in 1945 for criticizing Stalin in a private letter, spending eight years of his life in labor camps similar to the one he describes here. In 1962, he became famous with this novel's publication, a landmark event in the history of Soviet literature. This memorable work was the first public recognition of the existence of the labor camps and the hideous conditions endured by their inmates. **EF**

The Third Wedding

Costas Taktsis

Lifespan | *b.* 1927 (Greece), *d.* 1988
First Published | 1963
First Published by | Self-published
Original Title | *To trito stefani*

This is the story of two Athenian women, Nina and Ekavi, in the mid twentieth century, focussing especially on Nina's three weddings. We see how they become friends and how they respond to major historical events in Greece before and after the Second World War, including the German occupation and the Civil War. The narration ends in the early 1960s with Nina's third marriage. The adventures and sufferings of the characters are based on how ordinary Greeks experienced war, crime, loyalty, betrayal, and love, and the narration is transformed into an allegory of life itself.

Costas Taktsis uses simple but not simplistic language, enriching his extended monologues with everyday words and idioms in a vibrant and highly recognizable writing style. The language he uses is reminiscent of the vaudeville and folk cinema of Greece in the 1950s and '60s. The narration, consisting of numerous stories intertwined inextricably with each other and apparently without organization, seems to be written seamlessly with a single stroke of the pen.

The book offers far too much information on modern Greece, but Taktsis presents his story in an easygoing way, capturing the important minor details of Greek life. Inspired by ordinary people's fortunes and misfortunes, *The Third Wedding* is a celebration of life as experienced by everyone. To this end, Taktsis is a master artist who is able to silence himself in order to let life speak. **SMy**

Dog Years

Günter Grass

Lifespan | *b.* 1927 (Poland)
First Published | 1963, by Luchterhand (Neuwied)
Original Title | *Hundejahre*
Nobel Prize for Literature | 1999

The third novel in Günter Grass's Danzig trilogy, completing the sequence begun by *The Tin Drum* and *Cat and Mouse*, *Dog Years* continues the author's critical examination of recent German history. Once again, the unnerving perspective of unnaturally grown-up children is exploited to cast a subversive light upon the adult world, although the text grows to embrace a far wider range of viewpoints.

The foundation of the narrative is the prewar childhood friendship of Walter Matern with the artistic scarecrow-maker Eddie Amsel in Danzig. As the work expands and diversifies in a riot of stories and stories-within-stories, the theme of the friends' relationship remains its structural backbone. Other narrative lines take over the foreground, including the tale of the epistolary lover Harry Liebenau and of the dog Prinz, who becomes Adolf Hitler's favorite hound. Prinz's escape from the Führer's Berlin bunker is one of the book's comic highlights.

Dog Years is even more daring than its predecessors in its repetitive intertwining of myth, fact, and fantasy. Its experimentation with language, including parodies of the tortured diction of German philosopher Heidegger ("The final struggle of the German people will be conducted with regard to the Nothing attuned to distantiality."), are often very funny, but end up clouding the point of Grass's complex and surreal vision. The result is a bloated, often frustrating book, yet overflowing with humor, fresh ideas, and narrative surprises. **RegG**

The Bell Jar

Sylvia Plath

Lifespan | *b.* 1932 (U.S.), *d.* 1963 (England)
First Published | 1963
First Published by | W. Heinemann (London)
Pseudonym | Victoria Lucas

Casually described by Sylvia Plath in a letter to her mother as a "pot boiler," *The Bell Jar* has become one of the most notorious depictions of a mental breakdown in American literature. First published in 1963 under the pseudonym Victoria Lucas, the novel provides a thinly disguised autobiographical account of Plath's teenage years. It covers the life of Esther, from her spell as a guest editor of a teen magazine to her failed suicide attempt and the crude care of mid-twentieth-century American psychiatry.

Initially celebrated for its dry self-deprecation and ruthless honesty, *The Bell Jar* is now read as a damning critique of 1950s social politics. Plath makes clear connections between Esther's dawning awareness of the limited female roles available to her and her increasing sense of isolation and paranoia. The contradictory expectations imposed upon women in relation to sexuality, motherhood, and intellectual achievement are linked to Esther's sense of herself as fragmented. Esther's eventual recovery relies on her ability to dismiss the dominant versions of femininity that populate the novel. Yet concern with the stifling atmosphere of 1950s America is not limited to examination of gender. The opening sentence—"It was a queer sultry summer, the summer they electrocuted the Rosenbergs"—very precisely locates the novel in Cold War McCarthyism and makes implicit connections between Esther's experiences and the other paranoias and betrayals that characterized the decade. **NM**

Inside Mr. Enderby

Anthony Burgess

Lifespan | *b.* 1917 (England), *d.* 1993
First Published | 1963
First Published by | W. Heinemann (London)
Pseudonym | Joseph Kell

This novel, the first in a trilogy, makes the case for Anthony Burgess as the preeminent comic novelist of the 1960s and 1970s, succeeding Waugh and surpassing Kingsley Amis. Burgess's substance and staying power derive from an intense interest in language, both literary and spoken, and from inspired technical ingenuity. Burgess's ear for pub speech, for example, permits verbal misunderstandings to develop into startling outcomes, always to the disadvantage of the baffled, too-talkative but tough-minded poet Enderby. Inside Mr. Enderby are his guts. He farts and belches incessantly, the exact sounds carefully transcribed by Burgess, a connoisseur of wind. The body's disgustingness is evoked in Rabelaisian mode, as is the domestic filth in which Enderby lives. His other "inside" is his poetry, written with trousers down on the toilet. A series of accidents leads from poetry to marriage to a mental hospital. An epigraph from Jules Laforgue ("Tout le monde est dehors") indicates he should get out more, so *Enderby Outside* appeared in 1968. The trilogy was completed in *A Clockwork Testament* (1974).

Burgess writes as a Catholic, and guilt about sex and masturbation are pervasive, as is an innocent prefeminist satire of women. Near death, Enderby's bodily eructations return in language of astonished disgust: "Enderby was suffocated by smells: sulphuretted hydrogen, unwashed armpits, halitosis, feces, standing urine, putrefying meat—all thrust into his mouth and nostrils in squelchy balls." **AMu**

The Girls of Slender Means

Muriel Spark

Lifespan | *b.* 1918 (Scotland), *d.* 2006 (Italy)
First Published | 1963
First Published by | Macmillan & Co. (London)
Shortened Version | *Saturday Evening Post* (1963)

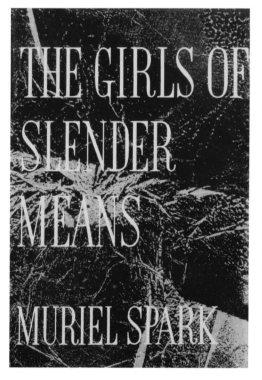

"Long ago in 1945 all the nice people of England were poor."

⊙ Although *The Girls of Slender Means* is set in London, Sparks was living in New York at the time when she wrote the novel.

Brilliantly constructed, this slender novel combines multiple ironies of tone with a series of allegorical levels of storytelling that develop the different narrative possibilities suggested by the title. Out of the adventures of several more or less slender young ladies coping with postwar austerity, Spark spins a remarkable reworking of Gerard Manley Hopkins's *The Wreck of the Deutschland*. That this unlikely model for an amusing short novel should figure so unobtrusively and effectively indicates some of the underlying seriousness with which Spark blends comic and religious levels of meaning. Apparently trivial details show up fundamentals, without any loss to the seductive surface of plotting and social wit.

Set in the ruins of London toward the end of the Second World War, the novel appears at first to engage a delightfully carefree world of girls living in a residential club for unmarried women and variously on the make. This circumscribed context provides an optic through which to view the wider historical context. Spark's satirical eye is quick to deflate the romantic purposes of youth, male and female, along with withering passages of brief literary pastiche. More than one girl becomes involved with a certain Nicholas Farringdon, and there is plenty of pith and verbal rapacity to amuse and delight. Amid rivalries and the development of peacetime corruption, the plot heads toward an apocalyptic conclusion. The way circumstances bring death suggests the virtues of staying slender, while reminding us that even in the midst of life we are in death, with all that this implies for reflections on mortality.

Less decisive readers might care to reflect on Spark's formal ingenuity in offering a metaphysical parable as rigorously well made as it is light and entertaining. A treat for the jaded literary palette. **DM**

The Spy Who Came in From the Cold

John Le Carré

Before John Le Carré, the British espionage novel was dominated by the dashing spy, a man of action, either amateur or professional, who reflects a confident civilization—a Richard Hannay or a James Bond. With *The Spy Who Came in From the Cold*, Le Carré introduces a much grimmer, antiheroic perspective, a world where there is no clear sense of the democratic West's moral superiority over the communist East.

Set largely in Cold War Germany, the novel is a story of deception at all levels. Dismayed by the East German intelligence service's success in capturing his agents, Lamas, who runs a British operation from Berlin, agrees to become a double agent so that he can sow confusion in East German intelligence by proposing that its head is in the pay of the British. According to plan, Lamas becomes dissolute, leaves "the Service"—Britain's overseas intelligence agency MI6—and is eventually recruited by the East Germans in the hope of obtaining information about British operations. Part of the book's quality is Le Carré's ability to convey the shabby, unglamorous world of the spy while maintaining a wonderful sense of tension and intrigue. Spying here is an elaborate game, a complex operation of trying to outwit the opposition. What is reality and what constructed fantasy remains unclear. In fact, Lamas, too, discovers that he is actually a pawn in a larger game.

What elevates this book beyond the superior thriller is its critique of the intelligence services' cynical manipulation of their own citizens in playing espionage games, questioning what they are supposed to be protecting. The human cost is high, and it is never obvious that there is any real intelligence to be obtained. Lamas's ultimate recognition of this, and his refusal to abandon an innocent girl, leads to his death. **TH**

Lifespan | *b.* 1931 (England)
First Published | 1963
First Published by | V. Gollancz (London)
Given Name | David John Moore Cornwell

"What do you think spies are: priests, saints, and martyrs?"

David Cornwell, better known as spy novelist John Le Carré, gives the camera a suitably stern and suspicious look in 1967.

Manon des Sources

Marcel Pagnol

Originally published as a two-part novel, *Jean de Florette* and *Manon des Sources* present an epic tragedy involving three generations of Provençal peasants. Cesar Soubeyran and his nephew, Ugolin, are all that is left of a family cursed with a history of misfortune. To Cesar, known as Papet, the rather simple Ugolin is the last supreme hope of the Soubeyran race. When a hunchback from the city inherits a nearby farm, Papet's exceptional talent for connivance and deception is mobilized. Conscious that acquiring the farm would be a means of restoring wealth and distinction to the Souberyan name, the uncle and nephew patiently plot to bring about the interloper's downfall. The hunchback's daughter, Manon, grows up in the time between the novel's two parts. Ugolin falls desperately in love with her, but, far from returning his love, her heart is set passionately on avenging the ill treatment of her father. The repercussions of unrequited love ensue, but it is not only Ugolin who suffers this fate.

Marcel Pagnol was born in the hills near Marseille where the novel is set. He spent long summer holidays in the region as a child, among the people who were to inspire his novel's characters. His story is interspersed with entertaining detours, offering vignettes of lives long steeped in the peasant tradition. Best known, in France at least, as a filmmaker and a playwright, it was perhaps Pagnol's awareness of the visual that allowed his simple prose style in *Jean de Florette* and *Manon des Sources* to be translated so beautifully into two successful movies by Claude Berri. Starring Daniel Auteuil, Emmanuelle Béart, Gérard Depardieu, and Yves Montand, these movies provide great accompaniments to the novel, but when it comes to a picture of rural French life, it is Pagnol's text that provides the richness of detail. **PM**

Lifespan | *b.* 1895 (France), *d.* 1974
First Published | 1963
First Published by | Editions de Provence (Paris)
Sequel to | *Jean de Florette*

"The spring no longer flowed."

⊙ Famous in France primarily as a playwright and a movie director, Pagnol is shown here with his wife, actress Jacqueline Bouvier.

◐ The bewitching Emmanuelle Béart plays Manon in Claude Berri's highly successful 1986 movie version of Pagnol's epic novel.

The Graduate

Charles Webb

Lifespan | *b.* 1939 (U.S.)
First Published | 1963
First Published by | New American Library (N.Y.)
Movie Adaptation Released | 1967

This 1963 novel is so much eclipsed by the 1967 movie with Anne Bancroft and Dustin Hoffman that we should recall that most of its iconic moments already exist in Webb's text. The advice to go into "plastics" does not, but the underwater diving-suit scene, Benjamin's embarrassment at booking a hotel room for sex, the un-naming of "Mrs. Robinson" (no first name), and Benjamin fighting off Elaine's parents and friends with a crucifix are all in the original. A mild attack on the values of the white American professional middle class, *The Graduate*, in both forms, has become a much admired populist satire.

Mrs. Robinson's alcoholism and silence might signal psychosis, but do not; Benjamin's post-university distress is short of existential dread; the malice of his parents and their friends is harmless in the face of true love. Written in the early 1960s, Webb's satire provided that necessary medium of social criticism on which the harder attitudes of the late 1960s were founded. As fiction, *The Graduate* is notable for its flat and understated but expressive prose. Much hinges on the difference between "What?" and "What." The question mark signals anguish or outrage and warns of imminent distress in personal relationships. "What" without the expected query makes a genuine inquiry of the other person and predicts positive consequences. At the iconic moment when Benjamin and Elaine escape from her wedding on the bus, she says "Benjamin?" and he replies "What." As the bus moves off no more is said. **AMu**

Cat's Cradle

Kurt Vonnegut, Jr.

Lifespan | *b.* 1922 (U.S.), *d.* 2007
First Published | 1963
First Published by | Holt, Rinehart & Winston (N.Y.)
Alternate Title | *Ice 9*

Felix Hoenikker, father of the A-bomb, is without sin. Rationality abjures abstracts such as morality; he is a man of hard science. Be it nuclear weapons or turtles, Hoenikker is a whirring brain needing occupation. Take away his turtles, and he can blow up Hiroshima. It is when hard science falls to soft humans that things get messy. But Hoenikker's "greatest" creation is Ice-nine, an isotope of water that freezes at room temperature, creating a chain reaction—like the A-bomb or the children's game of cat's cradle—elegant, never ending, and ultimately pointless. Whereas the A-bomb fell short of total annihilation, Ice-nine will do the trick. John, the narrator, while researching a book on the day the bomb was dropped on Hiroshima, stumbles across the Books of Bokonon. Bokonism baldly declares itself a bunch of "shameless lies"; truth plays no part in religion. The least it can do is offer some comfort. Vonnegut creates a religion in order to mock religion. He also targets technology, the big, destructive twentieth-century lie, which supplants it. The end of the world comes as a roaring whimper, the result of carelessness and laziness—technology and stupidity are a very dangerous alchemy indeed. In *Cat's Cradle*, Vonnegut reveals the meaning of life: there is none. But he is a master and can make even the end of the world funny. The serious implications come to us later, after we have our breath back. **GT**

> Kurt Vonnegut at home in 1969: a writer obsessed by memories of the destructiveness of war recollected in ironic tranquillity.

V.

Thomas Pynchon

Lifespan | *b*. 1937 (U.S.)
First Published | 1963
First Published by | Lippincott (Philadelphia)
William Faulkner Foundation Award | 1963

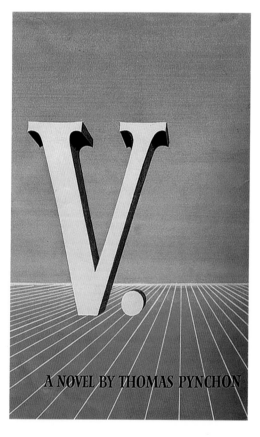

● The jacket of the first edition of *V.*, the novel that established Pynchon as an enigmatic cult hero of American literature.

V. marks the arrival of one of North America's most imaginative and challenging literary talents. The novel is constructed around two separate but interconnected narratives. The first of these concerns the ex-sailor Benny Profane, who bums his way around the eastern seaboard during the mid-1950s in search of odd jobs, kicks, and a sense of identity. In the course of his wanderings, Profane encounters a strange character named Herbert Stencil. Stencil is obsessed with the mysterious figure of V., a woman who manifests herself in different forms at violent flashpoints in twentieth-century history. Stencil's paranoid quest to decode the incarnations and abstractions of V.—who becomes less and less corporeal as the novel progresses—sets up an elaborate second narrative spanning the decades from 1880 to 1943. This wild, panoramic sweep takes in Egypt during the Fashoda crisis, rioting Venezuelan expatriates in Florence, the German occupation of south-west Africa, and much more.

Stencil is searching for a unifying order amid the violence and strife, what Pynchon calls "the century's master cabal," the "Plot Which Has No Name." But perhaps the real danger is to be found in the novel's "present"—a modern America profoundly transformed by the Second World War, about to hit boiling point through the social and cultural revolutions of the 1960s. *V.* establishes many of the themes that continue to occupy Pynchon: the use and abuse of power, the patterns of historiography, the status of marginalized communities, and altered states of perception. It is grandiose, architectural writing, yet also intimate and humane. *V.* recalls Joyce, Beckett, Kafka, and European Surrealism, but ultimately coheres into a remarkable, entirely new kind of contemporary American writing. **SamT**

Herzog

Saul Bellow

The novel that made Saul Bellow's name as a literary best seller is a comedy of manners and ideas, loss and partial redemption. The cuckolded academic Moses Herzog is neurotically restless, a pathological condition that notably manifests itself in his habit of composing unsent letters to the great and good of past and present times ("Dear Doktor Professor Heidegger, I should like to know what you mean by the expression 'the fall into the quotidian.' When did this fall occur?"). We follow Herzog's musings on the events that have brought him to this state, most notably his amatory betrayal at the hands of his former friend, Valentine Gersbach, and we follow him physically as he heads into Chicago for an abortive attempt at bloody revenge. Typically, he ends up arrested for possessing a firearm instead; however, in the process, we find, something may have begun to fall back into place in his life ("At this time he had no messages for anyone").

Indeed, the phrase "no messages" could well provide the epigraph for Moses Herzog because, for all its overt intellectualizing, this is not a novel that offers convenient, formulaic meanings. Rather, *Herzog* works as a whole; we need to take in both Herzog the character's fretful inner life and his comic wanderings, as part of a larger exploration of the boundaries of human choice ("There is someone inside me. I am in his grip."). The power of Bellow's novel comes not only from his famously imaginative prose, but also from what such exercises of the mind can reveal; it is a testimony to *Herzog* that readers may find themselves thinking more in terms of what its characters are and do than what they "represent." Herzog comes to recognize how life is always bigger than the shapes we impose on it, and, in following him, we may have a parallel experience. **BT**

Lifespan | *b.* 1915 (Canada), *d.* 2005 (U.S.)
First Published | 1964
First Published by | Viking Press (New York)
National Book Award | 1965

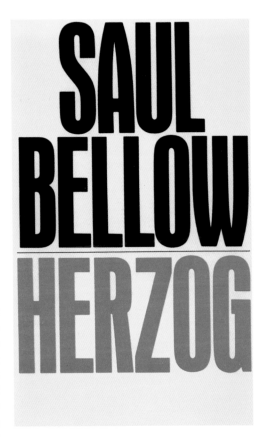

A U.S. edition of Bellow's novel—the name of the eponymous protagonist means "prince" in German.

The Ravishing of Lol V. Stein

Marguerite Duras

Lifespan | *b.* 1914 (Vietnam), *d.* 1996 (France)
First Published | 1964
First Published by | Gallimard (Paris)
Original Title | *Le Ravissement de Lol V. Stein*

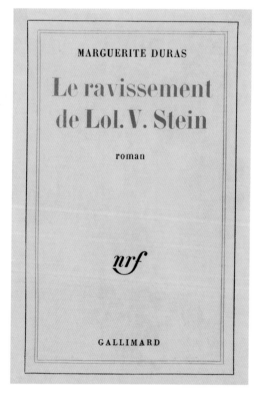

MARGUERITE DURAS

Le ravissement de Lol. V. Stein

roman

nrf

GALLIMARD

"Lol was funny, an inveterate wit, and very bright . . ."

⊙ A prominent figure in Parisian intellectual circles, Duras wrote the script for Alain Resnais's classic 1959 movie *Hiroshima, Mon Amour.*

Lol Stein is nineteen years old, and the stuff of local legend. She is engaged to Michael Richardson, we are told by an anonymous narrator, when into the ballroom step two strikingly beautiful women, Anne-Marie Stretter and her daughter. Richardson is transfixed, abandons Lol, and spends the rest of the night dancing in the arms of Anne-Marie Stretter, while Lol looks on. At dawn, the couple leave the ballroom, and Lol lets out a cry. One question that haunts the remainder of the novel is whether the events at the ball constituted a moment of rapture for Lol, or whether in fact it was rupture.

The action starts long after Lol's recovery from her supposed trauma, when she is married with three children and has recently returned to her home. She starts to run over the ball in her mind, then begins to orchestrate a repetition of the night's events: this time she is the outsider, and the unwitting couple are her old friend, Tatiana, and her lover, Jack Hold (who only now reveals himself as the narrator). Jack falls hopelessly in love with Lol, but, rather than urge him to leave Tatiana, she persuades him to keep on loving her, pushing all three beyond the usual economies of desire.

For psychoanalysts, the love triangle always contains rivals and can be resolved only by the elimination of one of them. Interestingly, Duras herself was involved in a ménage à trois with her husband, the poet Robert Antelme, and Dionys Mascolo; when Duras had Mascolo's child, Antelme (who also had a lover or two) eventually left, but that relationship was not to last either. Duras's novel explores the possibility of moving beyond this: the possibility of maintaining desire without rivalry. In doing so, it offers its readers one of the most powerful anti-Oedipal myths of recent times. **PT**

Arrow of God

Chinua Achebe

Set in Nigeria in 1921, this novel tells how the elderly Ezeulu, an Ibo community's polygamous high priest, endeavors to adapt to the power of the white colonial officials (whose black messenger terms him "witch-doctor"). In a bitter comedy of errors, an attempt by a well-meaning English District Officer to declare him an accredited chieftain results in his humiliation by a white deputy and his black emissary. Thereafter, Ezeulu seeks to humiliate his community by post-poning an impending harvest day; the people then turn away from him to the Christian mission, which encourages timely harvesting. Ezeulu withdraws into "the haughty splendor of a demented high priest."

The interest of *Arrow of God* lies partly in the novel's subtle plotting and largely in the vivid rendering of the complexities of the evolving indigenous society. We see how diversely the people respond to the challenges of colonialism. Ezeulu's community maintains traditional celebrations and intimate rituals, but also sanctions the ubiquitous exploitation of women by men; lepers are scorned; its religion veers between the profoundly intuitive and the superstitiously silly. Chinua Achebe's intelligent objectivity extends to the British community, too. If one official is naïvely arrogant, another tries to be fair-minded. If the English colonialists cause cultural disruption, they also terminate tribal warfare and build schools, roads, and hospitals. Achebe reminds us that British imperialism, however culpable, was far more constructive than the African imperialism of the nineteenth-century Benin dynasty.

Achebe writes with wit, humor, sharp realism, and imaginative empathy. His prose is refreshingly original, pungently spiced with translated idioms ("Unless the penis dies young it will surely eat bearded meat"), and coolly ironic. **CW**

Lifespan | *b.* 1930 (Nigeria)
First Published | 1964
First Published by | W. Heinemann (London)
Peace Prize of the German Book Trade | 2002

"What kind of power was it if it was never to be used?"

The "arrow" of the title refers to Ezeulu's image of himself as an arrow in the bow of his god, representing his will on Earth.

Three Trapped Tigers

Guillermo Cabrera Infante

Lifespan | b. 1929 (Cuba), d. 2005 (Britain)
First Published | 1964
First Published by | Seix-Barral (Barcelona)
Original Title | Tres tristes tigres

This, Infante's first novel, was awarded a prize in Spain in 1964 but was only published in 1967 after censorship; the complete version did not appear until 2005. Its defining title was a tongue-twister: a verbal display and an argumental hieroglyphic. It is the story of a ferocious melancholy fought with resourceful blows. But the protagonists are not the many people who wander through a leafy night, but their multiple voices. Translation tangles with the adventures of five friends (Cué, Códac, Silvestre, Eribó, and Bustrófedon) and the women they meet in the Havana of the 1950s, while change—loyal or deceptive—is the novel's subject and its method.

On the thread of a psychoanalytical session (a history of a singer of boleros and the nocturnal wanderings of two other characters), the book is constructed like a collage and a palimpsest, studded with written and oral monologues, stories that stand independently, and continuous open or hidden allusions to literature, music, and the cinema. The novel is a baroque literary display that enunciates its own poetry: ingenious wordplay, parodies of styles applied to historic events (such as the death of Trotsky), typographical experiments (pages in black, in white, or printed in mirror-image, with drawings). *Three Trapped Tigers* takes its genre toward a more complicated pattern, placing it in the avant-garde of the renewal of narrative fiction in the 1960s. **DMG**

Sometimes a Great Notion

Ken Kesey

Lifespan | b. 1935 (U.S.), d. 2001
First Published | 1964
First Published by | Viking Press (New York)
Movie Adaptation Released | 1971

Ken Kesey's second novel is a text that defines a period of twentieth-century U.S. history with originality, passion, and skill. Set in and around an Oregon logging camp, it explores the dynamics of one family, the Stampers, at odds with their town, at odds with their union, and—most of the time—at odds with each other. The tale revolves around the conflict between two brothers, Hank and Leland, two competing versions of manhood, played out in an environment redolent of the American frontier. Hank is big, brash, committed, and used to running the place, and the narrative begins with a conflict with the trade union. His younger half brother Leland then arrives, an East Coast college-educated dope smoker. Leland is unwilling to conform to Hank's straightforward rough-and-ready notion of manhood, or to his family's expectations. Kesey skillfully explores the dynamics of their relationship—their similarities, respect, and loyalty, and their destructive differences, particularly when competing in love. This is made all the more powerful as he switches between narrators, countering initial sympathies for Leland by showing the depths of Hank's struggle for the family and his own peace of mind.

An exploration of the American Dream and a fable of man pitted against nature, community, and big business, the novel is an important and unjustly neglected classic of American literature. **MD**

The Passion According to G. H.

Clarice Lispector

Lifespan | b. 1920 (Ukraine), d. 1977 (Brazil)
First Published | 1964
First Published by | Editôra do Autor (Rio)
Original Title | A paixão segundo G. H.

Ukranian-born Clarice Lispector lived in Brazil and wrote in Portuguese, but this work took more than twenty years to be translated into English. *The Passion According to G. H.* could hardly be considered conventional. To describe it using the language of plot and characterization would make little sense; in fact, it reads more like an existential inquiry than a narrative. For this reason, it is also a text that calls for careful, thoughtful reading, one that challenges and invites its reader, posing and exploring some of the fundamental questions that more normally appear in the often dry prose of philosophers.

The protagonist, known to us only as G. H. from the initials on her luggage, is propelled into a whirlpool of thoughts and emotions when she enters the room of her former maid, who has left a curious drawing on the wall. Further to the feelings that this evokes for G. H., there is an encounter with a dying cockroach, which becomes a central symbolic image around which the narrative sweepingly circles. Each chapter is beautifully linked through the repetition at the start of the previous section's final line, and the writing has the feel of a deeply personal internal monologue, encompassing questions and disquisitions on love and living, on the role of the past, and that of the future. Addressed to a personalized and also mysteriously undefined "you," this is a very intimate reading experience. **JC**

Back to Oegstgeest

Jan Wolkers

Lifespan | b. 1925 (Netherlands)
First Published | 1965
First Published by | Meulenhoff (Amsterdam)
Original Title | Terug naar Oegstgeest

A major theme in Jan Wolkers's works is sex. It serves not only as an escape, but also as a compensation for loneliness. Explicit sexual scenes are typical of his works and this characteristic has often drawn criticism. Other predominant themes are love of nature and criticism of religion.

All Wolkers's major themes converge in his autobiographical novel *Back to Oegstgeest*, which begins by describing his youth and first steps into the adult world. The narrator grows up in a family of ten children. The father is a strict Dutch Reformed Church grocery owner from the village of Oegstgeest; three times a day, he reads the Bible to his family. As a young man, the narrator has various jobs. Working as an animal keeper in a laboratory, he witnesses tests carried out by students on the animals. Later events are his brother's death and his life during the Second World War. The narrator's experiences with mortality coincide with his awakening sexuality and loss of faith.

Despite the protagonist's many setbacks and several horrific scenes, *Back to Oegstgeest* never condemns life. What makes the novel so captivating is the narrator's almost dogged attempt to retrieve a bygone world. The result is an impressive and evocative portrait of the prewar era, including kettles, steam trains, swimsuits for men, and grocery shops, served with a Calvinistic dressing. **JaM**

Closely Watched Trains

Bohumil Hrabal

Lifespan | *b.* 1914 (Moravia), *d.* 1997 (Czech Rep.)
First Published | 1965, by Ceskoslovensky spisovatel (Prague)
Original Title | *Ostre sledované vlaky*

In *Closely Watched Trains*, Hrabal tells the story of Milos Hrma, a gauche young apprentice working at a railway station in Bohemia in 1945. The Second World War is grinding to an end, and Milos has just come back from an enforced sabbatical brought about by his slashing his wrists. A sensitive young man, Milos is preoccupied by his inability to consummate his love for his girlfriend, Masha.

The novel describes the events of a day that will culminate in the acting out, by Milos and a colleague, of a plot intended to sabotage a passing German train. Despite his protagonist's dislike of the Germans, Hrabal emphasizes the human as well as the warlike character of the German soldiers traveling through the town. Milos is surprised that two SS soldiers on a train look as though they could be poets or men of leisure. He then sees a wounded German soldier crying for the mother of his children and recognizes the threads that connect people, whether they are Czechs or Germans.

The war, followed by the normalization of culture under Communist rule, meant that Hrabal, once a poet, was forty-nine before he had his first breakthrough as a writer of prose. *Closely Watched Trains*, told with a rare humor and humanity, is one of the finest examples of his craft. It was made into an Oscar-winning film in 1967 by Jirí Menzel. **OR**

🔵 In 1992 Czech photographer Miroslav Zajic ironically posed the ageing Hrabal as a gimcrack emperor on a Prague park bench.

The River Between

Ngugi wa Thiong'o

Lifespan | *b.* 1938 (Kenya)
First Published | 1965
First Published by | Heinemann Education (Lon.)
Original Language | English

The River Between, Ngugi's second novel, established his reputation as a major African writer. At one level, this is a simple love story set in the mid-colonial period, an African *Romeo and Juliet* in which two young people from opposing Gikuyu villages fall in love and attempt to transcend the ancient rift between their communities, with tragic results. On a more complex level, the novel engages with Kenya's precolonial and colonial history. It depicts the slow but steady infiltration of the country by the British; the alienation of local people from their land; the negative effects of Christian mission on local power structures, rituals, and relationships; and the deep disunity between different African factions that preceded the anticolonial struggle of the 1950s.

Centrally, the novel engages in the debate about female circumcision and reconciling this practice with Christian and European ones. Circumcision comes to symbolize Gikuyu cultural purity and anticolonial resistance to such an extent that the "unclean" status of the young heroine, Nyambura, seals the lovers' fate. In spite of its tragic consequences, circumcision is shown to be an important element of Kenyan national identity, a vital ritual in the face of colonial incursions and an increasingly absolute Christian education system. In describing the mythological origins of the Gikuyu people, and in setting his story in Kenyan hills as yet untouched by colonialism, Ngugi works to preserve African cultural differences within the English-language novel. **SN**

Garden, Ashes

Danilo Kis

Lifespan | *b.* 1935 (Serbia), *d.* 1989 (France)
First Published | 1965
First Published by | Prosveta (Belgrade)
Original Title | *Basta, pepeo*

"In her passionate brush with death, she had come to know the secret of everlasting life."

◉ Sophie Bassouls photographed Danilo Kis in Paris in 1985; the Yugoslavian writer spent the last ten years of his life in France.

Garden, Ashes is a remarkable portrayal of a middle-class Hungarian family during the Second World War. Seen through the eyes of the youngest son, Andi Scham, the story is focused on Andi's Jewish father, Eduard, as the family travels through Europe in order to escape persecution. A deeply eccentric and flamboyant character, Eduard is captivating and enigmatic, but also plagued by alcoholism and bouts of depression. As he becomes obsessed with the completion of his book, the third edition of the *Bus, Ship, Rail, and Air Travel Guide*, his behavior becomes increasingly erratic. It is not clear whether the cause is the burden of war, the pressures of their bizarre transient existence, or genuine madness.

Danilo Kis's dense and poetic prose is rich in detail as he explores Andi's childhood recollections. The narrative contains such intense and powerful evocations of childhood that often the story seems to slip into lyrical verse. But Eduard eventually disappears, and it is assumed that he has been despatched to a concentration camp.

Garden, Ashes, Kis's first novel, is a semi-autobiographical work—his own father was a Hungarian Jew who died at Auschwitz in 1944 when Kis was a child. However, the novel is not merely an account of the Second World War as a whole or of the Holocaust: its appeal is more universal. Auschwitz and concentration camps, incomprehensible to the young Andi, are never mentioned. The exhilaration and wonder of Andi's childhood experiences, although overshadowed by poverty and war, are far more vivid to him, and to us, than the family's wartime struggle. *Garden, Ashes* is a poignant story about a family living on the periphery of war, and a child's attempt to understand the world around him and to cope with the loss of his father. **RA**

Everything That Rises Must Converge

Flannery O'Connor

Like the sweet rot of fallen magnolia blooms, volatile notions of class and color, generational schisms, and convictions of belief permeate these stories, which rise from a time when the genteel South still tenuously hung onto outdated conventions and prejudices. This is a Manichean world full of grotesques and eruptions of unexpected cruelty. Characters rise and converge, through civil rights and through religious clarity. With the rising comes knowledge, but with the convergence comes collision—with old ideas, unexamined self-images, and the harsh light of truth. These are stories of dangerous epiphanies; sometimes finding grace is not a pleasant thing. And sometimes to find God you have to take a bullet in the chest, get thrashed with a broom, or get gored through the heart by a bull.

In one story, on a newly integrated bus, Julian, educated and stricken with class guilt, takes his mother to her slimming class at the "Y." She is mired in tradition and prejudice, and tension mounts when a black woman, with her own son, boards wearing the same new hat. Julian is so blinded by rage when his mother gives the black boy a penny that he cannot see her tragic chastening. In another story, Mrs. Turpin, self-righteous and superior, believes "it's one thing to be ugly and another to act ugly" and falls asleep at night by naming the classes of people. When she is throttled by a woman in a doctor's waiting room, she must contend with the idea that revelations can crumble the safety of the world.

Flannery O'Connor is, in turn, funny, trenchant, and brutal. The ignorant are punished; the well-intentioned even more so because of their insufficient strength to act. Her genius lies in writing profoundly moral stories where it is up to the reader to decide between right and wrong. **GT**

Lifespan | *b.* 1925 (U.S.), *d.* 1964
First Published | 1965
First Published by | Farrar, Straus & Giroux (N.Y.)
Full Name | Mary Flannery O'Connor

"The door closed and he turned to find the dumpy figure coming towards him."

○ *Everything That Rises Must Converge* was O'Connor's last work, pulling together many religious and social themes from her earlier fiction.

Things

Georges Perec

Lifespan | b. 1936 (France), d. 1982
First Published | 1965, by Julliard (Paris)
Original Title | *Les Choses: Une Histoire des années soixante*

Already the author of four unfinished and rejected novels when he erupted onto the literary scene in 1965, Georges Perec won the Renaudot prize for *Things: A Story of the Sixties*, his first published novel. The book recounts the intellectual decline of a young and likable couple of sociologists, Jerôme and Sylvie. Their search for happiness, promoted and stimulated by an affluent society, imperceptibly transforms them into a frustrated and resigned middle-class couple.

The story shocked the public, who saw in the novel a purely sociological representation of the so-called "consumer" society—not an appropriate subject for a work of literature. By his own admission, Perec wanted to describe the evolution of his own social milieu—that of the students who had fiercely opposed France's vicious war with Algeria and had become disillusioned and indifferent to politics by the war's end. He also wanted to bring literary theorist Roland Barthes's *Mythologies* (1957), in which Barthes used semiological concepts in the analysis of myths and signs in contemporary culture, to bear on his writing.

The unusual character of *Things* is due in great part to the coldness of the narrator-witness, who refuses to criticize, to judge, and to interpret the attitude of the protagonists. He merely records the things that they covet and accumulate in their apartment, describing them like "signs" or "images," by means of advertising formulas. **JD**

In Cold Blood

Truman Capote

Lifespan | b. 1924 (U.S.), d. 1984
First Published | 1966
First Published by | Random House (New York)
Full Name | Truman Streckfus Persons

Capote's most famous work is a pioneering example of both the "nonfiction novel" and the modern "true crime" story. It retells the story of the 1959 murders of the Clutter family in Kansas by a pair of drifting misfits, Dick Hickock and Perry Smith, and of the subsequent trial and execution of the killers. Capote also uses the polarities of this particular case as the starting point for a larger examination of the values of late 1950s and early 1960s America; the respectable Clutters are so wholesomely all-American that they could almost have been invented, while Smith and Hickock come over as brutal real life versions of the James Dean "rebel" culture. The world of the victims is painstakingly and sympathetically reconstructed, but Capote's real interest is in the emotional lives of Perry and Dick, and what might have led them into such murderous excess. Indeed, some argue that Capote was so fascinated by Perry Smith because he saw in him a possible alternative version of himself. Given that Capote wrote about the crime throughout the trial, it has even been suggested that the final verdicts were conditioned by the way in which his journalism had portrayed the killers. In this light, *In Cold Blood* offers a larger, more disturbing insight. Like Mailer's *The Executioner's Song* (1979), it embodies a debate about fact, fiction, and the overlaps and differences between their ethical responsibilities. **BT**

❯ A window display set up by Random House, Capote's publisher, in 1966 reflects the scale of the media interest his book aroused.

LIFE
MURDER SPAWNS
A MASTERPIECE
WEALTHY FARMER, 3 OF FAMILY SLAIN
HORROR SPAWNS A MASTERPIEC
Book Review
SAS FARM
BOOKS TODAY
4 Meaningless Murders,
In Cold Blood
SELECTED WRITINGS
The Muses
In Cold Blood
Truman Capote
In Cold Blood
Truman Capote

Death and the Dervish

Mesa Selimovic

Lifespan | *b.* 1910 (Bosnia), *d.* 1982 (Serbia)
First Published | 1966
First Published by | Svjetlost (Sarajevo)
Original Title | *Dervis i smrt*

Sheikh Ahmed Nuruddin is a dervish (an Islamic ascetic) in Ottoman-occupied Bosnia. He has lived most of his life in religious seclusion and it is his internal monologue that makes up a great deal of Mesa Selimovic's epic novel. Ahmed's deliberate avoidance of the turmoil of everyday life is put to an end by the arrest and subsequent death of his brother toward the beginning of the novel. This death leads him to question previous certainties and brings him into conflict with the local authorities. He becomes part of the political system himself and, unable to act decisively, comes to an unhappy end.

Death and the Dervish contains little dialog and Selimovic tells his seemingly sparse story through the voice of the highly introspective Ahmed. Occasionally exasperating, Ahmed is thankfully supported by a delightfully eccentric cast of supporting characters, including his friend Hassan, the family oddball who also happens to be in love with a Dalmatian Christian.

Selimovic, whose written Serbo-Croat greatly influenced today's Bosnian standard language, poured a great deal of the turmoil he felt over his own brother's death into the novel. While he also drew on the political events of his day in his work, *Death and the Dervish* is an invocation of another time that, in its Kafkaesque portrayal of a man sucked in and destroyed by a repressive system, addresses universal themes that go beyond Selimovic's troubled homeland. **OR**

Silence

Shusaku Endo

Lifespan | *b.* 1923 (Japan), *d.* 1996
First Published | 1966
First Published by | Kodansha (Tokyo)
Original Title | *Chimmoku*

Novelist Shusaku Endo was a cultural oddity: a Japanese Catholic. Influenced by European Catholic novelists such as Graham Greene and Georges Bernanos, his work expresses an anguished faith on the edge of disbelief, as well as a horror at the dark thread of cruelty running through Japanese history.

Silence, set in the early seventeenth century, is widely acknowledged as Endo's masterpiece. The Japanese shogunate has embarked on the ruthless extirpation of Christianity by torture and massacre. News reaches the Vatican that a highly respected Jesuit missionary, Father Ferreira, has renounced the faith under duress. Portuguese priest Sebastian Rodrigues, who regards Ferreira as his spiritual mentor, is sent to Japan to contact him. It is a risky mission that soon goes awry. Betrayed to the authorities by the Judas-like Kichijiro, Rodrigues is imprisoned and tortured. To save himself he must symbolically renounce his faith by treading on an image of Christ. When he refuses, the authorities begin martyring other Christians in front of his eyes. Rodrigues eventually meets Ferreira, who urges him to make an act of apparent apostasy.

The spare and dramatic narrative unfolds with stark power the horrors of persecution and the bitterness of the priest's dilemma. In Rodrigues, Endo succeeds in depicting a good man who is wholly credible and likeable, embodying the author's vision of a Christianity focussed on the suffering of Jesus rather than his glory. **RegG**

To Each His Own

Leonardo Sciascia

Lifespan | b. 1921 (Sicily), d. 1989
First Published | 1966, by Adelphi Edizioni (Milan)
Alternate Title | A Man's Blessing
Original Title | A ciascuno il suo

Leonardo Sciascia grew up in Sicily under the influence of Fascism. Beginning his career as a schoolteacher, he later became one of Italy's most controversial politicians and eventually a Radical Party MP in the Italian and European Parliaments. A love of his homeland and loathing of organized crime and political corruption would become driving inspirational forces in his writings.

In *To Each His Own*, a small-town chemist named Manno receives a death threat in the mail and, writing it off as a joke, is subsequently murdered together with his hunting companion, Dr. Roscio. The investigation focuses on Manno's death, with Dr. Roscio being declared an innocent bystander. Professor Laurana, a local schoolteacher, sets out to solve the mystery after coming across a disregarded clue. His investigation begins to bear fruit but his findings prove problematic. In a twist of fate, it turns out to be the chemist who was the unlucky bystander and Roscio who becomes the center of Laurana's investigation. With a skillful eye and a bit of cunning, Laurana persistently and systematically breaks down and unravels a network of erotic deception and skillful political calculation.

A detective story that seeks to understand the psychological grip and far-reaching influences of the never mentioned but always implied Cosa Nostra, or Mafia, *To Each His Own* is also a poignant critique of a society steeped in a tradition of silence and fueled by lies, complicity, and bloodshed. **SMu**

"To get involved in politics was a waste of time; if you didn't know that much, either you found politicking profitable or you'd been born blind. "

⊙ Suitably for a novelist from Sicily, island of the Mafia, Sciascia specialized in mystery stories where crime and politics intersect.

The Crying of Lot 49

Thomas Pynchon

Lifespan | *b.* 1937 (U.S.)
First Published | 1966
First Published by | Lippincott (Philadelphia)
Rosenthal Foundation Award | 1966

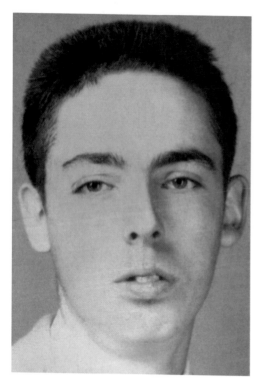

"The reality is in this head. Mine."

⬤ Thomas Pynchon in 1955: his determined refusal of all publicity means that only a few photos of the author are known to exist.

Joyously brief compared with the rather too-drawn-out literary pyrotechnics of Pynchon's longer novels, this is the postmodernist's perfect thriller, guaranteed to fox the literal-minded sleuth, while deliciously deft with its play of possible interpretations. Where many sophisticated novels resist plot summary because plot is an entirely secondary concern, this confection weaves a rich tapestry of narrative threads.

As befits a novel with a protagonist called Oedipa, this box of puzzles wears its enigmas with the smile of a sphinx. Set somewhere approximating California, the book's names work both as clues and as a comedy of connotations. From bands called Sick Dick and the Volkswagens to a cast of characters that includes Mike Fallopian, Dr. Hilarius, Genghis Cohen, and Professor Emory Bortz, Pynchon strains the limits of literary invention. The names mirror the larger structure of narrative gaming, interweaving conspiracy theories, more structural social critique, and doses of slapstick, including spoof mop-top popsters, The Paranoids, and a pastiche Jacobean revenge tragedy. Pynchon's spoofs are researched to within an inch of plausibility. The Paranoids' lyrics, for example, are sufficiently convincing that the group begins to take on an imaginary existence as lifelike as that of their nonfictional prototypes. Oscillations between ideological absurdity and mediated superficiality sketch out a wasteland of seemingly empty but wildly proliferating signs, and the story careers from thought experiments to anarchist miracles.

As well as providing the idle dullness of stamp collectors with a most intriguing rationale, there is an almost Borgesian history of the modern world. The blueprint for a generation of clever-clever novels that combine highbrow and pop cultural sensibilities, this is the one with which to start. **DM**

Giles Goat-Boy

John Barth

Giles Goat-Boy opens with various publishers' written qualms (charting their various deteriorating mental states) and a faux cover letter that was attached to this orphan—if not feral—manuscript. Publishing is just one of the many targets for Barth's vitriolic comic genius; others are technology, sexual mores, jingoism, and the idea of the noble savage. It is giddy and profane, a ribald tilt-a-whirl packed tight with wit as dry as the academic density that it mocks.

The story concerns the journey of Billy Bockfuss, saved as a baby from the belly of a supercomputer and raised at the teat of a goat. With the turbulence of adolescence Billy grows ambivalent, not wanting to leave his beautiful goathood to become an uncertain, hairy-in-all-the-wrong-places human being. But the ewes are unresponsive, and his needs are as relentless as spring. He adopts life as a human, first as George the Undergraduate and finally as the messianic George the Heroic Grand Tutor, savior of New Tammany College. In a retelling, rife with odd usages and neologisms, of the myths and legends of humanity—from the New Testament to Cold War internecine politics—the entire language is corrupted, transmuted, a patois of academic terminology becoming the lingua franca. The campus becomes a microcosm of the world: the East Campus is the Soviet Union, the Great Founder is God Almighty, copulation is commencement exercise, and Enos Enoch is Jesus Christ. Academic verbiage is used as everyday colloquialisms; "flunk" is a multipurpose vulgarity (as in "flunk it" or "this flunking gate").

In Barth's hands the story becomes a living thing, like electricity. It is both a satire and a celebration of language, with phrases like succulent nuggets of hard candy: rich, delicious, to be savored. It is doubtful that it is like anything you have read before. **GT**

Lifespan | *b*. 1930 (U.S.)
First Published | 1966, by Doubleday (New York)
Full Title | *Giles Goat-Boy; or, The Revised New Syllabus*

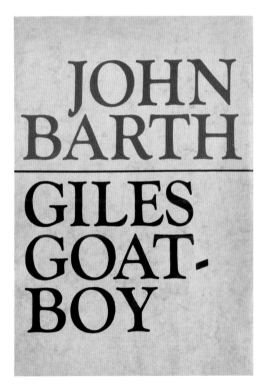

"George is my name; my deeds have been heard of ..."

⊛ Barth intended the name "Giles" to be pronounced with a hard "G," as he "liked the alliteration with the word 'Goat.'"

Marks of Identity

Juan Goytisolo

> "... we are made of stone and we will remain stone why do you blindly seek disaster forget about us and we will forget about you your birth was a mistake bear with it "

● Spanish author Goytisolo lives in Morocco; his work often celebrates the Muslim and Jewish roots of Spanish culture.

Lifespan | *b.* 1931 (Spain)
First Published | 1966
First Published by | Joaquín Mortiz (Mexico City)
Original Title | *Señas de identidad*

Three despairing thoughts open this novel: one by Quevedo ("Yesterday has gone, tomorrow has not yet come"), another by Larry, and a final one by Cernuda ("better yet, destruction, fire," which almost became the title of the novel). The main character, Álvaro Mendiola, who is Spanish, bourgeois, and anti-Franco, recounts his life as he finishes a bottle of Fefiñanes wine (it is summer and he is in the garden of his family house). Through his memory pass his childhood recollections of the civil war, his anti-Franco militancy, the Spanish resistance fighters whom he met in his exile in France, his experiences in the Cuban revolution (greatly cut in later editions, after the author's break with Castro), his eventful romantic life and its many breakups, his discovery of homosexuality, and his search for what little remained of the rebellious spirit in 1970s Spain.

Mendiola's interior monologue and sarcastic outbursts, the author's use of second-person narrative as an objectification of moral self-awareness, and even—in the final pages—the fluency of the poem in free verse all form a profound puzzle for the reader. The novel began a trilogy that continued with *Count Julian* (1970) and *Juan the Landless* (1975). Banned in Spain, *Marks of Identity* became the bible of a generation and a symbol of the author's break with the traditional, Catholic, repressive idea of his country. Applied to the need to know about the hidden past, its title became emblematic of Spain's political transition. **JCM**

The Vice-Consul

Marguerite Duras

Lifespan | b. 1914 (Vietnam), d. 1996 (France)
First Published | 1966
First Published by | Gallimard (Paris)
Original Title | Le Vice-Consul

The Vice-Consul might be categorized as a nouveau roman, in that it rejects conventions of realist fiction, such as morality and psychology, in favor of the visual description of action. Two stories emerge. The first depicts the solitary journey of a young Vietnamese peasant girl, who is turned out of her home by her mother when she becomes pregnant. The second revolves around several figures associated with the French Embassy in Calcutta, most notably the Vice-Consul of Lahore. The Vice-Consul creates a scandal that preoccupies the French diplomatic community when he fires gunshots indiscriminately at lepers and dogs living in the Shalimar gardens. He also falls in love with Anne-Marie Stretter, the Ambassador's enigmatic, promiscuous wife.

Duras's minimalist style handles issues of love, sexual desire, jealousy, motherhood, hunger, violence, waiting, and boredom with beautiful and exceptional subtlety. Through the story of the Vice-Consul's scandalous shooting, she explores the effects of confronting human suffering, illness, and poverty in a way that exposes rational reaction as highly suspect and even fraudulent. One of the most fascinating aspects of this novel is the texture and layering of its narrative voice. The novel's structure places the reader in a disturbing position, inspiring consideration of questions such as "Who is writing?" and "Whose story are we reading?" Duras ensures that we do not forget that we are experiencing a literary construct and not a representation of reality. **PMB**

The Magus

John Fowles

Lifespan | b. 1926 (England), d. 2005
First Published | 1966
First Published by | Little, Brown & Co. (Boston)
Revised Edition | 1977

The Magus, although not John Fowles's first published work, was in fact his first novel, begun in the 1950s. An absorbing book, redolent with the atmosphere of a gray, decaying London and a resplendent Greece, it charts the stage-managed masque both endured and enjoyed by the novel's protagonist, Nicholas Urfe. Nicholas is, in many ways, a fundamentally unlikable character. A middle-class English everyman of the postwar period, he is self-absorbed, naïve, and a sexual predator. Yet it is impossible not to empathize with both his humanity and the extraordinary ordeal he undergoes. Indeed, the events surrounding his encounters with Conchis and the beautiful twins are as compelling and intoxicating for the reader as they are for Nicholas himself.

The novel is steeped in Jungian ideas about the psychological. The overall effect is powerful, but ambiguous, interrogating ideas of freedom, absolute power, and knowledge, as well as the concept and experience of love. It does not seek to provide an answer to the questions it raises, and as such it is both exhilirating and disturbing, as well as frustrating at times. Yet the book's engagement with humanity's longing for transcendence in both life and art is fascinating.

Fowles's foreword to the revised edition (1977) speaks of his uncomfortable relationship with the text, which he feels to be deeply flawed. In this debate it is impossible not to side with the readers who have given The Magus its lasting popularity. **DR**

The Master and Margarita

Mikhail Bulgakov

Lifespan | *b.* 1891 (Ukraine), *d.* 1940 (Russia)
First Published | 1966, in *Moskva* journal
First Published (Book) by | YMCA Press (Paris)
Original Title | *Master i Margarita*

⊙ Bulgakov's Margarita, as represented in this painting by Serbian artist Gordana Jerosimic, is hauntingly mysterious and erotic.

❯ A poster for a performance based on Bulgakov's masterpiece, staged in Moscow in 2000 on the sixtieth anniversary of his death.

In 1966, almost thirty years after the author's death, the magazine *Moskva* published the first part of *The Master and Margarita* in its November issue. The book had circulated underground before surfacing into the public arena. Had it been discovered during Bulgakov's lifetime, the author would probably have "disappeared" like so many others—despite the dubious honor of being named as Stalin's favorite playwright for a short period. *The Master and Margarita* has survived against the odds and is now recognized as one of the finest achievements in twentieth-century Russian fiction. Sentences from the novel have become proverbs in Russian: "Manuscripts don't burn" and "Cowardice is the most terrible of vices" are words with a special resonance for the generations who endured Soviet totalitarianism's worst excesses. Its influence can be detected further afield—from Latin American magic realism to Rushdie, Pynchon, and even the Rolling Stones ("Sympathy for the Devil" is said to be inspired by Bulgakov).

The novel is composed of two distinct but interconnected narratives. One is set in modern Moscow; the other in ancient Jerusalem. Into these Bulgakov inserts a cast of strange and otherworldly characters that includes Woland (Satan) and his demonic entourage, an unnamed writer known as "the master," and his adulterous lover, Margarita. Each is a complex, morally ambiguous figure whose motivations fluctuate as the tale twists and turns in unexpected directions. The novel pulsates with mischievous energy and invention. By turns a searing satire of Soviet life, a religious allegory to rival Goethe's *Faust*, and an untamed burlesque fantasy, this is a novel of laughter and terror, of freedom and bondage—a novel that blasts open "official truths" with the force of a carnival out of control. **SamT**

Wide Sargasso Sea

Jean Rhys

Lifespan | *b.* 1890 (Dominica), *d.* 1979 (England)
First Published | 1966
First Published by | Andre Deutsche (London)
WH Smith Literary Award | 1967

Wide Sargasso Sea is Jean Rhys's literary response to Charlotte Brontë's 1847 novel, *Jane Eyre*. Rhys takes as her starting point Brontë's animalistic, sexualized depiction of Bertha Mason, Edward Rochester's dangerously insane first wife. In rewriting this literary classic, Rhys allows Antoinette to speak (Bertha is revealed as Rochester's imposed name for his wife) and also explores the uneven desires and fears that have dominated relationships between the Caribbean and Europe. The novel is divided into three parts: in the first, Antoinette gives an account of her unhappy childhood; in the second, Rochester describes his uneasy first marriage; and in the third, we are witness to the confused dreams and thoughts of Antoinette after she has been imprisoned in England. This structure allows Rhys to make explicit connections between the story of *Jane Eyre* and the violent colonial history underpinning it.

Rhys sets the events in the novel against slavery's ending in the Caribbean and positions Antoinette—whose mother was from Martinique—between the black and European communities. Her vulnerability is used by Rhys to explore the colonial relations identity that Brontë could only imply. The doomed arranged marriage between Antoinette and Rochester is sexually charged and yet profoundly precarious because of the incomprehension and mistrust that both bring to it. In this parallel narrative, Antoinette is no longer merely an insanely vengeful wife, but a tragic victim of a complex historical moment. **NM**

The Third Policeman

Flann O'Brien

Lifespan | *b.* 1911 (Ireland), *d.* 1966
First Published | 1967
First Published by | MacGibbon & Kee (London)
Given Name | Brian O'Nolan

There is a fascination with the bicycle in the Irish experimental novel. Flann O'Brien's comic masterpiece *The Third Policeman*, written in 1940 but unpublished until 1967, treats the bicycle with an obsessive philosophical interest, at once absurd and hilariously plausible. The story starts off in a humdrum world of Irish pubs, farms, and petty ambitions. Following a brutal murder, this realist beginning unravels, and the first-person narrator wanders into a two-dimensional, perplexing, and incomprehensible world. He shows up at a bizarre police barracks, where he finds the two policemen, MacCruiskeen and Pluck, and is introduced to "Atomic Theory" and its relation to bicycles. The title's third policeman, Sergeant Fox, bears a striking similarity to the man the narrator has killed and operates the machinery that generates "eternity" which, it turns out, is just down the road. The narrator's obsession throughout is with fictitious philosopher De Selby, who is a skeptic about all known laws of physics. His eccentric ideas on the delusory nature of time and space are repeatedly footnoted in a wonderful parody of academic scholarship and intellectual pretension. It places the novel in a distinctly Irish strain of comic writing associated with the likes of Jonathan Swift, in which po-faced scholasticism and internally plausible reasoning lead to bizarre conclusions. For first-time readers, the surprise ending casts events in this delightfully weird but deeply intelligent novel in a wholly new light. **RM**

Miramar

Naguib Mahfouz

Lifespan | b. 1911 (Egypt), d. 2006
First Published | 1967
First Published by | Maktabat Misr (Cairo)
Nobel Prize for Literature | 1988

Naguib Mahfouz's *Miramar* portrays a slice of Egyptian life in the immediate aftermath of the army coup of July 1952. "The Revolution" is one of the main characters of the novel; encountering it changes people's lives, and makes or unmakes their fortunes. The action is set around a pension called "Miramar" on the Alexandrian seafront—the lodgers belong to different social classes and generations, and espouse disparate ideologies reflecting the hybridity and diversity of Egyptian identity.

The plot of the novel transpires through the characters' monologues, which shift between past and present to furnish us with the histories of both the narrators and their communities. Details accumulate to build the narrative and solve the riddle of the death of Sarhan El-Beheiry, the symbol of the hope and promise of the Revolution. Mahfouz's portrayal deviates from the officially sanctioned narrative of a post-Revolutionary Egypt enjoying the fruits of liberty, equality, and stability. He delineates a society terrified of "Uniforms," of arbitrary arrests and detentions, of sudden confiscations and random sequestration.

One of *Miramar*'s greatest achievements is its depiction of the emergent attitudes to gender, class, politics, and religion in a turbulent period of Egypt's history—attitudes that have evolved to shape the social and political realities of today. It offers a penetrating, albeit bleak, view of the rich and complex tapestry of Egyptian society. **JH**

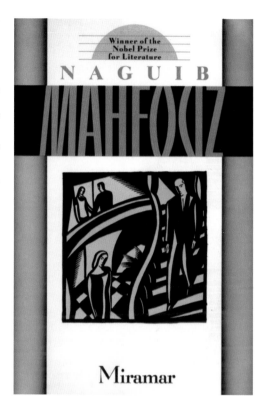

"'The Revolution has stolen the property of a few and the liberty of all.'"

⬥ The cover of a 1993 English edition of Mahfouz's novel stresses the Nobel Prize that belatedly won him a Western readership.

Z

Vassilis Vassilikos

VASSILIS VASSILIKOS

GALLIMARD

Lifespan | *b.* 1934 (Greece)
First Published | 1967
First Published by | Gallimard (Paris)
Movie Adaptation Released | 1969

Part *All The President's Men*, part *JFK*, part *Missing*, this political thriller combines investigative reporting with a hard-hitting exposé of the 1960s Greek military junta. Vassilikos pulls no punches in showing how the corrupt regime orchestrated the assassination of a popular Greek left-wing politician named Gregoris Lambrakis. He was a hero to a voiceless people, but the right wing saw him as pro-Communist and an anti-American troublemaker. He was assassinated on a Salonika street in 1963 and 400,000 came to the funeral in silent protest. Very soon after that, "Z"—*zei* meaning he lives—was seen scrawled everywhere in Athens.

In this thinly veiled fictionalized account (the names are changed) the author retraces the few seconds surrounding a politician's suspicious death after allegedly being run over in a hit-and-run accident. Through his study of the investigative documents of the time and his understanding of his native Salonika, where the murder takes place, Vassilikos uncovers a crudely sanctioned plot involving a drive-by beating up by hired thugs in plain view of the police and civilian spectators. What emerges through the pages of this absorbing novel is the bravery of ordinary people cowered by a brutal dictatorship that routinely resorts to a network of corruption, illegality, and violence to silence dissent. Vassilikos went on to co-write the Oscar-winning movie directed by Costa-Gavras—as riveting now as when it first came out in 1969. **JHa**

> *"In writing Z I wanted to show, more than the precise case of Z, the mechanism of political crime in our time."*
>
> *Vassilis Vassilikos, 1967*

🔹 Vassilikos is a prolific writer with more than 100 books to his credit, but *Z* has remained by far his most celebrated work.

Pilgrimage

Dorothy Richardson

Lifespan | *b.* 1873 (England), *d.* 1957
First Published | 1967
First Published by | J. M. Dent & Sons (London)
Published Separately | 1915–1938

Pilgrimage was Dorothy Richardson's life work, in many senses of the term. Its thirteen volumes recount the experiences of the years between 1891 and 1912 through the consciousness of her autobiographical/fictional persona, Miriam Henderson. It opens with the seventeen-year-old Miriam on the eve of her departure to Germany, where she will work as a pupil-teacher; her middle-class family's financial losses, like those of her creator, plunge her into the world of work. In the central volumes of the series, Miriam is in London, living on a pound a week, a "New Woman" embracing the intellectual and personal freedoms of the city and the new century. The later volumes take Miriam out of London and into rural existence, as she pursues her journey and the "adventure" of the questing, and writing, self.

When she began to write *Pilgrimage* in 1913, at the age of forty, Richardson understood that, at the center of her novel, her heroine must be alone in her narration. Miriam's consciousness is all we have, though the narrative moves between third- and first-person narration, and as readers we are fully immersed in the world she touches, feels, hears, and sees. The publication of the collected volumes by Dent did not persuade Richardson that *Pilgrimage* was complete. It was a project, perhaps, that could not be brought to a conclusion. As she was to write of the work: "To go ahead investigating, rather than describing, was what seemed to me from the first minute must be done." **LM**

The Manor

Isaac Bashevis Singer

Lifespan | *b.* 1904 (Poland), *d.* 1991 (U.S.)
First Published | 1967
First Published by | Farrar, Straus & Giroux (N.Y.)
Nobel Prize for Literature | 1978

A historical saga (complete with a sequel, *The Estate*), *The Manor* chronicles the trials of a Polish merchant and his family "on the way up" in the late nineteenth century. Singer introduces his shrewd Jew, Calman Jacoby, a trader in wheat who is left in charge of the "manor" of the title—a former Polish count's estate confiscated by the czar after the unsuccessful Polish Rebellion of 1863. Jacoby prospers at a time when Jews were beginning to play an active role in Polish industry, business, arts, and society. Jacoby's dilemma is how to take the social opportunities brought by industrial revolution, urbanization, and entrepreneurship while staying faithful to deeply engrained Jewish customs and religious rituals.

The spiritual and the social do not sit comfortably together for Calman in this modernizing milieu, especially when it comes to the social standing expected by his wife, Zelda, and the need to get their four daughters wedded. Marriage and dowry are everything—"One's own children were born of pain, but grandchildren were sheer profit"—but his daughters' marriages are not straightforward and Calman is caught up in many experiences that pull him between the strictures of Judaism and the attractions of Mammon.

Written in 1953–55, in Yiddish, as with most of Singer's novels it was first serialized in the Jewish *Daily Forward* on which he worked as journalist (with his novelist brother Israel) after emigrating to the United States from Warsaw in 1935. **JHa**

One Hundred Years of Solitude

Gabriel García Márquez

Widely acknowledged as Gabriel García Márquez's finest work, *One Hundred Years of Solitude* tells the story of the fictional Colombian town Macondo and the rise and fall of its founders, the Buendía family. Revealed through intriguing temporal folds, characters inherit the names and dispositions of their family, unfolding patterns that double and recur. The mighty José Arcadio Buendía goes from intrepid, charismatic founder of Macondo to a madman on its fringes. Macondo fights off plagues of insomnia, war, and rain. Mysteries are spun out of almost nothing. This beguilingly colorful saga also works out a wider social and political allegory—sometimes too surreal to be plausible, at times more real than any conventional realism could afford. An exemplification of so-called magic realism, this allegorical texture incorporates a sense of the strange, fantastic, or incredible. Perhaps the key sociopolitical example is the apparent massacre by the army of several thousand striking workers whose dead bodies seem to have been loaded into freight trains before being dumped in the sea. Against the smoke screen of the official version, the massacre becomes a nightmare lost in the fog of martial law. The disappeared's true history takes on a reality stranger than any conventional fiction, demanding fiction for the truth to be told. While the novel can be read as an alternative, unofficial history, the inventive storytelling brings to the foreground sensuality, love, intimacy, and different varieties of privation. Imagine the wit and mystery of the *Arabian Nights* and *Don Quixote* told by a narrator capable of metamorphosing from Hardy into Kafka and back in the course of a paragraph. García Márquez may have spawned clumsy imitations whose too clever inventions merely tire, but this is a strange and moving account of solitude. **DM**

Lifespan | *b.* 1928 (Colombia)
First Published | 1967, by Sudamericana (B. Aires)
Original Title | *Cien años de soledad*
Nobel Prize for Literature | 1982

"'The farce is over, old friend'"

⬤ This rare hardcover edition evokes the forest around Macondo, in which a galleon is found in the novel's early pages.

◗ In this photograph by Isabel Steva Hernandez, García Márquez appears physically oppressed by a copy of his famous novel.

No Laughing Matter

Angus Wilson

Lifespan | *b.* 1913 (England), *d.* 1991
First Published | 1967
First Published by | Secker & Warburg (London)
Original Language | English

When Angus Wilson submitted *No Laughing Matter* to his publishers, they were sufficiently bemused for him to send a thematic synopsis to guide them through a second reading. At first, the outline's territory would have been familiar even to Jane Austen: according to Wilson, the book is the story of "three brothers and three sisters" from a "shabby genteel . . . middle-class family." By its end, however, Wilson's summary has name-checked Guernica, Hitler, Stalin, the Suez crisis, *Look Back in Anger*, Kandinsky, Ben Hur, and the challenges of providing honorably for an extended household of same-sex Moroccan lovers.

Clearly, this is not a conventional family saga. The book's scale can be inferred from the list of "Principal Players," "Supporting Roles," and "Additional Cast" with which it is prefaced. Yet one of its joys is its evocation of the ties and rivalries of the Matthews family; Wilson dramatizes a century of change without sacrificing his fine observations of class, gender, and sexuality. More than that, the Matthews family *is* the twentieth century, as experienced by middle-class Britons adjusting to the loss of empire. In retrospect, the book can be seen as both the high point of the traditional family-based English novel and the beginning of magic realism. Mixing naturalism, hyperrealism, and fantasy, it is a missing link in British fiction, connecting Alan Hollinghurst to Jane Austen and E. M. Forster. **VQ**

Day of the Dolphin

Robert Merle

Lifespan | *b.* 1908 (Algeria), *d.* 2004 (France)
First Published | 1967
First Published by | Gallimard (Paris)
Original Title | *Un animal doué de raison*

In this thriller, morality, justice, and even humanity appear to have deserted most of the characters. Set in the United States in the early 1970s, the combined effects of the Vietnam War, modern technological developments, and an arms race spiraling out of control have left the government and security services a cynical and weary elite.

At the center of this corruption Robert Merle places Professor Sevilla, a marine biologist, who is looking into the possibilities of communication between humans and dolphins. It is in the animal innocence of the dolphins that Merle locates the remaining way forward for a hopelessly corrupt world. Attempting to communicate with Ivan the dolphin and his mate, Bessie, Sevilla is reminded of altruism, hope, and love by what Merle ironically terms "the humanity of the dolphins." Inevitably, however, the idyll is threatened when both sides of the Cold War begin to view the dolphin as useful as an "undetectable submarine and an intelligent torpedo."

Combining the creativity of science fiction with the suspense of a perfectly crafted spy novel, *Day of the Dolphin* poses some deep questions about the human capability for good and evil. Fascinating, at times disturbing, and overall deeply moving, Merle's novel encourages us to question the assumptions behind not only political decisions but the conventional thriller as well. **AB**

The Electric Kool-Aid Acid Test

Tom Wolfe

Lifespan | *b.* 1931 (U.S.)
First Published | 1968
First Published by | Farrar, Straus & Giroux (N.Y.)
Full Name | Thomas Kennerly Wolfe, Jr.

The Electric Kool-Aid Acid Test is one of the most notable works of the American "New Journalism"—which, in the writing of Tom Wolfe, Hunter S. Thompson, Norman Mailer, and Joan Didion, creatively blurs the boundaries between the techniques of fiction and those of journalistic reporting. In his account of novelist Ken Kesey and his roving band of political performance artists, the Merry Pranksters, Wolfe tries, as he claims, "to re-create the mental atmosphere or subjective reality" of the experience. As the Pranksters' bus travels around, leaving a trail of LSD trips and improvised "happenings" in its wake, Wolfe's book unfolds like a verbal pop art painting. It offers an extraordinary verbal collage of the Pranksters' world, taking in hippie slang, comic book impressionism, and cinematic jump cuts. Wolfe's style bends and skews to fit itself to the contours of how it might have felt to "be there" with them, making it a necessary document of the rise and eventual fall of a particular era and mentality. *Hell's Angels*, Thompson's more historically accurate account of the same events, offers a sobering counterweight.

The Electric Kool-Aid Acid Test hangs together so well stylistically that one cannot always tell where history ends and Wolfe's journalistic riffs begin. It is an exhilarating and exhausting experience, but, like the movie of Woodstock, it cannot define its times, only respond to them. **BT**

" . . . the usual in the head world of San Francisco, just a little routine messing up the minds of the citizenry . . ."

⊙ Fashionable 1960s photographer Jack Robinson captured Wolfe in suit, tie, and waistcoat in the decade of jeans, beads, and kaftans.

Eva Trout

Elizabeth Bowen

Lifespan | *b.* 1899 (Ireland), *d.* 1973
First Published | 1968
First Published by | A. Knopf (New York)
First UK Edition | 1969, by Jonathan Cape (London)

Eva Trout is Bowen's final and, in some ways, most demanding masterpiece. It shares with her earlier great works the brilliantly funny and disquieting incisiveness of her descriptions of people and places, feelings and ideas, love and loss, but it moves out to weird new depths. It is a marvelously fishy book. In some ways, apparently still inhabiting the social ambience and language of earlier decades, it is also one of the most remarkable, elusive, and yet strangely representative literary works of the 1960s.

Eva Trout tells the story of an improbably large or "outsize" young woman who inherits enough money to do virtually anything. The protagonist somehow acquires a child in the United States, a deaf and mute boy called Jeremy, and back in England falls in love with Henry, a Cambridge undergraduate a good deal younger than herself. In a surreal, compelling finale at Victoria Station, about to depart for a fake wedding and honeymoon with Henry, she is shot dead by Jeremy. A sense of anarchic possibility affects everything, including Bowen's syntax: you often can hardly guess where or how a sentence is going to land. There is a profound impression of diffusion and seeking new, multiple channels of feeling and communication. *Eva Trout* casts bizarre, fascinating, and comical reflections on the sense that, as a character remarks, "Life is an anti-novel." **NWor**

🔵 Patrick Hennessy painted this severe yet oddly magical portrait of Bowen at her Irish family estate, Bowen's Court, in the 1950s.

The Cathedral

Oles Honchar

Lifespan | *b.* 1918 (Russia)
First Published | 1968
First Published by | Harper & Row (New York)
Original Title | *Sobor*

Oles Honchar's *The Cathedral* is a key work of the Ukrainian literary movement of the 1960s, which challenged the norms of "socialist realism," both in the artistry of its work and in its focus on the historic and cultural heritage of Ukraine.

The story is set in a town on the Dnieper river, the location of a Soviet-style heavy metallurgical works but still redolent of its independent Ukrainian Cossack history. This past is symbolized by a derelict cathedral built by a group of Cossacks-turned-monks in the eighteenth century. The cathedral is being used as a grain store, and the authorities are proposing to demolish it and replace it with a market hall. To the protagonist of the story, Mykola, a student of metallurgy, the cathedral sums up the spiritual values ignored by the Soviet worldview. As the threat to the cathedral increases, the townspeople become aware of the personal significance it has for each of them. The dispute over whether to destroy or preserve it becomes an allegory of the struggle between historical identity and the ideologues' vision of a "Soviet person."

The novel is, however, far more than allegory, and more than a brilliant portrayal of a town in the grim Soviet era—almost devoid of young men, a young woman struggling to obtain the necessary papers to leave the collective farm and become a student, industrial pollution, mindless bureaucracy. The novel is a lasting proclamation of the fact that "where there is no vision, the people perish." **VR**

A Kestrel for a Knave

Barry Hines

Lifespan | *b.* 1939 (England)
First Published | 1968
First Published by | Michael Joseph (London)
Movie Adaptation Released | 1969

More lyrical than deadpan social reportage, more impressionistic than might be presumed, with opening scenes of a Yorkshire town under the grip of mining pit monotony, Barry Hines's portrait of one teenager's survival with the companionship of his kestrel singularly defies generic categorization. Ambitiously, Hines divides the novel's timescale between the hardship of the present and the pull of sudden remembrance. His uncompromising journey thus shadows Billy Casper's routine paper round and his subsequent day at school. These successive events are interspersed with flashback episodes, rewinding to Billy's first discovery of the hawk to whom he will become devoted, against the meanness and futility of the mundane. Hines becomes our guide to Billy's austere mining community, evoking the tenderness the boy develops by training his hawk. From chick, to leash, to exercising her with a lure as an adult raptor freely off the glove, falconry itself opens up an ultimately fragile space of resistance to Barnsley's everyday necessities.

The novella subsequently appeared as the remarkable movie *Kes* (1969), directed by Ken Loach. Loach's working methods at that time chime with a kind of Italian neorealism, and the movie steadfastly refuses to embellish the rhetorical economy that for Hines had remained so crucial. **DJ**

◐ David Bradley played teenage falconer Billy Casper in Ken Loach's hard-hitting 1969 movie *Kes*, based on Hines's novella.

In Watermelon Sugar

Richard Brautigan

Lifespan | *b.* 1935 (U.S.), *d.* 1984
First Published | 1968
First Published by | Four Seasons Foundation
Full Name | Richard Gary Brautigan

To be in watermelon sugar is a state of mind. Or a state of grace. Or a hallucination. Most people in watermelon sugar live in iDEATH, a village that is constantly reshaping itself. It is a place full of statues (there is one of a potato, another of grass), where the sun shines a different color every day, and where everyone has a job (whether it be writing a book about clouds, tending the watermelon fields, or simply planting flowers). And everything in iDEATH is made out of watermelon sugar, pine, and stones. Or trout. There were once tigers in iDEATH, who spoke beautifully, but had to eat people or die. They were very pleasant about it. They even helped the young narrator with his arithmetic as they ate his parents. But there is a disturbance in watermelon sugar. Margaret, her heart broken by the narrator, has fallen under the influence of inBOIL, a disgruntled alcoholic who left iDEATH and started making whiskey. He and his band of like-minded drunkards mean to prove to those in watermelon sugar that they do not know what iDEATH really means. They arrive at the Trout Hatchery and dismember themselves with jackknives, bleeding to death, having made their point. What may have seemed nonsensical begins to make perfect sense.

Brautigan's language casts a spell. Repetitive and hypnotic, his prose is a transcendental mantra. Gradually, painlessly, the reader soon finds himself in watermelon sugar. More than just a document of the 1960s, it is a passport to revisiting that time. **GT**

The German Lesson

Siegfried Lenz

Lifespan | *b.* 1926 (Germany)
First Published | 1968
First Published by | Hoffman & Campe (Hamburg)
Original Title | *Deutschstunde*

"It was all simply too much. I was swamped."

⬥ Like Günter Grass and Heinrich Böll, Lenz was concerned with the impact of Germany's totalitarian past on the postwar era.

Siggi Jepsen, an inmate in a juvenile offenders' institution, has to write an essay on "The Joys of Duty". He writes about his father, Jepsen, who, during the Second World War, held the post of police chief in a village in the north of Germany. In Siggi's account, his father is charged with implementing the Nazi policy against "degenerate art"; in this role, he is required to enact a prohibition against the local painter Nansen (a character based on the Expressionist painter Emil Nolde, 1867–1956), who has been his friend since their youth. Jepsen carries out his orders, even going so far as to destroy some of Nansen's work. Siggi refuses to help his father, and instead becomes the painter's ally, hiding his pictures and warning him when danger threatens.

When the war is over, matters acquire a strange dynamic of their own. Although Jepsen no longer holds the authority of his post, he is unable to stop persecuting the painter, and Siggi is equally unable to give up the role of protector. When some of Nansen's paintings are destroyed in a fire, and Siggi suspects his father, his frustration leads him to steal other pictures from an exhibition—the action that has landed him in the juvenile offenders' institution.

What Siggi achieves in his own private "German lesson"—the examination of his private history—is also applicable, on a broader scale, to what Lenz regards as the task of German literature as a whole: to work through the past in order to understand the present. In *The German Lesson*, Lenz is particularly interested in the concept of duty: as it affects the father, who must do what he is told; as it affects Nansen, who is commanded by his conscience and vocation; and as it affects Siggi, who is caught between the two. *The German Lesson* is a plea for the questioning of authority. **MM**

The Quest for Christa T.

Christa Wolf

Christa Wolf is undoubtedly the most significant author to have lived and worked in the German Democratic Republic (the former East Germany). She was a convinced socialist and a member of the ruling party, yet her work nevertheless demonstrated a sensitivity to some contradictions of the system. She frequently investigated the difficulty of maintaining a sense of personal identity and integrity in a society in which the emphasis was always on the collective.

The novel presents a dense, nonlinear narrative in which the organizing principle is the narrator's "quest" to reconstruct the life of a friend, Christa T., who has recently died of leukemia. The focus is upon Christa T.'s struggle to balance her eccentric character with the political conformism expected of her and her intense desire for a private, personal existence with a willingness to serve the community. The narrator, who functions as an alter ego for Wolf, combines her own fragmentary memories of her friend with extracts from diaries, letters, and other sources. From the beginning she concedes that the project can never be complete, that one can never wholly "know" another person, and that in a sense it is as much about getting to know herself as it is about her dead friend. The narrator's highly self-conscious investigation becomes a meditation upon familiar themes for Wolf: politics and morality, memory and identity, and the underlying purpose of writing. Unsurprisingly, the novel prompted a good deal of controversy in East Germany, and authorities even went so far as to instruct bookstores to sell it only to well-known literary professionals. Despite this, or perhaps because of it, the novel established her as an important figure in the cultural life of the eastern bloc. **JH**

Lifespan | *b.* 1929 (Germany)
First Published | 1968
First Published by | Mitteldeutscher Verlag (Saale)
Original Title | *Nachdenken über Christa T.*

"It was I who ended up knowing most about her."

◉ A critical but committed supporter of East German Communism, Christa Wolf opposed the reunification of Germany in 1990.

Do Androids Dream of Electric Sheep?

Philip K. Dick

Lifespan | b. 1918 (U.S.), d.1982
First Published | 1968
First Published by | Doubleday (New York)
Movie Adaptation | Blade Runner (1982)

The novels of Philip K. Dick are a continual and often surprising source of inspiration for the mundane fantasies of Hollywood. *Total Recall* (1990) (from the short story of 1966 "We Can Remember It for You Wholesale"), *Minority Report* (2002), *Paycheck* (2003), and *A Scanner Darkly* (2006) have all graced blockbuster screens. The complexities of *Do Androids Dream of Electric Sheep?* inspired Ridley Scott's groundbreaking *Blade Runner* (1982), but the movie is still a pale shade of the text.

The book questions the nature of humanity through the figure of Rick Deckard, a man who hunts "replicants"—androids designed to be "more human than human." The nominal "sheep" of the title is an artificial creation that dies through Deckard's neglect, a source of intense shame to him. This lack of empathy, fundamental to Dick's distinction between human and replicant, suggests the interminably argued point that Deckard himself may be one of the replicants he hunts. Deckard's growing ethical confusion about "retiring" the replicants is highlighted by the book's extension into the quasi-religious undertones of persuasion and vicarious empathy. The religion of Mercerism—from which replicants are prohibited—is a typical Dick invention. Mercer is a false idol, and the text not only asks what it means to be human, but also, in an expression of Dick's philosophy, questions the viability of reality itself. **SS**

2001: A Space Odyssey

Arthur C. Clarke

Lifespan | b. 1917 (England)
First Published | 1968
First Published by | Hutchinson (London)
Original Movie Released | 1968

A "book-of-the-movie" every bit as superbly crafted as the Stanley Kubrick movie of the same name, *2001: A Space Odyssey* was not written after the movie was made, but rather in tandem with it. The fabric of both movie and text were woven simultaneously, with Clarke and Kubrick collaborating to create one of the most enduring and influential science fiction works ever envisioned.

Clarke's novel sometimes seems overly specific in its technical detail, especially in instances where the passage of time has made his projected futuristic developments date badly. It is important (and remarkable) to remember, however, how many of Clarke's predictions have been realized, and how respected he is not simply as an author, but also as one of the foremost visionaries of the space age. It is in the final part of *2001* that his vision truly bursts forth. The all-powerful computer HAL 9000, which controls the exploratory spacecraft *Discovery*, turns the human emotions of its creators back on themselves, becoming a terrifying psychotic. The magnificent climax of Clarke's *2001* leaves the reader in little doubt as to why it is considered one of the best novels of its type, and shows why it has garnered such a central place in our imaginings of the future. **DR**

❯ Stanley Kubrick's enigmatic movie version of Clarke's science fiction work has tended to overshadow the author's novel.

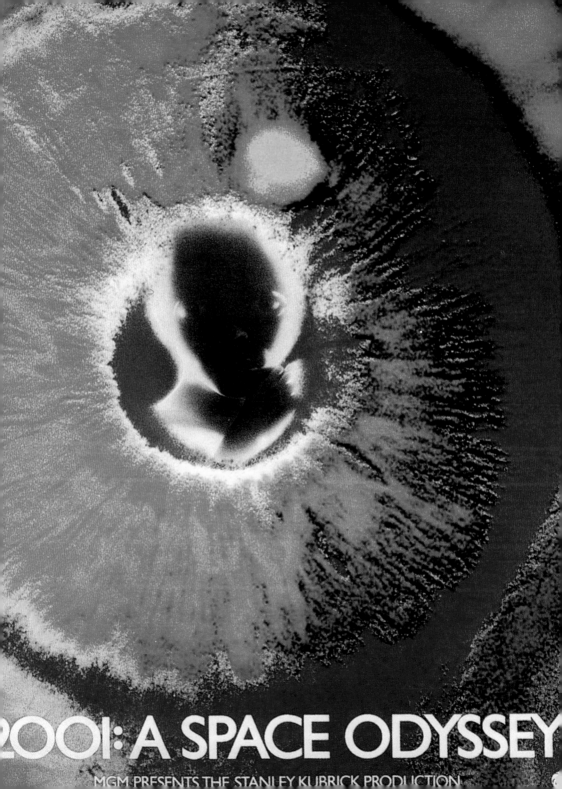

2001: A SPACE ODYSSEY

MGM PRESENTS THE STANLEY KUBRICK PRODUCTION

Belle du Seigneur

Albert Cohen

Lifespan | b. 1895 (Greece), d.1981 (Switzerland)
First Published | 1968
First Published by | Gallimard (Paris)
Original Language | French

Comic and tragic in almost equal measure, *Belle du Seigneur* is many things, but remains essentially a love story. The tone is set from the beginning, as the opening scene finds protagonist Solal, posturing in the guise of Don Juan, fresh but firm in his resolve to seduce another man's wife: the incorrigibly vain Ariane d'Auble. The other man in question is Adrien Deume, an ingratiating social climber under Solal's employ, whom Solal smoothly outmaneuvers by exploiting his position as Under-Secretary-General of the League of Nations. He does succeed in his endeavor, though not without consequence, and a passionate if rather contrived love affair unfurls as he and Ariane elope. However, their initial happiness soon subsides as the threat of boredom, coupled with their respective sacrifices, reveals the fragility of their love, and they hobble toward an unhappy finale. Different characters' perspectives are given in first-person stream-of-consciousness-style passages, adding texture, and often humor, to the novel. The incorporation of certain autobiographical elements means that beneath the blithe veneer of sprawling text are sharp observations on society mores.

Despite being highly rated in France and recognized as a significant contributor to French Jewish fiction, it is fair to say that Albert Cohen has been largely forgotten, perhaps unfairly. **TW**

⬥ Born on the Greek island of Corfu, Albert Cohen adopted Swiss nationality in 1919, but his most deeply felt identity was Jewish.

Cancer Ward

Aleksandr Isayevich Solzhenitsyn

Lifespan | b. 1918 (Russia), d. 2008
First Published | 1968, by Il Saggiatore (Milan)
Original Title | *Rakovy korpus*
Nobel Prize for Literature | 1970

Strongly autobiographical, like most of Solzhenitsyn's work, *Cancer Ward* takes place in the post-Stalinist 1960s in a provincial hospital in Central Asia. It was published abroad in 1968, after prolonged and unsuccessful efforts to place it in the Soviet literary journal *Novyi Mir*. It constructs a whole social world by unmediated shifts of perspective and of narrative focus from one character to the next. However, it seems less interested in the overtly political and philosophical questions raised by the Soviet system of camps and oppression than in focusing on the way a distorted society affects the lives of individuals.

The protagonist, Kostoglotov, is, like Solzhenitsyn, a former political prisoner, who is faced with a life-threatening cancer for which he needs radiotherapy, with potentially devastating consequences for his sexual life. Not long released from the camps into internal exile, this represents a brutal shattering of his hopes for what remains of his life after the Gulag has robbed him of his youth and early manhood. Kostoglotov develops an unlikely relationship with a lonely middle-aged female doctor, and the main plot of the novel explores their tentative and ultimately unrealized emotional intimacy. It is the enmeshing of their personal stories into a whole tableau of other characters and their voices, however, that makes the novel's impact so striking. It tells of self-deception and careerism; of youthful desire and innocence; of anger, faith, and resignation. Most of all, it tells of broken lives in a society still shaped by the Gulag. **DG**

Myra Breckinridge

Gore Vidal

Lifespan | *b.* 1925 (U.S.)
First Published | 1968
First Published by | Little, Brown & Co. (Boston)
Full Name | Eugene Luther Gore Vidal

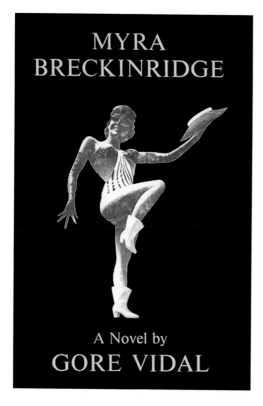

MYRA
BRECKINRIDGE

A Novel by
GORE VIDAL

⊙ Gore Vidal devoted much of his literary career to attacks on
sexual hypocrisy and the corruption of American political life.

◎ Raquel Welch as Myra reveals the nub of the plot in a saucy
scene from the disastrous 1970 Hollywood version of Vidal's novel.

Myra Breckinridge is a reeling tour de force, a bawdy full-frontal attack on decency and polite behavior. Shocking in its time—not least for its content and rude prose—it is even more so, considering Gore Vidal had run for Congress eight years before. This is not the kind of book one expects from a politician. Myra is a sublime creation. She is a voracious dominatrix, a brazen superhero, a big slut, a voluptuous omnivore: "Myra Breckinridge is a dish, and never forget it, you motherfuckers, as the children say nowadays." Myra used to be Myron, a meek film critic, but after a radical act of self-creation—a sex change in Copenhagen—Myra comes to Hollywood to take on the forces of male domination and become "woman triumphant." More feminine than a proper woman, more masculine than an intact man, she is a woman so liberated she may be a mockery of feminism. She certainly calls into question sexual stereotypes and reflexive morality.

The focus of Myra's gleeful battle is Uncle Buck Loner. Buck is a he-man who runs an academy for burgeoning Hollywood stars and starlets. Myra tries to fool him into thinking she is Myron's widow—which, in a way, is true—so that she can claim Buck's estate as her inheritance. She is convincing, knowing things only Myron could. Buck does not believe her, insisting that Myron was a "fruit." He does not part with his money easily and staves off her lawsuit by hiring her to teach Empathy and Posture. She wreaks havoc—an Amazon let loose in a china shop of American innocents. Sadly, there is a problem. Something goes wrong with her sex change, and she reverts to being Myron. She may not have succeeded in becoming woman triumphant, but she—and Vidal—have indisputably triumphed in bringing American hypocrisy and self-obsession forever to its knees. **GT**

The First Circle

Aleksandr Isayevich Solzhenitsyn

Lifespan | *b.* 1918 (Russia), *d.* 2008
First Published | 1968
First Published by | Harper & Row (New York)
Original Title | *V kruge pervom*

Aleksandr Solzhenitsyn's novel, initially published in a shorter version in the hope of passing Soviet censorship, was revised into a "final" version, first published in Russian ten years later, in 1978. His novel is at the same time a portrait of late Stalinist society and a philosophical inquiry into the nature of patriotism. The book is set mainly in a special privileged prison for engineers, scientists, and technicians forced to work on inventing gadgets for Stalin's police apparatus. It describes Soviet society not only from the point of view of the prison inmates, but also from that of their families, their non-inmate colleagues, and their jailers. It is Solzhenitsyn's special talent to speak convincingly in many different voices, immersing us completely in each character's inner world.

The First Circle of the title refers mainly to the privileged nature of the special prison, which forms a Dantean first circle in the hell of the Gulag. In the final version the phrase is also used in a different sense, when one of the characters speaks of his own people or nation as "the first circle" and the outside world as "the next one." The relationship between inner and outer in this sense, and the loyalties owed to each one, is an important element in the plot of the book. Yet it is the great merit of *The First Circle* that the characters discussing these questions never become pure mouthpieces, but are given to the reader as full and complex human beings inhabiting their own interconnected worlds. **DG**

A Void / Avoid

Georges Perec

Lifespan | *b.* 1936 (France), *d.* 1982
First Published | 1969
First Published by | Editions Denoël (Paris)
Original Title | *La Disparition*

A Void / Avoid, Gilbert Adair's remarkable translation of the title of Georges Perec's extended lipogram—a literary exercise that involves writing without a given letter of the alphabet—adds a further layer of self-reflexivity to a novel that does nothing but point (obliquely) to what is missing. Writing without the letter "e" requires mastering avoidance techniques, and here Perec proves himself a virtuoso, mobilizing the often forgotten resources of the French language so as to inscribe within it a new "e"-less idiom. But Perec's novel is far more than an elaborate linguistic game. It is proof that it is possible to do without the letter "e," a demonstration that affirms the expressive possibilities of (even a deficient) language that—as the second sense of Adair's title suggests—is deeply troubling. In *A Void / Avoid*, there is something missing, a hole or vacuum that threatens to suck in all the other letters. An indispensable vowel, what Perec calls "a basic prop," turns out to be dispensable. What then cannot be removed?

The question takes on added urgency when the experiment in the removal of a vowel is repeated in the obliteration of a people. The missing letter is the clue not only to the genesis of the novel, but also to the plot's series of disappearances. The forbidden "e" turns out to be a kind of malediction, an invisible bodily mark that condemns the characters, one by one, to death. An exercise in style brilliantly executed, this is a ludic detective fiction in which the key to the mystery is visible everywhere and nowhere. **KB**

them

Joyce Carol Oates

Lifespan | b. 1938 (U.S.)
First Published | 1969
First Published by | Vanguard Press (New York)
National Book Award | 1970

Deliberately labeled with a lowercase "t", *them* was written early on in Joyce Carol Oates's prolific career, and remains one of her most original and best executed works. It focuses on the working-class lives of Loretta Wendall and her children, Maureen and Jules, in inner-city Detroit between 1937 and 1967.

One of the novel's most challenging features is the way it takes the representation of the naturalistic novel to the limits. It opens with a famous author's note claiming that the text was based on the life of one of Oates's students at the University of Detroit. This note gives way to a naturalistic narrative about the lives of the Wendalls, juxtaposing a forceful psychological portrayal of each of the characters with the violent realities of their everyday life. Halfway through the novel, however, the main narrative is unexpectedly interrupted—with several letters from Maureen to "Miss Oates." Maureen questions her teacher about the role of literature and Miss Oates's suggestion that literature gives form to life. Maureen, who has prostituted herself and been beaten by one of her mother's lovers, asks contemptuously if literary form can really give order and coherence to a life such as hers. Maureen's impassioned letters voice an irrepressible anger toward the type of literature that can only be understood and savored in the safe middle-class world inhabited by Miss Oates and her kind. Through the very process of writing, Miss Oates is no longer part of the working-class experience she describes—she is no longer one of them. **SA**

Ada

Vladimir Nabokov

Lifespan | b. 1899 (Russia), d. 1977 (Switzerland)
First Published | 1969
First Published by | McGraw-Hill (New York)
Alternate Title | *Ardor*

Ada, or *Ardor*, is Vladimir Nabokov's irrepressively inventive novel, which can, for want of a better description, be called a family chronicle. Using Tolstoy as a cultural touchstone and point of departure, Nabokov embarks upon an extraordinary epic prose adventure involving, invoking, and expanding upon a diffuse intertextual network. In common with *Lolita*, *Ada* is the story of an intense but taboo sexual relationship. The incestuous union between Ada and Van, raised as cousins but biologically brother and sister, is presented in such a way that the reader is not encouraged to feel the sense of moral condemnation that might be expected.

Ada is undoubtedly one of Nabokov's most challenging novels, which above and beyond its subject matter, confuses, bewilders, and delights the reader in turn. Quite apart from the sheer intricacy and ingenuity of his writing, the novel confounds expectations of time and place. The events of the novel unfold not on Earth but within the alternative geography of Antiterra, playing with our perceptions of what is real and what is realistic, and as the elderly Ada and Van reflect upon their relationship the narrative is complicated by the continued but unsignaled temporal shifts.

In its treatment of a forbidden romance, the novel follows the couple over eighty years. The unique combination of myth and fairy tale, eroticism and romance is matched only by the singularity of Nabokov's writing style. **JW**

The Godfather

Mario Puzo

Lifespan | *b.* 1920 (U.S.), *d.* 1999
First Published | 1969
First Published by | Putnam (New York)
Movie Trilogy Released | 1972, 1974, 1990

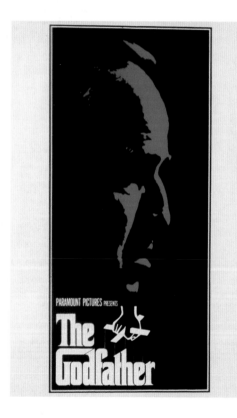

● Coppola's *Godfather* movies retained the strengths of the novel, sustaining moral weight and a somber atmosphere.

● Author Mario Puzo is given something of the arrogant, menacing look of a Mafia godfather in this 1969 photo by Bernard Gotfryd.

Few novels have forced themselves into the cultural imagination as brutally as Mario Puzo's *The Godfather*. Arriving on the bestseller list at a highly contentious moment in U.S. history, when political institutions and social practices were being scrutinized and questioned as never before (or, arguably, since), *The Godfather* raised the stakes.

The novel poses questions about the origins and legitimacy of power by interrogating the notion that, as Balzac's epigraph puts it, "Behind every great fortune there is a crime." Here is a novel that purports to show you how things "really" work, while also playing games with the reader. Making the bad guys seem good, the novel redefined the gangster genre. Puzo's strategy of rhetorical inversion, overturning conventional moral presuppositions of right and wrong, enforces a new understanding of the manipulative and treacherous capacities of language. Twisting distinctions between hero and villain, Puzo's enthralling story of the Corleone's "family business" and Italian-American immigrant culture serves to affirm the "outlaw" character of America in general.

Although *The Godfather* has filtered into the culture mostly through the movie trilogy and other derivations, the novel remains the driving force behind the mobster culture industry. It is the novel that gives us such legendary sayings as "I'll make him an offer he can't refuse" and "a lawyer with his briefcase can steal more than a hundred men with guns." Above all, in spite and perhaps because of the clear, accessible prose, the novel testifies to the myth-making potential of contemporary writing. Puzo's depictions of Italian Americans have been seen as both celebratory and defamatory: either way, Puzo's *The Godfather* remains remarkably influential, compelling, and readable. **JLSJ**

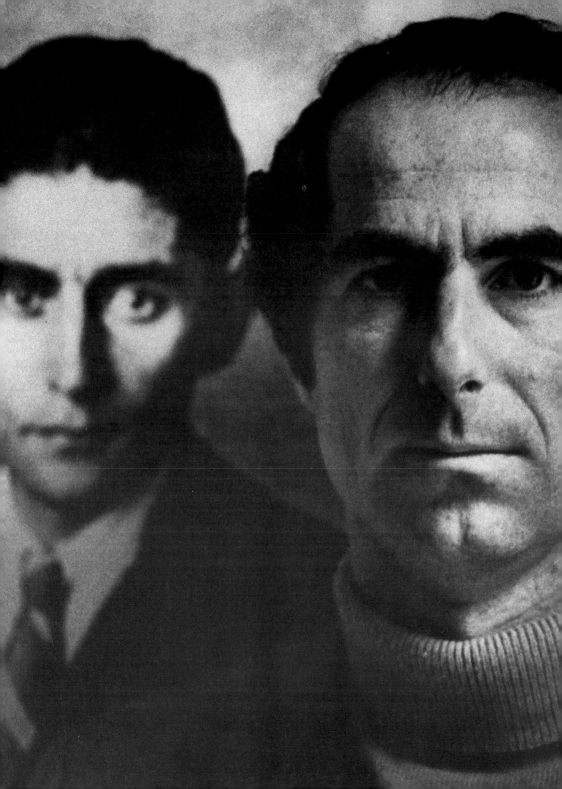

Portnoy's Complaint

Philip Roth

Lifespan | b. 1933 (U.S.)
First Published | 1969
First Published by | Random House (New York)
Full Name | Philip Milton Roth

When *Portnoy's Complaint* first appeared in 1969, it was immediately hailed as scandalous. This was partly because of its explicit sexual content, which is considerable and inventive, but it was also because this content was linked to a kind of diagnosis of the American male of the times. Portnoy's situation—his fixation on his mother; his difficulties with members of the opposite sex; his occasionally maudlin self-pity—described and defined a syndrome with which all too many of Roth's (male) readers were familiar. Into this mix also goes Portnoy's Jewishness, here seen as a kind of exaggeration of the repressive orthodoxies against which the book and Portnoy himself impotently rail. In a sense, it is not a book with a story to tell, but rather one with a condition to portray. Portnoy is trapped in a world that cannot fulfill his bizarre and extreme fantasies. Yet the reader does not blame Portnoy; if nothing else, he at least has occasional flashes of insight into his condition, and Roth writes with a great deal of wit and panache.

Perhaps because of the further increase in sexual explicitness since the 1960s, *Portnoy's Complaint* now looks less extreme than it did at the time; despite this, its capacity if not to shock, then at least to deeply embarrass, is undiminished. In the end the book's real strength lies in the figure of Portnoy himself and the universality of his complexes and humiliations. **DP**

🔾 Roth is posed in front of a photo of Franz Kafka, a fellow Jewish writer whom he regards as a major inspiration for his work.

Jacob the Liar

Jurek Becker

Lifespan | b. 1937 (Poland), d. 1997 (Germany)
First Published | 1969
First Published by | Aufbau-Verlag (Berlin)
Original Title | *Jakob der Lügner*

Jacob the Liar manages to do what might seem to be impossible, to tell the story of the Holocaust through humor. Largely based on Jurek Becker's own childhood experiences in the Jewish ghetto, the novel takes the form of a memoir from its only survivor, who is compelled to tell the story not of the tragic deportation of his friends and family, but of the moments of calm that preceded the tragedy.

The narrative focuses on Jacob Heym, who, in order to cheer up his friends, convinces them that he has a clandestine radio that picks up news from the Allied powers. As the lies spiral out of control—at one point Jacob even has to improvise an entire speech by Winston Churchill—Becker shows the reader the effect that this new hope has on the population. Even though the rumors are all false, the hope that they bring allows people to carry on their lives, creating a touching web of interactions, as people fall in love, deal with family members, and socialize with friends. While we know all along that Becker's novel cannot end happily, the horror of the empty train cars waiting to be filled with the town's population is mitigated by the strength of connections that bind the people together.

Originally a screenplay, *Jacob the Liar* is written in a lucid, clear, and often funny tone with moments of touching beauty. Becker's take on the holocaust novel will leave the reader sobered and mindful, but also aware of the continuing possibility of human joy, even in the worst of circumstances. **AB**

The French Lieutenant's Woman

John Fowles

Lifespan | *b.* 1926 (England), *d.* 2005
First Published | 1969
First Published by | Jonathan Cape (London)
WH Smith Award | 1969

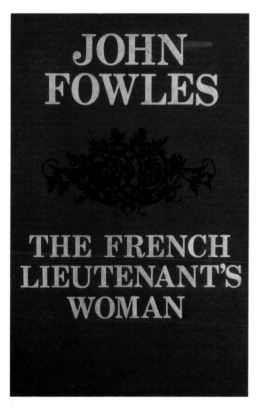

◉ Cover artist, Fletcher Sibthorp, later became predominantly
known for his large-scale figurative and dance pieces.

◉ Meryl Streep plays the eponymous heroine in Karel Reisz's 1981
film version of the novel, which was scripted by Harold Pinter.

In *The French Lieutenant's Woman,* John Fowles set out to do what should have been an impossibility: to reconcile the scope of Victorian realism with the cynicism of a self-reflective experimental narrative. That Fowles realized his purpose in a novel that is a magnificent blend of story, history, and literary critique is testament both to his skill as a writer, and to the ambition of his humanism. The novel is a pastiche of Victorian realism—undermining the latter's formal claim to comprehensiveness and truth by drawing attention to what was rendered unspeakable by a complacent sense of narrative propriety. Yet it is also full of respect and almost envy for the fundamental premise of nineteenth-century realism: that human reality is representable, and that the novel has an explanatory function with a moral duty to be as truthful as possible.

In this tale of a nineteenth-century gentleman, Charles Smithson, who falls in love with the enigmatic, jilted Sarah Woodruff, the twentieth-century narrator plays with his reader's expectations. He scorns especially the illusion of narrative omniscience and omnipotence and flirts with the endless possibilities of interpretation. He also utilizes an essentially Dickensian narrative license to address the reader as familiar and intimate. The "dear reader" addressed here is expected to tolerate—and welcome—a range of devices. Footnotes give information on sources in the style of a scholar and a gentleman. There are long historical digressions, copious quotations from Victorian classics, and digs at the twentieth century's own complacencies. Still, just as the reader addressed by Dickens or George Eliot was credited both with an interest in knowing and a capacity to understand others, so, too, Fowles works to make us see the ties that bind us all. **PMcM**

Slaughterhouse Five

Kurt Vonnegut, Jr.

> *"All time is all time. It does not change. It does not lend itself to warnings or explanations. It simply is. Take it moment by moment, and you will find that we are all . . . bugs in amber."*

🔵 Like his novel's hero, Billy Pilgrim, in 1969 Vonnegut was "living in easy circumstances on Cape Cod," where this photo was taken.

Lifespan | *b.* 1922 (U.S.), *d.* 2007
First Published | 1969, by Delacourte Press (N. Y.)
Alternate Title | *The Children's Crusade: A Duty-Dance with Death*

Kurt Vonnegut's *Slaughterhouse Five* is a dazzling, indispensable achievement in twentieth-century writing, juggling broad thematic and structural complexities alongside a narrative that combines autobiography with a story of time-traveling aliens taken straight from some particularly imaginative science fiction, and with an apparent ease that makes the joins impossible to spot.

In this absurdist classic, Billy Pilgrim, a German-American and a former infantry scout in the Second World War, is a man "unstuck in time" after he is abducted by aliens. Who is this single man to make decisions upon universal solutions, let alone trouble us with his workings? Time, memory, and the literary combination of invention and experience are at the book's center, but Vonnegut rejects any undue artifice in his language.

The absurdities of war and those of time-traveling aliens appear to Billy Pilgrim on an even footing, as we follow him through all the many phases of his life in a novel that absolutely refuses to subscribe to any incarnation of rigid authority. Having fought in the Second World War, been imprisoned, seen thousands dead, and witnessed the devastating Allied fire-bombing of Dresden, the author has produced from his experiences a representation of the literal result of all such authority being simultaneously let go. **SF**

Blind Man with a Pistol

Chester Himes

Lifespan | *b*. 1909 (U.S.), *d*. 1984 (Spain)
First Published | 1969
First Published by | Morrow (New York)
Alternate Title | *Hot Day, Hot Night*

The final, completed novel of a series featuring two black Harlem police detectives, Coffin Ed Johnson and Grave Digger Jones, *Blind Man with a Pistol* takes the detective fiction genre as far as, and beyond, its breaking point. In previous novels, Himes found a way of reconciling his coruscating anger at the open-ended nature of racial discrimination and injustice in the United States with the genre's demands for explanations and closure. Writing from Paris about New York, the results were an often beguiling mix of surreal violence, political protest, and police procedural. In *Blind Man with a Pistol*, Himes is no longer interested in performing such a convoluted juggling act. Rather, the debilitating effects of living in a racist, white-controlled world finally mean that Coffin Ed and Grave Digger, already set against the black community they police and the white justice system they reluctantly serve, can no longer fulfill their function as detectives.

Entering the novel invisible and nameless, they leave it, frustrated and impotent, while a blind, black man fires his pistol indiscriminately into a crowded subway car. Marginalized within the white-controlled police department they served for their entire careers, they end up shooting rats on a derelict Harlem construction site. *Blind Man with a Pistol* is a bleak antidote to the hopeful yearnings of the Civil Rights movement. **AP**

Pricksongs and Descants

Robert Coover

Lifespan | *b*. 1932 (U.S.)
First Published | 1969
First Published by | E. P. Dutton (New York)
Original Language | English

Coover takes as his source the fables and myths of our collective psyche, the folk tales and television programs and nameless anxieties that keep us awake at night. A master of legerdemain, he plays with the familiar, contorting it into something more complexly sinister than even the grimmest of fairy tales. There are Disneyland woods and breadcrumb trails, where birds join in on children's songs about God's love. Why are the children singing? Childish imbecility? To comfort the old man? What is the old man gazing at with such sadness? Distant regrets? His destination? Small details burn with inchoate sexual energy. A carnival sideshow is a riotous self-contained universe, where the fat lady becomes thin and the thin man beefs up, through vanity, for each other's love, creating a chaos of multiple voices and absurdist anarchy.

The language is refracted through a prism; phrases seem familiar or new, depending on the facet Coover shows us. Meanings, chronologies, become fundamental elements that coalesce like quick fades in a movie—sometimes a montage of color; sometimes a sound cue in an empty frame. Coover makes the archetypal real and the mundane archetypal. Bedtime stories teem with real shadows, deep phobias are made manifest, and biblical characters are confused. He is the ringleader of a universe that operates with the dark and heavy logic of delta-wavelength sleep. **GT**

Tent of Miracles

Jorge Amado

Lifespan | *b.* 1912 (Brazil), *d.* 2001
First Published | 1969
First Published by | Livaria Martins Editora (Rio de J.)
Original Title | *Tenda dos milagres*

With this novel, Jorge Amado, Brazil's greatest twentieth-century novelist, wrote his most ambitious political satire and also his richest articulation of the complexity of Afro-Brazilian culture. Mainly set in the crumbling colonial labyrinths of Pelhourinho, a black district in the heart of Salvador Bahia, the novel confronts the legacy of Pedro Archanjo, Amado's most seductive, yet ambiguous, fictional creation. He is a mestizo—an autodidact, author of cookbooks, poet, part-time ethnographer, carnival king, black rights activist, worshipper, and lover of women. Archanjo is also, in the eyes of the Brazilian white cultural elite, a drunk, a seducer, a libertine, a scoundrel, and an intellectual charlatan.

The novel opens as Arachanjo dies drunk and alone in a gutter in the small hours of the morning while the Second World War rages. Some fifty years later, James D. Levenson, Nobel Laureate from East Coast American academe, discovers the now-forgotten Archanjo's publications, and goes to Bahia to cash in on the cultural gold mine he has unearthed. An exploration of why Black Brazil matters follows, and of the ways in which North America and Europe only see it through stereotypes, parody, and patronization. Amado's approach is tolerant and celebratory of cultural and sexual miscegenation. Black and white people are "gonna go on being born and growing up and mixing and making more babies, and no son-of-a-bitch is gonna stop 'em!" You can't argue with that. **MW**

The Case Worker

György Konrád

Lifespan | *b.* 1933 (Hungary)
First Published | 1969
First Published by | Magveto (Budapest)
Original Title | *A látogató*

The Case Worker recounts the events that take place during a busy working day of a social worker: his insoluble conflict between personal and impersonal loyalty, and his powerlessness in the face of extreme misery. György Konrád's first novel was immediately condemned by the authorities in Hungary for its harsh realism and its exposure of the darker side of contemporary Hungarian society.

The author himself was a social worker for seven years, and the novel draws heavily on his experiences. The narrator, also the main character, produces reports of his work in charge of children at a state welfare organization. His files are filled with cases of neglected, abused, abandoned, delinquent, and retarded children, along with parents dead by suicide. Doing this job and still maintaining his humanity becomes a vain effort. As the narration progresses, the novel becomes a powerful and very disturbing image of the social substrata not only in Budapest but also in the universal metropolis.

The novel fuses sociological and literary concerns. The stark realism of physical, moral, and intellectual degeneration in cities is recounted in lyrical language. An advocate of individual freedom, Konrád was under a publication ban during most of the 1970s and 1980s; it was only when Communism began to collapse in Hungary in 1989 that his books began to appear in Budapest. However, this extraordinary novel assured him a prominent place in world literature long before that. **AGu**

Moscow Stations

Venedikt Yerofeev

Lifespan | *b.* 1938 (Soviet Union), *d.* 1990
First Published | 1969
First Published in | Samizdat
Original Title | *Moskva-Petushki*

In the Soviet Union, quality alcohol was hard to find, but Venedikt Yerofeev's cult novella shows a way out of such an impasse. It teems with recipes for deadly alcoholic beverages; diagrams (much in the spirit of the planned Soviet economy) showing the average alcohol consumption on an average work day; lyrical insights—"First love or last sorrow, is there a difference?"; descriptions of fated love affairs between comsorgs (an organizer and secretary of the Comsomol) and honest working girls; and discussions of Russian literature, homosexuality, and other exigencies of Soviet day-to-day life. *Moscow Stations* is a drink novella, with Yerofeev as the sole originator of the genre.

Much like a "road movie," the story follows a journey that is contemporaneous with the character's inner journey from one melancholy rumination to the other, destined from the very outset to lead nowhere. "On the road," so to speak, the narrator encounters a plethora of Russian folk willing to discuss their often wildly absurd life experience, which in no way corresponds to the purported ideals of Soviet life. Yerofeev, who himself was kicked out of five universities due to "ideological unsuitability," writes an immensely entertaining and ultimately sad story that runs against the grain of an ideology that claims to have all the answers. The narrator's truth-seeking therefore has to take the form of incessant question asking, and finally—in a theological twist of affairs—Christlike suffering. **IJ**

Heartbreak Tango

Manuel Puig

Lifespan | *b.* 1932 (Argentina), *d.* 1990 (Mexico)
First Published | 1969
First Published by | Sudamericana (Buenos Aires)
Original Title | *Boquitas pintadas*

Starting with an obituary reporting the death of Juan Carlos Etchepare in 1947, a complex story of jealousy and meanness begins to unfold, the main episodes of which come to a head at the end of the 1930s in the fictional town of Coronel Vallejos. The plot of *Heartbreak Tango* consists of perfectly choreographed triangles: Nélida and Mabel compete for the love of Juan Carlos, but they drop him when they find he is tubercular and poor; Pancho, a friend of Juan Carlos, falls in love with a maid called Raba and leaves her pregnant, only to seduce Mabel, who will cost him his life. Extending this geometry of passions are the mother and the treacherous sister of Juan Carlos, Celina; and the widow with whom the ailing Don Juan will end his days. The novel ends in 1968 when Nélida dies, taking with her the knowledge that was linking all these stories together.

Manuel Puig developed a new form of popular literature, employing kitsch resources such as the strip cartoon and tango lyrics. In doing this he displays a dazzling panoply of voices (particularly female ones): letters; diary entries, medical notes, and police records; advertising slogans and radio commercials; confessions, conversations with double meanings, telephone conversations; and interior monologues using a supposedly objective third person. Playing on his readers' taste for gossip, Puig knows how to deliver a virulent criticism of the deep hypocrisy that eats away at the little worlds of human society, which are usually the closest. **DMG**

Seasons of Migrations to the North

Tayeb Salih

Lifespan | *b.* 1929 (Sudan)
First Published | 1969
First Published by | Heinemann (London)
Original Title | *Mawsim al-hijrah ila'l-shamal*

Mustafa Sa'eed's sojourn in England has brought academic success, but he has also served time in prison for the deaths of a number of his English sexual partners. Back in the Sudan and married, he dies suddenly, apparently taking his own life. The narrator's fragmentary recreation of Sa'eed's life portrays him as a dislocated figure, hiding violent urges of the colonizer that have survived many generations and passed through to the children of the once colonized nation.

It appears that the narrator—also a successful returnee from the north—may also unwittingly hide an unavowed colonial violence. This is implied further when Sa'eed's widow kills both herself and her new husband, events that the narrator intimates he could have prevented. It is the narrator's complicity in a situation outside his volition that finally leads to his trying to break the cycle of violence in which he has found himself embroiled.

The novel's presentation of colonial violence through local sexual violence makes it a rather uncompromising read, but this relationship yields an extraordinarily disturbing sense of how different kinds of brutality can coalesce in the postcolonial nation. While the novel was banned by the Sudanese government in 1989, it is hailed as the "most important Arabic novel of the twentieth century" by the Syria-based Arab Literary Academy. **ABi**

Here's to You, Jesusa!

Elena Poniatowska

Lifespan | *b.* 1933 (France)
First Published | 1969
First Published by | Ediciones Era (Mexico City)
Original Title | *Hasta no verte, Jesús mío*

Based on actual interviews by Poniatowska, Jesusa Palancares is a synthesis in the first person of the history of Mexico in the twentieth century, and a discourse on behalf of women who have had enough of hard times and want to find good ones. The author is simply the silent interviewer who filters Jesusa's continuous monologue. Jesusa tells the story of how she came to take control of her destiny. Left an orphan by her mother, she travels with her father, eventually joining the revolutionary forces. Surviving the war, she takes up many trades in the country and in the capital—barmaid, servant, furniture maker, and washerwoman, always dragged along by historic events, including the Cristero Rebellion and the expropriations of the 1940s.

While Jesusa's character is indomitable and she refuses to submit, whether to men or to adversity, it is the touchstone of an often desolate reality. Jesusa's life is touched by the esoteric after she discovers the Obra Espiritual, a kind of sect that teaches the immediate presence of the most far. Fatalistic and rebellious, nothing stops her; only age and tiredness put an end to her way of life and her discourse. Through subtle handling of the spoken word and the ingenious assembly of sequences that are not always linear, the book reflects the rise of modern Mexico, and it is a perfect example of autobiography by the person interviewed. **DMG**

Fifth Business

Robertson Davies

Lifespan | *b*. 1913 (Canada), *d*. 1995
First Published | 1970, by Macmillan (Toronto)
Trilogy | *The Deptford Trilogy*: *Fifth Business* (1970);
The Manticore (1972); *World of Wonders* (1975)

Fifth Business, the first novel in Robertson Davies's acclaimed Deptford trilogy, won him international recognition as a storyteller. The novel is particularly noted for its adept dramatization of the spiritual and psychological theories of Carl Jung, who posits that we interpret the world through our recognition of archetypes: We all have our villains and our saints, and understand our role in relation to these.

Dunstan Ramsay, the novel's protagonist, comes to understand himself as Fifth Business, neither "Hero nor Heroine, Villain nor Confidante," but nonetheless essential to the story's unfolding. As a ten-year-old, Dunstan ducks a snowball intended for him that instead hits the Baptist pastor's wife. The pastor's wife goes into premature labor and loses most of her wits; later she becomes the town scandal and ruins her family's reputation. Boy Staunton, the boastful brat who threw the snowball, is permitted to bury the secret and his share of the blame until it buries him years later. And Dunstan bears the full burden of guilt well into middle age. Along the way he picks up wisdom from various sources—a saintly apparition, a Jesuit hedonist, and a magician's sidekick. These lead to a Jungian understanding of God as an essential psychological concept, uniting both the saintly and villainous sides of the unconscious—both of which one needs to reveal and confront to maintain a moral life. **MaM**

Play It As It Lays

Joan Didion

Lifespan | *b*. 1934 (U.S.)
First Published | 1970
First Published by | Farrar, Straus & Giroux
Movie Adaptation | 1972

Joan Didion's novel of 1960s dissolution centers on the character Maria Wyeth, an actress who freewheels through her life in a haze of insular celebrity and anaesthetics. With a stylistic debt to American Modernists like Hemmingway, Didion refrains from abstraction and focuses instead on Maria's messy world on the fringes of half-formed social-convenience networks.

There is a pop-nihilism throughout. "Playing it as it lays" comes to Maria as advice from a deceased world, from parents who are as outmoded as her hometown, which was levelled to make way for a missile range. Maria is a character unbounded and helpless, and her decline gains momentum through a loveless marriage, the suicide of a friend, and a traumatic abortion that becomes the focus of the book. Maria is eventually incarcerated in the same mental institution as her daughter—Maria's only link to a world of unalloyed emotional life.

Didion's forbears settled the Sacramento Valley in the 1850s and a version of the pioneering spirit pervades the directionless drift of Maria, typified by her relentless freeway driving. This slice of 1960s abjection, written at the end of that decade, avoids moral lessons or resolution in preference for unadulterated exposure. It succeeds thanks to Didion's skill at creating character out of her highly stylized sentences. **DTu**

Jahrestage

Uwe Johnson

Lifespan | *b.* 1934 (Germany), *d.* 1984 (England)
First Published | 1970, by Suhrkamp (Frankfurt)
Full Title | *Jahrestage: Aus dem Leben von Gesine Cresspahl*
(*Anniversaries: From the Life of Gesine Cresspahl*)

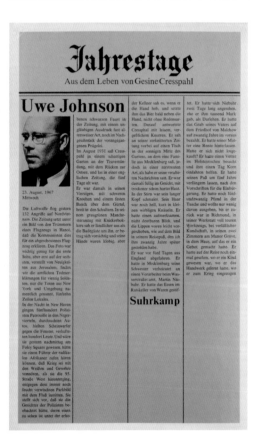

Johnson found life in both East and West Germany intolerable,
preferring an unsettled exile in England and the United States.

Jahrestage is Uwe Johnson's masterpiece, a magisterial sweep through German history from the days of the Kaiser and ending in 1960s New York. Born in a part of eastern Germany that became Polish territory, Johnson left East Germany for West Germany, before eventually settling in Kent, England. There, while recovering from a breakdown, caused by the discovery that his wife was spying on him for German Democratic Republic secret services, he finished *Jahrestage*.

Published in four volumes, *Jahrestage* (meaning *Anniversary*) describes 365 days in the life of Gesine Cresspahl. Gesine lives in New York with Marie, her daughter from a past relationship with Jakob Abs, the protagonist of Johnson's earlier novel *Mutmaßungen über Jakob*. The ten-year-old Marie makes Gesine talk about the past: in the narrative that follows, one year in New York becomes the lens through which German history is filtered. Gesine moves back in time, to her family in a small village in Mecklenburg. The story is interwoven with that of the rise and fall of the Third Reich, and links back to the time of Wilhelm II and the Weimar Republic, before returning to the present in a divided Germany. Marie takes the information in her stride; Gesine realizes that she will always be a stranger in the United States, but prefers exile to a return to Germany.

Jahrestage is technically fascinating because of its complex use of overlapping time levels that shape the narration, but the formidable length of the novel has put off many readers. A recent film version by Margarethe von Trotta (2000) is helping to restore Johnson to his place among the most important writers of postwar Germany, on the same level as Günther Grass and Heinrich Böll. **MM**

A World for Julius

Alfredo Bryce Echenique

A World for Julius could be defined, essentially, as a novel of education and the confusing journey towards maturity. Between the ages of five and twelve, the youngest child of an upper-class family in Lima, who loses his father soon after he is born, truly discovers the world and learns how people's behavior is determined by their surroundings. Alfredo Bryce Echenique traces the movement of his young protagonist, Julius, through a series of social worlds; a world of the faded old palaces of the descendants of the viceroys; the world of dazzling new palaces built by speculators who spend their days shuttling between parties and playing golf; the world of expensive colleges, where the pleasures of music and caresses are learned, but also the pain of blows and humiliations; and the world of the hovels of the servants and the tenements of a more impoverished and alienated middle class. Through these experiences, the child discovers death (that of his unknown father, his favorite sister, and the most motherly of the maids) and also the meaning of friendship and love (meager in the case of his mother, stepfather, and his siblings; sincere and sometimes moving in the case of the maidservants).

Bryce Echenique's novel ends ambiguously—refusing to reveal which of these multiple worlds will turn out to be the dominant one for Julius, to which of them the adolescent will be delivered, and whether he has actually learned enough to carry them on his shoulders. Typical of the author is his mastery of a very free use of speech, bold changes of perspective, and an autobiographical tone that varies between the ironic and the sentimental. These characteristics gave his writing a new direction that placed him firmly in the boom generation of Spanish-American fiction. **DMG**

Lifespan | *b.* 1939 (Peru)
First Published | 1970
First Published by | Barral Editores (Barcelona)
Original Title | *Un mundo para Julius*

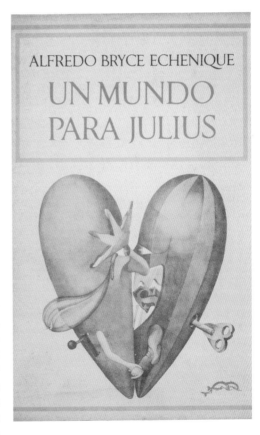

Peruvian author Bryce Echnique turns an ironic gaze upon the experience of growing up in a wealthy South American family.

I Know Why the Caged Bird Sings

Maya Angelou

I Know Why the Caged Bird Sings is the first of five volumes of singer, poet, actress and writer Maya Angelou's autobiography and is a milestone for African-American writing. In her distinctive lyrical prose, Angelou recounts the first seventeen years of her life, discussing her unsettled childhood in America in the 1930s and her changing relationships. When her parents separate, Maya and her brother Bailey, three and four years old respectively, are sent from their parental home in California back to the segregated South, to live with their grandmother, Momma, in rural Arkansas. Momma provides a strict moral center to their lives. At the age of eight, Maya goes to stay with her mother in St. Louis, where she is molested and raped by her mother's partner. With her brother she later returns to stay with Momma before returning again to live with her mother and her mother's husband in California. The book ends with the birth of Maya's first child, Guy.

Angelou became a prominent figure in the American Civil Rights Movement, fighting for African-American rights during the 1960s. She became a close associate of Malcolm X, and later of Dr. Martin Luther King. When King was assassinated in 1968, Angelou was inspired by a meeting with James Baldwin and cartoonist Jules Feiffer to write *I Know Why the Caged Bird Sings* as a way of dealing with death of her friend, and to draw attention to her own personal struggles with racism. Against the backdrop of racial tensions in the South, Maya Angelou confronts the traumatic events of her own childhood, and explores the evolution of her own strong identity as an African-American woman. Her individual and cultural feelings of displacement are mediated through her passion for literature, which proves both healing and empowering. **JW**

Lifespan | *b*. 1928 (U.S.)
First Published | 1970
First Published by | Random House (New York)
Given Name | Marguerite Ann Johnson

⬆ Maya Angelou struts her stuff by an artfully arranged fire for the cover photography of her music album *Miss Calypso*.

◀ An exuberant Maya Angelou, self-discovered through her passion for literature, radiates joy and life on a San Francisco beach.

The Bluest Eye

Toni Morrison

Lifespan | b. 1931 (U.S.)
First Published | 1970
First Published by | Holt, Rinehart & Winston (N.Y.)
Nobel Prize for Literature | 1993

This is Toni Morrison's first novel and recounts the life of the Breedlove family after they move from the country to set up home in Lorain, Ohio (also the author's birthplace). The Breedloves' dislocation, and the descent into madness of their daughter, Pecola, becomes a powerful metaphor for the difficulties of trying to inhabit a space of black identity that is not already part of a racist mythology.

The novel suggests that the categories of gender, race, and economics are enmeshed in determining the fate of the eleven-year-old tragic heroine. Pecola's obsessive desire to have the bluest eyes is a symptom of the way that the black female body has become dominated by white masculine culture. Morrison offers a typically powerful critique of the way that black subjectivity continues to be repressed in a commodity culture. The complex temporal structure of the novel and the restless changes in point of view are in part an attempt to imagine a fluid model of subjectivity that can offer some kind of resistance to a dominant white culture. The adolescent black sisters who relate the narrative, Claudia and Freda MacTeer, offer a contrast to the oppressed Breedlove family in that here they exercise both agency and authority.

In this early novel, Morrison's writing not only captures the hidden cadences of speech; she writes with a keen sensitivity to the protean quality of words. She offers a poetry infused with the promise of alternative modes of being in the world. **VA**

The Sea of Fertility

Yukio Mishima

Lifespan | b. 1925 (Japan), d. 1970
First Published | 1965–1970
First Published by | Shinchosha (Tokyo)
Original Title | Hōjō no umi

Published in four volumes, The Sea of Fertility is Mishima's final work. It first appeared in serial form in the Japanese literary magazine Shincho. Volume One, Spring Snow, is set in the sequestered world of Tokyo's imperial court in around 1910 and depicts the hopeless love between the young aristocrat Kiyoaki Matsugae and his lover, Satoko. Kiyoaki keeps a distance from Satoko, until her engagement to a son of the Emperor makes the impossibility of their love all too real. At this point, their desperate but passionate affair begins, witnessed by Shigekuni Honda, Kiyoaki's closest friend. When Kiyoaki dies, Honda embarks on a search for his reincarnation.

The protagonists in the later volumes (Runaway Horses and The Temple at Dawn) bear the shade of Kiyoaki—as a political fanatic in the 1930s, as a Thai princess before and after the Second World War, and, in the final volume (The Decay of the Angel), as an evil orphan in the 1960s. The idea of this reincarnation nourishes Honda until the final volume. The ending suggests that human life is irretrievable and its end inevitable. In a stunning finale, Honda finally realizes the impossibility of reliving the past and reviving the dead. The novel, which some consider to be the Japanese version of Proust's In Search of Lost Time, provides us with a fabulous insight into life and the experience of memory. **KK**

❯ Yukio Mishima poses as a samurai ready to commit ritual suicide by disembowelling—which he eventually did, in November 1970.

Rabbit Redux

John Updike

Lifespan | b. 1932 (U.S.), d. 2009
First Published | 1971
First Published by | Alfred Knopf (New York)
Pulitzer Prizes | 1982, 1991

Rabbit Redux, John Updike's second novel in his four-volume "Rabbit" series, takes place in 1969, ten years after the end of *Rabbit, Run*. Set in the small town of Brewer, Pennsylvania, the Rabbit series describe the life of Harry Angstrom, nicknamed "Rabbit," as he progresses from high school basketball star to young husband and father, and finally through middle age and into retirement.

Updike's Everyman, now in his thirties, is uncomfortably aware of being on the verge of middle age. Set against the surreal background of the *Apollo 11* moon landing, *Rabbit Redux* charts, through Rabbit's own chaotic personal life, the positive and damaging changes to small-town America, brought about by the collision of traditional values and hierarchies and the irresistible rise of 1960s counterculture. When his apparently conformist marriage begins to crumble, Rabbit must acknowledge the wider events that are occurring in the lives of those around him, pitting him against his working-class Midwestern roots. Rabbit's certainties about life begin to crumble, threatening his relationships with his family and colleagues. However, Rabbit is granted unexpected spiritual growth that changes his life.

Rabbit Redux not only describes but lovingly captures the feeling of the 1960s, plunging the reader into a world characterized by confused sensuality and political chaos, but also a touching and expansive hope for the future. **AB**

Cataract

Mykhaylo Osadchyi

Lifespan | b. 1936 (Soviet Union), d. 1994 (Ukraine)
First Published | 1971
First Published by | Smoloskyp (Paris/Baltimore)
Original Title | Bilmo

This book is one of the seminal texts of Soviet underground literature of the 1960s. It describes the arrest and imprisonment of the author, Ukrainian journalist and poet Mykhaylo Osadchyi, on various charges of anti-Soviet and pro-Ukrainian activities—"crimes" that he had been unaware of committing until he was arrested for them.

In general, Ukraine's underground literature had less impact internationally than similar works from Russia. This was partly due to the difficult logistics of smuggling it out of the country, but also because both the world human rights community and most professional Sovietologists considered that in the case of Soviet matters analysis should focus on the "center"—Moscow and Leningrad. The strength of ethnic self-identification and desire for cultural autonomy and political independence in the non-Russian republics was largely disregarded.

Cataract (the title refers to the disorder that obscures vision) is not simply a factual account of the writer's trial and arrest, but also of his prison dreams and fantasies—dreams that some readers have seen as symptoms of incipient insanity, but which are better perceived as allegorical of the degradation and denigration of the individual psyche under the Soviet system, in everyday life no less than in prison or labor camp. Brilliantly written by an insightful writer, *Cataract* not only documents a specific historic situation but is also an enduring proclamation of the human spirit in adversity. **VR**

Group Portrait With Lady

Heinrich Böll

Lifespan | *b.* 1917 (Germany), *d.* 1985
First Published | 1971
First Published by | Kiepenheuer & Witsch (Cologne)
Original Title | *Gruppenbild mit Dame*

What Heinrich Böll creates in his Nobel Prize-winning novel is an ensemble of transitory identities. The novel leads into the German past between 1890 and 1970. Psychological insights from the perspectives of various characters are heterogeneous and convincing. We encounter young intellectuals, a Jewish nun, a female freedom fighter, a notorious upstart, a political opportunist, and stupefied Nazis. Yet, one person remains a matter of pure conjecture: Leni Pfeiffer. She is the lady in the center of the portrait around whom the series of interviews, letters and personal stories revolve. Leni is seen through the eyes of the narrator, who tends to mystify his blond and allegedly naïve protagonist. Nevertheless, her character resists cliché; her insistence on overcoming racial and social limits points to a subversive, intelligent character.

Böll's writing is bound up with the aims of Gruppe 47 (Group 47)—a literary association founded by Alfred Andersch and Walter Richter in West Germany in 1947. These authors responded to the gulf that had been opened between them and those German intellectuals who had fled Nazi rule. Initially, the authors of the Gruppe 47 felt the need to cleanse their language of Nazi propaganda by advocating a sparse realism. In *Group Portrait With Lady*, the naturalistic narrative indicates the complexity of real life, particularly toward the end of the novel, when the narrator reveals his partiality by actively participating in the events. **MC**

"Leni no longer understands the world, in fact doubts whether she has ever understood it."

🔵 The cover of the German edition presents the men in the group as faceless and pale, drawing attention to the dark figure of Leni.

Fear and Loathing in Las Vegas

Hunter S. Thompson

"We were somewhere around Barstow on the edge of the desert when the drugs began to take hold." Thompson's novel has one of the most recognizable first lines in modern fiction. It tells the story of the narrator's chemical-fueled sojourn in and around Las Vegas in the manic company of his Samoan attorney, on an assignment to cover an off-road dune-buggy-and-motorbike race called the Mint 400 for a New York sporting magazine. Having spent his advance on a trunkload of illegal drugs, the pair begin their adventure at a crazed pitch, abandoning any sense of personal responsibility. This frenzy intensifies when they hit the city and, among other questionable decisions, decide to hole up in a hotel which is hosting the National District Attorneys' Conference on Narcotics and Dangerous Drugs.

The heroes' self-indulgence is simply American over-consumption turned up many notches in a parodic take-off of thoughtless consumerism. At the same time, the journey is an extreme but somehow admirable celebration of traditional American freedoms, in Nixon's first term as president, while the war in Vietnam is being waged, and scandalously punitive jail sentences are being handed out at home for draftcard burners and marijuana smokers. *Fear and Loathing* is experienced through doors of perception, which are set so fantastically awry that no one can be said to know for sure what just happened, what is happening, and what might happen. The book provides an invigorating and hilarious demolition job on the ultimate postmodern city, suggesting that the best way to resist Vegas's rapacious demands is to screw yourself up so entirely beforehand that you are altogether unable to respond in the way which the city commands that you do. **RP**

Lifespan | *b.* 1939 (U.S.), *d.* 2005
First Published | 1971, by Random House (N.Y.)
Full Title | *Fear and Loathing in Las Vegas: A Savage Journey to the Heart of the American Dream*

"'How about some ether?'"

◉ Thompson enjoys a cigar in 2003, two years before his death by suicide; at his funeral, his ashes were fired from a cannon.

◉ A caricature of Thompson's friend Johnny Depp playing the author in Terry Gilliam's 1998 movie version of *Fear and Loathing*.

The Book of Daniel

E. L. Doctorow

The Book of

Daniel

E.L.DOCTOROW

'A masterpiece...I would place Mr Doctorow's achievement as a political novelist above that of any contemporary except Solzhenitsyn'

GUARDIAN

"'Few books of the Old Testament have been so full of enigmas as The Book of Daniel.'"

● The cover of the Pan paperback edition, published in London in 1973, blends the Communist red and Jewish yellow stars.

Lifespan | *b.* 1931 (U.S.)
First Published | 1971
First Published by | Random House (New York)
Full Name | Edgar Lawrence Doctorow

The Book of Daniel examines the nature and effectiveness of different forms of political protest in the United States, and the passage from the Old Left of the 1940s and 1950s to the New Left of the 1960s. For the narrator, Daniel Isaacson, it is about the difficulties of coming to terms with the political and familial legacy of his parents—Ethel and Julius Rosenberg in all but name—who were executed by the state for allegedly passing nuclear secrets to the Soviet Union in 1953.

The novel asks how political power manifests itself in the hands of individuals and institutions, and what can be done to oppose the concentration and abuse of power by government and corporations. In a choice between the "gutsy and pathetic" radicalism of his father, and the flaccid, hubristic counter-cultural pronouncements of Artie Sternlicht, who promises to "overthrow the United States with images," Daniel finds only disillusionment and dead ends. The former is naïve and easily crushed by the state. The latter finds its fullest realization in Disneyland, a theme park world that proposes "a technique of abbreviated shorthand culture for the masses." Daniel must address the different fragments of his life in order to reconcile the political legacy of his parents' activism with his own disenchanted view of the world. This account of protest and family succumbs neither to the optimistic belief that personal struggle conquers all nor the pessimistic belief that all political struggle is futile. **AP**

Lives of Girls & Women

Alice Munro

Lifespan | b. 1931 (Canada)
First Published | 1971
First Published by | McGraw-Hill Ryerson (New York)
Television Adaptation | 1994

Lives of Girls and Women was Alice Munro's first attempt at a novel after her award-winning short story collection, Dance of the Happy Shades. Despite the disavowal printed in most editions, the material is highly autobiographical, Del Jordan's circumstances reflecting Munro's own upbringing in semi-rural Ontario. The adolescent Del is torn between bookishness and an intense hunger for physical experience, rejecting her mother's belief in sexual repression as the means to female liberation.

The book consists of a series of free-standing chapters, halfway between a traditional novel and a short-story collection. The episodic form suits the material perfectly, as Munro explores the impulse to turn our lives and those of others into a set of tales, conforming to our own self-image, fantasies, and the neat resolutions we expect from fiction. The section, "Epilogue: The Photographer," refers to a novel Del has begun, turning her neighbors' lives into a gothic yarn. An encounter with one of her fictional characters' real-life prototypes makes her rethink her whole attitude. In a phrase that has become Munro's own artistic manifesto, she learns that ordinary lives are "dull, simple, amazing and unfathomable—deep caves paved with kitchen linoleum." Del has learned to empathize with others instead of treating them as raw material. That same appreciation of the contradictions of the everyday brings to life the small-town streets and the natural landscape, along the banks of the Wawanash river. **ACo**

House Mother Normal

B. S. Johnson

Lifespan | b. 1933 (England), d. 1973
First Published | 1971
First Published by | Collins (London)
Full Title | House Mother Normal: A Geriatric Comedy

B. S. Johnson's novel is a razor-sharp parody of the world of geriatric state-care. Cruelty between proprietor and patient is normalized as an accepted routine for nursing the elderly under meager sponsorship. House Mother Normal is structured by descent, both psychological and moral. The novel unfolds as a series of monologues from the most able-minded resident, Sarah Lamson, whose disabilities are largely rheumatic, to the ninety-four-year-old Rosetta Stanton, whose physical and cognitive ailments are too numerous to list. Rosetta has been addressed by the authorities as a case unworthy even of pity simply because "she has everything everyone else has," and her utterances randomly scatter the page, drained of all intention or reference.

This is a challenging and uncomfortable position in which to be placed as reader. Johnson offers us a privileged, almost forensic, access to the mind of each of his speakers. Little is inevitable in this anarchic care home as we move, in the case of each occupant, through the vicissitudes of their recollections, interrupted only by the House Mother's grim party game of pass-the-parcel, which she has organized solely for her own sadistic gratification. Johnson compels us to acknowledge our freedom as observers who can go on thinking and speculating at will—who have the freedom, potentially, to choose not to be at the mercy of institutional abuse—while each of the narrators lapse between pain and slumber. **DJ**

In a Free State

V. S. Naipaul

Lifespan | *b.* 1932 (Trinidad)
First Published | 1971, by Deutsch (London)
Full Name | Vidiadhar Surajprasad Naipaul
Booker Prize | 1971

Winner of the 1971 Booker Prize, *In a Free State* contains two short stories and a novella enveloped by a diary-form prologue and epilogue. One of V. S. Naipaul's best-known novels, it is a profound examination of dislocation and the meaning and limitations of freedom in a context of displacement.

In the first story, an Indian servant finds himself in Washington after his boss is posted there as a diplomat. He ends up as an illegal immigrant and marries to become naturalized. In the second narrative, an Indian from the West Indies follows his brother to England and is left fending for himself. In both cases, freedom arrives only with the loss of those anchors that once provided meaning and security in their home countries.

The longest narrative of the collection, "In a Free State," is set in an unnamed, newly independent country in Africa. Bobby, a homosexual colonial civil servant with a penchant for seducing young black men, and Linda, a colonial radio host's wife, who harbors a disgust for Africans, travel by car to the Southern Collectorate, an autonomous region of the country still controlled by the king. During the journey, a series of antagonistic encounters take place with local inhabitants that progress from insults and vandalism to physical violence. The old colonial confidence that surrounds the start of the journey is gradually eroded and the brutal reality of what the new free state implies for the expatriate community begins to appear. **ABi**

Surfacing

Margaret Atwood

Lifespan | *b.* 1939 (Canada)
First Published | 1972
First Published by | McClelland & Stewart (Toronto)
Movie Adaptation Released | 1981

Surfacing, Margaret Atwood's second novel, draws on elements of the thriller, the ghost story, the travelogue, and the pioneer narrative. It strikes a perfect balance between around-the-campfire suspense and intellectual insight. *Surfacing* is the story of an unnamed narrator who returns to her birthplace on a remote island in Québec after her father mysteriously disappears. She is accompanied by three lifelong city-dwellers: her partner, Joe, and an obnoxious married couple, Anna and David. After arriving on the island, dark secrets "surface" like sunken objects from the lake that surrounds it. The weaknesses, vanities, and prejudices of each character are slowly squeezed out by the experience of isolation. As the pressures of both past and present intensify, the narrator regresses into a paranoid, animalistic state, and eventually imagines herself in a shamanic union with nature after discovering an underwater cave painted with Native American glyphs.

Surfacing is a novel preoccupied by the question of boundaries: of language, of national identity, of "home," of gender, and of the body. One of its most engaging features, however, is the depiction of a rural Canada transformed by commercialization and tourism. The novel shows that it is not only refugees or armies who cross borders but the whole gigantic machinery of capital and the mass media. This is a novel of belonging and displacement told with remarkable precision and economy. **SamT**

G

John Berger

Lifespan | *b.* 1926 (England)
First Published | 1972
First Published by | Weidenfeld & Nicolson (London)
Booker Prize | 1972

G is a chronicle of the sexual exploits of a nameless protagonist (helpfully identified in the novel as "the protagonist") at the turn of the century. Set against the backdrop of Garibaldi and the failed revolution of Milanese workers in 1898, the novel provides an intimate portrait of the numerous dalliances of this aspiring Don Juan, who is seemingly impervious to the calamities that are occurring outside the bedroom. *G* is an exploration of how the domain of private experience can ultimately also translate into a recognition of broader social belonging.

What is most immediately striking about the novel is the experimental narrative style. As the story is recounted largely from the perspective of the narrator and the women who yield to his seductions, "the protagonist" largely becomes the layered accumulation of these perceptions rather than a fully defined character from the outset. The novel is notable for its attention not merely to what occurs during sexual intimacy, but also how this is structured through a perception of intersubjectivity. Eroticism arises from the way the characters fashion their experience of consciousness through an awareness they have of the experience while actually performing it. This narrative absorption in the realm of the senses, rather than insulating the reluctant hero further from a world of contact with others, becomes the mainspring for an aroused consciousness of the oppression and injustice that is taking place around him. **VA**

The Summer Book

Tove Jansson

Lifespan | *b.* 1914 (Finland), *d.* 2001
First Published | 1972, by A. Bonnier (Stockholm)
Original Language | Swedish
Original Title | *Sommarboken*

The writer and artist Tove Jansson is best known as the creator of the much-loved Moomin children's stories. *The Summer Book* was one of ten novels she wrote for adults and is regarded as a modern classic in Scandinavia, where it has never been out of print.

Based loosely on the author's own experiences, *The Summer Book* spans a season during which an elderly artist and her six-year-old granddaughter, Sophia, while away the long days together on a tiny island in the Gulf of Finland. It is a magical, elegiac, quietly humorous book that slowly draws the reader into the lives of Sophia (whose mother has recently died), her grandmother, and her largely absent "Papa." The color and depth of the characterization moves the narrative forward, despite the fact that very little actually happens. The old woman and the young girl spend their days pottering around their tiny, idyllic island summer home, collecting driftwood, discussing death, putting down new turf, and infuriating each other. Descriptions, such as that of the texture of moss that has been trodden on three times, are written in minute, leisurely detail and through these descriptions the reader comes to understand the special relationship between the grandmother and granddaughter. Jansson's style is unsentimental and, as the book meanders through summer, the two learn to adjust to each other's fears and idiosyncrasies, allowing a deep, understated love to unfold that extends beyond the family to both the island and the season. **LE**

The Twilight Years

Sawako Ariyoshi

Lifespan | *b.* 1931 (Japan), *d.* 1984
First Published | 1972
First Published by | Shinchôsha (Tokyo)
Original Title | *Kôkotsu no hito*

Ariyoshi's poignant, humane novel addresses a topic of pressing concern in societies with ever-increasing life expectancy: the impact of ageing relatives upon their families. With consummate skill, Ariyoshi draws the reader into the life of Akiko, a working mother in 1970s Japan. Her busy everyday routines are blown apart by the unexpected death of her mother-in-law, which leaves her father-in-law, Shigezo, as an incipiently senile dependent. Shigezo is a contemptuous and bad-tempered egotist but now, because she is a woman, it falls to her to care for him.

Ariyoshi has plenty to say about gender and generational relations in a rapidly changing Japan, but the focus never shifts far from the almost unbearable experience of mental and physical decline in the aged. Despite painting an unsentimental and unflinching portrait of the awfulness and degradation of ageing, Ariyoshi miraculously draws a positive feeling out of the experience. Akiko finds a kind of pride and fulfillment in her absolute commitment to keeping the useless old man alive, while the mind-blank Shigezo seems to discover a serenity on the threshold of death denied him in his choleric selfish life. *The Twilight Years* is one of those profoundly useful books that confronts the worst life can bring and convinces you that, for no crude or obvious reason, it all somehow remains worthwhile. **RegG**

"But for a working wife, speed and nutritional value came before taste."

◔ Sawako Ariyoshi's novel has become a set text for students addressing the problems of a graying, ageing society.

The Optimist's Daughter

Eudora Welty

Lifespan | *b.* 1909 (U.S.), *d.* 2001
First Published | 1972
First Published by | Random House (New York)
Pulitzer Prize | 1973

Eudora Welty's understated novel relates events surrounding the death of 71-year-old Judge McKelva following an eye operation. The novel begins by sketching out various antagonisms that intensify once the judge, the "optimist" of the title, is no longer there to neutralize them. His young second wife, Fay, takes pains to assert her authority as "Mrs. McKelva"; Laurel, his adult daughter, tries to manage the funeral formalities while remembering her family's past; and the townswomen frame the activity in a flurry of speculative talk. Laurel and Fay struggle against each other almost constantly, for reasons of temperament and perceived familial status. In the end, however, the fact that Laurel has long ago left her hometown and forfeited her insider status renders her palpably ignorant of who her father is and what has motivated his retired life.

Laurel represents a genteel Southern woman, whereas Fay is characterized as a grasping, coarse figure. Yet both women are young widows by the end of the novel, and the village women interpret Laurel's choice to remain in Chicago after her husband's death as an indication of Laurel's own version of Fay's self-centeredness. The fact that the novel closes with the village women's amused disbelief over the judge's poor choice of Fay as his second wife, seems to suggest the parties may not be so dissimilar as they like to imagine. **AF**

Invisible Cities

Italo Calvino

Lifespan | *b.* 1923 (Cuba), *d.* 1985 (Italy)
First Published | 1972
First Published by | G. Einaudi (Turin)
Original Title | *Le città invisibili*

Invisible Cities is constructed as a series of imaginary travel anecdotes told to the Tartar emperor Kublai Khan by the Venetian explorer Marco Polo. Fifty-five prose pieces each describe a different fabulous city and each contains a conceptual or philosophical puzzle or enigma. Zemrude, for example, is a city that changes according to the mood of the beholder. It is divided into upper and lower parts, windowsills and fountains above, gutters and wastepaper below. The upper world is known chiefly through the memory of those whose eyes now dwell on the lower. In Diomira, one feels envious toward those other visitors for whom the city instils melancholy. Zoe, a city of "indivisible existence," where every activity is possible everywhere, becomes indistinct: "Why, then, does the city exist?"

Tucked between some of the descriptions are brief but telling episodes in which the relationship between the interlocutors is developed. Kublai Khan finds in the Venetian's stories something to transcend his earthly, temporal empire. In their art he discerns, "through the walls and towers destined to crumble, the tracery of a pattern so subtle it could escape the termites' gnawing." For his part, Polo invents cities on a redemptive principle. He says, "I am collecting the ashes of the other possible cities that vanish to make room for it, cities that can never be rebuilt or remembered." **DH**

Gravity's Rainbow

Thomas Pynchon

Lifespan | *b.* 1937 (U.S.)
First Published | 1973
First Published by | Viking Press (New York)
National Book Award | 1974

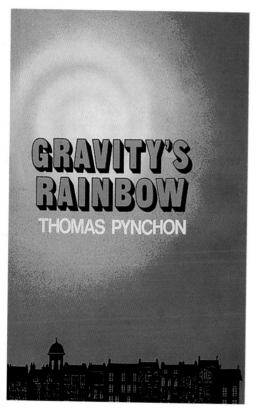

🔊 Pynchon's massive work opens with London under attack from V-2 rockets during the closing stages of the Second World War.

It would be as futile to attempt a plot summary of *Gravity's Rainbow* here as it would be to say that *Ulysses* is about two men and their day in Dublin. Indeed, Thomas Pynchon's extraordinary novel is already famous (or perhaps infamous) for its linguistic experimentation, its esoteric knowledge systems, and the way in which it so visibly dismantles its own sense of space and time. Nevertheless, much of the novel can be located in Europe during the years just preceding the end of the Second World War and the years of fragile peace just after. The central motif that binds the work together is the German V-2 rocket bomb, a weapon one hears only after it has already hit its target (the rocket travels faster than the speed of sound). The V-2 becomes a mystic object, a Kabbalistic text, an apocalyptic phallus, an emblem of "the World's suicide." Behind the scenes, shadowy (but very real) companies such as IG Farben and Shell Oil form another order of power—as if the whole war had been staged in order to find uses for their technologies and to expand their markets.

It is almost impossible to convey the scope of Pynchon's writing in a few words. *Gravity's Rainbow* is a proliferating, encyclopedic work with multiple points of entry and exit. There are literally thousands of allusions and enigmas in which to lose oneself: references to comics, B-movies, popular and classical music, drugs, magic and the occult, engineering, physics, Pavlovian psychology, economic theory—the list goes on. It remains a milestone in American fiction; a massively ambitious, carnivalesque epic that tracks the realignment of global power through the theater of war. For all the novel's complexity and darkness, it is Pynchon's commitment to oppressed and unrecorded voices, to justice, to partnership, and to community that shines through. **SamT**

The Honorary Consul

Graham Greene

Charley Fortnum, the alcoholic British Honorary Consul in a remote region of northern Argentina, has been kidnapped by mistake. Rebels from over the border in Paraguay intended to capture the American Ambassador. Fortnum may not have been the target, but he is now the hostage, and will be killed in four days' time unless a number of political prisoners are released in Paraguay. The General—Alfredo Stroessner, who ruled Paraguay from 1954 until 1989—holds power only by virtue of American patronage. But Fortnum is more of a nuisance than an asset to the British authorities, and British influence is anyway negligible.

Fortnum's only friend is Dr. Eduardo Plarr, who arrived in Argentina twenty years previously as a teenage refugee with his Paraguayan mother, leaving his English father behind. As a child in Paraguay, Plarr went to school with two of the kidnappers, and when the sedatives they have given their hostage react badly with the alcohol in his system, they call on the doctor for help. But Plarr's motives are suspect, even to himself: his father is one of the prisoners the rebels want released; he is also sleeping with Fortnum's wife.

Like many of Greene's novels, *The Honorary Consul* is concerned with the intersections of politics, religion, and sex. But the burden of Catholic guilt is carried not, as in previous books, by the protagonist, but by the leader of the kidnappers, a defrocked priest. And if Plarr seems unusually world-weary for a man in his thirties, his cynicism can be traced not only to the age of the author (Greene was nearly seventy when he wrote the novel) but to the age in which he lived. *The Honorary Consul* was published the year that Allende was overthrown in Chile by General Pinochet and the CIA. **TEJ**

Lifespan | *b.* 1904 (England), *d.* 1991 (Switzerland)
First Published | 1973
First Published by | Bodley Head (London)
Full Name | Henry Graham Greene

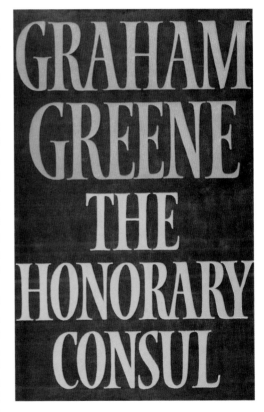

◉ The title of Greene's novel is, of course, ironic, with its suggestion of "honor" in a world that seems quite devoid of that quality.

Crash

J. G. Ballard

Lifespan | *b.* 1930 (China), *d.* 2009 (England)
First Published | 1973
First Published by | Jonathan Cape (London)
Movie Adaptation Released | 1996

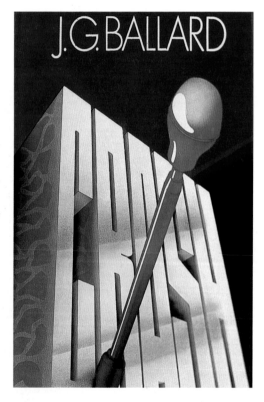

🔵 The striking jacket of the first edition of Ballard's novel gives eye-catching prominence to an undisguisedly phallic gearstick.

🔵 This wrecked Pontiac was one of the exhibits at the "Atrocity Exhibition," which was staged by Ballard in London in 1970.

J. G. Ballard's *Crash* is the story of the narrator's relationship with Vaughan and of Vaughan's obsession with the actress Elizabeth Taylor. Contemporary desire, the violence of the look, has a new vehicle, the car. There are bodies everywhere; sex and chassis, metal and skin. Photographs, radio transmissions, cameras, motor shows—all these are the new manifest content of our waking dreams. Disturbingly, the novel's characters appear to have no internal life in any traditional novelistic sense, since every excess is exposed on film or, finally, by actions. Gestures of apparent intimacy become a search for new wounds, barriers are smashed, and damage is a revered quality.

Ballard's novel, "the first pornographic book dominated by twentieth-century technology" according to Maxim Jakubowski, is an exception within an exceptional body of work. It contains none of the more explicit, worldwide catastrophes of his earlier works. This breakdown is something we can all identify with; it has already happened, inside us. Given that the narrator is named Jim Ballard, the novel jumps other barriers, providing a link with his later, lightly fictionalized, autobiographies, especially *The Kindness of Women*, where it is unnervingly possible to identify certain characters from *Crash*.

Nevertheless, the novel remains classic Ballard; the shocking insights are unerring, the perversions intensely sane and personalized. Frighteningly, it all makes sense, although not everyone would be prepared to admit they belong to this world: "The author of this book has gone beyond psychiatric help," a publisher's reader stated. This inadvertently perceptive comment invites the question—where has he ended up? Ballard considered the assessment "the greatest compliment you can be paid." **JS**

The Castle of Crossed Destinies

Italo Calvino

Lifespan | b. 1923 (Cuba), d. 1985 (Italy)
First Published | 1973
First Published by | G. Einaudi (Turin)
Original Title | Il castello dei destini incrociati

In Italo Calvino's essay collection, *Six Memos for the Next Millennium*, he argued passionately for the qualities in literature that future generations should cherish: lightness, quickness, exactitude, visibility, and multiplicity. *The Castle of Crossed Destinies* exemplifies all of these qualities, though perhaps, above all, visibility. As Calvino has said: "This book is made first of pictures—from tarot cards—and secondly of written words."

The two short books that make up *The Castle of Crossed Destinies* both follow the same pattern: a traveler arrives at his destination (a castle in one book, a tavern in the next), to discover that everyone there, including himself, has been struck dumb. The guests tell their stories to each other by means of tarot cards. The resulting tales are like a distillation of all the stories ever told. They include tales of the alchemist who sold his soul, of Roland crazed with love, tales of St. George and St. Jerome, of Faust, Oedipus, and Hamlet. Calvino's own invention, "The Waverer's Tale," tells the story of a man unable to choose in a world that continues to inflict the torment of choice upon him. In the tarot decks of Bonifacio Bembo and of Marseille, Calvino discovers, or rediscovers, the oldest story-generating machine of them all. **PT**

🔾 This confident portrait photo of Italo Calvino was taken in the author's home by French photographer Sophie Bassouls in 1974.

The Siege of Krishnapur

J. G. Farrell

Lifespan | b. 1935 (England), d. 1979 (Ireland)
First Published | 1973
First Published by | Weidenfeld & Nicolson (London)
Booker Prize | 1973

Set during the Indian Mutiny of 1857, *The Siege of Krishnapur* is concerned with a large group of characters. It might even be viewed as a kind of nineteenth-century pastiche, but it is odder and funnier than that. Beyond the siege, the novel's main point of reference is the Great Exhibition of 1851, when all the new technology invented by the Victorians was brought together and proudly displayed in London. Krishnapur's taxman, Mr. Hopkins, is an enthusiast who brings examples of the new technology to India, although most of it is eventually fired at the attacking sepoys.

The fighting is an opportunity for debates between the padre, who stresses God's existence even as he helps fire a cannon, the rationalist magistrate who believes in phrenology, and competing views of medical research. Dr. McNab correctly understands how to treat cholera, but his rival refuses treatment and dies. The novel is a mosaic of mid-Victorian languages in dispute. The languages of belief, of rationalist skepticism, and quite bad poetry embody new (and old) perceptions. Women are modernized and liberated by the siege; Lucy, trapped in Krishnapur, becomes expert in making cartridges and when the siege is raised and they are no longer needed, she weeps. The anti-imperialist uprising provokes debates about occupation of countries that are as relevant now as then. **AMu**

A Question of Power

Bessie Head

Lifespan | *b.* 1937 (South Africa), *d.* 1986 (Botswana)
First Published | 1973
First Published by | Davis-Poynter (London)
Paperback | Heinemann African Writers Series

A Question of Power raises fascinating questions about the relationship of fiction to autobiography. Like Bessie Head herself, the novel's protagonist, Elizabeth, has fled apartheid South Africa for Botswana; the daughter of a black father and a white mother imprisoned for insanity, she was brought up by a foster-mother she believed to be her birth mother until adolescence. Elizabeth, like Head, undergoes an experience in Botswana that could be variously described as spiritual journey or mental breakdown.

The novel shifts continually between two narratives. One concerns Elizabeth's life in a Botswanan village. The other strand tells the story of Elizabeth's debilitating visions of the monklike figure Sello and the sadistic seducer Dan. Head never allows her reader to know whether these figures are supernatural apparitions of ancient souls or the figments of a disordered mind. Not least of the haunting presences in the novel is South Africa itself. *A Question of Power* is perhaps most profoundly concerned with what Head calls "the problem of evil." Elizabeth's wrestling with the visions comprises a meditation upon the nature of evil. The final outcome of her journey is the realization that life must be sacred. Perhaps the greatest triumph of this fine novel is that to read it is to feel oneself go just a little mad—to have thrown into disarray one's certainties about the boundaries between fiction and autobiography, reality and unreality, madness and cure. **VM**

Fear of Flying

Erica Jong

Lifespan | *b.* 1942 (U.S.)
First Published | 1973
First Published by | Holt, Rinehart & Winston (N.Y.)
Full Name | Erica Mann Jong

An uninhibited tale of sexual liberation and self-discovery, as well as being a self-consciously feminist text, *Fear of Flying* tells the story of a twice-married, over-psychoanalyzed woman writer named Isadora Wing, who models herself on predecessors such as Mary Wollstonecraft and Virginia Woolf, and leaves her psychiatrist husband at an international conference in order to take up with an inappropriate lover. They travel around Europe in a drunken daze, making love and feeling guilty in equal measures, before the lover leaves Isadora. Isadora returns to her husband, having learned, in the space of twenty-four hours of solitude, to stand on her own two feet.

A flawed, articulate heroine, Isadora is unable to incorporate feminism fully in her life. Escape fantasies loom large in her imagination, and are intimately bound up, for her, in being a woman. The novel is peppered with both graphically sexual flashbacks and didactic statements of feminism; the combination does not always work. While Erica Jong attempts to portray sexual infidelity as liberating, Isadora's emotional dependence on the men in her life undercuts this message. *Fear of Flying* breaks many taboos, but the novel ultimately leaves the status of the institution of marriage intact. It is this ambivalence toward feminism that makes this a key text in the feminist canon. **HM**

❯ Young and vivacious, Erica Jong interpreted feminism as a woman's right to the pursuit of unbridled heterosexual pleasure.

The Dispossessed

Ursula K. Le Guin

Lifespan | *b.* 1929 (U.S.)
First Published | 1974
First Published by | Harper & Row (New York)
Full Title | *The Dispossessed: An Ambiguous Utopia*

The Dispossessed is the fifth in Le Guin's Hainish Cycle of novels but concerns the earliest events in its chronology. While a science fiction novel on the surface, *The Dispossessed* gives up the genre staples of light-speed travel and space battles in favour of a more "realistic" mode, alongside a simultaneous rendering of a complex temporality in theme and plot. The novel tells of two parts of the physicist Shevek's life on two different planets, described in alternating chapters. The plot concerns his experience of separately flawed systems as he lives first in the socially libertarian but scientifically restrictive Anarres, then on the capitalist Uras where he is free to work towards the completion of his research into a General Temporal Theory.

The Cold War parallels in Le Guin's description of the two planets are self-evident, but the positive and negative characteristics of each society oscillate as much as the complex temporality that the novel attempts to establish. This is both a complex work of science fiction and a complex political text, refusing to draw simple, black-and-white conclusions about the differing states Shevek attempts to innovate within. Instead, Le Guin uses the novel to draw distinctions and comparisons in a manner that mirrors the temporal concepts at the heart of the story; the respective benefits and impediments that the two systems produce are presented alongside each other in a way that highlights the process of evaluation over the conclusions. **SF**

The Diviners

Margaret Laurence

Lifespan | *b.* 1926 (Canada), *d.* 1987
First Published | 1974
First Published by | McClelland & Stewart (Toronto)
Given Name | *Jean Margaret Wemyss*

In the year of its publication, *The Diviners* was awarded the Governor General's award, the highest honor for literary arts in Canada. In the same year, however, and throughout the decade that followed, it was also denounced from pulpits and banned by school boards as blasphemy, pornography, and insidious warfare on the sanctity of marriage.

Margaret Laurence's last novel, the fifth in her Manawaka cycle set in rural Manitoba, is now prescribed reading in Canadian classrooms. Its well-loved heroine, Morag Gunn, is a towering figure of courage and independence, challenging the racial and sexual mores of her time. *The Diviners* is also emblematic of its generation, however, for its early grappling with the meaning of "identity." Morag is an orphan who attempts to weld a heritage out of snapshot memories of her parents and her foster father's epic tales of her ever-resilient Scottish ancestors. But she is also fascinated by the heritage of other displaced people she knows, finding understanding and a strange kind of love with a Métis boy, whose forebears were pushed aside by hers. Over the years, their lives intersect and diverge and intersect again, as she becomes a writer, and he a singer, both divining the past for a sense of belonging. Eventually, they share a child, who later seeks her own identity in much the same painful way. *The Diviners'* no-nonsense prose, starkly honest depictions of small-town life, and witty, moving heroine lodge in the memory as lifelong allies. **MaM**

The Lost Honor of Katharina Blum

Heinrich Böll

Lifespan | *b.* 1917 (Germany), *d.* 1985
First Published | 1974
First Published by | Kiepenheuer & Witsch (Cologne)
Original Title | *Die Verlorene Ehre der Katharina Blum*

The Lost Honor of Katharina Blum is possibly best known now as the basis for Volker Schlöndorff's and Margarethe von Trotta's acclaimed 1975 film of the same name. On the surface, the novel appears to be a morality tale with a simple lesson about the evil of the unscrupulous sensationalism of the mass media. This is born out by the fact that it was written after Heinrich Böll himself was made the subject of a virulent hate campaign by the populist right-wing tabloid *Bild* after he criticized the newspaper in the liberal weekly *Der Spiegel*.

Katharina Blum is a normal young woman who lives a somewhat reclusive life, working as a housekeeper. At a party she meets and falls in love with Ludwig Gotten, wanted by the police for an unspecified crime. The pair spend the night together at Katharina's flat, but when the police storm the building in the morning, Ludwig has vanished. Over the next four days, Katharina's life is taken apart by the police and her name is dragged through the mud by a mass tabloid clearly modeled on *Bild*. She decides to give a private interview to the tabloid reporter responsible, and when he makes a sexual pass at her, she shoots him dead. Böll's text is more than simply an outraged response to the excesses of a specific tabloid. It contains an awareness of the power and the dangers of language, as well as a warning about the violence that even supposedly objective words can do if respect for facts is not accompanied by respect for people. **DG**

"... she rings the front door bell at the home of Walter Moeding, Crime Commissioner, ... and she declares to the startled Moeding that at about 12:15 noon that day she shot and killed Werner Totges..."

⊙ A poster for the original German version of Schlöndorff and Von Trotta's highly acclaimed 1975 movie adaptation of Böll's novel.

Dusklands

J. M. Coetzee

Lifespan | b. 1940 (South Africa)
First Published | 1974
First Published by | Ravan Press (Johannesburg)
Nobel Prize for Literature | 2003

Dusklands is composed of two short narratives. The first deals with Eugene Dawn's work on "The Vietnam Project," devising and analyzing mythographies that will both allow America to justify its own position in that war, and undermine the Viet Cong's resistance. The second is the self-told, brutal tale of Jacobus Coetzee, one of the "heroes who first ventured into the interior of Southern Africa, and brought back news of what we had inherited."

The parallels and crossovers of these two narratives make for unsettling, stark juxtapositions. The lines between the physical, mental, and cultural methods of colonial domination are blurred, and the psychology of the imperialist is laid disturbingly bare. Underneath this tantalizing exploration, never quite on the surface, lies a strong interrogation of the way in which history is itself constructed. Yet despite this density of theoretical allusion and exploration, the text is never sterile. J. M. Coetzee's prose is characteristically direct and vivid. Conjured from the spare passages are visions of horror and empathy, falsehood, and truth. From the twenty-four pictures of the Vietnam War that Dawn carries round in a lunch pail, to the horrific "vengeance" meted out by Jacobus Coetzee, *Dusklands* is viscerally gripping. It is a novel that manages to be a breathtakingly direct attack on its targets, but also an unnerving reminder of the spreading tentacles of complicity, and of the presence in all our stories of the things that we would rather were not told. **DR**

The Fan Man

William Kotzwinkle

Lifespan | b. 1938 (U.S.)
First Published | 1974
First Published by | Avon (New York)
First UK Edition | A. Ellis (Henley-on-Thames)

Books take us to many exotic and strange places, but few are stranger than the sublime depths of the mind of Horse Badorties, the Fan Man. William Kotzwinkle plants us into the psychedelic rollercoaster of Horse's dirt and drug-addled brain. We wander with Horse through the "abominated filthiness" of his Lower East Side apartment, a "pad" stacked so high with garbage and cockroach nests that he needs to get another pad on the same floor. "The rent will be high but it's not so bad if you don't pay it."

Not a paragraph passes without Horse's focus abruptly shifting onto a new plan. Swept along on this exuberant torrent, we are left exhausted and not a little disoriented. We travel with Horse in his cardboard Ukrainian slippers and his Commander Schmuck Imperial Red Chinese Army hat as he embarks on his greatest scheme: recruiting teenage runaway "chicks" for his apocalyptic Love Chorus. He is constantly waylaid by his frenzied craving for a Times Square hotdog, the procurement of an air-raid siren from a junkyard, or, startlingly, Dorky Day (a ritualistic mind-cleaning where Horse utters "Dorky" 1,382 times in a single chapter). This marijuana-fuelled rhapsody, combined with a grab-bag of Eastern philosophy, is a hippie celebration of all things hippie, at a time when hippies were regarded, without nostalgia, as dirty, lazy, and deluded (all of which Horse gleefully is). A week in the head of Horse Badorties is exhilarating. And your mind will never be the same, man. At least, not legally. **GT**

The Port

Antun Šoljan

Lifespan | b. 1932 (Yugoslavia), d. 1993 (Croatia)
First Published | 1974
First Published in | Znanje (Zagreb)
Original Title | Luka

In his novel The Port, Antun Šoljan turns politics into fiction. His theme is the relationship between a government and the individual: how a government can control a person's dreams and also destroy them without his realizing it. When a government sees profit in something—in this novel it is oil—there is nothing that can stop it in reaching its goal. Conversely, that government can be ruthless if the promise of profit disappears.

The story is set in a small town called Murvice on Croatia's Adriatic coast. Šoljan's protagonist is engineer Slobodan Despot; his only connection with the town is that his father was born there, but he hopes one day to spend his retirement in the port. Engineer Despot is in charge of a government project called "Port." Creating the port is his dream. He will finally build something magnificent and help the whole region, or so he thinks.

Despot is just an ordinary, rather bored man, but as the story develops his life is gradually destroyed. His dream gets no support from his wife, government officials start to use him for their dirty work, and stress begins to eat him from the inside. Far from building a bridge to connect nations, he loses himself in fantasy and spends his days in drinking and sex until the whole project falls into the water. The government cancels the project and pulls out, and the poor engineer loses his sanity. The Port's message is bleak, but it has comedy and also provides insight into what was Yugoslavian life. **MCi**

Ragtime

E. L. Doctorow

Lifespan | b. 1931 (U.S.)
First Published | 1975
First Published by | Random House (New York)
Musical Adaptation | 1998

The first paragraph of Ragtime lasts nearly two pages, the sentences tumbling out one after another. Look at the passage again and you'll find that it consists of a series of short, declarative statements, almost all of them based on past tenses of the verb "to be": "It was . . . ," "There were . . . ," "He was . . . ," "She had been . . . ." The effect is to consign the things described to an irretrievable past: the sentences gather, like the fragments of a mosaic, to form a picture of American life in the early 1900s—an era whose sensibilities, E. L. Doctorow seems to suggest, belong now to history. As the novel develops out of the threads begun in this opening passage, the stories of real historical figures—Henry Ford, Theodore Roosevelt, Emma Goldman, Freud, Houdini, and countless others—intersect with the fictional destinies of a white bourgeois American family, called simply Mother, Father, Mother's Younger Brother, and so on, and an equally emblematic immigrant Jewish family, Mameh, Tateh, and The Little Girl. Among the stories that stand out against the panorama is that of Coalhouse Walker, a successful ragtime pianist, who has his new Model T Ford vandalized by racist firemen. He leaves the car to rot in the road where it stands, but his protest escalates, finally ending in a hail of bullets outside the home of Pierpont Morgan, the weathiest man in America. The stories are rich, vivid, and involving; but what will stay with you is the writing, the eddying jazz in Doctorow's prose. **PMy**

The Commandant

Jessica Anderson

Lifespan | *b.* 1916 (Australia)
First Published | 1975
First Published by | Macmillan (London)
Miles Franklin Literary Award | 1978, 1980

Patrick Logan, the Commandant, is an unquestioning disciplinarian, convinced that a strict regime is the only way to run his remote penal colony at Moreton Bay (present-day Brisbane). In the space of just a few months in 1830, he is forced to question his values in a country where social and political changes are afoot, spurred on by a free press. The penal colony is only reachable by boat, so news travels slowly. When it does, it is not good news for Logan. Escaped prisoners have reached Sydney and tales of a barbaric commandant have appeared in the press. Logan is not concerned with the maneuvering taking place between press, governor, and British interest. But when visitors, including Captain Clunie (working for the governor to ascertain the situation) and his more liberal-minded sister-in-law, Frances O'Briene (through whose eyes the story is mostly told), arrive at the colony, the tale unfolds with an added urgency and debate.

Jessica Anderson shows how in fact both protagonists are "outsiders"—Frances, with her mildly radical ideas, will not conform to upper-class colonial society, while the commandant is "out of touch" with the political milieu of London and Sydney. He has become the wrong man in the wrong place at the wrong time, unable to deal with it, and ultimately meeting his death as a result. But nothing is simple in novelist Anderson's complex treatment, and the reader is left to question the motives and morality of all involved in a land they barely understand. **JHa**

The Year of the Hare

Arto Paasilinna

Lifespan | *b.* 1942 (Finland)
First Published | 1975
First Published by | Weilin & Göös (Helsinki)
Original Title | *Jäniksen vuosi*

Editor Kaarlo Vatanen is fed up with life, numbed by the extreme boredom of his everyday routine. He is middle-aged, cynical, and unhappy. Returning home from an assignment with his photographer, their car hits a hare. Vatanen follows it into the forest and finds it with a broken hind leg. Struck with emotion, he decides to look after the poor creature. The odd couple eventually make a journey together that becomes an extraordinary rural adventure.

Vatanen's misery lifts as he becomes liberated by his simple life of traveling and working in the forest, with Arto Paasilinna's effortless style seeming to smooth away any practical difficulties he might face. The odyssey through Finland brings a new lust for life, a friendship with no need for words, and certainly a mutual dependence. The countryside offers an escape from the stupidity and unbending bureaucracy of the city, and a haven for those who are different. Paasilinna often touches on the absurdities that occur when the norm tries to neutralize the weird, always to very amusing effect.

Paasilinna uses his burlesque sense of humor to navigate through delicate subjects such as death, mental illness, suicide, unemployment, rebellion, and alcoholism, yet never descending into banality. This ability has made him a loved author not only in Finland but around the world. **TSe**

⊙ Paasilinna, shown here in 1965, grew up in the forests of Lapland; his acute knowledge of rural Finland is at the heart of his writing.

Humboldt's Gift

Saul Bellow

Lifespan | *b.* 1915 (Canada), *d.* 2005 (U.S.)
First Published | 1975
First Published by | Viking Press (New York)
Pulitzer Prize | 1976

The winner of the 1976 Pulitzer Prize, this novel is narrated in the first person. It is essentially a portrait of the artist, Charlie Citrine, a successful writer who is prompted by the death of his friend, Humboldt, into reflecting upon his own meager talents. The novel provides an episodic rather than sequential account of Citrine's travails: not only is he in thrall to a Chicago mobster, Citrine is crushed by divorce and is ultimately even abandoned by his mistress.

However, it is in Citrine's admiration for Humboldt that the novel becomes an extended lament for men of feeling who are annihilated by the testosterone-fueled credo of greed and self-aggrandizement that characterizes American society. As an increasingly disillusioned Citrine begins to realize how his own character has been shaped by these forces, the novel identifies the decadents: sexual guru Kinsey, corporate capitalism, an intellectually bankrupt philosophical discourse, and the rise of feminism all make for some rather unlikely bedfellows.

Bellow hoped that this novel would "hold up a mirror to our urban society and to show its noise, its incertitudes, its sense of crisis and despair, its standardization of pleasures." Armed with his dazzling prose style and blessed with a gift for social satire, Bellow achieves this task with conviction and intelligence. **VA**

◐ Bellow, aged sixty-one, cheerfully engages in one of the routine tasks of a writer's life with a book signing in his native Chicago.

Woman at Point Zero

Nawal El Saadawi

Lifespan | *b.* 1931 (Egypt)
First Published | 1975
First Published in | Dar al-Adab (Beirut)
Original Title | *Emra'a 'inda nuqtat al-sifr*

Woman at Point Zero is a finely executed novel of outrage and an indictment of the position of women in Egypt. It charts the history of Firdaus from her childhood as a village girl, sexually abused by her uncle, forced to marry into a violent relationship, and then pushed into prostitution. She is finally arrested for murdering a pimp and sentenced to death.

In little more than a hundred pages, the novel creates a resonant and overarching sense of relentlessness and despair. It is narrated from a prison cell, and it is Firdaus's early life, rather than her incarceration and the events leading up to it, that appears most restrictive and brutal. The circumstances of her pain may change but she remains within a closed system in which she is no more than an exchangeable sexual commodity. The repetition of key passages in the novel, in which certain individuals are substituted for others, emphasizes this element of her substitutability. There is a disturbing irony in the fact that her death, with which the novel ends, must be seen as preferable to any possibility of release.

This sense of claustrophobia is increased by Saadawi's focus on eyes throughout the novel. Firdaus's existence is very much subordinated to the threatening glare of others who prey on her body visually and sexually. There are, to be sure, intimations of the possibility of non-appropriative sexual relations. But they seem distant and fleeting, seeming to arise from an inaccessible past. **ABi**

Willard and His Bowling Trophies

Richard Brautigan

Lifespan | *b.* 1935 (U.S.), *d.* 1984
First Published | 1975, by Simon & Schuster (N. Y.)
Full Title | *Willard and His Bowling Trophies:*
A Perverse Mystery

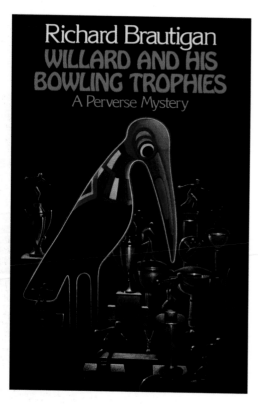

Brautigan's novels expressed the anxieties, aspirations, and humor of the American West Coast counterculture.

Roger Ressmeyer snapped Brautigan in his office in North Beach, San Francisco, in 1981, hitting the wastebasket with rejected words .

In *Willard and His Bowling Trophies*—subtitled *A Perverse Mystery*—Richard Brautigan, San Francisco's Haight-Ashbury muse, ventures into genre fiction. As a mystery it is marginal, but it is definitely perverse.

Bob, his very existence and psyche devastated by a persistent case of venereal warts (it is San Francisco in the 1970s, after all), has taken up amateur sadism in order to preserve his relationship with his wife, Constance. Constance, who gave him the warts in the first place, mourns for the loss of her old Bob, and is frustrated by this mere shell of her former husband. Willard is a large, exotically painted papier mâché bird. The bowling trophies (which are, in fact, stolen) that he presides over are located in Pat and John's apartment downstairs. Their sex life is fine. Unknown to either couple is the ever-widening, ever more violent swath of crime spreading across America as the monstrous Logan brothers ruthlessly search for their stolen bowling trophies. Formerly clean-cut exemplars of middle-American masculinity—healthy, law-abiding, good at bowling—they are now driven by rage and an obsession that leads from petty theft to armed robbery to, eventually, murder. It takes them three years—"America was a very large place and the bowling trophies were very small in comparison"—before they wind up at the house on Chestnut Street.

A novel about the arbitrary devastation wrought by fate, about the disintegration of meaning and purpose in the nadir of 1970s America, *Willard and His Bowling Trophies* is made hypnotic by Brautigan's unique style. His short, expository, sterile sentences—simple language, like an explanation to a child—act like a rhythmic metronome, leaving the reader breathless, mesmerized. And laughing. **GT**

Fateless

Imre Kertész

Lifespan | *b.* 1929 (Hungary)
First Published | 1975
First Published by | Szépirodalmi Könyvkiadó
Original Title | *Sorstalanság*

Initially rejected for publication, *Fateless* was eventually published in 1975 in Communist Hungary. At its publication, the novel, singled out for the Nobel Prize in 2002, was met with complete silence. No doubt this is due to the main concern of Imre Kertész's writing, which explores the struggle of an individual confronted with the faceless brutality of history. György Köves, a fifteen-year-old Jewish boy, is sent first to Auschwitz and then to Buchenwald. On arrival at the camp, Köves lies about his age and thus unknowingly avoids the gas chamber. Written in the first person, the novel describes the mechanisms of survival under horrific conditions.

Kertész, himself a Holocaust survivor, described the novel as being autobiographical in form, yet not an autobiography. The linearity of narration, and the frequent use of the present tense draw the reader into concentration camp life as it unfolds, including the tediousness, the physical pain, and, as Köves shockingly asserts on his return to Hungary after the end of war, the "happiness." *Fateless* thus avoids objectivity and any simple moral judgment.

Fateless asks questions in the wake of Auschwitz that need to be answered in the present, since, as Kertész insists, the Holocaust cannot be written about in the past tense. What does it mean to be Jewish? How do we become free? Auschwitz is the zero point of European culture—it marks the death of God, the beginning of solitude, and, surprisingly, the potential to fulfill a promise of liberty. **IJ**

> *"Still, even the imagination is not completely unbounded, or at least is unbounded only within limits, I have found."*

⦿ Holocaust survivor Kertész is photographed in 2005 on a visit to Berlin, a city where the death camps are now memorialized.

The Dead Father

Donald Barthelme

Lifespan | *b.* 1931 (U.S.), *d.* 1989
First Published | 1975
First Published by | Farrar, Straus & Giroux (N. Y.)
Jesse H. Jones Award | 1976

A seminal work of Postmodernist fiction, *The Dead Father* ostensibly tells the tale of the journey of a Dead Father (who "is only dead in a sense") across the countryside in search of an object called The Golden Fleece. This monolithic father (an imposing and ridiculous 3,200 cubits long) is towed by a crew of nineteen men. The Golden Fleece will rejuvenate the Dead Father and, he is assured, restore him to his former position of authority as the father of all culture. Erratic and tyrannical, the Dead Father spends his time seducing women, lamenting his lost youth, and, whenever he is so inclined, slaughtering indiscriminately those unfortunate enough to be within striking distance. It soon transpires, however, that he is being conducted not toward a place of rejuvenation but toward his burial.

In this merciless assault upon "authority", Donald Barthelme systematically slays the sacred cows of Western culture: Freudiansim is lampooned, high priests of Modernism such as Eliot and Joyce are parodied, and any notion of an objective "truth" discarded. His freewheeling narrative is comprised of seemingly inconsequential digressions that only provisionally coalesce around a meaningful plot. With its wholesale departure from reason, its flight from naturalism, and its emphasis on the textuality of text, this novel serves up a heady concoction. Readers curious as to why Postmodern fiction has proved to be so contentious need look no further than this exuberant and challenging novel. **VA**

Correction

Thomas Bernhard

Lifespan | *b.* 1931 (Netherlands), *d.* 1989 (Austria)
First Published | 1975
First Published by | Suhrkamp (Frankfurt)
Original Title | *Korrektur*

In this demanding masterpiece, Thomas Bernhard recounts the self-destruction of an eccentric and brilliant scientist, Roithamer, who is fanatically obsessed with achieving perfection in his design and building of a giant cone-shaped home for his sister. The novel consists of two parts. The first part is narrated by Roithamer's friend, a mathematician, who has returned to Austria from England following Roithamer's suicide in order to sort out his papers. The second part is a selection from Roithamer's papers. It traces the development of Roithamer's work and explores his solipsistic nihilism, cultural exile, and passionate love and hatred of Austria.

Correction is Bernhard's most sustained expression of his fascination with Wittgenstein. Roithamer shares many biographical details with Wittgenstein, but more important is the latter's rejection of his social and cultural background and inheritance, his ascetic genius, and the purity and rigor of his thought and philosophical method. Roithamer's compulsive pursuit results in his sister's death, a death he has brought about despite his great love for her. In killing his sister, he kills himself. She represents a more complete emotional and artistic self than the hyper-intellectual Roithamer.

The novel's strength lies largely in the energy of the tormented prose. It is a perfectly paced, complex study of the dangers of intellectual obsession and Bernhard's most serious working of the issues that he dealt with throughout his writing career. **AL**

A Dance to the Music of Time

Anthony Powell

This series of twelve novels, each short enough to read in a day and comprehensible if read in isolation, is an English response to Proust's *À la recherche du temps perdu*. Nick Jenkins, the mild hero of Powell's magnum opus, like Proust's narrator, observes the comic and amazing antics of his contemporaries from his schooldays at Eton in the 1920s to old age in the 1970s. The first three volumes (sometimes published together as "Spring") deal with school, university, and early life in London. The next three ("Summer") take us up to the war and through, among other things, love. The third set ("Autumn") deals with the farcical and fascinating events of 1939–1945 as seen from the entirely personal, worm's-eye view of a junior officer. The final three volumes ("Winter") find Jenkins involved in the mixed scenarios of his middle and later age: a literary conference in Venice, and English country life.

However, as with Proust, the joy of these addictive novels does not lie in their plots or in the portrait they give, such as it is, of half a century of largely upper-class English life. Powell's success comes from his comedy, his characterizations, and his style—the first two of these being indivisible from the third. Beautifully written, his assessments of the private experiences of his hero comfort us and steady our view of the world. Everything, in his quiet but elegant prose, becomes matter for comedy and puzzlement. Prime among his triumphs of character is the monstrous egoist, Kenneth Widmerpool, who features in each of the novels, appearing always in a new and more repellent incarnation until his final comeuppance in the last volume. Widmerpool might be taken as the perfect symbol of a century gone mad; Nick Jenkins, who soldiers quietly on, goes some way toward restoring the balance. **PM**

Lifespan | *b.* 1905 (England), *d.* 2000
First Published | 1951–1975
First Published by | Heinemann (London)
Full Series Includes | Twelve volumes

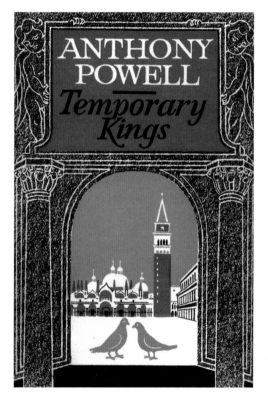

The eleventh volume in *A Dance to the Music of Time*, here pictured with its original UK hardback jacket.

Powell, pictured here in the 1930s, was influenced by interwar Modernism as well as by the tradition of English social comedy.

W, or the Memory of Childhood

Georges Perec

Lifespan | b. 1936 (France), d. 1982
First Published | 1975
First Published by | Éditions Denoël (Paris)
Original Title | W, ou le souvenir d'enfance

Georges Perec's compelling fictional autobiography alternates between two very different, apparently unrelated narratives. In the first, the narrator is told a curious story about a boy lost at sea, and an island called W, where a fictional society is organized around sport. The second story is autobiographical: still in the first person, Perec, who was born into a family of Polish Jews in 1936, narrates episodes from his childhood and boarding school years in the south of France. The customs and organization of the imagined Olympian society are presented with the accuracy and precision of a factual account. The facts of Perec's life, however, appear as mutable and as open to revision as fiction. Perec claims not to have any childhood memories, and false memory, doubt, and uncertainty beset his memoir. Dates, measurements, statistics, certificates and other official documentation of fact, however precise, do nothing to describe the inexpressible horror of Auschwitz, where Perec's mother was sent in 1943. The imaginary account of life on W, where the athletes are identified by a sign stitched to their shirts, where failure to achieve is punished by food deprivation, where a kind of utopia slowly converts to a Nazi death camp—goes some way toward filling in the blanks. With W or the Memory of Childhood Perec effectively reinvents the autobiographical form for the twentieth century. **KB**

Autumn of the Patriarch

Gabriel García Márquez

Lifespan | b. 1928 (Colombia)
First Published | 1975
First Published by | Plaza & Janés (Barcelona)
Original Title | El otoño del patriarca

Autumn of the Patriarch is García Márquez's most demanding and most experimental novel. It is also the most underrated—a novel all too often eclipsed by his more commercially successful work, and the cause of much confusion among critics: the novel is described by Garcia Márquez himself as "a poem on the solitude of power." At its center is a nameless South American dictator whose political genius is offset by his profound sense of loneliness and paranoia. The Patriarch is a synthesis of the various autocrats and lunatics who have held office during the twentieth century. He is a creature of pure cruelty and pure despair, holding sway over a long-suffering population through the mythic aura he has created for himself. After revolutionaries discover the Patriarch's decomposing body in his palace, a fantastical space of unimaginable riches, Márquez unleashes a great torrent of words, rebuilding the public and private life of the deceased tyrant from the fragments he has left.

The novel unfolds through six sections of almost entirely unpunctuated prose, often recalling Molly Bloom's soliloquy in the final chapter of Joyce's *Ulysses*. Space and time are consistently disrupted, with the narrative taking unexpected detours into real historical events and wild flights of fancy. The novel is a remarkable study in charisma, corruption, violence, and the apparatus of political power. **SamT**

Patterns
of Childhood

Christa Wolf

Lifespan | *b.* 1929 (Germany)
First Published | 1976
First Published by | Aufbau Verlag (Berlin)
Original Title | *Kindheitsmuster*

At the heart of *Patterns of Childhood* is the nature of the complex relationship between the adult and the child she once was. Can the one really leave the other behind? And will a child who has received all her earliest impressions in Nazi Germany ever be free from the period's influence?

Nelly Jordan, the autobiographical narrator of *Patterns of Childhood*, sets out to reflect on these questions when she revisits her home town, L, now the Polish G. The last time Nelly saw L was as a child, at the climax of the Second World War, as she fled from the Russian advance. The visit is a catalyst for painful memories: images she has suppressed rise again as she looks at a childhood under the Nazis with the eyes of a grown-up citizen of East Germany. Nelly's shocking conclusion is that the casual fascism in the day-to-day existence of her family and those they knew then is not so far removed from the cowardice and hypocrisy of the socialist G.D.R. of the time at which she was writing. A country of Nazis cannot overnight be turned into one populated by socialist heroes. Change, if it happens at all, will happen incrementally. *Patterns* is remarkable for its recognition that it is necessary to look at Germany's past with total honesty, notwithstanding the discomfort this entails. Christa Wolf's resolution in challenging the ideology of the G.D.R. earned her admiration and respect in Germany and beyond. **MM**

"You imagine a nation of sleepers, a people whose dreaming brains are complying with the given command: Cancel cancel cancel."

◉ Christa Wolf, who is famous for openly criticizing the leadership of East Germany during the G.D.R. era, now lives in Berlin.

Blaming

Elizabeth Taylor

Lifespan | b. 1912 (England), d. 1975
First Published | 1976
First Published by | Chatto & Windus (London)
Original Language | English

Elizabeth Taylor's final novel, *Blaming*, is a detached account of emotional rigidity, sympathetic yet unsparing in its portrait of the upper middle class. As the story begins, Amy copes with the death of her husband on a cruise around the Mediterranean. She is accompanied back to London by a chance acquaintance, Martha, a young American novelist. There is an obvious incompatibility between the restrained Englishwoman and the demonstrative American. But, looking beyond cultural stereotypes, Taylor reminds us that even the nicest people can be petty-minded. This mean-spiritedness is often manifested through penny-pinching—resentment over a taxi fare or lights left on in the house. Taylor shows how thoughtless actions sometimes have devastating consequences, drawing the reader into her character's shame, embarrassment, and remorse.

"Tragedy" seems too grandiose a term for a book so grounded in the mundane; and the closing pages do bring a happy ending of sorts. But this is tragedy in its truest sense, a mesmerizing spiral of unintended consequences. The writing is enriched by life-enhancing comedy—most notably the passages concerning Amy's fogeyish son, James, and her shrewd granddaughters, Isobel and Dora. While Taylor is an acute observer of social conventions in the early 1970s, the novel has a fluid, timeless quality that transcends its specific milieu. **ACo**

Cutter and Bone

Newton Thornburg

Lifespan | b. 1929 (U.S.)
First Published | 1976
First Published by | Little, Brown & Co. (Boston)
Full Name | Newton Kendall Thornburg

A lost masterpiece of the Vietnam era, Newton Thornburg's *Cutter and Bone* traces the domestic fallout of a period of protest that promised social and political revolution but ultimately produced little change. At the novel's heart is the relationship between Alex Cutter, an alcoholic, disillusioned, crippled Vietnam veteran, and Bone, a self-interested gigolo. When Bone witnesses a figure dumping a woman's corpse in a trashcan, and identifies the killer as conglomerate tycoon J. J. Wolfe, the two men decide to pursue Wolfe for profit and justice.

Thornburg makes sure that the reader is never certain about anything. Is Cutter really as self-interested as he pretends or does his antipathy for Wolfe conceal an underlying political motive? Is the fire that kills his wife and baby the result of Cutter's own negligence or his pursuit of Wolfe? Grieving for himself and for his country, which has sold its soul to corporations and has lost its way in Southeast Asia, Cutter's mission to bring down Wolfe is either the last act of an heroic man with nothing to lose or the product of a deranged mind. The novel is an extended suicide note in which Cutter's disillusionment is mitigated only by a bittersweet acknowledgement that the world is as lost as he imagines it to be. **AP**

❯ John Heard played the mutilated Vietnam veteran Alex Cutter in *Cutter's Way*, Ivan Passer's 1981 movie version of Thornburg's novel.

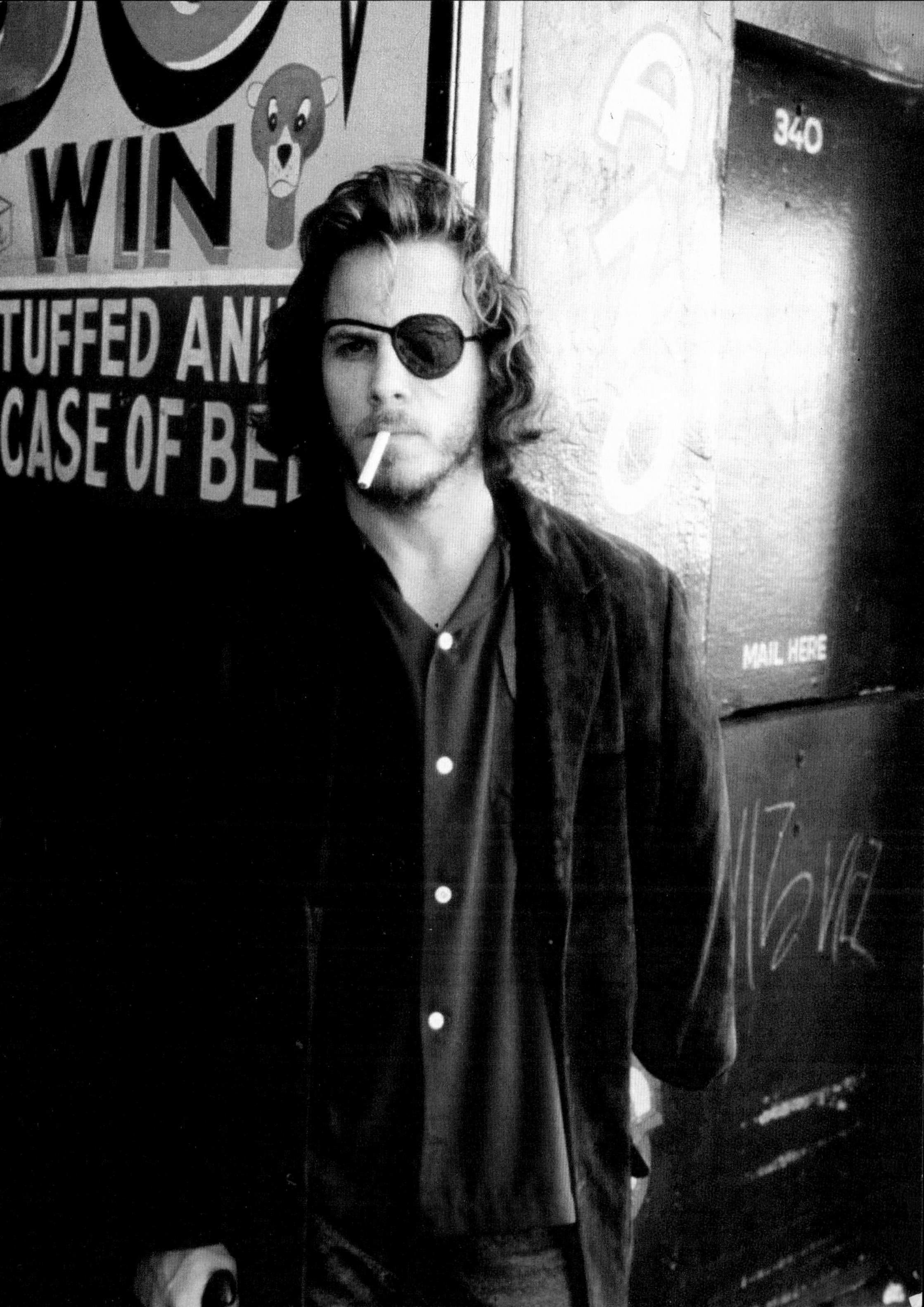
WIN
TUFFED ANI
CASE OF BE
340
MAIL HERE

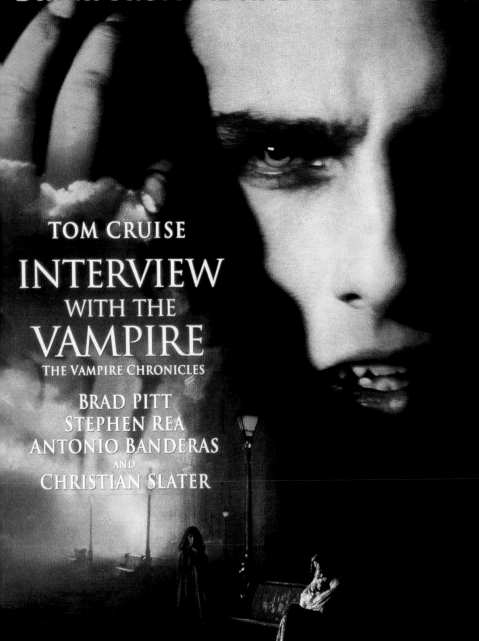

DRINK FROM ME AND LIVE FOREVER

TOM CRUISE

INTERVIEW
WITH THE
VAMPIRE
THE VAMPIRE CHRONICLES

BRAD PITT
STEPHEN REA
ANTONIO BANDERAS
AND
CHRISTIAN SLATER

GEFFEN PICTURES PRESENTS
A FILM BY NEIL JORDAN · TOM CRUISE · BRAD PITT · STEPHEN REA · ANTONIO BANDERAS AND CHRISTIAN SLATER
"INTERVIEW WITH THE VAMPIRE" KIRSTEN DUNST VAMPIRE MAKEUP AND EFFECTS BY STAN WINSTON EDITOR MICK AUDSLEY PRODUCTION DESIGNER DANTE FERRETTI
DIRECTOR OF PHOTOGRAPHY PHILIPPE ROUSSELOT MUSIC COMPOSED BY ELLIOT GOLDENTHAL CO-PRODUCER REDMOND MORRIS SCREENPLAY BY ANNE RICE BASED ON HER NOVEL
PRODUCED BY STEPHEN WOOLLEY AND DAVID GEFFEN DIRECTED BY NEIL JORDAN

Interview With the Vampire

Anne Rice

Across a long series of books, Anne Rice has substantially reworked the ancient legends of the vampire into a more modern mold. Her vampires take on many of the qualities of Dracula, but she portrays a more eroticized and more violent world than Bram Stoker, one that is brought up to date and resituated in her home town of New Orleans.

The central figure of *Interview With the Vampire* is Louis, who has been a vampire for two hundred years and is gifted, or cursed, with immortal life. As he tells his story, we begin to understand what such a life might be like. Vampires see the world through different senses—their world is at once more brutal and yet more startlingly vivid than it can ever be to mere human perception. Louis himself, however, is plagued by doubt: doubt as to how he has come into this condition, doubt as to what combination of gods and devils are actually responsible for his plight. Furthermore, he is a vampire with a conscience. Unwilling to feed off humans, he tries to assuage his uncontrollable appetite in other ways. It is a measure of the strength of the book that this improbable situation never veers into being mawkish or sentimental; the reader is brought to understand both the terrors and the attractions of being an outcast, not only from humankind but also to a large extent from the other vampires who are, perforce, his only kind.

Permeating this dilemma are the bright lights and shadows of New Orleans, a city at once ancient and modern, broodingly pagan and showily contemporary. In *Interview With the Vampire*, a novel of brilliant chiaroscuro, we find ourselves immersed in a nighttime world that sometimes seems to be the negative image of the world we perceive through our limited human senses. **DP**

Lifespan | *b.* 1941 (U.S.)
First Published | 1976
First Published by | Alfred A. Knopf (New York)
Given Name | Howard Allen O'Brien

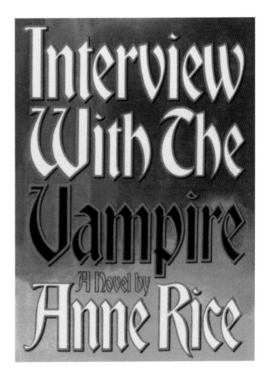

"The vampire smiled."

◆ Anne Rice is a popular writer of erotic fantasy fiction, most of which is set in her native New Orleans.

◆ Rice herself wrote the screenplay for the 1994 movie version of her novel, directed with lush, decadent style by Neil Jordan.

The Left-Handed Woman

Peter Handke

Lifespan | b. 1942 (Austria)
First Published | 1976
First Published by | Suhrkamp (Frankfurt)
Original Title | Die linkshändige Frau

Peter Handke was very much the enfant terrible of Austrian literature in the late 1960s and 1970s, whose wide-ranging output explores political, aesthetic, psychological, and philosophical issues unflinchingly, even aggressively. This novella, a story of existential crisis narrated in spare, icy prose, is a fine example of his rigorous Modernism. Disaffected housewife Marianne, in a moment of spontaneous self-assertion, decides to split up with her husband, the father of her eight-year-old son. Over the course of several days of self-imposed near-isolation, she attempts to rediscover a sense of independence and identity beyond marriage and motherhood.

Handke discourages subjective identification with characters. Marianne, for example, is referred to by the narrator simply as "the woman," her son Stefan for the most part as "the child." The narrator avoids descriptive detail and interior monologues, and translates the characters' inner confusion into a narrative of disjointed dialogue and awkward silences. The message is that personal identity is fragile and difficult to maintain; it is threatened even by everyday acts of naming and description. The symbolic idea of "left-handedness" evokes this desire for individuality, for the right to be different, and the text concludes on a reservedly optimistic note when Marianne asserts: "You haven't betrayed yourself. And no one will humiliate you any more." **JH**

Kiss of the Spider Woman

Manuel Puig

Lifespan | b. 1932 (Argentina), d. 1990 (Mexico)
First Published | 1976
First Published by | Seix-Barral (Barcelona)
Original Title | El beso de la mujer araña

Kiss of the Spider Woman is Manuel Puig's most acclaimed novel, and also the most original despite the simplicity of its approach. Two prisoners share a cell in the Argentina of the military dictatorship: Molina, a homosexual window dresser, a frivolous, egocentric character, imprisoned for corruption of a minor, and Valentín, who is there for "subversion" and is obsessed by the woman he has abandoned to follow the revolutionary struggle. To distract them from the periodic torture sessions to which they are subjected by the political police, Molina begins to tell Valentín tales of the old romantic movies that he loves. At first reluctant, Valentín joins Molina in his world of glamor and sentimentality, impatiently looking forward to the next story. Molina, for his part, comes to commits himself to Valentín's cause.

Here film becomes a powerful metaphor, as the situations of the characters in Molina's movie plots find parallels in the relationship between the two men, which passes from indifference to friendship, and from compassion to love. The novel at the same time forms a fascinating intersection between the question of "compromise," so prominent in the debates of the 1970s, and the prerogatives of fantasy and imagination. **SR**

❯ Willam Hurt gives an Oscar-winning performance as homosexual Luis Molina in Hector Babenco's 1985 movie version of Puig's novel.

Almost Transparent Blue
Ryu Murakami

Lifespan | b. 1952 (Japan)
First Published | 1976
First Published by | Kodansha (Tokyo)
Original Title | Kagirinaku tomei ni chikai buru

Rendered in excruciating, often repugnant detail, Ryu Murakami's *Almost Transparent Blue* describes the day-to-day existence of a group of nihilistic youths living near an American army base in an unnamed Japanese port town. The narrator, Ryu, and his friends have rejected the formulaic lifestyle of the "straights"—including job security, family, and most importantly, moral constraints. Rather, they devote their shared existence to drugs, sexual orgies, and music. Seemingly without a plot, the novel outlines the boredom, alienation, and subsequent depravity of a generation lacking purpose.

Written when he was only twenty-three, Ryu Murakami's *Almost Transparent Blue* refuses to spare the reader's sensibilities. The audience is forced to partake in a catalog of graphic sexual violence and drug-induced frenzies, unable to avert its gaze from the unpalatable. But beneath the meticulous descriptions of the grotesque is a stark portrait of a universal loneliness, reminiscent of Albert Camus or Franz Kafka. Straying away from the introspective trend of postwar literature, this enfant terrible of the Japanese art world annihilates the Japan of snowcapped mountains and cherry blossoms, exposing the underbelly of a culture in flux. Dividing readers and critics alike, *Almost Transparent Blue* won the prestigious Akutagawa Literary Prize in 1976, and became an instant bestseller. **BJ**

In the Heart of the Country
J. M. Coetzee

Lifespan | b. 1940 (South Africa)
First Published | 1977
First Published by | Secker & Warburg (London)
Nobel Prize for Literature | 2003

In the Heart of the Country, J. M. Coetzee's second novel, is a tale of madness, lust, and fantasy in the heart of the South African veld. Magda is the spinster daughter of a widowed white farmer on an isolated farm. When her father seduces the young bride of their African servant Hendrik, Magda collapses into jealousy, alienation, and an ambivalent desire for the love and sexuality she has never known. Feeling herself to be dried-up, barren, sexless, and unused, Magda believes that she has been spoiled for all others by her lifetime of isolation with her distant and oppressive father—a "spoiling" that in her fantasies becomes an act of paternal rape.

Coetzee's stark, dense prose achieves a kind of dark poetry as Magda struggles to fill in the void of her life with words. In enforced seclusion from history, time stretches before and behind Magda without meaning or event, and through her incessant weaving of stories she strives to pull this life into some kind of significance. Language fails, and her mind begins to consume itself. *In the Heart of the Country* is the story of a woman that history has abandoned, but the book does not itself abandon history in its journey into the inner psyche. Shocking, challenging, and disturbing, this is one of the earliest of Coetzee's fictional explorations of the webs of sexual and racial oppression bequeathed to South Africa by its history of colonial rule. **VM**

The Engineer of Human Souls

Josef Skvorecky

Lifespan | *b.* 1924 (Czechoslovakia)
First Published | 1977
First Published by | Sixty-Eight (Toronto)
Original Title | *Príbeh inzenyra lidskych dusí*

The Engineer of Human Souls centers on protagonist Danny Smiricky, a Czechoslovak writer in exile in Canada who has lived under both the Nazi and Communist regimes. Considered by the Czech authorities to be a controversial and divisive writer, Danny is continually hounded by the secret police. The plot zigzags between past and present as incidents in Danny's life trigger flashbacks from his past life in Nazi-occupied Czechoslovakia. He adopts various guises during his comedic adventures and escapes as a fugitive in order to avoid persecution.

While it is a hilarious satirical black comedy, the novel is also a somber portrait of life as a Czech immigrant in postwar Canada. The seven chapters closely relate to writers who are included in the course that Danny is currently teaching at a university in Toronto, all of whom—Poe, Hawthorne, Twain, Crane, Fitzgerald, Conrad, and Lovecraft—feature largely throughout the novel.

Josef Skvorecky was born in 1924 in Bohemia, Czechoslovakia. His first novel, *The Cowards*, written in 1958, was condemned by the Communist Party. After the Soviet invasion of 1968, Skvorecky and his wife left for Canada, where he worked as a lecturer and founded the Sixty-Eight Publishers, who published banned Czech and Slovak books. Skvorecky has received numerous awards and was appointed to the Order of Canada in 1992. **RA**

Quartet in Autumn

Barbara Pym

Lifespan | *b.* 1913 (England), *d.* 1980
First Published | 1977
First Published by | Macmillan (London)
Booker Prize Nominee | 1977

A successful novelist in the 1950s, Barbara Pym was abandoned by publishers in the 1960s, her subtle, gently humorous novels regarded as unsellable in the new brash cultural climate. In 1977, her admirers, who included the poet Philip Larkin, succeeded in attracting public attention to the long-neglected novelist. *Quartet in Autumn* was published—her first novel to appear for sixteen years—to critical acclaim.

Quartet describes the lives of four office workers approaching retirement: Marcia, Lettie, Norman and Edwin. All four live alone. Marcia is a woman veering from dottiness towards outright madness. She has developed an obsession with the surgeon who performed her mastectomy. Although she buys tinned food regularly she never eats, slowly dying of malnutrition while the tins accumulate. Lettie is sane and sensitive but painfully isolated, humiliated and patronized by all around her. The irascible Norman, "like a tetchy little dog," passes his life snapping at people and cars, while Edwin is a self-satisfied incense-sniffer, seeking out the most gratifying church services to attend.

The plot is a web of missed encounters: The nearest approach to an emotional relationship between the characters is Marcia's fleeting interest in Norman. *Quartet in Autumn* is saturated in loneliness and death; this is a book for readers ready to face some of the darkest truths of life. **RegG**

The Hour of the Star

Clarice Lispector

Lifespan | b. 1920 (Ukraine), d. 1977 (Brazil)
First Published | 1977
First Published by | Livraria José Olympio Editora
Original Title | A Hora da estrela

Clarice Lispector is known internationally as one of the great exponents of the short story, and the delicacy, evanescence, and unremitting intensity of her work do not translate easily into more extended narrative modes of fiction. In her final novel, *The Hour of the Star*, she is stretched to her formal limits. This novel operates in familiar territory for Lispector and traces the tragic life and sudden death of a poor young black Brazilian woman, Macabéa, who travels from the backwoods of Alagoas to Rio, where she ekes out a precarious existence as a barely functioning secretary. Lispector's peculiar abilities to evoke the inner lives of oppressed, uneducated, and inarticulate women are triumphantly displayed here. Her strategies for giving a voice to the voiceless include a constant humor, sometimes laconic, sometimes shot through with a wild despair.

Lispector's tremulous narrative evokes a game of life and death, in which it is the author's sacred duty to redeem her characters from oblivion. Lispector as narrator talks of her relationship with Macabéa, and gives some sense of the passionate fragility with which she negotiates her sacred task as author: "As the author I alone love her. I suffer on her account. And I alone may say to her: 'What do you ask of me weeping that I would not give to you singing?'" Lispector dedicated this book to a series of great composers, clearly aware that her work is as untranslatable as beautiful music. Lispector must be read, not written about. **MW**

Song of Solomon

Toni Morrison

Lifespan | b. 1931 (U.S.)
First Published | 1977
First Published by | Alfred A. Knopf (New York)
Given Name | Chloë Anthony Wofford

Song of Solomon opens with a desperate and lonely man attempting to fly, watched by a woman who is in the early stages of labor. The novel goes on to tell us the story of this baby, the first black child to be born inside the Mercy Hospital on Not Doctor Street. His laboring mother was allowed into the hospital because of the commotion following the failed flight from its roof and because his father had been the town's first doctor. The circumstances of this child's birth—the desires, disappointments, and dispossessions that infuse it—are the questions that he grows up to eventually resolve.

The child, Macon Dead Jr., is the son of the richest black family in a Midwestern town, and has a privileged, if largely loveless, childhood. His parents are long estranged. It is only when Macon becomes familiar with his paternal aunt's family that he learns of a family history rich in secrets and stories that he needs to gain access to. His desire for manhood takes him on a quest and he returns to the South and to the folklore from which he has been estranged. Macon finds a family history that explains him to himself and lets him, finally, possess his name. It is not until he returns home, however, and realizes the damage that his former privileged casualness has wreaked, that he learns the responsibilities that come with this knowledge. **NM**

❯ Toni Morrison has always been a politically committed author; she once stated that no "real artists have ever been non-political".

The Wars

Timothy Findley

Lifespan | b. 1930 (Canada), d. 2002 (France)
First Published | 1977
First Published by | Clarke, Irwin & Co (Toronto)
Governor General's Award for Fiction | 1977

The Wars was a bestseller and is the third novel in a total of eleven. Timothy Findley's Canadian childhood and adolescence were marked by family conflict, the events and aftermath of the Second World War, and an early realization of his homosexuality. Through these seminal experiences can be traced the recurring themes of his work—mental illness, sexuality, war, and the sufferings of the vulnerable.

The Wars is a Postmodern narrative made up of a series of personal testimonies, letters, and diary entries interspersed with the reflections of the researcher who has brought them all together. He is attempting to construct a cohesive history of Robert Ross, a nineteen-year-old Canadian who enlisted as an officer in the First World War, and the effect is a convincing documentary-style text.

Findley portrays the damage wrought on a sensitive middle-class boy whose innocence is stripped brutally from him through a series of traumatic events. Amid the carnage, love grows, not only for a fellow officer and a glamorous girl back home, but for the most blameless victims of all—the animals. Robert's rape at the hands of his comrades is emblematic of the nature of war in general—the rape of humanity. Finally broken by the insanity that surrounds him, Robert commits the last desperate and ambiguous act toward which the trajectory of the narrative speeds. Is this an act of cowardly insanity or clear minded heroism? A rejection of life or its beautiful affirmation? **GMi**

Dispatches

Michael Herr

Lifespan | b. 1940 (U.S.)
First Published | 1977
First Published by | Alfred A. Knopf (New York)
First UK Edition | 1978, by Pan Books (London)

Ostensibly journalism, Dispatches is above all great literature. The book charts the year Michael Herr spent in Vietnam (1967–68), where he witnessed some of the most brutal fighting and significant events of the war, including the Tet offensive and Khe Sanh siege. It is a carefully structured, finely wrought work that reads at times like a memoir, but with the impact and intensity of live action reporting. There is little by way of conventional journalism, but only a frank, raw account of what it felt like to be there.

Herr is unsentimental yet sympathetic in his treatment of the "grunts," the regular soldiers. He brilliantly captures the verve and wit of their slang as well as the fear, boredom, and drug-fueled insanity of the Vietnam experience. His astonishing prose ranges from a soldier's crude cynicism, "that's just a load, man. We're here to kill gooks. Period," to lyrical evocations of the jungle where "your cigarettes taste like swollen insects rolled up and smoked alive, crackling and wet." The book is an exploration of man's seemingly intractable need for thrill-seeking and the terrible fact that war is the ultimate hit. It does not shy away from the absolute horror of the war and yet it also shows how nothing can possibly match the feeling of being so alive. This is all too clearly illustrated to the reader by the disquieting fact that the book is utterly compelling to read. **AL**

❯ Michael Herr, accompanied by photographer Larry Burrows, covers the Vietnam War as a journalist in Saigon in May 1968.

The Shining

Stephen King

Stanley Kubrick's adaptation of *The Shining*, starring Jack Nicholson, is well established as classic cinema. The immense popularity of the film, however, has perhaps eclipsed the achievement of Stephen King's novel as an exceptional and thrilling piece of storytelling. When Jack Torrance takes the job as caretaker of the remote Overlook Hotel for the winter, he thinks it will provide the perfect setting in which to soothe damaged bonds between himself, his wife, Wendy, and his son, Danny, and to put an end to his long-lingering unfinished play. Nothing could be further from the truth. Marital tension, alcoholism, the destructiveness of feelings of guilt, writer's block, telepathy—not to mention wasps' nests—all converge in King's Jack Torrance more subtly and even more disturbingly than Kubrick manages to depict on screen. Perhaps one of the most impressive aspects of this novel, however, is the way that King handles and narrates the experience of a psychic/telepathic five-year-old boy who has a direct link to his father's growing insanity. As a character, Danny is neither clichéd nor overblown.

What is fascinating about this book is the balance it provokes between internal and external worlds, and the questions it raises about whether madness comes from the inside out or vice versa. It is also a novel about voices, the telepathic voices received and transmitted by Danny, but also voices as they come in the shape of histories: the history of Wendy and Jack's marriage; their private histories; the sinister history of the Overlook that Jack discovers in a scrapbook in the basement. Histories in *The Shining* become dangerous and destructive. It is, without a doubt, among the most sophisticated of King's novels and is filled with some of the most disturbing and intriguing of all King's characters. **PM**

Lifespan | *b.* 1947 (U.S.)
First Published | 1977
First Published by | Doubleday (New York)
Movie Adaptation Released | 1980

> *"'I don't believe you care much for me, Mr. Torrance. I don't care. Certainly your feelings toward me play no part in my own belief that you are not right for the job.'"*

▲ Kubrick's adaptation of *The Shining* was not well received on its first release in 1980, but is now revered as a classic horror movie.

◀ Photographed by Alex Gotfryd in the 1970s, Stephen King looks more like an academic than a writer of horror stories.

Delta of Venus

Anaïs Nin

Lifespan | *b.* 1903 (France), *d.* 1977 (U.S.)
First Published | 1977
First Published by | Harcourt Brace Jovanovich (N.Y.)
Original Language | English

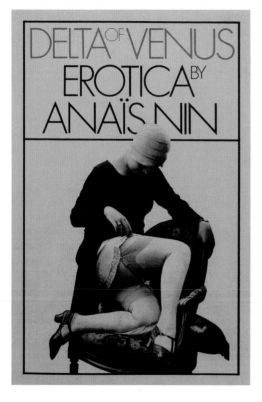

🔵 Graphic designer Milton Glaser featured a vintage pornographic photograph on the cover of the first US edition.

🔵 Audie England starred in Zalman King's 1995 movie *Delta of Venus*, a steamy if aesthetically dubious piece of cinematic erotica.

Anaïs Nin's *Delta of Venus* is a collection of strikingly Freudian erotica written for the titillation of an aged but wealthy collector at the rate of a dollar a page. Each story is a self-contained erotic episode or series of episodes, but the whole has the mark of a novel since some characters, notably the prostitute, Bijou, recur in several places. The action occurs throughout in a stylized urban and suburban Paris as distinctive and amorphous as that in Baudelaire's *Le Spleen de Paris*. The evocation of evenings in the cold studios of failing artists, the fumes of drugs, the sound of cheap music, and the rain in the gutters make Nin's tales of sexual encounter her own most impressive prose-poem: a kind of *Le Cul de Paris*.

Unlike the formulae of mainstream pornography, Nin's work touches upon homosexuality, incest hermaphroditism, interracial affairs, fetishism, and pedophilia, and its depiction of heterosexual love-making is remarkable for the genre. Everyone who takes part in the erotic cycle of tension and release, and the class of prudes who attempt to remove themselves from it, is on the road to or from a personal pathology. The characters are in helpless thrall to infatuations, repressions, and deep-seated hatreds that can only be allayed in their brief obliteration through orgasm. Bijou, however, is Nin's most remarkable creation, a voluptuous cipher and part-owner of a body placed permanently on display, endlessly enticing to men and women alike. Her total immersion in the performance of sex scarcely allows for an inner life worth having, but the unavailability of a "real" Bijou, set against the descriptions of her total sexual availability, proves much more intriguing than the recklessly conventional introspection and motivations of the other protagonists in the book. **RP**

The Beggar Maid
Alice Munro

Lifespan | *b.* 1931 (Canada)
First Published | 1978
First Published by | Macmillan of Canada (Toronto)
Original Canadian Title | *Who Do You Think You Are?*

Brought up in relative poverty, largely by Flo, her stepmother, Rose is educated out of her class. She is courted and won by Patrick, the scion of a wealthy family, who venerates her as the beggar maid in a pre-Raphaelite painting. Rose's loyalties are divided between her married life in the Vancouver suburbs and the harsh values she has left far behind geographically, but which are too deeply internalized to ever be fully rejected.

Alice Munro is best known as a short-story writer, and the gestation of *The Beggar Maid* was marked by conflicts with publishers who, at the start of her international career, were expecting her to switch to writing novels. What she produced in *The Beggar Maid* is something between a successful hybrid of the two forms, a sequence of stories marking out the stages in Rose's life so far. There is continuity, but also gaps in between. The marriage disintegrates, and Rose takes up a nomadic lifestyle as an actor and teacher, her choice of profession mirroring Munro's suggestion that we are all playing a series of roles.

In later episodes, such as "Simon's Luck," Munro explores the excruciating torments brought by the sexual revolution of the 1960s, as the old inhibitions are thrown out, only to be replaced by less explicit, more ambiguous rules of conduct. No one can summon desire as strongly as Munro, or the shame of disappointment. Munro's finely nuanced writing gives us no easy answers, no heroes or villains, just an understanding of the fickle turns of fate. **ACo**

Requiem for a Dream
Hubert Selby Jr.

Lifespan | *b.* 1928 (U.S.), *d.* 2004
First Published | 1978
First Published by | Playboy Press (Chicago)
Original Language | English

The destruction of the characters in Hubert Selby Jr.'s *Requiem for a Dream* is made all the more tragic because they bring their demise on themselves. The novel depicts the attempts of the four protagonists to escape the normality of their lives—by selling drugs, in the case of Harry, Tyrone and Marion, and by appearing on a television game show, in the case of Harry's mother Sara. Both modes of escape are rooted in addiction; to the heroin that the younger characters take but also want to sell, to the slimming pills that Sara takes in preparation for her dreamed-of television appearance, and to television and dreams as inextricably related entities.

The most striking horror of *Requiem for a Dream* is the degree to which the characters are able to ignore the evidence of their senses in order to continue towards the dream they have allocated themselves. This is seen most clearly in Sara's mental and physical deterioration through her abuse of slimming pills and amphetamines, and in Harry's willful blindness to the impracticalities of selling heroin as an addict, and to the severe infection that leads to him losing his arm. It is the anesthetizing process that all of Selby's protagonists effect on themselves, and on each other, that renders them unable to escape the paths they set in motion. As the novel unfolds it becomes clear that this is not solely an internal process, but one that is performed on them by their society, where chasing a dream at all costs is encouraged constantly. **SF**

The Singapore Grip

J. G. Farrell

Lifespan | *b.* 1935 (England), *d.* 1979 (Ireland)
First Published | 1978
First Published by | Weidenfeld & Nicolson (London)
Full Name | James Gordon Farrell

Set in Singapore just before the Japanese invasion in the Second World War, *The Singapore Grip* is the final book in Farrell's *Empire Trilogy* that began with *Troubles* and the *Siege of Krishnapur*. In each book, Farrell takes a critical view of the British Empire, representing its demise through a cast of characters, both fictional and historical, whose lives are irrevocably changed by events beyond their control.

The money that Farrell received from the Booker Prize for the *Siege of Krishnapur* helped him fund a trip to Singapore in 1975, where he began the meticulous research into the history and people of the era about which he was to write. For the Blackett family, Singapore in 1939 was a world of tennis and cocktail parties. But as Walter Blackett, the head of Singapore's oldest and most powerful rubber firm, Blackett and Webb, struggles to contain strikes by his workers, there are signs of a change in the air.

As Blackett struggles to break the strikes and fend off his daughter's unsuitable beaux, the fixed boundaries between classes and nations begin to crumble. In Farrell's account of Singapore's fall to the Japanese and the end to British superiority in the region, he creates a vivid portrait of Singapore at a historical watershed. The novel is lengthy and leisurely, but full of suspense and humor. Quietly and humorously critical of the conventions and ideologies of empire, Farrell anticipates a style of postcolonial writing that came to be embodied by authors such as Timothy Mo and Salman Rushdie. **LE**

"Singapore was not built up gradually. . . . It was simply invented one morning early in the nineteenth century . . ."

◉ The title of the novel refers to a slang phrase describing a sexual technique sometimes employed by prostitutes.

The Sea, The Sea

Iris Murdoch

Lifespan | *b.* 1919 (Ireland), *d.* 1999 (England)
First Published | 1978
First Published by | Chatto & Windus (London)
Booker Prize | 1978

Charles Arrowby is a washed-up thespian who retires to a dilapidated house by the sea to write his memoirs. Former colleagues and lovers descend upon his coastal retreat and stir up some unhappy memories, but it is with the appearance on the scene of Mary Hartley, with whom Charles has enjoyed an unconsummated fling many years previously, that the story threatens to take a more tragic turn. Alternately pathetic and absurd, Arrowby's self-absorption is ridiculed by the narrator in a number of comic set pieces. But his efforts to evade the past are doomed to failure and Arrowby's development into a character worthy of our sympathy must be accompanied by a painful self-understanding.

The sea referred to in the novel's title is not only the source of the dominant strain of imagery; it is itself a major protagonist. As a force of indeterminacy and flux, it is a counterpoint in the narrative to the deluded and narcissistic efforts of Arrowby to freeze the past into an image of his own myth-making. In a way that bears closest affinity to *The Tempest*, Arrowby's Prospero-like pretensions to orchestrate the lives of those who trespass upon his island is an egotistical tyranny that also must be surrendered in time for the denouement.

Iris Murdoch's gift for elevating even the most seemingly banal of events into the focus of enduring philosophical and ethical questions is nowhere more convincingly wrought than in this novel by a writer at the peak of her powers. **VA**

Life: A User's Manual

Georges Perec

Lifespan | *b.* 1936 (France), *d.* 1982
First Published | 1978
First Published by | Hachette (Paris)
Original Title | *La Vie, mode d'emploi*

Dwarfing its contemporaries like "a Pompidou Center amongst bus shelters," as one reviewer put it, Georges Perec's gargantuan work won the prestigious Médicis Prize in 1978. The novel seeks to write the teeming minutiae of everyday life as well as provide engaging narrative. It is also an astonishing exercise in form. The book is a portrait of a Parisian apartment block. We move around the building, each room allocated a chapter. Ever a fan of puzzles and games, Perec uses mathematical formulae to generate prepared lists of objects each of the ninety-nine chapters should contain, while a tortuous chess problem determines the route of the narrative.

The central conceit is equally labyrinthine. A rich Englishman named Percival Bartlebooth sets out to organize his life around a fifty-year project: "an arbitrarily constrained program with no purpose outside its own completion." His aesthetic endeavor entails the production and destruction of a number of paintings, resulting in nothing. Lest this nullity seems to reflect Perec's own aesthetic gesture, we must be aware that his writing is experimental, not existential. A member of the Oulipo ("Workshop for Potential Literature") group since 1967, Perec keeps to Oulipian maxims, seeking to reunite literature with the disciplines from which it has been separated, like mathematics or game theory. **DH**

> ◗ Georges Perec, genial as well as a genius, had the gift of making experimental writing an entertaining experience for the reader.

The Back Room

Carmen Martín Gaite

Lifespan | *b.* 1925 (Spain), *d.* 2000
First Published | 1978
First Published by | Destino (Barcelona)
Original Title | *El cuarto de atrás*

This novel, which won the Spanish National Prize for Literature in 1978, was the beginning in Martín Gaite's work of an intimate journey with autobiographical roots, not unrelated to her earlier novels but moving forward from them. The mixture of fiction and reality, the coexistence of a character part fantastic and part demonic ("the man in black") with personal memories, and the formalized structure of the story with much dialog, lead to innovative and imaginative results. Written in the first person and dedicated to Lewis Carroll, the novel opens by singing the praises of the "world of dreams." But it is not revealed whether it is reality or the writer's imagination that sees the arrival of the mysterious character during a tempestuous night of insomnia—when she was trying to write a novel—with whom she talks about memories, writing, fears, love, and literature.

Martín Gaite recreates the irrational imprecision of daily life as it happens, often without being understood, in stories that are linked together in some surprising ways. At dawn, the confused writer is awakened by the arrival of her daughter; she is no longer on the sofa but lying on her bed. Who telephoned, what happened? In the room is a little gilt box brought by the visitor, and sheets of paper with the title "The Back Room," the completed novel. Closing the circle, this novel begins with the same words as the story that we have just read. Is this a true fiction, or a life dreamed? This is a strange work of unresolved mystery. **M-DAB**

The Virgin in the Garden

A. S. Byatt

Lifespan | *b.* 1936 (England)
First Published | 1978
First Published by | Chatto & Windus (London)
Given Name | Antonia Susan Drabble

The Virgin in the Garden is the first part of a tetralogy (latterly known as the *Frederica Quartet*) that was completed in 2002. The four novels, set between the 1950s and 1970s, take as their anchor point the life of Frederica Potter, her family, and friends. Beginning in Yorkshire in 1953, the year of Elizabeth II's coronation, *The Virgin in the Garden* recounts Frederica's coming of age. The novel's center is the staging of a verse drama about the Virgin Queen, *Astraea*, written by Alexander Wedderburn to celebrate the coronation. Frederica's competitive nature drives her to desire only the title role in Wedderburn's play. Stephanie, Frederica's sister, although as intellectually capable as Frederica, instead chooses domesticity by marrying the local vicar. The comedy of Frederica's attempts to lose her virginity is adept and amusing, as is the sense of both time and place that A. S. Byatt conjures. The lightness of the social comedy of Frederica's story is offset by a rather dark subplot involving the mental deterioration of Frederica's younger brother, Marcus.

Many critics have noted parallels between the relationship of Frederica and Stephanie and Byatt's own relationship with her sister, the writer Margaret Drabble. As the tetralogy developed, Byatt played down the novels' historicity and their comedy (the third novel, *Babel Tower*, reads more like a thriller than a social comedy). She also went on to develop a more sophisticated model of what the historical novel ought to be in *Possession* (1990). **VC-R**

The Cement Garden

Ian McEwan

Lifespan | *b.* 1948 (England)
First Published | 1978
First Published by | Jonathan Cape (London)
First U.S. Edition | Simon & Schuster (New York)

As is the case for many of Ian McEwan's novels, *The Cement Garden* elaborates upon short stories published in his two inaugural collections: *First Love, Last Rites* (1975) and *In Between the Sheets* (1978). Both stories and novel are preoccupied with sexual maturation and initiation, incest, and violation, yet these surface continuities are ultimately less significant than their deeper proximities of form and structure. *The Cement Garden* shares the economy of the short story, with its calibrated presuppositions, pressure-cooker plot, and claustrophobic prose.

Set during a hot, indeterminate post-war summer, the novel describes the inexplicable yet inevitable actions of four children following the deaths of their parents. In an atmosphere of disturbing intimacy, the children begin to explore their adolescent sexuality, both alone and with each other. McEwan proceeds by juxtaposition rather than justification or discursive explanation. Events are simply placed alongside their responses, with a disconcerting gap where the reassurance of explanation might otherwise reside. In this world, morality is not merely forestalled: it is a dialect with which the story's language does not quite coincide. Instead, events follow their own logic, which we, as outsiders, can only translate. As a result, the final, incestuous sexual coupling of its climax becomes a perverse celebration, provoking the regeneration not only of the children's shared memories, but also their family. **DT**

"I am only including the little story of his death to explain how my sisters and I came to have such a large quantity of cement at our disposal."

⊙ McEwan was one of the first graduates of Malcolm Bradbury's creative writing course at the University of East Anglia.

Hitchhikers' Guide to the Galaxy

Douglas Adams

Lifespan | b. 1952 (England), d. 2001 (U.S.)
First Published | 1979
First Published by | Pan (London)
Series Published | 1980–1992

Douglas Adams's "trilogy in four parts" began life as a BBC radio series in 1978. This, the first book, combines the science fiction genre with pithy, tongue-in-cheek humor and some underhand satire directed at everything from bureaucracy and politics to bad poetry and the fate of all those biros . . . . When the Earth is destroyed to make way for an intergalactic motorway, hapless Everyman Arthur Dent finds himself journeying through the galaxy with his friend, Ford Prefect, who turns out not to be from Guildford but from Betelgeuse Five. Ford's job is as a writer for the eponymous *Hitchhiker's Guide to the Galaxy*, a brilliant fusion of travel book and electronic guide. Insights from the guide punctuate the narrative, providing hilarious explanations of the workings of the universe. The well-observed and eccentric characters, and a suitably bewildered Arthur, provide a rare kind of chemistry in a work of fiction that is well plotted, well paced, and surprisingly sophisticated.

Adams combines extraordinary inventiveness with an understanding of science, shamelessly flouted in the name of chuckle-out-loud wit. He affectionately mocks the planet while putting it firmly back in the center of the universe. **AC**

Adams (left) and comic book publisher Nick Landau hold a copy of Adams's book and an LP recording of the radio series.

If on a Winter's Night a Traveler

Italo Calvino

Lifespan | b. 1923 (Cuba), d. 1985 (Italy)
First Published | 1979
First Published by | G. Einaudi (Turin)
Original Title | Se una notte d'inverno un viaggiatore

If on a Winter's Night a Traveler is a novel about the urgency, desire, and frustration bound up in the practice of reading novels. Italo Calvino devises a clever narrative containing a library shelf of incomplete novels—enticing fragments from imagined books that are brutally interrupted by the contingencies of faulty binding or missing pages. For this novel is also about all that can go wrong on that hazardous journey between a writer and a reader who sits down to read a novel. That reader is me—potentially you. But it is also a character called the Reader, whose initial desire to get hold of an undamaged copy of Italo Calvino's latest novel (which happens to be titled *If on a Winter's Night a Traveler*) is soon confused with his desire for Ludmilla, another reader. Theirs is the framing narrative, interspliced with the fragments of the other novels they read—each passing itself off as the sequel to the fragment they (and we) have just read. This complex organization allows Calvino to write ten brilliant extracts from ten very different novels, this tour of reading taking us on a journey across genres, periods, languages, and cultures.

Above all, this novel is a manifesto for the pleasures and the adventures of reading alone as well as a celebration of the thrill of mutual recognition experienced when two readers discover that they have read and loved the same book. **KB**

So Long a Letter

Mariama Bâ

Lifespan | *b.* 1929 (Senegal), *d.* 1981
First Published | 1979, by Les Nouvelles Editions Africaines (Dakar)
Original Title | *Une si longue lettre*

Infidelity is a commonplace in Western fiction, but *So Long a Letter* is not really a commonplace Western novel; here the betrayal is not simply a private tragedy, but a publicly accepted way of structuring family life. Passionate, melancholy, and gently mocking, *So Long a Letter* is a declaration of love as well as a denunciation of polygamy. Written as one long letter from Ramatoulaye, a Muslim woman in Senegal, to a close friend, this novel depicts her memory not only of a long, happy marriage shattered by desertion and then death, but of thoughts on a changing society—postcolonial Senegal—where education and the rights of women rub uneasily against culture and religious tradition.

Mariama Bâ was the daughter of a politician who insisted that she pursue her education. This was despite the misgivings of her maternal grandparents, who raised her following her mother's death. The struggle between modernity and tradition was therefore present in Bâ's own childhood, and remained a constant theme in a life devoted to teaching, writing, and working for the feminist movement in Senegal.

So Long a Letter is undoubtedly one of the most energetic depictions of the female condition in African literature, and, as such, it is essential reading for those who seek an insight into feminist concerns in a rapidly changing African postcolonial context. The novel was awarded the first Noma Award for Publishing in 1980. **RMa**

Burger's Daughter

Nadine Gordimer

Lifespan | *b.* 1923 (South Africa)
First Published | 1979
First Published by | Jonathan Cape (London)
Nobel Prize for Literature | 1991

Nadine Gordimer's *Burger's Daughter* is a novel that explores the impossibility and the necessity of a private life. In South Africa in the late 1960s and 1970s, private life is a luxury, belonging only to those whites who can blind themselves to the fact that their "normality" is underpinned by other peoples' suffering. For Rosa Burger, a private life comes also to be a necessity, a strategy for survival after the death of her father in prison, a means whereby she can resist the absorption of herself into his reputation and his South Africa.

Both of Rosa's parents were Afrikaner Marxists—freedom fighters, figures for whom politics was no respecter of the thin line demarcating the supposed sanctity of the private domain. By the novel's end, Rosa Burger is also in prison. But in the defeat of her painful attempt to carve out a life of her own, there is a strange liberation.

Gordimer articulates a critique of what passes for "freedom" through the anguish of a white woman trapped in a past not of her making. The untold histories, interlaced with the story of her struggle, are the stories of migrant miners, factory workers, homeless servants, and landless peasants. This corrodes sympathy, leaving the reader no choice but to read on, to be glad this novel was written, and to regret the need for it to be written. **PMcM**

> Gordimer, here at her Johannesburg home in 1981, expresses the dilemmas of a white woman in a racially divided country.

A Bend in the River

V. S. Naipaul

Lifespan | *b.* 1932 (Trinidad)
First Published | 1979
First Published by | Deutsch (London)
Nobel Prize for Literature | 2001

◉ In the UK cover art pictured here, a small vessel makes its way through the uncharted waters of a "great river" in a vast land.

Shortlisted for the Booker Prize in 1979, V. S. Naipaul's *A Bend in the River* is set in an unnamed central African state, closely modeled on Mobutu's Zaire, and is narrated by Salim, a Muslim of Indian descent who travels from his family's home on the East African coast to run a sundries shop in a crumbling town "on the bend in the great river." The Europeans have largely departed; this is a dangerous new land.

Salim is surrounded by people of all sorts: a tribal woman who visits his shop and deals in charms and potions; an old Belgian priest who collects African masks and carvings; and upwardly mobile entrepreneurs, including a fellow Indian who sets up a Bigburger joint in town. Salim has a protégé, a young African called Ferdinand; he sends him to school and watches him transform himself from a rural nobody into a politically engaged government administrator. Always felt but never foregrounded in the narrative are the turbulent events—guerrilla uprisings, corruption, killings—of a nation that is seeking an identity. The president, always referred to as the Big Man, creates his own darkly Africanized myth of himself, aided by a white historian with whose wife Salim has a violent affair.

Everyone's lives are interconnected, and their complications are driven by larger forces: the clash of cultures, the weight of history. *A Bend in the River* shares with Naipaul's other novels a deep skepticism about the direction of non-European civilization, but, at the same time, he manages to avoid glorifying the previous colonial administration of such countries. Rather than focusing exclusively on the larger political struggles of these newly independent nations, what really resonates in Naipaul's work are the stories of individuals and their personal calamities and triumphs. **DSoa**

A Dry White Season

André Brink

Schoolteacher Ben Du Toit is one of those "nice," unassuming, middle-class Afrikaners enjoying the privileged lifestyle of servants and swimming pools that South Africa's apartheid in the 1970s afforded the whites. But his world begins to fall apart when he innocently takes up his gardener's plea to help find his son who has disappeared after protesting with other black school kids in Soweto.

In an increasingly harrowing investigation, Ben gets sucked into a world of corruption, cover-up, bigotry, and murder that goes deeper into the corridors of power. In his searching for the truth, Ben has to come to terms with the fact that he is alienating many in his community, even his family, by not "letting it go," while at the same time he is mistrusted by the blacks he is trying to help. The search is not straightforward and André Brink exposes how the wheels of state repression never stop grinding, at a human and personal level, and eventually grind our hero under. Ultimately he points the finger at the iniquities of South Africa's apartheid policy.

André Brink was no stranger to controversy when he wrote this novel. His earlier books written in his native Afrikaans (such as *Looking on Darkness*, 1977) had begun to explore the breakdown of human values brought on by the injustices of apartheid. His opinions did not exactly make him popular with his fellow Afrikaners, nor with the government—who banned his books under censorship laws. Brink was forced to translate from Afrikaans and write his works in English to allow his political message to reach a wider audience. *A Dry White Season* certainly did that, not least because it became an international movie (1989), starring Donald Sutherland, South African Janet Suzman, and cinematic heavyweight Marlon Brando. **JHa**

Lifespan | *b.* 1935 (South Africa)
First Published | 1979
First Published by | W. H. Allen (London)
Movie Adaptation Released | 1989

André Brink used Afrikaans, the language of the South African apartheid regime, to criticize white racism and state oppression.

The Book of Laughter and Forgetting

Milan Kundera

Lifespan | *b.* 1929 (Czechoslovakia)
First Published | 1979
First Published by | Gallimard (Paris)
Original Title | *Kniha smíchu a zapomnení*

Kundera
Le livre du rire et de l'oubli

folio

◉ Following the blacklisting of his works in his native Czechoslovakia, Kundera fled to France in 1975, where this novel was published.

◗ After Kundera became a French citizen in 1981, his work slowly drew away from concern with his politically troubled Czech past.

Milan Kundera compares the structure of this novel to variations upon a musical theme. This is an apposite analogy because the novel profoundly challenges our expectations of the form. It is separated into seven sections that cannot be assimilated within the conventions of a linear or cohesive narrative, and it is interspersed with historical information and Kundera's own autobiographical recollections.

Tamina, the novel's principal character, leaves Czechoslovakia with her husband to escape the realities of the Communist regime. When he dies soon afterward, she struggles with an overwhelming anxiety that she will forget him. The importance of remembering is a preoccupation of the novel, and of Kundera's wider work. It is his conviction that erasure and forgetting are political tools that are exploited by the Communist state, sometimes literally, as when dissenting party members are airbrushed out of propaganda photographs. The events of the novel take place against the backdrop of Czechoslovakia in the postwar period. Under the leadership of Alexander Dubcek, the country was working to make socialism more "human." The 1968 Soviet invasion put paid to that ambition, however, and led to disillusionment with the political process.

The Book of Laughter and Forgetting is recognizably the work of Kundera but, perhaps more than any of his other works, it is suffused with an ineffable strangeness that is at once provocative and forbidding. As with his other writing, this novel raises questions about the representation of female characters, and is open to accusations of latent misogyny. These are valid objections that may engender fruitful considerations of this novel as forming a historical document as much as a work of experimental fiction. **JW**

Fool's Gold

Maro Douka

Lifespan | *b.* 1947 (Greece)
First Published | 1979
First Published by | Kedros (Athens)
Original Title | *E Archaia Skoura*

Maro Douka's first novel, *Fool's Gold*, uses the 1967 coup d'état in Greece as its starting point and the infamous dictatorship of the colonels as its background and inspiration. Myrsini Panayotou, an Athenian girl about to start university, learns of the dictatorship and becomes more and more involved with the underground resistance. Douka uses this scenario to introduce us to a varied cast of characters who all come from a very different social background to Myrsini. Myrsini's family, bourgeois sophisticates, are forever having affairs and entertaining important people while, at the same time, falling for the latest fad or jumping on the latest fashionable bandwagon.

Douka's novel is, as you would expect, highly political, and the writer's sharp wit is aimed as much at posing leftists and the bourgeois middle class as it is at the dictatorship. She writes from Myrsini's perspective but moves sharply into the first person of the characters around her protagonist, presenting the internal monologues of the supporting cast as they are imagined by Myrsini. The reader is given an interesting, if a little heavy-handed, picture of the Greek class system and those who represent it best.

But *Fool's Gold* is not simply a novel about class and politics. It is also a Bildungsroman, for it relates the story of Myrsini's spiritual, as well as political, education. In the end, it is her feelings for her fiancé that make it difficult to reconcile her human instincts with her idealistic philosophy. **OR**

Smiley's People

John Le Carré

Lifespan | *b.* 1931 (England)
First Published | 1979
First Published by | Alfred A. Knopf (New York)
Given Name | David John Moore Cornwell

Smiley's People captures the dark, unglamorous world of espionage in the last days of the Cold War. John Le Carré maintains his fine sense of plotting and pace that is the hallmark of the accomplished thriller. George Smiley, a British intelligence agent, is called from retirement to discover why a former Soviet defector has been murdered. The novel portrays the hunt to destroy Carla, the ruthless and formidable grand master of Soviet espionage who featured in *Tinker, Tailor, Soldier, Spy*. Smiley gradually uncovers an intricate web that leads him to realize that Carla has a weak link: a parental concern for a daughter who is mentally ill. In many respects, this novel is Le Carré's bleakest depiction of a world that has seemingly lost its ideals. There is no longer even a vestige of ideological struggle between East and West; espionage here is conducted for private purposes. At the same time, he depicts politically displaced figures who have suffered enormous indignity seeking justice. The book powerfully articulates that individuals of integrity can make a difference in a morally anarchic world.

It is the human cost of the Cold War that fascinates Le Carré; both sides have generated an environment that seems to lead to psychological instability. Smiley emerges with credit because he almost wishes not to succeed: he recognizes that there is something repugnant about blackmailing Carla, that he must stoop to using methods Western values are supposed to oppose. **TH**

Southern Seas

Manuel Vásquez Montalbán

Lifespan | *b.* 1939 (Spain), *d.* 2003 (Thailand)
First Published | 1979
First Published by | Planeta (Barcelona)
Original Title | *Los mares del sur*

The scene is Barcelona on the day before the first democratic municipal elections. The haute bourgeoisie is recovering its pride, at a time when being a businessman seemed something to be ashamed of, as one of its members puts it. The investigator Pepe Carvalho, sentimental liberal, absolute hedonist, compulsive gastronome, insatiable reader, and burdened with a guilty conscience (he burns the books that he has read), declares in his turn: "We private eyes are the barometers of established morality." And he adds that "this society is rotten. It doesn't believe in anything." But the businessman whose death he is investigating, Carlos Stuart Pedrell, appears to have believed in something: he wanted to disappear to the South Seas, following in the footsteps of the painter Gauguin to the island of Tahiti.

Carvalho's investigation, as he searches for the reasons behind Pedrell's death, introduces him not only to the glamorous, sophisticated world of Barcelona's haute bourgeoisie, but also into the world of proletarian immigrants, because the secret of his death lies in one of their dormitory towns, San Magin, which—through a quirk of fate—was built by one of the dead man's companies. The novel is among the best (or perhaps the best) of Manuel Vásquez Montalbán's Carvalho books, with several nods to the best traditions of Hollywood film noir, and it also creates a portrait of the Barcelona of the time that would be hard to excel. **JCM**

> *"The policeman looked aside for a moment, and Darkie gave him a solid right-hander. A path opened for him in the night . . ."*

⬦ The cover art features a detail from Gauguin's Tahitian painting *Where Do We Come From? What Are We? Where Are We Going?*

The Name of the Rose

Umberto Eco

Lifespan | *b.* 1932 (Italy)
First Published | 1980, by Bompiani (Milan)
Movie Adaptation Released | 1986
Orginal Title | *Il nome della rosa*

With a narrative apparatus as complex as it is beautiful, Umberto Eco's *The Name of the Rose* gives the reader both a clear defense of the study of signs and an intricate detective story. Both facets are framed by the unfinished story, a prenarrative, of a scholar who finds in a number of manuscripts a story worth telling. Perhaps because the space this prenarrative is given is so slight compared to the density of what is to follow or perhaps because of the tone of the scholar, these first few pages remain with the reader as the text goes back to the source of the manuscripts in the early fourteenth century.

A young Benedictine novice, Adso of Melk, tells of his travels with a learned Franciscan, William of Baskerville, to a troubled Benedictine monastery. This monastery, a cruel enclosed arena of conflicts and secrets, is ruled by books. The Benedictines who inhabit it live for books. As, one by one, six of them are murdered, William of Baskerville searches for the truth of their internal mute warfare by finding and reading the signs of jealousy, desire, and fear.

The Name of the Rose asks its readers to share Baskerville's task of interpretation, to respect the polyphony of signs, to slow down before deciding upon meaning, and to doubt anything that promises an end to the pursuit of meaning. In this way, Eco opens up the wonder of interpretation itself. **PMcM**

🔵 Eco tries hard not to look ridiculous, posed by photographer David Lees with the rose of his novel's title in a medieval setting.

Clear Light of Day

Anita Desai

Lifespan | *b.* 1937 (India)
First Published | 1980
First Published in | Heinemann (London)
Given Name | Anita Mazumdar

Born of an Indian father and a German mother, Anita Desai has said that while she "feels about India as an Indian, she thinks about India as an outsider." In this fascinating and finely detailed novel, set in a crumbling mansion in Old Delhi, she describes the tense and fractious relationships within a deeply divided family and sets them against the seismic historical events of India's partition, the death of Gandhi, and the ensuing struggle for political power.

The two central characters are the estranged sisters Bim and Tara, brought together again on the occasion of their niece's wedding. Bim, the elder sister, has remained at home to care for her autistic younger brother and an elderly alcoholic aunt. Tara escaped from both the house and the traditions that ruled it by marrying a diplomat and going to live abroad. The two women recall their childhood past and attempt some degree of reconciliation in spite of the diverging paths their lives have since taken. But Tara finds Bim embittered and defensive, unable to forgive what she regards as betrayal of her family.

Anita Desai has described history as "a kind of juggernaut," and in many of her novels the protagonists are swept along by historical and social forces that they struggle in vain to control. In *Clear Light of Day*, she examines the effects of a complex and turbulent history on contemporary Indian society, and focuses on the way that this has impacted on the lives of the two women and their very different quests for fulfillment. **TS**

Confederacy of Dunces

John Kennedy Toole

Lifespan | *b.* 1937 (U.S.), *d.* 1969
First Published | 1980
First Published by | Louisiana State University Press
Pulitzer Prize | 1981 (posthumous)

"When a true genius appears in the world, you may know him by this sign, that the dunces are all in confederacy against him." The quote is by the satirist Jonathan Swift, and the unlikely genius at the center of John Kennedy Toole's grotesquely comic novel is the corpulent Ignatius J. Reilly, a man of huge appetites and extraordinary erudition. Intent on spending his time in his bedroom, binge-eating, ranting, and recording his musings on a jumbled pile of writing pads, he is forced, through an unfortunate turn in circumstances, to venture out into the world of work. He is drawn into a series of misunderstandings and misadventures as he struggles to deal with the horrors of modern life. Orbiting around him are the dunces, the eccentric inhabitants of a splendidly described low-life New Orleans. The atmosphere of decay adds a discordant undertone to the comedy, and there are disquieting insights into the hypocrisy and discrimination lurking behind the city's grinning carnival mask.

John Kennedy Toole struggled for years to find a publisher for the novel. It was only years after his suicide that his mother convinced the novelist Walker Percy to read the manuscript, and it was his enthusiasm for the book that led to its publication. It went on to become a bestseller. This is a timelessly funny and fast-moving novel, spiralling through a uniquely unhinged world in which, according to Ignatius J. Reilly, "the gods of Chaos, Lunacy and Bad Taste" have gained ascendancy over humankind. **TS**

Rituals

Cees Nooteboom

Lifespan | *b.* 1933 (Netherlands)
First Published | 1980
First Published by | Arbeiderspers (Amsterdam)
Original Title | *Rituelen*

Cees Nooteboom has been described as the Netherlands's answer to Nabokov or Borges. *Rituals* is neither outspokenly Postmodern nor especially magic realist, but it is certainly not linear or predictable.

Concerning Inni Wintrop, a thinker privileged with a prosperous life and too much time on his hands, the novel conjures an impressionistic literary landscape, where events and people mirror each other but are never fully explained. Perhaps Wintrop's self-confessed dilettantism cannot allow for answers, only endless and restless questioning, yet it is not his life that lies at the heart of the novel as much as the story of two men by the name of Taads; father Arnold and son Philip. Both end up committing suicide. Nooteboom uses the divergent circumstances of their lives and deaths to explore how different generations face similar crises of intellectual and spiritual faith.

Cees Nooteboom is neither burdensomely philosophical nor anthropological in his approach; ramblings on the nature of God and existence are leavened by the macabre whimsy of a circumcision or satirical soundings on the art world. Much of the language, too, is crisply and poetically precise, whether conveying existential doubt or paying homage to Amsterdam's engrossing cityscape. *Rituals* became Nooteboom's first major success in the English-speaking world; in the case of such an idiosyncratically "European" novel, perhaps this is telling of its assured greatness. **ABI**

Smell of Sadness

Alfred Kossmann

Lifespan | *b.*1922 (Netherlands), *d.*1998
First Published | 1980
First Published by | Querido (Amsterdam)
Original title | *Geur der droefenis*

Smell of Sadness is the magnum opus of the Dutch novelist Alfred Kossmann, written after he explored many boundaries of both the literary and journalistic worlds. From an early age, Kossmann was a fascinated observer of his own life and that of others, and his attitude to life was channeled into various literary forms of expression. In 1946, he made his debut as a poet with *Het vuurwerk* (*The Fireworks*), which he followed with both novels and journalism. Kossmann also published numerous extensive travel stories that combined firsthand observations and autobiographical reflections.

Smell of Sadness is an amalgam of all aspects of Kossmann's authorship, and it includes many autobiographical elements. The novel describes forty years in the life of writer Thomas Rozendal, who as a teenager claims that life "isn't hard but extremely boring." Decades later, he is compelled to accept that existence is meaningless. An atmosphere of futility and mortality emerges: one character commits suicide, another becomes insane, a third is run over by a truck. And Thomas? He lets life pass by with bewildering resignation and remains incapable of experiencing it fully. All the characters have grown up during the war and have led mostly tragic lives as a result of incomprehensible events and developments. Kossmann tells his story through interwoven memories, facts, fabrications, and dreams. Reality is distorted by an impressive literary mix, emanating a "smell of sadness." **JaM**

Broken April

Ismail Kadare

Lifespan | *b.* 1936 (Albania)
First Published | 1980, in *Gjakftohtësia*
First Published by | Naim Frashëri (Tirana)
Original Title | *Prilli i Thyer*

Set in Albania between the World Wars, in a nation on the brink of European modernity, *Broken April* focuses on the story of Gjorg Berisha's involvement in a blood feud, the conduct of which is strictly governed by the Kanun, an ancient code of honor that has dominated Albanian culture for generations. Gjorg's family have been involved in a seventy-year-old feud with a neighboring family, the Kryeqyqes. The novel begins when Gjorg assassinates a member of the Kryeqyqe family, in revenge for the earlier murder of his own brother. The murder inevitably makes Gjorg himself the next victim in the vicious cycle of recrimination and bloodshed.

The Kanun decrees that there is a thirty-day period of truce after a murder occurs, and before it can be avenged with the killing of its perpetrator. It is this period that the novel covers, from the moment that Gjorg murders his victim, in mid March, to the moment that Gjorg will be delivered to the implacable justice of the Kanun, in mid April. During this period, Gjorg is neither alive nor dead, but suspended in empty time.

Written with an extraordinary simplicity and elegance, this is a haunting and haunted tale. The space between life and death that the novel maps out is given a dreamlike articulation that is infused with the spirit of Homer, Dante, and Kafka. Kadare is also stunningly original, inventing a newly ancient language in which to express the contradictions of contemporary life in eastern Europe. **PB**

Midnight's Children

Salman Rushdie

Midnight's Children is narrated by Saleem Sinai, who was born at midnight on August 15, 1947: the moment of the creation of India as an independent nation. Saleem's life comes to embody that of the young nation. Rather than allowing the novel or this protagonist to stand as representative of the country, Salman Rushdie explores the complex fantasies and failures that the myth of nationalism offers.

All of the children born during the hour of midnight are uniquely gifted, the closer to midnight the more powerful the gift. This cohort of the fantastic and the surreal—children who can move through time, multiply fishes, become invisible—is an imaginary expression of India's rich potential. Of the group, two are born on the stroke of midnight, and are its potential leaders: Saleem, who can see into the hearts and minds of others, and Shiva, who is given the converse gift, the gift of war, and becomes a brutish killer. The adversarial relationship between the two is crucial to this huge and sprawling narrative, which is set against the backdrop of the first years of independence. Saleem comes from a privileged and well-connected family, whereas Shiva, a motherless street child, has nothing. Midway through the novel, however, we discover that these two children were swapped at birth and that neither is who they are assumed to be. The anxieties around paternity, dispossession, authenticity, and trust that this knowledge raises come to reverberate throughout the novel and are constantly read back against the partitioned history of India itself.

This masterly novel, which transfixes the reader with its imaginative scope, humor, dizzying wordplay, and heartbreaking pathos is an exciting blend of magic realism and political reality, Rushdie's heartfelt tribute to his native land. **NM**

Lifespan | *b.* 1947 (India)
First Published | 1980
First Published by | Jonathan Cape (London)
Booker Prize | 1981

Salman Rushdie, shown here in 1988, became an internationally famous writer as a result of the success of *Midnight's Children.*

Indians celebrate independence from Britain in Calcutta on August 15, 1947, the day of the birth of Rushdie's narrator, Saleem.

Waiting for the Barbarians

J. M. Coetzee

Lifespan | b. 1940 (South Africa)
First Published | 1980
First Published by | Secker & Warburg (London)
Nobel Prize for Literature | 2003

Critics frequently attempt to read into J. M. Coetzee's dense, elliptical narratives allegories of the South African state during and after the period of apartheid. *Waiting for the Barbarians* is certainly open to such an interpretation.

Set in an unnamed empire, in an unspecified location, at an imprecise time, the novel relates the tale of a magistrate. He comes up against the machinery of a brutal state by attempting, in some small way, to recompense a "barbarian" girl for the torture inflicted upon her by the inscrutable Colonel Joll. The magistrate collects wooden slips retrieved from the desert containing an ancient and unreadable script. He concludes that these fragments of writing form an allegory that arises not from the slips themselves but from the order and manner in which they are read. In this way, *Waiting for the Barbarians* is a more general meditation on the act of writing and on the potential failures of writing to communicate meaning. Here the "barbarians" seem to represent a testimony of suffering that cannot be articulated. The woman that the magistrate rescues says little and he largely infers her consciousness, seeking to read a narrative of the empire from her wounds. Similarly, through the magistrate's abasement, Coetzee offers a portrait of political commitment as something that is simultaneously total and also empty of ideology. **LC**

Summer in Baden-Baden

Leonid Tsypkin

Lifespan | b. 1926 (Belarus), d. 1982 (Russia)
First Published | 1981, in *Novyy Amerikanets* (N.Y.)
Original Title | *Leto v Badene*
First UK Edition | 1987, by Quartet (London)

This extraordinary novel, first published in 1981, just before the author died, was recently brought to the attention of the reading public by the critic Susan Sontag just before her own death.

The novel dramatizes Fyodor and Anna Dostoevsky's tempestuous relationship, focusing on a summer trip the couple took to Baden-Baden in 1867. However, the story of Anna and Fyodor is also folded inside an autobiographical account of Leonid Tsypkin's own travels, and folded again into scenes and moments from Dostoevsky's writing, and from the wider Russian literary heritage.

As the reader becomes lost between the real and the imagined, the beautiful and the ugly, in this multiframed novel, Tsypkin's wild, uncontainable prose starts to take over, to produce its own crazed reality. Tsypkin's prose is unlike any other, an entirely new and vivid invention. In the rhythms of his writing, as he imagines his way toward the insanity of Dostoevsky's love for Anna, he catches the very movement of Dostoevsky's thought, of his paranoia, his desperation, and his brilliance.

Summer in Baden-Baden gives Dostoevsky to us in a new way, and in doing so it promises to redraw the map of contemporary fiction. That it should be rescued from the dark by a woman at the end of her life, in an act that is itself a testament to the love of literary fiction, is almost uncannily fitting. **PB**

The House with the Blind Glass Windows

Herbjørg Wassmo

Lifespan | b. 1942 (Norway)
First Published | 1981
First Published in | Gyldendal (Oslo)
Original Title | Huset med den blinde glassveranda

Set in a small Norwegian fishing village still struggling in the aftermath of German Nazi occupation, *The House with the Blind Glass Windows* tells the story of eleven-year-old Tora. The illegitimate daughter of a dead German soldier, Tora shares a run-down tenement flat with her mother and drunken stepfather, Henrik. Socially ostracized by the stigma of her birth, Tora also suffers constant sexual and mental abuse from her stepfather while her mother is at work.

Wassmo's fragmented prose conveys Tora's increasing despair as she struggles to deal with her bleak situation. Although in desperate need of protection, Tora is scared of burdening her mother with the truth. She escapes into a fantasy world of safety and comfort, imagining her real father coming to rescue her. Wassmo lightens this brutal narrative and graphic content with gentle and melodic prose.

The House With The Blind Glass Windows was the first volume of Wassmo's Tora trilogy. The novel is not just a tale of woe; with the friendship and support of a few neighboring women, Tora finds the strength to survive. While centrally a novel about the victimization of women, *The House with the Blind Glass Windows* also celebrates Tora's triumph. This is a powerful tale about women's solidarity, as together they struggle against gender inequality, poverty, and postwar depression. **RA**

Leaden Wings

Zhang Jie

Lifespan | b. 1937 (China)
First Published | 1981, by The People's Literature Publishing House
Original Title | Chenzhong de chibang

Zhang Jie's novel tells the stories of a group of characters who have in common their connection to the Dawn Motor Works, a large Chinese industrial corporation. The central theme is the radical change brought about by modernization and how this change affected Chinese society. Jie's intimate observations of daily life in modern China lay bare the effects that cultural and political revolution had on the peripheral characters of industrial society, giving us a unique insight into the lives of factory workers and their wives and children.

With extensive use of dialog and a tantalizing lack of narrative conclusion, the short, open-ended stories glimpse fragments of a changing culture. Despite recent developments, prejudices rooted in a feudal past still reign; reformers face formidable obstacles from officials who built their careers under the old system, and women are still regarded as second-class citizens. We are left curious as to the outcome of the various characters, but also with a wider picture of their social and political unease.

In the midst of the Cultural Revolution, Zhang Jie was ordered to participate in re-education at a special school in Beijing. She later worked for almost twenty years at the Ministry of Industry for Mechanical Engineering, not starting to write until after the Cultural Revolution; this novel was one of the first of its era to be translated in the West. **RA**

The War at the End of the World

Mario Vargas Llosa

Lifespan | *b.* 1936 (Peru)
First Published | 1981
First Published in | Seix-Barral (Barcelona)
Original Title | *La guerra del fin del mundo*

Still addressing the various faces of evil in his eighth novel, Mario Vargas Llosa presents a remarkable, apocalyptic tale, at the same time establishing a turning point in his work. For the first time, the Peruvian author leaves the country of his birth and his own times to tell the story of real-life events that took place in Brazil at the end of the nineteenth century. This was the messianic experience of Antonio Consejero, a visionary holy man who, by preaching against the Republic and modernity, spoke up for the dispossessed of northeast Brazil and challenged the Republican government. Inevitably, the Brazilian army destroyed Canudos, the city in which Consejero and his supporters intended setting up a thousand-year kingdom.

Vargas Llosa created a novel of remarkable documentary power, inspired by a work that he considered fundamental, *Rebellion in the Backlands*, by Euclides da Cunha. He organized his story into a strict structural pattern consisting of an alternation of parallel stories. The result is a meticulous account of the rise, career, and destruction of a fascinating monster. A vehement critic of fanaticism and utopianism, Vargas Llosa here recovered the ambition of his novels of the 1960s. The work gave a tremendous boost to a new treatment of the historical novel that was beginning to achieve recognition in the Hispanic world. **DMG**

Lanark: A Life in Four Books

Alasdair Gray

Lifespan | *b.* 1934 (Scotland)
First Published | 1981
First Published by | Canongate (Edinburgh)
Saltire Society Book of the Year | 1981

When Alasdair Gray made his debut with *Lanark*, he seemed to reset the benchmarks for invention in Scottish fiction. Gray continued a twofold legacy, inheriting the impulse for typographic innovation from Jonathan Swift and Joyce, while sustaining a Blakean vision of radical social possibilities latent within the texture of everyday Glaswegian life. Traversing between Unthank and Glasgow, the narrative spans two urban underworlds as it traces the attempts by Lanark and Duncan Thaw to resist the drudgery of workaday routine.

Throughout *Lanark,* the reader's attention is drawn to the value of the physical book by its material layout. From chapter to chapter, Gray's iridescent etchings of imaginary topographies offset his written documentary of cynicism as an affliction of Scotland's youth. The portrayal in words of urban disaffection provokes illustrations that prospect Scotland's regeneration. With both cities portrayed as perpetual transit zones, shifting between stagnation and restitution, the reader is encouraged to interact with Gray's typographical designs (just as his protagonists mature on their journeys of self-discovery). It is this state of interactivity that testifies to the indispensability of the printed page. **DJ**

> ◉ Drawn by the author himself, this rare illustration typifies Gray's clever use of fantasy and typography in his work.

Rabbit is Rich

John Updike

Lifespan | b. 1932 (U.S.), d. 2009
First Published | 1981
First Published by | Alfred A. Knopf (New York)
Pulitzer Prize | 1982

Rabbit is Rich, the third novel in John Updike's acclaimed four-part Rabbit series, jumps forward another ten years to 1979. Set in the fictional small town of Brewer, Pennsylvania, it again takes up the story of Harry Angstrom, nicknamed "Rabbit," who, now in his forties, is enjoying a prosperous career as a used-car salesman. Happily settled with his wife, and renegotiating difficult relationships as his son grows older and marries, Rabbit has seemingly grown into the role of "solid citizen" mocked by Sinclair Lewis's *Babbitt*, which serves as an epigraph to the book. Set against the background of the worldwide oil crisis of the late 1970s, the novel's action turns on the ironies implied by Rabbit's change of occupation from a working-class linotyper to an upwardly mobile dealer in used cars. Selling Toyotas to newly gas-conscious middle-class drivers has become Rabbit's own ticket into the middle-class world of country clubs and cocktails. His pleasure in achieving the riches implied by the title is balanced by the book's sensitive portrayal of the loss of American working-class jobs.

Rabbit is Rich charts the emotional upheavals of Rabbit's personal life against the background of an America that was just on the cusp of what would become the grim anxieties of the 1980s. Updike's lyric prose and thoughtful characterizations are as strong as ever. As Rabbit ages, the sensitive portrayal of the emotional connections that underpin everyday life achieves a new poignancy. **AB**

Couples, Passerby

Botho Strauss

Lifespan | b. 1944 (Germany)
First Published | 1981
First Published in | Hanser Verlag (München)
Original Title | *Paare, Passanten*

In this collection of six vignettes by German writer and playwright Botho Strauss, couples both longstanding and temporary, frustrated in their neverending but fruitless search for meaning and emotional connection, cling together only to find greater loneliness and despair.

Loss of humanity, solipsism, and essential selfishness under the pressure of history and technology are frequent themes in the work of Strauss, an acute social conservative profoundly displeased with what he sees as the cultural drift of his country and uninterested in the way of life in the new Germany. Strauss's alienated individuals are likely to collide briefly, pointlessly, or violently.

The stories in this collection depict a people losing their humanity under the pressures of modernization and the past; they describe robotlike characters with holes where their souls should be, carrying out the tasks of their daily lives—working, talking, sinning—amid spiritually void and intellectually desolate surroundings. By sketching the lifelessness of his modern Germany, Strauss attempts to point toward a truer, more authentic mode of life and expression. That he writes in the shadow of Germany's twentieth-century history adds an obvious edge to his work and directs the interested reader's attention toward his aesthetic vision. His mini-portraits and short-takes flow from the anonymously guilty Volk of the Third Reich to the individuals of the Cold War and beyond. **LB**

July's People

Nadine Gordimer

Lifespan | *b.* 1923 (South Africa)
First Published | 1981
First Published by | Jonathan Cape (London)
Nobel Prize for Literature | 1991

This apocalyptic novel is set during the imaginary civil war that follows upon an invasion of South Africa from Mozambique in 1980. The cities are alight and the houses burning, as Maureen and Bam Smales and their children set out in a pickup truck, "the yellow bakkie," with their servant, July, to escape to safety in his distant village.

Confronted with the gritty realities of village life, Maureen prospers, whereas Bam, lost without his rifle, is a defeated man. In their newly dependent situation, Bam's relationship with July becomes increasingly difficult as the white couple gradually lose touch with their culture day by day: Maureen poses like a model across the bakkie, and July fails to recognize the moment or the meaning. Desire and duty are now largely shaped by economic considerations, and the white liberal assumption of a shared human nature is brought into question. Nadine Gordimer's complex prose performs extraordinary feats of allusion and implication to juxtapose past certainties with present doubt, and scarcely a single paragraph is set in an undisturbed present. These profound questions are hardly capable of resolution. When a helicopter lands in the village, Maureen rushes out to it, not knowing if it belongs to the army or to the revolutionaries, and there the novel ends, itself unresolved. Untrue to history and the actual moment of change in South Africa, *July's People* nevertheless provides a truthful dissection of white liberal vulnerability. **AMu**

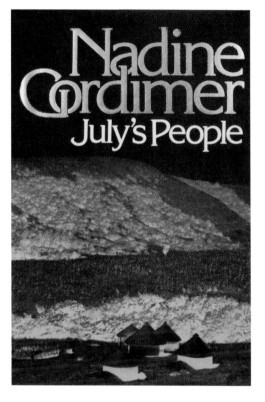

"The black man looked over to the three sleeping children bedded down on seats taken from the vehicle. He smiled confirmation: 'They all right.'"

◉ The novels and short stories of Nadine Gordimer often focus on race relations in her native South Africa.

On the Black Hill

Bruce Chatwin

Lifespan | *b*. 1940 (England), *d*. 1989 (France)
First Published | 1982
First Published by | Jonathan Cape (London)
Whitbread Literary Award | 1982

For an author who spent much of his short life traveling and writing about traveling, *On the Black Hill* is a curious book to have written. It concerns eighty years in the lives of Benjamin and Lewis, identical twins from the Welsh border country, who remain for that entire period either within or near an isolated farm on which they live and subsequently work. Apart from a very brief period in the army, from which Benjamin is dishonorably discharged, they avoid the draft for the First World War, they never marry, and after the death of their parents, they sleep in their parents' bed for over forty years.

The novel looks back over the lives of the twins, and is recounted in a distinctive realist prose. Bruce Chatwin favors the short single clause summary sentence over more complex, longer structures. He also relegates complexity of plot in favor of detailed character portrayal, avoiding both crude simplification or sentimental excess.

On one level, the novel contains all the appeal of a traditional rural drama: a hot-headed father who mistreats his educated wife and disrupts her attempts at schooling the twins, rural family feuds involving violence, a suicide, army brutality, the demise of a noble family due to corruption. But the book is also a study in the local and sedentary, and the tensions created within traditional lifestyles by motion and flight, as created by Lewis's interest in aviation and the opposite sex, and the brief and difficult moments where the twins are parted. **ABi**

The House of the Spirits

Isabel Allende

Lifespan | *b*. 1942 (Peru)
First Published | 1982
First Published by | Plaza & Janés (Barcelona)
Original Title | *La casa de los espíritus*

The vivacity of the imagination that shines through the fantastic story of Isabel Allende's *The House of the Spirits* is difficult to describe as being anything other than magical. The novel playfully traverses the boundary between the real and the incredible, while never losing its solid grounding in the history and political reality of Chile.

The House of the Spirits is a deeply personal novel. Begun as a letter to Allende's dying grandfather, it tells the story of the Trueba family, with the rise to power of Isabel's own uncle, Salvador Allende ("The Candidate" in the text), and his subsequent death in the coup of 1973 as its tragic backdrop. The atrocities that surround this bloody moment of Chilean history are strikingly evoked, and what has seemed an enchanting fairy tale becomes a dark and powerful narrative. The chronicle of these events may be the most striking element of the book, and has much to do with its (deserved) acclaim, but it is the exuberant presentation of the Trueba clan that is its emotional heart. Allende's tender and sentimental, caustic and biting assessments of thinly veiled figures from her own life are brilliantly evocative. The empathy inspired by the tale of this extraordinary family is gripping, and the deep involvement engendered by Allende's writing makes the tragic and horrifying end personally moving. **DR**

> Isabel Allende is the niece of Chilean president Salvador Allende, killed in the coup that brought General Pinochet to power in 1973.

Lfd. Nr.	H.Art u.Nam.	H.Nr.	Name und Vorname	Geburts- datum	Beruf
361	Ju.Po.	6920 8	Hahn Dawid	2o.lo.97	Werkzeugschlosse
362	" "	9	Immerglück Zygmunt	13.6. 24	Stanzer
363	" "	lo	Katz Isaak Josef	3.12.08	Klempnergehilfe
364	" "	1	Wiener Samuel	11. 5.o7	Tischlergehilfe
365	" "	2	Rosner ¨eopold	26, 6.o8	Maler
366	" "	3	Gewelbe Jakob	22. 9.97	Photografmeister
367	" "	4	Korn Edmund	7. 4.12	Metallarbeiter
368	" "	5	Penner Jonas	2. 2.15	Stanzer
369	" "	6	Wachtel Roman	5.11.o5	Industriediamant
370	" "	7	Immerglück Mendel	24.9.o3	Eisendrehergesel.
371	" "	8	Wichter ¨eiwel	25. 7.26	ang.¨etallverarb.
372	" "	9	Landschaft Aron	7. 7.o9	" "
373	" "	6922o	Wandersmann ¨arkus	14. 9.o6	Stanzer
374	" "	1	Rosenthal Izrael	24.lo.o9	Schreibkraft
375	" "	2	Silberschlag ¨ersch	7. 4.12	Ang.Metallverarbe
376	" "	3	Liban Jan	29. 4.24	Wasserinst.Gehil¨
377	" "	4	Kohane Chiel	15. 9. 25	Zimmerer
378	" "	5	Senftmann Dawid	6. 9.o9	Ang.Metallverarbe
379	" "	6	Kupferberg Izrael	4. 9.98	Schlossermeister
380	" "	7	Buchführer Norbert	12. 6.22	Lackierer Geselle
381	" "	8	Horowitz Schachne	3.1288	Schriftsetzermei
382	" "	9	Segal Richard	9.11.23	Steinbruchmineur
383	" "	6923o	Jakubowicz Dawid	15. 4.26	"
384	" "	1	Sommer Josef	21.12.14	ang.Metallverarb.
385	" "	2	Smolarz Szymon	15. 4.o4	"
386	" "	3	Rechem Ryszard	3o. 5.21	Automechank.Gs.
387	" "	4	Szlamowicz Chaim	16. 5.24	Stanzer
388	" "	5	Kleinberg Szaija	1. 4.2o	Steinbruchmineur
389	" "	6	Miedziuch Michael	3.11.16	Fleischergeselle
390	+ "	7	Millmann Bernhard	24.12.15	Stanzer
391	" "	8	Königl Marek	2.11.11.	Ang.Mettallverarb
392	" "	9	Jakubowicz Chaim	lo. 1.19	Steinbruchmineur
393	" "	6924o	Domb Izrael	23. 1.o8	Schreibkraft
394	" "	1	Klimburt Abram	1.11.13	Koch
395	" "	2	Wisniak Abram	3o	¨ehrling
396	" "	3	¨chreiber Leopold	15.lo.25	Schlossergeselle
397	" "	4	Silberstein Kacob	1. 1.oo	Galvanis¨urmeiste:
398	" "	5	Eidner Pinkus	2o.12.14	Dampfkesselheizer
399	" "	6	Goldberg ¨erisch	17. 5.13	ang.¨etallverarb.
400	" "	7	¨einer Josef	16. 5.15	Automechanikcer
4o1	" "	8	¨einer Wilhelm	21.lo.17	Stanzer
4o2	" "	9	Löw Zcycze	28. 6.97	Kesselschmied Mei¨
4o3	" "	6925o	Löw Jacob	3. 3.oo	" "
404	" "	1	Pozniak Szloma	15. 9.16	Bäcker
4o5	" "	2	Ratz Wolf	2o. 6.o9	Metallverarb.
4o6	" "	3	Lewkowicz Ferdinand	12. 3.o9	Arzt Chrirug
4o7	" "	4	Lax Ryszard	9. 7.24	Automechaniker Ge
4o8	" "	5	Semmel Berek	5. 1.o5	Tischler Gehilfe
4o9	" "	6	Horowitz ¨sidor	25. 9.95	ang.Installateur
41o	" "	7	Meisels Szlama	2.2.16	Fleischergeselle
411	" "	8	Kormann Abraham	15. 1. o9	Buchhalter
412	" "	9	Joachimsmann Abraham	19.12.95	Stanzer
413	" "	6926o	Sawicki Samuel	9. 4.17	Koch
414	" "	1	Rosner Wilhelm	14. 9.25	Schlossergehilfe
415	" "	2	Hirschberg Symon	23. 7.o8	Stanzer
416	" "	3	Goldberg Bernhard	lo.lo.16	Koch

Schindler's Ark

Thomas Keneally

Schindler's Ark begins with a "note" from Thomas Keneally describing the chance encounter with Leopold Pfefferberg, a "Schindler survivor," that prompted him to write the story of Oskar Schindler, "bon vivant, speculator, charmer." An industrialist and member of the Nazi Party, Schindler risked his life to protect Jews in Nazi-occupied Poland.

Winning the Booker Prize on its publication in 1982, *Schindler's Ark* is a "novel" deeply embedded in the trauma of modern European history, a story that, Keneally insists, attempts to avoid all fiction. Driven to understand Schindler's "impulse towards rescue," to explore the enigma that, on this telling, still haunts "Schindler's Jews", the book combines historical research with imaginative reconstruction to portray the complex and provocative character of Oskar Schindler. In the process, Keneally draws his readers into the world of those condemned by the Nazis as a form of "life unworthy of life." He examines the volatile mix of political violence and sexual sadism that prompts one of the most unsettling questions in the book: "What could embarrass the SS?" At the same time, in taking the decision to represent the Holocaust, Keneally writes his way into the controversy that surrounds that project: not only how "true" is this portrayal of Schindler, but who is licensed to bear witness to the Holocaust? What literary form can memorialize the reality of those events? In 1993, the release of Steven Spielberg's award-winning *Schindler's List* (the U.S. title of Keneally's book) reinforced that controversy. In particular, as part of the so-called "Holocaust boom," Spielberg's film refracts what remains, in one critical view, the untroubled, but profoundly troubling, sentimentality of Keneally's narrative: its novelistic depiction of history through the life of one man. **VL**

Lifespan | *b.* 1935 (Australia)
First Published | 1982, by Hodder & Stoughton (Lon.)
Alternate Title | *Schindler's List*
Booker Prize | 1982

◉ Spielberg's epic movie version of the Schindler story has inevitably tended to overshadow Thomas Keneally's book.

◉ A copy of Oskar Schindler's original list of twelve hundred Polish Jews to be saved from death in the Holocaust.

A Pale View of Hills

Kazuo Ishiguro

Lifespan | *b.* 1954 (Japan)
First Published | 1982
First Published by | Faber & Faber (London)
Original Language | English

A Pale View of Hills is narrated by Etsuko, a war-ravaged widow from Nagasaki who is living in England. Her memories of the past and of her daughter Keiko, who committed suicide, are prompted by the arrival in England of her second child, Niki. Not only does Etsuko try unsuccessfully to articulate a meaningful response to her daughter's death, the reader is also never fully certain about the events that took place in the hot summer in Nagasaki to which her narrative returns time and again. Ishiguro is less interested in offering an account of the central trauma that defines a character's identity than in demonstrating how the very act of storytelling is never straightforward.

As past and present interweave in increasingly enigmatic ways, the novel raises as many questions as it answers. Ishiguro's narrative style urges the reader to consider the ways that subjectivity is both provisional and improvised, and how identity, rather than the pre-existing stories we come to tell about ourselves, may be something that is perhaps always in process. Just as the horror of Nagasaki broods over the narrative without ever being mentioned directly, so too the interplay between memory, identity, and trauma in this haunting debut novel challenges any naive conception of language as a clear window onto a world of objective truth. **VA**

ⓖ Born in Nagasaki, Ishiguro was brought to England aged five; as a child, he was the only one of his family who spoke fluent English.

Wittgenstein's Nephew

Thomas Bernhard

Lifespan | *b.* 1931 (Netherlands), *d.* 1989 (Austria)
First Published | 1982
First Published by | Suhrkamp (Frankfurt)
Original Title | *Wittgensteins Neffe: eine Freundschaft*

In *Wittgenstein's Nephew*, an intellectual, sick, and obsessive narrator reflects on the tragic life and unfortunate death of a close friend, who is also an intellectual and sick and obsessive. The narrator is Thomas Bernhard himself and in this, his most personal novel, he reveals a compassionate humanity that is so glaringly absent from his work in general.

The novel is written as a tribute to Bernhard's friendship with Paul Wittgenstein, nephew of the famous Austrian philosopher. It opens with Wittgenstein and Bernhard staying in the same Viennese hospital, in separate wards. Wittgenstein suffers from a recurring mental illness and Bernhard from a recurring pulmonary condition. From this beginning, Bernhard creates an honest and touching account of Wittgenstein's life, his gradual demise, and Bernhard's reaction to it. He reflects on illness, intellectual and artistic passion, and the two men's hatred for the complacency of Austrian society. Bernhard sees Wittgenstein as a victim of his patrician family's suffocating conformity and Austrian society's blinkered provincialism. He considers Wittgenstein an intellectual equal to his uncle, who he believes would have shared a similar fate had he not escaped to England.

Wittgenstein's Nephew is an affectionate account of the value of friendship and a meditation on the perilous link between intellectual energy and insanity, which addresses issues of isolation, illness, and death without being sentimental or morose. **AL**

The Color Purple

Alice Walker

Lifespan | *b.* 1944 (U.S.)
First Published | 1982
First Published by | Harcourt Brace Jovanovich (N.Y.)
Pulitzer Prize | 1983

"You better not never tell . . ."

◉ A feminist as well as a civil rights activist, Walker has been criticized for an allegedly negative portrayal of African-American men.

❯ A scene from Spielberg's 1985 movie version of *The Color Purple*, a film adaptation that failed to match the impact of the book.

The Color Purple documents the traumas and gradual triumph of Celie, a young African-American woman raised in rural isolation in Georgia, as she comes to resist the paralyzing self-concept forced on her by those who have power over her. Celie is repeatedly raped by her father, and gives birth twice as a result of the abuse, but assumes the children have been killed when her father secretively disposes of them. When a man proposes marriage to Celie's sister, Nettie, their father pushes him to take Celie instead, forcing her into a marriage as abusive as her early home. Nettie soon flees that home, first to Celie and her husband and then out into the wide world. By the time of her reunion with Celie almost thirty years later, Nettie has met and traveled to Africa with an African-American missionary couple, whom she discovers to be the adoptive parents of Celie's children. In Africa, Nettie lives among the Olinka, whose patriarchal society and indifference toward the role of Africans in the slave trade underline the prevalence of exploitation.

Celie narrates her life through letters to God. These are prompted by her father's warning to tell "nobody but God" when he makes her pregnant for a second time at the age of fourteen, and she writes to God with the unselfconscious honesty of someone who thinks nobody is listening. As she builds relationships with other black women, and especially with those women engaging forcefully with oppression, however, Celie draws strength and insight from their perspectives and develops a sense of her own right to interpret herself and her world. Her independence develops symbiotically through her expanded firsthand and secondhand experience of the world until she is able to construct her relations to others according to her own values. **AF**

A Boy's Own Story

Edmund White

Lifespan | b. 1940 (U.S.)
First Published | 1982, by E. P. Dutton (N.Y.)
Trilogy | A Boy's Own Story (1982); The Beautiful
Room is Empty (1988); A Farewell Symphony (1998)

A Boy's Own Story is a coming-out novel significant not only for its timing, being one of the first, but also for its frank portrayal of a young teenager's anxious self-conception, growing up gay in 1950s America. Based to some extent on Edmund White's own story, the narrator is eccentric and slightly creepy. However, the boy's precociousness, combined with his physical self-disgust and ambivalent sexual shame, make the novel a quintessential narrative of teenage angst and self-discovery.

The veneer of seedy sexual exploration defines the boy's journey toward young adulthood in a conservative social climate that pathologized homosexuality. Though never in doubt of his orientation, the boy undergoes psychoanalysis in an attempt to cure his "impossible desire to love a man but not to be a homosexual." This impossible desire is fulfilled in the final pages of the novel by his shocking betrayal of a teacher he lures into a sexual liaison. This event dramatically marks the boy's entry into an adult world of sex and power.

White lyrically evokes a poignant longing for love and highlights the disorienting lack of romantic narratives for gay people. In stubbornly creating, articulating, and undermining its own fantasies, the novel is effectively a Postmodern fairy tale of a brutally repressed desire. At the time of its publication, it affirmed a history and a material and psychic presence for the gay community at a moment of crisis with the emergence of Aids. **CJ**

If Not Now, When?

Primo Levi

Lifespan | b. 1919 (Italy), d. 1987
First Published | 1982
First Published by | G. Einaudi (Turin)
Original Title | Se non ora, quando?

By the time of his death in 1987, Primo Levi had established his reputation as a writer of the Holocaust, a survivor who bore witness to the horrors of Auschwitz. Perhaps inevitably, the broader range of his writing has been relatively neglected (science fiction, poetry, and drama).

Described as Levi's most conventional novel, If Not Now, When? tells the story of a band of Jewish partisans, and their acts of resistance against the Germans as they journey through Eastern Europe toward Italy from 1943 to 1945. "For the most part," Levi notes, "the events I depict really did take place. . . . It is true that Jewish partisans fought the Germans." Levi continues to bear witness, but this time in the shape of a novel: imaginary characters, omniscient narrator, period reconstruction, description of landscape. Levi views it as "a story of hope," even if set against the backdrop of massacre. In fact, at key moments, Levi refuses to tell that story of death and extermination: characters disappear ("Immediately hidden from sight by the curtain of snow, they vanish from this story"), and events are not depicted ("But what happened in the courtyard of the Novoselki monastery will not be told here"). Described by Philip Roth as less imaginative in technique than Levi's other books, If Not Now, When? was defended by Levi as an account of Ashkenazi civilization: "I cherished the ambition," he once acknowledged, "to be the first (perhaps the only) Italian writer to describe the Yiddish world." **VL**

The Book of Disquiet

Fernando Pessoa

Lifespan | *b.* 1888 (Portugal), *d.* 1935
First Published | 1982, by Ática (Lisbon)
Pseudonym | Bernardo Soares
Original Title | *Livro do Desassossego*

The Book of Disquiet is presented as the "factless autobiography" of Bernardo Soares, a solitary assistant bookkeeper whom Pessoa has met in a Lisbon restaurant. In a fragmentary text broken up into hundreds of short sections—some bearing titles such as "The Art of Effective Dreaming for Metaphysical Minds"—Soares reflects on art, life, and dreams, observes the changing weather and street scenes of central Lisbon, meditates upon the futility of existence, and recommends techniques for living a pointless life.

Fernando Pessoa is best known as a Modernist poet who published his poems as the work of "heteronyms"—pseudonymous personae with fictional biographies and radically different writing styles. Soares is a "heteronym" closer to the author himself than any of the others. He shares Pessoa's sense of being "the empty stage where various actors act out various plays." The published text has been assembled from fragments of prose scribbled on scraps of paper and the backs of envelopes that were found in a trunk after Pessoa's death. Several versions exist, based on different selections and arrangements of the material; in principle, readers are welcome to create their own book by following their own path through the text. As the core of the author's stance is the rejection of "real life" and action in favor of dreams and sensations, not much happens externally. But the life of the mind is celebrated in texts that are vigorous, rich, aphoristic, and paradoxical. **RegG**

Baltasar and Blimunda

José Saramago

Lifespan | *b.* 1922 (Portugal)
First Published | 1982, by Caminho (Lisbon)
Original Title | *Memorial do Convento*
Nobel Prize for Literature | 1998

Many magical realist novels fail to live up to either half of that label, but José Saramago's *Baltasar and Blimunda* successfully creates an imaginary world in which the wildest fantasies take on the objectivity of everyday reality, while real historical events have the heightened quality of fairy tale or nightmare.

The novel is set in Portugal in the early eighteenth century. An absolute monarchy ruthlessly exploits an impoverished population, over whom the inquisition exercises a reign of terror. Baltasar is a soldier who has lost a hand in one of the king's wars, Blimunda a woman with magical powers whose joyful and independent life is contrasted with the cruelly constrained lives of the women of the royal family. The rendering of the couple's relationship is a masterly depiction of erotic love.

Two historic projects dominate the novel's structure. One is the construction, on the king's orders, of the vast convent of Mafra—now a major tourist attraction. Saramago depicts the building of the convent, on which thousands of laborers worked in conditions of near slavery, as an act of oppression on an epic scale. The other project is the attempt of a Jesuit priest, Bartolomeu Lourenço de Gusmão, to invent manned flight—another historical fact.

There is finally no escape from historical reality for any of the central characters. The lovers are doomed by their circumstances. Yet Saramago, a left-wing humanist, leaves us in no doubt that their lives have been worthwhile even in defeat. **RegG**

The Sorrow of Belgium

Hugo Claus

Lifespan | *b.* 1929 (Belgium), *d.* 2008
First Published | 1983
First Published by | De Bezige Bij (Amsterdam)
Original Title | *Het Verdriet van België*

Covering the years 1939 to 1947, this intense and vivid novel is set in anti-Semitic West Flanders, where young Louis Seynaeve emerges from childhood and adolescence amid the deprivations and moral conflicts of the Second World War.

The story begins in the convent school where Louis and his friends form a secret society in resistance to the stern rule of the Sisters, and where his imagination vies with his ignorance to satisfy a hunger to know and understand the world—a complex of fragmented loyalties, rumors of war, and impending invasion by the Germans. This first part, "The Sorrow," has a child's confused perspective, with its unintentional comedy uncannily rendered. In the second section, "Of Belgium," the saga of the Seynaeve family continues under Nazi occupation. Friends and relatives become complicit with the new regime, Louis's parents actively participating— his father as publisher of propaganda, his mother as secretary and mistress to an officer. As a wartime chronicle, this rich and dense novel is unusual for its eccentric characters and lively dialogue, and for being a portrait of the artist at the same time— Louis's brilliant tendency toward invention results in his developing into a novelist by the book's end.

Hugo Claus is one of only a handful of Belgian writers to live solely by his creative output, which includes works of poetry, drama, movie scenarios, and short stories, as well as longer fiction, essays, and translations, and an opera libretto. **ES**

The Piano Teacher

Elfriede Jelinek

Lifespan | *b.* 1946 (Austria)
First Published | 1983, by Rowohlt (Berlin)
Original Title | *Die Klavierspielerin*
Nobel Prize for Literature | 2004

Elfriede Jelinek's oeuvre is embroiled in her critique of capitalist and patriarchal society, and her construction of human intimacy. The prose is relentless in its exploration of the unlived sexuality of voyeurism, addressing as it does the woman's appropriation of the male rights to sexual looking.

In this unnerving, painful portrayal of a woman's sexuality, the protagonist, Erika Kohut, is a woman given over to the uncertain pleasures of looking— from peepshow to porn film, to the couple on whom she spies in the meadows of the Vienna Prater. But Jelinek also binds the looking to the experience of heterosexual sadomasochism at its most violent edge: "Erika seeks a pain that will end in death." As Erika attempts to contract the terms of her own torture with her student lover, Walter Klemmer, Jelinek embeds her sexuality in her unsettling tie to her mother, to a form of maternal love that demands, above all, the daughter's submission: "never could she [Erika] submit to a man after having submitted to her mother for so many years."

Contributing to a literature committed to the exploration of sexual dissidence, Jelinek also brings her readers up against the anxiety that has haunted feminist responses to women's sadomasochism. Refusing either to condemn or to celebrate Erika's desires, Jelinek sustains her critical gaze, even against the usual pleasures of reading and writing: "I strike hard," she has commented, "so nothing can grow where my characters have been." **VL**

The Life and Times of Michael K

J. M. Coetzee

Lifespan | *b.* 1940 (South Africa)
First Published | 1983
First Published by | Secker & Warburg (London)
Booker Prize | 1983

This novel uses the enduring South African pastoral ideal to challenge the myths that sustained the apartheid regime. Michael K, a hare-lipped non-white who is brought up in a home for unfortunate children in apartheid-era South Africa, becomes a gardener in the Sea Point district of Cape Town, where his mother works as domestic help. When she begins to die, he tries to return her to the farm in the Karoo where she was born, but she dies in transit. Michael continues his journey alone to scatter her ashes on the abandoned farm. He stays on, growing pumpkins and living a simple existence off the land. Meanwhile a civil war is raging. Accused of aiding the insurgency, Michael is arrested and interned in a labor camp, where he refuses to eat. He escapes and returns to Sea Point, where he lives as a vagrant.

The second part of the novel is a diary, written by the medical officer of the internment camp, in which the officer recounts his attempts to get Michael to yield something of significance. But very little passes Michael's misshapen lips: food is rarely consumed and speech rarely emanates. Michael's refusal to be part of any system undermines all the officer's own certainties in his own hierarchical world.

This is a remarkable tale of a simple man. The richness of the novel lies in the enigma and resistance that Michael poses both to the authorities and to the reader. J. M. Coetzee is careful to preserve the unknowable quality of Michael K by eschewing any overarching interpretive framework **ABi**

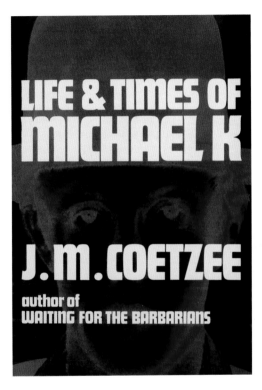

"He is a simpleton, and not even an interesting simpleton. He is a poor helpless soul who has been permitted to wander out on the battlefield ... of life ..."

◉ Coetzee once described himself as an author who represents "people slipping their chains and turning their faces to the light."

Waterland

Graham Swift

Lifespan | *b.* 1949 (England)
First Published | 1983
First Published by | Heinemann (London)
Guardian Fiction Award | 1983

When narrator Tom Crick's wife, Mary, kidnaps a child from a local supermarket, it creates a firestorm of publicity. In the lead-up to his final days as a secondary school history teacher, Crick examines his own history and childhood to try to work out just how things went so wrong. He recalls the silent, inscrutable, mentally disabled brother who eventually committed suicide; his own feeling of guilty implication in the death of a neighborhood boy; and the dangers he and Mary faced when trying to procure an abortion after their teenaged sexual experimentation. The procedure, alluded to as a fearful quasi-religious rite presided over by high priestess Martha Clay, widely supposed to be a witch, renders Mary sterile and permanently traumatized. Even the lyrical story of Crick's parents' romance does not escape the sinister shadow of a silent crime and its tragic fallout.

The metaphor of land reclamation plays a significant role in Crick's assessment of the consolations of storytelling and historical narrative. Crick sees history not as the march of progress, but something more like the constant, cyclic battle against the encroaching waters of England's East Anglia Fens. As Crick debates the value of history with one particularly insistent student, he advances the idea that narrative cannot be justified by appealing to its beneficial consequences, but to its power to fend off nothingness—the only resource people have against despair. **AF**

LaBrava

Elmore Leonard

Lifespan | *b.* 1925 (U.S.)
First Published | 1983
First Published by | Arbor House (New York)
Full Name | Elmore John Leonard, Jr.

Elmore Leonard's razor-sharp portrayals of the underbelly of American urban life have forged his reputation as one of the sharpest, funniest, toughest, and most insightful contemporary American writers. *LaBrava* is certainly the best example of Leonard's effortless mastery of a form he would come to make his own: part mystery, part suspense, part crime, part thriller, part urban treatise.

Enter Joe LaBrava, an ex-Secret Service agent and photographer whose style, like Leonard himself, "is the absence of style," or rather whose work is without artistic pretensions. LaBrava befriends Jean Shaw, an aging movie actress famous for her femme fatale roles in the 1950s, who is herself plotting with Richie Nobles, a grinning redneck psychopath, to defraud a friend of hers, Maurice, of $600,000. Nobles, in turn, has fallen in with Cundo Rey, a Cuban go-go dancer whose preference for leopard jockstraps barely conceals his own pecuniary ambitions. What delights about *LaBrava* is Leonard's ear for dialogue and the skillful way in which he brings these characters into collision with each other, shifting points of view in order to generate suspense. As the characters strive to twist circumstances to suit their own ambitions, they take on a life of their own, but in spite of the novel's self-referential nods (whereby Jean Shaw's movies bleed into the "reality" of the plot), Leonard resolutely avoids Postmodern trickery. In the end, this is not a dissertation on literary artifice but a cracking good read. **AP**

The Christmas Oratorio

Göran Tunström

Lifespan | *b.* 1937 (Sweden), *d.* 2000
First Published | 1983
First Published by | Bonniers (Stockholm)
Original Title | *Juloratoriet*

Big in Sweden, and bigger still after a 1996 movie adaptation directed by Kjell-Åke Andersson, *The Christmas Oratorio* is a finely wrought and sweeping drama from a gifted writer. As with his other fiction, especially *The Thief* (1986), Göran Tunström explores, in a lyrical and economical style, the themes of lost childhood and the search for identity in the dynamics of an extended family.

The Christmas Oratorio is effectively a succession of tragedies—composed by Tunström as a variation on the theme of mourning—that befall three generations of the Nordensson family across three continents. Their lives are all shaped by the slowly expanding ripples of one tragic event, "like frozen music that may take ages to thaw out."

That event goes back to the 1930s: Sidner, the pivotal character, tells his son how he saw his own mother, Solveig, crushed to death by cows in a freak accident. She had been cycling to a remote country church to sing in Bach's *Christmas Oratorio*. This part of the story, like much of his other writings, takes place in the pastoral setting of Värmland, Tunström's birthplace. Sidner's father, Aron, runs off without him to New Zealand (where Tunström himself lived for a while), beginning a new relationship that is haunted by his dead wife, while Sidner ends up with an older woman. These are tragic, poignant, and perplexing love stories and father–son relationships beautifully observed by an author who deserves a wider readership. **JHa**

Göran Tunström

Juloratoriet

"Every act in the past yielded a thousand other possibilities, all trickling along toward their own future."

🔺 The Swedish cover of Tunström's *The Christmas Oratorio* attempts to suggest the novel's major themes of love, loss, and memory.

Fado Alexandrino

António Lobo Antunes

Lifespan | *b.* 1942 (Portugal)
First Published | 1983
First Published by | Publicações D. Quixote (Lisbon)
Jerusalem Prize | 2005

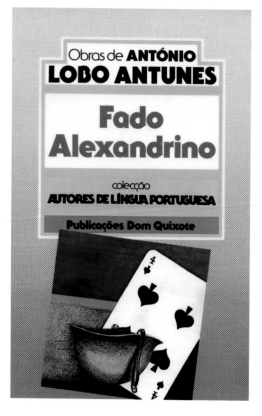

In Portuguese, *fado* relates to either traditional singing or to one's destiny. *Fado Alexandrino*, made up of three sections, each containing twelve chapters, encapsulates both meanings of the word in the shape of thirty-six verses concerned with the fate of Angola before, during, and after the revolution of April 25, 1974.

António Lobo Antunes, a former psychiatrist, was sent to war in Angola in 1971. In the two years that he was there as a lieutenant and army doctor, he apprehended the reality not only of war itself but particularly that of his companions' perception of war. In his prose, war becomes a process that, while omnipresent, invokes a feeling of alienation from self and other on the part of its direct participants. Every individual tries continually to reattain what is lost at the most mundane, everyday level, as a way of conferring meaning to communal experience.

Fado Alexandrino is merciless in depicting a dystopian scenario of impotence—both sexual and political—that demands an emotional predisposition from the reader to want to explore more. Why so? Because, in an imaginative and beautifully constructed use of language, Lobo Antunes guides us through what is most mundanely profound in a nation trying to come to terms with its identity just before, during, and after one of the most crucial events of its history. At a superficial level, the novel is about five ex-militants who have dinner and discuss their professional, social, and personal lives in the period of 1972–82. However, in intertwining space and time—frequently within a set dialog— Lobo Antunes weaves a complex structure that encompasses issues of race, class, and money but, above all, deglorifies the effort of war through the narration of individual life stories. **ML**

◉ Lobo Antunes's depiction of Portugal is grounded in a personal experience of colonial warfare and revolutionary upheaval.

The Witness

Juan José Saer

With the outward appearance of a historical novel, *The Witness* is actually an existentialist fable on the awareness of life. It is the story of an anonymous orphaned cabin boy who, in the early sixteenth century, travels from Spain to the New World. He and his traveling companions are besieged by Indians when they arrive and he is the sole survivor of the raid. He lives for ten years as a prisoner of a tribe of cannibals and, once freed, makes the story of this experience the center of his existence. It is an allegory on the radical strangeness of human beings and on the responsibility of the individual toward the world. Cannibalism ceases to seem a monstrous sign of alienation and becomes a metaphor for the obligation of indigenous peoples toward a universe whose balance must be preserved. The apparent report ends like an anthropological treatise and horror gives way to understanding: the essence of the human being is problematical, and only the subjective conscience allows a meaning to be given to existence.

The prime responsibility of the unnamed narrator is to preserve the memory of these Indians. Although they are radically different to him, they are also similar to him in his state as an orphan, which is that of a man ignorant of his origins, the subject of chance events, and, in short, able to learn about himself only through his immediate experience. The memory of the eclipse of the moon with which the novel ends is also presented as an allegory of this complete darkness. The balance between objectivism and lyricism, the freedom in the treatment of linguistic truth and of the point of view, and the changes of narrative pace make this book a model example of a new treatment within the genre of the historical novel. **DMG**

Lifespan | *b.* 1937 (Argentina), *d.* 2005 (France)
First Published | 1983
First Published by | Folios (Buenos Aires)
Original Title | *El entenado*

◉ Considered one of the finest Argentinian novelists of recent times, Saer lived in France for the last twenty-seven years of his life.

Shame

Salman Rushdie

Lifespan | *b.* 1947 (India)
First Published | 1983
First Published by | Jonathan Cape (London)
Full Name | Ahmed Salman Rushdie

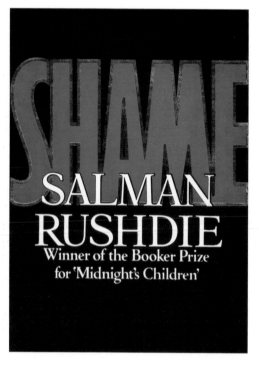

"'Come quickly, your fatherji is sending himself to the devil.'"

◉ The red lettering on the jacket of the first edition symbolizes the central theme of the novel—that violence is born out of shame.

Following the discussion of India's partition in *Midnight's Children* (1981), *Shame* focuses on the nation that emerged from that partition, Pakistan. It has a "peripheral" hero who watches from the wings, the disreputable Omar Shakil. He is the child of three sequestered sisters who all consider themselves the boy's mother. The novel is set in the remote border town of Q in a country that is not quite Pakistan but a place "at a slight angle to reality." The narrative is frequently disrupted with asides and newspaper reports, blurring the division between fiction and history, and creating a satire of the Pakistan of Zulfikar Ali Bhutto and Zia al Haq, in their fictional equivalents, Iskander Harappa and Raza Hyder.

The narrative follows the feud between Iskander Harappa, the prime minister, who is a gambler and womanizer, and Raza Hyder, who usurps his power in a coup. Set against this political struggle, the Hyder and Harappa families are inextricably bound up in a series of sexual and marital intrigues, which largely center on the female characters, particularly Sufiya Zinobia, the daughter of Harappa who eventually marries Omar Shakil. Zinobia is the embodiment of the barely translatable Urdu word *sharam,* rendered in English as "shame." As the brainsick daughter who should have been a son, she also symbolizes Pakistan, the miracle that went wrong. It is the beast of shame hidden deep inside Zinobia that finally surfaces to exact retribution on the whole cast of characters.

A daring blend of historical commentary, political allegory, and a fantastical fictional style that owes a stylistic debt to Gabriel García Márquez, *Shame* is a fitting successor to *Midnight's Children*, displaying the same capacity for comic excess, complex narrative, and biting political critique. **ABi**

Money: A Suicide Note

Martin Amis

John Self, the empty Everyman of *Money*, is one of Martin Amis's more powerful and memorable creations. Set in the summer of 1981, the novel's opening sees Self escape the nationalist romance of the Royal Wedding and his own failing and violent love affair by flying to New York. There he embarks on a corporately financed yet profoundly pleasureless binge of drugs, alcohol, violence, and sex.

The novel offers a darkly satirical celebration of the insatiable but righteous greed of Reaganite America and its counterpart in Thatcherite Britain. *Money* also invites us to identify with John Self, who makes a thoroughly unpleasant but oddly likeable hero. Self has been lured from Britain and his successful career in advertising—that most archetypal of 1980s industries—by the promise of Hollywood fame, and it is the money pressed upon him by the movie's financiers that he so recklessly spends throughout the novel. However, the reader soon becomes aware that Self's profound loss of control is quickly leading him to a moment of humiliating hubris. As the novel unravels we realize that Self has been the victim of a hugely elaborate corporate hoax that will leave him financially destitute. By the novel's end we see that he has lost not only his ambition, his livelihood, his father, and friends, but also, more poignantly, the salvation offered by his unlikely and redemptive lover. The final irony of the novel, although it offers little solace to Self, is that he inadvertently thwarts the hoax that ruins him. His limited participation in the movie that was destined never to be made involves hiring a lowly British novelist—Martin Amis himself—whose rewriting of the ludicrously unfilmable screenplay began the chain of events that ultimately led to the plot's unraveling. **NM**

Lifespan | *b.* 1949 (England)
First Published | 1984
First Published by | Jonathan Cape (London)
First U.S. Edition | 1985, by Viking (New York)

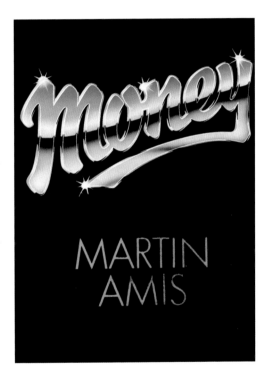

"I'm drinking tax-exempt whisky from a toothmug . . ."

⊘ Designed by Mon Mohan and Dick Jones, the jacket of the first edition of the book evokes 1980s-style material wealth.

Flaubert's Parrot

Julian Barnes

Lifespan | *b.* 1946 (England)
First Published | 1984
First Published by | Jonathan Cape (London)
Pseudonym | Dan Kavanagh

Funny and erudite, this is a novel about quiet passion and the delusion of academic celebrity. It is a love story, spectacularly unrequited, between a lonely amateur scholar and the object of his affection, Gustave Flaubert. And it is a detective story—though less Chandler than Borges.

Geoffrey Braithewaite stumbles onto what seems to him a great unsolved literary mystery: which of two stuffed parrots is the one that sat on Flaubert's desk—the parrot featured in *Un Coeur Simple*? Ultimately pointless, it is a parody of the ineffectuality of academia and the hermetic viciousness of overspecialization. It explores the nature of creativity, of criticism, and of creating heroes. Beauty can be fragile: do we risk destroying it through intimate dissection or is part of the magic in the mystery? The novel is less about Flaubert (and even less about the parrot) than about Braithewaite and the danger that, in getting too close to one's heroes, one is getting uncomfortably close to oneself. "All art is autobiographical," claims Lucien Freud, and that includes the art of biography. Braithewaite is a tragic figure: numb to life, his own memories and feelings go unregarded, so empty he must devote himself not to another human being but to something far safer.

A dusty retired doctor consumed by a dead French writer seems unlikely to be fertile ground for humor—but the novel is full of wit and insight. It brims with detail, including three biographies of Flaubert (one unctious, one critical, one objective), the appearance of real-life Flaubert expert Enid Starkie, and even a mock university exam. It also contains whimsical material like Braithewaite's *Dictionary of Accepted Ideas*. This is a fascinating jigsaw puzzle of a book. **GT**

◉ Shortlisted for the Booker Prize in 1984, the novel began three years earlier on the sighting of two stuffed parrots in Normandy.

◑ Photographed here in 1990, Barnes became an admirer of Flaubert's work at fifteen, when he first read *Madame Bovary*.

Professor Martens' Departure

Jaan Kross

Lifespan | b. 1920 (Estonia)
First Published | 1984
First Published by | Eesti Raamat (Tallinn)
Original Title | Professor Martensi ärasõit

In 1907, F. Martens, Professor for International Law and official of the Russian Ministry of Foreign Affairs, travels from his native Estonian summer home back to St. Petersburg. Along this journey, out of Martens's reminiscences, daydreams, and conversations with real and hallucinated fellow travelers emerges the trajectory of a life that led from a provincial orphanage to international renown. This life is strangely intertwined with that of another Martens, also a famous lawyer, who lived almost a century before him in Germany. It is a life dominated by a combination of learning, ambition, and the wounded self-love of one who made his way among those who never accepted him as one of their own.

Jaan Kross did not have to invent the bitterness, hurt vanity, and contempt that characterizes Martens, or his reaction at being passed over for the Nobel Peace Prize—they can be found in the real Martens's diaries. But it is Kross's idea to let Martens, at the end of his life, conclude an imaginary "contract of honesty" with his wife and to set his vanity and self-importance against a sustained attempt at self-examination—and to show that self-awareness does not make the slightest bit of difference; that vanity, ambition, and the compromising of ideals can coexist and even feed on the ability to see through one's own self-deceptions. It is this profound insight that gives the book its universal appeal. **DG**

Blood and Guts in High School

Kathy Acker

Lifespan | b. 1947 (U.S.), d. 1997 (Mexico)
First Published | 1984
First Published by | Grove Press (New York)
First UK Edition | Pan Books (London)

Kathy Acker's *Blood and Guts in High School* reinterprets the familiar rite-of-passage novel. The result is a narrative that combines the troubled life of Janey (an American teenager who hates school, is bored by her part-time job, and gets into trouble with the police) with the profane, the shocking, and the surreal. Its opening tone is that of the familiarly banal daytime talk show as it depicts Janey and her father as adults wrangling with the guilt and responsibility attendant upon a failed sexual relationship. The reader's inability to determine Janey's age, or to distinguish between what is either a metaphorical comment on gender politics or a literal and disturbingly normalized representation of incest, characterizes the profoundly disquieting experience that the book as a whole imparts.

As the novel progresses, the depiction of Janey's life becomes increasingly preposterous, frightening, and comic. The narrative of her sexual liberation and subsequent enslavement is interpolated with hand-drawn images of her dreams, pieces of her homework, and childish translations of rudimentary Arabic. This unruly and challenging text is an affront to the assumption that literary texts should be neat, complete, and somehow true. In the face of this, Acker places the sexual and anarchic energy of a young woman firmly at odds with the stifling patriarchal order she so literally caricatures. **NM**

Larva: Midsummer Night's Babel

Julián Ríos

Lifespan | b. 1941 (Spain)
First Published | 1984
First Published in | Libres del Mall (Barcelona)
Original Title | Larva: Babel de una noche de San Juan

The neo-avant-garde movement of the 1970s, inspired by French structuralism and the counter-culture movement, produced its best fruit and at the same time reached its limits in Larva, a novel that consists of a frenetic, opaque, linguistic festival reserved for the enjoyment of a minority of readers. The distortions affect both the writing and the graphic arrangement of the text so that the slight story is scarcely visible through the dense tangle of multilingual wordplay and constant cult allusions.

The model for Julián Ríos was Finnegans Wake, by James Joyce, and, as in that novel, the basic technique is the combination of one or several words with another, usually with humorous effect: thus, Herr Narrator is a "ventrilocuelo" (a play on "ventriloquist") and the protagonists Milalias and Babelle "escriviven" ("write-and-live") their alcohol-fuelled erotic adventures on a midsummer's night in London. To the carnivalesque metamorphosis and interweaving of words and the flood of hidden references, as well as the Cervantes-like alternation of narrators, must be added the singular division of the text—the even pages contain the ironic, cloudy narration of facts; the odd pages, the notes and commentaries that they engender, and, at the end, the "Pillow Notes," the comments of Babelle about the story of Milalias. The work is a tribute to the structural heterodoxy of Rayuela by Cortázar. **DRM**

Nights at the Circus

Angela Carter

Lifespan | b. 1940 (England), d. 1992
First Published | 1984
First Published by | Chatto & Windus (London)
Given Name | Angela Olive Stalker

Angela Carter's dazzling aerialist, the tough and beguiling Fevvers, a winged-woman who defies gravity and sexual ideology, takes center stage of a novel that explores the eccentric limits of gender and geography. With the narrative's three-part excursion from London to St. Petersburg, finally reaching the vast expanses of Siberia, we journey with reporter Jack Walser, assigned to shadow the fortunes of Fevver's carnivalesque circus community. In his position as commentator, he is at once convivial and satirical.

The novel is filled with burlesque ebullience, a carnival riot of voices, dialects, and stories, through which Carter explores the reality of the perpetual masquerade with shrewd discretion. Performers from the circus emerge each night disheveled, wearied by the outward selves that they are compelled to assume. Carter brings a degree of rationality, of subtle reticence, to her narrative, enabling her to exploit the self-parodic energies of magic realism. But she does not compromise pragmatism in her depiction of self-transformation, charting Fevvers' uneven journey, "turning, willy-nilly, from a woman into an idea." Tirelessly defying generic consistency, Carter's work invites us to assume a pleasurable if disarming repose, which swings between complicity and detachment, while at the same time thwarting our preconceptions. **DJ**

Neuromancer

William Gibson

Lifespan | *b.* 1948 (U.S.)
First Published | 1984
First Published by | Ace Books (New York)
Video Game Adaptation | 1988

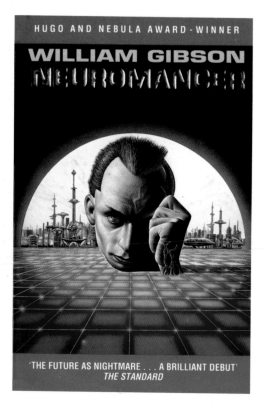

HUGO AND NEBULA AWARD-WINNER

WILLIAM GIBSON

NEUROMANCER

'THE FUTURE AS NIGHTMARE . . . A BRILLIANT DEBUT'
THE STANDARD

◉ The first cyberpunk novel has sold more than 6.5 million
copies worldwide and won three major science fiction awards.

◉ William Gibson, seen here walking through New York's Chinatown
in 1991, has never had any special affinity with computers.

Neuromancer is a landmark novel, not only in the science fiction genre, but also in the contemporary social imagination as a whole. With extraordinary prescience, William Gibson invented the basic concept of "cyberspace" (a three-dimensional representation of computer data through which users communicate and do business, alongside a whole host of more dubious activities) long before the Internet and other virtual technologies were integrated into everyday life. It is a book that has inspired a generation of technophiles.

The plot revolves around a "computer cowboy" known as Case—a data thief who "jacks in" to the virtual world until his nervous system is badly maimed by a client he has double-crossed. Unable to interface with a "deck," he ekes out a precarious living in the lawless zones of Chiba City, Japan. However, Case is offered the chance of regaining his old powers by the mysterious Armitage—a businessman whose motives remain unclear until the final, exhilarating denouement. Gibson creates a world of televisual twilight and fiber optic shocks, all realized in lavish detail with a rich, sometimes disorienting vocabulary of jargon and slang. It is a world of techno-hustlers, strung-out junkies, bizarre subcultures, surgically enhanced assassins, and sinister "megacorps"—a world that increasingly resembles parts of our own.

Neuromancer is an enduring work because it combines the pace and urgency of the best thrillers with the scope, invention, and intellectual rigor of Orwell or Huxley. Perhaps its most compelling and disquieting feature, however, is Gibson's refusal to make any clear-cut moral distinctions between virtual and organic life—between human and cyborg, between program and reality. **SamT**

The Wasp Factory

Iain Banks

Lifespan | *b.* 1954 (Scotland)
First Published | 1984
First Published by | Macmillan (London)
Full Name | Iain Menzies Banks

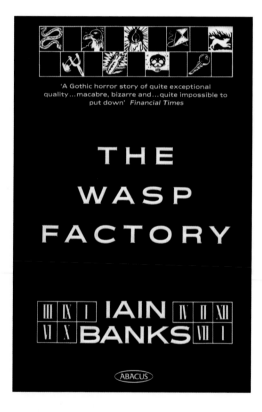

'A Gothic horror story of quite exceptional quality...macabre, bizarre and...quite impossible to put down' *Financial Times*

THE WASP FACTORY

IAIN BANKS

ABACUS

◐ The destructive impact of Thatcherite policies on British society resonate throughout this highly political novel.

◑ When asked to express himself for an exhibition in Aberdeen, Scotland, in 2001, Iain Banks submitted this self-portrait.

Like many of Iain Banks's novels, much of the impact of *The Wasp Factory* comes from its surprise ending and from the hyperbolic qualities of its content. It is a story of exceptional cruelties inflicted upon animals and humans alike.

The narrator, Frank Cauldhames ("cold homes"—a name with appropriate metaphoric content), spends his time carrying out idiosyncratic rituals: inventively killing animals and capriciously murdering siblings and cousins. Haunted by his apparent castration by the family dog, Frank's life is formed around a bizarre exaggeration of masculinity. Frank imagines himself, unmutilated, as a tall, dark, lean hunter; he despises women, eschews sex, but childishly revels in the adolescent drinking and the pissing games invented by his friend, Jamie. Frank's father is an eccentric libertarian who, having failed to register Frank at birth, allows Frank's behavior to continue almost unchecked. It is only at the end of the novel that the reader realizes that both Frank and his half-brother, Eric, are the products of their father's experimentation and impersonal cruelty. A surprising revelation comes during the cataclysmic conclusion to the novel when the insane Eric returns home driving a herd of burning sheep.

As a whole, the novel develops a deeply layered mythology based upon a series of masculine clichés: the potency of bodily fluids; the cosmic superiority of men over creation, which is manifested as violence toward animals; and the totemic effectiveness of their corpses. However, despite its occasionally exaggerated fantasies, the true value of *The Wasp Factory* is in the quality and style of Banks's writing, which is both beautiful and arresting. His skill is in characterization and his depiction of Frank as both psychotic and believably mundane. **LC**

Iain Banks

Democracy

Joan Didion

Lifespan | b. 1934 (U.S.)
First Published | 1984
First Published by | Simon & Schuster (New York)
Original Language | English

Democracy opens with a nuclear weapons test in the Pacific and ends with the American withdrawal from Vietnam. Between these geopolitical poles is played out the more personal story of Inez Victor, wife of presidential hopeful Harry Victor. Under the glare of political publicity Inez deals with her father's bitter recriminations and eventual murderous bent, her daughter's very middle-class heroin habit, and an affair with C.I.A. agent Jack Lovett.

These events are filtered through a fractured narrative voice and the novel can read like a subgenre of Gonzo-journalism. Stylized repetition extends the plot by revealing different trajectories the novel could have taken. With tongue in cheek, Joan Didion describes how the novel's style could be discussed in a literature studies classroom and gives creative-writing advice. These fragments of different realities often work most effectively when reproducing the vocabulary of oblique behind-the-scenes political maneuvering, blurring boundaries between public and private personality, which Inez uses to navigate her various lives. For all the cryptic playfulness, Didion has personal warmth at the center of the novel in the form of Inez. A complicit victim, she claims the major casualty of a publicly lived life is "memory."

Democracy is an explicitly experimental novel and Didion's fusion of genres and literary devices gives a fascinating insight into both her creativity and the backrooms of American politicking. **DTu**

The Lover

Marguerite Duras

Lifespan | b. 1914 (Indochina), d. 1996 (France)
First Published | 1984, by Éditions de Minuit (Paris)
Original Title | L'Amant
Prix Goncourt | 1984

Set in Sa Dec, French Indochina, in the 1930s, this ostensibly autobiographical novel details fifteen-year-old French girl Hélène Lagonelle's relationship with a wealthy Chinese man twelve years her senior. This taboo sexual relationship unfolds against the backdrop of her unstable and largely unhappy family life. Living with her depressive mother and two older brothers, Hélène and her family exist in a poverty induced by her eldest brother's drug and gambling addictions. His sadistic treatment of her, and the disturbing pleasure he derives from her mother's abuse of her, lend the novel an unsettling dimension that is perhaps underplayed by the adult voice of the narrator. While her family disapprove of the interracial relationship, they benefit financially from it, and their awkward meetings with her lover throw into relief the tensions generated by the French colonial regime and the differences in their status and cultural backgrounds. Challenging sexual stereotypes, Hélène instigates the relationship, she is the partner able to detach the physical from the emotional, and, despite being a child and financially insecure, she is ultimately the one with the upper hand in the relationship.

With its shifts between the first and third person, the use of flashbacks, and its impressionistic, disrupted style, Duras's writing is very cinematic, influenced as she was by the French nouveau roman of the 1950s. The novel was turned into a movie in 1993, directed by Jean-Jacques Annaud. **JW**

The Year of the Death of Ricardo Reis

José Saramago

Lifespan | *b.* 1922 (Portugal)
First Published | 1984
First Published by | Editorial Caminho (Lisbon)
Original Title | *O ano da morte de Ricardo Reis*

Ricardo Reis was one of the pseudonyms used by the celebrated Portuguese poet Fernando Pessoa (1888–1935), for example, in his poetry collection, *Odes de Ricardo Reis* (1946). In José Saramago's novel, Reis, a doctor and unpublished poet, returns to Lisbon after many years abroad in Brazil. This is the year following Pessoa's death, and Reis meets the ghost of Pessoa, with whom he holds a number of dialogs on matters great and small.

Against the backdrop of the rise of fascism in Europe and Salazar's oppressive regime in Portugal, Saramago skillfully employs a panoply of literary methods to bring issues under scrutiny. Most important among these are questions of identity: who precisely is Ricardo Reis and what is his relationship to Pessoa? There is also the gently implied but finally irresistible suggestion that there is a thin line between the monarchism, social conservatism, and stoicism of Reis, and the successful rise of Salazar.

Notwithstanding its weighty concerns, it remains an eminently readable novel. The narrative is intimate, almost conversational. The plot has conventional elements: Reis has an affair with a hotel chambermaid and falls in love with an aristocratic woman from Coimbra. Large parts of the novel are taken up with walks though the streets of Lisbon, giving the book a flavor of a Portuguese *Ulysses*. And, like Joyce's masterpiece, the more one brings to this erudite novel, the richer it becomes. **ABi**

"Lisboa, Lisbon, Lisbonne, Lissabon, there are four different ways of saying it . . . And so the children come to know what they did not know before, and that is what they knew already, nothing . . ."

This photograph of Saramago was taken by Horst Tappe in 1998, the year the novelist won the Noble Prize for Literature.

Empire of the Sun

J. G. Ballard

Lifespan | *b.* 1930 (China), *d.* 2009 (England)
First Published | 1984
First Published by | V. Gollancz (London)
Movie Adaptation | 1987

During a career spanning nearly fifty years, J. G. Ballard published many science fiction and futuristic novels. With *Empire of the Sun*, however, he discussed what seems a very different topic, namely his own incarceration as a child in a Japanese concentration camp during the Second World War. The story charts the fall of Shanghai to Japanese occupying troops, the capture of the protagonist, Jim, and his various complicated means of managing his survival in the Lunghua camp. Though predominantly from Jim's perspective, there are terrifying moments when we see Jim as the other camp inmates do and realize the madness within him. The book culminates when the world lights up as the first atom bomb is dropped on Japan, after which Jim escapes.

A major strength of the book lies in the way we are drawn into a frightening closeness to Jim, a boy who is obviously being forced to mature beyond his years under circumstances of chronic degradation. Because of his youth, he is perhaps more resilient than the others, but we are left in no doubt as to the trauma of his imprisonment. Many of the motifs of the book—the sudden atomic explosion, the lonely lives and deaths of airmen, the presence of torn and mangled bodies—occur throughout Ballard's work. *Empire of the Sun*, a remarkably achieved work in its own right, also serves as a key to the preoccupations of the rest of Ballard's fiction. **DP**

The Busconductor Hines

James Kelman

Lifespan | *b.* 1946 (Scotland)
First Published | 1984
First Published by | Polygon (Edinburgh)
Original Language | English

With his first novel, *The Busconductor Hines*, James Kelman extends the short story mode, which initially earned him recognition, into what is his funniest and most likable book. Robert Hines, the eponymous hero, is a bus conductor on the verge of an existential collapse. The episodic events of the novel develop through an innovatively woven mix of idiomatic and colloquial registers, which offers an acute representation of spoken Glaswegian, moving fluidly between a first-person narration centered on Hines and third-person description. One signature stylization is the introduction of emphasis in the middle of words, as in "malnufuckingtrition," "exploifuckingtation," or "C. B. bastarn I."

The world of Hines is one of domestic incidents, family life on limited resources, the trials of work, and occasional reveries that reveal an intellectual imagination attuned to the reality of his situation without the trappings of populist ideology. Hines is quick to reject the typical strategies of capitalist common sense, instead offering an amusingly skeptical take on the lives available. Indeed, the novel is notably free of the world of media and what passes for popular culture. Time spent watching television is mentioned, but as if it were a piece of furniture, the inspection of which constitutes a kind of emptying loss of consciousness. Public transport workers, in particular, will enjoy this novel. **DM**

Dictionary of the Khazars

Milorad Pavić

Lifespan | *b.* 1929 (Yugoslavia)
First Published | 1984
First Published by | Prosveta (Belgrade)
Original Title | *Hazarski Recnik*

Part encyclopedia, part intellectual puzzle, part deconstruction (or spoof of same), part myth, part hodgepodge, *Dictionary of the Khazars* is not a traditional novel that respects the conventions of beginning/middle/end. In addition to its other oddities, the book was published in male and female editions, with seventeen lines of differing text that distinguish them from each other. The author himself encourages readers to make of it what they please, without regard to chronology.

It is almost impossible to relate the teeming abundance of such a non-narrative, although there is a plot of sorts. This concerns the attempt of three modern-day scholars to locate the last remaining copies of a lexicon otherwise destroyed during the Inquisition. The dictionary is composed of three distinct but intertwined and cross-referenced versions—one each for the Christian, Muslim, and Jewish interpretations—of the fate of the long-lost Khazars, a Turkish people who once lived in the Balkan region, and the biographies of those involved in the so-called Polemic.

But it is the dictionary entries in themselves that supply the pleasure of the book. Enjoy the whimsy, the inventive imagery, the surrealistic complexity, and the delights afforded by the imaginative application of language itself. No one could charge Milorad Pavić with a lack of generosity. **ES**

"Whoever opened the book soon grew numb . . ."

⬡ The cover of the Hamish Hamilton edition of the book, shown here, is based on the original Rita Muhlbauer jacket design.

The Unbearable Lightness of Being

Milan Kundera

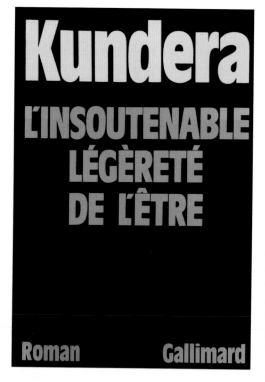

Lifespan | *b.* 1929 (Czech Republic)
First Published | 1984
First Published by | Gallimard (Paris)
Original Czech Title | *Nesnesitelná lehkost bytí*

"Her drama was a drama not of heaviness but of lightness. What fell to her lot was not the burden, but the unbearable lightness of being."

⬤ Kundera's most famous novel expresses his intention to move on from involvement with his home country's political problems.

This is a novel about exile and persecution in the former Czechoslovakia, written by a man who knew a great deal about both conditions. The novel considers the quality of lightness, where nothing means anything, and the heaviness that forms Nietzsche's philosophy of eternal return.

It is the dangerous year of 1968 in Prague. Tomas is a surgeon who embraces lightness. He is willfully free of all heaviness, shunning labels and ideals. Sabina is the epitome of lightness, an artist who, like Tomas, believes in unfettered individualism. Tereza is heaviness. Escaping from provincial life, she believes in the romantic ideal of Tomas. Her love is a binding thing—not bad, just heavy. She also has fervent political ideals, whereas Tomas is held down by none. As their three lives collide, the viability of lightness is questioned. What is our responsibility to ourselves, to others?

When the Soviet tanks roll in to crush the Prague Spring, Tomas and Tereza flee to Switzerland. But Tereza decides to return, leaving Tomas to make a choice. He accepts heaviness and follows her to certain persecution, unwilling to be a pawn of either the Communists or the insurgents. It is unbearable that each choice can only be made once with one possible result, and that we can never know what other choices would have wrought. A novel that is not as much political as about the primacy of personal freedom, it is a bittersweet celebration of the individual; urgent and necessary. **GT**

Legend

David Gemmell

Lifespan | *b.* 1948 (England)
First Published | 1984
First Published by | Century (London)
Original U.S. Title | *Against the Horde*

David Gemmell's aging Druss the Legend represents one of the definitive characters in fantasy literature. With a man at the end of his life as the story's central protagonist, Gemmell's book is as much a meditation on a warrior long past his prime, as it is a rip-roaring fantasy. While its story may appear linear, it is the recourse to alternative perspectives and the complex split narrative—in which Druss is largely defined by the people who choose to follow him into his last battle—that sets it apart as a classic work of fantasy literature.

Legend, the first book in Gemmell's "Drenai" series, is always aware of its predecessors, with clear undertones of Robert E. Howard and Edgar Wallace, but it is also very much a novel of the 1980s, seeking always to present events in a more realist tone. The text is a classic example of a simplistic narrative rendered in a novel manner. Druss is at times an unsympathetic figure, yet he is always heroic, and his humanism renders him powerfully empathic. Druss demonstrates the complexities of a man who has become a warrior through circumstance rather than straight volition. At the same time, the unspoken code that he follows throughout his life makes him a powerful, and often fatherly figure, fulfilling the traditional role of reluctant hero by default rather than intent. Overall, *Legend* provides a fresh perspective in the genre by emphasizing the ordinariness of heroes, rather than resorting to inexplicable heroics. **EMcCS**

The Young Man

Botho Strauss

Lifespan | *b.* 1944 (Germany)
First Published | 1984
First Published in | Hanser Verlag (München)
Original Title | *Der junge Mann*

The loss of humanity under the pressure of history and technology is a frequent theme in the novels of Botho Strauss, an acute social conservative profoundly displeased with what he sees as the cultural drift of his country and uninterested in the way of life in the new Germany. Accordingly, the young man of the work's title, Leon Pracht, who has left the theater to write, is contemplative, brooding, and alienated from both society in general and those to whom he should be close. Pracht moves numbly through a series of encounters whose protagonists wake up in spaces where the laws of time always change, and where they become victims of erotic metamorphoses or spectators of their own repressed history.

The novel, characterized by an extraordinary stylistic subtlety and avant-garde ambition, has been regarded as a Bildungsroman, an allegorical novel and a romantic fantasy at the same time. The protagonist is a voyeur in the crowd of life, and his precise observation of both the everyday and the fantastic is underscored by his increasing detachment. His reflections and reactions paint a compelling portrait of contemporary society and of the individual struggling to find a place within (and without) it. *The Young Man* is generally considered to be one of the few Postmodern German novels, a work in which Strauss reveals the hidden truths and underlying misery of a technologically and historically burdened society. **LB**

Love Medicine

Louise Erdrich

Lifespan | *b.* 1954 (U.S.)
First Published | 1984
First Published by | Holt, Rinehart and Winston
National Book Critics Circle Award | 1984

Louise Erdrich's intricately woven narrative spans a fifty-year period in and around a North Dakota reservation. Beginning in the 1930s, when the Chippewa community was suffering from chronic high unemployment and poverty, and struggling to maintain their social and cultural practices, the novel follows characters from two main families through to the 1980s. The novel traces the complex intertwining of the characters' lives through marriage, infidelity, powerful blood-bonds, and the equally enduring unconventional alliances that emerge as a consequence of difficult circumstances.

Although *Love Medicine* has been likened to a collection of short stories with a shared cast of characters, to make this comparison is to misunderstand its nature—as a metafictional narrative it takes storytelling as its structure and theme. In Erdrich's exquisite rendering of unique and powerful voices, she references a vibrant oral culture and calls attention to politics of representation.

Erdrich does not engage directly with the tensions existing between the Native American population and the federal government. Rather, the narrative voices provide multiple perspectives on the bicultural influences that informed the Chippewa people's experiences. In particular, she explores the identities conferred by Catholicism, contrasting the experiences of the white nuns with Native American Catholics, and subtly highlights their differing investments in their faith. **JW**

White Noise

Don DeLillo

Lifespan | *b.* 1936 (U.S.)
First Published | 1985
First Published by | Viking Press (New York)
American Book Award | 1985

(Post)modern American consumer culture streams powerfully through Don DeLillo's landmark novel like a fatal sugar rush. The book presents a highly detailed yet utterly mass-mediated world wherein human skin is "a color that I want to call flesh-toned," television is a member of the family, and one can prayerfully murmur "Toyota Celica" in one's sleep. But the characters here are not the dupes of the system; they are its professional analysts. Set in a Midwestern college town, the central protagonists are Jack Gladney, professor of Hitler Studies at the College-on-the-Hill, his faculty wife, Babette, and their children from Brady Bunch-style previous marriages. Children, as DeLillo points out, are savvier, more adapted, and yet more disillusioned about modern culture than adults; fourteen-year-old Heinrich, for example, plays chess by mail with an imprisoned mass murderer.

Much of the novel, told from Jack's perspective, is domestic in orientation, detailing fragments of information and conversation in a way that is both alienating and comforting. It is unclear whether DeLillo affirms a human ability to create meaningful and intimate relationships from the most unpromising of materials or whether he laments a wholesale loss of "authenticity." *White Noise* inhabits the hyperreal with wit and warmth, but deals too with a more sinister reality that crashes into the later part of the book, a shadow that no amount of shopping and chattering will obviate. **DH**

Half of Man Is Woman

Zhang Xianliang

Lifespan | b. 1936 (China)
First Published | 1985
First Published in | Wenlian Chuban (Beijing)
Original Title | Nanren de yiban shi nüren

Largely an autobiographical novel, and one of the few Chinese novels of the 1980s that has also won critical attention and commercial success outside China, *Half of Man Is Woman* continues the story of an imprisoned intellectual, Zhang Yonglin, that was begun in an earlier novel, entitled *Mimosa*.

Like the author himself, the protagonist has fallen victim to the 1955 "anti-rightist" movement and is imprisoned in a labor camp. Zhang Yonglin is sent to guard a rice paddy, where one day he sees a young inmate of a women's labor camp bathing in the flooded field. While he hides behind the reeds on the banks, his gaze is transfixed on the woman's naked body. Eight years later, he works on a state farm where the two meet again. They marry, but on their wedding night Zhang realizes that years of denial have left him impotent. Tormented by his own physical inadequacy, he also has to witness how his wife starts an affair with the party secretary. When during a flood he single-handedly fills a breach, he is commended for bravery and finally regains his manhood after his wife renews her affection.

Published at a time of political thaw during the mid-1980s, the book indicts a political system that has rendered parts of its population mentally and physically impotent. Dialogs of the protagonist with philosophers, mythical figures, and even animals bespeak the influence of the magical realism of some Latin-American writers, but also the desire of writers to reconnect to their Chinese origins. **FG**

Reasons to Live

Amy Hempel

Lifespan | b. 1951 (U.S.)
First Published | 1985
First Published by | Knopf (New York)
Original Language | English

In this collection of stories, the tragedies happen offstage. As in life, tragedies are seldom terminal and life goes on. These are stories about just getting on—they are stories about grace. In "Nashville Gone to Ashes," a widow tends to an ark of pets when her veterinarian husband dies. This includes the ashes of her husband's beloved saluki—the Egyptian temple dog—who ought to have an Egyptian name. The pick of the litter was named Memphis. They misunderstood and named theirs Nashville. Embedded in the daily details, the narrator takes her husband's bed, so that when she looks over, the empty bed she sees is her own.

In "Tonight is a Favor to Holly," the narrator waits for a blind date. The story ends before the date begins because it is actually about the tenuous bond between the narrator and her friend Holly, adrift in the sunshiny limbo of Los Angeles's beach communities, where "just because you have stopped sinking doesn't mean you're not still underwater."

These are the stories of people who cope in the little ways they know how, keeping themselves occupied with the tender and absurd details of living. As one character states, "We give what we can, that's as far as the heart will go." The stories illustrate the intricate smokescreens of minutiae hiding the current of grief that might swallow us up, if it were acknowledged. Fragile as the surface tension on water, so enthralling and so funny, one almost overlooks the exquisite sadness. Almost. **GT**

The Handmaid's Tale

Margaret Atwood

In *The Handmaid's Tale*, Atwood creates a dystopic future in which the population has become threateningly infertile and women are reduced to their reproductive capabilities. Patriarchy takes on a new, extreme aspect; one that oppresses in the name of preservation and protection, one in which violence is perpetrated by the language of ownership and physical delineation. In this nightmare society women are unable to have jobs or money, and are assigned to various classes: the chaste, childless Wives; the housekeeping Marthas; and the reproductive Handmaids, who turn their offspring over to the Wives. The tale's protagonist, Offred—so named to denote the master to whom she belongs—recounts her present situation with a clinical attention to her body, now only an instrument of reproduction. A counterpoint is provided through moving glimpses into her past life: memories of a sensual love for her lost family.

Set in a future Cambridge, Massachusetts, and partly inspired by New England's puritan American society, Atwood transforms the institutions and buildings of a familiar landscape into a republic called Gilead. Atwood's prose is chillingly graphic, achieving the sense that all of life's past physical pleasures have been reduced to mechanical actions, throwing the value of desire into sharp relief. Through her imagined world, she shows sexual oppression not so much taken to its extreme conclusion, as sexuality obliterated from the desiring body; an act every bit as violent as sexual violation. Atwood expertly handles the different forms that power manages to take within the handmaids' emotional dilemmas, as she describes the timeless tensions evoked by the body's immediate needs and our ability to look beyond desire to greater political ends. **AC**

Lifespan | *b.* 1939 (Canada)
First Published | 1985
First Published by | McClelland & Stewart (Toronto)
Governor General's Award for Fiction| 1986

Shortlisted for the Booker Prize

◉ The cover illustration shows women wearing the uniform imposed on handmaids in Atwood's fictional totalitarian society.

◉ Stephanie Marshall plays Offred in Poul Ruder's operatic adaptation staged by the English National Opera in 2003.

Hawksmoor

Peter Ackroyd

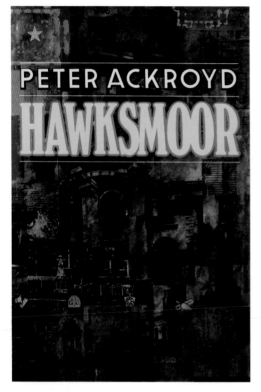

Lifespan | *b.* 1949 (England)
First Published | 1985
First Published by | Hamish Hamilton (London)
Whitbread Award | 1985

Hawksmoor, Peter Ackroyd's breakthrough as a novelist, is set in London in two different time frames —the early eighteenth and late twentieth centuries. It is a detective novel that deliberately subverts any coherent concepts one might have of either detection or history.

In the twentieth-century narrative, detective Nicholas Hawksmoor is assigned to investigate a series of murders after the bodies of tramps and small boys are discovered at seven churches dotted around the city. In reality, Nicholas Hawksmoor was an eighteenth-century architect who designed six of London's churches. In the world of the novel, however, the eighteenth-century architect of these London churches is given the name of Nicholas Dyer. One of Ackroyd's main achievements in *Hawksmoor* is the ventriloquism that he performs in recreating the earlier period. He narrates the design and erection of the buildings as well as a similar series of murders committed by Dyer, who, it is revealed, has covertly introduced occult designs and motifs into his churches.

History, rather than being represented as purely linear, is shown here to have a distinctly spatial aspect. Time and history are drawn together in the voices of the two characters in the novel; each chapter united by a repetition of the closing words of the previous chapter. Indeed, the novel turns upon the notion of repetition, which, in turn, leads to one of the most spectacular and peculiar endings to any novel. **VC-R**

> *"And so let us beginne; and, as the Fabrick takes its shape in front of you, alwaies keep the Structure intirely in Mind as you inscribe it."*

◉ *Hawksmoor* delves into the history of London, a subject Ackroyd would further explore in his famous biography of the city.

Perfume

Patrick Süskind

Lifespan | *b.* 1949 (Germany)
First Published |1985, by Diogenes (Zürich)
Full Title | *Perfume: The Story of a Murderer*
Original Title | *Das Parfum*

Set in eighteenth-century France, Patrick Süskind's novel tells the story of Jean-Baptiste Grenouille, born with a supernatural sense of smell and the complete absence of any odor of his own. The style of *Perfume* is distinguished by its emphasis on smell, in which every scene is recounted, via Grenouille's nose, through the layered complexity of its olfactory detail. Süskind paints a series of elaborate pictures of the smells of everyday objects (such as the depth and variety of aromas emitted by wood) and of the manipulation of smell by eighteenth-century perfumery.

What could become just a literary gimmick is prevented from being such by a focus on the psychology of the characters. A veritable psychopath, Grenouille is convinced that his acute sense of smell elevates him above ordinary humanity. He conceives a fantasy of himself as the capricious ruler of men, bestowing upon the masses the most delicate of fragrances, before surrendering to his own gratification. However, in a world constructed of scents, Grenouille becomes obsessed with his own lack of odor, since this effectively renders him a cipher, able to discern the substance of everything but lacking a substance of his own. Intent on creating a scent for himself, Grenouille embarks on the murderous process of capturing the most beautiful human scents: those of 'ripe' young women. But even the most exquisite aroma can only mask his essential odorlessness and his consequent insignificance within a fragrant universe. **LC**

Blood Meridian

Cormac McCarthy

Lifespan | *b.* 1933 (U.S.)
First Published | 1985, by Random House (New York)
Full Title | *Blood Meridian, or the Evening Redness in the West*

"See the child," orders the narrator at the beginning of *Blood Meridian*. Following this initial focus on a character that is known only as "kid" comes a voyage through Texas and Mexico after the U.S.–Mexico War of 1846. The kid's travels are an odyssey strangled by an unimaginable violence—a violence that knows no limits and is exclusive to no particular race, be it white or indigenous, Mexican, or North American.

Cormac McCarthy learned Spanish for this novel, to help him imagine the squalid exchanges between the gang of amoral scalp hunters with whom the kid works, and the people that emerge like ghostly ciphers on the desert horizons. The novel's chapters are introduced thematically, like a list of occurrences in an old travel narrative. And yet, *Blood Meridian* quickly becomes something more than a historical novel. McCarthy's achievement lies in his prose, which has been compared to the near-biblical style found in Melville and Faulkner. In *Blood Meridian*, McCarthy introduces one of his devil-incarnate characters—the nameless, nefarious judge. He is a creature of equally limitless wisdom and evil who, like a degenerate Ralph Waldo Emerson, calmly preaches chains of dictums such as "Your heart's desire is to be told some mystery. The mystery is that there is no mystery," while holding the great femur of "some beast long extinct." Ominously, the judge is a figure that cannot be made to disappear, a sinister reminder of the negative side of the American narrative of manifest destiny. **MPB**

Contact

Carl Sagan

Lifespan | *b.* 1934 (U.S.), *d.* 1996
First Published | 1985
First Published by | Simon & Schuster (New York)
Locus Award | 1986

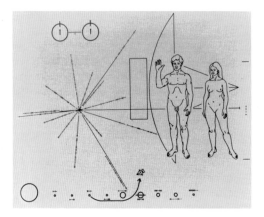

"Science fiction, You're right, it's crazy . . . You wanna hear something really nutty? I heard of a couple guys who wanna build something called an airplane . . ."

● The plaque Carl Sagan designed for the Pioneer space probe was meant to be comprehensible to any extraterrestrial intelligence.

◐ Sagan, in 1972, displays his space probe plaque, which failed to escape the sexism of its day—the man active, the female passive.

Carl Sagan, an astronomer who was inextricably tied to the search for extraterrestrial intelligence (the SETI program), was one of the most famous popular scientists of the last century, as respected by his fellow professionals as he was by the public. A major proponent of the search for extraterrestrial life, Sagan designed a special plaque for the exterior of NASA spacecraft. It bore a universal message for spacecraft bound outside the solar system, which could be understood by any extraterrestrial intelligence that might find it. He was also one of the first scientists, along with Frank Drake, to use a radio telescope to search for deliberate signals from nearby galaxies, estimating that our galaxy was home to over a million civilizations.

The highly successful novel *Contact*, which was adapted for screen a year after Sagan died, was Sagan's best-known foray into the world of fiction, bringing scientific principles to mainstream entertainment. Unsurprisingly, its overriding theme is that of extraterrestrial contact. The main character, astronomer Ellie Arroway, detects a signal from a nearby star, a repeating sequence of the first 261 prime numbers, which she deduces could only be sent from an intelligent civilization. It turns out that the message is more complex than initially realized; it actually contains a blueprint for an advanced space traveling machine. Religious fundamentalists, scientists, and governments argue over whether to build it and, in the end, a multinational team is chosen to make the trip. Throughout the story, Sagan intertwines complex mathematics with fiction, and through the knots in his story come hints of deep questions about the meaning of religion and spirituality, humanity, and social consciousness. **EF**

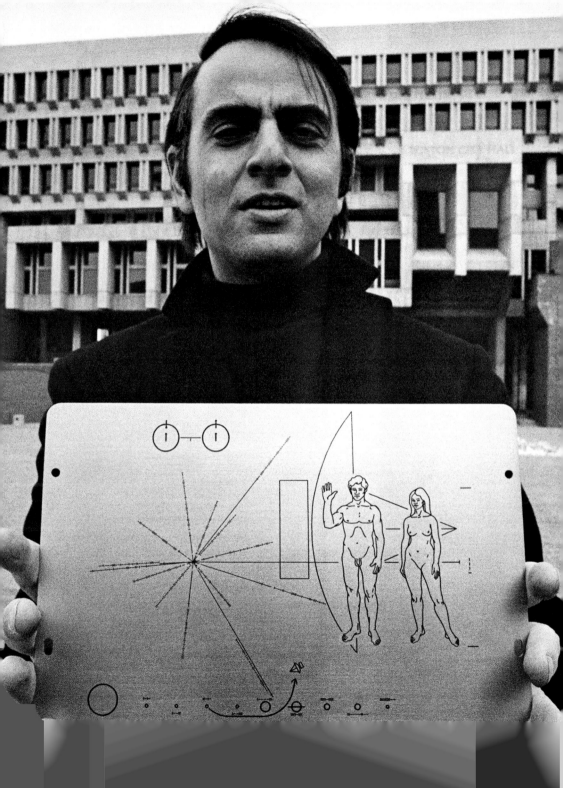

Simon and the Oaks

Marianne Fredriksson

Lifespan | *b.* 1927 (Sweden)
First Published | 1985
First Published by | Wahlström & Widstrand
Original Title | *Simon och ekarna*

Simon Larsson, aged eleven when the story begins, is given away by his biological mother when he is only three days old. Half Jewish with an unknown father, Simon is brought up by Karin and Erik Larsson at their working-class home in Sweden. With war threatening Europe, he befriends Isak, a Jewish boy brought to Sweden by his father to escape the Nazis. When Isak begins to recollect his traumatic past, Karin rescues him from deep depression. Simon and Karin often take refuge in a copse of oaks; only there can they work out their anger and anxieties. Simon discovers that Karin and Erik are not really his parents but his aunt and uncle, and on this day, the reader learns, he ceases to be a child.

Fredriksson's characters are developed to great depth; they experience paradoxical feelings, where guilt accompanies goodness, where loneliness is felt in company, and easy answers are hard to find. Here, taking the mother–child relationship as her central theme, she analyzes the causes of their emotions and actions. Her view tends toward the psychoanalytical and the religious, but without invoking a god; she brings out the hidden mysticism in the lives and struggles of ordinary people.

Marianne Fredriksson, a successful journalist and editor-in-chief, made her literary debut at fifty-three and is one of Sweden's most popular authors. Esteemed for her realism and accurate touch, her books are better known than those of Strindberg and have been translated into fifty languages. **TSe**

The Cider House Rules

John Irving

Lifespan | *b.* 1942 (U.S.)
First Published | 1985
First Published by | W. Morrow (New York)
Movie Adaptation | 1999

One of Irving's most political novels, *The Cider House Rules* explores the contentious issue of abortion, as well as those of addiction, racism, and rejection. Dr. Wilbur Larch is the ether-addicted and childless proprietor of the St. Clouds Orphanage in 1920s Maine. After many years witnessing unwanted children and deaths from backstreet abortions, Dr. Larch starts an illegal, and safe, abortion clinic at the orphanage. Homer Wells is one of the orphans, a bright and enterprising boy who appears to be inexplicably unadoptable, being returned again and again to the orphanage from would-be families. Larch realizes Homer will probably spend his life in the orphanage and decides to train him to take over his profession as St. Clouds's illegal abortionist.

But Homer does not agree with abortion, and decides instead to take a trip with a young couple, from which he never returns. Dr. Larch must come to terms with Homer's reluctance both to follow his professional footsteps and to return to St. Clouds, while Homer's life develops complications of its own as love, and the Second World War, intervene. In dealing with the racism of the time, the novel's title derives from a list of rules Homer posts in the Cider House. These are supposed to keep order and safety among the black migrant workers who come to pick apples, but Homer is unaware that these rules are resented by the workers. Along with Homer, we come to realize that the real rules of the Cider House, and of life, are never written down. **EF**

Annie John

Jamaica Kincaid

Lifespan | b. 1949 (Antigua and Barbuda)
First Published | 1985
First Published by | New American Library (N.Y.)
Given Name | Elaine Cynthia Potter Richardson

Fizzing with all the energy and contradictions of adolescence, *Annie John* is a coming-of-age tale set on the stunning Caribbean island of Antigua. Bright and insatiably curious, Annie is fascinated by the doings of her neighbors in her small seaside community. Enveloped in her mother's love and tenderness, Annie's childhood is happy and peaceful—until notes of discord creep in just before she starts high school. In cool, pared-down prose, Kincaid depicts the horrors of a mother–daughter relationship in freefall, Annie's disillusionment with respectable pastimes and friendships, and a slide toward delinquency and psychosomatic crisis.

As with much of Kincaid's writing, *Annie John* is richly informed by her own childhood in Antigua. The author experienced a Caribbean way of life that maintained respect for traditional medicines and belief in the restlessness of the dead and the power of dreams. Similarly, Kincaid struggled against the multiple binds of empire, restrictive gender roles and an education system dulled by convention.

Annie John is imbued with the strange, pure colors of Caribbean magic realism. It is a shining example of Caribbean women's writing, outlining with startling clarity themes that we find pursued, with varying levels of success, by other writers, namely the troubled mother–daughter relationship that mirrors the motherland–colony problem, the mental distress of the dominated woman, and the urge to escape from the cage via migration. **RM**

The Parable of the Blind

Gert Hofmann

Lifespan | b. 1931 (Germany), d. 1993
First Published | 1985
First Published by | Luchterhand (Darmstadt)
Original Title | Der Blindensturz

Pieter Breughel's painting *The Parable of the Blind* depicts six blind men walking in line, one following the other; disturbingly, the leader has stumbled into a pond and lies sprawled on his back as the others approach. Narrated in the first-person plural voice, the collective "we" in which these blind men think Hofmann's novel retells the big day on which they have come to visit the famous artist, so that he can paint them. On the way, they are taunted by villagers, fall asleep in barns, and lose their bearings several times, before eventually finding their way, bruised and confused, to the pond beside which the famous artist lives.

In these frail, exposed, and vulnerable blind men, the reader is brought face to face with bare life. Part of the poignancy of the narrative is that while the blind men pin their hopes on the meeting with the painter, they never in fact encounter him face-to-face. To make matters worse, they are forced to walk into the pond again and again, so that they can be painted in a situation that, if anything, exaggerates the helplessness of their predicament.

In Hofmann's masterful hands, Breughel's painting becomes a parable of not just the blind—who here stand for Everyman—but of the ambiguous power relationship between the artist and his models. By imagining how these unfortunate individuals came to be painted, Hofmann fixes permanently on the strange, shifting world of those who cannot see in a world where sight is all that matters. **PT**

Love in the Time of Cholera

Gabriel García Márquez

Lifespan | b. 1928 (Columbia)
First Published | 1985, by Bruquera (Barcelona)
Original Title | El amor en los tiempos del cólera
Nobel Prize for Literature | 1982

On the day of the funeral of Fermina Daza's husband, her former fiancé, Florentino Ariza—poet, prodigious lover, and president of the River Company of the Caribbean—reiterates his undying love for her. Appalled, Fermina rejects him: fifty-one years, nine months, and four days after his first unceremonious rejection by her. She then orders him to never show his face again. The body of the novel catapults the reader back more than fifty years to the beginning of Florentino and Fermina's courtship, as well as their subsequent lives, and a multitude of other characters' stories are interwoven. The final chapter returns to the present, recounting Florentino's infinitely more successful second wooing of his beloved.

Love in the Time of Cholera is an epic love story. At the same time, it is utterly unsentimental, leaving its reader with a sense of the astonishing power of patience and determination to overcome all obstacles, more than some romantic eternal power of love. Peopled by ghostly apparitions, cursed dolls, and sinister parrots, the book contains enough delightful moments of everyday unreality to confirm Garcia Márquez's place among the most outstanding of magic realist writers. More aware of the weight of history and the scourges of urban living, this is darker but no less captivating than *One Hundred Years of Solitude*, its great predecessor. **SD**

Ancestral Voices

Etienne van Heerden

Lifespan | b. 1954 (South Africa)
First Published | 1986
First Published by | Tafelberg (Cape Town)
Original Title | Toorberg

The dead walk freely through the pages of this modern South African classic, where the sins of the fathers are visited on their descendants in the arid landscape of the Karoo. Part thriller, part soap opera, and entirely riveting, *Ancestral Voices* traces the downfall of the Moolmans, a pioneering Afrikaans family, who have farmed the abundant land of Toorberg (Magic Mountain) for a hundred years. When the patriarch's illegitimate only grandson dies mysteriously in a borehole dug in a fruitless search for water, a magistrate comes to town to investigate.

He finds himself judging not only the living, but the dead, too. The roots of this tragedy lie in the Moolman men's drive to dominate. In each generation they reject those who choose a different path. First to fall is Floris, who commits the unforgivable sin of crossing the color line and beginning the Skaamfamilie—the Shame Family. Ironically, from this family comes the true inheritor of the Founder Abel's driving force, Pastor Oneday Riet, who leads the dispossessed colored people.

The curse on the Moolmans, representatives of an entire race, is illustrated with powerful, resonant symbolism. Not one is free of the shame of the injustices heaped upon the family black sheep. Etienne van Heerden weaves the past and present together to give a clear vision of the Afrikaner inheritance in the twilight years of apartheid. **LD**

The Beautiful Mrs. Seidenman

Andrzej Szczypiorski

Lifespan | *b.* 1924 (Poland), *d.* 2000
First Published | 1986
First Published in | Instytut Literacki (Paris)
Original Title | *Poczatek*

Warsaw under Nazi occupation is a place of sudden death and unexpected redemption, where Jews live like trapped rats in the ghetto or eke out a fugitive existence on the streets. Everyone has a new, often contradictory identity. Henio, a young Jew on the run, forsakes safety to return to his people in the ghetto. Sister Weronika baptises rescued Jewish children into the Catholic faith. Meanwhile, the beautiful Irma Seidenman, a Jewish doctor's widow, lives quietly with forged papers in the city's Aryan sector, until an informer betrays her to the Gestapo, and her life depends on the loyalty of strangers.

In *The Beautiful Mrs. Seidenman*, Andrzej Szczypiorski investigates the conundrum of human belonging: who decides who we become? Some of Sister Weronika's child converts resettle in Israel, others become Polish patriots, rabidly anti-Semitic. Mrs. Seidenman, who renounced her own Jewishness to survive the war, is driven into exile by the anti-Jewish purges of 1968. Although she chose to live as a Pole in Poland, she can never be Polish enough to be safe. Perhaps Henio, who freely chose his own death in the ghetto, made a better choice? Twenty years after the war, Jewish soldiers renew the cycle of killing and hatred in the Arab settlements of Palestine. Perhaps, Szczypiorski warns in this moving and provoking novel, the mask of violence is the only immutable human identity. **MuM**

The Drowned and the Saved

Primo Levi

Lifespan | *b.* 1919 (Italy), *d.* 1987
First Published | 1986
First Published by | G. Einaudi (Turin)
Original Title | *I Sommersi a i salvati*

Published a year before his death, *The Drowned and the Saved* is Primo Levi's final return to the tormenting question of how to write about the experience of Auschwitz, the "abyss of viciousness" we are so tempted to forget. In particular, he returns to the question explored in *If This is a Man* (1947); how to bear witness to the death camps when the "true witnesses"—those put to death—have been obliterated. Survivors, Levi reflects in his chapter on "Shame," are an "anomalous minority": "we are those who by their prevarications or abilities or good luck did not touch bottom."

Throughout the book, Levi brings to bear the resources of memory, anecdote, and reflection on the questions of survival, communication, and judgement that are part of the legacy of the death camps. "Almost everybody," Levi insists, "feels guilty of having omitted to offer help," a statement that pulls his readers into the drama of accusation, and self-accusation, that prolongs the suffering of the camps throughout a lifetime. It is a burden of guilt that, Levi suggests, is vital to the totalitarian system; its most extreme example the Sonderkommandos of the extermination camps, the squads of prisoners selected to run the crematoria. Levi's work is to bring readers toward the paralysis of judgement that results from trying to hear the message of the horrific atrocities perpetrated in the camps. **VL**

Watchmen

Alan Moore and Dave Gibbons

Lifespan | b. 1953 (England), b. 1949 (England)
First Published | 1986
First Published by | DC Comics/Titan Books (N.Y./Lon.)
Hugo Award | 1987

A meditation on the Nietzschean Superman. A murder mystery. An alternate world sci-fi epic. A psychological study of power and corruption. A comic.

The year 1986 marked a significant turning point for the graphic novel. Alongside Frank Miller's reinvention of Batman came Alan Moore's twelve-part saga of superheroes and their troubles. Set in America in 1985, Nixon is president for a third term, and costumed adventurers have been outlawed by the 1977 Keene Act. Two are still operational: the Comedian, a tough, vicious soldier with a dark past, and Dr. Manhattan, the victim of an atomic accident, whose extraordinary powers give America the decisive edge in the Cold War. The other superheroes are arguably happier in their enforced retirement. Except for Rorschach, the sociopath, whose response to the Keene Act was to deliver the dead body of a multiple rapist to New York's police along with a note saying "Never." But then the Comedian is killed. Someone has a plan. The Cold War is not over but escalating. Who can rise above it? And at what cost?

With a broad cast of characters, *Watchmen* shows a humanity in the face of Armageddon. Moore knows the attractions and the pitfalls of comics, and has no time for a simple tale of heroes and villains. In addition to Moore's narratives, Dave Gibbons's art can bring a tear to the eye. Today, the term "graphic novel" is both overused and ill-defined. *Watchmen* remains the standard and the challenge. **JS**

Extinction

Thomas Bernhard

Lifespan | b. 1931 (Netherlands), d. 1989 (Austria)
First Published | 1986
First Published by | Suhrkamp (Frankfurt)
Original Title | *Auslöschung: ein Zerfall*

Thomas Bernhard's final novel, *Extinction*, is a powerfully sustained monologue on the subject of family, Austria, the scars of Nazism, and the impossibility of escaping cultural inheritance. It is a final reckoning of the formal and thematic concerns Bernhard worked on throughout his career.

Franz-Joseph Murau is an Austrian intellectual living in Rome, where he has taken refuge from Austria and his family in the "infinite paradise" of literature and the arts. The novel begins when Murau receives a telegram informing him that his parents and older brother have been killed in a car accident, leaving him heir to the family estate, Wolfsegg. As he prepares to leave for the funeral, he reflects on his family, his hatred for them, and the lack of remorse he feels for their untimely deaths. The second half of the novel takes place at Wolfsegg, where he is forced to confront the burden of individual and collective history. Murau charges both his family and a large part of Austrian society with complicity in Nazi crimes and berates them for their complacent and hypocritical treatment of the past. Declamatory but never self-righteous, Murau is constantly aware of his own failings and the bitter tirades never descend into facile moralizing. Such insistent diatribes form part of a provocative attempt to awaken Austria from its historical amnesia. Far from a parochial concern, his savage indictment of Austria is directed at all forms of repressive dogma, and is an incitement for cultures to remain open to continuous reevaluation. **AL**

An Artist of the Floating World

Kazuo Ishiguro

Lifespan | *b.* 1954 (Japan)
First Published | 1986
First Published by | Faber & Faber (London)
Whitbread Award | 1986

In his second novel, Ishiguro examines the "floating world" of postwar Japan, as it struggles to come to terms with social upheaval and changing cultural values. Told through the personal tale of Masuji Ono, an artist and propagandist for Japanese imperialism during the Second World War, the novel examines the country's prewar history and the difficulties it faces in coming to terms with the mistakes of the past.

The story begins three years after Japan's defeat. Ono's wife and son have been killed, leaving him to examine his role in the imperialist movement that led the country to disaster. He is involved in negotiations over his younger daughter's proposed marriage. The groom's family had abruptly canceled his other daughter's wedding, a year previously. Ono begins to question whether his artistic support of Imperial Japan has put his daughters' futures at risk. Yet while he attempts to keep his personal history under wraps, he is reluctant to exchange his prewar values for dubious modern ones.

Ishiguro, who left Nagasaki aged five and moved to Britain, vividly evokes the time and place of postwar Japan. His style mimics that of classical Japanese literature, the rigid prose reflecting the inflexibility of the aging artist. As in his subsequent novel, *The Remains of the Day*, Ishiguro creates an essentially expressive individual, who is forced by circumstance to repress his feelings. He writes like the painter of the title, creating a canvas on which his characters are set amid a wealth of intricate details. **LE**

> *"'Of course, circumstances oblige us to consider the financial aspect, but this is strictly secondary.'"*

◉ *An Artist of the Floating World* is set in Ishiguro's birthplace, Nagasaki, following the detonation of the atomic bomb.

Memory of Fire

Eduardo Galeano

Lifespan | b. 1940 (Uruguay)
First Published | 1982–1986
First Published in | Siglo XXI (Mexico C)
Original Title | Memoria del fuego

Eduardo Galeano, an essayist and journalist from Uruguay, took nine years to write the trilogy Memory of Fire, which consisted of Genesis, Faces and Masks, and Century of the Wind. The opus is difficult to define because it is neither a poem, nor a chronicle, nor an essay, nor an anthology, nor a novel, but rather a work inspired by various literary forms. It stands alone as a deeply personal and incisive narrative on the history of the two American continents.

The story of America is recreated in short, poignant chapters. The line-up of events and political intrigues, told one after another, is breathtaking and awe-inspiring. Each one contributes yet more telling detail to an all-encompassing historical mosaic spanning centuries. Historical figures as disparate as Columbus, Moctezuma, Charles V, Simón Bolívar, Napoleon, Darwin, Washington, Voltaire, Lenin, Allende, Rockefeller, Rigoberta Menchú, Frida Kahlo, Chaplin, and Evita are each given their individual voice and brought to life.

There is nothing impartial or objective about this work. All the scenes, significant or not, are narrated with ferocity and in full. Unapologetic, Galeano aligns himself with the conquered. He excels in making his readers remember the foundations of modern America, where a rich indigenous past was exchanged for injustice, oppression, poverty and underdevelopment. In 1989, Galeano won the American Book Award for the trilogy, which was hailed as a masterpiece. **AK**

The Old Devils

Kingsley Amis

Lifespan | b. 1922 (England), d. 1995
First Published | 1986
First Published by | Hutchinson (London)
Booker Prize | 1986

The Old Devils is regarded as one of Kingsley Amis's finest novels, and it is the only book to rival 1954's Lucky Jim in popularity. The targets of Amis's satire this time are Peter, Charlie, and Malcolm—the "Old Devils"—a close-knit group of aging Welshmen who, along with their wives, spend their lives in idle gossip and drinking.

When Alun Weaver, a "professional Welshman" and his seductive wife, Rhiannon, appear on the scene, the Old Devils must re-evaluate their way of life and face hard truths about their own standing in the community. As always, Amis's understated realism and keen eye for the ridiculous minutiae of middle-class life produces a novel that occasionally makes for uncomfortable reading, where any sort of pomposity or pretence is immediately exposed to mockery. Despite this, the reader is also encouraged to feel a grudging sympathy with the curmudgeonly antics of the Old Devils, and it is in this combination that Amis's talent really lies. This savage comic novel nevertheless contains a strong strain of human sympathy, as the buffoonish characters cannot help but win the reader's admiration.

Amis's writing in the late period of his career has often been criticized for its famous misanthropy and frequently offensive conservatism. In The Old Devils, he exposes the fallacy of this charge, combining the exquisite poise and control of his early satires with a gentleness and genuine humanity that make this novel a pleasure to read. **AB**

Matigari

Ngugi Wa Thiong'o

Lifespan | *b.* 1938 (Kenya)
First Published | 1986
First Published by | Heinemann (Nairobi)
Original Language | Kikuyu

Matigari returns from the mountains, after years of struggle against colonial settlers, to find his country and home bequeathed to the heirs of the opponents he has defeated. But in place of a victorious and proud homecoming, he finds an oppressive and corrupt neocolonial order and an acquiescent population. The struggle for justice must begin again, and Matigari becomes the instigator of various events that, in their retelling, take on the power of myth. Matigari awakens a taste for rumor that loosens the tongues of the poor. Truth and political maneuvering have become difficult to distinguish between, and the president's "voice of truth," which blurts incessantly over the radio, is no longer immune from questioning.

Set "once upon a time, in a country with no name," Ngugi avoids determinacy of time or place. But in weaving together allusions to recent Kenyan history with pre-independence ideals from the Gikuyu oral traditions, the novel creates a sense of loss and historical obligation alongside a characteristically sharp critique of post-independence Kenya. Some months after the novel's first publication, intelligence reports in Kenya stated that a figure known as Matigari was traveling across the country preaching about peace and justice. Orders were given for his immediate arrest. The situation uncannily mirrors the last part of the novel, where it is the inability to pin down any meaning to Matigari that prohibits his capture and assimilation. **ABi**

Anagrams

Lorrie Moore

Lifespan | *b.* 1957 (U.S.)
First Published | 1986
First Published by | Knopf (New York)
Given Name | Marie Lorena Moore

This debut novel from one of America's foremost short-story writers displays all the brilliance of her early stories, only delightfully longer. This is a commonplace fable of ordinary lives confused by the fact that they are not extraordinary. It opens with a mischievous literary anagram. We are given successive versions of the first chapter, each slightly different, shuffled. Details fluctuate and merge until Lorrie Moore comes up with the right one. Not just a self-reflexive trick, the gambit captures the theme of the narrative: the attempts of the characters to rearrange details of their lives, their outlooks, and their partners to create something that makes sense. Benna, alternately, is a nightclub singer, an unemployed aerobics instructor, and an art history professor. In one incarnation she wonders, "perhaps there are really only a few hundred people in the whole world and they all have jobs as other people." Gerard is her friend, her neighbor, her ex-lover, her student. How do the characters fit their lives and how do they fit their lives best? How do we create ourselves, our lives, to be successful?

In elaborate yet casual prose, *Anagrams* is about friendship, connection, barely missed connections, love, and loneliness. The characters try to be a part of things but can't find the courage to try hard enough. There are no grand evils here, only the careless indignities of everyday life; simple pathos, more of a shrug than a scream. At its heart is Moore's incisive humor coupled with compassion. **GT**

Lost Language of Cranes

David Leavitt

THE · LOST
LANGUAGE
OF · CRANES

A · NOVEL · BY · THE · AUTHOR · OF
FAMILY · DANCING
DAVID · LEAVITT

"No matter what he pretended, he knew, he was going where he was going."

⬤ The first edition cover refers to an article read in the library about a child who mimics cranes and is then rejected by his parents.

Lifespan | *b.*1961 (U.S.)
First Published | 1986
First Published by | Knopf (New York)
First UK Edition | 1987, by Viking (London)

David Leavitt's first novel, an impressive debut, explores the terrible secrets that families keep from one another, and the consequences of their discovery. Set in 1980s New York against the terrifying backdrop of the Aids epidemic, the novel recounts the coming out of Philip Benjamin to his parents, Owen and Rose. His disclosure has an immediate impact on their comfortable, settled lives. His mother feels a kind of shocked "grief," driven by her fear of the sexual danger that her son is to negotiate as a homosexual. For his father, "it is the end of the world." Confronted by Philip's "news," Owen is utterly inconsolable, confused by the upheavel in his family, and overwhelmed by his inability to cope with his own undisclosed homosexuality, realized only in clandestine Sunday afternoon visits to gay porn theaters.

The novel progresses through Philip's sexual and emotional development in his relationship with his lover, Eliot, who feels thwarted by the effeminacy of Philip's desire. Their relationship provides a counterpoint to that of Philip's parents. By far the most adept aspect of the novel, Leavitt examines the way in which Owen and Rose's marriage changes once she realizes that they have been living a lie for the last three decades. Without slipping into cliché where other writers might, Leavitt's assiduous, scrupulous style here conveys the fissures that all too easily appear between generations and within families. **VC-R**

The Taebek Mountains

Jo Jung-rae

Lifespan | *b*. 1943 (Korea)
First Published | 1986
First Published by | Hangilsa (Seoul)
Original Title | *Taebaek sanmaek*

The Taebek Mountains is a ten-volume epic novel by one of South Korea's most respected and bestselling writers. It spans a period of Korean history that saw intense ideological conflicts between the political right and left following the establishment of the South Korean government in 1948—these conflicts continued until the end of the Korean War.

The novel focuses on the fate of Beolgyo, a small town in southwest Korea, focusing on the period from 1948–1950. This proves to be a tumultuous time for ordinary civilians, as control of the town shifts from faction to faction. The struggles are frequently violent: each time the balance of power shifts, it is the townspeople who suffer.

Within a cast of almost five hundred characters, the saga follows a number of protagonists, including Yeom Sang-ku, a violent inspector general who takes the lead in ferreting out the leftists; his brother, Yeom San-jin, a leftist military party chairman; Kim Beom Woo, a middle-of-the road anti-Communist; Seo Min-young, a landowner who decides to share his land with his tenants; and So-hwa, a Korean shaman who represents traditional Korean values. The novel skillfully conveys intimate personal dramas played out in a climate of suspicion and terror.

The Taebek Mountains has sold more than six million copies. Jo has revealed that people often ask him which part of his novels are fiction and which are fact, "I answer with a grin that in a good novel there is no distinction between them." **HO**

Ballad for Georg Henig

Viktor Paskov

Lifespan | *b*.1949 (Bulgaria)
First Published | 1987
First Published in | Bŭlgarski pisatel (Sofia)
Original Title | *Balada za Georg Henih*

Viktor Paskov's *Ballad for Georg Henig* is a bittersweet fable about love, love's failure, and the mesmerizing power of music. Set in Bulgaria in the 1950s, the novel is told through the eyes of ten-year-old Viktor, a failed child prodigy whose proudest possession is a one-eighth-size violin. It was custom made by Georg Henig, a Czech violin maker, now dying, alone and poor, neglected by his former students and clients.

Viktor's parents married for love, but life on a musician's salary has killed their illusions. Viktor's mother resents their poverty and fantasizes about owning a sideboard, her symbol of domestic bliss. Viktor's father, a trumpeter at the Musical Theatre, lives for his music and does not understand his wife's yearning for possessions. To save their marriage, and his wife's sanity, he decides to build a sideboard in Henig's workshop. Young Viktor comes to love the old man and learns to ask new questions: who is God, what does poverty really mean, and is the new sideboard driving his parents further apart?

The novel is saved from sentimentality by Paskov's portrayals of banal evil: the alcoholic who menaces his children with an axe, the vile neighbors whose dog savages Henig. Paskov ponders the question of how artistic and ethical integrity can survive in essentially philistine societies. Young Victor finally poses himself the novel's central conundrum: if a master craftsman like Henig cannot make a good instrument in six days, how can God expect the world to be a success? **MuM**

Enigma of Arrival

V. S. Naipaul

Lifespan | *b.* 1932 (Trinidad)
First Published | 1987
First Published by | Viking (London)
Nobel Prize for Literature | 2001

The setting of a Wiltshire valley near Stonehenge in the heart of Thomas Hardy's mythical "Wessex" is typical of a landscape deeply inscribed in the English literary imagination. At the start of the novel, this rural idyll is obscured by incessant rain and the narrator's romanticized image of England that he has gleaned from his literary studies in Trinidad. Through five sections that interweave time and space, a picture of England slowly emerges, which seriously disrupts the narrator's original vision of an undisturbed culture. At every juncture, the appearance of England's ancient purity is contaminated by change, and the lasting impression is one of incongruity. Even Jack, the landlord who is the subject of the first part of the novel, turns out not to be firmly rooted in the apparent antiquity of the location but is, like the narrator, a later arrival.

Situated on the border between autobiography and fiction, *The Enigma of Arrival* belongs to a tradition of novels including Proust's *In Search of Lost Time* and Joyce's *Portrait of the Artist*. It tells the story of the narrator's settling in England, his arrival at an understanding of England filtered necessarily through his colonial heritage, and his eventual writing of this very novel. Here we see the realization that the changes wrought on the English landscape and lifestyles by the newcomers are, in essence, no different to the narrator's restyling of England for his own literary purposes: the colonies have already taken root in the colonizer. **ABi**

World's End

T. Coraghessan Boyle

Lifespan | *b.* 1948 (U.S.)
First Published | 1987
First Published by | Viking Press (New York)
PEN/Faulkner Award | 1988

World's End is T. Coraghessan Boyle's great novel, a grand symphony of themes, motifs, and variations. He roots it in the Hudson Valley, where the ancestral bond to the land—and actual ancestors—still suffocates the present. It is the story of the Van Brunts, a family abused by fate, and begins with a distant ancestor, Harmanus Van Brunt, the victim of the illusion of a better life who sails for New Amsterdam. Far from finding the promised land, he is beset by hardships and blights that could make the God of the Old Testament cringe. And so begins the curse, the bad luck, and loss of limbs. But these Van Brunts are not inculpable. They betray their own sons, their own fathers, wives, cousins, and in-laws. They succumb to passion and caprice. They are human; they are Americans. The future is adumbrated by the past, the past plays off the future. There can't be losers without winners, however, and the winners are the Van Warts. Seventeenth-century patroons and tormenters of the Van Brunts, their ancestries are symbiotically entwined. They rule, and always will. But it does all end hopefully—or at least with the possibility of an end to the damage.

In *World's End*, Boyle tackles three hundred years of history and myth in America, and does it with verbal sleight of hand and wickedly subversive wit. It is a breathtaking feat of prose. **GT**

❯ T. Coraghessan Boyle sits on the steps of his house in Santa Barbara, California, which was designed by Frank Lloyd Wright.

The Pigeon

Patrick Süskind

Lifespan | b. 1949 (Germany)
First Published | 1987
First Published by | Diogenes (Zürich)
Original Title | Die Taube

This short, tightly written novella is pervaded by a dark intensity. Patrick Süskind has been admired for his exploration of psychological themes and possesses a skill for closely drawing society's outsider individuals and their peculiarities. Jonathan Noel, a somewhat eccentric Everyman, is a bank guard in his fifties who leads an almost automated existence of monotonous uniformity. He has withdrawn from all but the most perfunctory necessities of social interaction. Instead of depending upon people, who in his youth had consistently let him down or disappeared, Noel relies for stability on the simplicity of uneventfulness and the security of familiar surroundings and routines.

The novella takes place over twenty-four hours, beginning with an early morning encounter with a pigeon outside the studio apartment Noel has occupied for over thirty years. Looking into the bird's eye, which seems devoid of life, Noel is precipitated into what is commonly and crudely known as a midlife crisis. The event is to disrupt and deeply disturb not only his regimen but also his carefully maintained internal equilibrium. For the first time in his life, he finds himself inattentive at work and unable to return home; for the first time, he questions the meaningfulness of the existence he has built for himself. Powerful for its potential universality, this short tale is also a persuasive examination of how an apparently trivial, if unusual, occurrence can force the self into new perspectives. **JC**

Of Love and Shadows

Isabel Allende

Lifespan | b. 1942 (Peru)
First Published | 1987
First Published by | Plaza & Janés (Barcelona)
Original Title | De amor y de sombra

Born in Peru, Isabel Allende moved to Chile when her parents separated. In 1973, when General Pinochet assassinated her uncle, then president Salvador Allende, and began an era of military dictatorship that saw 11,000 Chileans perish in torture chambers, she inherited her family's political legacy. While most of her family fled or were imprisoned, Isabel launched into the humanitarian work that enabled her to record interviews with the regime's surviving victims, stating that "some day we would have democracy back and our evidence would help bring to justice the murderers and torturers."

Allende's second novel, *Of Love and Shadows*, refers to the real discovery of bodies of *disaparecidos*, disappeared people, in a mineshaft in 1978. The novel's plot—a young fashion journalist falls in love with a photographer with whom she discovers the bodies of victims of Pinochet's security forces—closely resembles Allende's own transition from frivolous journalism to a more weighty career as novelist and political activist.

The love story at the heart of this novel is as pivotal as the politics it expresses, if only because it appropriates the distinctly female sentimental literary genre of the *novella rosa*, largely ignored by literary critics, and yet read by the masses. The combination of politics and populism is potent in realizing Allende's mission to engage with a history that fails to appear in textbooks, and to honor the novel's closing sentiment: "We will be back." **JSD**

Beloved

Toni Morrison

Lifespan | b. 1931 (U.S.)
First Published | 1987
First Published by | Knopf (New York)
Pulitzer Prize | 1988

Beloved has become an influential force in articulating the profound horror of slavery's legacy in American culture. At the novel's absent center are the consequences of the actions of Sethe, a mother who commits infanticide rather than allow her child to be taken back into the slavery from which she has just escaped. In the narrative's opening, Sethe and her one remaining child live on in the house in which the crime occurred, now haunted by the hungry sadness of the dead child. The appearance of Paul D., who had shared Sethe's traumatic experience of slavery on the ironically named "Sweet Home" Farm, appears to banish the ghost, only for her to reappear as the woman she would have been if allowed to live. Her now malevolent physical presence forces Paul D. away from the family and begins to punish Sethe. By the novel's end, the community, which had been presented as complicit with the murder, regroups around the family and allows Sethe to be free and, finally, her lover to return.

The novel was critically acclaimed for finding an appropriate form for remembering the inhumane violence of slavery. Sethe's slow and partial recollection of the debased treatment she endured during slavery, the emotional and physical hurts that carried her to a defensive act of infanticide, are central to the recovery the novel allows her. Morrison's lack of recourse to either sentiment or identification make it one of the most startlingly powerful books in twentieth-century American literature. **NM**

All Souls

Javier Marías

Lifespan | b.1951 (Spain)
First Published | 1987
First Published in | Anagrama (Barcelona)
Original Title | *Todas las almas*

Three years after winning the Herralde de Novela prize with *The Man of Feeling*, Javier Marías published this work, the embodiment of an original, powerful novel, reflexive and flexible, given to speculation yet at the same time tempted toward more or less autobiographical truth.

From the start, the setting is suggested in the distance that lies between the narrator who is telling the story and the "I," a different, distinct, other who is the person who lived it. The book is dedicated to his predecessors (Vicente Molina Foix and Félix de Azúa), among others, and Marías openly draws upon his experience as a teacher at Oxford University to recreate an almost private world, populated by characters with secret or only half-told stories, cults, and often adventurers wearing fancy dress (perhaps because "in Oxford nobody ever says anything clearly"). Some of these elements reappear in one form or another in later books, but already in this novel can be found valid rules for constructing stories around fictitious identities, the weight of words, and memory used in the construction of identity. The porous pliability of the language is turned to the unfolding of various pieces of knowledge, while the search for this or that title in secondhand bookstores, the reflexive conversations, and the theoretical debates about poetry or painting come together in a novel without apparent difficulty. With a slippery density of feeling, the book is certainly also enigmatic. **JGG**

The New York Trilogy

Paul Auster

Lifespan | *b.* 1947 (U.S.)
First Published | 1987, by Faber & Faber (London)
Trilogy | *City of Glass* (1985), *Ghosts* (1986),
The Locked Room (1986)

City of Glass
Paul Auster

The New York Trilogy, volume 1

◉ The first novella in *The New York Trilogy*, *City of Glass* was first
published in 1985, when it was presented as detective fiction.

◗ Paul Auster, photographed here in Paris, France, in 1990, lived in
France for four years after graduating from Columbia University.

The New York Trilogy comprises three novellas that explore the possibility of meaningful coincidence, necessity, and accident through the conventions of detective fiction and ordinary people's investigations of their mysterious worlds. *City of Glass* features a mystery writer, Daniel Quinn, with an insatiable love for the genre and its artificiality who, after answering two wrong number calls for the Paul Auster Detective Agency, decides to impersonate Auster and take the case. However, he is soon plunged into homeless ruin through his monomaniacal pursuit of a man who tried to beat his infant son into abandoning derivative, "human" language and letting a divine language pour forth. Yet, along with his inevitable desperation and hardship, Quinn seems to develop a Zen-like, uncluttered awareness as his world shrinks drastically. The characters of *Ghosts*, caught up in a highly stylized, surrealistic game of who's watching who, are named after colors, lending a quasi-allegorical air to the action. Black's inaction pushes Blue, the man hired to spy on him, both to read voraciously and nearly lose his mind. *The Locked Room*, itself named after a subgenre of detective fiction, watches an unnamed first-person narrator slowly take over the life of a disappeared childhood friend. He marries his wife and shepherds the publication of his previously unknown literary masterpiece, only to be contacted by said friend and informed that the whole scenario has been intricately orchestrated.

The New York Trilogy is full of terrifying brushes with the zero point that is both complete potentiality and the collapse of identity. The effect of deprivation forms an intriguing subtext to all three stories, not least with respect to their own sparse language and brevity, as the worlds of the novellas gradually drift or lurch toward nothingness. **AF**

Black Box

Amos Oz

Lifespan | *b.* 1939 (Jerusalem)
First Published | 1987
First Published by | Am Oved (Tel Aviv)
Original Title | *Kufsah Shorah*

"Activism is a Way of Life."

◉ The cover of the original Hebrew edition of Oz's *Black Box*;
"Oz" is an adopted name, being the Hebrew word for "strength."

A series of letters, notes, and telexes provide the documentation of a marriage breakdown as it happens; in a sense, these materials become the data inside a marital "black box." The reader is left to decode with real feeling the disintegration of Ilana and Alex's relationship in Israel and their struggle to settle the issues of their wayward son, Boaz. It is a tangled relationship into which Ilana's second husband, Michel, an alternately funny, sad, and fanatical Jew, and others are drawn to complete a dysfunctional ensemble joined by marriage or profession. The correspondence allows Amos Oz to use different voices and tones to capture the frailty, sexuality, absurdity, and ambivalence of human existence in a religiously, politically, and socially charged environment. The tone of the book is sometimes desperate, sometimes seedy, but also comic and lyrical in turn.

As with his other tales of modern Jewish life, most famously *Mikha'el Sheli* in 1968 (*My Michael,* 1972), Oz uses the interaction between his characters—the complexities, guilt, and feelings of persecution inherent within their relationships—to open up a discourse on his country's modern history, politics, and religious splinterings. Oz does not apologize for these but lets the characters play out his ironic take on modern Israeli life, with all its splits and strains. Writing in Hebrew (as with all his works), Oz gives an honest and often wry account of the conflicts inherent in being an Israeli. Like many of his generation, Oz is skeptical of the optimistic certainties of the founding settlers. Having served in the Israeli Army, been a part-time teacher, lived on a kibbutz, and studied at Oxford and in the United States, he certainly imparts an unusually broad perspective on the issues he tackles. **JHa**

The Bonfire of the Vanities

Tom Wolfe

An ambitious brick of a book, Tom Wolfe's first excursion out of the realm of journalism and into novel writing is a savage indictment of the excesses of 1980s Wall Street capitalism. Sherman McCoy, a wealthy, upwardly mobile bondtrader at a prestigious city firm, is involved in a car accident in the South Bronx, in which his mistress, Maria Ruskin, runs over and fatally injures a young black man, Henry Lamb. The novel charts the fall of the once-mighty Sherman, and the range of vested interests that contribute to his public disgrace, arraignment, and trial. While some people emerge triumphantly from the events the novel charts, morally there are no winners. Wolfe cynically suggests—and his own right-wing viewpoint is in evidence here—that the city's political and legal systems, as well as its media, are all complicit in the complicated structures of class and race warfare he describes. The posthumous conversion of Lamb into an idealized "honors student," for example, happens as a result of the career ambitions of the louche journalist Peter Fallow, who wins fame, fortune, and a Pulitzer Prize from his reporting of the accident.

Whatever one's view of Wolfe's politics, it is hard not to admire his prose. His minutely detailed accounts of Park Avenue apartments, the maze of Bronx streets, in which a panicked Sherman finds himself lost, the Southern drawl of Maria, and the impassioned accents of the Harlem-based black rights activist, the Reverend Bacon, render the sheer variety of New York with relish. This is a city seething with ethnic hostilities and class envy, driven by the desire to get rich quick; here sex, money, and power rule almost everyone. Wolfe makes good on his claim to offer a twentieth-century rival to the Victorian blockbusters of Dickens and Thackeray. **CC**

Lifespan | *b.* 1931 (U.S.)
First Published | 1987
First Published by | Farrar, Straus & Giroux (N.Y.)
First UK Edition | 1988, by Jonathan Cape (London)

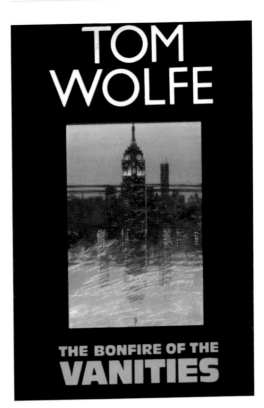

"They'll come see you!"

⊙ Shown here is the UK edition, with jacket design by Mark Holmes. The novel was first serialized in *Rolling Stone* magazine.

The Black Dahlia

James Ellroy

James Ellroy's *The Black Dahlia*, the first of a quartet of novels to pick the scab off L.A.'s dark underbelly between the late 1940s and mid-1950s, is both a straightforward police procedural and a complex, disquieting meditation on voyeurism and sexual obsession. At its heart is the horrific murder of Elizabeth Short, a.k.a. the Black Dahlia, a young woman who arrives in Hollywood looking for stardom and romance, and finds only prostitution, pornography, and death. To track down her killer, police detective Bucky Bleichert must piece together the final days of her life, an act of recovery that brings him to confront not just powerful figures from the law enforcement and business communities, but also his own barely suppressed demons.

Later, Bleichert's discovery of the murder "scene" in a building that, quite literally, supports part of the famous Hollywood sign, brings together the novel's primary areas of concern: pornography, spectacle, and the construction industry. Just as the rebuilding of Los Angeles in the post-Second World War era involves physically scarring the landscape for profit, the spectacular cutting of Elizabeth Short is linked to the commercial ambitions of a sexually deviant property developer. In all of this, unlike Raymond Chandler's archetypal detective, Bleichert cannot remain emotionally and sexually detached: his own obsession with the murdered woman ruins both his marriage and his promising career. The scene where he lures a prostitute back to a motel room littered with photographs of Elizabeth Short's horribly mutilated corpse, and forces the terrified woman to dress up as the Black Dahlia, is as disturbing as it is effective. Though the killer is eventually revealed, it is the supersaturation of violence, sexual depravity, and corruption that endures. **AP**

Lifespan | *b.* 1948 (U.S.)
First Published | 1987
First Published by | Mysterious Press (New York)
Given Name | Lee Earle Ellroy

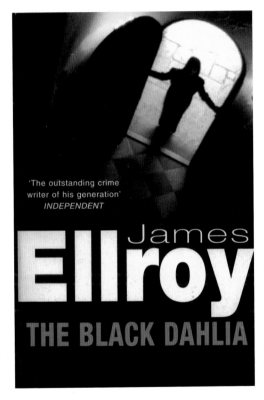

'The outstanding crime writer of his generation'
INDEPENDENT

James **Ellroy**

THE BLACK DAHLIA

The unsolved murder of Ellroy's mother, Geneva, in Los Angeles in 1958, shaped Ellroy's life and led him to write crime novels.

Elizabeth Short was twenty-two years old when her mutilated dead body was found in a Los Angeles parking lot in 1947.

The Afternoon of a Writer

Peter Handke

Lifespan | *b.* 1942 (Austria)
First Published | 1987
First Published by | Residenz Verlag (Salzburg)
Original Title | *Nachmittag eines Schriftstellers*

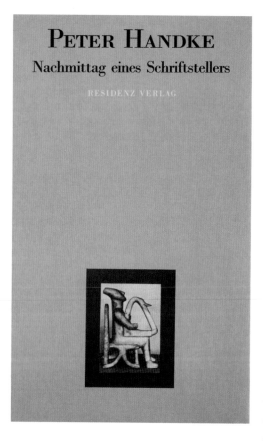

PETER HANDKE

Nachmittag eines Schriftstellers

RESIDENZ VERLAG

⬤ Both a novelist and a playwright, Handke co-wrote the
Wim Wenders movie *Wings of Desire*, also released in 1987.

"Afternoon" in Peter Handke's *The Afternoon of a Writer* is, on the one hand, a definite temporal category. The writer finishes his day's work in a house saturated with the dull, melancholy sunlight of a winter's afternoon. But, on the other hand, "Afternoon" is also a spatial and sensual arena, a matter of the body's movements in habitual spaces, when the body itself is impelled by its own needs rather than by the purposeful structures of work. "Afternoon" in this sense is the aftermath of labor, a period and a sensibility marked by a certain freedom, yet also by a fatigue that transmutes that freedom into something semiconscious; a precious yet barely endurable return to a self stripped of external purpose or motivation.

Handke's writer in *The Afternoon of a Writer* is a man who lives, works, eats, and walks on his own, but this physical isolation only barely protects the privacy he nourishes and cherishes. Seduced, yet at the same time repelled, by the abstract chatter of words and images that engulf a city street, the writer embarks on a walk, hesitates, plunges in, and is lost.

Uneasily self-conscious about calling himself a writer, he is a man for whom art is a daily, sweaty activity and an overarching proud goal. Confronted with the depth of the writer's solitude and the consequent richness of his relations to language and to observation, the world "outside" cannot but pale a little. Handke indeed encourages such an opposition by refusing to name the city the writer walks in; its streets are anonymous and the language or languages spoken on them are unspecified. An opposition is not an unbridgeable chasm, however, and it is the beauty of this small book to make the writer—and the reader—hunger for the things of the world. **PMcM**

The Radiant Way

Margaret Drabble

Margaret Drabble's acclaimed novel is the first book in a sweeping trilogy that follows the lives of three women who, like Drabble herself, found themselves at Cambridge University in the 1950s. Opening at a party on New Years' Eve, 1979, *The Radiant Way* begins by examining the life of Liz Headland, whose apparent success in family, career, and London social life have resulted in twenty years of settled contentment. However, as the 1980s begin, Liz's certainties about life begin to crumble in a dramatic fashion, and she finds herself again thinking of her childhood and adolescence in the provincial north of England, before Cambridge provided her with a passport to the welcome sophistication of London. Interwoven with Liz's story are those of her two Cambridge friends: Alix, whose naïve political convictions and cheerful romanticism make her frighteningly vulnerable to the emotional and financial vagaries of adult life, and Esther, whose mysterious reserve, amusing at Cambridge, has since grown to extreme lengths that worry her friends. All three are confident, happy women, but the life-changing events of the 1980s, culminating in a suggestion of violence previously unimaginable within their comfortable lives, force them to reconsider their success in life and to find value once again in their long friendship.

Here, as usual, Drabble explores the issues of freedom, ambition, and love that face working women in a subtle and often ironically funny way. The otherwise mundane details of characters' lives are interwoven with the surreal background of London during exciting cultural change and political uncertainty. Both an ironic feminist Bildungsroman and a magnificent state-of-England novel, this remains one of Drabble's finest and most absorbing books. **AB**

Lifespan | *b.*1939 (England)
First Published | 1987
First Published by | Weidenfeld & Nicolson (London)
First U.S. Edition | Alfred A. Knopf (New York)

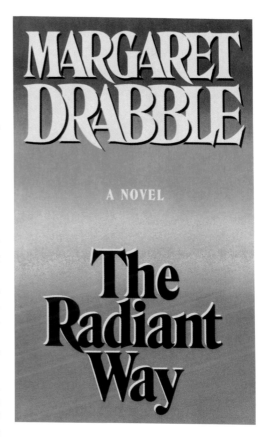

⊙ Margaret Drabble received a C.B.E in 1980, and was later promoted to a Dame in the 2008 Birthday Honors.

Kitchen

Banana Yoshimoto

Lifespan | *b.* 1964 (Japan)
First Published | 1987, by Fukutake (Tokyo)
Given Name | Mahoko Yoshimoto
Original Title | *Kitchin*

キッチン

Banana Yoshimoto

吉本ばなな

"Now only the kitchen and I are left. It's just a little nicer than being left all alone."

When *Kitchen* first appeared in Japan with this discreet cover, its sensational impact provoked "Bananamania" among the young.

In the two novellas that comprise *Kitchen*, Japanese writer Banana Yoshimoto (pen name of Mahoko Yoshimoto) explores the inextricable link between longing and mourning. When Mikage Sakurai in the title novella, "Kitchen," is left an orphan by the death of her grandmother, she accepts the offer from college classmate Yuichi Tanabe, and his mother/father, Eriko (a post-operative transsexual), to move temporarily into their home. Within a quirky world of gay nightclubs, gender reassignment surgeries, and culinary experimentation, the three attempt to carve out an alternative nuclear family. However, a tragic murder threatens to destroy Yuichi and Mikage's newfound equanimity, uniting them in hopelessness, grief, and, finally, love.

The fragile boundary between death and desire is also subtly analyzed in the second novella, "Moonlight Shadow." Overwhelmed by the premature death of her lover, Hitoshi, Satsuki takes up jogging to avoid coming to terms with her loss. However, she finds herself unable to refuse when a mysterious woman she meets on a bridge offers her the chance to lay her grief to rest. Written in simple, elegiac prose, "Moonlight Shadow," like "Kitchen," depicts characters that suddenly find themselves adrift in a cold and unfamiliar universe, and their subsequent search for meaning.

Banana Yoshimoto, daughter of renowned 1960s New Left philosopher Ryumei (Takaaki Yoshimoto) and sister of popular cartoonist Haruno Yoiko, has received much critical acclaim in both her native Japan and abroad. Although written when she was only twenty-three and working as a waitress in Tokyo, this debut novel was awarded two of Japan's most prestigious literary awards, and has since been translated into over twenty languages. **BJ**

Dirk Gently's Holistic Detective Agency

Douglas Adams

In *Dirk Gently's Holistic Detective Agency,* Douglas Adams returns to earth with a highly unconventional detective story. The author deals with all the big questions that informed his earlier series, the *Hitch Hiker's Guide to the Galax.* As ever with Adams, things are not what they seem: a playful and comic interweaving of the science fiction, ghost story, and whodunit genres serves to mask a darker and altogether more haunting set of themes.

Private detective Dirk Gently undertakes to track down the murderer of the millionaire founder of a computer empire. The case enables this most unusual sleuth to employ his trademark holistic method. His longheld belief in the underlying interconnectedness of all things yields results. The conventions of the detective genre are inverted: the clues follow Dirk and reveal themselves to him one after another. But there is plenty left for him to do, for the central mystery that Dirk Gently is trying to solve is none other than discovering the origins of life on earth and unveiling the forces behind the course of history. Although Gently is painted as an absurd and slightly tragic figure, it is through him that Adams accesses some of the more profound currents of thought circulating in the 1980s. This is one of few novels to investigate the ideas of chaos or complexity theory. In rescaling his canvas from the intergalactic *Hitch Hiker's Guide to the Galaxy* to the terrestrial for *Dirk Gently's Holistic Detective Agency,* Adams reflects an emerging popular awareness of the connections found in and among a globalizing world. As his characters grapple with a malevolent enemy, they become conscious that their choices, even those made with the best of intentions, have an unintended but far-reaching impact on the interconnected webs of life. **AC**

Lifespan | *b.* 1952 (England), *d.* 2001 (U.S.)
First Published | 1987
First Published by | Heinemann (London)
First U.S. Edition | Simon & Schuster (New York)

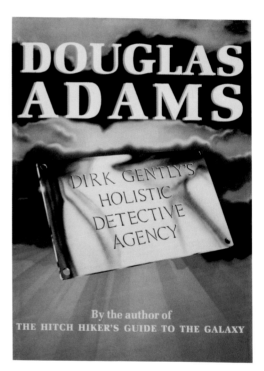

DOUGLAS ADAMS

DIRK GENTLY'S HOLISTIC DETECTIVE AGENCY

By the author of
THE HITCH HIKER'S GUIDE TO THE GALAXY

" Let's think the unthinkable, let's do the undoable."

⊙ Adams described his novel as a "thumping good detective-ghost-horror-who dunnit-time travel-romantic-musical-comedy-epic."

Cigarettes

Harry Mathews

Lifespan | *b.* 1930 (U.S.)
First Published | 1987
First Published by | Weidenfeld & Nicolson (N. Y.)
First UK Edition | 1988, by Carcanet (Manchester)

Harry Mathews is the only American member of the Oulipo, the Paris-based group of writers who experimented with inventions in literary combinatorics, mathematically derived rules imposed upon sentences, poems, and whole novels. Mathews's best-known contribution to the forum is the Mathews Algorithm, a way of recombining arbitrary elements of plot in order to discover unthought-of sequences.

This may or may not be the organizing principle behind *Cigarettes*, which is set over a period of thirty years among New York's generally idle rich—the kind of people Mathews grew up among. Each chapter is a subtle transformation of those surrounding it, where similar events are seen from a different point of view, and each is devoted to the power play between a particular pairing of characters—Owen, who is blackmailing Allen, whose daughter Priscilla has an affair with Walter, who is the mentor of Phoebe, who forges a portrait of Elizabeth, who everyone loves. There are multiple miscommunications and deceptions—between lovers, business partners, parents, and children—and talismanic objects move through the text, from one person to another, connecting them all. It is impossible to avoid the feeling—typical of Mathews—that something intricate is going on beneath the surface. But even that surface is phenomenally rich, and it displays a great range of forms and registers, all engineered with faultless precision. **DSoa**

Nervous Conditions

Tsitsi Dangarembga

Lifespan | *b.* 1959 (Zimbabwe)
First Published | 1988
First Published by | Women's Press (London)
Commonwealth Writer's Prize (Africa) | 1988

Nervous Conditions is a colorful personal memoir, but also a clear-eyed snapshot of colonial Rhodesia in the 1960s. Tambu's branch of the family are subsistence farmers, and her early life on the homestead is marked by hard work and a deep sense of injustice. She is a canny observer of the Shona patriarchy in operation, but will not, like her mother, resign herself to the "poverty of blackness on the one side and the weight of womanhood on the other." Her father deems that there is no point sending Tambu to school, as she cannot "cook books" to feed a husband. But she realizes early that education will be her escape; though clearly a gifted student, she succeeds through chance and sheer determination.

The novel's title is taken from its epigraph, itself a quotation from Jean-Paul Sartre's introduction to Frantz Fanon's *The Wretched of the Earth*: "The condition of native is a nervous condition." Once at the mission school, Tambu enters a different world: the world of her successful uncle and his family, each member of whom has been marked by time spent in England. Tambu sees firsthand, in her cousin Nyasha's eating disorder, in her uncle's nervousness and excessive control—the tensions produced by the colonial condition, by being caught between two worlds. This is the minefield Tambu must negotiate in her formal education, but it is exacerbated by larger questions about black female identity articulated through the unique experience of the four women of her utterly engaging story. **ST**

The First Garden

Anne Hébert

Lifespan | b. 1916 (Canada), d. 2000
First Published | 1988
First Published by | Éditions du Seuil (Paris)
Original Title | Le premier jardin

The First Garden takes as its epigraph William Shakespeare's "all the world's a stage," a quotation that the main character, the fading actress Flora Faranges, takes all too literally, interpreting her life through the medium of a series of dramatic roles. After years of living in France, Flora is offered a role in a play and returns to her native Quebec, where the remembrance of her troubled past and her problematic relationship with her estranged daughter rise up to haunt her, despite her outward success. While rehearsing for the play, she begins to spend an increasing amount of time with the much younger Raphael, a relationship that begins a chain of events that lead her back to the horrifying events of her early childhood.

Hébert's short, dreamlike scenes convey the intricacies of Flora's consciousness to the reader with an immediacy that is almost disturbing; the novel skips around in time and place so that we, like Flora, discover memories gradually through psychological association and reverie. The First Garden details the painful minutiae of failed family life—Flora's failure with her daughter, Maud, echoes her own troubled relations with her adoptive parents, whose bourgeois facade has hidden a horrifying truth about her early childhood.

A short, savage novel, The First Garden takes an unsparing look at how people "act out" at the expense of others, and spells out the repercussions that such behavior can have. **AB**

The Last World

Christoph Ransmayr

Lifespan | b. 1954 (Austria)
First Published | 1988
First Published in | Fischer (Frankfurt)
Original Title | Die letzte Welt

Ransmayr's novel takes as its starting point Ovid's banishment from Rome and his youthful friend Cotta's search for him in the remote Black Sea port of Tomi (in modern Bulgaria). The narrative soon becomes a visionary alternative to history when the landscape impersonates Ovid's vanished poem Metamorphoses. Cotta meets or hears about inhabitants of Tomi who reveal themselves as modern counterparts of mythic figures in the poem. The village prostitute, who repeats the words of those talking to her, is called Echo; Dis and Proserpina, gods of Hades, are now Thies, a refugee German gravedigger, and his quarrelsome fiancée; the deaf-mute weaver is Arachne; and Fama is a gossip who runs the local store. These encounters and other events furnish the pieces of a puzzle that Cotta molds into a dramatic and bewitching story.

Acclaimed as a modern masterpiece, The Last World is especially praised for its dense magical images, for which it has been compared to the magic realism of Garcia Marquez. But this parable of vivid images and unsettling force goes beyond the assertion that great authors cannot be silenced and that myth permeates our lives. Ransmayr's universe is not just a metamorphosis of the Metamorphoses, it is also a timeless poetic world, a political fable that allows its author to deal subtly and indirectly with themes of universal and contemporary interest, such as exile, censorship, dictatorship, and the threat of ecological disaster. **LB**

Oscar and Lucinda

Peter Carey

Lifespan | *b.* 1943 (Australia)
First Published | 1988
First Published by | University of Queenstown Press
Booker Prize | 1988

🔵 *Oscar and Lucinda*, here shown with its UK cover, won the Booker Prize in 1988. A movie version was made in 1997.

Peter Carey is probably Australia's best-known postcolonial writer. *Oscar and Lucinda* is set in mid-nineteenth-century England and Australia. Oscar Hopkins is the son of a preacher, an effeminate Englishman with hydrophobia. Lucinda Leplastrier is an Australian heiress who, fighting against society's expectations of the confinement of her gender, buys a glass factory with her inheritance. Both suffer childhood traumas, Oscar's the result of his relationship with his controlling, religious father, and Lucinda's centered around a doll, a present from her mother. In adulthood, both protagonists develop a passion for gambling and it is this love of risk that unites them when they finally meet, on a boat bound for New South Wales. Between the two there develops an uneasy and unspoken affection. Finally, they set out to transport a glass church across godforsaken terrain and the love developing between them, instead of blossoming, becomes isolated inside their skins.

Several important themes run through the book—not least the idea of love as the ultimate gamble, the high-risk play to which Oscar and Lucinda ironically cannot commit themselves. Carey explores the idea of gender confinement at a time and place in history where society was happiest with strictly defined roles. Lucinda discovers again and again that if she manages to step outside the boundaries placed upon her by society, she will be excluded. Finally, the novel is an acerbic comment on colonialism as the couple attempt to transport a glass church unharmed across native land. In the end it is glass (so similar to his feared water) that, although providing Lucinda with her fortune, plays a hand in the tragic conclusion and in the eventual destruction of the Australian outback. **EF**

The Swimming-Pool Library

Alan Hollinghurst

When Alan Hollinghurst published *The Swimming-Pool Library*, he was already well engaged in the literary scene, having published two collections of poetry and being on the staff of the *Times Literary Supplement*. This, his first novel, is an exuberant narrative of gay life set in 1983, which portrays the hedonism of "the last summer of its kind there was ever to be," before the Aids crisis had really taken hold. By turns enraptured with the present and nostalgic for the past, the novel revels in the company of men and ubiquitous gay sex, while conducting the reader to a finely pitched denouement.

Two lives are contrasted here, that of Lord Nantwich, an ex-colonial administrator in Africa, and William Beckwith, a young gay man of independent means. After saving the aging peer's life, William is subsequently persuaded to write Nantwich's biography and comes into possession of his diaries. These provide a parallel narrative, and it becomes apparent that, though the two men are generations apart, their lives contain disquieting similarities. Racism and queer-bashing endure—even fifteen years after the legalization of homosexuality, the harassment of gay men persists as the arrest of William's best friend by an undercover policeman, himself gay, uncannily echoes the circumstances in which Nantwich served a prison sentence in the 1950s. For all the licentious liberty, the machinery of oppression is never far away in this novel, and further, the whiff of nostalgia for the alluring eroticism of the outlaw highlights the underlying complexity of desire. The shadowing of contemporary gay liberation with the dangers of the illicit homosexual life is a reminder, lest we become complacent, of our connection and debt to past defeats as well as present victories. **CJ**

Lifespan | *b.* 1954 (England*)*
First Published | 1988
First Published by | Chatto & Windus (London)
Somerset Maugham Award | 1989

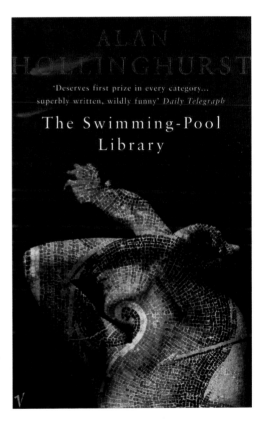

'Deserves first prize in every category... superbly written, wildly funny' *Daily Telegraph*

The Swimming-Pool Library

◉ On its publication, Edmund White hailed the novel as "the best book about gay life yet written by an English author."

The Satanic Verses

Salman Rushdie

Lifespan | *b.* 1947 (India)
First Published | 1988
First Published by | Viking (London)
Fatwa Issued | 1989

◉ The fatwa declared by Ayatollah Khomeini on Rushdie extended to his translators and publishers, several of whom were attacked.

❱ In a pro-Iranian rally in southern Beirut in 1989, a girl stands ready to kill Rushdie before a poster of Ayatollah Khomeini.

This is the book that triggered riots around the world in 1988 and 1989, brought a fatwa (death sentence) upon its author from Ayatollah Khomeini of Iran, and forced Rushdie into hiding for over a decade. The "Rushdie Affair" represents a seminal moment in literary history, in which a host of religious and political tensions crystallized explosively around one novel and its Indian-born, British-educated author.

Written in a playful, magic realist style, *The Satanic Verses* is a transcultural view of the world as perceived by two Indian migrants, Saladin Chamcha and Gibreel Farishta. In the moment of genesis that opens the novel, both men fall into Britain, angel-like from the sky, when their plane is bombed by terrorists. British racism and the colonial legacy affect these characters in different ways, driving Gibreel into delusional, psychotic dream sequences in which he appears as the Angel Gabriel, bringing divine revelations to the Islamic Prophet. Meanwhile, the sycophantic Anglophile, Saladin, becomes more devilish by the minute in a physical mutation he cannot control. A multitude of Black and Asian British characters probes postcolonial migrant experience in the novel. Mixing words, worlds, histories, fictions, dreams, delusions, and prophesies, Rushdie's style is an exercise in cosmopolitanism.

In Gibreel's dream sequences, set in and around Mecca, Rushdie asks what makes a "new idea," Islam, stick fast, while a multitude of other ideas fail to take hold of the imagination. The answer to this question lies in the Prophet's "ramrod-backed" conviction that his idea is absolute and pure. In fictionalizing the Prophet's life, however, and by inserting a psychotic character into the role of angel, Rushdie offended millions of Muslims worldwide and provoked a sense of outrage that persists today. **SN**

Wittgenstein's Mistress

David Markson

Lifespan | *b.* 1927 (U.S.)
First Published | 1988
First Published by | Dalkey Archive Press (Illinois)
First UK Edition | 1989, by Jonathan Cape (London)

It must be a fantasy most, if not all, of us had at some point in our lives: you are the last person left alive on earth. This is what happens to Kate, the protagonist of David Markson's novel *Wittgenstein's Mistress*. Or does it? "In the beginning, sometimes I left messages in the street," the work begins, but the reader never learns anything about what precedes this beginning other than through Kate's interior monologue. The story that unfolds leaves open two basic possibilities: Kate can be trusted, in which case she lost a son in a fire she probably caused, and now is, for some unknown reason, the last representative of humankind; or she cannot be trusted, in which case she lost a son in a fire she probably caused, and subsequently went mad, now imagining she is the last representative of humankind.

This theme of trust, in others and oneself, and its relationship with language is what fully justifies the book's title. It is, in fact, a fictional interpretation of Wittgenstein's thought, and the turmoil and torment of Kate's voice reads like an uncanny echo of what lies behind Wittgenstein's philosophical texts. As her knowledge of the past and her personal memory becomes ever more unreliable, we realize that there can be no knowledge of the present and no sense of self without it. The brilliance of this underrated author lies in the subtlety with which doubt creeps in and finally engulfs the reader as well. **DS**

Paradise of the Blind

Duong Thu Huong

Lifespan | *b.* 1947 (Vietnam)
First Published | 1988
First Published by | Phu nu (Hanoi)
Original Title | *Nhung thiên duong mù*

This sensuous, evocative novel is a journey into the shattered heart of Communist Vietnam: its potency is such that Huong's work is still effectively banned in her homeland. The story is told from the perspective of Hang, a young migrant worker in a Russian textile factory, as she travels across Russia to see the Communist uncle whose actions caused her loved ones unremitting and almost unforgivable suffering, yet who remains, thanks to the cultural strength of family ties, at the core of their existence.

Lovingly detailed yet excrutiating in its painful honesty, *Paradise of the Blind* brings a sensual intensity to the daily life of rural Vietnam and the harsh routines of the city fringes—you can almost smell the offerings on the family altar, taste the texture of duck's blood custard, or feel the slime of the duckweed that clogs the village ponds. Hang's widowed mother, her spinster aunt, and her Communist uncle all do their best, in their very different ways, to live by the conflicting rules of a peasant society hurled headfirst into cultural revolution, at immense cost to themselves.

Huong digs deep below the picture-postcard images of paddy fields, bamboo, and water buffalo, conical hats and bicycles, into a country of old religions, ancient hatreds, and huge transition. This is a novel of wonderful, elegiac power that delivers powerful insights into a changing Vietnam. **TSu**

Foucault's Pendulum

Umberto Eco

Lifespan | *b.* 1932 (Italy)
First Published | 1988
First Published by | Bompiani (Milan)
Original Title | *Il pendolo di Foucault*

Everything is open to interpretation in this novel, which is why we should not overlook the fact that the narrator is the namesake of Dorothea's scholarly husband in *Middlemarch*. Umberto Eco's Causabon also wants to rewrite the messy confusion of world history as a single, coherent narrative, but, unlike Eliot's Causabon, who is convinced of the truth of his project, Eco's character is well aware that his story is just one version.

Foucault's Pendulum is a vast, sprawling novel all about the desire for meaning. Causabon, Belbo, and Diotallevi work together at Garamond Press, researching a book on the histories of secret societies. In what starts out as an elaborate joke, they feed all the explanations and interpretations they can find into Belbo's computer, and end up recreating the Plan of the Knights Templar. The Plan is the ultimate conspiracy theory: each apparently unconnected historical event takes on new significance in the context of a synthesized story in which everything accounts for everything else. This is a dangerous game, and one that will eventually catch up with its players. *Foucault's Pendulum* is a novel that has all the elements of a detective fiction, apart from the final (dis)closure; an alternately compelling and frustrating narrative in which everything points to a greater truth outside of itself—only that truth is, precisely, the fiction. **KB**

"Above her head was the only stable place in the cosmos . . . and she guessed it was the Pendulum's business, not hers."

⊙ The novel was translated into English by William Weaver and published the following year in the U.S. and the U.K.

Gimmick!

Joost Zwagerman

Lifespan | *b.* 1963 (Netherlands)
First Published | 1989
First Published in | De Arbeiderspers (Amsterdam)
Given Name | Johannes Jacobus Zwagerman

"When I'm dead, you can do what you want with my books; remove them from the shops, burn them— gone is gone."

Joost Zwagerman

⊙ Joost Zwagerman, photographed by Maartje Geels in 2005, is an essayist and poet as well as the author of a handful of novels.

After a highly acclaimed prose debut at age twenty-three, *Gimmick!* three years later became Joost Zwagerman's conclusive breakthrough. In this novel, set in Amsterdam in 1989, the author lets main character Walter "Raam" van Raamsdonk talk us through seven months of contemporary and decadent consumer society lifestyle. Raam and his friends, Groen and Eckhart, are elite young Dutch artists. Spending their evenings at the nightclub De Gimmick, Groen and Eckhart produce their works to earn money for sex, drugs, and rock'n'roll—since everything has been done before, why not? Raam, on the other hand, has been unable to make art ever since he was left by his girlfriend. Trying to stay in the game in a spoiled world, Raam crumbles.

With snide commentary, Zwagerman takes on the yuppie culture, trying to discover a raw, real life beneath it. Combining spontaneity with literary refinement and his praised sense of nuance, Zwagerman allows his characters to speak for themselves. Raam's world of cocaine, money, a broken heart, and failed affairs is bound up with questions of personal authenticity in a postmodern world, the fear of losing oneself in love for someone or something else, and the unavoidable loss of innocence. Is the fabulously fabricated inferior to true experience; is there a difference at all? Who are you, and what do you want? At the end of the novel, Raam is resting in bed with a woman, bleeding from his nose: "I want a taxi," he says. **MvdV**

Obabakoak

Bernardo Atxaga

Lifespan | *b.* 1951 (Spain)
First Published | 1989, by Erein (San Sebastián)
Original Language | Basque
Given Name | Joseba Irazu Garmendia

Bernardo Atxaga's novel, its title translated loosely by the author as "Stories from Obaba," was awarded the National Prize for Literature in Spain one year after it was first published in the Basque language, Euskera. True to its name, the work comprises a series of short stories, all of which spring from the memories and imaginations of the inhabitants of Obaba, a mythical setting in the Basque Country. These exquisitely compassionate, funny, and often moving tales guide the reader on a journey through an imaginative landscape of both the world and the human mind, from Bavaria to Baghdad, encountering along the way an indigenous tribe of the Upper Amazon, mountain climbers in Switzerland, and a fanatical murderer in China, together with the childhood memories of the narrators and protagonists themselves.

Obabakoak's appeal lies not only in its narrative diversity but also in its juxtaposition of personal and universal themes: the individual plight of the author and the history of literature; the Basque Country, with its minority language, and the rest of the world, with its abundance of ancient and widespread languages. At a time when Basque nationalism and separatism are at the heart of a long-standing controversy, Atxaga's take on his homeland is refreshingly depoliticized, focusing instead upon the individual's relationship with the land and the community, while retaining the universality invoked by the protagonists' flights of imagination. **LBi**

Inland

Gerald Murnane

Lifespan | *b.* 1939 (Australia)
First Published | 1989
First Published by | Heinemann (Melbourne)
Patrick White Award | 1999

Inland belongs to the genre of metafiction, the literary method prematurely ignited by Laurence Sterne in the 1700s and adopted by writers such as John Barth, Robert Coover, and John Fowles in the late twentieth century. Essentially a mode of writing concerned with the process of its own making, metafiction dares to refer to both its author and reader, to the unavoidable instability of its "truth," and to its reliance on extraneous writings that inform its own existence.

Instead of having a linear plotline with a tangible narrator, the novel acts as a window on to several shifting worlds, occasionally and vaguely locatable in America, Australia, and Hungary. Borrowing various personas, from reclusive Magyar author to Australian adolescent, the narrator explores human themes such as life, death, sexual impulse, nature and man's imprint upon it, and the importance of recording it all with the written word.

Highly autobiographical in places, *Inland* exposes the inner workings of the author's artistry, demonstrating how a writer's imagination and memory merge to give a novel its form. In keeping with Gerald Murnane's actual life story, a life spent almost constantly "inland" in Australia, this novel illustrates the possibility of crossing borders and seas via the act of writing. In its detail, as well as its omissions, *Inland* offers an alternative philosophy, underlining most of all the literary power to create parallel lives through a harnessed imagination. **LK**

A Prayer for Owen Meany

John Irving

Lifespan | *b.* 1942 (U.S.)
First Published | 1989
First Published by | W. Morrow (New York)
Full Name | John Winslow Irving

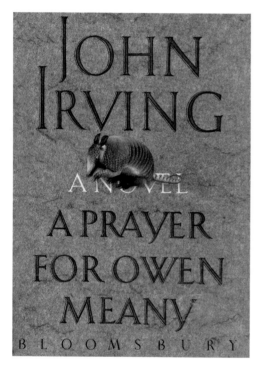

"I am doomed to remember a boy with a wrecked voice . . ."

⊙ Just like the narrator in the novel, John Irving's mother always refused to reveal the identity of his father.

John Irving's novels characteristically revolve around intricate plots and memorable comic characters, leaving his work balanced somewhere between literary and popular fiction. *A Prayer for Owen Meany* is widely considered to be his finest work.

A rich and deeply comic account of faith, doubt, and memories, the novel also reflects on American culture, and is probably Irving's most autobiographical. In Toronto in 1987, a troubled and past-obsessed John Wheelwright narrates the story of his early life, remembering the time he spent during the 1960s and 1970s with his friend, Owen Meany. He remembers Owen as a weird, luminous-skinned dwarf, whose underdeveloped vocal chords shaped the sound of his bizarre, nasal voice (which is represented in the text in capital letters) and led him to bear the brunt of many cruel pranks. He also remembers Owen as the person who accidentally killed his mother.

John writes on the first page that Owen Meany is the reason he is a Christian; the rest of the book serves to narrate the story of how and why this happened, of how John discovers his own spiritual faith. The main theme of the book is the relationship between faith and doubt in a world—or at least in the world according to John—in which there is no obvious evidence for the existence of God. The most important symbol is Owen himself, who embodies the relationship between the natural and the supernatural that is at the heart of the novel. For all his strangeness, Owen represents the spiritual condition of humankind; the difference between Owen and most other people is that he knows he is the instrument of God. Owen's fatalistic faith centers on his prophetic knowledge of his own heroic death, for which he prepares all his life. **EF**

Like Water for Chocolate

Laura Esquivel

Each of the twelve chapters of Laura Esquivel's delightful love story, set in Mexico, bears the name of a month and opens with a recipe. This fascinating combination of ingredients results in a book as earthy and full of flavor as the cuisine it describes. Thus the recipes become as integral a part of *Like Water for Chocolate* as food is to our daily lives. It is the story of Tita, the youngest daughter of the all-female De La Garza family, who is forbidden to marry by the matriarch Mama Elena because of a Mexican tradition that dictates that the youngest daughter must care for her mother until her death.

Inevitably, Tita falls in love with Pedro, who then decides to marry Tita's ugly older sister, Rosaura, in order to at least remain physically close to his true love. The marriage marks the start of a twenty-two-year-long conflict, filled with passion, deceit, anger, and love, during which the two lovers are forced to circle one another, their passion remaining unconsummated. In her position as head cook on the family ranch, Tita produces food that is imbued with her own feelings of love and longing—food that affects both everyone who eats it and ultimately the outcome of the story.

The culinary backdrop to the lovers' tale features mouthwatering recipes for Wedding Cake, Quail in Rose Petal Sauce, and Chilies in Walnut Sauce, which, as well as whetting the appetite, provide a metaphorical commentary on the characters. The delicate blending of these recipes with the tale of romance produces an extraordinary novel with an unusual and distinct flavor, at once vibrant and sensual, funny and passionate, bittersweet and delicious. Like Tita's Chocolate and Three King's Day Bread, this original and compelling novel is impossible to resist. **LE**

Lifespan | *b.* 1950 (Mexico)
First Published | 1989
First Published by | Editorial Planeta Mexicana
Original Title | *Como agua para chocolate*

"From that day on, Tita's domain was the kitchen . . ."

⊙ Pictured here in 2001 in her home in New York, Laura Esquivel's first novel was made into a movie, which was released in 1993.

The History of the Siege of Lisbon

José Saramago

Lifespan | *b.* 1922 (Portugal)
First Published | 1989, by Editorial Caminho (Lisbon)
Original Title | *História do Cerco de Lisboa*
Nobel Prize for Literature | 1998

As in all his extraordinary novels, here José Saramago writes with the absolute minimum of punctuation. The result, something akin to the serial music of Schoenberg, is a reinvention of the historical novel as we know it, which makes most efforts in this direction look clumsy and heavy-handed. By a conjurer's sleight of hand, Saramago transports his reader straight to the heart of another world.

Raimundo Silva, proofreader for a Lisbon publisher, decides on a whim to put a negative into a history text, effectively recasting Portugal's past: during the siege of Lisbon in the twelfth century, the Crusaders did *not* come to the help of the king of Portugal against the Saracens. Rather than causing Silva to lose his job, his act of insubordination grabs the attention of his new superior, Dr. Maria Sara, who is fifteen years his junior. She persuades him to actually write this new history, and as he begins to create his revisionist tale, the two fall in love. Characteristically, Saramago lets us into their love affair via glimpsed moments of awkwardness, humor, and tenderness.

In the whole of twentieth-century writing, there can be no purer example, and certainly no funnier one, of what novelist Christine Brooke-Rose has referred to as "palimpsest history"—that is, the novel that offers us an overwriting of history and, in the process, the reinvention of our world. **PT**

The Trick is to Keep Breathing

Janice Galloway

Lifespan | *b.* 1956 (Scotland)
First Published | 1989
First Published by | Polygon (Edinburgh)
MIND/Allen Lane Book of the Year | 1990

A frank account of female psychological crisis, *The Trick is to Keep Breathing* is by turns soul-destroying and bleakly comic. When the lover of the ironically named Joy Stones dies in an accident, she senses his spirit in an omnipresent aromatic cloud, until she finds the overturned, leaking aftershave bottle under the bed. This scene of self-delusion provides a quintessential model of a stereotypical femininity that, in a desperate quest for love and intimacy, is complicit in its own oppression. It is not only Michael who dies, but Joy herself experiences a kind of living death along with him when she becomes socially invisible as the mistress of a still-married man, excluded from the rituals of mourning. In her subsequent anguish, Joy becomes anorexic and literally almost disappears. Her body feels remote and fragmented in an experience of psychic fracture only intensified by her time in a psychiatric unit.

Embodying Joy's breakdown, the novel fragments, dissolves, and reconstitutes itself in myriad of different forms: extracts from magazines, recipes, horoscopes, letters, and self-help books—all the accessories of insecure femininity. In navigating this haphazard textual landscape, we appreciate the destructiveness of Joy's predicament and the absurdly precarious nature of woman's position in the world. Eventually Joy regains a coherent sense of self when she realizes that life, like swimming, is a trick to be learned. **CJ**

The Great Indian Novel

Shashi Tharoor

Lifespan | b. 1956 (England)
First Published | 1989
First Published in | Arcade Publishing (New York)
Commonwealth Writers' Prize | 1991

Self-consciously announcing its aspiration to epic status from its very title, *The Great Indian Novel* sets itself the daunting task of, as one of the characters puts it, telling "the story of an entire nation." For this task Shashi Tharoor enlists the aid of the epic Indian stories of the *Mahabharata*, basing his novel around the interaction of ancient myth with modern Indian political and historical realities. The result is a dazzling, sensitive, and often riotously funny ride through a semi-imaginary twentieth-century India, an alternative created in loving parody of its original.

Told as a memoir by Ved Vayas to his scribe, Ganapathi, the novel follows the complex political machinations of a family seemingly formed by combining the most famous among India's political leaders and mythological creations, ranging from Nehru to Indira Ghandi to Krishna within the space of a few pages. Clever and self-aware, the novel also plays with the cultural heritage of the Indian novel in English; characters from *A Passage to India* and Kipling's renamed "The Bungle Book" wander in and out. Despite its ironic humor and slippery political allegiances, the novel treats its subject with both reverence and a critical eye, emphasizing, in the grand sweep of its satire, both the importance of this story of national birth and the sense that, as Tharoor puts it, "in our country the mundane is as important as the mystical." **AB**

The Melancholy of Resistance

László Krasznahorkai

Lifespan | b. 1954 (Hungary)
First Published | 1989
First Published by | Magveto Kiadó (Budapest)
Original Title | Az ellenállás menakóliája

The Melancholy of Resistance is the first work by the reclusive Hungarian novelist László Krasznahorkai to be translated into English. A small, anonymous, and impoverished Hungarian town is utterly transformed when a traveling circus arrives on a winter's night carrying the desiccated corpse of an enormous whale. After the exhibit is parked in the central square, a wave of suspicious rumors and paranoia sweeps the town, eventually descending into rioting and violence. But the whale is only a Trojan horse. Behind the scenes, a horribly deformed dwarf known as the Prince has ordered the town to be destroyed, and he expertly manipulates the townspeople into a state of fear and nihilism. Struggling against this tide of senseless aggression are Valuska, a naïve young man treated as a kind of village idiot by the locals, and his mentor, Mr. Eszter, a strange figure who is obsessed by the idea of retuning a piano to its "original" harmonies using mathematically pure intervals.

This is a deeply strange, unsettling, intensely detailed, and richly atmospheric work. It is a novel of long shadows, bitter cold, and sinister whispers—all rendered in treaclelike prose. Perhaps the novel can be read as an allegory for the upheavals of eastern Europe; perhaps it is a meditation on folk culture and the formation of social consciousness; perhaps it is an attempt to reclaim the gothic from the clutches of kitsch; perhaps it is all this and more. **SamT**

The Remains of the Day

Kazuo Ishiguro

Lifespan | *b.* 1954 (Japan)
First Published | 1989
First Published by | Faber & Faber (London)
Booker Prize | 1989

ff
KAZUO ISHIGURO
The Remains of the Day

"What a terrible mistake . . ."

⊙ Time is running out for both Stevens and the British Empire on the jacket of the first edition, shown here.

Stevens is the butler of thirty-four years at Darlington Hall, right in the dying heart of the British class system. He is precise, rigid, and will broach no effusion. His father, also a butler, taught him that to be great, dignity is key. He staves off any inchoate passions and thwarts any slackening of the cold precision with which he runs the house. Four years after Darlington's death, Stevens travels to persuade the former housekeeper, Miss Kenton, to return to work for a new master, a wealthy American named Farraday. Farraday is as brash and casual as Stevens is staid and frigid. Stevens is not comfortable with "banter." Miss Kenton had been as conscientious as Stevens, but her warmth ran counter to his severity. Their squabbles were petty and endearing, surges sublimating affection. When she reveals her life may have turned out better had she married Stevens, he is deeply shaken, though reticent. This lost possibility goes not only unacted upon but undiscussed.

Stevens's journey to visit Miss Kenton gives him an opportunity to reminisce about his life and work. He longs for times of pomp and decency and grows melancholic about a world that is gone, a world in which he knew his place. He has become an anachronism, an outdated tradition. Finally he confronts the truth that Lord Darlington, though a perfect gentleman, was a Nazi supporter. Stevens had always been loyal to the point of blindness, but his long overdue lucidity leaves him bereft. He recognizes that his life has been one of misplaced trust and unplaced affection. He finally locates dignity—too late—where he previously ignored it, in Miss Kenton's honesty. This is a breathtaking feat of voice, by turns hilarious and poignant. Ishiguro casts a merciless eye on British society, but never with cruelty, always with affection. **GT**

London Fields

Martin Amis

Martin Amis's *London Fields* is a darkly ironic inversion of the whodunit plot in which the central protagonist, Nicola Six, conspires with the narrator to create two potential "murderees." The sour and witty novel uses this sense of suspense to explore the possibility of the end of time.

Nicola Six is the fulcrum for this cataclysmic possibility. She uses the weaknesses of her failed suitors—the vicious, criminally minded working-class Keith and the gentle, guileless upper-class Guy—to associate herself with a crudely feminized version of nuclear holocaust. She sends Guy on a fruitless search for her orphaned friends "Enola Gay and Little Boy" and taunts a confused Keith with her bikini-clad body while lecturing him about the etymology of the word "bikini." The narrative takes place in the final weeks of the twentieth century when ominous clouds threaten an environmental catastrophe, and "Faith," the American President's wife, fights for her life. These literal evocations of the end of the world are set within an ambivalent fear of the death of culture itself. The deeply self-conscious form of the novel itself only reinforces this fear. Keith's slavish dependence upon an impoverishing mass culture is contrasted against mocking references to high literary culture, including a lengthy parody of a passage from D. H. Lawrence's *The Rainbow*. Samson Young, the narrator, is slowly dying throughout the novel and by its end he is dead. The novel's closing anxious reference to Samson's more successful doppelgänger (Mark Asprey or "M.A.") renders the novel's author uncertain. Indeed this uncertainty seems generally characteristic of the novel, as it delves unflinchingly into the darker side of urban life without ever quite reconciling itself to anything as obvious as critique. **NM**

Lifespan | *b.* 1949 (England)
First Published | 1989
First Published by | Jonathan Cape (London)
First U.S. Edition | 1990, by Harmony (New York)

"Keith Talent was a bad guy."

This novel is the second in a loose trilogy that begins in 1984 with *Money* and ends in 1995 with *The Information*.

Moon Palace

Paul Auster

Lifespan | *b.* 1947 (U.S.)
First Published | 1989
First Published by | Viking Press (New York)
Full Name | Paul Benjamin Auster

Moon Palace is a meditation on the obstacles that can frustrate and derail fatherhood: the novel is littered with men ignorant of, overeager for, or ambivalent toward their prospective or actual paternity. The protagonist, Marco Stanley Fogg, has never known his father and was raised by his mother until her death when he was eleven years old. He went on to live with his Uncle Victor in a congenial but emotionally casual household. On Victor's death, Fogg inherits his massive book collection, which he sells piece by piece to fend off eviction, homelessness, and ruin. Kitty Wu, the child of an elderly, polygamist father, rescues Fogg, and they fall in love. He finds work recording the life story of Thomas Effing, a bizarre, reclusive painter, but this period of stability is short-lived. Fogg forms a crotchety bond with Effing, who becomes an adopted spiritual mentor, and Fogg later discovers that Effing is, in fact, his paternal grandfather. Through Effing's will, Fogg is finally reunited with his biological father, with whom he shares an intense but brief connection. Kitty's pregnancy takes on symbolic dimensions for Fogg, who sees an opportunity to redeem his own disheartening experiences, but their love cannot survive the mutual sense of betrayal generated by his controlling behavior. Ultimately Fogg is left alone, yet perhaps with a newfound clarity. **AF**

◐ Paul Auster has lived in Brooklyn, New York, since 1980, preferring this district to Manhattan. Here he is at home with his typewriter.

Sexing the Cherry

Jeanette Winterson

Lifespan | *b.* 1959 (England)
First Published | 1989
First Published by | Jonathan Cape (London)
First U.S. Edition | Atlantic (New York)

Set in seventeenth-century London, *Sexing the Cherry* brings to life a tumultuous time of imperial exploration, revolution, and the discovery of a perversely shaped tropical fruit. The Dog Woman, a living mountain of flesh, camps with an assortment of raucously disturbing neighbors, scores of home-bred dogs, and her adopted son Jordan, the child she found in the Thames whom she raises as her own. She is of superhuman scale: by virtue of her extreme size and deeply held ethical convictions, the Dog Woman is a sovereign avenging force in the lawless bustle of her world, achieving by might anything she cannot achieve by argument or persuasion. She comes to lament having named young Jordan after a body of moving water when he falls in love with discovery on seeing the explorer Tradescant's exhibition of bananas. Jordan eventually sets off on an expedition that is as much metaphysical as it is geographical. The final section of the novel, identified as taking place "some years later," reincarnates Jordan and the Dog Woman as a Royal Navy sailor and an environmental scientist-turned-activist, who recapture their primal bond.

Winterson's trademark style is here at its most glittering. With stories of twelve dancing princesses, or "word cleaners," dispatched to cleanse cities' atmospheres of their logomaniacal citizens' pollution, the narrative complicates notions of reality and fantasy until they dissolve. Myth, fable, fairy tale, and history are cannibalized until a new genre is achieved. **AF**

Like Life

Lorrie Moore

Lifespan | *b.* 1957 (U.S.)
First Published | 1990
First Published by | Alfred A. Knopf (New York)
Given Name | Marie Lorena Moore

"'Is this a TV show?'"

◉ Moore's stories are set in the Midwest, a part of the United States where in the author's words, "there were gyms but no irony."

Lorrie Moore's *Like Life* met with excellent reviews on its publication, and it is no secret that Moore crafts her stories like a gem cutter wields a chisel. In this collection of eight short stories, most of them take place in the Midwest, a noticeably innocent swath of America less prone to self-examination than, say, to snowmobiling and deer hunting. "There were gyms but no irony . . . people took things literally, without drugs."

These are stories about people who watch, baffled, as life seems to go easily for others. "Sometimes she thought she was just trying to have fun in life, and other times she realized she must be terribly confused." Mary is dating two men. It all seems daring and utterly modern. And, of course, that's the impression she gives in postcards to envious friends. But she is slowly unraveling, wearing only white and sitting in public parks reading "bible poetry." Harry is a playwright who, through naïve enthusiasm and hunger for success, gives his life story, his life's work, to a predatory television producer over drinks. Zoe is a teacher at a small university in rural Illinois, a land so blond that just because she has dark hair, she is presumed to be from Spain. She tries to make a home, like others do, and buys an oriental rug. The salesgirl tells her the pictograms mean "Peace" and "Eternal Life." But how can she be sure? How can she ever know that they don't in fact say, for instance, "Bruce Springsteen"? Plagued with uncertainty, she has no choice but to return the rug.

These are characters who are fragile, hilarious, and heartbreaking in their familiarity. The title of Moore's collection of stories—*Like Life*—could hardly be more apt. We laugh until it catches in our throats, out of recognition, but never mockery. **GT**

The Buddha of Suburbia

Hanif Kureishi

The Buddha of Suburbia's comedy often takes political correctness as its target as it follows its seventeen-year-old narrator, Karim Amir, growing up in London's suburbs in the 1970s. His father Haroon, a civil servant, is encouraged to pursue his less conventional interests by his mistress Eva, and he assumes the status of a New Age guru, a "Buddha" of suburbia. The affair has a devastating effect upon Haroon's wife, Karim's mother, Margaret, who becomes marginalized and depressed. The support Margaret receives from her sister proves invaluable, and the attention from her brother-in- law quite unhelpful, but their attitudes throw into relief their patronizing views. Throughout the disintegration of his parents' marriage, Karim is bolstered by the support of his friends. Jamilla, a strong-willed and confident young woman, challenges many of the traditions of her Asian upbringing and her experimental sexual relationship with Karim continues after her engagement to another man. Eva's son, Charlie, is also a significant figure. Their sexual relationship opens Karim's eyes to the uninhibited zeitgeist but does not ultimately lead beyond friendship.

The novel engages with many of the nebulous aspects of identity that are negotiated during the transition into adulthood. Karim experiments with drugs, explores his bisexuality and considers the interrelationship of the two histories that have contributed to his sense of Englishness. To a large extent, the book traces Karim's attempts to escape conservative social, political, and sexual attitudes by following his movement away from the suburbs to the city. In this sense, it is a novel about Karim's coming of age, and of his search for an identity separate from that of his family. The novel was adapted into a successful BBC drama. **JW**

Lifespan | b. 1954 (England)
First Published | 1990
First Published by | Faber & Faber (London)
Whitbread First Novel Award | 1990

"Englishman I am . . ."

◉ Hanif Kureishi has often courted controversy, spurning both traditional moral stances and the pieties of political correctness.

The Shadow Lines

Amitav Ghosh

Lifespan | *b.* 1956 (India)
First Published | 1990
First Published by | Ravi Dayal (New Delhi)
Sahitya Akademi Award | 1989

Winner of the Sahitya Akademi Award, India's most prestigious literary prize, *The Shadow Lines* is a chronicle of three generations that stretches from Calcutta to Cairo, London to Dhaka. The unnamed narrator jumps back and forth through time and space to explore the intertwined lives of his Bengali family and the British Price family, who have known each other since the time of the Raj. While the mystery at the center of the novel revolves around the fate of the narrator's second cousin (and mentor) Tridib in the city of Dhaka in 1964 (the date of Bangladesh's Partition), the details and effect of his tragedy span over twenty years and color the lives of all of the other characters of the novel. Intricately weaving together the memories and stories of various characters, *The Shadow Lines* acts as a microcosm of a nation rent by politics, exposing the borders (the shadow lines), both physical and metaphorical, that can divide individuals.

Born in Calcutta in 1956, Amitav Ghosh is one of the most highly respected Indian authors writing in English today. He has been awarded the Arthur C. Clarke Award, the Pushcart Prize, and France's Prix Medici Etranger, among other accolades. Although his previous books have also centered on exile, diaspora, and cultural displacement, *The Shadow Lines* offers an elaborate and highly developed exploration of these themes, rendered in a powerful, yet subtle, prose. Ghosh is also the author of numerous novels, essays, and travelogues. **BJ**

> *"But . . . it seems something of a mystery to me now, why they put up with him: he was never one of them . . ."*

Although his novels are mostly set in his native India, Ghosh lives in New York; this photo was taken at Columbia University in 1996.

The Midnight Examiner

William Kotzwinkle

Lifespan | *b.* 1938 (U.S.)
First Published | 1990
First Published by | Houghton Mifflin (Boston)
First UK Edition | 1990, Black Swan (London)

Howard Halliday is an editor at Chameleon Publications, publisher of *Bottoms*, *Knockers*, *Brides Tell All*, and *The Midnight Examiner*. Fueled by peppermint caffeine tablets and his love for Amber Adams, the beauty editor, he leads his staff on a manic ride through the sleaziest tidepool of publishing.

Howard longs for a proper job. As do his eccentric staff. There is Fernando, the layout artist prone to catatonic seizures and obsessed with drawing his masterpiece, "Big Womans," on Howard's kitchen wall. Nathan Feingold shoots pigeons—and staff—with hot-sauce-tipped darts from his blowgun. Forrest Crumpacker is hired against his will to head the new religious magazine and forcibly ordained as a mail-order bishop. Hattie Flyer is disfigured by the beauty products their papers sell. Hip O'Hopp, alcohol-sodden, was once a reporter on real newspapers; now he wants to find some Chinese woman to marry so he won't wind up alone on the sidewalk with a bottle. They spend their days turning everything into a lurid headline ("UFO Found in Girl's Uterus"; "I Was A Hooker Until I Met Jesus"). They spend their nights drinking. When erstwhile model Mitzi Mouse "accidentally" shoots a crime lord while filming a porno movie, the forces of Chameleon come to her rescue. Armed with boomerangs, Nathan's blowgun, and a fishing pole—with invaluable assistance from Madame Veronique's hoodoo magic—they go to battle. This is an affectionate farce, impossible to put down. **GT**

The Things They Carried

Tim O'Brien

Lifespan | *b.* 1946 (U.S.)
First Published | 1990
First Published by | Houghton Mifflin (Boston)
First UK Edition | Collins (London)

Though this Vietnam War text is purportedly a work of fiction, Tim O'Brien, and his first-person narrator "Tim O'Brien," never stop playing with readers' assumptions about the possibility of achieving truth through careful description. O'Brien earlier wrote a Vietnam memoir (*If I Die in a Combat Zone*, 1973), but here he self-consciously probes the conventions that we typically rely on to distinguish fiction from memoir, non-fiction from storytelling, and fact from interpretation. The copyright page states that the book's ". . . incidents, names, and characters are imaginary," but it faces O'Brien's (or is it "O'Brien'"s?) "loving" dedication to "the men of Alpha Company," a striking juxtaposition once we realize these "men" are the book's primary characters. This tension permeates the text as "Tim O'Brien" wrestles with how best to convey his experience of Vietnam: must a war story literally be true in order to be a "true war story"? If one mode of narrative cannot satisfactorily evoke an event, should another be called upon?

O'Brien's narrative goes from profound sorrow to self-mockery to dark humor and back again. This sense of narrative uncertainty creates a feeling of anxiety and mistrust that O'Brien indicates was the existential condition of American soldiers. O'Brien uses various mismatches between experience and description against his readers, who may find themselves longing for the deceptive luxury and easy comfort of uncritical narrative the way "O'Brien" and his fellow soldiers long for home. **AF**

Stone Junction

Jim Dodge

Lifespan | *b.* 1945 (U.S.)
First Published | 1990
First Published by | Atlantic Monthly Press (N. Y.)
Full Title | *Stone Junction: An Alchemical Potboiler*

Stone Junction chronicles the life and times of one Daniel Pearce, born in 1966 to Analee, a sixteen-year-old runaway. Jim Dodge's novel is a vibrant, antiauthoritarian romp that combines page-turning urgency with a serious examination of the margins of American society.

From a remote shack in the wilderness, Daniel and Analee fall in with an organization known as AMO (an Alliance of Magicians and Outlaws). As Daniel grows up, he is placed into the custody of a series of wonderfully eccentric teachers who provide an unorthodox education. He is taught meditation, outdoor survival, sex, drugs, safe-cracking, impersonation, and poker.

However, a second plotline interrupts Daniel's learning curve in the form of a whodunit. His mother is suspiciously killed on a mission for AMO when he is aged just fourteen. The two narratives come together when Daniel learns the art of invisibility from the Great Volta (who is one of the prime suspects in Analee's death).

At the novel's climax, Daniel is sent to steal a mysterious, six-pound diamond from a maximum security compound. But, as with all the best mysteries, things are not as they seem. In Dodge's own words, *Stone Junction* is an "alchemical potboiler"—a defiant celebration of magic and the outlaw tradition in an age where living and communicating in the margins becomes increasingly difficult. **SamT**

> *"Sister, I've devoted half my life to survival because I've found life mean . . ."*

◉ Stone Junction is the third of Jim Dodge's three novels; he has also written a collection of poetry and short prose.

◗ Dodge in a suitably zany pose in 1984—his novel *Stone Junction* was described by author Thomas Pynchon as "a nonstop party."

Amongst Women

John McGahern

Lifespan | *b.* 1934 (Ireland)
First Published | 1990
First Published by | Faber & Faber (London)
Irish Times Literary Award | 1991

John McGahern's lyrical, resonant, and subtle meditations on rural Irish life have a long and loving gestation, appearing every ten or twelve years. *Amongst Women* tells the story of power relations within a rural Irish family, set within the history and the thwarted promise of the independent Irish state.

Michael Moran, an old IRA man who fought in the Anglo-Irish War, feels utterly alienated and detached from the independent Ireland that he helped to create. Disdaining a part in the new political or social order, he sits in patriarchal dominance at the center of his big farmhouse, Great Meadow. Luke, the oldest son, flees to England, away from Moran's overbearing authority. His other children, three daughters and another son, regularly return to Great Meadow. Moran is deeply loved by his daughters and his second wife, Rose, but his mood swings and desperately fragile pride have long impeded them and deflated their aspirations. He holds down his daughters in order to protect the suffocating unity of the family. The struggle between wife, daughters, and patriarch is compellingly recreated, as Moran's grip on power weakens alongside his grip on life. For all his authoritarianism and implacable surliness, Moran is a tormented, complex, vulnerable man in existential crisis. The story is laced with poetic language and generously humane depictions of frailty. It is at once an expression of a postcolonial condition, generational change, and shifting gender relations in rural Catholic Ireland. **RM**

Get Shorty

Elmore Leonard

Lifespan | *b.* 1925 (U.S.)
First Published | 1990
First Published by | Delacorte Press (New York)
Movie Adaptation | 1995

Hollywood has been a significant influence on Leonard's writing, not simply because he began his career as a writer of westerns and many of his subsequent novels have been turned into mostly unsuccessful motion pictures. Nor can this influence be measured in terms of the cinematic references that pepper his novels; long before Tarantino, Leonard's characters discussed movies with passion and humor. Movies pervade Leonard's novels insofar as his characters see themselves as performing roles—killer, lover, robber, cop—and their relationship to these roles has been shaped by their interaction with the movies.

When Chili Palmer, a debt collector and one in a long line of "no-bullshit" Leonard heroes, follows a dry cleaner who has "scammed" an airline and absconded to Hollywood, he agrees to chase up another bad debt, this time owed by a Hollywood producer. Quickly realizing that everyone is playing a role, Chili reinvents himself as a producer, pitching a version of what has occurred so far in the novel. Above all, the resulting scam, which involves drug dealers, limousine drivers, and movie players, is handled with a comic but assured touch. In an irony worthy of Leonard himself, the movie version of *Get Shorty*, a story about the stupidity and vacuity of Hollywood filmmakers, became the best and most successful of all Leonard adaptations. **AP**

◉ John Travolta plays phony producer Chili Palmer in Barry Sonnenfeld's acclaimed movie version of Leonard's scam novel.

The Daughter

Pavlos Matesis

Lifespan | *b.* undisclosed
First Published | 1990
First Published by | Kastaniotis Editions (Athens)
Original Title | *I mitera tou skilou*

Modern Greek history is not very well known: the Second World War, the famine then the political instability, the Civil War. *The Daughter* tells a story of two women during these times. The narrator, Rarau, a delusional actress suffering frequent seizures, tells the story of her family during the wartime German occupation of Greece, when her mother sleeps with an Italian officer to save her children from famine. Afterward, with the "so-called Liberation," such women ("the collaborators") are publicly punished and humiliated; her mother never speaks again. Rarau takes her to Athens, where initially they become beggars. Rarau does not mind the begging; wanting to be an actress, it helps her to get used to the stage. Later she becomes successful as an extra in the many theatrical productions staged around Greece. In the end, she is happy, she claims.

The Daughter is a unique book inasmuch as it dares to deal with Greece in a blasphemous and unpatriotic way. God is disowned several times in the book: "Where was He when my children were dying from hunger?"; and so is Greece, "the so-called Nation." Rarau is crazy, an unreliable narrator, but there is a Greek proverb that fits well: one learns the truth only from children and madmen. She tells us the story of her country with a disarming naivety, introducing an almost surreal mosaic of characters and incidents in the process. Matesis does not feel the need to glorify his country or his main character: loving them as he does is sincerity enough. **CSe**

Vertigo

W. G. Sebald

Lifespan | *b.* 1944 (Germany), *d.* 2001 (England)
First Published | 1990
First Published by | Eichborn (Frankfurt)
Original Title | *Schwindel, Gefühle*

This was the first novel published by the now highly acclaimed author W. G. Sebald. *Vertigo* defies generic conventions, combining elements of fiction, reportage, travel writing, autobiography, and the photographic essay to create a distinctive literary form that is without precedent. Divided into four parts, the novel follows the narrator's travels through Italy and southern Germany. We accompany the narrator on a spiritual pilgrimage whose purpose is to raise the dead so that the living might interrogate them on the meaning of life.

Although highly discursive and meandering, several key themes emerge over the course of the narrator's descriptions of the lives, loves, and losses of Marie Henri Beyle (Stendhal), Giacomo Casanova, and Franz Kafka, among many others. Chief among these themes is the chimerical and unreliable nature of memory, its tendency to invent and even obscure the past as much as it recalls it. The mastery of *Vertigo* is in its skillful interbraiding of multiple narrative strands, its breathtaking revelations of the mysterious coincidences and points of crossover that bind together disparate lives, times, and places. While there is a decidedly sinister ambience evoked by the hallucinatory journeys of the narrator, there are also moments of unmistakable playfulness and humor, an underappreciated facet of Sebald's prose. *Vertigo* is further enhanced by the numerous photographs of paintings, diagrams, drawings, and documents that are interspersed throughout. **CG-G**

American Psycho

Bret Easton Ellis

Lifespan | *b.* 1964 (U.S.)
First Published | 1991
First Published by | Vintage (New York)
First UK Edition | Picador (London)

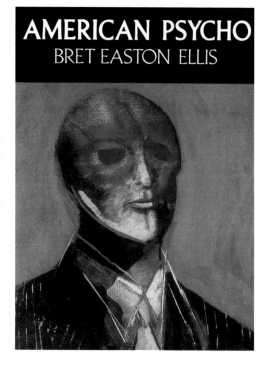

American Psycho is, above all, an ugly book. It is an extraordinarily graphic description of obscene violence, which is spliced with reviews of music by Phil Collins and Whitney Houston, and with endless, repetitive descriptions of 1980s main street fashion. The novel's protagonist, Patrick Bateman, is a psychopath who also works on Wall Street. He conducts business meetings, goes to upmarket restaurants, and commits rape and murder. The novel registers no difference between these activities. Depravity, it suggests, is so finely woven into the fabric of contemporary life that it is no longer possible to see it or depict it, to know when capitalism stops and brutalization begins.

There is no attempt to take a moral stance on Bateman, or the culture to which he belongs. But the extremity of the violence, coupled with the uninflected way in which it is described, produces a strange, ethereal dimension to the writing, which is as close as the novel can come to an ethics, or to an aesthetic. As Bateman struggles to understand why he has been summoned to this particular damnation, he is unable to formulate to himself his own misery, or his own confusion. As a result, the novel produces a longing for ethical certainty, for some kind of clear perspective on a culture that has become unreadable, and unthinkable. This is a longing that speaks of a kind of innocence, even in the midst of depravity, and for this reason alone, *American Psycho* must continue to be read. **PB**

> *"'Abandon all hope ye who enter here' is scrawled in blood red lettering on the side of the Chemical Bank near the corner of Eleventh and First . . ."*

⊙ The inhumane face attached to the Wall Street suit on the jacket of the novel epitomizes the character of the novel's serial killer.

The Laws

Connie Palmen

Lifespan | *b.* 1955 (Netherlands)
First Published | 1991
First Published by | Prometheus (Amsterdam)
Original Title | *De wetten*

*"With regret and remorse,
I see his face cloud over,
his excitement shrink . . ."*

◉ Palmen's first novel, *The Laws*, made her a best-selling author
in her own country and earned her an international reputation.

Marie Deniet, a Catholic country girl who has lost her faith and replaced it with a worship of language and ideas, makes a narrative inventory of her relationships with the seven important men in her life. Each of them provides her with a story that contributes to her self-definition; also, they are themselves defined by their stories as astrologer, epileptic, philosopher, priest, physicist, artist, and psychiatrist. Bolstered by her confidence in the power of words, Marie sets about ordering existence and dispelling the chaos of meaninglessness that threatens a world that has lost its heaven. Her progress through a universe that seems indebted to human wit and reasoning is arrested and rendered illusory by the complications lurking behind a man's love, the same kind of event with which the cycle of meaning-engendering loves began in her adolescence. Through the disintegration of her dream of love with the sculptor Lucas Asbeek, Marie learns that tales do not accord with reality, that language is not the omnipotent deity that replaced her lost God, and that life outside predetermined story lines has strength and independence.

At a time when artifice seems to provide the web onto which we each weave our own small realities, questioning the possibilities of art and language is synonymous with questioning the meaning of life itself, and forging a new kind of reality equals a work of art. Marie's failure to completely succumb to the allurement of validation through language, and her final painful withdrawal from the laws made by the men who repeatedly created her story, coincides with her realization that language gives meaning only when it is used as a meeting ground with others, since "that which is individual and alone has no meaning." **MWd**

Faceless Killers

Henning Mankell

A man and his wife are brutally murdered. There is no trace of a perpetrator, no discernible motive, and no witnesses. The few clues to be found all lead nowhere, but something tells police detective Kurt Wallander to keep on looking . . .

In this first novel featuring the latterly well-known Wallander, we are invited behind the scenes of a small town in southern Sweden, which upon closer inspection proves to be less of an idyll than it seems. The hunt for the killer proceeds at a furious pace, and soon Wallander finds himself investigating circles with racist and xenophobic tendencies.

Written in 1991, *Faceless Killers* reflects a Swedish society facing economic crisis, high unemployment, political populism, and a brief but much publicized appearance of a declared xenophobic party in parliament. The darker undertones pervading society are reflected in the portrayal of a bleak and rainy small town, its dejected police force, and generally passive inhabitants. Distrust permeates not only the murder investigations but society in general, and an increased polarization of opinions shapes the environment in which Wallander is obliged to operate. Although not an overtly political novel, *Faceless Killers* nevertheless takes a stand against increasing intolerance, so a moral element is added to a riveting plot told by a highly skilled storyteller.

Faceless Killers is the first in a series of nine Wallander novels, and the book proved to be Henning Mankell's international breakthrough. Although a must-read in its own right, it also deserves our attention as a representative of the inexorable rise of the modern crime novel in late twentieth-century Scandinavia, part of a fictional crime wave arguably led by Mankell and closely followed by Norwegian contemporary Karin Fossum. **GW**

Lifespan | *b.* 1948 (Sweden)
First Published | 1991
First Published by | Ordfront (Stockholm)
Original Title | *Mördare utan ansikte*

"I meant, of course, that it was particularly fiendish individuals who did this . . ."

⊙ Famous for the Kurt Wallender detective novels, Mankell spends much of his time in Mozambique, where this photo was taken.

Astradeni

Eugenia Fakinou

Lifespan | b. 1945 (Egypt)
First Published | 1991
First Published by | Kedros (Athens)
First English Edition | 1992, by Kedros (Athens)

Astradeni is not a political novel like many modern Greek works. It is set in 1978 and deals with the huge wave of immigration from rural areas to Athens and its consequences for the country and its people.

The family of eleven-year-old schoolgirl Astradeni move from Symi, a small island of the Dodecanese, to Athens. They do not fit in: they are poor, they speak a dialect, and they are scared of cars. Their life in Athens consists mainly of defeats: Astradeni's father cannot get a decent job, her mother stays at home alone crying, while Astradeni herself has no friends at school and cannot even go outside to play, there being no yard anywhere—"there is not enough room" in Athens. Astradeni's only victory throughout the book concerns her name. Her new teacher in Athens does not understand it, claims that it is not Christian, and arbitrarily uses "Urania." But Astradeni means "she who binds the stars," and in the end the girl manages to persuade the school headmaster to force her teacher into using her name.

In Astradeni herself, Eugenia Fakinou introduces a childishly naive but disarmingly honest narrator who elicits sympathy in her tales of the vast movement of poor peasants to Athens and their fierce resistance to assimilation: "But why are they calling us peasants? We're islanders." The unfairness of this life is what Astradeni best conveys, expressing the despair of a free-spirited girl who is caged in an apartment where she cannot play and a school where people do not even use her own name. **CSe**

Regeneration

Pat Barker

Lifespan | b. 1943 (England)
First Published | 1991
First Published by | Viking (London)
First U.S. Edition | 1992, by E. P. Dutton (New York)

With the Regeneration trilogy Pat Barker extended the formal and thematic frontiers of contemporary historical fiction. This first book is a psychologically penetrating novel that revises the account of events at Craiglockhart War Hospital, Edinburgh, in 1917, involving the neurologist Dr. Rivers and traumatized soldier and poet Siegfried Sassoon.

In her "Author's Note" Barker warns, "Fact and Fiction are so interwoven in this book that it may help the reader to know what is historical and what is not." Yet it is precisely her braiding together of actuality and dramatization that sustains arresting insights for the reader. She uses the novel to trace the progression of Sassoon's complicated commitment to pacifism, and to investigate the cruelty of institutional psychiatry epitomized by Dr. Lewis Yealland's horrific techniques for treating so-called hysterical disorders. When evoking the scenes of that brutality, Barker's style remains impersonal and taut. The navigation between pared-down dialogue and interior reflection invites an uneasy sympathy for Rivers. The reader is enticed to collude with his struggle to reform the clinical approach to "shell shock." But the fluctuating affects of this disorder are everywhere inscribed upon the inhospitable social landscape that unfolds for sufferers like Sassoon on their return. Regeneration reveals the First World War's indelible and manifold legacy and compels us to re-examine the relationship between public authority and personal memory. **DJ**

Typical

Padgett Powell

Lifespan | *b.* 1952 (U.S.)
First Published | 1991
First Published by | Farrar, Straus & Giroux (New York)
Original Language | English

One of the most inventive writers to emerge in New Southern Writing—hailed by his peers, from Donald Barthleme to Saul Bellow—Padgett Powell takes the reader on a stylistic tour de force in *Typical*. The voice of America is the true subject of these stories, in particular the language of the South. It is a South of long-neck Buds and shotguns in the back windows of pickup trucks; of the peculiar joy in defeat of backwater trailer parks. Powell captures the music in the language, colorful to the point of poetry.

From the stream of self-excoriation of the narrator in "Typical," who has come to terms with being "a piece of crud . . . an asshole," to Aunt Humpy in "Letter from a Dogfighter's Aunt, Deceased," who corrects the grammar of her trash family from beyond the grave, Powell explores the soul of a South too complacent to rise again. In "Florida" and "Texas," he paints entire emotional landscapes with lists. In "Mr. Irony," the writer searches for his voice under the tutelage of Mr. Irony, "a therapist of self-deprecation." "Limn with humility," Mr. Irony extols. The narrator—the writer—ultimately fails to master irony and absents himself from the story. "Dr. Ordinary," where every sentence begins with "He found . . ." and "General Rancidity," where each sentence begins with "He ran . . ." are bravura performances. That such technical acrobatics manage to rise above mere novelty to create sublime explorations of self-knowledge without regret is a testament to Powell's genius. **GT**

Mao II

Don DeLillo

Lifespan | *b.* 1936 (U.S.)
First Published | 1991
First Published by | Viking (New York)
PEN/Faulkner Award | 1992

Don DeLillo's *Mao II* adopts the title of a Warhol portrait and brings to the foreground the role of images in the interdependence of individualism, social traditions, and terrorism. This story of reclusive writer Bill Gray's progressively deeper political involvement opens with a mass wedding conducted by Reverend Sun Myung Moon. The narrative perspective continually vacillates between the soon-to-be-spouses and invited, or interloping, observers in the stands. Bill has spent many years in virtual hiding, holed up in a compound with his affairs managed by a disconcertingly insistent fan-turned-executor. When Bill agrees to meet portrait photographer Brita, and later to act in support of a poet kidnapped in Beirut, he stops interminably writing, reworking, and unwriting the same narrative. His emergence ultimately leads to direct involvement with the poet's struggle.

Mao II is preoccupied with the figure of the terrorist, particularly in relation to the isolated writer, and the dynamics of crowds. In the wake of Salman Rushdie's metaphorical abduction by Ayatollah Khomeini's 1989 fatwa, the writer is no longer the artistic counterpart of the terrorist, but also his potential adversary or victim. Bill's fiercely guarded isolation, in part an act of resistance against the culture of consent in late capitalist America, becomes more like a terrorist abduction of the self. In the process, the writer's and the terrorist's shared but unrealizable dream of complete autonomy is exposed. **AF**

Wild Swans

Jung Chang

Lifespan | *b.* 1952 (China)
First Published | 1991
First Published by | HarperCollins (London)
Full Title | *Wild Swans: Three Daughters of China*

WILD SWANS

Three Daughters of China

'*It is impossible to exaggerate the importance of this book.*'
Mary Wesley

JUNG CHANG

◉ *Wild Swans* is still banned in mainland China, but has sold over ten million copies across the rest of the world.

In *Wild Swans,* Jung Chang recounts how three generations of her family's women fared through the political storms of China in the twentieth century. Her grandmother, whose feet were bound according to ancient Chinese custom, was the concubine of an Emperor. Her mother struggled during Mao's revolution before rising, like Chang's father, to a prominent position in the Communist Party, only to be denounced during the Cultural Revolution. Chang herself was brought into the world a Communist and also followed Mao enthusiastically, before the harsh excesses of his policies and the destructive purges that crushed millions of innocent Chinese, including her parents, created the shadow of doubt. Working as a "barefoot doctor," Chang saw the worst effects of Mao's rule and eventually fled to the United Kingdom in 1978.

This intensely personal memoir is written in powerful yet delicate prose. An important work in terms of its examination of the effects of grand historical movements on the individual soul, as well as providing a vivid depiction of life in twentieth-century China, it covers a particularly eventful period of Chinese history.

Wild Swans traces the demise of Imperial China, the Japanese wartime occupation, the rise of the nationalist movement, the devastating civil war between the nationalist Kuomintang and the Communists, the Communist takeover, Mao's Great Leap Forward (starving tens of millions to death), and finally the Cultural Revolution, which uprooted the nation's identity and broke its collective spirit.

This is a revelatory book, and readers must constantly remind themselves that they are reading a work of fact rather than one of fiction—which at some points is a terrible thought. **EF**

Arcadia

Jim Crace

Visions of a garden-city, of a pastoral idyll preserved at the core of a modern commercial center, hold Jim Crace's aging millionaire in thrall. Alone with his fortune on his eightieth birthday, Victor resolves to pay tribute to the vibrant yet rugged fruit market at the city's heart by building a vaulted glass enclosure as an epitaph in place of its current traders. The quest to realize this architectural ambition is overseen by a reporter who with sympathy recounts the way Victor's idyllic monument is eventually overturned by the trading community it romanticizes, and with disastrous consequences. Crace offers a shrewd yet sensitive commentary on a wishful effort to resuscitate an urban environment simply by refurbishing its visible topography within the confines of nostalgia.

If Crace can be seen as ironically appropriating long-established pastoral conventions, he does so to evoke one of civilization's oldest debates, one that pits the urge to preserve the natural world against the ever-present need for redevelopment, the importance of rurality and that of commercial modernity. *Arcadia*'s voyage unfolds in a pristine style that remains as sensuous as it is polemical; drawing us into that "amiable and congested tension of the streets which kept the traffic and pedestrians apart," Crace's evanescent descriptions immerse the reader in a bustling marketplace whose aestheticization he then later interrogates.

As elsewhere in his oeuvre, Crace furnishes an anonymous setting in such a way that personifies its physical terrain: it is as though this fictional place itself is auditioned from the outset as a fellow protagonist among the novel's events, events whose volatile succession the marketplace does ultimately survive, but scarcely unscathed. **DJ**

Lifespan | *b.* 1946 (England)
First Published | 1992
First Published by | Jonathan Cape (London)
E. M. Forster Award | 1992

 In the year of *Arcadia*'s publication, Crace was awarded the E. M. Forster Award by the American Academy of Arts and Letters.

Hideous Kinky

Esther Freud

This novel is semi-autobiographical and based on the author's own experience of traveling with her mother, Bernadine Coverley, in North Africa, between the ages of four and six. Weaving between the vivid descriptions of life on the move, the desert, and its cast of exotic characters, is a deeply moving and poignant tale of what it is like, as a child, to be part of an unconventional family. For Freud herself, the daughter of the artist Lucien, and the great-granddaughter of the famed Sigmund, childhood was unlikely ever to be normal. The novel beautifully evokes the bohemian life that she and her sister, the fashion designer Bella Freud, unwittingly witnessed as children, while all the while craving a more stable upbringing.

Hideous Kinky is the story of Julia, a hippie mother, and her daughters, Lucia and Bea, who travel to Morocco. Early on in the trip the girls decide that many of the sights they witness are best described in the words of the title. Events are narrated through the voice of five-year-old Lucia, who observes their exotic foreign surroundings with mixed emotions. One moment she is seduced by the vast desert skies and the magic of colorful street markets, but the next she is craving a normal, English upbringing, complete with childhood staples such as regular school and set bedtimes. As their mother immerses herself in Sufism, in her quest for personal fulfillment and spiritual enlightenment, the girls' longing for stability amidst the shifting desert sands intensifies. In this, her first novel, Freud not only paints a vivid and compelling picture of a country that was the Mecca of the hippie movement of the 1970s, but also tells a touching story about childhood, with a simplicity and lightness that both moves and enchants. **LE**

Lifespan | *b.* 1963 (England)
First Published | 1992
First Published by | Hamish Hamilton (London)
Movie Adaptation | 1998

'Fresh and clear, funny and sharp' – Margaret Forster in the *Spectator*

HIDEOUS KINKY

⬆ The image on the cover of the Penguin edition, shown here, was drawn by the author's father, Lucien Freud.

◀ Esther Freud, pictured here in 2004, was named as one of the Best of Young British Novelists by *Granta* magazine in 1993.

Memoirs of Rain

Sunetra Gupta

Lifespan | b. 1965 (India)
First Published | 1992
First Published in | Grove Press (New York)
Sahitya Akademi Award | 1996

Sunetra Gupta's debut novel was published to acclaim from critics who likened her sinuous, poignant prose to that of Virginia Woolf. The events of *Memoirs of Rain* take place over a weekend, during which Moni, the Bengali-born wife of an English writer, prepares to escape the quiet anguish of her unhappy marriage and return to India with her daughter.

Like Woolf's Mrs. Dalloway, Moni is superficially occupied with arrangements for a party, but her mind continually wanders as she remembers the tentative beginnings of her relationship with her husband, Anthony, and her uneasy adjustment to life in London. The passion of youth contrasts painfully with Anthony's subsiding infatuation and later guilty indifference, and his barely concealed infidelity is the source of Moni's despair. Although it is Moni's point of view that informs most of the narrative, the stream-of-consciousness technique (again echoing Woolf) confuses and conflates wife and mistress, past and present, real and imaginary, while the intensely lyrical rhythms of descriptive passages are accentuated by extracts from the poetry of Bengali poet Rabindranath Tagore, interwoven with the text in translations by the author.

A searching examination of a fading affair and the exploration of a particularly feminine form of self-expression are bound up in the juxtaposition of two cultures. As the literary importance of Indian diasporic writers continues to grow, Gupta's elegant, thought-provoking debut remains remarkable. **VB**

Asphodel

H. D.

Lifespan | b. 1886 (U.S.), d.1961(Switzerland)
First Published | 1992
First Published by | Duke University Press
Given Name | Hilda Doolittle

Asphodel is a remarkably complex, innovative, and hugely underrated work of Modernist fiction. The story follows the European travels of Hermione Gart, a young American who experiences artistic and sexual awakenings in the years leading up to the First World War. Themes of marriage, infidelity, and illegitimacy all connect the novel with the Jamesian literary tradition. More radically, however, the novel also explores one failed and one hopeful lesbian relationship. H. D. attempted to deter publication of this autobiographical novel—written in 1922 and unpublished for seventy years—by penciling "DESTROY" across the title page of the manuscript; it has been presumed that this was due to *Asphodel's* lesbian theme. Perhaps also psychological trauma and the stillbirth of Hermione's first child were themes that were just too close to home.

As a feminist novel, this is the story of female expatriation, an experience that is immeasurably different from that of young expatriate men. As a novel that reinscribes the psychological experience of war, it presents a landscape where both interior and exterior spaces are violated. If for the Modernists, the world of the mind was the only safe space to retreat to, then where does one go when even interior space has been violated by the public trauma of war, or the private trauma of stillbirth? **VC-R**

❷ Hilda Doolittle, photographed here in the 1910s, was prominently known simply by her initials, H. D.

The Butcher Boy

Patrick McCabe

Lifespan | *b*. 1955 (Ireland)
First Published | 1992
First Published by | Picador (London)
Irish Literature Prize for Fiction | 1992

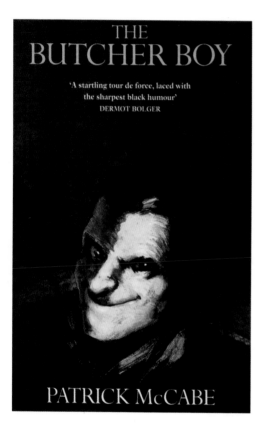

THE
BUTCHER BOY

'A startling tour de force, laced with
the sharpest black humour'
DERMOT BOLGER

PATRICK McCABE

◉ *The Butcher Boy* is one of five novels that Patrick McCabe has published; he also writes radio plays and children's books.

The Butcher Boy is as exciting as it is horrific, as comic as it is disturbing. The story is told in tightly controlled flashback from Francie Brady's wooded hideout, where we learn the whole town is after him "on account of what I done on Mrs. Nugent."

Set in the Irish Republic in the early 1960s, Francie is the neglected only child of an alcoholic father and a suicidal mother. His troubled family is very unlike that of the well-to-do Mrs. Nugent and her namby-pamby son, Phillip. Francie's imagination is saturated with comic books, American movies, television, and the mischief he gets up to with his only friend, Joe Purcell. The stifling town in which Francie lives, and his twisted family life, makes him love-starved, emotionally stunted, and ultimately unhinged. While Joe can grow into adolescence, Francie remains undeveloped and childlike, despite leaving school early and getting a job in an abattoir, an appropriate occupation for one obsessed by Mrs. Nugent's comparison of his family to "pigs."

Exploiting the tendency of the childish voice to imitate what it overhears, the narrative recycles adult cliché through the mind of a disturbed boy. Francie absorbs and invigorates the banal conversational idiom of life in a small Irish town, infusing it with energy and menace. The first-person narrative here races along in colloquial fluency, for despite the utter dysfunctionality of Francie's family life, his inner, fantasy life is explosive and dynamic. The more the world outside rejects him and fails to meet his needs, the more recourse he has to this fantasy world, so that the descent into madness and murder, however genuinely shocking, comes with its own childish logic. It is a powerfully original voice, deftly crafted into a compelling, shocking, and entertaining novel about damaged childhood. **RM**

Smilla's Sense of Snow

Peter Høeg

Six-year-old Isaiah is found lying face down in the snow at the foot of an apartment complex in Copenhagen, Denmark. The authorities record the death as an accident, but Smilla Jasperson, Isaiah's neighbor and surrogate mother, feels convinced that something more sinister lies behind the tragedy. An expert reader of snow and ice, Smilla is able to deduce from Isaiah's footprints that he jumped on purpose, something he only would have done had he been pursued. Her subsequent research leads her to the Arctic ice cap, as a stowaway on a cruise liner, as she slowly uncovers a conspiracy involving numerous members of Denmark's scientific elite intent on safeguarding their secret at any cost.

Smilla's Sense of Snow is narrated in the first person: we inhabit the perspective of a highly intelligent woman whose pluckiness and abrasive sense of humor at first belie the tremendous grief she feels as a result of Isaiah's death. As the story progresses, we learn more about Smilla's relationship with Isaiah, particularly the bond they shared as displaced Greenlanders forced to make a life for themselves in homogenous Denmark. The novel is a bracing critique of Denmark's colonization of Greenland as well as of the continuing prejudices harbored by many Danish toward Greenland's indigenous people.

What elevates this story to the status of a great novel is the eloquence with which Peter Høeg deftly interweaves a detective plot with striking character portraitures and philosophical musings. "Ice and life are related in many ways," Smilla tells us at the beginning of her story, and the rest of the novel ingeniously expounds on this relationship, juxtaposing adventure on the high seas with finely crafted meditations on love and loss. **CG-G**

Lifespan | *b.* 1957 (Denmark)
First Published | 1992, by Rosinante (Copenhagen)
Alternate Title | Miss Smilla's Feeling for Snow
Original Title | *Frøken Smillas fornemmelse for sne*

Peter Høeg has written six novels, all published in Denmark by Rosinante. This novel was made into a movie by Bille August.

The Dumas Club

Arturo Pérez-Reverte

Lifespan | *b.* 1951 (Spain)
First Published | 1992
First Published by | Alfaguara (Madrid)
Original Title | *El club Dumas*

The Dumas Club is the novel by Pérez-Reverte most admired by his critics, perhaps because it is the most meta-literary of all his works, or perhaps simply because its chosen subject is the world of antiquarian books.

In any case, this explicit tribute to Alexander Dumas contains, in equal measure, any and all of the ingredients needed to turn a story of intrigue, mystery, and action into an excellent book appealing to contemporary tastes: a plausible protagonist (the unheroic Lucas Corso, antiquarian book dealer and faithful heir of the skeptical characters of the traditional detective novel); enigmas to be resolved (authenticating a forged manuscript chapter of *The Three Musketeers*; investigating the existence of examples of a medieval work—*The Ninth Gate*—burned, with its printer, on its appearance in 1667); the universe of assistants (Irene Adler, the young beauty who decides to help Corso); and the opposition (the evil and metaliterary Balkan/Richelieu, Rochefort, and Milady/Liana), all involved in an investigation that develops in an exotic international setting; the intelligent segmentation of the story through ellipsis and insinuation to increase the suspense and the crossing of trails and countertrails; and, finally, the no-less skillful inclusion of erudite information (that comes from the buccaneering world of antiquarian books), satisfying readers by presenting difficulties and then leading them well through the decipherment of the tangle. **JCA**

Written on the Body

Jeanette Winterson

Lifespan | *b.* 1959 (England)
First Published | 1992
First Published by | Jonathan Cape (London)
First U.S. Edition | 1993, Knopf (New York)

Set against the comic relation of the narrator's previous sexual liaisons, *Written on the Body* tells the story of the narrator's deeply serious love affair with a married woman called Louise. Although, in this book Jeanette Winterson eschews the explicit engagement with sexual and gender politics that characterized her infamous first novel, *Oranges are Not the Only Fruit* (1985), her decision to make the gender of the narrator in *Written on the Body* ambiguous has prompted much debate. Various textual clues—including the evidently easy bisexuality of the narrator, and the ease with which Louise's husband allows them to carry on their affair under the eaves of the marital home—suggest that the narrator is female. While the novel might therefore be read as an acutely observed reflection on female sexuality, the mystery of the narrator's gender might also indicate a more radical undermining of assumptions about gender and sexuality.

The novel begins and ends with more abstract poetic reflections on love, testifying to Winterson's skill as one of the few contemporary prose writers who can both write a compelling narrative about the vicissitudes of love and sex and construct sentences with the precision and beauty of the poetic. Sharing the magic realism of contemporary novels such as Angela Carter's *The Passion of New Eve* and Salman Rushdie's *Midnight's Children*, the story is a poetic and philosophical reflection on the body—a complex, interwoven palimpsest of who we are. **SD**

The Crow Road

Iain Banks

Lifespan | *b.* 1954 (Scotland)
First Published | 1992
First Published by | Scribner (London)
Adapted for Radio (BBC) | 1996

Iain Banks's *The Crow Road* begins with one of the most memorable paragraphs in modern literature: "It was the day my grandmother exploded. I sat in the crematorium listening to my Uncle Hamish quietly snoring in harmony to Bach's *Mass in B Minor*, and I reflected that it always seemed to be death that drew me back to Gallanach." This is the voice of Prentice McHoan, the middle son of an affluent Scottish family whose narrative forms the greater part of the book, while the rest is told in the third person, a kind of domestic saga of the McHoan, Watt, and Urvill families.

Away at university, Prentice finds himself returning to his family home (or rather, after a falling-out with his father over religious belief, to the home of his Uncle Hamish). Another uncle, Rory, hasn't been seen in eight years. As the mystery of Uncle Rory's fate takes greater and greater hold on the text, Prentice takes on the role of fallible detective, charged with making sense of all that happened to the generations before him and piecing together fragments to form a single truth.

The Crow Road is a novel about death: desire and its relationship to death, the body in life and death, and the exhuming of buried secrets. By the end of the book, despite the concentration on a bleak and stark Scottish landscape, the real map is created within Prentice's mind, as he reaches inside himself to discover the lost truths of a generation and the fragility of memory. **EF**

Indigo

Marina Warner

Lifespan | *b.* 1946 (England)
First Published | 1992
First Published by | Chatto & Windus (London)
First U.S. Edition | Simon & Schuster (New York)

Novelist, literary critic, and historian, Marina Warner is a chameleon of the pen, and *Indigo* derives from all these aspects of her interest. Skipping between the fifteenth-century British appropriation of an imaginary Caribbean island, with many references to Shakespeare's *The Tempest*, and the story of the founding family's heirs in the twentieth century, *Indigo* draws upon several facets of English history.

Warner draws out all the more sinister colonial implications of Prospero's enslavement of Ariel and Caliban, and revives the witch Sycorax, mentioned fleetingly in *The Tempest* as Caliban's mother. She is the island wise woman and herbalist, learned in the art of extracting indigo and dying cloths. As the British misunderstand and all but destroy the local population, Sycorax's daughter escapes death, if not the ravages of the community established by the conquerors. Alongside this narrative of colonial tyranny is the tale of London-born Miranda, a descendant of the island's colonial governor, who eventually finds her way to the Caribbean island that her family helped to alter dramatically. Warner also manages to poignantly portray the struggle of Miranda to understand and come to terms with her relatives. However, while the tale is played out within a single family, the message is clearly wider: the legacy of colonialism and its crimes do not disappear but are part of the fabric and history of our culture and those they have impacted in a way that is extremely real and present. **JC**

The English Patient

Michael Ondaatje

Michael Ondaatje writes the most remarkable prose. Beautifully crafted sentences flow effortlessly through his work, hypnotic in their perfection. *The English Patient* is a spellbinding novel, both because of this endlessly rich language, and for the story itself, filled as it is with sadness and tragedy.

Set in the closing days of the Second World War, the novel moves between war-ravaged Italy, and the prewar African desert of Ladislaus de Almásy's memory, the terribly burned "English Patient" of the title. Scarred beyond recognition, and dying, he is cared for by a young nurse, Hana, in a partially ruined and deserted villa. Into the lives of this strange couple come Kip, a young Indian sapper in the British Army, and Caravaggio, a charming Italian-Canadian thief, who has been broken by his experiences of war. The tale of Almásy's doomed affair with a married woman, and its tragic end, weaves around the lives of Hana, Caravaggio, and Kip, pouring forth from the strange living corpse that the English Patient has become. The horror of war is distant, but central, as Hana and Kip begin a tentative love affair. The characters are warm, human, likable, yet morally flawed, damaged, and overwhelmingly ambiguous.

In one of the finest scenes in the novel, the uneasy peace of the villa is shattered when Kip hears the news of the bombing of Hiroshima and, shocked and outraged, abandons the villa. It presents the damage and the terrible strain on each character in a way that manages to be both a microcosm of the novel as a whole, and its perfect conclusion. Division and unity, ally and enemy, the boundaries become confused and indistinguishable, running into each other like the sands of the English Patient's memories. This novel is a virtuoso performance from Ondaatje and an endlessly pleasurable read. **DR**

Lifespan | b. 1943 (Sri Lanka)
First Published | 1992
First Published by | McClelland & Stewart
Booker Prize | 1993 (joint)

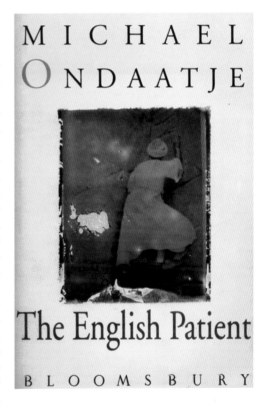

The cover picture of Indian sapper Kip on the U.K. edition is strongly reminiscent of Kipling's *Kim*.

Ralph Fiennes plays disciple of Herodotus, Count Ladislaus de Almásy, in the 1996 movie adaptation by Anthony Minghella.

Possessing the Secret of Joy

Alice Walker

Lifespan | *b.* 1944 (U.S.)
First Published | 1992
First Published by | Harcourt Brace Jovanovich (N.Y.)
First UK Edition | Jonathan Cape (London)

Possessing the Secret of Joy is an angry, impassioned defence of femininity, and of the female body, against the horrific violence of female genital mutilation. The novel focuses on the story of Tashi, an Americanized member of Walker's fictional African people, the Olinka. Tashi opts in adult life to have herself circumcised, or, as she calls it, "bathed." For Olinkans, "bathing" involves not only the excision of the clitoris, but also the removal of the labia, and the stitching closed of the vagina.

Tashi is demonstrating her allegiance to Olinka tradition and her fierce devotion to a culture that is under threat. As the novel progresses, however, she comes to believe that her genital mutilation is a symptom of a more general, transcultural oppression of women by men. In dramatizing Tashi's choice between her nation and her sexuality, Walker sets up an extremely difficult and troubling set of oppositions; the powerful claims of allegiance to African nationalism cannot be reconciled with equally powerful demands of feminism. The novel seeks to understand female suffering at the hands of patriarchal culture and a universal horror at the form that such suffering has taken. It is the possibility of a resistance to patriarchal oppression that turns out, here, to be the real secret of joy. Whatever its difficulties, as a poem of resistance to the violence of misogynist cultures in both Africa and the West, this novel is unforgettable. **PB**

All the Pretty Horses

Cormac McCarthy

Lifespan | *b.* 1933 (U.S.)
First Published | 1992
First Published by | Alfred A. Knopf (New York)
National Book Award | 1992

All the Pretty Horses, the first novel in Cormac McCarthy's "Border Trilogy," centers on John Grady Cole, a 16-year-old cowboy old enough to choose his way of life, but too young to realize this choice in the face of familial and institutional resistance. When John's mother sells the family ranch, John and his best friend, Lacey Rawlins, leave for Mexico. Along the way they cross paths with the even younger character Blevins—a meeting that will dramatically alter each of the boys' lives in different ways.

The novel's cultural landscape is in a state of transition, as the open Texan spaces are encroached upon by electric fences dividing land into smaller and smaller parcels. One feels that the fast-food homogeneity already colonizing the rest of the country waits just around the corner. At the outset of John and Lacey's journey, Mexico plays a familiar part in this scenario: As the young men leave their home behind, they imagine a rugged land that will form a suitable backdrop to their nostalgic fantasies of cowboy life. When they become workers at a large hacienda, however, they find themselves the subordinates of one of Mexico's powerful elite. An island of opulence surrounded by back-breaking poverty, the hacienda does not protect John and Lacey from the intrigue resulting from their association with Blevins, and John's love for the *hacendado*'s daughter promises future trouble. **AF**

The Triple Mirror of the Self

Zulfikar Ghose

Lifespan | b. 1935 (Pakistan)
First Published | 1992
First Published by | Bloomsbury (London)
Original Language | English

The question of national origin and identity is never simple in Zulfikar Ghose's work. In *The Triple Mirror of the Self*, his most accomplished novel, themes of exile, migration, and identity loss are woven into an elaborate, mythic journey in time and space. Divided into three sections, the novel opens in a jungle in South America, where a group of strange characters have come together to form a pseudo-primitive commune of exiles and misfits. As the mountains of South America fade into the Hindu Kush, the novel changes tack and touches on a ship sailing to Europe, a university in the United States, and finally pre-1947 India, where a young boy is learning difficult lessons about identity as a Muslim in a group of friends soon to be split by Partition.

The Triple Mirror of the Self explores how we think about our own national identity when our nation is taken away. The reader never really pins down the central character, whose identity shifts throughout the narrative. Through the novel's dreamy, evocative prose and deliberately obscure chronology, the reader is encouraged to see boundaries blur through the medium of a single extraordinary life. *The Triple Mirror of the Self* suggests that a coherent identity is nothing more than a series of infinite reflections; for Ghose, however, the interaction of these reflections makes up what is most beautiful and valuable about the human experience. **AB**

Uncle Petros and Goldbach's Conjecture

Apostolos Doxiadis

Lifespan | b. 1953 (Australia)
First Published | 1992, by Kastaniotis (Athens)
Original Title | *O Theios Petros kai i Eikasia tou Goldbach*

In this novel the narrator's uncle, a gifted Greek mathematician called Petros Papachristou, becomes obsessed with solving Goldbach's Conjecture, one of the great problems in mathematics. Searching for a proof, Uncle Petros throws away a promising career in academic mathematics, and at the novel's end the reader remains uncertain whether he ever solved the problem. The narrator, a young man, inherits his uncle's fascination with the conjecture, but only as an excuse to construct a fiction. At the same time he describes, in his own charming manner, what all people experience at least once in their lifetime: a face-to-face encounter with major existential questions. The plot unravels like a mathematical problem, drawing the reader into a tale of life, love, and sacrifice, with Uncle Petros battling against human irrationality, isolation, and loss of ideals.

Doxiadis is a talented storyteller and a gifted mathematician who knows how to present mathematics in an easygoing and fascinating way. His book combines fiction and fact in equal measure, helped along by a plethora of unexpected events, colorful language, clever plotting, and an eye for irony. Doxiadis's achievement is to open up the worlds of mathematics and science, even for those who have always been mystified by them, and show that everyone can find interesting challenges even in the most unexpected fields. **PMy**

The Discovery of Heaven

Harry Mulisch

Lifespan | *b.* 1927 (Netherlands), *d.* 2010 (Netherlands)
First Published | 1992, by De Bezige Bij (Amsterdam)
Movie Adaptation | 2001
Original Title | *De Ontdekking van de Hemel*

Although Harry Mulisch is less well known in the English-speaking world, he is a prolific writer and a prominent figure in twentieth-century Dutch literature. On the basis of its physical heft alone, *The Discovery of Heaven* is a book to be reckoned with, while its theme consists of nothing less than the failure of humanity's covenant with God. One premise of the novel is that the scientific method is a trick of Lucifer's, one that has succeeded incredibly well. As the narrative unfolds, two supremely talented men, Max Delius, an astronomer, and Onno Quist, a linguist, meet by chance one dark night and become friends. Later, on a trip to Cuba, they jointly and repeatedly impregnate a young cellist named Ada Brons, who had earlier been involved with each of them in turn. Though she suffers a serious accident and dies, her baby survives. Named Quinten Quist, his mission is to retrieve the Ten Commandments and return them to heaven because of mankind's utter inability to fulfill God's will on earth. Delius, meanwhile, makes a stupendous astronomical discovery, before being killed by a meteorite. If the plot sounds contrived, that is the result of the intervention of angels or, more precisely, demiurges, who concoct the plan to create a human being to reclaim the Biblical tablets.

This monumental and controversial effort, cosmic in scope and comic in tone, has been heralded internationally and may be considered a contemporary instance of myth creation. **ES**

> *"At the stroke of midnight I contrived a short-circuit. Anyone walking along . . . would have seen all the lights in the detached mansion suddenly go off . . ."*

⬤ Harry Mulisch, photographed here in 1993, received the once-in-a-lifetime Award for Dutch Literature in 1995.

Life is a Caravanserai

Emine Sevgi Özdamar

Lifespan | b. 1946 (Turkey)
First Published | 1992, by Kiepenheuer & Witsch
Original Title | Leben ist eine Karawanserai hat zwei
Türen aus einer kam ich rein aus der anderen ging ich raus

The book with the unconventional title (*Life is a Caravanserai Has Two Doors I Came in One I Went Out the Other*) breaks conventions throughout. That unpunctuated running together of phrases starts us off as we will go on. The first sentence continues: "First I saw the soldiers, I was standing there in my mother's belly between the bars of ice . . ." Clearly, *Caravanserai* is not your usual memoir: in the process of describing childhood in the Turkey of the turbulent 1950s and 1960s, we can switch between the protagonist in her mother's womb and the train carriage in which the mother stands surrounded by soldiers just as easily as the book continuously shifts its diction, register, and perspective.

The marriage of stylistic and thematic concerns is absolute: while the narrative is about the way in which female identity can be newly constructed in a laden political and social context, the stylistic experiments at first seem disorienting, but come to create a poetic and challenging sort of logic of their own. The boundaries of linguistic categories are fluidly reinvented as subjective, national, and gender roles are rethought. The book is wonderfully anarchic: both in the verbal marvels that disrupt its own narrative texture (from the Arabic prayer for protection and forgiveness that runs throughout to Joycean renderings of the sounds of a crunching apple), and also in its physical openness and pungency, replete with dozens of farts, all kinds of bodily fluid, and a vivid catalog of smells. **MS**

Before Night Falls

Reinaldo Arenas

Lifespan | b. 1943 (Cuba), d. 1990 (U.S.)
First Published | 1992
First Published by | Tusquets (Barcelona)
Original Title | Antes que anochezca

Written against time and published posthumously, Arenas's autobiography is a furious denunciation of the Castro regime in Cuba, but, above all, it relates the circumstances that influence the life of a homosexual intellectual in a world marked by repression. Sex, politics, and writing are tied together in a linear story of resounding frankness and amazing dynamism. From Arenas's childhood in Cuba to his flight to New York, where he knows he is about to die, homosexuality is the basis of his every experience. Its recognition is almost simultaneous with the loss of illusions raised by the revolution; it reveals the moral perversion of the political system; it is seen as the mechanism of collective rebellion; it is the pretext that brings the protagonist to prison; and, ironically, it opens the way to freedom (as an "undesirable") through the Port of Mariél exodus.

Arenas tells of his detention, his escape, his almost dreamlike clandestine life in a park, his terrible incarceration, his defeat, his denunciation of his work, the further surveillance he underwent, and his final flight. Everything was made worse because writing was the whole of Arenas's life. This secret journey leads from a literary childhood but without reading to international conferences, moving through his early triumphs in the revolutionary atmosphere, his relationships with Virgilio Piñera, Lezama Lima, and his companions of the "lost generation," and his continuous efforts to save his texts before he reached the end. **DMG**

The Secret History

Donna Tartt

Lifespan | *b.* 1963 (U.S.)
First Published | 1992
First Published by | Alfred A. Knopf (New York)
First UK Edition | Viking (London)

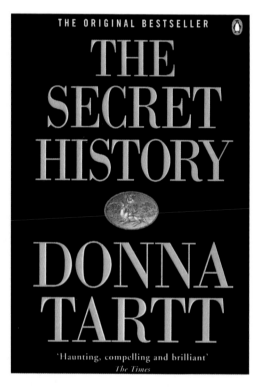

THE ORIGINAL BESTSELLER

THE SECRET HISTORY

DONNA TARTT

'Haunting, compelling and brilliant'
The Times

"... how I longed to be an orphan when I was a child!"

◉ After the sensational success of Tartt's first novel, *The Secret History*, she was determined to remain "a writer, not a TV personality."

Good publicity can give a book a bad name. Donna Tartt's first novel, begun when she was still at college and bought for $450,000 by Knopf after a bidding war, quickly became a bestseller and made its author a reluctant star. The critics were not impressed: they thought the book leaden, pretentious, and thinly characterized. In some ways, they were taking it too seriously; in others, perhaps, not seriously enough.

The Secret History is a page-turner, certainly, but there is more to the novel than plot alone. Telling his story as if it were still unfolding, though in fact he is recalling events long since past, the narrator, Richard Papen, leaves behind his unsatisfying teenage years in Plano, California, to enroll at Hampden, a small, exclusive college in Vermont. He is soon captivated by a group of five rich, otherworldly classics students and their mercurial tutor, Julian Morrow, and gradually becomes enmeshed in the clique. He learns that the group—Henry, Francis, Bunny, and the twins Charles and Camilla—have been attempting to recreate a frenzied bacchanal, the consequences of which culminate in Bunny's death. The remainder of the novel charts the slow splintering of the group's friendships under the pressures of fear, remorse, and sickened self-knowledge.

The Secret History is a study of ruin, of lives blighted forever by adolescent hubris. It is also about charisma: the reader is seduced, along with Richard, by the charming and dissolute Francis, by Julian's sublime sensibility, and the twins' ethereal self-containment, and, above all, by Henry, who is by turns benevolent and warm, aloof and forbidding, but always, in the end, opaque. A strange confection, Tartt's melancholy murder mystery is quality trash for highbrows: the storytelling retains its grip to the final page and beyond. **PMy**

The Adventures and Misadventures of Maqroll

Álvaro Mutis

Lifespan | b. 1923 (Colombia)
First Published | 1993, by Siruela (Madrid)
Original Title | *Empresas y tribulaciones de Maqroll el Gaviero*

Under this overall title and around an enigmatic figure, a saga of seven novels unfolds, originally published between 1986 and 1993. Maqroll is a hero of the earth and sea, in the tradition of those Conrad or Hugo Pratt, at the edge of the conventional, beyond time and space. He multiplies his destinies: he transports logs or he runs a bar in the mountains (*The Snow of the Admiral*); he co-manages a brothel (*Ilona Arrives with the Rain*) or he restores an old steamship (*The Tramp Steamer's Last Port of Call*); he takes part in arms smuggling (*A Beautiful Death*) or he tries to bring an old mine back into production (*Amirbar*). Many more adventures are described, as are the innumerable characters Maqroll encounters in his travels, among whom Ilona, the girl from Trieste, and the Lebanese Abdul Basur stand out.

Elegiac and almost magical, in this journey every meeting is always a reunion and a prediction of departure, everything is inevitable, and everything (except death) is avoidable. A philosopher alternating between disillusionment and the pleasure of the journey, a tireless reader, a notable diarist, letter writer, and invocatory poet, Maqroll is, above all, a literary hero. He leaves an ironic, fragmentary, incomplete dossier of documents and declarations, unified by a fictionalized Mutis. The collection is a dazzling verbal comic strip that, at any moment, appears capable of being expanded. **DMG**

> *"He is always semi-inebriated, a condition that he skillfully maintains by a process of steady drinking . . ."*

◉ Mutis's generous, good-humored novellas reflect his fascination with sea voyages and his total lack of interest in political issues.

Remembering Babylon

David Malouf

Lifespan | b. 1934 (Australia)
First Published | 1993
First Published in | Chatto & Windus (Sydney)
NSW Premier's Literary Award | 1993

Set in the mid nineteenth century in Queensland, *Remembering Babylon* is the story of an English baby who is thrown from the ship that brought him from England to Australia. The castaway in question, Gemmy, is raised by a group of Aboriginal people for sixteen years before returning to civilization via a small community of Scottish immigrant farmers.

Backed onto a fence by a stick-brandishing eleven-year-old Scot, Lachlan Beattie, and his cousins, Gemmy's first appearance in the novel is carefully engineered by Malouf, who places him between European colonizers and the Aboriginal land. Indeed, his role as an "in-between creature," a self-proclaimed "B-b-british object" with an understanding for and alliance with Aboriginal life, brings into focus the novel's principal preoccupation with the problem of identity for the colonial subject.

Gemmy's appearance in this small community is so threatening, his knowledge of "the other" so closely rendered, that the settlers are forced to question their own inherent sense of superiority. Settlers who ally themselves with Gemmy are quickly estranged from their community. Gemmy's eventual forced departure from the community invites readers to remember Babylon, the cradle of civilization that provided both motivation and justification for the colonial project that created him, and that frames Gemmy's narrative. **JSD**

The Holder of the World

Bharati Mukherjee

Lifespan | b. 1940 (India)
First Published | 1993
First Published by | Alfred A. Knopf (New York)
Original Language | English

In this, the sixth novel by Indian-born American writer Bharati Mukherjee, the story is told by Beigh Masters, a twentieth-century asset hunter who is trying to trace a legendary diamond from Mughal India. Beigh uncovers the story of Hannah Easton, the American lover of an Indian Raja. Born in the backwoods of New England in 1670, Hannah's life takes her through a strict Puritan upbringing in Salem to the shorebound life of a seafarer's wife in England. Searching for adventure, she finds herself segregated behind the walls of White Town in Mughal India, before being carried off by a Hindu Raja. Hannah finds herself trapped by, and yet alienated from, each of the cultures in which she finds herself. Only when she becomes the Raja's lover does Hannah finally gain the freedom to act as she wishes rather than as her society dictates.

In the story that frames Hannah's tale, Beigh's investigations of Hannah's life through objects, diaries, and pictures is contrasted with her partner Venn's computer simulation of a recent day using modern paraphernalia. The conclusion that the former creates a richer and more valid evocation of the past is underlined when Beigh physically steps into Hannah's world through a computer simulation. *The Holder of the World* is thus a vibrant narrative of migration and alienation that crosses the boundaries of time and culture. **CIW**

The Virgin Suicides

Jeffrey Eugenides

Lifespan | *b.* 1960 (U.S.)
First Published | 1993
First Published by | Farrar, Straus & Giroux (New York)
Movie Adaptation | 1999

● Jeffrey Eugenides, here photographed by Robert Maas in 1993, was born in Detroit, Michigan, of mixed Greek and Irish descent.

Part detective story, part Bildungsroman, part tragedy, *The Virgin Suicides* starts from a premise so shocking it is almost inconceivable (though supposedly drawing its basic facts from a real-life case). Jeffrey Eugenides's adult narrator recalls the "year of the suicides," in which all five of the Lisbon family's daughters ultimately succeed in committing suicide. The novel brings together "evidence" such as the girls' journals and notes, the collected memories of the narrator and his clique, and interviews conducted around the time of the narrative—yet the atmosphere is thick with confusion.

Several aspects of the Lisbon girls' lives seem to collude in the air of mystification. Neighborhood boys have always romanticized them into a monolithic blond fantasy of unreachability, while neighbors create a whispering backdrop for familial eccentricities. After the first suicide, the remaining four girls become isolated at school by the awkward pity of their peers and teachers. For all the persistence with which the narrator pursues the "truth" behind the suicides, he is never able to illuminate the mystery that enshrouds the girls and their self-inflicted, eternal silence. Never having attempted to look beyond his own interpretation of the girls' mental state, the narrator can only allude to his contributing role in their deaths. The sense that the suicides are simply physical enactments of their complete effacement by their environment is reinforced by the paranoia of their mother, Mrs. Lisbon, about spiritual propriety and pollution. Dutch elm disease hysteria provides a metaphor for the hypochondriacal fear of pandemic at the heart of suburban American culture, where killing something healthy is the preferred resolution to fear of the possibility of contamination. **AF**

The Stone Diaries

Carol Shields

The Stone Diaries is a panoramic novel, a masterful odyssey through the trials, minor joys, and ennui of the nearly century-long life of Daisy Goodwill. Starting with her tragic birth in rural Manitoba in 1905 and ending with her death in Florida, the story is told in chapters, spaced a decade apart, that visit childhood, marriage, remarriage, motherhood, independence, grief, and finally old age and death. We glimpse in the distance, from these windows into Daisy's life, the changing face of the twentieth century. We also see the evolution of women's position in society.

But is this purely a women's book? It is about a woman, and the mundane crises of being a woman, but, more fundamentally, it is about being human. It is a complex narrative—made more complex in that it is ostensibly a first-person "autobiography," but one that alerts us to its unreliability at every step of the way. It offers us multiple versions of Daisy's life—some from before she was born, some after she has died—from a variety of characters. But through all of the different subjective viewpoints, through entire sections made up of letters and newspaper columns on gardening, oddly the one point of view most often absent is that of Daisy. This is a novel about the difficulty of finding an identity, and—considering the position of women—the complication that we are most often defined by others.

Throughout the decades, two motifs reflect minor triumphs and ordinary devastation: the resolute rigidity of stone and the irrational growth of plants. But plants win. Where loss, ossifying grief, or age would be a dead end to other heroines, Carol Shields repeatedly gives us renewal. She shows that life—in surprising ways—finds a way to bloom. There is dignity in the ordinary. There is hope. **GT**

Lifespan | *b.* 1935 (U.S.), *d.* 2003 (Canada)
First Published | 1993
First Published by | Random House (New York)
Pulitzer Prize | 1995

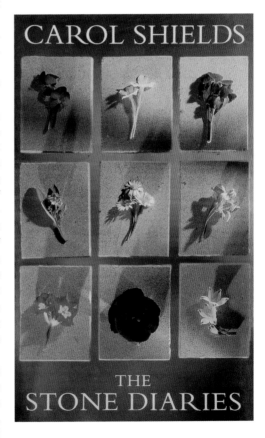

○ The cover design of the first Canadian edition presents the two recurring symbols that occur in the book: flowers and stone.

A Suitable Boy

Vikram Seth

"You too will marry a boy I choose," announces Mrs. Rupa Mehra to her younger daughter, Lata, at the start of Vikram Seth's colossal novel. Lata, however, is unconvinced, and at the heart of the story is the decision she has to make. Will she comply with her mother's wishes and marry Haresh Khanna, the most "suitable" of the three men who are courting her, a shoe factory manager with great enthusiasm for his work who was introduced by a family friend? Will she marry the poet Amit, her brother's brother-in-law, who proposes after they become friends during Lata's university holidays? Or will she defy her mother and marry the most unsuitable boy of them all, Kabir, a Muslim fellow university student, with whom she has fallen in love? The story of the search for a husband follows the fortunes of four families during one year, 1951, four years after Indian independence. It is set against the background of the passage of land reform legislation, religious festivals such as the Pul Mela, and the considerable Hindu–Muslim tensions that lurk beneath the surface and occasionally erupt into violence.

Why read such a long book, shorter than *War and Peace* by only some fifty pages? In Seth's novel, there are none of the weighty meditations of Tolstoy, nor is the intention behind the novel one of a grand epic. Instead, there is a lightness of touch in his prose that moves effortlessly through his vast cast of characters, spanning the frivolous world of the anglicized elite, the tensions of academia and politics, and the grinding poverty of the villages and slums. Surprisingly, the novel is a remarkably accomplished example of restraint and temperance in narrative. It avoids excess despite its enormous scope, and there is a respect for character and detail that is now rare among modern writers. **ABi**

Lifespan | *b.* 1952 (India)
First Published | 1993
First Published by | Phoenix House (London)
Commonwealth Writers Prize | 1994

Seth's epic novel is set in India, the country of his birth, although the author has lived primarily in the U.K. and U.S. since his teens.

Seth, jauntily posed above copies of his novel, looks a thoroughly suitable boy—a writer of serious but never heavyweight fiction.

What a Carve Up!

Jonathan Coe

Lifespan | *b.* 1961 (England)
First Published | 1993
First Published by | Viking (London)
John Llewellyn Rhys Prize | 1994

In this, Jonathan Coe's fourth and overwhelmingly most successful novel, Michael Owen is the hapless biographer of the Winshaw family, a gallery of monsters whose greed and unscrupulousness have enabled them to profit from, and indeed to have made possible, the Thatcherite climate of 1980s Britain. As we move from formative episodes of Michael's life to his account of the Winshaws' rise to positions of power and influence, we discover, along with him, that the family has determined the course of his life in unimaginably far-reaching ways. In the end, a traumatized Michael is transported to the Winshaws' family home, where he and they live out a *Carry On* movie spoof called *What a Carve Up!*, in which Michael's dreams are fulfilled and the Winshaws, in turn, receive their just deserts.

In calling Coe's dazzling novel "Postmodern," critics presumably have in mind its metatextual playfulness—its unreliable narrator, its mingling of literary forms, and the apparently arbitrary interconnectedness of its characters and plots. However, it sits just as happily in the tradition of Victorian social realism, in which personal destinies and sociopolitical contexts are entwined in ways revealed by the story. Many of Coe's novels are detective stories in disguise, beginning with loose ends and gradually tying them into elegant knots. Here, the story's resolution is as satisfying as its literary tricks are delightful, but do not be deceived: at heart, this novel is a furious social satire. **PMy**

Deep River

Shusaku Endo

Lifespan | *b.* 1923 (Japan), *d.* 1996
First Published | 1993
First Published in | Kodansha (Tokyo)
Original Title | *Fukai kawa*

By the end of his life, when this novel was written, Japanese Catholic novelist Endo had become a cultural celebrity in his country, regarded by some as the moral and spiritual conscience of the nation. *Deep River* sums up the personal conflicts and public reflections of a lifetime. The river of the title is the Ganges in northern India, visited by a group of Japanese tourists undergoing varieties of life crisis. One is a Second World War veteran haunted by memories of the horrors of the campaign in Burma, another a guilt-ridden businessman looking for the reincarnation of his wife, dead of cancer. Endo's religious concerns find expression in the person of Otsu, a Japanese Catholic rejected by the official European-based church, who has followed his own version of the faith in India. And there is Misuko, a woman seeking forgiveness for once seducing Otsu in a frivolous attempt to undermine his faith.

While presenting observations of India and its beliefs from a Japanese perspective, Endo remains preoccupied with his lifelong concerns: Japan and Catholicism. His criticism of the materialism and lack of spirituality of Japanese society is stern, but so is his rejection of the European Catholic hierarchy's pretensions to define and control the Christian faith. Endo proposes a vision of religion that is inclusive, tolerant, and all-embracing, and all his major characters find some form of reconciliation, self-acceptance, or fulfillment. Japanese director Kei Kumai made a movie of *Deep River* in 1995. **RegG**

The Twins

Tessa de Loo

Lifespan | *b.* 1946 (Netherlands)
First Published | 1993
First Published by | De Arbeiderspers (Amsterdam)
Original Title | *De tweeling*

The twins Anna and Lotte, separated in early childhood, first by the death of both parents in rapid succession, then by illness, family feuds, and finally by the Second World War, meet accidentally, aged seventy-four, at a health resort. The unexpected encounter produces opposite emotions in the two women: Anna, the German sister, who had been mistreated by her adoptive family as a child, and who had since lost, to war and circumstances, everybody who gave her anchorage and a feeling of belonging, fervently embraces her newfound sibling. Lotte, raised in Holland by an estranged branch of the family, has a longstanding hatred for her former homeland, and she receives her sister's joyous advances with suspicion and disdain.

Tessa de Loo gives voice to the millions of Germans standing convicted before the tribunal of history of passively acquiescing to genocide. With Anna, a picture of the ordinary citizen takes shape, and it is very different from the one approved by history. Questions with wider ethical reach stand in counterpoint with this theme. How much of our energy and resources are we allowed to expend on ourselves, and how much should we save for others, even in the face of dire personal need and adversity? Can affection be rekindled, and childhood bonds renewed, across over half a century of neglect and misunderstanding? This novel provides no clear answers, but the problems it poses revolve in the mind long after the last page is finished. **MWd**

"What was a German doing here, in Spa, where every square . . . had a monument with lists of the fallen of two World Wars carved in stone?"

◉ The cover of the first edition of De Loo's novel, the tale of two lives that illuminates a dark period of European history.

Looking for the Possible Dance

A. L. Kennedy

Lifespan | *b.* 1965 (Scotland)
First Published | 1993
First Published by | Secker & Warburg (London)
Somerset Maugham Award | 1993

'A fine, imaginative and powerful novel. I like A.L. Kennedy's commitment, her energy, her dialogue, and moments of this book are most moving and lyrical ... an exciting young writer.'

Jennifer Johnston

Looking for
the possible dance

⊙ A. L. Kennedy is a Christian and has expressed her faith politically through an involvement in antiwar and antinuclear protests.

Looking for the Possible Dance is an almost everyday story of life, love, and sacrifice in the fraught world of male–female relations. In charting Margaret's resistance to the limited womanly roles of daughter, wife, and mistress, the novel demonstrates the fragility of men and their desperate and resented dependence on the women in their lives, a dependence that must breed hate alongside love.

During a train journey from Glasgow to London, Margaret recounts the events that have brought her to this moment. Her beloved but possessive father has died, and she has lost her job at a community center because her boss, who indulged himself in an imaginary and unreciprocated affair with her, has engineered false accusations against her. Her lover, Colin, has been severely disabled by a gangland attack, in which he was nailed to a warehouse floor in a gruesome crucifixion, a punishment for exposing loan sharks in the community. Having earlier refused to marry him, Margaret now has to decide whether to return to that relationship on his terms, reciprocating his public sacrifice with her own private one. In a typically ambiguous conclusion, Kennedy sends her heroine home, completing the journey of discovery that takes her back where she started. Anxious love and uneasy fear coexist in Margaret, suspending her in this finely balanced narrative of duty and desire. Only dancing offers a glimpse of social harmony, but even this affirmation of the possibility of new relations is finally denied. The present soulless reality is sustained by violence: the public brutality of men's relationships with men and the private coercion of men's relationships with women. In this novel, the dance of life provides little opportunity to escape a routine that creates love and resentment in equal measure. **CJ**

Birdsong

Sebastian Faulks

Birdsong is "a story of love and war." A mixture of fact and fiction, the book was born of the fear that the First World War was passing out of collective consciousness. At one level, it upholds the promise: "We Shall Remember Them," and Faulks's fictional soldiers give an identity to the "lost" of the war—both the dead and "the ones they did not find." Through unashamed emotional manipulation, Faulks solicits heartrending sympathy. He redefines heroism by presenting valor, not as gung-ho bravado, but as fear and the stoic endurance of pointless suffering.

Stephen Wraysford's notebooks, containing his war diaries, are found by his granddaughter, Elizabeth, in 1978. In reading Wraysford's history, Elizabeth relives his past and finds her own identity —a way "of understanding more about herself." The explicit intensity of Stephen's sexual passion for his mistress, Isabelle, stands as vicarious sexual experience for those, like Stephen's friend, Weir, who lost their lives without experiencing sex. And the graphic horror of the Belgian trenches is seared into the reader's consciousness to provide a vicarious national identity for a generation that has never experienced combat. By glimpsing how we might respond in extreme situations that arise only in national crises, *Birdsong* enables readers to learn, as Elizabeth learns, more about themselves. But the novel is not nationalistic, for Stephen is saved by a German soldier, and they weep together "at the bitter strangeness of human lives." Ultimately, the novel acknowledges that any attempt to tell the truth about war lies beyond language, for that truth is too awful both to tell and to comprehend. The "birdsong" of the title stands for the voice of a lost generation and also represents the voice of art, which attempts, and necessarily fails, to capture it. **AR**

Lifespan | *b.* 1953 (England)
First Published | 1993
First Published by | Hutchinson (London)
First U.S. Edition | 1994, by Vintage (New York)

Sebastian Faulks is a popular writer who seeks to engage the emotions of contemporary readers with historical subjects.

The Shipping News

E. Annie Proulx

"His thoughts churned like the amorphous thing that ancient sailors . . . called the Sea Lung . . ."

The landscape of Newfoundland is central to the unfolding story and the development of the characters that inhabit it.

Lifespan | *b.* 1935 (U.S.)
First Published | 1993
First Published by | Scribner (New York)
Pulitzer Prize | 1994

Quoyle is a thirty-six-year-old reporter from New York with a traumatic and stressful life—his parents have committed suicide, and his wife died in a car accident while she was with another man. His aunt has always wanted to return to the land of her history and she convinces Quoyle and his daughters to move with her to Newfoundland. He overcomes his fear of water to accept a job as the shipping correspondent on a local paper. A series of strange events soon beset Quoyle. In the town, he notices a graceful woman whose child has Down's syndrome, and they form a bond that nearly leads to intimacy. Quoyle's ancestors, who lived nearby, were reputedly pirates and violent murderers. He visits their burial ground and on his way home finds a suitcase with a head in it. Less disturbing but more worrisome is the fact that every so often Quoyle finds a length of knotted twine lying around his house.

In the end, there is the triumph of life over death as Quoyle survives a boat wreck. *The Shipping News* was reputed to have been an experiment in writing a novel with a happy ending, after Proulx had received feedback that her first novel seemed dark. But this happy ending is neither euphoric or easy—it seems that the only form of happiness Proulx can bestow on her characters is an absence of trauma and pain, and the resolution of this strange and unsettling novel is filled with unease. **EF**

Waiting for the Dark, Waiting for the Light

Ivan Klima

Lifespan | b. 1931 (Czechoslovakia)
First Published | 1993
First Published in | Cesky spisovatel (Prague)
Original Title | Cekani Na Tmu, Cekani Na Svetlo

What does it mean to be free? How can we be expected to cope with a world where old limits have disappeared? And which of the many lives we live, choices we make, and identities we adopt is really our true self? Klima, himself extensively censored during the Cold War, investigates these big questions with a paradoxical authority, stylistic sureness of touch, and potent insight that empower his refusal to draw conclusions or to moralize. A surrealist, almost magical-realist, imagination is blended with deft satire and black humor. While the experience handled by Klima—1989's Velvet Revolution—is obviously Czech, the setting is trans-national and the messages are universal.

The novel tells the story of Pavel, a commitment-phobic cameraman working for a restrictive and corrupt regime. He distorts the truth on a daily basis and dreams of a freedom where his talents and his true self have free rein. When he gains that "impossible" freedom, the novel explores who he becomes and the ever-complex mismatch between ideals and actions. Multiple narratives interweave in Pavel's story: a president in an imagined labyrinth of senility, an abstract screenplay that Pavel one day hopes to write, a blurred tale of long-lost love, even a hostage drama. But the heart of the novel is Pavel himself: compromised, mediocre, aimless, flawed, yet ultimately very human. **TSu**

The Invention of Curried Sausage

Uwe Timm

Lifespan | b. 1940 (Germany)
First Published | 1993
First Published by | Kiepenheuer & Witsch (Cologne)
Original Title | Die Entdeckung der Currywurst

In The Invention of Curried Sausage, successful and prolifc author Uwe Timm packs in enough material for a work four times its length. It distills challenging subject matter—the end of the Second World War, adultery, Nazism—to its emotional essence, the seemingly inconsequential, yet potent symbol of postwar German cultural integration—the ubiquitous Currywurst.

Timm's investigation of the invention of this delicacy is sparked off by childhood memories of eating the sausage at Lena Brücker's fast-food stand. Brücker claims to be the genuine inventor, but before revealing the details of her culinary discovery, she must excavate her past for the events that led to it. Timm, the narrator, pretends that his sole motivation for interviewing Brücker is to solve the riddle of the sausage, when in reality it is more a device for untangling the riddles of war, duty, and love. Our encounter with the accidental recipe is preceded by Brücker's affair with Bremer, a fugitive soldier hiding from the Nazi authorities. She betrays the unwritten rules of love by lying to him in order to keep their relationship afloat.

The curried sausage becomes a twentieth-century analogy to folklore's stone in the soup. The deftly handled personal and cultural issues give the novella its overriding flavor, while the sausage provides the spicy seasoning. **ABI**

Disappearance

David Dabydeen

'David Dabydeen's poetry has already demonstrated that he has an original and idiosyncratic voice. His fiction now shows him to be the best of the younger generation of Caribbean novelists, writing powerfully of the immigrant experience.' **Penelope Lively**

Disappearance

"I think there was a belief that if you went to England and worked, you could become wealthy." David Dabydeen

⊙ Chris Shamwana designed the jacket for Dabydeen's novel, which reflects his experience as a Guyanese living in Britain.

Lifespan | *b.* 1955 (Guyana)
First Published | 1993
First Published by | Secker & Warburg (London)
Original Language | English

The narrator, a young Guyanese engineer, is sent to Dunsmere Cliff on the Kent coast to oversee the building of a containing wall to save the village from collapse into the sea. A serious and contemplative man, he boards in the home of a fiery old Englishwoman who is fascinated by Africa, where she had spent many years of her life. As the old woman probes into the narrator's African ancestry, the question at the heart of the novel, whether one can ever "get rid of the past," begins to trouble the narrator. He begins to understand the nature of the village, discovering that under its apparent Englishness is a latent violence that connects it to its imperial past. What results is a powerful meditation on the condition of England, seen as a land of monuments and national narratives that serve finally to mark what has disappeared, or what was never really properly acknowledged: the imperial encounters, the violence that created great civic works, and the deaths of slaves.

A novel employing epigraphs from both the philosopher Jacques Derrida and former prime minister Margaret Thatcher ought perhaps to demand one's attention for this reason alone. But it is the way in which Dabydeen incorporates the theoretical idea that absences articulate more than presences into the fabric of recent British national sentiments that gives this short novel a seriousness and resonance that transcends its lightness of touch. **ABi**

On Love

Alain de Botton

Lifespan | *b.* 1969 (Switzerland)
First Published | 1993
First Published by | Macmillan (London)
Alternate Title | *Essays in Love*

As its title suggests, *On Love* is in the same genre of philosophical essay that received its fullest expression in the work of Michel de Montaigne. But it is also a thoroughly modern love story.

This skillful combination of the intellectual and the emotional, the philosophical and the novelistic, makes *On Love* a delightful and original work. With references to Wilde, Heidegger, Hegel, Marx, Nietzsche, Kant, Wittgenstein, Plato, Mill, Heraclitus, Freud, and Flaubert, among others, *On Love* is unashamedly intellectual. But its narrator uses erudition in order to reflect with wit and insight upon the universal experiences of falling in and out of love: that feeling when we first fall in love that we were meant to be together; the way we idealize the beloved; the subtext of seduction; the lack of authenticity involved in wanting to be whoever you think your beloved wants you to be; the disjunction between mind and body when making love; the insecurity of the lover when the beloved eventually returns their affection; and the way in which being a lover reaffirms everything about oneself and is in fact the mirror in which one sees oneself. The novel's philosophical reflections are interwoven with the story of the narrator's love affair with a woman called Chloë, who he meets on a Paris–London flight. This is not a novel for the incurably romantic, but it is a sharp and sustained dissection of love that also achieves the irresistible seduction of a well-told love story. **SD**

"It is one of the ironies of love that it is easiest confidently to seduce those who we are least attracted to."

⊙ Alain de Botton's philosophical novel is known as *On Love* in the U.S. and as *Essays in Love* in the U.K.

Captain Corelli's Mandolin

Louis de Bernières

Lifespan | *b.* 1954 (England)
First Published | 1994
First Published by | Secker & Warburg (London)
Commonwealth Writers Prize | 1995

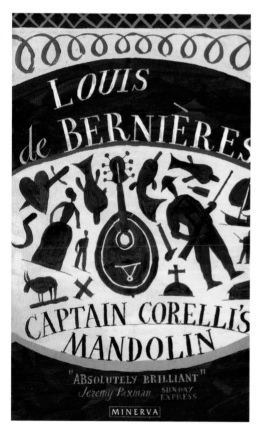

Louis de Bernières writes in the great tradition of Gabriel García Márquez—vast, sprawling narratives that take in a whole world, that evoke and depict a community and the interrelatedness of its inhabitants from the birth to the death of its most long-lived members. Such a technique creates novels of remarkable depth, breadth, and humor.

The main narrative of *Captain Corelli's Mandolin* focuses on Pelagia and her father Dr. Iannis, two inhabitants of the beautiful Greek island of Cephallonia. Against the backdrop of the Second World War and the Italian and German occupation of the island, the novel traces the love that develops between Pelagia and a musically gifted Italian soldier, Captain Corelli. The novel is inhabited by a multiplicity of other characters and its seventy-three sections are narrated from multiple perspectives, ranging from omniscient narrative to secret letters, from the historical writings of Iannis to the imagined megalomaniacal ravings of Mussolini. With its combination of all these narratives—at once beautiful, funny, sad, horrific, and, above all, human—the novel can, at first, seem a little disjunctive and alienating. However, as its momentum builds, the reader is caught up in a multifaceted narrative that testifies with sagacity and humor to the way in which the lives of disparate individuals are at the same time infinitely separate and yet also intimately linked. Despite the wealth of historical description, the novel is not intended to be a textbook of world events against which personal stories are set. Rather, the novel eschews the pretence to objectivity of official history and, more effectively than any textbook, evokes the horror, pain, and strange small miracles that happen during war to "the little people who are caught up in it." **SD**

Captain Corelli's Mandolin achieved major bestseller status only gradually, as news of its readability spread by word of mouth.

How Late It Was, How Late

James Kelman

How Late It Was, How Late is a novel of existential alienation. Awarded the 1994 Booker Prize for fiction, the resulting public consternation culminated in the charge of "literary vandalism" by the editor of *The Times*. Consequently the novel became more famous for its "bad" language than its remarkable innovations in form and style.

Told from the viewpoint of an unemployed Glasgow man, this is the story of Sammy Samuels, who wakes up blind after a police beating. Thereafter he struggles to navigate the labyrinthine city and welfare state as he attempts to claim benefit for his "dysfunction," all the while meditating on his predicament. The Kafkaesque sensibility of the book conjures up a shadowy establishment arbitrarily wielding an oppressive authority. For Kelman, however, the instrument of this horror is language itself, and he rids his novel of a traditional English narrative framework to let Sammy speak for himself in the Glaswegian vernacular. In a further liberating move, the text slips back and forth between the first- and third-person narrative voice, effacing the boundary between narrator and character and eliminating this traditional linguistic hierarchy. Sammy becomes narrator and narrated, subject and object, an unstable identity that signals a crisis in Sammy's sense of self, a sense of alienation that is amplified by the repetition of words, actions, and events. Sammy is thus trapped in the present moment—a moment stripped of meaning, direction, and opportunity for action. In the postindustrial Scottish context this predicament points to a particularly masculine crisis. However, the dehumanizing forces of society are resisted here with enormous emotional complexity, intellectual insight, and disarming humor. **CJ**

Lifespan | *b.* 1946 (Scotland)
First Published | 1994
First Published by | Secker & Warburg (London)
Booker Prize | 1994

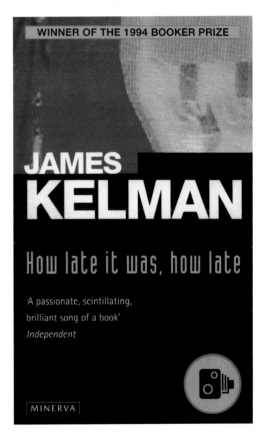

WINNER OF THE 1994 BOOKER PRIZE

JAMES KELMAN

How late it was, how late

'A passionate, scintillating, brilliant song of a book'
Independent

MINERVA

Despite his humor and imaginative verve, Kelman alienated mainstream readers with an insistent use of "bad" language.

City Sister Silver

Jáchym Topol

Lifespan | *b.* 1962 (Czechoslovakia)
First Published | 1994
First Published by | Atlantis (Brno)
Original Title | *Sestra (Sister)*

"We were the People of the Secret. And we were waiting."

🔼 A subversive poet and songwriter in the last years of communist rule, Topol is now seen as an intriguing young Czech novelist.

Jáchym Topol is undoubtedly one of the bravest and most vibrant Czech voices to emerge since the Velvet Revolution in 1989. Son of the playwright Josef Topol and brother of Filip (the frontman for the rock band Psí vojáci), Topol was the youngest signatory of the dissident initiative Charter 77 and has been involved in the artistic and political underground for his entire adult life. *City Sister Silver* is perhaps the only literary work to give the postrevolutionary period a sustained treatment. It is also one of the first works to explore the literary potential of colloquial Czech—reveling in the slang and profanities of a language often suppressed by decades of occupation. In many ways, *City Sister Silver* can be read as a declaration of independence for the modern Czech imagination.

The novel begins at the early stages of the Revolution with an account of the flight of East German refugees from Prague and establishes its primary narrator—an alienated, poetic soul named Potok who falls in with a crew of semi-criminals who are looking for business opportunities amid the chaotic energy of the new era. From this point on, however, time "explodes." *City Sister Silver* is a fantastical trip through European history, veering drunkenly between passages of clipped social realism, news events, madcap dream sequences, and esoteric mythology. It is a difficult experience for a reader unfamiliar with Czech culture, but one that reflects the acute uncertainties—moral, social, political, economic, linguistic, religious—of the post-revolutionary moment. Running parallel to the drift and flux, however, is a moving love story as Potok searches for, and eventually finds, his "sister," or soul mate. This is a beautiful, bewildering, and consistently inventive work. **SamT**

Pereira Declares: A Testimony

Antonio Tabucchi

The story is recounted to the narrator—as we are reminded by the phrase "declares Pereira" ritually introducing each chapter—by Pereira, the editor of the cultural page of the *Lisboa* newspaper. Tabucchi's love for Portugal is tangible in the novel's descriptions of Lisbon glittering under the sun or shivering under the ocean breeze. It is the summer of 1938 and, while dictatorships in the rest of Europe are already strongly established, Portugal is still witnessing the early manifestations of Salazar's regime. *Pereira Declares* is a story about the power of words and how they can make people politically and ethically responsible. At the opening, Pereira is a rather heavy, inward looking widower who converses depressingly with a photograph of his dead wife. Untouched by the erosion of democracy and the violent silencing of protest under Salazar's dictatorship, Pereira is divided between his worries about his heart condition and his intellectual concerns about death. From the beginning, the smell of death permeates the novel. When Pereira discovers a philosophical essay on the topic by the young revolutionary Monteiro Rossi, Pereira is awakened to echoes of the collective extermination of Jews and the beating of workers. The violent murder of Monteiro at the hands of Salazar's police convinces Pereira to take a political stance.

Death is a political metaphor for the absence of freedom. Symbolically, out of death comes life and Pereira's decision to fight for it. The novel closes on a transformed Pereira, feeling younger and lighter and committed to fight political repression with the use of words. Before fleeing Portugal, his last piece in *Lisboa* is not just another timid book review but a fearless accusation of government responsibility for the death of his friend Monteiro. **RPi**

Lifespan | *b.* 1943 (Italy), *d.* 2012 (Portugal)
First Published | 1994, by Feltrinelli (Milan)
Original Title | *Sostiene Pereira: una testimonianza*
Campiello Prize | 1994

"But he, Pereira, was meditating on death."

Italian author Tabucchi is a professor of Portuguese literature and has spent much of his life in Lisbon, the setting of this novel.

The Wind-Up Bird Chronicle

Haruki Murakami

Lifespan | b. 1949 (Japan)
First Published | 1994
First Published by | Shinchosa (Tokyo)
Original Title | Nejimaki-dori kuronikuru

The narrator of *The Wind-Up Bird Chronicle*, Haruki Murakami's heftiest novel, has recently quit his job. Toru Okada spends his days at home in a Tokyo suburb, while his wife goes out to work. Then a series of strange events disrupts his life: the cat goes missing, he receives sinister erotic phone calls from a woman he does not know, and he inherits an empty box from an old fortune-teller. Then, one day, his wife does not come home.

The novel takes on the form of an ambiguous quest, with many intriguing clues. Okada meets a teenage girl who, like him, does not have much to do all day. A platonic friendship develops. She points him in the direction of a garden with a dried-up well in it. An old soldier tells him a story of how, during the war, he spent several days at the bottom of a well in Mongolia. Okada takes to meditating in the well in the garden, where the borders between alternative realities become porous.

"Most Japanese novelists," Murakami has said, "are addicted to the beauty of the language. I'd like to change that. . . . Language is . . . an instrument to communicate." His flat style is more remarkable in Japanese, because the flatness itself is more striking, but it lends itself well to translation. **TEJ**

⊙ Murakami's Japan is the everyday contemporary urban world, but strangely penetrated by mysteries and historical reflections.

Our Lady of the Assassins

Fernando Vallejo

Lifespan | b. 1942 (Colombia)
First Published | 1994
First Published by | Alfaguara (Bogotá)
Original Title | La virgen de los sicarios

After thirty years abroad, Fernando, writer and grammarian, returns to Medellín, a city that has been degraded by violence. There he falls in love with Alexis, one of the young hit men who are risky sexual playthings to be found at the parties of the cynical well-to-do. The wearied, misanthropic Pygmalion finds a terrifying yet fascinating purity in the murderous child. He travels the city with him and realizes that the dead mark the route—because Alexis has resolved every conflict with bullets.

Fernando Vallejo has written some of the most brilliant prose of recent times, in all registers, from Catholic liturgy to the most brutal narco-murderous slang and grotesque, irrational horror. Yet shooting a wounded dog is the only crime and the only act of piety that he will admit to. When the end comes, Alexis dies protecting Fernando, who is desolated. However, he takes little time in replacing his lover with Wilmar, without knowing that it was he who killed Alexis. When he discovers this, and before discovering what it might do to their relationship, Wilmar, too, is killed by anonymous bullets.

This monologue of love, death, and scorn for the world is explicitly aimed at a polymorphous destination, an ignorant foreigner in hell, a necessary counterpoint to justify the ironic didacticism of the narrator. The book reveals one of the most powerful voices of Spanish-American fiction today. **DMG**

Land

Park Kyong-ni

Lifespan | *b.* 1926 (South Korea)
First Published | 1969–1994
First UK Edition | 2002, by Kegan Paul (London)
Original Title | *Toji*

This five-part saga relates the tragic story of four generations of the Choi family of rich landowners—from 1897 to Korea's liberation from Japan in 1945—revealing in the process many little-understood aspects of Korean life and history.

In Part 1 (1897–1908), Park describes the collapse of the Choi family and the seizing of their property by Cho Joon-ku, a remote relative. Also covered is the childhood of Seo-hee, a daughter of the family, who eventually travels to Jendao in Jilin Province, China, with some villagers who hate Cho Joon-ku. Part 2 (1911–1917) is concerned with Seo-hee's life and success in Jendao. Seo-hee marries Gilsang, a former servant of the Choi family, before returning home. The reader is introduced to the Korean independence movement, and conflicts in the expatriate Korean community are exposed. In Part 3 (1919–1929), Seo-hee succeeds in driving out Cho Joon-ku. Meanwhile, the narrative touches on the predominant issues and difficulties of Korean intellectuals under Japanese colonial rule.

In Part 4 (1930–1939), as Seo-hee's sons, Hwan-kuk and Yoon-kuk, grow up, Park delves deeper into Korean history, culture, and art. She explores how Korea evolved greater self-knowledge as Japanese oppression resulted in growing disorder in Korean society. Part 5 (1940–1945) is focused on the Koreans who sought liberation. It climaxes with the news of Japan's surrender, when Seo-hee feels as if a heavy iron chain on herself has finally been removed. **Hoy**

Whatever

Michel Houellebecq

Lifespan | *b.* 1958 (Réunion)
First Published | 1994, by M. Nadeau (Paris)
Given Name | Michel Thomas
Original Title | *Extension du domaine de la lutte*

Whatever is a study in contemporary alienation. In straightforward, almost journalistic prose, the first-person narration documents the lonely life of a computer engineer. He is well-off, but finds no satisfaction in his job or any of the products that it allows him to buy. He manages to do a passable imitation of a functioning individual, but is unable to form attachments to either things or people.

The original French title, which translates as "Extension of the Domain of the Struggle," provides an insight into the novel's main theme. The insidious advance of capitalist values has infiltrated every aspect of our lives. Even the realms of love and sex are subject to the same forces of competition and exchange as the marketplace. This creates a sexual underclass, represented in the novel by the narrator and his ugly colleague Tisserand, still a virgin at age twenty-eight, although not through want of trying. Drunk, bored, and on the verge of a breakdown, the narrator tries halfheartedly to talk Tisserand into murdering the latest in a long line of women who have turned him down, as if to redress the imbalance he perceives in the sexual economy.

Michel Houellebecq's approach adopts a highly deterministic outlook, where one is merely the sum of the quality of one's genetic inheritance and the strength of one's socio-economic position. This view of contemporary European society may be what makes Houellebecq one of the most popular and influential novelists currently writing. **SS**

Troubling Love

Elena Ferrante

Lifespan | *b.* undisclosed (Italy)
First Published | 1995
First Published by | Edizioni e/o (Rome)
Original Title | *L'amore molesto*

Narrated in a deeply observed, excruciatingly blunt style, this story is set in a beguiling but often hostile Naples, whose chaotic, suffocating streets become one of the book's central motifs. After her mother's untimely and mysterious death, Dalia, an illustrator originally from Naples who has lived in Bologna for years, returns to her native city. Dalia cannot believe that her mother, who she remembers as a positive, exuberant woman, might have committed suicide. Searching for the truth about her mother also inevitably becomes a search for the truth about her family and herself, and the knot of lies and emotions that has bound them together.

A reconstruction of her mother's last days sheds light on willfully-forgotten events from Dahlia's own life, forcing her to reinterpret her past. In a raging, tormented narrative voice, she remembers how her relationship with her mother collapsed after her aggressive, possessive father accused her of having an extramarital affair. Dalia, however, is not ready to face the whole truth about her mother and herself. For this reason, when the mystery of her mother's final days is about to be resolved, Dalia decides to return to Bologna, leaving Naples—its streets and its unbearable knots of lies and truths—behind.

Ferrante's novel has been widely acclaimed for the way it combines a psychologically subtle and effective use of simple language, an insightful prose, and lucid analysis of a mother–daughter relationship in contemporary Italian society. **LB**

The Late-Night News

Petros Markaris

Lifespan | *b.* 1937 (Turkey)
First Published | 1995
First Published by | Gabrielides (Athens)
Original Title | *Nychterino deltio*

The Late-Night News is the first book in Petros Markaris's series of mysteries featuring Athenian police inspector Costas Haritos. An apparently simple crime of passion in the Albanian immigrant community of Athens becomes much more high-profile when celebrated TV journalist Yanna Karayoryi takes an interest. When Yanna is murdered moments before making an on-air revelation about the case, Inspector Haritos embarks on a complex investigation that leads ultimately to the discovery of an international network of child traffickers.

Although Haritos, as narrator, is not a likeable character, the reader begins to sympathize with his aggressive and pessimistic outlook. He has reached age fifty and dramatic changes in his world have left him uneasy and cynical. He knew where he was when Greece was still a military dictatorship, and before his daughter left home. Now Haritos is passed over for promotion because he does not know how to operate in the complex world of democratic Greece. At home, he has an uncomfortable relationship with his wife; now that they are alone, they no longer know how to relate to each other.

In this winding and sometimes over-complex narrative, Markaris gives the reader a broad look at contemporary Greek society, ranging in scope from the sexual politics of Haritos's relationship with his wife and daughter to Athenian traffic congestion, and from the corruption of Greek politics old and new to the legacy of the fall of communism. **CIW**

The End of the Story

Lydia Davis

Lifespan | *b.* 1947 (U.S.)
First Published | 1995
First Published by | Farrar, Straus & Giroux (New York)
First UK Edition | 1996, by High Risk (London)

True to its title, *The End of the Story* begins at the end of the love affair at its heart. Flashing forward a year, the nameless narrator, a writer and university teacher, goes on to tell us of her failed attempts to find "him" (also nameless) in a strange city. Tracing him to his last known address, she finds unfamiliar names above the doorbell. With more than a nod to Proust (of whom Davis is a distinguished translator), the narrator spends the novel ringing the doorbell of the past in the vain hope of finding truth on the other side. The hope is all the more urgent in that she is writing a novel about the affair, the very novel we are reading (or is it?).

Like many contemporary novels, *The End of the Story* is in large part about itself, about the painful process of its own making. Yet it is not a novel seeking to subvert conventional modes of storytelling from some self-conscious and superior ironic perspective. Rather, it is about the strange paradox under which all writers (and indeed non-writers) labor, namely that the very attempt to clarify our experience can end up obscuring it. Thus, the narrator starts to doubt the apparent solidity of her memory—did she really fall in love by candlelight? Indeed, was that really what she was feeling?

The crystalline simplicity and precision of Davis's prose only intensifies this sense of the profound elusiveness of life and love. We can tell our stories, her novel painstakingly shows us, only after they happen—that is, after they are lost to us. **JC**

Love's Work

Gillian Rose

Lifespan | *b.* 1947 (England), *d.* 1995
First Published | 1995
First Published by | Chatto & Windus (London)
Full Title | *Love's Work: A Reckoning With Life*

Sigmund Freud described love and work as the foundations of human happiness. The philosopher and social theorist Gillian Rose's autobiographical text, *Love's Work*, intertwines them in order to explore the love of work (the work of thought, of philosophy) and the work, and workings, of love. The book opens with Rose's first meeting with Edna, a New Yorker in her nineties, who has lived with cancer since the age of sixteen. *Love's Work* thus begins with an exploration of the meanings of survival and the necessity of living "skeptically." Contradiction, difference, and the ways in which we negotiate them are at the heart of the book and are strongly figured for Rose in the relationship between Protestantism and Judaism (her family's religion), the appeal to "inwardness" or to a law that compels obedience but not belief. This is a story about "education," but one in which the meanings of this term are continually tested.

It is not until several chapters into the book that Rose reveals to the reader that, as she writes, she has advanced cancer. She has already described the destruction wrought by an unhappy love affair, which has to be embraced in order that "I may have a chance of surviving . . . I hear the roaring and the roasting and know that it is I." The reader, confronted with his or her own preconceptions of the disease, is challenged to think in new ways about living and dying, the comedy of life and the tragedy of philosophy, and their ultimate inseparability. **LM**

A Fine Balance

Rohinton Mistry

Lifespan | *b.* 1952 (India)
First Published | 1995
First Published by | McClelland & Stewart (Toronto)
Commonwealth Writers Prize | 1996

Rohinton Mistry's *A Fine Balance* is set in India in the mid-1970s. Two tailors, Ishvar and his nephew Omprakash, leave their small village under tragic circumstances to work in the city. Their employer is the widowed Dina Dalal, who is also supplying accommodation for her friends' student son, Manek. These four lives become intertwined and tremulous friendships are made amid the chaos of Indian life under the State of Emergency, declared in 1975.

The epic scale of the novel confronts the ruthless brutality of class and caste as the protagonists are left vulnerable to the vagaries of poverty and discrimination. This is a historical novel, which meticulously recreates Indira Gandhi's India, and the author uses this context to present a paradoxically humane vision of inhumanity.

Rigorously unsentimental and full of black humor, *A Fine Balance* takes the reader through a vicious and sometimes carnivalesque world of poverty and utter powerlessness. The novel's harrowing denouement is as shocking and as distressing as anything in twentieth-century literature. Perhaps Mistry's greatest achievement is his clear-sighted depiction of relentless, impersonal brutality. What we are given is a heartbreaking story of lives torn apart not by individual weakness but by institutional inequity and the horrors of corrupt power. This is a beautiful and devastating novel whose genius lies in its refusal to allow the reader to escape to either pathos or cynicism. **PMcM**

"Dina pretended to be upset, saying he had never praised her meals with superlatives. He tried to wriggle out of it."

Rohinton Mistry has lived in Canada since 1975, but his novels and short stories have been set in India, the country of his birth.

The Reader

Bernhard Schlink

Lifespan | *b.* 1944 (Germany)
First Published | 1995
First Published by | Diogenes (Zürich)
Original Title | *Der Vorleser*

Falling ill on his way home from school, fifteen-year-old Michael Berg is rescued by Hanna Schmitz, a streetcar conductor twice his age. When he returns later to thank her, a passionate and volatile relationship ensues. Torn between his youth and his desire for Hanna, Michael is nonetheless devastated when she mysteriously disappears. While the affair is short-lived, the experience fundamentally affects the way in which he shapes his own identity. Subsequently, Michael's sense of self is shattered when he encounters Hanna, years later, on trial for Nazi war crimes. As he watches her refuse to defend herself, he slowly realizes that she is hiding a secret she considers more humiliating than murder. Simultaneously a student of law and her former lover, Michael must attempt to reconcile the horrendous crimes of which she is accused with the memory of the woman he loved. After Hanna dies years after she and Michael renew their acquaintance, he visits an elderly Jewish woman who had been one of the prisoners guarded by Hanna during the war. Hanna has asked Michael to give this woman all of her savings but the woman refuses the money, unwilling to "sell" Hanna her forgiveness.

Bernhard Schlink, himself a professor of law and a practicing judge, grapples with the complex ethical questions that inevitably emerge after the horror of genocide. But instead of concentrating on its victims, Schlink shifts his focus to the inheritors of the Nazi legacy. *The Reader* asks its readers to consider to what extent we can hold the postwar generation responsible for the sins of its fathers and mothers, and if such atrocities can even be redressed. Does the demonization of the Nazis serve to chastise their behavior, or is it a selfish measure to create a false division between them and us? **BJ**

◉ Schlink was already well known in Germany as a writer of popular crime fiction before he published *The Reader*.

Santa Evita

Tomás Eloy Martínez

Santa Evita is the story of the investigation into what happened to the body of the legendary Argentine First Lady Eva Perón (1919–52) in the years following her death. Embalmed immediately after passing away (at the age of thirty-three from what was later disclosed to be cervical cancer), the relic leaves Argentina when the widowed leader is exiled in 1955, and becomes a strange and embarrassing phenomenon for the new regime. Kidnapped, multiplied by a number of accurate wax replicas, sent to Europe, later recovered and returned to the country, its posthumous history is confused and elusive. The peregrinations of the corpse as it passes into legend are collected together by a narrator who is explicitly identified with the author, the body's final guardian, a prisoner of the same curse that emanates from this deceased woman.

Combining documentary fiction, adventure story, and a heterodox hagiography, the novel is also the work of a writer who wants to exorcise an obsession. Like an embalmer, Tomás Eloy Martínez wants to stop the deterioration of a body and its story. Critical of Argentina as a necrophiliac nation, the story expresses its allegorical range from the very first pages, sometimes by parodic attacks that reveal the fragile boundary that exists between fiction and reality. The writing does not attempt to conceal the ways in which the transcription of interviews, or the quotations and commentary of fictional and historical sources, is inevitably affected by manipulation. Experimenting with various means of textual representation (such as scripts, conversations, and letters), and being open about the task of rewriting and creating an impossible ending, the story develops the effigy of a future Eva, uncorrupted and for ever renewed. **DMG**

Lifespan | *b.* 1934 (Argentina)
First Published | 1995
First Published by | Planeta (Buenos Aires)
First U.S. Edition| 1996, by Alfred A. Knopf (New York)

A journalist and academic as well as a novelist, Martínez is fascinated by power politics and by Argentina's recent history.

Morvern Callar

Alan Warner

Lifespan | *b.* 1964 (Scotland)
First Published | 1995
First Published by | Jonathan Cape (London)
First U.S. Edition | 1997, by Anchor (New York)

It is just before Christmas, and there is something lying on the kitchen floor that Morvern Callar is putting off dealing with—the dead body of her boyfriend. Her first reaction is, understandably, to consider ringing for an ambulance, but she smokes a Silk Cut (the first of many), turns away from "His" body, and leaves for a night of untroubled alcoholic, narcotic, and sexual excess. This, it turns out, is to be expected from our heroine. As the reader is drawn into the fallout from this suicide and Morvern's complex reactions to it, we encounter a brilliantly eccentric succession of West Highland misfits debauched in their apathy, and "the Port," a dreamlike town on the coast where they are all marooned.

Yet this is definitively Morvern's novel, and—just as in Lynne Ramsay's recent film adaptation—it is her dispassionate voice and her eclectic music tastes that dominate. Warner does not pretend to offer insights into Morvern's soul, but she is governed by her own sense of morality: it is this, in fact, that raises her above the druggies, townies, and no-hopers she encounters on her travels. She simply and genuinely adapts to situations as they arise; she takes advantage of circumstances; ultimately she gains a different perspective upon her life and those around her as a result. Taking in the unrepentant hedonism of rave culture of the early nineties, Club Med holidays, and British tourism, this was a defining text for a generation. This powerful and original voice remains unsurprisingly vital. **MD**

The Unconsoled

Kazuo Ishiguro

Lifespan | *b.* 1954 (Japan)
First Published | 1995
First Published by | Faber & Faber (London)
Original Language | English

Few readers will know a book as mesmerizing as Kazuo Ishiguro's unique *The Unconsoled*. The text is oriented around (if it can be said to be oriented at all) the uncanny sense that we as readers, and Ryder the narrator, have somehow been here before. The novel opens with Ryder entering a hotel in an unnamed Central European city for a performance at the Civic Concert Hall, probably the most important concert of his life. Ryder is confident in the knowledge that he is the greatest pianist of his generation, but he suffers from severe and disorienting bouts of amnesia.

The music-obsessed city in which he finds himself is as much a city of the mind as a physical space: as he wanders the streets, he encounters people he knows intimately, and people similarly seem to know him. His past continually intrudes on the present, and with deft surrealist touches Ishiguro allows the fictional world of the novel to overflow its bounds. Space becomes compressed and expanded, time loses meaning, and Ryder finds himself entangled in a situation where he only knows that he has the solution, although what that answer is, he has no idea. The narrative plays tricks with Ryder and with the reader, combining his limited sense of his own past and events around him with a prescient third-person narrative that allows him apparently impossible insights. A virtuoso performance, this thrillingly original text demands engagement from its readers and is a richly rewarding experience. **MD**

Alias Grace

Margaret Atwood

Lifespan | *b.* 1939 (Canada)
First Published | 1996
First Published by | McClelland & Stewart (Toronto)
Giller Prize | 1996

Alias Grace is a lyrical work of historical fiction based around the story of servant girl, Grace Marks, who is one of Canada's most notorious female criminals. Grace tells her story in a vivid, bitter voice, from her childhood in Ireland through life as part of the underclass in colonial Victorian Canada to her conviction for murdering her employer in 1843 at the age of sixteen. The story is told to Dr. Simon Jordan, a mental illness specialist who is engaged by a group of reformers and spiritualists seeking a pardon for the young woman. As he brings Grace closer and closer to the day she cannot remember, he comes to learn about the strained relationship between her employer, James Kinnear, and his housekeeper and mistress, Nancy, and of the alarming behavior of Grace's fellow servant, James McDermott.

As always, Margaret Atwood includes elements of social and feminist comment in her work, exploring the relationships between sex and violence in a historically repressed society. The author also reflects, in people's reactions to Grace, the period's ambiguity about the nature of woman. Some factions of society felt that women were weak and therefore that Grace must have been a victim who was forced into a desperate act. Others believed that women were intrinsically more evil than men. This dichotomy between the demonic and pathetic woman is subtly reflected in the character of Grace who, having spent time in a lunatic asylum, claims to have no memory at all of the murders. **EF**

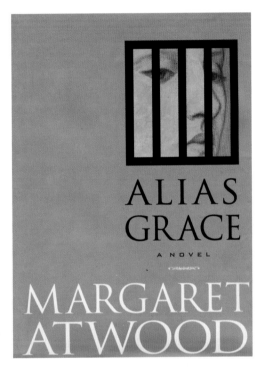

"It's 1851. I'll be twenty-four years old next birthday. I've been shut up in here since the age of sixteen. I am a model prisoner, and give no trouble."

⊙ The design for the jacket of Atwood's novel aptly reflects the themes of imprisonment and the mystery of human motivation.

The Clay Machine-Gun

Victor Pelevin

Lifespan | *b.* 1962 (Russia)
First Published | 1996
First Published by | Vagrius (Moscow)
Original Title | *Chapaev i Pustota*

The main character of this novel is Petr, a comrade of Chapayev, a Soviet Civil War hero made famous by a 1930s propaganda movie that spawned a whole series of irreverent "Chapayev jokes." Hard drinking and hard living in the turbulent early 1920s, Petr has recurrent alcohol and cocaine-induced dreams, which, in a reversal of ordinary flashback techniques, take him and the plot to a post-Soviet insane asylum, where the stories of three inmates are revealed during their therapy. Overarching all this is a Buddhist vision centered on Chapayev-turned-spiritual teacher, which explores the meaning and dissolution of reality.

The Clay Machine-Gun weaves together its various strands and characters in a way that is nothing less than random. Its language and motives, taken variously from post-Soviet daily life, outdated ideology, history, literature, Zen philosophy, and pop culture, may seem incongruent. Yet they all form part of a plot constructed with the absurd stringency of a children's play, where there can be no loose ends left untied, and every element must be connected into a tapestry of the strange, the exaggerated, and the delusional, creating the impression of some larger meaning. The charm of Victor Pelevin's book is the playful way in which it denies yet enjoys meaning, and the sheer joy of invention it exudes. It is a bit like one very long, very complex, and, above all, very good joke; and, like all good jokes, it has a great deal to say about the "real world." **DG**

Infinite Jest

David Foster Wallace

Lifespan | *b.* 1962 (U.S.), *d.* 2008
First Published | 1996
First Published by | Little, Brown & Co. (Boston)
First UK Edition | 1997, by Abacus (London)

Where does one begin with a book of over a thousand pages, of which the last ninety-six feature three hundred and eighty-eight detailed (but also wildly funny) footnotes? A plot synopsis is sadly doomed to inadequacy. Set in the near future, *Infinite Jest* is the title of a film made by the maverick avant-garde filmmaker James O. Incandenza, which is apparently so funny that the viewer ultimately expires in a state of uncontrollable hilarity. When both film and filmmaker disappear, all manner of sinister individuals, government agencies, and foreign governments attempt to track them down, and the ensuing chaos incorporates the recovering addicts of Ennet House (a Boston dependency clinic), and the Enfield Tennis Academy. These last two locations provide two opposing points of focus for the text. One allows Wallace to explore the centrality of addiction to consumer culture and the place of narcotics within that culture. The other is an extraordinary vision of a hothouse sporting school, which produces children for an industry that will disregard most of them.

Infinite Jest satirically attacks the vacuous predilections of contemporary American culture mercilessly, while shamelessly reveling in them. Wildly inventive, linguistically original, extravagantly detailed, and playful, this text is the one you would take with you to a desert island. **MD**

◉ Wallace's zany satire and fascination with conspiracy places him in the same modern American tradition as DeLillo and Pynchon.

Hallucinating Foucault

Patricia Duncker

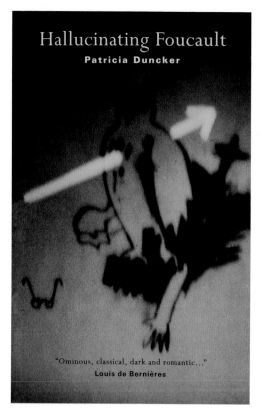

Hallucinating Foucault
Patricia Duncker

"Ominous, classical, dark and romantic..."
Louis de Bernières

Lifespan | *b.* 1951 (Jamaica)
First Published | 1996
First Published by | Serpent's Tail (London)
First U.S. Edition | Ecco Press (Hopewell)

Hallucinating Foucault is a dark and tragic novel. It is also beautiful, romantic, and funny. Like its characters, it is a deeply idiosyncratic work that is both disturbing and seductive. While negotiating themes of death, sexuality, crime, and madness, this novel is in fact primarily about love—for both books and people. It is about the surreal disjunction between an author and his work, and the madness of the reader, who loves the book and its creator at the same time and yet distinctly.

In a first-person retrospective narrative, the novel tells the story of a young student writing his doctoral thesis on the works of a (fictional) gay French novelist, Paul Michel. Early in his research, the narrator is drawn into a love affair with a captivating Germanist, who compels the narrator to travel to France to seek out Michel; the novelist has been incarcerated in psychiatric institutions since his violent bout of madness following Michel Foucault's death in June 1984. In making the journey, the narrator embarks on a love affair that will change his life, if not his work, forever.

A masterfully told story, *Hallucinating Foucault* leaves its own readers with that profound sense of loss felt when the final lines of a book signal ejection from a world that has both captivated and contained them. Reading Duncker's first novel, a tale of the kind of love that can exist between reader and author, cannot be anything but the beginning of a personal love affair with her work. **SD**

> *"The love between writer and a reader is never celebrated. It can never be proved to exist."*

◉ Patricia Duncker's debut novel tells the story of a French novelist who is so devastated by Foucault's death that he goes insane.

Fugitive Pieces

Anne Michaels

Lifespan | *b.* 1958 (Canada)
First Published | 1996
First Published by | McClelland & Stewart (Toronto)
Orange Prize | 1997

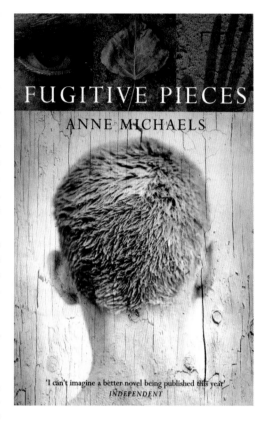

Winner of several prestigious awards and critically acclaimed, *Fugitive Pieces* recounts the life of a Jewish boy, Jakob, rescued from a Polish city during the Holocaust and taken by Athos, a Greek scholar, to the island of Zakynthos. In a hilltop refuge, surrounded by botany, geological artifacts, and classic poetry, Jakob soaks up knowledge while he grieves for his murdered parents and lost sister.

From the start, this is a novel with a difference. Written by an already successful poet, the prose is richly textured, resonant, and rhythmic. Michaels employs the vocabularies of archaeology, geology, and literature to build a unique sense of personal and political history, as we witness the developing relationship between Jakob and his savior. We follow the journey of Athos and Jakob to a Canada imbued with a new sense of its immigrant population. Still haunted by the death of his family, Jakob continues the literary career encouraged in him by Athos. The key to Jakob's redemption comes through his poetry and the late awakening of the sensual possibilities of his own body. In the last section of the novel, the repercussions of the emotional traumas that Jakob has absorbed throughout his life are shown by their redemptive effects on a reader of his poetry. Michaels presents the interlocking of lives across cultures through the passing on of a written knowledge that has the power to heal. She does not balk from the complex notion that beauty applies equally to devastation and to love. **AC**

"Grief requires time. If a chip of stone radiates its self, its breath, so long, how stubborn might be the soul."

⊙ The cover of the Bloomsbury edition of *Fugitive Pieces* underlines the imaginative quality of the book, a poet's first novel.

Forever a Stranger

Hella Haasse

Lifespan | *b.* 1918 (Java)
First Published | 1996, by Oxford University Press
Originally Published by | Collectieve Propaganda
voor het Nederlandse Boek, in 1948 (as *Oeroeg*)

Hella Haasse is one of the Netherlands's most esteemed, venerable, and prolific authors, although English-language translations of her works have been mysteriously slow to arrive. *Forever a Stranger* was her first prose work, written at the age of thirty, and it made her name. Written as the deeply controversial Dutch military operations against the Indonesian struggle for independence were beginning, this spare and incisive ninety-page story of friendship between a Dutch boy and an Indonesian boy is at once a moving and engaging narrative, a telling historical fable, and a treatise on "irrevocable, incomprehensible differentness."

The original Dutch title was *Oeroeg*, after the Indonesian boy with whom the (unnamed) Dutch narrator is friends. The story covers their inseparable childhood, through to an adolescence of increasing alienation and displacement governed by the immovable judgement: "Some day you'll have to live without Oeroeg. . . . You're European!" The implications of this difference are followed through to the final confrontation: "Am I forever to be a stranger in the land of my birth?"

Forever a Stranger and Other Stories is tellingly aware of the ways that language, personal identities, and national destinies intersect, and are at odds. Although the finer points of these qualities were lost in *Oeroeg*'s translation to the big screen (*Going Home,* 1993), the continuing power Haasse's tale has over Dutch culture is evident. **MS**

A Light Comedy

Eduardo Mendoza

Lifespan | *b.* 1943 (Spain)
First Published | 1996
First Published by | Seix-Barral (Barcelona)
Original Title | *Una comedia ligera*

Ten years after his *The City of the Prodigies*, Eduardo Mendoza returns to the novel of large scale and multiple personalities with his typical mature, light, invisible irony. Mendoza acts, thinks, and suffers with his characters as if he were living in something like a dramatic muddle, perhaps a light comedy that ends up being torn apart by a murderer. The thriller-like detective story is secondary because it is mainly introduced to shake up certainties and to convey the atmosphere of the end of an era. The novel crosses the city of Barcelona from place to place and the combination of both the coarse surroundings and the sophistication of the bourgeois at leisure create a rich parody of mid twentieth-century Barcelona society, with its police, Falangist leaders, black marketeers, and dimwits of good family.

The delicate comedies of protagonist Carlos Prullàs, with their word-games and theatrical contrivances, seem like something for another audience and another period, while the new times demand, as his good friend Gaudet declares, a different theater "of social realism and the avant-garde." Without knowing it, the world of the theater embodies the imminent shake-up that will define the future. It also reveals the end of an era and the impossibility of Prullàs being able to adapt: "Everything was ready to change radically in society." An irreversible change in his life waits to cast a shadow of melancholy over the hedonism and peace of his soft, leisurely summer days. **JGG**

Fall on Your Knees

Ann-Marie MacDonald

Lifespan | *b.* 1958 (Canada)
First Published | 1996
First Published by | Knopf (Toronto)
Commonwealth Writers' Prize | 1997

Earl Birney, Canada's pioneer of modernist poetry, once famously declared that Canada suffered from a distinct lack of ghosts: "it's only by our lack of ghosts we're haunted." In *Fall on Your Knees*, her first novel, Canadian playwright and actress Ann-Marie MacDonald does much to redress this balance.

Set on Nova Scotia's Cape Breton Island, this is the story of the Piper family, which begins when James Piper, a poor piano tuner of Gaelic origin, elopes with Materia Mahmoud, the daughter of a wealthy Lebanese family. The family's roots are as varied as the forty ethnicities that populate the island, and their isolation as remote as Canada's.

The four Piper daughters delineate the story's central axis of family love. Kathleen, the couple's first-born child, is poised to take her place on the world stage as an opera diva, and provides us with a stark juxtaposition of family love and murder. Her sister Mercedes is the story's saint figure, born to sacrifice herself for others. Frances, the family's self-proclaimed bad girl, is motivated by a fear that she will not be loved by her family, and Lilly, whose story begins before her birth, is the product of the family's dark secret, populating the novel with its ghosts.

This is a disturbing tale of family love and of sin, guilt, and redemption. But it also confronts Canada's inherited blank cultural space through a distinctly Freudian inquisition into the relationship between the familiar and the unfamiliar, through the constant renegotiation of geography and identity. **JSD**

Silk

Alessandro Baricco

Lifespan | *b.* 1958 (Italy)
First Published | 1996
First Published by | Rizzoli (Milan)
Original Title | *Seta*

One day, Hervé Joncour leaves his small town of Lavilledieu and starts regular journeys to Japan in search of silkworm eggs to bring back to Europe, where the silk industry is beginning to thrive. It is 1861, the year, as the author informs us, when Flaubert was writing *Salammbô*, electricity was still only a future project, and on the other side of the ocean, Lincoln was engaged in a Civil War.

Hervé's journeys to Japan are ritualized in their repetitiveness and in the appointments with the unknown characters who provide the Frenchman with eggs in return for gold chips. No dialogue accompanies the repeated gestures, in the same places on the same days of the year. Hervé grows increasingly used to the long silences of the people he meets, witnesses the wars that European countries wage against Japan in the attempt to open the borders of the silk trade, and describes the ensuing consequences of the war with simplicity. But, as impalpable as silk, love embraces Hervé, who exchanges furtive glances with a mysterious Asian woman with Western features, who gives him a secret love message that he will take back to Lavilledieu with his precious load, always on the same day of the same month. Love becomes dream and an urge to explore when Hervé's journeys to Japan end. The memory of his ethereal love and the desire to interpret the message, the only precious token left of the Orient, are a caress for Hervé even when his wife dies. **RPi**

The God of Small Things

Arundhati Roy

Lifespan | *b.* 1961 (India)
First Published | 1997
First Published by | India Ink (New Delhi)
Booker Prize | 1997

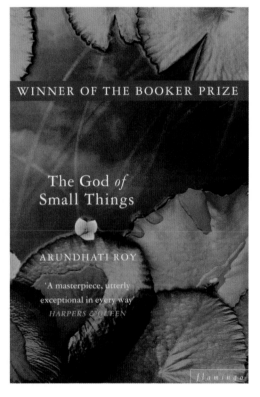

The pivotal point of Roy's novel is a tragic drowning, obliquely suggested in the beautiful but oddly disquieting cover image.

Photographed here in Delhi in 1997, Arundhati Roy has now abandoned writing fiction to devote herself to politicial activism.

Set in Kerala in the 1960s, this Booker Prize winner follows Ammu's family through both ordinary and tragic events, focusing most memorably on her "two-egg twins," Estha and Rahel. The accidental death by drowning of a visiting English cousin is to have a pivotal effect on their young lives. The novel is told in nonlinear time through a jigsaw of vivid encounters and descriptions, recounted in exquisite prose. The reader pieces together a childhood world, interrupted by adult tragedies and the effect these have on Velutha, the twins' boatman friend who belongs to India's "untouchable" caste. Arundhati Roy's style has drawn comparison to Salman Rushdie, yet her prose is distinctly rhythmic and poetic, and the overall effect is unique in its sensuality. A less likely, but perhaps more apt reference point might be E. M. Forster's *A Passage to India*, in the way the strange and lawless beauty of the natural world is evoked as both the counterpoint and the cause of human order and its sometimes brutal interpretations. Roy's strength lies in the quirky clarity with which she renders the mind of the child and the emotional force she creates in the various relationships.

The novel's political concerns revolve around the notion of who decides "who should be loved and how much," with Roy's imaginative transgressions designed not so much to shock as to move the reader. A political figure who championed the cause of the oppressed and spent time in jail in 2002 for opposing the authority of the Indian court, Roy's politics are concerned with the small powers of the human, powers that are shocking in their ability to redeem and destroy. She sacrifices neither structure, complexity, nor beautiful prose to convey her beliefs. This book is a challenge to others who have attempted to tell us what love means. **AC**

Margot and the Angels

Kristien Hemmerechts

Lifespan | *b.* 1955 (Belgium)
First Published | 1997
First Published by | Atlas (Amsterdam)
Original Title | *Margot en de engelen*

◉ The cover of an edition of Hemmerechts's novel stresses the emotional darkness of her story of a young runaway.

◑ Hemmerechts photographed by Marco Okhuizen in 2004: an author who explores desire with humane sympathy.

In an era when many male authors have fallen prey to the seductions of magical realism and ludic Postmodernism, women writers of outstanding talent have continued to remind us of the power of the novel to explore human relationships and emotional life in the context of everyday contemporary reality. Kristien Hemmerechts's work shows just how far such a superficially traditional approach can lead us into innovative territory.

The plot of *Margot and the Angels* is simple enough. Margot is a runaway teenager. She leaves her Dutch home without explanation, asking her parents not to contact her, and ends up in the English port city of Hull. Hemmerechts charts the differing impacts of this decision upon her father and mother, who eventually resolve to search for her. Margot eventually becomes involved with a religious sect, the angels of the title, as the plot evolves to its inexorably grim conclusion.

Working with great economy of style, Hemmerechts strips bare her characters' romanticism and self-delusions. Margot's father, for example, is a man who has always preached the need for people to lead their own lives, but is thrown into emotional torment by his daughter's declaration of independence. The physical desires of the female characters are delineated with startling matter-of-factness, as is the aspiration to escape from the body's clamoring needs.

Hemmerechts's prose exhibits the traditional virtues of balance, control, and clarity, and the framework of her plot is satisfactory carpentry. Yet in her vision of life there is an utter lack of complacency and her insights are full of the unexpected, insistently reshaping our image of how "ordinary" people think, feel, and act. **RegG**

The Life of Insects

Victor Pelevin

Lifespan | b. 1962 (Russia)
First Published | 1997, by Vagrius (Moscow)
First Serialized | 1994, in *Znamya* (Moscow)
Original Title | *Zhizn' Nasekomyk*

This is a bizarre collection of interconnected vignettes about life in a shabby Crimean Black Sea resort, where people change from insects into humans and back in seemingly random mutations. In fact, the oscillation between human and insect does not form part of the narrative, but rather a change of optical apparatus on the part of the narrator. It sometimes takes the reader a while to understand which lens he is looking through at any given moment, and this produces an effect that is both unsettling and amusing.

In using and subverting the fable genre, Pelevin gives us a picture of contemporary Russian society. This ranges from straightforward satire, as in the joint venture negotiations between Russian and American mosquitoes out to make money, to the invention of an entire mythology and world view for dung beetles, to a surprisingly poignant portrayal of an ordinary swarming female ant's inner life. There are plenty of intriguing allusions, double entendres, and incongruous, yet carefully constructed, allegories and metaphors. But there is more to the novel than pure intellectual playfulness, and a concrete and wistful account of the human condition emerges. Somehow, and unaccountably, one puts down this novel convinced of having learned something true about life in post-Soviet Russia. The absurd acquires verisimilitude perhaps because it takes absurdity to break through the opacity of language in describing the world. **DG**

Memoirs of a Geisha

Arthur Golden

Lifespan | | b. 1957 (U.S.)
First Published | 1997
First Published by | | Knopf (New York)
Movie Adaptation | 2005

Written in the first person, Arthur Golden's *Memoirs of a Geisha* traces the fictional story of Nitta Sayuri and how she overcomes her humble fishing village roots to become one of Japan's most celebrated geishas. Chiyo is the stunningly pretty child of impoverished parents who is taken away at the age of nine and sold into the slavery of a geisha house in the Gion district of Kyoto. Renamed Sayuri, she undergoes cruel treatment as she transforms herself into a desirable geisha, skilled in the arts of pouring sake, dancing, singing, and pleasing men.

Through Sayuri's eyes, a secretive, vicious, competitive world is revealed where women are measured by the attention of men, where virginity is auctioned off to the highest bidder, and where there is no such thing as trust or love. But with the Second World War comes the realization that the old Japanese ways are disappearing. By then a well-known geisha, Sayuri is forced to reinvent herself in order to survive.

The book is important for its glimpses into a way of life that has all but disappeared. It also provides a disturbing view of the place of women in Japanese society and culture. Sayuri was respected as a geisha but not as a woman, and it was only through resourcefulness and beauty that she managed to transcend the boundaries of her position. Arthur Golden's novel is also a story about a young girl's survival at the expense of her dreams, and how society's expectations smother love. **EF**

Underworld

Don DeLillo

Lifespan | *b.* 1936 (U.S.)
First Published | 1997
First Published by | Scribner (New York)
First UK Edition | 1998, by Picador (London)

Underworld is a vast, encyclopedic novel, which reaches back from the brink of the twenty-first century to the early 1950s, and to the beginnings of the Cold War. Told as the private story of the central character and sometimes narrator, Nick Shay, as well as the public story of the Cold War, the narrative offers to bring the hidden connections that have driven the second half of the twentieth century into the light.

In a liquid, versatile, and immaculate prose, Don DeLillo's narrative burrows back through the decades, both toward the shrouded space of Nick's personal secret, and toward the unconscious, abject places from which postwar history itself emerges. One of the most remarkable things about this extraordinary, revelatory novel is that its search for a universal voice with which to reveal the secrets of history leads it, repeatedly, to those historical, political, and personal moments that cannot be spoken of, to those secrets that cannot be given away.

Written at the end of a century, and at the end of a millennium, *Underworld* offers a way of understanding our collective past. It excavates the arcane workings of our culture, articulating connections between the overt and the hidden mechanisms of state power. At the same time, its awed intuition of the unseen forces that continue to drive history toward redemption or annihilation looks forward to a new millennium. **PB**

"If you know you're worth nothing, only a gamble with death can gratify your vanity."

⊕ DeLillo is fascinated by the underside of events—he wrote that "history is the sum total of all the things they aren't telling us."

Crossfire

Miyabe Miyuki

Lifespan | *b.* 1960 (Japan)
First Published | 1998
First Published by | Kobunsha (Tokyo)
Original Title | *Kurosufaia*

"Reaching out to touch it, the water was cold. And black, like night."

⊙ Miyabe Miyuki's crisp, hard-hitting urban crime novel weaves the supernatural into the habitual pattern of murder and detection.

The third translated novel from Miyabe Miyuki, one of Japan's most popular writers, exposes complex interior worlds and a dark and unforgiving metropolis—a Tokyo that lies both before and beyond cyberpunk. *Crossfire* uses the structure and vocabulary of the detective story to lay open a place where values are uncertain, where rationality is useless, and where people live side by side yet remain blind to one another.

The heartrending story of Junko Aoki, a semi-voluntary vigilante born with the supernatural power to create and control fire, is told in counterpoint with that of the middle-aged arson detective—Chikako Ishizu—who is drawn deeper and deeper into her case. While these two women and their damaged male accomplices crisscross the urban desert of contemporary Tokyo, Miyabe gently explores the nature of right and wrong, of justice and injustice, of punishment and revenge. She exposes the emptiness and isolation at the heart of the cosmopolitan city at the end of the twentieth century, and adumbrates a curve of Japanese culture leading back into the murky aftermath of the Second World War and forward into the dark, casual criminality of a place where the once staunch mores have long been in decline.

In this very accessible book the pyrotechnics stay firmly in the narrative. There are no linguistic or stylistic fireworks, just controlled plotting and impactful storytelling. Yet Aoki's firestarting is wonderfully, deeply imagined and there is a poignancy to her loneliness and isolation—even to the routine daily grind of her hunter, the mumsy Ishizu. This is a beautifully fashioned book of simplicity and depth that drags you irresistibly onward toward its bitter denouement. **TSu**

The Poisonwood Bible

Barbara Kingsolver

Set in the Congo, this novel is narrated by Orelanna Price and her four daughters and tells the story of her husband, the overzealous Baptist preacher Nathan Price. As a child, Barbara Kingsolver lived in the Congo with her healthworker parents, but it was only in adulthood that she learned of the political situation that had seized the Congo while she lived there, when the United States secretly sabotaged the country's independence. She wrote this novel to address and publicize these issues.

The missionary's four children—Rachel, Ruth May, Leah, and the crippled mute Adah—react differently to their father's work, but when poisonous snakes appear in their house, planted by the village's religious leader, they try to convince their father to let them leave. He refuses, and Ruth May is killed, prompting her mother to leave the village with the other three daughters. Rachel goes on to marry three men and inherit a hotel in the Congo; Leah marries the village schoolteacher and dedicates herself to working for African independence; and Adah takes on science as her religion and becomes an epidemiologist. The mother lives the rest of her life wracked with guilt.

The novel represents a powerful indictment of Western colonialism and post-colonialism, of cultural arrogance and simple greed. Each of the narrators must struggle to deal with their guilt over Ruth May's death, but also with the guilt of their implication in the ruin of a country and, on a wider scale, Western guilt over its colonial past. The novel's title comes from the poisonwood, an African tree that Nathan Price is warned not to touch; he ignores the warning and suffers painful swelling. There can be no simpler allegory for Kingsolver's message about Price's missionary zeal. **EF**

Lifespan | *b.* 1955 (U.S.)
First Published | 1998
First Published by | HarperFlamingo (New York)
Pulitzer Prize Finalist | 1998

BY THE BESTSELLING AUTHOR OF PIGS IN HEAVEN

THE POISONWOOD BIBLE BARBARA KINGSOLVER

"Ants. We were walking on, surrounded, enclosed, enveloped, being eaten by ants."

The anti-colonial subject matter of *The Poisonwood Bible* reflects the author's overriding concern with promoting social change.

Veronika Decides to Die

Paulo Coelho

Lifespan | *b.* 1947 (Brazil)
First Published | 1998
First Published by | Objetiva (Rio de Janeiro)
Original Title | *Veronika decide morrer*

 Much of Paulo Coehlo's work has been based on his personal struggle to discover a religious path in an oppressive world.

 Coelho has sold seventy million copies of his spiritually uplifting books, which have been translated into every major language.

With a steady stream of boyfriends, a secure job in a library, a room to call her home, caring friends and family, Veronika is a normal young woman leading a normal life. Yet she decides to kill herself, leaving behind a note that deplores global ignorance as to the whereabouts of Slovenia. As she regains consciousness in Ljubljana's psychiatric hospital, Villete, she learns that she has one week to live as her heart is now apparently damaged. The novel follows Veronika's shift from seeking death to her awareness that there are facets of her world that make life worthwhile. In Villete, she blossoms. Since the insane have no behavioral norms, she embraces the freedom to behave in any way she wants. This newfound autonomy prompts her to hit a man who annoys her, to masturbate in front of a stoic schizophrenic, to reconnect with her passion for playing the piano, and ultimately to discover love with Eduard, a man hospitalized by his parents because he wants to be an artist.

The character Eduard is one of several elements that link Coelho himself with the fictional world of the novel. He actually enters the narrative in the third chapter, where he reveals his own stays in Brazilian asylums, committed by his parents because of his artistic inclinations. It is this direct personal knowledge that makes the novel so stark in its simplicity. Details of electroconvulsive therapy, insulin shock, and other treatments imposed on the insane lead us to reconsider the meaning of sanity.

In a world of increasing uniformity, conformity, and isolation, the novel reflects its late twentieth-century provenance with its blend of world religious sentiment, its self-help angle, and its advocacy that life can have meaning if we do not heed the social mores that stifle the human spirit. **CK**

The Hours

Michael Cunningham

Lifespan | *b.* 1952 (U.S.)
First Published | 1998
First Published by | Farrar, Straus & Giroux (New York)
Pulitzer Prize | 1999

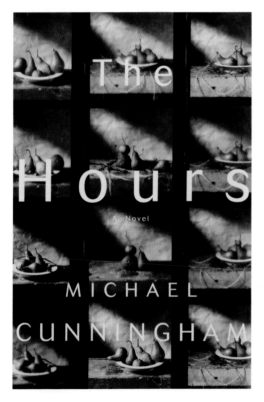

"I begin to hear voices . . ."

⊙ Cunningham won the Pulitzer Prize, PEN/Faulkner award, and the
Gay, Lesbian, Bisexual and Transgendered Book Award, all in 1999.

An intricate reworking of Virginia Woolf's classic 1925 stream-of-consciousness novel, *Mrs. Dalloway*, which describes a day in the life of a London socialite as she prepares for a party, Michael Cunningham's *The Hours* splits Clarissa Dalloway's internal monologue into the third-person narratives of three women. Clarissa Vaughan is a middle-aged lesbian living in contemporary New York. To help establish the links with Woolf's precursor, she is nicknamed "Mrs. Dalloway" by Richard, a prominent gay poet with whom she has shared a sexually ambiguous friendship. In another time and place, Los Angeles housewife Laura Brown reads *Mrs. Dalloway* and other novels to fight the emptiness of suburban motherhood in the late 1940s, and finds herself deeply shocked by her own moment of lesbian desire. Meanwhile a fictionalized Virginia Woolf frets over the writing of *Mrs. Dalloway* itself. As Clarissa prepares a party to celebrate Richard's receiving a prestigious literary award, Laura tries to invest herself in her young son, and Woolf struggles to navigate illness in order to complete the work around which Cunningham's novel is structured.

Cunningham reproduces Woolf's anatomy of the mourning of lost possibility—her heroine Clarissa Dalloway remains haunted by the unexplored lesbian connection. Clarissa Vaughan's successful long-term relationship and urban social freedom become the mundane background against which her youthful relationship with Richard and a single, ecstatic kiss shine all the more intensely. The uncertain way in which the eventful (suicide, kiss) complements ongoing ordinariness permeates the novel, as it meditates on the alchemical process through which temperament and experience act on each other to create our worlds. **AF**

All Souls Day

Cees Nooteboom

Arthur Daane, the central character of Cees Nooteboom's *All Souls Day*, is a man with time on his hands; indeed, he has specifically arranged it that way. He spends his days wandering through post-Wall Berlin, ruminating and reflecting as he negotiates his way through a city's past, and his own.

Ten years earlier, his wife and young son were killed in a plane crash, and since then Arthur has tried to live with the burden of his freedom and has carefully structures his life to allow him to do so. As a documentary filmmaker, he is accustomed to being an observer; however, when he meets a young woman who bears the scars of trauma on her face, he is called upon to engage in life more directly. Love—and, ultimately, another random act of violence—shock him out of his anonymity and propel him forward. The story is told at a rambling, walking pace, with scenes that read like verbal snapshots interposed with long discussions among a handful of Arthur's friends, who are as inclined to intellectual discourse as he is.

As much a romance as a kind of dialog with the dying twentieth century, Nooteboom's novel of ideas contemplates the catalog of horrors, losses, and destruction wrought in recent history—a contemporary reader will be chastened by considering all that has transpired since it was written. Indeed, the book opens with Arthur contemplating the relative sound of the word "history" in German and Dutch, realizing that the word itself gives no hint of the nature of the events it represents. With occasional, more far-reaching, narration offered by some of the souls already above and beyond the scope of time, *All Souls Day* is a sober inquiry into the meaning of life, art, and historical events, both personal and public. **ES**

Lifespan | *b.* 1933 (The Netherlands)
First Published | 1998
First Published by | Atlas (Amsterdam)
Original Title | *Allerzielen*

"Arthur had seen the light."

◉ Nooteboom has been mentioned several times in the context of the Nobel Prize for Literature, and has been shortlisted once.

The Heretic

Miguel Deliber

Lifespan | *b.* 1920 (Spain)
First Published | 1998
First Published in | Destino (Barcelona)
Original Title | *El hereje*

The starting point of Miguel Delibes's novel is October 31, 1517—the day in which Martin Luther nails to a church door in Wittenberg, Germany, his ninety-five theses on papal abuses and the sale of indulgences by church officials. It is also the day in which Cipriano Salcedo is born in Valladolid, Spain. The atmosphere of this historical novel is marked by the Roman Catholic intolerance and repression that ensues in Valladolid (where Delibes was born) in response to the awakening of Castilian Lutheranism.

At the heart of this transfixing narrative is Salcedo, a bourgeois Catholic man tormented by problems of conscience. Neither his religious doctrine nor the priests in charge of his education provide convincing answers to his theological questions. Unknown to him, these point to the Reformation: why should he, Salcedo, confide his sins to a priest in confession?; why does Mass distract him rather than elevate him?; why does he have to expiate his sins in Purgatory; didn't Christ suffer enough for all of humanity? His quest to define his relationship with God is largely ignored by a society that is becoming increasingly fanatical. He feels isolated, which leads him to a fraternity of new believers who provide him with a sense of belonging, but with devastating consequences.

The Heretic states persuasively our rights to religious freedom and tolerance, a particularly poignant message today. In 1999 it was the winner of the National Narrative Prize in Spain. **AK**

Elementary Particles

Michel Houellebecq

Lifespan | *b.* 1958 (Réunion)
First Published | 1998, by Flammarion (Paris)
Alternate Title | *Atomized*
Original Title | *Les Particules élémentaires*

This was the novel that first brought Michel Houellebecq's bleak worldview to an international audience. Western civilization has failed on a grand scale and human beings are miserable and lonely, barely capable of communication or emotion. Houellebecq charts the ascent of the modern leisure society with persuasive cultural analysis, concluding that the injunction to pursue personal pleasure and happiness is itself repressive and painful.

The book's central characters, Michel and Bruno, are brothers separated until middle age. Michel is a brilliant yet emotionally isolated scientist, Bruno a hopeless libertine. Sex is the arena in which the novel's argument is played out. Michel cannot form sexual relationships—he declines the affection of his beautiful childhood sweetheart Annabelle—while Bruno's escapades in New Age holiday camps, swingers' clubs, and as an occasional flasher provide a comic stage for Houellebecq's dissertation on the momentary utopias and abjections of the sexual act. The supremacy of the biological imperative leads to a series of conclusions about men and women. Women are self-sacrificing signifiers of mortality, men condemned to the destiny of their glandular promptings. This is no elegy to humanity—Houellebecq cannot wait to see the back of us. The question, though, is, does he really mean it? **DH**

❯ Houellebecq has been accused of misogyny and racism, but the main thrust of his books is a much broader distaste for human life.

Dirty Havana Trilogy

Pedro Juan Gutiérrez

PEDRO JUAN GUTIÉRREZ

Trilogía sucia de La Habana

ANAGRAMA
Narrativas hispánicas

"Now I was training myself to take nothing seriously . . . It's the only way to avoid suffering . . . "

● Juan Pedro Gutiérrez's semi-autobiographical trilogy forged his reputation as a master of "Cuban dirty realism."

Lifespan | *b.* 1950 (Cuba)
First Published | 1998
First Published by | Anagrama (Barcelona)
Original Title | *Trilogía sucia de La Habana*

These sixty narratives, drawn from the life of the poor, form a continuous apocalyptic fresco of Havana in the early 1990s. Nearly everything is told by a single narrator, Pedro Juan, a cynical former journalist and writer. A sharp, erudite rogue, or, rather, a hyper-eroticized ascetic, he sees everything from the vantage point of his attic in Central Havana. On foot, on a bicycle, or in buses and dilapidated trains, he looks for the opportunity to participate in everything or to struggle against it. But everything is reduced to misery and distress. Also everything is sex: the only nourishment for the body and the only spiritual relief in this capital of sorrow where, if "temperance" is a virtue, it is because it minimizes organic and psychological disorders.

But in this trilogy there is a distinct sign of a strengthening ethic: the multiple climaxes of desolation are immediately followed by new forms of hope—perhaps the only thing that is not dragged down in this world. The ability to see beyond (the benefit of an apparently useless objective, or privileged overseas utopias) and the will to survive in ever more extreme situations make these characters superhuman. With an allegedly anti-literary style (yet stylish in its economy of phrase, risky jargon, and visionary power), Gutiérrez has constructed and described an urban landscape unknown in Spanish-American literature. **DMG**

Savage Detectives

Roberto Bolaño

Lifespan | *b.* 1953 (Chile), *d.* 2003 (Spain)
First Published | 1998
First Published by | Anagrama (Barcelona)
Original Title | *Los detectives salvajes*

The first publication of *Savage Detectives* shook the international literary scene. The novel has been compared to the greatest Latin American novels of the twentieth century and has been widely awarded. Roberto Bolaño's book relates a long journey, a quest with elements of a Homeric odyssey, a generational Diaspora, and a beatnik delirium.

The novel starts in Mexico City. The year is 1976, and a teenager's diary tells how his life changes when his passion for literature leads him to enter a phantasmagorical avant garde group. Arturo Belano and Ulises Lima are the founders and also the savage detectives who, on New Year's Eve 1976, embark on a desperate voyage in search for an enigmatic Mexican woman writer who disappeared shortly after the Revolution. That is the starting point of a twenty-year journey that takes them through all five continents. Always told in the first person, the narrative is nonetheless related from a variety of perspectives. In the process, we are introduced to a wide range of characters and this constitutes a significant aspect of the novel's appeal.

Before the novel was published, Bolaño was a cult figure for a happy few. With this work, sales shot up. Bolaño was seriously ill, and he knew it. During the five years he had left, he wrote frenetically, leaving a monumental legacy. *Savage Detectives* is the perfect introduction to his literary world. **CA**

ROBERTO BOLAÑO

Los detectives salvajes

Premio Herralde de Novela

ANAGRAMA
Narrativas hispánicas

"You never finish reading, even if you finish all your books, just as you never finish living . . ." Roberto Bolaño

◉ *Savage Detectives* made Roberto Bolaño the unanimous winner of the coveted Rómulo Gallegos International Novel Prize in 1999.

Disgrace

J. M. Coetzee

Lifespan | *b.* 1940 (South Africa)
First Published | 1999
First Published by | Secker & Warburg (London)
Booker Prize | 1999

"Follow your temperament."

◉ Of South African origin, Coetzee became an Australian citizen in 2006. He was awarded the Nobel Prize for Literature in 2003.

◗ Coetzee stirred up controversy with his apparently bleak and pessimistic vision of the condition of post-apartheid South Africa.

South Africa after the end of apartheid is a country in which social and political structures that had once seemed immutable have crumbled, and many among the once-dominant white population are forced to make difficult adjustments. David Lurie, a fifty-two-year-old professor at a fictional university in Cape Town, is less troubled by the demise of institutionally sanctioned racism than by the entry of the country into a global culture that devalues his lifelong devotion to literature, to Romantic literature in particular. When an ill-judged seduction of one of his students results in a disciplinary hearing, he cannot bring himself to go through with the required public breast-beating and gives up his job, plunging into an unknown future.

J. M. Coetzee's novel, which had begun in the vein of campus satire, turns darker with Lurie's visit to his daughter, Lucy, on her small farm in the Eastern Cape. In an attack by three black men, Lucy is raped and Lurie burned; Lurie's appalled sense of a fundamentally changed world is exacerbated by his daughter's refusal to make her violation public, or to abort the child that she has conceived. His response is to dedicate his time to an animal shelter, where the region's unwanted dogs are put down, and to work on an opera that becomes less performable as it develops. Distanced from his daughter, he nevertheless hopes for a new relationship of "visitorship."

Disgrace caused fierce debates in South Africa over its portrayal of the new social and political order. Yet the novel's ethical stance is more challenging than its painful realism about some of the country's problems. Does Lurie's dedication to animals and to musical creation represent some kind of redemption after a life of self-centered sexual predation? **DA**

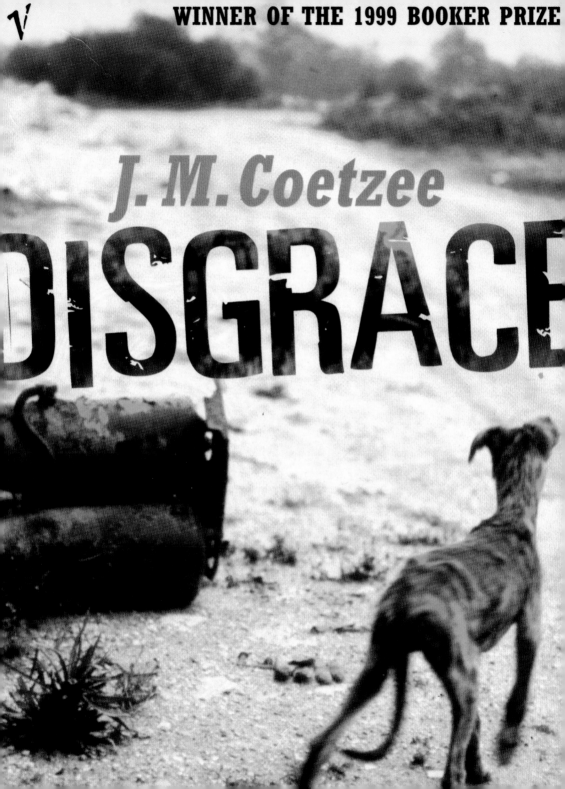

J. M. Coetzee
DISGRACE

As If I Am Not There

Slavenka Drakulić

Lifespan | *b.* 1949 (Yugoslavia)
First Published | 1999
First Published in | *Feral Tribune* (Split)
Original Title | *Kao da me nema*

The Croatian journalist Slavenka Drakulić is one of the most insightful and evenhanded observers of recent Balkan history. Her novel *As If I Am Not There* is set in Bosnia in the years 1992 and 1993. The narrative tells of the horrifying experiences endured by S.—a schoolteacher of mixed Serbian and Bosnian heredity—when Serbian forces enter her village. S. spends months in an all female compound of a Serbian concentration camp where she is subjected to continual sexual violence and beatings. The novel culminates with her arrival in Scandinavia as a refugee—pregnant, homeless, and ambivalent about her unborn son, conceived during a gang rape in the camp. What is more, S. is unable to find an individual or a community who will listen to her story without judgment.

Told in sparse, unflinching detail, without recourse to literary tricks, this is a haunting novel. Simply narrated but morally complex, *As If I Am Not There* establishes some powerful links between warfare, masculinity, sexual violence, and the female body, but avoids offering simplistic conclusions. Most strikingly, the novel refuses to demonize Serbia in its depiction of the war, and the use of initials to identify characters means that questions of nationality and religion are handled with great subtlety. In effect, the initials ask us to see each character in his or her own light, as an agent and an actor, as flexibly rational, but possessing the potential for terrifying irrationality. **SamT**

Pavel's Letters

Monika Maron

Lifespan | *b.* 1941 (Germany)
First Published | 1999
First Published by | S. Fischer Verlag (Frankfurt)
Original Title | *Pawels Briefe*

In this reconstruction of family history, Monika Maron explores the lives of her parents and grandparents under three German regimes; the Weimar Republic, National Socialism, and the German Democratic Republic. Part of a wider genre that examines twentieth-century German history through the lens of family history, the narrative focuses primarily on the tragic story of Pavel, Maron's Jewish grandfather, who perished at the hands of the Nazis in 1942. Maron's perception of her grandfather has been colored by her GDR upbringing and by the values of her mother, who is unable to come to terms with her daughter's emigration and literary success in the former West Germany. Maron attempts to gain a fresh perspective on her grandparents' lives in Poland and West Berlin before 1939, by piecing together conversations with her mother, old family photographs, and visits to Poland.

Maron's aim for her reconstruction of family history is both straightforward and ambitious: "not to find anything specific, but just to go there and imagine what their life was like, to search for the thread that connects my life to theirs." The book is set in the wake of the fall of the Berlin wall, and, as such, is as much a confrontation with the former East German state as it is with the legacy of National Socialism. Written in a simple, episodic style, *Pavel's Letters* is both an intimate family history, and a moving, universal tale set against the history of twentieth-century Europe. **KKr**

In Search of Klingsor

Jorge Volpi

Lifespan | *b.* 1968 (Mexico)
First Published | 1999
First Published by | Seix Barral (Barcelona)
Original Title | *En busca de Klingsor*

The Second World War has just come to an end and American physicist turned soldier-spy Francis P. Bacon is given the job of uncovering the identity of Klingsor, a man who supposedly controlled the direction and nature of scientific research in Nazi Germany. Bacon enlists the help of German mathematician Gustav Links and the mysterious Irene, who he promptly falls in love with. Links is the narrator of the story and the narrative includes his and Bacon's separate lives before and during the war.

Volpi uses these foundations to take the reader on a journey into the scientific and political climate of the 1930s and 1940s. In their pursuit of Klingsor, Bacon and Links meet with some of the finest physicists of the age: Schrödinger, Bohr, and prime suspect Werner Heisenberg. Volpi moves the plot of the spy thriller to its devastating climax while, at the same time, considering the weightier issues of relativity, certainty, and chance, re-imagining the characters and struggles of the physicists who battled to build the first atomic bomb.

Unlike many novels with such a wide scope, *In Search of Klingsor* is never overly earnest or sanctimonious. Rather, it moves on at a pace that allows for the development of the mystery while at the same time introducing the reader to the scientific thought of the day. Volpi has said that he writes thrillers to relax, but in his exploration of game-playing, chance, and rage, it is clear that his ambition stretches beyond mere relaxation. **OR**

Seix Barral Premio Biblioteca Breve 1999

Jorge Volpi
En busca de Klingsor

"I should clarify that I, Gustav Links—a man of flesh and blood just like you—am the author of these words. But who am I, really?"

⊙ Jorge Volpi's stylish, science-heavy, Nazi-hunt thriller escapes categorization as specifically Mexican fiction.

The Museum of Unconditional Surrender

Dubravka Ugresic

Lifespan | *b.* 1949 (Yugoslavia)
First Published | 1999
First Published by | Fabrika knjiga (Belgrade)
Original Title | *Muzej bezuvjetne predaje*

"I absorb people's misfortune"

🔘 Living in exile from her native Croatia, Ugresic uses sophisticated
literary techniques to explore deeply felt personal experience.

Roland the Walrus, which died on August 21, 1961, had the surrealistic contents of its stomach put on display in the Berlin Zoo. The narrator reads the list of contents and finds herself, as we find ourselves, trying to find some structure, some inner logic to their randomness. This becomes one of the central metaphors of an extraordinary novel of exile, remembrance, and loss. The Berlin flea markets, the contents of an old handbag, photograph albums, and a series of seemingly random events are all described in a prose of quiet beauty and melancholy.

Through the interconnected stories and encounters with various artists and friends, Dubravka Ugresic creates a collage effect full of multiple layers of meaning and interconnectivity. The characters she describes—real or imagined—allow her to explore the relationship between memory and identity and, in particular, the different methods used to cope with the lack of both. Ugresic went into exile in 1993 and left a country tearing itself apart. The wars and bloodshed that followed turned friend against friend, renewed old hatreds, and forced thousands to leave the country.

The novel attempts to capture the slow and constant sense of loss and displacement caused by exile, and the disappearance of anything one could call home. Its scattered, Postmodern method of narration moves between magic realism, diary entries, essayistic prose, and even a recipe for caraway soup. This allows the author to recognize herself as a kind of museum exhibit, as are all those who have left behind a home that no longer exists. She refers many times to the two different types of exile, those with photographs (ties to the past) and those without, and the novel is Ugresic's attempt to create and explore her ties. **JM**

Fear and Trembling

Amélie Nothomb

No one ever said that bridging the gap between East and West would happen easily. In this novel about a Belgian employee of a Japanese corporation dealing in everything from Canadian optical fibers to Singaporean soda, the problems of reconciling the new faith in a global village with traditional, insular societal norms are conveyed with satiric delight.

Fear and Trembling relates the experience of Amélie as she begins a one-year contract on the bottom rung of a massive Japanese corporation. Having been partly raised in Japan, she is simultaneously native and foreigner, but her nativeness serves to ostracize her as much as her foreignness (she is punished for understanding Japanese). The novel describes the process by which her Western background counts against her and she finds herself facing one degrading and very public demotion after another in an effort to emphasize her inability to be truly integrated into the company's culture: she is moved from mindless photocopying to the full-time cleaning of a restroom used only by herself and her immediate superior, Fubuki Mori, an exquisitely beautiful and dangerously proud woman for whom Amélie develops a self-destructive infatuation. The attitude of the company toward Amélie is encapsulated in the book's title. Apparently, the traditional attitude that Japanese expected foreigners to adopt on meeting their emperor was one of "fear and trembling."

Amélie Nothomb's attack on what is presented as crazed labor relations in a massive Japanese corporation is not entirely vituperative—she exhibits a sympathy to people obedient to their sense of honor and tradition. In this satiric and thoughtful novel, East and West are both ridiculed with a certain fondness for the foibles of every individual. **JuS**

Lifespan | b. 1967 (Japan)
First Published | 1999, by A. Michel (Paris)
Original Language | French
Original Title | Stupeur et tremblements

"I was senior to no one."

⊙ Daughter of a Belgian ambassador, Nothomb has thrived on the media exposure brought by precocious cultural celebrity status.

Two days later Richard Brinsley Sheridan entered the little bookshop

Ireland, having been alerted by a scrawled message an h

him. "My dear sir. An honour." Sheridan bowed. "We

"Where is the young man of the hour?" Sherida

found it difficult to turn as William descended the stairc

"I am William Ireland, sir."

"May I shake your hand, sir? You have done a serv

announced
pronounced each word as if he were addressing others u

believe who recommended Vortigern as a great subject

in Holborn Passage. Samuel

before, was waiting to greet

immensely

: all ~~very~~ proud."

as a large figure, and he

"Is it you?"

a great purpose"

ha ~~great service~~.' Sheridan

en. "It was Mr Dryden, I

a drama."

Peter Ackroyd, *The Lambs of London*, 2004

2000s

Bartleby and Co.

Enrique Vila-Matas

Lifespan | *b.* 1948 (Spain)
First Published | 2000
First Published by | Anagrama (Barcelona)
Original Title | *Bartleby y compañía*

Becoming a cult author with *A Brief History of Portable Literature* (1985), Enrique Vila-Matas gained wider recognition with this novel, which won an award in France as the best essay of 2000. He used the mysterious protagonist of Bartleby, Herman Melville's scrivener, as an emblem of those writers who, at a certain moment, prefer to abstain from publishing their work and give in to the power of saying "No." To examine this enigmatic "Bartleby syndrome," the author invents an alter ego, Marcelo, a solitary office worker, inspired by Kafka and Pessoa among others. In the summer of 1999, Marcelo starts a diary in which are recorded cases of "writers touched by the Evil" of silence, in "footnotes commenting on a text which is invisible."

The novel consists of eighty-six essay notes by Marcelo in which a fascinating army of inhibited and secret creators appears, people who prefer not to write or to make their writing known, from Socrates and Rimbaud to Juan Rulfo, J. D. Salinger, Thomas Pynchon, B. Traven, and Robert Walser, the final one a key name in the later work of Vila-Matas. Reality and fiction invade each other's boundaries, as do the text and his footnotes, the narrative and the essay, since the dissolution of conventional literary categories is one of the aesthetic intentions of the author, perhaps even the main intention. The result of this systematic subversion is a fascinating blend of imagination, writing, and reading in which the reader becomes involved. **DRM**

Celestial Harmonies

Péter Esterházy

Lifespan | *b.* 1950 (Hungary)
First Published | 2000
First Published by | Magveto (Budapest)
Original Title | *Harmonia caelestis*

Esterházy is a scion of Hungary's most prominent aristocrat clan, and, a decade after the end of Central European Communism under which the Esterházys lived in reduced circumstances, *Celestial Harmonies* is an attempt to reinscribe the family chronicles. It is massive in both its weight and in the reach of its anecdotes, judgements, and apercus. Even when the book is being deliberately evasive, the reader feels a shock of recognition at the extent to which private and public significances are entwined here, as Esterházy rolls out cameos for figures like Haydn, Béla Bartók, Winston Churchill, and Napoleon III.

Celestial Harmonies is divided into two very different halves. While "Book Two" gives us "Confessions of an Esterházy Family" in a narrative of the author's immediate ancestors, "Book One" is a playful, capricious, and somewhat insane catalog of "Numbered Sentences from the Lives of the Esterházy Family," in which a singular protagonist takes on a myriad of historical identities, stretched across several hundred years and many forms. No mistaking, this is a deeply odd book; possible English-language counterparts might be the more hallucinatory parts of *Ulysses*. If *Celestial Harmonies* seems sometimes oppressively Old World, Alpha-Male, hierarchical, and willful, it makes up for it with the anarchic brilliance of its imagination. **MS**

❯ Péter Esterházy, a descendent of one of Hungary's most aristocratic families, has transformed Hungarian fiction writing.

Under the Skin

Michel Faber

Lifespan | *b.* 1960 (The Netherlands)
First Published | 2000
First Published by | Canongate Press (Edinburgh)
First U.S. Edition | Harcourt (New York)

Michel Faber's first novel focuses on the life and work of its main female character, Isserley, who trawls the Scottish Highlands in an old Corolla searching for well-built and muscular male hitchhikers. To reveal her purpose in doing so would be to ruin a novel whose shocking power is derived primarily from its perfect orchestration of beautiful description, cunning deception, suspense, and macabre revelation. Suffice to say that reading this novel will force you to confront the arbitrariness of divisions between the human and the animal, as well as the often overlooked ethics of our culture's industrial-scale slaughter and consumption of meat. But it does so within the context of a compelling and original story that defies simple generic classification—it is a thriller, a science fiction novel, and a lyrical portrayal of one individual's struggle to make sense of the world.

The novel is saturated with powerful, evocative descriptions of the landscape. For Isserley, the breathtaking beauty of nature is compensation for the hardships of her life and work, but she has undergone immense personal sacrifice and pain to gain the freedom to appreciate it. Herein lies Faber's elegiac yearning for delight in the natural world and a recognition of our privilege to be living in it, attitudes that the reader senses he feels might be irretrievable or unachievable in the face of the urbanization, consumption, waste, and destruction of contemporary global capitalism. **SD**

The Human Stain

Philip Roth

Lifespan | *b.* 1933 (U.S.)
First Published | 2000
First Published by | Houghton Mifflin (New York)
PEN/Faulkner Award | 2000

The Human Stain brings together two common preoccupations—a hero with a secret and an affair between an older man and a younger woman—in the character of Coleman Silk, the boxer-turned-professor whose story is narrated by his neighbor, Nathan Zuckerman. Silk is vilified by his university following false allegations of racism and retires to his home, discovering Viagra and beginning an affair with Faunia, an illiterate maid who is grieving over the death of her children and is being pursued by a violent Vietnam veteran ex-husband.

Through flashbacks to his childhood, we discover that Silk has been covering up an enormous secret—he is a black man who has rejected the racism he has experienced from both blacks and whites. Silk's liberation—both personal and sexual—after his involvement with Faunia is startling, and Nathan, at first simply a curious observer, begins to develop a relationship with Silk himself.

While *The Human Stain* questions the possibility of objectivity in a world of emotions, the book is primarily about guilty secrets, assumptions, and perceptions. Silk may appear to be the archetypal man fallen from grace, but there is far more at work here than simple parables. It is a sly glance at American social politics, replete with judgment, shame, and hypocrisy, and at the stain left on life by humanity itself. And at the end, it is a book that, although ostensibly about the black and white of things, is inherently a thousand shades of gray. **EF**

White Teeth

Zadie Smith

Lifespan | *b.* 1975 (London)
First Published | 2000
First Published by | Hamish Hamilton (London)
Whitbread First Novel Award | 2000

White Teeth opens with the attempted suicide of Archie Jones. Archie is a war veteran, unable to make a decision without the toss of a coin, and basically irrelevant. His suicide foiled, he wanders into a New Year's party. He meets a toothless angel, a Jamaican goddess named Clara. She is a Jehovah's Witness and Archie's fresh start. They beget Irie, a hybrid, put-upon, and quintessential Brit of the new sort; multiethnic, rootless, and disenchanted.

Samad Iqbal is a Bengali waiter at an Indian restaurant. He met Archie in the war, and also has a fresh young wife. A traditionalist, he, too, is trying to come to terms with postwar England. His twin sons do not make it easy. He has to kidnap one and take him to Bangladesh to prevent him from becoming too English. Anchored in the twin histories of Archie and Samad, *White Teeth* is an epic diorama spanning decades of postcolonial England. A narrative shot through with accident, fate, and disappointment, it is about immigration and hybridity, religion and politics, and what it means to be English in an increasingly impersonal landscape.

White Teeth, a virtuoso debut from a then twenty-four-year-old writer, is crawling with vibrant characters, each with a distinct voice that sings with authenticity. Smith writes with equal facility about teenage love or the trenches of the Second World War; she knows the hearts of her characters and treats them with humor and compassion. The maturity and scope of her talent seems preternatural. **GT**

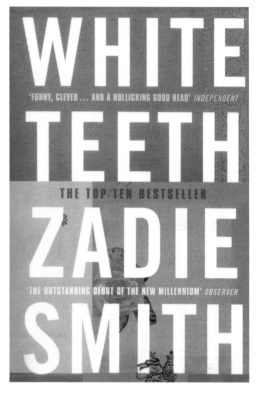

'FUNNY, CLEVER ... AND A ROLLICKING GOOD READ' *INDEPENDENT*

THE TOP-TEN BESTSELLER

'THE OUTSTANDING DEBUT OF THE NEW MILLENNIUM' *OBSERVER*

"He had flipped a coin and stood staunchly by its conclusions. This was a decided-upon suicide. In fact it was a New Year's resolution."

⬥ Zadie Smith's English father and Jamaican mother met at a party, just as Archie Jones and Clara were made to do in her novel.

Spring Flowers, Spring Frost

Ismail Kadare

Lifespan | *b.* 1936 (Albania)
First Published | 2000
First Published by | Onufri (Tiranë)
Original Title | *Lulet e ftohta të marsit*

Spring Flowers, Spring Frost is set in contemporary Albania and tells the story of Mark Gurabardhi, an artist who is struggling to live and work after the fall of his country's communist regime. Ismail Kadare's novel is carefully structured between balanced opposites—between movement and stasis, between sleep and wakefulness. Everywhere in the novel there are signs of rebirth, and everywhere these signs are balanced against omens of talismanic death, betokened most powerfully in the resurrected "book of blood," or Kanun, that has regulated ritual murder in Albania since medieval times.

These oppositions create an extraordinarily jarring effect. Elements from contemporary Europe sit side-by-side with stories and rituals that are derived from deep in the Albanian cultural memory. These oppositions suggest a deadlock, an impasse between a bankrupt mythical history and an equally bankrupt present. Mark cannot feel at home, either in the Albanian past, or in the present dominated by global capital. The novel vividly depicts this nightmarish impasse. But in the quietly poetic movement of Kadare's prose we can glimpse a new set of possibilities: a new art, and a new Albania, for which there is not yet a language. **PB**

○ Ismail Kadare won his international reputation as an outspoken and talented critic of the dictatorship of Enver Hoxha.

The Devil and Miss Prym

Paulo Coelho

Lifespan | *b.* 1947 (Brazil)
First Published | 2000
First Published by | Objetiva (Rio de Janeiro)
Original Title | *O demônio e a Senhorita Prym*

The Devil and Miss Prym concludes Paulo Coelho's trilogy "And on the Seventh Day." Each of the three books is concerned with a week in the lives of ordinary people, who find themselves suddenly confronted by love, death, and power and are forced to face their own inner conflicts and make choices that will affect their very futures.

In *The Devil and Miss Prym*, a stranger descends on Viscos, a small town in France, depicted both as paradise on earth and a dead-end, lifeless place. This contradiction illustrates the author's belief that we choose our own attitudes to life; either affecting reality by making it better for ourselves or failing to find happiness in even the most perfect conditions. Into the village comes a stranger, the Devil of the title, with a mission to discover within a week the answer to the question: are humans essentially good or evil? He finds his Eve in the local barmaid, Chantal Prym, and tempts her to commit evil. In welcoming the mysterious foreigner, the whole village becomes an accomplice to his sophisticated plot. The novel illustrates how the actions of a moment can affect the entire course of our lives and makes us question how we respond to those moments of no return. In a world where we are quick to condemn murderous regimes and "axes of evil," this is a book that reminds us that all humans are fallible and that each and every one of us has the capacity for good or evil. **LE**

The Feast of the Goat

Mario Vargas Llosa

Lifespan | *b.* 1936 (Peru)
First Published | 2000
First Published by | Alfaguara (Madrid)
Original Title | *La Fiesta del Chivo*

Novels describing the rise, fall, and personal lives of South American dictators can hardly be said to be a new development in Latin American literature. Established authors of the "dictator" genre—most notably Gabriel García Márquez with *Autumn of the Patriarch* and *The General in His Labyrinth*—typify their writing by drawing on myth and allegory. However, in *The Feast of the Goat*, Mario Vargas Llosa shows his readers the private world of the conspirators, invites them to the dinner table of the victims, and mocks the urine-stained trousers of the notorious seventy-year-old General Rafael Trujillo by exploring the last day of the dictator's thirty-one-year tyrannical rule of the Dominican Republic.

The novel has three storylines which interweave and form the overall structure. The story of Urania Cabral—the daughter of Trujillo's former secretary-of-state, who returns to her homeland after gaining an education in the United States—represents the Dominican Republic's political relationship with the rest of the world, but is also used to describe both the suffering of the Dominican citizens, and their blind faith and complicity in the exploitative regime. The second plotline is that of the conspirators, the once-upon-a-time Trujillo loyalists. Finally, there is Trujillo himself. Obsessed with cleanliness as much as with the bladder problem that challenges the machismo of his powerful public persona, even Trujillo is a character that suffers from compromise.

Llosa once claimed that in writing about this particular dictator, he was effectively writing about all dictators, wherever they are found, and about the essential nature of the power they wield. But Llosa's meticulous research on the streets of the republic, interviewing real people for this novel, makes it a tense, unnerving, and uncomfortably direct read. **JSD**

◆ Mario Vargas Llosa was a conservative candidate for the Peruvian presidency in 1990—an unusually ambitious aim for a novelist.

I'm Not Scared

Niccolò Ammaniti

Niccolò Ammaniti's *I'm Not Scared* is set in southern Italy during the ferocious heat wave of 1978. The narrator, Michele Amitrano, is now an adult, but he looks back on his nine-year-old self, when he was living in Acqua Traverse, a village of four hovels in a desolate countryside.

It is summer and there is a tremendous, sticky, unbearable heat, which only a small group of boys can bear, spending most of their days exploring their surroundings on their bikes, and setting each other dares as they do so. Michele, like almost all the young men who are the central characters of Ammaniti's novels, has an exaggerated sensibility, innocent yet mature, which separates him from the petty, unthinking logic of the herd. While "Skull" claims the others' rough respect as the leader, inflicting a load of forfeits on the rest of the gang, Michele does not take part in what increasingly seems to be a form of juvenile tyranny; in fact, he takes on another's forfeit, agreeing to explore an abandoned farmhouse. Once there, Michele discovers something in the building that changes his world, and this twist wrenches the book out of the relatively innocent world of childhood into the sinister, incomprehensible world of adults.

I'm Not Scared is the very best kind of coming-of-age novel—one in which the progression from childhood to adulthood is not presented as a necessary "putting away of childish things" in favor of the increased experience of maturity, nor as a naive celebration of the innocence of children in contrast with the cruelty of adults. If anything, Ammaniti suggests that children and adults have more in common than most people think. The novel bears this philosophy lightly, however, carrying it on the back of what is, fundamentally, a thrilling story. **FF**

Lifespan | *b.* 1966 (Italy)
First Published | 2001
First Published by | Einaudi (Turin)
Original Title | *Io non ho paura*

⊙ *I'm Not Scared* is based on the true story of a kidnapped boy and was made into a film in 2003, directed by Gabriele Salvatores.

Atonement

Ian McEwan

The first part of the novel begins in the summer of 1935 as thirteen-year-old Briony Tallis attempts to direct her three cousins in a self-penned play to celebrate the homecoming of her adored older brother, Leon. The children's lives should be idyllic in their upper-middle-class, interwar setting, but real-life events soon enrapture Briony more than her play. She witnesses a moment of sexual tension between her older sister Cecilia and Robbie Turner, the housekeeper's son, whose education Cecilia's father has been funding. Assuming he is forcing Cecilia into a sexual encounter, and later intercepting a letter Robbie sends to Cecilia declaring his lust, Briony decides that Robbie is an evil beast. When her cousin Lola is mysteriously attacked, Briony wrongly points the finger at Robbie, who is arrested and jailed. Cecilia, heartbroken at her lover's confinement and never ceasing to believe in him, leaves to become a nurse in London and refuses to speak to Briony.

The second part of the novel follows Robbie five years later, now in the army, as he is exposed to the horrors and suffering of the Dunkirk evacuations. In the third, and final, part, Briony becomes a war nurse in London and begins to come to terms with her guilt over what she did to Robbie and Cecilia, now finally together.

In the epilogue, McEwan paints Briony as an aging novelist, revisiting her past in fact and fiction and casting doubt over the truthfulness of her stories, which brings into question the author's struggle to relinquish control over the reaction of his readers. This novel is not only about love, trust, and the war. It is also about the pleasures, pains, and challenges of writing, the burden of guilt, and, above all, the danger of interpretation. **EF**

Lifespan | b. 1948 (England)
First Published | 2001
First Published by | Jonathan Cape (London)
National Book Critics Circle Award | 2001

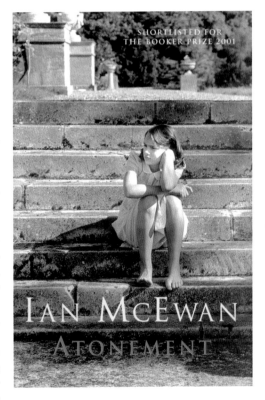

SHORTLISTED FOR THE BOOKER PRIZE 2001

IAN McEWAN
ATONEMENT

⊙ *Atonement*'s cover photograph by Chris Fraser Smith captures the feverish cerebral activity of McEwan's protagonist, Briony.

◁ Keira Knightley plays Cecilia, and Saoirse Ronan plays the thirteen-year-old Briony, in a 2007 film adaptation of *Atonement*.

Soldiers of Salamis

Javier Cercas

Lifespan | *b.* 1962 (Spain)
First Published | 2001
First Published by | Tusquets (Barcelona)
Original Title | *Soldados de Salamina*

"It was the summer of 1994 . . ."

◉ With *Soldiers of Salamis*, a thriller-like investigation of the fascist past, Cercas achieved huge popular and critical success in Spain.

It is not easy to pinpoint the precise factors that contribute to a novel being both a brilliant popular success and one that is also capable of attracting the emphatic appreciation of high-brow writers and critics such as Mario Vargas Llosa, Alberto Manguel, and George Steiner. But the clarity of Javier Cercas's *Soldados de Salamina* (*Soldiers of Salamis*) is certainly one of the reasons this deceptively innocent look at both sides of the Spanish Civil War, set simultaneously during the war and the present day, has attracted such a following.

The narrator begins an investigation of the life of a Spanish Falangist leader, Rafael Sánchez Mazas, but the work ends up as a moral fable. It reflects on the virtuous instinct that causes a militiaman who discovers Mazas to spare his life in the war (Mazas then continues to fight until 1945, when he enters Paris with the tanks of the liberation forces). The attempt to understand, without prejudice, the nature of the interaction between the two men is combined with another more secret adventure: the moral and personal maturing of the narrator. Like the author, he is a Spanish journalist named Javier Cercas, and he achieves, during the course of his investigations into why the two sides are fighting, not only a better understanding of the world but also of himself. The tension of the story builds up to an explosive and sentimental end. Concealed, and then confounded, is a belief arising from having, at last, found the militiaman who spared the life of Rafael Sánchez Mazas, and a private feeling of having learned something fundamental: that the instinct for virtue can be a gift bestowed by people furthest from one's political persuasion, although in this case the militiaman offers both moral and political reasons. **JGG**

Austerlitz

W. G. Sebald

W. G. Sebald's novel *Austerlitz* opens with a chance encounter in a railway station in Antwerp between its unnamed narrator and the eponymous Austerlitz, who has set out to explore his roots in Europe after discovering that he is actually the son of Jews from Prague. Austerlitz has been brought up as Daffyd Elias by an austere Welsh minister and his wife, and kept in total ignorance of his real name and early childhood living with his biological family in Prague. It turns out that he was evacuated to Wales before the Second World War, where his amnesiac, dislocated life as Daffyd Elias began. The ensuing discussion between the men at the station, focusing on the relationship between architecture and historical time, lasts for several hours, and then is rejoined as the two meet up repeatedly, and always by chance, over a number of years. Their relationship remains cold and distant, until Austerlitz decides to tell the narrator his life story, a story that he is still in the process of remembering.

The novel follows Austerlitz's attempt to plumb the depths of his memory, seeking, like Austerlitz himself, to reclaim a time lost in the shadows of the Second World War—a time made inaccessible by the horrors perpetrated by the Nazis. The recovery of these memories begins when Austerlitz wanders into a disused room in London's Liverpool Street Station, and has a vague feeling that he has been there before. He realizes that the general feeling of desolation that plagues him in his daily life might come from being cut off from his origins; until he discovers his past, his life will remain unfulfilled. The narrative style performs with an uncanny fidelity the process of remembering, of diving into the darkness of repressed personal and cultural memory. To read the novel is to experience the regaining of time. **PB**

Lifespan | *b.* 1944 (Germany), *d.* 2001 (England)
First Published | 2001
First Published by | C. Hanser (Munich)
Original Language | German

"Our Antwerp conversations"

⊙ Sebald, photographed here shortly before his death, was haunted by a grim vision of humanity's "insatiable urge for destruction."

Life of Pi

Yann Martel

Lifespan | *b.* 1963 (Spain)
First Published | 2001
First Published by | Knopf Canada (Toronto)
Hugh MacLennan Prize for Fiction | 2001

"My suffering left me sad . . ."

🔵 *Life of Pi*'s dust jacket clearly demonstrates Pi's stark options:
keeping a tiger under control or facing the animals overboard.

This book, which won the Man Booker Prize in 2002, is the story of Pi Patel, the sixteen-year-old son of a zookeeper from Pondicherry, India. Pi is a religious zealot—the problem being that he is not quite sure which religion he is zealous about, attracting different beliefs "like flies" to become a practicing Christian, Muslim, and Hindu all at the same time. Planning a move to start a new life in Canada, Pi's father packs up the belongings and the menagerie, and the family set off aboard a freighter. After a terrifying shipwreck, Pi finds himself the sole survivor adrift in the Pacific Ocean, trapped on a twenty-six-foot lifeboat with a wounded zebra, a spotted hyena, a seasick orangutan, and a Bengal tiger named Richard Parker. After Richard Parker dispatches the others, Pi must use all his zoological knowledge, wits, and faith to stay alive. The two remain drifting, hungry and exposed to the elements, for 227 days. Pi recounts the harrowing journey but hidden in his account is an examination of the strengths and weaknesses of religion and writing, and the essential difference between truth and fiction. Pi realizes he must learn to become the tiger's master, with the interaction between the two forming rich metaphors for spirituality and belief—to some extent, each of the (possibly imaginary) animals could represent a different facet of the hallucinating Pi. The underlying current of the book is that Pi must master his own dark side, his fear, despair, and desperation at his condition and the loss of his family. In a philosophical twist at the end, after Richard Parker disappears and Pi is rescued, Pi placates doubting officials with a more credible version of his survival story. This is the version he is convinced they want to hear, and the reader is reminded yet again of how hard it is to tell whether a story is true. **EF**

The Corrections

Jonathan Franzen

It is ambition that makes Jonathan Franzen's third novel, *The Corrections*, an important novel. It sets out to be important, to declare unapologetically and often ferociously that the novel itself, literature in all its tenuous glory, is important.

The significance of the novel genre for Franzen lies not with the stories it can tell but with the fact that it can tell any story at all, that the novel as a form enables the making visible of that stream of connections and unities that constitute a life, whereas life itself, pummeled with distractions and weak with forgetting, hides nine-tenths or more of the work that creates and sustains it.

The Corrections asks as much of its readers as it asks of itself. The ambition that drives it to melt down and merge the interlocking relations, careers, and madnesses of a midwestern, middle-class, middle-aged American family, is an ambition its readers must take on themselves if they are to make it through pages that simultaneously have the cognitive shape of a hangover and a high.

The pace of *The Corrections* is frenetic, simply because it has to be: it is an encyclopedic work, meticulously detailed about the areas of American life it brings under its gaze. These are so multifarious, their significances so varied yet so irrefutable, that the novel creates something of the multi-colored polyphony of history itself.

Published in the United States a week before the atrocity of 9/11—when terrorists crashed two planes into the World Trade Center causing huge loss of life—there is plenty in this novel to support the view that America is bent on dancing with death. The scope and exuberance of *The Corrections'* appetite for the world, however, makes it an oddly affirmative and even joyful novel. **PMcM**

Lifespan | *b.* 1959 (U.S.)
First Published | 2001
First Published by | Farrar, Straus & Giroux (New York)
National Book Award for Fiction | 2001

'Jonathan Franzen has built a powerful novel out of the swarming consciousness of a marriage, a family, a whole culture.' **Don DeLillo**

JONATHAN FRANZEN

THE CORRECTIONS

WINNER OF THE NATIONAL BOOK AWARD 2001

"The anxiety of coupons . . ."

⊙ The understated dust jacket of the original edition has nothing in common with the book's attention-grabbing paperback cover.

Platform

Michel Houellebecq

Lifespan | *b.* 1958 (Réunion)
First Published | 2001
First Published by | Flammarion (Paris)
Original Title | *Plateforme*

"In fact, nothing disturbs me."

◉ Chip Kidd is the designer credited for the dust jacket of the
hardback edition, with its oblique allusion to Thai prostitution.

This Swiftian analysis of Western decadence and its global impact interweaves narrative with the thought of Baudrillard, Comte, and a trademark essay style voiced through the central protagonist, Michel. Houellebecq offers an argument justifying Third World prostitution through market forces. Prefaced by a citation from Balzac that states, "The more contemptible his life, the more a man clings to it," the book also concerns Michel's quest for redemption through love.

At the novel's outset, middle-aged bachelor Michel discovers his father has been murdered, a fact that, far from forming a psychological angle to the plot, simply allows him to resign his dull job at the Ministry of Culture and indulge in foreign travel. Once abroad, his taste for Thai prostitutes, nurtured already by peep shows and prostitutes in Paris, is only offset by his distaste for more worthy, conventional tourists. He meets Valérie, with whom, back in Paris, he begins an affair. Valérie, it transpires, is an executive for a large travel agency and, with her boss, Jean-Yves, she and Michel develop the "platform" of the novel's title: a travel agency dealing specifically with sex tourism.

Houellebecq's thesis is that, no longer empire builders or "civilizers," modern Europeans barely deserve to survive: their only use is to redistribute the wealth of their industrious forebears. In the absence of more concrete principles, the exchange of sex, rationally, should follow the exchange of money: "a concept in which neither race, physical appearance, age, intelligence, nor distinction plays any part." Scathingly ironic, magisterially scurrilous, and thoroughly dangerous, the novel is a timely provocation for both liberal orthodoxies and Islamic morality, as its devastating conclusion shows. **DH**

Snow

Orhan Pamuk

When Ka, a poet, returns to Turkey after years of political exile in Germany, he is sent as a journalist to the remote city of Kars on the Turkish border. He is to report on the local election, which is likely to be won by fundamental Islamists, and to investigate a sudden outbreak of suicides among young women fighting for the right to wear their Islamic head scarves. As a blizzard cuts the city off from the outside world, tensions between secularists and fundamentalists come to a head in a violent coup. Ka enters the city with the mindset of one who has been brought up in a secular, Westernized Turkish family, and has lived for many years in the West. He is ready to listen to everyone, but is dismissive of fundamentalism, seeing such beliefs as backward. But, drawn into the events around him, Ka will leave the city, once the blizzard is over, an utterly changed man, with his heart broken.

This is a tense political thriller, cut through with moments of black farce. The reader is bombarded with different views, as Ka meets fundamentalists, secularists, writers, religious leaders, and the "head scarf girls" themselves. The book considers not only the clash between Turkey's various political and cultural groups, but also contemplates the basic gap between East and West, the nature of religious belief, and how art is created.

Turkish author Orhan Pamuk, winner of the 2006 Nobel Prize for Literature, has described *Snow* as "my first and last political novel." First published in Turkey in 2002, *Snow* caused controversy among Pamuk's compatriots, with some critics viewing him as being too Westernized to paint a fair portrait of his country. It brought Pamuk international acclaim, however, for his honest portrayal of Turkey's complex political and cultural situation. **CIW**

Lifespan | *b.* 1952 (Turkey)
First Published | 2002, as *Kar*
First Published by | İletişim (Istanbul)
Nobel Prize for Literature | 2006

"The silence of snow . . ."

⊙ In 2005 Pamuk faced criminal charges, now dropped, after alleging the Turkish state committed genocide against Armenians in 1915.

Nowhere Man

Aleksandar Hemon

Lifespan | *b.* 1964 (Yugoslavia)
First Published | 2002
First Published by | Nan A. Talese (New York)
Original Language | English

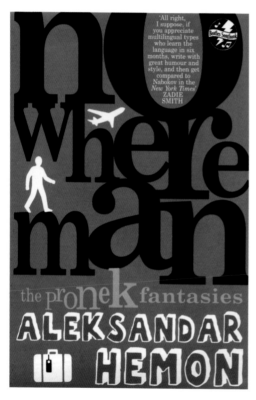

'All right, I suppose, if you appreciate multilingual types who learn the language in six months, write with great humour and style, and then get compared to Nabokov in the *New York Times*'
ZADIE SMITH

"Today was the interview."

⊙ Josef Pronek's journey from Sarajevo to the United States is referred to in the novel's quirky hardback dust jacket artwork.

Aleksandar Hemon arrived in the United States from Sarajevo in 1992, and started writing in his adoptive language three years later. The most striking feature of his writing is his wonderfully innovative use of the English language. Like his postcolonial antecedents, Hemon's work expands the limits of English and challenges the cultural authority of the standard forms of the language.

Nowhere Man, Hemon's first novel, comprises of six interrelated narratives, each with its own style. These different narrative voices recount moments in Josef Pronek's life in Sarajevo prior to the outbreak of the Yugoslav war, in the Ukraine, and in Chicago. They range from the self-consciously scholarly idiom of the graduate student, littered with Shakespearean quotations, to imperfect English as Josef struggles to express himself in his adopted language. Salman Rushdie has commented that translation is a physical movement from one cultural space to another. Hemon vividly represents the exertion that this physical movement requires by depicting the effort that Josef must expend in order to make himself understood. Words strain out of him like the imperfect distillation of ideas. The novel is most striking in those passages where he forces the reader to contemplate the English language afresh by stretching the literal meaning of English words into contexts in which they are not usually applied. For instance, he talks of a light switch "pending in the darkness," which, although consistent with the literal meaning of pending (in the sense of hanging or waiting), is so idiomatically unusual and fresh that it estranges speakers of standard English from their own language. By compelling us to reflect upon his word choices, Hemon's writing forces us to reconsider the very contours of language itself. **LC**

Everything Is Illuminated

Jonathan Safran Foer

Jonathan Safran Foer's *Everything Is Illuminated* is a strikingly ambitious first novel that has enjoyed a rare combination of commercial success and critical acclaim. The story revolves around a young Jewish American author (also named Jonathan) who, with little more than a faded photograph, travels to the Ukraine in search of Augustine—a woman who may have saved his grandfather from the Nazi occupation. Much of the novel is built around a series of retrospective letters to Jonathan from Alex Perchov, a Ukrainian in his late teens who Jonathan hires as his guide and translator. Alex's limited grasp of English ("my second tongue is not so premium," he admits) and misconceived use of a Thesaurus are rendered in a dazzling feat of linguistic invention. However, although his mistakes and malapropisms are often wildly comical, Alex is no simpleton and he grows in dignity and insight as the novel progresses. These letters are broken up by strange, magic-realist style episodes, which recount the history of Jonathan's ancestral village (or "shtetl") from the day of its founding at the beginning of the nineteenth century to the tragedy of the Final Solution.

Everything Is Illuminated is a willful conflation of fact and fantasy—an audacious vision of the Holocaust and its legacy presented through skewed translations, simple twists of fate, half-remembered conversations, fragile friendships, and competing narrative voices. It is a novel deeply concerned with the politics of memory, with how our relationship to the past is negotiated by the needs of the present. It is a novel about ancient secrets, about ignorance and knowledge, innocence and experience, atonement and guilt. It is both riotously funny and quietly devastating and may well signal the arrival of a major new voice in contemporary fiction. **SamT**

Lifespan | *b.* 1977 (U.S.)
First Published | 2002
First Published by | Houghton Mifflin (Boston)
Guardian First Book Award | 2002

"I am unequivocally tall."

● *Everything Is Illuminated* was inspired by Jonathan Safran Foer's own visit to the Ukraine in 1999 to research his grandfather's life.

The Namesake

Jhumpa Lahiri

Lifespan | *b.* 1967 (England)
First Published | 2003
First Published in | Houghton Mifflin (New York)
Original Language | English

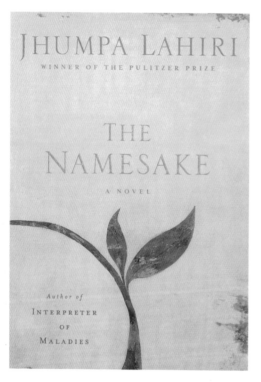

"Motherhood in a foreign land."

⊙ Born in England and raised in the U.S., Lahiri has managed to retain her Bengali cultural identity, which runs through her work.

Abandoning their tradition-bound life in Calcutta, recently married Ashima and Ashoke Ganguli move to a town outside of Boston, Massachusetts to pursue their version of the American dream. Unwilling to give up their Bengali culture, Ashima in particular struggles against Western assimilation, attempting to maintain ties with India. However, the births of their son, Gogol (named after the Russian writer), and their daughter, Sonia, who grow up American first, Bengali second, undermine their hope of respecting the customs of their former world. As they cling to the past, their children endeavor to overcome the schizophrenia of being at once inside of and marginalized from the only society they have ever truly known. Recording the immigrant experience in a direct and resonating prose, Jhumpa Lahiri's *The Namesake* illustrates how a clash of cultures may erupt between generations within a single family, and how, ultimately, home becomes a microcosm of the self.

An immediate best seller and winner of both the *New York Times* and *New York Magazine* Book of the Year Awards, *The Namesake* was Lahiri's much-anticipated first novel. Whereas the novel describes the experiences of second-generation Indian immigrants to America and the sense of being torn between the country of their birth and the country of their parents' birth, her debut work, a collection of short stories entitled *The Interpreter of Maladies* (1999), looked at the strain of leaving behind the familiarity of one's homeland for the strangeness of a completely foreign culture. This collection earned her the Pulitzer Prize for fiction in 2000—a prize rarely given to debut works or collections—as well as the PEN/Hemingway Award, and has been translated into twenty-nine languages. **BJ**

Vernon God Little

DBC Pierre

Winner of the 2003 Man Booker Prize, *Vernon God Little* is a black comedy written with a Texan drawl so intense you find yourself mouthing the words under your breath in order to catch their sense. The book is set in the town of Martirio (Spanish for "martyr"), the "barbecue sauce capital of Texas"—an ordinary town, full of average, self-obsessed people. Our hero, fifteen-year-old Vernon, is a survivor of a high-school massacre, carried out by his closest friend, Jesus. As police and media attention focus increasingly on Vernon, he begins to be seen as an accessory to the crime rather than a near-victim.

Vernon is powerless. He lacks the maturity to take control of his situation. He must do what the adults around him—teachers, his mother, the police—tell him; he mistakenly places a childlike trust in these people, and, again and again, they fail him. The author constantly plays with Vernon's middle name Gregory, calling him "Vernon Gone-to-hell Little" and "Vernon Gonzalez Little," each time reflecting the influence Vernon feels himself under. On death row, at the end of the book, Vasalle, the axe-murderer tells Vernon: "You're the God. Take responsibility." It is only when Vernon takes responsibility for the things that are happening to him that he can influence the direction of his own life and become "Vernon God Little."

DBC Pierre's novel targets all the usual ills of contemporary America—guns, teenage alienation, dysfunctional families, the justice system, gluttony—as well as offering a chilling portrayal of the way the media is able to twist events to its own ends. The book's dark comedy occasionally loses its way among these multiple targets, becoming puerile or farcical, but the plot swings along at such a pace and with such startling twists that this relatively minor quibble scarcely seems to matter. **CIW**

Lifespan | *b*. 1961 (Australia)
First Published | 2003
First Published by | Faber & Faber (London)
Man Booker Prize | 2003

"It's hot as hell in Martirio. . ."

◉ "DBC Pierre" is the pseudonym of Peter Warren Finlay; "DBC" stands for "Dirty But Clean," while "Pierre" is a childhood nickname.

The Successor

Ismail Kadare

Lifespan | *b.* 1936 (Albania)
First Published | 2003
First Published by | Shtëpia Botuese 55 (Tiranë)
Original Title | *Pasardhësi*

This novel, written by Ismail Kadare, winner of the inaugural Man Booker International Prize in 2005, is set in Tirana, the capital of Albania, and is based around the death of Mehmet Shehu, the "Successor" to the "Guide," communist dictator Enver Hoxha, who ruled Albania for fifty years and in 1981 was poised to surrender his power. The Successor's family having been arrested or eradicated, it remains unclear whether or not he was murdered or committed suicide. The mystery of his death is accompanied for most Albanians by a long-bred fear of inquiry.

It is this fear that Kadare's clear, precise, and unsentimental prose communicates, reinforcing the tension brought by the unresolved murder. Tension and fear produce the paranoia that consumes his Albanian characters: Suzanna, the Sucessor's daughter, who is traumatized by the termination of her engagement to Genc, due possibly to his alliances with the former regime; the pathologist who worries that in performing the Successor's autopsy, he is securing his own death; and the architect who builds the Successor's great house— bigger, he comes to realize, than that of the Guide.

By linking political fear to geographic isolation, Kadare brings his Albanian audience to the fore. It is in the character of a supernatural old aunt, whether spy or ghost, who appears to the family of the Successor after his death, that the narrative is conveyed to Albanians. Her prophecies are as transcendental as the past they must acknowledge before shedding their cloak of fear. **JSD**

Lady Number Thirteen

José Carlos Somoza

Lifespan | *b.* 1959 (Cuba)
First Published | 2003
First Published by | Mondadori (Madrid)
Original Title | *La Dama número trece*

In his novels José Carlos Somoza has alluded to very distinct literary genres: from mystery stories and erotic fiction to futurist fantasy and the scientific thriller. But for Somoza, the conventions of a genre are merely tools for developing a literary game around questions such as philosophy—*The Athenian Murders*—or art—*The Art of Murder*—or the power of poetry—*Lady Number Thirteen*, a novel that falls within the realm of the terror genre.

A professor of literature, Salomón Rulfo, suffers a recurrent nightmare in which he finds himself present at a triple murder in a house familiar to him, while a woman desperately asks him for help. Despite his doctor's attempted explanations, the dream seems incredibly vivid and Rulfo believes that the desperate woman will actually be killed. Rulfo decides to enter the house surreptitiously, to reexperience the setting of his dream. From that moment, he seems to enter another reality, in which "human language is not inoffensive" and people do not suffer simple misfortunes but live caught in a curse, in a "combination of powerful words."

Somoza was a psychiatrist before becoming a novelist and, as with his other novels, the mystery of *Lady Number Thirteen* revolves around psychological obsession. He writes with great power of conviction and, in a story full of supernatural portents, he persuades his readers to suspend their disbelief, taking them on a vertiginous succession of witches' sabbaths in sumptuous settings. The result, once again, is a novel as exciting as it is intelligent. **SR**

What I Loved

Siri Hustvedt

Lifespan | *b.* 1955 (U.S.)
First Published | 2003
First Published by | H. Holt & Co. (New York)
First UK Edition | Sceptre (London)

What I Loved examines the bonds aging art historian Leo Hertzberg created and lost with his closest friend Bill Wechsler throughout their twenty-five-year relationship. Bill's early painting of a young woman captivates Leo, and prompts him to seek out the unknown artist. An intellectually charged discussion in Bill's studio culminates in Bill giving Leo "permission" to see the shadow in the painting as his own, a gesture of intimacy that launches their fraternal affection. Throughout the intervening years, the men share improbable but evocative parallels. Bill and his wife, Lucille, move into the loft above Leo and his wife, Erica, and later Bill's model and second wife, Violet, comes to stay. The families welcome baby boys within weeks of each other. Both suffer the loss of their sons—precocious Matt Hertzberg in a childhood boating accident and Mark Wechsler in a perplexing yet persistent drift into mental disorder. By the time of the narrative, Leo is the lone remnant of a once robust world of personal and creative engagement. His quietly mournful voice unflinchingly describes the consequences of some catastrophic failures.

Populated with artists, academics, and poets, the world of Siri Hustvedt's novel bristles with an experimental energy against which the characters' domestic tragedies unfold. Bill's art stakes its claim at the periphery of the intelligible. Leo's patient readings of Bill's work ease it into articulateness, while testing the boundaries of interpretation in art, criticism, and our everyday lives. **AF**

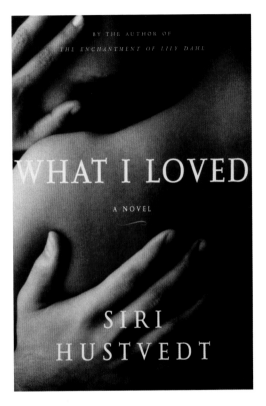

"The hand that had painted the picture hid itself in some parts of the painting and made itself known in others."

◉ In *What I Loved*, Siri Hustvedt returns to the theme of how events can shape our lives and determine who we become.

A Tale of Love and Darkness

Amos Oz

Lifespan | *b.* 1939 (Jerusalem)
First Published | 2003
First Published by | Keter (Jerusalem)
Original Language | Hebrew

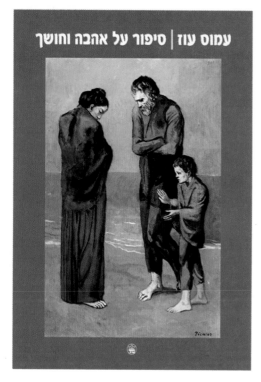

עמוס עוז | סיפור על אהבה וחושך

"My father could read sixteen or seventeen languages . . ."

⚉ Born Amos Klausner, Oz adopted his surname—Hebrew for "strength"—after joining the Kibbutz Hulda at the age of fifteen.

A Tale of Love and Darkness is Amos Oz's first autobiographical novel, and it won him numerous awards, including the Goethe Cultural Award and a nomination for the Nobel Prize. Opening with Oz's birth and ending with his mother's death three months before his bar mitzvah, Oz unfolds the story of his childhood and adolescence, his parents' lives, and the family's roots in a fluid, nonchronological account. The personal narrative, spanning five generations of Oz's family, is masterfully woven into a larger history—the fate of East-European Jews from the eighteenth to the twentieth century, the Zionist movement, the British mandate in Palestine, the siege on Jerusalem, the War of Independence, and the founding of Israel.

The core narrative, which binds together the myriad subplots, is that of Oz's mother, Fania. Her suicide is repeatedly broached throughout. Oz struggles painfully with his family's inherent compulsion for silence regarding emotions: "From the day of my mother's death to the day of my father's death, twenty years later, we did not talk about her once. Not a word. As if she never lived."

It is not until the very last pages of his memoir that Oz succeeds in finally shattering the "thousand dark years that separated everyone," and recounts the final days of his mother's life. It is in this poignant moment of the narrative that Oz's literary ingenuity comes into full play. Relying on his recollection of his aunt's and uncle's account, he glimpses his mother's death "as though an old moon was reflected in a windowpane from which it was reflected in a lake, from where the memory draws, not the reflection itself, which no longer exists but only its whitened bones," and (re)constructs an evocative, moving, and eloquent description. **IW**

Your Face Tomorrow

Javier Marías

Even without the projected third volume of Javier Marías's *Your Face Tomorrow*, the first two installments of this massive work, *Fever and Spear* and *Dance and Dream*, are enough to confirm the literary ability of a writer created in the magisterial mold of Juan Benet. Marías insists that *Your Face Tomorrow* is not a trilogy but a novel in three volumes and, as such, comparisons with Proust's *À la recherche du temps perdu* are inevitable. Without leaving the central themes of his novel, such as the weight of uncertainty in our life, or the distrust of the supposedly well known, Marías has opened new imaginative areas in his novels. In particular, his questions now concern the past and the credibility of narratives in which the past is described, and the many interests that threaten the possibility of a conclusive description of the past.

The novel describes the biased historical retelling of events in the Spanish Civil War (such as the case of Andreu Nin, killed by the communists), and the experiences of characters who, during the Second World War, were British espionage agents, coming from the highest spheres of the British universities: the protagonist of *Fever and Spear*, Jacques Deza, is working in London during the Civil War, where he is recruited to the British Secret Service by retired Oxford professor Sir Peter Wheeler. "Never tell anyone anything," this massive novel memorably begins, a reflection on the impossibility of knowing the trustworthiness of individuals, from the viewpoint of a protagonist whose trade consists of detecting possible genuineness. The novel uses speculation as a narrative device, and the style is always labyrinthine and involving, like a gauze weaved by a narrator while meditating and searching for certainties. **JGG**

Lifespan | *b.* 1951 (Spain)
First Published | 2002–04
First Published by | Alfaguara (Madrid)
Original Title | *Tu rostro mañana*

"One should never tell anyone anything . . ."

Sophisticated and unhurried, Marías slows down the action in his novels to expose rich seams of observation and reflection.

Cloud Atlas

David Mitchell

Shortlisted for the Man Booker Prize
Winner of the Richard and Judy Best Read of the Year

DAVID
MITCHELL

cloud atlas

'Superbly entertaining' *Daily Telegraph*
'A masterful feast' *Evening Standard*
'Shamelessly exciting' *Spectator*
'Remarkable' *Guardian*
'Stunning' *Daily Mail*

"If there be any eyrie so desolate . . . that one may there resort unchallenged by an Englishman, 'tis not down on any map I ever saw."

◉ The psychedelically styled cover, by Kal and Sunny, suggests an unfamiliar world after the downfall of science and civilization.

Lifespan | *b.* 1969 (England)
First Published | 2004
First Published by | Sceptre (London)
First U.S. Edition | Random House (New York)

Cloud Atlas is a glittering compendium of interlacing parables. Divided into six different accounts spanning several centuries, Mitchell ranges from the journal of a nineteenth-century explorer to the postapocalyptic memoir of a herdsman, Zachry. Each testament breaches time and space. Thus, in the second story, the financially destitute musician Robert Frobisher happens upon the explorer's journal and includes it in a letter to his lover Rufus Sixsmith; in the third story, Sixsmith is a scientific advisor blowing the whistle on a nuclear conglomerate's reactor; the report of the young journalist accompanying him then enters the custody of Timothy Cavendish, a publisher fleeing his underworld creditors. As Cavendish hides in a nursing home, Mitchell propels his reader into the future, where we encounter the plangent last testament of genetic fabricant Somni-451, detailing for the archives her life as an automaton under state control prior to execution.

Mitchell has recalled that "lurking in *Cloud Atlas'* primordial soup was an idea for a novel with a Russian-doll structure" that would allow him to house multiple narratives within each other. He notes Italo Calvino accumulated twelve plot layers with this device, yet "never 'came back' to recontinue his interruptions." Mitchell makes the return journey, allowing *Cloud Atlas* to "boomerang back through the sequence." And the novel's language is just as dynamic as its structure. Mitchell has secured this book with a rhapsody of contrasting dialects. **DJ**

The Swarm

Frank Schätzing

Lifespan | b. 1957 (Germany)
First Published | 2004
First Published by | Kiepenheuer & Witsch (Cologne)
Golden Feather Prize for Fiction | 2005

Frank Schätzing's eco-thriller begins off the Peruvian coast where a fisherman ponders his future vis-a-vis trawler fleets that decimate the world's fishing grounds. Shortly after, he disappears in the depths of the ocean. This is followed by other mysterious portents: whale attacks, the discovery of strange deep-sea worms, and devastating epidemics. It all turns out to be an attack on humanity in an attempt to halt the destruction of the planet's ecosystems. Masterminded by the Yrr, a single-cell maritime organism of superior intelligence, Nature eventually unleashes a huge tsunami that devastates Europe.

The Swarm's publication coincided not only with a number of natural disasters but also with America's war on terror, a war the novel alludes to: under the leadership of the presidential adviser Commander Li, the United States launches an expedition to seek contact with the Yrr. While European scientists urge Li to appease the Yrr through diplomacy, he plans to destroy it in order to establish humanity's dominance over the Earth. In a showdown that sees the sinking of the USS Independence and the death of Li and a number of other protagonists, contact with the Yrr is finally established and hostilities abate. The epilogue presents this truce as a final chance granted to humanity to avoid destruction.

The novel has been praised for its sound scientific background, although it has been dogged by allegations of plagiarism of scientific Web sites. In 2006, the movie rights were sold to Hollywood. **FG**

Suite Française

Irène Némirovsky

Lifespan | b. 1903 (Ukraine), d. 1942 (Poland)
First Published | 2004
First Published by | Éditions Denoël (Paris)
Prix Renaudot | 2004

Suite Française succeeds where all great literature succeeds—in the sharpness and delicacy with which it lays bare the frailties, longings, and triumphs of the human heart. The defeat of France early in the Second World War provides a tumultuous context within which Irène Némirovsky lays bare her cast of engaging yet seriously flawed characters.

Némirovsky charts the exterior and interior lives of several individuals and families in shock. Here and there the threads are brought together as the story of the rushed, fearful exodus from Paris unfolds, as the superiority and self-confidence of the bourgeoisie are slowly eroded and the basest of human emotions emerge in a time of extreme stress. The second section of the novel turns away from Paris to the life of a village under occupation. Even here, however, the theme of exodus is pursued, as people struggle both for and against the reassertion of normal life in an existence marked by uncertainty.

Much of the excitement surrounding this book has derived from the author's own life of exile, as the gifted daughter of rich European Jews who met her death at Auschwitz—a mistress of her craft, rediscovered when the manuscript of Suite Française was found and published half a century later. The hype may deter some. Yet this book is more than just an interesting publishing industry story; it deserves attention as a powerful testimony to events and emotions that were raw and real when they were first committed to paper. **RMa**

The Master

Colm Tóibín

Lifespan | b. 1955 (Ireland)
First Published | 2004
First Published by | Picador (London)
Novel of the Year | 2004

🔘 Tóibín's novel attempts to re-create the consciousness of Henry James—the eponymous Master—without mimicking his style.

🔘 Tóibín says that when he writes novels he is just anybody: "I'm not gay, I'm not bald, I'm not Irish . . . I'm the guy telling the story."

In *The Master,* Colm Tóibín re-creates the period in novelist Henry James's life between 1895, the year in which James endured the humiliating failure of his play *Guy Domville*, and 1899, closing with the visit of his brother William and his family to James's beloved Lamb House in the small fishing port of Rye on England's south coast. Time in Tóibín's novel is, for the most part, subordinated to space, and, more particularly, to the spaces of rooms and of houses. The novel creates a Jamesian world of consciousness without falling into pastiche, its narrative inflected by that of "the Master" but never lapsing into a parody of it.

The Master is a strongly episodic work, depicting in vivid detail a series of self-contained scenes and events: James's visit to Ireland, his painful negotiations with incompetent servants, and the surreal aftermath of the suicide of his close friend, the American novelist Constance Fenimore Woolson. Tóibín imagines his way into James's consciousness by describing his dreams and memories, which allow the novel to travel back to James's boyhood and youth, and to demonstrate the impact of a tragic series of deaths and losses throughout his life. Tóibín also seeks to show how experience, or occasionally the turning away from experience, transmuted itself into the stuff of James's fiction. The novel opens up, in ways both subtle and powerful, the question of authorial revelation and secrecy, the degree to which a novelist's work relies on their own lived experience, and the nature of James's desire, which is neither separable from the question of homosexuality nor fully explicable by it. Published at a time when many novelists are turning to biographical sources, *The Master* finds a new way for biography and fiction to meet, and to transform each other. **LM**

The Book about Blanche and Marie

Per Olov Enquist

Lifespan | *b.* 1934 (Sweden)
First Published | 2004
First Published by | Norstedts (Stockholm)
Original Title | *Boken om Blanche och Marie*

"It remembers the caresses . . ."

⊙ Enquist has been a dominant figure in Swedish culture since the
1960s; his novels are grounded in detailed historical research.

The Book about Blanche and Marie charts the lives of Blanche Wittman, the woman used by neurologist Jean-Martin Charcot in his demonstrations of hysteria at the Salpêtriére Hospital outside Paris, and Marie Curie, the Polish scientist, winner of the Nobel Prize, and co-discoverer of radium. When Blanche leaves the Salpêtrière, she becomes Marie's assistant and live-in companion. From this point of departure, Per Olov Enquist looks at the private lives led by major public figures, focusing in particular on the friendship that develops between Blanche and Marie, and on how Blanche copes with life as a multiple amputee. Blanche had one arm and both her legs amputated by the time of her death, having been exposed to massive quantities of radioactive material. She leaves behind three notebooks asking the question: What is love?

Enquist both lingers within his characters and stands resolutely outside of them; despite allowing them to ventriloquize through him, he vehemently asserts his independent presence as the author of the text. Appearing in the first person, Enquist discusses his obsession with the task at hand, and his inspiration and use of sources. Focusing on certain details and moments at random and then panning out again, Enquist provides us with intimate, fragmented snapshots of his subjects' lives.

The text is at once compulsive and opaque, and it is hard to fathom what derives from reliable historical sources and what is Enquist's own fantasy. This delicate, troubling novel marks a movement away from the violence and carnival of many postmodern novelists' treatment of history, and a movement toward a calmer, more tender, and yet equally open idea of how to bring historical fact within the realm of the novel. **LL**

2666

Roberto Bolaño

If it were a date, the title *2666* would perhaps seem to anticipate an inevitably posthumous work. Roberto Bolaño's massive novel, completed shortly before he died of a liver disorder in 2003 and coming in at more than 1,100 pages long, opens a seed of evil, and its five parts transform this seed into the elusive dream of a writer, Benno von Archimboldi. In the first part, four literary critics seek him in their texts while their lives become involved with him, eventually sensing him in the streets of Santa Teresa, a disguised version of the Mexican city of Ciudad Juárez. In the second, this same city is the cloister where the philosopher Amalfitano teaches, reads, reminds his wife that she left him, and wonders how to escape from there to Rosa, his adolescent daughter. In the third, a sports journalist called Fate arrives at Santa Teresa to report on a boxing match, but ends up becoming involved in the investigation of crimes against women that have occurred there. This thread leads to the fourth part, the real black heart of the novel: a ruthless, exhausting succession of murders, their dates, and their futile investigation. The end of the last part sees the reappearance of Archimboldi, the pseudonym of a German writer who appears to have traversed the twentieth century only to arrive at Santa Teresa.

An impossible challenge for the hurried reader, *2666* proves a mesmerizing experience. Perhaps the most incredible aspect of Bolaño's career is that, apart from one novel published in 1984, the rest of his considerable body of work was only published in the decade or so preceding his death. Consequently, *2666* stands as both the culmination of his life's work and as the promise of what Bolaño might have gone on to achieve, had he not succumbed to a tragically premature death. **DMG**

Lifespan | *b.* 1953 (Chile), *d.* 2003 (Spain)
First Published | 2004
First Published by | Anagrama (Barcelona)
Original Language | Spanish

"... a cult hero cut down ..."

New York Times *obituary, August 9, 2005*

⊙ Unfinished at the time of Bolaño's death, *2666* is divided into five parts, which were originally to be published as separate novels.

The Line of Beauty

Alan Hollinghurst

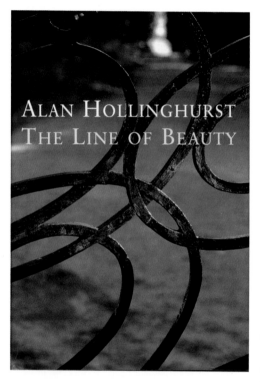

Lifespan | b. 1954 (England)
First Published | 2004
First Published by | Picador (London)
Man Booker Prize for Fiction | 2004

The Line of Beauty is Alan Hollinghurst's fourth novel. London life in the 1980s is viewed through the amoral eyes of Nick Guest, a young man who is seduced literally by the discovery of gay sex and metaphorically by the glamour of life among the powerful and the rich in Margaret Thatcher's Britain.

As a hanger-on in the household of a politician and the lover of the son of a Lebanese millionaire, Nick enjoys easy money, easy sex, and ubiquitous cocaine—one of the multiple possible references of the title's "line." A series of Thatcherite grotesques make their appearance and Thatcher herself features in one of the novel's comic highspots. No-holds-barred descriptions of gay sex are central to the author's purpose, which is underlined by giving Nick an obsession with Henry James; whereas James had to disguise his sexuality, Hollinghurst can flaunt it. The onset of AIDS darkens the novel's later stages, but the mood is far from despair or tragedy; Hollinghurst seems to identify with Nick's "love of the world that was shockingly unconditional."

Except for its sexual orientation, *The Line of Beauty* is a fairly conventional novel in the English literary tradition, written in an elevated, precise prose with an exact eye for character and a sharp ear for varying social registers of speech. Aesthetically pleasing, darkly humorous, and skillfully plotted, the novel delivers its intended pleasures to any reader ready to follow the author in uncritical acceptance of homosexuality in all its aspects. **RegG**

"He had a blind date . . . that evening, and the hot August day was a shimmer of nerves, with little breezy interludes of lustful dreaming."

⊙ For Hogarth, the line of beauty was a curve of aesthetic perfection; for Hollinghurst, it refers to everything from cocaine to a lover's body.

Measuring the World

Daniel Kehlmann

Lifespan | *b. 1975 (Germany)*
First Published | 2005
First Published by | Rowohlt (Reinbeck)
Original Title | *Die Vermessung der Welt*

This is a novel about two great German minds, the mathematician Carl Gauss (1777–1855) and the explorer Alexander von Humboldt (1769–1859). Their life stories have striking similarities and differences from the start. Gauss comes from impoverished circumstances, but his genius is obvious from early in his childhood; Humboldt is born to nobility and trained for greatness from the first. They represent two very different approaches to surveying the world of their time. Carl Gauss sees little of the physical world but much in his mind's eye; Humboldt travels far and wide in an attempt to see as much of the physical world as possible.

Kehlmann's style is almost sketchlike, offering telling detail but leaving much of the background to the imagination. He does not move slowly and methodically through the biographies, but lingers over some sections and skips over others, subtly portraying the limiting effect fame has on his subjects. Both men are considered to be "islands", living in worlds of their own making, obsessed with obtaining vast amounts of knowledge.

Kehlmann is fascinated by his two characters' obsessive behaviors and what the two great minds are willing to do to achieve their end goals. Each is, in his own way, locked into his own world, with Gauss not much of a social creature and Humboldt remaining largely oblivious of others. *Measuring the World* portrays the two historical figures with liveliness, extraordinary erudition, and sly humor. **LB**

The History of Love

Nicole Krauss

Lifespan | *b. 1974 (U.S.)*
First Published | 2005
First Published by | W. W. Norton & Co (New York)
Orange Prize for Fiction Shortlist Nominee | 2006

This sad and achingly beautiful book is a skillfully crafted exploration of loss and its aftermath: loss of a lover, son, husband, father, friend. With continually changing narrative voices, it weaves at least three stories seamlessly together with moments of surprising convergence, their unifying point being the "lost" manuscript, "The History of Love," written sixty years before by Polish émigré Leo Gursky, a paean to the only woman he ever loves, Alma.

Now an old man, Leo lives a solitary life in his New York apartment, continually revisiting the past and creating for himself a half-fantasy world in which he can survive his sorrows for a little longer. He finds solace in writing, this time a manuscript entitled "Words for Everything," because to set his life in words means his story is heard and he is not yet dead. Unbeknown to him, his manuscript "The History of Love" has been published and it plays a part in the love story of a young Israeli man and his wife, who name their firstborn Alma after "every girl in (the) book." The teenage Alma's struggle to manage her family's sorrow and way forward, following the death of her beloved father, sets her on a path that untangles the mystery of the life of the book, her namesake, and its author.

With immense tenderness and with moments of unexpected humor, Nicole Krauss shows the ability of the human spirit to survive in the wake of seemingly insupportable loss and in the process celebrates and validates the act of writing itself. **CN**

The Sea

John Banville

Lifespan | *b.* 1945 (Ireland)
First Published | 2005
First Published by | Picador (London)
Man Booker Prize | 2005

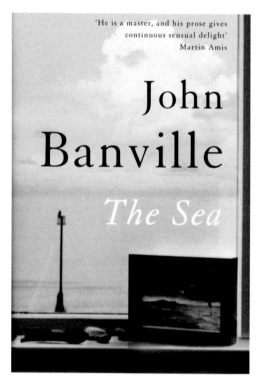

'He is a master, and his prose gives continuous sensual delight'
Martin Amis

John Banville
The Sea

"Happiness was different in childhood."

◉ *The Sea* was seen to be returning literary credibility to a prize often awarded to populist works when it won the Man Booker in 2005.

"Memory dislikes motion, preferring to hold things still." This poignant realization lies at the heart of John Banville's latest novel, which won the Man Booker Prize in 2005 in one of the tightest contests in years, narrowly beating out Kazuo Ishiguro's *Never Let Me Go* only when the chairman of the judging panel cast his deciding vote in Banville's favor.

The Sea tells the story of Max Morden's grief after the death of his wife, and his subsequent journey to the mysterious scene of a childhood romance. This trip is an attempt by Morden, an art historian, to reclaim the past as a work of art. His bereavement compels him to search for some early scene of love and loss, some original drama that remains proof against the tidal, erosive work of time.

Banville's prose often seems to have something of the miraculous to it, and the miracle in this novel is its capacity to use words to produce vivid images—to find beneath the constant movement of the everyday an attitude, or glance, or shape that seems suddenly, magically present. The novel depicts the ugliness of death and of bodily decrepitude, as it conjures the experience of loss with an uncanny intensity. But if this novel discusses death and the steady humiliation of dying, its greater concern is with the preservative power of memory, and of art, to catch something that does not die, something that is as immune to death as innocence. This novel is soaked in images and phrases drawn from works of art—from Bonnard, Whistler, and Vermeer; from Shakespeare, Proust, and Beckett. Morden's journey to early childhood is woven into this homage to art, seamlessly and exquisitely. Reading the novel is at once to feel what it is to die and to find oneself lifted from the choppy motion of time, into the quiet midst of an unmoving image. **PB**

The Elegance of the Hedgehog

Muriel Barbery

Renée Michel is not who she appears to be. For the rich inhabitants of 7 Rue de Grenelle, the concierge who has been there for years is a good woman, the archetypal building caretaker: there is nothing particularly striking about her appearance, and she can be both helpful and gruff. But behind her slightly tough exterior, the fifty-four-year-old Renée hides some surprising habits. At the back of her concierge's room, she indulges her passions for Russian literature (her cat is named Leo, in homage to the author of *Anna Karenina*), Japanese cinema, and Dutch painting and wonders about the nature of phenomenology. She is fascinated by those pure moments of grace when everything hangs in perfect but precarious balance.

Paloma Josse hides herself, too. She is twelve years old and lives with her parents in one of the very chic apartments in the building. An exceptionally gifted and rebellious child, she plans to kill herself and burn the family apartment on her thirteenth birthday. With wit and humor, she scrupulously records her deepest thoughts in a journal and tries to discover the secret of "still movement." For Paloma, adult life is a goldfish bowl, an empty and absurd place where false impressions reign.

The rest of the building is filled mainly with narrow-minded, bourgeois tenants who are rooted in their prejudices. However, the arrival of a wealthy Japanese widower, sophisticated and refined, upsets this world of deceptive appearances. Following the alternating points of view of the two protagonists, the novel is a philosophical journey, a reflection on the meaning of life that offers the reader multiple and unexpected sensations. Written in an elegant and lively style, it brings us spiritedly into a world that is rich, subtle, and funny. **SL**

Lifespan | *b.* 1969 (Morocco)
First Published | 2006
First Published by | Gallimard (Paris)
Original Title | *L'Élégance du hérisson*

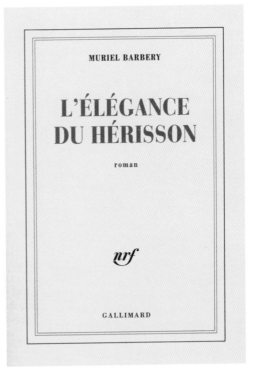

"Concierges do not read The German Ideology . . .*"*

● Muriel Barbery's novel captured the hearts of French readers, selling over a million copies in its first year.

Carry Me Down

M. J. Hyland

Lifespan | *b.* 1968 (England)
First Published | 2006
First Published by | Canongate (Edinburgh)
Man Booker Prize Shortlist Nominee | 2008

carry
me
down

"This is writing of the highest order."
—J. M. COETZEE

M. J. HYLAND
Author of *How the Light Gets In*

"I'm angry with her now . . ."

◉ Hyland originally intended John to be middle-aged but wrote a flashback to his childhood and realized he worked better as a child.

Carry Me Down is narrated in the present tense by eleven-year-old John Egan, who lives in Ireland in the early 1970s. This increasingly popular narrative perspective forces M. J. Hyland to work from a limited vocabulary, giving a clarity and pureness of tone and avoiding overt stylization. Hyland's style captures this young boy's various troubles, curiosities, and fears amid a disintegrating family and his awkward pre-pubescent self-discovery.

A major preoccupation of the novel is the rather grand theme of truth, as refracted through the autodidactic and secretive John, who believes he possesses a "gift" for truth-detection and expends much time and energy trying to prove it. To this end, he produces his own book of lies, a log of the misdirection and compromises he constantly needs to find his way around. He records his physical symptoms when lied to and pushes people to the limits of their patience and good will, ostensibly in order to test their honesty.

However, John's abstract systematizing and detective work come unstuck when faced with his family's deceit. Unversed in the emotional background behind the lies, John subjects those around him to forced confessions and revenge missions, never noticing the disparity between his motivations and actions, or the self-deceit he might have in common with those he attacks.

Hyland characterizes John as a limited and internalizing young boy on the verge of a skewed adolescence, but he gradually becomes a tool used to explore a wide range of forces beyond his understanding. At its core a novel about emotional development, *Carry Me Down* pits innocence and deceit against each other and finds the murky middle ground to be littered with vested interests. **DTu**

Against the Day

Thomas Pynchon

After the intricately woven conflation of fact and fantasy that characterized *Mason & Dixon*, *Against the Day* marks the emergence of what might be called Pynchon's "late style." Complex yet warmly accessible, eschewing the formal experimentation of *Gravity's Rainbow*, this is a vast, multitextured work set primarily in the two decades of geopolitical turbulence leading up to the First World War. Turbulence is an appropriate metaphor given one of the novel's central plot strands—the madcap, Jules Verne-style exploits of "The Chums of Chance," global adventurers of varying degrees of competence who traverse the skies in an airship captained by the indefatigable Randolph St. Cosmo. Within this loose framing device, Pynchon leads us on wondrous detours to silent-era Hollywood, Iceland, the Balkans, Göttingen, the Siberian tundra, and the spiritualist backrooms of late Victorian London.

In many respects, *Against the Day* exhibits all of the hallmarks of Pynchon's earlier writing—the ethical commitment to those who "couldn't buy a baby bonnet for a piss ant" if "a nightshirt for an elephant cost two cents"; the fascination with strange cosmologies, fragile folk cultures and outlaw(ed) traditions; the scorn for corporate skulduggery; the knotted relationship between "historical" and "narrative" time; the loopy fondness for talking animals and obscene songs. There are also, however, a number of new developments, particularly Pynchon's evocation of fin de siècle anarchism and political violence—a reckoning with the moral vortex of the blast radius that resonates deeply with our contemporary situation. Impossible to summarize, *Against the Day* is utterly unique yet unmistakably the work of one of America's greatest and most mysterious literary artists. **SamT**

Lifespan | *b.* 1937 (U.S.)
First Published | 2006
First Published by | Penguin (New York)
Original Language | English

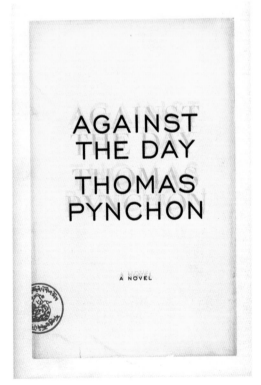

"They fly toward grace."

◉ Of *Against the Day*, Pynchon has said, "Maybe it's not the world, but with a minor adjustment or two it's what the world might be."

The Inheritance of Loss

Kiran Desai

This multigenerational story is set in India and New York, over which Britain hovers as the ghost of colonial past, casting long shadows over the present. In Kalimpong, the orphaned teenage girl Sai lives with her Cambridge-educated grandfather, a retired judge. Although neglected, Sai is cherished by the cook whose son, Biju, subsists as an immigrant in New York. The narrative moves between the two locations to interweave human stories with the politics of bourgeois neocolonialism, globalization, multiculturalism, and terrorist insurgency.

The Judge and Biju offer insights into different migrant experiences, in terms of class, historical, and geographical location. Yet both have been indoctrinated with a firm belief in the inherent superiority of the West. The Judge's sense of internal exile results from the humiliation of his colonial encounter, leaving him with a festering hatred for his culture. Biju's experience of cultural dislocation within the New York underclass is equally destructive. Local ethnic tensions are dramatized through Sai's doomed romance with tutor Gyan, who joins the Nepalese insurgents.

However, the novel's pessimistic vision of a multicultural future is peppered with penetrating humor. Through the immediacy of comic dialogue, Desai explores colonial history and postcolonial tensions. The shifting sensibility of modernity is articulated through the amusing superiority of the Jane Austen reading class, who pitch the BBC against CNN, and sneer at a country where jam is labeled Smuckers rather than "By appointment to Her Majesty the Queen."

Essentially a novel about longing and belonging, Desai captures the nuances of her flawed characters with tenderness and affection. **KDS**

Lifespan | *b*. 1971 (India)
First Published | 2006
First Published by | Hamish Hamilton (London)
Man Booker Prize | 2006

WINNER OF THE MAN BOOKER PRIZE 2006

KIRAN DESAI

THE INHERITANCE OF LOSS

'Affecting and endearing, full of laughter and tears'
BOYD TONKIN, *INDEPENDENT*

The Inheritance of Loss is Desai's second novel; her first, *Hullabaloo in the Guava Orchard*, won the Betty Trask Award in 1998.

Desai is the daughter of author Anita Desai, who has been shortlisted for the Man Booker three times but has never won.

Half of a Yellow Sun

Chimamanda Ngozi Adichie

Lifespan | *b.* 1977 (Nigeria)
First Published | 2006
First Published by | Fourth Estate (London)
Orange Prize for Fiction | 2007

The 1967–70 Nigerian–Biafran War—the subject of Adichie's second novel—started with the Nigerian Igbo ethnic group setting up their own state and ended with mass starvation caused by a Nigerian blockade. It is a conflagration that may not ring many bells with Westerners these days, but it was a burning issue of the time and motivated John Lennon to return his MBE in disgust at British involvement.

Adichie's 2003 debut *Purple Hibiscus* was highly regarded, but its horizons were limited by its first person narration and the fact that its protagonist was only fifteen years old. With *Half of a Yellow Sun*, Adichie goes panoramic, weaving a wide-ranging story seen through the eyes of three disparate characters across the course of nearly a decade: houseboy Ugwu, beautiful English-educated Olanna, and Richard, an awkward but radical Englishman infatuated by Olanna's semiestranged twin sister. Added to this is a book within a book, a retrospectively written account of the story the book tells, whose authorship is a sublime twist in the tale.

Adichie is clearly writing for an international market but is never heavy-handed as she imparts the minutiae of Nigerian life to the unfamiliar. Nor is she didactic, candidly acknowledging snobbery within the beleaguered Igbos' ranks. Inspired by many of the same things as her compatriot Ben Okri, Adichie spurns his magic realism for the more naturalistic devices of her hero Chinua Achebe, who was directly involved with the short-lived Biafran government. **SE**

The Gathering

Anne Enright

Lifespan | *b.* 1962 (Ireland)
First Published | 2007
First Published by | Jonathan Cape (London)
Man Booker Prize | 2007

This is one of three novels that Dublin-born Anne Enright wrote before *The Gathering*, the novel that won the prestigious Man Booker Prize in 2007.

The novel's story revolves around thirty-nine-year-old Veronica Hegarty, a mother of two who is in a state of shock after the death of her brother Liam. After years of struggling with alcoholism, Liam has drowned himself in Brighton. The majority of the novel is comprised of flashback sequences in which Veronica tries to locate the motivation for his suicide. Whether Veronica finds that cause is debatable. The genesis of Liam's suicide may or may not lie in an incident that occurred the summer that she and her siblings spent at their grandmother's house. And it may or may not have spiraled from the love triangle that her grandmother was involved in. It is the ambiguity that Enright crafts through her prose and her ability to shift the narrative from the inside of one character's head to the next that bear her mark as a master novelist.

The interior landscape that the novel inhabits is in stark contrast to the robust corporeal description that runs throughout. Veronica's experience of grief is thus something that is mapped out emotionally as well as physically as ". . . a confusing feeling—somewhere between diarrhea and sex—this grief that is almost genital." The themes of love and death here intersect on the body, ultimately evoking the lasting scar of love that remains to haunt us when those whom we love leave. **JSD**

The Brief Wondrous Life of Oscar Wao

Junot Díaz

Lifespan | *b.* 1968 (Dominican Republic)
First Published | 2007
First Published by | Riverhead Books (New York)
Pulitzer Prize for Fiction | 2008

The long-awaited first novel from Junot Díaz expands the short story about Oscar Wao—a lonely sci-fi nerd who falls hopelessly in love with women who never reciprocate his feelings—originally published in the *New Yorker* seven years previously. It tells of Oscar's sister, his mother, and his grandfather who, in defying the vicious Dominican dictator Rafael Trujillo, brought terrible suffering upon the family's subsequent generations.

According to the narrator, Yunior, this suffering was the result of a *fukú*, or curse, a superstition as old as the first European arrival on Hispaniola and blamed for anything from the Yankees losing a ball game to an inability to have male children. In the story of Oscar Wao (a mishearing of "Oscar Wilde"), the *fukú* is responsible for the death of Oscar's grandfather, Abelard, and two of his three beautiful daughters, as well as the suffering of the much younger third daughter (Oscar's mother). It is this same *fukú* that drives Oscar mad with love and puts an end to his short, desperate life.

The threads of the story that tell of Oscar's family, in particular those set in the Dominican Republic during Trujillo's reign of terror, are the most captivating, brought to life by Díaz's playful voice, which is liberally peppered with Spanish (and especially Dominican) slang and sci-fi references, a style representative of Gabriel García Márquez's "Macondo" turned "McOndo": magic realism for the diaspora generation. **PC**

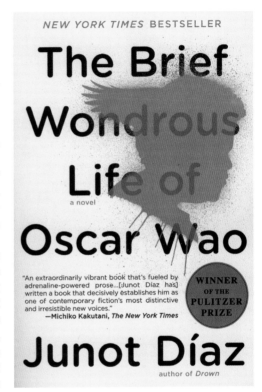

"They say it came first from Africa, carried in the screams of the enslaved; that it was the death bane of the Tainos . . . that it was a demon . . ."

⬆ Junot Díaz's long-anticipated first novel tells of Oscar's hopeless love life and his family's struggles.

The Blind Side of the Heart

Julia Franck

Lifespan | *b*. 1970 (East Germany)
First Published | 2007
First Published by | S. Fischer Verlag (Frankfurt)
Original Title | *Die Mittagsfrau*

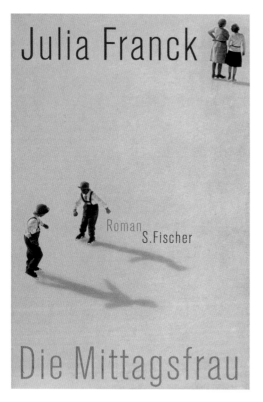

Julia Franck

Roman
S.Fischer

Die Mittagsfrau

"We're leaving. Peter nodded."

🔵 *The Blind Side of the Heart* tells the story of Helene, whose tragic
love life leads her eventually to abandon her seven-year-old son.

The Blind Side of the Heart, which won Julia Franck the coveted German Book Prize in 2007, tells the story of Helene, a woman whose life-journey takes her from Bautzen in Saxony at the beginning of the twentieth century, through the Berlin of the Roaring Twenties, to occupied Pomerania at the close of the Second World War. The story of Helene's life also encompasses the twentieth-century history of Germany, spanning two world wars, the Weimar era, and the rise of National Socialism.

The German title of the novel (*Die Mittagsfrau*, literally "Lady Midday") refers to the Wendish legend of a woman who would appear at the hottest part of the day in harvest time and condemn those she encountered to death unless they could promptly answer the questions that she posed to them. The title of Franck's novel thematizes the centrality of narration to life, particularly as *The Blind Side of the Heart* charts the progressive emotional petrifaction that results from increased repression and silence about a problematic personal history.

The tragic end of a love affair with a charismatic philosophy student plunges Helene into an amnesiac work ethic as a nurse, as well as into increasing emotional apathy. This in turn leads to her ill-advised marriage to an emphatic Nazi sympathizer, who falsifies Helene's papers to cover over her Jewish roots and changes her name to Alice. The prologue and epilogue that frame the story are narrated from the point of view of Helene's son, Peter, abandoned by his mother during the flight from Pomerania to Berlin at the close of the Second World War. He represents the millions of Germans who lived in the long shadow of the Nazi era—the physically absent mother in this instance figures as the master trope for an inaccessible and repressed past. **KKr**

Kieron Smith, Boy

James Kelman

Kieron Smith, Boy marks a new period in James Kelman's writing career, as it suggests a new general development in contemporary writing. The novel bears some resemblance to Kelman's 2004 novel, *You Have To Be Careful in the Land of the Free*, in that both novels are virtually plotless, and both are locked tightly within the consciousness of an isolated narrator. In the case of *You Have To Be Careful*, the narrator belongs to a familiar Kelman lineage, being a working-class Scotsman who finds himself out of step with his surroundings (here as an "unassimilatit non-integratit immigrant" living in the United States). But in *Kieron Smith, Boy*, Kelman writes from the perspective of a child who narrates the story of his family's relocation from Glaswegian tenements to a housing scheme on the outskirts of the city.

Kelman's adoption of a child's voice might put *Kieron Smith, Boy* in a tradition of novels that see the world through child's eyes. But Kelman achieves with his use of this voice something that is entirely unprecedented, and that amounts to nothing less than a reinvention of the novel form. In giving language to the thought of Kieron Smith, Kelman's prose conjures an intense and overwhelming intimacy with the movement of an imagination grappling with the outrageousness of ordinary young life. In reading the novel, one cannot resist asking oneself why this boy should share the inside of his mind with us in this way. What has allowed this miracle of frictionless telepathy to take place? To respond to this question is to recognize that Kelman has forged a language here that reshapes the relationship between reader and narrator, and that, in its poetic perfection, suggests a new way of encountering the movement of the mind. **PB**

Lifespan | *b.* 1946 (Scotland)
First Published | 2008
First Published by | Hamish Hamilton (London)
Original Language | English

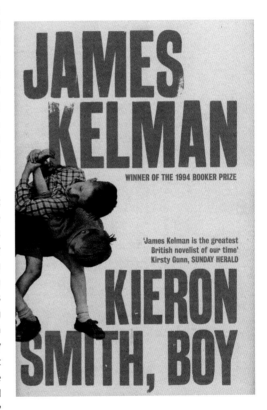

"Ye caught fish in it too."

⊙ James Kelman is notorious for dividing the critics, and *Kieron Smith, Boy* provoked heated debate.

Home

Marilynne Robinson

Home is a retelling of the events of Robinson's second novel, *Gilead*, from the perspective of the Boughton family. With it she cements her reputation as one of the most extraordinary novelists writing today, unique in her powerful combination of intellectual rigor and compassion for human frailty.

The plot is minimal. Glory Boughton returns to the house of her father, the ailing Reverend Boughton, at the age of thirty-eight after a failed engagement. Shortly after her arrival, her brother Jack, the much-loved, much-mourned black sheep of the family, sends word that he too will be coming home. The arrival of this prodigal son brings his dying father great joy, but Jack's sins prove too many and too much for the Reverend to forgive, and his last words to his most distant and beloved son, the son "whom he has favored as one does a wound," are spoken in petty frustration. Jack leaves and Glory is left as the inheritor of the old family home, preserving it for a time when Jack's mixed-race son might return in his place.

Set in a small town in the American Midwest against the background of the 1950s civil rights movement, *Home* is an astonishingly thorough and poignant meditation on the power and limits of faith and forgiveness, longing and loss, and the spiritual isolation of those souls who are seemingly predestined to find themselves alienated wherever they go—above all when they attempt to return home. Robinson's spare prose, at once simple and poetic, is unforgiving in its dissection of damaged individuals struggling toward a state of grace, but the seriousness with which she approaches both the theological and human implications of each gesture and encounter creates the possibility of transcendence, or of something like it. **JHu**

Lifespan | *b.* 1947 (U.S.)
First Published | 2008
First Published by | Farrar, Straus & Giroux (New York)
Orange Prize for Fiction | 2009

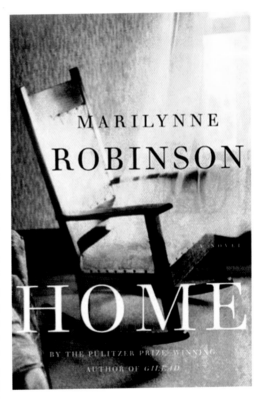

○ *Home* is only Robinson's third novel in twenty-eight years, but it has cemented her standing as one of the most important living writers.

◐ Marilynne Robinson in Paris while finishing her third novel in October 2007.

The White Tiger

Aravind Adiga

Lifespan | *b.* 1974 (India)
First Published | 2008
First Published by | Atlantic Books (London)
Man Booker Prize | 2008

Winner of the Man Booker Prize 2008

THE WHITE ARAVIND ADIGA TIGER

"I am tomorrow."

🔺 Aravind Adiga's breakout first novel depicts an India that is jarringly different from the country usually seen in the West.

The White Tiger, Aravind Adiga's debut novel, made a huge splash upon publication, garnering voluminous praise and making Adiga the second-youngest author ever to win the Man Booker Prize.

The book received this praise for the story it tells and the uniqueness of the protagonist's character and narrative voice. Balram Halwai, according to his name and his caste, ought to be a sweet-maker in the small village in rural India where he was born (referred to as the Darkness, in contrast to the Light of the big cities such as Delhi, Mumbai, and Bangalore). But there is nothing typical about Balram. He is an entrepreneur, and as the story unfolds—told over seven nights to Premier Wen Jiabao of China in an imaginary series of letters from Balram's tiny, chandelier-equipped office in Bangalore—we learn just what it means to be one of the new breed of entrepreneurs in India.

This is not the beautiful, exotic, magic-realist India of Salman Rushdie that is so often idealized by Western readers. Instead, this is a story of the dark, dirty, corrupt India that, along with China, is booming while the West stagnates. It is the story of India debunked, the story of one man's attempt to escape the dead end that is, according to Balram, the lot of the vast majority of the Indian population. In Balram's eyes, the people have been hoodwinked and sold into servitude by fellow countrymen against whose ruthlessness the only response is more ruthlessness. As he says, "Only a man who is prepared to see his family destroyed . . . can break out of the coop."

The White Tiger exposes the stale attitudes and deep-rooted injustices that keep Indian society running, yet shows that something is about to break under all the pressure. This is a very angry book that manages, remarkably, to be very funny indeed. **PC**

Cost

Roxana Robinson

Roxana Robinson had already written three novels—*Sweetwater* (2003), *This Is My Daughter* (1998), and *Summer Light* (1988)—in addition to three short story collections and a biography of Georgia O'Keeffe (1989) when she sat down to write *Cost*, a story of addiction that wonderfully explores the intricacies of family relationships and emotions.

Protagonist Julia Lambert is an art professor at Columbia University in New York. She has two adult sons, Steven and Jack, and two elderly parents, Edward and Katherine, and when *Cost* opens, Julia is entertaining said parents at her summer home in Maine. And she is feeling immensely frustrated with her childlike behavior toward them. It is into this fraught space that Steven, on his way up to the house, steps. Steven has just visited his younger brother and has learned that Jack is addicted to heroin. The discovery of this addiction—and the ensuing family intervention—shapes the plot of the book as we witness two characters from each generation cycle through their own personal anxieties in the face of Jack's demise.

Though it is Jack's addiction that drives the novel, the characters provide it with its conflict and momentum. Robinson has said that she plans biographies for each of her characters before she begins writing, and in *Cost* this is evident. It is the interiority of her characters' landscapes, described in intensely scrutinous writing and careful language that gives *Cost* its remarkable quality. Robinson has often been tagged as a chronicler of conservative WASP life, and *Cost* will undoubtedly be marketed as a book about heroin addiction. Both are misleading in the face of a novel about the depth of human anxiety, about discovering that the cost of losing one's family may just motivate us all. **JSD**

Lifespan | *b.* 1946 (U.S.)
First Published | 2008
First Published by | Sarah Crichton Books (New York)
Original Language | English

"Her memory was gone."

⌕ Roxana Robinson's fourth novel deals with the far-reaching consequences of a young man's addiction to heroin.

The Children's Book

A. S. Byatt

Lifespan | *b.* 1936 (England)
First Published | 2009
First Published by | Chatto & Windus (London)
Original Language | English

"His eyes were blue . . ."

🔵 *The Children's Book* explores the darker side of childhood in the late Victorian era.

Spanning twenty-five years from the last days of the Victorian era to the end of the First World War0, *The Children's Book* is a vastly ambitious novel that combines trenchant social analysis of turn-of-the-century utopianism in all its forms (Fabianism, Quakerism, the suffrage movement, and anarchism to name just a few) with a compelling depiction of the darker aspects of childhood. The intensities of youth, from the dreamlike sense of oneness with the natural world to the opaquely disturbing but endlessly powerful experience of infant sexuality and the Oedipal complex, are strikingly connected by Byatt to the development of English and German society in the run up to the Great War.

The novel opens with the discovery of a wild boy, Philip Warren, living in the basement of the South Kensington Museum after running away from a pottery town. He is taken in by a visiting author of modern fairy tales, Olive Wellwood, and sent to work as an apprentice to Benedict Fludd, a master ceramicist. The Wellwood household is a model of domesticity in the Fabian fashion: a sprawling farmhouse in Kent decked out in Arts and Crafts movement decor run over with children of varying parentage, with an open door policy to rebels, artists, and financiers alike. The Fludd house, conversely, is a nightmarish parody of domestic life in which a tortured genius patriarch smashes as many pots as he makes, ignores his drug-addicted wife, and has incestuous relations with his daughters. As the book progresses and secret histories come to light, it becomes clear that the terrors of the Fludd house are no less present at the Wellwoods' because art and family are both, always and inevitably, founded on betrayal. **JHu**

American Rust

Philipp Meyer

This assured first novel from Philipp Meyer presents from a number of first person perspectives the brutalized nature of life in a dying Pennsylvania steel town. Isaac English, a strange but smart twenty year old, and his high school football star friend Billy Poe have both stayed in Buell, Pennsylvania, after high school despite being offered the chance to leave. Now they dream of sending Isaac to California to study astrophysics with the help of the railroads and four thousand dollars that he has stolen from his disabled father. On the way out of town, however, they encounter three homeless men; Poe cannot resist a fight, and one of the strangers ends up dead. In following the fallout of this event from the perspectives not only of Isaac and Poe but also Poe's mother Grace, police chief and Grace's longtime lover Bud Harris, and Isaac's sister Lee, the reader is taken further and further into a world where economic calamity has rendered free will an illusion.

In the two decades that the main protagonists have been alive, 150,000 jobs have been lost in the Mon Valley region. While *American Rust* is vividly plotted, its real strength is in depicting the consequences of this catastrophic blow to the blue-collar middle class at every level: from the crippling demoralization of a man who wants to work and cannot, to the families condemned generation after generation to a life lived in unheated trailers eating only what they can kill, to communities unable to pay for basic services, existing in a landscape of rusting steelworks that nobody can afford to tear down. At a time when hundreds of thousands more well-paid manufacturing jobs are being lost across the United States, this prescient novel delivers an unsentimental indictment of the human costs of late capitalism. **JHu**

Lifespan | *b.* 1974 (U.S.)
First Published | 2009
First Published by | Spiegel & Grau (New York)
Original Language | English

"A small thin figure . . ."

◔ Meyer worked several different jobs, including stints as a banker and a paramedic, before writing *American Rust*.

1Q84

Haruki Murakami

Lifespan | *b.* 1949 (Japan)
First Published | 2009–2010
First Published by | Shinchosha (Tokyo)
Original Title | Ichi-kew-hachi-yon

Haruki Murakami's magnum opus, the three-volume *1Q84*, contains simultaneously a love story, a universe of parallel worlds, a reflexive meditation upon the productive power of fiction, and an exemplary model of a novel that works through process, rather than resolution. Framed through the alternating narratives of Aomame, Tengo and, in the final volume, the sinister Ushikawa, Murakami charts the characters' sequential incursions into a twin-mooned world parallel to Orwell's eponymous year, 1984. In this other world, an ambivalent, potentially malignant force manifests itself through the figures of the Little People, a supernatural race affiliated with the cult of Sakigake. As the novel progresses, a veil is lifted from each character to reveal their hidden life and the threats posed by the world of 1Q84 upon their ambitions: Aomame, the benevolent assassin with a promiscuous sex life; Tengo's authorial collusion with a young girl on an award-winning book; and Ushikawa's unlikely abilities as a detective. As the narratives converge, the reader is embroiled in a race against time to escape from the nightmare universe and defy the ominous prophecy of Sakigake's mysterious Leader.

Despite the formidable length of the work, Murakami's style is engaging and comprehensible. The resolution to the work, however, is problematic. In fact, the achievement, and enjoyment, of *1Q84* lies in the path it treads, rather than its destination; it is a flawed, yet brilliant, masterpiece. **MPE**

Cain

José Saramago

Lifespan | 1922–2010
First Published | 2009
First Published by | Editorial Caminho, Lisbon
Original Language | Portuguese

The last work of Portuguese Nobel laureate José Saramago takes as its hero the fratricidal Cain and as its villain the god of the Old Testament. After killing his brother Abel, Cain is condemned to be a wanderer in time as well as space, a convention that allows the author to transport him to the scene of a series of biblical stories from the sacrifice of Isaac and the building of the Tower of Babel to the destruction of Sodom and Noah's Ark. *Cain* at time strays outside the Bible, notably in a passionate liaison with the dangerous, man-devouring Lilith—a strikingly positive depiction of a woman of power and lust. Yet the majority of the book is a retelling of familiar tales, given a fresh twist by Cain's and the author's acidic commentary on God's cruelty, petulance, self-satisfaction, and irrationality.

Despite unconventional typography—dialogue is presented in solid paragraphs without quotation marks—*Cain* is an easy and amusing read, sprinkled with aphorisms and colloquial asides. Darkly visible through the lucid simplicity of its storytelling, however, is a complex and bitter view of the human condition. For Saramago, a lifelong communist, God stands for the human tyrants who render life on earth a torment. Cain's revolt against God is a rebellion against all the injustices of the world. Eventually, Cain returns to killing in a rage against God's vileness. Despite this bleak conclusion, a luminous warmth toward ordinary human beings balances the author's hatred of their oppressors. **RegG**

A Gate at the Stairs

Lorrie Moore

Lifespan | *b.* 1975 (U.S.)
First Published | 2009
First Published by | Alfred A. Knopf (New York)
Orange Prize for Fiction Shortlist Nominee | 2010

Tassie is a freshman in a small college town, a farmgirl newly plucked from her father's foundering empire of designer root vegetables. Trying to find an identity in the United States—or even just a template—is never easy, but it becomes even more ticklish in a nation recently tinged by September 11.

Tassie lives cautiously, "in a spirit of regret prevention," lazily juggling her curriculum of geology, Sufism, wine tasting, and soundtracks of war movies, coping with family, and honing her burgeoning sexuality. When she lands a job as a babysitter for Sarah Brink, a highly strung chef, Tassie realizes how slippery identity can be. When is an adoptive mother of a mixed-race baby not a modern career woman but someone sad and unhealable? When is a boyfriend not a Brazilian photography student, but a terrorist? When is a little brother no longer a little brother, but a soldier in an ill-defined war? Although the novel's action does not travel beyond the borders of Wisconsin, all of America is here: racial tension, class, climate change, and children: having them, being them, no longer being them, and the need for something we cannot quite understand about them.

Lorrie Moore is perhaps America's finest short story writer and here her skill at making few words work hard is astonishing. Her voice is full of satire and fun, denuding liberal smugness and Midwestern churlishness, but when things become not so satiric, not so funny, her true virtuosity shines. **GT**

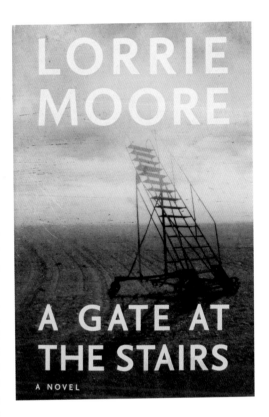

"The difference between opera and life, I'd noticed, was that in life one person plays all the parts."

⊙ Lorrie Moore's third novel is a witty, darkly funny, yet moving observation of small-town American life.

Freedom

Jonathan Franzen

Lifespan | *b.* 1959 (U.S.)
First Published | 2010
First Published by | Farrar, Straus & Giroux
Original Language | English

Jonathan Franzen's long anticipated follow-up novel to *The Corrections* (2001) is the story of the Berglund family—Walter and Patty, their children Joey and Jessica, and their difficult friendship with cool rock musician, Richard Katz. The novel traces their patchy fidelity to one another—as friends, parents, children, lovers—and follows with a startling precision the ways in which the rich joy of such fidelity is balanced against the need for new pleasures, the urge toward constant reinvention and extension of the self.

The novel, then, is about freedom, and the contradictions that surround its pursuit. Freedom is both our aim, the prized asset of our civilization, and a kind of solitude, or emptiness, as Patty finds when she discovers that she "pities herself for being so free." But if the novel offers a forensic analysis of the desire for freedom in a domestic setting, it always carries out its work in the global political context. The quality of the experience of freedom is influenced at all times by the wars that are being fought in its name at the beginning of the twenty-first century.

Reading *Freedom* is an effortless experience, like reading air. Franzen's narration of his characters' striving is so transparent and compelling that the story enters the reader's mind whole. Nonetheless, the novel continues to do its work long after it has been read. Franzen's enormous gift as a storyteller is that he tells us about our lives while also making us aware of the public networks and matrices within which we have our most private thoughts.

Freedom helps us to see how the fields of force that are producing world politics in the new century are also reshaping our most private experiences, both of our personal freedom, and of our loving commitment to others. **PB**

⊙ Jonathan Franzen's dissection of American middle-class life makes allusions to Tolstoy's classic novel *War and Peace.*

⊙ *Time* magazine hailed Franzen as a "Great American Novelist" when he featured on its cover on August 23, 2010.

Nemesis

Philip Roth

Lifespan | *b.* 1933 (U.S.)
First Published | 2010
First Published by | Houghton Mifflin Harcourt
Wellcome Trust Book Prize Shortlist Nominee | 2011

"Summers were steamy . . ."

🔘 Philip Roth uses a deadly outbreak of polio in wartime
New Jersey to examine the resolve of humanity under attack.

Brought up by his physically and morally strong grandfather to face down any evil, twenty-three-year-old Eugene "Bucky" Cantor is devastated to be turned away from volunteering for the armed forces when the United States enters the Second World War. A superior weightlifter and javelin thrower at college, Bucky is built like a marine but is crucially impaired by his poor vision, and so told to remain in Newark, New Jersey and complete his training as a physical education teacher.

When a polio epidemic sweeps the city, however, Bucky sees his chance to confront evil and redeem himself from failure. In his own private war with the disease, he discovers a difficulty that his friends on the Western Front are not facing: how do you fight an enemy that you know next to nothing about and that you cannot see?

Over the duration of a scorching hot summer, he is forced to stand by as, one by one, the boys at the playground he supervises die of polio, meanwhile doing all he possibly can to assuage the boys' fears and their parents' sense of panic and grief. Then comes the offer of a job at a summer camp in the mountains where his girlfriend is working, and Bucky is faced with a seemingly impossible choice: leave Newark for the clean air and the one he loves, or stay and fight a disease against which he is cruelly unarmed.

In this blasting, late novel about the terrors of contagion, Philip Roth contaminates the scene of his youth with the illegible savagery that defines violence in the twenty-first century. In *Nemesis* he takes the American man further than ever before in his fiction: into the politics of his being, and to the limit of what might be possible for him. **MJo**

The Marriage Plot

Jeffrey Eugenides

Like *The Virgin Suicides* (1993) and the Pulitzer Prize-winning *Middlesex* (2002), Eugenides's third novel is another coming-of-age story. Its subject is the love triangle between three students drawing to the end of their senior year at Brown in 1982. Mitchell Grammaticus loves Madeleine Hanna; Madeleine loves Leonard Bankhead; while Leonard, in line with the post-structuralist theory that Madeleine, an English Major, grapples with, is more interested in deconstructing the very idea of love, before breaking Madeleine's heart and winding up in a psychiatric unit.

This is a self-consciously literary novel. It begins with Madeleine's bookshelves, upon which lie the Austen, Eliot, and Brontës that inspire the thesis she is writing—"I Thought You'd Never Ask: Some Thoughts on the Marriage Plot"—and with these, his literary predecessors, in mind, Eugenides's novel is a postmodern twist on the classic Victorian narrative trope. Madeleine, from whose perspective the majority of the story is told, has to choose between the two men in her life, but it soon becomes apparent that, just as in the works of his contemporaries, such as David Foster Wallace and Jonathan Franzen, Eugenides's account of modern life, let alone matrimony, is not always a case of "happily ever after."

While Eugenides distinguished himself as a talented writer from the very start, *The Marriage Plot* is a significantly more accomplished novel than the work that precedes it. From the dreamlike internalization of *The Virgin Suicides*, through the sweeping multigenerational and intercontinental saga that is *Middlesex*, *The Marriage Plot*'s scope lies in its intertextuality and tightly plotted structure, firmly establishing Eugenides's position as one of America's foremost contemporary writers. **LSc**

Lifespan | *b*. 1960 (U.S.)
First Published | 2011
First Published by | Farrar, Straus and Giroux (NY)
Original Language | English

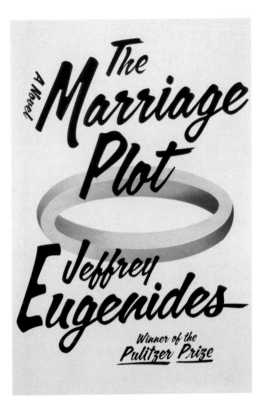

"The wood felt nice and cool."

◉ Jeffrey Eugenides sets his novel about a love triangle at his Ivy League alma mater, Brown University.

The Sense of an Ending

Julian Barnes

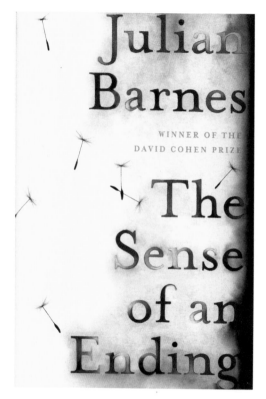

Lifespan | *b.* 1946 (England)
First Published | 2011
First Published by | Jonathan Cape (London)
Man Booker Prize | 2011

"History is that certainty produced at the point where the imperfections of memory meet the inadequacies of documentation."

⬥ In France, Julian Barnes is the only writer to have won both the Prix Médicis and the Prix Fémina.

On first appearances *The Sense of an Ending* is an old boys' venture: the story of a pseudo-intellectual clique at a London grammar school quoting Camus and Wittgenstein to each other, lording it over the fellow students they consider "vegetable matter." The entrance of new boy Adrian Finn into this group's lives is a similarly dusty trope; Adrian outdoes them at their own game by taking literature and philosophy seriously, with little regard for his image. "This was one of the differences between the three of us and our new friend," writes Tony, the novel's narrator. "We were essentially taking the piss, except when we were serious. He was essentially serious, except when he was taking the piss." In an exchange with the history master about the recent suicide of a student, Adrian contends that "nothing can make up for the absence of testimony, sir." Tony narrates the novel as a retired, aging man bearing witness to Adrian; he positions himself as a third party, writing testimony to the better thinker, the braver man.

Barnes constructs this traditional premise in order to unravel its power balance, until Tony is asking questions of not only himself and Adrian but the whole structure of biography. This is a novel about what we do with time and who we think we become. It is about what we mean when we say someone "took his life in his own hands." For all the complex, academic lines coursing through it, *The Sense of an Ending* is no sterile read; the very touchstones by which we orient our lives are drawn into it. **MJo**

A Visit from the Goon Squad

Jennifer Egan

Lifespan | b. 1962 (U.S.)
First Published | 2010
First Published by | Alfred A. Knopf (New York)
Pulitzer Prize | 2011

Jennifer Egan's Pulitzer Prize-winning novel is a masterful combination of experimental aesthetic form and compelling storytelling. Delivered in a series of self-contained episodes, the novel might be read as a series of short stories, each with its own distinct narrative voice and tone, but the substrata of connections holding these stories together create complex formal and narrative continuities that go right to the core of Egan's imaginative world.

The novel is loosely centered in the U.S. music scene and the life of music producer Bennie Salazar. Each story within the novel connects to Bennie in some way, although these connections are often oblique. The teenage members of a punk band, a disaffected Hollywood starlet, a suicidal teamster, an attempted rapist, a kleptomaniac; these lives are intertwined in a complex network of geographies and timeframes that suggest at once the proximity of human connectedness and its opposite. Lives fatally collide or tantalizingly brush past each other in a novel whose real subject is time (the eponymous "goon") and memory.

A Visit from the Goon Squad leaves you with the feeling that the world is larger than you had ever imagined, and yet closer and more real. In the midst of this complicated universe, Egan can distill everything into a moment of suspended time, a boy casting off his childhood self, learning to dance in the heat of an African night, which ripples exquisitely out to the further reaches of the novel. **HJ**

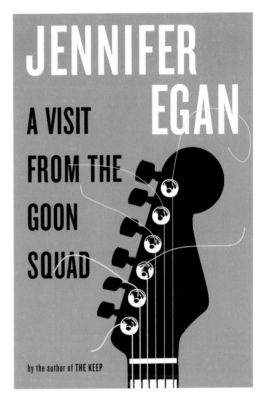

"Everybody sounds stoned, because they're e-mailing people the whole time they're talking to you . . ."

⊙ *A Visit from the Goon Squad* won the Pulitzer Prize, the National Book Critics Circle Award for Fiction, and the LA Times Book Prize.

There but for the

Ali Smith

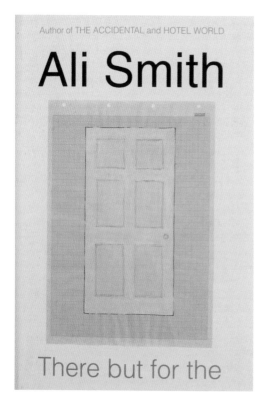

Author of THE ACCIDENTAL and HOTEL WORLD

Ali Smith

There but for the

"He's a pretty ordinary man
except that across his eyes
and also across his mouth
it looks like he's wearing
letterbox flaps."

○ Ali Smith's satire of contemporary culture turns on a dinner guest who locks himself in the spare room and refuses to leave.

Lifespan | *b.* 1962 (Scotland)
First Published | 2011
First Published by | Hamish Hamilton (London)
Original Language | English

Each of the words of the title of Ali Smith's *There But For The* serves as a heading to one of the book's four sections. Each of these sections features a different character: "There" is about a woman, Anna, who has just quit her job in "Senior Liaison"; "But" focuses on Mark, whose dead mother berates him in rhyme; "For" introduces May, an elderly but spirited woman in a nursing home; and, finally, "The" centers on Brooke, a precocious nine year old bursting with facts.

Each of these sections tells a distinct story; they seem at first to be unrelated. Gradually, however, it becomes clear that the tales are connected. The link is Miles, who is a guest at the Lees' annual alternative dinner party (to which they invite people who are "different" to those with whom they usually spend time). Part way through the dinner—which turns out to be a hotbed of concealed hostility and strained middle-class politesse—Miles leaves the table, goes upstairs, and locks himself in the spare room. He refuses to leave. Mrs Lee is horrified and distraught.

This prompts the reader to wonder: who is Miles? What point does he wish to make? When will he leave? Each section offers a partial answer. However, the book is about much more than resolving these questions. By turns serious, comic, playful, and sentimental, it is, more than anything, a celebration of language. It revels in the power and the possibilities of words, even words as unobtrusive as "there," "but," "for," and "the." **LMcN**

The Art of Fielding

Chad Harbach

Lifespan | *b.* 1976 (U.S.)
First Published | 2011
First Published by | Little, Brown (New York)
Original Language | English

Henry Skrimshander is a scrawny South Dakota teenager with an "impossibly concave" chest, but he has a gift: as shortstop, he never misses a ball, and he can make the throw to first with speed and accuracy every single time. When the novel opens, Henry is at the end of his high school baseball career and destined to disappear into obscurity—college coaches are only interested in size and batting power. He is rescued by Mike Schwartz, a player on an opposing team who is entranced by Henry's talent and who makes it his mission to see Henry succeed.

Henry's first three years at Westish College race by in an extended montage; he becomes so good a player that scouts begin to turn up at games with talk of six-figure signing bonuses. However, when a routine throw goes wrong, seriously wounding Henry's friend and roommate, Owen, it sets in motion a chain of events involving five characters whose lives become painfully entangled. While Henry falls into a debilitating paralysis of overthinking that threatens to ruin his game, Mike fights against the jealousy he feels toward his friend's success. Owen, meanwhile, finds himself the object of a dangerous crush that the sixty-year-old college president, Guert Affenlight—a dashing Melville scholar and lifelong bachelor—struggles to understand.

In spite of some predictable, not to say improbable, plot arcs, Harbach's warmhearted debut wins readers over with its fluent, engaging prose and suspenseful plotting. **PC**

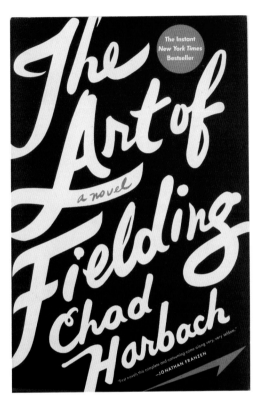

"Schwartz didn't notice the kid during the game. Or rather, he noticed only what everyone else did—that he was the smallest player on the field."

⬆ Chad Harbach's novel is an exploration of the timeless themes of love, desire, and commitment.

Author Index

Major Prize Winners

Man Booker Prize

1969 **Something to Answer For** P.H. Newby

1970 **The Elected Member** Bernice Rubens

1971 **In a Free State** V.S. Naipaul 648

1972 **G** John Berger 649

1973 **The Siege of Krishnapur** J.G. Farrell 657

1974 **The Conservationist** Nadine Gordimer

   Holiday Stanley Middleton

1975 **Heat and Dust** Ruth Prawer Jhabvala

1976 **Saville** David Storey

1977 **Staying On** Paul Scott

1978 **The Sea, The Sea** Iris Murdoch 694

1979 **Offshore** Penelope Fitzgerald

1980 **Rites of Passage** William Golding

1981 **Midnight's Children** Salman Rushdie 713

1982 **Schindler's Ark** Thomas Keneally 722–3

1983 **The Life & Times of Michael K** J.M. Coetzee 731

1984 **Hotel du Lac** Anita Brookner

1985 **The Bone People** Keri Hulme

1986 **The Old Devils** Kingsley Amis 766

1987 **Moon Tiger** Penelope Lively

1988 **Oscar and Lucinda** Peter Carey 786

1989 **The Remains of the Day** Kazuo Ishiguro 798

1990 **Possession** A.S. Byatt

1991 **The Famished Road** Ben Okri

1992 **The English Patient** Michael Ondaatje 827

   Sacred Hunger Barry Unsworth

1993 **Paddy Clarke Ha Ha Ha** Roddy Doyle

1994 **How Late It Was, How Late** James Kelman 849

1995 **The Ghost Road** Pat Barker

1996 **Last Orders** Graham Swift

1997 **The God of Small Things** Arundhati Roy 868

1998 **Amsterdam** Ian McEwan

1999 **Disgrace** J.M. Coetzee 886

2000 **The Blind Assassin** Margaret Atwood

2001 **True History of the Kelly Gang** Peter Carey

2002 **Life of Pi** Yann Martel 906

2003 **Vernon God Little** DBC Pierre 914

2004 **The Line of Beauty** Alan Hollinghurst 926

2005 **The Sea** John Banville 930

2006 **The Inheritance of Loss** Kiran Desai 935

2007 **The Gathering** Anne Enright 940

2008 **The White Tiger** Aravind Adiga 944

2009 **Wolf Hall** Hilary Mantel

2010 **The Finkler Question** Howard Jacobson

2011 **The Sense of an Ending** Julian Barnes 946

Orange Prize for Fiction

1996 **A Spell of Winter** Helen Dunmore

1997 **Fugitive Pieces** Anne Michaels 865

1998 **Larry's Party** Carol Shields

1999 **A Crime in the Neighbourhood** Suzanne Berne

2000 **When I Lived in Modern Times** Linda Grant

2001 **The Idea of Perfection** Kate Grenville

2002 **Bel Canto** Ann Patchett

2003 **Property** Valerie Martin

2004 **Small Island** Andrea Levy

2005 **We Need to Talk About Kevin** Lionel Shriver

2006 **On Beauty** Zadie Smith

2007 **Half of a Yellow Sun**

   Chimamanda Ngozi Adichie 936

2008 **The Road Home** Rose Tremain

2009 **Home** Marilynne Robinson 943

2010 **The Lacuna** Barbara Kingsolver

2011 **The Tiger's Wife** Téa Obreht

Pulitzer Prize

Novel 1918–1947; fiction 1948–present

1918 **His Family** Ernest Poole

1919 **The Magnificent Ambersons** Booth Tarkington

1920 No award

1921 **The Age of Innocence** Edith Wharton **286**

1922 **Alice Adams** Booth Tarkington

1923 **One of Ours** Willa Cather

1924 **The Able McLaughlins** Margaret Wilson

1925 **So Big** Edna Ferber

1926 **Arrowsmith** Sinclair Lewis

1927 **Early Autumn** Louis Bromfield

1928 **The Bridge of San Luis Rey** Thornton Wilder

1929 **Scarlet Sister Mary** Julia Peterkin

1930 **Laughing Boy** Oliver Lafarge

1931 **Years of Grace** Margaret Ayer Barnes

1932 **The Good Earth** Pearl S. Buck

1933 **The Store** T.S. Stribling

1934 **Lamb in His Bosom** Caroline Miller

1935 **Now in November** Josephine Winslow Johnson

1936 **Honey in the Horn** Harold L. Davis

1937 **Gone With the Wind** Margaret Mitchell **384–5**

1938 **The Late George Apley** John Phillips Marquand

1939 **The Yearling** Marjorie Kinnan Rawlings

1940 **The Grapes of Wrath** John Steinbeck **408–9**

1941 No award

1942 **In This Our Life** Ellen Glasgow

1943 **Dragon's Teeth** Upton Sinclair

1944 **Journey in the Dark** Martin Flavin

1945 **A Bell for Adano** John Hersey

1946 No award

1947 **All the King's Men** Robert Penn Warren

1948 **Tales of the South Pacific** James A. Michener

1949 **Guard of Honor** James Gould Cozzens

1950 **The Way West** A.B. Guthrie

1951 **The Town** Conrad Richter

1952 **The Caine Mutiny** Herman Wouk

1953 **The Old Man and the Sea** Ernest Hemingway **477**

1954 No award

1955 **A Fable** William Faulkner

1956 **Andersonville** MacKinlay Kantor

1957 No award

1958 **A Death in the Family** James Agee

1959 **The Travels of Jaimie McPheeters** Robert Lewis Taylor

1960 **Advise and Consent** Allen Drury

1961 **To Kill a Mockingbird** Harper Lee **546**

1962 **The Edge of Sadness** Edwin O'Connor

1963 **The Reivers** William Faulkner

1964 No award

1965 **The Keepers Of The House** Shirley Ann Grau

1966 **Collected Stories** Katherine Anne Porter

1967 **The Fixer** Bernard Malamud

1968 **The Confessions of Nat Turner** William Styron

1969 **House Made of Dawn** N. Scott Momaday

1970 **Collected Stories** Jean Stafford

1971 No award

1972 **Angle of Repose** Wallace Stegner

1973 **The Optimist's Daughter** Eudora Welty **651**

1974 No award

1975 **The Killer Angels** Michael Shaara

1976 **Humboldt's Gift** Saul Bellow **667**

1977 No award

1978 **Elbow Room** James Alan McPherson

1979 **The Stories of John Cheever** John Cheever

1980 **The Executioner's Song** Norman Mailer

1981 **A Confederacy of Dunces** John Kennedy Toole **710**

1982 **Rabbit is Rich** John Updike **718**

Acknowledgments

Quintessence Editions would like to thank the following people for their help in the preparation of this book:

Mark Abley, Bianca Jackson, and Simon Doubt for researching contributors; Martha Magor for researching quotes; Reg Grant for writing picture captions; Sonia Land at Sheil Land Associates for liaison with Peter Ackroyd; Liz Wyse, Cathy Meeus, and Siobhan O'Connor for copyediting; Victoria Wiggins and Helena Baser for editorial assistance; Elaine Shatenstein and Lisa Morris for proofreading; Ann Barrett and Kay Ollerenshaw for the index; Maria Gibbs for picture research and for compiling the picture credits; Simon Goggins, Nick Jones, and Rod Teasdale for design assistance; Phil Wilkins and Robert Gillam for additional photography; Irene Scheimberg, Marcus Deyes, Lucy Holliday, and Elisabeth de Lancey for the loan of books.

Quintessence Editions would also like to thank the following people and picture libraries:

Elbie Lebrecht at Lebrecht, Teresa Riley and Paul Jennings at Getty, Tessa Ademolu and Simon Pearson at Corbis, Jenny Page at Bridgeman, Lucy Brock at AKG, Angela Minshull at Christie's, Anna Barrett at Art Archive/Kobal, Emma Doyle at Peter Harrington Antiquarian Bookseller, and Simon Pask.

Picture Credits

Every effort has been made to credit the copyright holders of the images used in this book. We apologize in advance for any unintentional omissions or errors and will be pleased to insert the appropriate acknowledgment to any companies or individuals in any subsequent edition of the work.

2 Private Collection, Lauros/Giraudon/Bridgeman 22 TopFoto.co.uk 23 Lebrecht 26 TopFoto.co.uk 27 Charles Walker/TopFoto.co.uk 29 Private Collection/Archives Charmet/Bridgeman 30 PrivateCollection, Giraudon/Bridgeman 33 Mary Evans Picture Library/Alamy 35 Archivo Iconografico/Corbis 36 Real academia de la Historia, Madrid/Bridgeman 38 Roger-Viollet/TopFoto.co.uk 39 GettyImages 40 Bodleian Library Oxford/The Art Archive 42 Getty Images 43 Getty Images 44 Getty Images 45 Lebrecht 47 TopFoto.co.uk 49 Hermitage, St Petersburg/Bridgeman 50 Lebrecht 51 Victoria and Albert Museum London/Eileen Tweedy/The Art Archive 52 Sheryl Straight/www.eroticabibliophile.com 53 Bettmann/Corbis 55 Lebrecht 56 Mary Evans Picture Library/Alamy 59 Lebrecht 60 Getty Images 61 Getty Images 63 TopFoto.co.uk 64 Museo di Goethe Rome/Dagli Orti/ The Art Archive 65 Private Collection Paris/Dagli Orti/The Art Archive 66 Getty Images 67 Lebrecht 68 Private Collection, The Stapleton Collection/Bridgeman 71 Michael Nicholson/Corbis 72 AKG Images 73 AKG Images 75 The British Library/TopFoto.co.uk 77 Lebrecht 80 Lebrecht 87 The Art Archive 88 Time Life Pictures/Getty Images 91 Lebrecht 92 FIA RA/Lebrecht 93 Getty Images 95 Mary Evans Picture Library/Alamy 96 Getty Images 97 Getty Images 98 Burstein Collection/Corbis 100 Lebrecht 101 Getty Images 102 Lebrecht 103 Victor Hugo House Paris/Dagli Orti/The Art Archive 104 Lebrecht 105 Interfoto/Lebrecht 106 Leonard de Selva/Corbis 108 Lebrecht 109 British Museum/Eileen Tweedy/The Art Archive 111 Crawford Municipal Art Gallery, Cork/Bridgeman 112 Hollandse Hoogte/Lebrecht 115 Bibliothèque de l'Institut de France, Paris/Archives Charmet/Bridgeman 116 Getty Images 117 Getty Images 118 Stefano Bianchetti/Corbis 120 Lebrecht 121 Lebrecht 122 David Lyons/Alamy 123 Getty Images 124 Hulton-Deutsch Collection/Corbis 125 Getty Images 127 Brian Seed/Lebrecht 128 Getty Images 130 Bettmann/Corbis 131 The Art Archive 133 Culver Pictures/The Art Archive 134 The Art Archive 135 Lebrecht 136 TopFoto.co.uk 137 Culver Pictures/The Art Archive 139 TopFoto.co.uk 140 Bibliothèque des Arts Décoratifs Paris/Dagli Orti/The Art Archive 141 Lebrecht 142 Sammlung Rauch Interfoto/Lebrecht 143 TopFoto.co.uk 145 Getty Images 146 Getty Images 148 Getty Images 150 Getty Images 151 Bibliothèque des Arts Décoratifs Paris/Dagli Orti/The Art Archive 152 Getty Images 153 TopFoto.co.uk 154 Getty Images 155 Hulton-Deutsch Collection/Corbis 156 Lebrecht 157 Lebrecht 158 Time Life Pictures/Getty Images 159 Roger-Viollet/TopFoto.co.uk 160 Rex Features 162 Private Collection, Archives Charmet/Bridgeman 164 Bettmann/Corbis 167 Popperfoto/Alamy 168 Getty Images 169 The Art Archive 171 The Art Archive 172 Getty Images 173 Lebrecht 174 Getty Images 178 Getty Images 179 Private Collection/Bridgeman 181 Classic Image/Alamy 182 The Art Archive/Harper Collins Publishers 183 Musée Carnavalet Paris/Dagli Orti/The Art Archive 184 Rex Features 188 The Art Archive/Biblioteca Comunale Palermo/Dagli Orti 189 The Art Archive/Biblioteca Nationale do Rio de Janeiro/Dagli Orti 191 The Art Archive 192 Lebrecht 193 Roger-Viollet/TopFoto.co.uk 196 Stapleton Collection/Corbis 197 Lebrecht 198 Archivo Iconografico/Corbis 200 Getty Images 202 The Art Archive/Strindberg Museum, Stockholm/Dagli Orti 204 Lebrecht 206 Hollandse Hoogte/Lebrecht 207 Lebrecht 209 Lebrecht 210 Lebrecht 211 Corbis 213 Bettmann/Corbis 215 Chris Hellier/Corbis 216 Eileen Tweedy/The Art Archive 217 Historical Picture Archive/Corbis 218 Lebrecht 222 The Art Archive 223 Lebrecht 225 Artur Hojny Forum/Lebrecht 226 Lebrecht 227 AKG Images 228 Getty Images 231 Getty Images 233 Getty Images 236 Corbis 238 Private Collection/MD/The Art Archive 239 © Elizabeth Banks/The Art Archive 240 Private Collection/Marc Charmet/The Art Archive 241 Getty Images 242 Zoetrope/United Artists/The Kobal Collection 245 Getty Images 247 Getty Images 250 Time Life Pictures/Getty Images 252 Getty Images 253 Getty Images 255 E.O. Hoppé/Corbis 257 Domenica del Corriere/Dagli Orti (A)/The Art Archive 259 Getty Images 260 Popperfoto/Alamy 262 PVDE RA/Lebrecht 263 Archiv Friedrich Interfoto/Lebrecht 264 Private Collection, The Bloomsbury Workshop, London/Bridgeman 265 Bettmann/Corbis 270 The Art Archive 273 Asian Art & Archaeology/Corbis 274 Rex Features 276 Asian Art and Archeology, Inc/Corbis 277 E.O. Hoppé/Corbis 278 Asian Art & Archaeology/Corbis 280 Courtesy of Peter Harrington Antiquarian Bookseller. B. W. Huebsch 283 TopFoto.co.uk 284 Getty Images 287 Condé Nast Archive/Corbis 288 Getty Images 289 David Lees/Corbis 290 Lorenzo Ciniglio/Corbis 291 Courtesy of Peter Harrington Antiquarian Bookseller. Shakespeare & Co. 293 Private Collection/Archives Charmet/Bridgeman 294 Condé Nast Archive/Corbis 297 Getty Images 298 Mary Evans Picture Library/Alamy 299 Time Life Pictures/Getty Images 300 Burstein Collection/Corbis 303 Corbis 304 S. Fischer Verlag 306 Time Life Pictures/Getty Images 307 TopFoto.co.uk 308 Paris Europa/FICIT/HSA/The Kobal Collection 309 Getty Images 311 Getty Images 312 The British Library/HIP/TopFoto.co.uk 313 HIP/Ann Ronan Picture Library/Lebrecht 317 Lebrecht 319 Courtesy of Peter Harrington Antiquarian Bookseller. J. M. Dent & Sons 320 Getty Images 322 Kiepenheuer 324 Harlinque/Roger-Viollet/Lebrecht 325 Getty Images 327 Getty Images 328 Bettmann/Corbis 331 Getty Images 332 Getty Images 333 Getty Images; Penguin 334 Courtesy of Peter Harrington Antiquarian Bookseller. Hogarth Press 336 Bettmann/Corbis 337 Jean-Pierre Muller/AFP/Getty Images 338 Allianz/Capital/The Kobal Collection 339 Universal/The Kobal Collection 340 Condé Nast Archive/Corbis 342 Bettmann/Corbis 344 Bettmann/Corbis 346 Courtesy of Peter Harrington Antiquarian Bookseller. Arthur Press 347 Ferens Art Gallery, Hull City Museums and Art Galleries/Bridgeman 349 © 1961 Estate of Vanessa Bell, courtesy Henrietta Garnett/The Stapleton Collection/Bridgeman 351 John Springer Collection/Corbis 352 Biblioteca Nationale. Paris/Archives Charmet/Bridgeman 355 Hulton-Deutsch Collection/Corbis 356 Getty Images 357 Christie's Images 358 Lebrecht 359 Getty Images 362 Getty Images 363 Andy Warhol Foundation for the Visual Arts/Corbis 366 Images.com/Corbis 367 Christie's Images 368 Getty Images 369 Content Mine International/Alamy 370 Time Life Pictures/Getty Images 372 Musée de Saint-Denis, France/Archives Charmet/Bridgeman 373 Ludwig Museum, Cologne, Giraudon/Bridgeman 375 Courtesy of Peter Harrington Antiquarian Bookseller. A. Barker 376 Bettmann/Corbis 379 Oscar White/Corbis 380 TopFoto.co.uk 381 TopFoto.co.uk 383 CSV Archiv, Everett/Rex Features 384 MGM/Album/ AKG Images 385 Getty Images 386 Time Life Pictures/Getty Images 389 Getty Images 392 Getty Images 393 Getty Images 394 Courtesy of Peter Harrington Antiquarian Bookseller. G. Routledge & Sons 395 Constable & Co. 396 Associated British/The Kobal Collection 397 Courtesy of Peter Harrington Antiquarian Bookseller. W. Heinemann 399 Courtesy of Peter Harrington Antiquarian Bookseller. V. Gollancz 400 Private Collection/Archives Charmet/Bridgeman 401 Condé Nast Archive/Corbis 402 Persephone Books 404 Courtesy of Peter Harrington Antiquarian Bookseller. Hamish Hamilton 405 Warner Bros/The Kobal Collection 406 Viola Roehr v. Alvensleben, München/AKG Images 407 ABC/Allied Artists/The Kobal Collection 408 AKG Images 409 Time Life Pictures/Getty Images 410 TopFoto.co.uk 413 AKG Images 415 Bettmann/Corbis 416 Simon & Schuster 417 Ediciones Ercilla, Santiago 418 Courtesy of Peter Harrington Antiquarian Bookseller. Routledge & Kegan Paul 420 Roger-Viollet 421 Collection Albert Camus/Archives Charmet/Bridgeman 423 Bettmann/Corbis 425 Condé Nast Archive/Corbis 426 Penguin/Christie's Images 427 Courtesy of Peter Harrington Antiquarian Bookseller. W. Heinemann 429 Patrik Sjöling IBL Bildbyra/Lebrecht 431 Random House/The British Library/HIP/TopFoto.co.uk 432 TopFoto.co.uk 434 Penguin/ Christie's Images 435 M. Peric/Lebrecht 437 Getty Images 440 Sophie Bassouls/Corbis 441 Harper Collins/Christie's Images 442 AGIP RA/Lebrecht 445 Random House/Lebrecht 448 Time Life Pictures/Getty Images 452 Random House/Christie's Images 453 Random House/AKG Images 454 Rex Features 456 Courtesy of Peter Harrington Antiquarian Bookseller. Hamish Hamilton458 Random House; Christie's Images 459 Random House/Lebrecht 460 Getty Images 462 Getty Images 463 Simon & Schuster 464 Cuadernos Americanos 467 Getty Images 469 Time Life Pictures/Getty Images 472 Courtesy of Peter Harrington Antiquarian Bookseller. Little Brown & Co. 473 Random House/Christie's Images 474 Worldimage RA/Lebrecht 476 Harcourt/Christie's Images 477 Random House/Lebrecht 478 Time Life Pictures/Getty Images 479 Time Life Pictures/Getty Images 480 Lipnitzki/Roger-Viollet/TopFoto.co.uk 482 Courtesy of Peter Harrington Antiquarian Bookseller. Knopf 483 Courtesy of Peter Harrington Antiquarian Bookseller. Jonathan Cape 484 Time Life Pictures/Getty Images 485 Orion Publishing Group/Christie's Images 487 Underwood & Underwood/Corbis 488 Penguin/Christie's Images 492 Faber & Faber/Christie's Images 493 Two Arts/CD/The Kobal Collection 495 Time Life Pictures/Getty Images 498 Getty Images 502 The Kobal Collection 504 Hulton-Deutsch Collection/Corbis 505 MGM/The Kobal Collection 506 Random House/Christie's Images 507 Harper Collins/TopFoto.co.uk 508 Getty Images 511 Time Life Pictures/Getty Images 512 Time Life Pictures/Getty Images 515 Harper Collins/ Lebrecht 517 Rex Features 520 Penguin/ Christie's Images 521 Penguin/Lebrecht 523 TopFoto.co.uk 525 Getty Images 526 Getty Images 527 Getty Images 528 Time Life Pictures/Getty Images 530 Methuen 532 Getty Images 533 Paramount/The Kobal Collection 535 Getty Images 536 Getty Images 538 Seitz/Bioskop/ Hallelujah/The Kobal Collection 539 Random House/AKG Images 540 Harper Collins/Christie's Images 541 Loomis Dean/Time Life Pictures/Getty Images 542 VIC/Waterhall/The Kobal Collection 544 Darlene Hammond/Hulton Archive/Getty Images 545 Hulton Archive/Getty Images 546 Harper Collins/Christie's Images 547 Donald Uhrbrock/Time Life Pictures/Getty Images 548 Time Life Pictures/Getty Images 549 Lebrecht 552 Condé Nast Archive/Corbis 553 Christie's Images 554 Courtesy of Peter Harrington Antiquarian Bookseller. Wydawnic†on 555 Bettmann/Corbis 556 20th Century Fox/The Kobal Collection 557 Hulton-Deutsch Collection/Corbis 558 Time Life Pictures/Getty Images 563 AGIP RA/Lebrecht 565 Time Life Pictures/Getty Images 566 Time Life Pictures/Getty Images 567 Penguin 568 Courtesy of Peter Harrington Antiquarian Bookseller. Viking Press 569 Jonathan Cape 570 Sophie Bassouls/Corbis Sygma 572 Getty Images 573 TopFoto.co.uk 576 Macmillan & C. 577 Time Life Pictures/Getty Images 578 RENN/A2/RAI-2/The Kobal Collection 579 TopFoto.co.uk 581 Time Life Pictures/Getty Images 582 Harper Collins/Christie's Images 583 Random House/Lebrecht 584 Gallimard 585 W. Heinemann 588 Miroslav Zajic/Corbis 590 Corbis 591 Getty Images 593 Getty Images 596 Bettmann/Corbis 597 Doubleday 598 Lebrecht 600 Margarita from Bulgakov's "Master and Margarita." Jerosimic, Gordana (Contemporary Artist)/Private Collection/Bridgeman 601 Novosti/TopFoto.co.uk 603 Lebrecht 604 Gallimard 606 Colita/Corbis 607 Christie's Images 610 Crawford Municipal Art Gallery, Cork/Bridgeman 612 Woodfall/Kestrel/ Barnett, Michael/The Kobal Collection 614 Interfoto/Lebrecht 615 Interfoto/Lebrecht 617 MGM/The Kobal Collection 618 Getty Images 620 Little Brown & Co. 621 20th Century Fox/The Kobal Collection 624 Paramount/The Kobal Collection 625 Getty Images 628 Jonathan Cape 629 Christie's Images 630 Getty Images 636 Suhrkamp 637 Barral Editores 638 Bettmann/Corbis 639 Getty Images 640 Getty Images 641 Getty Images 643 Kiepenheuer & Witsch 644 Louis Monier/RA/Lebrecht 645 Lynn Goldsmith/Corbis 646 Pan Macmillan/Lebrecht 650 Getty Images 652 Penguin/Christie's Images 654 Random House/Lebrecht 654 Random House/Christie's Images 655 Sophie Bassouls/Corbis 659 Bioskop/Paramount-Orion/WDR/The Kobal Collection 665 Lebrecht 666 Bettmann/ Corbis 668 Simon & Schuster 671 © 1975 by Wendell Minor 669 Roger Ressmeyer/Corbis 670 Micheline Pelletier/Corbis 672 TopFoto.co.uk 674 Time Life Pictures/Getty Images 675 Getty Images 677 United Artists/The Kobal Collection 678 Warner Bros/Everett/Rex Features 679 Alfred A. Knopf 681 HB Filmes/Sugarloaf Films/The Kobal Collection 683 Rex Features 687 Christian Simonpietri/Corbis 688 Alex Gotfryd/Corbis 689 Everett Collection/Rex Features 690 Harcourt Brace Jovanovich 691 Corbis 693 Weidenfeld & Nicolson 695 Michel Clement/AFP/Getty Images 697 Getty Images 698 Getty Images 701 William Campbell/Corbis 702 TopFoto.co.uk 703 W. H. Allen 704 Gallimard/Lebrecht 705 Getty Images 707 Planeta 708 Time Warner Book Group UK 712 Getty Images 713 Rex Features 717 © 1981 Alisdair Gray. Reproduced by permission of the author c/o Rogers, Coleridge & White Ltd., 20 Powis Mews, London W11 1JN/Special Collections Dept, University of Glasgow 719 Jonathan Cape 721 Getty Images 722 Reuters/Corbis 723 Amblin/Universal/The Kobal Collection 724 Sophie Bassouls, 726 Getty Images 727 Warner Bros/The Kobal Collection 731 Secker & Warburg 733 Lebrecht 734 Publicacoes D. Quixote 735 Lebrecht 736 Random House/Lebrecht 737 Random House/Lebrecht 738 Random House 739 L. Birnbaum/Lebrecht 742 Harper Collins 743 Time Life Pictures/Getty Images 744 Time Warner Book Group UK 745 Rex Features 747 Horst Tappe/Lebrecht 749 Penguin/ Lebrecht 750 Gallimard 754 Getty Images 754 TopFoto.co.uk 755 Virago RA/Lebrecht 758 Getty Images 759 Jeff Albertson/Corbis 760 Faber & Faber 768 Knopf 771 Macduff Everton/Corbis 774 Faber & Faber/Christie's Images 775 Sophie Bassouls/Corbis 776 Lebrecht 777 Random House/Lebrecht 778 Bettmann/ Corbis 779 Random House 780 Residenz Verlag 781 Weidenfeld & Nicolson 782 Lebrecht 783 Heinemann 786 Faber & Faber 787 Random House 788 Penguin/Lebrecht 789 Getty Images 791 AGIP/RA/Lebrecht 792 Maartje Geels Hollandse Hoogte/Lebrecht/Lebrecht 794 Bloomsbury 795 James Leynse/Corbis 798 Faber and Faber 799 Random House/Lebrecht 800 Arnold Newman/ Getty Images 802 Faber & Faber 804 Time Life Pictures/Getty Images 806 Atlantic Monthly Press 807 Roger Ressmeyer/Corbis 809 MGM/Jersey Films/The Kobal Collection 811 Pan Macmillan 812 Corbino Hollandse Hoogte/Lebrecht 813 Gideon Mendel/Corbis 816 HarperCollins 817 Jonathan Cape. Jacket photograph: André Kertész, courtesy Michael M. Senft, One Bond/Masterworks N.Y, N.Y. © Estate of André Kertész 818 Rex Features 819 Penguin/Lebrecht 821 Bettmann/Corbis 822 Picador 823 Rosinante 826 Fotos International/Rex Features 829 Orion Publishing Group 841 Hollandse Hoogte/Lebrecht 833 Polfoto/Miriam Dalsgaard/TopFoto.co.uk 834 Louis Monier RA/Lebrecht 836 Robert Maass/Corbis 837 Random House 838 Times Newspapers/Rex Features 839 Orion Publishing Group 841 Hollandse Hoogte/Lebrecht 843 Secker & Warburg 843 Hutchinson 844 Scribner 846 Random House/Lebrecht 847 Macmillan 848 Random House 849 Random House & Ingeborg Pelster Amsterdam, Wichtrach/Bern 859 Sophie Bassouls/Corbis 861 Random House/Lebrecht 863 Steve Liss/Time Life Pictures/Getty Images 864 Serpent's Tail 865 Bloomsbury 868 "Book Cover", copyright © 1997, from The God of Small Things by Arundhati Roy. Used by permission of Random House, Inc. 869 Karan Kapoor/Corbis 870 Hollandse Hoogte/Lebrecht 871 Marco Okhuizen Hollandse Hoogte/Lebrecht 873 Scribner. Jacket photograph: © estate of André Kertész 874 Lebrecht 875 Faber & Faber 876 AFP/Getty Images 877 Paulo Fridman/Corbis 878 Farrar, Straus & Giroux 879 AFP/Getty Images 881 Ted Soqui/Corbis 882 Sceptre 883 Anagrama 884 Getty Images 885 Random House/Lebrecht 887 Seix Barral 888 Fabrika knjiga 889 Eric Fougère/VIP Images/Corbis 893 AFP/Getty Images 895 Penguin 896 Christopher Furlong/Getty Images 898 Allison & Busby. Cover: Ambrogio Lorenzetti. Alegoría del mal gobierno (fragmento) 899 Einaudi. Elaboracion grafica da foto Amit Bar/© Olympia 900 Focus/Everett /Rex Features 901 Random House 902 John Foley Opale/Lebrecht 903 Horst Tappe/Lebrecht 904 TopFoto.co.uk 905 Harper Collins 906 Random House/Lebrecht 907 Iletisim 908 Pan Macmillan/Lebrecht 909 Penguin 910 Houghton Mifflin. Jacket illustration © Kiran Desai, 2006; reproduced by permission of Penguin Books Ltd. 911 copyright © Robur/Corbis 914 Keter 915 WW Norton & Co Ltd 916 Hodder Headline 918 AFP/Getty Images 919 Getty Images 920 Sophie Bassouls/Corbis 921 © Opale/Lebrecht Music & Arts 922 Picador 924 Picador 925 Gallimard 926 Canongate 927 reproduced by permission of Penguin Books Ltd. 928 Nick Cunard/Rex Features 929 copyright © Jean Desai, 2006; reproduced by permission of Penguin Books Ltd. 931 copyright © Robur/Corbis, 2007; reproduced by permission of Penguin Books Ltd. 932 S. Fischer Verlag 933 copyright © James Kelman, 2008; reproduced by permission of Penguin Books Ltd. 934 Getty Images 935 Farrar, Straus & Giroux 936 Atlantic Books 937 Jacket design by Jennifer Carrow from COST by Roxana Robinson. Jacket design copyright © 2008 by Jennifer Carrow; jacket painting copyright © Roxana Alger Geffen. Reprinted by permission of Farrar, Straus and Giroux, LLC. 938 Random House 939 Random House 941 Alfred A. Knopf. Front-of-jacket photograph © Kamil Vojnar 942 Farrar, Straus & Giroux. Jacket art: ceruean warbler © Dave Maslowski; landscape ©2009 Heikki Salmi/Getty Images 943 Getty Images 944 Houghton Mifflin Harcourt. Cover design © Milton Glaser 945 Farrar, Straus and Giroux 946 Jonathan Cape 947 Alfred A. Knopf 948 Hamish Hamilton 949 Little, Brown. Jacket © 2011 Hachette Book Group Inc